Fundamentals of
Cost Accounting
Principles and Practice

by the same author:

- **Fundamentals of Management Accounting**

Fundamentals of

Cost Accounting

Principles and Practice

Dr. H.V. Jhamb

Associate Professor
Department of Commerce
Sri Guru Tegh Bhadur Khalsa College
University of Delhi

Ane Books Pvt. Ltd.

New Delhi ♦ Chennai

Fundamentals of Cost Accounting: Principles and Practice

H.V. Jhamb

Published by

Ane Books Pvt. Ltd.
4821, Parwana Bhawan, 1st Floor, 24 Ansari Road, Darya Ganj, **New Delhi** - 110 002, India
Tel.: +91(011) 23276843-44, Fax: +91(011) 23276863
e-mail: kapoor@anebooks.com, Website: www.anebooks.com

Branch Office :

- Avantika Niwas, 1st Floor, 19 Doraiswamy Road, T. Nagar, **Chennai** - 600 017, Tel.: +91(044) 28141554, 28141209 e-mail: anebooks_tn@airtelmail.in

ISBN : 978-93-8061-898-2

Printed at : R.K. Offset Process, New Delhi.

Dedicated to

my family and my parents

Preface

Essence of cost accounting is the use of accounting information for profit planning and control. In this era of global competition, it is crucial to study the various aspects of costs as business firms constantly strive to achieve financial efficiency for survival and growth. This exhaustive work *"Fundamentals of Cost Accounting"* describes the internal use of accounting information for controlling cost. It will enable the readers to grasp the cardinal axioms of this specialty and also instils a practical application sense to resolve real-life problems.

The text is lucidly written with lot of emphasis on providing conceptual clarity, while logically progressing on practical problem solving. The subject matter of this book is pragmatically woven around the accounting information for Profit Planning and Control by a firm and is divided into Six Units. Unit I starts with the overview of Cost Accounting in terms of its relationship with financial accounting and the main contents of the cost accounting information. Material Cost, an important element of product cost, is dealt in Unit II. Unit III is allocated to Labour Cost and Direct Expenses. Unit IV is assigned to Overheads and Activity Based Costing, while Unit V discusses the Methods of Cost Accounting. Unit V is concerned with the cost book-keeping and its system.

It provides a comprehensive coverage to suit the requirements of Undergraduate and Postgraduate courses such as B.Com., B.Com. (Hons.), M.Com., and professional courses such as BBA, CA, I.C.W.A., M.B.A., MIB, MHROD and even the managers who are interested in upgrading their understanding of cost controlling.

I am extremely grateful to my publishers M/s Ane Books Pvt. Ltd. and their entire team especially Mr. Sunil Saxena, Mr. Jai Raj Kapoor, Mr. Prem Raj Verma, Mr. Nishant and Mr. Inderjeet, for doing the enormous work throughout the writing of this textbook.

I sincerely thank my friends and colleagues for constantly encouraging me in bringing out a learner-friendly book on cost accounting.

Words fail to show my love, gratitude and respect for my parents and my family for their perseverance and patience throughout this arduous task.

I earnestly look forward to valuable feedback from my students and the faculty at large by way of comments and criticism. I assure you all that these suggestions will gratefully be acknowledged and duly incorporated in the next edition.

H.V. Jhamb

Contents

UNIT - III : LABOUR COSTING

UNIT - IV : OVERHEADS COSTING

1 Nature and Significance of Cost Accounting

Learning Objectives

It attempts to explain the relevance of cost accounting. In this chapter you will learn :

1. Limitations of financial accounting.
2. Necessity of cost accounting.
3. Meaning, nature, scope and objectives of cost accounting.
4. Costing, cost accounting and cost accountancy.
5. Difference between :
   (a) Financial accounting and cost accounting,
   (b) Cost accounting and management accounting.
6. Need and importance of cost accounting.
7. Installation of cost accounting system.
8. Methods and techniques used in cost accounting.
9. Functions of cost accounting.
10. Limitations of cost accounting.
11. Conventions of cost accounting.
12. Status of the cost accountant.

INTRODUCTION

Since time immemorial when trade, commerce and industry commenced on earth, accounting has been considered to be an essential tool to record business transactions. Even with the introduction of computers, which store and analyse the data kept in memory, the knowledge of accounting concepts is considered essential for data feeding and processing. Financial accounting is considered to be the father of accounting systems. But it has its own limitations and these limitations gave birth to Cost Accounting and Management Accounting systems. In this age, the main accounting systems are (1) Financial Accounting, (2) Cost Accounting, and (3) Management Accounting.

Financial Accounting: Limitations

Financial accounting is concerned with recording, classifying, analyzing and summarizing financial transactions and preparing financial statements with a view to disclosing profitability and financial status of the business. The financial accounting facilitates recording of cash and credit transactions of a business according to the nature of expenditure and income so as to enable the preparation of Profit and Loss Account for a period and the Balance Sheet on a specific date. The significance of such statements is in determining the gains and losses of the business over a period and its state of affairs on a particular date. The following are the limitations of financial accounts and statements: -

(1) Financial accounts are of historical character. They record the events, which have already occurred. They do not throw adequate light on future.

(2) Only monetary information finds place in financial records. Non-monetary information has no place in financial statements.

(3) Financial accounts generally disclose profitability of the entire organization. It provides overall information of the organisational performance. Financial statements fail to give picture of each Product, Process, Job, Segment and sub-segments.

(4) They fail to reveal efficiency and inefficiency in various segments and sub-segments of the organization. Financial profit is not a true measure of efficiency. Profits may be high despite inefficiencies and vice versa..

(5) Information available from these books is insufficient in ascertaining cost of products/services because costs are not classified as direct and indirect.

(6) It is difficult to know the behaviour of costs in financial accounting as expenses are not categorized into fixed and variable.

(7) Financial accounting contains historical cost information, which is accumulated at the end of the accounting period. The historical cost is not a reliable basis for predicting future earnings, solvency, or overall managerial effectiveness.

(8) Financial accounting does not provide necessary information to management in taking critical decisions about expansion/ diversification of business, dropping of a product line, starting a new product, alternative methods of production/processes or improvement in product design etc.

(9) Financial accounting does not provide cost data to predetermine the price/quotation of the product/contract or order to be manufactured or the service being rendered to the consumers.

(10) The recording and accounting for wages and labour is not done for different jobs, processes, products, departments. This creates problems in analyzing the cost associated with various activities and rewarding workers and employees for the above-normal performance.

(11) Financial accounting fails to answer the following questions:

  (i) Can the manufacturing cost be reduced? If so, to what extent and at what stage?

  (ii) Can the selling prices be increased or raised?

  (iii) How can the wastage in manufacturing be minimized?

  (iv) Is the current profit optimal? How can it be further raised? In case of loss, could this loss be reduced or turned into profits by controlling the costs?

  (v) Should the production be made more capital intensive or labour intensive? That is, should latest machines be introduced and manual labour replaced?

  (vi) What should be the optimum product-mix?

  (vii) Should the offer to execute an order at low rates be entertained?

Necessity of Cost Accounting

Cost accounting not only cured the malady of limitations of financial accounting but also helped the management and industry to achieve success in fields hitherto impossible.

Financial accounts safeguard the interests of the business, its proprietors, shareholders, present and prospective creditors and the government, especially Income-Tax, Excise and other authorities. Thus, financial accounts are used for the external users. Cost accounts render information for the guidance of the management for proper planning, operation, control, profitability and decision-making. In case of materials, financial accounts show whether purchases have been correctly accounted and paid for and closing stocks have been valued "at cost or market price, whichever is less" for the purpose of making Position Statement. Cost accounts, however, maintain detailed account for each material, report the management regarding effectiveness of material utilisation and inform the variances from budgets as regards price and consumption with the causes of variances. Similarly, treatment for labour utilisation and capital resources utilisation is done. Thus, cost accounting provides financial statements for managers for internal management whereas financial accounting is intended for external stakeholders. It may be observed that where financial accounts end, Cost accounts start. On making purchases of raw materials, financial accounts keep records of purchases and creditors meticulously but do not keep records of raw materials. The cost accounts keep additional detailed records in respect of each material showing receipts, issues and balance in terms of quantity and value. Thus, detailed records of utilisation in respect of all inputs of material, labour and other services are maintained in the cost department so as to determine cost of sales of each product/job and when the same is compared with the sales, the profit or loss for each product/job is arrived at (as against the TOTAL profit revealed by the financial accounts).

A Comparison

The difference between financial accounting and cost accounting is discussed hereunder:

Basis of Distinction	Financial Accounting	Cost Accounting
1. Purpose	The main purpose is to prepare Income Statement and Position Statement for reporting to the shareholders and the outside parties/agencies.	The main purpose is to provide detailed cost information to management for proper planning, decision-making and control.
2. Nature	It keeps historical records. Its nature is easily understood in the context of the purpose for which it was designed.	It considers both historical as well as predetermined costs, and extends to plans and policies to improve performance in future.
3. Manner (Subjective OR Objective)	It classifies records and analyses transactions in a subjective manner i.e. According to the nature of expenses.	It records expenditure in an objective manner i.e. according to purposes for which costs are incurred.
4. Statutory requirements	It is prepared to meet the requirements of Companies Act, 1956 and Income Tax Act, 1961.	It is kept voluntarily except where Cost Accounting Records Rules have been framed for the maintenance of cost accounting records.
5. Reporting	Financial reports are usually prepared on annual basis. Costs are reported in *total* in financial accounts.	Cost reporting is a continuous process and its periodicity may be weekly, monthly, or quarterly. The costs are split on a unit basis in cost accounts.
6. Stock Valuation	The valuation of Stock is done on cost or realisable value, whichever is less.	The valuation of Stock is mostly done on cost basis.

7. Analysis of Cost and Profit	It reveals the profit or loss of the entire business during a particular period.	It shows the detailed cost and profit data for each product, line, department, process, etc.
8. Control	The emphasis is on the recording of financial transactions and no importance is given to the control aspect.	It provides for an in-built system of control with the help of budgetary control and standard costing.

Meaning and Definitions

According to Charted Institute of Management Accountants (CIMA), London, Costing is "the techniques and processes of ascertaining costs". The definition of costing given by Wheldon is "the classifying, recording and appropriate allocation of expenditure for the determination of costs, the relation of these costs to sales value and the ascertainment of profitability."

Thus, costing is cost finding by any process or technique. It entails principles and rules to determine the followings:

(i) The cost of manufacturing a product; and

(ii) The cost of providing/rendering a service.

Cost accounting is a formal system of accounting for costs in the books of accounts by means of which cost of products or services is ascertained and controlled. According to Charted Institute of Management Accountants (CIMA), London, "Cost accounting is the process of accounting for costs from the point at which expenditure is incurred or committed to the establishment of its ultimate relationship with cost centres and cost units. In its widest usage, it embraces the preparation of statistical data, the application of cost control methods and ascertainment of profitability of activities carried out or planned."

Scope of Cost Accounting

Following functional activities are included in the scope of cost accounting:

1. **Cost Book keeping:** It entails maintaining complete record of all costs from their incurrence to their charge to departments, products and services, preferably on the basis of double entry system.
2. **Cost system:** Systems and procedures are devised for accounting for costs.
3. **Cost ascertainment:** The major function of cost accounting is the determination/ascertainment of cost of products, processes, jobs, etc. It is the basis of managerial decisions in regard to pricing, planning and control.
4. **Cost analysis:** It involves detailed investigation into the causes of actual costs varying from the budgeted costs and assigning responsibility for cost increases.

5. **Cost comparisons:** It is the comparison between cost from alternative technologies, cost of different products and activities, and cost of same product or service over a period of time.
6. **Cost control:** Making use of cost information for exercising control is another function of cost accounting. It involves minute examination of each cost in the light of benefit derived from its incurrence.
7. **Cost reports:** Preparation and presentation of cost reports is the ultimate function of cost accounting. These reports are used by the management internally at different levels. Cost reports constitute the basis for planning, control, performance appraisal and managerial decision-making.

Difference between Costing and Cost Accounting

The terms 'Costing' and 'Cost accounting' are quite often used interchangeably. There is, yet, a difference between the two. Costing is simply ascertainment of costs by using any method such as memorandum statements, arithmetical process. Cost accounting denotes the formal accounting mechanism by means of which costs are ascertained by recording them in the books of accounts. It can thus be stated that costing is merely finding cost of a product/service by any technique or method, the cost accounting means costing using double entry system.

Installation of a Cost Accounting System

A Cost accounting system is a set of plans, programmes, procedures and documentation designed to accumulate costs, assign them to products, processes and jobs, and report cost information to management at different levels. Installation of a costing system involves thorough examination of all aspects of organization including interrelations between segments and its place vis-à-vis outside environment having an impact on internal functioning. To start with, it is essential to make cost-benefit analysis. The benefits from the system must not be less than the amount incurred on it. The management must feel the need of such a system and it should be able to make full use of the information available from the system in the smooth conduct of the business. The system should be justified on the basis of its value to management.

Main Considerations

The under mentioned main considerations to be kept in mind while introducing a costing system in a manufacturing organisation are:

1. **The Product:** The nature of the product determines to a great extent the type of costing system to be put in force. A product requiring high value of material content requires an elaborate system of materials control. A product requiring high value of labour content requires an efficient time-keeping and wage system. The same applies to overheads.

2. **The Organisation:** Authority-responsibility relationship, the source from which the costing information is to be obtained and the reports to be submitted at various managerial levels should be carefully studied. The existing organizational set up should be minimally disturbed.
3. **The objective:** The objectives and information which the management seeks to acquire are to be given due thought.
4. **The Technical details:** Detailed study of technical aspects of the business is the pre-requisite for introducing a system of costing in the organization. Efforts should be made to get the cooperative assistance and support of the concerned supervisory staff and the workmen.
5. **Method of maintenance of costing records:** There are two accounting systems in vogue. A choice has to be exercised between Integral and Non-integral accounting systems. In integral accounting system no separate set of books of accounts is maintained but there is interlocking with financial transactions. In case of non-integral system, separate books of accounts are maintained for cost and financial transactions. At the end of the period the results shown by the methods are reconciled. In case of a big business house it will be appropriate to maintain a separate set of books for cost transactions.
6. **Accuracy of data:** The degree of accuracy desired should be determined in regard to costing data to be collected and analysed.
7. **Current practice:** The methods and procedures already in use in the organization should be studied thoroughly. The method of procuring materials and procedure for making payment must be analysed before introducing any change in the current mode of working.
8. **Flexible:** The costing system should be flexible and capable of adapting to the changing requirements of the business.
9. **Simple and Informative:** The system needs to be simple to implement; it must provide relevant information at the time when it is required. In this regard, following points must be given due consideration:
   (a) The system must be capable of providing necessary information systematically and on regular basis.
   (b) Full information about departmental activities in terms of output, processes and operations must be clearly presented and every item of expenditure must be properly classified.
   (c) Standard printed forms preferably of different colors may be used so as to make the information detailed, clear and intelligible.
   (d) Data, complete in all respects, should be provided in a simple manner so that measurement of variations between actual and standard costs is possible.

Other Considerations

In the process of installing a costing system the following practical difficulties may be encountered:

1. Lack of enthusiasm and support from top management because they are not fully convinced about the benefits accruable from such a system.
2. Resistance from production staff and people at different levels in other departments because they fear getting subjected to additional controls.
3. Resistance from accounting staff as they believe that their work would increase.
4. High cost of installing the system.
5. Shortage of well trained and well qualified staff.

From the above it is obvious that the employees need to be re-oriented and educated. They have to be told the advantages that will accrue to them and to the organization as a whole on account of efficient working of the system.

The following numerical example illustrates the limitations of financial accounting and the need of cost account:

Illustration 1.1 : *The financial accounts of B.C. Ray Company show a profit of ₹ 1,00,000 for the year ending March 31, 2007 as follows:*

Profit and Loss Account
(For the year ending March 31, 2007)

Dr Cr

Details	Amount (₹)	Details	Amount (₹)
To Materials Used	62,500	By Sales	2,50,000
To Manufacturing Wages	56,250		
To Chargeable Expenses	3,250		
To Production Expenses	28,000		
To Gross Profit c/d	1,00,000		
	2,50,000		2,50,000
To Administrative Expenses	12,500	By Gross Profit b/d	1,00,000
To Selling and Distribution Expenses	37,500		
To Net Profit (20% of Sales) = [2,50,000 × 0.2]	50,000		
	1,00,000		1,00,000

This company produces three products P-1, P-2 and P-3. The cost Accountant has analysed costs and submitted the following product-wise Statement of Profit and Loss.

Statement of Profit and Loss (Product –wise)
(For the year ended on March 31, 2007

Details	Total	Product		
		P-1	P-2	P-3
	Amount (₹)	Amount (₹)	Amount (₹)	Amount (₹)
Direct Material cost	62,500	25,000	25,000	12,500
Direct Wages	56,250	25,000	15,000	16,250
Direct Expenses	3,250	NIL	1,950	1,300
Prime cost	1,22,000	50,000	41,950	30,050
Production Overhead	28,000	11,200	8,400	8,400
Cost of Production	1,50,000	61,200	50,350	38,450
Administration Overhead	12,500	6,500	3,000	3,000
Selling and Distribution Overhead	37,500	12,500	10,000	15,000
Total cost	2,00,000	80,200	63,350	56,450
Sales	2,50,000	75,000	90,000	85,000
Profit or Loss	50,000	(5,200)	26,650	28,550
Profit % to Sales	20%	(6.93%)	29.61%	33.59%

The above detailed statement of cost and profit makes it clear that the contribution of product P-3 is ₹ 28,550 in a total profit of ₹ 50,000 i.e. 56% and product P-2 is contributing more than 53% of the total profit and the Product P-1shows a loss of ₹ 5,200 i.e.10.4%. Based on such analytical information, the management would like to investigate to find out the factors responsible for the loss due to the product P-1. If the product P-1 cannot be produced on profitable basis, the decision to stop its production can be taken in the interest of increasing overall performance of the organisation. From the above table, it is obvious that such information is not made available by financial accounts.

Advantages of Cost Accounting

The advantages to be derived depend upon the efficiency with which cost accounting system is installed and the extent to which the management is prepared to accept the system. The main advantages of cost accounting are as under:

1. **Accuracy of financial accounts:** It provides a reliable check on the accuracy of financial accounts with the help of reconciliation between the two at the end of the accounting period.
2. **Inventory control:** Perpetual inventory system, which is an integral part of cost accounting, helps in the preparation of interim Profit and Loss Account. Other inventory control techniques like ABC analysis, level setting, etc. are also used in cost accounting.

3. **Reveals profitable/unprofitable activities:** It reveals and segregates profitable and unprofitable activities. Based upon this information the management may take appropriate measures to reduce or eliminate wastages and inefficiencies which may be due to idle time, and under utilisation of plant capacity.
4. **Formulation of policies:**
   (i) It lays the basis of standard costing and budgetary control systems. Variance analysis and comparison of actual performance with budget estimates indicates area where economies can be achieved.
   (ii) Detailed costs of materials, labour and overheads reveal actual and potential sources of cost savings and reductions.
   (iii) It provides suitable data and information which help the management in taking decisions such as 'Make or Buy', 'Shut-down or continue', Selection of most profitable product-mix, acceptance or Rejection of a special Order, Introduction of a new product, etc.

Limitations of Cost Accounting

Cost accounting has limitations as no cost can be exact or accurate as it incorporates a large number of conventions, estimations and other flexible factors such as:

(i) Classification of costs into its elements,
(ii) Materials issue pricing is based on average or standard costs,
(iii) Arbitrary basis is used to apportion, and allocate overhead to cost centres and cost units,
(iv) Arbitrary basis is applied to allocate joint product costs,
(v) Segregation of semi-fixed costs into variable and fixed,
(vi) Improper classification of costs into "normal and abnormal" and "controllable and uncontrollable"
(vii) Use of predetermined overhead rates of recovery,
(viii) Adoption of marginal and standard costs, and
(ix) Inclusion or exclusion of certain items of expenses.

Thus, cost accounting is not an exact science but an art which has been developed through theories and accounting practices based on reasoning and common sense. The cost statement submitted by the cost accountant is not absolutely a statement of true costs as some have been allocated, some apportioned on arbitrary bases and few of them suitably amended in the light of conventions according to the judgment and opinion of cost accountants. Further, no one cost is suitable for all purposes and under all circumstances. Costing information submitted during recession is different from that under normal conditions, standard costs are different from actual costs, and costs for decision making are different from costs under normal circumstances. It may be concluded that it offers "different costs for different purposes".

Despite the above stated limitations, cost data help management in controlling the situation and making vital managerial decisions. Accuracy in costing is relative. Some figures are better than no figures. Nothing is perfect in this world. With these ideas in mind it may be emphasized that cost accounting approach is more dynamic and renders valuable assistance to the management in making critical decisions.

Status of Cost Department in an Organisation

In a typical manufacturing company the main divisions of managerial responsibility are:

(a) **Purchasing:** The Purchase manager is in charge of this function and he has to look after the interest of production and services.

(b) **Human resource:** The human resource Manager is responsible for recruitment and selection, training and development, placement, promotion, etc of suitable employees.

(c) **Production and Services:** The Production manager is in charge of this function and he has to perform his function as per plans and schedules.

(d) **Accounting:** This function includes financial accounting, cost accounting and management accounting and other related accounting services.

(e) **Marketing:** Marketing manager is in charge of this function and he has to perform various marketing functions such as sales promotion, selling and distribution, marketing research etc.

It is crystal clear from the above, that with the development of cost accounting techniques and the recognition of the usefulness of the cost analyses and reports, the cost department nowadays is an integral part of Accounting Division and all the accounting work is integrated for the purposes of cost ascertainment, cost control, preparation of final statements, managerial decision making and submission of information required by the management.

Critical Evaluation of Cost Accounting

The role of cost accounting is reognised in improving the performance (efficiency) of the organization. There are certain objections raised against the introduction of such a system in an industrial establishment.

1. **Expensive:** The installation of a Cost Accounting system is quite expensive which only large organizations can afford. It is also argued that the introduction of such a system will involve additional expenditure which will lead to the reduction of profits of the organization.

   A costing system must be treated as an investment and the benefits derived on account of this should be more than the expenditure incurred on it. It should not prove to be a drag on the finances of the organization. From an economic point of view, the maintenance of the records should be kept to the minimum considering the need and use of each record.

2. **Unnecessary:** It is felt that the introduction of cost accounting system involves duplication of work. It is based on the presumption that a good number of concerns are running prosperously without any system of cost accounting. This may be true in a few cases. However, in the globalised world of today, it is absolutely necessary to conduct business with utmost efficiency; the management needs to know detailed cost information on continuous basis for its decision making. Only a properly installed costing system can serve such a need of the management and thus help in the efficient conduct of the business.
3. **Inapplicable:** There is an argument that the modern methods of cost accounting are not applicable to certain types of industries. This argument is not correct. The fault lies in an attempt to introduce a ready made costing system in an industry. A costing system need to be specially tailored in accordance with the requirements of the concerned business.
4. **Variance in results:** The results shown by the cost accounts differ materially from those shown by the financial accounts. Preparation of reconciliation statement frequently becomes necessary to verify their accuracy. It may be pointed out that differences between results shown by cost accounts and financial accounts arise on account of over and under –absorption of overheads, methods of material pricing used and treatment of other incomes. An integrated system of accounts can help in elimination of such differences. The costing is necessary for each manufacturer as each manufacturing process requires the consumption of material, labour etc.

In this age of competition and globalization, a manufacturer must know the exact cost not only of each item of the product but also of each process involved in its production so that he may be in a position to avoid waste and so minimize its cost of operation. To make the system a success, the utility of the system need to be explained to the management and the active cooperation of the employees should be sought by convincing them that the system is for the betterment of *all.*

Techniques of Costing

In addition to the methods of costing, the following techniques of costing are used by the management for the purposes of controlling costs and making managerial decisions. These techniques can be applied along with any of the methods of costing.

1. **Marginal Costing:** it is a technique of costing in which allocation of expenditure to production is restricted to those expenses which arise as a result of production. It means direct material, direct wages, direct expenses, and variable overheads. Fixed overheads are excluded .This technique is useful in manufacturing industries with varying levels of output.

2. **Differential costing:** It is the technique of comparing cost of two alternatives for the purpose of deciding which alternative is the best. The technique makes a distinction between fixed and variable cost and also considers semi-fixed costs. It is a useful technique for 'Accept-Reject decisions' and for 'Selection of Alternatives'.
3. **Standard costing:** Standard costing is a system under which the cost of the product is ascertained in advance on the basis of certain pre-set standards. Standard cost is predetermined as target of performance and actual performance is measured against the standard. The difference between standard and actual cost is analysed to know the causes of the difference so that remedial measures could be suggested and executed.
4. **Historical costing:** It is the ascertainment of cost by actuals. It may be in the nature of (a) Post costing, or (b) Continuous costing.
   (a) **Post costing:** It implies ascertainment of cost after the production is completed. This is done by analyzing the financial accounts at the end of the period in such a way as to disclose the cost of the units which have been produced. This method is useful only for ascertaining cost of a product/service but not useful in exercising any control over cost. It can act as a guiding point for production in future provided working conditions remain same in the future.
   (b) **Continuous costing:** Cost is ascertained as soon as the job is completed or even when the job is in progress. This is done usually by charging the job or product with actual expenditure on materials and wages and estimated share of overheads. Thus, the cost ascertained is not exact. However, cost information could be provided to the management promptly thereby enabling to take the necessary remedial measures before it is too late. This method neither provides any standard for judging current efficiency nor does it disclose what the cost of the job ought to have been.
5. **Direct costing:** The approach of charging all direct costs to operation or products, leaving all indirect costs to be written off against profits in the period in which they arise, is termed as direct costing. This technique is different from marginal costing as some fixed costs can be considered as direct costs in appropriate circumstances.
6. **Absorption (Total) costing:** The approach of charging all costs, both variable as well as fixed, to operations, products or processes is termed as absorption costing. " a method of costing by which all direct costs and applicable overheads are charged in products or cost centre to find out the total cost of production. Absorbed cost includes production cost as well as administrative and other costs."
7. **Activity based costing:** It is primarily used for the apportionment of overhead costs in an organization having products that differ in volume

and complexity of production. The overhead costs are identified with each activity which acts as cost driver (which is the reason for the incurrence of overhead cost). Such cost drivers may be Purchase orders, Stores requisitions, Power consumed, Machine time etc. Having determined the overhead cost with each cost centre, cost per unit of cost driver can be ascertained. The overhead cost can then be assigned to jobs on the basis of number of activities required for their completion. The Activity Base Costing can be defined as a technique which involves identification of costs with each cost driving activity and making it as the basis for recovery of costs over different products or jobs. CIMA defines it as a technique of, "cost attribution to cost units on the basis of benefits received from indirect activities i.e. ordering, setting up, and assuring quality."

8. **Throughput Accounting:** it is "a method of performance measurement which relates production and other costs to throughput. In throughput accounting product costs relate to usage of key resources by various products. Throughput represents amount of material put through a process especially in a specified period of time."
9. **Uniform costing:** The standardized principles and methods of cost accounting are applied by a number of different companies and firms. The standardization may extend to the Method of costing, Accounting, classification including codes, methods of defining costs and charging depreciation, methods of allocating or apportioning overheads to cost centers/units. This technique makes inter-firm comparisons possible and realistic pricing policies can be adopted.

Costing systems and techniques can be used with any of the methods of costing discussed in the following pages.

Methods of Costing

Different methods of cost finding are applied as businesses vary in their nature and in the type of products or services they produce/provide. The cost of output needs to be ascertained with due regard to method of production and the unit of cost used. Specific Order costing and Operation costing are the main systems of cost finding.

(A) Specific Order Costing

It is employed in cases where the items of prime cost are traceable to specific jobs or orders. House building, ship building, etc are some of the examples of Specific Order costing. It includes Job costing, Batch costing and Contract costing. Each job/Batch/ Contract is authorized by specific order.

1. **Job costing:** Costs are collected and accumulated for each job, project or work order independently. Each job is a separate cost unit. Each job is distinct, and it is to be costed separately.
2. **Contract costing:** A contract is a big job in terms of cost involved and time required to complete it. Each contract is a separate cost unit. Each contract is distinct, and it is to be costed separately. Costs are collected and accumulated for each contract independently. A separate account is maintained for each individual contract. Each contract is like a mini Profit and Loss account. It gives costs and profitability of each contract. This method is used in house building, civil engineering works, plant installations, ship building etc. Thus, it can be stated that contract work is in general site-based.

   Job costing and contract costing are also known as 'Terminal Costing'.
3. **Cost plus costing:** In contracts where in addition to 'Cost' and an agreed sum or percentage to cover overheads and profit is paid to the contractor, the method is termed as cost plus costing. The term 'cost' includes material, labour, and expenses incurred directly in the process of production. The method is used usually in cases where the job is NEW for the contractor or where Government happens to be the contractee.
4. **Batch costing:** A batch is a group of similar products or a number of small orders processed or manufactured together as a single set/unit. Each batch is produced according to specific instructions and is to be costed separately. The cost per unit can be ascertained by dividing the total cost of producing the batch by the total number of identical units constituting the batch. Batch costing is applicable to Confectionary, Pharmaceuticals, Production of spare/machine parts, ready-made garments, processed food etc.

(B) Operation Costing

It consists of costing methods applicable to standardized goods and services entailing repeated and continuous operations or processes. All costs are first charged to individual operation or process. Cost of a product is ascertained by accumulating cost of its each process. Process costing and operating costing are examples of operation costing. In case it is impossible to trace the items of prime cost to a particular order because their identity is lost in manufacturing operations, the Process costing is used. In a refinery where several tonnes of oil are being produced at the same time, the prime cost of a specific order of say, five tonnes cannot be traced. The cost can be found out only by finding out the cost per tonne of total oil and then multiplying it by five.

1. **Process costing:** Output of one process is input for the next process. Each process produces identical units. Process Account for each process

is prepared. Total cost incurred at a process divided by total number of units produced at the process gives cost per unit at the process. As the products are manufactured in continuous processes, this is called continuous costing. Final output is obtained at the conclusion of the final process. There may be losses and wastages at different processes. Some of the products may be produced jointly. By-products may also arise in the course of manufacturing.

2. **Operation costing:** Production process of a product is separated into different operations. Each operation is costed separately. The system is used when large number of standardized units is produced under iterative or repetitive conditions. It involves simultaneous production of different parts of a product through the use of different operations. The cost unit may be a component or the operation involved in production. The total cost of all components or operations in obtaining the final finished product gives cost of the product.
3. **Unit costing (Output costing or Single costing):** The undertaking produces standardized products in large number. Manufacturing is continuous and the units produced are identical. The cost per unit is determined by dividing the total cost incurred by the total number of units produced. Detailed cost sheet is prepared periodically for each product. Unit costing method is applicable in mining, oil drilling, cement works, brick works, breweries, steel production etc. In these cases there is a natural or standard unit of cost. The production is costed as a single process. This is why this method is also called 'Single Operation Costing'.
4. **Operating costing (Service costing):** It is used for undertakings providing service rather than producing tangible products and for the service of departments of undertakings. Services could be Passenger/ Goods transport, Power Generation, Education, Hospital, Hotel, Water Works, Gas supply, etc. An appropriate cost unit is selected as per the nature of the service. It usually consists of a Compound/Composite cost unit such as Passenger-kilometer, Ton-kilometer, Per Guest per day, and Per Patient per bed per day.
5. **Departmental Costing:** It refers to a situation where cost of the output of each department as a cost centre is ascertained separately. Total cost of the department divided by the number of units produced in the department gives cost per unit. The method is useful when output or service performed by a department is uniform. A departmental rate per unit of output or service is ascertained and applied to all jobs passing through the department. Computation of cost of products may, thus, involve multiple costing.

6. **Composite costing (Multiple costing):** Some products are so complex (e.g. motor cars, aeroplanes, cycles, radio etc) that no single system of costing is applicable. Where total cost is ascertained by aggregating component costs which are collected by both job and process costing, the system is termed multiple or composite costing. It applies to agricultural machineries, general hosiery, electrical accessories, etc.

It may therefore, be inferred that the methods of batch, contract and cost plus costing are only the variants of the 'job costing', while the methods of unit, operation and operating costing are only the variants of 'Operation costing'. Following table showing different methods of costing is self explanatory:

Table showing Different Methods of Costing with Final Cost Units

Type of Product	Basic Costing	Alternative Term	Ascertainment of Cost	Name of Industry	Final Cost Unit
1. Product made to customer's order	JOB	Terminal, Batch or Contract	Each order or Job	Furniture Ship-Building Books Building Pharmaceuticals Case making Road Construction	Per Unit, Per Ship, Per Order, Per Book Per Contract, Per thousand litre, Pack Per case Per Km.
2. Single and Uniform	PROCESS	Single or Unit or Output	Average per unit produced	Colliery Brick works Milling Transport Paints	Per tonne Per thousand Per bag Per tonne-Kilometer Per litre, Pack
3. Varied type Produced by Series of processes	PROCESS	Single or Unit or Output	Average per unit at each process	Chemicals Soap-works Oil refinery Jam, Cocoa & Brewery	Per litre Per kg or litre Per kg , litre or tonne Per kg or litre
4. Varied type but highly complex in nature	Both JOB and PROCESS	Multiple or Composite	Each component costed and aggregated to give final cost of complete product	Motor cars Radio sets Aircraft Cycle	Per car Per set Per Craft Per cycle

LET US RECAPITULATE

1. Main accounting systems in the modern times are (i) Financial Accounting, (ii) Cost Accounting, and (iii) Management Accounting.
2. The financial accounting facilitates recording of cash and credit transactions of a business according to the nature of expenditure and income so as to enable the

preparation of Profit and Loss Account for a period and the Balance Sheet on a specific date.

3. Financial accounting does not provide cost data to predetermine the price/quotation of the product/contract or order to be manufactured or the service being rendered to the consumers.
4. The recording and accounting for wages and labour is not done for different jobs, processes, products, departments. This creates problems in analyzing the cost associated with various activities and rewarding workers and employees for the above-normal performance.
5. Financial accounts safeguard the interests of the business, its proprietors, shareholders, present and prospective creditors and the government, especially Income-Tax, Excise and other authorities.
6. Cost accounts render information for the guidance of the management for proper planning, operation, control, profitability and decision-making.
7. Cost accounting provides financial statements for mangers for internal management whereas financial accounting is intended for external stakeholders.
8. The installation of a costing system is quite expensive which only large organizations can afford.
9. In the globalised world of today, it is absolutely necessary to conduct business with utmost efficiency; the management needs to know detailed cost information on continuous basis for its decision making. Only a properly installed costing system can serve such a need of the management and thus help in the efficient conduct of the business.
10. The cost department nowadays is an integral part of Accounting Division and all the accounting work is integrated for the purposes of cost ascertainment, cost control, preparation of final statements, managerial decision making and submission of information required by the management.

OBJECTIVE TYPE QUESTIONS

I. Fill in the blank spaces with suitable word/s :

1. Any technique or process to ascertain the cost of a product or service is known as ....
2. Main function of cost accounting is reporting to ....
3. In cost accounting, abnormal costs are transferred to ....
4. Method of costing used in building construction is known as ....
5. In cement industry, Method of costing used is known as ....
6. In Cinemas, ... is used.
7. In .... costing, cost of a group of products is ascertained.
8. Method of costing used in continuous production industries is known as ....

9. Ascertainment of costs after they have been incurred is known as ....
10. Under .... costing technique, only variable costs are charged to product cost.
11. Method of costing used in textile mills is known as ....
12. .... is the formal mechanism by means of which cost of products are ascertained.

Answers :

1. Costing	**2.** Management
3. Costing Profit and Loss account	**4.** Contract costing
5. Process costing	**6.** Operating costing
7. Batch	**8.** Process
9. Historical	**10.** Marginal
11. Process costing	**12.** Cost Accounting

II. Indicate whether the following statements are True or False :

1. Cost accounting is a branch of financial accounting.
2. Cost accounting can be used only in manufacturing concerns.
3. Cost control is a part of cost accountancy.
4. Cost audit is a part of cost accountancy.
5. Costing, cost accounting and cost accountancy are synonymous.
6. Costing information has to be provided to shareholders in annual report..
7. Costing is cost finding by any technique or process.
8. Main purpose of cost accounting is to maximise profits.
9. A prosperous business does not need a costing system.
10. Cost accounting may be used in educational institutions like schools, colleges and universities.
11. Cost and expense are synonyms.
12. Cost accounting is a part of financial accounting.
13. Financial accounting is meant for external reporting while Cost accounting is meant for internal reporting.
14. Costing is exactly the same thing as Cost accounting.
15. Single costing and output costing are synonymous.
16. A firm manufacturing bicycles may use multiple costing.
17. When a number of firms make use of the same method of costing, it is known as unit costing.
18. Marginal costing is a technique of cost control.
19. In chemical works, process costing is used.
20. In ship building, process costing is used.
21. In painting and decoration work, batch costing is used.
22. Cost audit is a part of cost accountancy.
23. In electricity companies, job costing should be used.
24. Standard costing is used only in large manufacturing companies.
25. Standard cost is a historical cost.

Answers :

1. False	**2.** False	**3.** True	**4.** True
5. False	**6.** False	**7.** True	**8.** False
9. False	**10.** True	**11.** False	**12.** False
13. True	**14.** False	**15.** True	**16.** True
17. False	**18.** False	**19.** True	**20.** False
21. False	**22.** True	**23.** False	**24.** False
25. False			

THEORETICAL EXERCISES

1. Discuss briefly the meaning and role of cost accounting in a manufacturing concern.

2. Explain why is it necessary to devise different methods of costing for different industries and list the various methods employed.

3. What is a cost centre and how does it differ from a department of a factory?

4. Explain the concept of cost. How does it differ from expense?

5. What are the main advantages derived from the installation of a costing system in a manufacturing company?

6. Costing methods are classified according to nature of operations. Explain.

7. Explain the points of difference between Cost Accounting and Financial accounting.

8. What are the limitations of financial accounting? How cost accounting overcomes these limitations?

9. Explain the important objectives of cost accounting. **[DU, B.Com (Hons.) 1997]**

10. What is cost Accounting? Discuss briefly its important function in a business firm. **[DU, B.Com (Hons.) 1998]**

11. "Cost accounting has come to be an essential tool of the management." Comment on the Statement. **[DU, B.Com (Hons.) 2000]**

12. "Limitations of financial accounting have made the management to realize the importance of cost accounting." Comment on the Statement. **[DU, B.Com (Hons.) 2003]**

13. What are the main objectives of cost accounting?

14. "Need for cost accounting arises due to limitations of financial accounting". Discuss.

15. What arte the points of difference between financial Accounting and cost accounting? What are the characteristics of an efficient cost accounting system? Explain the considerations to be borne in mind while installing a cost accounting system?

16. Explain the important difficulties in installing a costing system.

17. "Cost accounting is a system of foresight and not a postmortem examination. It turns losses into profits, speeds up activities and eliminates waste". Discuss.

18. Discuss the role of a cost accountant in a manufacturing organization.

19. "Cost accounting has come to be an essential tool of the management". Discuss.

❑❑❑

2

Classification of Cost

Learning Objectives

It attempts to explain Cost and its Classification. In this chapter you will learn :

1. The concept of cost
2. Classification of cost
3. Elements of cost
4. Cost Sheet
5. Linking of costs with cost centres and cost units

The Concept of Cost

Generally, 'Cost' means a sacrifice measured in money. In cost accounting, it has a specific meaning. It is the amount of expenditure incurred on a specific thing or activity. "Cost is a measurement in monetary terms of the amount of resources used for some purpose." "Cost of an article has two components: Quantity and Price.

The term 'Cost' refers to the resources sacrificed or foregone to achieve a specific objective. It represents the expenditure which has been made or incurred for an economic benefit. There can be three situations in regard to such benefit: (i) It may have already been received; (ii) it is yet to be received; and (iii) the possibility of receiving the benefits may have been lost. The Company takes a fire insurance policy on its building on September 1, 2008 by paying a premium of ₹ 6,000. As on 31.03.2009 the company has already used the insurance cover for seven months. While the benefit of insurance cover for the remaining five months is yet to be received. In this case the total cost of the insurance policy is ₹ 6,000. However, the amount of expense is only ₹ 3,500 i.e. 6,000 × 7/12 and the amount of unexpired or deferred cost is ₹ 2,500. If it is found that in the next financial year 2009-10 the insurance company has gone into liquidation and it will not be possible to get the benefit for the next five months, the amount of unexpired cost will be treated as Loss.

Expense

When benefits are actually received, the cost becomes an expense. An expense is defined as a cost that has given benefit and has now expired. Unexpired costs that can give future benefits are categorized as assets e.g. prepaid insurance, rent paid in advance etc. The term 'Loss' refers to the excess of expenses over revenues for a period. It may also be the excess of cost of an asset over its related sale proceeds. This occurs when the asset is sold, discarded or destroyed.

A cost objective is any activity for which a separate measurement of costs is desired. Examples of cost objectives include the cost of a product, the cost of providing a service to a bank customer or hospital patient, the cost of operating a department or sales territory or indeed anything for which one wants to measure the resources used.

Cost Unit

'Cost Unit' or 'Unit of Activity' is "a unit of quantity of product, service or time or a combination of these in relation to which costs may be ascertained or expressed". In case of job costing, cost unit is a single specific order; in batch costing, it is a batch of homogenous products; in contract costing a contract itself is a cost unit; in process industries it is the process or operation whose cost is ascertained.

An appropriate cost unit should be selected keeping in view the followings:

- It should be natural to the business.
- It should be readily understood and accepted by all concerned.
- It should be same as followed through out the industry or service sector.
- It should be uniformly maintained over a period of time and should be same for similar products.
- It should be of same size which is used for selling the product in wholesale.
- The size of the cost unit is determined keeping the nature of the product or service. In case of gold, cost unit can be 10 gram, for chemicals it is per kilogram, for steel it is per ton. In case of bricks, it is 1,000 bricks. Per ton in case of gold will be too big cost unit, and 10 gram in case of steel will be too small.

Cost units are of two types :

(i) **Simple:** It measures just one characteristic such as length or volume or area or weight. Cost unit for measuring products is mostly simple cost unit.

(ii) **Composite:** It measures two or more characteristics simultaneously. Cost per passenger-kilometer or cost per ton-kilometer, or per patient, per bed, per day. Composite cost units are mostly applicable in case of services.

Cost Centre

A cost centre is a location, person or item of equipment in respect of which costs may be ascertained and related to cost units for control purposes. In order to obtain the cost of a product or service, expenses should be appropriately segregated and charged to cost centres. In a factory, cost centre may be production cost centre, service cost centre, and service_cum_production centre.

Production cost centre: it includes departments that arte directly engaged in manufacturing activity and contribute to the content and form of the finished product. Cutting, Assembly and Finishing departments are typical examples of a production cost centre.

Service cost centre: It provides service or assistance to other departments. It contributes indirectly to the production process and does not shape the finished product. Maintenance department, Steam department, Power department Personnel department are some of the examples of this category.

Service-cum-Production centre: It is a hybrid cost centre. Primarily, it is a service centre but at times it may undertake some production work also. A glaring example is that of a Tools Department producing dies and jigs as well as servicing tools.

Classification of Cost

It is the process of arranging items into groups according to their degree of similarity. It is the arrangement of items in logical groups having regard to their nature or the purpose of to be fulfilled. Thus, it could be subjective classification or objective classification. The subjective classification indicates nature of expenditure and the objective classification indicates where the expenditure is to be charged.

Objectives of Classification

1. Classification of costs into fixed and variable helps in break-even analysis.
2. It also helps in preparation of flexible budgets.
3. It helps the management in decision making.
4. The classification of costs into controllable and uncontrollable helps in controlling costs.
5. Classification of costs into product and period costs helps in computing product cost.

Costs may be classified according to nature and a number of other characteristics, such as (i) Nature or Element; (ii) Traceability; (iii) Function; (iv) Variability; (v) Controllability; (vi) Normality; (vii) Time; (viii) Decision-making; and (ix) Analytical.

(A) Element of Cost

A cost consists of three elements i.e. material, labour and expense. Each of these elements may be direct or indirect:

I. Direct Costs = Direct Material + Direct labour + Direct Expense

II. Indirect Costs = Indirect Material + Indirect labour + Indirect Expense

(i) Material Cost

Material cost is "the cost of commodities supplied to an undertaking." Materials may be direct or indirect.

(a) Direct Material: Material that can be conveniently and easily identified with and can be directly allocated to a particular product, job, process or department. Timber used in furniture, Refill used in pen, Paper used in a book, gold or silver used in jewellery are some of the indicative examples of direct material.

(b) Indirect Material: Material that cannot be conveniently identified with and cannot be directly allocated to a particular product, job, process or department. Nails used in furniture, Thread used in stitching, Lubricant oil and grease used in manufacturing are some of the examples of indirect material.

(ii) Labour Cost

(a) Direct labour: Labour cost that can be conveniently identified with and can be directly allocated to a particular product, job, process or department is known as direct labour. Carpenter in furniture unit, Baker in baking unit, Halwai in confectionery unit, Washer in Dry cleaning unit are some of the indicative examples of direct labour.

(b) Indirect labour: Labour cost that cannot be conveniently identified with and cannot be directly allocated to a particular product, job, process or department is known as indirect labour. Labour employed in security department, Labour employed in repairs and maintenance department, Labour employed in machine shop such as tool setters, fitters and cleaners, are some of the indicative examples of indirect labour.

(iii) Expenses

(a) Direct Expense: All direct costs other than direct materials and direct labour are marked as direct expenses. Such costs can be conveniently identified with and directly allocated to a product, job, processes or department. Cost of special mould and design, Excise duty / Royalty based on output produced are some of the indicative examples of direct expense.

(b) Indirect Expense: All indirect costs other than indirect materials and indirect labour are marked as indirect expenses. Such costs cannot be conveniently identified with and cannot be directly allocated to a product, job, processes or department. Telephone expenses, Rent and Taxes of the building, Repairs/insurance/depreciation of building, plant and machinery and furniture are some of the indicative examples of indirect expense.

(B) Traceability

Costs are classified as direct and indirect costs on the basis of their identification with particular jobs, products or processes.

(i) Direct cost: It is a cost which can be directly, identified with a product, process or department. Materials used and labour engaged in manufacturing an article are most common examples of direct costs.

(ii) Indirect cost: It is not traceable to any particular product, process or department, but is common to different products, processes or departments. Factory rent or insurance of factory building are typical examples of indirect costs.

The distinction between direct and indirect costs hinges upon whether or not the cost can be identified with the activity or other relevant cost unit. The nature of business and cost unit chosen determine which are direct and which are indirect costs. Direct costs are allocated whereas indirect costs are apportioned to different jobs, products or services on a suitable criterion.

(C) Functional Classification of Costs

Costs are classified according to the purpose for which they are incurred and leads to the grouping of costs according to the broad divisions of activity into production cost, administration cost, selling cost, distribution cost and research and development costs:

(i) **Production cost:** It is the cost of the process which begins with supplying materials, labour and services and ends with primary packing of the product. All the relevant expenses are collected and further sub-divided to arrive at the production cost. It includes cost of materials, labour, factory rent, power and lighting, depreciation of plant, etc.

(ii) **Administration cost:** It is the cost of formulating the policy, directing the organization, and controlling the operations of an undertaking, which is not directly related to research, development, production, distribution or selling activity or function. It includes accounts office expenses, audit fee, legal expenses, directors' remuneration, etc.

(iii) **Selling cost:** It is the cost of creating and stimulating demand and of securing orders. It includes remuneration of salesperson, advertisement, showroom expenses, cost of samples, etc.

(iv) **Distribution cost:** It is the cost of the sequence of operations which starts with making the packed product available for dispatch and ends with the reconditioned returned empty package available for reuse. It includes distribution packing, carriage outward costs, upkeep of delivery vans, etc.

(v) **Research and development costs:** It is the cost of searching for new or improved products. Development costs are the costs incurred between the decision to produce a new improved product and the commencement of full and formal manufacture of the product.

(D) Variability

Costs are classified according to their behaviour in relation to changes in volume of production. Within a normal range of output (level of activity), costs are (i) Fixed, (ii) Semi-fixed; and (iii) variable.

(i) **Fixed:** It is a cost which tends to be unaffected by variations in volume of output. Rent, insurance of factory buildings, depreciation, etc., remain constant irrespective of the number of units produced in different months. In marginal costing, fixed costs are not a part of product cost and are charged to Costing Profit and loss Account.

(ii) **Semi-fixed or Semi-variable:** It is that cost which is partly fixed and partly variable. A part of semi-variable cost remains fixed and the other part varies directly with the activity level. Step cost, which remains fixed within a range of activity and increases in steps, is another variety of semi-variable cost.

(iii) **Variable:** It is a cost which tends to vary directly with level or volume of activity or output. Direct materials cost, direct wages, and direct expenses and variable overheads are definitely variable costs.

(E) Normality

Costs can be classified into normal costs and abnormal costs. The distinction between normal and abnormal costs is important for cost ascertainment under all methods of costing.

Normal Costs: All costs which can be planned or budgeted are normal costs. These costs arise in the day to day operation of the business. They are anticipated. They are unavoidable if the business operations are to continue. They are of recurring nature. They are part of routine business activity. Direct material, direct labour, direct expenses and indirect factory expenses and other overhead costs which take place in routine operations are normal costs. Similarly, all those losses which can be anticipated and budgeted are normal losses. Normal losses recur with quite regularity and are unavoidable.

Abnormal Costs: All costs which cannot be planned or budgeted are normal costs/losses. These are totally unanticipated, and are not provided for. They are just like bolt from the blue. Losses arising out of fire, accidents, floods, theft, strikes, war, civil riots etc. are some of the examples of abnormal losses.

Accounting Treatment: All normal costs/losses must always be charged to the product or service because they can be anticipated, occur regularly and cannot be avoided. If they are not recovered from the product or service, the cost will be underestimated and the customer may be undercharged. It will affect the profitability of the firm. The firm may be forced to close down. Inclusion of normal costs/losses in the cost structure is also necessary for cost planning, cost control, budgeting and profit planning.

Normal may be charged to the product by distributing them over normal output. This process is grossing up. A wagon load of 28 tons of coal is purchased from the pit head at a price of ₹ 94,500. However, 27 tons of coal reaches because one ton usually gets pilfered in transit. The cost of 28 tons is to be distributed over normally recovered weight of 27 tons. Thus, cost per ton should be taken as ₹ 3,500 (i.e. 94,500/27) per ton and not ₹ 3,375 (i.e. 94,500/28) per ton. On some other occasion, the coal actually realized from the wagon coal of 28 ton is 25 tons, it implies there is an abnormal loss of two tons, and the cost per ton must be taken as ₹ 3,500 only. Abnormal loss of ₹ 7,000 (i.e. 3,500 × 2) is to be charged to costing Profit & Loss Account. If coal realized is 27.4 tons, even then the cost per ton shall remain ₹ 3,500 and abnormal gain of ₹ 1,400 (i.e. 3,500 × 0.4) is to be credited to Costing Profit & Loss Account. Thus, it is absolutely clear; cost per unit must always be computed as if only normal cost/loss has been incurred. It must never be influenced by an abnormal gain or abnormal loss.

(F) Controllability

Costs are classified according to whether or not they are influenced by the action of the designated member of the undertaking. These costs may be controllable, and uncontrollable.

(i) **Controllable cost:** It is said to be controllable when the amount of cost incurred can be influenced by the action of a specified member of an undertaking. The specified member may be a manger or a supervisor of the undertaking.

(ii) **Uncontrollable cost:** It is that cost which cannot be influenced by the action of a specified member of the undertaking is known as uncontrollable cost.

The distinction between controllable and uncontrollable costs depends upon a point of reference. An item of cost may be uncontrollable at one level of management but the same item may be controllable at another level of management. Almost all costs are controllable at some level of management. Such segregation of costs facilitates in fixing the responsibilities of different executives for unfavorable cost variances. An executive should be held responsible only for those costs which are under his control.

(G) Time Basis

Costs can be classified on the basis of time as historical cost and predetermined cost.

(i) Historical cost: It relates to events which have already happened. Costs are incurred and recorded only after the work has been accomplished. Accumulation of costs for a product produced, job performed or a contract fully or partially completed etc., are examples of historical cost.

Features of historical cost:

- It is based on recorded data.
- It is reliable as it is supported by documentary evidence.

- It is objective due to the very fact that occurrence of the event has been observed.
- Information relating to it is available in the financial records.

(ii) Pre-determined cost: It is established before the occurrence of the event, i.e. before the completion of production. It is based on analysis, guidelines, and forecasts. It represents what is expected to happen or what should happen. It is usually scientifically ascertained by using costing, engineering, and statistical techniques. Budgeted costs, estimates, standard cost, replacement cost, overhead recovery rates, etc. are all examples of pre-determined cost.

Historical as well as pre-determined costs are mutually complimentary. Historical costs measure the cost of past events. They are guide to future costs. They constitute the initial point for arriving at the pre-determined cost. Pre-determined costs are essentially required for planning, control, and performance appraisal.

(H) Decision-Making

For the purpose of managerial decision-making costs may be sub-divided into two broad categories: (i) Relevant, and (ii) Irrelevant. Relevant costs are those costs which are relevant for decision making (i.e. course to be adopted in the future) such as marginal cost, differential cost, opportunity costs, etc. Relevant costs are future-oriented incremental cash flows. Irrelevant costs are those costs which have no impact on the decision, e.g. absorbed fixed costs, sunk costs, committed costs, etc.

(i) Relevant cost: Such portion of total cost which differs under different alternatives. The dismantling cost of old machine is a relevant cost in the case of decision relating to replacement of old machine.

Some of the relevant costs are discussed:

(a) Marginal cost: It is the sum of variable costs (i.e. Prime cost + Variable Overheads). It is relevant for decision making as this will be incurred in future whereas fixed costs will remain unchanged and hence irrelevant. However, if fixed cost also changes, such fixed cost becomes relevant for decision making.

(b) Replacement cost: It is the cost of replacement at current market price and is definitely relevant for decision making. It is the cost at which there could be purchase of an asset or material identical to that which is being replaced.

(c) Out of pocket cost: It is the cost in terms of outflow of cash due to a particular managerial decision. It includes both the present as well as future outflow of cash due to a managerial decision. Depreciation does not involve cash and hence is not a part of out-of-pocket costs.

(d) Opportunity cost: It refers to the alternative foregone. It is the maximum possible earning from the next best possible use of the alternative. Thus, it is the cost in terms of the value of benefit sacrificed from the next best possible alternative. It is the value of sacrifice involved in accepting the alternative under consideration.

(e) **Imputed costs:** These are notional costs appearing in cost accounts only. Notional costs are those costs, for which neither any transaction has taken place, nor any payment has been made or is yet payable, but they represent a sacrifice or a resource use capable of being measured in terms of money. Writing of account books by the owner of the business, and use of personally-owned building for owned business are glaring examples of notional cost.
Where alternative capital investment projects are being evaluated, it is necessary to consider the imputed interest on capital before decision is arrived at as to which is the acceptable project.

(f) **Differential costs:** The difference in total costs between two alternatives is known as differential cost. In case the choice of an alternative results in increase in total costs, such increase in costs is known as 'Incremental costs'. In case the choice of an alternative results in decrease in total costs, such decrease in costs is known as 'Decremental costs'. While evaluating the profitability of a proposed change, the incremental costs are matched with the incremental revenue or decremental costs are matched with Decremental revenue. The proposed change is accepted only when it results in increase in relative profitability.

▣ **Example :** *A company is manufacturing 2,500 units of a product. The existing cost structure is as under:*

Selling price per unit: ₹ *40*
Variable cost per unit: ₹ *25*
Fixed costs: ₹ *30,000*

Following alternatives are placed before the management for decision making:

- ***Alternative I:*** *Accept an export order for another 500 units @* ₹ *30 per unit. The expenditure of the export order will increase the fixed costs by* ₹ *1,500.*
- ***Alternative II:*** *Reduce the production to 1,500 units and buy another 1,000 units from the market@* ₹ *27 per unit. This will result in decrease in fixed costs to* ₹ *25,000.*

Which alternative is preferable?

Solution : **Statement of Comparative Profitability**

Details	Existing Situation		Proposed Situation			
			Alternative I		Alternative II	
	Amount (₹)	Amount (₹)	Amount (₹)	Amount (₹)	Amount (₹)	Amount (₹)
Sales		1,00,000		1,15,000		1,00,000
Less: variable costs	62,500		75,000	1,06,500	64,500	89,500
Fixed costs	30,000	92,500	31,500		25,000	
Profit		7,500		8,500		10,500

Comments :

1. Existing Profit is ₹ 7,500.
2. Proposed situation-I gives a profit of ₹ 8,500. The incremental costs are ₹ 14,000 (i.e. 1,06,500 – 92,500) while the incremental revenue is ₹ 15,000. Hence, there is a net gain of ₹ 1,000 under the proposed situation-I as compared to existing situation.
3. In the proposed situation-II, the decremental costs are ₹ 3,000 (i.e. 92,500 – 89,500) while there is no change in revenue. Hence, there is a net gain of ₹ 3,000 as compared to the existing situation.
4. From the above, it is obvious that the company makes maximum profit under the proposed situation-II.

(ii) Irrelevant cost: Such portion of total cost which is same under different alternatives. It is unavoidable and is also known as sunk cost. Fixed cost is irrelevant in the case of decision of 'Make or Buy' or 'whether to purchase raw material or manufacture'.

Some of the irrelevant costs are discussed:

(a) **Sunk cost:** It is a past cost and is not relevant for decision making. It is caused by complete abandonment as against temporary shut-down. It is the written down the value of the abandoned plant less its salvage value.

(b) **Committed cost:** A cost which has been committed by the managerial decision in the past is irrelevant for a decision meant for future.

(c) **Absorbed fixed cost:** Fixed cost which does not change due to increase or decrease in activity is not relevant for decision making. Although fixed costs are absorbed in cost of production at a normal rate, such costs are irrelevant for managerial decision making.

(iii) Others :

(a) **Shut down cost:** It is the minimum fixed costs which an undertaking will have to incur during the period of temporary closure of the department, division or even the entire production activity of the organization. Certain fixed costs such as factory rent, insurance of the plant and machinery, have to be incurred. The shut down may require some additional costs, such as additional cost on security, maintaining public relations and advertisements explaining the shut down, etc. which were not required had the plant been operative.

(b) **Product cost/Inventoriable cost:** Product cost is associated with output and is considered to be reasonably attached to the units produced and matched against the revenues of the accounting period in which these units are sold. As it forms part of the value of inventories of finished and semi-finished unsold stock, it is also called inventoriable cost. Initially it is charged to the output, forms part of current assets of the business, and gets charged to an accounting year by becoming part of cost of goods sold in the year units of output are sold out. Direct material, direct labour and direct factory expenses are always taken as product costs. Variable factory overheads also constitute an integral part of product cost. Other costs may be treated as product cost or period cost depending on the method of accounting. Under absorption costing all costs are charged to the units produced, and this is why they are regarded as product cost. Only that part of total cost is charged to an accounting period which relates to goods sold during that period. Costs relating to unsold stock are carried forward to the next accounting period.

(c) **Period cost:** It is non-inventoriable cost because it is associated with a particular accounting period and is charged in *toto* against the revenues of the period in which such costs are incurred. No part of the period cost is carried forward to the next accounting year. It is not associated with output but is regarded as cost relating to the year in which such costs are incurred and are debited in its entirety to that year account irrespective of number of units produced and sold. Costs relating to research and development, office and administration, selling and distribution overheads and other fixed costs associated with lapse of time rather than output are regarded as period costs.

(d) **Conversion cost:** It is the cost of converting raw materials into finished product. It is the sum of direct labour, direct factory expenses and factory overheads. Thus, it is the production cost minus the direct material cost.

(e) **Explicit cost:** Cost which results from a transaction and is given in monetary terms. The payment has either been made for it or is yet to be made; there is no ambiguity in regard to its amount of costs. Most of the costs are of explicit nature, e.g., Wages, Salaries paid or payable, rent paid or payable, Commission on sales, etc.

(f) **Notional costs:** Notional costs are those costs, for which neither any transaction has taken place, nor any payment has been made or is yet payable, but they represent a sacrifice or a resource use capable of being measured in terms of money. Writing of account books by the owner of the business, and use of personally owned building for owned business are glaring examples of notional cost.

(g) **Implicit cost:** Implicit costs are those costs, for which neither any transaction has taken place, nor do they involve any payment in cash, but they do involve a sacrifice which is not capable of being measured in money, though it influences decision-making. It is the opportunity cost which cannot be measured in monetary terms. The relevant example is an option to doing some work may be just enjoying with friends or taking rest.

(h) **Common cost:** These are costs which are incurred collectively for a number of cost centres, and are to be suitably apportioned for ascertaining the cost of individual cost centre e.g. overheads incurred for a factory as a whole, combined purchase cost for purchasing several materials in one consignment, etc.

(i) **Joint cost:** It relates to two or more products produced from a common product process or element: material, labour or overhead or any combination thereof or so locked together that one cannot be produced without producing the other. While refining crude oil a number of products are produced, the costs incurred till these various products are separated from each other are termed as joint costs. It is joint till the point of split-off or separation.

The fundamental difference between joint cost and common cost is that joint costs are incurred only in case of process industries where a product cannot be produced independently i.e. the nature of manufacturing is such that out of the same process two or more products will be produced, while common costs may be incurred for all types of industries whether job or process. They may be incurred in addition to joint costs in the same industry.

(j) **Standard cost:** It is a predetermined cost which is computed in advance of production on the basis of specification of all the factors affecting cost and used in standard costing. It is a scientifically determined cost under specified set of circumstances. It is a management's well considered estimate prepared in advance of production of the cost of inputs that should be necessary to obtain a specific material, product or service.

(I) Analytical Approach

'Cost' is the sum of three groups or elements: (a) the purchase or transfer price of material, (b) the cost of hire of labour, and (c) the value of other disbursements made or expenditure incurred in achieving the desired product or result. The total expenditure consisting of material, labour and other expenses can be analysed as under:

Cost Structure

Element of Cost	Prime	Overheads	Total
Material	Direct Material Cost	Indirect Material Cost	Material Cost
Labour	Direct Labour Cost	Indirect Labour Cost	Labour Cost
Expenses	Direct Expenses	Indirect Expenses	Expenses
SUM =	Prime Cost	Overhead	Total Cost

Thus, Prime Cost is the sum of direct material cost, direct wages, and direct expenses; and Overhead is the sum of indirect material cost, indirect wages, and indirect expenses. Total cost is sum of prime cost and overhead.

(i) Prime Cost

It is the aggregate of direct material, direct labour and direct expenses.

Prime cost = Direct Material + Direct labour + Direct Expense

(ii) Overhead

It is the aggregate of indirect material, indirect labour and indirect expenses.

Overhead = Indirect Material + Indirect labour + Indirect Expense

(a) Works Overhead: It is the sum of indirect material cost, indirect wages, and indirect expenses incurred in the factory from the receipt of the order until its completion ready for dispatch.

(b) Administration Overhead: It is the sum of indirect material cost, indirect wages, and indirect expenses incurred in the direction, control and administration of an undertaking. The following groups of indirect items fall within the purview of administration overhead:

- Cost of indirect materials such as printing and stationery.
- Indirect wages such as office salaries including salaries of administrative directors, secretaries, accountants, credit approval, cash collection and treasurer's department.
- Rent, rates and insurance of general office; lighting, heating and cleaning of general office; bank charges. Depreciation and repairs of office building and equipment, legal charges, and audit fees, etc.

(c) Selling Overhead: It is the sum of indirect material, indirect wages, and indirect expenses incurred in promoting sales and retaining customers. The following groups of indirect items fall within the purview of administration overhead:

- Printing and stationery, mailing literatures, catalogues, price-lists, etc. constitute the category of indirect materials.
- Salaries, commission etc. of the salespersons, technical representatives and sales managers; selling department salaries constitute category of indirect wages.
- Indirect expenses such as advertising, rent, rates and insurance of showrooms and sales office, bad debts and collection charges, cash discount allowed, post-sale services, etc.

(d) Distribution Overhead: It is the sum of indirect material cost, indirect wages, and indirect expenses incurred with making the packed product available for dispatch and ends with making the reconditioned returned empty packages available for reuse. The following groups of indirect items fall within the purview of administration overhead:

- Packing cases, oil, grease, spare parts used in upkeep of delivery vehicles come under the category of indirect materials.

- Indirect wages such as wages of packers, delivery van drivers, dispatch clerks, etc.
- Carriage and freight outwards, rent rates, depreciation and insurance of warehouse, depreciation and running expenses of delivery vehicles, etc.

Cost Sheet or Cost Statement

Cost sheet or cost statement is that statement which is prepared to present the total costs of production in details during a given period. It provides information relating to cost per unit at different stages of completion of the product. Cost per unit is obtained by dividing the total cost by the number of units produced. A cost sheet will have separate columns for the total and the unit cost of each element of cost. Cost Sheet can be prepared on weekly, monthly or any other time period basis as desired by the management. At times standard cost data are also provided to facilitate comparison with the actual cost incurred. The cost sheet discloses the followings: (i) Prime Cost, (ii) Factory (Works) Cost, (iii)) Cost of Production, and (iv) Total Cost (Cost of Sales).

Advantages of Cost Sheet :

- It shows the total cost and cost per unit of the product produced during the given period.
- It facilitates control over the cost of production.
- It acts as a guide to the producer and helps him in formulating a definite and profitable production policy.
- It aids the management in fixing the selling price of the products.
- It helps the management in making a comparative study of the various components of cost with the past results and the pre-determined cost.

A specimen of Cost Sheet or Cost Statement is given hereunder:

Specimen of Cost Sheet

Cost Sheet for the period __________

Production_____Units

Details	Total Cost (₹)	Cost Per Unit (₹)
Direct Materials:		
Opening Stock…		
Purchases		
Freight on Purchases		
Less: Purchase Returns		
Net Purchases		
Less: Closing Stock….		
Less: Scrap		

(a) Direct Materials Consumed		
(b) Direct Wages		
(c) Direct Expenses		
I. Prime Cost (i.e. a + b + c)		
Add: ***Factory Overheads:***		
Indirect Materials		
Indirect Wages		
Loose Tools		
Rent and Rates (Factory)		
Lighting and Heating (Factory)		
Power and Fuel		
Repairs and Maintenance		
Cleaning		
Drawing Office Expenses		
Cost of Research and Experiments		
Depreciation of Factory Plant		
Works Stationery		
Welfare service expenses		
Insurance: Fixed assets etc.		
Stock and Finished goods		
Works Manager's salary		
II. Factory or Works Cost		
Add: ***Office and Administrative Overheads:***		
Rent and Rates (Office)		
Salaries (Office)		
Lighting and Heating		
Insurance of Office building and equipments etc.		
Telephone and Postages		
Printing and Stationery		
Depreciation of Furniture and Office Equipments, and Buildings		
Legal Expenses		
Audit fees		
Bank Charges		
III. Cost of Production or Cost of Goods Produced		
Add: ***Selling and Distribution Overheads:***		
Showroom Rent and Rates		
Lighting and Heating		
Salesmen's Salaries		

Commissions		
Traveling Expenses of Sales Representatives		
Sales Printing and Stationery		
Advertising		
Bad Debts		
Postage		
Depreciation and Expenses of Delivery Van including Delivery Van Driver's Salary		
Debt collection expenses		
Carriage freight outwards		
Samples and other free gifts		
IV. Cost of Sales		
Net Profit (or Loss) — Balancing Figure		
V. Sales		

Important Note: Items of expenses, which are in the nature of appropriation of profits, should not form part of the cost of a product. Such appropriations and expenses may be: Income Tax; Dividends to shareholders; Commission to Managing director/ Partners out of Profits; Capital Loss i.e. Loss arising out of sale of assets; Interest on Loan; Donations; Capital Expenditure; Discount on issue of shares and debentures; Underwriting expenses; Writing off goodwill, etc.

Total Cost Components

The ascertainment of total cost of a product or service passes through several stages. The successive stages, through which the costs flow give rise to major divisions of cost, are given below:

1. **Prime cost:** It consists of costs of direct material, direct labour, and direct expenses.
2. **Works cost:** It is the sum of prime cost and proportionate factory overheads.
3. **Cost of production:** It is the sum of works cost and proportionate office and administration overheads.
4. **Cost of goods sold:** It is the adjusted cost of production on account of opening and closing stock of finished goods.
5. **Cost of Sales (Total cost):** It is the sum of cost of goods sold and selling and distribution overheads.

Adjustments:

(a) **For Inventories:** Some adjustments are to be made on account of inventories at various stages of production:

1. *Stock of raw materials*: For the purpose of cost sheet, the value of materials consumed can be ascertained with the help of following formula:

   Value of materials consumed: = Opening stock of raw materials
   + Net Purchases + Expenses on purchase
   – Closing stock of raw materials

   Raw materials cost is always inclusive of all expenses incurred in getting raw materials to the factory.

2. *Stock of work-in-progress*: Incomplete units at the end of a period are called 'work-in-progress'. It may be valued at prime cost or works cost.

   = Works cost + Opening stock of work-in-progress
   – Closing stock of work-in-progress

3. *Stock of finished goods*: In order to find out the cost of goods sold, adjustment on account of stock of finished goods becomes necessary.

   = Cost of production + Opening stock of finished goods
   – Closing stock of finished goods

(b) For Other items:

1. *Scrap*: It is the incidental residue from certain types of goods manufactured. It is of small amount and low value, recoverable without further processing. Such recoverable value of scrap is deducted either from Production overheads or works cost.

2. *Spoilage and defectives*: It consists of goods that do not meet the production standards. Such goods are either sold for their salvage value or discarded without further processing. The cost of normal spoilage is borne by good units. The cost of abnormal spoilage is transferred to the Costing Profit and Loss Account.

   Goods that do not meet production standards and must be processed further to make them saleable as good units are called as defectives. Cost of rectification of normal defectives is charged to good units including those rectified. The entire cost of abnormal defectives is charged to Costing Profit and Loss Account.

3. *Sales tax (VAT)*: Sales tax or VAT is levied on sales. The firm has to deposit this amount with the tax authorities. It is deducted from the sales to arrive at Net Sales.

4. *Excise duty*: It is levied on production. It is treated as direct charge to production and is included in prime cost.

5. *Royalty*: It is a payment for the right to manufacture a product or the use of a process or technology. If royalty is paid on the basis of

production, it is a direct charge to production and included in prime cost. If royalty is paid on the basis of number of units sold, the amount is charged to selling overheads.

Computation of Profit

Profit may be computed as a percentage of cost or as a percentage of selling price. As a matter of convenience, it is advisable to take the given basis as equal to 100 and then proceed with the calculation work. Explanatory illustrations are given to emphasise the point:

▣ **Example 1 :**

Given,

Cost : *₹ 67,500*

Profit percentage : *8*

Basis of charge : *Cost*

Solution : Take cost = ₹100

Profit: ₹ 8 (i.e. 100 × 0.08)

Multiplier = 8/100 = 0.08

Profit on a cost of ₹ 67,500 is

= 67,500 × 0.08 ⇒ ₹ 5,400.

▣ **Example 2 :**

Given,

Cost : *₹ 67,500*

Profit percentage : *8*

Basis of charge : *Selling price*

Solution : Take Selling price = ₹100

Profit: ₹ 8 (i.e. 100 × 0.08)

Cost = 100 – 8 ⇒ ₹ 92

Multiplier = 8/92 = 2/23

Profit on cost price of ₹ 67,500 is

= [67,500 × (2/23)] ⇒ ₹ 5,869.57.

Verification :

Cost + Profit = Selling Price

67,500 + 5,869.57 = ₹ 73,369.57

Profit on a cost of ₹ 73,369.57is

= 73,369.57 × 0.08 ⇒ ₹ 5,869.57.

▣ **Example 3 :**

Given,

Selling price : *₹ 67,500*

Profit percentage : 8

Basis of charge : Cost

Solution : Take Cost price = 100

Profit: ₹ 8 (i.e. 100 × 0.08)

Cost + Profit = Selling Price

100 + 8 = ₹ 108

Multiplier = 8/108 = 2/27

Profit on a Selling of ₹ 67,500 is

= [67,500 × (2/27)] ⇒ ₹ 5,000.

Verification :

Selling Price – Profit = Cost

67,500 + 5,000 = ₹ 62,500

Profit on a cost of ₹ 62,500 is

= 62,500 × 0.08 ⇒ ₹ 5,000.

Linking Process

It is easy to charge direct costs to products, but difficult to charge indirect costs to products. The main stages in the process of linking such costs with cost centres and/or cost units are (a) cost classification, (b) cost allocation and apportionment, and (c) overhead absorption.

(a) Cost classification: Costs may be classified according to their nature and a number of other characteristics, such as function, variability, controllability and normality, etc.

(b) Cost allocation and apportionment: Cost allocation is the allotment of whole items of cost to cost centres or cost units. Cost apportionment is the allotment of proportions of items of cost to cost centres or cost units.

(c) Overhead absorption: It is the charging of overheads to cost units. It is the procedure involved in the allotment of overhead costs of a cost centre to the products or services on a suitable criterion, which that cost centre provides.

Illustration 2.1. *In a factory, a standard product is manufactured. From the following particulars, prepare a cost sheet showing total cost and profit made*:

Raw materials consumed ₹ 50,000 Labour ₹ 1,00,000.

Production overhead is charged at 60% of factory cost and office overhead is taken at 20% on total cost. The standard product sold during the period is 250 units @ ₹ 2,300 each.

Solution : **Cost Sheet**

(250 Units)

Details	Amount (₹)	Amount (₹)
Raw materials consumed	50,000	
Labour	1,00,000	
Prime cost		**1,50,000**
Add: Production overhead [0.6 (1,50,000/ 0.4)]		2,25,000
Factory cost		**3,75,000**
Add : Office overhead [0.2 (3,75,000/ 0.8)]		93,750
Cost of Goods Produced		**4,68,750**
Profit (Balancing figure)		1,06,250
Sales (250 × 2,300)		**5,75,000**

Illustration 2.2. *On June 30, 1997, a flash flood damaged the warehouse and factory of ABC Corporation completely destroying the work-in-progress inventory. There was no damage to either the raw materials or finished goods inventories. A physical verification taken after the flood revealed the following valuations:*

Details	*Amount (₹)*
Raw Materials	*62,000*
Work-in-progress	*?*
Finished Goods	*1,19,000*

The inventory on January 1, 1997 consisted of the followings:

Details	*Amount (₹)*
Raw Materials	*30,000*
Work-in-progress	*1,00,000*
Finished Goods	*1,40,000*
Total	*2,70,000*

A review of the books and records disclosed that the gross profit margin historically approximated 25% of sales. The sales for the first six months of 1997 were ₹ 3, 40,000. Raw Material purchases were ₹ 1, 15,000. Direct labour costs for this period were ₹ 80,000 and manufacturing overhead has historically been 50% of direct labour.

Compute the cost of work-in-progress inventory on June 30, 1997 by preparing a statement of cost and profit. **[DU, B.Com (Hons.) 1998]**

Solution : **Books of ABC Corporation**

Statement of Cost and Profit

Details		**Amount (₹)**
Raw Materials:		
Opening Stock of Raw Materials	30,000	
Add: Purchases	1,15,000	
Raw Materials Available for Consumption	1,45,000	
Less: Closing Stock of Raw Materials	62,000	
Raw Materials Consumed		83,000
Direct Labour		80,000
Prime Cost		**1,63,000**
Add: Manufacturing Overhead [0.5 × 80,000]		40,000
Current Factory Cost		2,03,000
Add: Opening work-in-progress		1,00,000
Less: Closing work-in-progress [*See Working note*]		69,000
Factory Cost		**2,34,000**
Add: Opening Stock of Finished Goods		1,40,000
Finished Goods available for Sale		3,74,000
Less: Closing Stock of Finished Goods		1,19, 000
Cost of Goods Sold = Cost of Sales		**2, 55,000**
Profit (Balancing Figure)		85,000
Sales		**3,40,000**

Working note :

1. Profit = (0.25 × 3,40,000) = ₹ 85,000

2. Calculation of Closing Work-in-Progress:

Details	**Amount (₹)**
1. Sales	3,40,000
2. *Less*: Profit	85,000
3. Cost of Sales	2,55,000
4. *Add*: Closing Stock of Finished Goods	1,19,000
5. Finished Goods available for Sale	3,74,000
6. *Less*: Opening Stock of Finished Goods	1,40,000
7. Factory Cost	2,34,000
8. *Less*: Cost before Closing Work-in-Progress	3,03,000
9. Closing Work-in-Progress [i.e. (8) – (7)]	**69,000**

Illustration 2.3. *The Standard Electrical Limited manufactures one product. A summary of its activities for the year 2008-09 is as under:*

Details		*Unit*	*Amount (₹)*
Sales		*40,000*	*10,00,000*
Material inventory:	*1.4.2008*		*50,000*
	31.3.2009		*40,000*
Work-in-Progress inventory:	*1.4.2008*		*70,000*
	31.3.2009		*90,000*
Finished goods Inventory:	*1.4.2008*	*8,000*	*80,000*
	31.3.2009	*12,000*	
Material Purchases			*1,90,000*
Direct Wages			*1,80,000*
Production Overheads			*1,40,000*
Selling and Distribution Expenses			*62,500*
General and Administration Expenses			*50,000*

Compute:

(i) The current manufacturing cost for the year 2008-09.

(ii) The total cost of goods manufactured (Finished), the number of units manufactured (Finished) and the cost per unit.

(iii) The cost of goods sold for the year presuming the company uses the LIFO inventory costing method for its finished goods inventory.

Solution :

Cost Sheet

(For the year 2008-09)

Output: 44,000 units

Details		**Amount (₹)**
Direct Materials:		
Opening Stock	50,000	
Add: Purchases	1,90,000	
Materials Available for consumption	2,40,000	
Less: Closing Stock	40,000	
Materials Consumed		2,00,000
Direct Wages		1,80,000
Prime Cost		**3.80.000**
Add: Production Overhead		1,40,000
Factory cost (Gross)		5,20,000
Add: Opening work-in- progress		70,000
		5,90,000

Less: Closing work-in- progress	90,000
Factory Cost (Net: Cost of goods manufactured)	5,00,000
Add: General and Administration Expenses	50,000
Cost of Production or Cost of Goods Produced	**5,50,000**
Add: Opening Stock of Finished Goods	80,000
Finished Goods Available for Sale	6,30,00
Less: Closing Stock of Finished Goods	1,30,000
Cost of Goods Sold	**5,00,000**
Selling and Distribution Expenses	62,500
Cost of Sales	**5,62,500**
Profit	4,37,500
Sales	**10,00,000**

Working Notes :

1. Number of units manufactured during the year:
   Sales + Closing stock of finished goods – Opening stock of finished goods = 40,000 + 12,000 – 8,000 ⇒ 44,000 units
2. Cost per unit of finished goods:
   = 5,50,000/44,000 ⇒ ₹ 12.50
3. Valuation of Closing Finished goods on LIFO Basis:

8,000 units @ ₹ 10	80,000
4,000 units @ ₹ 12.50	50,000
Total 12,000 units	1, 30,000

Illustration 2.4. *Cost of Sales of Product A is made up as under:*

Details	***Amount (₹)***
Materials used in Manufacturing	*54,000*
Materials used in Primary Packing	*10,000*
Materials used in Selling the Product	*1,500*
Materials used in Factory	*750*
Materials used in Office	*1,250*
Labour required in Producing	*10000*
Labour required for factory supervision	*2,000*
Direct expenses	*5,000*
Indirect expenses (Factory)	*1,000*
Administrative Expenses	*1,250*
Depreciation on Office Building and Equipment	*750*
Depreciation on Factory Building	*1,750*
Selling Expenses	*3,500*
Freight on Materials Purchased	*6,000*
Advertising	*1,250*

Assume that all goods manufactured are sold. What would be the selling price to obtain a profit of 20% on selling price?

Solution : **Fixation of Selling Price of a Product**

Details		Amount (₹)	Amount (₹)
Materials used in Manufacturing	54,000		
Materials used in Primary Packing	10,000		
Total Materials used		64,000	
Labour required in Producing		10,000	
Direct Expenses		5,000	
Prime cost			79,000
Factory Overheads:			
Materials Used in Factory		750	
Labour required for factory supervision		2,000	
Indirect Expenses		1,000	
Depreciation on Factory Building		1,750	
Freight On Materials Purchased		6,000	
Total Factory Overheads			11,500
Factory cost			90,500
Office Overheads:			
Materials used in office		1,250	
Administrative expenses		1,250	
Depreciation on office Building and Equipment		750	
Total Office Overheads			3,250
Cost of Production			93,750
Selling Overheads:			
Materials Used in selling		1,500	
Selling expenses		3,500	
Advertising		1,250	
Total of Selling Overheads			6,250
Cost of sales			1,00,000
Profit			25,000
Selling Price			**1,25,000**

Illustration 2.5.

Details	*Amount (₹)*	*Details*	*Amount (₹)*
Direct Materials	*1,20,000*	*Direct wages*	*3,0000*
Direct Expenses	*6,000*	*Wages of foremen*	*5,000*
Electric Power	*1,000*	*Store Keeper's wages*	*1,000*

Lighting: *Factory* 2000 *Office* 500	2,500	*Rent:* *Factory* 5,000 *Office* 3,000	8,000
Oil and water	500	*Carriage outwards*	500
Repairs and Renewals: *Factory Plant* 4000 *Office Premises* 500	4,500	*Depreciation:* *Factory Plant* 500 *Office Premises* 1500	2,000
Transfer to reserves	1,000	*Discount on issue of shares written off*	500
Consumable stores	2,000	*Manager's salary*	5,000
Director's fees	1,500	*Office stationery*	500
Telephone charges	500	*Postage and telegrams*	200
Salesmen salary	2,500	*Salesmen traveling Expenses*	300
Advertising	1,000	*Warehouse Charges*	500
Income tax	10,000	*Dividend Paid*	2,000
		Sales	2,30,000

Prepare Cost Sheet showing Prime Cost, Factory Cost, Cost of Production, Cost of Sales and Profit.

Solution : **Cost Sheet**

Details	Amount (₹)	Amount (₹)
Direct Materials	1,20,000	
Direct Wages	30,000	
Direct Expenses	6,000	
Prime cost		1,56,000
Factory Overheads:		
Store keeper's Wages	1,000	
Lighting	2,000	
Oil and water	500	
Repairs	4,000	
Foremen wages	5,000	
Rent	5,000	
Depreciation	1,500	
Consumable stores	2,000	
Total Factory Overheads		21,000
Factory Cost		1,77,000

Administrative Overheads:		
Lighting	500	
Repairs	500	
Directors' fees	1,500	
Telephone charges	500	
Postage and Telegram	200	
Electric Power	1,000	
Rent	3,000	
Depreciation	1,500	
Manager's Salary	5,000	
Stationery	500	
Total Administrative Overheads		14,200
adjustrightCost of Production		1,91,200
Selling and Distribution Overheads:		
Salesmen salary	2,500	
Advertising	1,000	
Carriage outwards	500	
Salesman Travelling expenses	300	
Warehouse Charges	500	
Total Selling and Distribution		4,800
Cost of Sales		1,95,000
Profit (Balancing Figure)		35,000
Sales		**2,30,000**

LET US RECAPITULATE

1. Cost is a measurement in monetary terms of the amount of resources used for some purpose.
2. The term 'Cost' refers to the resources sacrificed or foregone to achieve a specific objective. It represents the expenditure which has been made or incurred for an economic benefit.
3. An expense is defined as a cost that has given a benefit and has now expired.
4. The term 'Loss' refers to the excess of expenses over revenues for a period. It may also be the excess of cost of an asset over its related sale proceeds.
5. 'Cost Unit' or 'Unit of Activity' is "a unit of quantity of product, service or time or a combination of these in relation to which costs may be ascertained or expressed".
6. Cost unit may be simple or composite.
7. A cost centre is a location, person or item of equipment in respect of which costs may be ascertained and related to cost units for control purposes.

8. Cost classification is the arrangement of items in logical groups having regard to their nature or the purpose of to be fulfilled.
9. A cost consists of three elements i.e. material, labour and expense.
10. Material cost is "the cost of commodities supplied to an undertaking." Materials may be direct or indirect.
11. All direct costs other than direct materials and direct labour are marked as direct expenses.
12. Direct costs are allocated whereas indirect costs are apportioned to different jobs, products or services on a suitable criterion.
13. Fixed cost is a cost which tends to be unaffected by variations in volume of output.
14. Variable cost is a cost which tends to vary directly with level or volume of activity or output.
15. Historical cost relates to events which have already happened.
16. Relevant cost is that portion of total cost which differs under different alternatives.
17. Differential cost is the difference in total costs between two alternatives is known as differential cost.
18. Sunk cost is a past cost and is not relevant for decision making.
19. Shut down cost is the minimum fixed costs which an undertaking will have to incur during the period of temporary closure of the department, division or even the entire production activity of the organization.
20. Cost is said to be controllable when the amount of cost incurred can be influenced by the action of a specified member of an undertaking.
21. Product cost is associated with output and is considered to be reasonably attached to the units produced and matched against the revenues of the accounting period in which these units are sold.
22. Period cost is charged in its entirety against the revenues of the period in which such costs are incurred.
23. Conversion cost is the cost of converting raw materials into finished product.
24. Prime Cost is the sum of direct material cost, direct wages, and direct expenses.
25. Overhead is the sum of indirect material cost, indirect wages, and indirect expenses.
26. Total cost is sum of prime cost and overhead.
27. Cost sheet or cost statement is that statement which is prepared to present the total costs of production in details during a given period.
28. The cost of normal spoilage is borne by good units. The cost of abnormal spoilage is transferred to the Costing Profit and Loss account.
29. Goods that do not meet production standards and must be processed further to make them saleable as good units are called as defectives.
30. Profit may be computed as a percentage of cost or as a percentage of selling price.
31. Overhead absorption is the charging of overheads to cost units.

OBJECTIVE TYPE QUESTIONS

I. Fill in the blank spaces with suitable word/s :

1. On the basis of behaviour, costs are classified into .... and ....
2. Total of direct material cost, direct wages and direct expenses is .....
3. Total of indirect material cost, indirect wages and indirect expenses is .....
4. A cost that involves making of a payment is known as ....cost.
5. .... and ....are examples of variable costs.
6. .... and ....are examples of fixed costs.
7. .... is an example of out of pocket cost.
8. .... is an example of imputed cost.
9. Prime cost consists of direct material, direct wages and ......
10. Overhead is the aggregate of all .... costs.
11. ....is a cost which cannot be influenced by the action of a specified member of an undertaking.
12. .... Cost is an example of pre-production cost.
13. When a change is made in the level or method of production, the resultant change in cost is called ....
14. .... is a statement which gives detailed components of cost of a cost centre or cost unit.
15. .... costs are those which follow the item into inventory and .... costs are charged against current income.
16. .... is the practice of charging all costs, both fixed and variable, to operations, processes or products.
17. Timber used in making furniture is an example of ..... material.
18. An example of direct expense is ....

Answers :

1. Fixed, variable **2.** Prime cost **3.** Overhead
4. Out of pocket **5.** Direct material, Direct wages
6. Factory rent, manager's salary **7.** material cost
8. Interest on equity capital **9.** Direct Expenses **10.** Indirect
11. Controllable cost **12.** Research and development
13. Differential cost **14.** cost sheet **15.** product, period
16. Absorption costing **17.** direct
18. hire of special plant for a specific job

II. Indicate whether the following statements are True or False :

1. Variable cost per unit remains constant.
2. Fixed cost per unit remains constant.
3. Cost centre and cost unit are the same.

4. Administration costs are mostly fixed.
5. Abnormal cost is controllable.
6. Period costs are not assigned to products.
7. Cost of production is equal to prime cost plus works cost.
8. Committed cost is relevant for decision making.
9. Direct cost can be identified with and charged to a particular cost unit.
10. Total variable cost does not increase in proportion to output.
11. Decremental cost means the cost of an added unit.
12. Standard cost is what cost should be.
13. Sunk costs are relevant for decision making.
14. Marginal cost is helpful for decision making.
15. The term overhead and indirect expenses have the same meaning.
16. Conversion costs and overhead are interchangeable terms.
17. Direct materials are a variable cost of production.
18. An item of cost that is direct for one business may be indirect for another.
19. Period costs are invariable and are expensed out as and when the inventory is sold.
20. Conversion cost is equal to direct wages plus factory overhead.
21. Overhead includes only fixed cost.
22. Indirect materials are those materials the cost of which can be easily traced to the product.
23. Raw materials, work-in-progress, and finished goods are all inventory accounts.
24. Direct labour combined with direct materials is known as prime cost.
25. All costs are controllable.
26. Depreciation is an out of pocket cost.
27. Period costs are recorded as expense in the period in which these costs are incurred.
28. Fixed cost does not change in the same proportion in which output changes.
29. The rentals of a car which include a fixed daily rate plus an extra fee for each kilometer driven are an example of a step cost.
30. Change in fixed costs occurs outside the relevant range of activity.
31. Notional costs are not included while ascertaining cost.
32. Fixed cost does not change in the same proportion in which output changes.
33. The rental of a car which includes a fixed daily rate plus an extra fee for each kilometer driven is an example of a step cost. **[DU, B.Com (Hons.) 1999]**
34. Period costs are invariable and are expensed out as and when the inventory is sold. **[DU, B.Com (Hons.) 1999]**
35. Fixed costs are controllable.
36. Direct costs are those which are incurred for and conveniently identified with a particular cost centre or cost unit.
37. Salary of the works manager is an example of fixed cost.

38. Cost unit and cost centre have the same meaning.

39. Chargeable expenses are the sum of all direct and indirect expenses.

40. Research and Development cost is a discretionary fixed cost.

41. Supervisor's salary is a direct labour cost.

42. Prime cost is the aggregate of direct materials, direct wages and production overheads.

43. Plant depreciation is a committed cost.

44. Power used in the aluminum industry is a direct material cost.

45. Carriage outward is a selling overhead.

46. Carriage inward is a direct expense.

47. The purpose of ascertaining cost by cost centres is to control the cost.

48. Depreciation of plant is a sunk cost.

49. Rental value of own building is an example of imputed cost.

50. Interest on equity capital is an imputed cost.

51. Increase in total variable cost is due to increase in fixed cost.

52. Abnormal costs are charged to costing profit and Loss account.

Answers :

1. True	**2.** False	**3.** False	**4.** True
5. True	**6.** True	**7.** False	**8.** False
9. True	**10.** False	**11.** False	**12.** True
13. False	**14.** True	**15.** False	**16.** False
17. True	**18.** True	**19.** False	**20.** True
21. False	**22.** False	**23.** True	**24.** True
25. False	**26.** False	**27.** True	**28.** True
29. False	**30.** True	**31.** False	**32.** True
33. False	**34.** False	**35.** False	**36.** True
37. True	**38.** False	**39.** False	**40.** True
41. False	**42.** False	**43.** True	**44.** False
45. True	**46.** False	**47.** True	**48.** False
49. True	**50.** True	**51.** False	**52.** True

THEORETICAL EXERCISES

1. 'Costs may be classified in a variety of ways according to their nature and the information needs of management.' Explain and discuss this statement giving examples of the classifications required for different purposes.

2. State the primary objectives of installation of a costing system. Apart from technical costing problems, what practical difficulties would you meet and how would you overcome them?

3. Explain concisely 'Engineered costs' and 'discretionary costs. What is the right approach to control these?

4. Explain the classification of cost into controllable and uncontrollable.

5. Explain the nature of product and period cost. How do they affect net income of a business enterprise? **[DU, B.Com (Hons.) 1997]**

6. "Product cost is a general term that denotes different costs allocated to products for different purposes." Describe three purposes. Explain the composition of 'Product cost', for the purpose of external financial reporting along with its rationale. **[DU, B.Com (Hons.)1998]**

7. The term 'cost' must be qualified according to its context. Comment. **[DU, B.Com (Hons.) 2002]**

8. Distinguish between the followings:
   (1) Expired cost and Unexpired cost
   (2) Direct and Indirect costs **[B.Com (Hons.), DU, 1998, 2000]**
   (3) Distinguish between cost centre and cost unit
   (4) Distinguish between fixed costs and variable costs. **[DU, B.Com (Hons.) 1999]**
   (5) Prime Cost and Conversion cost **[DU, B.Com (Hons.) 1999]**
   (6) Controllable and Uncontrollable costs **[DU, B.Com (Hons.) 1999]**

9. Explain the significance of 'Decision-Making costs'. **[DU, B.Com (Hons.) 1999]**

10. Elucidate the meaning and formulation of 'Product cost' for the purpose of income measurement and determination of financial position. **[DU, B.Com (Hons.) 1999]**

11. What purposes do cost centres serve? Are cost centres and cost unit related to each other? If yes, How? **[DU, B.Com (Hons.) 2002]**

12. Explain in brief the following concepts:
   (i) Product costs; **[DU, B.Com (Hons.) 2001]**
   (ii) Relevant Range;

13. Explain the followings:
   (a) Notional Salary for proprietors' supervision
   (b) Packing expenses
   (c) Sunk costs

14. Match the following:

Cost	Meaning
1. Total Fixed cost	1. What Cost should be
2. Total Variable cost	2. Incurred Cost
3. unit variable cost	3. Increases with Output
4. unit fixed cost	4. What costs are expected to be
5. Standard cost	5.Decreases with rise in output
6. Period cost	6. Cost of conversion
7. Actual Cost	7. Remains constant in total
8. Labour and Overhead	8. Cost not assigned to product
9. Incrémental Cost	9. Remains constant per unit
10. Budgeted Cost	10. Added value of a new product

[DU, B.Com (Hons.) 2003]

Answers :

Cost	Meaning
1. Total Fixed cost	1. Remains constant in total
2. Total Variable cost	2. Increases with Output
3. unit variable cost	3. Remains constant per unit
4. unit fixed cost	4. Decreases with rise in output
5. Standard cost	5. What Cost should be
6. Period cost	6. Cost not assigned to product
7. Actual Cost	7. Incurred Cost
8. Labour and Overhead	8. Cost of conversion
9. Incremental Cost	9. Added value of a new product
10. Budgeted Cost	10. What costs are expected to be

15. What is a cost centre and how does it differ from a department of a factory?

16. Explain the concept of cost. How does it differ from expense?

NUMERICAL EXERCISES

1. Prepare a cost sheet with the help of the following giving all relevant components. Give statement of cost and profit valuing closing stock on the basis of LIFO, FIFO and Weighted average separately.

Details	Amount (₹)
Opening Stock :	
Raw materials	10,000
Work-in-progress	30,000
Finished goods (1,000 units)	80,000
Total purchases of materials	1,00,000
Direct labour	3,00,000
Direct power	20,000
Indirect power	6,000
Indirect materials	24,000
Other factory expenses	30,000
Show room expenses	40,000
Selloing commission @ 5% on sales	
Other selling expenses	15,000
Office and administration overhead	60,000
Sales (12000 units)	12,00,000
Closing Stock :	
Raw material	15,000
Work-in-progress	18,000
Finished goods (4,000 units)	

[Ans. ......]

2. From the books of M/s Bradman Enterprises, the following details have been extracted for the year ending march 31, 2007:

Details	Amount (₹)
Stock of materials - Opening	1,88,000
Closing	2,00,000
Materials purchased during the year	8,32,000
Direct wages paid	2,38,000
Indirect wages	16,000
Salaries to administrative staff	40,000
Freights - inwards	32,000
Freights - outward	2,000
Cash discounts allowed	14,000
Bad debts written off	18,800
Repairs to plant and machinery	42,400
Rent, rates and taxes - factory	1,200
Rent, rates and taxes - office	6,400
Traveling expenses	12,400
Salesman's salaries and commission	33,600
Depreciation written off : Plant and commission	28,400
Depreciation written off : Furniture	2,400
Director's fees	24,000
Electricity charges (factory)	48,000
Fuel (for boiler)	64,000
General charges	24,800
Manager's salary	48,000

The manager's time is shared between the factory and the office in the ratio of 20: 80. From the above details you are required to prepare a cost sheet showing:

(a) Prime cost; (b) factory overhead; (c) factory cost;
(d) general overhead; and (e) total cost. **[Ans. ……]**

3. On December 31, 2007, a flash flood damaged the warehouse and factory of APS Corporation completely destroying the work-in-progress inventory. There was no damage to either the raw materials or finished goods inventories. A physical verification taken after the flood revealed the following valuations:

Details	Amount (₹)
Raw materials	82,000
Work-in-progress	NIL
Finished goods	2,09,000

The inventory on January 1, 2007 consisted of the followings :

Details	Amount (₹)
Raw materials	40,000
Work-in-progress	80,000
Finished goods	1,80,000
Total	3,00,000

A review of the books and records disclosed that the gross profit margin historically approximated 20% of sales. The sales for the last six months of 2007 were ₹ 5,50,000. Raw Material purchases were ₹ 2,65,000. Direct labour costs for this period were ₹ 1,20,000 and manufacturing overhead has historically been 65% of direct labour. Compute the cost of work-in-progress inventory on December 31, 2007 by preparing a statement of cost and profit. **[Ans. ₹ 32,000]**

4. The following inventory data relate to XYZ Ltd. :

Details	Beginning Inventories (₹)	Ending Inventories (₹)
Finished goods	1,10,000	95,000
Work-in-progress	70,000	80,000
Raw materials	90,000	95,000

Additional information :

Details	Amount (₹)
Cost of goods available for sale	6,84,000
Total goods processed during the period	6,54,000
Factory overheads	1,67,000
Direct materials used	1,93,000

Requirements :

(i) Determine Raw Material Purchases.

(ii) Determine the Direct Labour cost incurred.

(iii) Determine the Cost of Goods Sold.

[Ans. (Purchases : ₹ 1,98,000; Direct Labour cost : ₹ 2,24,000; Cost of Goods Sold : ₹ 5,89,000)]

❑❑❑

3

Material Control

Learning Objectives

It attempts to explain material management and control. In this chapter you will learn :

1. Meaning of materials, and distinction between direct material and indirect material.
2. Meaning of stores.
3. Need and types of material control.
4. Ingredients of a sound material control system.
5. Purchasing :
   (a) Generalized vs. decentralized
   (b) Materials requirement planning (MRP)
   (c) Purchase procedure
6. Storing :
   (a) Objectives of store-keeping
   (b) Centralized vs. decentralized,
   (c) Classification & codification, and recording of stores.
7. Inventory systems : Periodic and perpetual.
8. Discrepancies and accounting treatment.

INTRODUCTION

Material is the substance from which the product is made. Materials are the basic substances that are transformed into finished goods. Production of every product requires some form of basic materials. Materials constitute the substances or the integral parts of which product is made. They may be classified into three broad categories:

(i) **Raw materials:** It is those materials which are in their natural or raw form. Sugarcane for the sugar factory, oil seeds for the oil Mill, cotton for a Cotton textile Mill are some of the indicative examples of this nature of materials which include those materials that are not one hundred percent complete in all respects. It requires some processing before it could be sold as the final-finished product.

(ii) **Semi-finished materials:** It includes materials which are not 100% complete in all respects. It implies that some processing still remains to be done before the product could be sold. A furniture manufacturer may purchase unpolished furniture from the market and may sell it after polishing it.

(iii) **Finished materials:** It consists of finished components which are used as raw materials for manufacturing a product. Tyres and batteries are finished materials for automobile manufacturers.

The term 'Material' refers to such commodity which is supplied in its crude or original form. Products are fabricated and services rendered through it. Material is the substance from which the product is made. Materials in general are raw in nature and need further processing. They may be categorized as (a) Raw materials, (b) Components, (c) Consumable materials, (d) Maintenance materials, and (e) Tools.

Material cost may be either direct or indirect :

Direct Materials: There are three characteristics of direct materials:

(1) They are easily traced to the product.

(2) They represent a major segment (material) of the finished product.

(3) They can be identified directly with production of the product.

Indirect Materials: These include all other materials used in production and are considered to be a part of factory overhead cost.

MATERIALS CONTROL

Materials control is a system which ensures the provision of the right quantity of material of the right quality at the right time with the minimum amount of investment. It is the systematic control over the procurement, storage and usage of materials so as to maintain an even flow of materials and avoiding at the same time excessive investment in inventories. The functions of a good system of material control include scheduling the requirements, purchasing, receiving and inspecting, maintaining stock records and stock control. In fact, material control is a matter of coordination amongst the following departments:

1. Purchase;
2. Receiving and Inspection;
3. Store-keeping;
4. Production control; and
5. Stock control.

Material control is affected by the establishment of functional organization and the assignment of responsibility through the use of standard forms; accounting records and entries, and also reports affecting materials from the initiation of purchase requisition till the material is consumed and manufactured goods are stocked in warehouses.

Material control is to be exercised at three stages:

(i) Control on policies, systems and procedures connected with the procurement of materials;

(ii) Control on storage of materials; and

(iii) Control on issue and usage of materials.

It may be pointed out that these controls aim at ensuring that:

(a) Production process is not hampered due to non-availability of materials at right time and of right quality;

(b) Investment in materials is kept at minimum level so that cost of materials per unit of output is kept at minimum.

With a view to contribute to the corporate objectives, the chief buyer should plan the procurement strategies to include the following "rights", namely:

(1) Right Quantity
(2) Right Source
(3) Right Quality
(4) Right Material
(5) Right Price
(6) Right Time
(7) Right Contract and legal aspects
(8) Right Place of delivery
(9) Right Packing
(10) Right Transport
(11) Right systems, procedures, etc.
(12) Right Methods of handling
(13) Right materials intelligence covering economic, socio-political, financial, regulatory, natural, technological and inflationary environment, etc.

Need for Material Control: To make any cost accounting system to be effective, it is necessary to have a proper control of materials and supplies from the moment orders are placed with suppliers until they have been effectively utilized in production. Since materials are equivalent to cash, and since they make a significant portion of total cost of a product, it is essential that materials should be properly safe guarded and correctly accounted for. Control over materials is also necessary to ensure a steady supply of each item of materials. The success of a business concern largely depends upon efficient purchasing, storage, usage and accounting of materials.

Advantages of material control: Following advantages accrue due to a good system of material control:

1. Wastage in the use of materials is eliminated.
2. Risk of loss from fraud and theft is reduced.
3. Perpetual inventory and other records facilitate the preparation of proper and accurate reports for the management.
4. Cost of storage is reduced.
5. Investment in inventories is reduced.

Objectives of material control: Following are the detailed objectives of material control under the basic premise of continuous supply of materials for uninterrupted flow of production and meeting material requirement at the minimum possible cost:

1. **Continuous availability of materials:** Materials of all types should always be available for production. Panicky purchases should be avoided.
2. **Optimum investment in materials:** It is to ensure that the requirements of materials are met with minimum investment in materials. Over stocking of items should be avoided.
3. **Economy in purchasing:** Materials are to be purchased at the lowest possible price without compromising on quality, regularity and reliability of supplies.
4. **Strict quality control:** The order for right quality of raw materials should be authorised. Materials should be tested at the time of receipt and the concerned person should put his signatures so that responsibility could be fixed had the quality been compromised.
5. **Minimum handling cost:** Materials should be stored at such a place and in such a manner that (a) materials could be located at ease, (b) minimum effort is involved in making materials available to the user department, and (c) time taken in tracing the materials and making them reach the user department should be minimum.

6. **Reliable flow of information about materials:** It is ensured that material' records as to stock position, maximum and minimum levels, special problems and the list of reliable suppliers is updated on regular basis. This helps in placing orders of right size, at the right time and to the right supplier.
7. **Minimise wastes:** The system aims at minimizing wastages of materials in handling at the time of receipt in stores, their issue and use in the user department. Norms of wastages of each item of materials should be fixed in advance. Further, it is ensured that pilferages of materials do not take place.
8. **Authorised payment for materials:** It is to ensure that no payment is made for materials which have not been duly ordered, though received, or for materials which have not been received, or for materials which have been received but are not in tune with the ordered quality of materials.
9. **Authorised issue of materials:** Issue of materials without proper authorization need not be permitted.
10. **Control on leakages and pilferages, and other losses:** The system should help minimise spoilages and obsolescence. In this case also, norms should be fixed for each item of the material.
11. **Detect slow or non-moving items of materials:** A proper system should be developed to detect on regular basis the items of materials which are moving slow or are not-moving at all. It is advisable to dispose of not-moving materials to avoid further storage costs.

Thus, there is a need to make a perfect synchronization between the availability of materials and their utilisation.

Material control entails materials planning, materials purchasing and receiving, storage of materials, issue of materials, and material accounting and reporting. Following points must be kept in mind while installing and operationalising a material control system.

Materials Planning: It includes the followings:

(i) Suitable classification and codification of all items of materials.

(ii) Ascertainment of material requirement in advance.

(iii) Adoption of Perpetual Inventory system.

(iv) Role of centralized buying of materials.

(v) Ascertainment of economic order size, maximum, minimum and reorder levels of each item of materials, and their periodical review.

(vi) Adoption of ABC technique for selective and focus control on high value-cum-low volume items of materials.

(vii) Adoption of VED technique for controlling spare parts.

Materials purchasing and receiving: It includes the followings:

(i) Preparation of material purchase budget for each item of material required.

(ii) Scheduling of purchase of materials.

(iii) Updating of the list of reliable suppliers of different materials.

(iv) Devising a system of calling quotations and opening thereof.

(v) Devising a system of comparing quotations and making a choice.

(vi) Devising a system of receiving and inspection of each item of materials and comparing them with the purchase order and challans. It also involves assigning responsibility for receiving the materials, checking the quantity and testing the quality.

Storage of materials: It includes the followings:

(i) Location and layout of stores in the factory premises.

(ii) Maintenance of Stores Ledger containing a ledger account for each item of material.

(iii) Making of surprise checking of materials in the bin and comparing with the bin card attached to it.

(iv) Calculate inventory turn over ratio for each type of material.

(v) Guard against pilferage and spoilage.

(vi) Ensure that issues are made quickly and with least inconvenience.

Issue of materials: It includes the followings:

(i) Issue of materials to the users against a duly authorised numbered material requisition slip.

(ii) Preparation of Bill of materials by every user of materials.

(iii) If necessary, use Material Transfer Note for direct transfer of materials from one job to another.

(iv) Maintenance of complete record of normal as well as abnormal losses of materials.

(v) Ensure immediate return of surplus materials with the user department to the store.

(vi) Selection of a method of valuing issue of materials.

Materials accounting and reporting: It includes the followings:

(i) Maintenance of complete record of all purchases, issues, returns, transfers and losses of materials.

(ii) Maintenance of a system of internal check and internal audit of records of materials.

(iii) Ensure timely payment for the purchase of materials only after due comparison of supplier's bill with the copy of purchase order along with receiving and inspection report.

(iv) Maintenance of control accounts and subsidiary ledgers for obtaining summarised information regarding purchases, issues, returns, and spoilages, etc.

(v) Preparation of reports on purchases, issues and stocks on regular basis for managerial purposes.

(vi) Preparation of special reports on spoilage, returns to suppliers, obsolete items, defectives and abnormal losses on regular basis for managerial purposes.

MATERIALS MANAGEMENT

Materials management is the function responsible for coordination of planning , sourcing, purchasing, moving, storing, and controlling materials in an optimum manner so as to provide pre-decided services to the customer at a minuim cost. It is to work in close coordination with production, marketing and finance departments. The importance of materials management can be gauged by the fact that materials management has evolved as a separate subject of study. In some of the industries especially heavy engineering industry, materials constitute more than sixty percent of the total cost of production. However, with changes in manufacturing environment, the share of the overheads in the total cost of production is increasing and correspondingly the proportion of materials cost is coming down. This has not reduced the importance of materials management; rather newer techniques have emerged to suit the advanced manufacturing environment.

The objectives of materials management may be sub-divided into primary and secondary objectives. The primary objectives are:

(i) Lower cost of acquisition;

(ii) Maintaining continuity of supply with consistency of quality;

(iii) Minimising investment in inventories;

(iv) Assuring a high inventory turnover.

The secondary objectives are:

(i) Material cost reduction through simplification, standardization, value analysis, inventory control, etc.

(ii) Coordinating the functions of planning, scheduling, storage, materials handling, traffic, etc.

(iii) Development of personnel relating to materials management.

The operation of material control system involves monitoring the entire 'material cycle' starting from the initiation of material requirement, and passing through placement of purchase order, receiving and inspection, storage and issue and ending at the replenishment of material consumed. The procedures, documentation and systems are individual organisations' and divisions' specific.

This chapter intends to provide an overview of materials management techniques. Materials management involves:

1. Purchase of materials (Purchase function)
2. Receipt, Storage and Issue of materials (Stores function)
3. Inventory Control.

PURCHASE FUNCTION

To ensure the procurement of materials of requisite quantity at most economical rates, it is necessary to consider the followings:

1. **Centralised Purchasing:** All purchasing should be done by the purchasing department. However, for minor as well as emergency purchases departmental mangers may be permitted to make purchases.
2. **Requisite co-operation:** There has to be perfect co-operation between the purchase department and the user departments. Every department should send the details of materials well in advance.
3. **Co-operation between Purchasing and Finance department:** It is necessary for the purchase department to remain in constant touch with the finance department. This ensures procurement of requisite materials at the right time and at the right price.
4. **Proper procedure:** Though details of a purchase procedure may differ from firm to firm, it includes the following steps:
   (i) **Purchase requisition:** It is a formal request by the incharge of a department or any authorised officer to the Chief Buyer to purchase the specified materials (specimen given hereunder).

Purchase Requisition

No. 205 Dated: November 10, 2009

Please purchase for P-1 Department/Work order No. 308

S. No.	Stock. code No.	Details of item	Quantity	Remarks
1.	B.87	1.5" Brass screws	30 kg.	Material is required latest by December 1, 2009

Requested by ....

Approved by...........

The authorised persons may be

(a) **Storekeeper:** The storekeeper is expected to initiate the purchase procedure when standard materials reach reordering level.

(b) **Production Planner:** The production Planner is expected to initiate the purchase procedure for special items of materials required for the manufacture of a new product.

(c) **Plant Engineer:** The Plant Engineer is expected to initiate the purchase procedure for materials required for repairs and maintenance.

(d) **Department Incharge:** A Departmental Incharge is expected to initiate the purchase procedure for department specific-materials.

Purposes of a Purchase requisition: A purchase requisition aims at fulfilling the following purposes:

(1) It initiates the purchase of materials and sets the purchasing process in motion.

(2) It provides details of materials to be purchased.

(3) It provides dates for reference.

Usually, two copies of the Purchase requisition are made. The original copy is sent to the Purchase department and the second copy is retained in the requisitionist department.

(ii) Inviting quotations: The Purchase department starts the process of inviting tenders or quotations from the reliable suppliers for the supply of requisite quantity and quality of materials.

(iii) Preparing a schedule of quotations: A schedule of quotations, the specimen format of which is given as under, is prepared on the basis of tenders or quotations received. Basically, it is a comparative statement on the basis of which decision to appoint a supplier is made.

Schedule of Quotations

Material: 1.5" Brass screws November 21, 2009

Name of the Supplier	Rate per kg. (₹)	Time of Delivery	Terms of Delivery	Remarks
Radhey and Company	1,550	5 days	Free	
Mohan and Company	1,528	10 days	Free	
Krishana and Company	1,510	8 days	Free	Accepted

Purchase office assistant: Jagan

Purchase manager: R. Sahoo

(iv) **Approving the supplier:** In selecting a supplier certain factors in regard to price, quality of materials, terms of payment, mode and time of delivery and reliability of the firm are given due weightage. The Purchase committee does the scanning of the quotations in details and selects a reliable supplier.

(v) **Placing the purchase order:** This document prepared by the Purchase department is a written authorization to the supplier for a specified quantity and quality of materials at the stipulated terms and conditions as regard to time, mode and place of delivery and payment. This purchase order, the specimen format of which is given as under, is signed by the Purchase manager.

APS Limited
Purchase Order

To
Krishana and Company
Andheri(West) Mumbai

Order No. 1125
Requisition No. 205
Dated: November 22, 2009

S. No.	Details of item	Quantity	Rate (₹)	Amount (₹)
1.	1.5" Brass of screws	30 kg.	1,510	45,300

Place of Delivery: Free at our factory
Packing and dispatching instructions: Sealed wooden boxes
Date of Delivery: November 30, 2009
Terms of Payment: 40 days' credit

R. Sahoo
(Purchase manager)

The Purchase order is usually prepared in triplicate. The original copy is mailed to the supplier, the second copy is sent to the accounts department and the third copy is retained by the Purchase department for future reference. Some organisations prepare five copies instead of three. The fourth copy is sent to the store keeper or the department which initiated the purchase requisition and the receiving department respectively.

(vi) **Receiving of materials:** The receiving department is responsible for unpacking the goods received and verifying their quantity and condition. The quantity is checked against the purchase order copy and the supplier's advice note which is usually received along with the goods. The complete details of the goods received are entered in a Goods Received Note, a specimen format of which is given as under to serve the following purposes:

(i) The store keeper / requisitionist department is informed of the receipt of materials.

(ii) The accounting department gets informed that the requite materials have been received and that a payment voucher can be made;

(iii) It becomes a source of entry in the stores ledger.

APS Company Limited
Goods Received Note

Supplier:		No.:	
....		Date:	
Advice Note No.:		Purchase order No. :	
Quantity	**Description**	**No. of Packages**	**Gross Weight**
Quantity	Inspection Report		
Passed	Quantity rejected	Reasons for rejection	
Inspected by		Date:	Received by ....

(vii) Inspection and Testing of Materials: Goods received are to be inspected for quality to ensure that they comply with the specifications mentioned in the purchase order. An inspection report is prepared to show the results of the inspection-cum-testing. This report prepared separately or incorporated in the Goods Received Note is forwarded to the Purchase department.

(viii) Return of rejected materials: If materials received are not in accordance with the specifications mentioned in the purchase order or damaged, they are returned to the supplier along with a Debit Note. When such a claim is accepted by the supplier, he signifies his acceptance by issuing a Credit Note. The rejected materials may be returned to the supplier or they may be held back till instructions from the supplier. The Debit Note, a specimen format of which is given as under, is prepared by the Purchase department on the basis of inspection and Testing Report. Original copy is sent to the supplier and the second copy is sent to the accounting department for making adjustment entry and the third copy is retained by the purchase department for future reference.

APS Company Limited

Debit Note

To (supplier) .... No.: ....

.... Dated: ....

We are constrained to debit your account with the value of under-mentioned materials for the reasons cited herein. Meanwhile we wait for your instructions by return mail.

Quantity	**Description**	**Rate (₹)**	**Amount (₹)**

Reasons: .... Date of which received: ....

Purchase Order No.: .... Goods received Note No.: ....

Supplier's Invoice No.: ....

Signature: ....

(ix) Authorising Payment: Invoices received are numbered serially and entered in the Invoice Register. This invoice along with all supporting documents is sent by the Purchase department to the Accounts Department for making prompt payment to the supplier of the materials. The supporting documents are: (i) Purchase order, (ii) Goods Received Note, (iii) Inspection and Testing Report, and (iv) Debit or Credit Note. All the calculations regarding adjustments, rates, amount, cash and trade discounts, penalties, etc., are checked before a voucher authorising payment is prepared. All the relevant documents are marked with the Invoice Number to preclude the chances of making duplicate payment.

A crossed cheque in favour of the supplier is prepared. All the supporting vouchers are attached with the cheque for verification when it is presented to the signing authority. Duly signed cheque is then handed over or sent to the supplier.

Illustration 3.1 : *The management of M S T limited desires to introduce suitable procedures and forms in connection with purchase and receipt of materials. You are required to tabulate the procedure and forms to be used for this purpose.*

Procedure	Forms
1. Written request for materials from departments	Purchase Requisition
2. Locate the source of supply by reference to catalogues, price list etc.	Schedule of quotations
3. Make a binding contract with the selected supplier	Purchase order
4. Maintain follow-up system to ensure materials ordered are delivered in time	Letter (or by telephone call)
5. Received goods and inform other departments	Goods Received Note
6. Provide for inspection of goods	Inspection Note
7. Return to suppliers goods not according to specification	Rejection Report
8. Complete each transaction by checking the creditor's invoice in terms of contract	Purchase journal or Voucher register
9. Adjustment for excess or short receipt	Debit or credit note

STORAGE OF MATERIALS

Store keeping is the function involving proper keeping of stocks, identifying and classifying them according to their nature, type and sizes and also includes proper maintenance of stock records. Since materials are equivalent to cash, and since they make up an important part of total cost, it is essential that materials should be properly accounted for and safeguarded in a good stores department. Proper control over materials can make a substantial contribution to the efficiency of a business.

It is necessary to ensure that materials bought are kept in the store efficiently. Storage efficiency is crucial to efficiency in operations, cost economies and proper working capital management. Efficient storage system serves the objectives of storage functions which are as under:

(1) Ensure availability of all types of materials as and when required.

(2) Ensure that all materials records are accurate and up-to-date.

(3) Ensure that there is no unauthorised movement of materials into the stores, from the stores, or even within the stores.

(4) Ensure the effective prevention of pilferage, breakage, wastage or deterioration of stock of materials.

(5) Ensure optimal usage of store space.

(6) Ensure easy accessibility of each item in the stores.

(7) Ensure that stock-on-hand of each type of material is known.

(8) Ensure efficient handling of all items into the stores, out of the stores and within the stores.

(9) Ensure storage cost minimum without sacrificing efficiency and effectiveness of the storage function.

(10) Ensure complete accountability for all items of stocks.

Stores Records

Records relating to materials are available at number of places:

1. Purchase department maintains records of purchase requisitions received, materials ordered and orders supplied and orders in pending.
2. Receiving and Inspection department maintains records of materials inspected, received, returned and handed over to the storekeeper.
3. Accounts department has copies of purchase order, and receiving and inspection report, along with invoice sent by the suppliers for making payment.
4. The Storekeeper maintains physical records of materials entering the stores after due authorization, and leaving the stores on the basis of authorised material requisitions, and the balance of stores in hand.
5. The costing department maintains complete records of all movements of materials (into the store, from the store, from one department tot another; from one job to another, etc.) These records are not only in physical units but also in monetary value. Such records serve following two purposes:
   (i) Material control;
   (ii) Determine the material cost and charge it to various user departments, products, processes and jobs, etc.

Bin cards and Stores ledger are two important stores records.

(i) Bin card or Stock card: Bin refers to container or space where materials are kept.

APS Limited

Bin Card

Bin No.: .... Maximum Quantity: ....

Details: .... Minimum Quantity: ....

Code No.: .... Re-order Level: ....

Stores Ledger Folio: .... Ordering Quantity: ....

Location No.: ....

Date	GRN No.	Quantity	SRN No.	Quantity	Balance	Date of Checking	Order No.	Date of Order	Quantity	Date of Receipt

GRN No. means Goods Received Note Number
SRN No. means Stores Requisition Note Number

(ii) Two Bin System: This system requires the bin to be divided into two parts. One part of the bin contains the minimum quantity which should always remain there. Stocks over and above the minimum levels are contained in the larger part of the bin from which issues are made. Requisition for purchase is made just before the exhaustion of stock in the larger part of the bin. This system ensures better control against running out of stock and also facilitates verification of materials as there may no need to verify stock in the minimum part of the bin.

Stores Ledger

The Cost office maintains the stores ledger. A separate account is maintained for each type of material and other items of supplies and spares stocked in the stores. Separate stores ledgers may be kept for separate groups of materials in case of a large organisation. Stores ledger gives same information as is available from bin cards except that it gives monetary information also such, rate and amount of receipts, issues and balance of materials. Entries in stores ledger are made from goods received notes, suppliers' invoices, material requisition notes and material return notes.

Stores ledger Accounts have three main sections:

(a) Receipts with rate and amount,

(b) Issues with rate and amount, and

(c) the balance with the quantity, rate and amount.

Stores ledger may also contain columns for 'Materials ordered', 'Materials reserved for specific jobs, etc, and 'Stock verified' and signature of the person verifying the stocks. It is necessary that the stores staff should have no connection with the writing up of stores ledger, nor this ledger be left with the stores staff. This ledger should be written only by staff of the costing Department.

Stores Ledger Sheet

Description .... Code No. .... Unit ..... Maximum .... Ordering level ......
Bin No. .... Location .... Minimum ...... Ordering Qty. ....

Ordered	**Reserved**	**Received**	**Issued**	**Balance**	**Stock Verification**
Date	Date required	Date	Quantity	Quantity	Date
P.O. No.	Work order No.	Quantity	Rate (₹)	Rate (₹)	Initials
Quantity	Quantity	Rate (₹)	Amount (₹)	Amount (₹)	Remarks
		Amount (₹)			

Distinction between Bin Card and Stores Ledger:

Bin Card	Stores Ledger
1. It records only the Quantity of materials.	It records Quantity as well as value of the materials.
2. It is kept by the Store Keeper in the stores.	It is kept by the Cost Accounting department in the Accounts Office.
3. Entries in the Bin card are made before the transaction of receipt or issue of material takes place. (pre-transaction record)	Entry in the Stores Ledger is made after the transaction of receipt or issue of material has taken place. (post-transaction record)
4. It is kept in store.	It is kept generally, in costing department.
5. Each transaction of receipt and issue is individually posted in the bin card.	Store ledger transactions may be summarised and posted periodically.
6. Transfer of materials from one department/job to another does not appear in the bin card.	Transfer of materials from one department/job to another does appear in the stores ledger for costing purposes..

Classification and Codification of Materials

Classification of materials is important for storage accounting and codification. Codification of materials is possible only when materials have been classified according to their nature, quality, usage and at times according to their location.

Classification: According to ICMA terminology, classification refers to "the arrangement of items in a logical sequence having regard to their nature (subjective classification) or the purpose to be fulfilled (objective classification)". It is the process of arranging items in groups and sub-groups according to common characteristics. The subjective classification is useful for identification, storage, ordering and accounting of materials. The objective classification is significant for costing purposes.

In a manufacturing organisation, materials are generally classified as under:

(a) **Raw materials:** Basic materials used in production, such as cotton, wool, silk for textile production, oilseeds for extracting oils, etc.

(b) **Components:** They are to be used in end-products.

(c) **Consumable stores:** They are used in production process. Dyes and chemicals, lubricating oil, cotton waste, etc.

(d) **Tools:** They are jigs, screw drivers, wrenches, clamps, etc.

(e) Nuts and bolts and other such items.

(f) **Maintenance materials:** They are required for maintenance of plant and machinery, vehicles, building, etc.

(g) **Work-in-progress:** They are semi-finished products. They are not yet complete in all respects.

(h) **Office materials:** They are primarily printing and stationery.

(i) **Miscellaneous items:** They are such items which do not fall in the above categories.

Items falling in the above categories can be further classified into various sub-groups depending upon shape, size, quality and other relevant characteristics. Oil seeds may be sub-categorised as mustard seeds, cotton seeds, sunflower seeds, etc.

Codification: It is the process of assigning a symbol or number to items falling in different groups and sub-groups. According to ICMA terminology, codification is ' a system of symbols designed to be applied to a classified set of items'. Thus, classification facilitates identification of items on the basis of description while coding is the process of assigning symbol or code number. Code is precise and a substitute for long and imprecise description.

Advantages of coding: Coding of materials leads to following advantages:

1. It facilitates identification of items.
2. Effective communication between stores, purchasing, production control and costing departments is facilitated.
3. It reduces clerical work and economises use of stationery.
4. Data processing is facilitated. For mechanized accounting coding is a pre-requisite.
5. It facilitates maintaining organizational secrets as to material purchase, storage and usage.
6. It helps in overall material control.

System of coding: The system of coding differs from organisation to organisation depending upon its size, diversity and special requirements. Keeping this fact in view, it is necessary to decide as to the number of characteristics in a code. Larger the number of items and the number of characteristics, the larger will be the size of code and the symbols in a code. If the code has to represent main group, sub-group, the quality of item, the location and the use to which material is put, the code may have four parts:

(a) In the first part, the first two alphabets may represent main group and the third alphabet may represent sub group;

(b) The second part of the code may consist of one or two digits representing quality code;

(c) The third part may have two or more digits representing location code; and

(d) The fourth and final part may have two or more digits representing usage of material.

Example: Suppose main group is 'Brass' and sub-group is 'plates' denoted by P, the quality is first denoted by 1, the place where the materials are located has been assigned the number 16 and the use is for wire drawing and this usage has been assigned number 26. The code can be denoted as

(a) "BSP1.16.26" or

(b) "BSP. 1.16.26"; or

(c) in any other such manner.

Codes may be alphabetical, numerical or based on combination of the two.

Alphabetical:

Numerical:

Alpha-Numerical:

Inventory Systems

Inventory records relating to quantity and value may be maintained according to any of the systems: Periodic or Perpetual.

Periodic Inventory System: Stock-taking for each material is done only at the end of a specified period, usually at the end of the accounting year. All inventory items are physically counted and value is assigned to stock of each item according to pre-decided method of valuation. In many cases organisations have to suspend business operations for periodic stock-taking. This system of stock-taking is especially suited for small value and for slow moving items of inventory. By taking the following steps it can be made effective:

- Such stock-taking must be planned and organized well in advance with minutest details so that can be completed quickly and accurately and there is least disruption in production and sale operations.
- Written instructions should be issued with complete details regarding stock taking activity.
- Each team of officers is to be given the list of inventory items it has to check physically.
- Inventory tags are to be used to record units counted. These tags are to be tied to the relevant bins.
- Printed inventory sheet should be used; these should be summarised and completed by accounts or internal audit department.
- Physical inventory is to be compared with recorded inventory to ascertain discrepancies,
- Suitable rectification and adjustment is to be made in stores records.

Perpetual Inventory System: It is "the method of recording stores balances after each transaction of receipt and issue to facilitate regular checking and obviate closing down or suspending the operations for stock-taking". According to CIMA (London), perpetual inventory system is "a system of records maintained by the controlling department which reflects the physical movement of stocks and their current balance... A perpetual inventory is usually checked by a programme of continuous stock-taking, and the two terms are sometimes loosely considered synonymous. Perpetual inventory means the system of records, whereas continuous stock0taking means the physical checking of those records with actual stocks".

Entries for receipts and issues of materials are made in bin card and stores ledger immediately with each receipt and issue. Receipts are added to the existing stock and the issues are deducted so as to obtain the latest balance in units in bin cards and in units as well as value in stores ledger. This system facilitates checking on a regular basis and avoids suspension of business operations for stock taking.

Continuous stock-taking is an inseparable feature of perpetual inventory system. Perpetual inventory system includes continuous stock-taking. Continuous stock-taking is concerned with only physical verification of stores with the store records. It is not concerned with valuation of stocks. Perpetual inventory system cannot be practiced without continuous stock-taking but continuous stock-taking can take place without perpetual valuation of inventories.

An organisation may decide to adopt a system of continuous stock-taking for effective control on materials but practice periodic valuation of stocks.

Just in Time (JIT) Inventory System

Inventories are designed to act as buffers so that operations can proceed smoothly even if the suppliers are late with deliveries or the department is unable to operate for a short period because of the break-down or any other reason. Carrying of inventories entails costs in terms of storage, blocking of capital investment, insurance, etc. such costs can be reduced/ minimized by keeping the inventories at the lowest possible level.

JIT inventory system means all inventories are received in time. Raw materials are received 'just in time' to go into production, manufactured parts are completed 'just in time' to be assembled into products and products are completed 'just in time' to be shipped to customers. In JIT environment the flow of goods is controlled by what is known as "pull approach" as opposed to 'pushed forward' approach to the manufacture of products. The "pull approach" means at the final assembly stage, a signal is sent to the preceding work-stations as to the exact quantum of parts and materials that will be needed over the next few hours for the assembly of products, and only that quantum of parts and materials is provided. The same signal is sent back through each workstation so that a smooth flow of parts and materials is maintained with no inventory buildup at any point. The "pull approach" is different from "push approach" used in the traditional inventory systems. In the latter case, inventories of parts and materials are built-up and 'pushed forward' to the next workstation. This leads to blocking of funds and stock piling of parts which may not be used for days or even weeks together.

Essentials of JIT system: For the successful operations of JIT inventory system following essentials must be adopted:

(a) The organisation must have a few suppliers.

(b) The suppliers must be bound by long term contracts and willing to make frequent deliveries in small lots.

(c) Total Quality control (TQC) is to be developed. TQC means that no defects can be allowed over its parts or materials.

(d) Workers must be multi-skilled in JIT environment. Machine and equipments are arranged in small 'cells' where several tasks can be performed in relation to a product. The workers assigned to these cells are expected to operate all the equipments which are in their respective cells.

Advantages of JIT system: JIT system accrues the following advantages:

1. Inventories of all types can be reduced significantly . this leads to reduction in costs.
2. Storage space used for inventories can be made available for other more productive applications.
3. Total Quality control makes production of quality products possible.
4. Productivity of workers increases and machine set up time is reduced.

Thus, smooth flow of goods between work stations , decrees in total production time and maximization of profits of the company are the direct fruits of JIT system of inventory.

Stock Discrepancies

There can be discrepancy between the quantity shown in the stores ledger and the bin card and that verified by actual physical counting/measurement of stocks. The causes for such discrepancy can be categorised into avoidable causes and unavoidable causes.

Avoidable causes abnormal losses: With the application of reasonable amount of skill and care in material handling and recording, these causes can be controlled, which are as under:

- Improper storage; carelessness in counting, weighing and measurement;
- Losses due to evaporation, moisture, shrinkage, etc. beyond the anticipated level;
- Clerical errors leading to wrong recording;
- Pilferage beyond the normal level;
- Losses due to fire, accidents, etc.
- Theft.
- Loss due to carelessness in breaking bulk or cutting;

Unavoidable causes or normal losses: They are inherent in the nature of materials or material handling. Some of such losses are enumerated as under:

- Normal losses on account of evaporation, moisture, shrinkage, etc. inherent in the nature of certain type of materials.
- Normal pilferage;
- Normal storage losses;
- Normal Obsolescence;
- Normal losses in breaking bulk or cutting;
- Normal defectives and scraps;
- Normal losses due to accidents inherent in the nature of business activity.

Accounting treatment of Discrepancies

It is the responsibility of the management to strengthen and improve material handling, recording and internal check system to eliminate or minimise losses due to avoidable reasons. If insured the insurance premium becomes normal business cost. Normal material losses must be charged to the output achieved. This can be achieved in two ways:

1. The rate of issue of materials may be suitably inflated so that normal loss is scattered over the normal output.; or
2. The normal loss of materials is debited to Production overhead and credited in stores ledger so as to bring stores ledger balance in tune with the actual physical balance in stores. The following entry to this effect is made:

   Production Overheads Control A/c Dr

   To Stores ledger control A/c
3. Abnormal material losses, which can be avoided or insured, cannot be charged the output. It is debited to costing profit & Loss a/c and the Stores Ledger control account is credited to make it in tune with the actual physical quantity of stock. The following entry to this effect is made:

   Costing Profit & Loss A/c Dr

   To Stores ledger control A/c
4. In case the shortage of material is due to the fact that an issue of material has not been charged to the output, then the entry will be as under:

   Work-in-Progress Control A/c Dr

   To Stores ledger control A/c

The detection and treatment of all the above material losses is quicker if perpetual inventory system is adopted and adhered to.

Illustration 3.2 (Bin Card) : *The following information regarding Material M-1 is obtained from the stores records of a factory:*

Date	Details
December, 2007	
1	*Opening Balance: 1,000 Tonnes*
2	*Issued 285 Tonnes vide Requisition No. 273*
4	*Issued 415 Tonnes vide Requisition No. 285*
5	*Received from supplier vide Challan No. 77 of December 5, 2007: 600 tonnes. The supply was expected on this date.*
8	*Issued 460 Tonnes vide Requisition No. 341*
12	*Issued 150 Tonnes vide Requisition No. 364*
17	*Received from supplier vide Challan No. 98 of December 17, 2007: 500 tonnes. The supply was expected on this date.*
24	*Issued 345 Tonnes vide Requisition No. 428*
28	*Issued 145 Tonnes vide Requisition No. 447*
30	*Received from supplier vide Challan No. 171 of December 30, 2007: 625 tonnes. The supply was expected on this date. Received back by Credit Slip No. 37: 50 tonnes.*
31	*Issued 425 Tonnes vide Requisition No. 483*

Examination by the stock verifier on December 26, 2007 revealed a shortage of 30 tonnes.

The maximum amount of stock of material M-1 permissible at any time is 1,000 tonnes, and the minimum 250 tonnes. The ordering level is 500 tonnes.

Draw up the Bin Card (No. 47) for M-1 with all the necessary transactions in December 2007.

Solution : **Bin Card for Material M-1**

No.	47	Maximum stock	1,000
Unit:	Tonnes	Minimum stock	250
		Ordering level	500

Date 2007	Receipts		Issues		Balance	Stock Verification		
	Challan No.	Quantity	Requisition No.	Quantity	Quantity	Date 2007	Remarks	Initials
Dec. 1					1000	Dec. 26	Shortage	30 tonnes
Dec. 2			273	285	725			
Dec. 4			285	415	300			
Dec. 5	77	600			900			
Dec. 8			341	460	440			
Dec. 12			364	150	290			
Dec. 17	98	500			790			
Dec. 24			428	345	445			

Dec. 26			Shortage	30	415			
Dec. 28			447	145	270			
Dec. 30	171	628			895			
Dec. 30	Credit slip no. 37 (Received back)	50			945			
Dec. 31			483	425	520			

Illustration 7.3. *Raw materials 'x' costing ₹100 per kilogram and 'y' costing ₹.60 per kilogram are mixed in equal proportions for making product 'P'. The loss of materials in processing works out to be 25% of the output. The production expenses are allocated at 50% of direct material cost. The end product is priced with a margin of 100/3% over the total cost.*

Material 'y' is not easily available and a substitute raw material 'z' has been found for 'y' costing ₹ 50 per kilogram. It is required to keep the proportion of this substitute material in the mixture as low as possible and at the same time maintain the selling price of the end product at existing levels and ensure the same quantum of profit as at present.

You are required to compute what should be the ratio of mix of the raw materials 'x' and 'z'.

Solution : Statement of Cost and Price (per kg.) of product 'P'

Details	**Amount (₹)**
Material x : (0.625 kg × ₹100)	62.50
Material y: (0.625 kg × ₹60)	37.50
Total material cost	100.00
Add: production expenses (50% of material cost)	50.00
Total cost	150.00
Add: profit (1/3 of total cost or 1/4 of sales)	50.00
Selling price	200.00

Note: It is assumed that production expenses include labour cost as well.

Working Note:

(I) Loss of material = 25% of output

Let 1 kg be the output of product 'P'.

1.25 kg is the input of material x and y.

Proportion of material x and y in the output of 1kg of product P is:

x = 1.25 kg/2 = 0.625 kg. y = 1.25 kg/2 = 0.625 kg.

(II) Ratio of material 'x' and 'z' in the product 'P': Assume the minimum quantity of material 'z' in the product 'P' is Q kg. This means that 1.25 minus Q kg of 'z' is the required quantity of material 'x' for producing 1 kg of product 'P' to maintain the same level of profit and the selling price as calculated above. For this it is necessary that the total material cost in One kg of product 'P' should not exceed ₹100. Thus:

$$Q \text{ kg 'z'} \times ₹50 + (1.25 - Q \text{ of 'z'}) \text{ kg} \times ₹\ 100;$$

or

$$Q \text{ of 'z'} = 0.5\text{kg}.$$

Thus, the quantity of material 'x' = 1.25 kg – 0.50 kg = 0.75 kg.

Ratio of maximum material 'x' and minimum 'z' = 0.75: 0.50 or 3:2.

LET US RECAPITULATE

1. Material is the substance from which the product is made.
2. Materials are the basic substances that are transformed into finished goods.
3. Raw materials are those materials which are in their natural or raw form.
4. Semi-finished materials constitute those materials which are not 100% complete in all respects.
5. Finished materials compose of finished components which are used as raw materials for manufacturing a product.
6. Material cost may be either direct or indirect.
7. Materials control is a system which ensures the provision of the right quantity of material of the right quality at the right time with the minimum amount of investment.
8. To make any cost accounting system to be effective, it is necessary to have a proper control of materials and supplies from the point of time orders are placed with suppliers until they have been effectively utilized in production.

OBJECTIVE TYPE EXERCISES

I. Fill in the blank spaces with suitable word/s :

1. Stores Ledger is maintained by the .... department.
2. Bin card is a record of .... only.
3. Bin card is maintained by ....
4. .... is a document which records the return of unused materials.
5. .... is a document for recording the transfer of materials from one job/department to another.
6. The perpetual inventory records are .... and ....
7. Goods Received Note is prepared by the ....
8. .... items should be stored as near as possible to the department requiring them.

Answers :

1. Cost accounting	**2.** units	**3.** Store keeper
4. Material Return Note	**5.** Material Transfer Note	
6. Bin card, Stores Ledger	**7.** Receiving department	**8.** Bulky

II. Indicate whether the following statements are True or False :

1. When a stores ledger is maintained, there is no need to maintain bin cards.
2. The terms 'Materials' and 'Inventory' should not be used synonymously.
3. Stores ledger is maintained by the Store keeper.
4. Perpetual inventory system enables management to ascertain stock for materials at any time without the expense of physical stock taking.
5. Purchase Requisition Note is prepared by the purchasing department.
6. Annual stock taking confirms that the perpetual inventory system is functioning properly.
7. Bin card shows the quantity and value of a material at any moment of time.
8. Bin cards are not a part of accounting records.
9. The economic order quantity is the re-order quantity.
10. A list of all materials required for a particular job is called production order.
11. Stores ledger and Bin card are written up with the same basic document.
12. Codification of materials brings in ambiguity in the description of materials.
13. Re-ordering level is always fixed somewhere between maximum and minimum stock levels.
14. Bill of materials is a cash memo sent by the supplier along with the materials.
15. Stores Requisition Note is not a perpetual inventory record.
16. When is maximum stock level fixed, the stock in hand should never exceed this level.
17. In ABC analysis, 'A' group of items consist of those materials, the value of which is not high but which are used in large quantities.
18. In two bin system, two bins are maintained for each material.
19. ABC analysis is based on the principle of 'management by exception'.
20. Goods Received Note is not prepared by the Receiving department.
21. Bin card is same as stores ledger.
22. On the bin card, number of units and values are recorded.
23. Bin card shows the money value of material received, issued and the balance at any point of time.
24. Perpetual inventory system means continuous stock taking.
25. Purchase requisition is prepared by the purchasing department.
26. Perpetual inventory system and periodic inventory system are synonymous terms.

Answers :

1. False	**2.** True	**3.** False	**4.** True
5. False	**6.** False	**7.** False	**8.** True
9. True	**10.** False	**11.** True	**12.** False
13. True	**14.** False	**15.** True	**16.** False
17. False	**18.** True	**19.** True	**20.** False
21. False	**22.** False	**23.** False	**24.** False
25. False	**26.** False		

THEORETICAL EXERCISES

1. Under what circumstances is it necessary to use continuous stock taking for control over materials? State its advantages. **[DU, B.Com (Hons.) 2002]**

2. Briefly describe the perpetual inventory system and continuous stock taking. What are the advantages of perpetual inventory system?

3. Explain and illustrate the meaning and importance of 'Economic Order Quantity'.

4. What is Material control? Explain the purpose of material control.

5. What are the important requirements of a system of material control?

6. Write short notes on:
(i) Bill of Materials (ii) Economic order quantity
(iii) Perpetual Inventory system

7. Elucidate the procedure of a manufacturing concern from the time a need for material is determined until the material is stored and paid for.

8. Draw a Performa of 'Materials Transfer Note' and list its uses.
[DU, B.Com (Hons.) 2001]

9. Indicate the accounting treatment given to 'defectives' in cost accounts.
[DU, B.Com (Hons.) 2002]

10. Explain ABC system of inventory control. **[DU, B. Com (Hons.) 1999]**

11. State the basic requirements of a materials control system.
[DU, B.Com (Hons.) 2004]

12. Explain in brief the following concepts:
(i) Just-in-Time Purchases. **[DU, B.Com (Hons.) 2001]**

13. Distinguish between the followings:
(1) Material Requisition Note and Material Transfer Note
[B.Com (Hons.), DU, 1998]
(2) Bill of Materials and Purchase Requisition. **[DU, B.Com (Hons.) 2000]**
(3) Perpetual and periodic inventory systems. **[DU, B.Com (Hons.) 2001]**
(4) Bin Card and Stores Ledger **[DU, B.Com (Hons.) 2003]**

NUMERICAL EXERCISES

1. Raw materials 'x' costing ₹800 per kilogram and 'y' costing ₹.600 per kilogram are mixed in equal proportions for making product 'A'. The loss of materials in processing works out to be 25% of the output. The production expenses are allocated at 50% of direct material cost. The end product is priced with a margin of 1/3 over the total cost.

Material 'y' is not easily available and substitute raw material 'z' has been found for 'y' costing ₹ 400 per kilogram. It is required to keep the proportion of this substitute material in the mixture as low as possible and at the same time maintain the selling price of the end product at existing levels and ensure the same quantum of profit as at present.

You are required to compute what should be the ratio of mix of the raw materials 'x' and 'z'.

2. Compute Raw material cost of finished product from the following information:

Input of Raw cotton	= 300 Kg.	
Output (Cloth containing Cotton)	= 240 Kg.	
Cost per Kg.of Raw Cotton	= ₹30.00	**[Ans. ₹ 37.50]**

❑❑❑

4

Valuation of Materials

Learning Objectives

It attempts to explain as to how the incoming and outgoing materials are to be valued. In this chapter you will learn :

1. Method of valuing incoming materials.
2. How the cost of containers and discount modify the valuation of incoming materials.
3. Evaluate different methods of valuing the issues/outgoing materials.
4. A suitable method of pricing the issues under appropriate circumstances.
5. Prepare the stores ledger regarding both receipts and issues of materials.

INCOMING MATERIALS

The receipt of materials means incoming materials for conversion into production. The incoming materials are to be valued at invoice price subject to trade or quantity discount plus all expenses incurred up to the point of placing materials in a condition suitable for issuance from the stores. These expenses include:

(i) Transportation including cartage expenses;

(ii) Receiving, unpacking and inspecting costs;

(iii) Insurance and storage costs;

(iv) Accounting and purchasing costs.

The costs mentioned under point Number (ii) through (iv) form part of overhead costs. The basic price of materials is to be adjusted upwards considering the cost of containers and the discount availed.

Cost of Containers

The supplier of materials may charge separately for the containers that he has used for supplying materials. In case these containers are not returnable, their cost is to be added to the cost of materials received. If the containers are returnable at a price less than the cost charged, the difference should be added to the cost of materials received. In case they are to be accepted at full cost charged, their cost should not be added to the cost of incoming materials.

Discount

Discount is of three types:

(a) **Trade Discount:** It refers to the allowance which is permitted by the vendor to a purchaser who has to resell the articles. The allowance is permitted to compensate the purchaser for his costs of storage, breaking bulk, and selling and delivering small quantities.

(b) **Quantity Discount:** Such discount is allowed by the supplier to the buyer to encourage him to place large orders. Large orders from buyer give economies of large scale of production to the supplier. Part of this advantage is passed on to the buyer by allowing him the quantity discount.

Both trade and quantity discounts should be taken into account while valuing the incoming materials.

(c) **Cash Discount:** Such discount is allowed by the vendor to the buyer to encourage him to make prompt payment of cash. It is allowed only when the buyer makes the cash payment in the stipulated period. Since it is a financial matter, it is preferable to exclude it from the cost accounts.

Illustration 4.1 : *The Quality Limited quotes for Material M as under:*

Lot Size (Kg)	*Rate* (₹)
500	*20.00*
1,250	*14.00*
2,000	*12.00*

The supplier allows a trade discount of 25% and a cash discount of 4% if payment is made within two weeks. One container is required for every 50Kg of materials, and the containers are charged at ₹ 10 each but credited at ₹ 7.50 on return. The buyer decides to buy 2,000 Kgs of materials from the Quality limited. Transport charges amounting to ₹ 800 are charged by the supplier. Calculate the price of 2,000 Kgs of materials.

Solution :

Details		Cost per Kg. (₹)	Total cost (₹)
2,000 Kgs. Materials @ ₹ 12.00		12.00	24,000
Less: Trade Discount @ 25%		3.00	6,000
		9.00	18,000
Add: Charge for containers:			
For 50 Kg. One container			
For 2,000 Kg. 40 containers charged at ₹ 10 each	₹ 400		
Less: credit @ ₹ 7.50 per container	₹ 300	0.05	100
Add: Transport charges		0.40	800
Total Value for costing purposes		**9.45**	**18,900**

Note: Cash discount of ₹ 756 on the amount of ₹ 18,900 @ 4% is a matter of pure finance. Hence it has been excluded for costing purposes.

Illustration 4.2 : *The details relating to 6,000 Litres of a certain raw material purchased by the Kwality Limited during September were as under:*

(i) ***Lot Size (Litre)*** ***Rate*** (₹)

Lot Size (Litre)	Rate (₹)
Upto 4,000	*30.00*
Between 4,000 – 5,000	*28.00*
Between 5,000 – 6,000	*25.00*

(ii) Trade discount of 20%.

(iii) Additional charge for containers @ ₹ 10 for every 50 Litres of raw material. Credit allowed on return of containers @ ₹ 6 per container of 50 Litres capacity.

(iv) VAT @ 12.5% on raw material and 5% on the containers.

(v) Total freight paid by the Kwality limited ₹ 600.

(vi) Insurance @ 4% (on Net Invoice value) paid by the purchasing company.

(vii) Stores overhead absorbed @ 6% on total purchase cost of raw material.

The entire quantity was received and issued to production. The containers are returned in the due course. Draw up a suitable statement to show:

(a) Total cost of material purchased; and

(b) Unit cost of material issued to production.

Solution :

Details	Cost per Litre (₹)	Total Cost (₹)
6,000 Litres Materials @ ₹ 25.00	25.00	1,50,000
Less: Trade Discount @ 20%	5.00	30,000
	20.00	1,20,000
Add: Charge for containers: 120 container charged @ ₹ 10 each (6,000 Litres ÷ 50 Litres per container)	0.20	1,200
Add: VAT:		
12.5% on ₹ 1,20,000 (Raw material)	0.24	15,000
5% on ₹ 1,200 (Containers)	0.01	60
Net Invoice Value	20.45	1,36,260
Freight paid	0.10	600
Insurance @ 4% on ₹ 1,36,260	0.91	5,450
	21.46	1,42,310
Less: credit @ ₹ 6.00 per container	0.12	720
Purchase Cost	21.34	1,41,590
Add: Stores Overheads @ 6%	1.42	8,495
Total Value for costing purposes	22.76	1,50,085

OUTGOING MATERIALS

The issue of materials mostly for production purposes is known as outgoing materials. The question is at what price such materials are to be charged. There are various materials of outgoing issue of materials.

Methods of Pricing the Issue of Materials

Materials issued to different jobs/ work orders are to be charged with the value of materials. The inventory of materials consists of different consignments received at different dates and prices. It becomes necessary to decide about the price of issue which is to be charged to a job or a work order. Some of the important methods of valuing materials are as under:

I. Based on Cost Price:
   1. Specific Price Method
   2. First In First Out Method
   3. Last In First Out Method
   4. Highest In First Out Method
   5. Next In First Out Method
   6. Base Stock Method

II. Derived from Cost Price:
   1. Average Cost Method
   2. Market Price Method:

(i) Replacement Price Method

(ii) Realisable value Method

(iii) Re-use Price method

III. Based on Notional Price:

1. Inflated Price method
2. Standard cost method

Each of the method listed above is discussed in detail in the following paragraphs.

Specific Price Method

Materials are charged at the price at which they were originally bought. This requires identification of each lot purchased. This method is applied when the materials have been bought for the specific job/work order.

This method is useful where materials are purchased exclusively for special jobs/work orders/contracts. These jobs are charged at the specific prices at which the materials used were purchased. Materials purchased are job specific and are therefore, easily identifiable.

Merits:

1. It is especially useful in case of job order industries where materials are bought on job basis.
2. Actual price paid for the procurement of materials is charged to the jobs.
3. The question of difference in the value of stocks as per stores ledger and the actual value of stock in hand does not arise.
4. It provides appropriate matching of cost and revenue.

Demerits:

1. It has limited application i.e. job order industry.
2. In other industries, it may not be easy to identify which unit of material was procured at what price.
3. In other cases, use of this method would lead to serious problems. Each Works manager would like to get those units of materials issued which were procured at the lowest price. It may create disharmony in the production department, and also material handling problems.
4. Cost may cease to serve as a basis for price fixation and efficiency measurement.
5. This method is quite unsuitable in large organisations with huge stocks of materials.

Following illustration attempts to explain this method.

Illustration 4.3. (Specific Price Method)

Following is the record of receipt and issue of certain materials during the month of September, 2008:

Date	*Details*
2008	
September 1	*Purchased 800 Kgs for Job No. 91 @ ₹ 25 per kg.*
5	*Purchased 600 Kgs for Job No. 92 @ ₹ 27.50 per kg.*
12	*Issued 600 Kgs for Job No. 91*
17	*Purchased 500 Kgs for Job No. 93 @ ₹ 30 per kg.*
18	*Issued 500 Kgs for Job No. 92*
20	*Purchased 800 Kgs for Job No. 95 @ ₹ 32.80 per kg.*
20	*Issued 500 Kgs for Job No. 93*
24	*Purchased 800 Kgs for Job No. 94 @ ₹ 32.50 per kg.*
25	*Issued 800 Kgs for Job No. 94*
26	*Issued 800 Kgs for Job No. 95*
27	*Purchased 500 Kgs for Job No. 96 @ ₹ 33.00 per kg.*
28	*Issued 450 Kgs for Job No. 96*

Solution : **Stores Ledger Sheet (Specific Price Method)**

Date	Receipts				Issues				Quantity (unit)	Amount (₹)
	Job No.	Quantity (unit)	Rate (₹)	Amount (₹)	Job No.	Quantity (unit)	Rate (₹)	Amount (₹)		
2008 Sep. 1	91	800	25.00	20,000					800	20,000
5	92	600	27.50	16,500					1,400	16,500
12					91	600	25.00	15,000	800	21,500
17	93	500	30.00	15,000					1,300	36,500
18					92	500	27.50	13,750	800	22,750
20	94	800	32.80	26,240					1,600	48,990
20					93	500	30.00	15,000	1,100	33,990
24	95	800	32.50	26,000					1,900	59.990
25					94	800	32.80	26,240	1,100	33,750
26					95	800	32.50	26,000	300	7,750
27	96	500	33.00	16,500					800	24,250
28					96	450	33.00	14,850	350	9,400

Composition of closing stock:

Job No.	Balance (Units)	Rate (₹)	Amount (₹)
91	200	25.00	5,000
92	100	27.50	2,750
96	50	33.00	1,650
Total	350	—	9,400

First in First out Method (FIFO)

Issue of materials is priced in the order of their purchases. The material issued is priced at the earliest purchase price and the inventory is valued at the latest purchases. It does not mean that the issue of materials is actually in the order of first in first out; the physical flow of materials need not necessarily be in the order of their respective purchases. The FIFO method applies the price of the first batch of materials purchases for all issues, till the quantity of materials forming this batch is fully issued. Thereafter, the materials are issued at the next purchase price and so on. FIFO method assumes that materials purchased first are issued first. The actual physical movement of materials may or may not follow this pattern. This assumption results in the followings:

(a) Both issues and stocks are priced at actual cost.

(b) Production is charged at the earliest purchase price of materials used.

(c) Closing stock is valued at the latest purchase price of materials.

This method is especially useful in case of perishable materials used in food processing industry.

Merits :

1. FIFO is most appropriate in case of perishable materials because the pricing method will almost coincide with the actual physical movement of materials.
2. The method is simple to understand and apply.
3. All issues are priced at cost price so that the entire cost price of materials is recovered from production.
4. It results in lower book profit and lower tax liability during the period of falling prices.
5. Value of closing inventory of materials is at the latest purchases; thus the value of the closing stock is equivalent to market price.

Demerits :

1. There is no proper match of sales and cost of sales. Sales are always at current market price while material cost charged to production is at the earliest (Old) prices. This mismatch gains prominence if there is significant time lag between purchase of materials and their issue for production.
2. It results in higher book profit and higher tax liability during the period of rising prices as the closing stock of materials is valued at the latest prices which are higher.
3. For pricing one material requisition, more than one price figures may be involved. In such cases, the computations are prone to clerical errors.
4. The issue price differs from issue to issue. Consequently, Cost comparison gets distorted.

Following illustration attempts to explain this method.

Illustration 4.4. (FIFO Method)

From the following transactions prepare Stores Ledger Sheet using FIFO method of Issue of materials:

Date 2008	*Details*
November 1	*Opening Balance 1,000 units @ ₹ 20*
November 4	*Issued 400 units vide MRN 91*
November 5	*Purchased 1,500 units @ ₹ 22 vide GRN 25*
November 8	*Issued 750 units vide MRN 109*
November 12	*Purchased 1,250 units @ ₹ 26 vide GRN 32*
November 14	*Issued 850 units vide MRN 125*
November 15	*Issued 600 units vide MRN 138*
November 17	*Purchased 750 units @ ₹ 30 vide GRN 41*
November 20	*Purchased 500 units @ ₹ 32 vide GRN 44*
November 20	*Issued 900 units vide MRN 157*
November 21	*Issued 1,200 units vide MRN 162*
November 23	*Purchased 600 units @ ₹ 35 vide GRN 49*
November 24	*Issued 250 units vide MRN 168*
November 28	*Purchased 2,000 units @ ₹ 40 vide GRN 70*
November 30	*Issued 1,500 units vide MRN 185*

Solution : **Stores Ledger Sheet (FIFO Method)**

Date 2008 Nov.	Receipts				Issues				Balance	
	GRN.	Quantity (unit)	Rate (₹)	Amount (₹)	MRN.	Quantity (unit)	Rate (₹)	Amount (₹)	Quantity (unit)	Amount (₹)
1	Opening Balance	—	—	—	—	—	—	—	1,000	20,000
4					91	400	20	8,000	600	12,000
5	25	1,500	22	33,000					2,100	45,000
8					109	600	20	12,000		
						150	22	3,300		
						750		15,300	1,350	29,700
12	32	1,250	26	32,500					2,600	62,200
14					125	850	22	18,700	1,750	43,500
15					138	500	22	11,000		
						100	26	2,600		
						600		13,600	1,150	29,900
17	41	750	30	22,500					1,900	52,400

20	44	500	32	16,000					2,400	68,400
20					157	900	26	23,400	1,500	45,000
21					162	250 750 200 1,200	26 30 32	6,500 22,500 6,400 35,400	300	9,600
23	49	600	35	21,000					900	30,600
24					168	250	32	8,000	650	22,600
28	70	2,000	40	80,000					2,650	1,02,600
30					185	50 600 850 1,500	32 35 40	1,600 21,000 34,000 56,600	1,150	46,000

Note:

(1) The closing stock of 1,150 units is at the latest purchase price of ₹ 40 per unit.

(2) In case both the receipt and issue are given on the same date, the time of receipt and issue is not given, and the order of the two transactions cannot be established, it is preferable to record the receipt at the first instance.

Last in First out Method (LIFO)

The method assumes that the last item of materials purchased is the first to be issued. The price of the latest consignment is used for pricing the materials issued till it is exhausted, and then the next consignment pricing is used and so on through successive consignments.

Merits:

(i) It takes into account the current market conditions while valuing materials issued to different jobs/work orders. It evens out the effect of fluctuating prices in profit figures of the organisation as the cost of sales is the largest when the prices are rising and lowest when prices are falling.

(ii) During the period of rising prices, the burden of income tax is reduced.

(iii) Proper picture of profit or loss is obtained because current costs are correlated with current sales.

(iv) Actual cost of materials is charged to production and so there is no fictitious profit or loss on account of this method.

Demerits:

(i) The stock in hand is valued at the cost which might have become obsolete as compared to the current prices of the inventory.

(ii) It requires considerable amount of clerical work because of computing prices.

Illustration 4.5. (LIFO Method)

Continuing with the Illustration 2, prepare Store ledger sheet using LIFO method.

Solution : **Stores Ledger Sheet (LIFO Method)**

Name of the article .... Bin Number .... Folio Number ....
Type/Size .... Location .... Maximum Level ....
Code Number .... Minimum Level ....
Ordering Level ....

Date 2008 Nov.	Receipts				Issues				Balance	
	GRN.	Quantity (unit)	Rate (₹)	Amount (₹)	MRN.	Quantity (unit)	Rate (₹)	Amount (₹)	Quantity (unit)	Amount (₹)
1	Opening Balance	—	—	—	—	—	—	—	1,000	20,000
4					91	400	20	8,000	600	12,000
5	25	1,500	22	33,000					2,100	45,000
8					109	750	22	16,500	1,350	28,500
12	32	1,250	26	32,500					2,600	61,000
14					125	850	26	22,100	1,750	38,900
15					138	400 200 600	26 22	10,400 4,400 14,800	1,150	24,100
17	41	750	30	22,500					1,900	46,600
20	44	500	32	16,000					2,400	62,600
20					157	500 400 900	32 30	16,000 12,000 28,000	1,500	34,600
21					162	350 550 300 1,200	30 22 20	10,500 12,100 6,000 28,6 00	300	6,000
23	49	600	35	21,000					900	27,000
24					168	250	35	8,750	650	18,250
28	70	2,000	40	80,000					2,650	98,250
30					185	1,500	40	60,000	1,150	38,250

Note:

(1) Composition of closing stock of 1,150 units is as under:

GRN	Balance (Units)	Rate (₹)	Amount (₹)
70	500	40	20,000
49	350	35	12,250
Opening Balance	300	20	6,000
Total	1,150	—	38,250

(2) In case, the date of receipt and issue is the same, the time of receipt and issue is not given, and the order of the two transactions can not be established, it is preferable to record the receipt first.

Evaluation of FIFO and LIFO Methods of pricing during market oscillations:

Period of rising prices:

Period falling prices:

Highest in First out Method (HIFO)

Materials are issued to jobs at the rate of highest priced materials in store. This highest rate is charged until the materials purchased at that highest price are not exhausted as per records. After this the next highest price is used for pricing issues, and so on. Thus, highest cost paid for materials is charged to production and closing stock is valued at lowest priced materials. It is obvious that highest cost of materials is recovered first and the inventory valuation is kept at the lowest. This undervaluation of stocks amounts to creation of secret reserve. The method is used in cost-plus contracts or for determining monopoly prices. Otherwise, the method is not used. Following illustration explains the operation of the method.

Illustration 4.6. (HIFO Method)

From the following transactions, prepare Stores Ledger Sheet using HIFO method of Issue of materials:

Date 2008	*Details*
November 1	*Opening Balance 1,500 units @ ₹ 20*
November 4	*Issued 900 units vide MRN 91*
November 5	*Purchased 1,000 units @ ₹ 24 vide GRN 25*
November 8	*Issued 550 units vide MRN 109*
November 11	*Purchased 1,250 units @ ₹ 22 vide GRN 32*
November 14	*Issued 800 units vide MRN 125*
November 17	*Purchased 750 units @ ₹ 28 vide GRN 41*
November 20	*Issued 600 units vide MRN 157*
November 23	*Purchased 1,100 units @ ₹ 26 vide GRN 49*
November 26	*Issued 1,800 units vide MRN 168*

Solution : **Stores Ledger Sheet (HIFO Method)**

Date 2008 Nov.	Receipts				Issues				Balance	
	GRN.	Quantity (unit)	Rate (₹)	Amount (₹)	MRN.	Quantity (unit)	Rate (₹)	Amount (₹)	Quantity (unit)	Amount (₹)
1	Opening Balance	—	—	—	—	—	—	—	1,500	30,000
4					91	900	20	18,000	600	12,000
5	25	1,000	24	24,000					1,600	36,000
8					109	550	24	13,200	1,050	22,800
11	32	1,250	22	27,500					2,300	50,300
14					125	450	24	10,800		
						350	22	7,700		
						800		18,500	1,500	31,800
17	41	750	30	22,500					2,250	54,300
20					157	600	30	18,000	1,650	36,300
23	49	1,100	26	28,600					2,750	64,900
26					168	150	30	4,500		
						1,100	26	28,600		
						550	22	12,100		
						1,800		37,600	950	19,700

Composition of closing stock of 950 units is as under:

GRN	Balance (Units)	Rate (₹)	Amount (₹)
32	350	22.00	7,700
Opening Balance	600	20.00	12,000
Total	950	—	19,700

Next in First out Method (NIFO)

Materials are charged NOT at the actual price already paid for the materials but at a PRICE at which an order has been placed and the NEXT DELIVERY is expected. It means, issues are at the latest price at which the business has committed itself though materials have not been physically received till the time of issue. This way the output is charged at a price close to market price of materials at the time of production. The method is suitable for materials which are not much in demand but require replacement immediately after their issue, otherwise NIFO method is not much in use.

Illustration 4.7. (NIFO Method)

Date	Receipts	Date	Issues
2009		*2009*	
November 1	*Opening Balance 500 Units @ ₹ 24*	*November 4*	*MRN 521 250 units*
November 6	*GRN 47 400 units @ ₹ 25*	*November 11*	*MRN 532 300 units*
November 12	*GRN 58 450 units @ ₹ 23*	*November 17*	*MRN 542 200 units*
November 18	*GRN 70 200 units @ ₹ 26*	*November 21*	*MRN 555 300 units*
November 22	*GRN 78 320 units @ ₹ 24.5*	*November 25*	*MRN 568 280 units*
November 28	*GRN 87 380 units @ ₹ 27*		

Solution : **Stores Ledger Sheet (HIFO Method)**

Date 2008 Nov.	Receipts				Issues				Balance	
	GRN.	Quantity (unit)	Rate (₹)	Amount (₹)	MRN.	Quantity (unit)	Rate (₹)	Amount (₹)	Quantity (unit)	Amount (₹)
1	Opening Balance	—	—	—	—	—	—	—	500	12,000
4					521	250	25	6,250	250	5,750
6	47	400	25	10,000					650	15,750
11					532	300	23	6,900	350	8,850
12	58	450	23	10,350					800	19,200
17					542	200	26	5,200	600	14,000
18	70	200	26	5,200					800	19,200
21					555	300	24.5	7,350	500	11,850
22	78	320	24.5	7,840					820	19,690
25					568	280	27	7,560	540	12,130
28	87	380	27	10,260					920	22,390

Composition of closing stock of 920 units is as under:

GRN	Balance (Units)	Rate (₹)	Amount (₹)
47	150	25.00	3,750
58	150	23.00	3,450
78	20	24.50	490
87	100	27	2,700
Opening Balance	500	24.00	12,000
Total	920	—	22,390

Base Stock Method

It is assumed that minimum (base) stock is always maintained in stock and is not issued. This is in the nature of a fixed asset and is carried at original cost. Any quantity in excess of base stock is valued according to one of the other methods i.e.

FIFO, LIFO, Average etc. It may be pointed out that base stock method is not an independent method and has to be used in conjunction with some other method. It offers the advantage of simplifying valuation of inventory because base stock values are fixed. But the inventory valuation may not reflect the current market prices.

Illustration 4.8. (FIFO with Base stock)

Prepare Store ledger sheet showing pricing of materials based on FIFO with base stock of 400 units priced at ₹ 20 per unit, from the information given as under:

Date 2008	*Details*
November 1	*Opening Balance 1,000 units @ ₹ 20*
November 4	*Issued 400 units vide MRN 91*
November 5	*Purchased 1,500 units @ ₹ 22 vide GRN 25*
November 8	*Issued 750 units vide MRN 109*
November 12	*Purchased 1,250 units @ ₹ 26 vide GRN 32*
November 14	*Issued 850 units vide MRN 125*
November 15	*Issued 600 units vide MRN 138*
November 17	*Purchased 850 units @ ₹ 30 vide GRN 41*
November 20	*Purchased 500 units @ ₹ 32 vide GRN 44*
November 20	*Issued 900 units vide MRN 157*
November 21	*Issued 1,200 units vide MRN 162*
November 23	*Purchased 600 units @ ₹ 35 vide GRN 49*
November 24	*Issued 250 units vide MRN 168*
November 28	*Purchased 2,000 units @ ₹ 40 vide GRN 70*
November 30	*Issued 1,500 units vide MRN 185*

Solution : Stores Ledger Sheet (FIFO Method)

Date 2008 Nov.	Receipts				Issues				Balance	
	GRN.	Quantity (unit)	Rate (₹)	Amount (₹)	MRN.	Quantity (unit)	Rate (₹)	Amount (₹)	Quantity (unit)	Amount (₹)
1	Opening Balance	—	—	—	—	—	—	—	1,000	20,000
4					91	400	20	8,000	600	12,000
5	25	1,500	22	33,000					2,100	45,000
8					109	200	20	4,000		
						550	22	12,100		
						750		16,100	1,350	28,900
12	32	1,250	26	32,500					2,600	61,400

14					125	850	22	18,700	1,750	42,700
15					138	100	22	2,200		
						500	26	13,000		
						600		15,200	1,150	27,500
17	41	850	30	25,500					2,000	53,000
20	44	500	32	16,000					2,500	69,000
20					157	750	26	19,500		
						150	30	4,500		
						900		24,000	1,600	45,000
21					162	700	30	21,000		
						500	32	16,000		
						1,200		37,000	400	8,000
23	49	600	35	21,000					1,000	29,000
24					168	250	35	8,750	750	20,250
28	70	2,000	40	80,000					2,750	100250
30					185	350	35	12,250		
						1,150	40	46,000		
						1,500		58,250	1,250	42,000

Composition of closing stock of 1,250 units is as under:

GRN	Balance (Units)	Rate (₹)	Amount (₹)
70	850	40	34,000
Base stock	400	20	8,000
Total	1,250	—	42,000

Note: In case both the receipt and issue are given on the same date and neither the time of receipt and issue is given, nor the order of the two transactions can be established, it is preferable to record receipt first.

Average Cost Methods

Such methods are based on the assumption that the materials purchased in different lots are stored together and their identity gets lost. Therefore, these materials need to be charged to production at an average rate which may be a simple or a weighted average.

Simple Average Method

It is computed by adding ALL the different prices of materials in stock by the number of prices used in that total. This method does not take quantities into account. Assume, the following three lots of materials are in stock on the day of issue:

800 units purchased @ ₹ 28
500 units purchased @ ₹ 29
900 units purchased @ ₹ 31
700 units purchased @ ₹ 32

Simple Average Price = (28 + 29 + 31 + 32) ÷ 4 = ₹ 30

Simplicity is the only advantage of this method. As this method ignores the quantity aspect of valuation, it is called an unscientific method. This method does not charge materials at actual cost and thus, may result in unrealized profit or loss.

Illustration 4.9. (Simple Average Method)

From the following transactions, prepare Stores Ledger Sheet using Simple average method:

Date 2008	*Details*
January 1	*Purchased 2,000 units @ ₹ 25 vide GRN 32*
January 4	*Issued 600 units vide MRN 201*
January 5	*Purchased 1,000 units @ ₹ 27 vide GRN 35*
January 8	*Issued 900 units vide MRN 204*
January 11	*Purchased 500 units @ ₹ 29 vide GRN 38*
January 14	*Issued 800 units vide MRN 208*
January 16	*Purchased 750 units @ ₹ 31 vide GRN 45*
January 18	*Issued 450 units vide MRN 211*
January 19	*Purchased 1,500 units @ ₹ 33 vide GRN 48*
January 20	*Issued 1,400 units vide MRN 215*
January 22	*Purchased 1,250 units @ ₹ 35 vide GRN 51*
January 23	*Issued 1,300 units vide MRN 217*
January 24	*Purchased 850 units @ ₹ 34 vide GRN 54*
January 27	*Issued 1,000 units vide MRN 228*
January 28	*Purchased 2,600 units @ ₹ 36 vide GRN 65*
January 30	*Issued 2,860 units vide MRN 236*

Solution : Stores Ledger Sheet (Simple Average Method)

Date 2008 Nov.	Receipts				Issues				Balance	
	GRN.	Quantity (unit)	Rate (₹)	Amount (₹)	MRN.	Quantity (unit)	Rate (₹)	Amount (₹)	Quantity (unit)	Amount (₹)
1	32	2,000	25	50,000	—	—	—	—	2,000	50,000
4					201	600	25	15,000	1,400	35,000
5	35	1,000	27	27,000					2,400	62,000
8					204	900	26	23,400	1,500	38,600
11	38	500	29	14,500					2,000	53,100
14					208	800	27	21,600	1,200	31,500
16	45	750	31	23,250					1,950	54,750
18					211	450	29	13,050	1,500	41,700
19	48	1,500	33	49,500					3,000	91,200
20					215	1,400	30	42,000	1,600	49,200
22	51	1,250	35	43,750					2,850	92,950

23					217	1,300	33	42,900	1,550	50,050
24	54	850	34	28,900					2,400	78,950
27					228	1,000	34	34,000	1,400	44,950
28	65	2,600	36	93,600					4,000	138,550
30					236	2,860	35	100,100	1,140	38,450

Working Notes : The calculation of issue price on various dates is as under:

Date 2008	Details
January 4	₹ 25 as there is only one lot @ ₹ 25
January 8	(25 + 27) / 2 = ₹ 26
January 14	(25 + 27 + 29) / 3 = ₹ 27
January 18	(27 + 29 + 31) / 3 = ₹ 29
January 20	(27 + 29 + 31 + 33) / 4 = ₹ 30
January 23	(31 + 33 + 35) / 3 = ₹ 33
January 27	(33 + 35 + 34) / 3 = ₹ 34
January 30	(35 + 34 + 36) / 3 = ₹ 35

Problems arising out of Simple average method :

This method is considered unscientific, and can lead to absurd results. Following examples attempt to make this point clear:

(a) 900 units of a material are purchased @ ₹ 40 per unit and 200 units are purchased @ ₹ 32 per unit. Total purchase price of materials is 900 × 40 + 200 × 32 = ₹ 42,400. Suppose all the units of the material are issued for production at the simple average price of ₹ 36 {(40 + 32)/2}, at the issue amount of ₹ 39,600i.e. (1,100 × 36). Thus, material cost has been under absorbed by ₹ 2,800 (i.e. 42,400 – 39,600).

(b) 900 units of a material are purchased @ ₹ 32 per unit and 200 units are purchased @ ₹ 40 per unit. Total purchase price of materials is 900 × 32 + 200 × 40 = ₹ 36,800. Suppose all the units of the material are issued for production at the simple average price of ₹ 36 {(32 + 40)/2} at the issue amount of ₹ 39,600 i.e. (1,100 × 36). Thus, material cost has been over absorbed by ₹ 2,800 (i.e. 36,800 – 39,600).

(c) 900 units of a material are purchased @ ₹ 40 per unit and 200 units are purchased @ ₹ 60 per unit. Total purchase price of materials is 900 × 40 + 200 × 60 = ₹ 48,000. Suppose 1,000 units of the material are issued for production at the simple average price of ₹ 50 {(40 + 60)/2} i.e. 1,000 × 50 = ₹ 50,000. As per records the firm has a stock of one hundred units with negative value of ₹ 2,000; this is absurd.

From the above it is obvious that simple average method stands totally rejected, and it is rarely used.

Suitability: The method is particularly suitable when all purchases are of equal or more or less equal lot size as it obviates the computation problems of the weighted average method.

Weighted Average Method

It is computed by dividing the total cost of goods in stock by the total quantities in stock. Prices are averaged after giving multiplying the price with the respective quantities of the lot. The average cost at any point of time is simply the balance value divided by balance quantity. Whenever a new lot is purchased and received, a new weighted average cost is computed by adding the value of the new lot to the cost of stock in hand. The rate thus computed is used to charge ALL the issues till a new lot is purchased and received. It is obvious that this method of charging the issues is based upon Quantity available in stock and Value of that stock for issue.

Merits: Following are the main advantages of this method:

(1) Effect of widely varying prices of different lots consisting of the stock is even out.

(2) It is considered more scientific as the inventory is valued at one rate till next lot is purchased and received.

(3) It recovers FULL cost of materials from the production.

(4) It obviates the need for adjustments in stock valuation.

Demerits: Following are the main advantages of this method:

(1) The inventory is valued NOT at the latest price and therefore does not reflect the current economic value.

(2) In case receipts are numerous, calculation work becomes tedious, and at times weighted average price may run to decimal points.

(3) Fresh rate of issue needs to be calculated after every fresh receipt of materials.

(4) Issue rate is different from actual cost for individual issues.

Suitability: The method is particularly suitable when:

(a) There are considerable price fluctuations; and/or

(b) There are few receipts of materials accompanied with large number of issues.

Illustration 4.10. (Weighted Average Method)

Prepare stores ledger sheet from the preceding Illustration using weighted average method:

Solution : Stores Ledger Sheet (Weighted Average Method)

Date 2008 Nov.	Receipts				Issues				Balance	
	GRN.	Quantity (unit)	Rate (₹)	Amount (₹)	MRN.	Quantity (unit)	Rate (₹)	Amount (₹)	Quantity (unit)	Amount (₹)
1	32	2,000	25	50,000	—	—	—	—	2,000	50,000
4					201	600	25	15,000	1,400	35,000
5	35	1,000	27	27,000					2,400	62,000
8					204	900	25.8333	23,250	1,500	38,750
11	38	500	29	14,500					2,000	53,250
14					208	800	26.625	21,300	1,200	31,950
16	45	750	31	23,250					1,950	55,200
18					211	450	28.3077	12,738	1,500	42,462
19	48	1,500	33	49,500					3,000	91,962
20					215	1,400	30.654	42,916	1,600	49,046
22	51	1,250	35	43,750					2,850	92,796
23					217	1,300	32.56	42,328	1,550	50,468
24	54	850	34	28,900					2,400	79,368
27					228	1,000	33.07	33,070	1,400	46,298
28	65	2,600	36	93,600					4,000	1,39,898
30					236	2,860	34.9745	1,00,027	1,140	39,871

Working Notes : The calculation of issue price on various dates is as under:

Date 2008	Details
January 4	₹ 25 as there is only one lot @ ₹ 25
January 8	62,000 / 2,400 = ₹ 25.8333
January 14	53,250 / 2,000 = ₹ 26.625
January 18	55,200 / 1,950 = ₹ 28.3077
January 20	(91,962 / 3,000 = ₹ 30.654
January 23	92,796 / 2,850 = ₹ 32.56
January 27	79,368 / 2,400 = ₹ 33.07
January 30	1,39,898 / 4,000 = ₹ 34.9745

Periodic Simple Average Method

Issue rate is calculated only periodically (weekly, fortnightly, or monthly, etc.) and not at the time of each issue. For the specific period the issue rate remains constant. The work of computing the rate of issue is done at the end of the period. During the period only the quantities are entered in stores ledger as and when issues are made. The rate is computed by adding the prices at which different lots were purchased during the given period and dividing the sum total of these prices by the number of prices or the number of purchases during the given period. Price of opening stock is excluded both in the numerator as well as denominator.

Merits:

1. As compared to simple average method it is simpler as the issue rate is calculated once in a period.
2. It gives more representative issue rate than that obtained by simple average.

Demerits:

1. It is unscientific and suffers from all the defects of simple average.
2. The pricing of the issue has to wait till the end of the given period.

Illustration 4.11. (Periodic Simple Average Price Method)

Prepare stores ledger sheet from the preceding Illustration using Periodic Simple Average Method.

Working Note : *Periodic Simple Average Price:*

= Sum of Purchase prices during the Period/ number of Purchases during the period

= (25 + 27 +29 + 31 + 33 +35 + 34 +36)/8

250/8 ⇒ ₹ 31.25

Solution : Stores Ledger Sheet (Weighted Average Method)

Date 2008 Nov.	Receipts				Issues				Balance	
	GRN.	Quantity (unit)	Rate (₹)	Amount (₹)	MRN.	Quantity (unit)	Rate (₹)	Amount (₹)	Quantity (unit)	Amount (₹)
1	32	2,000	25	50,000	—	—	—	—	2,000	50,000
4					201	600	31.25	18,750	1,400	31,250
5	35	1,000	27	27,000					2,400	58,250
8					204	900	31.25	28,125	1,500	30,125
11	38	500	29	14,500					2,000	44,625
14					208	800	31.25	25,000	1,200	19,625
16	45	750	31	23,250					1,950	42,875
18					211	450	31.25	14,063	1,500	28,812
19	48	1,500	33	49,500					3,000	78,312
20					215	1,400	31.25	43,750	1,600	34,562
22	51	1,250	35	43,750					2,850	78,312
23					217	1,300	31.25	40,625	1,550	37,687
24	54	850	34	28,900					2,400	66,587
27					228	1,000	31.25	31,250	1,400	35,337
28	65	2,600	36	93,600					4,000	1,28,937
30					236	2,860	31.25	89,375	1,140	39,562

Periodic Weighted Average Method

Weighted average is computed periodically. It is computed at the end of a specified period. The weighted average is applied to all issues made during the given period. It is calculated by dividing the total cost of purchases of a material during a given period by the total quantity of material purchased during that period. The opening stock is not considered in the computation.

Merits: It has all the advantages of the simple weighted method. Besides these, (i) Calculation work is less, and (ii) issue price remains constant during the given period so that cost comparison s during the period reflect relative efficiency in a proper perspective.

Demerits: The additional disadvantage is that the preparation of stores ledger and computation of issue rate has to wait till the expiry of that given period.

Illustration 4.12. (Periodic Weighted Average Price Method)

Prepare stores ledger sheet from the preceding Illustration using Periodic Simple Average Method.

Working Note : *Periodic Simple Average Price:*

= Total cost of material purchased during the Period/ Total quantity of Purchases during the period

= 3, 30,500) /10,450 ⇒ ` 31.6268

Solution : Stores Ledger Sheet (Weighted Average Method)

Date 2008 Nov.	Receipts				Issues				Balance	
	GRN.	Quantity (unit)	Rate (₹)	Amount (₹)	MRN.	Quantity (unit)	Rate (₹)	Amount (₹)	Quantity (unit)	Amount (₹)
1	32	2,000	25	50,000	—	—	—	—	2,000	50,000
4					201	600	31.6268	18,976	1,400	31,024
5	35	1,000	27	27,000					2,400	58,024
8					204	900	31.6268	28,464	1,500	29, 560
11	38	500	29	14,500					2,000	44,060
14					208	800	31.6268	25,301	1,200	18,759
16	45	750	31	23,250					1,950	42,009
18					211	450	31.6268	14,232	1,500	27,777
19	48	1,500	33	49,500					3,000	77,277
20					215	1,400	31.6268	44,278	1,600	32,999
22	51	1,250	35	43,750					2,850	76,749
23					217	1,300	31.6268	41,115	1,550	35,634
24	54	850	34	28,900					2,400	64,534
27					228	1,000	31.6268	31,627	1,400	32,907
28	65	2,600	36	93,600					4,000	1,26,507
30					236	2,860	31.6268	90,453	1,140	36,054

Moving Simple Average Method

The moving simple average price is the average of the periodic simple average prices for a given number of periods. The period for which the material issues are to be valued will be the last period. The issues of materials are valued at the average price so computed. Thus, the method takes into account not only the current average price but also the average prices for a given number of preceding periods. This method is suitable when there are seasonal fluctuations in prices and the monthly purchases do not vary much. The method attempts to smoothen out the oscillations in price over a number of periods and therefore give better results than the simple periodic average. The demerit of this method is that it does not reflect current price conditions and it also involves lot of ministerial work at the end of the period.

Illustration 4.13. (Moving Simple Average Method)

Month (1)	Periodic Simple Average Price (₹) (2)	Total for 5 months (₹) (3)	Moving Simple Average (₹) (4) = {(3)/5}
April	40		
May	42		
June	41		
July	43		
August	44	(40 + 42 + 41 + 43 + 44) = 210	210/5 = 42.0
September	45	(42 + 41 + 43 + 44 + 45) = 215	215/5 = 43.0
October	47	(41 + 43 + 44 + 45 + 47) = 220	220/5 = 44.0
November	44	(43 + 44 + 45 + 47 + 44) = 223	223/5 = 44.6
December	48	(44 + 45 + 47 + 44 + 48) = 228	228/5 = 45.6
January	46	(45 + 47 + 44 + 48 + 46) = 230	230/5 = 46.0
February	50	(47 + 44 + 48 + 46 + 50) = 235	235/5 = 47.0
March	47	(44 + 48 + 46 + 50 + 47) = 235	235/5 = 47.0

Merits: The moving average method evens out the price oscillations. In column No. 2 the prices fluctuate between ₹ 40 and ₹ 50 whereas in column No.4 they fluctuate between ₹ 42 and ₹ 47 and that too have a rising pattern.

Demerits:

1. It involves more clerical work.
2. It results in a problem of over/under recovery of material cost.
3. The value of inventory will be quite high during the period of rising prices and vice versa.
4. The moving average of a particular period is affected by a number of periods in the past and may be out of tune with the current prices.

Compare the prices of the month December and February. In December, the periodic simple average price is ₹ 48 whereas the moving price is ₹ 45.6. The same pattern of pricing is observed in the month of February.

Moving Weighted Average Method: The process of calculation is exactly the same as in the case of moving simple average method except that periodic weighted average prices replace the simple average prices. The method is definitely superior to moving simple average pricing method.

Notional Pricing Method: The issue price of materials is not based on actual cost incurred in purchasing the materials, though this aspect is not exactly ignored.

Standard Price Method

All receipts of materials are recorded at the actual price paid but all issues are priced at a predetermined price which is termed as standard price. The standard price for each material is fixed after taking into account factors such as quantity of materials to be purchased, market conditions, freight and warehouse expenses, etc.

Merits: following are the specific advantages of this method:

1. It is relatively easy to operate because all issues of materials are priced at the same price. A lot of clerical work is saved.
2. The efficiency of the Purchasing Department can be judged. The method incurs a profit on issue but this is not due to approximation of computations but because of standard price being higher or lower than the actual price paid. The variance can be favorable if standard price exceeds the actual price paid, and it could be regarded as the efficiency of the Purchasing department.

Demerits:

1. Any error in determination of standard price leads to problems in price fixation and cost control.
2. Fixation of appropriate standard price may be difficult if price fluctuations are substantial and abrupt.
3. It is the notional price but NOT the actual price paid for materials.

Suitability: The method is particularly suitable for industries which maintain their cost accounts on standard costing system.

Illustration 4.14. (Standard Price Method)

From the following transactions, prepare Stores Ledger Sheet using Standard Price Method, the standard price is ₹ 30 per unit.:

Date 2008	*Details*
January 1	*Purchased 2,000 units @ ₹ 25 vide GRN 32*
January 4	*Issued 600 units vide MRN 201*
January 5	*Purchased 1,000 units @ ₹ 27 vide GRN 35*
January 8	*Issued 900 units vide MRN 204*

January 11	*Purchased 500 units @ ₹ 29 vide GRN 38*
January 14	*Issued 800 units vide MRN 208*
January 16	*Purchased 750 units @ ₹ 31 vide GRN 45*
January 18	*Issued 450 units vide MRN 211*
January 19	*Purchased 1,500 units @ ₹ 33 vide GRN 48*
January 20	*Issued 1,400 units vide MRN 215*
January 22	*Purchased 1,250 units @ ₹ 35 vide GRN 51*
January 23	*Issued 1,300 units vide MRN 217*
January 24	*Purchased 850 units @ ₹ 34 vide GRN 54*
January 27	*Issued 1,000 units vide MRN 228*
January 28	*Purchased 2,600 units @ ₹ 36 vide GRN 65*
January 30	*Issued 2,860 units vide MRN 236*

Solution : **Stores Ledger Sheet (Standard Price Method)**

Date	Receipts				Issues				Balance	
2008 Jan.	GRN.	Quantity (unit)	Rate (₹)	Amount (₹)	MRN.	Quantity (unit)	Rate (₹)	Amount (₹)	Quantity (unit)	Amount (₹)
1	32	2,000	25	50,000	—	—	—	—	2,000	50,000
4					201	600	30	18,000	1,400	32,000
5	35	1,000	27	27,000					2,400	59,000
8					204	900	30	27,000	1,500	32,000
11	38	500	29	14,500					2,000	46,500
14					208	800	30	24,000	1,200	22,500
16	45	750	31	23,250					1,950	45,750
18					211	450	30	13,500	1,500	32,250
19	48	1,500	33	49,500					3,000	81,750
20					215	1,400	30	42,000	1,600	39,750
22	51	1,250	35	43,750					2,850	83,500
23					217	1,300	30	39,000	1,550	44,500
24	54	850	34	28,900					2,400	73,400
27					228	1,000	30	30,000	1,400	53,400
28	65	2,600	36	93,600					4,000	1,47,000
30					236	2,860	30	1,00,100	1,140	46,900

Inflated Price Method

If the nature of the materials is such that some losses are unavoidable in the storage and handling of materials and additional costs are incurred in handling the materials, the issue price may be appropriately adjusted upwards (inflated) to recover extra handling costs and unavoidable losses. This process assumes that such expenses and losses are a direct charge to materials consumed. Inflated pricing is not a method but an accounting procedure for adjusting material losses and incidental expenses.

Illustration 4.15. *UV Limited has purchased a consignment of material I and material II. The following are the costs in purchasing:*

Details		***Amount*** (₹)
Material Material-I	*8,000 Litre @ ₹ 25 per litre*	*2, 00,000*
Material Material-II	*12,000 Litre @ ₹ 15 per litre*	*1, 80,000*
VAT @ 4%		*15,200*
Railway Freight		*4,000*
Total		*3, 99,200*

Other handling charges have been estimated to be ₹ 2,600. In addition Material-I involves special handling cost of ₹ 296 in stores.

Normal breakage in transit and in storage is estimated to be 6% in case of Material-I and 10% in case of material Material-II. Determine per Litre issue price for material Material-I and material Material-II so as to recover normal losses of materials as well as incidental costs to purchases and storage.

Solution :

Details	Material-I (₹)	Material-I (₹)	Total (₹)
Invoice Value	2,00,000	1,80,000	3,80,000
VAT @ 4% OR apportioned in the ratio of Value i.e. 10: 9	8,000	7,200	15,200
Railway freight apportioned in the ratio of Weight i.e. 2: 3	1,600	2,400	4,000
Special handling cost	296	NIL	296
Other handling Charges apportioned in the ratio of Weight i.e. 2: 3	1,040	1,560	2,600
Total	2,10, 936	1,91,160	4,02,096
Quantity Purchased (Litre)	8,000	12,000	
Normal Loss of material @ 6% and 10% Respectively (Litre)	480	1,200	
Materials effectively available for Issue (Litre)	7,520	10,800	
Issue Price (₹)	28.05	17.70	

Working Note: Issue Price of Material:

= Total cost of acquisition / Material quantity available for Issue

Material M-I: 2, 10,936 ÷ 7,520 ⇒ ₹ 28.05

Material M-II: 1, 91,160 ÷ 10,800 ⇒ ₹ 17.70

Market Price Method

Materials are issued for production at a price prevailing at the time of issue. In case ordering costs including transportation costs are low then market price is also the replacement cost of materials. Market price is used for the issue of materials for production while realizable value is used for valuing the inventory held for sale.

Merits: The main advantage of this method is that the material cost is based on the current market situation. Consequently, price fixation is in conformity with the latest market situation. The method can be easily used if following conditions are satisfied:

(i) Materials are of standard nature;

(ii) The price of the material is daily quoted on television, newspaper ,etc.,

(iii) There are no much fluctuations in the price during the day.

Demerits: The method suffers from the following disadvantages:

(i) Market price needs to be ascertained at the time of each issue.

(ii) Issue price may vary from issue to issue making cost comparisons misleading.

Suitability:

Replacement Cost Method

This is also known as Replenishment cost Method. In case ordering costs especially the transportation cost of materials is quite heavy, the replacement cost will be much higher the market price. This applies to materials such as coal, iron ore, etc. In such cases adoption of replacement cost is far better option than just the market price, because replenishment of materials includes all ordering costs.

Re-use Price Method

Materials may be found to be defective or not serving the purpose of the user department; they may be returned in the same condition in which they were originally issued or may be after initial processing. These returned materials when issued for an alternative purpose are priced at a value different from the purchase price. This price at which these materials are re-issued is known re-use price.

Selection of Material Pricing Method

Each method of pricing has its own advantages, limitations and suitability situation. Demanding upon the requirement of the organisation, different pricing methods are followed and even different methods can be adopted for different group of materials in the same organisation. Whatever method or methods are followed, they should be followed with consistency over a period time. Frequent changes in the method will distort cost computations as well as income determination. An appropriate method is that which gives good matching of costs against revenues and also produces meaningful cost figures for effective cost control and analysis.

LET US RECAPITULATE

1. The incoming materials are to be valued at invoice price subject to trade or quantity discount plus all expenses incurred up to the point of placing materials in a condition suitable for issuance from the stores.
2. Trade Discount refers to the allowance which is permitted by the vendor to a purchaser who has to resell the articles.
3. Quantity discount is allowed by the supplier to the buyer to encourage him to place large orders.
4. Cash discount is allowed by the vendor to the buyer to encourage him to make prompt payment of cash.
5. Material Requisition is a formal request by the user department to the store-keeper for the issue of materials.
6. A bill of materials is prepared for non-standardized jobs where exact material requirement differs from job to job and there is a need to make an advance estimate of cost expected to be incurred on the job.
7. The department returning the materials makes a Material Return Note or Stores Debit Note giving complete details of materials being returned.
8. Transfer of materials from one department to the other is done through material transfer note.
9. Material Abstract is a summary of Material Requisition, Material Return Note, and Material Transfer Notes during a certain costing period.
10. The inventory of materials consists of different consignments received at different dates and prices.
11. Under the Specific Price Method materials are charged at the price at which they were originally bought.
12. Under the First in First out Method, Issue of materials is priced in the order of their purchases.
13. Under the Last in First out Method, the price of the latest consignment is used for pricing materials issues till it is exhausted, and then the next consignment pricing is used and so on through successive consignments.
14. Under the Highest in First out Method materials are issued to jobs at the rate of highest priced materials in store.
15. Under the Next in First out Method materials are charged NOT at the actual price already paid for the materials but at a PRICE at which an order has been placed and the NEXT DELIVERY is expected.
16. Base stock is in the nature of a fixed asset and is carried at original cost.
17. Average Cost methods are based on the assumption that the materials purchased in different lots are stored together and their identity gets lost.
18. Simple Average Method is computed by adding ALL the different prices of materials in stock by the number of prices used in that total.

19. Weighted average Method is computed by dividing the total cost of goods in stock by the total quantities in stock.
20. Under the Periodic Simple Average Method, the issue rate is calculated only periodically (weekly, fortnightly, or monthly, etc.) and not at the time of each issue.
21. Under the Periodic Weighted Average Method, the issue rate is calculated by dividing the total cost of purchases of a material during a given period by the total quantity of material purchased during that period.
22. The moving simple average price is the average of the periodic simple average prices for a given number of periods.
23. All receipts of materials are recorded at the actual price paid but all issues are priced at a predetermined price which is termed as standard price.
24. Under the Market Price Method, materials are issued for production at a price prevailing at the time of issue.
25. Frequent changes in the method will distort cost computations as well as income determination.

SOLVED PROBLEMS

Problem 1. *From the following details of receipts and issues of the Material PT in a manufacturing unit from the store meant for the organization, prepare the Store ledger Sheet using "Weighted Average" method of valuing the issues:*

Date 2008	*Details*
September 1	*Opening Stock 2500 units @ ₹ 6 each*
September 4	*Issued 1,700 units to Production*
September 6	*Received 6,000 units @ ₹ 7.50 each*
September 8	*Issued 1,700 units to Production*
September 10	*Returned to stores 200 units by the Production Department (From the Issues of September 4)*
September 15	*Received 3,000 units @ ₹8.00 each*
September 18	*Returned to supplier 300 units out of the quantity received on September 6)*
September 21	*Received 1,200 units @ ₹8.50 each*
September 24	*Issued to Production 2,800 units.*
September 27	*Received 1,600 units @ ₹ 8.40 each*
September 29	*Issued 4,000 units to Production*

Solution :

Date 2008 Sep.	Receipt			Issues			Balance		
	Quantity	Rate (₹)	Amount (₹)	Quantity	Rate (₹)	Amount (₹)	Quantity	Rate (₹)	Amount (₹)
1							2,500	6.0000	15,000
4				1,700	6.0000	10,200	800	6.0000	4,800
6	6,000	7.5000	45,000				6,800	7.3235	49,800
8				1,700	7.3235	12,450	5,100	7.3235	37,350
10	200	6.0000	1,200				5,300	7.2736	38,550
15	3,000	8.0000	24,000				8,300	7.5361	62,550
18				300	7.5000	2,250	8,000	7.5375	60,300
21	1.200	8.5000	10,200				9,200	7.6630	70,500
24				2,800	7.6630	21,456	6,400	7.6630	49,044
27	1,600	8.4000	13,440				8,000	7.8104	62,484
29				4,000	7.8104	31,242	4,000	7.8104	31,242

Problem 2. *Show how the items given in the stores ledger card, using weighted average method for issue pricing:*

Date 2005	*Details*	*Unit*	*Price (per unit) (₹)*
January 1	*Opening Balance*	*300*	*20*
January 5	*Purchases*	*200*	*22*
January 11	*Issue*	*150*	*?*
January 22	*Purchases*	*200*	*23*
January 24	*Issue*	*150*	*?*
January 28	*Issue*	*200*	*?*

[B.Com (Hons.) DU, 2005]

Solution :

Date 2005 Jan.	Receipt			Issues			Balance		
	Quantity	Rate (₹)	Amount (₹)	Quantity	Rate (₹)	Amount (₹)	Quantity	Rate (₹)	Amount (₹)
1							300	20	6,000
5	200	22	4,400				500	20.8	10,400
11				150	20.8	3,120	350	20.8	7,280
22	200	23	4,600				550	21.6	11,880
24				150	21.6	3,240	400	21.6	8,640
28				200	21.6	4,320	200	21.6	4,320

Problem 3. *AV Limited provides you the following information. Calculate the cost of goods sold and ending inventory, applying the LIFO method of pricing raw materials under the Perpetual and Periodic inventory system.*

Date 2005	*Details*	*Unit*	*Price (per unit) (₹)*
January 1	*Opening Balance*	*200*	*20*
January 10	*Purchases*	*400*	*24*
January 12	*Issue*	*500*	*?*
January 16	*Purchases*	*300*	*22*
January 19	*Issue*	*200*	*?*
January 30	*Purchases*	*100*	*30*

Also explain in brief the reasons for a difference in profit, if any.

Solution :

Details	Perpetual Inventory Method [Unit × Rate = Amount (₹)]	Periodic Inventory Method [Unit × Rate = Amount (₹)]
I. Cost of Goods Sold: Jan. 12	[400 × 24 = 9,600] [100 × 20 = 2,000] 11,600	[100 × 30 = 3,000] [300 × 22 = 6,600] [300 × 24 = 7,200]
Jan. 19	[200 × 22 = 4,400] 4,400	
Total	700 16,000	700 16,800
II. Ending Inventory:	100 × 20 = 2,000 100 × 22 = 2,200 100 × 30 = 3,000	100 × 24 = 2,400 200 × 20 = 4,000
Total	300 7,200	300 6,400

Profit: As the cost of goods sold (Issued) is more under Periodic Inventory System, therefore, the profits under this system will be less and vice-versa. Alternatively, it can be so said that less the ending inventory (Periodic Inventory System), less is the amount of profit.

Problem 4. (Pricing of Issues)

From the following transactions extracted from the books of a manufacturing firm as on January 31,2004 compute (i) the consumption value of raw materials in the month and (ii) value of closing stock as on January 31, 2004 under the following methods of pricing issues: (1) FIFO, (2) LIFO, (3) FIFO WITH base Stock of 600 Units, (4) Simple Average, (5) Weighted Average, (6) Periodic Average, and (7) Periodic weighted Average. Show results in a tabular form.

Date 2004	*Details*	*Quantity*	*Rate per unit (₹)*
January 1	*Opening Stock*	*1,700*	*28*
January 5	*Purchase*	*1,450*	*31*
January 13	*Issues*	*2,200*	
January 18	*Purchase*	*1,700*	*34*
January 20	*Issues*	*1,250*	
January 24	*Purchase*	*950*	*37*
January 29	*Issues*	*700*	

Solution : (1) FIFO Method :

1. Analysis of Closing Stock:

700 Units @ ₹ 34 = ₹ 23,800
950 Units @ ₹ 37 = ₹ 35,150
Total: 1650 Units = ₹ 58,950

2. Consumption of Materials at a value of ₹ 1,26,550.

(2) LIFO Method :

1. Analysis of Closing Stock:

950 Units @ ₹ 28 = ₹ 26,600
450 Units @ ₹ 34 = ₹ 15,300
250 Units @ ₹ 37 = ₹ 9,250
Total: 1650 Units = ₹ 51,150

2. Consumption of Materials at a value of ₹ 1,34,350.

(3) FIFO Method with Base Stock 600 Units

1. Analysis of Closing Stock:

600 Units @ ₹ 28 = ₹ 16,800
100 Units @ ₹ 34 = ₹ 3,400
950 Units @ ₹ 37 = ₹ 35,150
Total: 1650 Units = 55,350

2. Consumption of Materials at a value of ₹ 1,30,150.

(4) Simple Average Method :

Date 2004 Jan.	Receipt			Issues			Balance	
	Quantity	Rate (₹)	Amount (₹)	Quantity	Rate (₹)	Amount (₹)	Quantity	Amount (₹)
1	1,700	28	47,600				1,700	47,600
5	1,450	31	44,950				3,150	92,550
13				2,200	29.5	64,900	950	27,650
18	1,700	34	57,800				2,650	85,450
20				1,250	32.5	40,625	1,400	44,825
24	950	37	35,150				2,350	79,975
29				700	35.5	24,850	1,650	55,125
Total	5,800		1,85,500	4,150		1,30,375		

1. Determination of Issue Rate:-

Jan. 13: (28 + 31) ÷ 2 = ₹ 29.5

Jan. 20: (31 + 34) ÷ 2 = ₹ 32.5

Jan. 29: (34 + 37) ÷ 2 = ₹ 35.5

2. Consumption of Materials at a value of ₹ 1,30,375

(5) Weighted Average Method:

Date 2008 Jan.	Balance			Issues			Balance		
	Quantity	Rate (₹)	Amount (₹)	Quantity	Rate (₹)	Amount (₹)	Quantity	Rate (₹)	Amount (₹)
1	1,700	28	47,600				1,700	28.0000	47,600
5	1,450	31	44,950				3,150	29.3810	92,550
13				2,200	29.3810	64,638	950	29.3810	27,912
18	1,700	34	57,800				2,650	32.3442	85,712
20				1,250	32.3442	40,430	1,400	32.3442	45,282
24	950	37	35,150				2,350	34.2264	80,432
29				700	34.2264	23,958	1,650	34.2264	56,474
Total	5,800		1,85,500	4,150		1,29,026			

1. Analysis of Closing Stock:

1650 Units @ ₹ 34.2264 = ₹ 56, 474

2. Consumption of Materials at a value of ₹ 1,29,026.

(6) Periodic Simple Average Method:

Rate of Issue = ₹ (31 + 34 + 37) ÷ 3 = ₹ 34

Value of Consumption = 4,150 × ₹ 34 = ₹ 1,41,100

Value of Closing Stock = Opening Stock + Purchases – Value of Consumption

= ₹ 47,600 + ₹ 1,37,900 – ₹ 1,41,100

= ₹ 44,400

(7) Periodic Weighted Average Method:

Date 2004	Units	Rate (₹)	Amount (₹)
Jan. 5	1,450	31	44,950
18	1,700	34	57,800
24	950	37	35,150
Total	4,100		1,37,900

Rate of Issue = ₹ 1,37,900 ÷ 4,100 = ₹ 33.6342

Value of Consumption = 4,150 × ₹ 33.6342 = ₹ 1,39,582

Value of Closing Stock = Opening Stock + Purchases – Value of Consumption

= ₹ 47,600 + ₹ 1,37,900 – ₹ 1,39,582

= ₹ 45,918

Problem 5. *The Stores Ledger of a manufacturing Unit of a company recorded for material S-25 for the month of August, 2008 the following information:*

Date August-2008	*Receipts*		*Issues*	
	Quantity (Units)	*Value (₹)*	*Quantity (Units)*	*Value (₹)*
5	500	1,600	—	—
8	200	1,200	—	—
12	—	—	400	1,600
17	250	1,000	—	—
20	200	2,400	—	—
25	—	—	500	3,000
26	500	4,000		
30			400	2,900

(*i*) *State the method of pricing that was employed in the Stores ledger; and*

(*ii*) *Complete the Stores ledger as per the method followed.*

Solution : On observation of the pricing of issues in the given question, it is obvious that weighted average price method has been employed by the costing department of the company.

Stores Ledger Sheet (Weighted Average Method)

Date Aug-08	Receipts			Issues			Balance		
	Quantity	Rate (₹)	Value (₹)	Quantity	Rate (₹)	Value (₹)	Quantity	Rate (₹)	Value (₹)
5	500	3.20	1,600	—		—	500	3.20	1,600
8	200	6.00	1,200	—		—	700	4.00	2,800
12	—		—	350	4.00	1,400	350	4.00	1,400
t7	250	4.00	1,000	—		—	600	4.00	2,400
20	200	6.00	2,400	—		—	800	6.00	4,800
25	—		—	500	6.00	3,000	300	6.00	1,800
26	500	8.00	4,000				800	7.25	5,800
30				400	7.25	2,900	400	7.25	2,900

Working Notes: Rate of Purchase = Value /quantity

August 5, 2008:

$$= 1{,}600 \div 500 \Rightarrow ₹\ 3.20$$

Balance as on August 8, 2008:

$$= 2{,}800 \div 700 \Rightarrow ₹\ 4.00$$

Rate of Issue = Value /quantity

August 12, 2008:

$$= 1{,}600 \div 400 \Rightarrow ₹\ 4.00$$

Problem 6. A. (Profit On issue method)

Discuss the effect of adopting the LIFO and FIFO on profits with the help of the following figures:

Date	Details
Jan. 01	*Opening balance 25 Units (December 28,purchase) @ ₹ 40*
Jan. 10	*Purchased 25 units @ ₹ 45*
Jan. 16	*Issued 25 Units*
Jan.31	*Closing balance 25 Units*
Feb. 03	*Purchased 25 units @ ₹ 50*
Feb. 14	*Issued 25 Units*
Feb. 28	*Purchased 25 units @ ₹ 56*

Sales during the two months amounted to ₹ 3,500.

Solution :

Date of Issue	FIFO Method (₹)	LIFO Method (₹)
Jan. 16 Feb. 14	25 × 40 = 1,000 25 × 45 = 1,125	25 × 45 = 1,125 25 × 50 = 1,250
Total	2,125	2,375
Profit	3,500 – 2,125 = 1,375	3,500 – 2,375 = 1,125

Profit = Sales revenue – Issue price

Problem 7. *The Stores Ledger of a manufacturing Unit of a company recorded for material S-32 for the month of April, 2008 the following information:*

Date April 2008	Receipts			Balance		
	Quantity (Unit)	Rate (₹)	Value (₹)	Quantity (Unit)	Rate (₹)	Value (₹)
1	—	—	—	250	4	1,000
8	500	4	2,000	250	4	3,000
				500	4	
13	750	8	6,000	250	4	9,000
				500	4	
				750	8	
17	—	—	—	250	4	7,000
				750	8	
20	—	—	—	250	8	2,000
25	1,000	10	10,000	250	8	12,000
				1,000	10	
28	—	—	—	500	10	5,000`
30	—	—	—	125	10	1,250

(i) *State the method of pricing that was employed in the Stores ledger; and*

(ii) *Complete the Stores ledger as per the method followed.*

Solution : On observation of the pricing of issues in the given question, it is obvious that FIFO pricing method has been employed by the costing department of the company. It is observed that the first issue April 17, 2008 of 500 units costing ₹ 4 has been made. ₹ 4 happens to be FIFO price. The second issue on April 20, 2008 confirms that issues are made on FIFO basis.

Stores Ledger Sheet (FIFO Pricing Method)

Date	Receipts			Issues			Balance		
April-08	Quantity	Rate (₹)	Value (₹)	Quantity	Rate (₹)	Value (₹)	Quantity	Rate (₹)	Value (₹)
1	—	—	—	—	—	—	250	4	1,000
8	500	4	2,000	—	—	—	250	4	3,000
							500	4	
13	750	8	6,000	—	—	—	250	4	9,000
							500	4	
							750	8	
17	—	—	—	500	4	2,000	250	4	7,000
							750	8	
20	—	—	—	250	4	1,000	250	8	2,000
				500	8	4,000			
						5,000			
25	1,000	10	10,000	—	—	—	250	8	12,000
							1,000	10	
28	—	—	—	250	8	2,000	500	10	5,000`
				500	10	5,000			
						7,000			
30	—	—	—	375	10	3,750	125	10	1,250

Problem 8. *Oil India is a bulk distributor of oil. A periodic inventory of oil on hand is taken when the books are closed at the end of each month. The following summary of information is available for the month of December.*

Sales ₹ *75,60,000*

General Administrative Cost ₹ *2,00,000*

Opening Stock 1,00,000 litres @ ₹ 24 per Litre: ₹ 24,00,000 purchases (including freight in)

Dec.1: 2,00,000 litres @ ₹ 22.80 per litre

Dec.30: 1,00,000 litres @ ₹ 24.24 per litre

Closing Stock:

Dec. 31: 1,30,000 litres

Compute the following by the FIFO, Weighted Average and LIFO method of inventory valuation:

1. *Value of Inventory on December 31;*
2. *Amount of cost of goods sold for December;*
3. *Profit or Loss for December.* **[B.Com (Hons.) DU, 2007 (Modified)]**

Solution : (I) FIFO Method:

Closing Inventory on December 31:

Details	Amount (₹)
Closing Inventory on December 31:	
1, 00,000 litres @ ₹ 24.24 per litre	24,24,000
30,000 litres @ ₹ 22.80 per litre	6,84,000
Value on Closing Inventory on December 31	31,08,000

Details	Amount (₹)
Cost of Goods Sold:	
Opening Stock	24, 00,000
Add: Purchases December 1	45,60,000
Add: Purchases December 30	24,24,000
Total Value of Goods Available for Sale	93,84,000
Less: Value Closing Stock on December 31	(31,08,000)
Cost of Goods Sold	62,76,000

Details	Amount (₹)
Calculation of Profit:	
Cost of Goods Sold	62,76,000
Add: General Administrative Cost	2,00,000
Total Cost	64,76,000
Profit (Balancing figure)	10,84,000
Sales	75, 60, 000

(II) Weighted Average Method:

Closing Inventory on December 31:

Details	Amount (₹)
Closing Inventory on December 31:	31,20,000
1, 30,000 litres @ ₹ 24 per litre	
The rate of ₹ 24 per litre is arrived in the following manner:	
First Receipt:	
[{(1,00,000 ×24) +(2,00,000× 22.80)}/ (1,00,000 + 2,00,000)] = 23.20	
Last Receipt:	
[{(30,000 ×23.20) +(1,00,000× 24.24)}/ (30,000 + 1,00,000)] =24	
Value on Closing Inventory on December 31	31,20,000

Details	Amount (₹)
Cost of Goods Sold:	
Opening Stock	24, 00,000
Add: Purchases December 1	45,60,000
Add: Purchases December 30	24,24,000
Total Value of Goods Available for Sale	93,84,000
Less: Value Closing Stock on December 31	(31,20,000)
Cost of Goods Sold	62,64,000

Details	Amount (₹)
Calculation of Profit:	
Cost of Goods Sold	62,64,000
Add: General Administrative Cost	2,00,000
Total Cost	64,64,000
PROFIT(Balancing figure)	10,96,000
Sales	75,60,000

(III) LIFO Method:

Closing Inventory on December 31:

Details	Amount (₹)
Closing Inventory on December 31:	7,20,000
30,000 litres @ ₹ 24.00 per litre	24,24,000
1, 00,000 litres @ ₹ 24.24 per litre	
Value on Closing Inventory on December 31	31,44,000

Details	Amount (₹)
Cost of Goods Sold:	
Opening Stock	24,00,000
Add: Purchases December 1	45,60,000
ultAdd: Purchases December 30	24,24,000
Total Value of Goods Available for Sale	93,84,000
Less: Value Closing Stock on December 31	(31,44,000)
Cost of Goods Sold	62,40,000

Details	Amount (₹)
Calculation of Profit:	
Cost of Goods Sold	62,40,000
Add: General Administrative Cost	2,00,000
Total Cost	64,40,000
PROFIT(Balancing figure)	11,20,000
Sales	75,60,000

Analysis Table (₹)

Details	FIFO Method	Weighted Average Method	LIFO Method
Value on Closing Inventory (As on December 31)	31,08,000	31,20,000	31,44,000
Cost of Goods Sold	62,76,000	62,64,000	62,40,000
Profit	10,84,000	10,96,000	11,20,000

Problem 9. *Given:*

Receipts	*1.10.2008*	*80 Litre @ ₹ 25 per Litre*
	11.10.2008	*80 Litre @ ₹ 30 per Litre*
Issues	*3.10.2008*	*60 Litre*
	13.10.2008	*60 Litre*

What is the value of 40 units of closing stock under each of the following methods?

1. *FIFO*
2. *LIFO*
3. *Simple Average Price*
4. *Weighted Average Price*

Solution : Value of stock under FIFO Method of Pricing is on the basis of Latest receipts. Thus the value of stock of 40 units is ₹ 1,200 i.e. 40 @ ₹ 30 per unit.

Value of stock under LIFO Method of Pricing is on the basis of Earliest Receipts. Thus the value of stock of 40 units is ₹ 1,100 i.e. 20 @ ₹ 25 per unit plus 20 @ Rs 30 per unit.

Value of stock under Simple Average Price Method of Pricing is on the basis of Latest Balance of items after the final issue at simple average pricing. Thus the value of stock of 40 units is ₹ 1,250 i.e. {(Received: (80 × 25) + (80 × 30)} {Issued: (60 × 25) + (60 × 27.50)} i.e. Balance = ₹ 4,400 – ₹ 3,150.

Value of stock under Weighted Average Price Method of Pricing is on the basis of Latest Weighted average price of Issue. Thus the value of stock of 40 units is ₹ 1,160 i.e. 40 @ ₹ 29 per unit.

OBJECTIVE TYPE EXERCISES

I. Indicate whether the following statements are True or False :

1. Under FIFO and LIFO, value of closing stock is same.

2. Purchase Requisition is prepared by the Purchase Department.

3. According to 'LIFO' Method of pricing, issues are close to current economic values.

4. Assuming inflation, if a company wants to maximise net income, it would select FIFO as the method of pricing raw materials. **[DU, B.Com (Hons.) 1999]**
5. Materials are issued at weighted average price under LIFO method.
6. LIFO and market price methods are not same.
7. FIFO method of pricing materials issue results in higher profits.
8. The adoption of LIFO method does not result in inflation of profits during the period of rising material prices.
9. Pricing of issues of materials has no impact on the value of closing stock.
10. Pricing of issues of materials is closely connected with actual physical movement of units of materials.
11. Issue prices have an impact on book profits.
12. Methods of pricing of issues aim at charging material cost to production.
13. In case of specific materials, issue rate is same as purchase rate.
14. Issue prices fluctuate more in case of weighted average method of pricing issues than under FIFO and LIFO.
15. Under FIFO method units of materials purchased first are physically issued first.
16. FIFO method does not usually give a good match between cost incurred and cost charged to product.
17. FIFO method is usually suitable in case of perishable materials.
18. LIFO gives higher value of closing stock during inflationary period than that if FIFO method of pricing of issues is adopted.
19. Under FIFO method book profits are higher than under LIFO method of pricing in a period of rising prices.
20. Under HIFO method value of closing stock is least.
21. Under standard price method of pricing issues, the payment made for material purchases always equals the charge to products for the consumption of materials.

Answers :

1. False	**2.** False	**3.** True	**4.** True
5. False	**6.** True	**7.** True	**8.** True
9. False	**10.** False	**11.** True	**12.** True
13. True	**14.** False	**15.** False	**16.** True
17. True	**18.** False	**19.** True	**20.** True
21. False			

II. Fill in the blank spaces with suitable word/s :

1. LIFO method of pricing of materials is suitable for ....
2. Under the .... method, materials are issued to production at a pre-determined price.
3. .... method of pricing the materials evens out the effect of fluctuations in purchase prices.

4. Under the ……… method, a new issue price is determined after each purchase.
5. Under the ……… cost method, the materials issued during a month are costed at the weighted average price as at the end of the prior month.
6. ……… is a document which is a classified record of material issues, returns and transfers.
7. In ……… method, stock is valued at the latest prices paid.
8. In ……… method of pricing, more than one issue price may have to be adopted for pricing a single requisition.
9. In base stock method of pricingthe material issues, the term 'base stock' represents the ……… .
10. Under ……… method of pricing, issues are close to current economic values.

Answers :

1. Bulky and non-perishable	**2.** Standard price
3. Weighted average price	**4.** Weighted average
5. Periodic weighted average	**6.** Materials issue analysis sheet
7. FIFO	**8.** LIFO or FIFO
9. Minimum Stock	**10.** LIFO

THEORETICAL EXERCISES

1. Briefly contrast the effects of using FIFO with the LIFO methods of pricing materials from stores.
2. Draw a Performa of 'Materials Transfer Note' and enlist its uses. **[DU, B.Com (Hons.) 2001]**
3. State concisely plus and minus points about standard cost method of pricing issues of materials.
4. Distinguish between Bill of Materials and Stores requisition. **[B.Com (Hons.), DU, 1997]**
5. What factors have to be considered for adopting a method for the pricing of materials? **[DU, B.Com (Hons.) 2000]**
6. What factors have to be considered for adopting a method for the pricing of materials issued to production? **[DU, B.Com (Hons.) 2004]**
7. Explain in brief the following concepts:
   (i) Discount on account of purchases **[DU, B.Com (Hons.) 2001]**
   (ii) Material Requisition
   (iii) Bill of materials
8. Write short notes on:
   (i) Weighted average method
   (ii) Standard price method

NUMERICAL EXERCISES

1. From the following details of stores receipts and issues of material "EXE" in a manufacturing unit, prepare the store ledger using weighted average method of valuing the issues:

Date	Details
Nov.1	Opening Stock 2000 units @ ₹ 5.00 each
Nov.3	Issued 1500 units to production
Nov.4	Received 450 units @ ₹ 6.00 each
Nov.8	Issued 1600 units to production
Nov.9	Returned to stores 100 units from production Department (out of the issues of Nov. 3)
Nov.16	Received 2400 units @ ₹ 6.50 each
Nov.1 9	Returned to supplier 200 units out of the lot received on Nov.4
Nov.20	Received 1,000 units @ ₹7.00 each
Nov.24	Issued to production 2100 units
Nov.27	Received 1,200 units @ ₹7.50
Nov.29	Issued to production 2,800 units

Note: Use rates up to two decimal points.

[Ans. Closing stock 3000 units ₹ 19588.00]

2. At the beginning of October 2006, Bestodent Brush Company had in stock 10000 brushes valued at ₹10 each.

Further purchases were made during that month as follows:

7th October 4000 brushes @ ₹ 12.50
14th October 6000 brushes @ ₹ 15.00
24th October 8000 brushes @ ₹ 16.50

Issued made to shop floor were as follows:

16th October 16000 brushes
28th October 10000 brushes

You are required to:

(a) Prepare stores ledger card for the month of October on the assumption that materials were issued on the first-in-first-out principle.

(b) State the value of closing stock at the end of October if issues are priced by the weighted – average method.

[Ans. (a) FIFO: Closing stock 2,000 units for ₹ 33000
(b) Weighted Average: Closing stock 2,000 units for ₹ 30000]

3. AV Limited provides you the following information. Calculate the cost of goods sold and ending inventory, applying the LIFO method of pricing raw materials under the Perpetual and Periodic inventory system.

Date 2008	Details	Unit	Price (per unit) (₹)
January 1	Opening Balance	500	20
January 10	Purchases	1000	24
January 14	Issue	1250	?
January 18	Purchases	750	22
January 22	Issue	500	?
January 30	Purchases	250	30

[Ans. Perpetual Inventory System: (1) Cost of goods sold: ₹ 40,000 for 1750 Units (2) Ending Inventory: ₹ 18,000 for 750 Units; Periodic Inventory System: (1) Cost of goods sold: ₹ 42,000 for 1750 Units (2) Ending Inventory: ₹ 16,000 for 750 Units]

4. In a manufacturing unit raw material passes through four processes I II, III, and IV and the output of each process is the input of the subsequent process. The loss in the four Processes I II, III, and IV are respectively 25%, 20%, 20%,and 50/3 % of the input. If the end product at the end of Process IV is 40,000 kgs, what is the quantity of raw materials required along with its cost to be fed at the beginning of Process I when the cost of the same is ₹ 5 per kg. **[DU, B.Com (Hons.) 1998]**

[Ans. Input in Process in Process I: 1, 00,000 units; ₹ 5,00,000]

5. From the following particulars, write up the priced stores ledger card:

Date	Details
August 1	Purchased 500 Kgs @ ₹ 25 per kg.
August 12	Purchased 300 Kgs @ ₹ 26.25 per kg.
August 15	Issued 600 Kgs
August 22	Purchased 400 Kgs @ ₹ 27.50 per kg.
August 25	Issued 300 Kgs
August 28	Purchased 500 Kgs @ ₹ 26.25 per kg.
August 31	Issued 200 Kgs

Adopt the 'Base stock method' of issue and ascertain the value of closing stock. Base stock quantity is 200 Kgs. Also compute the value of issued material using FIFO principle. **[Ans. value of closing stock: ₹ 15,500; value of issued material: ₹ 29,000]**

6. The purchases and issues of material M-3 in the month of August are as under:

Date	Details
August 1	Purchased 800 Kgs @ ₹ 25 per kg.
August 9	Purchased 700 Kgs @ ₹ 22.50 per kg.
August 12	Issued 600 Kgs
August 14	Issued 800 Kgs

August 17	Purchased 800 Kgs @ ₹ 25 per kg.
August 24	Purchased 500 Kgs @ ₹ 31.25 per kg
August 31	Issued 1,000 Kgs

The standard price per kg of material M-3 is ₹ 25, fixed for the year in view. Show the stores ledger entries and determine the price variance for the month of August, 2008.

[Ans. Material Price Variance: ₹ 1,375 (Unfavourable)]

7. The Stores Ledger of a manufacturing Unit of a company recorded for material S-25 for the month of August, 2008 the following information:

Date April-08	Receipts		Issues	
	Quantity (Units)	Value (₹)	Quantity (Units)	Value (₹)
4	100	160	—	—
6	40	120	—	—
12	—	—	70	140
16	50	100	—	—
20	40	240	—	—
26	—	—	90	270

(1) State the method of pricing that was employed in the Stores ledger; and

(2) Complete the Stores ledger as per the method followed.

[Ans. (1) Weighted Average Price method; and (2) Closing Stock: 70 units @ ₹ 3 per unit]

8. The Stores Ledger of a manufacturing Unit of a company recorded for material M-32 for the month of June, 2008 the following information:

Date April 2008	Receipts			Balance		
	Quantity (Unit)	Rate (₹)	Value (₹)	Quantity (Unit)	Rate (₹)	Value (₹)
1	—	—	—	500	2	1,000
8	1,000	2	2,000	500	2	3,000
				1,000	2	
13	1,500	4	6,000	500	2	9,000
				1,000	2	
				1,500	4	
17	—	—	—	500	2	7,000
				1,500	4	
20	—	—	—	500	4	2,000
25	2,000	5	10,000	500	4	12,000
				2,000	5	
28	—	—	—	1,000	5	5,000
30	—	—	—	250	5	1,250

(i) State the method of pricing that was employed in the Stores ledger; and

(ii) Complete the Stores ledger as per the method followed.

[Ans. (1) FIFO Price method; and (2) Closing Stock: 250 units @ ₹ 5 per unit]

9. The stock of material M-1 as at 1-4-2007 is 1200 units at ₹16 per unit. The following purchases and issues of this item were made subsequently.

Date 2007	Purchase		Issues	
	Units	Rate (₹)	Date	Units
April 6	1240	17	April 9	1200
April 20	1680	18	April 22	1200
April 27	960	19	April 30	1200
May 13	2400	20	May 15	1200
May 20	1200	21	May 22	1200
June 17	960	22	June 18	1200
June 28	720	23	June 28	1200

Prepare a statement, showing how the value of the above issues should be arrived at under the LIFO and FIFO methods.

[Ans. Closing Stock : (a) LIFO: 760 units {(40 × 17) + (240 × 18) + (480 × 20)} = ₹ 14,600;

(b) FIFO: 760 units {(40 × 22) + (720 × 23)} = ₹ 17,440]

❑❑❑

5

Investment in Materials

Learning Objectives

It attempts to explain the approach to optimize investment in materials. In this chapter you will learn :

1. Meaning and nature of safety stock.
2. Economic order quantity.
3. Stock levels.
4. Stock turnover ratio.
5. Special techniques of material control.

INTRODUCTION

One of the objectives of material control is to optimize investment in materials. It aims at making the best use of every rupee invested in inventories. Right quantity of materials is ordered to keep the material related costs to the minimum, replenishment of stock at right levels of stocks is done so that production and sales processes go on smoothly, avoid excessive investment in materials , and maintain necessary cushion in the form of safety stock. Thus, the importance of ordering materials in right quantities and maintaining the right level of stocks including necessary cushion of materials cannot be denied.

SAFETY STOCK

Safety Stock serves the same purpose in a business unit as shock absorber in a vehicle. It is maintained as a cushion to meet contingencies arising out of uncertainties on the supply/demand side. Larger the degree of uncertainties, greater is the need for safety stock. Requirement of safety stock cannot be computed with precision. It goes on changing from time to time depending upon changes relating to availability and use of materials. The level of safety stock can be estimated with the help of statistical tools, such as standard deviation and probability distribution, and with the help of sophisticated computerized calculations.

The attitude of the producer will have an effect on the level of safety stocks actually maintained. An overcautious producer will maintain larger safety stock. A producer, who is confident about his ability to meet contingencies, if at all they arise, will maintain lower safety stocks.

Cost of Too much Safety Stocks: Excess safety stocks entails the following costs:

1. Larger storage space resulting in higher rent cost;
2. Higher insurance premium;
3. High interest cost due to large investment in stocks;
4. Larger pilferage;
5. Larger obsolescence; and
6. Inefficiency and waste in the use of materials.

Cost of Too little Safety Stocks: Too little safety stocks involve following certain risks and costs:

1. Risk of interruption of production process involving heavy losses in terms of non-utilisation various overheads;
2. Panicky purchase at higher cost;
3. Stock-out costs impact long term profitability;
4. Emergency purchases of inferior quality of materials having adverse impact on quality if output.

Each producer has to exercise a balance between the costs of having plenty of safety stocks and scanty safety stocks. The objective is to minimise the total cost/risk entailed in stocking.

ECONOMIC ORDER QUANTITY

Economic Order Quantity i.e. EOQ refers to the size of purchase order for a material which results in making material available in a year at minimum total material related costs. Costs relating to materials are:

(i) Purchase price;

(ii) Storage costs;

(iii) Ordering costs;

(iv) Stock out costs (i.e. Opportunity costs)

In case it is assumed that price paid for materials does not change with the lot size, then the important material related costs are:

(i) Storage costs; and (ii) Ordering costs.

That order size is best which results in minimum sum total of storage costs and ordering costs. There is inverse relationship between order size and number of orders. Larger the size of order, smaller will be the number of orders, and vice versa.

Number of Orders = Annual material Requirement / Order Size

Order Size = Annual material Requirement / Number of Orders

Thus, EOQ is that order size which results in lowest material related cost for meeting a given material requirement in a period. The sum total of price paid for materials, ordering costs and storage costs are least. In case the price of material does not change with change in order size then EOQ is ascertained after considering ordering costs, storage/carrying costs and average consumption (Usage) of inventory.

Ordering Costs

The term "ordering costs" refer the followings:

(i) Cost of placing an order,

(ii) Cost of transportation,

(iii) Cost of receiving goods,

(iv) Cost of inspecting goods.

There is an INVERSE relationship between order size and ordering cost.

Size	Cost
Larger the order size	Lower the ordering costs because of fewer orders.
Smaller the order size	Higher the ordering costs because of more orders.

Storage/Carrying Costs

The term "Storage/ Carrying costs" refer the followings in relation to a given level of inventory:

(i) Cost of storage space,

(ii) Cost of handling materials,

(iii) Cost of insurance,

(iv) Cost of deterioration,

(v) Cost of store staff.

There is POSITIVE relationship between order size and Storage/Carrying cost.

Size	Cost
Larger the order size	Higher the Storage/ Carrying costs because of high average inventory.
Smaller the order size	Lower the Storage/ Carrying costs because of low average inventory.

EOQ Model solves one of the major problems of inventory management i.e. the order quantity problem; the question 'How much inventory should be ordered at a particular point of time?' is answered adequately by the EOQ Model.

Assumptions of EOQ Model

Following are the assumptions:

(i) Annual requirement of material can be estimated with reasonable accuracy.

(ii) Storage cost per unit of material per annum is constant.

(iii) Ordering cost per order is constant.

(iv) Daily consumption of materials is almost constant i.e. constant use of material.

(v) Zero lead time/delivery periods.

Determination of Economic Order Quantity

Any of the following three methods may be used to determine the economic order size of the order:

(1) Graphic Method;

(2) Tabular Method; and

(3) Algebraic method.

Method-wise process is given as under:

Graphic Method: The optimum quantity of inventory which should be ordered at a point of time is ascertained on achieving a trade off between ordering cost and carrying costs. Following steps need to be taken:

1. Take order size on X-axis and cost on Y-axis.
2. Draw carrying cost line going upwards indicating carrying cost increases as order size increases.
3. Draw ordering cost line sloping downwards indicating ordering cost decreases as order size increases.
4. Draw total cost line which first slopes downwards and then goes upwards after a certain minimum point.
5. Locate the point at which both carrying cost line and ordering cost line intersect each other and draw a perpendicular from this point on the X-axis.
6. Locate the point at which the perpendicular touches X-axis. This point gives the Economic order quantity.
7. Locate the point at which the perpendicular (if extended upwards) cuts the total cost line. This point gives the minimum total cost at the Economic order quantity.

Tabular(Trial and Error) Method: The ordering and carrying costs for different order sizes are computed and the order size with lowest total cost(ordering as well as carrying) of inventory is the EOQ. Carrying cost and ordering cost are equal at EOQ order size. Following is the format of the table to find out the EOQ order:

[EOQ Costs]

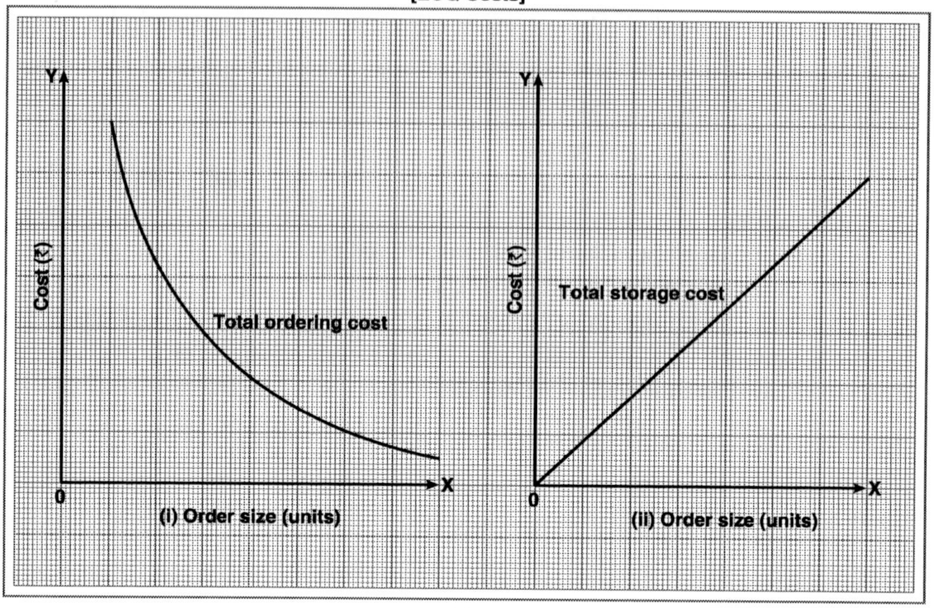

(a)

[Ascertainment of economic order quantity]

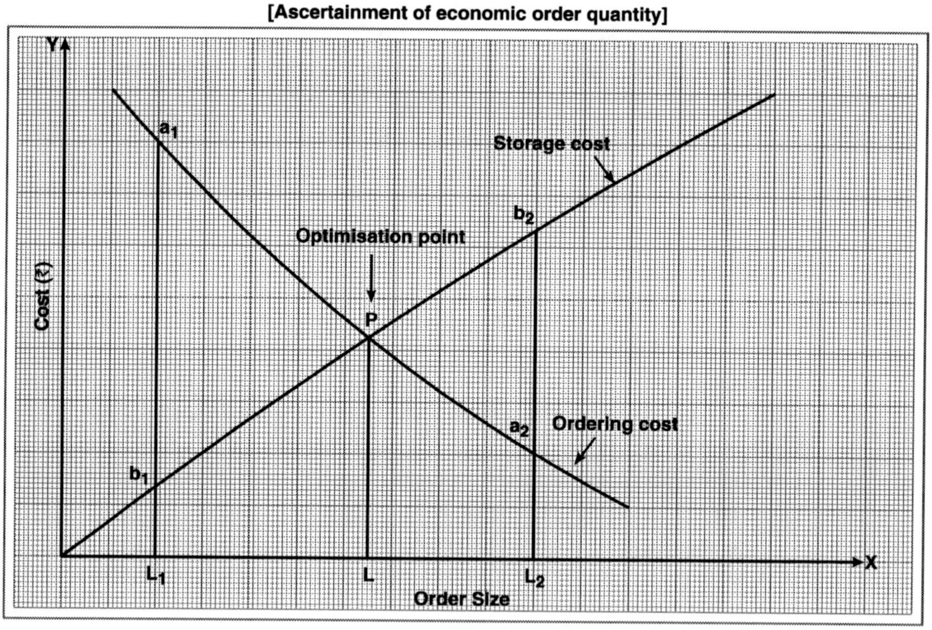

(b)

Graph 5.1

Determination of Economic Order Quantity (Order Size):

Details	Order Size - I	Order Size - II	Order Size - III	Order Size - IV	Order Size - V
A. Annual Usage (Units)					
B. Order Size (Units)					
C. Number of orders i.e. (A/B)					
D. Ordering cost per Order(₹)					
E. Total Ordering cost (₹) i.e. (C × D)					
F. Average inventory (Units) i.e. (Order size/2)					
G. Carrying cost per unit p.a. (₹)					
H. Total Carrying cost (₹) i.e. (F × G)					
I. Total cost (₹) i.e. (E + H)					

Note: Where quantity discount is offered by the supplier of inputs, the most economical purchase level is that order size at which the total cost (i.e. total annual ordering as well as carrying costs + Total purchase price of annual usage of inputs) is minimum.

Algebraic method: Following formula may be used to determine Economic order quantity:

$$EOQ = \sqrt{[2AB/C]}$$

where, A = Annual usage of inputs in units

B = Ordering cost per order

C = Carrying cost per unit per annum

Number of orders per Year = Total annual usage of inputs (in units)/ EOQ

Frequency of EOQ = 365 days / Number of orders per Year

Total annual ordering and carrying cost at EOQ Point = $\sqrt{[2ABC]}$

Stock Levels

In order to avoid under-stocking or over-stocking of items of materials, most of the large companies tend to fix stock levels on scientific basis. These levels are not permanent and must be reviewed to suit the changing circumstances. Following factors must be kept in mind while fixing the stock levels:

- Availability of storage space.
- Cost of storing.
- Amount of capital available.
- Estimated rate of consumption (item-wise).
- Procurement costs.
- Minimum order quantities imposed by suppliers.

- Risk of loss due to (i) Evaporation, (ii) Deterioration, (iii) Obsolescence, and (iv) Fall in market prices, etc.

Operation research and statistical techniques may be used in fixing the stock levels, which are (i) Maximum Level, (ii) Minimum Level, (iii) Re-order Level, and (iv) Re-order quantity.

Maximum Level (MxL)

It is the largest quantity of a particular material which should be kept in the store at any time. This much quantity in stock is necessary to avoid unnecessary blocking up of the capital in inventories, losses on account of deterioration and obsolescence of materials, extra overheads and temptations to thefts. Following points are considered in fixing the maximum level:

- Storage space.
- Availability of working capital.
- Rate of consumption of materials and time necessary in obtaining new materials.
- Economic order quantities.
- Cost of storage, insurance, interest on capital invested in stocks.

The formula to compute maximum level is as under:

MxL = Re-order Order Level + Re-Order Quantity
– (Minimum Usage × Minimum Re-order Period)

Minimum Level (MnL)

It is the lowest quantity of stock of materials which must be maintained in hand at all times so that the assembly line may not be stopped on account of non-availability of materials. Following points are considered in fixing the minimum level:

- Average rate of consumption of materials.
- Average time required to obtain delivery of fresh supplies.
- Re-order level.

The formula to compute minimum level is as under:

MnL = Re-order Order Level – (Normal Usage × Normal Re-order Period)

Re-order Level (RoL)

This is the point at which orders are to be placed for further supplies. it is somewhere between the maximum level and the minimum level in such a way that the quantity of materials represented by the difference between the reordering level and the minimum level is sufficient to meet the demand of the production till such time as the ordered materials and supplies are received i.e. the flow of production remains uninterrupted. It depends upon the followings:

- Maximum consumption
- Lead time i.e. the anticipated time lag between the dates of issuing purchase order and receipt of materials.

The formula to compute re-orders level is as under:

RoL = Maximum Re-Order Period × Maximum Usage

Re-order Quantity (RoQ)

It refers to the standard quantity of material which is normally placed on order when the stock reaches the re-order level. This term is synonymous with the economic order quantity.

The formula to compute re-order quantity is as under:

RoQ = Maximum level – Re-order level + (Minimum consumption × Minimum re-order period)

Danger level: This is a level at which normal issues are stopped and materials are issued for important jobs. This level is usually fixed below the minimum level. When it touches this level, urgent action becomes necessary for the replenishment of stock so that interruption in production process can be avoided. The formula to compute this level is as under:

= Normal consumption × maximum re-order period (under emergency conditions)

Stock Turnover

Stock turnover ratio indicates the frequency of consumption of stock in a given period, say, a year. It is an indicator of the rate of consumption. A high stock turnover ratio indicates fast moving materials and a low ratio indicates slow moving materials. Thus, higher the stock turnover, more efficient is the stock policy. It is a good measure of the efficiency of material utilization.The stock turnover ratio is equal to cost of materials consumed during a given period divided by average stock of materials during the same given period i.e.

Stock Turnover Ratio:

= Cost of materials consumed during a given period ÷ Average Stock of materials during the same given period

Stock turnover ratio may be computed in terms of days. It is number of days in the given period divided by stock turnover ratio i.e.

Stock Turnover Ratio (in Days):

= Number of days in the given period ÷ Stock Turnover Ratio

Illustration 5.1 : *The following information relates to the year 2009:*

Details	*Material: I*	*Material: II*
Opening Stock	*5,00,000*	*20,00,000*
Closing Stock	*3,00,000*	*16,00,000*
Net Purchases	*42,00,000*	*50,00,000*

Find out Stock Turnover Ratio.

Solution :

Details	Material: I	Material: II
Average Stock*	= (5,00,000 +3,00,000) ÷ 2 = ₹ 4,00,000	= (20,00,000 + 16,00,000) ÷ 2 = ₹ 18,00,000
Materials Consumed = Opening stock + Net Purchases – Closing stock	5,00,000 + 42,00,000 – 3,00,000 = 44,00,000	20,00,000 + 50,00,000 –16,00,000 = 54,00,000
Stock Turnover Ratio**	44,00,000 ÷ 4,00,000 = 11	54,00,000 ÷ 18,00,000 = 3
Stock Turnover Ratio (In days)***	= 365 / 11 ⇒ 33 Days	= 365 / 3 ⇒ 122 Days

*Average Stock = (Opening Stock + Closing Stock) ÷ 2

** Stock Turnover Ratio = Cost of materials consumed ÷ Average Stock

***Stock Turnover Ratio = 365 ÷ Stock Turnover Ratio

From the above computations it is obvious that Material: I is Fast Moving as compared to Material: II, which takes 122 days to consume the average stock.

Slow, Dormant and Obsolete Materials

Slow Moving materials: Such materials have a low turnover ratio; the rate of consumption is low as compared to their stock holding. Stocks of such should be maintained at the lowest levels.

Dormant materials: At present such materials have no demand; they may be required in future.

Obsolete materials: Such materials are those which have become useless with the lapse of time, due to change in design of the product, or methods of manufacture, etc. These materials are no longer in demand as there are better substitutes available in the market or the product in which such materials were required is no longer in demand.

It is the duty of the store-keeper to keep track of the slow moving materials and inform the concerned authorities so that alternative use of such materials could be found.

Factors responsible for slow moving, dormant and obsolete materials:

1. Failure of the store-keeper to report on slow moving items and recommend their use as substitutes.
2. No periodical review of the store ledger.
3. Failure of the production department to notify in time the contemplated change in the material requirements to material control department.
4. Failure of the purchase department to cancel outstanding orders for such materials.
5. Technical changes and use of substitute materials.
6. Purchase of obsolete items.

Control of slow moving, dormant and obsolete materials:

It is better to compute standard stock turnover ratio for each item of material. This is computed as under:

= Budgeted Consumption / Average Stock

The standard ratio is to be compared with the actual stock turnover ratio. If the actual stock turnover ratio is less than the standard, it means the item comes under the category of slow moving materials. Periodical reports on such item of materials be made and presented to the management for appropriate action. The report should include the rate of purchase and consumption of the stock (Item-wise).

Illustration : 5.2 (Material Input)

An article passes through three successive operations from the raw materials stage to the finished product stage. The following data are available from the production records of a particular month:

Operation No.	*No. of Pieces (Input)*	*No. of Pieces (Rejected)*	*No. of Pieces (Output)*
1	*75,000*	*25,000*	*50,000*
2	*82,500*	*7,500*	*75,000*
3	*60,000*	*10,000*	*50,000*

(i) Determine the input required to be introduced in the first operation in number of pieces in order to obtain finished output of 100 pieces after the last operation.

(ii) Calculate the cost of raw material required to produce one piece of finished product, given the following information.

Weight of the finished piece is 0.25 kg. And the price of raw material is ₹ 40 per kg.

Solution :

Operation No.	No. of Pieces (Input)	No. of Pieces (Rejected)	% Rejections to output	No. of Pieces (Output)
1	75,000	25,000	50	50,000
2	82,500	7,500	10	75,000
3	60,000	10,000	20	50,000

Input required for finished output of 100 Pieces:	No. of Pieces
Output of Operation No. 3	100
Loss in Operation No. 3 (20% of output of Operation No.3)	20
Input to Operation No.3 or output of Operation No. 2	120
Loss in Operation No. 2(10% of output of Operation No.2)	12
Output of Operation No. 2	132
Loss in Operation No. 2(50% of output of Operation No.1)	66
Input to Operation No.1	198

198 pieces of initial input are used to produce 100 pieces of finished output. The weight of one piece of finished output is 0.25 kg. Thus, the weight of input for one piece of output = 0.25 × 198 = 49.5 kg. The material required for one piece of finished product is 49.5/100 i.e. 0.495 and so the cost of input material @ ₹ 40 per kg comes to Rupees 19.8.Thus the total cost of materials required for the production of 50,000 units of output is 50,000 × 19.8 = ₹ 9,90,000.

Illustration : 5.3 (Tabular Approach)

A firm's inventory planning period is for one year. Its requirement for this period is 6400 units. Assume that the ordering cost comes to ₹ 100/- per order. The carrying costs are expected to be ₹8/- per unit per year for an item. Unit price is ₹80/-. The firm can procure inventories in various lots such as:

(i) 6400 units, (ii) 3200 units, (iii) 1600 units, (iv) 800 units, (v) 400 units, (vi) 200 units, and (vii) 100 units. Which of these order quantities is the economic order quantity?

Solution : Determination of Economic Order Quantity (Order Size): Tabular Approach

Details	I	II	III	IV	V	VI	VII
Cost of items purchased during the year (₹)	5,12,000	5,12,000	5,12,000	5,12,000	5,12,000	5,12,000	5,12,000
Order Size (unit)	6,400	3,200	1,600	800	400	200	100
Number of Orders (No.)	1	2	4	8	16	32	64

Average Inventory (unit)	3,200	1,600	800	400	200	100	50
Total Carrying Cost (₹)	25,600	12,800	6,400	3,200	1,600	800	400
Total Ordering Cost (₹)	100	200	400	800	1600	3200	6400
Total Cost (₹) (Carrying cost + Ordering cost)	25,700	13,000	6,800	4,000	3,200	4,000	6,800

The EOQ is 400 units.

Working Notes :

(i) Number of orders = Total Annual Inventory Requirement/Order Size

(ii) Average Inventory = Order Size/2

(iii) Total Carrying Cost = Average inventory × Carrying cost per unit

(iv) Total Ordering cost = Number of orders × Cost per order.

Illustration : 5.4 (Algebraic Approach)

A firm's Annual inventory requirement is 6, 400 units. Assume that the ordering cost comes to ₹ 100 per order. The carrying costs are expected to be ₹ 8 per unit per year for an item, which is 10% of its unit price. Find out EOQ.

Solution :

$$EOQ = \sqrt{[2AB/C]}$$

$$A = 6,400$$

$$B = 100$$

$$C = 8$$

$$EOQ = ?$$

$$= \sqrt{[(2 \times 6400 \times 100) \div (8)]}$$

$$= 400 \text{ Units.}$$

Illustration : 5.5

Given :

$$\sqrt{[2ABC]} = 3,200$$

$$B = 100$$

$$C = 8$$

$$EOQ = ?$$

Solution : Let the annual consumption be 'A'

$$\sqrt{[2A \times 100 \times 8]} = 3,200$$

$$1,600\ A = 3,200 \times 3,200$$

$$A = (3,200 \times 3,200)/1,600 = 6,400$$

$$EOQ = \sqrt{[2AB/C]} = \sqrt{[2 \times 6400 \times 100)/(8)]} = 400 \text{ Units.}$$

Illustration : 5.6 (Algebraic Approach)

From the following data find out economic order quantity for the item:

Total annual consumption	*= 3, 00,000 units*
Purchase Price per unit	*= ₹ 15.*
Ordering cost	*= ₹ 80 per order*
Cost of carrying inventory per unit p.a.	*= 20%*

Solution :

EOQ = √[2AB/C]

A = 3,00,000 units

B = ₹ 80

C = ₹ 15 × 0.2 = ₹ 3

EOQ = ?

= √[2 × 3,00,000 × 80)/(3)]

= 4,000 Units

Illustration : 5.7 (Stock Levels)

Medical Aids Company manufactures a special product "AID". The following details were compiled from the records of the company for the year 2007:

1. *Monthly demand of "AID" = 1,200*
2. *Cost of placing an order ₹ 125*
3. *Annual carrying cost per unit ₹ 19.50*
4. *Normal usage 60 units per week*
5. *Minimum usage 30 units per week*
6. *Maximum usage 90 units per week*
7. *Re-Order Period 4 to 6 weeks.*

Compute from the above:

A. *Re-Order Quantity*
B. *Re-Order Level*
C. *Minimum Order Level*
D. *Maximum Order Level*
E. *Average stock Level*

Solution :

Working Note: Normal usage is 60 units per week; for one year it amounts to 3,120 units (i.e. 52 × 60 units).

Re-Order Quantity = √[2AB/C]

A = 3,120 units

B = ₹ 125

C = ₹ 19.50

Re-Order Quantity OR EOQ = ?

(A) EOQ = √[2 × 3,120 × 125)/19.50] = 200 Units

(B) Re-Order Level = Maximum Re-Order Period × Maximum Usage
= 6 × 90 = 540 units

(C) Minimum Order Level:

Re-order Order Level – (Normal Usage × Normal Re-order Period)
= 540 – (60 × 5) = 540 – 300 = 240 Units

(D) Maximum Order Level:
= Re-order Order Level + Re-Order Quantity – (Minimum Usage × Minimum Re-order Period)
= 540 + 200 – (30 × 4) = 740 – 120 = 620 Units

(E) Average Stock Level:
= ½[Minimum Stock Level + Maximum stock Level]
= ½[240 + 620] = ½[860] = 430 Units

Special Techniques of Material Control

Following three techniques of material control are discussed hereunder:

(I) A-B-C Analysis

ABC system of controlling stock means stock control according to value method or proportional Parts Value analysis method. This is based on the general principle of 'Pareto Distribution' that there are a small percentage of items having relatively much larger significance.

'Category A' includes HIGH Value, LOW Volume items. It constitutes only a small percentage of total inventories in terms of Quantity (i.e. Number, Weight, or Volume) but represents large percentage share in total value of inventory.

'Category B' includes MEDIUM Value items. Their percentage share in total quantity is almost equal to their percentage share in total value of inventory.

'Category C' includes LOW Value, HIGH Volume items. Their percentage share in total quantity is quite, but their percentage share in total value of inventory is small.

The rational limits of different categories are:

Category	% of total quantity	% of total value of inventory
A	5 to 10	70 to 85
B	10 to 20	10 to 20
C	70 to 85	5 to 10

The following table and graph (Lorenz curve) gives three categories with the help of arbitrary proportions:

Material Categories based on ABC Analysis

Category	% share in total quantity (*i.e.*, units, weight or volume of total inventory)	% share of total value of inventories
A (high value, low volume)	10	70
B (medium value)	20	20
C (Low value, high volume)	70	10

[ABC Categorisation]

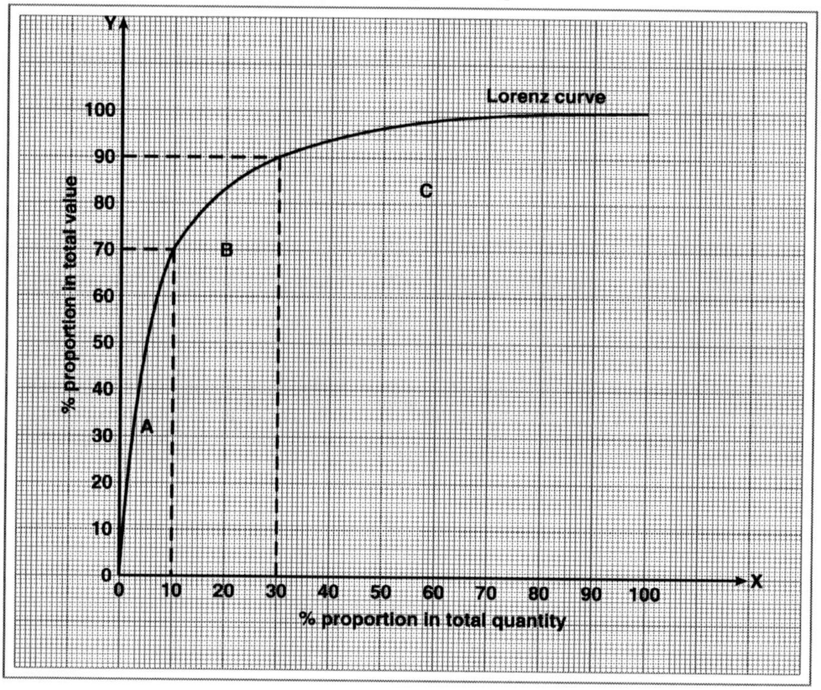

Graph 5.2

Illustration 5.8 : *Present the following information in graphical form according to A-B-C plan:*

Item	*Number of Units*	*Cost per unit (₹)*
M001	*250*	*300*
M002	*500*	*200*
M003	*1,000*	*100*
M004	*2,500*	*80*
M005	*4,500*	*20*
M006	*22,500*	*10*

Solution :

Item	Number of Units	% of Total Number	Cost per unit (₹)	Total Cost (₹)	% of Total Cost	Category
M001	250	0.800	300	75,000	9.375	A
M002	500	1.600	200	1,00,000	12.500	A
M003	1,000	3.200	110	1,10,000	13.750	A
M004	2,500	8.000	80	2,00,000	25.000	B
M005	4,500	14.400	20	90,000	11.250	B
M006	22,500	72.000	10	2,25,000	28.125	C
Total	31,250	100.000		8,00,000	100.000	

(II) VED Analysis

In ABC analysis materials are categorised into 'A', 'B' and 'C' on the basis of their value, spare parts are categorised into Vital, Essential and Desirable on the basis of their criticality to production. Vital Spares are those which are very critical for production; shortage of it can prove to be very costly for the organisation, the production process gets interrupted and leads to heavy losses. Essential Spares are those which are of great importance for few hours or a day the production department can continue the process of production. If they are out of stock for a long period of time, the production losses are bound to occur. Desirable Spares are those which are required for production but the workshop can mange without them for a short period of time, say a week, as they have substitutes or the production process can be modified in such a way that production can go on without these items of stores.

A spare may be less costly but critical for production. VED analysis ensures that due attention is paid on maintaining uninterrupted supply of vital spares.

(III) Input-Output Ratio

Input-output ratio is useful in measuring productivity of material, labour or capital or the composite productivity of all such resources at the micro/macro level. It is the ratio of quantity of materials used for actual output and the standard material input prescribed for actual output. Higher the ratio, lower is the productivity. It can be measured by using any of the alternatives.

Alternative I: If input and output are measured in the same units

$$\text{Input-output Ratio} = \frac{\text{Input of materials used for actual output}}{\text{Standard material input prescribed for actual output}}$$

Alternative II: If input and output are not measured in the same units

Input-output Ratio =

$$\frac{\text{Standard cost of actual input of materials used for actual output}}{\text{Standard cost of material input prescribed for actual output}}$$

Illustration : 5.9. *Present the following information in a table categorising according to A-B-C Plan:*

Item	*Number of Units*	*Cost per unit (₹)*
M001	*250*	*300*
M002	*500*	*200*
M003	*1,000*	*100*
M004	*2,500*	*80*
M005	*4,500*	*20*
M006	*22,500*	*10*

Solution :

Item	Number of Units	% of Total Number	Cost per unit (₹)	Total Cost (₹)	% of Total Cost	Category
M001	250	0.800	300	75,000	9.375	A
M002	500	1.600	200	1,00,000	12.500	A
M003	1,000	3.200	110	1,10,000	13.750	A
M004	2,500	8.000	80	2,00,000	25.000	B
M005	4,500	14.400	20	90,000	11.250	B
M006	22,500	72.000	10	2,25,000	28.125	C
Total	31,250	100.000		8,00,000	100.000	

Illustration : 5.10 (ABC Analysis)

Analyse the following items into A, B, and C categories on the basis of information given below, and prepare a report showing your findings with comments.

Category A: ₹ 80,000 and above (Total Value)

Category B: ₹ 20,000 and ₹ 79,999 (Total Value)

Category C: Below ₹ 20,000 (Total Value)

S. No.	*Component No.*	*Quantity*	*Unit Value (₹)*
1	*543*	*735*	*12.00*
2	*3,27,400*	*4,930*	*8.00*
3	*358400*	*1,765*	*16.00*
4	*491*	*44,655*	*0.40*
5	*31*	*6,195*	*0.60*

6	*751*	*500*	*1.00*
7	*1,411*	*90*	*2,052.00*
8	*91,101*	*18,850*	*10.00*
9	*95,100*	*3415*	*8.00*
10	*74,100*	*670*	*2.80*
11	*75,100*	*950*	*1.60*
12	*41,210*	*5*	*172.00*
13	*42,910*	*260*	*2.80*
14	*26,011*	*2,130*	*0.40*
15	*47,411*	*23,625*	*0.24*
16	*55,011*	*50*	*121.08*
17	*25,014*	*100*	*5.60*
18	*53,375*	*32,710*	*0.08*
19	*53,374*	*1,645*	*1.60*
20	*73,072*	*50*	*536.00*

Solution :

S. No.	Component No.	Quantity (Unit)	Unit Value (₹)	Total Value (₹)	Category A	Category B	Category C
1	543	735	12.00	8,820			8,820
2	3,27,400	4,930	8.00	39,440		39,440	
3	3,58,400	1,765	16.00	28,240		28,240	
4	491	44,655	0.40	17,862			17862
5	31	6,195	0.60	3,717			3,717
6	751	500	1.00	500			500
7	1,411	90	2,052.00	1,84,680	1,84,680		
8	91,101	18,850	10.00	1,88,500	1,88,500		
9	95,100	3,415	8.00	27,320		27,320	
10	74,100	670	2.80	1,876			1,876
11	75,100	950	1.60	1,520			1,520
12	41,210	5	172.00	860			860
13	42,910	260	2.80	728			728
14	26,011	2,130	0.40	852			852
15	47,411	23,625	0.24	5,670			5,670
16	55,011	50	121.08	6,054			6,054
17	25,014	100	5.60	560			560

18	53,375	32,710	0.08	2,617			2,617
19	53,374	1,645	1.60	2,632			2,632
20	73,072	50	536.00	26,800		26,800	
				5,40,428	3,73,180	1,21,800	45, 448

Analysis Table

Details	Total	Category A	Category B	Category C
Item (Number)	20	2	4	14
Item (%)	100	10	20	70
Value (₹)	5,40,428	3,73,180	1,21,800	45,448
Value (%)	100	69.05	22.54	8.41

[ABC Graph]
(Using Lorenz curve)

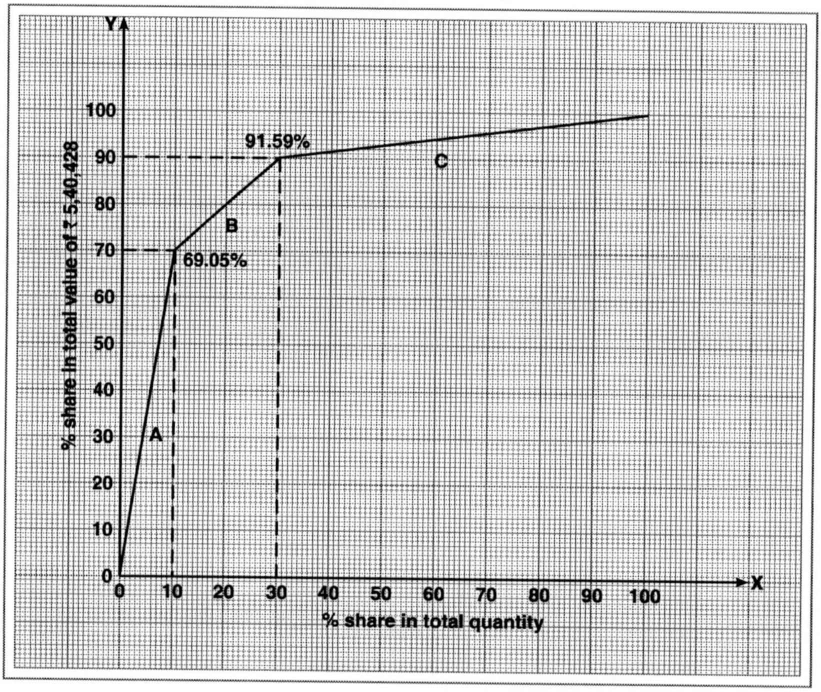

Graph 5.3

LET US RECAPITULATE

1. Investment in materials aims at making the best use of every rupee invested in inventories.
2. Importance of ordering materials in right quantities and maintaining the right level of stocks including necessary cushion of materials cannot be denied.
3. The attitude of the producer will have an effect on the level of safety stocks actually maintained.
4. EOQ refers to the size of purchase order for a material which results in making material available in a year at minimum total material related costs.
5. There is an INVERSE relationship between order size and ordering cost.
6. There is POSITIVE relationship between order size and Storage/Carrying cost.
7. EOQ= $\sqrt{[2AB/C]}$
8. Maximum Level is the largest quantity of a particular material which should be kept in the store at any time.
9. Minimum Level is the lowest quantity of stock of materials which must be maintained in hand at all times so that the assembly line may not be stopped on account of non-availability of materials.
10. Re-order Level is the point at which orders are to be placed for further supplies.
11. Re-order quantity refers to the standard quantity of material which is normally placed on order when the stock reaches the re-order level.
12. Stock turnover ratio indicates the frequency of consumption of stock in a given period, say, a year.
13. The stock turnover ratio is equal to cost of materials consumed during a given period divided by average stock of materials during the same given period.
14. Slow Moving materials have a low turnover ratio.
15. Obsolete materials are those which have become useless with the lapse of time, due to change in design of the product, or methods of manufacture, etc.
16. ABC system of controlling stock means stock control according to value method or proportional Parts Value analysis method.
17. In VED analysis, spare parts are categorised into Vital, Essential and Desirable on the basis of their criticality to production.
18. Input-output ratio is the ratio of quantity of materials used for actual output and the standard material input prescribed for actual output.

SOLVED PROBLEMS

Problem 1. *From the following information for the last two months, compute average stock level and Danger level for the Item 'X':*

Details	*Units*
Maximum Consumption	*300*
Minimum Consumption	*200*
Average Consumption	*225*

Re-Order Period (Max. Months): 6	
Re-Order Period (Min. Months): 2	
Re-Order Period (Max. Months): 1.5	
(for Emergency Purchases)	
Re-Order Quantity	*750*

Solution :

Minimum Level = ROL – (Average Consumption × Average Re-order period)

= [(300 × 6) – {225 × (6 + 2)/2}

= 1,800 – 900 = 900 Units.

Average Stock Level = Minimum Level + 0.5 ROQ

= 900 + 0.5 × 750

= 900 + 375

= 1,275 Units.

Danger Level

= Average consumption × Minimum re-order Period for emergency Purchases

= 225 × 1.5 = 337.5 Units.

Problem 2. (EOQ) *Hughes limited manufacturers of a special product, follows the policy of EOQ (Economic order quantity) for one of its components. The component's details are as follows:*

Purchase price for component	*₹ 200*
Cost of an order	*₹ 100*
Annual cost of carrying one unit in inventory:	*10% of purchase price*
Total cost of inventory and ordering per annum:	*₹ 4,000*

The company has been offered a discount of 2% on the price of the component, provided the lot size is 2,000 components at a time.

You are required to:

(a) Compute the EOQ

(b) Advise whether the quantity discount offer can be accepted. (Assume that the inventory carrying cost does not vary according to discount policy.)

(c) Would your advice differ if the company were offered 5% discount on a single order?

Solution : Inventory carrying cost per unit:

0.1 × 200 = ₹ 20

Let x be the EOQ,

Then we have average inventory holding as x/2 and annual carrying cost is (x/2) × 20, or ₹ 10x

If ordered quantity is EOQ, annual ordering cost is equal to annual carrying cost.

Therefore, annual carrying cost is ₹ 4,000/2 or ₹ 2,000

Thus, 10x = 2,000 or x = 200

Hence, EOQ = 200 units

Annual ordering cost is ₹ 4,000/2, or ₹ 2,000

Cost of an order is ₹100. therefore, number of orders = 2,000/100, or 20

Thus, annual requirements = EOQ × 20 or 200 × 20 or 4,000 units

Case I: Total inventory cost, if ordered quantity is EOQ as follows:

Cost of the component	₹200 × 4,000 or	₹8,00,000
Annual carrying cost		2,000
Annual ordering cost		2,000
Total cost		₹ 8,04,000

Case II: Total inventory cost, if ordered quantity is 2,000 units with discount of 2%is as follows:

Cost of the component ₹ {200 – (0.02 × 200)} × 4, 000 or ₹ 7,84,000	
Annual carrying cost (2000 / 2) × ₹ 20	20,000
Annual ordered cost (4,000 / 2,000) × ₹ 100	200
Total cost	₹ 8,04,200

Case III: Total inventory cost, if ordered quantity is 4,000 units, with discount of 5 % is calculated as follows:

Cost of the component: ₹ {200 – (0.05 × 200)} × 4,000 or	₹ 7,60,000
Annual carrying cost (4,000 / 2) × ₹ 20	40,000
Annual ordering cost (4,000 / 4,000) × ₹ 100	100
Total cost	₹ 8,00,100

Inference:

(a) EOQ is 200 units.

(b) Discount should be accepted, because the total inventory cost will be lower by ₹ 3,900 as compared to the total cost under EOQ policy.

Note: 'Total cost of inventory and ordering per annum' mentioned in the question is interpreted as 'total of annual carrying cost and ordering cost per annum'.

Problem 3. (EOQ) *Annual requirement of a particular item of inventory is 10,000 units. Inventory carrying cost per unit per annum is 20% and ordering cost is ₹ 40 per order. The price quoted by the supplier is ₹ 4 per unit. However, the supplier is ready to give a discount of 5% for orders of 1,600 units or more. Is it worthwhile to avail of the discount offer?* **[B. Com (Hons.) DU, 2006 (Modified)]**

Solution :

Working Note:

Purchase Price: In case of 5% discount on price

$$= 4.00 - (4.00 \times 0.05) \text{ or } 4.00 \times 0.95 = ₹\ 3.80$$

Carrying cost = $3.80 \times 0.2 = 0.76$

$$\text{EOQ} = \sqrt{[(2AB)/C]}$$
$$= \sqrt{[(2 \times 10{,}000 \times 40)/0.8]}$$
$$= 1{,}000 \text{ units}$$

Total Cost if Ordered Quantity is EOQ

(i.e. 1,000 units)

Details	Amount (₹)
Material cost (10,000 × 4)	40,000
Ordering cost [(10,000/1,000) × (40)]	400
Carrying cost [(1000/2) × (0.8)]	400
Total	40,800

Total Cost if Ordered Quantity is 1,500 units

At 5% discount on Price

Details	Amount (₹)
Material cost (10,000 × 3.80)	38,000
Ordering cost [(10,000/1,600) × (40)]	250
Carrying cost[(1600/2) × (0.76)]	608
Total	38,858

Decision: It is cheaper to buy in quantities of 1,500 units at 5% discount, as the company saves ₹ 1,942 by accepting such an offer of the supplier. Therefore, offer of discount should be availed.

Problem 4. (EOQ) *A company manufactures 5,000 units of a product per month. The cost of placing an order is ₹ 100. The purchase price of the raw material is ₹ 10 per kg. The re-order period is 4 to 8 weeks. The consumption of raw material varies from 100 kg to 450 kg per week; the average consumption being 275 kg. The carrying cost of inventory is 20% per annum. You are required to calculate reorder quantity, maximum level, minimum level and average level.*

[DU, B. Com (Hons.) 2006]

Solution :

$$\text{EOQ} = \sqrt{[(2AB)/C]}$$
$$= \sqrt{[\{2 \times (275 \times 52) \times 100\}/2]}$$
$$= 1{,}196 \text{ kg.}$$

Re-Order Level = Maximum Usage × Maximum Period

= 450 × 8 = 3,600 kg.

Maximum level:

= Re-Order Level + Reorder Quantity – (Minimum Usage × Minimum Period)

= 3,600 + 1,196 – (100 × 4)

= 4,396 kg.

Minimum level:

= Re-Order Level– ((Normal Usage × Normal Re-order Period)

= 3,600 – (275 × 6)

= 3,600 – 1650 = 1,950 kg.

Average level = [(Maximum level + Minimum level)/2]

= [(4,396 + 1,950)/2]

= 3,173 kg.

Working Note :

Carrying cost = 10 × 0.2 = ₹ 2 per unit per annum

Problem 5. (EOQ + ROL) *A company manufactures 4,000 units of a product per month. Cost of placing an order is ₹ 125. The purchase price of raw material is ₹ 10 per kg. The reordered period is 3 to 6 weeks. The consumption of raw material varies from 100 kg to 500 kg per week, the average consumption being 300 kg., the carrying cost of inventory is 20% p.a.*

You are required to calculate:

(i) Re-order quantity

(ii) Re-order level.

Solution : Re-order Quantity or Economic Order Quantity (EOQ):

EOQ = √[(2AB)/C]

A = 4,000 × 12 = 48,000 units

B = ₹ 125

C = ₹ 2 i.e. (10 × 0.2)

= √[(2 × 48,000 × 125) / 2]

= 2,450 units (approx.)

Re-order level = Maximum consumption × Minimum Re-order Period

= 500 × 6 = 3,000 units

Problem 6. *The following details are available in respect of a firm:*

(i) Inventory requirement per year: 9,000 units

(ii) Cost per unit(other than carrying and ordering costs): ₹ 15

(iii) Carrying cost per item for one year: 10%.

(iv) Cost of placing each order: ₹ 120

(v) *Alternative order size (units): 9,000, 6,000, 3,000, 1,500, 1,200, 1,000 and 600.*

Determine the EOQ and the cost.

Solution : Determination of Economic Order Quantity (Order Size) (Tabular Approach)

Details	I	II	III	IV	V	VI	VII
Cost of items purchased during the year (₹)	1,35,000	1,35,000	1,35,000	1,35,000	1,35,000	1,35,000	1,35,000
Order Size (unit)	9,000	6,000	3,000	1,500	1,200	1,000	600
Number of Orders (No.)	1	1.5	3	6	7.5	9	15
Average Inventory (unit)	4,500	3,000	1,500	750	600	500	300
Total Carrying Cost (₹) @ ₹ 1.50 per unit per annum	6,750	4,500	2,250	1,125	900	750	450
Total Ordering Cost (₹) @ ₹ 120 per Order	120	180	360	720	900	1,080	1,800
Total Cost (₹) = (Carrying cost + Ordering cost)	6,870	4,680	2,610	1,845	1,800	1,830	2,250

The EOQ is 1,200 units.

Working Notes :

(i) Carrying Cost per unit per annum = 0.1 × 15 = ₹ 1.50

(ii) Total Carrying Cost = Average inventory × Carrying cost per unit

(iii) Total Ordering cost = Number of orders × Cost per order.

Problem 7. *TSP Ltd. has received an offer of quantity discounts on its order of materials as under:*

Details (No.)	*Price per tonne (₹)*
Less than 1,000	*3,000*
1,000 and Less than 2,000	*2,950*
2,000 and Less than 4,000	*2,900*
4,000 and Less than 6,000	*2,850*
6,000 and Above	*2,800*

The annual requirement of the materials is 10,000 tonnes. The ordering cost per order is ₹ 3,000 and the carrying cost is estimated at 20% per annum.

You are required to compute the most economical purchase order.

Also find the order size if no discounts are offered and the price per tonne is ₹ 3,750.

Solution : Determination of Economic Order Quantity (Order Size) (Tabular Approach)

Details	Economic Purchase Level				
	I	II	III	IV	V
1. Annual Requirement (Unit)	10,000	10,000	10,000	10,000	10,000
2. E Order Size (Unit)	500	1,000	2,000	5,000	10,000
3. E/2 Average Stock (Unit)	250	500	1,000	2,500	5,000
4. Unit Rate (₹)	3,000	2,950	2,900	2,850	2,800
5. Average Stock Value (₹)	7,50,000	14,75,000	29,00,000	71,25,000	140,00,000
6. Number of Orders	20	10	5	2	1
7. Ordering cost@ ₹ 3,000 per order	60,000	30,000	15,000	6,000	3,000
8. Carrying cost@ 20% (₹)	1,50,000	2,95,000	5,80,000	14,25,000	28,00,000
9. Cost of Purchase (₹)	3,00,00,000	2,95,00,000	2,90,00,000	2,85,00,000	2,80,00,000
10. Total Material Cost (₹) [i.e. (7) + (8) +(9)]	3,02,10,000	2,98,25,000	2,95,95,000	2,99,31,000	3,08,03,000

$$\begin{aligned} EOQ &= \sqrt{[2AB/C]} \\ &= \sqrt{[2 \times 10{,}000 \times 3{,}000/750]} \\ &= \sqrt{80{,}000} \\ &= 282.84 \text{ tonnes (Approximately).} \end{aligned}$$

Problem 8. *A company manufactures a product having a monthly demand of 2,000 units. For one unit of finished product 2 Kgs of a particular material item is required. The purchase price of the material is ₹ 20 per kg. The ordering cost is ₹ 120 per order and the holding cost is 10% p.a. Calculate:*

(i) Economic Order Quantity, and

(ii) Annual cost of purchasing and storage of the raw material at that quantity.

Solution :

Working Notes :

Annual consumption (A): 2,000 × 2 × 12 = 48,000 Kgs.

Ordering Cost per order = ₹ 120

Carrying cost per unit p.a. = 20 × 0.1 = ₹ 2

$$\begin{aligned} EOQ &= \sqrt{[2AB/C]} \\ &= \sqrt{[2 \times 48{,}000 \times 120/2]} \\ &= \sqrt{57{,}60{,}000} \\ &= 2{,}400 \text{ Kg.} \end{aligned}$$

$$\begin{aligned} \text{Annual Cost} &= \text{Cost of ordering} + \text{cost of storage} \\ &= [(48{,}000/2{,}400) \times 120] + [(2{,}400/2) \times 2] \\ &= 2{,}400 + 2{,}400 = ₹\ 4{,}800. \end{aligned}$$

Problem 9. *A manufacturing company uses ₹ 50,000 materials per year. The administration cost per purchase is ₹ 50 and carrying cost is 20% of the average inventory. The company currently has an optimum purchasing policy but has been offered a 0.4 per cent discount if they purchase five times per year. Should the offer be accepted? If not, what counter offer should be made?*

Solution : The company may be currently placing order for economic order quantity because it is following an optimum purchasing policy. The current quantity of purchase per order is as under:

Current quantity of Purchase i.e. EOQ = √[2AB/C]

= √[2× 50,000×50/0.2] = ₹ 5,000

Number of times total requirement is being purchased:

= Total Requirement/EOQ

= 50,000/5000 = 10

Comparison of cost (₹):

Cost Element	EOQ Ordering	Non-EOQ Ordering
Material	50,000	49,800 {50,000 – 0.4% × 50,000}
Ordering	500 {10 × 50}	250 {5 × 50}
Carrying	500 {(1/2) × (50,000/10) × (0.2)}	996 {(1/2) × (49,800/5) × (0.2)}
Total	51,000	51,046

Note: For getting a discount of ₹ 200, the rate of discount is 0.4%. Therefore, for getting a further discount of ₹ 46, the additional rate of discount should be 0.1% {(0.4/200) *46}. Thus the rate of discount should be more than 0.5% to make the offer attractive. Let us compare the cost if the rate of discount is 0.6%:

Cost Element	EOQ Ordering	Non-EOQ Ordering
Material	50000	49700 {50000 – 0.6% ×50000}
Ordering	500 {10 × 50}	250 {5 × 50}
Carrying	500 {(1/2) × (50,000/10) × (0.2)}	994 {(1/2) × (49,700/5) × (0.2)}
Total	51,000	50,944

Problem 10. *From the following details, find out:*

(a) How much should be ordered each time?

(b) When should the order be placed?

(c) What should be the inventory level (ideally) immediately before the material order is received?

(i) Annual consumption: 30,000 units (360days)

(ii) *Cost per unit : ₹ 15*

(iii) *Ordering cost: ₹ 30 per order*

(iv) *Inventory carrying charge:16%*

(v) *Normal Lead time: 12 days*

(vi) *Safety stock: 30 Days consumption*

Solution : (a) EOQ = √[2AB/C]

= √[2 × 30,000 × 30/2.4] = 866 units

Each time order size should be for 866 units.

(b) Re-Order Level = Safety stock + lead time consumption

= 30 Days consumption + 12 Days consumption

= {(30 × 30,000)/360} + {(12 × 30,000)/360}

= 2500 + 1000 = 3500units

(c) Inventory level immediately before the material order is received should be equal to safety stock i.e. it should be equal to 30 days consumption.

Safety stock = 30 Days consumption

= {(30 × 30,000)/360}

= 2500 units.

Problem 11. *A company buys its annual requirement of 36,000 units in six installments. Each unit cost ₹ 10 and the ordering cost is ₹ 250. The inventory carrying cost is estimated at 20% of the unit value. Find the total annual cost of the existing inventory policy. How much money can be saved by economic order quantity?*

Solution : Calculation of the Annual cost of Existing inventory Policy

Details	Amount (₹)
Ordering cost for Six orders @ ₹ 250 per order	1,500
Carrying cost @ 20% [i.e. (36,000/6) × 10 × (1/2) ×.02]	6,000
Annual cost (Excluding purchase price of material)	7,500

Calculation of Economic Order Quantity

EOQ = √[2AB/C]

= √[2 × 36,000 × 250/2] = 3,000 units

Calculation of the Annual cost if ordering as per EOQ

Details	Amount (₹)
Ordering cost for 12 orders @ ₹ 250 per order	3,000
Carrying cost @ 20% [i.e. (36,000/12) × 10 × (1/2) ×.02]	3,000
Annual cost (Excluding purchase price of material)	6,000

Calculation of saving in cost if ordered as per EOQ

Details	Amount (₹)
Annual cost of existing inventory policy	7,500
Less: Annual cost by EOQ	6,000
Saving in cost by EOQ	1,500

Problem 12. *ABC Company buys in lots of 125 boxes which is a three month's supply. The cost per box is ₹ 125and the ordering cost is ₹ 250 per order. The inventory carrying cost is estimated at 20% of unit value per annum. You are required to ascertain:*

(i) The total annual cost of existing inventory policy.

(ii) How much money would be saved by employing the economic order quantity? **(B. Com. (Hons) DU, 2008)**

Solution : Calculation of the Annual cost of Existing inventory Policy

Details	Amount (₹)
Ordering cost for Four orders @ ₹ 250 per order	1,000.00
Carrying cost @ 20% [i.e. (500/4) × 125 × (1/2) ×.02]	1,562.50
Annual cost (Excluding purchase price of material)	2,562.50

Calculation of Economic Order Quantity

$$EOQ = \sqrt{[2AB/C]}$$

$$= \sqrt{[2 \times 500 \times 250/25]} = 100 \text{ units}$$

Calculation of the Annual cost if ordering as per EOQ

Details	Amount (₹)
Ordering cost for 5 orders @ ₹ 250 per order	1,250
Carrying cost @ 20% [i.e. (500/5) × 125 × (1/2) ×.02]	1,250
Annual cost (Excluding purchase price of material)	2,500

Calculation of saving in cost if ordered as per EOQ

Details	Amount (₹)
Annual cost of existing inventory policy	2,562.50
Less: Annual cost by EOQ	2,500.00
Saving in cost by EOQ	62.50

Problem 13. *A.S. Ltd. produces a product 'RED' using two components X and Y. each unit of 'RED' requires 0.4 kg of X and 0.6 kg of Y. Weekly production varies from 350 units to 450 units averaging 400 units. Delivery period for both the components is 1 to 3 weeks. The economic order quantity for X is 600 kgs and for Y is 1,000 kgs. Calculate:*

(i) Re-Order level of X;

(ii) Maximum level of X;

(iii) Minimum Level of Y. **(B. Com. (Hons) DU, 2008)**

Solution : Material X ::

Re-Order Level = Maximum Re-Order Period × Maximum Usage

= 3 × (0.4 × 450) = 540 kg

Maximum Order Level

= Re-order Order Level + Re-Order Quantity – (Minimum Usage × Minimum Re-order Period)

= 540 +600 – (350 × 0.4 × 1)

= 1140 – 140 = 1,000 kg

Material Y :

Minimum Order Level

= Re-order Order Level – (Normal Usage × Normal Re-order Period)

= (450 × 0.6 × 3) – (400 × 0.6 × 2)

= 810 – 480 = 330 kg

Problem 14. *Long Life Pharmacy produces Sanjivini tonic using two herbs H-1 and H-2. Each Litre of tonic requires 35 centiliters of H-1 and 65 centiliters of H-2. Weekly production varies from 500 litres to 600 litres averaging 550 litres. Delivery period for both the herbs is 2 to 6 weeks. The economic order quantity for H-1 is 800 litres and for H-2 is 1,500 litres.*

Compute:

(i) Re-order level of H-1;

(ii) Maximum Level of H-1;

(iii) Minimum Level of H-1.

(iv) Re-order level of H-2;

(v) Maximum Level of H-2;

(vi) Minimum Level of H-2.

Solution :

Re-order level of H-1

= (Maximum Consumption × Maximum Re-order Period)

= (600 × 0.35) × 6 = 1,260 Litres

Maximum Level of H-1:

= Re-order level + Re-order Quantity – (Minimum consumption × Minimum Re-order Period)

= 1,260 + 800 – (500 × 0.35 × 2)

= 1,260 + 800 – 350 = 1,710 Litres

Minimum Level of H-1:

= Re-order level – (Average consumption × Average Re-order Period)

= 1,710 – (550 × 0.35 × 4)

= 1,710 – 770 = 940 Litres

Re-order level of H-2

= (Maximum Consumption × Maximum Re-order Period)

= (600 × 0.65) × 6 = 2,340 Litres

Maximum Level of H-2:

= Re-order level + Re-order Quantity – (Minimum consumption × Minimum Re-order Period)

= 2,340 + 1,500 – (500 × 0.65 × 2)

= 2,340 + 1,500 – 650 = 3,190 Litres

Minimum Level of H-2:

= Re-order level – (Average consumption × Average Re-order Period)

= 2,340 – (550 × 0.65 × 4)

= 2,340 – 1,430 = 910 Litres

Problem 15. *In manufacturing its product P, a company uses two types of raw materials, M-1 and M-2 in respect of which the following information is supplied:*

One unit of P requires 16 Kg of M-1 and 6 kg of M-2 materials. Price per kg of M-1 is ₹ 25 and that of M-2 is ₹ 50. Re-order quantities of M-1 and M-2 are 16,000 kg and 7,600 kg. Re-order levels of M-1 and M-2 12,000 kg and 7,000 kg respectively. Weekly production varies from 200 units averaging 250 units. Delivery period of M-1 is 1 to 3 weeks and that of M-2 is 3 to 5 weeks. Compute:

(i) Minimum Stock level of M-1.

(ii) Maximum Stock level of M-2.

Solution : Minimum Stock level of M-1:

= Re-order level – (Normal Consumption × Normal Re-order Period)

= 16,000 – [(250 × 16) × 2]

= 16,000 – 8,000 = 8,000 Kg.

Maximum Stock level of M-2:

= Re-order level + Re-order Quantity –
(Minimum consumption × Minimum Re-order Period)

= 7,000 + 7,600 – [(200 × 6) × 3)]

= 7,000 + 7,600 – 3,600 = 11,000 Kg.

Problerm 16. *Find out re-order quantity if consumption is 80-100 units per day, delivery period is 3-5 days and maximum level is 660 units.*

Solution :

Re-order level = (Maximum Consumption × Maximum Re-order Period)

= (100 × 5) = 500 units

Maximum Level:

= Re-order level + Re-order Quantity –
(Minimum consumption × Minimum Re-order Period)

Re-order Quantity

= Maximum level – Re-order level + (minimum consumption × minimum re-order Period)

= 660 – 500 + (80 × 3)

= 660 – 500 + 240 = 400 units

Problem 17. *The following data pertain to Material M-I:*

Supply Period	*4 to 8 months*
Consumption Rate:	
Maximum	*600 units per month*
Minimum	*200 units per month*
Normal	*400 units per month*
Annual	*625 units per month*

Storage cost is 40% of stock value, ordering costs are ₹ 600 per order. Price per unit is ₹ 250.

Compute:

(i) Re-order level;

(ii) Maximum Stock Level;

(iii) Minimum Stock Level;

(iv) Average Stock Level.

Solution :

Working Notes :

Re-order Quantity or Economic Order Quantity (EOQ):

EOQ = √[(2AB)/C]

A = 625 × 12 = 7,500 units

B = ₹ 600

$$C = ₹\ 100 \text{ i.e. } (250 \times 0.4)$$
$$= \sqrt{[(2 \times 7{,}500 \times 600) / 100]}$$
$$= 300 \text{ units}$$

Re-order level = (Maximum Consumption × Maximum Re-order Period)
= (600 × 8) = 4,800 units

Minimum Stock level of M-1:
= Re-order level – (Normal Consumption × Normal Re-order Period)
= 4,800 – (400 × 6)
= 4,800 – 2,400 = 2,400 units

Maximum Level:
= Re-order level + Re-order Quantity – (Minimum consumption × Minimum Re-order Period)
= 4,800 + 300 – (200 × 4) = 4,300 units

Average Stock level
= Minimum Level + 0.5 Re-order Quantity
= 2,400 + 0.5 × 300
= 2,400 + 150 = 2,550 units

OR

$$\text{Average Stock level} = \frac{\text{Minimum Level} + \text{Maximum Level}}{2}$$
= (2,400 + 4,300) / 2
= 6,700 / 2 = 3,350 units

Problem 18. *From the following information for the last two months, compute Average Stock level and Danger level for the Item 'M-I':*

Details	***Unit***	***Month***
Maximum Consumption	*300*	
Minimum Consumption	*200*	
Average Consumption	*225*	
Re-Order Period (Max.)		*6*
Re-Order Period (Min.)		*2*
Re-Order Period (Max.) (for Emergency Purchases)		*1.5*
Re-Order Quantity	*750*	

Solution :

Working Note:

ROL = Maximum Re-order period × Maximum Consumption (usage)
= 6 × 300 ⇒ 1,800 units

Computation of Levels:

Minimum Level = ROL – (Average Consumption × Average Re-order period)

= [(300×6) – {225 × (6 + 2)/2}

= 1800 – 900 = 900.

Average Stock Level = Minimum Level + 0.5(ROQ)

= 900 + (0.5 × 750) = 1,275.

Danger Level = Average consumption × Minimum re-order Period for emergency Purchases

= 225 × 1.5 = 337.5

Problem 19. *Compute Input-Output Ratio from the following information:*

Input of Raw cotton = 250 Kg.

Output (Cloth containing Cotton) = 225 Kg.

Cost per Kg. of Raw Cotton = ₹ 27.00

Solution : Input /Output Ratio = 250/225 = 10/9

Raw Material Cost of Finished Product = 27 × 10/9 = 30.00.

Cost of Input = cost of finished Product

Cost of Input (250 × 27) = ₹ 6,750

Cost of Output (225 × 30) = ₹ 6,750

Problem 20. *A Lorry Load of materials of mixed grades is for ₹ 40,000. These were sorted into the following grades whose selling price is shown against each:*

Grade	*Unit*	*Selling Price per unit (₹)*
A	*5,000*	*6.00*
B	*3,000*	*5.00*
C	*2,000*	*2.50*

Find purchase rate per unit of each grade of the material, assuming all grades yield same rate of profit.

Solution : Working Note :

Profit = Total Revenue realized – Total cost incurred.

Total Revenue realized:

= [(5,000 × 6) + (3,000 × 5) + (2,000 × 2.5)]

= 30,000 + 15,000 + 5,000

= ₹ 50,000.

So, Profit = 50,000 – 40,000

= ₹ 10,000 which is 20% of Sales Value.

Statement of Purchase Price for each Grade

Grade	Unit	Selling Price per unit (₹)	Sales Value (₹)	Profit @ 20% of sales value	Cost of Purchase (i.e. 80% of sales Value	Purchase Rate per unit
(i)	(ii)	(iii)	(iv)	(v)	(vi)	(vii)=(vi)/(ii)
A	5,000	6.00	30,000	6,000	24,000	4.80
B	3,000	5.00	15,000	3,000	12,000	4.00
C	2,000	2.50	5,000	1,000	4,000	2.00
Total			50,000		40,000	

Problem 21. *Compute Raw material cost of finished product from the following information:*

Input of Raw cotton = 250 Kg.
Output (Cloth containing Cotton) = 225 Kg.
Cost per kg. of raw cotton = ₹ 27.00

Solution :

Cost per kg. of raw cotton = ₹ 27.00
Input /Output Ratio = 250/225 = 10/9
Raw Material Cost of Finished Product = 27 × 10/9 = 30.00

Problem 22. *A Lorry Load of materials of mixed grades for ₹ 40,000. These were sorted into the following grades whose selling price is shown against each:*

Grade	*unit*	*Selling Price per unit (₹)*
A	*5,000*	*6.00*
B	*3,000*	*5.00*
C	*2,000*	*2.50*

Find purchase rate per unit of each grade of the material, assuming all grades yield same rate of profit.

Solution : Working Note :

Profit = Total Revenue realized – Total cost incurred.

Total Revenue realized: = [(5,000 × 6) + (3,000 × 5) + (2000 × 2.5)]
= 30,000 + 15,000 + 5,000
= ₹ 50,000.

So, Profit = 50,000 – 40,000
= 10,000 which is 20% of Sales Value.

Statement of Purchase Price for each Grade

Grade	Unit	Selling Price (Per unit ₹)	Sales Value (₹)	Profit @ 20% of sales value	Cost of Purchase (i.e. 80% of sales Value	Purchase Rate (per unit)
(i)	(ii)	(iii)	(iv)	(v)	(vi)	(vii)=(vi)/(ii)
A	5,000	6.00	30,000	6,000	24,000	4.80
B	3,000	5.00	15,000	3,000	12,000	4.00
C	2,000	2.50	5,000	1,000	4,000	2.00
Total			50,000		40,000	

OBJECTIVE TYPE EXERCISES

I. Fill in the blank spaces with suitable word/s :

1. Two important opposing factors in determining the economic order quantity are ..... and ....
2. .... represents the quantity of material which is normally ordered when the materials reach ordering level.
3. The formula for fixing minimum stock level is ....
4. .... is that level of materials at which a new order for materials is to be placed.
5. Under the ABC technique 'A' stands for ....
6. Under Two-bin system of inventory control, the first bin contains enough stock to .... and the second bin contains the ....
7. Quantites of materials on hand as shown by the bin cards should agree with quantites shown by the ....
8. The average stock level is calculated by the formula ....
9. .... is a discount allowed on bulk purchases.
10. The two perpetual inventory records are .... and ....

Answers :

1. Cost of ordering, cost of carrying
2. Reorder Quantity
3. Reorder Level – (Normal consumption × Normal reorder period)
4. Re-order level
5. high value items
6. satisfy production needs, reserve quantity
7. stores ledger account
8. 50% (minimum Level + Maximum Level)
9. Quantity discount
10. Bin Card, stores ledger.]

II. Indicate whether the following statements are True or False :

1. Ordering costs consist of the costs of goods acquired from suppliers including freight and transportation costs.
2. Buying costs consist of the costs of preparing and issuing a purchase order.
3. There is difference between average inventory and inventory turnover.
4. The economic order quantity is that order quantity in which the carrying cost is equal to that of ordering cost.
5. The average inventory carried during the year is total demand for the year divided by two.

Answers :

1. False	**2.** False	**3.** True	**4.** True
5. False			

THEORETICAL EXERCISES

1. What is ABC technique of inventory control? Discuss its advantages.
2. Explain ABC system of inventory control. **[DU, B.Com (Hons.) 1999]**
3. Explain in brief the following concepts:
   (i) Ordering level;
   (ii) ABC analysis;
   (iii) VED analysis.
4. Write short notes on Economic order Quantity.
5. Explain and illustrate the meaning and importance of 'Economic Order Quantity'
6. What assumptions are involved in EOQ model?
7. Explain the nature of re-order level. What considerations should be borne in mind while ascertaining re0order level?
8. What arte the factors determining stock levels?
9. What are the types of stock levels? Explain each of them in brief.
10. Why do firms set the maximum level for each item of inventory?
11. Write short notes on:
    (i) Average stock level;
    (ii) Pricing of materials issues;
    (iii) Stores turnover.
12. What do you understand by inventory turnover? How is it measured? What are the implications of a high or low inventory turnover?
13. Explain what is meant by the maximum level, the minimum level, and the ordering level in maintenance of stock. What are the factors that govern fixing up of these levels?

NUMERICAL EXERCISES

1. Annual requirement of a particular item of inventory is 10,000 units. Inventory carrying cost per unit per annum is 20% and ordering cost is ₹ 40 per order. The price quoted by the supplier is ₹ 4 per unit. However, the supplier is ready to give a discount of 5% for orders of 1,500 units or more. Is it worthwhile to avail of the discount offer? **[B. Com (Hons.) DU, 2006]**

[Ans. It is cheaper to buy in quantities of 1,500 units at 5% discount, as the company saves ₹ 1,963 by accepting such an offer of the supplier. Therefore, offer of discount should be availed.]

2. Compute re-order quantity from the data given below:

Annual Usage of material	600 Units	
Cost per unit of material	₹ 2.40	
Buying cost per order	₹ 6	
Cost of carrying inventory	20%	**[Ans. 122 units (approx.)]**

3. Compute Economic order quantity from the data given below:

Annual Usage of material	1,00,000 Units	
Cost per unit of material	₹ 20	
Ordering cost	₹ 50 per order	
Carrying cost	8% of Average stock	**[Ans. 2,500 units]**

4. From the following particulars, find Economic order quantity (EOQ):

Annual Demand	= 3,200 Units	
Cost per unit of material	= ₹ 6	
Cost of one procurement	= ₹ 150	
Cost of carrying inventory	= 25% p.a.	**[Ans. 800 units]**

5. From the following information relating to a type of raw material, calculate Economic order quantity (EOQ):

Monthly Demand	= 200 Units	
Unit price	= ₹ 5	
Order cost per order	= ₹ 12	
Storage cost	= 2% p.a.	
Interest rate	= 10% p. a.	**[Ans. 310 units (approx.)]**

6. A company manufactures 5,000 units of a product per month. Cost of placing an order is ₹ 100. The purchase price of raw material is ₹ 10 per kg. The reordered period is 4 to 8 weeks. The consumption of raw material varies from 100 kg to 450 kg per week, the average consumption being 275 kg., the carrying cost of inventory is 20% p.a.

You are required to calculate:

(i) Re-order quantity

(ii) Re-order level **[Ans. (i) 2,450 units; (ii) 3,600 units]**

7. Sushen Pharmacy produces Sanjivini tonic using two herbs X and Y. Each Litre of tonic requires 40 centiliters of X and 60 centiliters of Y. Weekly production varies from 350 litres to 450 litres averaging 400 litres. Delivery period for both the herbs is 1 to 3 weeks. The economic order quantity for X is 600 litres and for Y is 1,000 litres.

Compute:

(i) Re-order level of X;

(ii) Maximum Level of X;

(iii) Minimum Level of Y. **[B.Com, DU, 1993]**

[Ans. (i) 540 Litres; (ii) 1,000 litres; (iii) 330 Litres]

8. In manufacturing its product P, a company uses two types of raw materials, M-1 and M-2 in respect of which the following information is supplied:

One unit of P requires 10Kg of M-1 and 4 kg of M-2 materials. Price per kg of M-1 is ₹ 10 and that of M-2 is ₹ 20. Re-order quantities of M-1 and M-2 are 10,000 kg and 5,000 kg. Re-order levels of M-1 and M-2 are 8,000 kg and 4,750 kg respectively. Weekly production varies from 175 units averaging 200 units. Delivery period of M-1 is 1 to 3 weeks and that of M-2 is 4 to 5 weeks. Compute:

(i) Minimum Stock level of M-1.

(ii) Maximum Stock level of M-2. **[Ans. (i) 4,000 kg. (ii) 5,550 kg.]**

9. Find out re-order quantity if consumption is 70-100 units per day, delivery period is 2-6 days and maximum level is 810 units. **[B.Com, DU, 1997]**

[Ans. 350 units]

10. Compute Re-order level and Re-order Quantity from the data given below in respect of Material Item L-605.

Re-order Period	4 to 6 weeks
Maximum Consumption	400 Units per week
Minimum Consumption	200 Units per week
Maximum level	3,000 units

[Ans. Re-order level > 2,400 units; Re-order Quantity > 1,400 units]

11. Calculate the Maximum stock level from the following data given:

EOQ	300 units
Usage Rate	25 to 75 units per week
Re-order Period	4 to 6 weeks

[B.Com, DU, 2002]

[Ans. 650 units]

12. Calculate the Maximum stock level from the following data given:

EOQ	500 units
Usage Rate	50 to 100 units per week
Re-order Period	5 to 8 weeks

[Ans. 1,050 units]

13. The following data pertain to Material M-I:

Supply Period	4 to 8 months
Consumption Rate:	
Maximum	600 units per month
Minimum	100 units per month
Normal	300 units per month
Annual	3,600 units

Storage cost is 50% of stock value, ordering costs are ₹ 400 per order. Price per unit is ₹ 64.

Compute:

(i) Re-order level;

(ii) Maximum Stock Level;

(iii) Minimum Stock Level;

(iv) Average Stock Level. **[B.Com, DU, 2002]**

[Ans. (i) 4,800 units; (ii) 4,700 units; (iii) 3,000 units; (iv) (a) 3,150 units' (b) 3,850 units.]

14. The details of two types of Materials M-1 and M-2 are given as under:

Rate of consumption: 50 units to 150 units per week of each material

Re-order Quantity: M-1: 1,200 units, and M-2: 2,000 units

Re-order Period: M-1: 2 to 6 weeks, and M-2: 4 to 8 weeks

[Ans. (Units)

Stock Level	M-1	M-2
Maximum	2,000	3,000
Minimum	500	600

15. The details of two types of Materials M-1 and M-2 are given as under:

Rate of Usage:

Minimum: 50 units per week of each material

Maximum: 150 units per week of each material

Normal: 100 units per week of each material

Re-order Quantity: M-1: 600 units, and M-2: 1,000 units

Delivery Period: M-1: 4 to 6 weeks, and M-2: 2 to 4 weeks

Calculate for each material:

(A) Minimum level, (B) Maximum Level, and (C) Ordering level. **[C.A. Inter]**

[Ans. (Units)

Stock Level	M-1	M-2
Ordering	900	600
Maximum	1,300	1,500
Minimum	400	300

16. Shagoon India Limited provides the following information in respect of material 'X':

Supply period : 5 to 15 days

Rate of consumption : Average : 15 units per day

: Maximum : 20 units per day

: Yearly : 5,000 units

Ordering costs are ₹ 20 per order

Purchase price per unit is ₹ 50

Storage costs are 10% of unit value

Compute:

1. Re-order level;
2. Minimum Stock Level;

3. Maximum Stock Level. **[B.Com (Hons.) DU, 2002]**

[Ans. (1) 300 units; (2) 150 units ;(3) 200 units]

[**Hint :** Re- Order Quantity: 200 units.]

17. From the following data prepare economic order quantity for the item:

Total annual consumption	= 1,20,000 units
Purchase Price per unit	= ₹ 1.50.
Ordering cost	= ₹ 80 per order
Cost of carrying inventory per unit p.a.	= 20%

[Ans. 8,000 Units]

18. Medical Aids Company manufactures a special product "AID". The following details were compiled from the records of the company for the year 2008:

A. Monthly demand of "AID" = 1,500
B. Cost of placing an order ₹ 100
C. Annual carrying cost per unit ₹ 15
D. Normal usage 50 units per week
E. Minimum usage 25 units per week
F. Maximum usage 75 units per week
G. Re-Order Period 2 to 4 weeks.

Compute from the above:

1. Re-Order Quantity
2. Re-Order Level
3. Minimum Order Level
4. Maximum Order Level
5. Average stock Level

[Ans. 186; 300; 150; 436 and 293]

19. Technical Aids Company manufactures a special product "TEKNO". The following details were compiled from the records of the company for the year 2007:

1. Monthly demand of "TEKNO" : 1, 000
2. Cost of placing an order: ₹ 100
3. Annual carrying cost per unit: 6.5%
4. Purchase Price of Input unit: ₹ 200
5. Normal usage 50 units per week
6. Minimum usage 25 units per week
7. Maximum usage 75units per week
1. Re-Order Period 4 to 6 weeks. For emergency 3 weeks.

Compute from the above:

A. Re-Order Quantity
B. Re-Order Level
C. Minimum Order Level
D. Maximum Order Level
E. Average stock Level
F. Danger level
G. Total cost p.a. if order size is (i) EOQ, (ii) 130 units, and (iii) 260 units.

[Ans. A. 200 units; B. 450 units; C. 200 units; D. 550 units; E.375 units or 300 units and F.150 units; G.(i): ₹ 5,22,600; G.(ii):₹ 5,22,845 and G.(iii):₹ 5,22,690.]

20. From the following particulars, calculate the economic order quantity and tabulate your results:
Annual requirement: 1,600 Units
Cost of material per unit: ₹ 40
Cost of placing and receiving one order: ₹ 50
Annual carrying cost of inventory: 10% of inventory value **[Ans. 200 units]**

21. Calculate the economic order quantity from the following:
(i) Consumption during the year: 600units
(ii) Ordering cost: ₹ 12 per order
(iii) Carrying cost 20%
(iv) Price per unit: ₹ 20 **(B. Com. Panjab)**
[Ans. 60 units]

22. A manufacturer buys certain equipment from outside suppliers at ₹ 30 per unit. Total annual needs are 800 units. The following further data are available:
(i) Annual return on investment: 10%
(ii) Rent, Insurance, taxes per unit per year: Re 1
(iii) Cost of placing an order: ₹ 100. **(M. Com. Calcutta)**
[Ans. 200 units]

23. From the following details, find out:
(a) How much should be ordered each time?
(b) When should the order be placed?
(c) What should be the inventory level (ideally) immediately before the material order is received?
(1) Annual consumption: 40,500 units (360days)
(2) Cost per unit : ₹ 20
(3) Ordering cost: ₹ 30 per order
(4) Inventory carrying charge:18%
(5) Normal Lead time: 10 days
(6) Safety Stock: 30 Days consumption
[Ans. (a) 900 units; (b) 4,500 units; (c) 1,125 units]

24. Find out the ordering level from the following information:
(a) Minimum stock: 1,250 units;
(b) Maximum stock level: 2,500 units;
(c) Time required for receiving the raw material: 16 days;
(d) Daily consumption of material 55 units. **[Ans. 2130 units]**

25. Calculate the (a) maximum level, (b) minimum level, and (c) re-ordering level from the following information:
(i) Re-order Quantity: 1,500 units
(ii) Re-order Period: 4 to 6 weeks
(iii) Maximum consumption: 400 units per week
(iv) Minimum consumption: 250 units per week
(v) Normal consumption: 300 units per week **(I.C.W.A. - inter)**
[Ans. (a) 2,900 units; (b) 900 units; (c) 2,400 units]

26. Two materials A, and B are used as follows :
(a) Minimum Usage: 50 units per week each;
(b) Maximum Usage: 150 units per week each;
(c) Normal Usage: 100 units per week each;
(d) Ordering Quantity: (i) A: 600 units, and (ii) B: 1,000 units
(e) Delivery Period: (i) A: 4 to 6 weeks (ii) B: 2 to 4 weeks
Calculate for each Material:
(1) Minimum level, (2) Maximum level, and (3) Ordering level. **(C.A. - inter)**
[Ans. A : (1) 400 units ; (2) 1,300 units ; (3) 900 units ; B : (1) 300 units ; (2) 1,500 units ; (3) 600 units]

27. The following information is available in respect of a Component C-41 :

Maximum Stock level:	12600 Units
Budgeted Consumption:	Maximum 2,250 units per month
	Minimum 1,200 units per month
Estimated Delivery Period:	Maximum 4 Months,
	Minimum 2 Months
You are required to calculate:	(i) Re-order level;
	(ii) Re-order quantity

[Ans. [(i) 9,000 units; (b) 6,000 units.]

28. A manufacturer buys certain equipment from outside suppliers at ₹ 100 per unit. Total annual needs are 1,200 units. The following further data are available:
1. Annual return on investment: 10%
2. Rent, Insurance, taxes per unit per year: Re 2
3. Cost of placing an order: ₹ 200. **[Ans. 200 units]**

29. The following data is given:
1. Minimum Usage: 25 units per week;
2. Maximum Usage: 75 units per week;
3. Normal Usage: 50 units per week;
4. Re-ordering Quantity: 300 units per week;
5. Re-ordering Period: (4 to 6 weeks
Calculate:
(1) Minimum level,
(2) Maximum level,
(3) Re-ordering level and
(4) Average Stock level.
[Ans. (1) 200 units; (2) 650 units; (3) 450 units, (4) 350 units]

30. The following data pertain to material X:
Supply Period: 4 to 8 months
Consumption Rate:
(1) Minimum Usage: 100 units per month;
(2) Maximum Usage: 600 units per month;
(3) Normal Usage: 300 units per month;
(4) Yearly: 3600 units

Storage costs are 12.5% of stock value
Ordering costs are ₹ 400 per order
Price per unit of material ₹ 256
Compute the Maximum Stock Level. **[Ans. 4700 units]**

31.

Details	Maximum	Average	Minimum
Daily consumption (Units)	75	50	25
Delivery period (day)	5	2	1

Ideal Order Size : 125 units
Re-order Level: 375 units
Determine Maximum stock level, and Buffer Stock level.

[Ans. (1) 475 units; (2) 275 units]

32. From the following information calculate E O Q and the number of orders to be placed in on e quarter of the year:
(i) Quarterly consumption of material: 2,000 Kg
(ii) Cost of placing one order: ₹ 50
(i) Cost per unit : ₹ 40
(ii) Storage and carrying cost: 8% on average inventory

(B. Com. (Hons) DU, 1997)
[Ans. EOQ : 500 units; Number of orders: 4]

33. Shagoon India Ltd. provides the following data in respect of material 'X':
Supply Period: 5 to 15 Days
Consumption Rate:
(i) Maximum Usage: 20 units per Day;
(ii) Average Usage: 15 units per Day;
(iii) Yearly: 5,000 units
Storage costs are 10% of unit value
Ordering costs are ₹ 20 per order
Price per unit of material ₹ 50
Compute:
(1) Re-order level
(2) Minimum level
(3) Maximum Level **(B. Com. (Hons) DU, 1998)**

[Ans. (1) 300 units; (2) 150 units; (3) 450 units]

34. P limited is engaged in the manufacture of industrial Pumps of a standard description. The company uses about 75,000 units of valves per year for its production and the usage is fairly constant at 6,250 valves per month. The valves cost ₹ 15 per unit bought in quantities and the carrying cost is estimated to be 20% of average inventory investment on the annual basis. The cost to place an order and process the delivery is ₹ 180. It takes 45 days to receive delivery from the date of an order and a safety stock of 3200 valves is desired.
You are required to determine:
(i) The most economical order quantity; and
(ii) The Re-order Point. **(B. Com. (Hons) DU, 2002)**

[Ans. (1) 3,000 units; (2) 12,575 units]

35. A company manufactures a product having a quarterly demand of 12000 units. For one unit of finished product 5 Kgs of a particular material item is required. The purchase price of the material is ₹ 75 per kg. The ordering cost is ₹ 800 per order and the holding cost is 8% p.a. Calculate:

(i) Economic Order Quantity, and

(ii) Annual cost of purchasing and storage of the raw material at that quantity.

[Ans. (1) 8000 units; (2) ₹ 48,000]

36. A producer has estimated annual purchase requirement of 30,000 units of a material. Unit price of material is ₹ 50. Annual cost of carrying inventory is 20%. Ordering cost for an order is ₹ 60. Find out Economic Order Quantity.

[B. Com. (Hons) DU, 2004 (Correspondance)]

[Ans. (1) 600 units]

37. EXE Ltd. has received an offer of quantity discounts on its order of materials as under:

Details (No.)	Price per tonne (₹)
Less than 500	1,200
500and Less than 1,000	1,180
1,000 and Less than 2,000	1,160
2,000 and Less than 3,000	1,140
3,000 and above	1,120

The annual requirement of the materials is 5,000 tonnes. The ordering cost per order is ₹ 1,200 and the carrying cost is estimated at 20% per annum.

You are required to compute

(a) The most economical purchase order; and

(b) What would be your answer to the above if there are no discounts offered and the price per tonne is ₹ 1,500? **[Ans. (a) 1,000 tonnes; (b) 200 tonnes]**

❑❑❑

6

Material Losses

Learning Objectives

It attempts to explain the nature and accounting treatment of material losses. In this chapter you will learn :

1. Meaning and nature material losses.
2. Various types of material losses.
3. Control of material losses.
4. Accounting treatment of material losses.

INTRODUCTION

It has been observed that usually in a manufacturing organisation there is a difference between the input of material put in a process and its output and the output is less than the input. This difference between the input and the output is known as "Material Loss" which may be of the following types:

1. Waste; 2. Scrap;
3. Spoilage; and 4. Defectives.

Losses of materials may arise during handling, storage or during the process of manufacturing. Material loss may be Normal Loss or Abnormal loss.

Normal Loss

Normal loss is that loss which necessarily occurs and thus is unavoidable. Loss by evaporation in case of liquid materials, Loss due to loading and unloading of materials, loss due to breaking of the bulk etc. are some of the indicative examples of normal loss. Normal loss can be controlled to a limited extent. All normal losses are treated as a part of the cost. The rates of usable materials in stock are inflated so that such losses are covered. There is another option available i.e. it may be transferred to factory overhead.

Abnormal Loss

Abnormal loss arises due to inefficiency in operations, acts of nature, and improper storage. Pilferage, breakage, fire accident, floods, use of inaccurate weighing instruments, etc. are some of the factors responsible for the occurrence of abnormal loss. Abnormal loss does not form part of the cost, and it is charged to costing Profit and Loss Account.

Control of Material Losses

It is necessary to control scraps, wastage and other material losses a regular basis. Following steps are suggested to control the material losses:

1. Use specialised material handling machines and equipments.
2. Check the accuracy of weighing instruments regularly.
3. Issue the materials on FIFO basis to avoid obsolescence loss.
4. Provide proper storage environment.
5. Develop systematic procedure in regard to the movement of materials; in no case unauthorised movement of materials be permitted.

Waste

It is that portion of the basic raw material which has been lost in the manufacturing process and which has no recoverable value. Gases, dust, smoke, evaporation are some of the examples of waste of materials. It may occur due to evaporation, breaking the bulk, loading and unloading, the leakage, inefficient handling, fire etc.

Control

Norms should be prefixed for each type of waste. Actual amount of wastage should be compared with the standard amount of wastage. Waste report, a specimen of which is given below, must be prepared at regular intervals. Special care needs to be taken to check abnormal wastage. One of the ways could be to hold regular meetings with the foreman and the staff.

Accounting Treatment

(i) **Normal wastage:** Waste within normal limits should be charged to good output. It would increase per unit cost of good units produced.

(ii) **Abnormal wastage:** Waste beyond normal limits is charged to Costing Profit and Loss account. This is to avoid any fluctuations in per unit cost of output.

SPG Limited
Waste Report

Department:				No.:
Cost Centre:				Date:
Process or Job No.	Actual Weight of Waste (kg)	Actual Percentage of Wastage to Production (%)	Normal Wastage of Percentage (%)	Remarks
Total				
Average Percentage				
Action Taken By				
Entered by				
				Signature of the Inspector

Illustration 6.1 : *4,000 Units of raw materials were introduced in a process at a cost of ₹ 28,000. 12.5% of the input introduced is considered to be waste having no recoverable value. The actual production was only 3,400 units. The other costs were as under:*

Direct Wages	*₹ 32,000*
Works overheads	*₹ 38,000*

Prepare a statement showing the cost per unit.

Solution :

Details	Unit	Amount (₹)
Raw Materials	4,000	28,000
Direct Wages		32,000
Works overheads		38,000
	4,000	98,000
Less: Normal Wastage	500	NIL
Works cost	3,500	98,000
Less: Abnormal Wastage =[(98,000 ÷ 3,500) × 100] or [100 × 28]	100	2,800
Cost of production [3,400 × 28]	3,400	95,200
Cost per Unit = 95,200 ÷ 3,400 ⇒ ₹ 28		

The net loss on account of abnormal wastage ₹ 2,800 (i.e. 2,800 – NIL) is to be transferred to Costing Profit and Loss Account. As is obvious from the above treatment, loss on account of normal wastage has been charged to good production; the cost per unit is ₹ 28 and not ₹ 24.50.

Scrap

Scrap is the incidental residue of material emerging due to certain manufacturing process or processes. It is in small quantity and of low value; it does not require further processing before its sale or disposal. It may arise due to turnings, borings, trimmings, moulding, etc., from metals on which machine operations are carried out. Scrap is always physically available while waste may or may not be present in the form of residue.

There are three types of scraps:

(a) Legitimate scrap i.e. which is predetermined and arise due to the nature of operations like turning, boring, punching, etc.

(b) Administrative scrap, i.e. scrap which arises due to administrative action such as change in method of production.

(c) Defective scrap, i.e. scrap which arises because of the use of inferior quality of material or bad workmanship or defective machine.

Control

It is possible to have control of scrap by:

- Setting standards for scrap;
- Assigning the responsibility for scrap;
- Maintaining proper records of scrap in the form of Scrap report, a specimen of which is given below.

SPG Limited

Scrap Report

Department: No.:

Cost Centre: Date:

Process or Job No.	Scrap Tag No.	Actual Scrap (kg/No.)	Actual Scrap (%)	Normal Scrap (%)	Abnormal Scrap		Action Recommended
					Quantity (kg/No.)	Value (₹)	

Action Taken By

Entered By

Signature of the Inspector

Accounting Treatment

Any of the following methods of treating scrap may be adopted:

(1) The sale value of scrap is credited to Costing Profit and Loss Account as an abnormal gain. This method is to be adopted when the quantum of scrap is almost negligible. However, this approach fails to ensure effective control over scrap as the detailed records are not maintained and the scraps are not identified to jobs or processes.

(2) Net sale proceeds of scrap are deducted from the material cost or factory overhead. Thus, the overall cost of material or overhead is reduced. The

method is suitable in cases where several production orders are taken up and it is not feasible to segregate the scrap for each order.

(3) The value realized from the sale of normal scrap is credited to the particular job/process/operation. The net loss on account of abnormal scrap is transferred to Costing Profit and Loss account. The method has the advantage of identifying the scrap with each operation/process or job.

Illustration 6.2 : *4,000 Units of raw materials are introduced in a process at a cost of ₹ 42,000. 12.5% of the input introduced is considered to be scrap having recoverable value @ ₹ 7 per unit. The actual production was only 3,400 units. The other costs were as under:*

Direct Wages	*₹ 32,000*
Works overheads	*₹ 38,000*

Prepare a statement showing the cost per unit, and a statement showing the net loss on account of abnormal scrap.

Solution :

Details	Units	Amount (₹)
Raw Materials	4,000	42,000
Direct Wages		32,000
Works overheads		38,000
	4,000	1,12,000
Less: Normal Scrap [500 × 7]	500	3,500
Works cost	3,500	1,08,500
Less: Abnormal Scrap =[(1,08,500 ÷ 3,500) × 100] or [100 × 31]	100	3,100
Cost of production [3,400 × 31]	3,400	1,05,400
Cost per Unit = 1,05,400 ÷ 3,400 ⇒ ₹ 31		

The net loss on account of abnormal scrap has been calculated as under;

Cost of abnormal Scrap (100 units @ ₹ 31)	₹ 3,100
Abnormal Scrap realized @ ₹ 7	₹ 700
Net Abnormal Loss	₹ 2,400

The net loss on account of abnormal scrap ₹ 2,400 is to be transferred to Costing Profit and Loss Account.

Spoilage

Spoilage relates to goods damaged beyond rectification and is to be sold without further processing. It occurs due to some defect in materials or operations which may or may not be inherent in the manufacturing process or operation.

Spoiled units are those that do not meet production standards and are either sold for their salvage value or discarded.

Difference between scrap and Spoilage:

Basis	Scrap	Spoilage
Processing	It is the result of processing of materials.	It occurs due to some defect in materials or operations.
Value	It has relatively low value	It varies between NIL to very high value if it could be sold as seconds.
Material loss	It involves material loss only.	It involves besides loss of materials, loss of labour and works overheads.

Control: Spoilage report is prepared on getting the information that the work has been spoiled. The actual spoilage is compared with the standard and remedial measures are suggested to prevent any abnormal spoilage. This report is prepared by the Inspector.

SPG Limited
Spoilage Report

Department: No.:
Cost Centre: Date:

Process or Job No.	Spoiled Units	Actual Spoilage (%)	Normal Spoilage (%)	Cost of Spoilage Less Salvage Value (₹)	Cost of Abnormal Spoilage (₹)	Causes and Actions
				Material Labour Overheads Total *Less:* Salvage Value Net Cost		
Total						

Action Taken By

Entered By

Signature of Inspector

Accounting Treatment

Spoilage is of two types (a) normal spoilage, and (b) Abnormal spoilage.

(a) Normal spoilage: It is natural and inherent result of the process and so uncontrollable. The cost of such spoilage is charged to good units of production. Normal spoilage is that which is expected to occur despite efficient production.

Normal spoilage can be applied to all jobs by including an estimate for normal spoilage in the factory overhead application rate, or it can be allocated only to the job in which it occurs by transferring the salvage value out of work-in-process inventory into a spoiled units' inventory.

(b) Abnormal spoilage: It is that which is in excess of what is acceptable; therefore, and the total cost of the abnormal spoiled units should be removed from work-in-process inventory, and any salvage value should be recorded in a Spoiled Units Inventory account. It is avoidable and controllable even in the short run. Its cost is to be charged to Costing Profit and Loss Account.

Illustration 6.3 : *40,000 units are introduced in a process at a cost of ₹ 12.50 per unit. The normal spoilage is estimated at 10% of the input, realizing ₹ 8 per unit. The actual output is 35,000 units. The other costs have been incurred as under:*

Direct Wages	*₹ 1,52,000*
Works overheads	*₹ 1,09,000*

Prepare a statement showing the cost per unit, and a statement showing the net loss on account of abnormal spoilage.

Solution :

Details	**Units**	**Amount (₹)**
Raw Materials @ ₹ 12.50 per unit	40,000	5,00,000
Direct Wages		1,52,000
Works overheads		1,09,000
	40,000	7,61,000
Less: Normal Spoilage [4,000 × 8]	4,000	32,000
	36,000	7,29,000
Less: Abnormal Scrap = [(7,29,000 ÷ 36,000) × 1,000] or [1,000 × 20.25]	1,000	20,250
Cost of production [35,000 × 20.25]	35,000	7,08,750
Cost per Unit = 7,08,750 ÷ 35,000 ⇒ ₹ 20.25		

The net loss on account of abnormal scrap has been calculated as under;

Cost of abnormal Scrap (1,000 units @ ₹ 20.25)	₹ 20,250
Abnormal Scrap realized @ ₹ 8	₹ 8,000
Net Abnormal Loss	₹ 12,250

The net loss on account of abnormal spoilage ₹ 12,250 is to be transferred to Costing Profit and Loss Account.

Note: The abnormal scrap or spoilage is assumed to be realized at the normal scrap or spoilage.

Defectives

Defective units do not meet production standards but are further processed to be sold as good units or as irregular units. It represents that portion of production which can be rectified and turned into good units by putting in extra material, labour and overheads. The main difference between spoilage and defectives is that spoilage is beyond rectification and sold as "seconds' or "thirds' while defectives can be rectified by reworking and sold as "firsts".

Control

On inspection if it is found that a portion of production is defective, a "Defective work report" must be prepared. The cost of rectification is estimated and a decision is taken whether or not to rectify the defective work. Appropriate steps should be taken to see that defective work remains within the pre-fixed standards.

SPG Limited
Defective Work Report

Department: No.:
Cost Centre: Date:

Process or Job No.	Defective Units	Normal Defectives	Abnormal Defectives	Cost of Rectification (₹)	Disposal Value of Defectives (₹)	Causes and Actions

Action Taken By
Entered By

Signature of Inspector

Accounting Treatment

Defectives are of two types (a) normal defectives, and (b) Abnormal defectives.

(a) Normal Defectives: The re-work costs for normal defective units are treated in a manner similar to those for spoiled units: either applied to all jobs by including an estimate in the factory overhead application rate, or applied only to the affected job.

If the defective units are clearly identified with a numbered job order and the defects are peculiar to the job, the cost to complete the defective units can be charged to the job. If the defective units occur irregularly, the cost of rectification is properly charged to factory overhead.

(b) Abnormal Defectives: Costs incurred to rework abnormal defective units are charged to an account called Loss from Abnormal defective units and are thus treated as period cost. They arise on account of abnormal circumstances and, therefore, should be charged to Costing Profit and Loss Account.

Illustration 6.4 : *5,000 units are introduced in a process at a cost of ₹ 20 per unit. The normal defective units are estimated to be 6% of the input. Actual output of good units is 4,250 units. The other costs have been incurred as under:*

Direct Wages ₹ 50,000

Works overheads ₹ 41,250

All defective units are required to be rectified by incurring additional cost@ ₹ 10 per unit

Prepare a statement showing the cost per unit, and a statement showing the cost of rectification of abnormal defective units.

Solution :

Details	Units	Amount (₹)
Cost of Basic input @ ₹ 20 per unit	5,000	1,00,000
Direct Wages		50,000
Works overheads		41,250
	5,000	1,91,250
Less: Defective units	750	NIL
	4,250	1,91,250
Add: Cost of rectification of Defective units = [300 × 10]	750	3,000
Normal cost of good units of output [1,94,250 ÷ 5,000] ⇒ ₹ 38.85	5,000	1,94,250

Accounting treatment of Rectification: The total cost of rectification of defective units amounts to ₹ 7,500 (i.e. 750 × 10). The cost of rectifying Normal defective units is only ₹ 3,000 (i.e. 300 × 10) which has been added to the cost of good units to arrive at the cost per unit of output. However, the cost of rectification of abnormal defective units being ₹ 4,500 (i.e. 450 × 10) is to be charged to the Costing Profit and Loss Account.

LET US RECAPITULATE

1. Difference between the input and the output is known as "Material Loss"
2. Losses of materials may arise during handling, storage or during the process of manufacturing.
3. Normal loss is that loss which necessarily occurs and thus is unavoidable.
4. Abnormal loss arises due to inefficiency in operations, acts of nature, and improper storage.
5. Waste is that portion of the basic raw material which has been lost in the manufacturing process and which has no recoverable value.

6. Scrap is the incidental residue of material emerging due to certain manufacturing process or processes. It is in small quantity and of low value; it does not require further processing before its sale or disposal.
7. Spoilage relates to goods damaged beyond rectification and is to be sold without further processing.
8. Spoiled units are those that do not meet production standards and are either sold for their salvage value or discarded.
9. Defectives represent that portion of production which can be rectified and turned into good units by putting in extra material, labour and overheads.

OBJECTIVE TYPE EXERCISES

I. State whether the following statements are True or False :

1. Waste has no realisable value.
2. Spoilage that occurs under efficient operating conditions and is ordinarily uncontrollable is called Normal spoilage.
3. Waste is that portion of a basic raw material lost in processing, having recovery value.
4. The incidental residual value from certain types of manufacture, usually of small amount and low value, recoverable without further processing is called scrap.
5. Waste can be realized but scrap cannot be realized.
6. The difference between spoilage and defectives is that the former cannot be rectified into good units while the latter can be.
7. There is no difference between waste and scrap.
8. All normal losses of material are charged to output.

Answers :

1. True	**2.** True	**3.** False	**4.** True
5. False	**6.** True	**7.** False	**8.** True

II. Fill in the blank spaces :

1. .... is that portion of a basic raw material lost in processing, having no recovery value.
2. Spoilage that occurs under efficient operating conditions and is ordinarily uncontrollable is called .... spoilage.
3. Spoilage that occurs under inefficient operating conditions and is ordinarily uncontrollable is called .... spoilage.
4. .... and .... are examples of scrap.
5. Units which must be sold for their salvage value are known as ....
6. .... units are further processed in order to be sold as good units.

7. .... spoilage is expected to occur despite efficient production.
8. The total cost of abnormal spoiled units should be (a) .... And any salvage value should be (b) ....
9. Rework costs for normal defective units can be (a) .... Or (b) ....

Answers :

1. Waste **2.** Normal **3.** Abnormal
4. Saw dust, trimmings **5.** Spoiled units **6.** defective
7. Normal
8. (a) removed from work-in-process inventory
(b) recorded in a Spoiled Units Inventory Account
9. (a) Applied to all jobs, (b) allocated to the job in which it occurs.

THEORETICAL EXERCISES

1. What is meant by material losses? What do the items constitute such losses? How are these accounted for?
2. Explain the nature of normal and abnormal material losses. How these two types of losses are treated in cost records?
3. Explain the meaning of scrap.
4. Explain 'spoilage' and state how it differs from 'defectives'.
5. Distinguish between waste and scrap.
6. What is the accounting treatment of waste?
7. Explain the treatment of normal and abnormal loss of materials and over / under recovery of overheads in cost ledger.
8. Distinguish between (i) Scrap and waste, and (ii) Spoilage and defectives.
9. Indicate the accounting treatment given to 'defectives' in cost accounts.
[DU, B.Com (Hons.) 2002]

❑❑❑

7

Labour Cost

Learning Objectives

It attempts to explain Labour cost. In this chapter you will learn :

1. Meaning and nature of labour cost.
2. Control of labour cost.
3. Method study; work study.
4. Job analysis, job evaluation and merit rating.
5. Accounting treatment of overtime.
6. Accounting treatment of idle time.
7. Difference between idle time and idle capacity.
8. Casual workers and outworkers.
9. Vacation and holiday pay.
10. Night shift allowance.
11. Labour turnover.

LABOUR COST

Labour Cost may be direct and indirect. Direct Labour cost is cost of all labour expended in altering the construction, composition or condition of the product. Direct labour cost is easily identified and allocated to cost units. It varies directly with volume of output and can be easily ascertained and controlled because of its close relationship with the output. Indirect Labour cost is the amount of wages paid to the workmen who are not so engaged in altering the composition of product. The basic distinction between direct and indirect labour in cost account depends not only on work done, but also on practicability and expediency. If a worker is engaged on a specific job for a considerable time so as to make the identification to the job practicable, the remuneration becomes direct. Unless both these conditions are satisfied, Labour cost may be considered indirect.

Direct Labour cost is the "cost of labour expended in altering the construction, composition or condition of a product." It is directly attributable and easily identified and allocated to the cost unit or cost centre. All wages of labourer directly engaged in production and wages paid to workers engaged in construction site constitute direct labour cost.

Direct Labour cost is charged to jobs and forms part of prime cost, whereas indirect labour cost becomes a part of overhead. Usually, a standing order is maintained for each type of indirect labour cost, such as salary of indirect labourers, overtime premium, night shift allowance, leave with pay and other fringe benefits. These standing orders form part of factory overhead and ultimately the process of apportionment and absorption of overhead link the indirect labour cost with production.

Indirect labour cost is the "cost of labour NOT directly engaged in production." It is not directly attributable to the cost unit or cost centre. Wages and salaries of employees in Purchase Department, Stores, Office and Time-Keeping Department, Foreman and Supervisors, Maintenance personnel etc. are obvious examples of indirect labour cost.

Direct wages being variable can be easily controlled. Indirect wages can be properly controlled by establishment of suitable labour budgets for each department and comparing the actual indirect labour cost with the budgeted indirect labour cost. For an effective managerial control over labour cost, the following techniques may be tried and adopted:

(1) *Production Planning:* It includes product/process engineering, planning, scheduling and routing. By means of adequate time and motion studies for each operation, standard times should be determined and care should be taken to see that actual time required conforms to the standard time.

(2) *Labour Budget:* Detailed production schedules and labour budget have to be prepared on the basis of data generated by production planning.

(3) *Labour Standards:* Standards set for labour cost are compared with actual data the variances are derived and prompt remedial measures are initiated.

(4) *Wage Incentive Schemes:* The efficiency reports of relevant departments help in ascertaining the effectiveness of wage incentive schemes.

(5) *Labour Performance Report:* Efficiency and Labour utilization reports help in installing managerial and labour cost control.

(6) *Labour Cost accounting:* A cost accounting system that enables the identification of direct labour cost with a product, job or process is to be devised for the organization. In order to institute an effective control over labour cost, wherever possible, automatic time recorders and punched card system be put into service so as to reduce clerical manipulations and cost.

Control of labour cost is the main objective of management and much can be achieved with the coordination of every member of the supervisory force from the top executive to the floor foreman. From functional point of view control of labour cost is affected by the coordination of managers of the following departments:

(a) Personnel,
(b) Time-Keeping,
(c) Payroll,
(d) Engineering and work study, and
(e) Cost accounting.

DEPARTMENT OF PERSONNEL

It is the responsibility of the Personnel Department to recruit, train and place the workers to the jobs they are best suited. It is also responsible for control and administration of the efficient utilization of the services of the human resource. The departments of Time keeping and Pay & Accounts are immediately informed of the appointment of a new worker in the Production or Finance or Marketing department of the organisation. Following illustration will make it clear the process of estimation of the requirement of the labour force for an organisation.

Illustration 7.1 : *The Bank has 1,250 staff in Group C, the lowest grade in the organisation, with the following age structure:*

Age	*Number*
Below 20	*800*
20-30	*400*
30 and Above	*50*
Total	*1,250*

Wastage rates and promotion prospects in the next three years are expected to be:

Age	*Wastage (%)*	*Promotion prospects (%)*
Below 20	*25*	*15*
20-30	*15*	*50*
30 and Above	*4*	*30*

The demand forecast shows that 1,600 Group C staff will be required in the next three years' duration. Assume that no promotion is due from Group D to Group C.

Solution :

Statement Showing Estimated Recruitment Requirements

Details		Number
Existing Staff		1,250
Less: Wastage (0.25 × 800) + (0.15 × 400) + (0.04 ×50)	= 262	
Promotion to Next Grade(0.15 × 800) + (0.5 × 400) + (0.3 × 50)	= 335	597
Add: Promotion from Lower grade	NIL	
Existing staff in the same grade in Three years time		653
Staff required in this grade in Three years time		1,600
Estimated recruitment requirements		947

Labour Placement Requisition

On receiving the Labour Placement requisition from the concerned department, the Personnel department goes through its own records to find out whether it has in its records the requisite number of personnel available for employment. Thereafter it writes to the Local employment Exchange, Technical colleges and Educational Institutions , advertises in News Papers, etc. Necessary action is taken to receive formal applications, interview and select persons. The concerned department is informed of the selection.

Labour Placement Requisition

Department.........   Requisition No. ....

Date : ....

Please arrange for workers of the following categories for my department with effect from ......

Number of persons required :

Category :

Job Specification:

Job Description:

Employee's History Record Card

The Personnel department keeps a record of each employee. The record is kept on a card which contains the details about the name, address, department, the name of the former employer, date of joining occupation, rate of pay and clock number, etc. Whenever the services of an employee are terminated, or he himself leaves the organisation on his own accord, the reasons for such termination or for the leaving are also recorded. This helps the management to find out solution of frequent labour turnover and to improve the working conditions in the workshop.

Necessary columns are provided usually on the reverse side of the employee's history card to insert information as to leave entitlement, leave availed, medical and other benefits taken by the employee. Adequate space is provided for recording the change of address, the progress of the worker, details regarding his promotion and transfer from one department to another.

Employee's History Record Card

Name .... Clock No. ....

Address ....

DOB .... Marital Status .... Children ....

Qualification: (a) Academic .... (b) Technical ....

Experience: (a) Previous .... (b) Existing ....

Date of Appointment .... Grade ....

Department .... Starting Basic Pay ....

Category .... Engaged as ....

Date of Leaving .... Previous employer ....

Reason for leaving .... Re-engaged ....

Details of Changes in Pay and Service

Date	Occupation	Grade	Pay	Reason for change (increment, transfer, promotion or demotion, etc.)
Enter				

DEPARTMENT OF ENGINEERING AND WORK STUDY

Performance of the following functions implies control over the working conditions and on production methods for different jobs/ operations/processes in different departments:

- Preparation of plans and specifications for each job, process and operation.
- Devising systems for supervising production within different departments.
- Ensuring safe working conditions.
- Promoting and sustaining efficient working conditions.
- Ascertaining areas requiring further research and development, and initiating and supervising research and development activities.
- Conducting work study i.e. time and motion studies.
- Making job analysis.
- Conducting job evaluation.
- Conducting merit rating of employees.
- Setting piece and time rates.

Some of the activities of the Engineering Department are explained hereunder:

Time Study

It involves determination of standard time for operations after standardization of methods. Standard time for each operation involved in a production activity, job or process is determined after giving due consideration to relevant factors such as labour movements, quality and sophistication of tools and equipment, work environment, training, efficiency and skill level of workers, degree of accuracy required in production.

Motion Study or Methods Study

It is to determine correct and efficient ways of performing different operations and completing jobs. It is concerned with improving methods of working. Unnecessary operations are weeded out and cumbersome operations are simplified. Motion study identifies best method of doing a job which results in maximum economy, least fatigue and improve productivity. Time and motion studies are conducted by observing workers at work and recording their movements.

Job Analysis

It involves observation and study of each job in order to ascertain

(a) Minute details of each job,

(b) Tasks involved in a job,

(c) Technical skills and qualifications required for the job,

(d) Capabilities, experience and aptitude required for each job, and

(e) Level of responsibility required of a worker for successful performance of the job.

Thus, job analysis helps establishing distinction between jobs, proper matching of jobs and workers and consequently helps in determining the number and type of workers to be recruited.

Job Evaluation

It aims at ascertaining relative worth of each job so that a systematic wage differential can be established for different jobs. Jobs involving similar duties, activities and responsibilities are paid at the same rate. The wage differential for workers on different jobs should match in their job content.

Merit Rating

It is the comparative appraisal of individual merits of an employee. It is the assessment of an employee's performance made by his superior. It is helpful to the management in following respects;

(i) Ascertaining the suitability of the worker for a particular job. The objective is achieved by linking merit rating with job evaluation.

(ii) Ascertaining an employee's merit for the award of promotion, increment, etc.

(iii) Introducing incentive wage payment, and simplification of the wage structure.

(iv) Analysing the employee's defects and bringing out the strong points and special abilities.

DEPARTMENT OF TIME-KEEPING

It embraces two functions:

1. *Time keeping:* It is the recording of time of workers for purpose of attendance and wage calculations.
2. *Time booking:* it is the reporting of each worker's time for each department, operation and job for the purpose of cost analysis and apportionment of labour costs between various jobs and departments.

Purpose of Time-Keeping

Recording of time serves the following purposes:

(i) Preparation of pay rolls, where workers are paid on time basis;

(ii) Enforce regularity, discipline and ensuring daily requirement of labour force in the factory;

(iii) Ensure proper distinction between direct and indirect costs, normal time and overtime, and regular and late comers.

(iv) Ensure internal administration, like increments, pension, provident fund, and gratuity and leave benefits.

(v) Find variations between the standard and actual labour hours worked/paid.

Methods of Time Keeping

Following are the usual methods of recording attendance of workers at the gate of the factory:

1. Manual Methods:

(i) Attendance Register, and (ii) Disc or token system.

2. Mechanical methods:

(i) Time recording Clock, and (ii) Dial time recorders.

Methods of Time Booking

In addition to recording the time of arrival and the departure of a worker in proper time records, it is also necessary to record time devoted by him on a job, order or process in the factory for the following reasons:

(a) Ascertain the cost of a job, order, or process;

(b) Ensure that the worker does not waste his time after entering the factory and goes straight to his job;

(c) Ascertain the cost of idle time.

Time may be recorded in appropriate records by manual or mechanical methods depending upon the size of the organisation. The records may be kept in any of the following manner:

1. Daily time sheet 2. Weekly time sheet 3. Job cards
4. Idle time card 5. Time – cum – Job Card 6. Labour cost card
7. Piece work card

Daily Time Sheet

A sheet is allotted to each worker in which he records time spent by him on each job during the day. The method is suitable in case of those workers who have to change their jobs quite frequently during a day. Maintenance workers are the obvious example. A specimen of Daily Time Sheet is given hereunder:

DAILY TIME SHEET

Employee's Name: .... Date: ....

Employee's ID No: ....

Job No.	Department	Time		Total Hours		Hourly Rate	Amount (₹)
		Start	Finish	Ordinary	Overtime		

Employee's signature: .... Foreman's signature: ....

Cost clerk's signature: ....

Weekly Time Sheet

This is meant for recording all jobs done during the week. This type of record is mainly suitable for intermittent jobs and is usually used for recording time in building or construction work. A proforma of a 'Weekly Time Sheet' is given below:

WEEKLY TIME SHEET

Employee's Name: .... DEPARTMENT: ....

Employee's ID No: .... Week Ending: ....

Day	Job No.		Job No.		Job No.		Total Time		Rate (₹)	Amount (₹)
	On	Off	On	Off	On	Off	Ordinary	Overtime		
							TOTAL			

Emplyee's signature: .... Foreman's signature: ....

Cost clerk's signature: ....

Job Card

A job card/ticket is maintained for every job. When a worker takes up a job, a job card bearing number of the job is given to him. He shall record in it the time of taking up and finishing the job. In most cases this is done by mechanical aids. As soon as a job is completed, the worker is given job card of another job to be done by him. In case the job is suspended or the worker does not get another job soon after the completion of a job, he should contact the time keeper so that appropriate booking of the waiting time may be made on the 'Idle Time card'. In a way the Job Card performs two functions:

(a) It authorizes a worker to carry out the operations detailed thereon;

(b) It enables the correct allocation of wages to jobs, operations or processes.

A proforma of a 'Job Card is given below:

JOB CARD

Work Order No. .... Job No. ....

Employee's Name .... Date ....

Employee's ID No. .... Time started ....

Job Description	Time On	Time Off	Total Hours Ordinary	Total Hours Overtime	Rate (₹)	Amount (₹)

Employee's signature .... Foreman's signature ....

Cost cler's signature ....

Idle Time Card

It is necessary to know the quantum of unproductive time in the factory and the reasons for it. It is the duty of the operator to record the time and the reasons for which he remained in the factory idle ('No work') in a separate card known as 'Idle Time card', the proforma of which is given below:

IDLE TIME CARD

Employee's Name: .... DEPARTMENT: ....

Employee's ID No: .... Date: ....

Causes of Idle time	Time From	Time To	Time Duration	Cost Rate (₹)	Cost Amount (₹)
Power Failure					
Break-down					
Waiting for job instructions					
Tools					
Materials					
Other Causes:					

Employee's signature: .... Foreman's signature: ....

Cost clerk's signature: ....

Illustration 7.2 : *The capacity usage ratio and the capacity utilization ratio in respect of a machine for a particular month is 75% and 85% respectively. The available working hours in a month are 240.*

The break-up of idle time is as under:

Waiting time	*8 hours*
Break-down	*6 hours*
Waiting for tools	*4 hours*

Calculate the idle time cost and present the same in a tabular form when the hourly fixed cost of running the machine is ₹ 40.

Solution : Total available Working Time:240 hours

Capacity Usage ratio:	75%
Normal capacity expected:	(0.75 × 240) = 180 hours
Unavoidable Idle time:	(240 – 180) = 60 hours
Capacity Utilization ratio:	85%
Actual time worked:	(0.85 × 180) = 153 hours
Capacity remained unutilized:	(180 – 153) = 27 hours
Idle time records reveal the followings:	
Waiting time	8Hours
Break-down	6 hours
Waiting for tools	4 hours
Total	18 hours
Idle time due to other reasons	27 – 18 = 9 hours

Report on Idle time

Details	Time (Hours)		Hourly Rate (₹)	Amount (₹)
Cost for Unavoidable time		60	40	2,400
Cost of Avoidable time:	8		40	320
Waiting for job	6		40	240
Break-down	4		40	160
Waiting for tools	9		40	360
Other reasons		27	40	1,080
Total idle time (240-153)		87		3,480

Time-cum-Job Card

A sheet is used to record both the attendance time and the work time of a worker. This facilitates the reconciliation of the gate time with work time. The use of such a card becomes convenient when the recording of time is done by means of time recording clocks. A proforma of such card is given below:

Time-cum-Job Card

Employee's Name: .... DEPARTMENT: ....
Employee's ID No: .... Date: ....

Day	Job No.	Clock Time In	Clock Time Out	Job Time On	Job Time Off	Total clock Time Ordinary	Total clock Time Overtime	Job Time	Idle Time
Monday									
Tuesday									
Wednesday									
Thursday									
Friday									
Saturday									

Total hours: .... Gross Wages: ₹ ....
Employee's signature: .... Less: Deductions: ....
Cost clerk's signagure: .... New Wages: ₹ ....

Foreman's signature: ....

labour Cost Card (Circulating Job Card)

If a Job/Work-Order requires the engagement of different workers on daily basis, a card may be kept for this particular Job/Work-Order. This job card known as Labour cost card shall be circulated amongst the workers when they are on working on this Job/Work-Order. The specimen card given below shows the total cost of labour engaged on a definite job and this is why it is known as labour cost card. This Card is maintained in addition to the job card issued to each worker.

LABOUR COST CARD
Job Number: ....
Week Ending ....

Day	Employee's Name	Details of work	Time On	Time Off	Total time Taken	Rate	Amount
Monday	1						
	2						
	3						
	4						
	5						
Tuesday	1						
	2						
	3						
	4						
	5						
Wednesday	1						
	2						

	3
	4
	5
Thursday	1
	2
	3
	4
	5
Friday	1
	2
	3
	4
	5
Saturday	1
	2
	3
	4
	5

Total Time Total Amount

Employee's signature: ………… Cost clerk's signagure :…………

Piece work Card

Piece-Work card is to be maintained for each worker if he is paid according to the work done and not on the basis of time.

PIECE WORK CARD

Work Order No: ………… DEPARTMENT: …………

Employee's Name: ………… Category: …………

Employee's ID No: ………… Week Ending: …………

Day	Job No.	Number of Units: Total	Rejected	Accepted	Inspector's Initials	Rate per unit (₹)	Amount (₹)
Monday							
Tuesday							
Wednesday							
Thursday							
Friday							
Saturday							

Employee's signature: ………… Checked by: …………

Foreman's signature: ………… Entered in Wages Abstract by: …………

Inspector's signature: …………

Matching of Attendance Time and Time Booked for Work

At the end of the wage period, the time shown by the time cards in respect of each worker should be compared with the time booked on the jobs as indicated by the job cards. This work is facilitated if a Time – cum – Job card is maintained. If time booked on jobs is less than the time recorded in the time cards, it implies idle time which may be checked with idle time cards. There is no need of maintaining separate job cards if the workers are mostly engaged throughout the period on the same process, job or contract. However, idle time cards may be maintained. The time recorded in the time cards minus the time recorded in the idle time cards will be the effective time booked to that process, job or contract in all such cases.

DEPARTMENT OF PAYROLL

Most companies have a separate payroll department whose function is to compute the total payroll indicating the Gross amount earned and the Net amount payable to employees after authorized deductions. It also makes the payment to the employees and maintains records of their earnings, their wage rate and job categories. Payroll accounting requires the availability of certain information relating to employee attendance, time, details of absenteeism, hourly rates of pay and details of other deductions on account of contributions to Provident fund, Employees State Insurance, and tax, etc.

The wage sheets are usually prepared department wise. Departmental wage sheets are summarised in a master wage sheet which forms the basis of payroll entry voucher in the general ledger in cost control account.

DEPARTMENT OF COST ACCOUNTING

The cost accounting department is responsible for recording separately the entries in respect of wages paid to direct and indirect labour. The direct labour costs are taken as prime cost of production, and indirect labour costs as overhead expenses. Analysis of labour costs into direct and indirect facilitates control over labour costs. It is the duty of the costing department to inform on regular basis the loss of labour time, wastage and inefficiencies, etc. It is also to compare the actual labour costs with the pre-fixed standard or budgeted costs and find out the cause of variances to the management.

WAGES ABSTRACT

Wages Abstract is a statement prepared by the costing Department wherein the allocation/allotment of wages by department, jobs, work orders or processes is analysed. This statement is usually prepared on weekly basis and the information relating to wages paid to workers for the different cost units or activities like jobs, work orders or processes etc. are incorporated therein. Time cards, Job cards, piece-work cards, wages sheets, etc, are the source documents used for such incorporation of data in the abstract.

For costing purposes, gross wages payable to the workers is to be distributed in direct and indirect categories at the first instance. In such an event two wages analysis sheets are to be prepared:

(i) Apportionment of wages between direct and indirect; and

(ii) Allocation of direct wages.

The first wagers analysis statement may be prepared on the basis of Time Card. Specimen proforma of the two are given hereunder:

WAGES ANALYSIS SHEET

Employee's Name	Time Card No.	Department	Direct Wages (₹)	Indirect Wages (₹)			Total (₹)
				Factory	Office	Selling and Distribution	

DIRECT WAGES ANALYSIS SHEET

Employee's Name (Emp-ID code)	Time Card No.	Job/Work order/Process No.					Total Wagdes for the week (₹)
		1(₹)	2(₹)	3(₹)	4(₹)	5(₹)	
						Total	

Prebared by ....

Checked by ....

Posted to ledger ....

IDLE TIME

It is that time for which wages are paid but no production is obtained. When workers are paid on time basis, some difference is bound to arise between the time for which they are paid and the time they actually spend upon production. It can be classified into Normal and Abnormal idle time.

Normal Idle Time

It pertains to that loss of time which is usually unavoidable and is bound to arise. Some of the reasons are (a) Time spent in setting the machines; (b) Adjusting the tools and jigs; (c) Moving from one job to another; (d) tea/coffee breaks; (e) personal needs, etc. it is crystal clear that wastage of time is unavoidable and its cost is, therefore, an expense which is to be directly charged to the job by upgrading or inflating the wage rate. If it is not feasible, cost of such normal idle time is to be treated as works overheads.

Abnormal Idle Time

If the reasons for the loss of time are abnormal and for which the employer must pay, the cost of such abnormal idle time is to be collected separately and written off to Costing Profit and Loss account. Some of the reasons could be power failure, strikes etc.

For the purpose of control, accounting treatment of idle time may be done in the following manner:

Idle Time Cost	Accounting Treatment
Normal :	
(a) Controllable: It arises due to normal causes but is controllable. It is treated as a part of cost and is treated as a part of works overhead. (Break-down of machinery, waiting for work or tools or instructions or materials).	It is debited to Production Overheads Control Account.
(b) Uncontrollable: It arises due to normal causes but is not controllable. (Set-up time for machines, interval between one job and another, personal needs).	It is treated as a part of cost and is directly charged to jobs by inflating wage rates.
Abnormal: It arises due to abnormal causes and is not treated as a part of cost.	It is debited to Costing Profit & Loss Account.

OVERTIME

If a worker spends more time over and above the normal working hours, it is known as overtime. The main causes of overtime are as under:

1. To meet the high level of production.
2. To make up production deficiency caused by strike, lock-out, official holidays.
3. To complete the emergent work or to execute the rush order.
4. To pull up backlog in production due to shutdown, power failure, break down of machinery etc.

Usually workers are paid at a higher rate than for normal time. According to Indian Factories Act, 1948, overtime has to be paid at double the normal rate of payment. Further, overtime comes at the end of the day when fatigue has set in.

thus, jobs done in overtime are rather costly because of higher wage rate, low efficiency and productivity and additional overhead expenditure such as lighting, extra depreciation, cost of supervision etc. Therefore, overtime must be resorted to only when it is extremely essential. Proper planning is required for keeping the overtime premium cost to the minimum. Factors like demand for the product, production capacity, seasonal conditions etc. should be given due consideration.

Accounting Treatment of Overtime

1. In case overtime premium payment is necessary on account of the necessity to increase the production level of the factory (Seasonal requirement), the cost of such wage bill should be treated as a Works overhead charge.
2. If overtime working becomes necessary on account of special request of the customer to get work done within a specified time, the cost of such overtime payment should be considered as a direct charge and recovered from the special job order only.
3. If the payment for overtime working is necessitated by abnormal factors such as break down of machinery, abnormal idle time, etc. then it should be treated as an abnormal expense and charged to costing Profit and Loss account.

CASUAL WORKERS AND OUTWORKERS

Casual Workers

Casual workers are those who are not on the list of regular employees, but are engaged casually whenever there is extra work-load in the factory; or whenever a regular worker is absent from the job for a temporary period because of sickness or any other reason. Such casual workers are usually paid on daily basis. The wages paid to them are treated as factory overheads if the time spent by them cannot be identified to specific jobs; and as direct labour if the direct identification of such time is possible. In the former case each worker is to be supplied with a 'Time Card' while in the latter case a 'Job Card' should be issued to each of them.

The employment of the casual workers must be properly regulated and authorized; the payment must be made by the Pay & Accounts Department in the presence of the foreman of the concerned department.

Outworkers

Workers who work outside the factory premises are known as out workers. They may be put any of the two categories:

(I) Workers who are not on the payroll of the factory

(II) Workers who are on the payroll of the factory

Workers who are not on the payroll of the factory

The factory supplies materials to such workers; however, they use their own tools, premises, etc. Strict supervision and control is required in such cases in respect of (a) materials issued to the workers for carrying to their homes, (b) delivery of manufactured products after the allotted time, and (c) the quality of work according to the directions given to them. There is no need to keep 'Time Cards' in such cases. Such workers are paid in general higher than those who work within the factory as they use their own premises, lighting, tools etc.

Workers who are on the payroll of the factory

They are on the regular employment of the business concern. They are sent to the customer's place to perform some specific duties such as sanitary work or plumber's work, etc. Time records of such employees are to be kept by the employer to record the time of arrival in the factory and time of going out. The workers may be given job cards in which the actual time taken by them in respect of jobs performed at various places should be recorded. It is preferable to have for each worker 'Out Work Time Sheet' specimen of which is given as under:

Out Work Time Sheet

Worker's ID No. .... Department ....

Worker's Name .... Week Ending ....

Day	Details of work	Time Start	Time Finish	Total Hours	Rate	Total cost
Monday						
Tuesday						
Wednesday						
Thursday						
Friday						
Saturday						
Sunday						

Workman ....

Foreman .... Costing done by ....

Control on Outworkers

In regard to the followings the control over outworkers need to be exercised:

(a) Complete record in terms of materials issued to each worker, materials used by them and materials returned.

(b) Standard should be laid down for the material use per unit of output.

(c) Strict control on the output of these workers must be maintained.

(d) System of fine should be devised for defectives and material wastages.

(e) Strict delivery schedule should be adhered to.

VACATION AND HOLIDAY PAY

Having served the organization for a certain length of period the employee generally receives paid vacations and holidays. Compensation of this variety is called nonproductive pay because an employee is receiving wages while making no contribution to output. Wages paid for holidays and leave period is treated as indirect expenses, and are charged to factory overhead. As a result, we are able to charge each month of service equally with proportionate amount of vacation pay.

Illustration 7.3 : Meira has worked for the Quality Production Ltd. for five years and is therefore, entitled to two weeks' paid vacation. Her weekly pay is ₹ 3,200. Make the entry to accrue Meira's vacation pay for the week, assuming she is not on vacation now.

Total vacation Pay:

= ₹ 3,200 per week × two weeks = ₹ 6,400

Weeks over which vacation pay is to be accrued: 52 weeks – 2 week vacation = 50 weeks

Weekly accrual: ₹ 6,400/50 weeks = ₹ 128 per week

The Journal Entry is:

Date	Details		L.F.	Amount (₹)	Amount (₹)
	Work-in-Process Inventory	Dr		3,200	
	Factory Overhead Control			128	
	(Vacation Pay) A/c	Dr			
	To Vacation Pay Payable A/c				128
	To Payroll Payable A/c				3,200

NIGHT SHIFT ALLOWANCE

Workers get extra payment if they are required to work at night. Payment for such work is known as Night shift allowance. The treatment of such payments is in the same way in which overtime premium is treated in cost accounts.

Illustration 7.4 : *Find out what an average worker costs the employer for a month of 208 hours, assuming 8 hours a day, from the followings:*

Average Basic wage per hour	*₹ 45*
Average D.A. per hour	*₹ 15*

Employer's contribution to Provident fund = (@ 8% of Basic wage and D.A.)

Employer's contribution to Employees State Insurance = (@ 2% of Basic wage and D.A.)

Other amenities per month	*₹ 380*
Number of other unpaid holidays (Festivals) in a year	*3*
Number of unpaid holidays in a year	*27*
Number of days on sick leave with half pay in a year	*12*

Solution : Computation of Monthly Earnings per worker

Details	Amount (₹)
Basic Wage (180 × 45)	8,100
D.A. (180 × 15)	2,700
Half Pay on account of sick Leave (12 × 30)	360
Employer's contribution to Provident fund (0.08 × 10,800)	864
Employer's contribution to Employees State Insurance (.02 × 10,800)	216
Value of other amenities per month	380
Total Earnings per Worker	12,620

Working Notes:

Number of hours per month	208
Less: Number of hours per month for unpaid holidays aggregating 30 days (27 + 3) in a year = (30 × 8)/12	(20)
	188
Less: Sick Leave hours per month (12×8)/12	(8)
Effective hours for the month	180

Illustration 7.5 : *Calculate the earnings of workers W-1 and W-2 from the following details for a month and allocate the earnings of each to Jobs J-1, J-2 and J-3.*

Details	*W-1*	*W-2*
Basic Wage	*25,000*	*25,000*
Dearness Allowance	*60%*	*64%*
Provident Fund (on wages inclusive of D.A.)	*8%*	*8%*
ESI (on Basic Wages inclusive of D.A.)	*2%*	*2%*
Overtime (hour)	*12*	—
Idle Time and Leave (hour)	—	*16*

The normal working hours for the month are 200. Overtime is paid at double the normal rate plus D.A. Employees' contribution to ESI and PF are at equal rates with the employer's contributions. The month has 25 working days of eight hours each and one paid holiday.

The two workers were engaged on jobs in the following proportions.

Worker	*J-1*	*J-2*	*J-3*
W-1	*40*	*35*	*25*
W-2	*50*	*20*	*30*

Overtime was done on Job no. J-2

Solution : **Earning of Workers**

Details	W-1	W-2
Basic Wage	25,000	25,000
Dearness Allowance	15,000	16,000
Overtime	4,800	———
Total Gross Wages	44,800	41,000
Less: Deductions:		
PF Contribution @ 8%	(3,200)	(3,280)
ESI Contribution @ 2%	(800)	(820)
Net Carry Home Wage	40,800	36,900

Labour cost for workers

Details	W-1	W-2
Gross Wages Excluding Overtime	40,000	41,000
Employer's contribution to PF and ESI	4,000	4,100
Total Labour cost Excluding Overtime	44,000	45,100
Labour cost per hour	220	225.50

Allocation of wages to Jobs: J-1, J-2 and J-3.

Details	Total Wages	J-1	J-2	J-3
Worker W-1:				
Regular Wages (8:7:5)	44,000	17,600	15,400	11,000
Overtime Wage	4,800	———	4,800	———
Worker W-2:				
Regular Wages (5:2:3)	45,100	22,550	9,020	13,530
Total Cost	93,900	40,150	29,220	24,530

Working Notes:

I. Computation of overtime cost:

Basic Wages	25,000
Dearness Allowance	15,000
Total	40,000

Regular Hourly Rate = 40,000/200 = ₹ 200.

Overtime Rate = 2 × Regular Hourly Rate

= 2 × 200 = ₹ 400.

Overtime Payment = 400 × 12 = ₹ 4,800.

II. Computation of Labour cost per hour:

W-1: 44,000/200 = ₹ 220

W-2: 45,100/200 = ₹ 225.50

III. Idle time and Leave have been considered as normal. Thus, the entire wages of ₹ 45,100 have been charged to jobs. Had the idle time and leave been considered as abnormal, the cost of such time i.e. 225.5 × 16 = ₹ 3,608 would have been debited to Costing Profit and Loss Account and the balance of ₹ 45,100 – ₹ 3,608 = ₹ 41,492 will be allocated to various jobs in the ratio of 5:2:3 i.e. ₹ 20,746, ₹ 8,298 and ₹ 12,448. Total wages chargeable to J-1 will be ₹ 38,346, to J-2 ₹ 28,498 and to J-3 ₹ 23,448.

Illustration 7.6 : *Mohan, an employee of SV Limited gets the following emoluments:*

Salary	*₹ 4,500*
Dearness Allowance (D.A.):	
On First ₹ 1,000 of Salary	*₹ 5,000*
On Next ₹ 1,000 of Salary	*₹ 3,000*
On Next ₹ 1,000 of Salary	*₹ 2,000*
On Next ₹ 1,000 of Salary	*₹ 1,000*
On Balance of every ₹ 1,000 of Salary or part thereof ₹ 500	
Employer's contribution to PF =	*8% of Salary and D.A.*
Employer's contribution to ESI =	*2.5% of Salary and D.A.*
Bonus:	*25% of Salary and D.A.*
Other Allowances:	*₹ 52,500*

Mohan works for 3,000 hours per annum, out of which 500 hours are non-productive but treated as normal idle time. Mohan worked for 20 effective hours on Job No. 335, where the direct material equals 'Mohan' earnings and the overhead applied is 120% of prime cost. The sale value of the job is quoted to earn a profit of 20% on such value. You are required to find out: (a) Effective hourly cost of 'Mohan' and (b) the expected sale value of Job No. 335.

Solution : Working Notes:

Computation of Effective Working Hours

Gross Hours	3,000
Less: Normal Idle time	(500)
Effective Working Hours	2,500

Statement of Mohan's Earnings and effective hourly cost of Mohan's work

Details		Amount (₹)
Salary (p.m.)		4,500
Dearness Allowance:		
On First ₹ 1,000 of Salary	₹ 5,000	
On Next ₹ 1,000 of Salary	₹ 3,000	
On Next ₹ 1,000 of Salary	₹ 2,000	
On Next ₹ 1,000 of Salary	₹ 1,000	
On Balance of every ₹1,000 of Salary Or part thereof	₹ 500	11,500

Salary and D.A. per month	16,000
Salary and D.A. per annum (16,000 × 12)	1,92,000
Employer's contribution to PF (0.08 × 1,92,000)	15,360
Employer's contribution to ESI (0.025 × 1,92,000)	4,800
Bonus (0.25 × 1,92,000)	48,000
Other allowances per annum(Fixed)	52,340
Total Earnings per annum	3,12,500

Effective Hourly cost of Mohan's Work

= 3,12,500/2,500

= ₹ 125 per hour

Cost Sheet of Job NO. 335

Details	Amount (₹)
Direct Wages (Mohan for 20 hours @ ₹ 125)	2,500
Direct Material (Equivalent to Mohan's wages)	2,500
Prime Cost	5,000
Add: Overheads@ 120% of Prime Cost (i.e. 5,000 × 1.2)	6,000
Works cost	11,000
Add: Profit 20% of Sales value or 25% of cost	2,750
Expected Sales value	13,750

Illustration 7.7 : *SV Limited provides the following information for its factory working six days in a week:*

(1) Hours as per Time card — *48*

(2) Hours booked to jobs as per job card — *38*

(3) Daily allowance for Lunch, Personal Needs, fatigue and Maintenance of machine — *45 (Minutes)*

(4) Wage Rate (₹) — *30 per hour*

(5) The time not booked was due break down of machinery, power failure, waiting for jobs, Materials and tools.

Required: How would you deal with the wage in cost account?

Solution : Idle Time:

= (Hours as per Time card) – (Hours booked to jobs as per job card)

= 48 – 38 = 10 hours

Normal Idle Time:

= (45/60) × 6 = 4.5 Hours

Abnormal Idle Time:

= (Total Idle Time) – (Normal Idle Time)

= 10 – 4.5 = 5.5 hours

Weekly Time:
= (Number of Working Days in a week) – (Number of working Hours per day)
= 6 × 8 = 48 hours

Weekly Payment:
= (Number of weekly working hours) × (Time Wage Rate)
= 48 × 30 = ₹ 1,440

Allocation of Weekly Wage Payment :

1. Charging to Jobs: (38 × 30) ₹ 1,140
2. Charging to factory overheads:
   Normal Idle time: (4.5 × 30) ₹ 135
3. Charging to Costing Profit and Loss A/c:
   Abnormal Idle time: (5.5 × 30) ₹ 165
   Total weekly Payment: ₹ 1,440

Illustration 7.8 : (Labour cost)

From the following details, prepare the labour cost sheet per man-day of Eight hours:

(1) Basic Salary	*₹ 200 per day*
(2) Dearness Allowance	*₹ 4 for every Point over 100,* *Cost of living index for working class:* *Current Cost of living index 600 points.*
(3) Leave Salary	*12.5% of (1) and (2)*

(4) Employer's Contribution to Provident fund: 10.0% of (1), (2) and (3)
(5) Employer's Contribution to ESI: 4.0% of (1), (2) and (3)
(6) Expenditure on amenities to labour: ₹ 2,110 per head per mensem.
(7) Number of working days in a month: 25 days of Eight hours each.

Solution : Statement of labour cost per Man-day of Eight Hours

Details		Monthly (25 Days) Amount (₹)	Rate per Man-Day of 8 hours (₹)
1. Basic Salary	(25 × 200)	10,000	200.00
2. Dearness Allowance	(500 × 4)	2,000	80.00
3. Leave Salary	(0.125 × 12,000)	1,500	60.00
4. Employer's Contribution to Provident fund	(0.1 × 13,500)	1,350	54.00
5. Employer's Contribution to ESI	(0.04 × 13,500)	540	21.60
6. Expenditure on amenities to labour		2,110	84.40
Total Cost per man-day of 8 hours		12,500	500.00

Illustration 7.9 : (Labour cost)

Following information is furnished by the Production Department of a Company:

Day of the week	*Hours worked*
Monday	*8*
Tuesday	*10*
Wednesday	*12*
Thursday	*9*
Friday	*10*
Saturday	*6*
Normal working Hours per Day	*8*
Normal Rate per Hour (₹):	*25*

Overtime Rate: Up to 9 hours in a day at Single Rate and over 9 hours At Double Rate or up to 48 hours in a week At Single Rate and over 48 hours at Double Rate, Which ever is more beneficial to the worker concerned.

Dearness Allowance: 125% of normal Wages

Bonus: 12.5% of Normal Wages and Dearness Allowance

Employer's Contribution to Provident fund: 10% of Normal Wages and Dearness Allowance

Employer's Contribution to ESI: 4% of Normal Wages and Dearness Allowance

Expenditure on amenities per worker per week: ₹ 800

Employee's Contribution to Provident fund and ESI is same as that of the employer.

Output in the week was 36 units.

The company allows statutory leave of two weeks per year with pay.

You are required to compute:

(1) Gross Wages earned and net Wages payable to a worker this week;

(2) Cost of labour per hour and per unit of output.

Solution : Statement showing Calculation of Normal and overtime Wages

Day	Actual Hours worked	Normal Hours	Normal Wages (₹)	Hours At Single Rate	Hours At Double Rate	Overtime Wages (₹)
Monday	8	8	160.00	———	———	———
Tuesday	10	8	160.00	1	1	60.00
Wednesday	12	8	160.00	1	3	140.00

Thursday	9	8	160.00	1	———-	20.00
Friday	11	8	160.00	1	2	100.00
Saturday	8	8	160.00	———-	———-	———-
Total	58	48	960.00	4	6	320.00

Total wages	Option I	Option II
A. Normal Wages	960.00	960.00
B. Overtime Wages	320.00	400.00
	1,280.00	**1,360.00**

Decision: Option II is to be preferred.

Statement showing the Gross Wages and Net Wages

Details			Amount (₹)
(i) Normal Wages	[48 × 20]		960.00
(ii) Overtime wages	[10 × 40]		400.00
(iii) Dearness Allowance	[960 × 1.25]		1,200.00
(iv) Bonus	[2,160 × 0.125]		270.00
(v) Gross Wages earned by a worker [(i) + (ii) + (iii) + (iv)]			2,830.00
(vi) Less: deductions from wages:			270.00
(a) Employee's Contribution to Provident fund	[2,160 × 0.1]	216.00	
(b) Employee's Contribution to ESI	[2,160 × 0.025]	54.00	
(vii) Net Wages payable to a worker [(v) – (vi)]			2,560.00

Statement showing the Labour Cost per Hour and per unit of Output

Details		Amount (₹)
(i) Normal Wages		960.00
(ii) Dearness Allowance		1,200.00
(iii) Bonus		270.00
(iv) Employer's Contribution to Provident fund	[2,160 × 0.1]	216.00
(v) Employer's Contribution to ESI	[2,160 × 0.025]	54.00
(vi) Leave Salary	[(2,160) × (2/52)]	83.08
(vii) Expenditure on amenities		800.00
(viii) Total Labour cost		3,583.08
(ix) Working hours		48
(x) Output (Units)		36
(xi) labour cost per hour [3,583.08 ÷ 48]		74.6475
(xii) labour cost per unit of Output [3,583.08÷36]		99.53

LABOUR TURNOVER

Labour turnover is the rate of displacement of the personnel employed in an organisation due to resignation, retirement or retrenchment. High labour turnover means instability of labour and it adversely affects their efficiency as well as the profitability of the organisation. The labour turnover proves to be very costly for the business and every effort should be made to reduce the frequency of labour turnover.

Factors Responsible for Labour Turnover

Avoidable Factors: These are the factors which are not within the control of the management:

(i) Personal betterment;

(ii) Sickness or accident;

(iii) Death or retirement;

(iv) Discharged due to insubordination etc.

(v) Marriage especially of female employees;

(vi) Seasonal nature of business;

(vii) Shortage of raw materials, power resulting in lowering production capacity;

(viii) Location change.

Unavoidable Factors: These are the factors which are within the control of the management. By taking appropriate preventive steps the management should attempt to reduce the rate of labour turnover. Some of unavoidable factors are:

(i) Lack of congenial and healthy environment in the factory;

(ii) Lack of proper facilities and amenities;

(iii) Lack of strategic planning;

(iv) Low wages and ill-treatment, etc.

(v) Relationship with fellow workers.

Measurement of Labour Turnover

Any of the following methods of measurement can be adopted, but as far possible consistency should be maintained for comparison purposes.

1. *Separation Method:* It is the division of total number of separations in a given period by the average number of workers on the payroll during the same period.

$$= \frac{\text{Total separations during the given period}}{\text{Average number of workers in the given period}}$$

2. *Replacement Method:* Only the actual replacement of the labour force is considered. It is the division of total number of replacements in a given

period by the average number of workers on the payroll during the same period.

$$= \frac{\text{Total number of replacements during the given period}}{\text{Average number of workers in the given period}}$$

3. *Flux Method:* It takes into account both the separations and the replacements while calculating the labour turnover, the formula of which is given hereunder:

$$= \frac{(\text{Total separation} + \text{Total number of workers joining excluding joining due to expansion})}{\text{Average number of workers in the given period}}$$

Cost of Labour Turnover

The cost of labour turnover is classified into two categories, (i) Preventive cost and (ii) Replacement cost.

(1) *Preventive cost:* These are the costs which are incurred in order to keep the workers satisfied and thus to act as a discouragement against leaving the organisation. Following are such costs:
   - (a) Personnel Administration costs: It relates to the efforts of the Personnel manager in maintaining harmonious relationship between the management and the staff.
   - (b) Cost of medical amenities;
   - (c) Cost of employee welfare services;
   - (d) Cost of retirement benefits.

(2) Replacement cost: It includes the followings:
   - (a) Increase in the expenses of the Personnel Department;
   - (b) Loss of output due to delay in obtaining new labour;
   - (c) Cost of training new labour;
   - (d) Increase spoilage;
   - (e) Cost of tool and machine breakages;
   - (f) Lower productivity on account of inefficiency of the new work force.

Treatment of Labour Turnover Cost

Preventive costs should be charged as an item of works overhead and apportioned to various departments on the basis of number of workers engaged in each department. Replacement costs should also be treated on the same criterion if it arises on account of the shortsightedness of the management. If it arises on account of the fault of a particular department, the same should be charged directly to that concerned department.

It may be pointed out that labour turnover cannot be completely avoided but its rate can be kept at the minimum level by taking such steps which improve employee morale and create the congenial atmosphere in the organisation.

Equivalent Rate of Labour Turnover

Labour turnover rate for a period less than one year can be calculated from annual turnover rate. Similarly, annual rate of turnover can be estimated from monthly/quarterly turnover rate. Such rate can be termed as 'Equivalent Monthly/ Quarterly Rate' or 'Equivalent Annual Rate'.

Equivalent Monthly Rate = Annual Turnover /12

Equivalent Quarterly Rate = Annual Turnover /4

Equivalent Annual Rate = Monthly Turnover × 12

OR

Equivalent Annual Rate = Monthly Turnover × 4

Average Workforce during a period:

$$= \frac{(\text{Opening Number of workers} + \text{Closing Number of workers})}{2}$$

Illustration 7.10 : *The following information relates to workforce in a large factory during the year 2007-08:*

Details	*Number*
Number of workers on April 1, 2007	*4,750*
Number of workers on March 31, 2008	*5,250*
Number of workers who quit the workshop on their own during 2007- 08	*400*
Number of workers who availed golden hand-shake opportunity	*100*
Number of workers employed during 2007- 08 including those employed due to expansion scheme	*1,600*

Calculate Annual Turnover Rate and Equivalent Quarterly Rate under different methods.

Solution :

Method	Formula	Calculation
Annual Turnover Rate 1. Separation Method	$\frac{\text{Total separations during the year}}{\text{Average number of workers}}$	$= \frac{(400 + 100)}{5{,}000}$ $= (500 \div 5{,}000) \times 100$ = 0.1 or 10%
2. Replacement Method	(Total Number of workers leaving the organisation requiring replacement) ÷ Average Number of workers	$= (400 \div 5{,}000) \times 100$ = 0.08 or 8%

3. Flux Method	(Total separation + Total number of workers joining excluding joining due to expansion) ÷ Average Number of workers	=[(400 + 100) + (1600 −1200)] ÷ 5,000 = (500 + 400) ÷ 5,000 = 0.18 or 18%
Equivalent Quarterly Rate		
1. Separation Method	$\frac{\text{Annual Turnover Rate}}{4}$	= 0.1 ÷ 4 = 0.025 or 2.5%
2. Replacement Method	$\frac{\text{Annual Turnover Rate}}{4}$	= 0.08 ÷ 4 = 0.02 or 2%
3. Flux Method	$\frac{\text{Annual Turnover Rate}}{4}$	= 0.18 ÷ 4 = 0.045 or 4.5%

Working Note:

(1) Annual Turnover Rate = (4,750 + 5,250) ÷ 2 = 5,000

(2) Workers Joining due to Expansion

= Total number of workers who joined – joined by way of replacement

= 1,600 – 400 = 1,200.

Illustration 7.11 : *An Analysis of the Time-Card of Mr. Mohan Das, a worker on one of the machines in the Workshop, shows that of the total 48 hours, he worked 44 hours (including 4hours overtime) on production and that there was 4 hours idle time due to power failure.*

The time rate of the worker is ₹ 12.5 per hour but overtime is paid 60% extra.

You are required to allocate the total wages paid to Mr. Mohan Das between 'direct' and 'indirect' labour.

Solution : Total Wages paid to Mr. Mohan Das inclusive of the followings:

Details		**Amount** (₹)
Time Wages for 48 hours @ ₹ 12.5 per hour (48 × 12.5)		600
Overtime Allowance for 4 hours @ ₹ 7.5 per hour (i.e. 60% of 12.5)		75
		675
Actual time spent on production is 44 hours:		
Wages to be charged as direct cost will be for 44 hours @ ₹ 12.5 per hour	550	
Overtime allowance to be treated as indirect labour cost		75
Loss on account of Abnormal Idle time, 4 hours @ ₹ 12.5 per hour		50
		675

LET US RECAPITULATE

1. Labour Cost may be direct and indirect.
2. Direct Labour cost is cost of all labour expended in altering the construction, composition or condition of the product.
3. Indirect Labour cost is the amount of wages paid to the workmen who are not so engaged in altering the composition of product.
4. Direct Labour cost is charged to jobs and forms part of prime cost, whereas indirect labour cost becomes a part of overhead.
5. Control of labour cost is the main objective of management and much can be achieved with the coordination of every member of the supervisory force from the top executive to the floor foreman.
6. It is the responsibility of the Personnel Department to recruit, train and place the workers to the jobs they are best suited.
7. It is also responsible for control and administration of the efficient utilization of the services of the human resource.
8. Time Study involves determination of standard time for operations after standardization of methods.
9. Motion study identifies best method of doing a job which results in maximum economy, least fatigue and improve productivity.
10. Job analysis helps establishing distinction between jobs, proper matching of jobs and workers and consequently helps in determining the number and type of workers to be recruited.
11. Job Evaluation aims at ascertaining relative worth of each job so that a systematic wage differential can be established for different jobs.
12. Merit rating is the assessment of an employee's performance made by his superior.
13. Time keeping is the recording of time of workers for purpose of attendance and wage calculations.
14. Time booking is the reporting of each worker's time for each department, operation and job for the purpose of cost analysis and apportionment of labour costs between various jobs and departments.
15. Daily Time sheet is allotted to each worker in which he records time spent by him on each job during the day. The method is suitable in case of those workers who have to change their jobs quite frequently during a day.
16. Weekly Time sheet is meant for recording all jobs done during the week.
17. A job card/ticket is maintained for every job. It performs two functions:
    (a) It authorizes a worker to carry out the operations detailed thereon;
    (b) It enables the correct allocation of wages to jobs, operations or processes.
18. Idle Time Card records the quantum of unproductive time in the factory and the reasons for it.

19. Time – cum – Job Card records both the attendance time and the work time of a worker.
20. Labour cost card is maintained in addition to the job card issued to each worker.
21. Piece-Work card is to be maintained for each worker if he is paid according to the work done and not on the basis of time.
22. The time recorded in the time cards minus the time recorded in the idle time cards will be the effective time booked to that process, job or contract in all such cases.
23. The direct labour costs are taken as prime cost of production, and indirect labour costs as overhead expenses.
24. Wages Abstract is a statement prepared by the costing Department wherein the allocation/allotment of wages by department, jobs, work orders or processes is analysed.
25. Idle time is that time for which wages are paid but no production is obtained.
26. Normal idle time pertains to that loss of time which is usually unavoidable and is bound to arise.
27. Abnormal idle time arises due to abnormal causes and is not treated as a part of cost.
28. Overtime is the spending of more time over and above the normal working hours.
29. Casual workers those who are not on the list of regular employees, but are engaged casually whenever there is extra work-load in the factory.
30. Workers who work outside the factory premises are known as out workers.
31. Wages paid for holidays and leave period is treated as indirect expenses, and are charged to factory overheads.
32. Workers get extra payment if they are required to work at night. Payment for such work is known as Night shift allowance.

SOLVED PROBLEMS

Problem 1. *From the following data prepare a statement showing the labour cost per day of 8 hours of engaging a particular type of labour:*

(a) *Monthly salary (basic plus dearness allowance) ₹ 4,000*

(b) *Leave salary payable to the workman 5% of (a)*

(c) *Employer's contribution to provident fund 10% of salary [Items (a) & (b)]*

(d) *Employer's contribution to state insurance 5% of salary [Items (a) & (b)]*

(e) *Pro rata expenditure on amenities to labour ₹ 670 per head per month.*

(f) *Number of working hours in a month 200.*

Solution : **Statement showing labour cost per hour**

Details	Rate	Monthly Amount (₹)
(a) Salary	₹ 4,000	4,000
(b) Leave salary	5% of ₹ 4,000	200
(c) P.F. contribution (employer's)	10% of ₹ 4,200	420
(d) E.S.I. contribution (employer's)	5% of ₹ 4,200	210
(e) Expenditure on amenities	₹ 670	670
Total labour cost for 200 hours		5,500

Hence, labour cost per Day = (5,500 ÷ 25) i.e. ₹ 220.

Problem 2. *A worker is paid ₹ 6,000 p.m. as basic wages and ₹ 2,000 as D.A. p.m. Employer's contribution to P.F. is 10% of his basic pay and D.A. Employer's contribution to E S I is 4% on basic pay. Monthly cost of non-monetary benefits to him is estimated as ₹ 500. Actual number of days (of 8 hours working per day) after adjustment for weekly offs, holidays and leave entitlement are estimated at 250 p.a. Normal idle time is 12%. Calculate wage rate per hour for costing purposes.*

Solution :

Details (Annual basis)	Amount (₹)
Basic Wages (6,000 × 12)	72,000
D.A. (2,000 × 12)	24,000
Contribution to P.F [{0.1 × (6,000 + 2,000)} ×12]	9,600
Contribution to E S I [{0.04 × (6,000)} ×12]	2,880
Cost of non-monetary benefits (500 × 12)	6,000
Total Labour Cost	1,14,480

Number of working days in a year:	250
Less: Normal Idle days (0.12× 250):	30
Effective annual labour days:	220
Effective annual Labour hours (8 × 220):	1,760

Effective Labour cost per hour of worker A: 1,14,480 ÷ 1,760 = ₹ 65.05

Problem 3. *From the following comparative statements for 2002 and 2003 :*

(a) *Find out whether the year 2003 showed an overall better performance or otherwise?*

(b) *Suggest possible causes of differences in performance.*

Details	*Year 2002*	*Year 2003*
Wages incurred (₹)	*6,00,000*	*12,60,000*
Units produced (No.)	*15,000*	*28,000*
Average number of workers	*200*	*360*

(Assume production of only one quality and same machinery conditions in both years)

Solution : (a) Overall performance:

Details	Year 2002	Year 2003	Remarks
(i) Labour cost per unit	₹ 40.00	₹ 45.00	12.5% rise
(ii) Average annual earning per man	₹ 3,000.00	₹ 3,500.00	16.67% rise
(iii) Annual output per man	75.0 units	77.8 units	3.73% rise

(b) Causes of difference: Although productivity per man has increased, labour cost has increased by 12.5% which is probably due to general rise in wages which have gone up by 16.67%.This increase in average earning may also be due to hiring of better skilled workers or overtime work for maintaining delivery schedules.

Problem 4. *A company's basic wage rate is ₹ 20 per hour and its overtime rates are:*

Evenings: Time and one-half.

Weekends: Double time.

During the previous year the following hours were worked:

Normal time 22,000 clock hours

Time plus one-half 2,000 clock hours

Double time 1,000 clock hours

The following times have been worked on these jobs:

Time	*Job A Clock hours*	*Job B Clock hours*	*Job C Clock hours*
Normal time	*300*	*500*	*400*
Evening time	*50*	*80*	*115*
Weekend overtime	*10*	*20*	*25*

You are required to calculate the labour cost chargeable to each job in each of the following circumstances:

(a) Where overtime is worked regularly throughout the year as company policy due to labour shortage.

(b) Where overtime is worked irregularly to meet the spasmodic production requirements.

(c) Where overtime is worked specifically at the customer's request to expedite delivery.

Solution :

	₹ per hour
Basic Rate	20
Evening overtime	30
Weekend overtime	40

Annual wages of previous year :

Details			Amount (₹)
Normal time	22,000 hrs. @ ₹20 per hr.	=	4,40,000
Evening time	2,000 hrs. @ ₹30 per hr.	=	60,000
Weekend overtime	1,000 hrs. @ ₹40 per hr.	=	40,000
Total	25,000 hrs		5,40,000

Average labour cost = ₹ 5,40,000 ÷ 25,000 hrs. = ₹ 21.60 per hour.

(a) In this case overtime becomes a part of the true labour cost:

			Amount (₹)
Job A	360 hrs. @ ₹21.60 per hr.	=	7,776
Job B	600 hrs. @ ₹21.60 per hr.	=	12,960
Job C	540 hrs. @ ₹21.60 per hr.	=	11,664
Total			32,400

(b) In this case all jobs would be charged at normal time- rate and overtime is treated as an item of production overhead:

Details			Amounr (₹)
Job A	360 hrs. @ ₹20.00 per hr.	=	7,200
Job B	600 hrs. @ ₹20.00 per hr.	=	12,000
Job C	540 hrs. @ ₹20.00 per hr.	=	10,800
Total			30,000

(c) In this case, the whole of overtime payments should be charged to the particular Jobs as follows:

			(₹)
Job A	300 hrs. @ ₹20.00 per hr.	=	6,000
	50 hrs. @ ₹30.00 per hr.	=	1,500
	10 hrs. @ ₹40.00 per hr.	=	400
Total			7,900
Job B	500 hrs. @ ₹20.00 per hr.	=	10,000
	80 hrs. @ ₹30.00 per hr.	=	2,400
	20 hrs. @ ₹40.00 per hr.	=	800
Total			13,200
Job C	400 hrs. @ ₹20.00 per hr.	=	8,000
	115 hrs. @ ₹30.00 per hr.	=	3,450
	25 hrs. @ ₹40.00 per hr.	=	1,000
Total			12,450

Problem 5. *Clinton Corporation has filed the following Income Statement for the year ended 31.3.2007:*

Details	*Amount* (₹)	*Amount* (₹)
Sales		*32, 00,000*
Less: variable costs :		
Material	*8,07,500*	
Direct labour	*5,59,000*	
Variable factory overhead	*4,80,000*	
Variable selling & distribution overhead	*1,91,000*	*20,37,500*
Contribution		*11,62,500*
Less: Fixed overhead		*6,62,500*
Net income before tax		*5,00,000*
Capital employed		*20,00,000*

The actual number of direct labour hours worked, in the year under review is 2, 07,000. As a consequence of delays in filling vacancies of employees who quit, 8,000 potential direct hours were not worked, and included in the actual hours worked were 5,000 hours of trainees, two-fifth time of which was unproductive. The costs incurred in consequence of re-employment were as follows: (a) separation costs ₹32,040; (b) Selection costs ₹ 40,160;(c) Recruitment costs ₹ 28,850; and (d) Training costs ₹ 38,950.

Calculate the profit lost or foregone on account of labour turnover (rounded off to the nearest rupee) and the potential return on capital and sales and turnover ratio.

Solution : **Statement showing contribution foregone**

	Hours
Actual hours worked	2,07,000
Less: unproductive training hours (40% of 5,000)	2,000
Actual productive hours	2,05,000
Potential labour hours not worked	8,000
Add: unproductive training hours	2,000
Effective labour hours lost	10,000

Contribution lost : [(11, 62,500 × 10,000) ÷ (2, 05,000)] ₹ 56,707

Savings in cost (₹)	
Separation costs	32,040
Selection costs	40,160
Recruitment costs	28,850
Training costs	38,950
	1,40,000

Statement of Profit foregone and other ratios

	Amount (₹)
Contribution lost	56,707
Savings in cost	1,40,000
Total profit foregone	1,96,707
Net profit before tax	5,00,000
Profit foregone	1,96,707
Potential profit	6,96,707
Actual sales	32,00,000
Sales foregone [(32, 00,000 × 10.000) ÷ (2, 05,000)]	1,56,098
Potential sales	33,56,098
Actual labour hours worked	2, 07,000
Labour hours lost	10,000
Potential labour hours	2,17,000
Potential Profit on capital employed (6, 96,707 ÷ 20, 00, 000)	34.84%
Potential Profit on Potential sales (6, 96,707÷ 33, 56,098)	20.76%
Turnover ratio: Labour hours lost / Potential labour hours = 10,000 ÷ 2,17,000	3.70%

(1) This question gives figures for replacement cost only and not preventive costs.

(2) Here, labour turnover ratio has been calculated on the basis of labour hours lost as number of separations or replacements has not been given.

Problem 6. *The management of Turnover Limited is worried about the increasing labour turnover in the factory and before analysing the causes and taking remedial steps; it wants to have an idea of the profit foregone due to labour turnover last year.*

Last year sales amounted to ₹ 12,07,5000 and the P/V ratio was 25%. The total number of actual hours worked by the direct labour force was 4.80 Lakhs. As a result of the delays by the Personnel department in filling vacancies due to labour turnover, 1,20,000 potentially productive hours were lost. The actual direct labour hours included 50,000 hours attributable to training new recruits, out of which forty percent of the hours were unproductive. The costs incurred consequent upon labour turnover revealed an analysis of the following:

Details	***Amount (₹)***
Settlement cost due to leaving	*62,500*
Recruitment costs	*36,750*
Selection costs	*22,750*
Training costs	*38,500*

Assuming that the potential production as a consequence of labour turnover could have sold at prevailing market prices, find the profit foregone last year on account of labour turnover.

Solution : Statement of Profit Foregone due to Labour Turnover

Details	Amount (₹)
Potential contribution foregone	7,87,500
Settlement cost due to leaving	62,500
Recruitment costs	36,750
Selection costs	22,750
Training costs	38,500
Profit foregone due to Labour turnover	9,48,000

Working Notes:

Actual hours worked	4,80,000
Less: Unproductive training hours (0.4 × 50,000)	(20,000)
Actual productive hours	4,60,000

Sales per productive hour = Sales/ Actual productive hours
= 120,75,000/4,60,000 = ₹ 26.25

Potential Total Productive hours lost	1,20,000
Sales value foregone = (26.25 × 1,20,000)	₹ 31,50,000

Potential contribution foregone: Sales foregone × P/V ratio
= 31,50,000 × 0.25 **₹ 7,87,500**

Problem 7. (Labour Turnover)

Compute the number of employees in the beginning and at the end of the year from the following information:

Labour turnover rate: 3%; Number of separations during the year: 12; Number of employees at the end were 100 in excess of employees in the beginning.

Solution :

$$\text{Labour Turnover Rate (Separation method)} = \frac{\text{Number of employees separated}}{\text{(Average number of employees on roll)}} \times 100$$

$$3 = (12 \div \text{Average number of employees on roll}) \times 100$$

$$3 \div 100 = 12 \div \text{Average number of employees on roll}$$

Average number of employees on roll = (12 ÷ 0.03) = 400

Average number of employees on roll =

$$\frac{\text{Employees at the beginning} + \text{Employees at the close}}{2}$$

$$\frac{BE + CE}{2} = 400$$

$$BE + CE = 800 \qquad \ldots(i)$$

$$CE - BE = 100 \qquad \ldots(ii)$$

Adding both the equations:

$$2CE = 900$$

$$CE = 900/2 = 450$$

$$BE = 450 - 100 = 350$$

Thus, the number of Employees at the Beginning is 350.

Problem 8. *Jobs are issued to operator X to make 186 units, and to operator Y to make 200 units for which a time allowance of 20 standard minutes and 15 standard minutes per unit respectively is credited. For every hour saved, bonus is paid at 50% of the base rate which is ₹ 20 per hour for both employees. The basic working week is 40 hours. Hours in excess are paid at double the time rate.*

X completes his units of work in 45 hours and Y completes his units of work in 38 hours (but works a full week). Due to defective materials, 6 units of X and 3 units of Y are subsequently scrapped, although all units produced are paid for.

You are required to calculate for each of X and Y:

(a) The amount of bonus payable;

(b) Total gross wages payable; and

(c) The wages cost per good unit made.

Solution :

Operator X

	Details	**Amount (₹)**
Basic wages	40 hours @ ₹ 20 per hour	800
Overtime	5 hours @ ₹ 40 per hour	200
		1,000
Bonus	186 units @ 20 min. per unit = 62 hours allowed	
	45 hours taken	
	17 hours saved @ ₹ 10 per hour	170
Gross wages payable		1,170

Good units produced (186 – 6) = 180 units

Wages cost of each good unit = ₹ 1170 ÷ 180

= ₹ 6.50 per unit

Operator Y

	Details	Amount (₹)
Basic wages	40 hours @ ₹ 20 per hour	800
Overtime	Nil	–
Bonus	200 units @ 15 min. per unit	
	= 50 hours allowed	
	38 hours taken	
	12 hours saved @ ₹ 10 per hour	120
Gross wages payable		920

Good units produced (200 – 3) = 197 units

Wages cost of each good unit = ₹ 920 ÷ 197 = ₹ 4.67 per unit.

Problem 9. *Given below is data relating to PV Limited for the month of May 2007.*

Details	*Amount (₹)*
Deduction for loan given to workers (staff advance)	*4,000*
Worker's contribution to Provident fund	*16,000*
Deduction for the use of canteen	*1,000*
Deduction for loan taken from Cooperative Credit and Thrift Society	*2,000*
Gross earnings of workers	*2,50,000*
Income tax	*6,000*
Worker's contribution to ESI (2%)	*5,000*
Employer's contribution to Provident fund (10%)	*25,000*
Employer's contribution to ESI (4%)	*10,000*
Time spent on manufacturing operations (80%)	–

Calculate (i) Total labour cost; (ii) Net wages payable;

Also journalise the entries in financial accounts and in cost accounts.

Solution : (i) Computation of Total labour Cost :

Details	Amount (₹)	Amount (₹)
(a) Gross earnings of workers		2,50,000
(b) Employer's contribution to ESI (4%)	10,000	
(c) Employer's contribution to Provident fund (10%)	25,000	
(d) Total i.e. (b) + (c)		35,000
Total labour cost		2,85,000

(ii) Computation of Net Wages Payable :

Details	Amount (₹)	Amount (₹)
Gross earnings of workers		2,50,000
Less: Deductions		
Loan recovery	4,000	
Worker's contribution to Provident fund	16,000	
Income tax	6,000	
Loan recovery by cooperative society	2,000	
Worker's contribution to ESI (2%)	5,000	
Canteen facility	1,000	
Total		34,000
Net wages payable		2,16,000

Journal Entries in Financial Books:

Date	Details	L.F.	V.N.	Debit Amount (₹)	Credit Amount (₹)
	Wages A/c Dr			2,85,000	
	To ESI A/c				15,000
	To Provident Fund A/c				41,000
	To Staff Advance A/c				4,000
	To Canteen Facility A/c				1,000
	To Income Tax A/c				6,000
	To Cooperative Credit and Thrift Society A/c				2,000
	To Wages Payable A/c				2,16,000
	(Being the gross wages due and net wages payable after making necessary deductions / recoveries)				
	ESI A/c Dr			15,000	
	Provident Fund A/c Dr			41,000	
	Income tax A/c Dr			6,000	
	Cooperative Credit and Thrift Society A/c Dr			2,000	
	Wages payable A/c Dr			2,16,000	
	To Bank A/c				2,80,000
	(Being the amount of payment to ESI, PF, Cooperative Society, Income tax and workers)				

Journal Entries in Cost Books:

Date	Details	L.F.	V.N.	Debit Amount (₹)	Credit Amount (₹)
	Wages Control A/c Dr To Cost Ledger Control A/c (Being the total labour cost accounted for in the cost ledger control A/c)			2,85,000	 2,85,000
	Factory Overhead Ledger Control A/c Dr Work in Progress Ledger Control A/c Dr To Wages Control A/c (Being the charging of wages to Factory Overheads and Work in Progress A/c)			57,000 2,28,000	 2,85,000

Problem 10. (Labour Turnover)

XYZ CO. Ltd. furnishes you with the following data:

Number of workers on the payroll at the beginning of the month 2,000

Number of workers on the payroll at the end of the month 2,340

During the month, 100 workers were discharged and 160 workers left the organization. The firm recruited 400 workers out of which 100 workers were taken in place of those who had left and the balance were assigned to the firm's expansion project.

You are required to compute labour turnover using (i) Accession method; (ii) Separation method; (iii) Replacement method; and (iv) Flux method

Solution : Working Notes:

Average number of employees on roll

$$= \frac{\text{No. at the end of period + No. at the beginning of the period}}{2}$$

$$= \frac{2{,}340 + 2{,}000}{2}$$

$$= 4{,}340/2 = 2{,}170$$

(i) Labour turnover rate (Accession method)

$$= \frac{\text{Number of Accessions during the period}}{\text{Average number of employees on roll}} \times 100$$

Accessions = No. at the end of period – No. at the beginning of the Period + No. that left during the period

= 2,340 – 2,000 + 260

= 600 No.

$\therefore$ Labour Turnover $= (600 \div 2{,}170) \times 100$

$= 27.65\%$

(ii) Labour turnover rate (Separation method)

$$= \frac{\text{Number of employees separated}}{\text{Average number of employees on roll}} \times 100$$

$= (260 \div 2{,}170) \times 100$

$= 11.98\%$

(iii) Labour turnover rate (Replacement method)

$$= \frac{\text{Number of employees replaced}}{\text{Average number of employees on roll}} \times 100$$

$= (100 \div 2{,}170) \times 100$

$= 4.61\%$

(iv) Labour turnover rate (Flux method)

$$= \frac{\text{Number of separations + No. of accessions}}{\text{Average number of employees on roll}} \times 100$$

$= (260 - 600 \div 2{,}170) \times 100$

$= (860 \div 2{,}170) \times 100$

$= 39.63\%$

Problem 11. (Labour Turnover)

From the following data calculate monthly labour turnover rate by

(i) Separation method; (ii) Replacement method; and (iii) Flux method

Number of workers on the payroll:

At the beginning of the month 700 and at the end of the month 800.

During the month, 10 workers left, 30 were discharged and 140 were recruited. Of those recruited 10 were replacements due to expansion.

[B.Com (Hons.) DU, 2007]

Solution : Working Notes:

Average number of workers on roll

$$= \frac{\text{No. at the end of period + No. at the beginning of the period}}{2}$$

$$= \frac{(700 + 800)}{2}$$

$= 1{,}500 \div 2 = 750$

(i) Labour turnover rate (Separation method)

$$= \frac{\text{Number of employees separated}}{\text{Average number of employees on roll}} \times 100$$

Number of employees separated : $10 + 30 = 40$

$= (40 \div 750) \times 100$

$= 5.33\%$

(ii) Labour turnover rate (Replacement method)

$$= \frac{\text{Number of employees replaced}}{\text{Average number of employees on roll}} \times 100$$

Number of employees replaced : 140 – 10 = 130

$$= (130 \div 750) \times 100$$
$$= 17.33\%$$

(iii) Labour turnover rate (Flux method)

$$= \frac{\text{Number of separations + No. of replacements}}{\text{Average number of employees on roll}} \times 100$$

$$= \frac{40 + 130}{750} \times 100$$
$$= (170 \div 750) \times 100$$
$$= 22.67\%$$

Problem 12. *Following are the particulars for April, 2008 relating to four employees working in Department 'D' of a factory, exclusively for Job No. 313:*

Name	*Designation*	*Wages (₹)*	*Frequency*
Ram	*Foreman*	*20,000*	*Per month*
Mohan	*Mechanic*	*300*	*Per day*
Krishna	*Operator*	*250*	*Per day*
Hari	*Workman*	*200*	*Per day*

The normal working hours per week of six days are 48 or 8 hours per day. Sundays are paid holidays. (There were no other holidays during the month).

Provident fund contribution was 10% of monthly wages by employee.

Provident fund contribution was 10% of monthly wages by employer.

Employee State Insurance contribution was 4% of monthly wages by employee and 6% of monthly wages by employer.

From the foregoing data, calculate:

1. *Net wages payable by the employer for the said month.*
2. *The total amount of provident fund contribution to be deposited by the employer.*
3. *The total amount of Employee State Insurance contribution to be deposited by the employer.*
4. *Total labour cost to the employer for the month of April,2008 chargeable to the Job No. 313;*
5. *The total cost of the Job requiring materials valued at ₹ 30,200 and Overhead at 60% of Prime cost.*

Solution : (Point-Wise):

Point No. 1: Computation of Net Wages Payable for the Month of April, 2008

Name	Designation	Calculation work	Wages (₹)
Ram	Foreman	20,000 × 1	20,000
Mohan	Mechanic	300 × 30	9,000
Krishna	Operator	250 × 30	7,500
Hari	Workman	200 × 30	6,000
Total	Gross		42,500
Less:	Deductions_	42,500 × 0.1 = 4,250	5,950
	Provident Fund (Employee's share)	42,500 × 0.04 = 1,700	
	ESI Contribution (Employee's share)		
	Net Wages Payable		36,550

Point No. 2: The total amount of provident fund contribution to be deposited by the employer:

Details	**Amount** (₹)
Employer's Share of Provident Fund (42,500 × 0.1)	4,250
Employee's Share of Provident Fund (42,500 × 0.1)	4,250
Total amount to be deposited by the Employer	8,500

Point No. 3: The total amount of Employee State Insurance contribution to be deposited by the employer:

Details	**Amount** (₹)
Employer's Share of E S I Contribution (42,500 × 0.06)	2,550
Employee's Share of E S I Contribution (42,500 × 0.04)	1,700
Total amount to be deposited by the Employer	4,250

Point No. 4: Total labour cost to the employer for the month of April, 2008 chargeable to the Job No. 313:

Details		**Amount** (₹)
Total Gross Wages		42,500
Add: Employer's Share of Provident Fund	4,250	
Employer's Share of E S I Contribution	2,550	
		6,800
Total Labour cost to Employer		49,300

Point No. 5: The total cost of the Job:

Details		**Amount** (₹)
Material	30,200	
Labour	49,300	
Prime cost		79,500
Overhead cost (79,500 × 0.6)		47,700
Total cost of the Job		1,27,200

Problem 13. *'X', an employee of ABC Co. gets the following emoluments and benefits:*

Details	*Monthly Amount (₹)/ (%)*
Basic Pay	*1000*
Dearness allowance	*200*
Bonus	*20% of Salary and D.A.*
Other allowances	*250*
Employee's contribution to P.F.	*10% of Salary and D.A.*

'X' works for 2400 hours per annum, out of which 400 hours are non-productive and treated as normal idle time. Find out the effective hourly cost of employee 'X'. **[DU, B.Com (Hons.) 2008]**

Solution :

Details	**Amount (₹) (p.a.)**
Basic Pay (1,000 × 12)	12,000
Dearness allowance (200 × 12)	2,400
Bonus [0.2 × (12,000 + 2,400)]	2,880
Other allowances (250 × 12)	3,000
Total	20,280

Normal hours = Total Working Hours – Idle Time

= 2,400 – 400 = 2,000

Effective hourly cost = 20,280 ÷ 2,000

= ₹ 10.14

Problem 14. *A worker is paid ₹ 25 per hour and the 6 days working week contains 48 hours. The daily allowance of approved absence from his place of work, maintenance of machine etc. is 15 minutes and his job card shows that his time chargeable during the week to various jobs is as follows:*

Job No. 810	*22 hours*
Job No. 815	*12 hours*
Job No. 830	*10 hours*

The unaccounted time is caused by a power failure. Show how his wages for the week would be dealt with in cost accounts.

Solution : Computation of Wages:

Wages payable for Six Days:

= 48 × 25 = ₹ 1,200.

Allocation:

Details	Amount (₹)
Chargeable to Job No. 810: (22 hours @ ₹ 25 per hour)	550.00
Chargeable to Job No. 810: (12 hours @ ₹ 25 per hour)	300.00
Chargeable to Job No. 810: (10 hours @ ₹ 25 per hour)	250.00
Normal Idle time (1.5 hours @ ₹ 25 per hour)	37.50
Abnormal Idle Time (Power failure) (2.5 hours @ ₹ 25 per hour)	62.50
Charged to Profit and Loss Account	
Total	1,200.00

Problem 15. (Suggestion box scheme)

A company uses an old method of machining a Component manufactured for sale. The estimates of operating details for the year 2010-11 are as under:

Number of Components to be manufactured and sold: 50,000

Raw materials required per component: 5 Kg. @ ₹ 16 per kg.

Average wage rate per worker: ₹ 240 per day of 8 hours

Average Labour efficiency: 80%

Standard time required to manufacture one component: 2.5 hours

Overhead Rate: ₹ 25 per clock Hour

Material handling expenses: 2.5% of the value of materials

The company has a suggestion box scheme and an award equivalent to four months' saving in labour cost is passed on to the employee whose suggestion is accepted. In response to this scheme, a suggestion has been received from an employee Mr. Krishnan to use a special Tool: T in the manufacture of the aforesaid component. The cost of the tool which has a life of one year is ₹ 35,000 and the use of the component will reduce the standard time by 15 minutes.

You are required to:

1. *Compute the amount of award payable to Mr. Krishnan whose suggestion has been accepted by the management.*
2. *Prepare a statement showing the annual cost of production before and after the implementation of the suggestion to use the Tool: T and find out the annual savings.*
3. *State the assumptions on which your calculations are based.*

Solution : Computation of the Amount of Award to Mr. Krishnan, an employee:

Wage rate per hour (240÷8)	₹ 30
Standard time required for one component	2.5 hours
Standard time required for 50,000 components (50,000 × 2.5)	1,25,000 hours

Average Labour efficiency	80%
Actual time (1,25,000÷0.8)	1,56,250 hours
Actual Labour cost (1,56,250 × 30)	₹ 46,87,500
Standard time required for one component	2.5 hours
Less: Saving in Standard time	15 minutes
Revised standard time required for one component	2.25 hours
Adjusted to 80% Efficiency	2.25 ÷ 0.8 = 2.8125 hours
Revised actual time (50,000× 2.8125)	1,40,625 hours
Revised Wages (1,40,625 × 30)	₹ 42,18,750
Annual savings in Wages (46,87,500 – 42,18,750)	₹ 4,68,750
Amount of award to the Employee Mr. Krishnan {4,68,750 × (4/12)}	₹ 1,56,250

Statement showing annual cost of production of 50,000 components

Details	Before Implementation (₹)	After Implementation (₹)
Raw Material (50,000 × 80)	40,00,000	40,00,000
Direct Wages @ ₹ 30 per hour	46,87,500	42,18,750
Prime cost	86,87,500	82,18,750
Overhead @ ₹ 25 per hour	39,06,250	35,15,625
Material handling (40,00,000 × 0.025)	1,00,000	1,00,000
Cost of Tool: T	NIL	35,000
Total cost	126,93,750	118,69,375
Gross savings in cost		8,24,375
Less: Award		1,56,250
Net Annual Savings		6,68,125

Assumptions:

1. No change in efficiency level.
2. Labour hours saved and surplus capacity created is being utilized profitably for other jobs.

OBJECTIVE TYPE EXERCISES

I. Fill in the blank spaces with suitable word/s :

1. Preventive cost and Replacement costs have .... relationship.
2. Job card is .... meant to record the attendance of the workers.
3. Abnormal idle time wages are .... in the cost of production.

4. Another term used for Time and Motion study is ....
5. One measure of reducing labour turnover is to ....
6. Two unavoidable reasons for idle time are .... and ....
7. Recording of arrival and departure time of workers is known as ....
8. Two basic forms used in accounting for labour costs are ....
9. The workers who are sent to sites or customers' premises for performing work are known as ....
10. Idle time arises only when workers are paid on .... basis.
11. .... is a process of recording the time spent by workers on different jobs.
12. Cost of normal idle time is charged to ....
13. The labour cost which can be identified with and allocated to cost centres or cost units is known as ....
14. .... is the rate of change in the labour force of an organisation.
15. An example of a variable labour cost is ...., of a fixed labour cost ...., and of a semi-variable labour cost is ....
16. Wages of a .... is an example of direct wages.

Answers :

1. inverse **2.** NOT
3. excluded **4.** work study
5. improve working conditions
6. time spent in machine maintenance and time which necessarily elapses between completion of one job and the start of the next job
7. time keeping **8.** time card and job card
9. out-workers **10.** time
11. time booking **12.** works overhead
13. direct labour cost **14.** Labour turnover
15. wages of machine operator, salary of works manager, salary of supervisor
16. machine operator

II. Indicate whether the following statements are True or False :

1. Overtime premium paid to all factory workers is usually considered direct labour. **[DU, B.Com (Hons.) 1999]**
2. Direct wages is a fixed cost.
3. Labour cost includes employer's contribution to Provident fund and Employees' state Insurance.
4. Cost to the employer of perquisites provided to the employees is part of labour cost.
5. Flux method of measuring labour turnover is the best method.
6. Indirect labour costs are not charged to output.
7. High labour turnover usually increases the labour cost.
8. Per unit direct labour cost can be used as an indicator of efficiency.

9. Existence of dummy workers reduces the labour cost.
10. Low wage rate will always lead to lower per unit labour cost.
11. Preventive costs and replacement costs have inverse relationship.
12. Job card is meant to record the attendance of the workers.
13. Labour cost card is the same thing as Job card.
14. Abnormal idle time wages are excluded in the cost of production.
15. Workers are remunerated according to time under piece wage system.
16. Time booking is not necessary when time keeping is accomplished.
17. Time keeping facilitates the preparation of payroll.
18. When time-cum-job card is maintained there is no need of keeping a separate time card.
19. Job evaluation is the comparative appraisal of workers on different jobs.
20. Cost of idle time due to labour strike should be treated as an item of factory overheads.
21. Direct wages is a variable cost.
22. When overtime arises due to general pressure of work, overtime premium should be charged to overhead.
23. Personnel department is responsible for computation and payment of wages of workers.
24. Job card is used for time keeping.
25. Salary paid to factory supervisor is indirect wages.

Answers :

1. True	**2.** False	**3.** False	**4.** True
5. False	**6.** False	**7.** True	**8.** True
9. False	**10.** False	**11.** True	**12.** False
13. False	**14.** True	**15.** False	**16.** False
17. True	**18.** True	**19.** False	**20.** False
21. True	**22.** True	**23.** False	**24.** Fasle
25. True			

THEORETICAL EXERCISES

1. What is meant by 'Idle Time' and state how it is treated in Cost Accounting?
2. How are the payments to workers in respect of the 'Over time' work and the 'set up' time treated in cost accounts? Explain.
3. What do you understand by labour turnover? How is it measured? What are its causes? What remedial steps would you suggest to minimize its occurrence?
5. Distinguish between normal and abnormal idle time. How would you deal with them in cost accounts?

6. What is idle time? Explain the causes leading to idle time and its treatment in cost accounts. Distinguish it from idle capacity.

7. For each of the payroll costs given below, state the accounting treatment that you would recommend, giving your reason:
   (a) Idle time in the finishing department because the assembly department delayed its production.
   (b) Overtime resulting from a customer saying, "I want this job done in a week, and if you have to work overtime, I do not mind".
   (c) Labour time involved in reworking five units out of a batch of fifty, on a process where 10% of the completed units are expected to be defective.

[DU, B.Com (Hons.) 2002]

8. How will you treat the following in Cost Accounts?
   (i) Learner's or apprentice wages
   (ii) Employer's contribution to ESI

9. How are payments to workers in respect of overtime work and 'set-up' time treated in Cost Accounting? **[B.Com (Hons.), DU, 1997]**

10. What is idle time? Explain the causes leading to idle time and its treatment in cost accounts. **[B.Com (Hons.), DU, 1998]**

11. Distinguish between the followings:
   (i) Job Evaluation and Merit Rating **[DU, B.Com (Hons.) 2001]**
   (ii) Overtime work and set up time
   (iii) Casual workers and Outworkers

12. Explain in brief the following concepts:
   (i) Job Ticket **[DU, B.Com (Hons.) 2001]**
   (ii) Time Booking
   (iii) Time Card

NUMERICAL EXERCISES

1. An Analysis of the Time-Card of Mr. Krishan Lal , a worker on one of the machines in the Workshop, shows that of the total 48 hours ,he worked 45 hours(including 4hours overtime) on production and that there was 3 hours idle time due to power failure.

   The time rate of the worker is ₹ 10 per hour but overtime is paid 50% extra.

   You are required to allocate the total wages paid to Mr. Krishan Lal between 'direct' and 'indirect' labour.

[Ans. Direct Labour cost ₹ 450; Indirect Labour cost ₹ 20; Abnormal Loss ₹ 30]

2. Find out what an average worker costs the employer for a month of 208 hours, assuming 8 hours a day, from the followings:

Average Basic wage per hour	₹ 60
Average D.A. per hour	₹ 20

   Employer's contribution to Provident fund: (@ 8% of Basic wage and D.A.)

Employer's contribution to Employees State Insurance : (@ 2% of Basic wage and D.A.)

Other amenities per month	₹ 440
Number of other unpaid holidays (Festivals) in a year	3
Number of unpaid holidays in a year	24
Number of days on sick leave with half pay in a year	15

[Ans. ₹ 17000]

3. Calculate the earnings of workers W-1 and W-2 from the following details for a month and allocate the earnings of each to Jobs J-1 and J-2 and J-3.

Details	W-1	W-2
Basic Wage	24000	24000
Dearness Allowance	50%	55%
Provident Fund (on Basic wages)	8%	8%
ESI (on Basic Wages)	2%	2%
Overtime (hour)	10	———
Idle Time and Leave (hour)	———	16

The normal working hours for the month are 200. Overtime is paid at double the normal rate plus D.A. Employees' contribution to ESI and PF are at equal rates with the employer's contributions. The month has 25 working days of eight hours each and one paid holiday.

The two workers were engaged on jobs in the following proportions.

Worker	J-1	J-2	J-3
W-1	40	30	30
W-2	50	20	30

Overtime was done on J-2. **[Ans. J-1:₹ —, J-2: ₹ ——, and J-3: ₹ —]**

4. The management of Turnover Limited is worried about the increasing labour turnover in the factory and before analysing the causes and taking remedial steps; it wants to have an idea of the profit foregone due to labour turnover last year.

Last year sales amounted to ₹ 8303300and the P/V ratio was 20%. The total number of actual hours worked by the direct labour force was 4.45 Lakhs. As a result of the delays by the Personnel department in filling vacancies due to labour turnover, 100000 potentially productive hours were lost. The actual direct labour hours included 30000 hours attributable to training new recruits, out of which half of the hours were unproductive. The costs incurred consequent upon labour turnover revealed an analysis of the following:

Details	Amount (₹)
Settlement cost due to leaving	43820
Recruitment costs	26740
Selection costs	12750
Training costs	30490

Assuming that the potential production as a consequence of labour turnover could have sold at prevailing market prices, find the profit foregone last year on account of labour turnover. **[Ans. ₹ 500000]**

5. A worker is paid 50 Paise per hour and the 5 days working week contains 42 hours. The daily allowance of approved absence from his place of work, maintenance of machine etc. is 12 minutes and his job card shows that his time chargeable during the week to various jobs is as follows:

Job No. 305	20 hours
Job No. 310	10 hours
Job No. 320	8 hours

The unaccounted time is caused by a power failure. Show how his wages for the week would be dealt with in cost accounts. **[DU, B.Com (Hons.) 2003]**

[Ans. Chargeable to Job No. 305: ₹ 10.00; Job No. 310: ₹. 5.00; Job No. 320: ₹ 4.00; Normal Idle Time: ₹ 0.50; and Abnormal Idle Time: ₹ 1.50]

6. PV Limited provides the following information for its factory working six days in a week:

(1)	Hours as per Time card	48
(2)	Hours booked to jobs as per job card	36
(3)	Daily allowance for Lunch, Personal Needs, fatigue and Maintenance of machine	40 (Minutes)
(4)	Wage Rate (₹)	20 per hour

(5) The time not booked was due break down of machinery, power failure, waiting for jobs, Materials and tools.

Required: How would you deal with the wage in cost account?

[B.Com DU, 2008]

[Ans. Chargeable to Jobs: ₹ 720; Chargeable to Factory Overheads (Normal Idle Time): ₹ 80; Chargeable to Costing Profit and Loss A/c (Abnormal Idle Time): ₹ 160]

❑❑❑

8

Pay Roll Accounting

Learning Objectives

It attempts to explain the payroll accounting. In this chapter you will learn :

1. Meaning and nature of payroll accounting.
2. Systems of payment of wages :
   (i) Time wage system
   (ii) Piece wage system : (a) Individual, (b) Group
3. Premium payment :
   (i) Overtime
   (ii) Shift premium
   (iii) Bonus
4. Accounting treatment of vacation and holiday pay
5. Incentive systems of wage payment :
   (i) Premium bonus system
   (ii) Differential piece work
   (iii) Combination of time and piece work
6. Group system of wage payment
7. Incentive schemes for indirect workers
8. Profit sharing and co-partnership

PAY-ROLL ACCOUNTING

Meaning Pay-Roll Accounting

Pay-Roll Accounting is that part of financial accounting which is concerned with the computation of gross wages and deductions from gross wages with a view to ascertain net wages payable to each employee during a particular period; and The preparation of Pay roll (or Wage Sheet) and Pay slip at periodic intervals, say weekly or monthly.

Meaning of Pay roll (or Wage Sheet)

Pay Roll is a periodic statement which entails:

(a) Gross wages earned by each worker: It is the sum of the components of wages which are (a) Basic Pay/Wages; (b) Dearness allowance; (c) House rent allowance; (d) City compensatory Allowance; (e) Traveling Allowance; (f) Overtime allowance ;(g) Overtime Premium and (h) Other allowances

(b) Deductions from Gross wages: It is the sum of deductions on account of (a) Provident Fund contribution; (b) Employees state Insurance Premium; (c) Fines; (d) Income tax; (e) recovery of advance, and (f) other deductions; and

(c) Net wages payable to each worker: It is the balance of Gross wages and Deductions i.e. Total deductions are deducted from the gross wages. Thus,

$$\text{Net Wages} = \text{Gross Wages} - \text{Deductions}$$

Alternative I :

Pay Roll / Wage Sheet

Department .... Week / Month ending ....

Profile			Components of Wages							
EmpId Name	Worked	Rate (₹)	Basic wages (₹)	Over-time allo-wance (₹)	Dear-ness allo-wance (₹)	House rent allo-wance (₹)	Trave-lling allo-wance (₹)	Bonus (₹)	Other allo-wance (₹)	Gross pay (₹)

Alternative II :

Wage Sheet

S. No.	Worker's ID	Worker's Name	Total Hours Wor-ked	Regu-lar Hours	Over-time hours	Bonus	DA	HRA	Gross Wage	Deductions ITax	PF	ESI	Others	Total	Net Wage
	Total														

Pay-Roll Assistant .... Checked by .... Authorised by ....

Format of Pay Slip

EmpId .... Department ....

Employee Name .... Wage Period ....

Details	Amount (₹)
Components of Wages:	
Basic Wages	
Overtime Premium	
Dearness Allowance	
House Rent allowance	
City compensatory Allowance	
Leave Pay	
Holiday Pay	
Other Allowances	
Gross Wages	
Deductions:	
P F Contribution	
E S I Contribution	
Income Tax	
Recovery of Loan/Advance	
Other deductions	
Total Deductions	
Net Wages Due	

WAGE STRUCTURE

An ideal wage structure should promote quantity and quality of output, improve employees' satisfaction and human relations, attract talent and maintain per unit labour cost at competitive levels. Three types of wage structures are in vogue: Time wage, Piece wage and various variants of these in the form of incentive plans.

Time Wage System

Workers are paid according to time spent at work place. They are paid on hourly, daily, weekly or monthly basis. The output of the worker during the period is not considered at the time of wage payment. There are five types of time wage systems. They differ only in respect of fixation of time rate. They are:

1. Flat Time Rate
2. High Day Rate
3. Measured Work Day Rate
4. Indexed Time Rate
5. Differential Time Rate

(1) Flat Time Rate

It is also known as Ordinary Time Rate. All workers of a particular grade and skill in a factory are paid wages at equal time rate. This time rate is ascertained keeping in view the average payment made in the industry in the same locality to the workers of same grade and skill. Flat time rate may be somewhat higher/lower than the industry average in view of special circumstances (including capacity to pay) of the organization.

Advantages:

- It is simple to understand and operate. Both the employer and the employee can easily calculate the periodic wage.
- It provides for assured wages to the employees.
- Quality of product is usually maintained because workers need not hurry through production.
- It facilitates Cash planning by the employer.
- Maintenance of elaborate employee-wise records of production is not required.

Disadvantages:

- Both efficient and inefficient workers are paid at the same rate. It implies that there is no inducement for better work performance. It demotivates the efficient and performing workers.
- Workers tend to work slowly during regular time so that employers are forced to make workers work overtime at a higher time wage rate.
- Strict supervision is necessary to get work done. It raises the supervisory cost.
- Workers are paid even for idle time. It stimulates laziness amongst workers.
- Perpetuation of laziness and inefficiency leads to delays in work schedules.

Suitability: The method is quite suitable if it entails

- Payment to highly professionalized and skilled workers.
- Payment to totally unskilled workers/ apprentices.
- Control of quality and speed of work by machines.
- Close supervision of workers.
- Quality of work being more important than quantity of work.
- Work of artistic importance and requires human ingenuity.
- Non-measurement of output of the employees such as workers working on repairs and maintenance, factory cleaning, and security staff etc.
- Frequent power failures, machine break downs, etc.

(2) High Day Rate

In order to attract efficient and motivated workers they may be paid a time rate higher than the industry average. This well paid workforce is required to achieve pre-determined standards of performance during regular working hours. Normally, overtime is not permissible.

(3) Measured Work Day Rate

The level of performance expected from different workers is pre-fixed by the employer. The daily or monthly wage rate is fixed in tune with the expected level of performance which the worker is required to achieve. It means higher wage rate is paid to workers with higher level of performance as an incentive for higher standards of performance.

(4) Indexed Time Rate

It is to ensure that the real wage of workers is not affected by inflation. The time rate of workers is indexed with cost of living index. Periodic wage increases due to increase in inflation.

(5) Differential Time Rate

Workers are paid different time rates according to their comparative ability, skill and speed. Efficient workers belonging to the same group are paid at a higher rate and less efficient workers are paid at a lower rate. It makes merit rating of workers necessary. Thus, the efficiency is rewarded and there is an in-built incentive to improve skills and achieve better performance.

Piece Wage System

Wages are paid at a fixed rate per unit of output. Wages are ascertained on the basis of work done without any regard to the time spent by the workers in the factory. The payment on the basis of units produced may be made at the end of each day, week, or a month. Piece wage system may be put into operation in the following manner:

1. Individual Piece work wage
2. Group Piece work wage
3. Balance of Debt System
4. Piece Rate with Guaranteed Time Rate

(1) Individual Piece Work Wage

This system involves payment of wages according predetermined rate per unit of output/ operation/ job performed by a worker.

(2) Group Piece Work Wage

This system involves payment of wages to a pre-arranged group of workers as a whole for the number of units produced or operations performed or job completed by the group. Group earnings are then shared amongst the group members on some mutually agreed criteria. Number of hours devoted by individual workers on group production may be one of the criteria. This system requires group effort and team spirit.

(3) Balance of Debt System

It ensures minimum time wage with a clause to recover the short-working. The worker is primarily paid on the basis of individual piece rate per unit of output / operation/ job performed. However, If in a particular payment period the wages due to him are less than the stipulated minimum time wage, he is paid a minimum time wage for that period subject to the condition that such excess payment will be recovered from his piece rate wages in the subsequent period.

(4) Piece Rate with Guaranteed Time Rate

It ensures minimum time wage with no clause to recover the short-working. The worker gets a pre-determined time wage or wage computed on piece rate basis, which ever is higher. There is no obligation to get such extra wage adjusted in future. Thus, a minimum time wage is always guaranteed to the worker with no regard to output. This system is far superior and it ensures higher safety to the worker without sacrificing the incentive to improve and perform better for higher wage.

Advantages of Piece Rate System: The system accrues the under mentioned advantages:

1. Incentive for better performance is ensured. An efficient worker is enabled to earn more than an ordinary worker.
2. Because of the in-built incentive for higher output per worker, it results in lower overhead cost per unit of output. Thus, there is higher margin of profit for the employer.
3. There is no idle time payment. This encourages workers to minimize idle time. The output increases and consequently the overhead costs come down.
4. Workers use tools and machinery carefully and try to minimize machine break-down and production interruptions as they aim at maximizing output.
5. As the workers remain self-motivated to produce more, supervision costs get reduced.
6. Workers have high motivation to suggest improvements in plant layout, machinery, technology and methods of production.

Disadvantages: The following are the main disadvantages of the Piece rate system of Wages:

1. Workers may increase the output at the cost of quality.

2. Slower workers get frustrated.
3. When piece workers are not physically fit to work, they are not able to earn wages. It has an in-built device for non-payment of wages on the norm' NO work, No payment'.
4. Workers may not care about wastage of materials, and consequently Input-Output ratio tends to decline.
5. Over speeding of machinery and its careless handling may increase repairs and maintenance cost.
6. Mishandling of materials and machinery will definitely lead to higher unit cost of output.
7. Low piece rate frustrates employees and a high piece rate increases cost of production. Fixation of fair and equitable rate for different products or operation and jobs is very tedious and it requires thorough in-depth study of tediousness, risk, skill and time required for different jobs.
8. Employers have a tendency to reduce piece rate if they find that employees have significantly improved upon their work efficiency; this results in exploitation of the workforce.

Suitability: Under the following conditions the method is applicable:

1. It is convenient to determine fair and equitable piece rate for each product, operation or job.
2. Work is of repetitive nature and output is standardized.
3. Quantity of output can be easily measured.
4. Quality of output can be controlled.
5. There is uninterrupted supply of materials, tools, power and other inputs.
6. Mishandling of materials and machinery, and other facilities can be controlled on regular basis.
7. Strict discipline on all workers can be enforced.
8. For outworkers the method is quite suitable.

Overtime Premium and Shift Premium

Work done beyond the regular or normal working hours is called overtime. Under the Factories Act, 1948 normal working is limited to nine hours in a day and 48 hours in a week. If a worker is asked to work more than this he is to paid at double the normal rate. Additional amount paid on account of overtime is called overtime premium.

Treatment of Overtime Premium

The treatment in costing books depends on the nature of work and the circumstances of occurrence of overtime, which can be as under:

1. *Indirect Labour:* Workers working overtime are performing indirect labour not identifiable with a particular cost unit; the entire overtime premium should be debited to Factory overheads.
2. *Abnormal Factors:* It should be debited to costing Profit & Loss Account.
3. *Very Occasional:* It is very small in magnitude and results occasionally, the overtime premium should be debited to Factory overheads.
4. *Special Job:* The special job necessitates overtime working. The entire overtime premium must be charged to that special job disregarding the working hours.
5. *Regular feature:* It should be distributed over total hours worked i.e. the entire wage rate should be grossed up. All units produced, whether during normal hours or during overtime should be charged uniformly at the grossed up rate.

Treatment of Night-Shift Premium

Sometimes workers are required to work night-shift for which they are paid extra amount in the form of night shift allowance. Such night shift allowance is to be treated in the same way as overtime payment.

Illustrations 8.1. (Overtime premium and Shift premium)

Alpha Bakers has eight bakers and a bakery supervisor on each of its two shifts. Bakers working from 8a.m. –5p.m. (with a 1-hour break) are paid ₹ 25/- per hour. Bakers working the 9p.m.-6a.m. shift (with a 1-hour break) are paid ₹ 30/- per hour. The supervisors are paid a salary of ₹ 2000/- per week. Due to the large volume of business, two of the daytime bakers worked until 8p.m. three evenings this week; they both received time and three-fifth for the extra hours worked. Prepare journal entries to distribute the weekly payroll.

Solution :

Day Shift Wages: ₹ 25 per hour × 48 hours per week = ₹ 1,200 per week for each worker 8 bakers × ₹ 1,200 per week = ₹ 9,600 per week for all bakers (direct labour).

Overtime:

(₹ 25 per hour × 3 hours per evening) × 2 bakers = ₹ 150 per evening

For three evenings = 150 × 3 = ₹ 450 (Direct labour)

Overtime premium:

(₹ 15 × 3 hours per evening) × 2 bakers = ₹ 90 per evening

For three evenings = 90 × 3 = 270 (overtime premium)

Night Shift Wages: ₹ 25 per hour × 48 hours per week = ₹ 1,200 per week for each worker 8 bakers × ₹ 1,200 per week = ₹ 9,600 per week for all bakers (direct labour).

Shift premium: ₹ 5 per hour × 48 hours per week = ₹ 240 per week for each worker 8 bakers × ₹ 240 per week = ₹ 1,920 per week for all bakers (Shift premium).

Supervisors: ₹ 2,000/- per week × 2 supervisors = ₹ 4,000 per week for both supervisors (Indirect labour).

Distribution:

Cost	Days (₹)	Nights (₹)	Total (₹)
Direct Labour	(9,600 + 450) = 10,450	9,600	19,650
Overtime premium	270		270
Shift premium		1,920	1,920
Indirect Labour	4,000		4,000

Journal Entry

Date	Details		L.F.	Amount (₹)	Amount (₹)
	Work-in-Process Inventory	Dr		19,650	
	Factory Overhead Control	Dr		6,190	
	To Payroll Payable				25,840

Shift premium, overtime premium and indirect labour are all elements of factory overhead. Under a perpetual system, these are all posted to one control account, which is a master balance for a subsidiary ledger.

Bonus

A bonus is an additional compensation generally given in recognition of exceptional productivity. Bonus may be a set amount or a percentage of profits, or a percentage of an employees' salary. Strictly stating, a bonus is a direct cost of production. However, because the purpose of cost accumulation is the establishment of a standard cost unit, bonuses are usually charged to factory overhead. A bonus should be charged to a liability each week/month (i.e. period of normal mode of remuneration) the eligible employee works. In practice this can be rarely done, so a single entry at the end of the period is preferred.

Illustrations 8.2. (Bonus)

Every employee of Shorts Ltd. is entitled to receive a bonus of 1.25% of the Company's preceding year's profits. Record the monthly payroll of one casting-line employee. Also find the accrual of the bonus, if monthly pay is ₹ six thousand. Assume that the profits for the preceding year were ₹ 9,36,000.

The Journal Entry is :

Date	Details		L.F.	Amount (₹)	Amount (₹)
	Work-in-Process Inventory	Dr		6,000	
	Factory Overhead Control (Bonus) A/c	Dr		975	
	To Bonus Payable A/c				975
	To Payroll Payable A/c				6,000

Note: (9,36,000 × 0.0125 = 11,700; > 11,700/12 = ₹ 975)

Illustrations 8.3. (Balance of Debt system)

From the following details compute the amount of wages payable to a worker Ms. Jones for each of the five days of the week based on 'Balance of Debt system':

Standard Rate per Hour	*₹ 40*
Standard Piece rate	*₹ 55*
Hours of work in a day	*8 hours*

Ms. Jones produced 4 pieces on the first day, 5 pieces on the second day, and 8 pieces on following three days.

Solution : Computation of Wages payable on Day basis

First Day:

Wages based on piece rate 4 × 55 = ₹ 220

Wages based on time rate 8 × 40 = ₹ 320

As the time wage is higher, she will be paid time wage of ₹ 320. The excess Payment of ₹ 100 (i.e. 320 – 220) will be recovered form subsequent wages of Ms. Jones.

Second Day:

Wages based on piece rate 5 × 55 = ₹ 275

Wages based on time rate 8 × 40 = ₹ 320

As the time wage is higher, she will be paid time wage of ₹ 320. The excess Payment of ₹ 45 (i.e. 320 – 275) will be recovered form subsequent wages of Ms. Jones.

Third Day:

Wages based on piece rate 8 × 55 = ₹ 440

Wages based on time rate 8 × 40 = ₹ 320

As the Piece wage is higher, she will be paid piece wage of ₹ 440 but a deduction of ₹ 120 (i.e. 100 + 20) will be made for excess payment on the first and second day. Thus the net payment on the third day is ₹ 320 (i.e. 440 – 120).

Fourth Day:

Wages based on piece rate 8 × 55 = ₹ 440

Wages based on time rate 8 × 40 = ₹ 320

As the Piece wage is higher, she will be paid piece wage of ₹ 440 but a deduction of ₹ 25{(100 + 45) – (100 + 20)} will be made for excess payment on the first and second day. Thus, the net payment on the third day is ₹ 415 (i.e. 440 – 25).

Fifth Day:

Wages based on piece rate $8 \times 55 =$ ₹ 440

Wages based on time rate $8 \times 40 =$ ₹ 320

As the Piece wage is higher, she will be paid piece wage of ₹ 440 with no deduction required.

Total wages for five days of the week:

Day	Amount (₹)
First	320
Second	320
Third	320
Fourth	415
Fifth	440
Total	**1,515**

Illustrations 8.4. (Group Piece Rate)

In a factory six workers work W-1, W-2, W-3, W-4, W-5, and W-6 together as a group and are paid on group rate. They also work individually for which they are paid at hourly time rate. They follow 48 hour week of which the time spent on group effort is: W-1& W-2: 40 hours each, W-3: 32 hours, W-4: 28 hours and W-5 & W-6: 20 hours each. The group piece rate is ₹ 26 and the group produced 626 units in the week just ended. The balance of the time has been booked by each worker on day work jobs. Their respective hourly rate is: W-1& W-2 ₹ 40 each, W-3 ₹ 64, W-4 ₹ 56, and W-5& W-6 ₹ 80 each. Each worker is entitled to Dearness allowance of 25% of wages earned. Compute Gross weekly earnings of each worker.

Solution : The group earnings is $626 \times 26 =$ ₹ 16,276. It is to be distributed to W-1, W-2, W-3, W-4, W-5, and W-6 in the ratio of their basic time earnings for the time spent on group effort which is as under:

Worker	Hour	Rate (₹)	Amount (₹)	Sharing proportion in group earning
W-1	40	40	1,600	50
W-2	40	40	1,600	50
W-3	32	64	2,048	64
W-4	28	56	1,568	49
W-5	20	80	1,600	50
W-6	20	80	1,600	50

Statement of Earnings

Worker (a)	Share in group work (₹) (b)	Time Rate Work (₹) (c)	Dearness allowance @ 25% of (b) + (c) (d)	Total Earnings (₹) (b) + (c) + (d) = (e)
W-1	[16,276 × (50/313)] = 2,600	(8 × 40) = 320	(2,920 × 0.25) = 730	3,650
W-2	[16,276× (50/313)] = 2,600	(8 × 40) = 320	(2,920 × 0.25) = 730	3,650
W-3	[16,276× (64/313)] = 3,328	(16 × 64) = 1,024	4,352 × 0.25 = 1,088	5,440
W-4	[16,276 × (49/313)] = 2,548	(20 × 56) = 1,120	3,668 × 0.25 = 917	4,585
W-5	[16,276 × (50/313)] = 2,600	(28 × 80) = 2,240	4,840 × 0.25 = 1,210	6,050
W-6	[16,276 × (50/313)] = 2,600	(28 × 80) = 2,240	4,840 × 0.25 = 1,210	6,050
Total	16,276	7,264	5,885	29,425

Accounting for Labour

All labour costs are entered in Wage Abstract. Suitable columns may be provided to categorize these wages as factory, administration and Selling overheads. Total wages are debited to Wages control account from where indirect wages are transferred to respective overheads control accounts and direct wages are transferred to work-in-Progress Control account.

Illustration 8.5 : *On the basis of following information, calculate the earnings of Krishana and Madhav under the Straight Piece rate system and Taylor's differential Piece rate System:*

Standard Production — *10 units per hour*

Normal time Rate — *₹ 25 per hour*

Differential Piece Rate to be applied:

(i) 80% of piece rate for below standard performance

(ii) 120% of piece rate for at or above standard performance

Actual performance:

Krishana produced 66 units in a day of 8 hours.

Madhav produced 90 units in a day of 8 hours.

Solution :

Working Notes:

Standard time allowed for 10 units = 1 hour; Time Rate = ₹ 25

Piece Rate per unit = 25/10 = ₹ 2.50

Low Piece Rate = (2.50 × 0.8) = ₹ 2.00

High Piece Rate = (2.50 × 1.2) = ₹ 3.00

Standard Output in 8 hours = (10 × 8) = 80 Units

Straight piece Rate System:

Krishana gets for 66 units @ ₹ 2.50 per unit = (66 × 2.5) = ₹ 165

Madhav gets for 90 units @ ₹ 2.50 per unit = (90 × 2.5) = ₹ 225

Differential Piece Rate System:

Krishana produced 66 units which is below standard, therefore

His earnings are ₹ (66 × 2.00) = ₹ 132

Madhav produced 90 units which is above standard, therefore

His earnings are ₹ (90 × 3.00) = ₹ 270

Illustration 8.6 : *Calculate the total monthly remuneration of three skilled workers W-1, W-2, and W-3 from the following data:*

(1) Standard Production per month per worker: 1,600 units

(2) Actual Production during the month: W-1 = 1,360 units; W-2 = 1,232 units; and W-3 = 1,552 units.

(3) Piece work rate: ₹ 25 per unit

(4) Additional production Bonus: ₹ 1,000 for each percentage of actual production exceeding 80% actual production over standard (79% = NIL; 80% = NIL; 81% > ₹ 1,000; 82% > ₹ 2,000; and so on).

(5) Dearness pay fixed ₹ 7,000 per month.

Solution :

Working Notes:

Worker	Efficiency Level (%)	Bonus (₹) [1,000 × (Actual – 80%]
W-1	(1,360 ÷ 1,600) × 100 = 85%,	5,000
W-2	(1,232 ÷ 1,600) × 100 = 77%	NIL
W-3	(1,552 ÷ 1,600) × 100 = 97%	17,000

Statement showing Earnings of Workers (₹)

Details	W-1	W-2	W-3
Piece Wages	34,000 [1,360 × 25]	30,800 [1,232 × 25]	38,800 [1,552 × 25]
Bonus	5,000	NIL	17,000
Dearness Pay	7,000	7,000	7,000
Total	46,000	37,800	62,800

INCENTIVE SYSTEMS

Meaning of Incentive

Incentive is the stimulation of effort and effectiveness by offering monetary inducements or enhanced facilities. It may be provided individually to every worker or collectively to a group of workers. The basic objective of incentive is to improve productivity and increase production as to bring down per unit cost of production.

I. Premium Bonus System :
   (a) Halsey and Halsey-Weir System;
   (b) Rowan System; and
   (c) Barth System
II. Differential Piece work :
   (a) Taylor System; and
   (b) Merrick System
III. Combination of Time and Piece work:
   (a) Emerson's Efficiency System;
   (b) Gantt Task and Bonus System;
   (c) Points system: (i) Beadaux System; (ii) Haynes System
   (d) Accelerated Premium System
IV. Group system of Wage Payment
V. Incentive schemes for Indirect workers
VI. Profit sharing
VII. Co-Partnership

Halsey and Halsey-Weir System

Halsey System

Salient Features:

1. Standard time is fixed for each work/task.
2. It guarantees hourly wages to the workers for actual time taken.
3. Bonus is paid if the time is saved i.e. actual time taken to complete the task is less than the standard time.
4. Bonus is equal to 50% of the time wages of time saved.

Computation of Earnings:

Total Earnings = Hourly Rate Wages + Bonus

= (Actual Time Taken × Time Rate) + 50% [Time saved ×Time Rate]

▣ **Example :** *Time allowed: 48 Hours; Actual Time Taken: 40 hours; Time Rate: ₹ 15.00 per hour.*

Solution :

$$= (40 \times 15.00) + [0.5(48 - 40) \times 15.00]$$
$$= 600 + 60 = ₹\ 660$$

Effective hourly earning = [Total Earnings/Actual Time Taken]

$$= 660/40 = ₹\ 16.50$$

Halsey-Weir System

Halsey-Weir system is the same as the Halsey system except that the bonus paid to workers is 30% of the time saved. Continuing with the preceding example total wages of a worker is computed as under:

$$= (40 \times 15.00) + [0.3(48 - 40) \times 15.00]$$
$$= 600 + 36 = ₹\ 636$$

Effective hourly earning = [Total Earnings/Actual Time Taken]

$$= 636/40 = ₹\ 15.90$$

Advantages:

1. It is easy to understand and simple to operate.
2. It guarantees hourly wages to the workers for actual time taken.
3. It provides an incentive for an efficient worker who completes his work in less than the standard time.
4. Efficiency improvement results in reduction in per unit labour cost.
5. Overhead cost per unit comes down with improvement in efficiency.
6. It provides an incentive to the employer to provide better production facilities as he is entitled to receive 50% (70%) share in savings attained by the worker.

Disadvantages:

1. Standard time for each job needs to be ascertained carefully, scientifically and objectively. Too tight standard may lead to frustration and unrest amongst workers.
2. Workers feel cheated as a part of value of time saved is shared with the employer.
3. Incentive is not so strong with piece rate system. The harder the worker works, the lesser he gets per piece.
4. It does not give full protection to employer against wrong rate setting.

Rowan System

Salient Features:

1. Standard time is fixed for each work/task.
2. It guarantees hourly wages to the workers for actual time taken.

3. Bonus is paid if the time is saved i.e. actual time taken to complete the task is less than the standard time.
4. Bonus is that proportion of time wages as time saved bears to the standard time.

Computation of Earnings:

Total Earnings = Hourly Rate Wages + Bonus

= (Actual Time Taken × Time Wage Rate) + [(Time saved/ Standard Time) × (Actual Time Taken × Time Rate)]

or

= (Actual Time Taken × Time Wage Rate) + [(Time saved/ Standard Time) × (Time Wages)]

Example :

Time allowed: *48 hours;*

Actual Time Taken: *40 hours;*

Time Rate: *₹ 15.00 per hour*

Solution :

= (40 × 15.00) + [{(48-40)/(48)} (40 × 15.00)]

= 600 + 100 = ₹ 700

or

= (40 × 15.00) + [{(48-40)/(48)} (600)]

= 600 + 100 = ₹ 700

Effective hourly earning = [Total Earnings/Actual Time Taken]

= 700/40 = ₹ 17.50

Advantages:

1. It guarantees hourly wages to the workers for actual time taken.
2. It provides more incentive to moderately efficient workers who save time up to 50% of the standard time.
3. Efficiency improvement results in reduction in per unit labour cost.
4. Overhead cost per unit comes down with improvement in efficiency.
5. It provides an incentive to the employer to provide better production facilities as he receives large share in savings achieved.
6. It protects the employer against wrong rate setting as the bonus can never reach 100% of time wages.

Disadvantages:

1. It is difficult to understand and complex to operate.
2. Standard time for each job needs to be ascertained carefully, scientifically and objectively. Too tight standard may lead to frustration and unrest amongst workers.
3. Workers feel cheated as a part of value of time saved is shared with the employer.
4. It does not provide adequate incentive for a very efficient worker who saves more than 50% of the standard time as the amount of bonus goes on declining after every decrease in time beyond 50% of standard time.
5. It does not give full protection to employer against wrong rate setting.

A Comparison between Halsey Plan and Rowan Plan

Time Saved	Bonus, Earnings Per Hour and Labour cost per unit
< 50% of Standard time	Bonus, Rate of increase in earnings Per Hour and Labour cost per unit are higher in Rowan plan than Halsey plan.
= 50% of Standard time	Bonus, Earnings Per Hour and Labour cost per unit are same under both plans.
>50% of Standard time	Bonus, Rate of increase in earnings Per Hour and Labour cost per unit are higher in Halsey plan than Rowan plan.

Barth System

Salient Features:

1. Standard time is fixed for each work/task.
2. It takes care of trainees, beginners and slow workers.

Computation of Earnings:

Total Earnings = Hourly Rate × √[Standard hours × Actual hours worked]

▣ **Example :**

Time allowed: *20 Hours;*

Actual Time Taken: *W-1: 25 hours; W-2: 20 hours; and W-3: 15 hours;*

Time Rate: *₹ 15.00 per hour*

Solution :

Earnings:

W-1 = ₹ 15 × √[20 × 25] = ₹ 335.41

W-2 = ₹ 15 × √[20 × 20] = ₹ 300.00

W-3 = ₹ 15 × √[20 × 15] = ₹ 259.81

Effective hourly earning = [Total Earnings/Actual Time Taken]

W-1 = 335.41 ÷ 25 = ₹ 13.42

W-2 = 300 ÷ 20 = ₹ 15.00

W-3 = 259.81 ÷ 15 = ₹ 17.32

Advantages: It is especially suitable for trainees and beginners and also for unskilled workers. For low production efficiency, earnings are higher, though earnings per hour are lower than the standard time rate of wage. For high production efficiency, earnings are less, though earnings per hour are higher than the standard time rate of wage

Disadvantages: It is not suitable for efficient workers because with the increase in efficiency, the rate of increase in the earnings falls.

Taylor's Differential Piece Rate System

Salient Features:

1. Standard time is fixed for each work/task.
2. Two piece rates are fixed:
   (i) a lower rate (i.e. 80 % of the Normal piece rate) for the worker who produces below the standard output;
   (ii) a higher rate (i.e. 120 % of the Normal piece rate) for the worker who produces standard output or more than the standard output.

Computation of Total Earnings

Worker	Total Earnings
(i)Who produces below the standard output	= Actual Output × normal Rate × 0.8
(ii)Who produces standard output or more than the standard output.	= Actual Output × normal Rate × 1.2

▣ **Example :**

Standard Output: 250 units; normal Piece rate: ₹ 2 per unit.

Actual output: W-1: 175 units; W-2: 250 units; W-3: 300 units.

Solution : Earnings of the workers:

W-1: 175 units × ₹ 2 × 0.8 = >₹ 280

W-2: 250 units × ₹ 2 × 1.2 = >₹ 600

W-3: 300 units × ₹ 2 × 1.2 = >₹ 720

Advantages:

1. It is easy to understand and simple to operate.
2. It provides incentive to efficient worker.
3. It helps the employer to increase the production by offering higher rates to more efficient workers.

4. It helps to reduce per unit overhead cost because of increased production.

Disadvantages:

1. It penalizes very severely the inefficient worker as a slight fall in output may result in a huge reduction in worker's earnings.
2. It does not guarantee the hourly wages and this insecurity affects the morale of the worker.
3. There will be difference in labour cost for two different levels of performance.
4. Higher and lower rates may be the source of conflict amongst workers.
5. Employer-employee relations suffer because of the standard being put at a very high level.

Merrick's Differential Piece Rate System

Features:

1. Standard time is fixed for each work/task.
2. Three piece rates are fixed as under:

Efficiency attained	Piece Rate (₹)
Up to 83 1/3 %	100% of Ordinary Piece rate
Above 83 1/3 % and up to 100%	110% of Ordinary Piece rate
Above 100%	120% of Ordinary Piece rate

Computation of Total Earnings :

Worker	Total Earnings (₹)
Produces up to 83 1/3 % of standard output	=Actual Output × Ordinary Piece rate
Produces Above 83 1/ 3 % and Up to 100% of standard output	=Actual Output × Ordinary Piece rate × 1.1
Produces above 100% of standard output	=Actual Output × Ordinary Piece rate × 1.2

▣ **Example :**

Standard Output: 250 units; normal Piece rate: ₹ 4per unit.

Actual output: W-1: 175 units; W-2: 250 units; W-3: 280 units.

Solution : Earnings of the workers:

W-1: 175 units × ₹ 4 = ₹ 700

W-2: 250 units × ₹ 4 × 1.1 = ₹ 1,100

W-3: 280 units × ₹ 4 × 1.2 = ₹ 1,344

Advantages: In addition to advantages of Taylor's Differential Piece Rate System, one more advantage of Merrick's Differential Piece Rate System is that it does not penalize the worker producing below standard output by applying the low piece rate.

Disadvantages: It has same disadvantages as Taylor's Differential Piece Rate System has except that it does not penalize the worker producing below standard output by applying the low piece rate.

Distinction between Taylor's Differential Piece Rate System and Merrick's Differential Piece Rate System

Basis of Distinction	Taylor's Differential Piece Rate System	Merrick's Differential Piece Rate System
Number of Piece rates in vogue	Two piece rates are fixed.	Three piece rates are fixed.
Penalty for workers producing below standard output	It does penalize the worker producing below standard output by applying the low piece rate.	It does not penalize the worker producing below standard output by applying the low piece rate.

Emerson's Efficiency System

Salient Features:

1. Standard time is fixed for each work/task.
2. It guarantees the day wages to the workers.
3. Bonus is paid if the level of efficiency attained exceeds 66 2/3 %.
4. It uses 32 different rates of bonus (up to 20% of basic wages) at different levels of efficiency ranging above 66 2/3 % to 100%.
5. Above 100% level of efficiency, bonus of 20% of basic wages plus 1% for every 1% increase in level of efficiency is provided.

Computation of Total Earnings:

level of efficiency	Total Earnings (₹)
Produces up to 66 2/3 %.of standard output	Only guaranteed time wages
Produces Above 66 2/3 % and Up to 100% of standard output	=(Actual hours worked × Hourly time rate) + An increase in bonus according to degree of efficiency on the basis of Step Bonus Rates which can go up to 20% of basic wages, for example at 80% level of efficiency, rate of bonus is 4%.
Produces above 100% of standard output	= (Actual hours worked × Hourly time rate) + bonus @ 20% of Basic wages + additional bonus @ 1% for every 1% increase in efficiency.

▣ **Example :** *Standard Output is 500 units. Daily Wage rate is ₹ 200. W-I produced 320 units, W-II produced 500 units and worker III produced 560 units.*

Solution : **Earnings under Emerson's Efficiency Plan**

Worker (I)	Actual output (II)	Level of efficiency (%) (III)	Guaranteed time wages (₹) (IV)	Bonus (₹) (V)	Earnings of the worker (₹) (VI)
W-I	320	64	200	NIL	200
W-II	500	100	200	$= 0.2 \times 200 = 40$	240
W-III	560	112	200	$= 0.32 \times 200 = 64$	264

Gantt Task and Bonus System

It is a combination of Time Rate, Piece Rate and Bonus Plan.

Salient Features:

1. Standard time is fixed for each work/task.
2. It guarantees the day wages to the workers.
3. Three rates of payments are fixed as follows:

Level of Output	Rate of Payment
(i) Less than the standard output	Guaranteed Time Rate
(ii) Equal to standard output	120% of Time Rate
(iii) More than the standard output	120% of Piece Rate

Computation of Total Earnings:

Level of Output	Total Earnings
(i) Less than the standard output	Actual Time × Time Rate per hour
(ii) Equal to standard output	Actual Time × (Time Rate per hour × 1.2)
(iii) More than the standard output	Actual Output × (Piece Rate × 1.2)

▣ **Example :** *Standard time allowed to produce 40 units: 8 Hours; Standard Wage rate ₹ 30 per hour; W-1, W-2, W-3 completed the task in 9 hours, 8 hours and 6 hours respectively.*

Solution : Earnings under Gantt Task and Bonus system:

Worker	Earnings (₹)	Earnings per hour (₹)
W-1	9 hours × 30 = 270	= 270/9 = 30.00
W-2	8 hours × 30 × 1.2 = 288	= 288/8 = 36.00
W-3	40 Units × 6 × 1.2 = 288	= 288/6 = 48.00

Note: Piece Rate = (8 / 40) × 30 = ₹ 6 per piece.

Hayne's System

Salient Features:

1. Standard time for the job is expected in terms of the standard man-minutes called as "MANT".

2. Each worker is paid according to hourly rate for the time spent by him on the job.
3. In the case of repetitive work the time saved is shared between the worker and the foreman in the ratio of 5:1.
4. If the work is of non-repetitive nature, the worker , the employer and the foreman share the value of time saved in the ratio of 5:4:1.

Accelerated Premium System

Earnings increase with output. The rate of increase of earnings itself goes up progressively with output. In fact the earnings increase in greater proportion than the increase in production. It acts as a strong incentive for skilled workers to earn high wage by increasing output and for production beyond standard.

Group Bonus System

It is a scheme in which bonus is calculated on the basis of collective production of a group of workers and is distributed among the individual members of the group on some agreed basis. It is usually introduced where performance of an individual worker cannot be assessed and the ultimate production is dependant on the collective effort of a group of workers. In the construction work, it is the team work that produces results.

Objective of Group Bonus Scheme

The Objectives of Group bonus scheme are enumerated as under:

1. Create collective interest and team spirit among workers;
2. Create collective interest among supervisors to improve performance;
3. Reduce wastage in materials and idle time;
4. Achieve optimum output at minimum cost;
5. Encourage individual members of the group /team where only the output of the team as a whole can be measured.

Illustration 8.7 : *From the following details, compute net incentive earned by each group:*

1. *A general production incentive of ₹ 12 per unit for any production in excess of 12,500 units to be distributed as under:*
   65% to Direct labour, 15% to Inspection staff, 12% to maintenance staff, 8% to supervisory staff.
2. *Inspection staff is penalized @ ₹ 25 per unit for any rejection by customer in excess of 1% of production.*
3. *Maintenance staff is penalized @ ₹ 25 per hour of machine break-downs.*
4. *Actual production 16,000 units. Rejection by customers 240 units, machine break down 40 hours.*

5. *Number of employees in each Group:*
   - *(i) Direct labour* 140
   - *(ii) Inspection staff* 08
   - *(iii) Maintenance staff* 20
   - *(iv) Supervisory staff* 06

Solution : Statement showing the Net Incentive earned by each Group

Details	Direct labour (₹)	Inspection staff (₹)	Mainte-nance staff (₹)	Supervisory staff (₹)	Total (₹)
General Production Incentive [65:15:12:8]	27,300	6,300	5,040	3,360	42,000
Less: Penalty: [80 × 25] (240 – 160) [40 × 25]	N I L	2,000	1,000	N I L	(3,000)
Net incentive	27,300	4,300	4,040	3,360	39,000
Net incentive per employee*	195.00	537.50	202.00	560.00	

*[Net Incentive Amount/ number of Employees]

Incentive Schemes for Indirect Workers

The output of indirect workers is difficult to ascertain and this tends to exclude them from incentive scheme. But a group bonus or payment by results for indirect workers is advisable because

(a) It is essential to avoid labour unrest as a result of paying time rate only to indirect workers while giving bonus to direct workers; and

(b) Indirect workers also contribute to productivity improvement.

(c) It encourages them to perform better.

Basis of Payment of bonus to indirect workers:

(i) On the basis of output of a group of direct workers whom they serve e.g. maintenance workers attached to a particular production department.

(ii) On the basis of output of the entire factory in case indirect workers provide general services.

(iii) On the basis of bonus of direct workers.

(iv) On any other equitable basis.

PROFIT SHARING AND CO-PARTNERSHIP

Sharing profits of a business with the workers and making them co-owner in the business serve the following objectives:

1. Infusing among the workers a sense pf belongingness with the organization;

2. Improving worker's interest, enthusiasm and motivation;
3. Stabilising labour force with the organization;
4. Relating reward to workers' productivity;
5. Achieving better human relations within the organization.

Profit sharing is statutory in all industries under the Payment of Bonus Act, 1965. The Act provides that all eligible employees are to be paid a minimum bonus of 8.33% of gross annual earnings irrespective of profits earned or losses incurred. A higher bonus up to a maximum 20% of gross earnings can be paid in case profits are adequate. Thus, the minimum bonus is an unavoidable charge on profits.

Profits can be shared with workers in any o the following forms:

(c) A fixed percentage of net profits may be distributed to workers in the ratio of their basic wage;

(d) Department-wise bonus may be paid to workers based on the profits earned by the department;

(e) Bonus may be related to worker's output; and

(f) Labour co-partnership.

Advantages: Following advantages accrue due to profit sharing and co-partnership:

(i) Productivity of workforce improves.

(ii) Worker's motivation level improves.

(iii) Labour turnover comes down.

(iv) Relations between workers and management improve.

(v) Worker is able to earn more due to his own effort and that of the group of workers in general.

(vi) There is better team work within the organization.

(vii) There is greater democratization in the management of the organisation.

Limitations:

(i) The fixation of formula for profit sharing itself results in dispute between workers and management.

(ii) Over a period of time, workers begin to consider bonus as their right irrespective of their productivity.

(iii) There is no direct relationship between individual's effort and efficiency and organizational profits.

(iv) In case profits are not earned due to wrong planning and other managerial failings, workers tend to get restive when they get low bonus.

Co-Partnership

Employees get the opportunity to share in the capital of the business and to receive a part of the profits that accrue to their share of ownership. The employees are given a loan for buying company's shares. In some cases, employees are free to deal with the shares in a normal way; in others, shares are regarded as 'employees" shares subject to certain restrictions. The employees get "dividends" and "bonus". In many cases these schemes provide for a minimum period of service as a condition of participation, and this tends to reduce labour turnover. Further, employee morale is enhanced to a great extent by the introduction of such schemes.

LET US RECAPITULATE

1. Pay Roll is a periodic statement which entails gross wages earned by each worker.
2. Net Wages is the balance of Gross wages and Deductions i.e. Total deductions are deducted from the gross wages.
3. In time wage system workers are paid according to time spent at work place. They are paid on hourly, daily, weekly or monthly basis.
4. In Flat Time Rate all workers of a particular grade and skill in a factory are paid wages at equal time rate.
5. In High Day Rate workers may be paid a time rate higher than the industry average. Normally, overtime is not permissible.
6. Measured Work Day Rate implies higher wage rate is paid to workers with higher level of performance as an incentive for higher standards of performance.
7. Indexed Time Rate implies that time rate of workers is indexed with cost of living index.
8. In differential time rate workers are paid different time rates according to their comparative ability, skill and speed.
9. In piece wage system workers are paid at a fixed rate per unit of output.
10. Individual Piece work wage system involves payment of wages according predetermined rate per unit of output/ operation/ job performed by a worker.
11. Group Piece work wage system involves payment of wages to a pre-arranged group of workers as a whole for the number of units produced or operations performed or job completed by the group.
12. Balance of Debt System ensures minimum time wage with a clause to recover the short-working.
13. Piece Rate with Guaranteed Time Rate implies that a minimum time wage is always guaranteed to the worker with no regard to output.
14. Overtime premium and Shift premium is to be treated as per the circumstances.
15. A bonus is an additional compensation generally given in recognition of exceptional productivity.
16. Total wages are debited to Wages control account from where indirect wages are transferred to respective overheads control accounts and direct wages are transferred to work-in-Progress Control account.

17. The basic objective of incentive is to improve productivity and increase production as to bring down per unit cost of production.
18. In Halsey Plan total earnings is the sum of Hourly Rate Wages and Bonus. Bonus is 50 %(30%) of time saved wages.
19. In Rowan Plan total earnings is the sum of Hourly Rate Wages and Bonus. Bonus is that proportion of time wages as time saved bears to the standard time.
20. Barth system of wage incentive is suitable for trainees and beginners and also for unskilled workers.
21. Taylor's Differential Piece Rate System helps the employer to increase the production by offering higher rates to more efficient workers.
22. Merrick's Differential Piece Rate System does not penalize the worker producing below standard output by applying the low piece rate.
23. In Accelerated Premium system earnings increase with output.
24. Group bonus system is usually introduced where performance of an individual worker cannot be assessed and the ultimate production is dependant on the collective effort of a group of workers.
25. Profit sharing is statutory in all industries under the Payment of Bonus Act, 1965.
26. In Co-Partnership employees get the opportunity to share in the capital of the business and to receive a part of the profits that accrue to their share of ownership.

SOLVED PROBLEMS

Problem 1. *A, an employee of XYZ co. gets the following emoluments and benefits:*

Salary	*₹ 250 per month*
Dearness allowance:	
On First ₹ 100 of salary	*₹ 400*
On Next ₹ 100 of salary	*₹ 100*
On balance every ₹ 100 of salary	*₹ 50 of part thereof*
Employer contribution to Provident Fund:	*8% of salary and D.A.*
E. S. I.	*4% of salary and D.A*
Bonus	*20% of salary and D.A*
Other allowances	*₹ 2,725 per annum*

A works for 2,400 hours per annum, out of which 400 hours are non-productive but treated as normal idle time. A works for 18 effective hours on Job No. 15, where the cost of materials equals A's earnings and the overhead applied is 100% of prime cost. The sale value of the job is quoted to earn a profit of 10% on such value.

You are required to find out: effective hourly cost of A, and

The expected sale value of Job No. 15. **[B.Com (Hons.) DU, 2009]**

Solution : **Emolument of 'A' per month**

Details		Amount (₹)
Salary		250
Dearness Allowance [400 + 100 +50]		550
PF: 8% of ₹ 800	64	256
ESI: 4% of ₹ 800	32	
PF: 20% of ₹ 800	160	
Other Allowances		2,725
Cost per month		3,781
Cost per annum (3,781 × 12)		45,372
Effective productive Hours: (2,400 – 400) = 2,000		
Effective Hourly cost of 'A': (45,372/2,000)		22.686
A's cost for the Job No. 15: (18 × 22.686)		408.348

Computation of Expected Sale Value of Job No. 15

Details	Amount(₹)
Cost of Materials	408.348
Cost of Labour	408.348
Prime cost	816.696
Overheads (100% of Prime cost)	816.696
06536 Works Cost	1,633.392
Profit (1/10 of Sales value) OR (1/9 of Cost)	181.488
Sale value	1,814.880

Problem 2. *From the following particulars, you are required to work out the earnings of a worker for a week under (i) Straight piece rate, (ii) Differential piece rate, (iii) Halsey Premium scheme (50% sharing, and (iv) Rowan premium scheme:*

Weekly working time (hour):	*48*
Wage Rate per hour:	*₹ 15*
Piece Rate per unit:	*₹ 5*
Normal time taken per piece (minute):	*20*
Weekly Normal output (piece):	*144*
Actual output for the relevant week:	*192*

Differential piece rate 80% of piece rate when output is below normal and 125% of piece rate when output is above normal.

Solution :

Computation of Workers' weekly earnings under different wage plans

Straight piece Rate:

= Weekly output × Piece Rate per unit

= 192 × 5 = ₹ 960.

Differential piece Rate:

Efficiency Level achieved = (144/192) × 100 = 133.33%

The efficiency level achieved is more than 80%. Hence, a high differential piece rate (i.e. @ 125%) is applicable i.e. 5 × 1.25 = 6.25 per piece.

Earnings = 192 × 6.25 = ₹ 1200

Halsey Premium scheme 50% sharing:

Standard Time for Actual Production = (48/144) × 192 = 64 (hours)

Time Saved = (64 – 48) = 16 hours

Earnings = (Hours Worked × Rate per hour) + (0.50% of time saved X Rate per hour)

= 48 × 15 + (0.5 × 16) × 15

= 720 + 120 = ₹ 840

Rowan Premium Scheme:

Earnings = Hours Worked × Rate per hour + [(Time Saved/Time Allowed) × Time Taken × Rate per hour]

= 48 × 15 + [(16/64) × 48 × 15]

= 720 + 180 = ₹ 900.

Problem 3. *The time allowed for a job is 40 hours. Actual time taken for completing the job individually by the job workers JW-1, JW-2, JW-3, JW-4, JW-5, JW-6, JW-7 and JW-8 is 36,32,30,24, 20, 18,16,and 12 hours respectively. The basic wage rate per hour is ₹ 25 for each worker. Tabulate the total earnings per hour worker-wise under (i) Halsey, and (ii) Rowan Schemes of incentive payments. What difference is noticed between the earnings per hour worked out under the two different schemes? Which scheme is considered beneficial to an efficient worker?*

Solution :

Worker	Standard Time	Time Taken	Halsey Plan	Rowan plan
JW-1	40	36	E=(TT X R) + 0.5 (ST – TT) X R E=(36 X 25) + 0.5 (4) (25) E= ₹ 950 Rate per hour= E/TT	E= TT X R + [(TS/ST) X TT X R] E=(36 X 25) + [(4/40) X 36 X 25] E= ₹ 990 Rate per hour= E/TT

			Rate per hour= 950/36= ₹26.39	Rate per hour= 990/36= ₹27.50
JW-2	40	32	E=(TT X R) + (ST – TT) X R X 0.5 E= (32 X 25) + (40 – 32) X 25 X 0.5 E= ₹ 900 Rate per hour= E/TT Rate per hour= 900/32= ₹28.125	E= TT X R + [(TS/ST) X TT X R] E=(32 X 25) + [(8/40) X 32 X 25] E= ₹ 960 Rate per hour= E/TT Rate per hour= 960/32= ₹30.00
JW-3	40	30	E=(TT X R) + (ST – TT) X R X 0.5 E= (30 X 25) + (40 – 30) X 25 X 0.5 E= ₹ 875 Rate per hour= E/TT Rate per hour= 875/30= ₹29.17	E= TT X R + [(TS/ST) X TT X R] E=(30 X 25) + [(10/40) X 30 X 25] E= ₹937.50 Rate per hour= E/TT Rate per hour= 937.50/30= ₹31.25
JW-4	40	24	E=(TT X R) + (ST – TT) X R X 0.5 E= (24 X 25) + (40 – 24) X 25 X 0.5 E= ₹ 800 Rate per hour= E/TT Rate per hour= 800/24= ₹33.33	E= TT X R + [(TS/ST) X TT X R] E=(24 X 25) + [(16/40) X 24 X 25] E= ₹840 Rate per hour= E/TT Rate per hour= 840/24= ₹35.00
JW-5	40	20	E=(TT X R) + (ST – TT) X R X 0.5 E= (20 X 25) + (40 – 20) X 25 X 0.5 E= ₹ 750 Rate per hour= E/TT Rate per hour= 750/20= ₹37.50	E= TT X R + [(TS/ST) X TT X R] E=(20 *25) + [(20/40) X 20 X 25] E= ₹ 750 Rate per hour= E/TT Rate per hour= 750/20= ₹37.50
JW-6	40	18	E=(TT X R) + (ST – TT) X R X 0.5 E= (18 X 25) + (40 – 18) X 25 X 0.5 E= ₹ 725 Rate per hour= E/TT Rate per hour= 725/18= ₹40.28	E= TT X R + [(TS/ST) X TT X R] E=(18 X 25) + [(22/40) X 18 X 25] E= ₹ 697.50 Rate per hour= E/TT Rate per hour=697.50/18= ₹38.75
JW-7	40	16	E=(TT X R) + (ST – TT) X R X 0.5 E= (16 X 25) + (40 – 16) X 25 X 0.5 E= ₹ 700 Rate per hour= E/TT Rate per hour= 700/16= ₹43.75	E= TT X R + [(TS/ST) X TT X R] E=(16 X 25) + [(24/40) X 16 X 25] E= ₹ 640 Rate per hour= E/TT Rate per hour= 640/16= ₹40

JW-8	40	12	E=(TT X R) + (ST – TT) X R X 0.5 E= (12 X 25) + (40 – 12) X 25 X 0.5 E= ₹ 650 Rate per hour= E/TT Rate per hour= 650/12= ₹54.17	E= TT X R + [(TS/ST) X TT X R] E=(12 X 25) + [(28/40) X 12 X 25] E= ₹ 510 Rate per hour= E/TT Rate per hour= 510/12= ₹42.50

Which scheme is considered beneficial to an efficient worker: It is crystal clear that Rowan Plan in the initial stages, and Halsey Plan, when the worker is extra-ordinary efficient and takes less than the 50% of the standard time is beneficial to the worker concerned.

Problem 4. (Rowan Plan)

In a factory bonus is paid according to the Rowan Plan. The allotted time for a job is 40 hours and the normal rate of wages is ₹ 25 per hour. The factory overhead charges are ₹ 10 per hour for the hours taken.

The factory cost of a work order executed by one worker is ₹ 32,375 and that by another worker is ₹ 31,092. The cost of material in each case is ₹ 20,000.

Calculate the amount of time taken by the respective workman to complete the work- order.

Solution :

Let X be the number of hours worked by a worker

[25X + {(40 –X)/40} × 25X] Labour + 10X Overhead

= ₹ 32,375 (Works Cost) – ₹ 20,000 (Material)

35X + (1,000X – 25 X 2) ÷ 40 = 12,375

1,400X + 1000X – 25 X 2 = 4,95,000

2,400X – 25 X 2 = 4,95,000

Dividing the Equation by 25

96X – X2 – 19,800 = 0

Changing the signs of the equation

X2 – 96X + 19,800 = 0

(X – 30) (X – 660) = 0

X is either 30 or 660.

As the standard time is 40, X should be taken as 30. It means the first worker took 30 hours time to complete the work order.

Similarly,

Attempt is made to find out the time taken by the second worker

[25X + {(40 –X)/40} × 25X] Labour + 10X Overhead

= ₹ 31,092 (Works Cost) – ₹ 20,000 (Material)

35X + (1,000X –25X2) ÷ 40 = 11,092

$$1{,}400X + 1{,}000X - 25X2 = 4{,}43{,}680$$
$$2{,}400X - 25X2 = 4{,}43{,}680$$

96X – X2 = 17,747.2 approximated to 17,750

Dividing the Equation by 25

$$96X - X2 - 17{,}750 = 0$$

Changing the signs of the equation

$$X2 - 96X + 17{,}750 = 0$$
$$(X - 25)(X - 710) = 0$$

X is either 25 or 710.

As the standard time is 40, x should be taken as 25. It means the second worker took 25 hours time to complete the work - order.

Verification:

Details	Worker I Amount (₹)	Worker II Amount (₹)
Direct Material	20,000	20,000
Direct Wages		
Overheads	7,500	6,250
Total	32,375	31,092

Wages of Worker I:

$$= (30 \times 25) + \{(40 - 30) \div 40\} \times 25$$
$$= 750 + 6.25 = ₹\ 756.25$$

Wages of Worker II:

$$= (25 \times 25) + \{(40 - 25) \div 40\} \times 25$$
$$= 625 + 9.375 = ₹\ 634.375$$

Problem 5. *Calculate the earnings of a worker under (i) Halsey Plan and (ii) Rowan Plan from the following particulars:*

Hourly Rate of wages guaranteed ₹ 4 per hour

Standard time for producing one unit of output is 15 minutes

Actual time taken by Krishna to produce 256 units is 48hours.

Solution : Computation of Earnings of Krishna under Halsey Plan:

Earnings = Hours Worked × Rate per hour+0.50% of Time saved × Rate per hour

$$= 48 \times 4 + [(0.5 \times 16) \times 4]$$
$$= 192 + 32 = ₹\ 224$$

Computation of Earnings of Krishna under Rowan Plan:

Earnings = Hours Worked × Rate per hour +

[(Time Saved) X Time Taken)] X Rate per hour (Time Allowed)

= 48 X 4 + [(16/64) X 48) X 4]

= 192 + 48 = ₹ 240

Problem 6. *Himachal Fur Coat factory has a bonus plan with the following structure: The fur cleaners (direct labour) receive one week's wages as a bonus at year- end. There are 25 workers in this category; each earns ₹ 1,248 per week.*

The Tailors (direct labour) are paid 6% of their salary as a bonus at year-end. The company has 10 tailors, each getting ₹ 2,500 per week.

Prepare separate journal entries to accrue the bonuses each week for each of the above categories of employees and distribute the weekly payroll in the same entry. Assume the company uses a perpetual cost accumulation system.

Solution : Details		**Amount (₹)**	
(a) Work-in-Process Inventory (1,248 × 25)	Dr	31,200	
Factory Overhead Control	Dr	600	
To Bonus Payable			600
To Payroll Payable			31,200
(1,248/52 = 24 × 25fur cleaners = 600)			
(b) Work-in-Process Inventory (₹ 2,500 × 10)	Dr	25,000	
Factory Overhead Control	Dr	1,500	
To Bonus Payable			1,500
To Payroll Payable			25,000
(₹ 2,500 per week × 0.06 = 150 × 10)			

Problem 7. *The basic rate of wage of a Quality Limited is ₹ 20 per hour and its overtime rates are:*

Evening time: Time and a half

Week ends: Double the time

During the Preceding year, the following hours were worked:

Normal time	*2,40,000 clock Hours*
Time and a Half	*40,000 clock Hours*
Double the time	*32,000 clock Hours*

The following times (Clock Hours) have been worked on four jobs:

Details	*J- 501*	*J- 502*	*J- 503*	*J- 504*
Normal time	*4,000*	*6,000*	*5,000*	*8,000*
Evening Overtime	*400*	*800*	*1,000*	*600*
Week end Overtime	*200*	*200*	*100*	*500*

You are required to calculate the labour cost chargeable to each job in each of the following circumstances:

(1) Where overtime is worked regularly throughout the year as the policy of the company due to labour shortage;

(2) Where overtime is worked specifically at the request of the customer.

Solution : Workings:

Basic rate of wage: RS. 20 (Given)

Evening Overtime: RS. 30 (20 x 1.5)

Week -end Overtime: RS. 40 (20 x 2)

Wages in the preceding year:

Details	computations	Amount (₹)
Normal time	2,40,000 x 20	48,00,000
Evening Overtime	48,000 x 30	14,40,000
Week end Overtime	32,000 x 40	12,80,000
Total	3,20,000 hours	75,20,000

Average Inflated time per hour: ₹ 23.50 [75,20,000 ÷ 3,20,000]

Labour cost for each job:

Case 1. Where overtime is worked regularly throughout the year as the policy of the company due to labour shortage:

Job No.	Time (Hour)	Rate per Hour (₹)	Amount (₹)
J- 501	4,600	23.50	1,08,100
J- 502	7,000	23.50	1,64,500
J- 503	6,100	23.50	1,43,350
J- 504	9,100	23.50	2,13,850

Case 2. Where overtime is worked specifically at the request of the customer:

Job No.	Time (Hour)	Rate per hour (₹)	Amount (₹)
J- 501	4,000	20	80,000
	400	30	12,000
	200	40	8,000
			1,00,000
J- 502	6,000	20	1,20,000
	800	30	24,000
	200	40	8,000
			1,52,000

J- 503	5,000	20	1,00,000
	1,000	30	30,000
	100	40	4,000
			1,34,000
J- 504	8,000	20	1,60,000
	600	30	18,000
	500	40	20,000
			1,98,000

Problem 8. *Specialty Product is the outcome of an engineering firm which engages five skilled workers. It is considering the introduction of some incentive scheme-Halsey Premium Plan or Rowan Premium Plan - of payment to raise the productivity at least by 25% to cope with the increased demand of its product. It is felt that if the proposed incentive scheme could bring about an average 20% increase over the existing earnings of the workers, it could act as a sufficient incentive for them to produce more and assurance to this effect has been given to the workers. As a result of this assurance, the increase in productivity has been observed by the following figures for the current Quarter:*

Hourly rate of wage (guaranteed) ₹ *40*

Average time for producing one piece by one worker at the previous performance: *1.25 hours*

(This may be considered as time allowed for the purpose of Incentive scheme)

Number of working Days in the Quarter: *75*

Number of working Hours per worker per day: *8*

Actual production during the relevant Quarter: *3,000 units*

You are required to:

(a) Calculate effective rate of earnings per hour under Halsey Premium Plan and Rowan Premium Plan;

(b) Calculate the savings to the firm in terms of direct labour cost per piece under the above Plans;

(c) Advise the manager of the firm about the selection of the Plan to fulfill the assurances given to the workers.

Solution : Answer Point wise:

Point (A):

Time allowed per unit: 1.25 hours

Units produced during the Quarter: 3,000

Thus, Total time allowed: 3,750 hours [i.e. 3,000 × 1.25]

Actual Time Taken: 3,000 hours [i.e. 75 × 8 × 5]

Time Saved: 750 hours [i.e. 3,750 – 3,000]

<u>Halsey Premium Plan:</u>

Time Wages: Time Taken × Standard Time wage rate

= 3,000 40 = ₹ 1, 20,000

Bonus: 0.5 × Time Saved × Standard Time wage rate

= 0.5 × 750 × 40 = ₹ 15,000

Total Earnings per Worker: (Time Wages + Bonus) / 5

= (1,20,000 + 15,000)/5 = ₹ 27,000

Effective Rate per Hour:

= Total Earnings per Worker/Actual hours worked per worker

= 27,000/600 = ₹ 45

<u>Rowan Premium Plan:</u>

Time Wages per worker: Time Taken × Standard Time wage rate

= 3,000 × 40 = ₹ 1,20,000

Bonus: (Time Saved/Time allowed) × Time Wages

= (750/3,750) × 1,20,000 = ₹ 24,000

Total Earnings per Worker: (Time Wages + Bonus) / 5

= (1, 20,000 + 24,000)/5 = ₹ 28,800

Effective Rate per Hour:

= Total Earnings per Worker/Actual hours worked per worker

= 28,800/600 = ₹ 48

Point (B):

Labour cost per piece without incentive:

= 40 × 1.25 = ₹ 50

Labour cost per piece under Halsey Premium Plan:

= (27,000 × 5)/3,000 = ₹ 45

Savings per piece = (50 – 45) = ₹ 5

Labour cost per piece under Rowan Premium Plan:

= (28,800 × 5)/3,000 = ₹ 48

Savings per piece = (50 – 48) = ₹ 2

Point (C):

Halsey Premium Plan brings about more savings in labour cost per unit than Rowan Premium Plan. However, Halsey Premium Plan does not fulfill the assurance given to the workers of 20% increase in their existing earnings as it provides only 12.5% [i.e.(3,000/24,000) * 100] increase. Rowan Premium Plan fulfills the assurance given to the workers of 20% increase in their existing earnings as it provides only 20% [i.e. (4,800/24,000) * 100] increase. Consequently, Rowan Premium Plan is recommended for acceptance by the firm.

Problem 9. *On the basis of following information. Calculate the earnings of W-1, W-2, W-3 and W-4 under Merrick Differential Piece Rate system. Also calculate labour cost per hour:*

Standard production per hour: *15 units*

Normal rate per unit in an 8 hour day: *₹ 90*

W-1 produced 80 units; W-2 produced 120 units; W-3 produced 105 units; W-4 produced 1126 units.

Solution : Rates under Merrick Differential Piece Rate system:

Up to 83%	Ordinary Piece Rate
Above 83% to 100%	110% of Ordinary Piece Rate
Above 100%	120% of Ordinary Piece Rate

Statement of Earnings

Details	W-1	W-2	W-3	W-4
Standard Production per day of 8 hours [15*8]	120	120	120	120
Actual Production	80	120	105	126
Efficiency level (%) [Actual Production/ Standard Production] *100	66.67	100.00	87.50	105.00
Piece Rate applicable* (₹)	90.00	99.00	99.00	108.00
Total earnings (₹)	7,200	11,880	10,395	13,608
Labour cost per hour	900	1,485	1299.375	1,701

Note: *

Rates Applicable under Merrick Differential Piece Rate system:

Up to 83%	[Ordinary Piece Rate] = ₹ 90.00
Above 83% to 100%	[110% of Ordinary Piece Rate] = 90(1.1) = ₹ 99.00
Above 100%	[120% of Ordinary Piece Rate] = 90(1.2) = ₹ 108.00

Problem 10. *The rate of pay of Mr. Red, a Workman, is ₹ 16 per hour. He works under the Rowan system of Payment of wages. In addition he receives a cost-of-Living Bonus of ₹ 225 per week of 45 hours. During a certain week he works on the following jobs:*

Job A for which 25 hours are allowed, in 20 hours.

Job B for which 32 hours are allowed, in 24 hours.

During the week his waiting time amounts to 6 hours.

Calculate the Mr. Red's earning and the amounts charged to each job and overhead.

Solution :

Job A	20 hours at ₹ 16 per hour	320	
	Bonus (5/25 x 20 x ₹16)	64	
	Cost of living bonus(20 hours x ₹5)	100	484

JOB B	24 hours at ₹16 per hour	384	
	Bonus (12/32 x 24 x ₹16)	144	
	Cost of living bonus (24 hours x ₹ 5)	120	648
	For waiting time,6 hours @ ₹ 16 per hour	96	
	Cost of living 6 hours @ ₹ 5	30	126
Gross Wages Earned			1,258

Problem 11. *Following are the particulars for April 2005 relating to five employees (A, B, C, D, and E) working in department 'K' of a workshop, exclusively for Job No. 21.*

Name	*Designation*	*Wage (₹)*	*frequency*
A	*Foreman*	*10,000*	*Month*
B	*Mechanic*	*250*	*Day*
C	*Machine operator*	*200*	*Day*
D	*Workman-1*	*150*	*Day*
E	*Workman-2*	*150*	*Day*

The normal working hours per week of six days are 48, at 8 hours per day. Sundays are paid holidays (There were no other holidays during the month).

(a) Provident Fund contribution was 8% of monthly wages by employee.

(b) Provident Fund contribution was 8% of monthly wages by employer.

(c) Employee State Insurance Contribution was 4% of monthly wages by

(d) Employee and 6% of monthly wages by employer.

From the foregoing data, calculate:

(1) Net wages payable by employer for the month of April 2005.

(2) The total amount of Provident fund contribution to be deposited by employer.

(3) Employee State Insurance Contribution to be deposited by the employer.

(4) The total Labour cost to the employer for the month of April, chargeable to the job; and

(5) The total cost of the job requiting materials valued at ₹ 42000 and Overheads at 60% of Prime cost.

Solution : Answer Point wise:

Net wages payable by employer for the month of April 2005:

Item		**Amount** (₹)
Gross Wages:		
	10,000	
	7,500	
	6,000	
	4,500	
	4,500	
		32,500

Deductions:

Provident Fund (8%r32,500)	2,600	
E.S.I. Contribution (4%r32,500)	1,300	(3,900)
Net Wages Payable		28,600

The total Provident fund contribution amount to be deposited by employer:

Item	**Amount** (₹)
Amount deducted as employees contribution to Provident	2,600
Employer's Contribution (8%r 32,500)	2,600
Total	5,200

Employee State Insurance Contribution to be deposited by the employer:

Item	**Amount** (₹)
Amount deducted as employees contribution to E.S.I.	1,300
Employer's Contribution (6%r32,500)	1,950
Total	3,250

The total Labour cost to the employer for the month of April, chargeable to the job No. 21:

Item		**Amount** (₹)
Gross Wages		32,500
Employer's Contribution: Provident fund	2,600	
E.S.I.	1,950	4,550
Total		37,050

Total Cost of the Job No. 21:

Element of cost	**Amount** (₹)
Material Cost	42,000
Labour Cost	37,050
Prime Cost	79,050
Overhead (60% of 79,050) (i.e. 79050 × 0.6)	47,430
Total Cost	1,26,480

Problem 12. The existing system of a certain factory is :

Details	***Workings***
Normal Working Work	*5 days of 9 hours each plus 3 late shifts of 3 hours each*
Rate of Payment	*Day Work: ₹ 24 per hour* *Late shift: ₹ 40 per hour*
Additional Bonus Payable	*₹ 60 per Day shift* *₹ 40 per Late shift*
Average output per worker for 54-hour week i.e. Including 3 late shifts	*160*

In order to increase output and eliminate overtime it was decided to switch on to a system of Payment by Performance. Following information is available:

Time Rate (as Usual):	*₹ 24 per hour*
Basic time allowed for 20 articles:	*5 hours*
Piece work Rate:	*Add 25% to the Time Rate*
Premium bonus:	*Add 60% to the Time Rate*

You are required to show :

Hours worked; (ii) Weekly earnings; (iii) Number of articles produced; and (iv) Labour cost per article for a worker under the following systems: (a) Existing time-Rate; (b) Straight Piecework; (c) Rowan system; (d) Halsey system.

Assume that 180 articles are produced in a 45-hour week under (b), (c), and (d) and that the worker earns half the time saved under the Halsey system. The additional bonus under the existing system will be discontinued in the proposed incentive scheme.

Solution : **Table showing Labour Cost per Article**

Payment Scheme	Hours worked	Weekly Earnings	Articles Produced	Labour cost per Article (₹)
(a) Existing Time-Rate	54	1,860	160	11.625
(b) Straight Piecework	45	1,350	180	7.500
(c) Rowan system	45	1,485	180	8.250
(d) Halsey system	45	1,404	180	7.800

Working Notes:

Existing Time-Rate

Details	Calculation	Amount (₹)
Weekly Wages	45 hours @ ₹ 24 per hour	1,080
	9 hours @ ₹ 40 per hour	360
	Day shift Bonus 5 × 60	300
	Late shift Bonus 3 × 40	120
	Total	1,860

Piece-Rate System

Details	Calculation	Amount (₹)
Basic Time	5 hours for 20 articles cost of 20 articles at hourly rates of ₹ 24 per hour *Add :* 25% Total	120 30 150 7.50
Rate per article	150/20 Quantity produced in a week (45 × 20) ÷ 5 = 180	 1,350
Earnings	180 × 7.50	

Rowan System

Details	Calculation	Amount (₹)
Basic Time	5 hours for 20 articles i.e. 15 minutes per article *Add:* 60% i.e. 3 hrs. or 9 minutes per article Total: 8 hrs. or 24 minutes per article Time allowed for 180 articles = 72 hrs. Actual time taken for 180 articles = 45 hrs.	
Earnings	E = (HW × RH) + {(TA – HW) / TA} × (HW × RH) = (45 × 24) + {(72 – 45) / 72} × (45 × 24) = 1,080 + 405	1,485

Halsey System

$$
\begin{aligned}
E &= (HW \times RH) + 0.5\,(TA - HW) \times RH \\
&= (45 \times 24) + 0.5 \times (72 - 45) \times 24 \\
&= 1080 + 324 \\
&= 1404
\end{aligned}
$$

Problem 13. *The following are the particulars given to you:*

Standard time	*40 Hours*
Time Rate	*₹ 50 per hour*

Prepare a comparative table under Halsey and Rowan Plan if time taken is 36 hours, 32 hours, 24 hours, 20 hours, 16 hours, and 12 hours. The table must show clearly the amount of bonus payable, the amount of total wages and labour cost per hour under the two methods. State at least one point of distinction between Halsey plan and Rowan plan in the light of your computations.

Solutions :

Scheme	Time Allowed (Hrs)	Time Taken (Hours)	Time Wage (₹)	Time Saved (Hrs)	Bonus (₹)	Total Wages (₹)	Labour cost per Hour (₹)
Case I.							
Halsey	40	36	1,800	4	100	1,900	52.78
Rowan	40	36	1,800	4 (10%)	180	1,980	55.00
Case II.							
Halsey	40	32	1,600	8	200	1,800	56.25
Rowan	40	32	1,600	8 (20%)	320	1,920	60.00
Case III.							
Halsey	40	24	1,200	16	400	1,600	66.67
Rowan	40	24	1,200	16 (40%)	300	1,500	62.50
Case IV.							
Halsey	40	20	1,000	20	500	1,500	75.00
Rowan	40	20	1,000	20 (50%)	500	1,500	75.00
Case V.							
Halsey	40	16	800	24	600	1,400	87.50
Rowan	40	16	800	24 (60%)	480	1,280	80.00
Case VI.							
Halsey	40	12	600	28	700	1,300	108.33
Rowan	40	12	600	28 (70%)	420	1,020	85.00

Comments:

1. When time saved is less than 50% of the time allowed, Rowan Plan allows higher amount of bonus as compared to Halsey Plan. In case time saved is more than 50% of the time allowed, Halsey Plan allows higher amount of bonus. If the time saved is exactly 50% of the time allowed, the permitted bonus under both the plan is SAME.
2. Labour cost per hour under Halsey Plan is highest when time saved is 70% (Case VI) as the bonus component is quite higher.

Problem 14. *Standard time for a job is 50 hours and guaranteed hourly time wage is ₹ 25. Mr. Shyam receives an effective hourly rate of ₹ 30 under Rowan Premium Plan due to efficiency in performance. Another worker Mr. Krishana has performed the similar job in the same time but he gets wages according to Halsey Premium Plan. Ascertain total wages for Mr. Krishana, and his effective hourly rate.*

Solution : **Rowan Premium Plan: (Mr. Shyam)**

$$\text{Total Wages} = (T \times R) + [\{(S - T)/ S\} \times (T \times R)]$$

Where

T = Time Taken (to be found out)

S = Standard Time

R = Guaranteed hourly rate

Thus,

$$T \text{ X Effective Rate per Hour} = (T \times R) + [\{(S - T)/ S\} \times (T \times R)]$$

$$T \times 30 = (T \times 25) + [\{(50 - T)/50\} \times (T \times 25)]$$

$$30 = 25 + [\{(50 - T) / 50\} \times (25)]$$

$$5 \times 50 = 1{,}250 - 25T$$

$$25T = 1{,}250 - 250$$

$$T = 1{,}000/25 = 40 \text{ hours}$$

Halsey Premium Plan: (Mr. Krishana)

$$\text{Total Wages} = (T \times R) + [0.5(S - T) \times R]$$

$$= (40 \times 25) + [0.5 \times (50 - 40) \times 25]$$

$$= 1{,}000 + 125$$

$$= ₹\ 1{,}125$$

Effective Rate per Hour = 1,125/40 = ₹ 28.125

Problem 15. *ABC Co. employs its workers for a single shift of 8 hours per day for 25 days in a month. The company has recently fixed the standard output of 44 units per day per worker for a mass production item and introduced an incentive scheme to boost output. Details of wages payable to the workers are as under:*

Item	*Rate (₹)*
Basic Wages	*5 per unit subject to a guaranteed Minimum wages of ₹ 150 per day worked.*
Dearness allowance	*60 per day worked*
Incentive Bonus:	
Up to 85% efficiency	*NIL*
Above 85% Efficiency	*₹ 80 for every 1% increase above 85%.*

The details of performance of two workers for a particular month are as follows:

Worker	*Number of Days worked*	*Output (unit)*
WX	*25*	*940*
WY	*20*	*750*

Calculate the total earnings of both the workers for the month.

Solution : **Statement of Earnings**

Details	Worker WX (₹)	Worker WY (₹)
Basic Wages:		
WX : 940 X 5	4,700	3,250
WY: 650 X 5		
Dearness allowance		
WX : 25 X 60	1,500	1,200
WY: 20 X 60		
Incentive Bonus:		
WX : 9 X 80	720	
WY: NIL		
Total Earnings	6,920	4,450

Working Notes:

Efficiency of Mr. WX = 940/ (25 × 40) = 94%

Efficiency of Mr. WY = 750/ (25 × 40) = 75%

Problem 16. *The following details apply to a factory where W-1, W-2, W-3, and W-4 do work:*

Normal Rate per Hour	*₹ 30*
Standard Time per Unit	*10 minutes*

In a 48 hour week, the output units were as under:

W-1	*W-2*	*W-3*	*W-4*
96	*240*	*288*	*360*

Required: *Calculate the cost per unit and earnings per worker under:*

Straight Time Rate system;

Straight Piece Rate system;

Taylor's differential Piece Rate system;

Merrick's differential Piece Rate system;

Gantt's Task Bonus system; and

Emerson's efficiency Bonus Plan.

Solution :

(i) Statement showing Earnings per worker and cost per unit

[Under Straight Time Rate system]

Worker (a)	Output Units (b)	Actual Time Taken (Hour) (c)	Rate per Hour (d)	Earnings per Worker (₹) (e) = [(c) × (d)]	Cost per Unit (₹) (f) = [(e)/(b)]
W-1	96	48	30	1,440	15.00
W-2	240	48	30	1,440	6.00
W-3	288	48	30	1,440	5.00
W-4	360	48	30	1,440	4.00

(ii) Statement showing Earnings per worker and cost per unit

[Under Straight Piece Rate system]

Worker (a)	Output Units (b)	Piece Rate Per Unit (c)	Earnings per Worker (₹) (d) = [(b) × (c)]	Cost per Unit (₹) (e) = [(d)/(b)]
W-1	96	5	480	5
W-2	240	5	1,200	5
W-3	288	5	1,440	5
W-4	360	5	1,800	5

Working Note:

Standard output per hour: 60/10 = 6 units

Normal Rate per Hour: ₹ 30

Piece Rate per Unit: [₹ 30/6 units] = ₹ 5

(iii) Statement showing Earnings per worker and cost per unit

[Under Taylor's differential Piece Rate system]

Worker (a)	Output Units (b)	Piece Rate Applicable (c)	Earnings per Worker (₹) (d) = [(b) × (c)]	Cost per Unit (₹) (e) = [(d)/(b)]
W-1	96	5	480	5
W-2	240	5	1,200	5
W-3	288	6	1,728	6
W-4	360	6	2,160	6

(iv) Statement showing Earnings per worker and cost per unit

[Under Merrick's differential Piece Rate system]

Worker (a)	Efficiency (%) (b)	Output Units (c)	Piece Rate Applicable (d)	Earnings per Worker (₹) (e) = [(c) × (d)]	Cost per Unit (₹) (f) = [(e)/ (c)]
W-1	33	96	5.00	480	5.00
W-2	83.33	240	5.00	1,200	5.00
W-3	100	288	5.50	1,584	5.50
W-4	125	360	6.00	2,160	6.00

(v) Statement showing Earnings per worker and cost per unit

[Under Gantt's Task Bonus system]

Worker & Output Units (a)	Standard Hours for Actual Output (b)	Time Rate per Hour (₹) (c)	Standard wages (₹) (d)	Bonus (₹) (e)	Guaranteed time Wages (₹) (f)	Actual or (f) w.e. h (₹) (g)	Cost per Unit (₹) (h) = [(g)/a)]
W-1: 96	16	30	480	NIL	1,440	1,440	15.00
W-2: 240	40	30	1,200	NIL	1,440	1,440	6.00
W-3: 288	48	30	1,440	288	1,440	1,728	6.00
W-4: 360	60	30	1,800	360	1,440	2,160	6.00

(vi) Statement showing Earnings per worker and cost per unit
[Under Emerson's efficiency Bonus Plan]

Worker (a)	Output Units (b)	Actual Time Taken (Hour) (c)	Time Rate Per Hour (d)	Guaranteed Time Wages (₹) (e)	Bonus (₹) (f)	Earnings per Worker (₹) (e) = [(e)+ (f)]	Cost per Unit (₹) (f) = [(e)/(b)]
W-1	96	48	30	1,440	NIL	1,440	15.00
W-2	240	48	30	1,440	72@	1,512	6.30
W-3	288	48	30	1,440	288	1,728	6.00
W-4	360	48	30	1,440	648	2,088	5.80

@ Rate of bonus is taken as 5% of time wages.

OBJECTIVE TYPE EXERCISES

I. Fill in the blank spaces with suitable word/s :

1. Differential piece work systems provide for higher rewards to .... workers.
2. In Taylor's differential piece rate system .... piece rates are set for each job.
3. Wage sheet is prepared by the .... department.
4. Overtime wages due to abnormal conditions like flood, earthquakes, etc. should NOT be charged to ....
5. In Halsey Bonus Plan, a worker gets a bonus equal .... of the time saved.
6. In Emerson's Efficiency Plan no bonus is payable to workers unless efficiency exceeds ....
7. When time saved is less than .... per cent of the standard time, Rowan Plan allows more wages to workers than Halsey Plan.
8. When overtime is worked due to seasonal pressure of work, the overtime premium should be treated as ....
9. When overtime is worked at the request of a customer due to urgency of work, overtime premium should be charged to ....

Answers :

1. efficient	**2.** two	**3.** Payroll
4. cost of production	**5.** 50%	**6.** 200/3%
7. 50	**8.** Factory overhead	**9.** job

II. Indicate whether the following statements are True or False :

1. Overtime wages due to seasonal pressure of work should be charged to costing profit and Loss account.
2. When time saved is more than 50% of standard time Rowan Plan does not allow more earnings to workers than Halsey Plan.
3. Amount of bonus is always different from that under Rowan Plan.
4. Minimum statutory bonus to direct workers should be treated as part of overheads and to indirect workers should be treated as part of direct cost.
5. Extra bonus over minimum statutory bonus should be excluded from cost accounts.
6. Group bonus encourages team spirit in case of smaller groups.
7. Profit sharing and co-partnership helps stabilising the work force.

8. Barth scheme is used in case of highly skilled workers.
9. Under Rowan Plan per unit labour cost decreases with increase in efficiency.
10. Piece rate is suitable for outworkers.
11. Workers are guaranteed a minimum time wage under Taylor's differential piece rate system.
12. Gantt Task and Bonus system guarantees a minimum time wage to workers.
13. Flat time rate is suitable in case of professional workforce.
14. Indirect labour should be paid on piece basis.
15. Piece wage should not be paid for defectives.
16. All incentive plans result in lower per unit labour cost.

Answers :

1. False	**2.** True	**3.** False	**4.** False
5. True	**6.** True	**7.** True	**8.** False
9. False	**10.** True	**11.** False	**12.** True
13. True	**14.** False	**15.** True	**16.** False

THEORETICAL EXERCISES

1. What are the advantages and disadvantages of Time rate and Piece Rate system of wage payment?
2. How would you deal with following in cost accounts?
   (a) Overtime wages; (b) Holiday with wages; (c) Bonus.
3. Write short notes on the following:
   (a) Pay roll accounting
   (b) Elements of wages
   (c) Profit sharing and co-partnership
   (d) Group bonus
   (e) Bonus to indirect workers
   (f) Differential piece rate
   (g) Merrick's differential or Multiple Piece rate system.
4. Distinguish between Halsey and Rowan Plans.
5. How do you calculate bonus under rowan plan?
6. Discuss the different methods of wage and bonus payment to labour.
7. Explain the nature of Gantt Task and Bonus System. What are its advantages and disadvantages?
8. Distinguish between 'incentive to indirect workers' and 'indirect incentives to direct workers'.

NUMERICAL EXERCISES

1. Calculate the earnings of a worker under (i) Halsey Plan and (ii) Rowan Plan from the following particulars:
   (i) Hourly Rate of wages guaranteed ₹ 5/- per hour
   (ii) Standard time for producing one unit of output 20 minutes
   (iii) Actual time taken by Krishna to produce 180units 48hours.

   [Ans. (i) 270/-; (ii) 288]
2. Himachal Fur Coat factory has a bonus plan with the following structure:
   The fur cleaners (direct labour) receive one week's wages as a bonus at year- end.

There are 25 workers in this category; each earns ₹ 1248 per week.
The Tailors (direct labour) are paid 6% of their salary as a bonus at year-end.
The company has 10 tailors, each getting ₹ 2500per week.
Prepare separate journal entries to accrue the bonuses each week for each of the above categories of employees and distribute the weekly payroll in the same entry. Assume the company uses a perpetual cost accumulation system.

3. Following are the particulars for April 2005 relating to five employees (A, B, C, and D) working in department 'Q' of a workshop, exclusively for Job No. 51.

Name	Designation	Wage (₹)	Frequency
A	Foreman	8000	Month
B	Mechanic	200	Day
C	Machine operator	150	Day
D	Workman	120	Day

The normal working hours per week of six days are 48, at 8 hours per day. Sundays are paid holidays (There were no other holidays during the month).
Provident Fund contribution was 8% of monthly wages by employee.
Provident Fund contribution was 8% of monthly wages by employer.
Employee State Insurance Contribution was 3% of monthly wages by Employee and 5% of monthly wages by employer.
From the foregoing data, calculate:
(a) Net wages payable by employer for the month of August 2004.
(b) The total amount of Provident fund contribution to be deposited by employer.
(c) Employee State Insurance Contribution to be deposited by the employer.
(d) The total Labour cost to the employer for the month of April, chargeable to the job; and
(e) The total cost of the job requiting materials valued at ₹ 16000 and Overheads at 40% of prime cost.

[Ans. (a) 19135; (b) 3440; (c) 1720; (d) 24295; (e) 56413]

4. XYZ Co. employs its workers for a single shift of 8 hours per day for 25 days in a month. The company has recently fixed the standard output of 40 units per day per worker for a mass production item and introduced an incentive scheme to boost output. Details of wages payable to the workers are as under:

Item	Rate (₹)
Basic Wages	3 per unit subject to a guaranteed Minimum wages of ₹ 80 per day worked.
Dearness allowance	40 per day worked
Incentive Bonus:	NIL
Up to 80% efficiency	
Above 80% Efficiency	50 for every 1% increase above 80%.

The details of performance of two workers for a particular month are as follows:

Worker	Number of Days worked	Output (unit)
A	25	820
B	18	500

Calculate the total earnings of both the workers for the month.

[Ans. ₹ 3,560; and ₹ 2,220]

5. The following details apply to a factory where W-1, W-2, W-3, and W-4 do work:
Normal Rate per Hour ₹ 25
Standard Time per Unit 12 minutes
In a 40 hour week, the output units were as under:

W-1	W-2	W-3	W-4
80	166	200	250

Required: Calculate the cost per unit and earnings per worker under:
(i) Straight Time Rate system;
(ii) Straight Piece Rate system;
(iii) Taylor's differential Piece Rate system;
(iv) Merrick's differential Piece Rate system;
(v) Gantt's Task Bonus system; and
(vi) Emerson's efficiency Bonus

[**Ans.** I. Cost per unit (₹)

Method	W-1	W-2	W-3	W-4
Straight Time Rate system	12.50	6.02	5.00	4.00
Straight Piece Rate system	5.00	5.00	5.00	5.00
Taylor's differential Piece Rate system	4.00	4.00	6.00	6.00
Merrick's differential Piece Rate system	5.00	5.00	5.50	6.00
Gantt's Task Bonus system	12.50	6.02	6.00	5.80
Emerson's efficiency Bonus	12.50	6.33	6.00	5.80

II. Earnings per worker (₹)

Method	W-1	W-2	W-3	W-4
Straight Time Rate system	1,000	1,000	1,000	1,000
Straight Piece Rate system	400	830	1,000	1,250
Taylor's differential Piece Rate system	320	664	1,200	1,500
Merrick's differential Piece Rate system	400	830	1,100	1,500
adjustrightGantt's Task Bonus system	1,000	1,000	1,200	1,450
Emerson's efficiency Bonus	1,000	1,050	1,200	1,450

6. Standard time for a job is 50 hours and guaranteed hourly time wage is ₹ 15. Mr. Mohan receives an effective hourly rate of ₹ 20 under Rowan Premium Plan due to efficiency in performance. Another worker Mr. Krishana has performed the similar job in the same time but he gets wages according to Halsey Premium Plan. Ascertain total wages for Mr. Krishana and his effective hourly rate. **[Ans. ₹ 625; ₹ 18.75]**

7. From the following details compute the amount of wages payable to a worker Ms. Riema for each of the five days of the week based on 'Balance of Debt system':
Standard Rate per Hour ₹ 60
Standard Piece rate ₹ 80
Hours of work in a day 8 hours
Ms. Jones produced 4 pieces on the first day, 5 pieces on the second day, 8 pieces on the third day, 8 pieces on the fourth day and 8 pieces on the fifth day.
[Ans. ₹ 480 for first three days; ₹ 560 on the fourth day and ₹ 640 on the fifth day; Total wage bill for five days ₹ 2,640]

8. From the following details compute the amount of wages payable to a worker Mr. Sohan Singh for each of the three days of the week based on 'Balance of Debt system':
Standard Rate per Hour ₹ 60

Standard Piece rate	₹ 80
Hours of work in a day	8 hours

Mr. Sohan Singh produced 3 pieces on the first day, 7 pieces on the second day, and 9 pieces on the third day.

[Ans. ₹ 480 on first two days; and ₹ 560 on the third day; Total wage bill for three days ₹ 1,520]

9. In a factory five workers work W-1, W-2, W-3, W-4, and W-5 together as a group and are paid on group rate. They also work individually for which they are paid at hourly time rate. They follow 48 hour week of which the time spent on group effort is: W-1& W-2: 45 hours each, W-3: 35 hours, and W-4 & W-5: 30 hours each. The group piece rate is ₹ 20 and the group produced 598 units in the week just ended. The balance of the time has been booked by each worker on day work jobs. Their respective hourly rate is: W-1& W-2 ₹ 40 each, W-3 & W-4 ₹ 64 each, and W5 ₹ 48. Each worker is entitled to Dearness allowance of 50% of wages earned. Compute Gross weekly earnings of each worker.

[Ans. ₹ 4567.5 each for W-1 & W-2, ₹ 6,708 for W-3, ₹ 6,408 for W-4, and ₹ 4,806 for W-5, and Total Gross weekly Wage Bill ₹ 27,057.]

10. From the following details, compute net incentive earned by each group:

1. A general production incentive of ₹ 10 per unit for any production in excess of 8,000 units to be distributed as under:
   70% to Direct labour, 10% to Inspection staff, 12% to maintenance staff, 8% to supervisory staff.
2. Inspection staff is penalized @ ₹ 20 per unit for any rejection by customer in excess of 1% of production.
3. Maintenance staff is penalized @ ₹ 20 per hour of machine break-downs.
4. Actual production: 11,000 units; Rejection by customers: 200 units; Machine break down: 40 hours.

[Ans. Earnings of the Group: ₹ 21,000; ₹ 1,200; ₹ 2,800; and ₹ 2,400]

11. The basic rate of wage of a Quality Limited is ₹ 20 per hour and its overtime rates are:

Evening time: Time and a half
Week ends: Double the time

During the Preceding year, the following hours were worked:

Normal time	2,40,000 clock Hours
Time and a Half	40,000 clock Hours
Double the time	32,000 clock Hours

The following times (Clock Hours) have been worked on four jobs:

Details	J- 501	J- 502	J- 503	J- 504
Normal time	4,000	6,000	5,000	8,000
Evening Overtime	400	800	1,000	600
Week end Overtime	200	200	100	500

You are required to calculate the labour cost chargeable to each job in each of the following circumstances:

(1) Where overtime is worked regularly throughout the year as the policy of the company due to labour shortage;

(2) Where overtime is worked specifically at the request of the customer.

[Ans. (I): Inflated Rate= ₹ 6.40 applied and labour cost of Job No. 1:₹ 21,760; Job No.2: ₹ 36,160; Job No. 3: ₹ 34,240; (II) Specific Rates: ₹ 6, ₹ 8, and ₹ 12 applied labour cost of Job No. 1:₹ 21,600; Job No.2: ₹ 35,400; Job No. 3: ₹ 36,000.]

12. The following are the particulars given to you:
Standard time 10 Hours
Time Rate ₹ 30 per hour
Prepare a comparative table under Halsey and Rowan Plan if time taken is 9 hours, 8 hours, 6 hours, 4 hours, and 3 hours. The table must show clearly the amount of bonus payable, the amount of total wages and labour cost per hour under the two methods. State at least one point of distinction between Halsey plan and Rowan plan in the light of your computations. **[B.Com. Banglore (Modified)]**

[**Ans.**

Details	Case I	Case II	Case III	Case IV	Case V	
Labour cost	Halsey	31.67	33.75	40.00	52.50	65.00
Per Hour (₹)	Rowan	30.00	36.00	43.00	48.00	51.00

13. Specialty Product is the outcome of an engineering firm which engages five skilled workers. It is considering the introduction of some incentive scheme-Halsey Premium Plan or Rowan Premium Plan - of payment to raise the productivity at least by 25% to cope with the increased demand of its product. It is felt that if the proposed incentive scheme could bring about an average 20% increase over the existing earnings of the workers, it could act as a sufficient incentive for them to produce more and assurance to this effect has been given to the workers. As a result of this assurance, the increase in productivity has been observed by the following figures for the current Month:

Hourly rate of wage (guaranteed) ₹ 20
Average time for producing one piece by one worker
at the previous performance: 2 hours
(This may be considered as time allowed for the purpose of Incentive scheme)
Number of working Days in the Month: 25
Number of working Hours per worker per day: 8
Actual production during the relevant Quarter: 625 units

You are required to:

(a) Calculate effective rate of earnings per hour under Halsey Premium Plan and Rowan Premium Plan;
(b) Calculate the savings to the firm in terms of direct labour cost per piece under the above Plans;
(c) Advise the manager of the firm about the selection of the Plan to fulfill the assurances given to the workers.

[I.C.W.A. (Inter); B.Com. Banglore Modified]

[Ans. Effective wage rate per hour: Halsey Premium Plan ₹ 22.50, and Rowan Premium Plan ₹ 24; Savings per piece: Halsey Premium Plan ₹ 4.00, and Rowan Premium Plan ₹ 1.60;Rowan Premium Plan is to be accepted]

14. On the basis of following information. Calculate the earnings of A, B, C and D under Merrick Differential Piece Rate system:
Standard production per hour: 12 units
Normal rate per unit in an 8 hour day: ₹ 60
A produced 64 units; B produced 96units; C produced 84 units; D produced 100 units. **[B.Com. Tirupati, Modified]**

[Ans. Total Earnings: A ₹ 3,840; B ₹ 6,336; C ₹ 5,544; D ₹ 7,200]

❑❑❑

9

Direct Expenses

Learning Objectives

It attempts to explain Direct Expenses as an element of prime cost. In this chapter you will learn :

1. Meaning and nature of direct expenses.
2. Different types of direct expenses
3. Accounting treatment of direct expenses.
4. Need to have control over direct expenses.

NATURE AND MEANING

Expenses, which are specifically incurred for a job or work order, are styled as 'Direct' or chargeable expenses. Such costs are other than materials and wages, and are incurred for a specific product or saleable service. It implies, direct expenses are neither material nor wages but constitute those costs which can be identified with a specific product, job or service. Since such costs are incurred specifically for a particular product, job, work order or unit of service, they are known as direct expenses. Identification with a particular job or work order is the only test to determine whether an expense, which is neither material nor labour, is direct. In the case of indirect costs, there is an element of apportionment.

Distinction between Overhead Expenses and Chargeable Expenses

Overhead expenses are indirect costs such as rent, insurance, showroom expenses etc. Overhead is an aggregate of indirect costs on account of indirect materials, indirect wages and indirect expenses.

Chargeable expenses are direct expenses which are incurred in a business. Overhead expenses consist of indirect materials, indirect wages and indirect expenses, whereas chargeable expenses do not include items like direct materials and direct wages. They include only direct expenses.

Some expenses though direct in nature, may be taken as indirect as a matter of convenience. These expenses are either of small or negligible value. A furniture manufacturer may take cost of glue, nails, nuts, and sand paper, etc., as indirect expenses though they may be capable of being allocated to a specific job, product or service.

Distinction between Direct Material and Direct Expenses

In relation to products, direct material is a material that forms an integral part of it and can be physically traced in some form in the finished product. Direct expenses in relation to products are cost of providing services or other kinds of special charge, but no trace of then can be obtained in the finished product like raw material. Thus, in manufacturing aluminium ingot, bauxite is the direct material, but electricity, though its cost is very high is the direct expense. Both direct material and direct expenses however, form part of the prime cost. In process industry all costs are allocated to processes as far as possible. Chargeable expenses are charged directly to process. Only overhead relating to Head office and such other common expenses are treated as overhead and apportioned on the basis of direct wages or prime cost.

Types of Direct Expenses

Some of the items of direct expenses are enumerated as under:

1. Inward carriage and freight charges on special materials.
2. Cost of Special moulds, designs and patterns.
3. Cost of defective work. Where several castings are necessary before an appropriate one is obtained, the cost of such castings is taken as direct expenses.
4. Experimental costs and expenditure on model and pilot schemes.
5. Cost of hiring special machinery or plant.
6. Cost of transport and conveyance to the site of the job or operation.
7. Cost of patent and royalties.
8. Fees paid to architects, surveyors and other consultants.
9. Cost of any special process not forming part of the normal manufacture.

Control over Direct Expenses

The number of items under the caption "Direct Expenses" is quite few. Further, direct expenses constitute a small portion of total cost of the product. Therefore, controlling of such costs is quite easy. A standard for such costs should be fixed in advance and the actual costs should be compared with the standards already set up. Variance, if any, should be identified along with the causal factors. Efforts should be made to reduce these variances.

Accounting Treatment of Direct Expenses

Direct Expenses may be booked under a common head "Direct Expenses Account". The expenses should be charged to specific jobs, products or services, as the case may be. In no case they are not to be mixed up with the Overheads.

LET US RECAPITULATE

1. Direct expenses are neither material nor wages but constitute those costs which can be identified with a specific product, job or service.
2. Identification with a particular job or work order is the only test to determine whether an expense, which is neither material nor labour, is direct.
3. In the case of indirect costs, there is an element of apportionment.
4. Chargeable expenses are direct expenses which are incurred in a business.
5. Overhead expenses consist of indirect materials, indirect wages and indirect expenses, whereas chargeable expenses do not include items like direct materials and direct wages. They include only direct expenses.
6. A standard for direct expense costs should be fixed in advance and the actual costs should be compared with the standards already set up. Variance, if any, should be identified along with the causal factors.
7. Some expenses though direct in nature, may be taken as indirect as a matter of convenience.

OBJECTIVE TYPE EXERCISES

I. Fill in the blank spaces with suitable word/s :

1. "Direct Expenses" and "Chargeable Expenses" are .... terms.
2. Hire charges paid for special machinery required for a specific job should be taken as an item of ....
3. In manufacturing aluminum ingots the cost of electricity for the processing is an item of ....
4. Depreciation of factory machinery is not an item of ....
5. Wages paid to a worker working on a .... job can be taken as "direct expenses cost".

Answers :

1. Synonymous **2.** Direct Expenses **3.** Direct Expenses
4. Direct Expenses **5.** specific

II. Indicate whether the following statements are True or False :

1. "Direct Expenses" and "Chargeable Expenses" are synonymous terms
2. The term "Overheads" includes direct expenses also.
3. Direct expenses can be conveniently and wholly allocated to a specific job, product or service.
4. Wages paid to a worker working on a specific work order can be taken as "direct expenses cost".
5. Depreciation of factory machinery is an item of indirect expenses.

Answers :

1. True	**2.** False	**3.** True	**4.** True
5. True			

THEORETICAL EXERCISES

1. What is a direct or chargeable expense? Give two examples.
2. Distinguish between Overhead expenses and Chargeable expenses.
   [DU, B.Com (Hons), 2001]
3. Distinguish between Direct Material and Chargeable expenses.
4. How direct Expenses are accounted for in Cost Accounting?

❑❑❑

10

Overheads : General

Learning Objectives

It attempts to explain overheads in general. In this chapter you will learn :

1. Meaning and nature of overhead cost.
2. Classification of overhead costs.
3. Fixed overheads.
4. Standing orders and codification of overheads.
5. Accumulation of overheads.
6. Treatment of specific items of overheads.

INTRODUCTION

Overheads by definition are indirect costs which cannot be conveniently allocated to cost units. Accounting and control of overhead costs is more complex than that of other elements of cost. There is a knotty problem of apportioning these indirect costs to cost centres and ultimately to cost units.

Nature of Overhead

Overhead is the aggregate of indirect material cost, indirect wages, and indirect expenses. The term 'indirect' indicates that the cost accountant is either unable or unwilling to allocate to specific cost unit and is generally apportioned to or absorbed by cost units on some appropriate bases. Indirect costs are also known as overheads or overhead costs. Overhead costs are not incurred exclusively for a specific cost unit. Overheads cannot be conveniently identified with a particular cost unit. They need to be allocated, apportioned and absorbed on some equitable criterion. Overhead costs are the operating costs of a business enterprise which cannot be traced directly to a specific unit of output. Overheads are all expenses other than direct expenses. C.I.M.A. gives a very simple definition of overheads as "an aggregate of indirect material cost, indirect wages, and indirect expenses". Overheads are those costs which do not result from the existence of individual cost units. It is obvious that overheads include indirect material, indirect labour, and indirect expenses. Some of the pertinent definitions are reproduced as under:

1. "Overhead may be defined as the cost of indirect material, indirect labour and such other expenses, including services as cannot conveniently be charged direct to specific cost units. Alternatively, overheads are all expenses other than direct expenses." Wheldon
2. "Overhead costs are those costs which can not be traced directly to a particular unit of output." Blocker and Weltmer
3. "Overheads are costs that have to be incurred, although they have no directly measurable observable relationship to specific activity, units, production or cost objectives." National Association of Accountants, U.S.A.

Thus, Overheads represent a necessary charge on cost units, though on an estimated basis.

Role of Overhead Costs

Due to the following reasons, allocation, apportionment, absorption and control on overheads is necessary:

1. In large organisations overheads are a significant share of total cost. Economy in total cost, therefore, presupposes an attempt to minimize overhead cost.
2. Distribution of overheads requires exercise of judgment. Therefore, due care needs to be exercised while adopting a basis for allocation, and apportionment of overheads.
3. Ascertainment of cost of a cost unit requires that a reasonable share of overheads is charged to cost units.
4. The quantum of overhead costs increases with the increase in size of the organisation.
5. Control of overheads is dependent on the use of direct material and direct labour cost.
6. Overheads can be charged on the basis of pre-determined overhead rates of recovery while direct costs are charged to products only after these have been incurred.
7. Direct costs are always fully absorbed while there could be under/over recovered overheads.
8. In most of the cases there is greater scope of economy of overhead costs than in direct costs.

Features of Overhead costs

1. Overhead costs by nature are common to a number of cost units and cost centres.
2. Most of the overheads do not change directly in proportion to change in volume of output.
3. They need to be distributed to cost centres and cost units as they are not identifiable with any specific cost units.
4. Overheads are distributed on some suitable criterion.
5. Distribution of overheads requires exercise of judgment and thus is an approximate charge to cost centres and cost units.

Overheads and Efficiency

In the following cases, an increase in overheads is indicative of inefficiency:

1. No improvement in quantity or quality of output.
2. No reduction in direct costs.
3. Per unit cost of production goes up.

However, in the following cases an increase in overheads is not indicative of inefficiency:

1. Increase in maintenance cost results in lower repairs, machine break-down and depreciation etc.
2. Increase in overhead costs due to higher level of mechanization results in higher reduction in labour cost.
3. Total production increases at a rate which is higher than the rate of increase in overhead costs.
4. There is more than commensurate improvement in the quality of products.
5. Expenditure on managerial controls and productivity improvements may lead to higher overhead costs but may simultaneously lead to reduction in overall cost.

COLLECTION AND ACCUMULATION OF OVERHEADS

Following are the main sources of overheads:

(1) *Invoices (Receipts):* To collect indirect expenses such as Rent, Insurance etc.

(2) *Stores Issue requisitions:* To collect indirect material cost.

(3) *Wage analysis Abstract:* To collect indirect wages.

(4) *Cash Book:* To collect indirect expenses.

(5) *Journal Entries:* To collect indirect charges such as depreciation, Own building rent, etc.

General Principles of recognizing Overheads

Following guidelines should be kept in view while deciding whether certain expenditure should be treated as overhead or not:

1. *Lack of identification:* Only those costs can be treated as overheads which fail in identifying themselves with a particular cost unit.
2. *Insignificant direct cost:* Certain cost of small value, such as nuts bolts nails screws, lubricants etc. Though identifiable with a particular cost unit may be treated as overhead cost. It is based on the principle of convenience.
3. *Benefit:* The cost centre should be charged for an overhead cost on the basis of benefit derived by it from that cost. Based on this principle, factory rent is charged to the departments in proportion of the area occupied by them.
4. *Responsibility:* A cost centre should be charged with only those costs which can be controlled or influenced by that departmental head.
5. *Exclude Non-cost Expenses or Payments:* Purely financial items such as cash discounts, subscriptions donations, and income-tax are not considered as overheads. Al expenses of capital nature are also excluded.
6. Overheads involve Cash Payments or Incurrence of liability or Diminution in Asset value or a Sacrifice measurable in terms of Money.

Classification of Overhead costs

Cost classification is the process of grouping of costs on the basis of similarities/dissimilarities and specific objectives. Overheads can be classified as under:

1. Fixed overheads, variable overheads and semi-fixed overheads. (Variability)
2. Controllable and non-controllable overheads. (Controllability)
3. Normal overheads and abnormal overheads. (Normality)
4. Overheads treated as product cost and overheads treated as period cost. (Treatment)
5. Relevant overheads and irrelevant overheads.(Relevance)
6. Manufacturing/Production, Office/Administration, and Selling and Distribution overheads.(Functional)

Importance of Classifying Overheads into Fixed and Variable

Such classification of overheads based on variability is widely made due to the following reasons:

1. *Cost-Volume-Profit (C-V-P) Relationship:* The (C-V-P) relationship is based on the segregation of fixed and variable costs in the total cost.

2. *Ascertainment of Break Even Level:* Break even is that level of output and sales at which total cost equals total revenue. This is where the contribution (Sales minus variable cost) is equal to fixed overheads. Thus, break even point cannot be ascertained without classifying cost s into fixed and variable.
3. *Fixation of minimum selling price:* The minimum price which a firm can charge is equal to marginal cost of the product i.e. Prime cost plus variable overheads. Therefore, it is necessary to ascertain fixed and variable overheads.
4. *Budget Making:* To make a budget it is necessary to know the nature and behaviour of the overhead cost in relation to output, and for this it becomes essential to classify the costs into variable, semi-variable and fixed overheads.
5. *Decision making at the Project stage:* At the project stage important decisions in regard to what to produce, and how much to create capacity are to be made.

   Each decision involves different sizes and compositions of fixed and variable costs which need to be analysed properly.
6. *Decision making at the Operating stage:* At the operation level, a number of decisions are to be made in regard to pricing, make or buy, continue production or shut down, etc. Decision regarding all these matters cannot be taken correctly without segregating overheads into fixed and variable.
7. *Absorption of overheads:* Separate rates for absorption of fixed and variable overheads are applied. Under or over absorption of overheads signify different situations necessitating different managerial decisions and actions. Under absorption of fixed overheads indicates idle capacity whereas under absorption of variable overheads signify inefficiency.
8. *Cost control:* It is only when such distinction of overhead costs into fixed and variable is made that operating mangers and supervisors know which costs they can influence and should, therefore, focus on.

In a factory if there is only one production department and same or similar jobs are done, the costing of the job is quite easy as there is no need for allocation/apportionment of overhead. All overheads accumulated should be charged on actual or estimated basis to find out the cost of production.

Illustration 10.1. *During the year ending on 31.3.2008 10,000 units of a product were produced. The production process is simple as there was only one production department and all factory overheads incurred are to be recovered at 180% of direct wages (Based on previous year's figures). From the data given, find out the factory cost of the product:*

Material cost: 20,000 kg @ ₹ 50 per kg	*10,00,000*
Direct Wages: 20,000 hours @ ₹ 25 per hour	*5,00,000*
Direct Expenses	*50,000*

Solution : Statement showing Factory cost for the year ending on 31.3.2008

Details	**Amount (₹)**
Material cost: 20,000 kg @ ₹ 50 per kg	10,00,000
Direct Wages: 20,000 hours @ ₹ 25 per hour	5,00,000
Direct Expenses	50,000
Prime Cost	15,50,000
Factory Overhead (180% of Direct Wages) (5,00,000 × 1.8)	9,00,000
Factory Cost	24,50,000

When there are two or more production cost centres and overhead rates vary significantly, it is desirable to collect the overhead expenses under suitable Standing order Numbers and prepare a primary and secondary distribution in order to find out the overhead recovery rate of each cost centre for charging to jobs/work orders executed through the respective cost centres.

DEPARTMENTALISATION OF OVERHEADS

The process of allocation and apportionment of overheads to cost centres or cost units is called Departmentalisation or primary distribution of overheads. The plant is divided into manageable units to which expenses are charged. It serves the following purposes:

(1) Closer control of overheads: It makes the incurrence of expenses the responsibility of the departmental head i.e. foreman or the supervisor.

(2) Accurate costing: It facilitates accurate costing of jobs and products.

(3) Proper utilization of services: It facilitates control and proper utilization of the services of the service centres.

(4) Absorption rates: It facilitates the making of appropriate rates of recovery of overheads.

(5) Valuation of Work-in-Progress: It makes possible the ascertainment of the cost of work-in-progress and transfer of goods from one process to another.

Following factors must be considered in deciding the kinds of departments required to control costs and to establish departmental overheads rates of recovery:

(i) Similarity of operations, processes and machinery in each department.

(ii) Location of operations, processes and machinery in each department.

(iii) Responsibility for production and costs.

(iv) Relationship of operations to the flow of product.

(v) Number of departments or cost centres.

Allocation of Overheads

It is the allotment of *whole* items of cost to cost centres or cost units. Expenses which originate directly and completely in a department are identified with the foreman/ supervisor responsible for the supervision of the department. Direct departmental overhead in production or service centres can be classified as under:

- Indirect material and factory supplies
- Labour fringe benefits
- Supervision, indirect labour and overtime
- Depreciation of the equipment
- Repairs and maintenance

Apportionment of Overheads

There are certain expenses such as rent, depreciation of factory buildings which are shared by all departments and cannot be charged directly to a specific department. These expenses do not originate with any specific department. They are incurred for all to use and so must be apportioned to all departments using appropriate criteria.

Distinction between Allocation and Apportionment

Allocation and apportionment are two successive stages in the process of distribution of indirect expenses. The distinction is basically conceptual. The points of distinction are as under:

1. If an item of overhead can be identified directly with a specific cost centre, it is allocated thereto. If such identification is not feasible, the cost of the item will have to be apportioned on some equitable criteria. In a way allocation ends with the cost centre, the process of apportionment is carried further down the line.
2. In allocation the whole of the item of indirect cost is charged to a cost centre whereas in apportionment only a part of the overheads is charged to the cost centre. Allocation is a direct process but apportionment is an indirect method for which equitable bases are to be selected.

Apportionment and Absorption

Overhead apportionment is the distribution of overheads over various production and service departments. It is described as "the allotment of proportions of items of cost to cost centres or cost units." Rent of the building is distributed over various departments on the basis of area occupied by various departments. This is known as apportionment of Building Rent based on Area occupied. Once overheads have been apportioned to various departments and the total overheads of each department are known, these are then absorbed by the cost units produced in the department. Absorption of overheads is, thus, charging of overheads to cost units. Simply stated, the apportionment is the distribution of overhead to various departments and the absorption of overheads is the distribution of departmental overheads to various cost units.

Classification of Overhead Costs

Cost classification is the process of grouping costs according to their similar characteristics and establishing a series of special groups according to which costs are classified or categorized. It entails two steps: (i) Determination of category in which the overhead costs is subdivided, (ii) actual process of classification of the various items of expense into one or the other groups/category. The method to be adopted for the classification of overhead costs depends upon the size of the business, nature of product or services rendered and policy of management. The various classifications are: (1) Functional classification, (2) Classification in regard to behaviour of expenditure, (3) Element –wise classification, and (4) Classification according to nature of expenditure.

A firm may adopt one or more of the above classifications. The overhead expenses of a firm may be first divided according to functions. The expenses pertaining to one group may further be classified into fixed, variable and semi-variable. Each of these groups may then be classified into the elements of cost and under each element, the expenses may be further sub-divided according to their nature i.e. depreciation, salary, repairs and maintenance etc.

Functional Classification

Under functional classification, expenses are classified with reference to major activity divisions of a concern. This is necessary for the segregation of the cost of each of the principal functional division of the firm and for having different method of accounting and control for the diverse nature of expenses in each division. The main groups forming the basis of classification are:

(a) Manufacturing overheads including Research & Development overhead,

(b) Administration overhead, and

(c) Selling and Distribution overhead.

(i) Manufacturing overheads including Research & Development overhead: It is also termed as factory overhead, works overhead or production overhead. It means indirect expenditure incurred in connection with production operations. It is the sum total of factory indirect material cost, indirect factory wages, and indirect factory expenses. Production overhead is the invisible segment of finished product. Lubricants, consumable stores, indirect wages, factory power and lighting, depreciation of plant and machinery, depreciation of factory building and furniture, insurance of factory plant and machinery, factory building, store keeping expenses, repairs and maintenance etc. are some of the examples of such overhead cost.

(ii) Administration overhead (Office or General overhead): Expenditures under this category are of general nature and consist of all costs incurred in the direction, control and administration (inclusive of secretarial, accounting and financial control, and legal work) of an undertaking which is not directly related to production or selling and distribution functions of the management. General management salaries, audit fees, office lighting, legal charges, office rent and rates, postage and telephone, stationery and printing, and salaries of the ministerial staff etc. are some of the examples of such overhead cost.

(iii) Selling and Distribution overhead: Selling overhead is the cost of seeking to create and stimulate demand and procuring orders. Advertising, salaries including sales commission of the sales personnel, showroom expenses, travelling expenses, bad debts, catalogues and price lists, samples etc. are some of the examples of such an overhead cost.

Distribution overhead cost includes all expenditures incurred from the time product is completed in the factory till it reaches the customer. It includes packing cost, carriage outward, delivery van expenses, warehousing costs, etc.

Selling overhead and distribution overheads are related to the marketing function and thus are combined into a single category of Selling and Distribution overhead. This overhead is also called "Post-Production overhead" as such costs are incurred after production work is over.

Classification based on behaviour of expenditure: Overheads are classified with reference to their tendency to vary with production/sales volume or level of activity or operations. Based on this behaviour, the expenses may be classified into: (a) Fixed overhead, (b) variable overhead, and (c) Semi-variable or Semi-fixed overhead. This classification is not absolute but is one of convenience. All costs are variable in the long- run; however, this classification is important for cost control and decision-making.

1. *Fixed overhead:* Fixed overheads are those costs which do not vary with the change in the volume of production upto a given range. Rent and Insurance of Building, plant and machinery and furniture, salary of manger etc. Fixed overheads have two characteristics:
   (i) Total fixed overheads do not vary with the change in the volume of production upto a given range.
   (ii) Fixed overheads per unit vary with change in the volume of production i.e. fixed overheads per unit decreases as the production increases and vice versa.

   Graphical Representation: (Graph 10.1)

[Fixed cost]

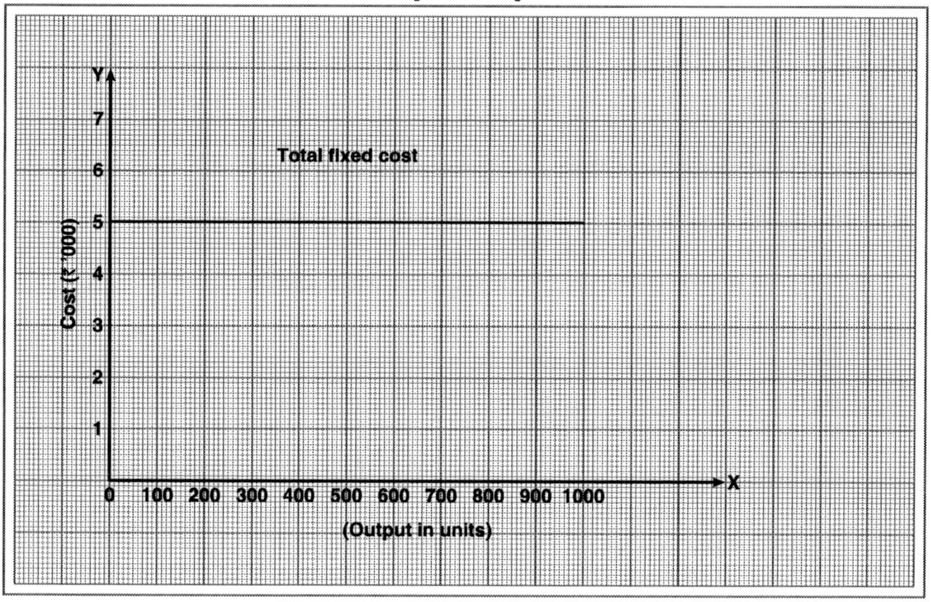

(a)

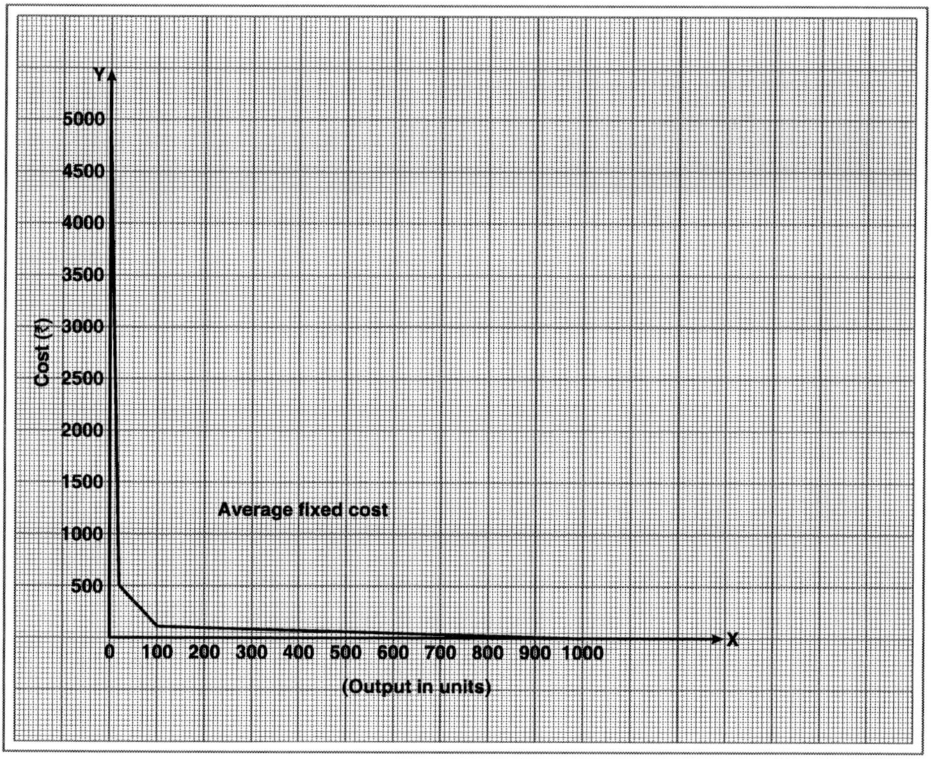

(b)

Graph 10.1

Numerical Example:

Output (unit) (A)	Total Fixed overheads (B) (₹)	Fixed overheads per unit (C) = (B)/(A) (₹)
0	5,000	5,000
1	5,000	5,000
10	5,000	500
100	5,000	50
500	5,000	10
1,000	5,000	5

2. *Variable overhead:* Variable overheads are those costs which vary in direct proportion to the volume of production. Variable overheads have two characteristics:
   (i) Total variable overheads vary in direct proportion to the volume of production i.e. total variable overheads decrease as the production decreases and vice versa.
   (ii) Variable overheads per unit remain fixed. They do not change with the change in the volume of output.

   Graphical Representation: (Graph 10.2)

   Numerical Example:

Output (unit) (A)	Total Variable overheads (B) (₹)	Variable overheads per unit (C) = (B)/(A) (₹)
0	0	20
1	20	20
10	200	20
100	2,000	20
500	10,000	20
1,000	20,000	20

3. *Semi-fixed overhead:* Semi-fixed overheads are those costs of which one part remains fixed up to a given range and the other part varies with the change in the volume of production but not in the same proportion. An expense may not change if output is upto 50% but may increase by 4% for every 10% increase in output over 50% capacity but upto 70%. Example: Telephone expenses; Depreciation; Repairs and maintenance; and delivery van expenses.

   Graphical Representation: (Graph 10.3)

[Variable cost]

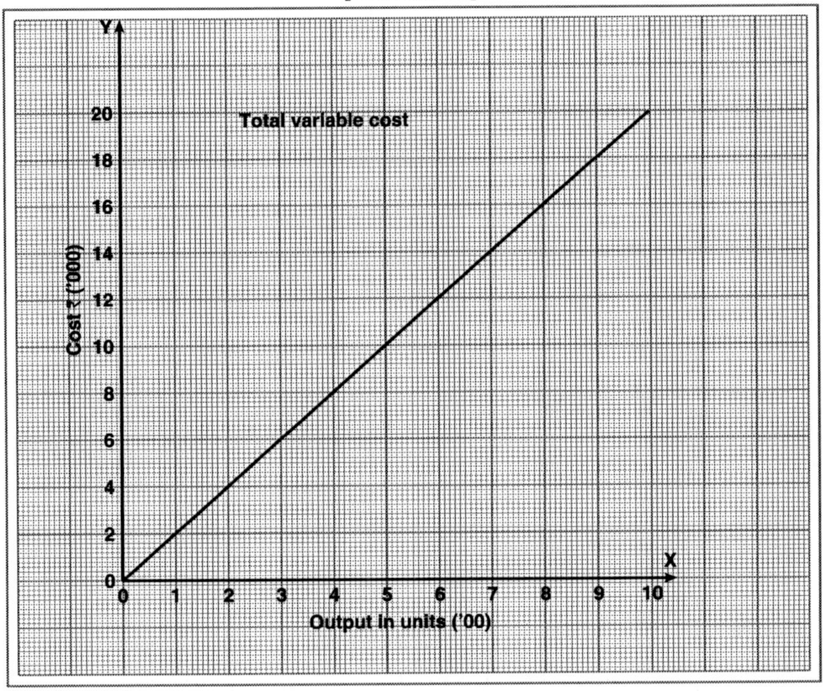

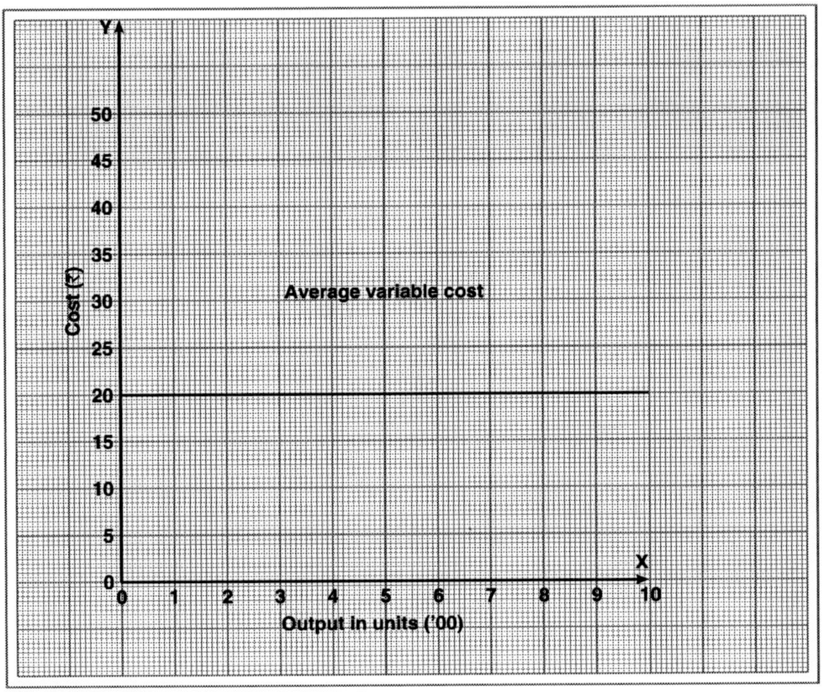

Graph 10.2

[Semi-variable cost]

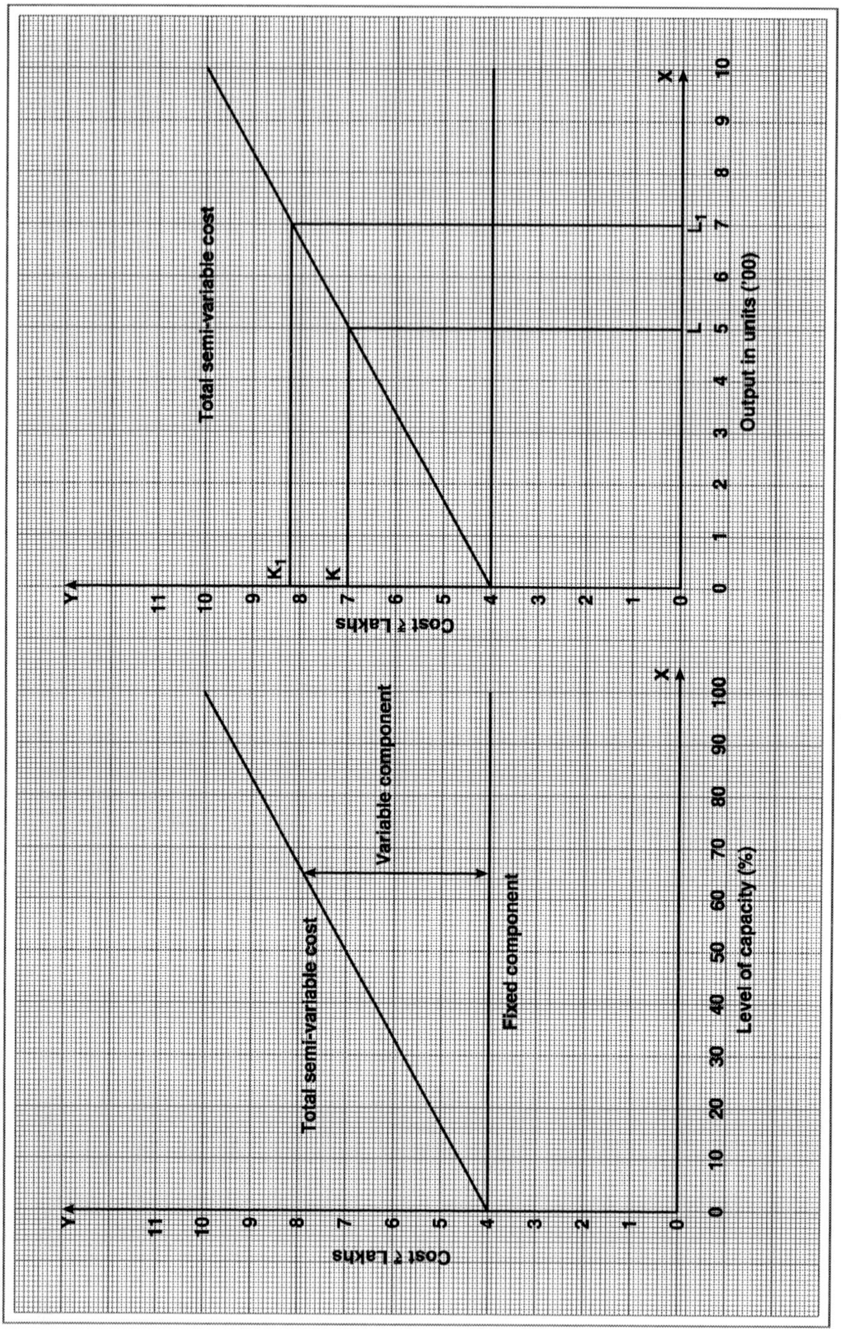

Graph 10.3

Numerical Example: Semi-variable overheads ₹ 6, 00,000 are constant up to 75% capacity (18,750 units) but increase by 20% over 75% but up to 85% and then increase by 30% over 85% but up to 100% capacity.

Capacity (%)	Output (unit) (A)	Total Semi-variable overheads (₹) (B)	Variable overheads per unit (₹) (C) = (B)/(A)
50	12,500	6,00,000	48.00
60	15,000	6,00,000	40.00
70	17,500	6,00,000	34.29
80	20,000	7,20,000	36.00
90	22,500	9,36,000	41.60
100	25,000	9,36,000	37.44

I-2 (Segregation of Variable and Fixed overhead)

UV Industries Limited is a single product organization having a manufacturing capacity of 7,500 units per week of 45 hours. The output data vis-à-vis different elements of cost for three consecutive weeks is as under:

Unit Produced	*Direct Material (₹)*	*Direct Labour (₹)*	*Total Factory Overheads (₹)*
3,000	*12,750*	*15,000*	*93,000*
3,500	*14,875*	*17,500*	*96,000*
4,500	*19,125*	*22,500*	*1,02,000*

Work out the selling price assuming an activity level of 80% weekly capacity utilization and a profit of 25% on selling price.

Solution : Working notes:

Incremental activity level: 4,500 – 3,000 = 1,500

Incremental factory overhead: ₹ (1,02,000 – 93,000) = ₹ 9,000

Estimated variable overhead per unit: 9,000 ÷1,500 = ₹ 6

Estimated fixed overhead: ₹ {1,02,000 – (6 × 4,500)} = ₹ 75,000

Computation of selling price at activity level of 6,000 units (i.e. 80% of 7,500):

Cost Element	Calculations	Amount (₹)
Direct Material @ ₹ 4.25	4.25 × 6,000	25,500
Direct Labour @ ₹ 5	5.00 × 6,000	30,000
Variable Overhead @ ₹ 6	6.00 × 6,000	36,000
Fixed Overhead		75,000

Total Works Cost		1,66,500
Profit	25% of S.P. or 1/3 of cost = [1,66,500 ×(1/3)]	55,500
Sale Value		2,22,000

Selling Price per unit = 2,22,000 ÷ 6,000 = ₹ 37.

Element-wise Classification

This classification is according to the nature and source of expenditure. The total expenses are split-up into (i) Indirect Materials, (ii) Indirect labour, and (iii) Indirect Expenses.

(i) Indirect Materials: Materials which cannot be allocated but which can be apportioned to or absorbed by cost centers or cost units. These are (a) stores used in maintenance of machinery, building etc like lubricants, cotton waste, bricks and cements; (b) Stores used by the service departments, and (c) Materials which due to their cost being small, are not considered worthwhile to be treated as direct materials.

(ii) Indirect labour: The wages of that labour which cannot be allocated but which can be apportioned to or absorbed by cost centers or cost units is known as indirect labour. Wages paid to labour which is employed other than on production constitute indirect labour costs. Maintenance workers, supervisors, departmental coolies, material handling and internal transport trainees and instructors, labour employed in time office and security office are some of the examples of indirect labour.

(iii) Indirect Expenses: These are the expenses which cannot be allocated but which can be apportioned to or absorbed by cost centers or cost units as rents rates insurance municipal taxes, general manager's salary, welfare expenses, telephone expenses, power and fuel. Two types of expenses come under this category: (a) Expenditure for which payments are made for services rendered or supplies made. (b) Such items which do not involve any payments and are mere adjustment transactions such as depreciation.

Overhead According to Nature of Expenses

The classification is done according to the nature and source of the expenditure. It is the logical outcome of the definition of the word 'Overhead'; expenses are categorised under three main groups given hereunder:

(i) *Indirect materials:* Material costs which cannot be allocated but which are to be apportioned to or absorbed by cost centres or cost units. Lubricants, fuel, tools for general use, etc. are some of the examples of indirect material costs.

(ii) *Indirect wages:* Such wages cannot be allocated but are to be apportioned to or absorbed by cost centres or cost units. Wages of cleaner/sweeper, idle time wages, maintenance and repair wages, leave pay, employer's contribution to ESI, etc. are some of the examples of such type of wages.

(iii) *Indirect Expenses:* Expenses which cannot be allocated but which are to be apportioned to or absorbed by cost centres or cost units are indirect expenses. Power, depreciation, insurance, taxes, rates and rent, etc. are some of the indicative examples of such nature.

Standing Order Numbers

In order to have quick and correct identification of overhead expenses, each group or sub-group of overheads should be assigned a distinct number. Such numbers/codes are known as Standing Order Number and are put in a manual maintained for this very purpose. The number and type of standing order numbers depend on several factors:

1. Size of the factory;
2. Diversity of production;
3. Geographical spread of production;
4. Types of expenses; and
5. Nature and degree of control required.

Ingredients of an effective system of Standing Order Numbers

The Cost-benefit Analysis must be done before it is introduced:

1. There should be no confusion or ambiguity regarding the Standing Order Number of overhead cost. Each Standing Order Number must be well defined.
2. Distinct/unique standing order number should be assigned to fixed overheads and variable overheads because separate rates of recovery are applied for the two.
3. The system should be in tune with the requirements of the organisation in terms of its size, nature and diversity.
4. The system should be comprehensive and cover all overhead costs.
5. The assigned number must be easy to remember.
6. Each overhead cost should be represented by a code to facilitate accumulation and distribution of overheads.

Codification of Overheads

Objectives: Codification of overheads should follow the same requirements as already listed for Standing order numbers. Coding is the technique of representing various costs and cost categories in numbers or alphabets or a combination of the two. It serves the following objectives:

1. Collection, Classification and Recording of overheads are facilitated.
2. Apportionment of similar overheads on similar basis is facilitated.
3. Departmentalization of overheads is facilitated.
4. Analysis of overheads becomes easier.
5. Computerization of cost data becomes easier.

Methods: Overheads may be coded according to one or more of the following systems:

1. *Serial Number System:* Each overhead cost is to be assigned a unique number. A group of numbers may be assigned for a particular group of overheads. Indirect materials may be assigned serial number between 0 and 20. For indirect factory expenses it may range between 21 and 50.
2. *Decimal System:* Decimal/s may be used with numbers. First number may be used to indicate the main group and decimal portion may be used for the sub-group/s. The code may be 1.5 indicating 1 as material and 5 as Lubricating oil, and the detailed code 1.5.2 may indicate 1 as material and 5 as Lubricating oil and 2 as the quality of the lubricating oil.
3. *Alphabetical system:* Alphabets are used as code. The alphabets are so chosen that they can be easily related to the relevant overhead cost, for example DP for Depreciation and W&S for Wages and Salaries.
4. *Alpha-Numericals:* Both alphabets and numbers may be used in a single code, for example DP1 for Depreciation of Machinery and for example DP2 for Depreciation of Furniture.

Illustration 10.2 : (Fixed Overheads computation)

The standard overhead rate for a department is ₹ 35 per hour. Based on the following details, work out the activity level at which the overhead rate has been pre-determined.

Details	*I*	*II*	*III*
Activity level (Hours)	*800*	*1,200*	*1,600*
Overhead Allowance (₹)	*28,000*	*33,600*	*39,200*

Solution :

$$\text{Variable Overheads per Hour} = \frac{\text{Change in Overhead Allowance}}{\text{Change in Activity Level}}$$

$$= 5{,}600 \div 400 = ₹\ 14 \text{ per hour}$$

Fixed Overheads:

= Total Overheads at an activity Level – Total Variable overheads at that activity level

= 28,000 – (800 × 14)

= 28,000 – 11,200 = ₹ 16,800

or

= 33,600 – (1,200 × 14)

= 33,600 – 16,800 = ₹ 16,800

Recovery of Fixed Overheads per hour:

= Standard overhead rate – Variable overhead rate

= 35 – 14 = ₹ 21

Activity level to recover fixed overheads of ₹ 16,800:

= Amount of Fixed overheads / Fixed Overheads per hour

= 16,800 ÷ 21 = 800 hours

Verification:

Activity Level: 800 Hours

Details	**Amount** (₹)
Fixed overheads	16,800
Variable overheads (800 × 14)	11,200
Total overheads allowance	28,000

Illustration 10.3 : (Fixed and variable Overheads)

A factory incurred the following expenses during the year 2007– 08:

Details			***Amount*** (₹)
Direct Materials			*600,00,000*
Direct Wages			*300,00,000*
Factory overheads:	*Fixed*	*75,00,000*	
	Variable	*150,00,000*	*225,00,000*
Total			*1125,00 000*

Estimated Expenses about the year 2008 – 09 are as under:

(i) *40% additional workers would be employed at 12.5% higher pay. These workers would be 20% more efficient.*

(ii) *Efficiency of the existing workers would increase by 8%.*

(iii) *Fixed overheads will increase by 20%.*

(iv) *Per unit cost of direct materials will come down by 10%.*

(v) *Variable overheads will increase in direct proportion to number of workers.*

Find out the total cost for the year 2008 – 09.

Solution : Working Notes: Material cost for the year 2008 – 09 increases in proportion to output; Output by the existing workers increases by 8% and that of the new workers by 48% because these 40% new workers are 20% more efficient. Total output in terms of material units are ₹ 6,00,00,000 + 8% of 6,00,00,000 and ₹ + 48% of 6,00,00,000 i.e. ₹ 6,00,00,000 + 48,00,000 + 2,88,00,000 = ₹ 9,36,00,000 subject to 10% fall in material prices i.e. The Direct material cost would be ₹ 8,42,40,000.

Estimated Total cost for the year 2008 – 09:

Details		**Amount** (₹)
Direct Material:		
[(600, 00 000 × 1.08) + (600, 00,000 × 0.4 × 1.2)] × 0.9		842,00,000
Direct Wages:		
[(300, 00 000 + (300, 00,000 × 0.4 × 1.125)]		435,00,000
Overheads:		
Fixed: [75, 00,000 × 1.2]	90,00,000	
Variable: [150, 00,000 × 1.4]	210,00,000	300,00,000
Total Estimated Expenses		1487,00,000

Illustration 10.4 : (Recovery of Overheads)

At 50% capacity utilisation the overhead recovery rate is ₹ 200 per unit. At 70% capacity the rate comes down to ₹ 160 per unit. What should be the recovery rate if the production attains 80% capacity utilisation? Calculate the recovery rate at 40%, 60%, 90% and 100% capacity.

Solution : Let the production at 100% capacity be 100 units so that 50 units at 50% capacity and 70 units at 70% capacity, and so on.

Total Overheads at 70% capacity i.e. for 70 units = ₹ 11,200 (= 70 × 160)

Total Overheads at 50% capacity i.e. for 50 units = ₹ 10,000 (= 50 × 200)

Variable overheads per percent i.e. per unit = Difference in total Overheads / Difference in Capacity Utilisation

= 11,200 – 10,000 / 70 – 50

= 1,200 / 20 = ₹ 60 per unit

Fixed Overheads:

= Total Overheads at an activity Level – Total Variable overheads at that activity level

= 11,200 – (70 × 60)

= 11,200 – 4,200 = ₹ 7,000

or

= 10,000 – (50 × 60)

= 10,000 – 3,000 = ₹ 7,000

Total Overheads at 80% activity Level:

= Fixed Overheads + Total Variable overheads at 80% activity Level

= 7,000 + (80 × 60)

= 7,000 + 4,800 = ₹ 11,800

Overheads recovery rate at 80% capacity Utilisation

= 11,800 / 80 = ₹ 147.50

Overheads recovery rate at different capacity utilisation levels

Capacity Utilisation (%) (Units)	40 40	60 60	90 90	100 100
Total fixed Overheads	7,000	7,000	7,000	7,000
Total variable Overheads	2,400	3,600	5,400	6,000
Total overheads	9,400	10,600	12,400	13,000
Overheads Recovery Rate	9,400/40 = ₹235	10,600/60 = ₹176.67	12,400/90 = ₹137.78	13,000/100 = ₹130

Illustration 10.5 : *Following data have been extracted from the records of a manufacturing company whose level of operations vary during different months:*

Level of Activity	*Minimum*	*Maximum*
Machine Hours	*40,000*	*1,00,000*
Manufacturing overheads (₹)	*6,00,000*	*10,80,000*

Determine the fixed and variable components of manufacturing overheads and compute the total manufacturing overheads for an activity level of 60,000 machine hours.

Solution : Variable overheads per Machine hour:

$$= \frac{\text{Difference in Total Overheads}}{\text{Difference in Capacity Utilisation}}$$

= 10,80,000 – 6,00,000/1,00,000 – 40,000

= 4,80,000/60,000 = ₹ 8 per machine hour

Fixed Overheads:

= Total Overheads at an activity Level – Total Variable overheads at that activity level

= 6,00,000 – (40,000 × 8)

= 6,00,000 – 3,20,000 = ₹ 2,80,000

or

= 10,80,000 – (1,00,000 × 8)

= 10,80,000 – 8,00,000 = ₹ 2,80,000

Total Overheads for 60,000 Machine hours:

= Fixed Overheads + Total Variable overheads for 60,000 Machine hours

= 2,80,000 + (60,000 × 8)

= 2,80,000 + 4,80,000 = ₹ 7,60,000

Profitability and overheads

Profitability of the business gets affected by the quantum and nature of overheads in the following manner:

1. An allocation of overheads which results in higher charge to a product reduces profitability of that product.
2. An increase in efficiency, in most of the cases, reduces per unit fixed overhead cost, and vice versa.
3. An increase in output reduces per unit fixed overhead cost, and increases profits at higher rate, and vice versa.

Illustration 10.6 : (Profitability and Overheads)

SV limited produces and sells three products P-1, P-2 and P-3. The details of cost and profitability are as under:

Details	*P-1*	*P-2*	*P-3*
Present output (units)	*10,000*	*15,000*	*25,000*
Prime cost per unit (₹)	*20*	*25*	*45*
Variable overheads per unit (₹)	*10*	*10*	*5*
Fixed overheads per unit (₹)	*5*	*7*	*10*
Total cost per unit (₹)	*35*	*42*	*60*
Selling price per unit (₹)	*60*	*70*	*80*
Profit per unit (₹)	*25*	*28*	*20*
Profit percentage on cost (%)	*71.43*	*66.67*	*33.33*

Fixed overheads are inevitable. With a view to increase profits, the company intends to discontinue the production of one of the three products. If production of one product is discontinued, that of the other can be increased by 60% each. Initially it was suggested that the production of product P-3 should be discontinued as it gives least per unit profit and least profit percentage on cost. Examine this suggestion and compare it with other alternatives to arrive at the most profitable alternative.

Solution : Working Notes :

Computation of Fixed cost:

Details	**Amount (₹)**
P-1: (10,000 × 5)	50,000
P-2: (15,000 × 7)	1,05,000
P-3: (25,000 × 10)	2,50,000
Total	4,05,000

Computation of Existing Profit:

Details	**Amount (₹)**
P-1: (10,000 × 25)	2,50,000
P-2: (15,000 × 28)	4,20,000
P-3: (25,000 × 20)	5,00,000
Total	11,70,000

Computation of Profit (as per Question):

Details	**Product:P-1 Unit:16,000 Amount (₹)**	**Product:P-2 Unit:24,000 Amount (₹)**	**Total Unit:40,000 Amount (₹)**
A. Sales:	9,60,000	16,80,000	26,40,000
(16,000 ×60)			
(24,000 ×70)			
Prime cost:	3,20,000		
(16,000 × 20)		6,00,000	9,20,000
(24,000 × 25)			
Variable Overheads:	1,60,000		
(16,000 × 10)		2,40,000	
(24,000 × 10)			4,00,000
Total variable cost	4,80,000	8,40,000	13,20,000
Total Fixed cost			4,05,000
B. Total cost			17,25,000
C. Total Profit			9,15,000

Alternative I to the Proposal given in the question:

Details	**Product:P-1 Unit:16,000 Amount (₹)**	**Product:P-3 Unit:40,000 Amount (₹)**	**Total Unit:56,000 Amount (₹)**
A. Sales:	9,60,000	32,00,000	41,60,000
(16,000 × 60)			
(40,000 × 80)			
Prime cost:	3,20,000		
(16,000 × 20)		18,00,000	21,20,000
(40,000 × 45)			
Variable Overheads:	1,60,000		
(16,000 ×10)		2,00,000	
(40,000 × 5)			3,60,000
Total variable cost	4,80,000	20,00,000	24,80,000

Total Fixed cost			4,05,000
B. Total cost			28,85,000
C. Total Profit			12,75,000

Alternative II to the Proposal given in the question:

Details	**Product:P-2 Unit:24,000 Amount (₹)**	**Product:P-3 Unit:40,000 Amount (₹)**	**Total Unit:64,000 Amount (₹)**
A. Sales: (24,000 × 70) (40,000 × 80)	16,80,000	32,00,000	48,80,000
Prime cost: (24,000 × 25) (40,000 × 45)	6,00,000	18,00,000	24,00,000
Variable Overheads: (24,000 × 10) (40,000 × 5)	2,40,000	2,00,000	4,40,000
Total variable cost	8,40,000	20,00,000	28,40,000
Total Fixed cost			4,05,000
B. Total cost			32,45,000
C. Total Profit			16,35,000

Comments: Highest total profit is earned in the Alternative No. II, i.e. Discontinuance of the product P-1. This leads to increase in level of activity i.e. production of product P-1 is 24,000 units and that of product P-3 is 40,000 units. Two factors are responsible for this situation:

(1) Total fixed cost remains constant at ₹ 4, 05,000; and

(2) Volume of output and sale is higher for Product P-2 and P-3; this results in higher contribution from these products.

CAPACITY AND OVERHEAD RATES

The rate of recovery of overhead is based upon many factors. These factors are the method of absorption based on volume of output, or direct material cost or direct wages or labour/machine hours etc. It also depends upon the quantum of overhead, size of labour force, degree of mechanization, the level of activity etc. One of the major factors having a direct bearing on the rate of overhead is the level of activity. Pre-determined rates of recovery of overheads are significantly influenced by the estimated level of activity. The rate of absorption of variable overheads will remain unaffected by the change in level of activity. This is not so with fixed overheads. Total fixed overheads remain the same irrespective of the level of operations/activity. However, the overhead rate varies with changes in the estimated volume of activity. Hence, it is absolutely necessary to consider the particular volume base of computing fixed overhead rate.

The capacity of a factory is its ability to produce a certain quantity of output with the given productive input resources. Capacity is measured in physical units such as number of units, kwh., metric tonnes, etc. The choice of activity level or volume may affect product costing, inventory valuation and profit. It is advisable to understand various concepts of capacity: Maximum capacity, Practical capacity, Capacity based on Sale expectancy, Actual capacity, Normal capacity and idle capacity.

(1) *Maximum capacity (Rated Capacity):* It is the capacity of a plant as indicated by its manufacturer. It is the maximum possible productive capacity of the plant. It is the installed capacity. It may be achieved subject to the plant working without any interruption or loss of operating time.

(2) *Practical capacity (Operating Capacity):* It is the capacity actually utilized after taking into consideration loss of operating time due to repairs, break-down of plant, Sundays and holidays, setting up time etc. It is the difference between the Maximum Capacity and the Loss of Operating time. Practical capacity is in general taken between 80 and 90 per cent of the maximum capacity. It is on this basis the predetermined rates of recovery of overheads are computed.

(3) *Capacity based on Sale expectancy:* It is the capacity to make and sell. This capacity level is decided keeping in mind the market demand of the product/ service. This level may be less than the practical capacity. The level it works is based on expected sales expectancy.

(4) *Actual capacity:* This is the level of activity or capacity actually achieved during a given period. It may be more or less than the practical capacity and capacity based on sales expectancy. Actual capacity can be known only at the end of the period.

(5) *Normal capacity:* It is the long –term average capacity that will satisfy average customer demand over a period of 3 to 5 years. Normal capacity takes into account seasonal/cyclical and trend factors. It is the capacity available for utilization during a normal period, if external factors such as lack of demand are not in operation.

(6) *Idle capacity:* It is that part of practical capacity which cannot be utilized. Non-availability of materials, shortage of skilled labour, lack of demand, and shortage of power are some of the factors responsible for non-utilisation of the available capacity. It is the difference between practical capacity and capacity based on sales expectancy.

Idle capacity is different from excess capacity. The question of excess capacity arises only when the firm has with it larger production capacity than what is necessary or what is expected to be used. It may arise because of non-synchronization of machines and equipment in the various production departments. The phenomenon of idle capacity is temporary while that of the excess capacity is more or less of permanent nature.

Idle Capacity Costs

These costs are mostly fixed in nature. Depreciation, repairs, maintenance, rent rates insurance and supervision are the elements of such cost. Such cost cannot be absorbed owing to underutilization of the plant capacity. It means the unabsorbed fixed overheads represent the cost of idle capacity. Such cost can be arrived by applying the following formula:

$$\text{Idle Capacity Cost} = \frac{[\text{Total overheads related to the Plant}]}{[\text{Normal capacity of the Plant}]} \times \text{Idle capacity}$$

OR

$$\text{Idle Capacity Cost} = \text{Rate of Recovery based on Normal Capacity} \times \text{Idle capacity}$$

Treatment of Idle Capacity Costs

The treatment of idle capacity cost depends upon the fact whether it is normal or abnormal. Normal idle capacity cost arises because of factors beyond the control of the Management. Repairs, maintenance, lack of demand, seasonal nature of product are the some of the factors which are unavoidable. Idle capacity cost arisen due to such factors may be absorbed by the product cost by inflating the Rate of Absorption. , otherwise a supplementary rate may be computed and applied. Factors such as lack of managerial planning and control, power failure, are avoidable and idle cost arisen due to such factors is known as abnormal. Idle cost arising due to depression is also abnormal. Such costs should not form part of product cost and be transferred to costing profit and loss account.

Illustration 10.7 : (Overhead rates and Capacity Utilisation):

From the following data calculate overhead rates based on (i) Maximum Capacity; (ii) Practical Capacity; and (iii) Capacity based on expected sales.

Details	*Maximum Capacity (100%)*	*Practical Capacity (90%)*	*Sales Expectancy Capacity (80%)*
Direct Labour Hours	*25,000*	*22,500*	*20,000*
Fixed Overhead	*2,25,000*	*2,25,000*	*2,25,000*
Variable overhead	*1,50,000*	*1,35,000*	*1,20,000*

If the actual capacity utilized be 19,400 labour hours, calculate amount of under/over absorbed of fixed overhead on the basis of each of above capacities.

Solution : Computation of Overhead Rates of absorption

Details	Maximum Capacity (100%)	Practical Capacity (90%)	Sales Expectancy Capacity (80%)
Direct Labour Hours	25,000	22,500	20,000
Variable overhead	1,50,000	1,35,000	1,20,000
Fixed Overhead	2,25,000	2,25,000	2,25,000
Variable overhead Rate (₹)	6.00	6.00	6.00
Fixed overhead Rate (₹)	9.00	10.00	11.25

Thus, variable Overhead rate remains same at all levels of activity and fixed overhead rate of absorption varies and depends on the specified capacity.

If the actual capacity utilized be 19,400 labour-hours, the amount of under absorption will be as under:

Details	Fixed overhead rate per Labour-hour (₹)	Overhead recovered on actual capacity i.e. 19,400 labour –hours (₹)	Under Recovery of Overhead (₹ 2,25,000– Recovered Amount) (₹)
A. Maximum Capacity	9.00	1,74,600	50,400
B. Practical Capacity	10.00	1,94,000	31,000
C. Expected Sales Capacity	11.25	2,18,250	6,750

Inference:

1. Under Recovery in A indicates that idle capacity cost is inclusive of all interruptions.
2. Under Recovery in B indicates that Idle capacity cost is due to lack of sales provided that no amount of the under recovered amount is attributable to other factors such as change in expenditure etc.
3. Under Recovery in C indicates that idle capacity cost is unutilized capacity due to expected sales not being materialized.

RESEARCH & DEVELOPMENT OVERHEADS

Keeping in view the prevailing competitive conditions, research and development is necessary not only for growth of the business but also for its survival. Large scale firms spend huge sums on research and development in order to carry out this function on continuous basis." Research Cost is the cost of searching for new and improved products, new application of materials, or new or improved methods". I.C.M.A. The research staff of the organization can carry out research work or it may be entrusted to an outside agency. Such costs of carrying out research include the cost of initial experimentation, all types of tests and subsequent small trial runs in order to prove the results of research. The main items of expenditure are salaries and wages of the research and testing staff, materials and facilities used in laboratory and research departments and payment to outside agencies.

Research may be of two types: (a) Basic research, and (b) Applied research.

(a) Basic Research: This is done to increase the knowledge in certain fields such as production, marketing etc. Such research is done in the hope that some useful applications will develop from it. Large companies the government and the education institutional go for such research. Basic research may be general or routine research. General research is meant for general purposes and is connected with any specific product. The benefit of such research cannot be assessed for a particular product. Routine research includes test for quality and specifications of input and output.

(b) Applied Research: It aims at producing results. It is usually limited to the study of field closely related to organisation's existing areas of business. Such research takes help of available knowledge or new facts uncovered by firm's basic research. Such research is done for improving the existing products, methods or equipments for exploring or establishing new products, processes methods or equipments for exploring or establishing new products which can provide more profits and for providing improved measures of health, safety and convenience. It may relate to raw materials and other resource utilisation and management of personnel and human relations.

Development Cost

"Development cost is the cost of the process which begins with the implementation of the decision to produce a new or improved product or to employ a new or improved method and ends with the commencement of formal production of that product or by that method". I.C.M.A.

Development starts where research ends as development expenditure is incurred to put the results of research on practical commercial basis. In fact, research indicates whether it is scientifically and technologically possible to manufacture a product according to a specified design. Development is the next stage when a small unit of production is made on trial or pilot run under practical conditions of production to see whether manufacture on large scale would be commercially viable. If the firm gets success, then the production on full scale is undertaken. Thus, Development forms a bridge between research and production though it is more close to the latter. The benefits of research are passed on to the development and the results obtained from development work are passed on to benefit production.

Features of Research and Development cost

(1) Research and development cost is incurred ahead of actual production. And it may not be charged to production.

(2) The benefit of this cost is spread over a number of years, so it is deferred revenue expenditure.

(3) Amount of expenditure involved in research and development is quite huge; it becomes difficult for a small firm to undertake the research and development work.

(4) At times research being unsuccessful gives no tangible result and huge expenditure incurred on research stands wasted.

(5) It is very difficult to fix proper standards against which efficiency of research and development expenditure is to be compared.

(6) There are varied objects for which the research and development is undertaken. So such costs require different treatments.

Objectives of Research and Development

(a) To acquire better knowledge and know-how.

(b) To find out new or improved products, new or improved methods of production and new applications of material so as to maximize profits.

(c) To find new uses for products.

(d) To improve the organization and layout of the business.

(e) To explore possibilities of a new and/or large market.

(f) To improve upon the existing products and processes so that it may give more profit at reasonable price and quality.

(g) To find methods by which better service may be rendered to the customers.

(h) To find out the possibilities of expansion/diversification of existing business.

Collection of Research and Development cost

Such costs are collected through the usual documents as material requisitions, labour time cards, invoices and vouchers. Special items such as royalty, patent rights. Cost of rectification etc is recorded through the vouchers.

A work order number is allotted for each research and development project.

Illustration 10.8 : (Treatment of R&D cost)

Alpha Devices Ltd. manufactures various surgical instruments/equipments. It has its own engineering Research Centre where applied research is carried on.

On April 1, 2001 three equipments were in process. During the year 2001, two more equipments were taken up for research and trial. The expenses booked on research during the yea2001-2002 are as under:

Details	*Amount (₹)*
Material Cost	*480000*
Labour Cost	*80000*
Factory Overheads	*16000*
Administration Overheads	*8000*
Regular and Routine Research	*25000*

The relevant expenditure on research is allocated on the basis of percentage shown against each product in the following table:

Product	*Opening Balance*	*Current Year Allocation (%)*
Multi-scanner	*6600*	*30.0*
Pulse reader	*25000*	*20.0*
Photo censor	*8400*	*12.5*
Blood analyzer	*Nil*	*22.5*
Cardiac pace-maker	*Nil*	*15.0*

On March 31, 2002 the results of various equipments were as under:

1. *Multi-scanner was successfully developed and trial production of 80 units was made. Expected future production will be 8000 units.*
2. *Pulse reader was a total failure.*
3. *Photo Censor is still under development.*
4. *Blood Analyser is under trial.*
5. *Cardiac pacemaker is successfully developed. The patent rights have been sold to M/s Medi-Appliances at 50% profit.*

Give your advice as to how the expenditure after allocation will be treated in the books of account of Alpha Devices Ltd. Also, state the treatment to be given to regular and routine research expenses.

Solution : Statement of Allocation of Research Expenditure

Details	Total	Product				
		Multi-scanner	Pulse reader	Photo censor	Blood analyzer	Cardiac pacemaker
Opening Balance	40,000	6,600	25,000	8,400	NIL	NIL
Expenses incurred	4,80,000					
During the year:						
Material Labour	80,000					
Factory overhead	16,000					
Administration	8,000					
overhead	5,84,000	1,75,200	1,16,800	73,000	1,31,400	87,600
Total	6,24,000	1,81,800	1,41,800	81,400	1,31,400	87,600

Statement showing treatment of Research expenditure allocation after Apportionment

Product	Amount (₹)	Details of treatment
Multi-scanner	1,81,800	Absorption Rate = (1,81,800/8,080) = ₹ 22.5 Charge cost of trial production to Costing Profit and Loss Account: = 80 × 22.50 = ₹ 1800. Recover the balance amount ₹1,80,000 (i.e. 1,81,800 – 18,00)
Pulse reader	1,41,800	The amount should be charged to costing Profit and loss Account as there has been total failure.
Photo censor	81,400	The amount should be carried forward in Work-in-Progress account as the product is under the development stage.
Blood Analyser	1,31,400	The amount should be carried forward in Work-in-Progress account as it is at the Trial stage.
Cardiac Pacemaker	87,600	The sale price of patent right will be as Cost + Profit Margin i.e. 87,600 + 0.5 × 87600 = ₹ 1,31,400 or 87,600 + 1.5 = ₹ 1,31,400

Note: (1) Research Expenditure should be charged to the Profit & Loss account in the year of incurrence. However, in the case of development expenses, it should be ensured that they are carried forward only if otherwise justified.

LET US RECAPITULATE

1. Overheads by definition are indirect costs which cannot be conveniently allocated to cost units.
2. Overhead is the aggregate of indirect material cost, indirect wages, and indirect expenses.
3. Overhead costs by nature are common to a number of cost units and cost centres.
4. Certain cost of small value, such as nuts bolts nails screws, lubricants etc. though identifiable with a particular cost unit may be treated as overhead cost.
5. Purely financial items such as cash discounts, subscriptions, donations, and income-tax are not considered as overheads.
6. Cost classification is the process of grouping of costs on the basis of similarities/dissimilarities and specific objectives.
7. In a factory if there is only one production department and same or similar jobs are done, the costing of the job is quite easy as there is no need for allocation/apportionment of overhead.
8. The process of allocation and apportionment of overheads to cost centres or cost units is called departmentalization or primary distribution of overheads.

9. Allocation of Overheads is the allotment of whole items of cost to cost centres or cost units.
10. Allocation and apportionment are two successive stages in the process of distribution of indirect expenses.
11. Overhead apportionment is the distribution of overheads over various production and service departments.
12. Absorption of overheads is charging of overheads to cost units.
13. Production overhead means indirect expenditure incurred in connection with production operations. It is the sum total of indirect factory material cost, indirect factory wages, and indirect factory expenses.
14. Expenditures under the category of administration overhead are of general nature and consist of all costs incurred in the direction, control and administration (inclusive of secretarial, accounting and financial control, and legal work) of an undertaking which is not directly related to production or selling and distribution functions of the management.
15. Selling overhead is the cost of seeking to create and stimulate demand and procuring orders.
16. Distribution overhead cost includes all expenditures incurred from the time product is completed in the factory till it reaches the customer.
17. Fixed overheads are those costs which do not vary with the change in the volume of production up to a given range.
18. Variable overheads are those costs which vary in direct proportion to the volume of production.
19. Semi-fixed overheads are those costs of which one part remains fixed up to a given range and the other part varies with the change in the volume of production but not in the same proportion.
20. Indirect Materials are those materials which cannot be allocated but which can be apportioned to or absorbed by cost centers or cost units.
21. Indirect labour means wages of that labour which cannot be allocated but which can be apportioned to or absorbed by cost centers or cost units is known as indirect labour.
22. Indirect Expenses are the expenses which cannot be allocated but which can be apportioned to or absorbed by cost centers or cost units.
23. In order to have quick and correct identification of overhead expenses, each group or sub-group of overheads is assigned a distinct number /code which is known as Standing Order Number.
24. Coding is the technique of representing various costs and cost categories in numbers or alphabets or a combination of the two.
25. An increase in output reduces per unit fixed overhead cost, and increases profits at higher rate, and vice versa.

26. Research Cost is the cost of searching for new and improved products, new application of materials, or new or improved methods.
27. Costs of carrying out research include the cost of initial experimentation, all types of tests and subsequent small trial runs in order to prove the results of research.
28. Development cost is the cost of the process which begins with the implementation of the decision to produce a new or improved product or to employ a new or improved method and ends with the commencement of formal production of that product or by that method.
29. Research Expenditure should be charged to the Profit & Loss account in the year of incurrence. However, in the case of development expenses, it should be ensured that they are carried forward only if otherwise justified.

SOLVED PROBLEMS

Problem 1. *Standard overhead rate is ₹ 54 per hour based on the following details provided to you, work out the activity level at which the overhead rate has been fixed.*

Working hours	*Overhead Allowance*
6,000	*3,00,000*
8,000	*3,60,000*
10,000	*4,20,000*

Solution : Variable overheads Rate per hour:

= Change in Amount of Expenses (₹)/Change in level of Activity

= 60,000/2,000

= ₹ 30 per hour

Fixed overhead = Total overheads – variable overheads

= 3,00,000 – (6,000 × 30)

= 3,00,000 – 1,80,000

= ₹ 1,20,000

Activity level at which overhead rate has been fixed:

= Fixed overhead/ Difference in two rates

= 1,20,000/24

= 5,000 working hours

Problem 2. *GP Industries Limited is a single product organisation having a manufacturing capacity of 15,000 units per week of 40 hours. The output data vis-à-vis different elements of cost for three consecutive weeks are given below:*

Production (Units)	*Direct Material (₹)*	*Direct Labour (₹)*	*Total Factory Overheads (₹)*
6,000	*30,000*	*48,000*	*84,000*
7,000	*35,000*	*56,000*	*90,000*
10,000	*50,000*	*80,000*	*10,800*

As a Cost Accountant, You are instructed by the management of the company to work out the selling Price assuming an activity level of 12,000 units per week and a profit of 20% on selling price.

Solution : Computation of rates of various elements of cost:

Direct Material:

30,000/6,000 = ₹ 5 per unit

Direct Labour:

48,000/6,000 = ₹ 8 per unit

Variable factory overheads:

Variable overheads Rate per Unit:

= Change in Amount of Expenses (₹)/Change in level of Activity

= 6,000/1,000 = ₹ 6 per Unit

Fixed overhead = Total overheads – variable overheads

= 84,000 – (6,000 × 6)

= 84,000 – 36,000 = ₹ 48,000

Computation of selling Price at a Level of 12,000 units of Production:

Details	Amount (₹)
Prime cost [5 + 8 + 6] = 12,000 × 19	2,28,000
Fixed cost	48,000
Total cost	2,76,000
Profit (1/5 of selling price I.e. 1/4 of Cost)	69,000
Total Sales value	3,45,000

Selling Price per unit

[3,45,000/12,000] = ₹ 28.75

Problem 3. *A Company sets up a factory overhead absorption rate of 85% of direct labour cost based on the following budget:*

Details	***Amount*** (₹)
Factory overhead costs	*90,000*
Direct labour hours	*750*

Labour rate per hour	*150*
Direct labour cost	*1,12,500*

In the current month, the method of operations was changed. The new operations require labour that will be paid ₹ 200 per hour; the operating time would be reduced by 20 percent.

What steps should be taken by the company's cost accountant to meet the situation? Give the necessary calculations also.

Solution :

Details	**Amount (₹)**
Factory overhead costs	90,000
Direct labour hours	750
Labour rate per hour	150
Direct labour cost	1,12,500

Factory overhead absorption rate in the previous month:

= (90,000/1,12,500) × 100 = 80% of direct labour cost.

Changes in current month

Labour wage rate (₹) = 200

Labour hours are 20% less than in previous month:

= [750 – (0.2 × 750) = 750 – 150 = 600 hours

Direct labour cost = 200 × 600 = ₹ 1,20,000

The new factory overhead absorption rate:

= (90,000/1,20,000) × 100 = 75% of direct labour cost.

The company's cost accountant should charge factory overhead at 75% of direct labour cost on current month and not at 80% as in previous month.

OBJECTIVE TYPE EXERCISES

I. Fill in the blank spaces with suitable word/s :

1. .... means allotment of overhead to cost unit.
2. .... means allotment of proportion of items of cost to cost centres or to cost unit.
3. Charging overheads to the product is known as ....
4. Charging overheads to cost .... is known as absorption of overheads.
5. Charging to cost centre those overheads that result only from the existence of the cost centre is known as ....
6. The technical term for charging of overheads to cost unit is known as ....
7. .... means that actual overheads are more than the absorbed overheads.
8. When the amount of overhead recovered is less than the actual amount of overheads, it is known as .... of overheads.

9. A factory manufacturing only one type of product adopts that method of absorption, which is ....

10. Charging to a cost centre those overheads that result only from the existence of the cost centre is known as ....

11. Machine Hour Rate method of recovery of overheads is used incase of departments where machine plays a .... role in production.

Answers :

1. Allocation	**2.** Apportionment	**3.** Absorption
4. units	**5.** Allocation of overheads	**6.** Absorption
7. Under-absorption	**8.** Under-absorption	
9. rate per unit of output	**10.** Allocation	**11.** Dominant.

II. Indicate whether the following statements are True or False :

1. Fixed overheads vary with the volume of production.
2. Allocation and apportionment of overheads means the same thing.
3. Direct assignment of factory overheads costs to each department is known as allocation of overheads.
4. The terms "allocation" and "apportionment" have the same meaning in costing.
5. Under absorption of overheads results in under-estimation of cost.
6. Under absorption of overheads decreases profits in costing books.
7. Apportionment of overheads means allotment of some items of cost which cannot be directly charged to cost units or centres.
8. When actual overheads exceed absorbed overheads, it is called over absorption.
9. Absorption means charging overheads to the product.
10. The use of actual overheads absorption rates results in delay in determining cost of products.
11. Salary of a foreman is a fixed overhead.
12. Manufacturing and administration overheads are different.
13. Overheads are also known as chargeable expenses.
14. Allocation of overhead implies the identification of overhead cost with particular cost centres to which they relate.
15. Absorption of overhead is the allotment of overhead to cost unit.
16. Variable overhead cost is a discretionary cost.
17. Fixed overhead cost is a committed cost.
18. Variable overhead cost is a period cost.

Answers :

1. False	**2.** False	**3.** True	**4.** False
5. True	**6.** False	**7.** False	**8.** False
9. True	**10.** True	**11.** True	**12.** True
13. False	**14.** True	**15.** True	**16.** False
17. False	**18.** False		

THEORETICAL EXERCISES

1. Indicate whether the following statements are True or False :
   1. Allotment of whole items of overhead to cost centre is known as apportionment of overhead. **[Ans. True]**
2. What do you mean by overheads? Why overheads are classified into fixed and variable overheads?
3. What do you mean by allocation, apportionment and absorption of overheads?
4. Why are overheads classified into fixed and variable categories? **[DU, B.Com (Hons.) 2000]**
5. Why do we employ pre-determined overhead rate of absorption? Under what circumstances is direct labour cost percentage method to be employed?
6. How will you treat Research and Development Costs in Cost accounts? **[DU, B.Com (Hons.) 2000]**
7. Distinguish between overhead and chargeable expenses. **[DU, B.Com (Hons.) 2001]**
8. Differentiate between apportionment and absorption of overheads. **[DU, B.Com (Hons.) 2003]**
9. Explain the general principles to be kept in mind while considering whether an item of expenditure is to be treated as overhead. **[DU, B.Com (Hons.) 2002]**
10. Explain in brief the following concepts:
    (i) Expenditure on Development **[DU, B.Com (Hons.) 2001]**
    (ii) Codification of overheads
11. How will you treat the following in Cost Accounts?
    (i) Interest on Capital
    (ii) Audit fees

NUMERICAL EXERCISES

1. Followwing data have been extracted from the records of a manufacturing company whose level of operations vary during different months:

Level of Activity	Minimum	Maximum
Machine Hours	30,000	80,000
Manufacturing overheads (₹)	4,00,000	6,00,000

Determine the fixed and variable components of manufacturing overheads and compute the total manufacturing overheads for an activity level of 50,000 machine hours. **[I.C. W. A (Inter) Modified]**

[Ans. (i) Fixed overheads: ₹ 2,80,000; (ii) Rate of recovery of variable overheads: ₹ 4 per machine hour; (iii) Total manufacturing overheads for 50,000 machine hours: ₹ 4,80,000.]

2. PV limited is produces and sells three products P-1, P-2 and P-3. The details of cost and profitability are as under:

Details	P-1	P-2	P-3
Present output (units)	4,000	5,000	6,000
Prime cost per unit (₹)	20	25	40
Variable overheads per unit (₹)	5	5	2
Fixed overheads per unit (₹)	2	3	8
Total cost per unit (₹)	27	33	50
Selling price per unit (₹)	40	50	58
Profit per unit (₹)	13	17	8
Profit percentage on cost (%)	48.15	51.51	16

Fixed overheads are inevitable. With a view to increase profits, the company intends to discontinue the production of one of the three products. If production of one product is discontinued, that of the other can be increased by 50% each. Initially it was suggested that the production of product P-3 should be discontinued as it gives least per unit profit and least profit percentage on cost. Examine this suggestion and compare it with other alternatives to arrive at the most profitable alternative.

[Ans. Preferable alternative is production of P-2 and P-3 as it fetches profit of ₹2,25,000 being the highest.]

3. A factory incurred the following expenses during the year 2007– 08:

Details			**Amount (₹ crore)**
Direct Materials			40
Direct Wages			20
Factory overheads:	Fixed	5	
	Variable	10	15
Total			75

Estimated Expenses about the year 2008 – 09 are as under:

(i) 30% additional workers would be employed at 10% higher pay. These workers would be 20% more efficient.

(ii) Efficiency of the existing workers would increase by 5%.

(iii) Fixed overheads will increase by 10%.

(iv) Per unit cost of direct materials will come down by 10%.

(v) Variable overheads will increase in direct proportion to number of workers.

Find out the total cost for the year 2008 – 09.

[Ans. Total Estimated cost for the year 2008 – 09 is ₹ 102.36 crore]

4. Standard overhead rate is ₹ 15 per hour based on the following details provided to you, work out the activity level at which the overhead rate has been fixed.

Working hours	Overhead Allowance (₹)
6,000	1,20,000
8,000	1,44,000
10,000	1,68,000

[I.C. W. A (Inter)]

[Ans. Variable overhead rate per hour: ₹ 12; fixed overheads: ₹ 48,000; activity level at which overhead rate has been fixed: 1,600 working hours]

5. Shyam Industries Limited is a single product organisation having a manufacturing capacity of 6,000 units per week of 40 hours. The output data vis-à-vis different elements of cost for three consecutive weeks are given below:

Production (Units)	Direct Material (₹)	Direct Labour (₹)	Total Factory Overheads (₹)
2,400	4,800	6,000	37,200
2,800	5,600	7,000	38,400
3,600	7,200	9,000	40,800

As a Cost Accountant, You are instructed by the management of the company to work out the selling Price assuming an activity level of 4,000 units per week and a profit of 20% on selling price.

[Ans. Variable overheads per unit: ₹ 3; fixed factory overheads: ₹ 48,000; Total Sales value: ₹75,000; Selling Price per unit: ₹ 18.75]

❑❑❑

11

Factory Overheads

Learning Objectives

It attempts to explain accounting for factory overheads. In this chapter you will learn :

1. Meaning, nature of factory overheads.
2. Process of allocation of cost.
3. Computation of machine hour rate and its application.
4. Process of reapportionment of cost of service departments.
5. Process of absorption of cost.
6. Treatment of over/under absorbed overheads.

NATURE

Factory overhead costs are operating costs of a business enterprise. Such costs cannot be traced directly to a specific unit of output. Factory overhead is the sum of indirect materials, indirect wages and indirect expenses. The term "overhead" is used interchangeably with "Factory/Manufacturing expense". However, the term "overhead" is preferable to manufacturing expenses, because manufacturing expenses often refer to all manufacturing costs, both direct and indirect. The term "overhead" may be used for all types of business enterprises while manufacturing expense is restricted in its use to manufacturing firms.

Allocation of Cost of Service Department to Producing Departments

There are two basic Factory departments in a manufacturing Company: (a) Producing departments and (b) Service departments. A Producing department is one where the conversion or production takes place. A Service department

(Stores or Maintenance) provides support to the producing departments. Since Service departments directly benefit the Producing departments, the expenses of the Service department should be allocated to the appropriate Producing departments (as a part of factory overhead costs). One of the following methods may be applied to allocate Service department costs to producing departments:

(I) Direct Method

(II) Step Method

(III) Algebraic Method.

(I) Direct Method

This is the most common method of allocating service department costs to producing departments because of its simplicity and ease of application. It involves allocation of Service department costs directly to Producing departments and inter-department service is altogether ignored.

Example 11.1

Assume the following data for the SV Ltd.:

Department	Amount (₹)
Service:	
S-1: Maintenance	16000
S-2: Canteen	7,000
Producing:	
P-1: Machinery	45,000
P-2: Assembly	83,000

The cost of the Maintenance department is allocated to the Producing Departments based on the number of Square Feet; the cost of Canteen department is allocated on the basis of number of employees.

Department	Direct Labour Hours	Area (Square feet)	Number of Employees
S-1: Maintenance	-	300	16
S-2: Canteen	-	900	12
P-1: Machinery	5,000	2,300	40
P-2: Assembly	20,000	5,700	160
Total	25,000	9,200	228

The Service Departments' costs allocation under the Direct Method and the calculation of Factory Overhead Rate per Direct Labour Hour is made as under:

Allocation of Costs (Using Direct Method)

Cost	Service Department		Producing Department	
	S-1: Maintenance	S-2: Canteen	P-1: Machinery	P-2: Assembly
Primary Distribution	16,000	7,000	45,000	83,000
Allocated to Producing Departments:				
S-1: Maintenance	(16,000)		4,600	11,400
S-2: Canteen		(7,000)	1,400	5,600
Balance after Allocation	NIL	NIL	51,000	1,00,000
Factory Overhead Rate per Direct Labour Hour			10.20	5.00

Working Notes:

(1) Allocation of Department S-1: Maintenance:

Allocation Rate = [Total Cost /Total Square Feet Area of Departments P-1 and P-2]

= 16,000 ÷ 8,000 i.e. Rate: 2 per Square Feet

P-1: 2,300 × 2 = 4,600

P-2: 5,700 × 2 = 11,400

Total Cost Allocated: 4,600 + 11,400 = 16,000

(2) Allocation of Department S-2: Canteen:

Allocation Rate = [Total Cost /Total Number of Employees of Departments P-1 and P-2]

= 7,000 ÷ 200 i.e. ₹35 per Employee

P-1: 40 × 35 = ₹ 1,400

P-2: 160 × 35 = ₹ 5,600

Total Cost Allocated: 1,400 + 5,600 = ₹ 7,000

(3) Factory Overhead Rate based on Direct Labour Hours for the Producing Departments:

= Total Cost after Allocation/ Direct Labour Hours

P-1: 51,000 ÷ 5,000 = ₹ 10.20

P-2: 1, 00,000 ÷ 20,000 = ₹ 5.00

(II) Step Method (Apportionment on Non-reciprocal Basis)

It involves apportionment of overheads of service departments on Non-reciprocal Basis. The service departments are not inter-dependent, and they are arranged in the descending order of their serviceability. The cost of the most serviceable department is first apportioned to other service departments. The service department which serves the next largest number of departments is taken up next and its cost including the prorated cost of the first service department is apportioned to other service and production departments except the first service department. In the same way, while apportioning the cost of the third service department in this order, the first two service departments are NOT considered. This process of apportionment of the cost of service departments is continued till the cost of the last service department is apportioned to the PRODUCTION DEPARTMENTS ONLY.

Allocation of Costs (Using Step Method) (₹)

Cost	Service Department		Producing Department	
	S-1: Maintenance	S-2: Canteen	P-1: Machinery	P-2: Assembly
Primary Distribution	16,000	7,000	45,000	83,000
Allocated to Producing Departments:				
S-1: Maintenance	(16,000)	1,618	4,135	10,247
S-2: Canteen		(8,618)	1,724	6,894
Balance after Allocation	NIL	NIL	50,859	1,00,141
Factory Overhead Rate per Direct Labour Hour			10.172	5.007

Working Notes:

(1) Allocation of Department S-1: Maintenance:

Allocation Rate = [Total Cost /Total Square Feet Area of Departments P-1 and P-2]

= 16,000 ÷ 8,900 i.e. Rate: ₹ 1.798 per Square Feet

S-1: 900 × 1.798 = ₹ 1,618

P-1: 2,300 × 1.798 = ₹ 4,135

P-2: 5,700 × 1.798 = ₹ 10,247

Total Cost Allocated: 1,618 + 4,135 + 10,247 = ₹ 16,000

(2) Allocation of Department S-2: Canteen:

Allocation Rate = [Total Cost /Total Number of Employees of Departments P-1 and P-2]

= 8618 ÷ 200 i.e. ₹ 43.09 per Employee

P-1: 40 × 43.09 = ₹ 1,724

P-2: 160 × 43.09 = ₹ 6,894

Total Cost Allocated: 1724 + 6,894 = ₹ 8,618

(3) Factory Overhead Rate based on Direct Labour Hours for the Producing Departments:

= Total Cost after Allocation/ Direct Labour Hours

P-1: 50,859 ÷ 5,000 = ₹ 10.172

P-2: 1,00,141 ÷ 20,000 = ₹ 5.007

Note: The cost of Maintenance Department has been allocated first.

(III) Algebraic Method (Simultaneous Equation Method)

This method is used when service departments are mutually dependent. Boiler house has to depend upon Pump room for supply of water and Pump room has to depend on the Boiler house for supply of steam power for driving the Pump. Thus both boiler house and Pump room depend upon each other for their services.

The problem in case of reciprocal services is that total overheads of service department S-1 include a share from the total overheads of service department S-2. Therefore, to determine total overheads of the service department S-1 one must know total overheads of the service department S-2 and to determine total overheads of S-2 one must know total overheads of S-1. This problem is solved with the help of simultaneous equation. Total overheads of each service department are ascertained with the help of simultaneous equations and then the overheads so determined are re-apportioned to Production departments on the basis of technical information. The following algebraic equations help in finding out the cost of service departments:

$$X = a + bY \quad \ldots(1)$$

$$Y = a + bX \quad \ldots(2)$$

Allocation of Costs (Using Algebraic Method) (₹)

Cost	Service Department		Producing Department	
	S-1: Maintenance	S-2: Canteen	P-1: Machinery	P-2: Assembly
Primary Distribution	16,000	7,000	45,000	83,000
Allocated to Producing Departments:	(16,643)	1,683	4,301	10,659
S-1: Maintenance	643	(8,683)	1,608	6,432
S-2: Canteen				
Balance after Allocation	NIL	NIL	50,909	1,00,091
Factory Overhead Rate per Direct Labour Hour			10.182	5.00455

Working Notes:

Let M = Total cost of Maintenance Department and C = Total cost of Canteen. The cost to be allocated to each department is then

M = 16,000 + (16 ÷ 216) C and C = 7,000 + (900 ÷ 8,900) M

By substitution we get

M = 16,000 + (16 ÷ 216) × {7,000 + (900 ÷ 8,900) M}

M = 16,000 + 518.52 + .00749 M

0.99251 M = 16,518.52

M = ₹ 16,643.

By inserting the value for M in the equation for department C, we get

C = 7,000 + (900 ÷ 8,900) 16,643 = 7,000 + 1,683 = ₹ 8,683.

Allocation of Department S-1: Maintenance:

(a) To Department S-1: 1,683 = (900÷8,900) ×16,643

(b) To Department P-1: 4,301 = (2,300÷8,900) ×16,643

(c) To Department P-2: 10,659 = (5,700÷8,900) ×16,643

Total Cost Allocated: 1,683 +4,301 + 10,659=16,643

Allocation of Department S-2: Canteen:

(a) To Department S-1: 643 = (16÷216) ×8,683

(b) To Department P-1: 1608 = (400÷216) ×8,683

(c) To Department P-2: 6432 = (160÷216) ×8,683

Total Cost Allocated: 643 +1,608 + 6,432 = 8,683

Factory Overhead Rate based on Direct Labour Hours for the Producing Departments:

= Total Cost after Allocation/ Direct Labour Hours

P-1: 50,909÷5,000 = ₹ 10.182

P-2: 1,00,091÷20,000 = ₹ 5.00455

Illustration 11.2. *The Value Added Limited has two service departments and two producing departments.*

Service Departments	***Total Cost*** (₹)
Department A, Factory Administration	*1,03,500*
Department B, Building and grounds	*96,000*
Producing Departments	
Department M, Machinery	*2,26,500*
Department Y, assembly	*1,90,400*

Additional Information:

Departments	*Estimated total Labour hours*	*Square Footage*
A. Factory Administration	*3,500*	*1,600*
B. Building and grounds	*1,500*	*2,000*
M. Machinery	*2,500*	*2,400*
Y. Assembly	*2,000*	*4,000*
Total	*9,500*	*10,000*

The costs of the factory administration are allocated based on estimated labour hours; buildings and grounds costs are allocated based on square footage. The producing departments compute these factory overhead rates based on machine hours, with 40,000 for machinery and 28,500 for assembly.

Allocate the costs of the service departments to the producing departments by using the following: (a) Direct Method, (b) Step Method (allocate the costs of factory administration first), and (c) Algebraic method. Calculate the Factory overhead rates for each producing department.

Solution : (a) Direct Method:

Allocation of Costs (₹)

Details	**Service Departments**		**Producing Departments**	
	A. Factory Administration	**B. Building and Grounds**	**M. Machinery**	**Y. Assembly**
Total Cost	1,03,500	96,000	2,26,500	1,90,400
Allocate to Producing departments M and Y	(1,03,500)	(96,000)	57,500	46,000
			36,000	60,000
Balance After allocation	NIL	NIL	3,20,000	2,96,400
Machine Hour	——	——	40,000	28,500
Absorption rate per machine hour	N.A	N.A	8.00 (3,20,000 ÷ 40,000)	10.40 (2,96,400 ÷ 28,500)

Working Notes:

(1) Allocation of Department A:

Allocation Rate:

= Total Cost / Total Estimated labour hours of Producing Departments M and Y

= 1,03,500 ÷3,600=₹ 28.75.

M: 2,000×28.75 = ₹ 57,500

Y: 1,600×28.75 = ₹ 46,000

Total Cost Allocated: 57,500 + 46,000 = ₹ 1,03,500

(2) Allocation of Department B:

Allocation Rate:

Total Cost / Total Square feet of Producing Departments M and Y

= 96,000 divided by 6,400= 15

M: 2,400×15 = ₹ 36,000

Y: 4,000×15 = ₹ 60,000

Total Cost Allocated: 36,000 + 60,000 =96,000

(3) Factory overhead rate (based on machine hours) for Producing Departments:

Allocation Rate: = Total Cost after Allocation / Machine Hours

M: 3, 20,000 ÷40,000=₹ 8.00

Y: 2, 96,400 ÷ 28,500= ₹ 10.40.

(b) Step Method:

Allocation of Costs (₹)

Details	**Service Departments**		**Producing Departments**	
	A. Factory Administration	**B. Building and Grounds**	**M. Machinery**	**Y. Assembly**
Total Cost	1,03,500	96,000	2,26,500	1,90,400
Allocate to Service Department B and Producing departments M and Y	(1,03,500)	25,875	43,125	34,500
Allocate to Producing Departments: M and Y	NIL	(1,21,875)	45,703	76,172
Balance After allocation	NIL	NIL	3,15,328	3,01,072
Absorption rate per machine hour	N.A	N.A	7.8832	10.5639

Working Notes:

(2) Allocation of Department A:

Allocation Rate:

Total Cost / Total Estimated labour hours of Service Department B and Producing Departments M and Y

=1, 03,500 ÷ 6,000 = ₹ 17.25

B: 1,500×17.25 = ₹ 25,875

M: 2,500×17.25 = ₹ 43,125

Y: 2,000×17.25 = ₹ 34,500

Total Cost Allocated: 25,875 +43,125 + 34,500 = ₹ 1,03,500

Allocation of Department B:

Allocation Rate:

Total Cost / Total Square feet of Producing Departments: M and Y

= 1, 21,875 ÷ 6,400 = ₹ 19.043

M: 2,400×19.043 = ₹ 45,703

Y: 4,000×19.043 = ₹ 76,172

Total Cost Allocated: 45,703 +76,172 = ₹ 1,21,875

(3) Factory overhead Rate (based on machine hours) for Producing Departments:

= Total Cost after Allocation / Machine Hours

M: 3, 15,328 ÷40,000 = ₹ 7.8832

Y: 3, 01,072 ÷ 28,500 = ₹ 10.5639.

(c) Simultaneous Equation Method or Algebraic Method:

Additional Information in relation to this algebraic method:

Services Provided by

Department	Factory Administration (Labour Hours)	Building and Grounds (Square Feet)
A.. Factory Administration	NIL	1,600
B. Building and Grounds	1,500	NIL
M. Machinery	2,500	2,400
Y. Assembly	2,000	4,000
Total	6,000	8,000

Solution (continued):

Let A = Total Cost of Factory Administration, and
B = Total Cost of Building and Grounds.

$$A = 1,03,500 + 1,600B/8,000$$

$$B = 96,000 + 1,500A/6,000$$

OR

$$A = 1,03,500 + 0.2B$$

$$B = 96,000 + 0.25A$$

By substitution we get

$$A = 1,03,500 + 0.2\,(96,000 + 0.25A)$$

$$A = 1,03,500 + 19,200 + 0.05A$$

$$0.95A = 1,22,700$$
$$A = 1,22,700 \div 0.95$$
$$A = ₹\ 1,29,158$$

By inserting the value for A in the equation for Department B, we get

$$B = 96,000 + 0.25\ (1,29,158)$$
$$B = 96,000+ 32,290 = ₹\ 1,28,290$$

Allocation of Costs (₹)

Details	Service Departments		Producing Departments	
	A. Factory Administration	B. Building and grounds	M. Machinery	Y. Assembly
Total Cost	1,03,500	96,000	2,26,500	1,90,400
Allocated to Service Department B and Producing departments M and Y	(1,29,158)	32,290	53,816	43,052
Allocated to Producing departments M and Y	25,658	(1,28,290)	38,487	64,145
Balance After allocation	NIL	NIL	3,18,803	2,97,597
Absorption rate per machine hour	N.A	N.A	7.97	10.442

Working Notes:

(4) Allocation of Department A:

Total Cost /Proportionate Estimated labour hours of Service Department B and Producing Departments: M and Y

$$= 1,\ 29,158 \div 6,000 = ₹\ 21.5263.$$

B: 1,500×21.5263=₹ 25,875

M: 2,500×21.5263=₹ 43,125

Y: 2,000×21.5263=₹ 34,500

Total Cost Allocated: 25,875 +43,125 + 34,500 = ₹ 1,03,500

(5) Allocation of Department B:

Total Cost / Proportionate Square feet of Service Department B and Producing Departments: M and Y

$$= 1,\ 28,290 \div 8,000 = ₹\ 16.03625$$

A: 1,600×16.03625=₹ 25,658

M: 2,400×16.03625=₹ 38,487

Y: 4,000×16.03625=₹ 64,145

Total Cost Allocated: 25,658 +38,487 + 64,145 = ₹ 1,28,290

(6) Factory overhead rate (based on machine hours) for Producing Departments:

Total Cost after Allocation /Machine Hours

M: 3, 18,803 ÷ 40,000=₹ 7.97

Y: 2, 97,597 ÷ 28,500=₹ 10.442

Illustration 11.3 : (Absorption rate based on various methods)

Standard Engineering Company accepts a variety of jobs which require both manual and machine operations. The budgeted profit and loss account for the period 2006-07 is as under:

Details		*Amount (₹)*
Sales		*300,00,000*
Cost:		
Direct materials	*40,00,000*	
Direct labour	*20,00,000*	
Prime cost	*60,00,000*	
Production overhead	*120,00,000*	
Production cost	*180,00,000*	
Administration, Selling and Distribution overhead	*60,00,000*	
Cost of Sales		*240,00,000*
Profit		*60,00,000*

Other budgeted data:

Labour hours for the period	*20,000*
Machine hours for the period	*12,000*
Number of jobs hours for the period	*150*

An enquiry has been received from a customer and the production department has prepared the following estimates for the job:

Details	***Amount*** (₹)
Direct material	*50,000*
Direct labour	*40,000*
Prime cost	*90,000*

Labour Hours required: 60

Machine Hours required: 40

You are required to:

(1) *Compute by different methods, six overhead absorption rates for absorption of production of overhead and comment on the suitability of each.*

(2) *Calculate the production overhead cost of the order on each of the above rates.*

Solution :

S. No.	Method of Absorption of Production overhead and computations	Overhead Absorption Rate (%)/(₹)
1.	Percentage of Direct Material Cost: (120,00,000÷ 40,00,000) × 100	300% or 3 times
2.	Percentage of Direct Labour Cost: (120,00,000÷20,00,000) × 100	600% or 6 times
3.	Percentage of Prime Cost: (120,00,000÷ 60,00,000) × 100	200% or 2 times
4.	Direct Labour Hour: (120,00,000÷20,000)	600
5.	Machine Hour: (120,00,000÷12,000)	1,000
6.	Production Unit/ Job: (120,00,000÷150)	80,000

Statement showing Production overhead cost of the job order under different methods

Details	Production overhead cost of the job order Amount (₹)
Percentage of Direct Material Cost: (50,000 × 3)	1,50,000
Percentage of Direct Labour Cost: (40,000 × 6)	2,40,000
Percentage of Prime Cost: (90,000 × 2)	1,80,000
Direct Labour Hour: (100 × 600)	60,000
Machine Hour: (80 × 1,000)	80,000
Production Unit/ Job: (80,000 × 1)	80,000

Comments:

1. In case of Percentage of Direct Material Cost, it may be suitable only if all the jobs use the same materials and labour, and machine time does vary minutely.
2. In case of Percentage of Direct Labour Cost, it may be suitable only if wage rates do not vary much.
3. Percentage of Prime Cost Method is quite simple but has the same disadvantages of Percentage of Direct Material Cost method and Percentage of Direct Labour Cost method.
4. The method of Direct Labour Hour/ Machine Hour provides rates of recovery of overheads based on time and hence generally considered equitable as most of the overheads vary with time.
5. Production Unit/ Job method is quite simple to understand and apply. However, this method is acceptable only when all the jobs are same; if they are different, this method is not appropriate for charging production overheads.

Illustration 11.4 : (Absorption rate based on various methods)

The following data relate to a manufacturing department for a period:

Details	Budgeted Data	Actual Data
Direct Material (₹)	5,00,000	7,00,000
Direct Labour (₹)	10,00,000	13,00,000
Production overheads (₹)	10,00,000	12,00,000
Direct Labour Hours	2,50,000	3,40,000
Machine Hours	1,25,000	1,60,000

Job MPT-12 was one of the jobs worked on during the period. The actual data relating to this job were:

Details	Actual Data
Direct Material (₹)	25,000
Direct Labour (₹)	15,000
Direct Labour Hours	1,000
Machine Hours	1,000

Required:

(i) Calculate the production overhead rate predetermined for the period based on:

(a) Percent of Direct Material cost, and

(b) Machine hour Rate.

(ii) Calculate the production overhead rate cost to be charged to Job MPT-12 based on the rates calculated (i) above.

(iii) Assuming that a Machine hour Rate of absorption is used, calculate the under/over absorption of Production overheads for the period.

Solution : Percent of Direct Material Cost:

= (Production overheads/ Direct material cost) ×100

= (10, 00,000 ÷ 5, 00,000) × 100 => 200%

Machine hour Rate:

= (Production overheads/ Machine hours) × 100

= (10, 00,000 ÷ 1, 25,000) => ₹ 8 per hour

Job MPT-12

Details	Percent of Direct Material Cost Method (₹)	Machine hour Rate Method (₹)
Direct Material	25,000	25,000
Direct Labour	15,000	15,000
Prime Cost	40,000	40,000

Production overheads: Direct Material Cost Rate (200% × 25,000)	50,000	
Machine hour Rate Method @ ₹ 8 per hour (1,000 × 8)		8,000
Cost of Production	90,000	48,000

Absorbed Overheads:

= Actual Machine Hours Worked × Machine Hour Rate

= 1, 60,000 × 8 => ₹ 12, 80,000.

Over absorbed overheads=Absorbed Overheads> Actual Overheads

Over absorbed overheads=Absorbed Overheads – Actual Overheads

= 12, 80,000 – 12, 00,000 => ₹ 80,000.

Illustration 11.5 : (Rate of Recovery- Overhead)

At 60% capacity utilization, the overhead recovery rate is ₹ 28. At 70% capacity, the rate gets reduced to ₹ 25 per unit. Find out what should be the absorption rate if production attains 90% capacity utilization.

Solution : Assume the total capacity = 100 units.

At 60% capacity utilization i.e. for 60 units, the rate is ₹ 28 per unit.

At 70% capacity utilization i.e. for 70 units, the rate is ₹ 25 per unit.

For incremental 10 units, incremental cost is ₹ {(25×70) – (28×60)}

= ₹ {1,750 – 1,680}

= ₹ 70

Estimated variable cost per unit = 70÷10 = ₹ 7

Estimated fixed cost = 70 × (25 – 7) = ₹ 1,260

Estimated total cost at 90% capacity utilization = 1,260 + (90 × 7)

= ₹ 1,890

Absorption rate at 90% = 1,890 ÷ 90 = ₹ 21

Illustration 11.6 : (Step- ladder method)

Johnson Manufacturing Company collects overhead costs under three production cost centers, denoted by X, Y and Z and two service cost centers i.e. A: (Canteen) and B: (Stores). The following list represents all the budgeted production overheads:

Rent and rates	*4,00,000*
Canteen food	*80,000*
Lighting	*40,000*
Stores staff wages	*36,000*
Insurance	*24,000*
	5,80,000

The following further information is available:

Details	*X*	*Y*	*Z*	*A*	*B*
Floor Area (m2)	*15,000*	*10,000*	*12,500*	*7,500*	*5,000*
Wattage of lighting	*1,000*	*1,500*	*750*	*500*	*250*
Ratio of insurance (%)	*30*	*30*	*20*	*5*	*15*
Number of employees	*30*	*35*	*40*	*10*	*20*
Value of material used	*6,000*	*3,000*	*5,250*	*750*	——

Apportion the cost to production cost centers using the step method.

Solution : **Primary Distribution**

Details	Total amount (₹)	Production Department			Service Department	
		X	Y	Z	A	B
Rent & Rates (6:4:5:3:2)	4,00,000	1,20,000	80,000	1,00,000	60,000	40,000
Canteen food	80,000				80,000	
Lighting (4:6:3:2:1)	40,000	10,000	15,000	7,500	5,000	2,500
Stores staff wages	36,000					36,000
Insurance (6:6:4:1:3)	24,000	7,200	7,200	4,800	1,200	3,600
Total	5,80,000	1,37,200	1,02,200	1,12,300	1,46,200	82,100

Secondary Distribution

Details	Total amount (₹)	Production Department			Service Department	
		X	Y	Z	A	B
Apportioned & Allocated	5,80,000	1,37,200	1,02,200	1,12,300	1,46,200	82,100
Department A (6:7:8:0:4)		35,088	40,936	46,784	(1,46,200)	23,392
Department B (8:4:7)		44,418	22,209	38,865		(1,05,492)
Total	5,80,000	2,16,706	1,65,345	1,97,949	Nil	Nil

Illustration 11.7 : (Direct Re-distribution Method)

Atkinson's Co. Ltd. has three production departments: a ,b, and g, and two service departments: m and w. The following estimated figures for a certain period have been made available:

	₹
Rent & Rates	*10,000*
Lighting and electricity	*1,200*
Indirect Wages	*3,000*
Power	*3,000*
Depreciation of machinery	*20,000*
Other expenses and sundries	*20,000*

The following details are provided by the firm:

Details	*Total*	*a*	*b*	*g*	*m*	*w*
Floor space (m^2)	*10,000*	*2,000*	*2,500*	*3,000*	*2,000*	*500*
Lighting point (No.)	*120*	*20*	*30*	*40*	*20*	*10*
Direct wages (₹)	*20,020*	*6,000*	*4,000*	*6,000*	*3,020*	*1,000*
Horsepower of machines	*300*	*120*	*60*	*100*	*20*	-
Cost of machinery (₹)	*1,00,000*	*24,000*	*32,000*	*40,000*	*2,000*	*2,000*
Working hours	——	*3,712*	*2,265*	*2,440*	——	——

The expenses of the service departments m and w are to be allocated as follows:

Department	*a*	*b*	*g*	*m*	*w*
m (%)	*20*	*30*	*40*	——	*10*
w (%)	*40*	*20*	*30*	*10*	——

You are required to calculate the overhead absorption rate per hour in respect of the three production departments. What will be the total cost of an article with material cost of ₹ 125 direct labour cost of ₹ 70 which passes through a,b and g for 2,3 and 4 hours respectively.

Solution : **Atkinson's Company Ltd.**

(A) Departmental Primary Distribution Summary

Item of cost (1)	**Apportionment Basis (2)**	**Total (₹) (3)**	**a (4)**	**b (5)**	**g (6)**	**m (7)**	**w (8)**
Rent & rates	Floor Area	10,000	2,000	2,500	3,000	2,000	500
Lighting & electricity	Light points	1,200	200	300	400	200	100
Indirect wages	Direct wages	3,000	900	600	900	450	150
Power	Horsepower of machines	3,000	1,200	600	1,000	200	——
Depreciation of machinery	Cost of machine	20,000	4,800	6,4000	8,000	400	400

Other expenses and sundries	Direct wages	20,020	6,000	4,000	6,000	3,020	1,000
Direct wages of service departments	Allocation	4,000	———	———	———	3,000	1,000
Total (₹)		61,220	15,100	14,400	19,300	9,270	3,150

(B) Secondary Distribution Summary

Details	a (₹)	b (₹)	g (₹)	m (₹)	w (₹)
Allocated and apportioned	15,100	14,400	19,300	9,270	3,150
Reapportioned of m	2,060	3,090	4,120	(9,270)	———
Reapportioned of w	1,400	700	1,050	———	(3,150)
Total (₹)	18,560	18,190	24,470	———	———

(C) Overhead Absorption Rate per hour

Details	a	b	g
Total overhead (₹)	18,560	18,190	24,470
Working hours	3,712	2,265	2,440
Rate per hour (₹)	5.00	8.031	10.029

(D) Statement of cost per unit

Cost Element	Amount (₹)	Total Amount (₹)
Material cost	125	
Direct labour cost	70	
Prime cost	195	195
Overhead :		74.21
a : 2×5	10.000	
b : 3×8.031	24.093	
g : 4×10.029	40.116	
Total overhead	74.209	
Total production cost		269.21

Illustration 11.8 : (Methods of Absorption: Unit of Production Method)

The following particulars are available in respect of a production cost center:

Products manufactured	*A*	*B*	*C*	*D*
Normal capacity (in units)	*40,000*	*25,000*	*20,000*	*10,000*
Unit weight (kg)	*5*	*4*	*2*	*1*

Factory overhead for the budget period is estimated at ₹10,50,000. Calculate overhead absorption rate per unit of production.

Solution :

	A	B	C	D
Normal capacity (in units)	40,000	25,000	20,000	10,000
Unit weight (kg)	5	4	2	1
Estimated total weight (kg)	2,00,000	1,00,000	40,000	10,000

Thus, estimated total overhead is to be spread over the total weight of 3,50,000 kg.

$$\text{Production overhead rate per kg} = \frac{10{,}50{,}000}{3{,}50{,}000} = ₹\,3$$

Converting this rate of ₹ 3 per kg into rate per unit of product:

Product	Calculation	Rate per unit (₹)
A	3×5	15
B	3×4	12
C	3×2	06
D	3×1	03

Illustration 11.9 : Compute machine hour rate from the following information:

(1) The machine room will work on 80% capacity throughout the year and that a break down of 12.5% is reasonable,

(2) There are three holidays at Deepawali; two days at Holi and two days at Christmas, exclusive of Sundays. The factory works eight hours a day and four hours on Saturdays.

(3) Number of machines (each of same type): Five

(4) Expenses per year:

	Amount (₹)
Power	*39,000*
Lubricating oil	*1,650*
Light	*8,000*
Repairs to machines	*18,075*
Salaries to foreman	*30,000*
Depreciation	*9,820*

Solution : **Computation of Machine-hour Rate**

Details	Total Amount (₹)	Amount per hour (₹)
(i) Standing Charges:		
Lighting	8,000	
Lubricating oil	1,650	
Salaries to foremen	30,000	
Total Annual standing charges	39,650	
Per hour standing charges (39,650 ÷ 7,840)		5.057

(ii) Machine Expenses:		
Repairs to machines (18,075 ÷ 7,840)		2.305
Depreciation (9,820 ÷ 7,840)		1.253
Power (39,000 ÷ 7,840)		4.974
Total Machine expenses per hour		8.532
(iii) Machine hour rate (per hour)		**13.589**

Working Notes :

Number of machine hours has been computed as under:

Total number of days in a year (Excluding Leap Year)			365
Less:	Saturdays	52	
	Sundays	52	
	Holidays (3 + 2 + 2)	07	111
Full working days			254
No. of hrs. on full working days @ 8 hours per day (254 × 8)			2,032
Add: number of hrs. on Saturdays @ 4 hours per day (52 × 4)			208
Total number of hours per machine			2,240
Capacity utilised (%)			80
Effective hours per machine (2,240 × 0.8)			1,792
Less: provision for break-down @ 12.5%			224
Total machine hours per machine			1,568
Total machine hours for five machines			7,840

ABSORPTION OF FACTORY OVERHEADS

Having apportioned overheads of all the service departments/centers to the production departments/centers, the next step is to charge the overheads of the production departments to products/ jobs/. This step of charging to products/jobs/ is termed as absorption of overheads. According to ICMA, the Absorption is "allotment of overhead to cost units." Consequently, the cost of each unit of product of the producing departments includes an equitable share of total overhead of that department.

Methods of Absorption

The rate, which is used to charge overhead cost to the products or jobs, is known as absorption rate. The following are the generally recognized methods of absorption or absorption rates:

(1) Percentage of Direct Materials: Factory overheads are charged on the basis of materials consumed by the products. The rate of absorption is calculated by dividing the estimated factory overheads for the period by the cost of direct materials consumed.

Percentage of Direct materials = (Overhead Expenses / Total Direct Material Cost) × 100

Example:

(a) Production overhead to be absorbed ₹ 35,000

(b) Direct Material cost incurred ₹ 50,000

Direct Material cost percentage rate = (a)/ (b)

= (35,000 / 50,000) × 100 = 70%

This rate is usually adopted where one product is being produced or where material prices are stable and equipment used remain unchanged. It is advisable to use this simple rate in case material cost forms a substantial component of cost of production. The method is quite simple. However, in most of the cases, there is no logical relationship between the direct material cost of a product and factory overheads incurred. Further, a product might be made from costly materials while the other requires less expensive materials; both the products require the same manufacturing process, and thus, incur approximately the same quantum of factory overheads. In that case, the product requiring costly material will be charged with more than its share of overheads. Further, this method ignores time factor, which is the most important factor because of its greater influence on overhead costs. This method is suitable for allocating material handling expenses to products.

(2) Percentage of Direct Labour costs: Direct labour cost is used as the basis of charging factory overheads. The rate of absorption is calculated by dividing the estimated factory overheads for the period by the cost of direct labour cost.

Percentage of Direct labour Cost = (Overhead Expenses / Total Direct Labour Cost) × 100

Example:

(a) Production overhead to be absorbed ₹ 25,000

(b) Direct Wages incurred ₹ 50,000

Direct Wages cost percentage rate = (a)/ (b)

= (25,000 / 50,000) × 100 = 50%

The method is simple to use. Wage analysis is the source document of direct labour cost. It is suitable in the following cases:

(i) Direct relationship exists between direct labour cost and factory overheads.

(ii) The hourly rates of payment for similar work are comparable.

(iii) Work is done mainly by machines.

This is easy to apply where the type of labour is uniform, the ratio of skilled and unskilled workers remains almost constant and the rates of wages do not fluctuate wildly all the time. This rate is suitable when standard costing is used. This method gives automatic consideration to time factor, as the higher the charge for wages, the longer must normally have been spent on that job. Relatively, this method of absorption is better as labour rates do not fluctuate like material prices.

However, there is very little relation between direct wages and overhead incurred. This gives unfair rate incase workers vary in ability i.e. some work at an average rate, while others work at high speed.

(3) Percentage of Prime cost: The rate of recovery of factory overheads is computed by dividing the factory overheads by the prime cost, which is the sum of direct material cost, direct labour cost and direct expenses.

Overhead Rate = (Overhead Expenses / Prime Cost) × 100

It is suitable in the following situation:

"Standard product is made requiring fixed quantity of material at a constant price, and the time taken in production is constant".

(4) Direct Labour hour rate: The basis of charging overheads is the direct labour hours worked. Overhead expenses are divided by total direct labour hours.

Direct Labour Hour Rate = Overhead Expenses / Total direct Labour Hours

It is suitable in the following situation:

"Cost centres are not extensively mechanized and the overheads are incurred mostly on time basis".

This method gives satisfactory results only when the estimated direct labour hours are adjusted for annual holidays, public holidays and anticipated normal idle time.

(5) Machine Hour rate:

Machine hour Rate = Overhead Expenses (Machine cost centre-wise)/ Number of effective Machine Hours

Effective Machine Hours = Normal working hours p.a. – Loss of hours due to repairs and maintenance and set-up, etc. If set-up time is considered productive, it should be added to machine hours and if it is considered unproductive, it needs to be excluded. The trial run hours may be treated as productive and should be added to machine hours.

Example:

(a) Production Overhead to be absorbed	₹ 35,000
(b) Number of machine Hours	₹ 2,500

MHR = (a)/ (b) = 35,000 / 2,500 = ₹ 14 per machine hour

Machine hour rate is usually computed department-wise. More than one rate may be computed, one for each machine or group of machines which are similar in regard to their make, type, capacity, wattage or horse power or technical factors.

Computation of Machine Hour Rate

Process to compute machine hour rate:

- Departmental overhead distribution summary;

- Total hours worked by a machine or group of machines;
- Appropriate basis of apportioning departmental expenses relating to more than one machine.

The criteria for the apportionment of the departmental expenses may be adopted as under:

Item of Expense	Criterion
Rent	Floor area occupied by the machine
Insurance on Building	Floor area
Consumable Stores; Lubricating Oil	As per stores requisition slips
Shop cleaners	Time spent on each machine
Insurance on Machinery	Value of each machine
Depreciation	Value of each machine
Power	H.P. of the Motor * Operation Time
Repairs and maintenance	Actual machine-wise
Supervision	Time spent on each machine

Preliminaries:

1. List all the machines;
2. Group them on the basis of their similarity;
3. Collect relevant information for each machine. The information is to be in regard to the cost of machine including installation charges, anticipated effective life of machines in years or working hours, the estimated salvage value, and the method of depreciation.
4. Collect information regarding all overheads to be allotted or apportioned to machines. This information could be in regard to factory rent, light, power, supervision cost, repairs and maintenance expenses, set-up time, oils and lubricants, etc.

Wherever possible, machine hours may be computed for fixed and variable overheads. This reveals the loss due to non-utilisation of machines. MHR is a scientific and accurate method of recovery of overheads resulting in ascertainment of costs with greater degree of accuracy especially when machines are predominant. Cost reports based on MHR help management in decision making.

(6) Rate per unit of Output: This could be actual or pre-determined rate of recovery of overheads. This is calculated by dividing the overhead to be absorbed by the number of cost units produced or expected to be produced.

Example:

(a) Production overhead to be absorbed ₹ 35,000

(b) Number of cost units produced ₹ 2,500

Rate per unit of Output = (a)/ (b) = 35,000 / 2,500 = ₹ 14 per unit

This method is usually associated with standard costing. This method works well in industries producing a single unit. The method is unsuitable where a variety of products are produced according to customer's specifications.

Under Absorption and over Absorption of Factory Overheads

Having ascertained the factory overhead absorption/recovery rate, it is used as the basis of charge of factory overhead costs to actual production. The rate is applied to production on an ongoing basis. Assume that the factory overhead rate of recovery is ₹ 80 per unit or ₹ 20 per machine hour. Ten thousand units of output were produced. Factory worked for forty thousand machine hours. If the basis of charge is output units then the total factory overheads charge would be ₹ 8,00,000 (10,000 × 80), and if the basis of charge is machine hours worked, the total of factory overhead charge would be ₹ 8,00,000 (40,000 × 20). In case factory overheads incurred are ₹ 8,60,000 or ₹ 7,60,000, difference between absorbed factory overheads and actual/incurred factory overheads is found out and if the difference is positive, it is a case of over absorption or a over recovery of factory overheads, and if the difference is negative i.e. adverse, it is case of under absorption or under recovery of factory overheads. In the foregoing illustration it is a case of under absorption (8,00,000 – 8,60,000) to the extent of ₹ 60,000 or it is case of over absorption to the extent of ₹ 40,000 (8,00,000 – 7,60,000). This difference is known as overhead variance, which may be disposed of by following either of the two methods:

(A) As a Period Cost: It is assigned to the current period income statement. The adjustment is made through Cost of goods sold account. Journal entries would be as under:

Date/ S.No.	Details		Dr Amount (₹)	Cr Amount (₹)
1.	Cost of Goods Sold A/c	Dr	60,000	
	To Factory Overhead Control A/c			60,000
	(For charging under-absorbed factory overheads)			
2.	Factory Overhead Control A/c	Dr	40,000	
	To Cost of Goods Sold A/c			40,000
	(For charging over-absorbed factory overheads)			

Note: This method is used when variance is trivial in magnitude.

(B) As a Cost of Production: The variance is treated as the cost of production of the current period and the amount is pro-rated to Work-in-Progress Inventory, Finished Goods Inventory and Cost of Goods Sold in proportion to the unadjusted factory overhead balance in each account. This method is quite appropriate when the variance is significant in magnitude. The aim is to allocate the under-or-over absorbed factory overhead costs to those accounts which were distorted by applying Incorrect recovery rate and to bring their closing balance near to what they would have been had the correct recovery rate had been applied. Journal entries would be as under:

Date/ S.No.	Details	Dr Amount (₹)	Cr Amount (₹)
1.	Work-in Progress Inventory A/c Dr Finished Goods Inventory A/c Dr Cost of Goods Sold A/c Dr To Factory Overhead Control A/c (For charging under-absorbed factory overheads)		
2.	Factory Overhead Control A/c Dr To Work-in Progress Inventory A/c To Finished Goods Inventory A/c To Cost of Goods Sold A/c (For charging over-absorbed factory overheads)		

Besides the magnitude of variance, the treatment would also depend on the nature of such variance. If the variance has been the result of abnormal factors/unusual events such as defective planning, it should be considered as a period cost and taken to the current year's cost of goods sold account. Otherwise, the foregoing treatment is to be made.

Illustration 11.10 : *In a manufacturing unit, factory overhead was absorbed at a predetermined rate of ₹ 30 per manday. The total factory overhead expenses incurred and the maydays actually worked were ₹50.5 lakh and 1.6 Lakh respectively. Out of the 42,500 units produced during a period, 34,000 were sold.*

On analyzing the causes, it was found that 40 percent of the unabsorbed overheads were due to defective planning and the rest were attributable to increases in overhead costs.

How would difference in overheads charged and the incurred be treated in cost accounts?

Solution : Working Notes:

Determination of Unabsorbed Factory Overheads:

Absorbed overheads: 1,60,000 × 30 = 48,00,000.

Actual overheads: 50,50,000.

Difference: Absorbed Minus Actual = 48,00,000 – 50,50,000 = (2,50,000)

Treatment of Unabsorbed Factory Overheads:

(1) 40% of unabsorbed overheads are attributable to defective planning, being abnormal in nature: ₹ 1,00,000 i.e. (0.4 × 2,50,000) is charged to Costing Profit and Loss Account.

(2) ₹ 1,50,000 i.e. (2,50,000 – 1,00,000) or (0.6 × 2,50,000) is to be apportioned between Cost of goods Sold (34, 000 Units) and Finished Goods in Stock (8,500 Units):

(a) Cost of Goods Sold (1, 50,000 × 0.8) = 1,20,000

(b) Finished Goods Stock (1, 50,000 × 0.2) = 30,000

LET US RECAPITULATE

1. Factory overhead costs are operating costs of a business enterprise.
2. A Producing department is one where the conversion or production takes place. A Service department (Stores or Maintenance) provides support to the producing departments.
3. Since Service departments directly benefit the Producing departments, the expenses of the Service department should be allocated to the appropriate Producing departments (as a part of factory overhead costs).
4. Direct Method involves allocation of Service department costs directly to Producing departments and inter-department service is altogether ignored.
5. Step Ladder method involves apportionment of overheads of service departments on Non-reciprocal Basis.
6. Algebraic (Simultaneous Equation) method is used when service departments are mutually dependent.
7. Absorption is "allotment of overhead to cost units.
8. In case of Percentage of Direct Material Cost, it may be suitable only if all the jobs use the same materials and labour, and machine time does vary minutely.
9. In case of Percentage of Direct Labour Cost, it may be suitable only if wage rates do not vary much.
10. Percentage of Prime Cost Method is quite simple but has the same disadvantages of Percentage of Direct Material Cost method and Percentage of Direct Labour Cost method.
11. The method of Direct Labour Hour/ Machine Hour provides rates of recovery of overheads based on time and hence generally considered equitable as most of the overheads vary with time.
12. Production Unit/ Job method is quite simple to understand and apply. However, this method is acceptable only when all the jobs are same; if they are different, this method is not appropriate for charging production overheads.
13. Direct Labour Hour Rate method gives satisfactory results only when the estimated direct labour hours are adjusted for annual holidays, public holidays and anticipated normal idle time.
14. MHR is a scientific and accurate method of recovery of overheads resulting in ascertainment of costs with greater degree of accuracy especially when machines are predominant.
15. Rate per unit of output is calculated by dividing the overhead to be absorbed by the number of cost units produced or expected to be produced.

SOLVED PROBLEMS

Problem 1. (Various Methods of Absorption)

Delhi Engineering Limited accepts a variety of jobs, which require both manual and machine operations. The budgeted Profit and Loss Account for the period 2003-2004 is as under:

Details	*Amount (₹)*	*Amount (₹)*
Sales		*300,00,000*
Less: Cost of Sales		
Direct Materials	*40,00,000*	
Direct Labour	*20,00,000*	
Prime Cost	*60,00,000*	
Production Overhead	*120,00,000*	
Production Cost	*180,00,000*	
Administrative, Selling and Distribution Overhead	*60,00,000*	*240,00,000*
Profit		*60,00,000*

Other Budgeted Information	*Hours/Number*
Machine Hours for the period	*25,000*
Labour Hours for the period	*30,000*
Number of Jobs for the period	*2,000*

An enquiry has been received recently from an esteemed customer and the production department has prepared the following estimate of the prime cost required for the job:

Direct material		*40,000*
Direct Labour		*35,000*
Prime Cost		*75,000*
Machine Hours required	*125*	
Labour Hours required	*80*	

You are required to calculate:

(i) Factory Overhead Rates of Absorption by different methods and comment on the suitability of each.

(ii) Production Overhead cost of the order based on each of the Absorption Rates calculated as in (I).

Solution : **Delhi Engineering Limited**

Computation of Production Overhead Absorption Rates

S. No.	Methods of Absorption	Formula	Calculations	Overhead Absorption Rate
1.	Direct Machine Hour Rate	$\frac{\text{Production Overheads}}{\text{Direct Machine Hours}}$	$\frac{120,00,000}{25,000}$	= ₹ 480
2.	Direct Labour Hour Rate	$\frac{\text{Production Overheads}}{\text{Direct Labour Hours}}$	$\frac{120,00,000}{30,000}$	= ₹ 400
3.	Percentage of Direct Material Cost	$\frac{\text{Production Overheads}}{\text{Direct Material Cost}} \times 100$	$\frac{120,00,000}{40,00,000} \times 100$	= 300%
4.	Percentage of Direct Wages Cost	$\frac{\text{Production Overheads}}{\text{Direct Wages Cost}} \times 100$	$\frac{120,00,000}{20,00,000} \times 100$	= 600%
5.	Percentage of Prime Cost	$\frac{\text{Production Overheads}}{\text{Prime Cost}} \times 100$	$\frac{120,00,000}{60,00,000} \times 100$	= 200%
6.	Job Rate	$\frac{\text{Production Overheads}}{\text{Number of Jobs}}$	$\frac{120,00,000}{2,000}$	= ₹ 6,000

Statement of Production Overhead Cost for the Job
(Under Different Methods)

Methods	Production Overhead Cost for the Job
1. Direct Machine Hour Rate	125 × 480 = 60,000
2. Direct Machine Hour Rate	80 × 400 = 32,000
3. Percentage of Direct Material Cost	300% × 40,000 = 1,20,000 or [40,000 × 3]
4. Percentage of Direct Wages Cost	600% × 35,000 = 2,10,000 or [35,000 × 6]
5. Percentage of Prime Cost	200% × 75,000 = 1,50,000 or [75,000 × 2]
6. Job Rate	1 × 6,000 = 6,000

Comments:

(1) Both the methods (Machine Hour Rate and Labour Hour Rate) are based on time. Both the methods are preferred because most of the overheads vary with time.

(2) Percentage of Direct Material Cost method is suitable only if all the jobs use the same materials and Labour, and machine time to perform the job does not vary much.

(3) Percentage of Direct Labour Cost method may be used if the labour rates for different jobs do not vary significantly. Is suitable only if all the jobs use the same materials and Labour, and machine time to perform the job does not vary much.

(4) Percentage of Prime Cost method is simple but has the disadvantages of both Percentage of Direct Material Cost method and Percentage of Direct Labour Cost method.

Job Rate Method is very simple and acceptable if all the jobs are of the same type and nature. If they are different, this method is not appropriate for charging Overheads.

Problem 2. *The factory overhead costs of four production departments of a company engaged in executing job orders, for an accounting year, are as under:*

Department	*Amount (₹)*
D-1	*40,200*
D-2	*10,800*
D-3	*5,600*
D-4	*5,000*

Overhead costs have been absorbed as under:

Department	*Basis of absorption*
D-1	*₹ 3 per Machine Hour for 14,000 hours*
D-2	*₹ 2.50 per Direct Labour Hour for 4,000 hours*
D-3	*75% of Direct Labour Cost of Rest 8,000.*
D-4	*₹ 5 per piece for 940 pieces.*

Find out department-wise the amount of under or over-absorbed factory overheads.

Solution : **Total Amount of Factory Overheads Absorbed**

Department	Total Amount Absorbed (₹)	Basis of absorption
D-1	42,000	₹ 3 per Machine Hour for 14,000 hours
D-2	10,000	₹ 2.50 per Direct Labour Hour for 4,000 hours
D-3	6,000	75% of Direct Labour Cost of ₹ 8,000.
D-4	4,700	₹ 5 per piece, for 940 pieces.
Total	62,700	

Amount of Under or Over Absorbed Factory Overheads

Department	Factory Overheads Absorbed (₹)	Factory Overheads incurred (₹)	Under-Absorbed (–)	Over-Absorbed (₹) (+)
D-1	42,000	40,200		1,800
D-2	10,000	10,800	800	
D-3	6,000	5,600		400
D-4	4,700	5,000	300	
Total	62,700	61,600		1,100

Problem 3. *A Company has three production departments and two service departments. The departmental distribution summary for a particular period has the following totals. You are required to compute the total share of overheads of the service departments to be distributed to production departments:*

Production departments: P-1: ₹ 800; P-2: ₹ 700; and P-3: ₹ 500. Total: ₹ 2,000.

Service departments: S-1: ₹ 234; and S-2: ₹ 300. Total: ₹ 534.

The expenses of the Service Departments are charged out on a percentage basis as follows:

	P-1	*P-2*	*P-3*	*S-1*	*S-2*
S-1(%)	*20*	*40*	*30*	——	*10*
S-2(%)	*40*	*20*	*20*	*20*	——

[B.Com (Hons.) DU, 2007]

Solution :

Suppose x = Overheads of S-1.   y = Overheads of S-2

$x = 234 + 0.2y$ $y = 300 + 0.1x$

Multiply both the equations by 10

$$10x - 2y = 2{,}340 \quad \ldots(i)$$

$$-x + 10y = 3{,}000 \quad \ldots(ii)$$

Multiplying equation (ii) by 10 and adding in (i)

$$10x - 2y = 2{,}340$$

$$-10x + 100y = 30{,}000$$

$$98y = 32{,}340$$

$$y = 32{,}340 \div 98 = ₹\ 330$$

Substituting the value of y in (i), we get

$$10x - 2(330) = 2{,}340$$

$$10x - 660 = 2{,}340$$

$$10x = 3{,}000$$

$$x = 3{,}000 \div 10 = ₹\ 300$$

Secondary overheads Distribution

Details	P-1	P-2	P-3
Total(given)	800	700	500
S-1: (0.2,0.4 and .3 of 300)	60	120	90
S-2: (0.4,0.2 and .2 of 330)	132	66	66
Total	992	886	656

Problem 4. *In a manufacturing unit, factory overhead was recovered at a predetermined rate of Recovery i.e. ₹ 40 per man- day. The total factory overhead expenses incurred and the man-days actually worked were ₹ 66.40 Lakh and ₹ 1.5 Lakh respectively. Out of the 50,000 units produced during a period, 36,000 were sold.*

On analyzing the causes, it was found that Forty per cent of the unabsorbed overheads were due to defective planning and the rest were attributed to increase in overhead costs.

How would unabsorbed overheads be treated in cost accounts?

Solution : Ascertainment of Unabsorbed Factory Overheads

Details	Amount (₹)
(a) Factory Overheads Absorbed: (1,50,000 × 40)	60,00,000
(b) Factory Overheads Incurred (Given)	66,40,000
(c) Factory Overheads Under-absorbed: [(a) – (b)]	6,40,000

Treatment of Unabsorbed Factory Overheads

Details	Amount (₹)
(a) 40% of Unabsorbed Factory Overheads are attributed to defective planning, being abnormal in nature, ₹ 2,56,000 (0.4×6,40,000) is charged to costing profit and loss account	2,56,000
(b) ₹ 384000(i.e. 6,40,000–2,56,000) is prorated between Cost of Goods Sold (36000 Units) and Finished Goods Inventory (14,000 Units):	3,84,000
Cost of Goods Sold [(3,84,000)×(18÷25)] = 2,76,480	
Finished Goods Inventory [(3,84,000×(7÷25)] = 1,07,520	
Total Factory Overheads Under-absorbed	6,40,000

Problem 5. *The following information is available in respect of a particular department of a concern for a month:*

Actual overhead expenses: ₹ 1,00,000 (including ₹. 20,000 paid one time on account of an old claim)

Actual machine hours worked: 10000 hours

Predetermined overhead recovery rate = ₹ 6 per machine hour

On analysis of under-absorbed overheads, it was noted that 70% of the under-absorption is due to defective planning and 30% is due to increase in expenditure. The department produced 20,000 units in the month, out of which 15,000 units were sold and 5,000 units remained in stock.

You are required to show how you will treat the under-or- over-absorbed overheads in cost accounts. **[B.Com (Hons.) DU, 2006 &2008]**

Solution :

Details	Amount (₹)
Actual overheads (1,00,000 – 20,000)	80,000
Less: Absorbed overheads (10,000 × 6)	60,000
Under absorbed overheads	20,000

Accounting Treatment:

	Amount (₹)
Transfer to Profit and Loss A/c:	
(20,000 × 0.7) =	14,000
Charge to Cost of Sales A/c:	
(20,000 × 0.3) × (15,000/20,000) =	4,500
Charge to Finished goods Stock A/c:	
(20,000 × 0.3) × (5,000/20,000) =	1,500
	20,000

Problem 6. (Inter-Department Services)

A Company has three production departments P-1, P-2, P-3 and two service departments S-1 and S-2. The following data are extracted from the records of the company for the Quarter ended on March 31, 2004:

Items of expenses	*Amount (₹)*
Indirect Wages	*50,000*
Rent and rates	*1,00,000*
General Lighting	*12,000*
Depreciation on Machinery	*2,00,000*
Power	*30,000*
Sundries	*2,00,000*

Additional Information (Department-wise)

Details	*Total Amount (₹)*	*P-1*	*P-2*	*P-3*	*S-1*	*S-2*
Direct Wages (₹)	*2,50,000*	*75,000*	*50,000*	*75,000*	*30,000*	*20,000*
H.P. of Machines used	*150*	*60*	*30*	*50*	*10*	———
Cost of Machines (₹)	*50,00,000*	*12,00,000*	*16,00,000*	*20,00,000*	*1,00,000*	*1,00,000*
Floor Area Used (Sq.Mtr.)	*10,000*	*2,500*	*2,000*	*3,000*	*1,500*	*1,000*
Lighting Point (No)	*80*	*16*	*20*	*24*	*12*	*8*
Production Hours Worked	———	*6180*	*4240*	*4580*	———	———
Service Departments Expenses (%):						
S-1		*25*	*30*	*35*	———	*10*
S-2		*35*	*20*	*25*	*10*	———

You are required to:

(a) Compute the overhead rate of production departments using the Repeated Distribution Method; and

(b) *Hence, determine the total cost of a product whose direct material cost and direct labour cost is respectively ₹ 4,000 and ₹ 2,400 and which would consume Four hours, Five hours and three hours in Departments P-1, P-2.and P-3 respectively.*

Solution : **Overheads Distribution Summary**

Items	Basis of Apportionment	Total Amount (₹)	P-1	P-2	P-3	S-1	S-2
(I) Primary Distribution:							
Direct Wages	Actual	2,50,000	75,000	50,000	75,000	30,000	20,000
Indirect Wages	Direct Wages (20%)	50,000	15,000	10,000	15,000	6,000	4,000
Rent and Rates	Floor Area 5:4:6:3:2 OR ₹ 10 per Sq. Mtr.	1,00,000	25,000	20,000	30,000	15,000	10,000
General lighting	Light Points 4:5:6:3:2 OR ₹150 per point	12,000	2,400	3,000	3,600	1,800	1,200
Depreciation on Machinery	Cost of Machinery: 4% of cost of Machinery	2,00,000	48,000	64,000	80,000	4,000	4,000
Power	Horse Power @ ₹ 200	30,000	12,000	6,000	10,000	2,000	———
Sundries	Direct Wages: @ 80%.	2,00,000	60,000	40,000	60,000	24,000	16,000
	Total	8,42,000	2,37,400	1,93,000	2,73,600	82,800	55,200
(II) Secondary Distribution:							
S-1	5:6:7:2 OR @ ₹ 828 per %	———	20,700	24,840	28,980	(82,800)	8,280
S-2	7:4:5:2 OR @ ₹634.8 per %		24687	14107	17633	7053	(63480)
S-1	5:6:7:2 OR @ ₹ 70.53 per %		1763	2116	2469	(7053)	705
S-2	7:4:5:2 OR @ ₹7.05 per %		274	157	196	78	(705)
S-1	5:6:7:2 OR @ ₹ 0.78 per %		22	26	30	(78)	———
(1)	Total Overheads	8,42,000	2,84,846	2,34,246	3,22,908	———	———
(2)	Production Hours Worked		6180	4240	4580		
(3): [(1)/(2)]	Overhead Rate of Absorption		46.09	55.25	70.50		

Statement of Total Cost of A Product

Details	Amount (₹)	Total Amount (₹)
Direct Material (Given)	4,000	
Direct Labour (Given)	2,400	
Prime Cost		6,400
Add: Overhead Cost	184.36	672.11
Department: (Hours × Rate Of Absorption)	276.25	
P-1: (4×46.09)	211.50	
P-2: (5×55.25)		
P-3: (3×70.50)		
Total Cost of Production		7,072.11

Problem 7. *A factory has three production departments (P1, P2 and P3) and two service departments (S1, and S2). Budgeted Overheads for the next period have been allocated/apportioned by the costing department among the five departments. However, the secondary distribution of the service department is still pending and following details are given to you to find out the absorption rate of the Production departments:*

Details	*P1*	*P2*	*P3*	*S1*	*S2*
Overheads apportioned/ allocated (₹)	*61,384*	*1,44,498*	*65,518*	*22,600*	*36,000*
Estimated Level (hours)	*6,000 (Labour)*	*15,000 (Machine)*	*7,500 (Labour)*	—	—
Inter-Department Service (%)					
(S1)	*20*	*40*	*20*	—	*20*
(S2)	*20*	*60*	*10*	*10*	—

Solution : Step 1: Computation of total cost of Service Departments using Simultaneous Equation Method:

Assume Total cost of Department S1= A and Total cost of Department S2= B

$$A = 22,600 + 0.1B \quad \ldots(1)$$

$$B = 36,000 + 0.2A \quad \ldots(2)$$

$$A = 22,600 + 0.1(36,000 + 0.2A)$$

$$A = 22,600 + 3,600 + 0.02A$$

$$0.98A = 26200$$

$$A = 26,200/0.98 = ₹\ 26,735$$

$$B = 36,000 + 0.2(26,735)$$

$$B = 36,000 + 5,347 = ₹\ 41,347.$$

Step 2: Allocation of Service Departments' cost to Production Departments

(₹)

Details	P1	P2	P3	S1	S2
Overheads apportioned/allocated (₹)	61,384	1,44,498	65,518	22,600	36,000
Allocation of Service Departments' cost to Production Departments: S-1	5,347	10,694	5,347	(26,735)	5,347
S-2	8,269	24,808	4,135	3,600	(41,347)
Balance After Allocation	75,000	1,80,000	75,000	NIL	NIL
Production Hours	6,000 (Labour)	15,000 (Machine)	7,500 (Labour)	NIL	NIL
Absorption Rates per hour (₹)	12.50	12.00	10.00	NIL	NIL

Problem 8. (Machine Hour Rate: Simple)

Ascertain the machine-hour rate from the following information:

Details	*Amount (₹)*
Cost of machine	*16,00,000*
Estimated scrap value on expiry of its useful life (10 years)	*1,00,000*
Rent and Rates for the shop per quarter	*30,000*
General lighting for the shop per month	*6,000*
Insurance premium for the machine p.a.	*42,000*
Repairs and maintenance expenses per annum	*30,000*
Power consumption: 10 units per hour @ ₹ 6 per unit	*60*
Estimated working hours per annum: 2,250(including setting – up time of 250 hours; no power is required during setting up time)	———
Shop supervisor's salary per month	*9,600*

The machine occupies one-third of the total area of the shop. The supervisor is expected to devote one-fourth of his time for supervising the machine.

Solution : Computation of Machine-hour Rate

Details	Amount (₹)	Amount per hour (₹)
(I) Standing Charges:		
Rent and Rates [(30,000×4)×(1/3)]	40,000	
General Lighting [(6,000×12)×(1/3)]	24,000	
Insurance Premium per annum	42,000	
Shop Supervisor's salary [(9,600×12)×(1/4)]	28,800	

Total Annual Standing Charges Per hour Standing Charges (1,34,800÷2,000)	1,34,800	67.40
(II) Machine Expenses:		
Repairs and Maintenance expenses (30,000÷2,000)		15.00
Depreciation [{(16,00,000–1,00,000) ÷ (10)} ÷ (2,000)]		75.00
Power Consumption per hour		60.00
Total Machine expenses per hour		150.00
(III) Machine Hour Rate (per hour)		217.40

Note: (I) Productive machine hours: 2,000 = (2,250 – 250).

(II) Machine expenses are in the nature of mixed and variable costs.

Problem 9. *The machine shop of a manufacturing concern has eight identical machines manned by four operators. The total cost of the machine is ₹ 16, 00,000. The following information relates to six monthly period ended March 31, 2008:*

Details	*Others/Amount (₹)*
Normal Available hours per month	*208*
Absenteeism (W/o Pay) hours per month	*18*
Leave (with Pay) hours per month	*20*
Normal Idle time hours per month	*10*
Average rate of wages per hour per operator	*45*
Production Bonus	*20% on wages*
Power and fuel consumption	*50,600*
Supervision and Indirect labour	*70,420*
Electricity and lighting	*27,500*
Repairs and Maintenance (per annum)	*3% of value of machine*
Insurance (per annum)	*84,000*
Depreciation (per annum)	*10% of original cost*
Allocated factory Overheads (per annum)	*3,46,960*

Compute Machine Hour Rate.

Solution : Computation of Machine Hour Rate

Details (Six Monthly)	**Amount (₹)**
Power and fuel consumption	50,600
Supervision and Indirect labour	70,420
Electricity and lighting	27,500
Repairs and Maintenance [16,00,000 × 0.03 × 0.5]	24,000
Insurance	42,000
Depreciation [16,00,000 × 0.10 × 0.5]	80,000

Other factory Overheads [3,46,960 × 0.5]	1,73,480
Wages	2,05,200
Bonus [2,05,200 × 0.2]	41,040
Total	7,14,240
Machine Hour Rate = 7,14,240 ÷ 7,680	93.00

Working Notes:

Number of working hours:

Monthly Hours = 208 – 18 – 20 = 160

Six Monthly Hours = 160 × 8 × 6 = 7,680

Amount of Wages:

Paid Hours = 208 – 18 = 190

Wages = 190 × 45 × 6 × 4 = ₹ 2,05,200.

Problem 10. (Machine Hour Rate: Comprehensive)

A machine costs ₹12,00,000 and is deemed to have a scrap value of 10% at the end of its effective life (12 years). Ordinarily, the machine is expected to run for 2,500 hours per year but it is estimated that ten percent of the time will be lost for normal repairs and maintenance and further 650 hours will be lost due to staggering. Other details in respect of machine shop are as under:

Details	***Amount (₹)***
Annual Wages, bonus and provident fund contribution of each of two operators (each operator is in-charge of three machines)	*1,50,000*
Rent of the shop (per year)	*1,20,000*
General Lighting of the shop (per month)	*6,000*
Insurance premium for one machine per annum	*28,000*
Cost of repairs and maintenance per machine per quarter	*6,000*
Shop supervisor's monthly remuneration	*15,000*
Power consumption of machine per hour 15 units @ ₹ 6 per unit	
Other factory overheads attributable to the shop per annum	*96,000*

There are six identical machines in the shop. The supervisor is expected to devote one-fifth of time for supervising the machine. Compute a comprehensive machine-hour rate from the above details.

Solution : Computation of Comprehensive Machine-hour Rate

Details	**Total Amount (₹)**	**Amount per hour (₹)**
(I) Standing Charges:		
Rent and Rates (1,20,000÷6)	20,000	
General Lighting (6,000×12) × (1/6)	12,000	
Insurance Premium per annum	28,000	

Shop Supervisor's salary [(15,000×12) × (1/5)]	36,000	
Other factory overheads (96,000÷6)	16,000	
Total Annual Standing Charges	1,12,000	70.00
Per hour Standing Charges (1,12,000÷1,600)		
(II) Machine Expenses:		
Repairs and Maintenance expenses (6,000×4) ÷1,600		15.00
Depreciation [(12,00,000 – 1,20,000) ÷ (12)] ÷1,600		56.25
Power Consumption per hour		90.00
Wages, bonus and provident fund (1,50,000÷3)=50,000÷1600		31.25
Total Machine expenses per hour		192.50
(III) Machine Hour Rate (per hour)		262.50

Note: (I) Productive machine hours: 1,600=(2,500 – 250 – 650).

(II) Machine expenses are in the nature of mixed and variable costs.

Problem 11. Comprehensive Machine hour rate)

SV Engg. Ltd. having ten different types of machines furnishes you the following data for the year 2007-2008 in respect of Machine No. M-4:-

1. *Cost of machine (10 years life) with zero scrap value* ₹ *1,25,000*
2. *Overhead expenses:*
   - *(i) Factory Rent (Annual)* 80,000
   - *(ii) Heating and Lighting (Annual)* 60,000
   - *(iii) Supervision (Annual)* 2,40,000
   - *(iv) Special Equipment for M-4* 12,000
   - *(v) Area of the Factory (Sq. feet)* 1,00,000
   - *(vi) Area occupied by M-4 (Sq. feet)* 4,000
   - *(vii) Power Cost Rs 6 per hour while in operation*
3. *Wages of machine operator* ₹ *120 per day of 8 hours including all fringe benefits. The operator attends to one machine when it is being set up and two machines while in operation.*
4. *Estimated Production hours (Annual)* 4,800

   Estimated set-up time (Annual) 200

Compute comprehensive machine hour rate and find out the cost of the following jobs:

	Job No. 21505	*Job No. 21812*
Set-up time (hours)	*25*	*15*
Operation time (hours)	*175*	*160*

Solution : Computation of Comprehensive Machine-hour Rate (₹)

Details	Per annum	Set-up cost per hour	Machine operation cost per hour
Direct Labour Cost: 120÷8=15		15.00	7.50
Machine Running Cost: Power			6.00
Standing Charges:	3,200	10.82	10.82
1. Factory Rent:			
[(4,000÷1,00,000) × 80,000]	2,400		
2. Heating and Lighting:	24,000		
[(4,000÷1,00,000) × 60,000]	12,000		
3. Supervision: (24,000÷10)	12,500		
4. Special Equipment	54,100		
5. Depreciation: (1,00,000÷8)			
Total Standing Charges			
Total cost per hour		25.82	24.32

Statement showing overhead cost absorbed by jobs

Details	Job No.21505	Job No.21812
Set-up: (i) 25hours × 25.82	645.50	387.30
(ii) 15hours × 25.82		
Operation: (i) 175hours × 24.32	4,256.00	3,891.20
(ii) 160hours × 24.32		
Total cost (₹)	4,901.50	4,278.50

Problem 12. [(Machine Hour Rate) Comprehensive]

From the details furnished below you are requested to compute a comprehensive machine hour rate:

Details	***Amount (₹)***
Original Purchase price of the Machine (subject to depreciation at 10% p.a. on original cost)	*3,00,000*
Normal working hours for the month (The machine works to only 75% of capacity)	*200 Hours*
Wages to Machine man (per day of 8 hours)	*120*
Wages to Machine Attendant (per day of 8 hours)	*80*
Monthly Supervision Charges apportioned for this machine	*1,500*
Annual Insurance of Plant and Building apportioned	*13,200*

Power Consumption p.m.	*750*
Electricity and lighting p.m.	*600*
Repairs and Maintenance (machine) including consumable stores p.m.	*900*
Other General Overheads p.a.	*24,000*

Production bonus payable to workers in terms of award= 40% of basic wages and dearness allowance. Workers are paid fixed dearness allowance @ ₹ 300 p.m.

Add 10% of basic wage and dearness allowance against leave wages and holidays with pay to arrive at a comprehensive labour wage for debit to production.

Solution : Computation of Comprehensive Machine Hour rate (₹)

Details	Per Month	Per Hour
Standing Charges:		50
Insurance of Plant and Building (13,200÷12)	1,100	
Supervision Charges	1,500	
Electricity and lighting	650	
Other General Overheads	2,000	
Depreciation	2,250	
Total (7,500÷150) = 50.	7500	
Variable Cost:		6
Repairs and Maintenance		5
Power		33
Wages of Machine man		23
Wages of attendant		
Machine Hour rate (Comprehensive)		117

Note: Item	Machine man	Attendant
Wages for 200 hours (200÷8=25 days) [120×25=3,000; 80×25=2,000.]	3,000	2,000
Dearness allowance	300	300
Total	3,300	2,300
Production Bonus: @ 40%. = [3,300 × 0.4]; [2,300 × 0.4]	1,320	920
Leave Wages	330	230
Total wages for the Month	4,950	3,450
Effective Wage Rate per Machine Hour = (0.75×200=150) i.e. (4,950÷150) and (3,450÷150)	33 and	23

Problem 13. (Idle Capacity)

The capacity usage ratio and the capacity utilisation ratio in respect of a machine for a particular quarter is 85% and 92% respectively. The available working hours in a quarter are 1,000 hours. The break-up of idle time is as under:

Waiting for jobs 26 hours; break-down 20 hours; waiting for tools8 hours. Calculate the idle time cost when the hourly fixed cost of running the machine has been worked at ₹ 17 with reference to available hours. Compute the cost of idle time.

Solution : Quarterly fixed cost for machine = ₹ 17 × 1000 = ₹ 17,000

Normal Capacity usage = 1,000 × 0.85= 850hours

Normal Idle Capacity = 1,000 – 850 = 150hours

Hourly fixed cost chargeable for machine running = 17,000÷850 = ₹ 20

Actual hours worked= 0.92 × 850 = 782 hours

Idle capacity or unutilized capacity = 850 – 782 =68 hours

Computation of Idle time cost

Details	Time	Amount (₹)
Waiting for Jobs @ ₹ 20	26	520
Break-down @ ₹ 20	20	400
Waiting for tools @ ₹ 20	8	160
Avoidable idle time @ ₹ 20 (68 – 26 – 20 – 8)	14	280
Total	68	1,360

Problem 14. *From the following data of a factory machine room compute machine hours per annum assuming that the machine room will work at 80% capacity throughout the year and that a break down of 5% of the total working hours is reasonable. There are five holidays excluding Saturdays and Sundays. The factory works 8 hours a day and 4 hours on Saturdays. Number of machines (each of same type) is 50.*

Solution : Computation of Machine Hours p.a.

Effective days = (Days in the year) – (Sundays, Saturdays and holidays)
= 365– (52 + 52 +5) => 256 days

Hours for full working Days (256 × 8) = 2,048

Add: Saturdays (52 × 4) = 208

Total 2,256

Effective working Hours = (2,256 × 50 ×0.85 × 0.95) => 91,086 hours.

Problem 15. *The following particulars refers to the machining process used in the treatment of material subsequently incorporated in a component forming part of an electrical appliance.*

(a) *The original cost of the machine used was ₹ 10,000. Its estimated life is 10 years and its scrap value at the end of its estimated life is ₹ 1,000. The estimated working time per year (50weeks of 44 hours) is 2,200 hours of which machine maintenance etc. is estimated to take up 200 hours. No other loss of working time is expected. Setting up time estimated at 100 hours (included in 2200 hours) is regarded as productive time.*

(b) *Electricity (Power) used by the machine during production is 10 units per hour at a cost of ₹ 1.50 per unit. Power is not consumed during maintenance or setting up.*

(c) *The machine requires a solution which is replaced at the end of each week at a cost of ₹ 50 each time.*

(d) *The estimated cost of maintenance per year is ₹ 1,200.*

(e) *Two attendants control the operation of the machine together with five other identical machines. Their combined weekly wages, insurance and employers contributions to the holiday pay amounted to ₹ 1,800.*

(f) *Departmental and General Works overheads allocated to this machine for the year amounted to ₹ 6,000.*

You are required to calculate the machine hour rate.

[B.Com (Hons.) DU, 2006 (Modified)]

Solution : **Computation of Machine Hour Rate**

Details		Amount (₹) Per hour
I. Annual Standing Charges:		10.50
1. General Works Overheads	6,000	
2. Wages (1,800 × 50) ÷6 =	15,000	
	21,000	
II. Machine Expenses:		
1. Depreciation (10,000 – 1,000) ÷20,000		0.45
2. Repairs and Maintenance (1,200 ×10) ÷20,000		0.60
3. Chemicals (50 × 50) ÷2,000		1.25
4. Power (1900 × 10 × 1.50)÷2,000		14.25
Total machine Expenses		16.55
III. Machine Hour Rate (I + II)		27.05

Problem 16. *A manufacturing unit has added a new machine to its fleet of five existing machines. The total cost of purchase and installation of the machine is ₹ 7,50,000. The machine has an estimated life of 15 years and is expected to realize ₹ 30,000 as scrap at the end of its working life. Other data are as under:*

(i) Budgeted working hours is 2,400 based on 8 hours per day for 300 days. This includes 400 hours for plant maintenance.

(ii) Electricity used by the machine is 15 units per hour at a cost of ₹ 2 per unit. No current is drawn during maintenance.

(iii) Estimated cost of the maintenance of the machine is ₹ 500 per week of 6 working days.

(iv) The machine requires special oil for heating which is replaced once every month at a cost of ₹ 2,500.

(v) 3 operators control the operations of the entire battery of 6 machines and the average wages per person amounts to ₹ 450 per week plus 40% fringe benefits.

(vi) Departmental and general works overheads allocated to the operation of 5 machines during the last year was ₹ 60,000.

During the current year, it is estimated that there will be an increase of 12.5% of this amount. No incremental overhead is envisaged for the installation of the new machine.

Compute the machine hour rate for the recovery of machine expenses.

[B.Com (Hons.) DU, 2008]

Solution : Computation of Machine Hour Rate
(Number of Machines: 6)

Details		Amount (₹)
Annual Standing charges:		
Departmental and General works Overheads		
(60,000 × 1.125)		67500
Operators Wages including fringe benefits		
[450×3×50) × (1.4)]		94500
Total Standing charges		162000
Standing charges Per machine hour		
[(1,62,000/6) ÷2000]		13.50
Machine charges:		
1. Electricity (15 × 2)	30.00	
2. Maintenance [(500/6) × (300) ÷ (2000)]	12.50	
3. Cost of Special Oil [(2,500×12) ÷2,000]	15.00	
4. Depreciation [{(7,50,000 – 30,000) ÷15}÷2,000]	24.00	81.50
Machine Hour Rate		95.00

Problem 17. (Overheads absorption)

A manufacturer found that his production costs for an accounting period had been as follows :

Direct Wages	*₹ 2,50,000*
Direct material costs	*80,000*
	3,30,000
Production overhead	*4,00,000*
Total cost	*7,30,000*

The direct costs of job No. 615 were:

Direct wages ₹5,000; direct material costs ₹ 11,500.

The job consists of erecting a small building.

You are required to calculate the works overhead chargeable to job 615, using the following methods : (a) Material costs rate; (b) Labour cost rate; (c) Prime cost rate. **[B.Com. Madurai, Venketeshwara modified]**

Solution : **Cost sheet of Job No. 615**

Cost Element	Material cost rate (₹)	Labour cost rate (₹)	Prime cost rate (₹)
Direct material	11,500	11,500	11,500
Direct wages	5,000	5,000	5,000
Prime cost	16,500	16,500	16,500
Chargeable production overheads:	57,500	8,000	20,000
(i) 5 times of ₹11,500			
(ii) 1.6 times of ₹5,000			
(iii) 40/33 times of ₹16,500			
Total cost	74,000	24,500	36,500

Working note:

1. Material Cost Rate $= \dfrac{\text{Production Overheads}}{\text{Material Costs}}$

$= 4{,}00{,}000 \div 80{,}000 = 5$

2. Labour Cost Rate $= \dfrac{\text{Production Overheads}}{\text{Labour Costs}}$

$= 4{,}00{,}000 \div 2{,}50{,}000 = 1.6$

3. Prime Cost Rate $= \dfrac{\text{Production Overheads}}{\text{Prime Costs}}$

$= 4{,}00{,}000 \div 3{,}30{,}000 = 40/33$

Problem 18. (Methods of absorption: unit of production method)

A company manufactures three products P-1, P-2 and P-3. For computation of overhead absorption rate it has assigned 8, 10, and 5 points to P-1, P-2 and P-3 respectively, to compensate the basic differences in the products. The normal capacity is as follows:

Product	*Units*
P-1	*2,500*
P-2	*8,000*
P-3	*1,000*

The budgeted overhead for the year is ₹ 4,20,000. Calculate overhead absorption rate.

Solution :

Product	Normal capacity (units)	Points assigned	Total Points
P-1	2,500	8	20,000
P-2	8,000	10	80,000
P-3	1,000	5	5,000

Overhead absorption rate per point = ₹ 4,20,000 ÷1,05,000 = ₹ 4

Converting this rate of ₹ 4 per point, into rate per unit we get:

Product	Rate per point (₹)	Points assigned	Rate per unit (₹)
P-1	4	8	32
P-2	4	10	40
P-3	4	5	20

Problem 19. (Overhead analysis sheet)

Following particulars have been extracted from the books of Osteo AG Co.:

Indirect materials		
Shop no.1	*₹ 12,000*	
Shop no.2	*18,000*	
Shop no.3	*6,000*	
Tool room	*3,600*	
Stores	*4,800*	
Factory office	*1,800*	*₹ 46,200*
Indirect wages		
Shop no.1	*12,600*	
Shop no.2	*17,600*	
Shop no.3	*16,000*	
Tool room	*11,100*	
Stores	*4,500*	
Factory office	*6,600*	*68,400*
Factory rent		*30,000*
Insurance		*6,000*
Depreciation 10 %		*36,000*
Power		*27,000*
Light and heat		*12,000*
Total		*₹ 2,25,600*

Further information regarding the operations is given below:

Departments	*Area (m²)*	*Book value of machinery*	*Direct labour*			
			Effective HP	*Hours*	*Cost (₹)*	*Machinery hours*
Production :						
Shop no.1	*800*	*90,000*	*90*	*1,50,000*	*1,80,000*	*1,20,000*
Shop no.2	*600*	*1,62,000*	*90*	*1,50,000*	*1,20,000*	*1,80,000*
Shop no.3	*1200*	*36,000*	——	*1,00,000*	*1,00,000*	——
Service :						
Tool room	*400*	*54,000*	*20*	——	*1,00,000*	——
Stores	*600*	*9,000*	——	——	——	——
Factory office	*400*	*9,000*	——	——	——	——
	4,000	*3,60,000*	*200*	*4,00,000*	*5,00,000*	*3,00,000*

You are required to prepare an 'overhead analysis sheet' for the departments of Osteo AG Co. for the year showing the basis for apportionment.

Solution : **Overhead Analysis Sheet**

(In ₹)

Expenses	**Total Amount**	**Basis**	**Factory Office**	**Stores**	**Tool Room**	**Shop No. 1**	**Shop No. 2**	**Shop No. 3**
Indirect materials	46,200	Direct	1,800	4,800	3,600	12,000	18,000	6,000
Indirect wages	68,400	Direct	6,600	4,500	11,100	12,600	17,600	16,000
Factory rent	30,000	Area	3,000	4,500	3,000	6,000	4,500	9,000
Insurance	6,000	Book value	150	150	900	1,500	2,700	600
Deprecia-tion	36,000	10% of book value	900	900	5,400	9,000	16,200	3,600
Power	27,000	HP	-	-	2,700	12,150	12,150	-
Light & heat	12,000	Area	1,200	1,800	1,200	2,400	1,800	3,600
Total	2,25,600		13,650	16,650	27,900	55,650	72,950	38,800
Factory office		Direct labour cost	(13,500)	——	2,700	4,860	3,240	2,700
Stores		Indirect material		(16,500)	1,500	5,000	7,500	2,500
Tool room		Machine			(31,200)	9,750	17,550	3,900
			Nil	Nil	Nil	73,760	98,540	47,300

Problem 20. (Comprehensive machine-hour rate)

Three machines P, Q and R, which are of different nature, are used in a department of a factory. From the following information, compute machine-hour rate of machine R:

(i) *Total cost of machine P, Q and R is ₹ 5,00,000, out of which cost of machine R is ₹ 1,00,000. Its estimated scrap value and working life are ₹ 10,000 and 18,000 hours, respectively;*

(ii) *Rent (total area 1,000 sq ft and machine R occupies 200 sq. ft):₹ 9,750 p.a.;*

(iii) *Lighting (total light points 12,out of which 2 points are used for machine R) ₹ 4,608 p.a;*

(iv) *Insurance for all machines ₹ 562.50 per quarter;*

(v) *Consumable stores for machines R: ₹ 600 per month;*

(vi) *Salary for supervisor (supervisor denotes 1/3 rd of his time for machine R): ₹7,500 per annum;*

(vii) *Repair and maintenance for the entire life of machine R: ₹9,000;*

(viii) *Machine R consumes 5 units of power per hour at a cost of ₹60 per 100 units;*

(ix) *Machine R will work 2,000 hours p.a. out of which normal idle time estimated at 8% of total working hours and time for routine maintenance estimated at 40 hours p.a.*

Solution :

Details	Per Annum (₹)	Per Hour (₹)
I. Standing charges:		
Rent	1,950	
Insurance	2,250	
Salary of supervisor	25,000	
Total standing charges [29,200 ÷1,800]	29,200	16.220
II. Running charges:		
Depreciation		5.000
Repairs and maintenance		0.500
Lighting		2.560
Consumable stores		4.000
Power		3.000
Total running charges		15.060
III. (I+II) Machine Hour Rate		31.280

Note : Effective working hours = [2,000 – (0.08 × 2,000) – 40] = 1,800 hours.

Problem 21. (Machine Hour Rate)

From the following data, work out the predetermined machine-hour rates for departments D-I and D-II of a factory:

Preliminary Estimates of Expenses

Details	*Total (₹)*	*Department D-I (₹)*	*Department D-II (₹)*
Power	*36,000*	———	———
Spare parts	*19,200*	*7,200*	*12,000*
Consumable stores	*15,000*	*6,000*	*9,000*
Depreciation on machinery	*75,000*	*25,000*	*50,000*
Insurance on machinery	*12,000*	———	———
Indirect labour	*1,00,000*	———	———
Building maintenance	*21,000*	———	———

The final estimates are to be prepared on the basis of above figures after taking consideration the following factors:

(a) *An increase of 12.5 per cent in the price of spare parts;*

(b) *An increase of 25 per cent in the consumption of spare parts for department –B only;*

(c) *Increase in straight line method of depreciation from 10 per cent on the original value of machinery to 12 per cent;*

(d) *20 per cent general increase in wage rates.*

The following information is available:

Estimated direct labour –hours	*1,00,000*	*1,50,000*
Ratio of kW ratings	*3*	*2*
Estimated machine-hours	*25,000*	*30,000*
Floor space (sq.ft)	*15,000*	*20,000.*

Solution : (a) Revised Estimates of Expenses (₹)

Items of expenses	**Total**	**Department D-I**	**Department D-II**
Power	36,000	——-	——-
Spare parts:			
Preliminary estimate	19,200	7,200	12,000
Increase in consumption of D-II (25%of 12,000)= [12,000 × 0.25]	3,000	——-	3,000
Increase in prices 10 % of ₹9,000 i.e. [9,000 * 0.1]	2,775	900	1,875
Revised estimate	24,975	8,100	16,875
Consumable stores	15,000	6,000	9,000
Depreciation of machinery:			
Preliminary estimate increase	75,000	25,000	50,000
Preliminary estimate	15,000	5,000	10,000
	90,000	30,000	60,000

Insurance on machinery	12,000		
Indirect labour:			
Preliminary estimate	100,000		
20% increase in wage	20,000		
Revised Estimate	120,000		
Building maintenance	21,000		

(b) Computation of Machine Hour Rate (₹)

Details	Basis of Apportionment	Total (₹)	Department A	Department B
Power	kW rating (3:2)	36,000	21,600	14,400
Spare parts	Allocated	24,975	8,100	16,875
Consumable stores	Allocated	15,000	6,000	9,000
Depreciation of machine	Allocated	90,000	30,000	60,000
Insurance of machine	Depreciation rate (1:2)	12,000	40,000	8,000
Indirect labour	Estimated direct labour hours (2:3)	1,20,000	48,000	72,000
Building maintenance	Floor area (3:4)	21,000	9,000	12,000
Total	Allocated & apportioned	3,18,975	1,26,700	1,92,275
Estimated machine hours			25,000	30,000
Machine Hour Rate (₹)			5.068	6.409

Problem 22. (Machine Hour Rate)

The cost of the machine is ₹ 66,000, and it has an estimated scrap value of ₹ 6,000 at the end of its effective life of 10 years. Annually the machine works on all the 365 days at a rate of 8 hours every day of which 120 hours p.a. are consumed by maintenance. About 1/7th of the total productive time is consumed in setting the machines. Various costs relating to the working of the machines are as follows:

(i) Two units of power are consumed every hour at the rate of ₹ 1.40 per unit.

(ii) Monthly cleaning and oiling expenses for the machines are ₹ 280.

(iii) Annual maintenance of machine amounts to ₹2,800.

(iv) Three operators combined together control of operations of ten identical machines and each of them gets a monthly salary of ₹ 2,100.

(v) Annual departmental overheads apportioned to the machines are: Fixed: ₹ 5,480; variable: ₹ 12,600.

Compute the machine hour rate in each of the following cases:

(a) Setting up time is regarded productive but power is not consumed during setting up time.

(b) Setting up time is not regarded productive but power is consumed during setting up time. **[B.Com (Hons.) DU, 2009]**

Solution :

MACHINE HOUR RATE

(Setting up time Productive and NO power consumption)

Details	Amount (₹) Per Annum	Amount (₹) Per Hour
Standing Charges:	3,360	6.857
Cleaning and Oil expenses (280 × 12)	2,800	
Maintenance	7,560	
Operators' salary [(3 × 2,100 × 12)÷10]	5,480	
Departmental overheads		
Standing charges Per Hour: (19,200 ÷ 2,800)		
Machine Expenses:		2.143
Depreciation [(66,000 – 6,000) ÷ (10 × 2,800)]		2.400
Power [(2×2,400 ×1.40) ÷2,800]		4.500
Variable Departmental overheads (12,600÷ 2,800)		
Machine Hour Rate		15.90

Working Notes :

Machine Hour per annum:	
Total Hours in a Year (365 × 8)	2,920
Less: Maintenance hours	120
Productive hours	2,800
Less: Setting up time (1/7 of Productive hours)	400
Actual Total Hours run on Production	2,400

MACHINE HOUR RATE

(Setting up time Non-productive but power is consumed)

Details	Amount (₹) Per Annum	Amount (₹) Per Hour
Standing Charges:	3,360	7.837
Cleaning and Oil expenses (280 × 12)	2,800	
Maintenance	7,560	
Operators' salary [(3×2,100 × 12) ÷10]	5,480	
Departmental overheads		
Standing charges Per Hour: (19,200 ÷ 2,450)		
Machine Expenses:		2.449
Depreciation [(66,000 – 6,000)/10 × 2,450)]		3.200
Power [(2×2,800 ×1.40) ÷2,450]		5.143
Variable Departmental overheads (12,600÷2,450)		
Machine Hour Rate		18.629

Working Notes :

Machine Hour per annum:

Total Hours in a Year (365 × 8)	2,920
Less: Maintenance hours	120
	2,800
Less: Setting up time	
(1/8 × 2,800 OR 1/7 of Productive time i.e. 2,450 hours)	350
Productive Hours	2,450

Problem 23. (Treatment of Over/Under Absorbed Overheads)

NCR Ltd. uses a historical cost system and applies overheads on the basis of pre-determined rates. The following data are available from the books of the company for the year ended March 31, 2008:

Details		*Amount (₹)*
Production Overheads		*10,00,000*
Production Overheads Applied		*8,56,000*
End Inventory:		*9,30,000*
Work-in-Progress	*6,20,000*	
Finished Goods	*3,10,000*	
Cost of Goods Sold		*27,90,000*

Apply under-absorbed overheads, showing the implications of each method on the profits of the company when:

(i) The entire overhead is treated as part of cost of sales, and

(ii) Under-absorbed overheads are to be prorated to cost of goods sold and End Inventory.

Solution : Computation of Under-absorbed Overheads

Details	Amount (₹)
Production Overheads	10,00,000
Production Overheads Applied	8,56,000
Under-absorbed overheads	1,44,000

Treatment of Application of Under-absorbed Overheads:

Method I: [The entire under-absorbed overheads are treated as part of the Cost of Sales]

Details		Amount (₹)	Amount (₹)
Cost of Sales A/c	Dr	1,44,000	
To Production Overheads A/c			1,44,000

Method II: [The entire under-absorbed overheads are to be prorated to both i.e. Cost of Goods Sold and End Inventory i.e. Unsold Closing Stock]

Cost of Goods Sold = Actual + Proportionate Under absorbed Overheads
= 27,90,000 + 96,000 => ₹ 28,86,000.

End Inventory i.e. Unsold Closing Stock:

Work-in-Progress = Actual + Proportionate Under absorbed Overheads
= 6,20,000 + 32,000 => ₹ 6,52,000.

Finished Goods = Actual + Proportionate Under absorbed Overheads
= 3,10,000 + 16,000 => ₹ 3,26,000.

Adjustment Entry

Details		Amount (₹)	Amount (₹)
Cost of Goods Sold A/c	Dr	96,000	
Work-in-Progress A/c	Dr	16,000	
Finished Goods Stock A/c	Dr	32,000	
To Production Overheads A/c			1,44,000

Effect on Profit: If Method I is adopted the profits get reduced by the total amount of ₹ 1,44,000. However, if the Method II is adopted, the profits get reduced by ₹ 96,000 only.

Working Note: Total under-absorbed production overheads are prorated over Cost of Goods Sold, Work-in-Progress and Finished Goods Stock in proportion of their actual costs i.e. ₹ 27,90,000, ₹ 6,20,000 and ₹ 3,10,000 i.e. 6:2:1.

Problem 24. *A company absorbs production overheads on the basis of pre-determined machine hour rate. For the month of March 2004 the budgeted machine hours were 8,500. During the month actual machine hours worked were 7,928, actual overheads were ₹ 1,46,200 and there was under-absorption of ₹ 7,460. Ascertain the budgeted level of overheads for the month.*

[DU, B.Com (Hons.) 2004]

Solution :

Absorbed Overheads = Actual Overheads – Under-absorbed overheads
= 1,46,200 – 7,460=> ₹ 1,38,740

Machine Hour Rate = Absorbed Overheads/ Actual Machine Hours
= 1,38,740 ÷ 7,928 = > ₹ 17.50

Budgeted Level of Overheads = Budgeted Hours × Machine Hour Rate
= 8,500 ×17.50 => ₹ 1,48,750

Problem 25. *X limited which recovers overheads at a pre-determined rate, provides you the following information;*

Overheads actually incurred (₹)	*6,00,000*
Overheads Recovered (₹)	*4,00,000*
Goods sold (Unit)	*30,000*
Stock of finished goods ((Unit)	*27,500*
Stock of Work-in-Progress (Unit)	*25,000 (20% complete)*

Unabsorbed overheads were due to rising price levels.

How would you treat under-absorbed overheads in cost accounts?

Solution :

Working Notes:

Total units of Production:

= Units sold + Units in closing stock + Equivalent units of work-in - progress

= 30,000 + 27,500 + (0.2 × 25,000)

= 30,000 + 27,500 + 5,000

= 62,500 Units.

Determination of Under-absorbed overheads:

Under-absorbed overheads = Actual overheads – Absorbed overheads

= 6,00,000 – 4,00,000

= ₹ 2,00,000

Determination of Supplementary Rate:

Supplementary Rate = (Under-absorbed overheads / Units of Production)

= 2,00,000 ÷ 62,500

= ₹ 3.20 per unit

As the under recovered overheads are due to the rising prices, it would be charged to the units of production.

Details	Computation	Amount (₹)
Cost of goods sold	30,000 × 3.20 = 96,000	96,000
Stock of finished goods	27,500 × 3.20 = 96,000	88,000
Stock of work-in- Progress	5,000 × 3.20 = 16,000	16,000
Total		2,00,000

Problem 26. *The budgeted working conditions for a cost centre are as follows:*

Normal working hours per week (hours)	*42*
Number of machines	*14*
Normal weekly loss of hours on maintenance etc. (hours per machine)	*5*
Number of weeks worked per year	*48*
Estimated annual overheads (₹)	*1,24,320*

Estimated direct wages rate (₹ per hour)		*4*
Actual results in respect of a 4 weeks period:		
Wages incurred (₹)	*9,000*	
Overheads incurred (₹)		*10,200*
Machine hours worked (hours)		*2,000*

You are required to calculate:

(a) The overhead rate per machine hour; and

(b) The amount of under/over absorption of wages and overheads.

[B.Com (Hons.) DU, 2009]

Solution :

Working Notes: Estimated Annual Machine Hours:

$= (42 \times 14 \times 48) - (5 \times 14 \times 48)$

$= 28{,}224 - 3{,}360 \Rightarrow 24{,}864$

Working Hours in a Four week period:

$= 42 \times 4 \times 14 = 2{,}352$ hours

Computation of Overhead Rate per machine hour:

= Estimated Annual Overheads / Estimated machine hours

= 1, 24,320 ÷ 24,864 => ₹ 5.

Application of rate:

Under/over recovery of Wages:

Wages recovered:

= 2,352 × 4 = ₹ 9,408

Less: Wages incurred: ₹ 9,000

Over-recovery: ₹ 408.

Under/over recovery of Machine overheads:

Machine overheads recovered:

= 2,000 × 5 = ₹ 10,000.

Overheads incurred: ₹ 10,200

Under-recovery: ₹ 200.

OBJECTIVE TYPE EXERCISES

I. Fill in the blank spaces with suitable word/s :

1. The most suitable basis for the allocation of service department costs to a production department is a basis which reflects the ....
2. Common examples of service departments are .... and ....
3. Service performed by one service department for another service department is termed .... services.

4. When the amount of under or over-recovered overhead is significant, it is disposed of by the use of ....

Answers :

1. service rendered	**2.** maintenance of power plant and purchasing
3. reciprocal	**4.** supplementary rate

II. Indicate whether the following statements are True or False :

1. Apportionment of overhead on reciprocal basis is known as step ladder method.
2. Under the ABC analysis of material control, 'A' stands for the highest number of items.
3. Machine hour rate method of absorption should be used in only those cost centres in which work is dominantly done by machines.
4. Reapportionment of service department's costs is known is known as secondary distribution of overhead.
5. When under or over recovered overheads is a significant amount, it should be transferred to Costing Profit and Loss Account.
6. Direct assignment of factory overhead cost to each department is known as apportionment.
7. Linking overheads to cost unit is known as overhead absorption.
8. Significant under-recovered overhead should always be prorated to work-in-progress, finished goods and cost of sales.
9. Over/under-absorbed is equal to the difference between actual factory overhead incurred and the factory overhead charged to production.
10. A company applies works overhead to production @ ₹ 150 per machine hour and actual machine hours were 1000 in the preceding month. Works overhead was under-recovered by ₹ 5,400. The actual overhead costs incurred during the month were ₹ 1,44,600.

Answers :

1. False	**2.** False	**3.** True	**4.** True
5. False	**6.** False	**7.** True	**8.** False
9. True	**10.** False		

THEORETICAL EXERCISES

1. Indicate whether the following statements are True or False :
   (1) Apportionment of overhead on reciprocal basis is known as step ladder method.
   (2) Under the ABC analysis of material control, 'A' stands for the highest number of items. **[Ans. (1) False, (2) True]**
2. How are services departments' costs distributed to the production department? **[DU, B.Com (Hons.) 2004]**

3. What are the causes of under/over absorption of factory overheads? How will you deal with them in cost accounts?

4. Explain how would you treat under-absorbed factory overheads in cost accounts?

5. State concisely why machine hour rate method is preferred for absorbing manufacturing overheads of those cost centres in which machine work predominates?

6. Discuss the secondary distribution of overheads. **[B.Com (Hons.), DU, 1997]**

7. What is the importance of 'machine hour' as a basis for the absorption of factory overheads? **[DU, B.Com (Hons.) 2004]**

8. Explain why pre-determined overhead absorption rates are preferred to overhead absorption rates calculated from factual information after the end of the financial period.

9. Explain various pre-determined overhead absorption rates used to absorb factory overheads.

10. Explain how you would treat under/over-absorption of overheads in Cost Accounts? **[DU, B.Com (Hons.), 1997]**

11. Explain in brief the following concepts:
(i) Machine Hour Rate **[DU, B.Com (Hons.) 2001]**
(ii) Departmentalisation of overheads

12. Distinguish between the followings:
(1) Over-absorbed and Under-absorbed overheads **[DU, B.Com (Hons.), 1998]**
(2) Blanket overhead rate and multiple overhead rates

13. Calculate the machine hour rate of a machine with information given below:

Details	No./Hours/Amount(₹)
Total number of weeks per quarter	13
Total number of hours per week	48
Stoppage due to maintenance	8 hours per month
Time taken for set-up	100 minutes per week
Cost of Machine	5,00,000
Repairs and Maintenance	75,000
Consumable Stores	95,800
Rent Rates and Taxes	20,000
Operator's wages	12,000 p.m.
Supervisor's Salary	25,000 p.m.
Cost of Power	12 units per hour @ ₹ 5 per unit

Notes :

1. Life of the machine is 10 years. Depreciation is provided on Straight line methods treated as variable cost.
2. Repairs and Maintenance and Consumable Stores are variable costs.

3. Power is consumed for production runs only and for set-up maintenance. But cost of power is to be borne by the total time excluding maintenance stoppages.
4. The supervisor is supervising work on three identical machines including the one now considered.
5. The company hires out excessive capacity in the machine shop for outside jobs. Assuming that hire charges are fixed at variable cost plus 25% what rate should be quoted by the company. **[ICWA (Inter) June 1999]**

NUMERICAL EXERCISES

1. The factory overhead costs of four production departments of a company engaged in executing job orders, for an accounting year, are as under:

Department	Amount (₹)
S	19300
G	4200
T	4000
B	2000

Overhead has been absorbed as under:

Department	Basis of absorption
S	₹1.50 per Machine Hour for 14000 hours
G	₹ 1.30 per Direct Labour Hour for 3000 hours
T	80% of Direct Labour Cost of ₹ 6000.
B	₹ 2/- per piece, for 950 pieces.

Find out department-wise the amount of under or over-absorbed factory overheads.

[Ans. Net Over-Recovery of Factory overheads: ₹ 2100]

2. A Company has three production departments P-1, P-2, P-3 and two service departments S-1 and S-2. The following data are extracted from the records of the company for the Quarter ended on March 31, 2004:

Items of expenses	Amount (₹)
Indirect Wages	15000
Rent and rates	50000
General Lighting	6000
Depreciation on Machinery	100000
Power	15000
Sundries	100000

Additional Information (Department-wise)

Details	Total Amount (₹)	P-1	P-2	P-3	S-1	S-2
Direct Wages (₹)	100000	30000	20000	30000	15000	5000
H.P. of Machines used	150	60	30	50	10	-
Cost of Machines (₹)	2500000	600000	800000	1000000	50000	50000
Floor Area Used (Sq.Mtr.)	10000	2000	2500	3000	2000	500
Lighting Point (No)	60	10	15	20	10	5
Production Hours Worked	-	6226	4028	4066	-	-
Service Departments Expenses (%):						
S-1		20	30	40	-	10
S-2		40	20	30	10	-

You are required to:

(a) Compute the overhead rate of production departments using the Simultaneous Equation Method; and

(b) Hence, determine the total cost of a product whose direct material cost and direct labour cost is respectively Rest. 600 and ₹ 400 and which would consume Four hours, Five hours and three hours in Departments P-1, P-2.and P-3 respectively. **[Ans. Rate of Absorption: 15, 22.5, and 30 respectively for P-1, P-2, P-3; and total cost of production: 1262.50]**

3. Ascertain the machine-hour rate from the following information:

Details	Amount (₹)
Cost of machine	450000
Estimated scrap value on expiry of its useful life (8 years)	50000
Rent and Rates for the shop per quarter	6000
General lighting for the shop per month	2000
Insurance premium for the machine p.a.	9000
Repairs and maintenance expenses per annum	12000
Power consumption: 10 units per hour @ Rest. 6/- per unit	60
Estimated working hours per annum: 2200(including setting –up time of 200 hours; no power is required during setting up time)	-
Shop supervisor's salary per month	7200

The machine occupies one-fourth of the total area of the shop. The supervisor is expected to devote one-fifth of his time for supervising the machine.

4. A machine costs ₹1500000 and is deemed to have a scrap value of 10% at the end of its effective life (15 years). Ordinarily, the machine is expected to run for 2400 hours per year but it is estimated that 150 hours will be lost for normal repairs and maintenance and further 750 hours will be lost due to staggering. Other details in respect of machine shop are as under:

Details	Amount (₹)
Annual Wages, bonus and provident fund contribution of each of two operators (each operator is in-charge of two machines)	150000
Rent of the shop (per month)	10000
General Lighting of the shop (per month)	6000
Insurance premium for one machine per annum	30000
Cost of repairs and maintenance per machine per quarter	9000
Shop supervisor's monthly remuneration	15000
Power consumption of machine per hour 12 units @ Rest. 6/- per unit	
Other factory overheads attributable to the shop per annum	96000

There are four identical machines in the shop. The supervisor is expected to devote one-sixth of time for supervising the machine. Compute a comprehensive machine-hour rate from the above details. **[Ans. ₹ 298]**

5. Alpha Engineering Limited accepts a variety of jobs, which require both manual and machine operations. The budgeted Profit and Loss Account for the period 2003-2004 is as under:

Details	Amount (₹)	Amount (₹)
Sales		4000000
Less: Cost of Sales		
Direct Materials	600000	
Direct Labour	400000	
Prime Cost	1000000	
Production Overhead	1500000	
Production Cost	2500000	
Administrative, Selling and Distribution Overhead	800000	3300000
Profit		700000

Other Budgeted Information	Hours/Number
Machine Hours for the period	10000
Labour Hours for the period	15000
Number of Jobs for the period	800

An enquiry has been received recently from an esteemed customer and the production department has prepared the following estimate of the prime cost required for the job:

Direct material		20000
Direct Labour		15000
Prime Cost		35000
Machine Hours required	120	
Labour Hours required	75	

You are required to calculate:

(1) Factory Overhead Rates of Absorption by different methods and comment on the suitability of each.

(2) Production Overhead cost of the order based on each of the Absorption Rates calculated as in (1).

[Ans. (1): MHR 150; LHR 100; percentage of direct material 250; percentage of direct wages cost 375; percentage of prime cost 150; job rate 1875; (2) 18000; 7500; 50000; 56250; 52500; 1875.]

6. The Roop Kamal Corporation estimates the following for the next period:

Details	Amount or Unit
Factory Overhead (₹)	4,00,000
Units Produced (Units)	50,000
Materials cost of units produced (₹)	8,00,000

Production will require 80,000 Labour hours at an estimated Labour cost of ₹ 2,00,000 Machine is estimated to run about 40,000 hours.

Determine the factory overhead rate to be used in applying factory overhead to production on each of the following bases: (a) Units of production, (b) Direct Labour Cost, (c) Direct Materials Cost, (d) Direct Labour Hours, and (e) Machine hours.

[Ans. (a) 8; (b) 200; (c) 50%; (d) 5; (e) 10]

7. PV Engg. Ltd. having Fifteen different types of machines furnishes you the following data for the year 2001-2002 in respect of Machine No. M-17:-

1. Cost of machine (10 years life) with zero scrap value ₹ 250000
2. Overhead expenses:
   - (i) Factory Rent (Annual) 120000
   - (ii) Heating and Lighting (Annual) 90000
   - (iii) Supervision (Annual) 360000
   - (iv) Special Equipment for M-17 18000
   - (v) Area of the Factory (Sq. feet) 100000
   - (vi) Area occupied by M-17 (Sq. feet) 5000
   - (vii) Power Cost ₹ 6/- per hour while in operation
3. Wages of machine operator ₹ 200 per day of 8 hours including all fringe benefits. The operator attends to one machine when it is being set up and two machines while in operation.
4. Estimated Production hours (Annual) 4800

   Estimated set-up time (Annual) 200

Compute comprehensive machine hour rate and find out the cost of the following jobs:

	Job No. 25105	Job No. 28112
Set-up time (hours)	60	20
Operation time (hours)	180	160

[Ans. MHR> Comprehensive: During Operation: ₹ 34.00; During Set-Up: ₹ 40.50; Job NO. 25105: ₹ 8550; Job NO. 28112: ₹ 6250]

8. The capacity usage ratio and the capacity utilisation ratio in respect of a machine for a particular quarter is 80% and 90% respectively. The available working hours in a month are 250 hours. The break-up of idle time is as under:

Waiting for jobs 7 hours; break-down 5 hours; waiting for tools 4 hours. Calculate the idle time cost when the hourly fixed cost of running the machine has been worked at ₹ 10 with reference to available hours. Compute the cost idle time. **[Ans. ₹ 250]**

9. Total overhead of Department SJ of a factory were ₹3600000 for the month January. The department produced three products – 100 units of X, 500 units of Y, and 200 units of Z. Direct costs incurred during the month were as follows:

		100X	500Y	200Z
Direct Material	₹	1800000	1400000	1300000
Direct Labour	₹	1500000	1700000	1800000
Direct Factory Expenses	₹	150000	200000	150000

Required:

(i) Direct Material Cost Rate and overheads chargeable to products based on this method,

(ii) Direct Labour Cost Rate and overheads chargeable to products on this basis,

(iii) Prime Cost Rate and overheads chargeable to products on this basis, and

(iv) Cost sheet for three products X, Y, and Z charging overheads on the basis of Prime Cost giving total cost as well as per unit cost. **[Ans. ....]**

10. Caribbean Manufacturing Limited has three departments which are regarded as production departments. Service departments costs are distributed to theses production departments using the step ladder method of distribution. Estimates of factory overhead costs to be incurred by each department in the forthcoming year are as follows. Data required for distribution is also shown against each department.

Department	Factory overhead (₹)	Direct labour hours	No. of employees	Areas in m^2
Production				
X	1,93,000	4,000	100	3,000
Y	64,000	3,000	125	1,500
Z	83,000	4,000	85	1,500
Service				
P	45,000	1,000	10	500
Q	75,000	5,000	50	1,500
R	1,05,000	6,000	40	1,000
S	30,000	3,000	50	1,000

The overhead costs of the four service departments are distributed in the same order: i.e. P, Q, R and S respectively on the following basis:

Department	Basis
P	Number of employees
Q	Direct labour hours
R	Area in m^2
S	Direct labour hours

You are required to:

(a) Prepare a schedule showing the distribution of overhead costs of the four service departments to the three production departments; and

(b) Calculate the overhead recovery rate per direct labour hour for each of the three production departments. **[Ans. 75, 45, 40]**

11. From the following data of a factory machine room compute machine hours per annum assuming that the machine room will work at 90% capacity throughout the year and that a break down of 10% of the total working hours is reasonable. There are seven holidays excluding Saturdays and Sundays. The factory works 8 hours a day and 4 hours on Saturdays. Number of machines (each of same type) is 40.

[Ans. 72,576 hours]

[B.Com (Hons.) DU, 2007]

12. From the following data of a factory machine room compute machine hours per annum assuming that the machine room will work at 85% capacity throughout the year and that a break down of 10% of the total working hours is reasonable. There are seven holidays excluding Saturdays and Sundays. The factory works 8 hours a day and 4 hours on Saturdays. Number of machines (each of same type) is 50.

[Ans. 85860 hours]

13. The following particulars refer to the machining process used in the treatment of material subsequently incorporated in a component forming part of an electrical appliance.

(a) The original cost of the machine used was ₹ 10,000. Its estimated life is 10 years and its scrap value at the end of its estimated life is ₹ 1,000. The estimated working time per year (50weeks of 44 hours) is 2200 hours of which machine maintenance etc. is estimated to take up 200 hours. No other loss of working time is expected. Setting up time estimated at 100 hours (included in 2200 hours) is regarded as productive time.

(b) Electricity used by the machine during production is 16 units per hour at a cost of 9 Paise per unit. Power is not consumed during maintenance or setting up.

(c) The machine requires a solution which is replaced at the end of each week at a cost of ₹ 20 each time.

(d) The estimated cost of maintenance per year is ₹ 1,200.

(e) Two attendants control the operation of the machine together with five other identical machines. Their combined weekly wages, insurance and employers contributions to the holiday pay amounted to ₹ 120.

(f) Departmental and General Works overheads allocated to this machine for the year amounted to ₹ 2000.

You are required to calculate the machine hour rate. **[B.Com (Hons.) DU, 2006]**

[Ans. ₹ 4.42]

14. The following data relate to a manufacturing department for a period:

Details	Budgeted Data	Actual Data
Direct Material (₹)	1,00,000	1,50,000
Direct Labour(₹)	2,00,000	2,50,000
Production overheads(₹)	2,00,000	2,15,000
Direct Labour Hours	50,000	65,000
Machine Hours	40,000	50,000

Job MPT-14 was one of the jobs worked on during the period. The actual data relating to this job were:

Details	Actual Data
Direct Material (₹)	6,000
0Direct Labour (₹)	3,000
Direct Labour Hours	750
Machine Hours	750

Required:

(A) Calculate the production overhead rate predetermined for the period based on:
  (i) Percent of Direct Material cost, and
  (ii) Machine Hour Rate.

(B) Calculate the production overhead rate cost to be charged to Job MPT-14 based on the rates calculated (A) above.

(C) Assuming that a Machine hour Rate of absorption is used, calculate the under/over absorption of Production overheads for the period.

[Ans. Percent of Direct Material cost: 200%; Machine hour Rate @ ₹ 5, over absorbed Overheads ₹ 35,000]

15. NCR Ltd. uses a historical cost system and applies overheads on the basis of pre-determined rates. The following data are available from the books of the company for the year ended March 31, 2008:

Details		Amount (₹)
Production Overheads		8,50,000
Production Overheads Applied		7,50,000
End Inventory:		7,20,000
Work-in-Progress	2,40,000	
Finished Goods	4,80,000	
Cost of Goods Sold		16,80,000

Apply under-absorbed overheads, showing the implications of each method on the profits of the company when:

(i) The entire overhead is treated as part of cost of sales, and

(ii) Under-absorbed overheads are to be prorated to cost of goods sold and End Inventory.

[Ans. Under absorbed Overheads ₹ 1,00,000; Method I: Profit is reduced by ₹ 1,00,000; Method II: Profit is reduced by ₹ 70,000]

16. A machine was purchased on 1st January 1998 for ₹ 5 Lakhs. The total cost of all machinery inclusive of the new machine was ₹ 75 Lakhs. The following further particulars are available:

Expected life of the machine 10 years

Scrap value at the end of 10 years ₹ 5,000

Repairs and maintenance for the machine during the year ₹ 20,000

Expected number of working hours of the machine per year 4,000 hours

Insurance premium annually for all machines ₹ 4,500

Power consumption for the machine per hour @ ₹ 6 per unit—15 units

Area occupied by the machine 100 sq. ft.

Area occupied by other machines 1500 sq. ft.

Rent per month of the department ₹ 800

Lighting charges for 20points for the whole department out of which three points are for the new machine ₹ 1500 per month.

Compute the machine hour rate for the new machine.

[DU, B. Com (Hons.) 1999(Modified)]

[Ans. Machine Hour Rate: ₹ 108.275]

17. The machine shop of a manufacturing concern has six identical machines manned by six operators. The total cost of the machine is ₹ 8,00,000. The following information relates to six monthly period ended September 30, 2000:

Details	Others/Amount (₹)
Normal Available hours per month	208
Absenteeism (W/o Pay) hours per month	18
Leave (with Pay) hours per month	20
Normal Idle time hours per month	10
Average rate of wages per hour per operator	22.50
Production Bonus	15% on wages
Power and fuel consumption	9,000
Supervision and Indirect labour	3,300
Electricity and lighting	1,200
Repairs and Maintenance (per annum)	3% of value of machine
Insurance (per annum)	42,000
Depreciation (per annum)	10% of original cost
Allocated factory Overheads (per annum)	75,670

Compute Machine Hour Rate. **[DU, B. Com (Hons.) 2001(Modified)]**

[Ans. Machine Hour Rate: ₹52.3125]

18. The budgeted activity and cost data for each half year of SV Ltd. were as follows:

Details	Amount (₹)
Direct Labour Hours	68,000
Direct Wages	42,500
Overheads: Fixed	37,400
Variable	64,600

During six months January to June the following actual results were achieved:

Details	Amount (₹)
Direct Labour Hours	65,000
Direct Wages	45,500
Overheads: Fixed	38,700
Variable	65,800

The existing method of absorbing overheads is by a direct wages percentage rate. A proposal has been made to change the overhead absorption to a direct labour hour rate analysed into fixed and variable overheads.

You are required for the period January to June to calculate under the new proposal (i.e. using direct labour hour rates of absorption):

(i) The budgeted direct labour hour rates of overhead absorption for fixed and variable overheads;

(ii) The absorbed overheads;

(iii) The over or under-absorbed overheads. **[B.Com (Hons.) DU, 2002]**

[Ans. Total Rate: ₹ 1.50 (0.55 + 0.95); Absorbed Overheads: ₹ 97,500; Under-Absorbed Overheads: ₹ 7,000]

19. The following information relates to the activities of a production department for the month of January:

Details	Hour	Amount (₹)
Materials Used		72, 000
Direct Wages		60, 000
Machine Hours	20, 000	
Labour hours	24, 000	
Overhead chargeable to the department		48, 000

On one order to be carried out in the month of February, the relevant data were:

Details	Hour	Amount (₹)
Materials		4, 000
Direct Wages		3, 300
Machine Hours	1, 200	
Labour hours	1, 650	

Prepare a comparative statement of cost of this order by using the following methods of absorption of overheads:

(i) Direct Labour Hour Rate;

(ii) Percentage of direct wages; and

(iii) Machine Hour Rate. **[B.Com (Hons.) DU, 2003]**

[Ans: Rate of Absorption: (i) ₹ 2; (ii) 80%; (iii) ₹ 2.40; Factory cost: (i) ₹ 10,600; (ii) ₹ 9,940; and (iii) ₹ 10,180.]

20. A company absorbs production overheads on the basis of pre-determined machine hour rate. The budgeted machine hours were 25,000 for the Quarter ending on 31.3.2004. During the Quarter actual machine hours worked were 23,800, actual overheads were ₹ 6,30,200 and there was over-absorption of ₹ 36,200. Ascertain the budgeted level of overheads for the Quarter.

[Ans. Machine Hour Rate ₹ 28; Budgeted Level of Overheads ₹ 7,00,000.]

21. X limited which recovers overheads at a pre-determined rate, provides you the following information;

Overheads actually incurred (₹)	1,50,000
Overheads Recovered (₹)	1,00,000
Goods sold (Unit)	12,000
Stock of finished goods ((Unit)	11,000
Stock of Work-in-Progress (Unit)	10,000 (20% complete)

Unabsorbed overheads were due to rising price levels.

How would you treat under-absorbed overheads in cost accounts?

[Ans. Supplementary Rate = ₹ 2 per unit]

22. The actual total expenditure of a light engineering factory was ₹ 6,75,912. Overheads were recorded at the rate of ₹ 2 per hour at normal capacity of the factory. Out of 10,000 units produced, only 8,000 units were sold. 500 units were in work-in-progress. Actual hours worked were 2,84,756. Sixty percent of the difference between the actual and applied overheads was due to fluctuations in material prices and labour rates. There was a fire in the factory during this accounting period and the company lost ₹ 50,000 of which the buildings accounted for ₹ 30,000 and the balance represented loss of materials stored in the Godown. A sum of ₹ 10,000 was paid as wages to workmen during the strike period. The balance amount represented the difference between the actual and applied overheads due to operational efficiency of inefficiency.

Calculate the under/over absorption of production overheads for the period and state the appropriate treatment in Cost Accounts. (Journal Entries not required).

[DU, B.Com (Hons.), 1999]

[Ans. Under Recovered Overheads ₹ 1,06,400; Supplementary Rate ₹ 6.384]

23. From the following data calculate overhead rates based on (i) Maximum Capacity; (ii) Practical Capacity; and (iii) Capacity based on expected sales.

Details	Maximum Capacity (100%)	Practical Capacity (90%)	Sales Expectancy Capacity (80%)
Direct Labour Hours	15000	13500	12000
Fixed Overhead	270000	270000	270000
Variable overhead	150000	135000	120000

If the actual capacity utilized be 12800 labour hours, calculate amount of under/over absorbed of fixed overhead on the basis of each of above capacities.

24. A company's production costs for the year ending 30/6/2003 are given below:

Item	Production department			Office	Stores	Work-shop	Total
	P_1	P_2	P_3				
Direct wages	20,000	25,000	30,000	-	-	-	75,000
Direct materials	30,000	35,000	45,000	-	-	-	1,10,000
Indirect materials	2,000	3,000	3,000	1,000	2,000	2,000	13,000
Indirect wages	3,000	3,000	4,000	10,000	10,000	5,000	35,000
Area in m^2	200	250	300	150	100	250	1,250
Book value of machinery	30,000	35,000	25,000	-	-	15,000	1,05,000
Total HP of machineries	15	20	25	-	-	5	65
Machine hours worked	10,000	20,000	15,000	-	-	5,000	50,000

Common expenses	Total
Rent	₹ 12500
Insurance	₹ 1050
Depreciation	15% of the value of machinery
Power	₹ 3800
Light	₹ 1250

You are requested to prepare an Overhead Analysis- Sheet for the department showing clearly the basis of apportionment, wherever necessary.

25. SVC Ltd. has the following information relating to absorbed and actual factory overheads for the current quarter:

Details	Amount (₹)
Factory Overheads Incurred	5,49,000
Factory Overheads Absorbed	7,14,600
Absorbed Factory overheads are in the following accounts:	
Cost of Goods sold	5,76,000
Closing Work-in-Progress	63,000
Closing Finished Goods Stock	75,600

You are required to allocate the under or over recovered factory overheads to relevant accounts and make necessary journal entries at the end of the quarter.

❑❑❑

12 Non-Production Overheads

Learning Objectives

It attempts to explain accounting for administration overheads as well as selling and distribution overheads. In this chapter you will learn :

1. Meaning and nature of administrative overheads.
2. Problem of distribution of administrative overheads.
3. Different approaches to apportion administrative overheads.
4. Accounting treatment of administrative overheads.
5. Meaning and nature of selling and distribution overheads.
6. Methods of apportionment of selling and distribution overheads.
7. Accounting treatment of selling and distribution overheads.

INTRODUCTION

Administrative overheads, Selling and Distribution (i.e. S&D) overheads, and other non-manufacturing expenses are remotely connected with current manufacturing activities. In financial accounting all such expenses are treated as period costs. However, for the purpose of decision- making, those expenses are usually linked to cost objects or cost centres.

Administrative Overheads

Office and Administration overhead pertain to general management and administration of an undertaking. It is the indirect expenditure incurred in formulating the policy, directing the organization and controlling the operations of the undertaking. All costs relating to policy making, top level administration and general management, overall planning and control, maintenance and running of routine office and handling of accounting and legal matters are included in administrative overheads. Such costs are of general nature. These expenses relate to the administration of an undertaking. They are not related to specific activity of production, sales, publicity or distribution. These costs are incurred for the benefit of organization as a whole. Administration overheads do no include costs of administering manufacturing activities. Those costs are treated as part of production overhead. Usually for a multi-unit firm, only corporate office expenses are treated as administration overheads while expenses associated with administrative activities at manufacturing units are treated as manufacturing/ production overheads. Although administration is a function essential to support manufacturing, selling, distribution and research& development activities, no direct relationship can be established between those activities and administration overheads. Administration overheads are related to activities, which determine the future of the firm rather than influencing the current operations. Salary of general manager and managing director, salaries of general office staff, office rent, depreciation of office machines, legal charges, accounting and audit expenses are some of the examples of Administration overhead.

Salient features of Administrative overheads:

(1) They are incurred for a business as a whole.

(2) They remain almost fixed despite changes in production level.

(3) In the short run, they are non-controllable.

(4) They are not identifiable with any specific cost unit. In many cases they may not be identified even with a cost centre.

(5) Compared with production overheads and selling overheads they are generally of smaller amount.

(6) Absorption of such overheads involves an element of subjectivity.

Treatment of Administrative Overheads

There are three approaches to account for the administration overheads:

(a) According to this approach, since the major activities, manufacturing and selling are befitted by administration overheads, the latter should be apportioned between the two activities on some suitable /equitable basis.

(b) The second view is that administration is an independent function and is as important as the other major functions. Since no direct relationship can be established between administration overhead and products or jobs manufactured and sold, and because these costs are largely fixed in nature, they should be treated as period costs and charged directly to Costing Profit and loss Account.

(c) The third approach is that administration overhead should be added as a separate item to the cost of manufacturing and selling the jobs or products.

The second approach is widely preferred by the professional accountants. AS-2, Inventory Valuation, permits only this method for accumulating for administration overheads.

Thus, Administrative overheads can be treated in the following three ways in cost accounts:

(A) Transfer to Costing Profit & Loss Account: This is the most appropriate method of accounting for administration overheads. Administration overheads for the period are transferred to the Costing Profit & Loss Account at the end of the accounting period. Administration activities, although essential for the survival and growth of the firm, do not contribute to current operations; so there is no logic for charging those expenses to manufacturing and selling. The main argument against this method is that if the administration overheads are eliminated from the cost of jobs, /products/ territories or salesmen etc, net profit for each segment cannot be ascertained properly. However, this argument is not tenable because administration overheads do not represent cost of resources used in producing or selling goods/services. In evaluating performance of a particular segment, operating results and operating assets are used, rather than net profit for the segment.

Some argue that charging administration overheads to Profit & loss Account results in inadequate control. There can be no argument against the view that each item of administration costs should be subjected to control procedure, but the control procedure can be independent of the accounting plan. AS-2, Inventory Valuation, recognizes this method only for valuation of inventories.

(B) Apportion to Production and Selling functions: A part of administration overheads is treated as factory overhead and is distributed to production and service cost centers. The other part is assigned to Selling and Distribution activities and is distributed amongst sales-service departments and sales territories. In this manner, administration overheads allocated to production and selling functions of the organization lose their identity. However, it leads to following problems:

(a) It is difficult to find equitable bases to apportion administration overheads between the manufacturing, selling, and distribution activities. In general, bases selected are arbitrary and so results are unreliable.

(b) Again, it is difficult to find suitable criteria to apportion the apportioned part of administration overheads to manufacturing into production and service departments.

(c) Similarly, it is difficult to identify equitable criteria for distribution of that part of administration overheads, which are assigned to selling activities between sales-service departments and sales territories.

The element of subjectivity can be reduced if each of administration overheads is analysed individually to measure the services received by each function. Criteria, which are commonly used, are as under:

Expense Item	Basis of Apportionment
Office rent, rates and taxes	Floor area
Correspondence	Number of letters drafted/prepared
Legal Expense (Personnel Matters)	Number of employees
Personnel Department Expenses	Number of employees
Computers/Typing	Number of letters and other documents made/typed
Depreciation of office building	Floor area

Under this method, that part of the administration overhead, which is apportioned to manufacturing activities, is treated as product cost. The other part apportioned to selling activities treated as period cost and along with other selling costs is transferred to the profit and loss account.

(C) Separate item of cost: Administration overhead is treated as a separate function and is shown as a separate element of the cost of finished goods sold. Periodic cost of sales analysis sheet is prepared to show manufacturing cost, selling and distribution costs and administration costs separately.

The most difficult problem in using this method is in selecting appropriate criteria for assigning those costs to units produced or units sold. Various bases, which are usually used to assign administration overheads, are:

(a) Net Sales Value;

(b) Number of units Sold;

(c) Selling Costs;

(d) Manufacturing Costs;

(e) Number of units manufactured; and

(f) Gross Profit on Sales.

Administration overheads are more likely to be related to sales rather than production and so the first three criteria, which emphasise the selling function, are considered more equitable than other criteria.

Administration overheads should be added to the cost of units sold and not to the cost of units lying in store, whether finished stock, or work-in-progress stock. According to AS-2 "Those overheads other than production overhead should be included as part of inventory cost only to the extent they clearly relate to putting the inventories in their present location and condition". This requirement of AS-2 clearly indicates that administration overheads should be included in inventory cost only under exceptional circumstances because there is little or no direct relationship between administration function and production function. Only in rare circumstances administration overheads clearly relate to bringing inventories in their present location and condition. The application rate is usually computed by dividing the total administration overhead by the base selected for assignment.

$$= \frac{\text{Administration Overhead for the period}}{\text{Net sales value for the period}} \times 100$$

If Administration Overhead for a specified period is ₹ 2,40,000 and the Sales Value for the same period is ₹ 15,00,000, the application rate will be (2,40,000 ÷ 15,00,000) ×100=16% of net sales. If net sales value of one order executed is ₹ 1,20,000, the administration overhead of ₹19,200 (being 16% of ₹ 1,20,000) is to be added to the cost of sales.

It is preferable to use a predetermined rate for the absorption of administration overhead.

Control of Administration Overheads

It requires collection of expenses under correct cost account numbers for each administration department separately. Then allocation and apportionment of overheads to various administration departments is done. Overheads collected for an accounting period are compared with: (a) Previous year's overheads, (b) Budgets and (c) Standards.

Previous year's data do not provide the right benchmark because they include inefficiencies of the past year and fail to consider the intervening changes. Budgets provide a better criterion for evaluation. The budget for administration overheads is prepared as a part of the master budget and actual expenses are compared with the same.

Some accountants suggest the use of standards for control purposes. Although it may not be possible to establish standards for all the executives, many tasks can be standardized. Steps involved in such standardization are: (a) Classification of tasks into two groups: those which can be standardized and those which cannot be standardized. (b) Selecting a unit measurement for each task (c) Undertaking the time and motion study of each operation (d) Determining the costs for each operation and (e) Establishing a reporting system.

Standardisation has the advantage that it helps to group similar activities, provides an incentive for better performance because each employee is aware that his performance will be measured against the standard. Although administration overheads are largely fixed in nature, once the volume of activity exceeds the higher limit of the 'relevant range' expenses increase. It is a fact that once an item of overhead touches a higher level; it becomes difficult to bring down the same even when the activity level comes down. So the pre-requisite of an effective control is to put restraint on the tendency to increase administration overheads.

Selling and Distribution Overheads

Selling overheads are costs of creating and stimulating demand and securing-cum -executing orders. Costs of manufacturing and distributing finished products are excluded from selling overheads. According to C.I.M.A., selling overhead is the cost incurred in promoting sales and retaining customers. Sales promotion expenses are incurred to promote sales of an organisation. These expenses depend on type, extent and duration of sales promotion which in turn depends on the business/marketing policy of the organisation. These expenses include advertisement expenses (incurred in posters, newspapers, signboards, Neon-signs, exhibitions, cinemas, TV shows etc) and distribution of free samples etc. If the advertisement is heavy and the benefit arising out of it may accrue over a longer period, such expenditure may be treated as deferred revenue expenditure and charged off to Profit and Loss Account over a period of three to five years. If it is not large amount, the whole of it may be charged off to Profit and Loss Account in the same year under the head selling overheads.

Distribution overheads are costs of moving finished products to central and local storage, moving finished products to the customers, moving finished products to and from the prospective customers as in the case of goods on sale or return basis and making empties reusable.

When a product is placed in a saleable condition, production function ends and distribution function begins. Overheads related to distribution function are known as distribution overhead. Many professional accountants prefer to deal with selling and distribution overheads together. Salaries, commissions, traveling expenses of salesmen and technical representatives, sales office expenses, bad debts, brokerage or third- party commissions, cost of operating the marketing information system including market research, expenses on advertisement and publicity cost of catalogues and price lists, and cost of maintenance of showrooms are some of the examples of sales overhead. Carriage and freight outwards, depreciation, cost of repair and maintenance, insurance charges and operating costs of distribution vehicles, cost of secondary packing, warehousing expenses, expenses on insurance of finished goods and wastage of finished goods are the examples of distribution overhead.

Accounting for Selling and Distribution Overheads

It involves the following steps:

(A) Collection of overheads under well-defined cost accounting numbers is the beginning of accounting for selling and distribution overheads. The cost account number indicates nature and object of expenditure. The following are the examples of account headings for selling and distribution overheads: (i) Advertising; (ii) Commission to salesmen (iii) Bank charges on bank guarantees obtained for bid-bonds (iv) Catalogue and price lists (v) Printing and stationery (vi) After-sales service (vii) Rent, rates and taxes (viii) Insurance (ix) Postage, telegram, telephone (x) Discount (xi) Fancy Packing (xii) Repairs, maintenance and running costs of Vehicles.

(B) Selling and distribution overheads may be classified as (i) fixed, (ii) semi-fixed, and (iii) variable overheads. Analysis of expenses under such classification is absolutely necessary for effective control and decision- making purposes.

(C) Allocate and apportion those expenses to various functions, territories and customers. These may be grouped under the following headings: (a) Advertising and Sales Promotion; (b) Direct Selling; (c) Transportation; (d) Warehousing and Storage; and (e)Credit and Collection.

Grouping varies among organizations depending upon organization structure and marketing structure. Each group is treated as a separate cost center and the method of allocation and apportionment of expenses to those cost centers is on the similar pattern as that of manufacturing overheads. Further, proper accounting requires charging of selling and distribution costs to the central marketing unit of the organization and territories. Expenses allocated and apportioned to central market unit are reapportioned to territories based on the following criteria:

Selling Overheads	Apportionment Criteria
Advertising Expense	Sales value/Physical units
Cataloguing cost	Sales value/ number of customers
Insurance charges	Property value
Depreciation	Capital value of asset

Some of the expenses can be traced to each function and each territory and so can be allocated directly. And these are: Direct Selling expenses; Traveling expenses of salesmen; Sales commission; Bank charges for the issue of bank-guarantees; outward transport cost; Depreciation, cost of repairs and maintenance, and insurance charges of buildings and office equipments; Depreciation, cost of repairs and maintenance, and insurance charges of buildings and vehicles.

Illustration 12.1 : *Following information is available for a certain month:*

Details	*Zone I*	*Zone II*	*Zone III*
Selling Expenses	*9,600*	*4,200*	*6,500*
Distribution costs	*4,000*	*2,000*	*3,000*
Number of units Sold	*16,000*	*5,000*	*10,000*
Sales	*1,20,000*	*35,000*	*65,000*

The Company adopts sales basis and quantity basis for application of selling and distribution costs respectively. Compute (a) Zone-wise overhead Absorption rates separately for selling and distribution costs and (b) the amount of selling and distribution costs chargeable to a consignment of 2,500 units of a product, sold in each Zone at ₹ 6.50 per unit.

Solution : Determination of Overhead Absorption Rates:

1. Selling Cost Absorption Rate = $\frac{\text{Selling Expenses}}{\text{Sales}} \times 100$

2. Distribution Cost Absorption Rate = $\frac{\text{Distribution Expenses}}{\text{No. of Units sold}} \times 100$

Overhead Absorption Rates Zone-wise

Zone	Selling Cost Absorption Rate	Distribution Cost Absorption Rate
I	(9,600 ÷ 1,20,000) × 100 = 8% of Sales	(4,000 ÷ 16000) = OR Re. 0.25 per Unit
II	(4,200 ÷ 35,000) × 100 = 12% of Sales	(2,000 ÷ 5,000) = OR Re. 0.40 per Unit
III	(6,500 ÷ 65,000) × 100 = 10% of Sales	(3,000 ÷ 10,000) = OR Re. 0.30 per Unit

Computation of Selling Cost and Distribution cost Chargeable to a Consignment of 2,500 Units for a Sales Value of ₹ 16,250.

Details	Zone I	Zone II	Zone III
Selling Cost	1,300	1,950	1,625
Distribution Cost	625	1,000	750
Total Selling and distribution cost	1,925	2,950	2,375

Illustration 12.2 : *Quality Limited sells its products throughout the country through its four zonal sales offices. The budgeted expenses for the year 2008-09 are given below:*

Expenditure			*Amount (₹)*
Sales Manager's Salary			*3,00,000*
Expenses relating to Sales Manager's Office			*2,10,000*
Traveling Salesmen's salaries			*6,00,000*
Traveling Expenses			*1,00,000*
Advertisements			*80,000*
Warehouse:	*A*	*30,000*	
	B	*50,000*	
	C	*20,000*	
	D	*36,000*	*1,36,000*
Insurance on Inventories			*35,000*
Commission on Sales@ 4% on sales			*8,40,000*

Additional Information:

Zone	*Sales (₹ Lakh)*	*Salesmen (No.)*	*Total Distance Covered (kms.)*	*Allocation of advertisement (%)*	*Average stock (₹ Lakh)*
A	*63*	*6*	*6,000*	*30*	*10.5*
B	*84*	*8*	*14,000*	*35*	*14.0*
C	*28*	*2*	*4,500*	*15*	*7.0*
D	*35*	*4*	*5,500*	*20*	*3.5*

Compute Zone-wise Selling overheads, as a percentage to sales, based on above details.

Solution : **Selling Overhead Distribution**

Expense	Basis of Allocation	Ratio	Total (₹)	Zone A	Zone B	Zone C	Zone D
Sales Manager's Salary	Sales	9:12:4:5	3,00,000	90,000	1,20,000	40,000	50,000
Sales Manager's Office Expenses	Sales	9:12:4:5	2,10,000	63000	84000	28000	35,000
Salesmen's Salaries	Number of Salesmen	3:4:1:2	6,00,000	1,80,000	2,40,000	60,000	1,20,000
Traveling Expenses	Distance Covered	12:28:9:11	1,20,000	24,000	56,000	18,000	22,000
Advertisement	Budgeted Ratio	6:7:3:4	80,000	24,000	28,000	12,000	16,000
Warehouse Rent	Actual	———	1,36,000	30,000	50,000	20,000	36,000
Insurance on Inventories	Average Inventory	3:4:1:2	35,000	10,500	14,000	7,000	3,500
Commission on Sales	Sales	9:12:4:5	8,40,000	2,52,000	3,36,000	1,12,000	1,40,000
Total Overheads			23,21,000	67,35,000	9,28,000	2,97,000	4,22,500

Amount of Sales			21,00,0000	63,00,000	84,00,000	28,00,000	3,50,0000
Percentage of Sales i.e. (Overhead/ Sales × 100)			11.05	10.69	11.05	10.61	12.07

Illustration 12.3 : (Selling Overheads)

Beeta Ltd., a manufacturing company, having an extensive marketing network throughout the country, sells its products through four zonal offices viz., North, South, East and West. The budgeted expenditure for the year is given below:

Details	*Amount (₹)*
Sales Manager's Office expenses	*3,00,000*
Sales Manager's Salary	*2,00,000*
Traveling Salesmen Salaries	*8,00,000*
Traveling Expenses	*90,000*
Advertisements	*75,000*
Godown Rent:	*1,70,000*
North 37,500	
South 63,000	
East 24,500	
West 45,000	
Insurance of Inventories	*50,000*
Commission on sales @ 4% of sales	*15,00,000*

Additional Information:

Zone	*Sales (₹ Lakh)*	*No. of Salesmen*	*Total distance covered (Kms)*	*Percentage Allocation of Advertise-ment*	*Average Inventory held (₹ Lakh)*
North	*112.5*	*5*	*15,000*	*30*	*15*
South	*150.0*	*6*	*35,000*	*30*	*20*
East	*50.0*	*3*	*14,000*	*20*	*10*
West	*62.5*	*2*	*11,000*	*20*	*5*

Compute zone-wise Selling Overheads as a percentage of sales.

Solution : Allocation and Apportionment of Selling Overhead

Details	**Criterion**	**Total ₹**	**Zone**			
			North	**South**	**East**	**West**
Sales Manager's Office expenses	Sales	2,00,000	60,000	80,000	26,667	33,333
Sales Manager's Salary	Sales	3,00,000	90,000	1,20,000	40,000	50,000

Traveling Salesmen's Salaries	No. of Salesmen	8,00,000	2,50,000	3,00,000	1,50,000	1,00,000
Traveling Expenses	Distance Covered	90,000	18,000	42,000	16,800	13,200
Advertisement	Allocation Ratio given	75,000	22,500	22,500	15,000	15,000
Godown Rent	Allocation	1,70,000	37,500	63,000	24,500	45,000
Insurance on Inventories	Average Stock	50,000	15,000	20,000	10,000	5,000
Commission on Sales	Sales	15,00,000	4,50,000	6,00,000	2,00,000	2,50,000
Total		29,85,000	8,83,000	11,67,500	4,56,300	4,78,200

Zone-wise Selling Overheads as a percentage of sales

Details	Total (₹)	Zone			
		North (₹)	South (₹)	East (₹)	West (₹)
Selling Overheads	29,85,000	8,83,000	11,67,500	4,56,300	4,78,200
Sales	375,00,000	112,50,000	150,00,000	50,00,000	62,50,000
Selling Overheads as a percentage of Sales	7.960	7.849	7.783	9.126	7.651

Illustration 12.4 : *A Company produces three types of products M, N, and P. The sales territory of the company is divided into three Zones Z-1, Z-2, and Z-3. The estimated sales (₹) of or the year are as under:*

Product	*Territory*		
	Z-1 (₹)	*Z-2 (₹)*	*Z-3 (₹)*
M	*60,000*	*25,000*	
N	*40,000*		*1,00,000*
P		*85,000*	*50,000*

Budgeted Advertising cost is as under:

Product	*Territory*			
	Total	*Z-1 (₹)*	*Z-2 (₹)*	*Z-3 (₹)*
Local	*14,500*	*3,750*	*5,500*	*5,250*
General	*9,000*			
Sum	*23,500*			

Find out the advertising cost percent on sales for each product and the zone showing how you will present the statement to the management.

Solution : Solution is given stage-wise:

Stage-I: Allocation and apportionment of advertisement expenses to sales zones

Details	Criterion	Total	Zone		
			Z-1	Z-2	Z-3
Local Cost	Given	14,500	3,750	5,500	5,250
General Cost	Sales	9,000	2,500	2,750	3,750
Sum		23,500	6,250	8,250	9,000

Stage-II: Apportionment of Advertisement expenses to the products

Zone	Criterion	Total	Product		
			M	N	P
Z-1	Sales	6,250	3,750	2,500	
Z-2	Sales	8,250	1,875		6,375
Z-3	Sales	9,000		6,000	3,000
		23,500	5,625	8,500	9,375

Stage-III: Statement showing Advertisement expenses

Zone	Total Sales (₹)	Total Expenses (₹)	% of sales	Product					
				M		N		P	
				Sales (₹)	Expenses (₹)	Sales (₹)	Expenses (₹)	Sales (₹)	Expenses (₹)
Z-1	1,00,000	6,250	6.25	60,000	3,750	40,000	2,500		
Z-2	1,10,000	8,250	7.50	25,000	1,875			85,000	6,375
Z-3	1,50,000	9,000	6.00			1,00,000	6,000	50,000	3,000
Total	3,60,000	23,500	6.53	85,000	5,625	1,40,000	8,500	1,35,000	9,375
% of Sales					6.62		6.07		6.94

Illustration 12.5 : (Selling and Distribution Expenses)

A company produces a single product in three sizes Sz-1, Sz-2, Sz-3. Prepare a Statement showing the selling and distribution expenses apportioned over these three sizes applying the appropriate basis for such apportionment in each case from the details indicated. Express the total of the costs so apportioned to each size as:

(a) Cost per unit, and (b) As percentage of sales turnover.

The expenses are:

Expenses	*Amount (₹)*	*Basis of apportionment*
Sales Salaries	*4,00,000*	*Direct charge*
Sales commission	*2,40,000*	*Sales turnover*
Sales Office expenses	*83,840*	*Number of orders*
Advertisement- General	*2,00,000*	*Sales turnover*

Advertisement- specific	*8,80,000*	*Direct charge*
Packing	*1,20,000*	*Total volume in cubic feet of product sold*
Delivery expenses	*1,60,000*	*Total volume in cubic feet of product sold*
Warehouse expenses	*40,000*	*Total volume in cubic feet of product sold*
Credit collection expenses	*51,840*	*Number of orders*

Data Available relating to the three sizes are as under:

Details	***Total***	***Sz-1***	***Sz-2***	***Sz3***
Number of Sales persons all paid same salary	*10*	*4*	*5*	*1*
Units sold	*52,000*	*17,000*	*20,000*	*15,000*
number of orders	*4,000*	*1,750*	*2,000*	*250*
% of specific advertising	*100*	*30*	*40*	*30*
Sales turnover (₹)	*80,00,000*	*23,20,000*	*32,00,000*	*24,80,000*
volume in cubic feet per unit of finished product	*—*	*5*	*8*	*17*

Solution : Statement of Apportionment of Selling and Distribution Expenses

Item	**Basis of apportionment**	**Total (₹)**	**Sz-1 (₹)**	**Sz-2 (₹)**	**Sz-3 (₹)**
Sales Salaries	Direct charge (based on number of sales persons)	4,00,000	1,60,000	2,00,000	40,000
Sales commission	Sales turnover i.e. 3% on sales turnover	2,40,000	69,600	96,000	74,400
Sales Office expenses	Number of orders	83,840	36,680	41,920	5,240
Advertisement- General	Sales turnover i.e. 2.5% on sales turnover	2,00,000	58,000	80,000	62,000
Advertisement- specific	Direct charge (3:4:3)	8,80,000	2,64,000	3,52,000	2,64,000
Packing	Total volume in cubic feet of product sold (Composite Ratio*)17:32:51	1,20,000	20,400	38,400	61,200
Delivery expenses	Total volume in cubic feet of product sold (Composite Ratio*)17:32:51	1,60,000	27,200	51,200	81,600
Warehouse expenses	Total volume in cubic feet of product sold (Composite Ratio*)17:32:51	40,000	6,800	12,800	20,400
Credit collection expenses	Number of orders	51,840	22,680	25,920	3,240
a. Total selling and distribution expenses		21,75,680	6,65,360	8,98,240	6,12,080
b. Units sold		52,000	17,000	20,000	15,000
1. Cost per unit sold (a/b)		41.84	39.14	44.91	40.81
c. Sales turnover (₹)		80,00,000	23,20,000	32,00,000	24,80,000
2. Percentage of Sales turnover i.e. (a/c) ×100		27.2	28.68	28.07	24.68

Working Note : Calculation of Composite Ratio*

Sz-1 = 5 × 17,000 = 85,000

Sz-2 = 8 × 20,000 = 1,60,000

Sz-3 = 17 × 15,000 = 2,55,000

In the ratio of 85,000 : 1,60,000 : 2,55,000 or 17 : 32 : 51

LET US RECAPITULATE

1. Office and Administration overhead pertain to general management and administration of an undertaking.
2. Office and Administration overhead is the indirect expenditure incurred in formulating the policy, directing the organization and controlling the operations of the undertaking.
3. Administration overheads are related to activities, which determine the future of the firm rather than influencing the current operations.
4. Administration is an independent function and is as important as the other major functions. As the administrative costs are largely fixed in nature, they should be treated as period costs and charged directly to Costing Profit and loss Account.
5. Selling overheads are costs of creating and stimulating demand and securing-cum -executing orders.
6. Distribution overheads are costs of moving finished products to central and local storage, moving finished products to the customers, moving finished products to and from the prospective customers as in the case of goods on sale or return basis and making empties reusable.
7. When a product is placed in a saleable condition, production function ends and distribution function begins.
8. Collection of overheads under well-defined cost accounting numbers is the beginning of accounting for selling and distribution overheads. The cost account number indicates nature and object of expenditure.
9. Selling and distribution overheads may be classified as (i) fixed, (ii) semi-fixed, and (iii) variable overheads. Analysis of expenses under such classification is absolutely necessary for effective control and decision- making purposes.
10. Proper accounting requires charging of selling and distribution costs to the central marketing unit of the organization and territories. Expenses allocated and apportioned to central market unit are reapportioned to territories based on the suitable criteria.

SOLVED PROBLEMS

Problem 1. *Following data is available for a company for the month of August, 2008:*

Details	*Area*		
	A-1	*A-2*	*A-3*
Selling Expenses (₹)	*80,000*	*32,000*	*60,000*
Distribution cost (₹)	*40,000*	*20,000*	*30,000*
Units sold (Number)	*20,000*	*16,000*	*10,000*
Sales (₹)	*8,00,000*	*4,00,000*	*5,00,000*

The company adopts sales basis and quantity basis for the application of Selling costs and Distribution costs respectively. Compute:

(a) The area-wise overhead recovery rates separately for selling cost and distribution cost;

(b) The amount of selling and distribution costs chargeable to a consignment of 5,000 units of a product sold in each area @₹ 30 per unit.

Solution : Area-wise Rate of Recovery for Selling and Distribution costs

Area	Selling cost as a percentage of sales	Distribution cost per unit sold
A-1	= (80,000 ÷ 8,00,000) × 100 = 10%	= 40,000 ÷ 20,000 = ₹ 2.00
A-2	= (32,000 ÷ 4,00,000) × 100 = 8%	= 20,000 ÷ 16,000 = ₹ 1.25
A-3	= (60,000 ÷ 5,00,000) × 100 = 12%	= 30,000 ÷ 10,000 = ₹ 3.00

Note : Selling cost as a percentage of sales

= (Selling expenses/ Sales value) × 100

Distribution cost per unit sold

= (Distribution Cost / Number of units Sold)

Selling and distribution cost chargeable to the consignment of 5,000 units

Details	Area		
	A-1	A-2	A-3
Sales (5,000 × 30)	1,50,000	1,50,000	1,50,000
Selling cost as percentage of Sales @ 10%, 8% and 12% respectively.	15,000	12,000	18,000
Distribution cost per unit @ ₹ 2.00, 1.25,3.00 respectively.	10,000	6,250	15,000
Total chargeable selling and distribution cost	25,000	18,250	33,000

Problem 2. *Madhav Trading Company has three salesmen A, B and C in Zone: North. Following information is obtained for the month of May, 2004:*

Details	*Amount (₹)*
North Zone Expenses	*15,000*
Net Sales	*1,20,000*
Cost of sales: 60% of net sales	
Salary of Salesmen	*25,000*
Commission of Salesmen	*5,000*
Travelling Expenses of Salesmen	*4,500*
Postage and stationery	*1,500*
Telephone and telegraphs	*2,000*

From the following additional information, prepare a (Sales Performance Statement) (₹)

Salesman	*Sales*	*Salary*	*Commission*	*Travelling Expenses*	*Postage & Stationery*	*Telephone & Telegraph*
A	*75,000*	*12,000*	*2,400*	*2,200*	*1,300*	*1,000*
B	*60,000*	*8,000*	*1,400*	*1,400*	*700*	*400*
C	*45,000*	*5,000*	*1,200*	*900*	*500*	*600*
Total	*1,80,000*	*25,000*	*5,000*	*4,500*	*2,500*	*2,000*

Solution : Allocation and Apportionment of Selling and Distribution Overhead (₹)

Details	Total	Salesman: A	Salesman: B	Salesman: C
Salary	25,000	12,000	8,000	5,000
Commission	5,000	2,400	1,400	1,200
Travelling Expenses	4,500	2,200	1,400	900
Postage and stationery	2,500	1,300	700	500
Telephone & Telegraph	2,000	1,000	400	600
Direct Cost:	38,000	18,900	11,900	8,200
Zonal Overhead on the basis of Net Sales	15,000	6,250	5,000	3,750
Total Selling & Distribution Cost:	54,000	25,150	16,900	11,950

Statement of Sales Performance (₹)

Details	Total	Salesman: A	Salesman: B	Salesman: C
Sales	1,80,000	75,000	60,000	45,000
Less: Cost of Sales@ 60%	1,08,000	45,000	36,000	27,000
Gross Profit	72,000	30,000	24,000	18,000
Less: S&D Cost	54,000	25,150	16,900	11,950
Net Profit	18,000	4,850	7,100	6,050
% Net Profit to Turnover	10	6.47	11.83	13.44
% S&D Cost to Turnover	30	33.53	28.17	26.56

Accounting by Sales Orders

If management is desirous to find out profit on sales orders, all direct expenses for the particular order should be arranged directly. The order will be charged with the selling and distribution costs of the particular territory. Thus costs must ultimately be related to territory and a territorial rate is obtained on the basis of sales of the territory.

Problem 3. *A Sales order of ₹ 25,000 has been received from North Zone. The direct selling and distribution costs for the order are to be ₹ 750/- Selling and distribution cost for the North zone are ₹ 50,000while sales are ₹ 40,0000. Gross Profit on Sales is 35%. Find the net profit for the sales order.*

Solution :

Details		**Amount (₹)**
Sales Price of the Order		25,000
Less: Cost of Sales@ 65%		16,250
Gross Profit		8,750
Less: S&D Cost:		
Direct	750	
Apportioned (North Zone)		
@ 12.5% of 25000	3,125	3,875
Net Profit		4,875

Accounting by Line of Products

Direct costs are charged directly to each line, whereas other costs are apportioned to products on the basis of net sales or other equitable bases. Analysis by lines of products helps management to know which line is profitable, whether to discontinue a particular line or to push the sales of the most profitable line for profit maximization.

Problem 4. *S V Ltd., which sells four products, proposes to discontinue the sale of one of them. The following information is available regarding its income, costs and activity for the year 2004:*

Details	*Product*			
	A	*B*	*C*	*D*
Sales (₹)	*8,00,000*	*13,50,000*	*6,50,000*	*12,00,000*
Cost of sales at purchase price	*4,80,000*	*12,00,000*	*4,00,000*	*7,50,000*
Area of storage (sq. m.)	*60,000*	*40,000*	*70,000*	*30,000*
Number of parcels sent	*1,00,000*	*1,30,000*	*1,20,000*	*1,50,000*
Number of invoices sent	*10,000*	*17,500*	*7,500*	*15,000*

Overhead Costs and bases of apportionment are:

Fixed cost:	***Amount*** **(₹)**	***Basis of apportionment to Products***
Rent and Insurance	*80,000*	*Sq. meter*
Depreciation	*30,000*	*Parcel*
Salesmen's Remuneration	*1,60,000*	*Sales Value*
Sales office Salaries	*1,30,000*	*No. of Invoices*
Variable Costs:		
Packing Wages and Materials	*50 Paise per Parcel*	
Commission	*5% of Sales*	
Printing and Stationery	*one rupee per invoice.*	

Prepare a Statement of Profit and Loss showing percentage of profit or loss for each product; and compare the profit if the firm discontinues sale of Product B, with the profit if it discontinues Product C.

Solution :

Stage I:

Comparative Profit and Loss Account

Details	**Total**	**Product**			
		A	**B**	**C**	**D**
Sales	40,00,000	8,00,000	13,50,000	6,50,000	12,00,000
Less: Cost of sales	28,00,000	4,50,000	12,00,000	5,00,000	6,50,000
Gross profit	12,00,000	3,50,000	1,50,000	1,50,000	5,50,000
Less: Variable S&D costs	5,00,000	1,00,000	1,60,000	80,000	1,60,000
Contribution	7,00,000	2,50,000	(10,000)	70,000	3,90,000
Less: Fixed S&D costs	4,00,000	88,000	1,23,300	80,700	1,08,000
Net profit (Loss)	3,00,000	1,62,000	(1,33,300)	(10,700)	2,82,000
% Net profit (Loss)		20.25	(9.87)	(1.65)	23.50

Stage II:

Details	Product B Discontinued	Product C Discontinued
Contributions From:		
Product A	2,50,000	2,50,000
Product B		(10,000)
Product C	70,000	
Product D	3,90,000	3,90,000
Total Contribution	7,10,000	6,30,000
Less: Fixed Cost	4,00,000	4,00,000
Net Profit	3,10,000	2,30,000

Decision: It is better to discontinue Product B.

Problem 5. *A company intends to make a study of the relative profitability of two products: P-1 and P-2. In addition to direct costs, indirect selling and distribution costs to be allocated between the two products are as under:*

Details	***Amount*** (₹)
Insurance charges for inventory (Finished)	*4,55,000*
Storage costs	*8,40,000*
Packing and Forwarding Charges	*18,00,000*
Salesmen Salaries	*34,00,000*
Invoicing costs	*11,25,000*

Other details are:

Details		***Product A***	***Product B***
Selling price per unit	(₹)	*1,200*	*2,400*
Cost per unit	(₹)	*800*	*1,500*
(Exclusive of indirect selling costs)			
Annual Sales	*(Units)*	*25,000*	*20,000*
Average Inventory	*(Units)*	*2,500*	*2,000*
Number of Invoices	*(No.)*	*5,000*	*4,000*

One unit of Product A requires a storage space twice as much as Product B. The cost to pack and forward one unit is the same for both the products. Salesmen are paid salary plus commission @4% on sales and equal amount of efforts are put forth on sales of each of the products.

Required:

(i) Set up a schedule showing the apportionment of the indirect selling and distribution cost between the two products.

(ii) Prepare a statement showing the relative profitability of the two products. **[C A (Modified)]**

Solution : Working Notes:

(i) Average Inventory value of P-1 and P-2:

P-1 = (2,500 × 1,200) = ₹ 30,00,000

P-2 = (2,000 × 2,400) = ₹ 48,00,000

Ratio = 5:8

(ii) Average Inventory storage space of P-1 and P-2:

P-1 = (2,500 × 2) = 5,000

P-2 = (2,000 × 1) = 2,000

Ratio = 5:2

Schedule showing apportionment of Selling and Distribution costs

Item	Basis of Apportionment	Total (₹)	Product	
			P-1 Amount (₹)	P-2 Amount (₹)
Insurance	Average Inventory value (5:8)	4,55,000	1,75,000	2,80,000
Storage cost	Average Inventory storage space (5:2)	8,40,000	6,00,000	2,40,000
Packing and forwarding	Sales Units (5:4)	18,00,000	10,00,000	8,00,000
Salesmen Salaries	Amount of effort (Equal) i.e. 1:1	34,00,000	17,00,000	17,00,000
Salesmen commission	Sales value (5:8)	31,20,000	12,00,000	19,20,000
Invoicing Cost	Number of Invoices (5:4)	11,25,000	6,25,000	5,00,000
Total			53,00,000	56,40,000

Profitability Statement

Details	Product P-1 Amount (₹)	Product P-2 Amount (₹)
Annual Sales	300,00,000	480,00,000
Less: Cost of Sales	200,00,000	300,00,000
Gross Profit	100,00,000	180,00,000
Less: Selling and distribution overhead apportioned	53,00,000	56,40,000
Profit	47,00,000	123,60,000
Profit as a percentage of Sales	15.67	25.75

Problem 6. *The manufactures Limited produces three products P-1, P-2, and P-3. The sales territory of the company is divided into three areas*

Product	*Territory*		
	T-I Amount (₹)	*T-II Amount (₹)*	*T-III Amount (₹)*
P-1	*25,000*	*10,000*	*NIL*
P-2	*15,000*	*NIL*	*40,000*
P-3	*NIL*	*35,000*	*25,000*

Budgeted advertising cost is as under:

Details	*Area*			*Total*
	T-I Amount (₹)	*T-II Amount (₹)*	*T-III Amount (₹)*	
Local cost	*2,000*	*3,600*	*2,600*	*8,200*
General	*N I L*	*N I L*	*N I L*	*4,500*

Find out the advertising cost percentage on sales for each product and territory showing how you would present the statement.

Solution : General advertising cost is common to all territories. It is apportioned on the basis of sales.

Percentage of General advertising g cost to sales:

= (Total general advertising cost / total sales of all territories) × 100

= (4,500 ÷ 1,50,000) × 100 = 3%.

Apportionment of General Advertising Cost

Territory	**Product**	**Sales**		**General advertising cost@ 3% of sales**	
		Amount (₹)	**Amount (₹)**	**Amount (₹)**	**Amount (₹)**
T-I	P-1	25,000		750	1,200
	P-2	15,000	40,000	450	
T-II	P-1	10,000		300	1,350
	P-3	35,000	45,000	1,050	
T-III	P-2	40,000		1,200	1,950`
	P-3	25,000	65,000	750	
		Total			4,500

Local advertising costs are apportioned to products on the basis of sales value in those specific territories.

Percentage of Local Advertising Cost to sales:

= (Local Cost / Territory Specific Sales) × 100

T-I = (2,000 ÷ 40,000) × 100 = 5%.

T-II = (3,600 ÷ 40,000) ×100 = 8%.

T-III = (2,600 ÷ 65,000) × 100 = 4%.

Apportionment of Local Advertising Cost

Territory	Product	Sales		Local advertising cost@ Territory specific Rates	
		Amount (₹)	Amount (₹)	Amount (₹)	Amount (₹)
T-I	P-1	25,000		1,250	2,000
	P-2	15,000	40,000	750	
T-II	P-1	10,000		800	3,600
	P-3	35,000	45,000	2,800	
T-III	P-2	40,000		1,600	2,600
	P-3	25,000	65,000	1,000	
		Total			8,200

Statement of Advertising cost (Amount in ₹)

Product	Territory									Grand Total (₹)	Percentage of Sales
	T-I			T-II			T-III				
	General	Local	Total	General	Local	Total	General	Local	Total		
P1	750	1,250	1,250	300	800	1,100				3,100	(3,100/35,000) × 100 = 8.86
P2	450	750	750				1,200	1,600	2,800	4,000	(4,000/55,000) × 100 = 7.27
P3				1,050	2,800	3,850	750	1,000	1,750	5,600	(5,600/60,000) × 100 = 9.33
Total	1,200	2,000	3,200	1,350	3,600	4,950	1,950	2,600	4,550	12,700	8.47

Percentage of Sales (territory -wise):

(3,200/40,000) ×100 = 8% (4,950/45,000) × 100 =11% (4,550/65,000) ×100 =7%

Problem 7. *The Standard Company manufactures and sells three products P-1, P-2, and P-3 in North, South and Central parts of the country. Sales are conducted by S-1, S-2, S-3, S-4, S-5, and S-6. The sales (₹) for the July, 2008 are:*

Territory	*North*		*South*		*Central*	
Salesman	*S-1*	*S-2*	*S-3*	*S-4*	*S-5*	*S-6*
P-1	*5,00,000*	*10,00,000*	*10,00,000*	*15,00,000*		
P-2	*40,00,000*	*25,00,000*			*15,00,000*	*20,00,000*
P-3			*22,50,000*	*2,50,000*	*13,75,000*	*11,25,000*

Each salesman is given a monthly remuneration of ₹ 10,000. In addition salesmen get a sales commission of 2% on sales of P-1, 4% on sales of P-2, and 5% on sales of P-3. Manufacturing cost of products P-1, P-2 and P-3 is ₹ 20, 00,000, ₹ 62, 50,000 and ₹ 30, 00,000 respectively.

The Company maintains a Head office which incurred overheads of ₹ 1,80,000, and maintains territorial office in each territory. Overheads of the territorial offices are: North ₹ 60,000, South ₹ 1, 20,000 and Central ₹ 96,000.

Head office expenses are apportioned to each product on the basis of manufacturing cost and expenses of territorial offices are charged to product in the ratio of sales.

Prepare statements showing profitability of each product in different territories.

Solution : Working Notes:

I. Head office expenses:

Head office expenses (%):

= (Total Head Office Expenses/ Total manufacturing cost) × 100

= (1,80,000/1,12,50,000) × 100 = 1.6%

This rate is applied to Manufacturing cost to apportion the head office expenses amongst the products.

II. Apportionment of Territorial Expenses:

North: (5,00,000 + 10,00,000) : (40,00,000 + 25,00,000)

15,00,000 : 65,00,000 i.e. 3:13

₹ 60,000 distributed For Product P-1: ₹ 11,250 and P-2: ₹ 48.750.

South: (10,00,000 + 15, 00,000) : (22,50,000 + 2,50,000)

25,00,000 : 25,00,000 i.e. 1:1

₹ 1, 20,000 distributed For Product P-1: ₹ 60,000 and P-3: ₹ 60,000.

Central: (15,00,000 + 20,00,000): (13,75,000 + 11,25,000)

35,00,000 : 25,00,000 i.e. 7:5

₹ 96,000 distributed For Product P-2: ₹ 56,000 and P-3: ₹ 40,000.

III. Apportionment of Sales Remuneration:

₹ 20,000 payable to S-1 and S-2 is apportioned to P-1 and P-2 in the ratio of

(5, 00,000 + 10,00,000) : (40,00,000 + 25,00,000)

15,00,000 : 65,00,000 i.e. ₹ 3,750 and ₹ 16,250

₹ 20,000 payable to S-3 and S-4 is apportioned to P-1 and P-3 in the ratio of

(10, 00,000 + 15,00,000) : (22,50,000 + 2,50,000)

25,00,000 : 25,00,000 i.e. ₹ 10,000 and ₹ 10,000.

₹ 20,000 payable to S-5 and S-6 is apportioned to P-2 and P-3 in the ratio of

(15,00,000 + 20,00,000) : (13,75,000 + 11,25,000)

35,00,000 : 25,00,000 i.e. ₹ 11,667 and ₹ 8,333.

Cost and Profit statement for Product P-1

Territory	North			South			Grand Total
Salesman Details	**S-1 Amount (₹)**	**S-2 Amount (₹)**	**Total Amount (₹)**	**S-3 Amount (₹)**	**S-4 Amount (₹)**	**Total Amount (₹)**	**Amount (₹)**
I. Sales	5,00,000	10,00,000	15,00,000	10,00,000	15,00,000	25,00,000	40,00,000
Manufacturing cost	2,50,000	5,00,000	7,50,000	5,00,000	7,50,000	12,50,000	20, 00,000
Head office Expenses	4,000	8,000	12,000	8,000	12,000	20,000	32,000
Territorial office Expenses	3,750	7,500	11,250	24,000	36,000	60,000	71,250
Salesmen Remuneration	1,250	2,500	3,750	4,000	6,000	10,000	13,750
Sales commi-ssion (2%)	10,000	20,000	30,000	20,000	30,000	50,000	80,000
II. Cost of sales	2,69,000	5,38,000	8,07,000	5,56,000	8,34,000	13,90,000	21,97,000
III. Profit	2,31,000	4,62,000	6,93,000	4,44,000	6,66,000	11,10,000	18,03,000

Cost and Profit statement for Product P-2

Territory	North			Central			Grand Total
Salesman Details	**S-1 Amoun (₹)**	**S-2 Amount (₹)**	**Total Amount (₹)**	**S-5 Amount (₹)**	**S-6 Amount (₹)**	**Total Amount (₹)**	**Amount (₹)**
I. Sales	40,00,000	25,00,000	65,00,000	15,00,000	20,00,000	35, 00,000	100,00,000
Manufacturing cost	25,00,000	15,62,500	40,62,500	9,37,500	12,50,000	21,87,500	62, 50,000
Head office Expenses	40,000	25,000	65,000	15,000	20,000	35,000	1,00,000
Territorial office Expenses	30,000	18,750	48,750	24,000	32,000	56,000	1,04,750
Salesmen Remuneration	10,000	6,250	16,250	5,000	6,667	11,667	27,917
Sales commi-ssion (4%)	1,60,000	1,00,000	2,60,000	60,000	80,000	1,40,000	4,00,000
II. Cost of sales	27,40,000	17,12,500	44,52,500	10,41,500	13,88,667	24,30,167	68,82,667
III. Profit	12,60,000	7,87,500	20,47,500	4,58,500	6, 11,333	10,69,833	31,17,333

Cost and Profit statement for Product P-3

Territory	South			Central			Trand Total
Salesman Details	S-3 Amoun (₹)	S-4 Amount (₹)	Total Amount (₹)	S-5 Amount (₹)	S-6 Amount (₹)	Total Amount (₹)	Amount (₹)
I. Sales	22,50,000	2,50,000	25,00,000	13,75,000	11,25,000	25,00,000	50,00,000
Manufacturing cost	13,50,000	1,50,000	15,00,000	8,25,000	6,75,000	15,00,000	30, 00,000
Head office Expenses	21.600	2,400	24,000	13,200	10,800	24,000	48,000
Territorial office Expenses	54,000	6,000	60,000	22,000	18,000	40,000	1,00,000
Salesmen Remuneration	9,000	1,000	10,000	4,583	3,750	8,333	18,333
Sales Commi-ssion (5%)	1,12,500	12,500	1,25,000	68,750	56,250	1,25,000	2,50,000
II. Cost of sales	15,47,100	1,71,900	17,19,000	9,33,533	7,63,800	16,97,333	34,16,333
III. Profit [(I)-(II)]	7,02,900	78,100	7,81,000	4,41,467	3,61,200	8,02,667	15,83,667

OBJECTIVE TYPE EXERCISES

I. Fill in the blank spaces with suitable word/s :

1. Administration Overhead are usually absorbed as a percentage of ....
2. Selling and distribution overheads are .... same as administration overheads.
3. The code number given to Administration overhead item is termed as ....
4. Insurance to cover sold goods while in transit .... a selling overhead.
5. Bad debt is an example of .... overhead.

Answers :

1. Works cost **2.** Not
3. Cost Account Number **4.** NOT
5. selling overhead

II. Indicate whether the following statements are True or False :

1. Selling and distribution overheads are same as administration overheads.
2. Administration overheads are usually absorbed as a percentage of prime cost.
3. Selling and distribution overheads are absorbed on the basis of percentage on selling price or a rate per unit.
4. Cost of After-Sales services is a part of selling and distribution overhead.

5. Administration overheads are non-controllable at lower level of management.

Answers :

1. False **2.** False **3.** True **4.** True
5. True

THEORETICAL EXERCISES

1. Define administration overheads and state briefly the treatment of such overheads in cost accounts. **[C.A. Inter, 1996]**
2. Write short note on Administration overhead. **[I.C. W.A. Inter, 1995]**
3. Explain the term 'Administration Overheads' and briefly discuss three methods of treatment thereof in cost Accounts. **[I.C. W.A. Inter, 1992]**
4. Explain concisely the best method to absorb selling and distribution overheads.
5. How selling overheads are allocated to products?
6. "While manufacturing overheads are part of costs, selling overheads are the results of policy." Do you agree?
7. Explain in brief the following concepts:
   (i) Selling overheads **[DU, B.Com (Hons.) 2001]**
   (ii) Distribution overheads

NUMERICAL EXERCISES

1. Following data is available for a company for the month of August, 2008:

Details	Territory		
	T-1	T-2	T-3
Selling Expenses (₹)	76,000	42,0 00	62,400
Distribution cost (₹)	40,000	18,000	20,000
Units sold (Number)	16,000	6,000	10,000
Sales (₹)	7,60,000	2, 80000	5,20,000

The company adopts sales basis and quantity basis for the application of Selling and Distribution costs respectively. Compute:

(a) The territory-wise overhead recovery rates separately for selling cost and distribution cost;

(b) The amount of selling and distribution costs chargeable to a consignment of 4,000 units of a product sold in each area @₹ 25 per unit.

[I.C.W.A. (Inter) (Modified)]

[Ans. Rates Of recovery: Selling costs: 10%, 15%, 12%; and distribution costs (per unit): ₹ 2.50; ₹ 3.00; and ₹ 2.00]

2. The manufactures Limited produces three products P-1, P-2, and P-3. The sales territory of the company is divided into three areas

Product	Territory		
	T-I Amount (₹)	T-II Amount (₹)	T-III Amount (₹)
P-1	25,000	10,000	N I L
P-2	15,000	N I L	40,000
P-3	N I L	35,000	25,000

Budgeted advertising cost is as under:

Details	Area			Total
	T-I Amount (₹)	T-II Amount (₹)	T-III Amount (₹)	
Local cost	2,000	3,600	2,600	8,200
General	N I L	N I L	N I L	4,500

Find out the advertising cost percentage on sales for each product and territory showing how you would present the statement. **[I.C.W.A.]**

[Ans.

Product-wise (%)		Territory-wise (%)	
A	6.29	North	6.00
B	5.64	South	7.00
C	6.45	West	5.55
Overall	6.10	Overall	6.10

3. The Standard Company manufactures and sells three products P-1, P-2, and P-3 in North, South and Central parts of the country. Sales are conducted by S-1, S-2, S-3, S-4, S-5, and S-6. The sales (₹) for the July, 2008 are:

Territory	North		South		Central	
Salesman	S-1	S-2	S-3	S-4	S-5	S-6
P-1	20,000	40,000	40,000	60,000		
P-2	80,000	60,000			60,000	70,000
P-3			90,000	10,000	55,000	45,000

Each salesman is given a monthly remuneration of ₹ 1,000. In addition salesmen get a sales commission of 4% on sales of P-1, 5% on sales of P-2, and 6% on sales of P-3. Manufacturing cost of products P-1, P-2 and P-3 is ₹ 20, 00,000, ₹ 62, 50,000 and ₹ 30, 00,000 respectively.

The Company maintains a Head office which incurred overheads of ₹ 36, 000, and maintains Territorial office in each territory. Overheads of the territorial offices are: North ₹ 10,000, South ₹ 27,000 and Central ₹ 23,000.

Head office expenses are apportioned to each product on the basis of manufacturing cost and expenses of territorial offices are charged to product in the ratio of sales.

Prepare statements showing profitability of each product in different territories.

[Ans. Profit from P-1: ₹ 69,500; Profit from P-2: ₹ 35,970; and Profit from P-3: ₹ 30,630.]

4. A company is making a study of the relative profitability of two products: A and B. In addition to direct costs, indirect selling and distribution costs to be allocated between the two products are as under:

Details	**Amount (₹)**
Insurance charges for inventory (Finished)	78,000
Storage costs	1,40,000
Packing and Forwarding Charges	7,20,000
Salesmen Salaries	8,50,000
Invoicing costs	4,50,000

Other details are:

Details		Product A	Product B
Selling price per unit	(₹)	500	1,000
Cost per unit	(₹)	300	600
(Exclusive of indirect selling costs)			
Annual Sales	(Units)	10,000	8,000
Average Inventory	(Units)	1,000	800
Number of Invoices	(No.)	2,500	2,000

One unit of Product A requires a storage space twice as much as Product B. The cost to pack and forward one unit is the same for both the products. Salesmen are paid salary plus commission @5% on sales and equal amount of efforts are put forth on sales of each of the products.

Required:

(1) Set up a schedule showing the apportionment of the indirect selling and distribution cost between the two products.

(2) Prepare a statement showing the relative profitability of the two products.

[C.A.]

[Ans. Profit on product A @ 10.9% and Profit on product B @ 22.09%]

5. Alpha Limited produces three types of products A, B and C. The sales territory of the company is divided into three zones X, Y and Z.

The estimated sales and the advertising cost for the next year areas under:

Product	**Territory**		
	A	**B**	**C**
X	50000	20000	
Y	30000		80000
C		70000	40000

Budgeted Advertising cost is as under:

Product	Total	Territory		
		X	Y	Z
Local	23800	6400	9000	8400
General	11600			
Sum	35400			

Prepare a statement showing territory wise advertising cost expressed as a percentage of sales. The allocation of advertising cost should be based on sales as given above.

[Ans. X : 12%, Y : 14%, Z : 11%]

6. Raghav Trading Company has three salesmen M,N and Q in Zone: South. Following information is obtained for the month of August, 2004:

Details	Amount (₹)
South Zone Expenses	15000
Net Sales	200000
Cost of Sales: 60% of net sales	
Salary of Salesmen	25000
Commission of Salesmen	@4% of Sales
Travelling Expenses of Salesmen	4500
Postage and stationery	2500
Telephone & Telegraphs	2000

From the following additional information, prepare a sales performance statement:

Salesman	Sales	Salary	Commission @ 4% of Sales	Travelling Expenses	Postage & Stationery	Telephone & Telegraph
M	85000	12000		1200	1100	1000
N	70000	8000		2000	900	400
Q	45000	5000		1300	500	600
Total	200000	25000	8000	4500	2500	2000

[Ans. Overall: 11.50%, 28.50%; M: 10.50%, 29.50%; N: 12.36%, 27.64%; and Q: 12.06%, 27.94%]

7. Standard Limited sells its products throughout the country through its four zonal sales offices. The budgeted expenses for the year 2009-10 are given below:

Expenditure	Amount (₹)
Sales Manager's Salary	3,75,000
Expenses relating to Sales Manager's Office	2,62,500
Traveling Salesmen's salaries	7,50,000
Traveling Expenses	1,25,000

Advertisements		1,00,000
Warehouse: A	37,500	
B	62,500	
C	25,000	
D	45,000	1,70,000
Insurance on Inventories		43,750
Commission on Sales@ 4% on sales		10,50,000

Additional Information:

Zone	Sales (₹)	No. of Salesmen	Total Distance Covered (kms.)	Allocation of Advertisement (%)	Average Stock (₹)
A	63,00,000	6	6,000	30	10,50,000
B	84,00,000	8	14,000	35	14,00,000
C	28,00,000	2	4,500	15	7,00,000
D	35,00,000	4	5,500	20	3,50,000

Compute Zone-wise Selling overheads, as a percentage to sales, based on above details.

❑❑❑

13 Activity Based Costing

Learning Objectives

It attempts to explain the new approach based on activities of assigning overhead costs to products. In this chapter you will learn :

1. Meaning, nature and objectives of activity based costing.
2. Activity, cost object, cost driver, cost pool.
3. Difference between traditional approach and new approach.
4. Process of activity based costing.

MEANING AND NATURE

Activity based costing (ABC) is a modern tool of charging overhead costs in which costs are first traced to activities and then to products or jobs. It is a technique which involves identification of costs with each cost driving activity and making it as the basis of absorption of costs over different products or jobs. Its main focus is on activities performed in the production of goods or services. Activities become the target points for cost computation. Costs are charged to products or services based on individual products' consumption of each activity (i.e. benefits received from indirect activities). Products/jobs/services consume activities and activities consume resources. Thus, overheads are first assigned to activities and then recovered by cost objects on the basis of activities consumed by these cost objects.

Thus, Activity based costing is " Cost attribution to cost units on the basis of benefits received from indirect activities, i.e. ordering, setting up, assuring quality, etc." C.I.M.A., London.

Activity based costing is an improvement over the traditional system of accounting for overheads. The following steps are involved in the traditional method of accounting for the overheads:

1. Allocation of overheads cost centre-wise;
2. Apportionment of common overheads to different cost centres;
3. Re-apportionment of overheads collected under service centres to production centres; and
4. Assignment of overheads collected under production cost centres to units produced.

Thus, overheads are aggregated at production cost centre level and are assigned to units produced. Assignment is based on average rate(s) determined by dividing the overhead expenses by the volume of units produced or a surrogate for them. In general, Labour-hour or machine-hour is used as a surrogate for the volume of units produced. Traditional method of accounting for the overheads assumes that 'volume' or 'units' produced is the only cost driver. Use of an average rate based on volume for assigning overheads to products distorts the product cost, if the firm produces a variety of products, the demand of different products on resources is not uniform.

ABC system aims at reducing the distortion. It recognizes the fact that there are many cost drivers including Volume. The system attempts to improve the accuracy of product cost and traces Selling and Distribution overheads to Customers and Market. Thus, Customer Profitability is determined. ABC system focuses on ACTIVITIES required to produce each product or to render each service based on each product's or service's USE of the activities.

Activity-Based-Costing (ABC) is that costing in which costs are first traced to activities and then to products. ABC system focuses on activities performed to produce products/render service. Activities become the points of attention and cost accumulation is activity-based. The system assumes that activities are responsible for the incurrence of costs and products create the demands for activities. Costs are assigned to products based on individual product's/service's use of each activity. By emphasizing activities, ABC attempts to ascertain the factors responsible for each critical/key activity, cost of such activities and the relationship between activities and products produced. Thus, there are two primary stages in ABC:

(1) *Tracing costs to activities:* Activities are identified and then classified into different categories that have relationship with the different parts of the production process. These activities may be direct labour related activities, machine related activities, and various support activities such as ordering, receiving, materials handling, production scheduling, packing and dispatching.

(2) *Tracing activities to Products:* Factory overhead costs of the activities are determined and classified into homogeneous cost pools. A homogeneous cost pool is a collection of overhead costs that are logically related to the tasks being performed. Cost pool is activity centre around which costs are accumulated.

To understand the intricacies of ABC, following terms used in ABC system are explained:

(1) *Activity:* It is a particular task or unit of work with a specific purpose. In business, it could be (a) Placing of a Purchase Order, (b) Receiving and Inspection of materials, (c) Setting up of a Machine, (d) Post-sale services, etc.

(2) *Cost Object:* It is an item for which cost measurement is required. A product, a service, a work-order, a job, a customer, location etc. are cost objects.

(3) *Cost driver:* It is a causal factor that brings a change in the cost of an activity. Cost driver is of two types: resource cost driver, and activity cost driver.

  (i) *Resource cost driver:* It is a measure of the quantum of resource consumed by an activity. For example, Number of purchase orders placed will determine the cost of purchasing the materials.

  (ii) *Activity cost driver:* It is a measure of the frequency and intensity of demand placed on the activites by cost objects. It is meant to assign activity costs to cost objects consuming the activity.

(4) *Cost pool:* It is also termed as cost centre.

It is necessary to identify the factors influencing the cost of the activity. These factors are known as cost drivers. It may be pointed out that direct costs do not need cost drivers as they can be traced directly to a product/service. Direct costs are themselves cost drivers. But all other factory costs need cost drivers. Cost drivers signify factors, forces or events that determine the costs of the activities. Cost drivers are links and they can link a pool of costs in an activity centre to the product.

Cost Drivers

The following are the three different types of cost drivers:

(1) Transaction drivers;

(2) Duration drivers; and

(3) Intensity drivers.

Transaction drivers determine number of times (frequency) an activity is performed i.e. number of set-ups, number of receipts, and number of products supported. Transaction drivers provide accurate results provided the activity whenever performed uses resources uniformly. The use of 'number of set-up' provides accurate result only if each set-up takes the same time and uses the same quantum of the same resources. In most manufacturing set-ups, which produce different types of products, it is rare that each set up takes up the same time to perform and uses same quantum of resources. In those cases when different set-ups take different time to perform, the use of set-up hours is more relevant than the number of set-ups. Set-up hour is an example of Duration drivers.

Activity	Activity type	Activity cost driver
Machine Run	Unit Level	Machine Hours
Inspection	Unit Level/Batch Level	Number of units/batches
Machine Set-up	Batch Level	Set-up Hours/ Number of set-ups
Shipping Set-up	Batch Level	Number of shipping
Receiving Materials	Batch Level	Number of materials receipts
Handling Materials	Batch Level	Number of Loads
Moving Materials	Batch Level	Number of production runs
Packing	Batch Level	Number of packing orders
Designing Products	Product-sustaining	Design hours/ parts square feet
Modifying Product characteristics	Product-sustaining	Number of engineering change notices
Administering Parts	Product-sustaining	Number of parts
General Administration	Facility support	Machine/labour hours or Amount of value addition
lparMaintaining Machine	Facility support	Number of maintenance hours

In ABC system, facility level activities and costs are treated as period costs as they are found difficult to assign to different products. The costs associated with the Unit level, Batch level and Product level categories are assigned to products using cost drivers that reflect causal relationship between activity consumption and cost.

A comparison between ABC and Traditional costing system:

1. In traditional costing system, overhead costs are assumed to be influenced by only units produced. It implies, in traditional costing system, costs of batch level, product level, and facility level activities are fixed costs. Variable overheads are directly assigned to products using the base number of units produced. In ABC, variable overhead is directly traced to individual products. ABC improves product costing procedure because it recognises that many so called fixed overhead costs vary in proportion to changes other than production units. By establishing the link between cost drivers and fixed overhead costs, they are finally traced to individual products.

2. Both the costing systems follow two stage allocation procedure. In traditional costing, in the first stage, overhead costs are allocated to production departments. But in ABC, in the first stage, overhead costs are assigned to each major activity and not to departments.
3. In traditional costing, Overheads are pooled/collected department –wise. But in ABC, many activity-based cost pools are created. In traditional costing, overhead costs of service departments are allocated/ reapportioned to production departments and therefore, in this costing system finally only fewer cost pools exist. But ABC creates separte cost pools for service activities as well and costs of these service departments are assigned directly to specific products through the application of cost driver rates. Thus, in ABC there is no need to reapportion overheads of service departments.

Merits of ABC System

The application of Activity based costing gives rise to the following advantages:

(1) *Focus on cost:* The focus is on the causes of the cost.

(2) *Accuracy:* Product costing is accurate because of the deep understanding of the cost behaviour.

(3) *Value added activities:* Only value added activities are considered. It helps in identifying the non-value added activity or wasted efforts and thus eliminates such activities.

(4) *Rational decisions:* It makes available the improved cost-basis both at head office and plant level for better decision making.

(5) It traces costs to areas of managerial responsibility, processes, customers, departments besides the product costs.

(6) In advanced manufacturing environment and technology where support functions overheads constitute a large share of total costs, ABC provides more realistic product costs.

(7) ABC uses multiple cost drives, many of which are transaction based rather than product volume. Further, ABC is concerned within and beyond the factory to trace more overheads to the products.

Demerits of ABC System

Followings are the demerits of the ABC system:

1. It has numerous cost pools and multiple cost drivers and therefore can be more complex than the traditional product costing systems. It can prove costly to mange ABC system.
2. Some difficulties emerge in the implementation of the ABC system, such as selection of cost drivers, assignment of common costs, varying cost driver rates etc.

3. It has different levels of utility for different organisations such as large manufacturing firm can use it more usefully than the small were firms. It is likely that smaller firms depending on cost-plus pricing can take advantages from ABC as it gives accurate product cost. But those firms which use market based prices may not favour ABC. The level of technology and manufacturing environment prevailing in different firms also affect the application of ABC system.

OPTIMALITY OF THE SYSTEM

The decision to use ABC is to make cost benefit analysis of this system. The benefits depend upon many factors such as level of competition, number of products manufactured and product diversity. It is usually felt that those firms which operate in a competitive environment do require correct product cost data for taking sound decisions with regard to determination of selling prices and taking better cost management measures. The complexity of product mix plays a greater role in ascertaining whether the cost of two or more activities can be combined and traced to a product by means of a single cost driver and still these costs can be assigned to products accurately. There is a need to increase the number of activity centres, cost pools and cost drivers in order to achieve the goal of more accurate product costs. However, it does not imply that a company should go for ABC system simply because that product diversity is large and non-unit-based costs constitute a large part of total overhead costs. One has to evaluate the trade off between measurement costs and cost of errors. Measurement costs are the costs associated with the measurement required by the cost systems. Error costs are the costs associated with making poor decisions based on inaccurate product costs. These two costs conflict each other and move in the opposite direction. More complex cost systems produce lower error costs but have higher measurement costs. For some organisations, the optimal cost system may not be an ABC system even though it is more accurate system. Depending upon the trade off, the optimal cost system may very well be a simpler, traditional, unit-based system.

ABC IN SERVICE ORGANISATIONS

In manufacturing companies, direct material and direct labours which are the important cost components can be traced to individual products. Indirect costs are thus likely to be a much smaller proportion of total costs in such manufacturing companies. In service organisations, most of the costs are treated fixed and indirect and therefore, irrelevant for most decisions. No attempt is made to prepare profitability analysis in service organisations. There is great need of making use of ABC system in service organisations. Earlier, service organisations were government owned or operated in highly regulated, protected and non-competitive environment. Thus the service organisations were not under any pressure to improve profitability by eliminating non-value added or non-profit activities. The prices of services were simply increased to cover cost increases including for inefficiencies. No effort was made to design a cost system that accurately measures the costs and profitability of individual services.

However, due to privatization, deregulation and increasing competition , the service organisations need to have cost and management accounting systems which can help them to accurately measure cost and resulting profitability for their services, customers and markets. Therefore ABC system would prove advantageous to service organisations to understand their cost base and make decisions on value-added/ non-value added activities. The following is the list of activities and cost drivers to apply ABC system:

Activity	Cost Driver
Provide ATM services	Number of ATM transactions
Clear debit items	Number of debits processed
Clear credit items	Number of credits processed
Issue cheque books	Number of cheque books issued
Computer processing	Number of Computer transactions
Prepare statements of account transactions	Number of statements issued
Administrative mortgages	Number of mortgages maintained

Illustration 13.1 : *Multi-Activity Limited manufactures two products K and P. The product K is a low volume item and its sales are only 8,000 units per annum. The product P is a high volume item and its sales are 20,000 units per year. Both products require two and a half direct labour hours for completion. The firm works 70,000 hours each year as given below:*

Product	*Unit @ 2.5 hours*	*Hours*
K	*8,000 × 2.5*	*20,000*
P	*20,000 × 2.5*	*50,000*
Total		*70,000*

Details of cost for material and labour (in ₹) for each product per unit are given below:

Cost Element	*Product K*	*Product P*
Direct Materials	*50*	*35*
Direct Labour(@ ₹ 10 per hour)	*25*	*25*

Annual total manufacturing cost for both the products= ₹ 8,75,000.

The firm has analysed its operations and has determined that five activities act as cost drivers in the incurrence of overhead costs. Data relating to the five activities are given below:

Activity	*Traceable cost (₹)*	*Number of Events or transactions*		
		Total	*Product K*	*Product P*
Machine set-ups	*2,50,000*	*5,000*	*3,000*	*2,000*
Quality Inspections	*2,00,000*	*8,000*	*5,000*	*3,000*
Production Orders	*81,000*	*600*	*200*	*400*
Machine-hours (worked)	*2,69,000*	*40000*	*12,000*	*28,000*
Material receipts	*75,000*	*750*	*150*	*600*
Total	*8,75,000*	—	—	—

Required: Compute Cost per unit product-wise using:

(a) Direct Labour Hour rate Method of Recovery of Overhead costs.

(b) Activity based Costing technique for absorption of overhead costs.

Solution :

(A) Computation of Product cost using Direct Labour Hour Rate Method

Working Notes:

$$\text{Rate of Recovery} = \frac{\text{Manufacturing Overhead Costs}}{\text{Direct Labour Hours}}$$

$= 8{,}75{,}000 \div 70{,}000 =$ ₹12.50 per Direct Labour Hour

Using this rate of recovery, the cost of manufacturing of each of the products is as under: (in ₹)

Cost Element	**Product**	
	K	**P**
Direct Materials	50	35
Direct Labour	25	25
Manufacturing Overhead (2.5hours@ ₹ 12.5)	31.25	31.25
Total Cost of Manufacture	106.25	91.25

(B) Computation Of Product cost using Activity Based Costing

(1) Overhead rates activity-wise

Activity	**Traceable cost Amount (₹)**	**Total Number of Events or Transactions**	**Rate per Event/transaction Amount (₹)**
Machine Set-ups	2,50,000	5,000	50.000
Quality Inspections	2,00,000	8,000	25.000
Production Orders	81,000	600	135.000
Machine-hours worked	2,69,000	40,000	6.725
Material Receipts	75,000	750	100.000
	8,75,000	—	—

(2) Overhead cost per unit of product

Details	Product K		Product P	
	Events	Amount (₹)	Events	Amount (₹)
Machine Setups@ ₹ 50	3,000	1,50,000	2,000	1,00,000
Quality Inspections @ ₹ 25	5,000	1,25,000	3,000	75,000
Production Orders@ ₹135	200	27,000	400	54,000
Machine-hours worked@ ₹ 6.725	12,000	80,700	28,000	1,88,300
Material Receipts@ ₹100	150	15,000	600	60,000
Total	——	3,97,700	——	4,77,300
No. of units produced	——	8,000	——	20,000
Overhead cost per unit (₹)	——	49.715	——	23.865

(3) Computation of total cost of product (A comparison)

Details	Activity Base		Direct Labour Hour Base	
	Product K	Product P	Product K	Product P
Direct Materials	50.000	35.000	50.000	35.000
Direct Labour	25.000	25.000	25.000	25.000
Production Overheads	49.715	23.865	31.250	31.250
Total cost of Manufacture	124.715	83.865	106.250	91.250

Illustration 13.2 : *SV Limited produces three products P1, P2, P3 for which the standard cost and quantities per unit are as under:*

Details	*P1*	*P2*	*P3*
Output (Unit)	*10,000*	*20,000*	*28,000*
Direct Material per unit (₹)	*125*	*100*	*80*
Direct wages per unit (₹)	*75*	*100*	*120*
Labour hour per unit (Hours)	*5*	*6*	*8*
Machine hours per unit (Hours)	*6*	*6*	*9*
Number of Purchase requisitions	*1,500*	*2,250*	*2,500*
Number of Machine set-ups	*300*	*320*	*380*

Manufacturing Overhead costs apportioned:

Department	*Hours*	*Amount (₹)*
D1(Labour Intensive)	*2,50,000*	*30,00,000*
D2 (Machine Intensive)	*6,25,000*	*37,50,000*
Total		*67,50,000*

Manufacturing Overhead costs apportioned:

Activity	*Amount (₹)*	*Number of Batches*
Receiving and Inspection	*35,00,000*	*6,250*
Production scheduling and set-up	*32,50,000*	*1,000*
Total	*67,50,000*	

Prepare cost statement under

(i) Traditional Method of absorption; and

(ii) Activity based costing method.

Also compare the result obtained by the above mentioned methods.

Solution : (i) Computation of Product cost using Traditional Method

Working Notes:

$$\text{Rate of Recovery} = \frac{\text{Manufacturing Overhead Costs}}{\text{Hourly Basis}}$$

$$\text{Department D1: } \frac{\text{Manufacturing Overhead Costs}}{\text{Direct Labour Hours}}$$

$$= 30{,}00{,}000 \div 2{,}50{,}000 = ₹\ 12 \text{ per Direct Labour Hour}$$

$$\text{Department D2: } \frac{\text{Manufacturing Overhead Costs}}{\text{Machine Hours}}$$

$$= 37{,}50{,}000 \div 6{,}25{,}000 = ₹\ 6 \text{ per Machine Hour}$$

Statement of cost (Per unit)

Details	P1 (₹)	P2 (₹)	P3 (₹)
Direct Material	125	100	80
Direct wages	75	100	120
Overhead costs:			
Department D1:			
P1: (5 × 12)			
P2: (6 × 12)	60	72	96
P3: (8 × 12)			
Department D2:			
P1: (6 × 6)			
P2: (6 × 6)	36	36	54
P3: (9 × 6)			
Total cost per Unit	296	308	350

(ii) Computation of Product cost using Activity Based Costing Method

Working Notes:

$$\text{Rate of Recovery} = \frac{\text{Manufacturing Overhead Costs}}{\text{Cost Driver}}$$

Receiving and Inspection Activity:

$$\frac{\text{Manufacturing Overhead Costs}}{\text{Number of Batches}}$$

= 35,00,000 ÷ 6,250 = ₹560 per Batch

Production scheduling and set-up Activity:

$$\frac{\text{Manufacturing Overhead Costs}}{\text{Number of Batches}}$$

= 32,50,000 ÷ 1,000 = ₹3,250 per Batch

Statement of cost (Per unit)

Details	P1 (₹)	P2 (₹)	P3 (₹)
Direct Material	125.00	100.00	80.00
Direct wages	75.00	100.00	120.00
Overhead costs:			
Receiving and Inspection Activity:			
P1: (1,500 ×560) ÷10,000	84.00		
P2: (2,250 × 560) ÷20,000		63.00	
P3: (2,500 × 560) ÷ 28,000			50.00
Production scheduling and set-up Activity:			
P1: (300 ×3,250) ÷10,000	97.50		
P2: (320 × 3,250) ÷20,000		52.00	
P3: (380 × 3,250) ÷ 28,000			44.11
Total cost per Unit	381.50	315.00	294.11

Details	Activity Base			Traditional		
	P1 (₹)	P2 (₹)	P3 (₹)	P1 (₹)	P2 (₹)	P3 (₹)
Direct Material	125.00	100.00	80.00	125.00	100.00	80.00
Direct wages	75.00	100.00	120.00	75.00	100.00	120.00
Manufacturing Overheads	(84.00 + 97.50) = 181.50	(63.00 + 52.00) = 115.00	(50.00 + 44.11) = 94.11	(60.00 + 36.00) = 96.00	(72.00 + 36.00) = 108.00	(96.00 + 54.00) = 150.00
Total	381.50	315.00	294.11	296.00	308.00	350.00

Illustration 13.3 : *A company, manufacturing two products, furnishes the following data for the year 2008-09:*

Product	*Annual output (units)*	*Total machine hours*	*Total number of purchase orders*	*Total number of set-ups*
P-1	*5,000*	*20,000*	*160*	*20*
P-2	*60,000*	*1,20,000*	*384*	*44*

The annual overhead costs are as under (₹):

Volume related activity costs	*5,60,000*
Set-up related costs	*8,20,000*
Purchase related costs	*6,08,000*

You are required to calculate the costs per unit of each product P-1 and P-2 based on:

(a) Traditional method of charging overheads

(b) Activity based costing method

Solution : (a) Traditional method of charging overheads:

Volume related activity costs	5,60,000
Set – up related Costs	8,20,000
Purchase related Costs	6,08,000
Total costs (₹)	19,88,000

Total machine hours (20,000 + 1, 20,000) = 1,40,000

Total costs per hour (₹19, 88,000 ÷ 1, 40,000) = ₹ 14.20

Cost per unit of P-1 = (20,000 × ₹14.20) ÷ 5,000 = ₹ 56.80

Cost per unit of P-2 = (1, 20,000 × ₹14.20) ÷ 60,000 = ₹ 28.40

(b) Activity based costing method of charging overheads:

Volume related activity costs per machine hour:

₹ 5,60,000 ÷ 1, 40,000 = ₹4.00

Set –up costs per set –up: ₹8, 20,000÷ 64= ₹12, 812.50

Purchase related costs per purchase order: ₹6,08,000÷ 544 = ₹1117.647

Cost per unit of product (₹)

Details	Cost Driver	P-1	P-2
Volume related costs	Machine hours	80, 000	4, 80,000
Set – up costs	Number of set-ups	2,56,250	5,63,750
Purchase related costs	Number of purchase orders	1,78,824	4,29,176
	Total costs	5,15,074	14,72,326
Cost per unit		103.01	24.54

Illustration 13.4. *Shemrok limited manufactures compact disc-players for different well-known companies. The compact disc players differ significantly in their complexity and their manufacturing batch sizes. The following costs were incurred in the year 2008.*

(a) *Process designing including drawing process charts and engineering process changes for products, ₹16,00,000.*

(b) *Procurement costs of placing purchase orders, receiving materials and paying suppliers related to the number of purchase orders placed, ₹8,00,000.*

(c) *Direct material costs, ₹10,00,000*

(d) *Costs for setting up machines, ₹6, 00,000*

(e) *Direct manufacturing labour costs, ₹15,00,000*

(f) *Machine related overhead costs such as depreciation, maintenance, production engineering, ₹12,00,000. These resources relate to operating the machines;*

(g) *Plant management, plant rent, and insurance ₹8, 00,000.*

Required: *Classify each of the above mentioned costs as output Unit – level, Batch –level, Product –sustaining or Facility – sustaining. Explain each answer.*

Solution :

Details	Classification	Explanation
Designing: ₹16,00,000	Product sustaining	Designing supports an individual product rather than each individual unit produced
Procurement cost: ₹8,00,000	Batch level	Procurement related activities support batches of units procured rather than each individual unit procured
Direct material cost: ₹10, 00,000	Unit level	Direct material cost represent resources sacrificed on activities performed on each individual unit
Set –up costs: ₹6,00,000	Batch level	Activities related to setting up machine support batch of units in a production
Direct labour costs: ₹15, 00,000	Unit level	Direct labour performs activities on each individual unit of production
Machine related overheads: ₹12,00,000	Unit level	Machine operation is an activity that is an activity that is performed on each individual unit of production
Plant management: ₹8,00,000	Facility sustaining	Plant management and related activities support the facility as a whole.

LET US RECAPITULATE

1. Activity Based costing is a technique which involves identification of costs with each cost driving activity and making it as the basis of absorption of costs over different products or jobs.
2. Activities become the target points for cost computation.
3. Costs are charged to products or services based on individual products' consumption of each activity (i.e. benefits received from indirect activities).
4. Traditional method of accounting for the overheads assumes that 'volume' or 'units' produced is the only cost driver.
5. ABC system recognizes the fact that there are many cost drivers including Volume.
6. Cost drivers signify factors, forces or events that determine the costs of the activities.
7. Cost drivers are links and they can link a pool of costs in an activity centre to the product.
8. Transaction drivers determine number of times (frequency) an activity is performed.
9. Set-up hour is an example of Duration drivers.
10. Both the costing systems follow two stage allocation procedures.

SOLVED PROBLEMS

Problem 1. *Wipro limited produces two types of stereo units. Activity data is as under:*

Activity usage	*Product costing data*		
	Deluxe	*Regular*	*Total*
Units produced p.a.	*4,000*	*40,000*	*44,000*
Prime cost (₹)	*54,000*	*3,96,000*	*4,50,000*
Direct labour hours	*5,000*	*35,000*	*40,000*
Machine hours	*15,000*	*1,05,000*	*1,20,000*
Production runs	*8*	*4*	*12*
No. Of moves	*100*	*50*	*150*

Activity cost data:

Activity	*Activity cost (₹)*
Setting of equipment	*75,000*
Material handling	*45,000*
Using power	*90,000*
Testing	*54,000*
Total	*2,64,000*

Required:

1. *Calculate the Utilisation ratios for each activities*
2. *Group activities based on consumption ratios and activity level*
3. *Calculate the rate for each pooled group of activities*
4. *Calculate unit product cost using the pool rates calculated under point 3.*

Solution : 1. Utilisation ratios

Overhead activity	Deluxe	Regular	Activity driver
Setups	2/3	1/3	Production runs
Material handling	2/3	1/3	No. Of moves
Using power	1/8	7/8	Machine hours
Testing	1/8	7/8	Direct labour hours

2. Group activities

(a) Batch level: setups and material handling

(b) Unit level: power and testing

3. Pool Rate

Batch level pool		Unit level pool	
Activity	**Amount (₹)**	**Activity**	**Amount (₹)**
Set ups	75,000	Power	90,000
Material handling	45,000	Testing	54,000
Total	1,20,000	Total	1,44,000
Runs	12	Machine hours	1,20,000
Pool rate	10,000/run	Pool rates	1.2/machine hr

4. Product cost computation

Details		Deluxe (₹)	Regular (₹)
Prime cost (given)		54,000	3,96,000
Overhead cost:			
Batch level pool	: Deluxe 10000 × 8	80,000	
	: Regular 10,000 × 4		40,000
Unit level pool	: Deluxe 1.2×15,000	18,000	
	: Regular 1.2×1,05,000		1,26,000
Total manufacturing cost		1,52,000	9,22,000
Units produced		4,000	40,000
Unit cost (i.e. Total cost ÷ Number of units)		38.00	23.50

Problem 2. *Goldie Test laboratories do heat testing (HT) and stress testing (ST) on materials. The firm aggregates all operating costs of ₹20, 00,000 and divides it by total test hours, estimated at 1, 00,000 to determine the overhead absorption*

rate of ₹20 per hour. HT uses 60,000 test hours and ST uses 40,000 test hours. In view of enough variation in test procedures and cost structures, the firm has decided to introduce the variation in test procedures and cost structures, the firm has decided to introduce the activity based costing (ABC) to determine the service costs into four activity cost categories.

(i) Direct labour costs are estimated at ₹4,00,000. These costs can be directly traced to HT and ST. direct labour cost is estimated at ₹3,00,000 for HT and ₹1,00,000 for ST.

(ii) Equipment related costs such as rent, maintenance costs and energy cost are assigned to HT and ST based on test hours. These costs are estimated at ₹ 6,00,000.

(iii) Set up costs are estimated at ₹8,00,000. These costs are assigned to HT and ST based on the number of set- up hours. Set –up hours for HT and ST are estimated at 20,000 hours and 5,000 hours

(iv) Costs of designing tests are estimated at ₹2,00,000. These costs are assigned to HT and ST based on the time required designing the tests. Design hours for HT and ST are estimated at 3,000 hours and 2,000 hours.

Required:

(i) Classify each activity cost as output unit level, batch level, product or service sustaining or facility sustaining.

(ii) Calculate the cost per test hour for HT and ST. explain the difference between rates determined under ABC system and ₹20 per hour determined under the existing system.

(iii) Comment on the accuracy of service costs determined under the ABC system and those determined under the existing system.

Solution : (i) Classification of activities

(a) Direct labour: ₹ 4,00,000 unit level activity

(b) Equipment related costs: ₹6,00,000 unit level activity/facility sustaining activity

Operating costs (e.g. energy) are incurred to run the equipment is a unit level activity. Rent and costs of maintenance relate to facility sustaining activity, because those resources are consumed to support facilities. However, break down maintenance may be classified as product or service sustaining activity, if the complexity of product is a cost driver for maintenance costs. Usually maintenance costs are assigned to products or service based on technical estimate.

(c) Set up costs unit level activity 8, 00,000. Setting up machine is a batch level activity.

(d) Cost of designing: ₹2,00,000. Designing is a product or service sustaining activity.

(ii) Cost per test hour

Details	HT (₹)	ST (₹)	Total (₹)
Direct level costs	3,00,000	1,00,000	4,00,000
Equipment related costs	3,60,000	2,40,000	6,00,000
Set up costs	6,40,000	1,60,000	8,00,000
Designing	1,20,000	80,000	2,00,000
Total	14,20,000	5,80,000	20,00,000

Cost per test hour

HT: (14, 20,000÷60,000) = ₹23.67 per test hour

ST: (5, 80,000÷40,000) = ₹ 14.50 per test hour

(iii) ABC system provides more accurate result as compared to result obtained by using a single rate because ABC system uses multiple cost drivers.

Problem 3. *Cromwell limited manufactures variety of steel chairs. It uses ABC system to determine its product costs. The company's activity areas and related data are as follows:*

Manufacturing activity area	*Budgeted conversion costs for the year 2006 (₹)*	*Costs driver used as application base*	*Conversion cost per unit of application base (₹)*
Material handling	*4,00,000*	*Number of parts*	*0.80*
Cutting	*40,00,000*	*Number of parts*	*5.00*
Assembly	*20,00,000*	*Direct labour hours*	*80.00*
Painting	*25,00,000*	*Number of painted units*	*50.00*

In June 2006, the company produced two types of chairs, office chairs and restaurant chairs. Their quantities, direct material costs, and other data follow:

Item	*Units produced*	*Direct material costs (₹)*	*Number of parts*	*Assembly direct labour hours*
Office chair	*7,500*	*30,00,000*	*1,00,000*	*10,000*
Restaurant chair	*1,500*	*6 ,00,000*	*10,000*	*1,000*

Required:

(a) Determine the total manufacturing costs and unit costs of the office chairs and the restaurant chairs.

(b) *Suppose upstream activities, such as product design, were analyzed and applied to office chairs at ₹50 each and restaurant chairs at ₹ 20 each. Similarly downstream activities, such as distribution, marketing, and customer service, were analysed and applied to office chairs at ₹600 each and restaurant chairs at ₹130 each. Determine the full product cost per unit.*

Solution : (a)

Details	Application Basis	Office chair	Restaurant chair
Direct material	Allocation	30, 00,000	6,00,000
Material handling	Number of parts	80,000	8,000
Cutting	Number of parts	5,00,000	50,000
Assembly	Direct labour hours	8,00,000	80,000
Painting	Number of units	3,75,000	75,000
Total manufacturing cost (₹)		47,55,000	8,13,000

Cost per unit (₹)

Office chairs (47,55,000 ÷ 75,001) = ₹634

Restaurant chairs (8,13,000 ÷ 1,500) = ₹542

(b) Full product costs

Details	Office chair (₹)	Restaurant chair (₹)
Upstream activities	50	20
Manufacturing	634	542
Downstream activities	600	130
Total	1,284	692

Problem 4. *ABC Limited manufacturing two products furnishes the following data for the year ending 31st March, 2007:*

Product	*Annual Output (Unit)*	*Total Machine Hours (per Unit)*	*Total Number of Purchase Orders Handled*	*Total Number of set-ups*
A	*5,000*	*20,000*	*160*	*20*
B	*60,000*	*1,20,000*	*384*	*44*

Annual Overheads are as under:	*Amount (₹)*
Volume related costs	*5,50,000*
Set up related costs	*8,20,000*
Purchase related costs	*6,18,000*
Total	*19,88,000*

You are required to calculate cost per unit of each product A and B based on:

(i) A traditional method of charging overheads.

(ii) Activity based costing method. **[B.Com (Hons.) DU, 2006 and 2007]**

Solution : Traditional costing approach:

Rate per Machine Hour = Total Overheads / Total Machine Hours

= 19, 88,000/ 1, 40,000 => ₹ 14.20

Overheads absorbed:

Product	Annual Output Unit	Machine Hours	Overheads absorbed (₹)	Overhead cost per unit of output = (Overheads absorbed/Annual output) (₹)
A	5,000	20,000	20,000 × 14.20 = 2,84,000	56.80
B	60,000	1,20,000	1,20,000 × 14.20 = 17,04,000	28.40
		Total	19,88,000	

Activity Based Costing Approach:

Computation of Rates:

I. Rate per Machine Hour

= Volume related Overheads / Total Machine Hours

= 5, 50,000÷1, 40,000 => ₹ 3.9286

II. Rate per Set-up = Set-up Overheads / Total Number of Set-ups

= 8, 20,000÷64 => ₹ 12,812.50

III. Rate per Order = Purchase Order Overheads / Total Number of Orders

= 6, 18,000÷544 => ₹ 1,136.0294

Overheads Absorbed (₹):

Product	Machine hour (I)	Setup (II)	Handling Orders (III)	Total (IV)	Absorption per unit of output
A	20,000 × 3.9286 =78,571	20×12,812.50 =2,56,250	160×1,136.0294 =1,81,765	5,16,586	5,16,586÷5,000 = ₹ 103.32
B	1,20,000 × 3.9286 = 4,71,429	44×12,812.50 =5,63,750	384×1,136.0294 =4,36,235	14,71,414	14,71,414÷60,000 = ₹ 24.57
Total	5,50,000	8,20,000	6,18,000	19,88,000	

Working Notes:

Total Machine Hours = 20,000 + 1, 20,000 =>1, 40,000

Total Number of set-ups = 20 + 44 =>64

Total Number of Purchase Orders Handled= 160 + 384 =>544

Problem 5. *A Company manufacturing two products L and M furnishes the overhead data for the year:*

Product	*Annual Output (Unit)*	*Machine Hours (per Unit)*	*Direct Labour Hours (per Unit)*	*Total Number of Orders Handled*	*Total Number of setups*
L	*5,000*	*3*	*1*	*15*	*10*
M	*7,000*	*1*	*2*	*60*	*40*

Required: *Calculate the production overheads to be absorbed by one unit of each of the products L and M using the following costing methods:*

(i) A traditional costing approach using direct labour hour rate to absorb overheads.

(ii) An activity based costing approach, using suitable cost drivers to trace overheads to products. **[B.Com (Hons.) DU, 2008]**

Solution : Traditional costing approach:

Direct labour Hour Rate = Total Overheads / Total Direct Labour Hours

= 2,85,000 ÷19,000 => ₹ 15

Overheads absorbed (₹):

Product	Annual Output (Unit)	Direct Labour Hours	Overheads absorbed (₹)	Direct labour Hour Rate per unit of output: (₹) (Overheads absorbed/ Annual Output)
L	5,000	5,000 × 1= 5,000	5,000 × 15 = 75,000	15
M	7,000	7,000 × 2= 14,000	14,000 ×15 = 2,10,000	30
		Total	2,85,000	

Activity Based Costing Approach:

Computation of Rates:

I. Rate per Machine Hour = Machine Overheads / Total Machine Hours

= 2, 20,000÷22,000 => ₹ 10

II. Rate per Set-up = Set-up Overheads / Total Number of Set-ups

= 20,000÷50 => ₹ 400

III. Rate per Order = Order Overheads / Total Number of Orders

= 45,000÷75 => ₹ 600

Overheads absorbed (₹):

Product	Machine hour (I)	Setup (II)	Handling Orders (III)	Total (IV)	Absorption per unit of output
L	5,000 ×3×10 = 1,50,000	10×400=4,000	15×600=9,000	1,63,000	1,63,000÷5,000 = ₹ 32.60
M	7,000 ×1×10 = 70,000	40×400=16,000	60×600=36,000	1,22,000	1,22,000÷7,000 = ₹ 17.43
Total	2,20,000	20,000	45,000	2,85,000	

Working Notes:

Total Direct Labour Hours = (5,000 ×1) + (7,000 × 2)
= 5,000 + 14,000 =>19,000

Total Machine Hours = (5,000 ×3) + (7,000 × 1)
= 15,000 + 7,000 =>22,000

Problem 6. *A company manufacturing two products furnishes the following data for the year 2008-09:*

Product	*Annual output (units)*	*Total machine hours*	*Total number of purchase orders*	*Total number of set-ups*
A	*8,000*	*32,000*	*232*	*25*
B	*96,000*	*1,92,000*	*568*	*55*

The annual overheads are as under:

Volume related activity costs	*5,60,000*
Set-up related costs	*8,20,000*
Purchase related costs	*6,08,000*

You are required to calculate the cost per unit of each product A and B based on:

(i) Traditional method of charging over heads; and

(ii) Activity based costing method

Solution : (i) Traditional method of charging over heads:

Volume related activity costs	5,60,000
Set – up related sots	8,20,000
Set – up related costs	6,08,000
Total costs	₹ 19,88,000

Total machine hours (32,000 + 1, 92,000) = 2,24,000

Total costs per hour (₹19, 88,000 ÷ 2,24,000) = ₹ 8.875

Cost per unit of A = (32,000 × 8.875) ÷ 8,000 = ₹ 35.50

Cost per unit of B = (1,92,000 × 8.875) ÷ 96,000 = ₹ 17.75

(ii) Activity based costing method of charging overheads:

Volume related activity costs per machine hour:

(5, 60,000 ÷ 2,24,00) = ₹2.50

Set –up costs per set –up: (8, 20,000 ÷ 80) = ₹10,250

Purchase related costs per purchase order: (6, 08,000 ÷ 800) = ₹760

Computation of Cost per unit of Product (₹)

Details	Cost Driver	A	B
Volume related costs	Machine hours	80, 000 (32,000×2.5)	4,80,000 (1,92,000×2.5)
Set – up costs	Number of set-ups	2,56,250 (25×10,250)	5,63,750 (55×10,250)
Purchase related costs	Number of purchase orders	1,76,320 (232×760)	4,31,680 (568 ×760)
	Total costs	5,12,570	14,75,430
Cost per unit	(Total costs ÷ Number of Units)	64.07	15.37

OBJECTIVE TYPE EXERCISES

I. Fill in the blank spaces with suitable word/s :

1. The cost driver rates are applied to ……… .
2. The aggregate cost can be calculated by multiplying the cost driver rate with the ……… of activities.
3. An activity ……… be a very small job.
4. The number of pools depends upon the cost ……… activities.
5. The term 'cost driver' is used under ……… costing system.
6. The cause and effect relationship is not considered under ……… system of costing.

Answers :

1. products	**2.** number
3. can	**4.** driving
5. ABC	**6.** traditional

II. Indicate whether the following statements are True or False :

1. The cost driver rates are applied to products.
2. The aggregate cost can be calculated by multiplying the cost driver rate with the number of activities.
3. An activity cannot be a very small job.
4. The number of pools depends upon the cost driving activities.
5. The term 'cost driver' is used under traditional costing system.
6. The causal relationship is not considered under ABC system.

Answers :

1. True	**2.** True	**3.** False	**4.** True
5. False	**6.** False		

THEORETICAL EXERCISES

1. What do you understand by activity-based costing? Discuss how it can be implemented in any industry with which you are familiar?
2. Give an overview of activity-based costing and indicate the impact of the same in ascertaining cost of products or services.
3. What is a cost driver? What is the role of cost driver in tracing costs to products?
4. What are the benefits of Activity-based Costing?
5. How ABC system different from traditional costing system? Illustrate.
6. Discuss the different stages in Activity-based costing.
7. "ABC systems only apply to manufacturing companies." Do you agree? Explain.
8. What are the basic steps required for activity-based costing?
9. Discuss between activity-based costing and traditional costing system.
10. What are the key reasons for product cost differences between traditional costing system and ABC systems?

NUMERICAL EXERCISES

1. Skyline limited manufactures four productsk,l,h and w using the same plant and processes. The following information relates to a production period:

Product	Volume	Material cost per unit (₹)	Direct labour per unit (hr.)	Machine time per unit (hr.)	Labour cost per unit (₹)
κ	500	200	0.50	0.20	20
λ	5000	200	0.50	0.20	20
η	600	800	2.00	1.00	100
ω	7000	900	1.50	1.50	150

Total production overhead recorded by the cost accounting system is analysed under the following headings:

(a) Factory overhead applicable to machine-oriented activity: ₹3, 74,240.

(b) Set –up costs: ₹ 45,000.

(c) Cost of ordering materials: ₹ 20,000.

(d) Handling materials: ₹75, 000.

(e) Administration of spare parts: ₹80, 000.

These overhead costs are absorbed by products on a machine @ ₹ 48.71 per hour, giving an overhead cost per product of:k = ₹9.74; l = ₹9.74; h = ₹48.71; w = ₹73.07. However, investigation into the production overhead activities for the period reveals the following totals:

Product	Number of set-ups	Number of materials order	Number of times materials was handled	Number of spare parts
κ	1	1	2	3
λ	5	4	10	6
η	2	1	3	1
ω	7	4	10	6

You are required:

(a) Compute overhead cost per product using activity based costing.

(b) Comment briefly on the differences disclosed between overheads traced by the present system and those traced by activity based costing. **[Ans. ....]**

2. SV limited manufactures four products, namely P-1, P-2, P-3, and P-4 using the same plant and processes. The following information relates to a production period:

Product	Volume	Material cost Per Unit (₹)	Direct Labour Per Unit (Hour)	Machine time Per unit (Hour)	Labour cost Per unit (₹)
P-1	500	250	0.50	0.20	25.00
P-2	5,000	250	0.50	0.25	25.00
P-3	800	1,050	2.00	1.00	150.00
P-4	8,000	1,250	1.50	1.50	200.00

Total Production Overhead recorded by the Cost Accounting System is analysed under the following headings:

(a) Factory Overhead applicable to machine -Oriented Activity ₹ 4,52,800.

(b) Set-up Costs ₹ 64,000.

(c) Cost of ordering materials ₹ 27,500.

(d) Cost of Handling Materials ₹ 88,000.

(e) Administration of Spare Parts ₹ 1, 00,670.

These Overhead costs are absorbed by products on a Machine hour rate of ₹ 51.80 per hour, giving an overhead cost per unit of Product P-1= ₹ 10.36; P-2= ₹ 10.36; P-3 = ₹51.80; and P-4 = ₹ 77.70. However, investigation into the production overhead activities for the period reveals the following totals:

Product	No. of Set-ups	No. of Materials Order	Frequency of Materials handled	No. of Spare parts
P-1	1	1	2	3
P-2	2	4	10	7
P-3	5	1	3	2
P-4	8	5	10	8

You are required:

1. Compute Overhead cost per product using activity based costing.
2. Comment briefly on the differences disclosed between overheads traced by the existing system and those traced by activity based costing.

❑❑❑

14 Unit or Single Output Costing

Learning Objectives

It attempts to explain the process of finding out the cost of a unit of product. In this chapter you will learn :

1. Meaning, nature and objectives of output costing.
2. Cost sheet or production statement.
3. Estimated cost statement of cost and profit.
4. Treatment of normal scrap.
5. Treatment of work-in-progress.

NATURE AND MEANING

The term "Single or output costing" is used where exclusively one homogeneous product or a few grades of the same product i.e. a single product or only a few category of similar articles are manufactured, e.g., paper, cement, sugar, steel, quarries, brickworks and breweries. Thus, it is a method applicable in case of industries where the products can be expressed in identical quantitative units and manufacturing is continuous. The cost incurred over a period is divided by the total output for ascertaining the cost per unit.The unit cost of the product is obtained by dividing the total cost of production by the number of units manufactured. The total cost of the product is ascertained in a cost sheet format. All costs are charged to that product as only one product is manufactured embracing a single process. In case several categories of the product are manufactured, it may be necessary to apportion the overhead costs relating to more than one category of the product. The cost units may be expressed in terms of number, weight, volume and time.

Following is a list of some industries and the corresponding cost units adopted by them.

Type of Industry	Cost unit
Brick making	Bricks made per 1,000
Steel manufacturing	Per tonne
Cement, Coal, Collieries, Quarries	Per tonne
Paper	Per kg- tonne
Bolts, nuts	Gross or per 1,000
Paint manufacturing	Per Litre
Gas Works	Per 1,000 cubic meters produced
Electricity undertakings	Per kilowatt-hour

From the above it is obvious that this method is followed in industries with the following characteristics:

(1) Production consists of a single product or a few products.

(2) Large number/quantity of identical units is produced with identical costs.

(3) Production is performed on continuous basis.

(4) Production is almost of standard quality.

(5) Cost unit is physical and natural, e.g. number of bricks, tons of cement, meters of cloth, liters of milk/Kerosene.

Thus, the industries using this method of costing are: Brick works, Milk dairies, Sugar mills, Paper mills, Mines and Quarries, Steel mills, Breweries, Chemical production, etc.

The computation of cost is done in the form of cost sheet/production statement and production account.

COST SHEET/PRODUCTION STATEMENT

A Cost Sheet or production statement is the statement that provides a logical, detailed and systematic presentation of various elements of cost information obtained through the cost records. It also includes sales as well as profit data. The term production statement may signify statement of units produced. Such a statement may be designated as a statement of cost and profits. For the sake of comparison and cost control, the corresponding figure for the preceding period or standard cost figure may also be provided in the cost sheet or production statement.

Purpose of Preparing Cost Sheet

1. It gives total cost of goods produced and sold as well as cost per unit.
2. The detailed break-up of the cost is pin pointed.
3. The detailed break-up of the cost is used for comparative analysis and efficiency.

4. Estimated cost sheet serves as an important tool for budgeting and cost control. Estimated cost sheet is essential for submitting tenders and quotations.
5. Cost sheet in percentages facilitates inter-firm and inter-temporal comparisons.
6. It becomes the basis for determining the selling price.

Production Account

The Production Account depicts Sales, Stocks, and Profit besides the Cost in a ledger account format. It is an account giving details of cost of production, cost of sales and profit made during a particular period. Such a compilation is made at periodic intervals: every month or quarter. The details are presented in T-form, based on double entry system, with debit and credit sides. It is also known as 'Manufacturing Account' which consists of two parts. The first part shows the cost components and the total cost of current production. The latter part shows the cost of sales, selling price, and the profit (or Loss for the relevant period.

Specimen of a Production Account is given as below:

(A) *Summarised :*

Production Account

(For the Period ....) Output : ...... unit

Details	Unit	Per unit Amount (₹)	Amount (₹)	Details	Unit	Per unit Amount (₹)	Amount (₹)
To Materials consumed A/c				By Closing work in Progress A/c			
To Wages A/c				By Cost of Production c/d			
To Direct Expenses A/c							
To Works overheads							
To Administration overheads							
To Opening work in Progress A/c							
Total				Total			
To Cost of Production b/d				By Sale			
To opening Stock of Finished Goods				By Closing Stock of Finished Goods			
To Profit							
Total				Total			

(B) *Detailed* :

Production Account

(For the Period ....) Output : ...... unit

Details	Debit Amount (₹)	Details	Credit Amount (₹)
To Opening stock of Raw Materials To Direct Material To Direct Labour To Direct Expenses		By Closing stock of Raw Materials By Net value of Normal Scrap realised By Prime Cost c/d	
Total		Total	
To Prime Cost b/d To Opening stock of Work in Progress To Factory Overheads		By Closing Stock of Work in Progress By Factory Cost c/d	
Total		Total	
To Factory Cost b/d To Office and Administrative Overheads		By Cost of Goods Produced c/d	
Total		Total	
To Cost of Goods Produced b/d To Opening Stock of Finished Goods		By Closing Stock of Finished Goods By Cost of Goods Sold c/d	
Total		Total	
To Cost of Goods Sold b/d To Selling and Distribution Overheads To Profit		By Sales	
Total		Total	

Estimated Cost Sheet

An estimated cost sheet is prepared before the production is commenced. The estimated cost sheet is subsequently compared with actual costs so that costs can be controlled and be kept within specified limits. Besides, the estimated costs can be used as the basis for fixing selling price and taking decisions regarding profit planning, production, administration and marketing by management. Estimation of costs is done on the basis of current situation and future envisaged circumstances likely to have impact on different elements of cost. Such estimates of costs are always required for submitting tenders or quotations to obtain a specific work order.

Treatment of Scrap

Scrap is the incidental residue from certain manufacturing processes generally of small amount and low value, recoverable without further processing. The amount recovered from the sale of scrap is to be deducted either from the Manufacturing overheads or gross works cost.

In case certain materials (before being put to use) are found to be defective and therefore sold, the value of materials consumed should be reduced by the cost of such materials. Any loss on sale of such materials is to be charged to costing profit and loss account.

Treatment of Spoiled and Defective work

Spoilage consists of goods damaged beyond rectification. Defectives consist of goods damaged but yet capable of being rectified. Loss on account of normal spoilage is borne by good units. Cost of rectification of normal defectives is charged to all good units including those rectified. Loss on account of abnormal spoilage or rectification cost of abnormal defectives is directly charged to the costing Profit and Loss Account. It can be understood by taking an example.

Example :

Input 4,000 units @ ₹ 25 per unit

Direct wages ₹ 50,000; Factory overheads ₹ 80,000.

12.5% of the units introduced are considered as normal spoilage which realized @ ₹ 16 per unit. Another 12.5% of the input is considered to be normal defectives. Actual spoilage amounts to 600 units while actual defectives are 800 units. The cost of rectifaction of defective units is ₹ 15 per unit.

Treatment of Inventories

Inventory may be of three types:

(A) Treatment of Raw Materials: In order to arrive at the value of raw materials consumed/used, the opening inventory of raw materials is added to the current period purchases of raw materials and the closing stock of raw materials is deducted.

Raw materials consumed:

= Opening inventory + Purchases of raw materials – Closing inventory

(B) Treatment of work-in- Progress: In order to arrive at the value of Works Cost, the current manufacturing cost (i.e. Prime cost + Factory overheads) is modified by adding the opening work-in-progress and deducting the closing work-in-progress.

Networks Cost:

= Current Manufacturing cost + Opening inventory of work-in-progress – Closing inventory of work-in-progress

(C) Treatment of Finished Goods: In order to arrive at the value of Cost of Goods Sold, the opening inventory of finished goods is added to the current period cost of production (i.e. Works Cost + Office and Administration overheads) and the closing stock of finished goods is deducted.

Cost of Goods Sold:

= Cost of Production + Opening inventory of finished goods – Closing inventory of finished goods

Illustration 14.1 : *A Standard Firm has purchased a plant to manufacture a new product, the cost details are as follows: -*

Details	*Units/ Amount (₹)*
Estimated Quarterly Sales (Units)	*7,500*
Materials (per unit)	*50.00*
Direct Labor (per unit)	*15.00*
Manufacturing Overheads (per annum)	*1,55,500*
Administrative Overheads (per annum)	*1,81,000*
Selling Expenses (percentage of Sales)	*12.50*

Calculate the Selling Price if Profit per unit is ₹ 20.

Solution : **Computation of Selling Price per Unit**

Details	**Amount (₹)**
Cost of Production:	
(Based on annual Output i.e. 7,500 × 4=30,000)	
Material	15,00,000
Direct Labour	4,50,000
Manufacturing Overheads	1,55,500
Administrative Overheads	1,81,000
Total Cost of production	22,87,500

Profit = ₹ 20 × 30,000= 6, 00,000

Selling Expenses= 12.5% of Sales

Hence, Total Cost of Sales = 22, 87,500 + 12.5% of Sales

Let X be Total Sales

$$X = \text{Total Cost of Sales} + \text{Profit}$$
$$X = 22,87{,}500 + 0.125X + 6,00{,}000$$
$$0.875X = 28,87{,}500$$
$$X = 28,87{,}500/0.875$$
$$X = 33,00{,}000$$

Selling Price per unit = 33, 00,000/30,000

= ₹ 110.

Selling Expenses = 4, 12,500 (i.e. 33, 00,000 × 0.125)

Illustration 14.2 : *A Firm presently sells equipment for ₹ 42,000. Increase in prices of Input of Labour and Material is expected to be 20% and 12.5% respectively in the year 2008. Material cost constitutes 40% of cost of sales and labour cost 32% of cost of sales. The balance of 28% relates to Overheads. If the existing selling price were to be retained, despite the increase in labour and material prices, the firm would face a 20% decrease in existing amount of profit on the equipment.*

You are required to arrive at a selling price as to give the same percentage of profit on increased cost of sales, as before. Prepare a statement of Profit/Loss per unit, showing the new selling price and cost per unit in support of your quotation of price.

Solution :

Selling Price= ₹ 42, 000

Let us assume the existing Total cost of sales as X.

Details	Existing Condition	Anticipated Condition
Direct Material	0.40X	0.48X (i.e. 0.4 × 1.2)
Direct Labour	0.32X	0.36X (i.e. 0.32 ×1.125)
Overheads	0.28X	0.28X
Total Cost of Sales	X	1.12X
Profit	(42000 – X)	(42000 – 1.12X)

From the above, the following equation can be formed:

$$(42{,}000 - X) - (42{,}000 - 1.12X) = 0.2(42{,}000 - X)$$
$$1.12X - X = 8{,}400 - 0.2X$$
$$1.32X - X = 8{,}400$$
$$0.32X = 8{,}400$$
$$X = 26{,}250$$

Hence the present Cost of Sales is Rupees 26, 250.

Statement of Profit or Loss

Details	Existing Amount (₹)	Anticipated Amount (₹)
Material	10,500	12,600
Labour	8, 400	9,450
Overheads	7,350	7,350
Cost of Sales	26,250	29,400
Profit (60% of Cost of Sales)*	15,750	17,640
Selling Price	42,000	47,040

Note:

*15, 750 ÷ 26, 250=0.6 i.e. Sixty percent of Cost of Sales.

*In the Anticipated situation, the profit amounts to Rupees 12, 600 (i.e. 42, 000 – 29, 400), which is 80% (i.e. 12, 600÷15, 750) of the existing Profit. To have the same percentage of profit i.e. 60% of the anticipated cost of sales the selling price needs to be ₹ 47, 040.

Illustration 14.3 : *SV Ltd. specializes in the manufacture of dinning tables of standard size, of which they can make 20,000 in a year. The cost per dinning table worked out as under for the year 2006-2007 when they made and sold 12,500 units:*

Details	*Amount (₹)*
Materials	*800*
Labour	*320*
Fixed Overhead Recovered @ 60% Of Material cost	*480*
Total Cost	*1,600*

Prices are fixed by adding a standard margin of 12.5% to the total cost arrived as above.

In the year 2007-2008 due to fall in cost of materials, total cost worked out is as under:

Details	*Amount (₹)*
Materials	*500*
Labour	*320*
Fixed Overhead recovered @ 60% of material cost	*300*
Total Cost	*1,120*

SV Ltd. maintained their standard margin of 12.5% on the cost. Sales were at the same level as in 2006-2007. You are asked to:

(i) Determine profit or loss for the year.

(ii) Compute the price, which should have been charged in 2007-2008 to yield the same profit or loss as in 2006-2007.

(iii) Show the defects, if any, in the costing and /or pricing system and suggest a proper system to be followed in future.

Solution : (i) Statement of Profit or Loss for the year 2006-2007 and 2007-2008

(Number of units: 12,500)

Details	Year: 2006-07		Year: 2007-08	
Sales (12,500×1,600×1.125); (12,500×1,120×1.125)		225,00,000		157,50,000
Less: Cost Incurred				
Materials	100,00,000		62,50,000	
Labour	40,00,000		40,00,000	
Fixed Overheads Recovered	60,00,000		37,50,000	
Total cost		200,00,000		140,00,000
Profit		25,00,000		17,50,000
Unabsorbed Overheads		Nil		(22,50,000)
Profit/(Loss)		25,00,000		(5,00,000)

(ii) Selling Price, which should have been quoted in the year 2007-2008:

Details	Amount (₹)	Amount (₹)
Materials	62,50,000	
Labour	40,00,000	
Fixed Overheads	60,00,000	
Total Cost		162,50,000
Profit as in 2006-2007		25,00,000
Desired Sales Value		187,50,000
Hence, the Desirable Price Quotation: (187,50,000÷12,500)		1,500

(iii) Both the costing and pricing systems of SV Ltd. are defective. That is why in the year 2007-2008 it incurred a loss of Rupees Five Lakhs despite the material cost having gone down. The basic defect lies in the pricing method, which should be based on the standard costing system. However, the standard cost for the year 2007-2008 is likely to be different than that for the year 2006-2007.

Illustration 14.4 : *From the following details, prepare a weekly cost sheet showing profit on the main product of PL Petroleum Ltd:*

Details	*Quantity (Liters)*	*Amount (₹)*
Crude Oil Used	*7,00,000*	*56,00,000*
Petrol Produced (Main Product)	*2,38,000*	

Sale of Petrol		*83,30,000*
By-Products:		
(i) Lubricating Oil	*70,000*	*15,40,000*
(ii) Fuel Oil	*3,22,000*	*40,25,000*
(iii) Kerosene	*52,500*	*5,25,000*
Raw Materials Consumed		*8,68,000*
Salaries and General Charges		*9,00,000*
Wages Incurred		*18,80,000*
Repairs and Renewals		*9,59,400*

Solution : **Cost Sheet for the Week Ending on…**

Details	Quantity (Litres)	Total Cost (₹)	Cost per Unit (₹)
Crude Oil Used (Input)	7,00,000	56,00,000	8.00
Raw Materials		8,68,000	
Wages Incurred		18,80,000	
Repairs and Renewals		9,59,400	
Salaries and General Charges		9,00,000	
Total cost of production (Main Product and By-Products)		102,07,400	
Less: Sale proceeds of by-products:			
Lubricating Oil @ ₹ 22	(70,000)	(15,40,000)	
Fuel Oil @ ₹ 12.50	(3,22,000)	(40,25,000)	
Kerosene @ ₹ 10	(52,500)	(5,25,000)	
Wastage	(17,500)	NIL	
Total Sale of By-Products		60,90,000	
Cost of production of Main Product (Petrol): (102,07,400 – 60,90,000)	2,38,000	41,17,400	17.30
Profit (Balancing Figure)		42,12,600	17.70
Sales Revenue		83,30,000	35.00

Note: Wastage has been assumed to be normal.

Illustration 14.5 : *The Modern limited furnishes the following details relating to the manufacture of a standard product during August 2008:*

Raw Materials consumed	*₹ 75,000*
Direct labour charges	*₹ 45,000*
Machine Hours worked	*800 @ ₹ 15*
Administration Overheads	*20% on Works cost*
Selling overheads	*₹ 4 per unit sold*
Units produced	*12,000*
Units Sold	*11,000 @ ₹ 40*

Required:

(i) Cost sheet showing details and cost per unit;

(ii) Cost per unit sold, and profit for the period.

Solution : **Cost Sheet**

(For August, 2008) Output : 12,000 units

Details	Per Unit (₹)	Total (₹)
Raw Materials consumed	6.25	75,000
Direct labour	3.75	45,000
Prime cost	10.00	1,20,000
Production Overheads (800 × 15)	10.00	1,20,000
Works Cost	20.00	2,40,000
Administration overheads (0.2×2,40,000)	4.00	48,000
Cost of goods Produced (12,000)	24.00	2,88,000
Less: Closing stock:		
As on 31.8.2008 (1,000 ×24)		(24,000)
Cost of goods sold (11,000)	24.00	2,64,000
Selling overheads (11,000 × 4)	4.00	44,000
Cost of sales	28.00	3,08,000
Profit	12.00	1,32,000
Sales (11,000×40)	40.00	4,40,000

Illustration 14.6 : *The following extract of costing information relates to a standard commodity 'Palm' for the year ending on 31.3.2009:*

Details	*Amount (₹)*
Purchase of Raw Materials	*3,05,400*
Direct Labour	*2,50,000*
Rent, rates, insurance and works On-cost	*1,00,000*
Carriage Inward	*6,000*
Opening stock:	
Raw materials	*50,000*
Finished product (200 Tons)	*40,000*
Closing stock:	
Raw materials	*55,000*
Finished product (400 Tons)	*?*
Work-in-Progress: Opening	*12,000*
Work-in-Progress: Closing	*40,000*
Factory supervision	*22,000*
Sale of finished Product @ ₹ 280 per unit	*?*

Advertising, discount allowed and selling costs ₹20 per ton sold. 3,200 tons of the product were produced during the given period. Prepare a Production statement to ascertain:

(a) the cost of the output of the period and the cost per ton of production;

(b) the net profit.

Solution : Working Notes:

Quantity Sold = Opening stock + Product Manufactured – Closing stock

= 200 + 3,200 – 400=>3,000 Units

Production Statement

(For year ending on 31.3.2009) Output: 3,200 units

Details		Per Unit (₹)	Total (₹)
Opening stock of raw			
Materials			50,000
Add: purchases			3,05,400
Less: Closing stock			55,000
Raw Materials consumed			3,00,400
Direct labour			2,50,000
Prime cost		172.00	5,50,400
Production Overheads:			
Rent, rates, insurance and			
Works on-cost	1,00,000		
Carriage Inward	6,000		
Factory supervision	22,000	40.00	1,28,000
Works Cost			6,78,400
Add: Opening Work-in-Progress			12,000
Less: Closing Work-in-progress			(40,000)
Works cost(Net)		203.25	6,50,400
Administration overheads		NIL	NIL
Cost of Goods Produced (3,200)		203.25	6,50,400
Add: Opening stock (200 units)			40,000
Less: Closing stock (400 × 203.25)			(81,300)
Cost of Goods Sold (3,000)		203.03	6,09,100
Selling overheads (3,000 × 20)		20.00	60,000
Cost of sales		223.03	6,69,100
Profit		56.97	1,70,900
Sales (3,000×280)		280.00	8,40,000

Illustration 14.7 : *Prepare Cost statement as well as Production account from the following information in regard to the production of special type of Paper:*

Direct Materials:

Paper pulp: 625 tonnes @ ₹ 800 per tonne

Other materials: 125 tonnes @ ₹ 500 per tonne

Direct Labour:

100 Skilled Work-Men @ ₹ 25 per hour for 25 days of 8 hours a day

60 unskilled Work-Men @ ₹15 per hour for 25 days of 8 hours a day

Direct Expenses:

Special Equipment: 65,000

Special dyes: 26,000

Factory Overheads:

Variable @ 125% and Fixed @ 75% on Direct Wages

Administrative Overheads: 12.5% of Factory Cost.

Selling and Distribution Overheads: 20% on Factory Cost.

500 tonnes of Special Paper was manufactured and sold @ ₹ 8,500 per tonne and ₹ 33,500 was realized by the sale of waste material during the course of manufacture. The scrap value of the special equipment and dyes after utilization in manufacturing work is nil.

Solution : **Cost Sheet for the period ending on...**

(Output: 500 tonnes)

Details	Total Cost (₹)	Cost per tonne (₹)
Direct Materials Used:		
Paper pulp (625 × 800)	5,00,000	1,000
Other materials (125 × 500)	62,500	125
Direct Labour:		
Skilled (100×25×8×25)	5,00,000	1,000
Unskilled (60×15×8×25)	1,80,000	360
Direct Expenses:		
Special Equipment	65,000	130
Special dyes	26,000	52
Prime Cost:	13,33,500	2,667
Add: Factory overheads:		
Variable (1.25×6,80,000)	8,50,000	1,700
Fixed (0.75×6,80,000)	5,10,000	1,020
Less: Sale Proceeds of waste material	(33,500)	(67)
Total Net factory overheads	13,26,500	2,653
Factory Cost:	26,60,000	5,320

Add: Administrative Overheads:		
12.5% of Factory Cost (0.125×26,60,000)	3,32,500	665
Cost of Production	29,92,500	5,985
Add: Selling and Distribution overheads:		
20% of Factory Cost (0.2×26,60,000)	5,32,000	1,064
Cost of Sales	35,24,500	7,049
Profit (Balancing Figure)	7,25,500	1,451
Sales	42,50,000	8,500

Production Account for the period ending on...

Details	Dr Amount (₹)	Details	Cr Amount (₹)
Direct Materials:		Prime Cost c/d	13,33,500
Paper pulp (625×800)	5,00,000		
Other Materials (125×500)	62,500		
20Direct Labour:			
Skilled (100×25×8×25)	5,00,000		
Unskilled (60×15×8×25)	1,80,000		
Direct Expenses:			
Special Equipment	65,000		
Special dyes	26,000		
Total	13,33,500	Total	13,33,500
Prime Cost b/d	13,33,500	Sale Proceeds of waste Material	33,500
Factory overheads:		Factory Cost c/d	26,60,000
Variable (1.25×6,80,000)	8,50,000		
Fixed (0.75×6,80,000)	5,10,000		
Total	26,93,500	Total	26,93,500
Factory cost b/d	26,60,000	Cost of Production c/d	29,92,500
Administrative Overheads:			
12.5% of Factory Cost (0.125×26,60,000)	3,32,500		
Total	29,92,500	Total	29,92,500
Cost of Production b/d	29,92,500	Cost of Sales c/d	35,24,500
Selling and Distribution overheads: 20% of Factory Cost (0.2×26,60,000)	5,32,000		
Total	35,24,500	Total	35,24,500
Cost of Sales b/d	35,24,500	Sales	42,50,000
Profit	7,25,500		
Total	42,50,000	Total	42,50,000

Illustration 14.8 : *Form the following cost records of Standard Chemicals Ltd.; you are required to prepare Production account for the year ending on March 31, 2009:*

Details	*Amount (₹)*
Opening Balances:	
Raw Materials	*6,00,000*
Work-in-Process	*2,40,000*
Finished Goods	*4,20,000*
Wages:	
Direct	*4,00,000*
Indirect	*50,000*
Sales	*16,50,000*
Purchase of Raw Materials	*5,40,000*
Carriage on purchase of raw materials	*20,000*
Factory Rent, Rates and Power	*1,25,000*
Depreciation of Plant and Machinery	*29,000*
Repairs of Machinery	*11,000*
Office Rent and Taxes	*50,000*
Advertising	*25,000*
Salesmen salaries and commission	*55,000*
Sale of scrap	*7,000*
Closing Balances:	
Raw Materials	*7,00,000*
Work-in-Process	*3,00,000*
Finished Goods	*2,20,000*

Solution : **Production Account**

(For the Quarter Ending on December 31, 2009)

Details	Dr Amount (₹)	Details	Cr Amount (₹)
Opening Stock of Materials	6,00,000	Prime Cost c/d	8,60,000
Purchases	5,40,000		
Carriage on Purchases	20,000		
Materials Available for use	11,60,000		
Less: Closing Stock of Materials	7,00,000		
Materials Used	4,60,000		

Direct Wages	4,00,000		
Total	8,60,000	Total	8,60,000
Prime Cost b/d	8,60,000	Factory Cost c/d	7,68,000
Factory Overheads: -			
Indirect Wages	50,000		
Factory Rent, Rates and Power	1,25,000		
Depreciation of Plant and Machinery	29,000		
Repairs of Machinery	11,000		
Add: Opening Work-in-Process	2,40,000		
Less: Closing Work-in-Process	(3,00,000)		
Sale of Scrap	(7,000)		
Total	7,68,000	Total	7,68,000
Factory Cost b/d	7,68,000	Cost of Production c/d	8,18,000
Office Rent and Taxes	50,000		
Total	8,18,000	Total	8,18,000
Cost of Production b/d	8,18,000	Cost of Goods Sold c/d	10,18,000
Opening Stock	4,20,000		
Finished Goods available for Sale	12,38,000		
Less: Closing Stock of Finished Goods	2,20,000		
Total	10,18,000	Total	10,18,000
Cost of Goods Sold b/d	10,18,000	Cost of Sales c/d	10,98,000
Advertising	25,000		
Salesmen Salaries and Commission	55,000		
Total	10,98,000	Total	10,98,000
Cost of Sales b/d	10,98,000	Sales	16,50,000
Profit	5,52,000		
Total	16,50,000	Total	16,50,000

Illustration 14.9 : *The details obtained from the records of M/s Bonnie Industries for the year 2008 are given below, from which you are required to prepare a cost sheet and a statement showing estimated cost for 1,000 units for the year 2009:*

Details	*Amount* (₹)
Opening Stock:	
Raw materials	*3,50,000*
Finished Goods	*50,000*
Purchases	*5,25,000*
Factory Wages	*9,50,000*
Factory Overheads	*1,75,000*
Office overheads	*1,00,000*
Closing Stock:	
Raw materials	*49,000*
Finished Goods	*4,00,000*
Sales	*19,44,000*

At the end of the year, the number of units produced was 5,000.

On the basis of the above, the firm intends to supply 1,000 units in the year 2009. It is estimated that the prices of raw materials and labour may rise by 12.5% and 20% respectively. Assume that the same percentage of profits on sales will be maintained.

Solution :

Statement of Cost and Profit
(Output: 5,000Units)

Details		**Amount** (₹)
Raw Materials:		
Opening Stock	3,50,000	
Add: Purchases	5,25,000	
	8,75,000	
Less: Closing Stock	(49,000)	8,26,000
Factory Wages		9,50,000
Prime Cost		17,76,000
Add: Factory Overheads		1,75,000
Factory Cost		19,51,000
Add: Office overheads		1,00,000
Cost of Production		20,51,000
Add: Opening Stock of Finished Goods		50,000
Goods Available for Sale		21,01,000
Less: Closing Stock of Finished Goods		4,00,000
Cost of Goods Sold		17,01,000
Profit (Balancing figure)		2,43,000
Sales		19,44,000

Statement of Quotation of Price
(For 1,000 units)

Details	Amount (₹)
Material Cost @ ₹ 185.85 per unit	1,85,850
Factory Wages @ ₹ 228 per unit	2,28,000
Prime cost	4,13,850
Factory overheads @ ₹ 35 per unit	35,000
Factory cost	4,48,850
Office overheads@ ₹ 20 per unit	20,000
Cost of Production i.e. Total cost	4,68,850
Profit @ 12.5% of Sales	66,980
Selling Price	5,35,830

Working Notes:

Cost of production per unit:

= 20, 51,000 ÷ 5,000 =>₹ 410.20

Percentage of Profit on Sales:

= (2, 43,000 ÷ 19, 44,000) × 100 =>12.5%

Estimated material cost per unit:

= (8, 26,000 × 1.125) ÷5,000 => ₹ 185.85

Estimated labour cost per unit:

= (9, 50,000 × 1.20) ÷ 5,000 => ₹ 228.

Illustration 14.10 : *The following data is available from the cost ledger of Konkan industries for the Year 2008:*

Details	*Amount (₹)*
Plant Maintenance	*1,20,000*
Lighting	*30,300*
Depreciation on Plant	*18,720*
Rates and Taxes for the Works	*39,000*
Staff Salaries	*1,53,600*
Management Salaries	*1,05,600*
Power (for this Plant)	*51,000*
Rental for Leasehold Equipments	*46,080*
Indirect Wages	*1,78,080*
Rectification cost of Defectives(Normal)	*40,500*
Consumable Stores	*85,500*
Selling Expenses	*1,44,000*
General charges	*75,000*
Sale proceeds from scrap	*21,000*

During the year total production was 1,50,000 units. The break –up of the prime cost per unit was: Materials: ₹ 16.50 and wages ₹ 13.50. The average Selling price was ₹ 44.00 per unit and the entire quantity produced during the years was sold out. With effect from January 1, 2009, the selling price was reduced by ₹ one per unit. It was envisaged that production could be enhanced during the year 2009 by 100/3% without incurring any overtime or extra-shift work, or additional selling expenses.

You are required to prepare statements showing:

(i) Actual cost for the year 2008;

(ii) Estimated cost and Profit for 2009 assuming that the entire production will be sold out during the year.

Assumptions, if any, required to be made in the above exercise should be clearly stated.

Solution : **Statement of Cost and Profit**

(For the Year 2008) Output: 1,50,000 units

Details	Per unit		Total	
	₹	₹	₹	₹
Materials		16.50		24,75,000
Wages		13.50		20,25,000
Prime Cost		30.00		45,00,000
Variable Factory charges:				
Power	0.34		51,000	
Rectification cost	0.27		40,500	
Consumable stores	0.57		85,500	
	1.18		1,77,000	
Less: Sale of Scrap	(0.14)	1.0400	(21,000)	
Fixed Factory charges:				
Indirect Wages	1.1872		1,78,080	
Plant Maintenance	0.8000		1,20,000	
Lighting	0.2020		30,300	
Depreciation of Plant	0.1248		18,720	
Rates and Taxes for works	0.2600		39,000	
Rental for Leasehold Equipments	0.3080		46,200	
		2.8820		
Total Factory Overheads		3.9220		5,88,300
Works Cost		33.9220		50,88,300

Office and Selling charges:				
Staff Salaries	1.0240		1,53,600	
Management Salaries	0.7040		1,05,600	
General Charges	0.5000		75,000	
		2.2280		
Selling Expenses		0.9600	1,44,000	
Total Office and Selling charges		3.1880		4,78,200
Cost of Sales		37.1100		55,66,500
Profit		6.8900		10,33,500
Sales		44.0000		66,00,000

Statement of Estimated Cost and Profit

(For the Year 2009) Output: 2,00,000 units

Details	Per unit		Total	
	₹	₹	₹	₹
Prime Cost @ ₹ 30per unit		30.0000		60,00,000
Variable Factory charges (Net) @ ₹ 1.0400		1.0400		2,08,000
Variable Cost		31.0400		62,08,000
Fixed Charges:				9,10,500
Works	2.1615		4,32,300	
Office	1.6710		3,34,200	
Selling	0.7200	4.5525	1,44,000	
Cost of Sales		35.5925		71,18,500
Profit		7.9075		14,81,500
Sales		43.0000		86,00,000

Illustration 14.11 : *The Managing Director of a small manufacturing concern consults you as to the minimum price at which he can sell the output of one of the departments of the company, which is intended for mass production in future. The Company's records show the following particulars for this department for the preceding year:*

Details	*Amount (₹)*
Production and Sale...(100 Units)	*40 ,000*
Materials	*13,000*
Direct Labour	*7,000*
Direct Charges	*2,000*
Production Overheads	*8,000*

Administrative Overheads	*2,800*
Selling Overheads	*3,200*
Profit	*4,000*

It is ascertained that 45% of the Production Overheads fluctuate directly with production and 60% of the Selling Overheads fluctuate with sales. It is anticipated that the department would produce 600 units per annum and that direct labour charges per unit will be reduced by 20%, while the fixed Production overheads will increase by ₹ 3,600. Administrative Overheads and fixed selling overheads are expected to show an increase of 25% but otherwise no changes are expected.

Solution : Working Notes:

Material cost per Unit: Material cost ÷ Number of units produced
= 13,000 ÷ 100 => ₹ 130

Direct Labour cost per Unit: Direct Labour cost ÷ Number of units produced
= 7,000 ÷ 100 => ₹ 70

Direct Labour cost per Unit (Expected): ₹ 70 ×0.8=> ₹ 56

Production overheads:

Variable per unit: [(8,000 × 0.45) ÷ (100) =>₹ 36.

Fixed: [8,000 – 3,600] = ₹ 4,400

Estimated Fixed Production Overheads: 4,400 + 3,600 => ₹ 8,000

Selling overheads:

Variable per unit: [(3,200 × 0.6) ÷ (100) =>₹ 19.20.

Fixed: [3,200 – 1,920] = ₹ 1,280.

Estimated Fixed Selling Overheads: [1,280 × 1.25] => ₹ 1,600.

Estimated Administrative Overheads: [2,800 × 1.25] => ₹ 3,500.

Profit: (4,000 ÷ 40,000) ×100= 10%

OR

Profit per unit: (4,000 ÷ 100) ×= ₹ 40

Statement of Quotation of Minimum Price
(For 600 units)

Details		Amount (₹)
Material Cost @ ₹ 130 per unit		78,000
Direct Labour cost @ ₹ 56 per unit		33,600
Prime cost		1,11,600
Production overheads:		
Fixed	4,400	
Variable @ ₹ 36 per unit	21,600	26,000

Factory cost		1,37,600
Administrative overheads		3,500
Cost of Production i.e. Total cost		1,41,100
Selling overheads:		
Fixed	1,600	
Variable @ ₹ 19.20 per unit	11,520	13,120
Total cost or Cost of sales		1,54,220
Profit @ 10% of Sales [(1,54,220)× (1/ 9)]		17,135
Sales**		1,71,355

·If Profit per unit is applied, the minimum price increases to ₹ 297.03 per unit.

** Selling Price per unit = Sales ÷ Number of units

= 1,71,355 ÷ 600=> ₹ 285.59

LET US RECAPITULATE

1. The term "Single or output costing" is used where exclusively one homogeneous product or a few grades of the same product are manufactured.
2. The unit cost of the product is obtained by dividing the total cost of production by the number of units manufactured.
3. The total cost of the product is ascertained in a cost sheet format.
4. The cost units may be expressed in terms of number, weight, volume and time.
5. It is a method applicable in case of industries where the products can be expressed in identical quantitative units and manufacturing is continuous.
6. It applies to paper, cement, sugar, steel, quarries, brickworks and breweries.
7. Cost sheet is a statement of various elements of cost.
8. The Production Account depicts Sales, Stocks, and Profit besides the Cost in a ledger account format.
9. The Production Account gives details of cost of production, cost of sales and profit made during a particular period.
10. An estimated cost sheet is prepared before the production is commenced.
11. The estimated cost sheet is subsequently compared with actual costs so that costs can be controlled.
12. The amount recovered from the sale of scrap is to be deducted either from the Manufacturing overheads or gross works cost.
13. Cost of rectification of normal defectives is charged to all good units including those rectified.
14. Raw materials consumed is equal to Opening inventory + Purchases of raw materials – Opening inventory.
15. Current manufacturing cost is the sum of Prime cost + Factory overheads.
16. Net Works Cost is equal to current manufacturing cost + Opening inventory of work-in-progress – Closing inventory of work-in-progress.
17. Cost of Goods Sold is equal to Cost of Production + Opening inventory of finished goods – Closing inventory of finished goods.

SOLVED PROBLEMS

Problem 1. *Delta Engineering Limited produces a uniform type of product and has a manufacturing capacity of 3,000 per week of 48 hours. From the cost records of the company, the following data are available relating to output and cost for three consecutive weeks:*

Week Number	*Units Manufactured*	*Direct Material (Amount ₹)*	*Direct Labour (Amount ₹)*	*Factory Overheads (Amount ₹)*
1	*1,500*	*18,000*	*6,000*	*60,000*
2	*2,000*	*24,000*	*8,000*	*70,000*
3	*2,250*	*27,000*	*9,000*	*75,000*

Assume that the company charges a profit of 25% on selling, find out the selling price per unit if the weekly output is 2,500 units.

Solution : It is necessary to segregate the factory overheads into Fixed and Variable and for this following working notes are necessary:

Week	Units Manufactured	Factory overheads (₹)
1	1,500	60,000
2	2,000	70,000
Difference	500	10,000

Variable Overheads per Unit = Difference in Cost ÷ Difference in units

Variable Overheads per Unit = 10,000 ÷ 500= ₹ 20.

Fixed Overheads:

Total Factory Overheads for 1,500 units= ₹ 60,000

Less: Variable Overheads (1,500×20) = ₹ 30,000

Total Fixed Factory Overheads= ₹30, 000

Alternatively

Total Factory Overheads for 2,000 units= ₹ 70,000

Less: Variable Overheads (2,000×20) = ₹ 40,000

Total Fixed Factory Overheads= ₹30, 000

Computation of Selling Price per unit at Production Level of 2,500 units per week

(Cost Sheet for 2,500 units)

Details	Total Cost Amount (₹)	Cost per Unit Amount (₹)
Direct Material: @ (18 000 ÷ 1 500)	30, 000	12
Direct Labour @ (6 000 ÷ 1 500)	10, 000	04

PRIME COST	40, 000	16
Variable Factory Overheads	50, 000	20
Fixed Factory Overheads	30, 000	12
Total Factory Overheads	80,000	32
Total Cost	120, 000	48
Add: Profit (1/4 of Selling Price or 1/3 of Total Cost)	40, 000	16
Sales	160, 000	64

Problem 2. *Kanpur Shoe Company manufactures two types of shoes M and B. Production costs for the year ended March 31, 2004 were as follows:*

Cost Element	*Amount (₹)*
Direct Material	*40,00,000*
Direct Wages	*28,00,000*
Production Overheads	*12,00,000*
Total	*80,00,000*

There was no work-in-progress at the beginning or at the end of the year. It is ascertained that:

(i) The cost of direct materials in type M shoes is twice as much as that in type B.

(ii) The direct wages for type B shoes were 60% of those type M shoes.

(iii) Production overhead was the same per pair of M and B type.

(iv) Administrative overhead for each type was 150% of direct wages.

(v) Selling cost was ₹ 4 per pair.

(vi) Production during the year:
Type M 50,000 pairs of which 40,000 were sold.
Type B 1, 50,000 pairs of which 1, 30,000 were sold.

(vii) Selling Price was ₹ 120 for type M and ₹ 90 for type B.

Prepare a statement showing cost and Profit.

Solution : Working Notes:

1. Direct material cost has been calculated as follows:

Assume

Direct material cost per pair for Type B = X

Therefore,

Direct material cost per pair for Type M = 2X

Thus,

Total direct Material cost for type B =1, 50,000 X

Total direct Material cost for type M =1, 00,000 X

Thus,

$$1,50,000\ X + 1,00,000\ X = 40,00,000$$
$$2,50,000\ X = 40,00,000$$
$$X = ₹\ 16 \text{ per pair}$$

Thus,

Direct material cost per pair for Type B = ₹ 16 per pair

Direct material cost per pair for Type M = ₹ 32 per pair

2. Direct Labour cost has been computed as under:

Assume

Direct Labour cost per pair for Type M = X

Therefore,

Direct Labour cost per pair for Type B = 0.6X

Thus,

Total direct Labour cost for type M = 50,000 X

Total direct Labour cost for type B = 90,000 X

Thus,

$$50,000\ X + 90,000\ X = 28,00,000$$
$$1,40,000\ X = 28,00,000$$
$$X = ₹\ 20 \text{ per pair}$$

Thus,

Direct Labour cost per pair for Type M = ₹ 20 per pair

Direct Labour cost per pair for Type B = ₹ 12 per pair

3. Production overhead per pair = 12, 00,000 ÷ 2,00,000

= ₹ 6 per pair

Statement of Cost and Profit

Details	Type M Units Produced (50,000) (₹)	Type B Units Produced (1,50,000) (₹)	Total (₹)
Sales [(40,000 × 120) ; (1,30,000 × 90)]	48,00,000	117,00,000	165,00,000
Cost of Goods Sold:			
Direct Material	8,00,000	48,00,000	56,00,000
Direct Wages	10,00,000	18,00,000	28,00,000
Prime cost	18,00,000	66,00,000	84,00,000
Add: Production Overheads	3,00,000	9,00,000	12,00,000
Works Cost	21,00,000	75,00,000	96,00,000

Add: Administrative Overhead	15,00,000	27,00,000	42,00,000
Cost of Production	36,00,000	102,00,000	138,00,000
Less: Closing stock of Finished Goods	7,20,000	13,60,000	20,80,000
COST OF GOODS SOLD	28,80,000	88,40,000	117,20,000
Add: Selling Overheads	1,60,000	5,20,000	6,80,000
COST OF SALES	30,40,000	93,60,000	124,00,000
PROFIT	17,60,000	23,40,000	41,00,000

Problem 3. *Cost of Sales of Product A is made up as under:-*

Details	***Amount (₹)***
Materials used in Manufacturing	*54,000*
Materials used in Primary Packing	*10,000*
Materials used in Selling the Product	*1,500*
Materials used in Factory	*750*
Materials used in Office	*1,250*
Labour required in Producing	*10,000*
Labour required for factory supervision	*2,000*
Direct expenses	*5,000*
Indirect expenses (Factory)	*1,000*
Administrative Expenses	*1,250*
Depreciation on Office Building and Equipment	*750*
Depreciation on Factory Building	*1,750*
Selling Expenses	*3,500*
Freight on Materials Purchased	*6,000*
Advertising	*1,250*

Assume that all goods manufactured are sold. What would be the selling price to obtain a profit of 20% on selling price?

Solution : Fixation of Selling Price of a Product

Details	**Amount (₹)**	**Amount (₹)**
Materials used in Manufacturing	54,000	
Materials used in Primary Packing	10,000	
Total Materials used	64,000	
Labour required in Producing	10,000	
Direct Expenses	5,000	
Prime cost		79,000

Factory Overheads:		
Materials Used in Factory	750	
Labour required for factory supervision	2 ,000	
Indirect Expenses	1,000	
Depreciation in Factory building	1,750	
Freight On Materials Purchased	6,000	
Total		11,500
Factory cost		90,500
Office Overheads:		
Materials used in office	1,250	
Administrative expenses	1,250	
Depreciation on office Building and Equipment	750	
Total		3,250
Cost of Production		93,750
Selling Overheads:		
Materials Used in selling	1,500	
Selling expenses	3,500	
Advertising	1,250	
Total		6,250
Cost of sales		1,00,000
Profit		25,000
Selling Price		1,25,000

Problem 4.

Details	*Amount (₹)*	*Details*	*Amount (₹)*
Direct Materials	*1,20,000*	*Direct wages*	*30,000*
Direct Expenses	*6,000*	*Wages of foremen*	*5,000*
Electric Power	*1,000*	*Store Keeper's wages*	*1,000*
Lighting:		*Rent:*	
Factory 2,000		*Factory 5,000*	
Office 500	*2,500*	*Office 3,000*	*8,000*
Oil and water	*500*	*Carriage outwards*	*500*
Repairs and Renewals:		*Depreciation:*	
Factory Plant 4,000		*Factory Plant 500*	
Office Premises 500	*4,500*	*Office Premises 1,500*	*2,000*
Transfer to Reserves	*1,000*	*Discount on issue of shares written off*	*500*
Consumable Stores	*2,000*	*Manager's salary*	*5,000*
Director's fees	*1,500*	*Office stationery*	*500*

Telephone charges	*500*	*Postage and telegrams*	*200*
Salesmen salary	*2,500*	*Salesmen traveling Expenses*	*300*
Advertising	*1,000*	*Warehouse Charges*	*500*
Income tax	*10,000*	*Dividend Paid*	*2,000*
		Sales	*2,30,000*

From the above information prepare Cost Sheet showing Prime Cost, Factory Cost, Cost of Production, Cost of Sales and Profit.

Solution :

Details	Amount (₹)	Amount (₹)
Direct Materials	1,20,000	
Direct Wages	30,000	
Direct Expenses	6,000	
Total	1,56,000	
Prime cost		1,56,000
Factory Overheads:		
Store keeper's Wages	1,000	
Lighting	2,000	
Oil and water	500	
Repairs	4,000	
Foremen wages	5,000	
Rent	5,000	
Depreciation	1,500	
Consumable stores	2,000	
Total Factory Overheads	21,000	21,000
Factory Cost		1,77,000
Administrative Overheads:		
Lighting	500	
Repairs	500	
Directors' fees	1,500	
Telephone charges	500	
Postage and Telegram	200	
Electric Power	1,000	
Rent	3,000	
Depreciation	1,500	
Manager's Salary	5,000	
Stationery	500	
Total Administrative overheads	14,200	14,200
Cost of Production		1,91,200

Selling and Distribution Overheads:		
Salesmen salary	2,500	
Advertising	1,000	
Carriage outwards	500	
Salesman Travelling expenses	300	
Warehouse Charges	500	
Total Selling and Distribution Overheads	4,800	4,800
Cost of Sales		1,95,000
Profit		35,000
Sales		2,30,000

Problem 5. *A work order for 600 units of a commodity has to pass through four different machines of which the machines hour rates are:-*

	₹
No. I	*5*
No. II	*12*
No. III	*16*
No. IV	*10*

The following expenses have been incurred on the work order. Materials ₹ 32,000 and wages ₹ 9,000.

Machine	*I*	*worked for*	*50 hours*
Machine	*II*	*Worked for*	*75 hours*
Machine	*III*	*Worked for*	*60 hours*
Machine	*IV*	*Worked for*	*25 hours*

After the work order had been executed, materials worth ₹ 1,000 were returned to stores.

Office overheads are to be estimated @ 75% of works cost: 10% of the production is going to be discarded, being unsatisfactory for which 60% of the amount can be realised from sale in the junk market. Find out the selling price per unit if 20% profit on selling price is desired.

Solution : Statement Showing Cost and Selling Price for 600 Units

Material used	32,000		
Less: Returns	(1,000)		31,000
Wages			9,000
Prime Cost			40,000
Work Overhead: Hours × Rate			
Machine No. I 50 × 5		250	
Machine No. II 75 × 12		900	
Machine No. III 60 × 16		960	
Machine No. IV 25 × 10		250	2,360

Work Cost			42,360
Office Overheads:			
75% of works cost (42,360 × 0.75)			31,770
Cost of production			74,130
Less: Sale of discarded units			
10% discarded	7,413		
60% to be realized	(4,448)		
Loss	2,965		(2,965)
Adjusted Cost of Production			71,165
Profit 20% on selling price or 25% on cost			17,791
Sales			88,956

Selling price per unit = Total Sales value ÷ No. of units of the work order

= 88,956 ÷ 600 = 148.26 (approx.)

Note: 600 units of the work order is the final output that is after the discarded units have been adjusted for.

Problem 6. *A small manufacturing unit sold its output in 2006-2007 for ₹15,000 at ₹12 per unit. The total fixed charges of the establishment amounted to ₹2, 000 per annum and the variable cost per unit of production was ₹8.*

The management wants to reduce the selling price to ₹ 10.50 per unit and to maintain the same amount of profit as before. How many more units should be produced and sold to give effect to this decision?

Solution :

Number of units produced = Total sales value / Selling price of one unit

= ₹15, 000 ÷ 12 = 1,250 units

Cost of Production = Fixed charges + variable cost

= 2 000 + (8 × 1,250)

= ₹12,000

Profit = ₹15, 000 – ₹ 12, 000 = ₹ 3, 000

Suppose increased output is P

The cost of producing P units will be = Fixed charges + variable cost

= 2, 000 + (8 P)

Sale Proceeds = ₹10.5 P

Sales Price – Cost price = Profit

10.5 P – (2,000 + 8P) = 3,000

10.5 P – 8 P = 5,000

2.5 P = 5,000

P = 5,000/2.5

P = 2,000 units

Additional Units
= Number of units required to be Sold – Present Number of units Sold
= 2,000 – 1,250 = 750 units.

Decision: The increased output is, therefore, 2,000 units. Thus, to earn the same amount of profit of ₹3, 000 at the selling price of ₹10.50 per unit, 750 more units of P should be produced.

Problem 7. *Following costs were incurred in producing 1,200 M.T. of M.S. rods:*

Details	***Amount (₹)***
Materials	*5,25,000*
Labour	*1,87,500*
Processing charges	*1,87,500*
Total cost	*9,00,000*

Of the total output, 12.5 % was defective and had to be sold after a discount of 10 % of the normal price. The scrap arising out of the production realized a sum of ₹13, 620. The sale price is calculated to yield 15% profit on sales. You are required to find out the normal price as well as the discounted price of M.T. of M.S. rods.

Solution : **Cost of production of M.S. rods**

Details	**Amount (₹)**
Materials	5,25,000
Labour	1,87,500
Processing charges	1,87,500
Total cost	9,00,000
Less: sale value of scrap material	13,620
Net cost of production	8,86,380
Profit @ 15% of sales i.e. 15/85 of cost (OR 3/17) [8,86,380 × 3/17]	1,56,420
Sales	10,42,800
Equivalent unit of sales:	
Total production (MT)	1,200
Less: Defective @ 12.5%	150
Good production (MT)	1,050
Add: equivalent of defective production @ 90 % of 150	135
Equivalent good production (MT)	1,185

Price of good production = ₹10,42,800 ÷ 1,185 = ₹ 880

Discounted price of defective production @ 10% discount is ₹792.

Problem 8. *SV Works can produce 75,000 units per year at its optimum (100%) capacity. The estimated costs of production are as under:*

Direct material *₹ 12 per unit*
Direct labour *₹ 8 per unit*
Indirect Expenses(Factory):
Fixed *₹ 8,40,000 per year*
Variable *₹ 20 per unit*
Semi-Variable *₹ 84,000 per year up to 50% capacity and an extra expenses of ₹ 21,000 for every 20% increase in capacity or part thereof.*

The factory produced only against orders and not for own stock. If the production programme of the factory is as indicated below, and the management desires to ensure a profit of ₹ 5,37,600 for the year, work out the average selling price at which each unit should be quoted:

First Four months of the year *50% of capacity*
Remaining Eight months *80% of capacity*

Assume that Selling & distribution and Administration overheads are estimated to be 20% of the works cost.

Solution : Working Notes:

Output:

First Four months at 50% of capacity:

= 75,000 × 0.5 × 4/12 => 12,500 units

Next Eight months at 80% of capacity:

= 75,000 × 0.8 × 8/12 => 40,000 units

Total units produced:

=12,500 + 40,000=>52,500 units

Statement of Production (Output: 52,500 units)

Details			Amount (₹)
Direct materials (52,500 units @ ₹ 12 per unit)			6,30,000
Direct Wages (52,500 units @ ₹ 8 per unit)			4,20,000
Prime Cost			10,50,000
Add: Manufacturing overheads			
Fixed		8,40,000	
Variable (52,500 units @ ₹ 20 per unit)		10,50,000	
Semi-Variable:			
First Four months at 50% of capacity			
={(84,000) × (4/12)}	28,000		
Next Eight months at 80% of capacity			
={(1,26,000) × (8/12)}	84,000		
(i.e. 28,000 + 84,000)		1,12,000	20,02,000

Cost of Production	30,52,000
Add: Selling & distribution and Administration overheads (30,52,000 × 0.2)	6,10,400
Cost of Sales	36,62,400
Profit (desired)	5,37,600
Estimated sales revenue for 52,500 units: 42,00,000	42,00,000
Selling price per unit: 42,00,000 ÷ 52,500 = ₹ 80.	

Problem 9. *The following inventory data relate to XYZ Limited:*

Details	*Inventory*	
	Opening (₹)	*Closing (₹)*
Finished goods	*1,10,000*	*95,000*
Work-in-Progress	*70,000*	*80,000*
Raw Materials	*90,000*	*95,000*

Additional Information:

Details	*Amount (₹)*
Cost of goods available for Sale	*6,84,000*
Total goods processed during the year	*6,54,000*
Factory Overheads	*1,67,000*
Direct materials Used	*1,93,000*

Requirements:

(i) Determine raw materials purchased;

(ii) Determine the direct labour cost incurred;

(iii) Determine the cost of goods sold. **[B.Com (Hons.), DU]**

Solution : Working Notes:

Direct Material Used

= Opening Stock of raw materials + Raw material Purchases – Closing Stock of raw materials

Raw material Purchased

= Direct Material Used + Closing stock of raw materials – Opening Stock of raw materials

= 1,93,000 + 95,000 – 90,000 => ₹ 1,98,000

Cost of Goods Produced

= Opening Work-in-Progress + Current Cost of goods manufactured – Closing Work-in-Progress

OR

Current Cost of Goods manufactured

= Total Goods Processed in the Current period – Opening Work-in-Progress = 6,54,000 – 70,000 => ₹ 5,84,000.

Cost of Goods available for Sale

= Opening Stock of Finished Goods + Cost of Goods Produced

Cost of Goods Produced

= Cost of Goods available for Sale – Opening Stock of Finished Goods

= 6,84,000 –1,10,000=> 5,74,000.

Cost o f Goods sold

= Cost of Goods available for Sale – Closing Stock of Finished Goods

= 6,84,000 – 95,000=> ₹ 5,89,000.

Prime Cost = Current Cost of Goods manufactured – Factory Overhead

= 5,84,000 –1,67,000=> ₹ 4,17,000.

Direct Labour cost = Prime Cost – Direct Material Used

= 4,17,000 – 1,93,000 =>₹ 2,24,000.

Statement of Cost

Details	**Amount (₹)**
Opening Stock of Raw materials	90,000
Add: Purchase of Raw materials	1,98,000
Raw Materials Available for Use	2,88,000
Less: Closing Stock of Raw materials	(95,000)
Direct Materials Used	1,93,000
Direct Wages	2,24,000
Prime Cost	4,17,000
Add: Factory overheads	1,67,000
Current Cost of Goods manufactured	5,84,000
Add: Opening Stock of work-in-Progress	70,000
Goods Processed during the period	6,54,000
Less: Closing Stock of work-in-Progress	80,000
Cost of Goods Manufactured	5,74,000
Add: Opening Stock of Finished Goods	1,10,000
Cost of Goods available for Sale	6,84,000
Less: Closing Stock of Finished Goods	95,000
Cost of Goods sold	5,89,000

Problem 10. *Following details are available about a standard company for the year 2008:*

Item of Expense	*Amount* (₹)
Cost of materials	*15,00,000*
Wages	*12,50,000*
Factory overheads	*7,50,000*
Administration Overheads	*8,40,000*
Selling overheads	*5,60,000*
Distribution overheads	*3,50,000*
Profit	*10,50,000*

A work order No. 901 is to be executed in the first quarter of the next year and the estimated expenses are:

Materials ₹ 40,000, wages ₹ 25,000

Assuming that next year the rate of factory overheads are likely to be 20% more, distribution overheads decrease by 10% and the selling and administration overheads will increase by 15%, at what price should the product be charged so as to earn the same rate of profit as in the current year.

Factory overheads are based on wages and administration, selling and distribution overheads on works cost. **[B.com (H) Calcutta, Banglore (Modified)]**

Solution : Working Notes:

Basic Ratios:

Factory overheads:

= (Factory overheads ÷ Wages) ×100

= (7,50,000 ÷ 12,50,000) ×100 => 60%.

Administration overheads:

= (Administration overheads ÷ Factory cost) ×100

= (8,40,000 ÷ 35,00,000) ×100 => 24%.

Selling overheads:

= (Selling overheads ÷ Factory cost) ×100

= (5,60,000 ÷ 35,00,000) ×100 = >16%.

Distribution overheads:

= (Distribution overheads ÷ Factory cost) ×100

= (3,50,000 ÷ 35,00,000) ×100 => 10%.

Profit overheads:

= (Profit ÷ Total Cost) ×100

= (10,50,000 ÷ 12,50,000) ×100 => 20%.

Statement of Cost
(For the current year 2008)

Details	Amount (₹)
Direct materials	15,00,000
Direct Wages	12,50,000
Prime Cost	27,50,000
Add: Manufacturing overheads: (60% of Direct Wages) i.e. (0.60 ×12,50,000)	7,50,000
Factory (Works) Cost	35,00,000
Add: Administration overheads: (24% of Factory Cost) i.e. (0.24 ×35,00,000)	8,40,000
Cost of Production	43,40,000
Add: Selling overheads: (16% of Factory Cost) i.e. (0.16 ×35,00,000)	5,60,000
Add: Distribution overheads: (10% of Factory Cost) i.e. (0.10 ×35,00,000)	3,50,000
Total cost or Cost of Sales	52,50,000
Profit: (20% of Total Cost) i.e. (0.20 ×52,50,000)	10,50,000
Sales	63,00,000

Statement of Estimated Cost and Profit
(For the Work Order No. 901 in the Year 2009)

Details	Amount (₹)
Direct materials	40,000
Direct Wages	25,000
Prime Cost	65,000
Add: Manufacturing overheads: {60 (1.2) = 72} (72% of Direct Wages) i.e. (0.72× 25,000)	18,000
Factory (Works) Cost	83,000
Add: Administration overheads: {24 (1.15) = 27.6} (27.6% of factory cost) i.e. (0.276 × 83,000)	22,908
Cost of Production	1,05,908
Add: Selling overheads: {16 (1.15) = 18.4} (18.4% of factory cost) i.e. (0.184 × 83,000)	15,272

Add: Distribution overheads: {10 (0.9) = 9.00} (9% of factory cost) i.e. (0.09 × 83,000)	7,470
Total cost or Cost of Sales	1,28,650
Profit (20% on Total Cost) i.e.(0.2 ×1,28,650)	25,730
Sales	1,54,380

Problem 11. *Find out the selling price of an article whose costs for production and sale of 12,500 units are:*

Material ₹ 51,200; Labour ₹ 40,000; overheads ₹ 1,60,000.

The fixed portion of capital employed is ₹ 80,000 and the varying portion is 40% of sales turnover. A profit of 9% on net capital employed after payment of tax @ 40% of the earnings is desired. **[I.C.W.A. (Inter)]**

Solution : Let Selling Price be ₹ 'X' per unit

Cost of Sales = Material + Labour + overheads

= 51,200 + 40,000 + 1,60,000 => ₹ 2,51,200

Desired Earnings after tax = 9% on net capital employed after charging tax @ 40% tax.

Thus,

Desired Earnings Before tax =15% [i.e. 0.09/0.6] on net capital employed

Total Sales = Cost of Sales + Profit

12,500X = Cost of Sales + 0.15 of capital employed

12,500X = 2,51,200 + 0.15 (80,000 + (0.4(12,500X)))

12,500X = 2,51,200 + 12,000 + 750X

11,750X = 2,63,200

X = 2,63,200/ 11,750=> ₹22.40

Problem 12. *The expenses of a Machine Cost Centre for a particular month are as under:*

(i) Power	*₹ 80,000*
(ii) Repairs and maintenance	*₹ 32,000*
(iii) Machine operator's Wages	*₹ 16,000*
(iv) Supervision	*₹ 40,000*
(v) Depreciation	*₹ 72,000*

Other Particulars are as under:

Product	*Rate of Production*	*Production (units)*
P-1	*40 units per hour*	*2,000*
P-2	*20 units per hour*	*800*
P-3	*12 units per hour*	*600*
P-4	*8 units per hour*	*480*

The entire production is to be offered to government on cost plus 30% basis. Material costs per unit are: P-1 ₹ 50; P-2 ₹ 80; P-3 ₹ 130; P-4 ₹ 400. Prepare a statement showing Product-wise cost and Offer price.

Solution : Statement of cost of a Machine Cost Centre for a Month

Details	Amount (₹)
Power	80,000
Repairs and maintenance	32,000
Machine operator's Wages	16,000
Supervision	40,000
Depreciation	72,000
Total	2,40,000

Statement of Product-wise cost for the Month

Product	Output (units)	Output per hour	Effective Machine Hours	Total Allocated overheads @ 1,200 (₹)	Allocated overheads (per Unit) (₹)	Material cost per Unit (₹)	Total Cost (₹)
P-1	2,000	40	50	60,000	30	50	80
P-2	800	20	40	48,000	60	80	140
P3	600	12	50	60,000	100	130	230
P-4	480	8	60	72,000	150	400	550

Statement of Product-wise Offer Price

Product	Cost per unit (₹)	Profit @ 30% of cost (₹)	Offer Price (₹)
P-1	80	24	104
P-2	140	42	182
P-3	230	69	299
P-4	550	165	715

Problem 13. *The Tirupati Electrical Ltd. manufactures one product. A summary of its activities for 2007 is as follows:*

Details	*Quantity (Kg)*	*Amount (₹)*
Sales	*2,00,000*	*200,00,000*
Materials Inventory:		
1.1.2007		*10,00,000*
31.12.2007		*8,00,000*

Work-in-Progress Inventory:		
1.1.2007		*13,75,000*
31.12.2007		*18,00,000*
Finished Goods Inventory:		
1.1.2007	*40,000*	*16,00,000*
31.12.2007	*60,000*	——
Materials Purchases		*38,00,000*
Direct Wages		*36,25,000*
Manufacturing overheads		*27,00,000*
Selling Expenses		*12,50,000*
General and Administration Expenses		*10,00,000*

Calculate:

1. *The current manufacturing cost for the year 2007.*
2. *The total cost of goods manufactured (finished), the number of units manufactured (finished) and the cost per unit.*
3. *The cost of goods sold for the year presuming the company uses the LIFO inventory costing method for its finished goods inventory.*

Solution :

Details		**Amount (₹)**
Direct materials consumed:		
Opening Stock	10,00,000	
Add: Purchases	38,00,000	
Direct materials Available for consumption	48,00,000	
Less: Closing Stock	(8,00,000)	40,00,000
Direct Wages		36,25,000
Prime Cost		76,25,000
Add: Manufacturing overheads		27,00,000
Current Manufacturing Cost		103,25,000
Add: Opening Work-in-Progress		13,75,000
		117,00,000
Less: Closing Work-in-Progress		(18,00,000)
Cost of Goods Manufactured		99,00,000

Cost of Goods Sold (LIFO Basis)

Details	**Unit**	**Amount (₹)**
Opening Stock of Finished Goods	40,000	16,00,000
Add: Cost of Goods Manufactured	2,20,000	99,00,000
Cost of Goods Available for Sale	2,60,000	115,00,000

Less: Closing Stock of Finished Goods [(40,000×40) + (20,000 ×45)]	(60,000)	25,00,000
Cost of Goods Sold	2,00,000	90,00,000

Statement of Profit

Details	Unit	Amount (₹)
Cost of Goods Sold	2,00,000	90,00,000
Add: General and Administration Expenses		10,00,000
Add: Selling Expenses		12,50,000
Cost of Sales		1,12,50,000
Profit(Balancing figure)		87,50,000
Sales		200,00,000

Working Notes:

Units Manufactured:

= (Finished Goods sold + Closing Stock of Finished Goods) – (Opening Stock of Finished Goods)

= (2,00,000 + 60,000) – (40,000) = 2,20,000.

Problem 14. (Missing Items)

A firm has purchased a plant to manufacture a new product, the cost details for which are given below:

Estimated Annual sales	*30,000 units*
Estimated costs:	
Material	*₹ 50 per unit*
Direct labour	*₹ 20 per unit*
Overheads (factory)	*₹ 3,00,450 per year*
Administrative expenses	*₹ 2,80,800 per year*
Selling expenses	*12.5 % of Sales*

Calculate the selling price if profit per unit is ₹ 20.

Solution : **Statement of Cost and Profit**

Details	Amount (₹)
Material (30,000 × 50)	15,00,000
Direct labour (30,000 × 20)	6,00,000
Factory Overheads	3,00,450
Administrative expenses	2,80,800
Cost of Goods Produced	26,81,250
Selling expenses	4,68,750

Cost of Sales	31,50,000
Profit	6,00,000
Sales	37,50,000

Working Notes:

Profit = ₹6,00,000 [30,000 × 20]

Selling expenses are 12.5 % of Sales

Hence,

Total Cost of sales = 26,81,250 + 12.5 % of Sales

Let total Sales be 'S'

S = Total Cost of sales + Profit

S = 26,81,250+ 0.125S + 6,00,000

0.875 S = 32,81,250

S = (32,81,250/0.875) => ₹ 37,50,000

Selling Price per unit = Total Sales Value / number of unit Produced and Sold

= 37,50,000 ÷ 30,000 => ₹ 125.

Problem 15. *Following details have been obtained from the cost records of Siema Paints limited:*

Item	*Opening Amount (₹)*	*Closing Amount (₹)*
Raw Materials	*3,75,000*	*4,58,000*
Work-in-Progress	*1,40,000*	*1,75,000*
Finished goods	*2,70,000*	*1,55,000*
Other Items	***Amount (₹)***	
Direct Wages	*2,62,500*	
Sales	*10,80,000*	
Indirect wages	*15,000*	
Purchase of Raw Materials	*3,50,000*	
Traveler's wages and commission	*35,000*	
Office rent and Taxes	*14,000*	
Factory rent, Rates and Power	*80,000*	
Depreciation of Plant and Machinery	*21,000*	
Expenses on Purchases	*8,000*	
Carriage outwards	*15,000*	
Advertising	*20,000*	

Prepare a Production account giving the maximum possible break-up of costs and profit.

Solution : Production Account for the year ended on ......

Details	Debit Amount (₹)	Details	Credit Amount (₹)
To Opening stock of Raw Materials 3,75,000 *Add:* Purchases 3,50,000 7,25,000 *Less:* closing Stock of Materials 4,58,000 Raw Materials Consumed	2,67,000	By Prime Cost c/d	5,37,500
To Direct wages	2,62,500		
To Expenses on Purchases	8,000		
Total	5,37,500	Total	5,37,500
To Prime Cost b/d	5,37,500	By Works cost (Net)c/d	6,18,500
To Indirect Wages	15,000		
To Factory Rent ,Rates and Power	80,000		
To depreciation on Plant and Machinery	21,000		
Gross Factory cost	6,53,500		
Add: Opening work-in-Progress	1,40,000		
Less: Closing work-in-Progress	1,75,000		
Total	6,18,500	Total	6,18,500
To Works cost (Net) b/d	6,18,500	By Cost of Production c/d	6,32,500
To Office rent and Taxes	14,000		
Total	6,32,500	Total	6,32,500
To Cost of Production	6,32,500	By Cost of Goods Sold c/d	7,47,500
Add: Opening stock of finished goods	2,70,000		
Goods available for Sale	9,02,500		
Less: closing stock of finished goods	1,55,000		
Total	7,47,500	Total	7,47,500
To Cost of Goods Sold b/d	7,47,500		

Add: Selling and distribution expenses: Carriage Outward 15,000 Advertising 20,000 Traveler's wages and commission 35,000 Total Selling and distribution Overheads	70,000	By Cost of Sales c/d	8,17,500
Total	8,17,500	Total	8,17,500
To Cost of Sales b/d To Profit (B. figure)	8,17,500 2,62,500	By Sales	10,80,000
Total	10,80,000	Total	10,80,000

Problem 16. *A company is manufacturing building bricks and fire bricks. Both the products require two processes: brick forming and heat treating.*

Time required for the two types of bricks are:

	Building bricks	*Fire bricks*
Forming per 100 bricks	*3 Hours*	*2 Hours*
Heat treatment per 100 bricks	*2 Hours*	*5 Hours*

Budgeted total cost of the two departments in one month is:

Forming ₹ *21,200*

Heat treatment ₹ *48,800*

Budgeted production during the month is:

Building bricks (No): 1,30,000 *Fire bricks (No): 70,000*

Prepare a statement of manufacturing costs for the two varieties of bricks.

Solution : Working Note:

Statement showing the computation of Time in Hours and Rate per Hour

Details	Building Bricks	Fire Bricks	Total Time	Total cost(₹)	Rate per hour (₹)
A. Total production (Number)	1,30,000	70,000			
B. Forming time per 100 (Hours)	3	2			
C. Total Forming time (Hours) [(A × B) ÷100]	3,900	1,400	5,300	21,200	4
D. Heating Time per 100 (Hours)	2	5			
E. Total Heating time (Hours) [(A × D) ÷100]	2,600	3,500	6,100	48,800	8

Statement of Manufacturing Cost (For Two varieties of Bricks)

Process	Building Bricks for 1,30,000 in Number				Fire Bricks for 70,000 in Number			
	Total Time (Hours)	Rate per Hour (₹)	Total Cost (₹)	Cost per 100 in Number (₹)	Total Time (Hours)	Rate per Hour (₹)	Total Cost (₹)	Cost per 100 in Number (₹)
Brick-Forming	3,900	4	15,600	12	1,400	4	5,600	8
Heat Treating	2,600	8	20,800	16	3,500	8	28,000	40
Total	6,500		36,400	28	4,900		33,600	48

Problem 17. *Following details have been obtained from the cost records of Siema Chemical Works:*

Details	*Quantity (Kg)*	*Amount (₹)*
Stock on April1, 2007:		
Raw materials	*5,000*	*40,000*
Finished mixture	*1,250*	*35,000*
Factory Stores		*1,45,000*
Purchases:		
Raw materials	*4,00,000*	*36,00,000*
Factory Stores		*4,85,000*
Sales:		
Finished Mixture	*3,82,625*	*183,60,000*
Factory scrap		*1,63,400*
Factory Wages		*35,73,000*
Power		*4,08,000*
Depreciation of Machinery		*5,60,000*
Salaries:		
Factory		*14,44,400*
Office		*7,44,400*
Selling		*8,30,000*
Expenses:		
Direct		*4,12,600*
Office		*3,64,000*
Selling		*3,60,000*
Stock on March 31,2008:		
Raw materials	*3,000*	
Finished mixture	*1,125*	
Factory Stores		*1,11,000*

The stock of finished mixture at the end of March, 2008 is to be valued at the factory cost of the mixture for the year. The purchase price of raw materials remained unchanged throughout the year 2007-08.

Prepare a statement giving the maximum possible information about cost and its break-up for the year 2007-08.

Solution :

Details			Amount (₹)
	(Units)		
Opening Stock of Raw Materials	5,000		40,000
Add: purchases	4,00,000		36,00,000
Material Available for production	4,05,000		36,40,000
Less: Closing stock	(3,000)		(27,000)
Material Consumed	4,02,000		36,13,000
Factory Wages			35,73,000
Direct Expenses			4,12,600
Prime Cost			75,98,600
Factory Overheads:			
Factory Stores consumed (1,45,000 + 4,85,000 – 1,11,000)		5,19,000	
Power		4,08,000	
Depreciation of Machinery		5,60,000	
Factory Salaries		14,44,400	29,31,400
Less: Factory scrap sold		(19,500 Units)	(1,63,400)
Factory cost (3,82,500 units)= (4,02,000 – 19,500)			103,66,600
Office Overheads:			11,08,400
Office Salaries	7,44,400		
Office Expenses	3,64,000		
Cost of Production	(3,82,500 units)		114,75,000
Add: Opening stock of Finished Mixture	(1,250 units)		35,000
Goods Available for Sale	(3,83,750 units)		115,10,000
Less: Closing stock of Finished Mixture	(1,125 units)		(33,750)
Cost of Goods Sold	(3,82,625 units)		114,76,250
Selling and distribution Overheads:			
Salaries	8,30,000		
Selling Expenses	3,60,000		11,90,000
Cost of Sales			126,66,250
Profit (Balancing Figure)			56,93,750
Sales (3,82,625 units)			183,60,000

Working Notes:

1. Value of Closing stock of raw materials:

= [(36, 00,000 ÷ 4, 00,000) × 3,000] =>₹27, 000.

OR

= [3,000 @ ₹ 9 per unit]

2. Value of Closing stock of Finished Mixture:

= [(114,75,000 ÷ 3, 82,500) × 1,125] =>₹33, 750.

OR

= [1,125@ ₹ 30 per unit]

3. Goods Produced = [(Sold + Closing stock) – (Opening stock)

= [(3,82,625 + 1,125) – (1,250)=> 3,82,500.

4. Factory Scrap Units: Material Consumed – Goods Produced

= 4, 02,000 – 3,82,500=>19,500.

Problem 18. *The cost structure of an article, the selling price of which is ₹ 45,000 is as follows:*

Direct Materials: 50%; Direct labour: 20%; and overheads: 30%.

An increase of 15% in the cost of materials and of 25% in the cost of labour is anticipated. These increased costs in relation to the present selling price would cause 25% decrease in the amount of present profit per article.

You are required to: (i) prepare a statement of profit per article at present, and (ii) the revised selling price to produce the same percentage of profit on sales as before.

Solution : Let total cost = X and profit = Y

Therefore, X + Y = ₹ 45,000 ...(i)

Details	Present cost (i)	Increase (ii)	Anticipated cost (i) + (ii) = (iii)
Direct materials	0.5x	(.15× .5x) = 0.075x	0.575x
Direct labour	0.2x	(.25× .2x) = 0.050x	0.250x
Overheads	0.3x	-	0.300x
Total cost	X	0.125x	1.125x

Due to increase in the cost, the existing profit is reduced by 25%

Sales – Anticipated cost = existing profit – 25% of existing profit

= Y – 0.25Y = 0.75Y

45,000 – 1.125 X = 0.75 Y

–1.1 25 X – 0.75 Y = –45,000

1.125 X + 0.75 Y = 45,000 ...(ii)

By solving equation No. (i) and (ii)

X = ₹30,000; and Y = ₹15,000

Thus old total cost is ₹30,000 and existing profit is ₹ 15,000

Statement of present cost

Materials	50% of ₹30,000	=	15,000		
Labour	20% of ₹30,000	=	6,000		
Overheads	30% of ₹30,000	=	9,000		
	Total cost (x)			=	30,000
	Profit (y)			=	15,000
	Selling price			=	45,000

Thus existing profit is (15,000 ÷45,000) × 100 = 100/3 % of Sales; or (15,000 / 30,000) × 100 = 50% of Cost.

Computation of Revised Selling Price

Details	**Amount (₹)**
Revised total cost (30000 × 1.125)	33,750
Revised profit (100/3 % of sales or 50% of cost)	
= 33,750 × 50%	16,875
Revised Selling Price	50,625

Verification: Increase in Selling price = Revised Selling Price – Existing Selling Price = 50,625– 45,000 =>₹ 5,625 which is 0.125 Of the existing Selling Price [i.e. (5,625÷45,000)]

Problem 19. *A Company makes two distinct types of vehicles, V-1, and V-2. The total expenses during a period as shown by the books for the assembly of 800 of the type V-1 and 1,200 of the type V-2 are as under:*

Item of Expenses	***Amount (₹)***
Materials	*4,20,000*
Direct Wages	*39,000*
Stores Overheads	*52,500*
Running expenses of the machines	*12,000*
Depreciation	*8,000*
Labour amenities	*7,800*
Works general overhead	*1,36,500*
Administration and Selling Overhead	*67,580*

The other data available is:

	V-1: V-2
Material cost Ratio per unit	*3:5*
Direct labour Ratio per unit	*2:3*
Machine utilization Ratio per unit	*1:2*

Solution : Working Notes:

A. Material cost has been apportioned on the basis of cost ratio per unit multiplied by the units produced:

V-1: V-2

(800 × 3): (1,200 × 5)

2,400: 6,000

2:5

B. Direct Wages have been apportioned on the basis of cost ratio per unit multiplied by the units produced:

V-1: V-2

(800 × 2): (1,200 × 3)

1,600: 3,600

4:9

C. Stores Overheads have been apportioned on the basis of Material cost:

$(52{,}500 \div 4{,}20{,}000) \times 100 = 12.5\%$

D. Running expenses and Depreciation have been apportioned on the basis of Machine utilization Ratio multiplied by the units produced:

V-1: V-2

(800 ×1): (1,200 × 2)

800: 2,400

1:3

E. Works overhead and labour amenities have been apportioned as a percentage of Wages as under:

Works overhead: $(1{,}36{,}500 \div 39{,}000) \times 100 = 350\ \%$

labour amenities: $(7{,}800 \div 39{,}000) \times 100 = 20\ \%$

F. Administration overhead have been apportioned as a percentage of Works Cost as under:

$(67{,}580 \div 6{,}75{,}800) \times 100 = 10\%$

Cost Statement for the period...........

Details	Total (₹)	Vehicle V-1 (800 Units) (₹)	Vehicle V-2 (1,200 units) (₹)
Materials	4,20,000	1,20,000	3,00,000
Direct Wages	39,000	12,000	27,000
Prime cost	4,59,000	1,32,000	3,27,000
Works overhead:	52,500	15,000	37,500
Stores Overheads	12,000	3,000	9,000
Running expenses of machines	8,000	2,000	6,000
Depreciation	7,800	2,400	5,400
labour amenities	1,36,500	42,000	94,500
Works general overhead			
Works cost	6,75,800	1,96,400	4,79,400

Administration and Selling overhead	67,580	19,640	47,940
Total Cost	7,43,380	2,16,040	5,27,340
Cost per unit		270.05	439.45

Problem 20. *On September 30, 2008, a flash flood damaged the warehouse and factory of PV limited completely destroying the work-in-progress inventory. There was no damage to either the raw materials or finished goods inventories. A physical verification taken after the flood revealed the following valuations:*

Inventory	***Amount (₹)***
Raw materials	*2,10,000*
Work-in-progress	*N I L*
Finished goods	*2,40,000*

On April 1, 2008, the inventories consisted of the followings:

Inventory	***Amount (₹)***
Raw materials	*1,30,000*
Work-in-progress	*2,50,000*
Finished goods	*3,70,000*
Total	*7,50,000*

A review of the books and records disclosed that the gross profit margin historically approximated 20% of sales. The sales for the first six months of 2008 were ₹ 15,60,000.

Raw Material purchases were ₹ 6,15,000. Direct labour costs for this period were ₹ 4,35,000 and manufacturing overheads has historically been 40% of direct labour.

Compute the cost of work-in-progress inventory lost on September 30, 2008 by preparing a statement of cost and profit. Show complete working.

Solution :

Account (Estimated) for half year ending on September 30, 2008

Details	Amount (₹)	Details	Amount (₹)
Opening Stock: Raw materials 1,30,000 Work-in-Progress 2,50,000 Finished goods 3,70,000	7,50,000	Sales	15,60,000
Raw Materials Purchased	6,15,000	Closing Stock: Raw materials 2,10,000 Work-in-Progress (Balancing figure) 2,76,000 Finished goods 2,40,000	7,26,000
Direct labour	4,35,000		

Manufacturing Overheads (0.4 × 4,35,000)	1,74,000		
Gross Profit (0.2 × 15,60,000)	3,12,000		
Total	22,86,000	Total	22,86,000

Statement of cost and Profit for half year ending on September 30, 2008

Details		Amount (₹)
Opening Stock of Raw materials	1,30,000	
Add: Purchase of raw materials	6,15,000	
Raw materials available for consumption	7,45,000	
Less: Closing Stock of Raw materials	2,10,000	
Raw Materials consumed		5,35,000
Direct Labour		4,35,000
Prime Cost		9,70,000
Manufacturing overheads (0.4 × 4,35,000)		1,74,000
Works Cost (Gross)		11,44,000
Add: Opening Stock of Work-in-Progress		2,50,000
Less: Closing Stock of Work-in-Progress		(2,76,000)
Works Cost (Net) OR Cost of Goods Produced		11,18,000
Add: Opening Stock of Finished goods		3,70,000
Cost of goods available for Sale		14,88,000
Less: Closing Stock of Finished goods		(2,40,000)
Cost of Goods sold		12,48,000
Gross Profit		3,12,000
Sales		15,60,000

Problem 21. *In a factory, the expenses of factory are charged on fixed percentage basis on wages and office overhead are computed on the basis of percentage of works cost. Following information is supplied to you:*

Details		*Work-Order I*	*Work-Order II*
Materials	(₹)	*25,000*	*36,000*
Wages	(₹)	*20,000*	*28,000*
Selling Price	(₹)	*89,700*	*1,23,760*
Percentage of Profit on cost		*15*	*12*

Find out percentage of Factory overheads and Office Overheads. Prepare Cost Sheet for Work-Order I and Work-Order II.

Solution : Work-Order I:

Cost of Production = Selling price/ 1.15

= 89,700/ 1.15 => ₹ 78,000

Work-Order II:

Cost of Production = Selling price/ 1.15

= 1,23,760/ 1.12 => ₹ 1,10,500

Cost of Production = Materials + Wages + Factory overheads + Office overheads

Let Factory overheads =X% of Wages; and Office overheads = Y% of Works cost

Work-Order I:

$$78{,}000 = 25{,}000 + 20{,}000 + \{(X/\ 100) \times 20{,}000\} + \{(Y/\ 100) \times (45{,}000 + 200X\}$$

$$33{,}000 = 200X + 450\ Y + 2XY$$

Dividing by 2, We get

$$16{,}500 = 100X + 225Y + XY \qquad ...(1)$$

Work-Order II:

$$1{,}10{,}500 = 36{,}000 + 28{,}000 + \{(X/\ 100) \times 28{,}000\} + \{(Y/\ 100) \times (64{,}000 + 280X\}$$

$$46{,}500 = 280X + 640\ Y + 2.8XY$$

Dividing by 2, we get

$$23{,}250 = 140X + 320Y + 1.4\ XY \qquad ...(2)$$

Multiplying Equation (1) by 14 and (2) by 10, we get

$$2{,}31{,}000 = 1{,}400\ X + 3{,}150\ Y + 14XY \qquad ...(3)$$

$$2{,}32{,}500 = 1{,}400\ X + 3{,}200\ Y + 14XY \qquad ...(4)$$

Subtracting (3) from (4), we get

$$1{,}500 = 50Y$$

$$Y = 1{,}500 \div 50 => 30$$

Substituting the value of Y in Equation (1)

$$16{,}500 = 100X + 225(30) + X\ (30)$$

$$16{,}500 = 100X + 6{,}750 + 30X$$

$$9{,}750 = 130X$$

$$X = 9{,}750 \div 130 => 75$$

Thus, Factory overheads are 75% of Wages and Office overheads are 30% of Works cost.

Cost Sheet for Work-Order I and Work-Order II

Details	Work-Order I (₹)	Work-Order II (₹)
Materials	25,000	36,000
Wages	20,000	28,000
Prime cost	45,000	64,000
Factory overheads @ 75% of Wages i.e. [0.75 × 20,000] ; [0.75 × 28,000]	15,000	21,000
Works Cost	60,000	85,000
Office overheads @ 30% of Works Cost i.e. [0.3 × 60,000]; [0.3 × 85,000]	18,000	25,500
Cost of Production	78,000	1,10,500
Add: Profit (15% and 12% respectively) i.e. [0.15 × 78,000]; [0.15 × 1,10,500]	11,700	13,260
Selling Price	89,700	1,23,760

Problem 22. *Following costs were incurred in producing 1,200 MT of M. S. Rods: Materials ₹10,80,000; Labour ₹ 4,00,000; Processing charges ₹8,40,000.*

Of the total output, 10% has to be sold after a discount of 10% off the normal price. The scrap arising out of the production realized a sum of ₹ 35,040. The sale price is calculated to yield 12.5% profit on sales. You are required to find out the normal price as well as the discounted price per MT of M.S. Rods.

Solution : Working Notes:

Effective units of Good production:

	M.T.
Total Production	1,200
Less: defective Production	120
Good Production	1,080
Add: defective production equivalent of good production @ 90% of 120	108
Total Effective units of Good production	1,188

Statement of Cost and Profit of M/S. Rods

Details		Amount (₹)
Materials	10,80,000	
Labour	4,00,000	
Processing charges	8,40,000	
Total cost		19,20,000
Less: Sale value of Scrap		(35040)
Cost of Production		18,84,960
Profit @ 12.5% of Sales OR (0.125/0.875) of cost of production i.e. 1/7 [(18,84,960) × (1/7)]		2,69,280
Total Sales Value		21,54,240
Price of Good Production= (Total Sales Value /Effective units of Good production) = (21,54,240 ÷ 1,188) => ₹ 1,813.33 per M.T.		1,813.33
Discount Price of Defective Production: = (1,813.33 × 0.9) =₹ 1,632.00 per M.T.		1,632.00

Problem 23. The cost structure of an article, the selling price of which is Rs. 45,000 is as follows: The direct material, the direct labour and overhead costs are 50%, 20%, and 30% respectively of the cost of sales.

An increase of 15% in the cost of materials and of 25% in the cost of direct labour is anticipated. These increased costs in relation to the present selling price would cause 25% decrease in the amount of present profit per article.

You are required:

(i) to prepare a statement of profit per article at present, and

(ii) the revised selling price to produce the same percentage of profit on sales as before.

Solution : Cost of sales + Profit = Sales

Cost of sales = X; Profit = Y

X + Y = 6,000

Details	Existing cost structure	Expected cost structure
Material	0.50	(0.50 × 1.08) = 0.54
labour	0.20	(0.20 × 1.05) = 0.21
Overhead	0.30	0.30
Cost of sales	X	1.05X

Increase in the cost of Sales = 0.05X

Reduction in the Profit 25% of Y = 0.25Y
(assuming there is no change in the selling price)
Thus,

$$\text{Increase in cost} = \text{Reduction in Profit}$$

So,

$$0.05X = 0.25Y$$
$$X = 5Y$$

Substituting the value of X in the equation,

$$X + Y = 6{,}000$$
$$5Y + Y = 6{,}000$$
$$6Y = 6{,}000$$
$$Y = 6{,}000/6 \Rightarrow ₹\ 1{,}000$$

Thus the cost of sales in the existing cost structure

$$X + 1{,}000 = 6{,}000$$
$$X = 5{,}000$$

Percentage of profit on cost:

$$= (1{,}000/5{,}000) \times 100 \Rightarrow 20\%$$

Existing cost of sales = ₹ 5,000
Expected cost of Sales = (5,000 × 1.05) => ₹ 5,250
Expected profit with no change in the existing selling price = ₹ 750
(i.e. 6,000 – 5,250)
Reduction in the existing profit= ₹ 250
(i.e. 1,000 – 750)
This reduction in existing profit is equal to 25% of the existing profit
(i.e. {(250/1,000) × 100}

To maintain the existing percentage of profit of 20% on the cost of sales as calculated above, it is necessary to add 20% profit to the expected cost of sales:

Details	**Amount(₹)**
Expected cost of Sales=	5,250
Add: Profit @20% of 5,250 [5,250 × 0.2]	1,050
Selling price (Proposed)	6,300

Verification:

Details	Computations	Existing Amount (₹)	Expected Amount (₹)
Material	(0.50 × 5,000) (1.08 × 2,500)	2,500	2,700

labour	(0.20 × 5,000) (1.05 × 1,000)	1,000	1,050
Overhead	(0.30×5,000) (Unchanged)	1,500	1,500
Cost of sales		5,000	5,250
Profit	(0.20 × 5,000) (0.20 ×5,250)	1,000	1,050
Sales		6,000	6,300

Problem 24. *A firm makes two distinct types of Products P and M. The costs incurred during the year for production of 1500 units and 2000 units of P and M respectively, are as under:*

Details	*Amount (₹)*	*Details*	*Amount (₹)*
Direct Materials	*11,00,000*	*Stores Overhead*	*55,000*
Direct Wages	*1,50,000*	*Indirect Labour*	*18,000*
Depreciation	*11,000*	*Other works overhead*	*4,20,000*
Administrative Overhead	*1,42,080*	*Running Expenses of Machine*	*22,000*

Other Relevant Data:

	P: M
Material Cost Ratio per Unit	*1:2*
Direct Labour cost Ratio per Unit	*2:3*
Machine Utilisation Ratio per unit	*1:2*

Compute the cost of each product per Unit giving reasons for the basis of apportionment adopted for different overheads.

Solution : Cost Sheet of Products P and M for the year ending ……
(Output: P 1500 Units; and M 2000 Units)

Details	Product P		Product M		Total Cost	
Direct Material		3,00,000		8,00,000		11,00,000
Direct Wages		50,000		1,00,000		1,50,000
Prime Cost		3,50,000		9,00,000		12,50,000
Works Overhead:	15,000		40,000		55,000	
Stores Overhead	3,000		8,000		11,000	
Depreciation	6,000		16,000		22,000	
Running Expenses	6,000		12,000		18,000	
Indirect Wages						
Other Works Overhead	1,40,000		2,80,000		4,20,000	
Works-on-cost	1,70,000	1,70,000	3,56,000	3,56,000	5,26,000	5,26,000
Works Cost		5,20,000		12,56,000		17,76,000
Administration Overhead		4,16,000		1,00,480		1,42,080
Total Cost		5,61,600		13,56,480		19,18,080
Cost per Unit		374.40		678.24		N.A.

Working Notes:

1. Material cost is apportioned in the cost ratio per unit multiplied by the units produced:

   P: M i.e. 1,500X1: 2,000X2 OR 1,500: 4,000 OR 3: 8.

2. Direct wages are apportioned in the same manner as given in point 1:

   P: M i.e. 1,500X2: 2,000X3 OR 3,000: 6,000 OR 1: 2.

3. Stores overhead are recovered on the basis of percentage to material cost:

   $$(5{,}500 \div 11{,}00{,}000) \times 100 = 5\%.$$

4. Running expenses and depreciation are apportioned on the basis of machine utilization ratio multiplied by units produced:

   P: M i.e. 1,500X1: 2,000X2 OR 1,500: 4,000 OR 3: 8.

5. Works overhead and indirect wages have been absorbed on the basis of percentage to wages as under:

   Works overhead = $(4{,}20{,}000 \div 1{,}50{,}000) \times 100 = 280\%$;

   Indirect wages = $(18000 \div 150000) \times 100 = 12\%$.

6. Administration overheads are recovered on the basis of percentage to works cost:

   $$(1{,}42{,}080 \div 17{,}76{,}000) \times 100 = 8\%.$$

OBJECTIVE TYPE EXERCISES

I. Fill in the blank spaces with suitable word/s :

1. In output costing, cost of products is estimated by preparing a statement, called ....

2. In a cost sheet, stock of finished goods is adjusted at the stage of ....

3. In a cost sheet, opening stock of work-in-progress is added and closing stock of work-in-progress is deducted from ....

4. Prime cost + Works Overhead = ...

5. Chargeable expenses are a part of ....

6. In cost sheet, realisable value of scrap is deducted form ....

7. Two examples of factory overhead are .... And ....

8. When details of a cost sheet or production statement are shown in a T-shape account, it is called.............

9. When profit is 60% of sales, it is ....% of cost.

10. When profit is 60% of cost, it is ....% of sales.

Answers :

1. Cost sheet	**2.** Cost of production
3. Works cost	**4.** Works cost
5. Prime cost	**6.** Factory overhead or Works cost
7. Factory Rent/ Insurance and Factory supervision	
8. Production account	**9.** 150%
10. 37.5%	

II. Indicate whether the following statements are True or False :

1. When details of a cost sheet or production statement are shown in T-shape account, it is called Production account.
2. In a cost sheet, realisable value of scrap is deducted from overhead.
3. Cost sheet is always prepared after the cost has been incurred.
4. Conversion cost includes direct material, direct labour and factory expenses.
5. Unit costing method is adopted where large number of identical units is produced.
6. Work-in-progress is always valued at prime cost.
7. Cost sheet is always prepared either on monthly basis or annual basis.
8. Selling expenses are included while calculating cost of goods sold.
9. Cost of basic packing is part of distribution cost.
10. Cost per unit is increased by unabsorbed overheads.
11. Cost sheet and production statements are very similar in content.
12. Computation per unit cost should be related to normal capacity.
13. Factory scrap should be deducted from factory overheads.
14. Interest on money borrowed for purchase of materials should be added while calculating cost of direct materials.
15. Loss on sale of materials wrongly purchased should be just ignored while preparing cost sheet.
16. Cost sheet must not be influenced by abnormal losses.
17. Estimated cost sheet is prepared for submitting quotations.

Answers :

1. True	**2.** True	**3.** False	**4.** False
5. True	**6.** False	**7.** False	**8.** False
9. False	**10.** False	**11.** True	**12.** True
13. True	**14.** False	**15.** False	**16.** True
17. True			

THEORETICAL EXERCISES

1. What is output costing? In which type of industries is it used?
2. Explain the nature of single output costing.
3. Describe briefly the procedure of presenting costs under single costing. Explain giving an example.
4. Explain in brief the following concepts:
   (i) Cost Unit
   (ii) Prime cost
   (iii) Cost of goods produced
5. How would you treat sale of scrap in a cost sheet?
6. List three such items that are excluded from cost accounts.
7. What is unit costing? How does it differ from job costing?
8. What is cost sheet? In what respect is it different from a production account?
9. What is the object of preparing cost sheet?
10. Distinguish between the following:
    (i) Prime cost and conversion cost;
    (ii) Prime cost and Factory cost;
    (iii) Factory cost and Cost of goods produced;
    (iv) Cost of goods produced and Cost of goods sold;
    (v) Cost of goods sold and Sales.
11. How will you deal with the following while preparing statement of cost and profit?
    (i) Net value of normal scrap of direct materials
    (ii) Net value of normal scrap of indirect materials
    (iii) Opening and closing stock of raw materials
    (iv) Opening and closing stock of Work-in-Progress
    (v) Opening and closing stock of Finished goods

NUMERICAL EXERCISES

1. The following details have been obtained from the cost records of SV Ltd.:

Details	Amount (₹)
Stock of Raw Materials on November 01, 2004	90,000
Stock of Raw Materials on November 30, 2004	1,09,800
Direct Wages	63,000
Indirect Wages	3,300
Sales	2,53,200
Work-in-Progress on November 01, 2004	33,600
Work-in-Progress on November 30, 2004	42,000
Purchase of Raw Materials	79,200

Factory rent, rates and power	18,000
intblDepreciation of plant and machinery	4,200
Expenses on purchases	1,800
Carriage outwards	3,000
Advertising	4,200
Office rent and taxes	3,000
Travellers' wages and commission	7,800
Stock of finished goods on November 01, 2004	64,800
Stock of finished goods on November 30, 2004	37,200

Prepare a Production Account giving the maximum possible break-up of cost and profit.

2. A firm has purchased a plant to manufacture a new product, the cost data for which is given below:

Details	Rate/ Unit	Details	Rate/ Unit
Estimated Annual Sales	30,000 Units	Overheads	42000 p.a.
Estimated Costs: Materials	₹ 5 per unit	Administrative Expenses	36000 p.a.
Direct Labour	₹ 0.75 per unit	Selling Expenses	20% of Sales

Calculate the Selling Price if profit per unit is ₹ 1.60

[Ans. Selling Price 21.50 per unit]

3. Following are the particulars of 14 H.P. Motors produced by Usha Motors Manufacturing Ltd. for the year ended on March 31, 2004:

Details	Amount (₹)	Details	Amount (₹)
Opening Stock of Raw Materials	70,000	Closing Stock of Raw Materials	1,05,000
Purchases	16,80,000	Production Overheads	3,13,600
Carriage	84,000	Establishment & General Charges	2,43,408
Wages	9,80,000		

1. Find out the works cost and total cost of a motorcar, the percentage the works overhead bears to the Wages and percentage that establishment charges bear to the works cost.
2. Work out what price the Company should quote for a motor, which it is estimated will require an expenditure of ₹ 9,000 in raw material and ₹7,500 in wages, so that it would yield profit of 25% on total cost. **[Ans. 25,515]**

4. M/S Usha Industries Limited is the manufacturer of specialized torches. The following data relate to thee manufacture of torches during the month of May 2004:

Details	Amount (₹)
Raw Materials Consumed	50,000
Direct Wages	30,000
Machine Hour Worked: 8,000	
Machine Hour Rate	5
Administration Overheads	25% of Works Cost
Selling and Distribution Overheads	2.50 per unit
Units Produced: 5,000.	
Units Sold @ ₹ 36 per unit: 4,800	

[Ans. Prime cost ₹ 80,000; Works Cost ₹ 1,20,000; Cost of Production ₹ 1,50,000; Cost of Production of goods sold ₹ 1,44,000; Cost of Sales 1,56,000; Sales 1,72,800; Profit ₹ 16,800]

5. The Managing Director of a small manufacturing company consults you as to the minimum price at which he can sell the output of one of the departments of the company, which is intended for mass production in future. The Company's records show the following details for this department for the preceding year:

Details	Amount (₹)
Production and Sale...(100 Units)	40,000
Materials	12,000
Direct Labour	8,000
Direct Charges	2,000
Production Overhead	8,000
ghtAdministrative Overheads	2,800
Selling Overheads	3,200
Profit	4,000

It is ascertained that 45% of the Production Overheads fluctuate directly with production and 60% of the Selling Overheads fluctuate with sales. It is anticipated that the department would produce 500 units per annum and that direct labour charges per unit will be reduced by 25%, while the fixed Production overheads will increase by ₹ 3600/-. Administrative Overheads and fixed selling overheads are expected to show an increase of 25% but otherwise no changes are expected.

[Ans.]

6. Kanpur Shoe Company manufactures two types of shoes M and B. Production costs for the year ended March 31, 2004 were as follows:

Cost Element	Amount (₹)
Direct Material	40,00,000
Direct Wages	28,00,000
Production Overheads	12,00,000
Total	80,00,000

There was no work-in-progress at the beginning or at the end of the year. It is ascertained that:

(i) The cost of direct materials in type M shoes is twice as much as that in type B.
(ii) The direct wages for type L were 60% of those type M shoes.
(iii) Production overhead was the same per pair of M and B type.
(iv) Administrative overhead for each type was 150% of direct wages.
(v) Selling cost was ₹ 4/- per pair.
(vi) Production during the year:
Type M 50,000 pairs of which 40,000 were sold.
Type M 1,50,000 pairs of which 1,30,000 were sold.
(vii) Selling Price was ₹ 140 for type M and ₹ 90 for type B.

Prepare a statement showing cost and Profit

7. Following are the particulars of 2.4 H.P. motors produced by Hyundai Motor Manufacturing Company for the year ended 31st December:

Opening stock of raw materials	₹ 5,0000
Works overheads	1,96,000
Purchases	12,00,000
Establishment & general charges	1,70,480
Carriage	60,000
Wages	7,00,000
Closing stock of raw materials	75,000

1. Find out the works cost and total cost of motor, the percentage the works overhead bears to the wages and percentage that establishment charges bear to the works cost.
2. Work out what price the Co. should quote for a motor, which it is estimated will require on expenditure of ₹6100 in raw materials and ₹ 5,000 in wages, so that it would yield profit of 25% on total cost.

[B.Com. (Hons.) Delhi modified]
[Ans. 16,875]

8. The books and records of Fernandez Manufacturing Company present the following data for the month of March 2004:

Direct labour cost	₹ 40,000
Cost of goods sold	₹1,40,000

Inventory accounts showed these opening and closing balances :

	March 1	March 31
Raw materials	20,000	21,500
Work –in-progress	20,000	30,000
Finished goods	35,000	45,000

Other data: Selling expenses ₹ 8,500, General and administrative expenses ₹ 6,500; Sales for the month ₹ 2,00,000.

You are required to prepare a statement showing cost of goods manufactured and sold and profit earned. **[CA (Inter.) Adapted]**

[Ans. 51,500]

9. Following costs were incurred in producing 1600 M.T. of M.S. rods:

	₹
Materials	2,87,200
Labour	1,00,000
Processing charges	1,00,000
Total cost	**4,87,200**

Of the total output, 12.5 % was defective and had to be sold after a discount of 20 % of the normal price. The scrap arising out of the production realized a sum of ₹9840. The sale price is calculated to yield 15% profit on sales. You are required to find out the normal price as well as the discounted price of M.T. of M.S. rods.

[Ans. Normal Price: ₹ 918; Discounted Price: ₹ 734.40]

10. Following details have been obtained from the cost records of Joseph Chemical Works:

Details	Quantity (Kg)	Amount (₹)
Stock on January, 2007:		
Raw materials	2,000	2,000
Finished mixture	500	1,750
Factory Stores		7,250
Purchases:	1,60,000	1,80,000
Raw materials		24,250
Factory Stores		
Sales:		
Finished Mixture	1,53,050	9,18,000
Factory scrap		8,170
Factory Wages		1,78,650
Power		20,400
Depreciation of Machinery		28,000

Salaries:		
Factory		72,220
Office		37,220
Selling		41,500
Expenses:		
Direct		18,500
Office		18,200
Selling		18,000
Stock on December 31,2007:		
Raw materials	1,200	
Finished mixture	450	
Factory Stores		5,550

The stock of finished mixture at the end of December, 2007 is to be valued at the factory cost of the mixture for the year. The purchase price of raw materials remained unchanged throughout the year 2007.

Prepare a statement giving the maximum possible information about cost and its break-up for the year 2007.

[Ans. Prime cost: ₹ 3,77,800; Factory Cost: ₹ 5,16,200; Cost of production: ₹ 5,17,620; Cost of Goods Sold: 5,71,852; Profit ₹ 2,86,648]

11. The Tirupati Electrical Ltd. manufactures one product. A summary of its activities for 2007 is as follows:

Details	Quantity (Kg)	Amount (₹)
Sales	80,000	8,00,000
Materials Inventory:		
1.1.2007		40,000
31.12.2007		32,000
Work-in-Progress Inventory:		
1.1.2007		55,000
31.12.2007		72,000
Finished Goods Inventory:		
1.1.2007	16,000	64,000
31.12.2007	24,000	———
Materials Purchases		1,52,000
Direct Wages		1,45,000
Manufacturing overheads		1,08,000
Selling Expenses		50,000
General and Administration Expenses		40,000

Calculate:

1. The current manufacturing cost for the year 2007.
2. The total cost of goods manufactures (finished), the number of units manufactured (finished) and the cost per unit.
3. The cost of goods sold for the year presuming the company uses the LIFO inventory costing method for its finished goods inventory.

[Ans. Current Manufacturing Cost: ₹ 4, 13,000; Cost of Goods manufactured: ₹ 3, 96,000; Cost of Goods Sold (LIFO Basis): 3, 60,000; Profit ₹ 3, 50,000.]

12. The details obtained from the records of M/s Bonnie Industries for the year 2006 are given below, from which you are required to prepare a cost sheet and a statement showing estimated cost for 1,000 units in future:

Details	Amount (₹)
Opening Stock:	
Raw materials	1,40,000
Finished Goods	20,000
Purchases	2,10,000
Factory Wages	3,80,000
Factory Overheads	70,000
Office overheads	40,000
Closing Stock:	
Raw materials	19,600
Finished Goods	1,60,000
Sales	7,56,000

At the end of the year, the number of units produced including the closing stock and the number of units sold was 4,000.

On the basis of the above the industry wanted to supply 1,000 units in future. It is estimated that the prices of raw materials and labour may rise by 15% and 10% respectively. Assume that the same percentage of profits on sales will be made.

[B.Com. (Hons.) Delhi ,2004 (External)]

[Ans. Cost of production per unit ₹ 205.10; Quotation ₹ 2, 52,211]

13. Flex Shoe Company manufactures two types of shoes M and P. Production costs for the year ended March 31, 2004 were as follows:

Cost Element	Amount (₹)
Direct Material	15,00,000
Direct Wages	8,40,000
Production Overheads	3,60,000
Total	27,00,000

There was no work-in-progress at the beginning or at the end of the year. It is ascertained that:

(i) The cost of direct materials in type T shoes is twice as much as that in type P.
(ii) The direct wages for type P shoes were 60% of those type T shoes.
(iii) Production overhead was the same per pair of T and P type.
(iv) Administrative overhead for each type was 150% of direct wages.
(v) Selling cost was ₹ 1.50 per pair.
(vi) Production during the year:
Type T 40,000 pairs of which 36,000 were sold.
Type P 1, 20,000 pairs of which 1, 00,000 were sold.
(vii) Selling Price was ₹ 44 for type T and ₹ 28 for type P.

Prepare a statement showing cost and Profit.

[Ans. Cost.: Type T ₹ 13,50,000; Type P ₹ 22,50,000 ; Profit : Type T ₹2,34,000 ; Type P ₹ 5,50,000.]

14. The managing director of a company producing consumer durables seeks your assistance in the matter of fixation of selling price for one of its products called 'X'. The cost structure of product 'X', the unit selling price is ₹ 45,000, is as under:

Details	**Amount**
Direct materials	50%
Direct labour	20%
Overheads	30%

An increase of 15% in the cost of materials and 25% in the cost of Labour is anticipated. These increased costs in relation to the presnt selling price would cause a 25% decrease in the amount of present profit per unit of 'X'.

You are required to :

(i) Prepare a Statement of profit per unit as at present;
(ii) Find out the revised selling price to produce the same percentage of profit to sales as before. **[DU, B.Com (Hons.) 2002]**

[Ans. ₹ 50,625]

15. PV Works can produce 60,000 units per year at its optimum (100%) capacity. The estimated costs of production are as under:

Direct material	₹ 3 per unit
Direct labour	₹ 2 per unit
Indirect Expenses:	
Fixed	₹ 1,50,000 per year
Variable	₹ 5 per unit
Semi-Variable	₹ 50,000 per year up to 50% capacity and an extra expenses of ₹ 10,000 for every 25% increase in capacity or part thereof.

The factory produced only against orders and not for own stock. If the production programme of the factory is as indicated below, and the management desires to ensure a profit of ₹ 1,00,000 for the year, work out the average selling price at which each unit should be quoted:

First Three months of the year 50% of capacity
Remaining Nine months 80% of capacity
Ignore Selling & distribution and Administration overheads. **(C.A. Adapted)**

[Ans. Selling price ₹ 17.24 per unit)

16. A Company makes two distinct types of vehicles, V-1, and V-2. The total expenses during a period as shown by the books for the assembly of 600 of the type V-1 and 800 of the type V-2 are as under:

Materials	1,98,000
Direct Wages	12,000
Stores Overheads	19,800
Running expenses of the machines	4,400
Depreciation	2,200
Labour amenities	1,500
Works general overhead	30,000
Administration and Selling Overhead	26,800

The other data available is:

	V-1: V-2
Material cost Ratio per unit	1:2
Direct labour Ratio per unit	2:3
Machine utilization Ratio per unit	1:2

[B.Com (H), DU and I.C.W.A.)

[Ans. Cost per unit: V-1 ₹ 138.78 and V-2 ₹ 264.28]

17. The following data is available from the cost ledger of Acme industries for the Year 2004:

Details	Amount (₹)
Plant Maintenance	25,000
lighting	6,300
Depreciation on Plant	8,100
Rates and Taxes for the Works	3,900
Staff Salaries	32,000
Management Salaries	22,000
Power (for this Plant)	10,600
Rental for Leasehold Equipments	9,600
Indirect Wages	37,100
Rectification cost of Defectives(Normal)	8,400
Consumable Stores	17,600
Selling Expenses	30,000
General charges	15,600
Sale proceeds from scrap	4,200

During the year total production was 1,20,000 units. The break –up of the prime cost Per unit was: Materials: ₹ 2.20 and wages ₹ 1.80. The average Selling price was ₹6.75 per unit and the entire quantity produced during the years was sold out. With effect from January 1, 2005, the selling price was reduced to ₹ 6.40 per unit. It was envisaged that production could be enhanced during the year 2005 by 100/3% without incurring any overtime or extra-shift work, or additional selling expenses.

You are required to prepare statements showing:

(i) Actual cost for the year 2004;

(ii) Estimated cost and Profit for 2005 assuming that the entire production will be sold out during the year.

Assumptions, if any, required to be made in the above exercise should be clearly stated. **[I.C.W.A.]**

[Ans. Profit on the estimated output of 1,60,000 units: ₹ 1,51,200.]

18. The PET Chemicals Company supplies you the following details from its cost records:

Details	Amount (₹)
Stock of Raw materials on 01.9.2005	75,000
Stock of Raw materials on 30.9.2005	91,500
Direct Wages	52,500
Indirect Wages	2,750
Sales	2,00,000
Work-in-Progress on 01.9.2005	28,000
Work-in-Progress on 30.9.2005	35,000
Purchases of Raw materials	66,000
Factory rent, rates and power	15,000
Depreciation of plant and machinery	3,500
Expenses on purchases	1,500
Carriage outward	1,000
Advertising	5,000
Office rent and taxes	2,500
Travellers' wages and commission	6,500
Stock of finished goods on 01.9.2005	54,000
Stock of finished goods on 30.9.2005	31,000

[B.Com, Delhi]

[Ans. Prime cost ₹ 1,03,500; Works cost ₹ 1,17,750; Cost of Goods produced ₹ 1,20,250; Cost of goods sold ₹ 1,43,250; profit ₹ 44,250.]

19. From the books of account of M/s. ZYX Enterprises, the following details have been extracted for the year ending March 31, 2005:

Details	Amount (₹)
Stock of Raw materials: Opening	1,88,000
Stock of Raw materials: Closing	2,00,000
Direct Wages Paid	2,38,400
Indirect Wages	16,000
Salaries to Administrative staff	40,000
Freight:	32,000
Inward	20,000
Outward	
Sales	15,79,800
Cash discount allowed	14,000
Bad debts Written Off	18,800
Repairs of Plant and machinery	42,400
Purchases of Raw materials	8,32,000
Rent, rates and Taxes:	
Factory	12,000
Office	6,400
Travelling Expenses	12,400
Depreciation Written Off:	
Plant and machinery	28,900
Furniture	2,400
Fuel (for Boiler)	64,000
Electricity charges (Factory)	48,000
Director's Fees	24,000
Sale of scrap	500
Manager's Salary	48,000
General charges	24,800
Salesmen's salaries and commission	33,600

The manager's time is shared between the factory and the office in the ratio of 1:4. From the above details you are required to prepare a cost sheet to show: (a) Prime cost; (b) Factory cost; (c) Cost of goods produced; (d) Total cost; and (e) Profit.

[I.C.W.A.]

[Ans. Prime cost ₹ 10,90,400; Factory cost ₹ 13,10,800; Cost of Goods produced ₹ 14,46,800; Cost of Sales ₹ 15,31,600; profit ₹ 48,200.]

20. M/s. YZX Engineering works Limited manufactured and sold 1,250 machines in 2008. Following are the details obtained from the records of the company:

Details	Amount (₹)
Cost of materials	1,20,000
Direct Wages Paid	2,00,000
Manufacturing expenses	80,000
Salaries to Managerial staff	1,00,000
aultSales	80,00,000
Rent, rates and Insurance	20,000
Selling Expenses	50,000
General Expenses	60,000

The Company plans to manufacture 2,000 machines in 2009. You are required to submit a statement showing the price at which machines would be sold so as to show a profit of 12.5% on the selling price. The following additional information is supplied to you:

(a) The price of material would rise by 25% over the preceding year's level.

(b) Wages will rise by 6.25%.

(c) Manufacturing expenses per unit will rise in proportion to the combined cost of material and wages.

(d) Selling expenses per unit would remain same.

(e) Other expenses will remain unchanged by the rise in output.

[Ans. Prime cost ₹ 5,80,000; Factory cost ₹ 7,25,000; Cost of Goods produced ₹ 9,05,000; Cost of Sales ₹ 9,85,000; profit ₹ 1,40,714.]

21. The expenses of a Machine Cost Centre for a particular month are as under:

(i) Power ₹ 50,000
(ii) Repairs and maintenance ₹ 10,000
(iii) Machine operator's Wages ₹ 2,000
(iv) Supervision ₹ 6,000
(v) Depreciation ₹ 40,000

Other Particulars are as under:

Product	Rate of Production	Production (units)
A	30 units per hour	1,800
B	10 units per hour	500
C	6 units per hour	300
D	4 units per hour	260

The entire production is to be offered to government on cost plus 25% basis. Material costs per unit are: A ₹ 40; B ₹ 60; C ₹ 100; D ₹ 300. Prepare a statement showing product-wise cost and Offer price. **[I.C. W.A. (Modified)]**

[Ans. Offer Price: A ₹ 70; B ₹ 135; C ₹ 225; D ₹ 525.]

22. A firm has purchased a plant to manufacture a new product, the cost dedtails for which are given below:

Estimated Annual sales	24,000 units
Estimated costs:	
Material	₹ 4 per unit
Direct labour	₹ 0.6 per unit
Overheads	₹ 24,000 per year
Administrative expenses	₹ 28,800 per year
Selling expenses	15% of Sales

Calculate the selling price if profit per unit is ₹ 1.02.

[I.C.W.A. (Modified)]
[Ans. ₹ 9.20 per unit]

23. On June 30, 1996, a flash flood damaged the warehouse and factory of ABC Corporation completely destroying the work-in-progress inventory. There was no damage to either the raw materials or finished goods inventories. A physical verification taken after the flood revealed the following valuations:

Inventory	**Amount (₹)**
Raw materials	62,000
Work-in-progress	N I L
Finished goods	1,19,000

On January1, 1996, the inventories consisted of the followings:

Inventory	**Amount (₹)**
Raw materials	30,000
Work-in-progress	1,00,000
Finished goods	1,40,000
Total	2,70,000

A review of the books and records disclosed that the gross profit margin historically approximated 25% of sales. The sales for the first six months of 1996 were ₹ 3,40,000.

Raw Material purchases were ₹ 1,15,000. Direct labour costs for this period were ₹ 80,000 and manufacturing overheads has historically been 50% of direct labour.

Compute the cost of work-in-progress inventory lost on June 30,1996 by preparing a statement of cost and profit. Show complete working. **[B.Com (Hons.) DU]**

[Ans. ₹ 69,000]

24. Nilgiri Airconditioning Company produces refrigerators and sells each for ₹ 4,000 during a certain season of the accounting year. The direct material, the direct labour and overhead costs are 60%, 20%, and 20% respectively of the cost of sales.

In a subsequent accounting year, the direct material cost increases by 15% and direct labour cost by 17.5%. due to these increases in costs, there would be a 50% decrease in the amount of profit if the same selling price is to be maintained.

Compute the new selling price to enable the company to maintain the same percentage of profit as that earned during the preceding year.

[B.Com (Hons.) DU; C.A. Inter]
[Ans. ₹ 4,500]

25. The cost structure of an article, the selling price of which is ₹ 45,000 is as follows: The direct material, the direct labour and overhead costs are 50%, 20%, and 30% respectively of the cost of sales.

An increase of 15% in the cost of materials and of 25% in the cost of direct labour is anticipated. These increased costs in relation to the present selling price would cause 25% decrease in the amount of present profit per article.

You are required: (i) to prepare a statement of profit per article at present, and (ii) the revised selling price to produce the same percentage of profit on sales as before.

[B.Com (Hons.) DU; C.A. Inter (Modified)]

[Ans. ₹ 50,625]

26. A manufacturer sold its output in 2008-09 for ₹ 1,40,000 @ ₹ 28 per unit. Total Fixed charges amounted to ₹ 28,750 per annum and the variable cost per unit was ₹ 18. The producer desires to reduce the selling price by ₹ 2 per unit and maintain the same profit as before. What should be the production and sale to implement this decision?

[Ans. 6,250 units]

27. Fatima Company limited manufactures electric fans which are sold at ₹ 800 per piece. The total cost is composed of 40% direct materials, 30% wages, and 30% overhead.

An increase in material price by 25% and in wage rate by 10% is expected in the forthcoming year; as a result of which the profit at current selling price may decrease by 39% of present profit.

With the above information, you are required to prepare (i) a statement showing current and future profit at present selling price, and (ii) how much selling price is to be increased to maintain the present rate of gross profit. Show working in details.

[B.Com , Bharathidasan]

[Ans. ₹ 904]

28. In a factory, the expenses of factory are charged on fixed percentage basis on wages and office overhead are computed on the basis of percentage of works cost. Following information is supplied to you:

Details		Work-Order I	Work-Order II
Materials	(₹)	25,000	36,000
Wages	(₹)	20,000	28,000
Selling Price	(₹)	91,500	1,24,200
Percentage of Profit on cost		20	15

Find out percentage of Factory overheads and Office Overheads. Prepare Cost Sheet for Work-Order I and Work-Order II. **[Ans. 80% of Wages; 25% of Works cost]**

29. Following costs were incurred in producing 800 MT of M. S. Rods:

Materials ₹2,80,000; Labour ₹ 1,00,000; Processing charges ₹1,00,000.

Of the total output, 10% has to be sold after a discount of 10% off the normal price. The scrap arising out of the production realized a sum of ₹8,760. The sale price is calculated to yield 12.5% profit on sales. You are required to find out the normal price as well as the discounted price per MT of M.S. Rods. **[Ans. ₹ 680; ₹ 612]**

30. A company produces a boat that sells for ₹1, 800. An increase of 7.5% in the cost of materials and 6.25% in the cost of labour is expected. What must be the selling price to produce the same percentage of gross profit as before? The only data available are:

The material cost has been 50% of the cost of sales.

The labour cost has been 20% of the cost of sales.

The overhead cost has been 30% of the cost of sales.

The anticipated increased costs in relation to the present sales price would cause a 25% decrease in the amount of the present profit.

Prepare a statement of profit and loss per unit, showing the new selling price desired and the new cost per unit. **[I.C.W.A.]**

[Ans. ₹ 1,890]

31. Standard Limited sells its products throughout the country through its four zonal sales offices. The budgeted expenses for the year 2009-10 are given below:

Expenditure			Amount (₹)
Sales Manager's Salary			3,75,000
Expenses relating to Sales Manager's Office			2,62,500
Travelling Salesmen's salaries			7,50,000
Travelling Expenses			1,25,000
Advertisements			1,00,000
Warehouse:	A	37,500	
	B	62,500	
	C	25,000	
	D	45,000	1,70,000
Insurance on Inventories			43,750
Commission on Sales@ 4% on sales			10,50,000

Additional Information:

Zone	Sales (₹)	No. of Salesmen	Total Distance Covered (kms.)	Allocation of Advertisement (%)	Average Stock (₹)
A	63,00,000	6	6,000	30	10,50,000
B	84,00,000	8	14,000	35	14,00,000
C	28,00,000	2	4,500	15	7,00,000
D	35,00,000	4	5,500	20	3,50,000

Compute Zone-wise Selling overheads, as a percentage to sales, based on above details.

32. The following details are available from the books of Kanishka manufacturer's limited for the year ending 31st December:

Details	Amount (₹)
Direct wages	6,00,000
Purchase of materials	7,20,000
Other materials	36,000
Carriage (miscellaneous)	8,640
Wages of foremen and storekeepers	48,000
Other indirect wages	6,000
Cost of research and experiments	30,000
Office manager's salary	72,000
Employee's state insurance	6,000
Power , fuel and haulage	54,000
Drawing office expenses	36,000
Printing and stationary	12,000
Counting house salary	12,000
Sales	18,00,000
Opening stock: raw materials	1,20,000
Work in progress	28,800
Finished products (units) 6,000	
Closing stock: raw materials	1,33,440
Work in progress	96,000
Finished products (units) 12,000	
Income tax	22,000
Donation	5,000

Selling the distribution expenses are to be charged at ₹1 per unit. During the year units produced were 96,000. Prepare a cost sheet showing the different elements of cost and the profit.

33. Parish international Co. has just completed operations for the year 2004. The company's assistant accountant (who is very inexperienced) prepares the following profit & loss account for the year's activities:

Details	Amount (₹)	Amount (₹)
Sales		32,00,000
Less: Operating expenses:		
Insurance	40,000	
Gas, Electricity, and water	1,00,000	
Direct labour cost	6,00,000	
Indirect labour cost	1,20,000	
Depreciation on factory equipment	1,60,000	
Raw material purchased during the year	12,00,000	
Rent	4,00,000	
Selling and administration Overheads	3,20,000	
Total Operating expenses		29,40,000
Net Profit		2,60,000

You have been asked to assist the company in preparing a correct profit and loss account for the year 2006. The following additional information is available:

(1) The company is a manufacturing firm that produces a product for sales to outside customers.

(2) 80 percent of the rent paid applies to the factory operations and the remainder to selling and administrative activities.

(3) No raw, materials were on hand on 1st January. However, raw materials of the value of ₹ 1,50,000 purchased during 2006 were still on hand on the 31st December. The remainder was used in production during the year.

(4) 70 percent of the insurance and the 90% of the gas, electricity and water paid apply to selling and administration activities.

(5) Work in progress and finished goods inventories were:

	1st January	31st December
Work-in-progress	₹ 4,20,000	4,80,000
Finished goods	₹ 5,40,000	4,00,000

You are required to prepare-

(a) A statement of cost of goods manufactured in 2006, and

(b) A corrected profit and loss account for the year ended 31st December, 2006.

34. The cost structure of an article, the selling price of which is ₹75, 000 is as follows:

Direct materials: 50%; Direct labour: 20%; Overheads: 30%.

An increase of 20% in the cost of materials and of 25% in the cost of labour is anticipated. These increased costs in relation to the present selling price would cause 30% decrease in the amount of present profit per article.

You are required to:

(i) Prepare a Statement of Profit per article at present, and

(ii) The revised selling price to produce the same percentage of profit on sales as before. **[Ans. ₹ 50,625]**

35. A company produces a boat that sells for ₹ 2,400. An increase of 71/2% in the cost of materials and 61/4% in the cost of labour is anticipated. What must be the selling price to produce the same percentage of gross profit as before? The only data available are:

The material cost has been 50% of the cost of sales.

The wages cost has been 20% of the sales.

The overhead has been 30% of the cost of sales.

The anticipated increased costs in relation to the present sales price would cause a 25% decrease in the amount of the present gross profit.

Prepare a statement of profit and loss per unit, showing the new selling price desired and new costs per unit. **[Ans. 25,207]**

36. The following balances have been obtained from the books of Grimpen limited for the year ending December 31:

Details	Amount (₹)
Stock on 1st January:	
Manufactured Goods	974
Raw Materials	300
Depreciation of Plant	1,300
Discount allowed	374
Printing and stationery	93
Purchases:	
Manufactured Goods	1,274
Raw materials	8,726
Repairs to plant	250
Office rent and rates	650
Coal	579
Carriage inwards	391
Office salaries	940
Carriage outwards	233
General expenses	317
Factory rent and rates	2,271
Manufacturing wages and salaries	11,029
Traveling expenses	279
Sales	29,942
Stocks on 31st December:	
Manufactured Goods	2,794
Raw Materials	200

Goods manufactured are to be debited to the sales department at current market prices, viz. ₹27150. You are required to prepare accounts in such a form as to disclose

(i) Cost of raw materials consumed,

(ii) Prime Cost,

(iii) Factory cost,

(iv) Gross Profit on manufacture,

(v) Cost of own manufactured goods to sales department,

(vi) Gross Profit on sales, and

(vii) Net Profit that may be considered rational from the accounting point of view.

37. A Factory which manufactured pens in three qualities, produced during the year 2007:

24,000 Pens of quality A;
20,000 Pens of quality B;
10,000 Pens of quality C.

The Stocks of Finished Goods on 1st January 2007 were:

Quality A: 1,520;
Quality B: 800, and
Quality C: 1,200.

Sales during the year 2007 were:

Quality A: 24,960 at ₹7.50;
Quality B: 19,200 at ₹ 6.75; and
Quality C: 10,200 at ₹ 6.00.

The following information is available from the account books:

Work-in-progress on 1-1-2004	₹30,000
Work-in-progress on 31-12-2004	36,000
Cost of raw materials used in manufacture	87,000
Cost of stores used in manufacture	12,000
Manufacturing wages	1,56,000
Depreciation (works)	18,000
Works on cost	33,000

From the above details, prepare manufacturing and trading accounts for the year ended 31st December 2007, showing the amount of gross profit carried to profit and loss account. Assume that the rate of gross profit is the same for all the three qualities of pens. **[Ans. ....]**

❑❑❑

15

Job and Batch Costing

Learning Objectives

It attempts to explain the process of charging of job/work order and a batch. In this chapter you will learn :

1. Meaning, nature and objective of job/batch costing.
2. Pre-requisites for job costing and procedure of job/batch costing.
3. Method of recording cost of a job or a batch.
4. Accounting treatment of completed jobs.

This chapter has been divided into two sections: section I deals with Job costing and section II deals with Batch costing.

SECTION I

JOB COSTING

Job order costing is that form of specific order costing which applies where work is undertaken to customer's requirements and each order is of comparatively short duration. The job is usually carried out within the factory and moves through processes and operations as a continuously identifiable unit. Besides, it applies to repair work to properties and also the method may be used in the costing of internal capital expenditure jobs.

Salient Features:

(i) The job is for a specific customer and is of the 'one 0ff' type. The job is not exactly the same as anything produced before and may never be produced again. Each job is separately identifiable and has its own special characteristics. Each job is a separate cost unit and each job needs to be costed independently. This is why it is necessary to assign a specific job order number.

(ii) It is most suitable when the products differ in types of material and work performed. Each product is made according to the customer's specifications and the price quoted is closely tied to the estimated cost.

(iii) There is no predetermined flow line for the job and therefore, careful routing and scheduling is essential for successful compliance.

(iv) The job can be identified at each stage of production, from start to finish.

(v) The production cycle is short as compared to the production cycle of long –term contracts.

(vi) In general, jobs are costed after the completion of jobs. But whenever required, estimated job cost sheet can be prepared for submitting tenders for the jobs.

(vii) The three basic elements of cost i.e. direct material, direct labour and factory overhead are accumulated according to the assigned job numbers.

(viii) The amount involved in work-in-progress varies from time to time depending upon the number and size of jobs in progress.

(ix) The unit cost for each job is obtained by dividing the total units for the job into the total cost. Selling and administration costs are NOT considered as part of the job and are shown separately on the cost sheet and income statement.

Organisations that commonly use job-costing system are engaged in manufacturing general engineering products, such as high-capacity pumps, compressors and pressure vessels, steel structures, and ship building. Consulting firms use job-costing method. Printing companies and ship building firms usually make use of job order costing.

Job costing is used in that type of production where work is done against orders and instructions from customers. A separate account is prepared for each job to ascertain its cost and profit. For this purpose each job is given a unique job number. Direct materials and wages are charged to each job on actual basis while overheads are charged on the pre-determined rate by one of the methods of absorption of overhead. In this way total cost of a job is ascertained. This total cost is compared with the sale price of the job to ascertain profit or loss on the job.

Pre-requisites for Job Costing

Following pre-requisites are meant to ensure that the system is efficient and effective:

(i) Cost centres should be well defined.

(ii) Appropriate system of material issues and material pricing should be in vogue.

(iii) Appropriate system of time booking and piece work recording should be maintained on continuous basis.

(iv) Appropriate overhead rates of recovery should be ensured for different jobs.

(v) Proper records of documents giving job-wise details are to be maintained efficiently. Documents may relate to work order, Bill of Materials, Requisitions for the issue of Jigs and Tools, and such type.

(vi) Appropriate accounting system that gives job-wise details must be devised by the management.

(vii) It is necessary to identify each job and segregate its related costs. Each individual order or batch is assigned a unique Number.

(viii) Material requisitions, labour costs and other charges carry the specific assigned job number and a cost sheet is used to summarise the applicable job costs. The profit or loss can be computed for each job and the unit cost can be computed for purposes of inventory costing.

Procedure of Job Costing

Design of a costing system must ensure proper basis of cost control and determination of cost of a Job. Job costing entails following steps and documents:

1. *Quotation for the Job:* Quotation based on direct costs, variable and fixed overheads, firm's policy of profit margin and intensity of competition is submitted for the competitive bid.
2. *Receipt of order:* If the customer is satisfied with the quotation submitted and the delivery schedule, he may place the order for the job with the firm.
3. *Job Number:* On the receipt of the order, a unique job number is assigned, which serves as a reference number for keeping a track of the job and its proper costing.
4. *Production Order:* The Production Control Department prepares a detailed production order authorising all concerned departments to start work on the job. The detailed works order contains a list of specifications and requirements relating to the Job. A number of copies of this works order is prepared to be dispatched to (a) Production supervisors of all concerned departments; (b) Store Keeper for the issuance of materials ; (c) Tool room as an advance intimation of tools required; and (d) Cost control department for keeping a track of jobs to be costed and controlled.

APS Company Limited
Production Order

Serial No. :	Customer's reference No. : ....
Code No. :	Quantity under order : ....
Bill of material No. : (attached)	Date ordered : ....
Description of job :	Date to commence : ....
Tool List No. :	Date of finish : ....
Operation Nos. :	Machine No. : ....

Clock times	Operation number	Department number	Operation		Quantity	
			Number	Details	Made	Rejected

Checked by .... Approved by ....

Note: On the other side of the production order, detailed costs of materials, labour and overhead may be collected so as to determine the profit or loss of the order.

5. *Projection of Cost and Delivery Schedule:* The cost estimates are prepared on the basis of similar jobs executed in the immediate past after making due allowance for cost escalations. Delivery schedule is ascertained after preparing the Production Plan which is based on the detailed analysis of work involved and available production facilities.
6. *Follow-up:* It is essential that the job is completed on time and for this it is necessary that the flow of materials, supplies, tools, is maintained as per time schedule laid down. Persons responsible for completion of jobs must keep a track that job schedules are adhered to at each stage of its completion.
7. *Bill of Materials:* A list of materials, stores and tools required for the execution of the job is prepared by the Department of Planning and Design. This list is sent in advance to the Stores and the concerned Works supervisors; this is done to ensure that the execution of the job does not suffer for non-availability of such items.
8. *Job cost Sheet:* This form is used to summarise the direct materials, direct labour, and factory overhead charged to a particular job. The form varies according to the needs of the particular company. A separate job cost sheet based on detailed expenditure incurred on the job is prepared for each job executed. A Job Card accompanies the job to each department where the entries are made in regard to time spent on the job and direct costs incurred. Total of all direct costs incurred on the job in different departments constitutes the prime cost of the job. Overheads

are recovered by the Costing department on the basis of pre-determined overhead rates of recovery to arrive at total cost of the job. The rate may be based on the direct labour hours, direct labour cost, machine hours etc. Where there are two or more departments, it is usually desirable to have separate overhead rates for each department or separate bases may be used. Selling price is arrived at after adding profit margin as per firm's policy. If the price is pre-fixed, then profit is the difference between selling price and cost incurred/charged to that job. In order to have additional information for the particular job readily available, many companies provide a summary on the cost sheet that includes the selling price as well as estimated selling and administrative expenses so that the estimated profit can be shown.

APS Company Limited
Job Order Cost Sheet No. : ......

Description :	Job No. : ....
Customer :	Quantity : ....
Design No. : (attached)	Date of delivery : ....
Material No. :	Date (Commenced) : ....
Reference No. :	Date (Finished) : ....

Date	Reference	Details	Material	Labour	Overhead

Summary of costs	Estimated (₹)	Actual (₹)	Details
Direct material cost			Units produced : ......
Direct wages production			Cost/unit (₹) : ......
Overhead			Remarks : ....
Production cost			
Admn. S & D			Prepared by : ......
Overheads			
Total cost			Checked by : ......
Profit/Loss			
Selling price			

Cost Documents

(a) Materials: Materials Requisitions, Bill of Materials, and Materials Issue Analysis sheet.

(b) Labour: Works Operation schedule, Job Card, and Wage Analysis Sheet.

(c) Overheads: Use of Standing Order Numbers facilitates charging of overhead costs to individual jobs.

Recording Costs on Jobs

Direct Material costs: Direct Materials are charged to the job on which they are used. Materials used in manufacturing and /or accomplishing jobs are called as direct materials.

Direct Labour costs: "Job time ticket" is the basis of charging labour costs identified with specific jobs. At the start of work on a work-order, the beginning time is noted on the ticket; and when the job is complete, the closing time is mentioned and the time spent is recorded. Earnings are then computed using the employee's hourly rate of payment.

Direct Expenses: Direct expenses are job specific and these are recorded for the job they are incurred.

Overhead: Overhead costs are charged to work-in-progress on the basis of pre-determined recovery rate computed in the pre-production period. Generally, it is derived from the budgeted figures.

Illustration 15.1 : *(Job Order Cost Sheet): The A.J. Manufacturing Company produces expensive furniture by special order. One order was started and completed during March. There was no other production. Factory overhead is applied at a rate of ₹ 20 per direct labour hour. Cost information for the month was as follows:*

Job No.1020

Details		***Amount*** (₹)
Direct Materials		*46,000*
Direct labour Cost		*42,000*
Hours	*3,000*	
Factory overhead:		
Indirect materials		*40,000*
Other factory overhead		*12,000*
Total		*52,000*

Job No. 1020 was ordered by the S.J. Company. They requested 250 rocking chairs. The selling price was ₹700 per chair, and selling and administrative expenses relating to job No. 1020 were ₹7,000.

Prepare a Job Order Cost Sheet. (Assume the order was placed on March 1, 2008 and the job was completed on March 31, 2008.)

Solution :

A.J. Manufacturing Co.

Job Order Cost Sheet

Customer : S.J. Co. | Job No. : 1020

Date Ordered : 01-03-2008 | Product : Rocking Chairs

Date Completed : 31-03-2008 | Quantity : 250

Direct Materials

Date	Description	Quantity	Cost	Amount
31/03	Lumber			46,000
			Total	46,000

Direct Labour

Date	Description	Hours	Rate	Amount
31/03		3,000	14	42,000
			Total	42,000

Factory Overhead

Month	Dept.	Hours	Rate	Amount
March		3000	20	60,000
			Total	60,000

Cost Summary

Selling price		1,75,000
Factory costs :		
Direct materials	46,000	
Direct labour	42,000	
Factory overhead	60,000	1,48,000
Gross profit		27,000
Selling & Admin.		7,000
Profit		20,000

Accounting Treatment of Completed Jobs

On the completion of a job/work-order, its cost is ascertained by aggregating prime cost and absorbed costs. The cost sheet is then marked 'Completed" and removed from the Job Ledger. A transfer entry is made in the Finished Goods Ledger.

For incomplete job the total cost incurred till date becomes cost of work-in-progress. The value of closing work- in- progress is determined from the work-in-Progress account. The closing work-in-Progress is carried to the next period as the opening stock of work-in- progress. The current period expenditure incurred on the job is added to this opening stock of work-in- progress.

Illustration 15.2 : *Power Manufacturing Corporation uses a job order cost system during 2008. These costs were incurred on the following open jobs:*

Job Number	*Direct Materials Cost (₹)*	*Direct Labour*		*Work-in-Process on January 1,2008*			
		Hours	*Cost (₹)*	*Direct Materials Cost (₹)*	*Direct labour Cost (₹)*	*Factory overhead Cost (₹)*	*Total Cost (₹)*
L-1716		*200*	*2,000*	*3,750*	*15,000*	*20,000*	*38,750*
J-1910		*3,000*	*24,000*	*12,500*	*20,000*	*10,000*	*42,500*
H-720	*42,200*	*500*	*3,940*				
G-911	*27,450*	*600*	*3,000*				
B-618	*14,200*	*90*	*450*				

Factory Overheads have been applied @ ₹ 20 per direct labour hour.

Sales:

Job Number	*Amount (₹)*
L-1716	*70,000*
J-1910	*1,32,500*
H-720	*90,000*
G-911	*67,500*
Total	*3,60,000*

Jobs completed during the year: L-1716, J-1910, H-720, and G-911.

Selling and Administration Expenses: ₹ 64,000.

Compute (1) The cost of completed Jobs; (2) The ending work-in-process inventory ; and (3) and the net income for the year 2008.

Solution : (Point-wise)

(1) The cost of completed Jobs:

Job Number	Opening Work-in-process (₹)	Direct Materials Cost (₹)	Direct Labour Cost (₹)	Factory overhead cost (₹)	Total Cost (₹)
L-1716	38,750		2,000	4,000	44,750
J-1910	42,500		24,000	60,000	1,26,500
H-720		42,200	3,940	10,000	56,140
G-911		27,450	3,000	12,000	42,450
Total	81,250	69,650	32,940	86,000	2,69,840

(2) The ending work-in-process inventory:

Job Number	Opening Work-in-process (₹)	Direct Materials Cost (₹)	Direct Labour Cost (₹)	Factory overhead cost (₹)	Total Cost (₹)
B-618		14,200	1,800	450	16,450

(3) Net income for the year 2008:

Details	**Amount (₹)**
Sales	3,60,000
*Less:*Cost of Goods sold	2,69,840
Gross Profit	90,160
*Less:*Selling and administration Expenses	64,000
Net Income	26,160

Estimating in Job Costing

The cost department needs to prepare an estimate of the cost of each job before a price is quoted. Past data in the form of cost sheets of similar jobs, and a careful forecast of material, labour and overhead costs are the bases of the cost estimate for the job. If the job is accepted, specification of materials and the job requirements with complete instructions for operations are recorded on a production order to accompany the work through the plant and simultaneously estimated costs are recorded on the job cost sheet so that a comparison of actual costs and estimated costs can be made at various stages of its completion.

Journal Entries for Job Order Cost System

The appropriate journal entries for a job order cost system are made in the following illustration.

Illustration 15.3 : *Quality Manufacturing Company uses a job order cost system and compiled the following data during 2008 for Job 403:*

Details	*Amount (₹)*
Materials and supplies Purchased	*3,02,500*
Direct materials used	*2,37,500*
Supplies used (Indirect materials)	*25,000*
Direct Labour	*1,87,500*
Indirect labour	*43,750*
Utility costs for the year Payable	*81,250*
Miscellaneous Overhead Payable	*50,000*
Depreciation: Equipment	*27,500*
Depreciation: Building	*10,000*
Applied factory overhead (120% of direct labour costs)	
Cost of goods manufactured	*6,50,000*
Sales	*7,50,000*
Cost of goods sold	*4,07,500*
Selling and administration expenses	*1,37,500*

Solution :

No.	Details		Debit Amount (₹)	Credit Amount (₹)
1.	Materials Inventory A/c	Dr	3,02,500	
	To Accounts Payable A/c			3,02,500
2.	Work-in-Progress A/c (Job No. 403)	Dr	2,37,500	
	Factory overhead Control A/c	Dr	25,000	
	To Materials Inventory A/c			2,62,500
3.	Work-in-Progress A/c (Job No. 403)	Dr	1,87,500	
	Factory overhead Control A/c	Dr	43,750	
	To Payroll Payable A/c			2,31,250

4.	Payroll Payable A/c	Dr	2,31,250	
	To Bank A/c			2,31,250
5.	Factory overhead Control A/c	Dr	1,68,750	
	To Accounts Payable A/c[81,250 + 50,000]			1,31,250
	To Accumulated Depreciation: Equipment A/c			27,500
	To Accumulated Depreciation: Building A/c			10,000
6.	Work-in-Progress A/c (Job No. 403)	Dr	2,25,000	
	To Factory Overhead (Applied)A/c [1,87,500 × 1.2]			2,25,000
7.	Finished Goods Stock A/c	Dr	6,50,000	
	To Work-in-Progress A/c (Job No. 403)			6,50,000
8.	Cost of Goods Sold A/c	Dr	4,07,500	
	To Finished Goods Stock A/c			4,07,500
9.	Accounts Receivable	Dr	7,50,000	
	To Sales A/c			7,50,000

Net income: (Computation):

Details	**Amount (₹)**
Sales	7,50,000
Less: Cost of Goods sold	4,07,500
Gross Profit	3,42,500
Less: Selling and administration Expenses	1,37,500
Net Income	2,05,000

Illustration 15.4 : *The information obtained from the books and records of a Work-Shop at the end of the accounting period as on 31.3.2005 is as under:*

Details	***Completed Jobs***	***Incomplete Jobs***
Direct Materials Supplied from Stores	*1,25,000*	*50,000*
Direct Wages	*1,60,000*	*65,000*
Direct (Chargeable) Expenses	*15,000*	*5,000*
Direct Materials Returned to Stores	*3,000*	——

Works Overheads are 75% of Direct Wages. Administrative Overheads are 30% of Factory Cost and Selling & Distribution Overheads are 10% of Cost of Production.

The Complete jobs realised ₹ 6, 30,000. Prepare:

(1) Work-in-Progress Ledger Control Account;

(2) Completed Job Ledger Control Account; and

(3) Cost of Sales Account.

Solution : **Consolidated Work-in-Progress Control A/c**

Dr Cr

Details	Amount (₹)	Details	Amount (₹)
To Direct Materials Consumed	50,000	By Balance c/d	2,19,375
To Direct Wages	65,000		
To Direct (Chargeable) Expenses	5,000		
Prime Cost	1,20,000		
To Factory Overheads(65,000 × 0.75)	48,750		
Factory Cost	1,68,750		
Administrative Overheads (1,68,750 × 0.30)	50, 625		
Cost of Production	2,19,375		2,19,375
To Balance b/d	2,19,375		

Completed Job Ledger Control A/c

Dr Cr

Details	Amount (₹)	Details	Amount (₹)
To Direct Materials Consumed (1,25,000 – 3,000)	1,22,000	By Customers' A/c	6,30,000
To Direct Wages	1,60,000		
To Direct (Chargeable) Expenses	15,000		
Prime Cost	2,97,000		
To Factory Overheads (1,60,000 × 0.75)	1,20,000		
Factory Cost	4,17,000		
To Administrative Overheads (4,17,000 × 0.30)	1,25,100		
Cost of Production	5,42,100		
To Selling and Distribution Overhead (5,42,100 × 0.10)	54,210		
To Net Profit transferred to Profit & Loss A/c	33,690		
Total	6,30,000	Total	6,30,000

Cost of Sales A/c

Dr Cr

Details	Amount (₹)	Details	Amount (₹)
To Direct Materials Consumed (1,25,000 – 3,000)	1,22,000	Balance c/d	5,96,310
To Direct Wages	1,60,000		
To Direct (Chargeable) Expenses	15,000		
Prime Cost	2,97,000		
To Factory Overheads (1,60,000 × 0.75)	1,20,000		
Factory Cost	4,17,000		
To Administrative Overheads (4,17,000 × 0.30)	1,25,100		
Cost of Production	5,42,100		
To Selling and Distribution Overhead (5,42,100 × 0.10)	54,210		
Cost of Sales	5,96,310		5,96,310

Illustration 15.5 : *The following information relates to the activities of a Production Department in a factory for the week ending on 31.10.2005:*

Materials Consumed		*₹ 1,20,000*
Direct Wages		*₹ 1,00,000*
Departmental Overheads		*₹ 80,000*
Labour Hours Worked	*20,000*	
Hours of Machine in Operation	*16,000*	

Relevant data for the Job No. 541carried out in the department is as under:

Materials Consumed		*₹ 12,200*
Direct Wages		*₹ 8,800*
Labour Hours Worked	*1,250*	
Hours of Machine in Operation	*800*	

Prepare a comparative statement of cost of this job, by using the following three methods of absorption of Overheads:

(a) Direct Labour Hour Rate;

(b) Direct Labour Cost Rate; and

(c) Machine Hour rate.

Solution : **Cost Statement of Job No. 541**

Details	Method		
	Direct Labour Hour Rate (₹)	Direct Labour Cost Rate (₹)	Machine Hour Rate (₹)
Materials consumed	12,200	12,200	12,200
Direct wages	8,800	8,800	8,800
Prime Cost	21,000	21,000	21,000
Overheads:			
(i) 1,250 hours @ ₹ 4 per Labour hour	5,000		
(ii) Direct wages : (8,800 × 0.80)		7,040	
(iii) 800 Machine hours @ ₹ 5 per machine hour			4,000
Factory Cost	26,000	28,040	25,000

Working Notes :

Direct Labour Hour Rate = (Overheads/ Direct Labour Hours)
= (80,000 ÷ 20,000)
= ₹ 4 per direct Labour hour

Direct Labour Cost Rate = (Overheads/ Direct Labour Cost)
= (80,000 ÷ 1, 00,000) × 100
= 80% Direct Labour Cost

Machine Hour Rate = (Overheads/ Machine Hours)
= (80,000 ÷ 16,000) = ₹ 5 per direct Labour hour

SECTION II

BATCH COSTING

Meaning and Nature

According to C.I.M.A. Batch costing is "that form of specific order costing which applies where similar articles are manufactured in batches either for sale or use within the undertaking." Each batch of output is a separate cost unit and cost is determined batch-wise. Each batch consists of a number of identical units of a product so that total batch cost is divided by number of units produced in a batch to get cost per unit.

In job costing, production is to satisfy a specific order and not for stock. In batch costing production is generally for stock though a batch of production is generally undertaken where there is an immediate demand for a part of the batch output. It is useful in case of production of pharmaceutical, automobiles, shoes, garments, instrumentation and engineering products.

Features : Main features of batch costing are enumerated as under:

1. Each batch is a cost unit.
2. All units produced in the batch are identical.
3. Cost of each batch is ascertained separately.
4. Batch production is in general for stock purposes.
5. The method of batch production is used where small parts are produced in significantly large number.
6. Each batch generally involves a set up cost.
7. Set up cost for each batch is more or less same irrespective of size of the batch.
8. Larger the size of the batch, lower is cost per unit.
9. Cost and profit per unit can be known without preparing cost sheet for each unit of product.

Procedure: Each batch is a separate cost unit and is assigned a specific batch number. All direct costs are identified with the batch and are entered in the Batch Cost Card. Material requisitions are entered batch wise and the labour is engaged batch wise. Record is kept as to which worker worked for which batch for how many hours. Overheads are recovered from different batches by applying appropriate overhead rates of recovery. Total cost incurred on the batch divided by the number of units produced in the batch gives cost per unit of output. A new batch of output is undertaken when existing stocks reach below the specified level of the stocks of the product.

Batch Size

It is important to determine the optimum size of the batch. The optimum size is one which results in minimum total cost i.e. the aggregate of set up cost and the stock holding cost is least. Economic size of the batch is the result of two sets of costs: Set up Cost and Holding Cost.

(1) Set up Cost: It is the initializing cost of production of the NEW batch. It involves

(a) setting the machines and tools for a particular batch,

(b) cleaning the plant and machinery,

(c) wastage of materials due to change in machine feeding,

(d) defectives at the start of a batch production,

(e) cost of time lost in change over from one batch to another, and

(f) loss of speed of work, etc.

(2) Holding Cost: It includes cost of capital blocked in inventories and storage costs like rent, insurance, pilferage, obsolescence etc. Larger the batch size, larger will be the average inventory held and thus higher will be the total holding cost for the period.

EBS can be determined with the help of the following formula:

$$(EBS) = \sqrt{[2\ A\ S/C]}$$

EBS = Economic Batch Size

A = Annual Demand

S = Setting up and order processing costs (per batch)

C = Inventory carrying cost per unit per annum

Illustration 15.6 : *Compute the Economic Batch Size of Production for a firm using batch costing with the following information:*

Annual Demand for the Component: 12,500 units

Setting up and order processing costs: ₹ 40

Cost of manufacturing one unit: ₹ 200

Annual Rate of Interest 6 %; and other Storage costs 2% per unit per annum.

Solution : Working Notes:

Carrying Cost = 6%+2% = 8% of ₹ 200 i.e. ₹ 16 per unit per annum [i.e. 200 × 0.08]

(EBS) = √[(2 A S)/ C]

= √[(2× 12,500× 40) ÷(16)] = 250 units per batch

Illustration 15.7 : *PV limited is committed to supply 2,000 screws per month on a steady daily basis. It is estimated that it costs fifteen paise as inventory holding cost per screw per month and that the set up cost per run of its manufacturing ₹ 486.*

(i) What should be the optimum run size for screw manufacture?

(ii) What should be the interval between two consecutive optimum runs?

(iii) Find out the minimum inventory holding cost.

Solution : Answer (i):

Workings:

Annual Demand or Requirement of Product in units

= 2,000 × 12 = 24,000 Units

Set Up cost = ₹ 486

Carrying Cost = 0.15 × 12 = ₹ 1.80 per unit per annum

EBS = √[(2 A S)/ C]

= √[(2× 24,000× 486) ÷ (1.8)] = 3,600 units per batch

Answer (ii):

Interval time between two consecutive runs:

= (EBS / Annual Production) × Number of months in a year

= (3,600 ÷ 24,000) × 12

= 1.8 Months

OR

= (EBS / Production) × Number of Days in a year

= (3,600 ÷ 24,000) × 365

= 54.75 => 55 Days

Answer (iii): Minimum Inventory cost per annum:

= [(Annual Production / EBS) × Set up cost] + [average inventory) × Carrying cost per unit per annum]

= [(24,000 ÷3,600) × 486] + [3,600÷2) × 1.8]

= 3,240 + 3,240 =>₹ 6,480.

Illustration 15.8 : *The demand of an item is uniform@ 50 Units p.m. The fixed cost is ₹ 30 each time a production run is carried out. The inventory carrying cost is ₹ 10 per unit per annum. Determine how often to make a production run and of what size? (Assume a year to be equal to 360 days).*

Solution : Working Notes:

Annual Demand of a Product = (50 × 12) = 600 Units

Set up cost = ₹ 30 per run

Carrying cost = ₹ 10 per unit per annum

EBS = √[(2 A S)/ C]

= √[(2× 600× 30) ÷ 10] = 60 units per batch

Number of production runs a year = (Annual Demand of a Product/ EBS)

= 600 ÷ 60 =>10

Interval between two runs:

= Number of Days in a year / Number of production runs a year

= 360 ÷ 10 => 36 days

Illustration 15.9 : *SV Limited has received an order for supply of 80,000 units of an electronic chip. The batch size has to be in multiples of 1,000 units. The set up cost is ₹ 720 per batch. Variable cost is ₹ 200 per chip. Interest charge is 10% per annum. The customer collects the entire production of the Electronic chip immediately after the batch production is complete.*

Required:

(i) Compute the total cost per annum for batch size of 1,000; 2,000; 4,000; 5,000; 8,000; and 10,000 units under consideration and suggest a batch size which will be most economical;

(ii) Compute economic batch size if the customer is prepared to accept batch of any size, not necessarily in multiples of 1,000units;

(iii) Compute the total set-up cost plus holding costs per annum for the batch size calculated in (ii) above.

Solution : **Computation of Annual cost (₹)**

Batch Size (a)	Set-up cost (b)	Holding cost (c)	Total cost (d)
1,000	(80,000 ÷ 1,000) × 720 = 57,600	(1,000 ÷ 2) × 20 = 10,000	67,600
2,000	(80,000 ÷ 2,000) × 720 = 28,800	(2,000 ÷ 2) × 20 = 20,000	48,800
4,000	(80,000 ÷ 4,000) × 720 = 14,400	(4,000 ÷ 2) × 20 = 40,000	54,400
5,000	(80,000 ÷ 5,000) × 720 = 11,520	(5,000 ÷ 2) × 20 =50,000	61,520
8,000	(80,000 ÷ 8,000) × 720 = 7,200	(8,000 ÷ 2) × 20 = 80,000	87,200
10,000	(80,000 ÷ 10,000) × 720 = 5,760	(10,000 ÷ 2) × 20 = 1,00,000	1,05,760

[No constraint of being in multiple of 1,000 units]

EBS = √[(2 A S)/ C]

= √[(2× 80,000× 720) ÷(20)] = 2,400 units per batch

Total set-up cost = Number of batches ×set-up cost per batch per annum

= (80,000 ÷ 2,400) ×720 = ₹ 24,000

Total storage cost = (Batch size ÷ 2) × Storage cost per unit

= (2,400 ÷ 2) × 20 = ₹ 24,000

Total annual cost = Total set-up cost + Total storage cost

= ₹ 24,000 + ₹ 24,000 = ₹ 48,000

Illustration 15.10 : *Batch No. B-11/06 incurred the following costs:*

Department P: 500 Labour hours @ ₹ 14

Department T: 700 Labour hours @ ₹ 12

Direct Materials ₹ 10,600

Factory overheads are recovered on the basis of Labour hours and the rates are ₹ 32 per hour for department P and ₹ 20 per hour for department T.

The firm uses a cost plus system for fixing selling prices and expects a 30% gross profit (Sales value minus factory cost). Administrative overheads recovered @ 12.5% of Selling Price. 1,600 units were produced in Batch No. B-11/06, calculate

(a) The Selling Price per Unit;

(b) Total Amount of Administrative overheads recovered by Batch No. B-11/06; and

(c) The notional profit per unit.

Solution : **Cost Sheet of Batch No. B-11/06**

Details	Amount (₹)	Amount (₹)
Direct Materials	7,000	10,600
Labour:	8,400	
Department P: 500 Labour hours @ ₹ 14		
Department T: 700 Labour hours @ ₹ 12		15,400
Prime cost		26,000
Factory Overheads:		
Department P: 500 Labour hours @ ₹32	16,000	
Department T: 700 Labour hours @ ₹ 20	14,000	30,000
Factory Cost		56,000
Administrative Overheads: 12.5% of ₹ 80,000		10,000
Total Cost		66,000
Profit		14,000
Selling Price		80,000

1. Selling Price per unit: Sales Value/ No. of units per batch

= 80,000 ÷ 1,600= ₹ 50 per unit.

2. Administrative overheads recovered = ₹ 10,000.

3. Notional profit per unit: ₹ 14,000 ÷ 1,600= ₹ 8.75.

Working Notes:

1. Sales Value: 56,000 ÷ 0.7 = 80,000.

2. Gross Profit: Sales Value – Factory cost

i.e. 80,000 – 56,000 = 24,000

which is equal to 30% of the Sales Value of ₹ 80,000.

Illustration 15.11 : *PV limited manufactures product XL-501in batches of 100 units by a series of operations in the Fabrication and Assembly departments of a factory. The following details relate to 45 batches manufactured by the firm during September 2008:*

Fabrication Department:

Materials: Issued 2,420 Kg. of alloy costing ₹ 125 per kg. 200 Kg of alloy was returned to stores at the end of the month. Off-cuts and scraps realized ₹ 2,500.

Labour: Normal rate of wages is ₹ 25 per hour. Time office recorded 2,460 hours for September 2008. This included 240 hours overtime work paid at the double the normal rate.

Assembly Department:

Materials: Cost of components used ₹ 3,23,600.

Labour: Workers are paid a piece rate of ₹ 10 per unit for production up to 3,000 units. For excess production over 3,000 units and up to 4,000 units the rate is 25% more and for excess over 4,000 units the rate is 50% more. During September 2008 there was stoppage of work for 10 hours due to bread down of machinery and for this stoppage ten workers in the department were paid @ ₹ 25 per hour.

Calculate the average prime cost per unit of XL-501 manufactured in September 2008.

Solution : Statement showing the average prime cost per unit of XL-501 during September 2008

Details			Amount (₹)	Amount (₹)
Direct Materials:				
Fabrication Department:				
Alloy 2,420 Kg @ ₹ 125 per Kg.		3,02,500		
Less: (i) 200 Kg returned @ ₹ 125 per Kg.	25,000			
(ii) Sale of Off-cuts and scraps	2,500	(27,500)	2,75,000	
Assembly Department:				
Cost of Components used			3,23,600	
Total Direct Material cost				5,98,600
Direct Labour:				
(a) Fabrication Department:				
2,460 Hours @ ₹ 25			61,500	
(b) Assembly Department:				
3,000 units @ ₹ 10		30,000		
1,000 units @ ₹ 12.50		12,500		
200 units @ ₹ 15		3,000	45,500	
Total Direct Labour cost			1,07,000	
Total Prime cost				7,05,600
Average Prime cost per batch [7,05,600 / 45]				15680
Average Prime cost per unit [15680/ 100]				156.80

Note: Overtime Premium Payment and Payment for the break down period (idle time) have been excluded from the computation of prime cost as they do not represent normal cost. Thus, they should form part of overheads.

LET US RECAPITULATE

1. Job order costing is that form of specific order costing which applies where work is undertaken to customer's requirements and each order is of comparatively short duration.
2. A separate account is prepared for each job to ascertain its cost and profit; Each individual order or batch is assigned a unique Number.
3. Proper records of documents giving job-wise details are to be maintained efficiently.
4. A separate job cost sheet based on detailed expenditure incurred on the job is prepared for each job executed.
5. Batch costing is that form of specific order costing which applies where similar articles are manufactured in batches either for sale or use within the undertaking.
6. Each batch is a cost unit.
7. Each batch generally involves a set up cost.
8. The method of batch production is used where small parts are produced in significantly large number.
9. Cost and profit per unit can be known without preparing cost sheet for each unit of product.
10. The optimum size of a batch is one which results in minimum total cost i.e. the aggregate of set up cost and the stock holding cost is least.

SOLVED PROBLEMS

Problem 1. *A shop floor supervisor of a small factory presented the following cost for Job No. 214 to ascertain its selling price:*

Details	*Amount (₹) (Per unit)*
Material	*700*
Direct Wages: 18 Hours @ ₹ 25 (Department X 8 hours; Department Y 6 hours; Department Z 4 hours)	*450*
Chargeable Expenses (Special Store Item)	*50*
Add: 100/3% for overheads	*400*
Prime Cost	*1,200*

Analysis of the Profit and Loss account for the Year 2007-08 shows the following:

Details	*Amount (₹)*	*Details*	*Amount (₹)*
To Material Used	*15,00,000*	*By Sales Less returns*	*25,00,000*
To Direct Wages:			
Department X 1,00,000			
Department Y 1,20,000			
Department Z 80,000	*3,00,000*		
To Special Store Items	*40,000*		
To Overheads:			
Department X 50,000			
Department Y 90,000			
Department Z 20,000	*1,60,000*		
To Gross Profit c/d	*5,00,000*		
Total	*25,00,000*	*Total*	*25,00,000*
To Selling Expenses	*2,00,000*	*By Gross Profit b/d*	*5,00,000*
To Net profit	*3,00,000*		
Total	*5,00,000*	*Total*	*5,00,000*

It is also noted that average hourly rates for the three departments X, Y and Z are similar.

You are required to:

(i) Draw up a job cost sheet;

(ii) Calculate the entire revised cost sheet of Job No. 214 using 2007-08 actual figures as the basis;

(iii) Add 20% to the total cost to determine selling price of the job.

[I.C.W.A; C.S (Modified)]

Solution :

Basic calculations: Overhead rates are to be computed on the basis of the data of 2007-08. The rates calculated for the various departments are as under:

Department (1)	Overheads (₹) (2)	Direct Labour Hour (Hours)* (3)	Rate per Hour (₹) (4) = (2) ÷ (3)
X	50,000	1,00,000 ÷25 = 4,000	12.50
Y	90,000	1,20,000 ÷25 = 4,800	18.75
Z	20,000	80,000 ÷25 = 3,200	6.25

* Direct Labour Hour = Direct Wages ÷ Direct Labour Hour rate

Revised Cost Sheet of Job NO. 214

Details	Amount (₹)	Amount (₹)
Material		700.00
Direct Wages:		
Department X [8 × 25]	200	
Department Y [6 × 25]	150	
Department Z [4 × 25]	100	450.00
Chargeable Expenses		50.00
Prime cost		1,200.00
Overheads:		
Department X [8 × 12.50]	100.00	
Department Y [6 × 18.75]	112.50	
Department Z [4 × 6.25]	25.00	237.50
Total Cost		1,437.50
Profit (1,437.50 × 0.2)		287.50
Selling Price		1,725.00

Problem 2. *Two fitters, a labourer and a boy undertake a job on piece rate basis for ₹ 9,000. The time spent by each of them is 80 ordinary working hours. The rates of pay on time rate basis are ₹ 30.00 per hour for each of the two fitters, ₹ 20.00 per hour for the labourer and ₹ 10.00 per hour for the boy. Calculate:*

(i) The amount of piece work premium and the share of each worker, when the piece work premium is divided proportionately to the wages paid and

(ii) The selling price of the above job on the basis of following additional data:

Cost of direct material ₹ 15,000; Works overhead @ 25% of prime cost, selling overhead @ 12.5% of works cost and profit @ 20% on cost of sales.

Solution :

Computation of Wages:

Details	**Amount (₹)**
Two fitters @ ₹ 30.00 per hour for 80 hours each	4,800
One labourer @ ₹ 20.00 per hour for 80 hours each	1,600
One Boy @ ₹ 10.00 per hour for 80 hours each	800
Total	7,200
Piece work premium:	
Total wages agreed on piece rate basis	9,000
Less: Wages calculated on time basis (computed above)	7,200
Piece work premium	1,800

Share of each worker in the quantum of piece work premium Amount:
(This will be shared by workers in the ratio of 6:2:1 as under)

Two fitters @ ₹ 600 Each	1,200
One labourer @ ₹ 400	400
One Boy @ ₹ 200	200

Computation of Selling Price for the Job

Details	Amount (₹)
Direct Material	15,000
Direct Wages	9,000
Prime Cost	24,000
Works overhead [24,000 ×0.25]	6,000
Works Cost	30,000
Selling Expenses [30,000 × 0.125]	3,750
Cost of Sales	33,750
Profit [33,750 × 0.20]	6,750
Selling Price	40,500

Problem 3. (Job Order Costing)

The Goodland Company received an order from a customer on May 13, 2003 for 1,600 tea pots, model# 16. The price is ₹ 30 each and delivery is promised in three months. Job No. 807 was assigned to the order.

Direct Materials:

Direct Materials costs for the job, obtained from materials requisition, are as under:

Department A:	*June 8, 800 bases @ ₹ 8.*	*₹ 6,400*
	June 14, 800 bases @ ₹ 9	*₹ 7,200*
Department B:	*July 11, 1,000 handles @ ₹ 3*	*₹ 3,000*
	July 20, 600 handles @ ₹ 5	*₹ 3,000*

Direct Labour:

Department A:	*June 17, Forming 20 hours @ ₹ 100*	*₹ 2,000*
	June 17, Polishing 16 hours @ ₹ 110	*₹ 1,760*
Department B:	*June 17, Assembly 24 hours @ ₹ 80*	*₹ 1,920*
	June 17, Assembly 16 hours @ ₹ 90	*₹ 1,440*

Factory Overhead: Factory overhead is absorbed when the job is completed or at the end of a period for jobs in process. The pre-determined factory overhead rate is based on direct labour hours for each department as follows: Department A, ₹ 50 per hour; Department B, ₹ 60 per hour.

Selling and Administration expenses are based on 12.5% of selling price.

Solution : Statement of Cost for Job No. 807

Details	Amount (₹)
Direct materials :	
Department A (800×8 + 800×9) = 13,600	
Department B (1,000×3 + 600×5) = 6,000	
Total direct material consumed	19,600
Direct wages :	
Department A: [(20×100) + (16×110)] = 3,760	
Department B: [(24×80) + (16×90)] = 3,360	
Total Direct wages expended	7,120
Prime cost	26,720
Factory overheads :	
Department A [(20+16) × 50] = 1,800	
Department B [(24+16) × 60] = 2,400	
Total factory overheads	4,200
Factory cost	30,920
Selling and Administration (48,000 × 0.125)	6,000
Cost of Sales	36,920
Profit (Balancing Figure)	11,080
Sales value (1,600× 30)	48,000

Problem 4. *From the records of a manufacturing Company, the following budgeted details are available:*

Details		*Amount (₹)*
Direct Materials		*2,43,500*
Direct Wages:		
Machine Shop(12,500 Hours)	*75,000*	
Assembly Shop(8,000 Hours)	*64,000*	*1,39,000*
Works Overhead:		
Machine Shop	*1,00,000*	
Assembly shop	*42,800*	*1,42,800*
Administrative Overhead		*1,05,000*
Selling and Distribution Overhead		*2,10,000*
Total		*8,40,000*

Assuming that the company follows absorption method of costing, you are required to:

(1) Prepare a Schedule of Overhead Rates from the information available. And

(2) Work out the cost estimate for the following Job based on Overhead Rates so determined:

Direct Material 30 Kg. @ ₹ 18 per Kg. ; and 20 Kg. @ ₹ 20 per Kg.

Direct Wages: Machine Shop 35 Hours and Assembly Shop 40 Hours (On the basis of Hourly rate of Machine Shop and Assembly Shop)

Solution : **Schedule of Overhead Rate**

Details	Amount (₹)
Direct Materials	2,43,200
Direct Wages:	
Machine Shop (12,500 × 6) = 75,000	
Assembly shop (8,000 × 8) =64,000	1,39,000
Prime cost	3,82,200
Works Overhead:	
Machine Shop (12,500 × 8) =1,00,000	
Assembly shop (8000 × 5.35) = 42,800	1,42,800
Works Cost	5,25,000
Administration Overheads 20% of Works cost: (5,25,000 × 0.2)	1,05,000
Cost of Production	6,30,000
Selling and Distribution Overheads 1/3 of cost of Production: {6,30,000 × (1/3)}	2,10,000
Total Cost of Sales	8,40,000

Workings:

1. Works Overhead rate:

   (Basis: Direct Labour hours)

   Machine Shop: Works overhead Amount / Direct Labour hours

   = 1,00,000 ÷12,500 => ₹ 8 per direct labour hour

   Assembly Shop: Works overhead Amount / Direct Labour hours

   = 42,800 ÷ 8,000 => ₹ 5.35 per direct labour hour

2. Administration Overhead rate:

   (Basis: Works cost)

   (Administration Overhead / Works Cost) × 100

   = (1,05,000 ÷5,25,000) × 100 => 20% of works cost

3. Selling and Distribution Overhead rate:
   (Basis: Total Product Cost)
   (Selling and Distribution Overhead / Total Product Cost) ×100
   = (2,10,000 ÷ 6,30,000) × 100 => 100/3 % or 1/3 of works cost

Estimate of Cost of Job

Details		Amount (₹)
Direct Materials:		
(30×18)=	540	
(25×20)=	500	1,040.00
Direct Wages:		
Machine Shop (35@ 6)=210		
Assembly Shop (40@ 8)=320		530.00
Prime Cost		1,570.00
Works Overhead:		
Machine Shop (35× 8) = 280		
Assembly Shop (40×5.35)=214		494.00
Works Cost		2,064.00
Administration Overhead (2,064.00 × 0.2)		412.80
Cost of Production		2,476.80
Selling and Distribution Overhead {2,476.80 × (1/3)}		825.60
Total Cost of Job		3,302.40

Problem 5. *It is observed that the selling price of Job No. 4213 has been computed on the following basis:*

Materials	*624*
Direct Wages: 25 hours @ ₹ 12 per hour	*300*
(Department X: 12 hours+ Department Y: 5 Hours + Department Z: 8 hours)	
Prime Cost	*924*
Add: (100/3) % on Prime Cost	*308*
Total	*1,232*

An analysis of the preceding year's Profit & Loss account shows the following:

Dr **_Profit & Loss Account_** *Cr*

Details	***Amount (₹)***	***Details***	***Amount (₹)***
Direct Materials Consumed	*15,50,000*	*Sales*	*27,00,000*
Direct Wages:			
Department X: 1,00,000			
Department Y: 1,20,000			
Department Z: 80,000	*3,00,000*		
Works Overhead:			
Department X: 50,000			
Department Y: 80,000			
Department Z: 20,000	*1,50,000*		
Gross Profit c/d	*7,00,000*		
	27,00,000		*27,00,000*
Selling Expenses	*5,50,000*	*Gross Profit b/d*	*7,00,000*
Net Profit	*1,50,000*		
Total	*7,00,000*	*Total*	*7,00,000*

You are required to:

(1) Prepare Job Cost statement;

(2) Compute and make the revised costs using the Preceding year's data as the basis;

(3) Add to the total job cost 12% for profit and fix the final selling price.

Solution : **Job cost Sheet: Job No. 4213**

Details			**Amount (₹)**
Direct Materials		624.00	
Direct Wages		300.00	
Prime Cost			924.00
Add Factory Overhead:			
Department X: (144 × 0.5)	= 72		
Department Y: (60 × 2/3)	= 40		
Department Z: (96 × 0.25)	= 24		136.00
Factory Cost			1,060.00
Selling Expenses (1,060 × 0.275)			291.50
Cost of Sales			1,351.50
Add Profit (1,351.5 × 0.12)			162.18
Selling Price			1,513.68

Working Note: Factory Overhead can be calculated as a rate per direct labour hour or as a percentage of direct wages. A percentage of direct wages has been taken to prepare the new job cost sheet.

Department X: (50,000 ÷ 1,00,000) × 100 = 50%

Department Y: (80,000 ÷ 1,20,000) × 100 = (200/3) % Or 2/3

Department Z: (20,000 ÷ 80,000) × 100 = 25%

Problem 6. *Leo Limited undertakes to supply 2,000 units of a component per month for three months of April, May and June 2005. Every month a batch order is opened against which materials and labour cost are booked at actual. Overheads are levied at a rate per labour hour. The selling price is contracted at ₹ 35 per unit.*

From the following data, present the cost and profit per unit of each batch order and the overall position of the order for 6,000 units.

Month	*Batch Output (Number)*	*Material cost (₹)*	*Labour cost (₹)*
April 2005	*2,000*	*10,000*	*20,000*
May 2005	*2,400*	*24,000*	*24,000*
June 2005	*1,600*	*8,000*	*16,000*

Labour is paid at rate of ₹ 10 per Labour hour. The details are:

Month	*Overheads (₹)*	*Labour Hours*
April 2005	*60,000*	*4,000*
May 2005	*45,000*	*4,500*
June 2005	*75,000*	*5,000*

Solution :

Leo Limited

Statement of cost and profit per unit of each batch

(For the period April, 2005 to June, 2005)

Details	**April 2005 Amount (₹)**	**May 2005 Amount (₹)**	**June 2005 Amount (₹)**	**April to June 2005 Amount (₹)**
Batch Output (Number)	2,000	2,400	1,600	6,000
Sales Value @ ₹ 35per unit	70,000	84,000	56,000	2,10,000

Cost:				
Materials	10,000	24000	8,000	42,000
Wages	20,000	24000	16,000	60,000
Overheads	30,000	24000	24,000	78,000
Total	60,000	72000	48,000	1,80,000
Profit per Batch	10,000	12,000	8,000	30,000
Cost per unit	30	30	30	30
Profit per unit	5	5	5	5

Working Notes:

Month {a}	Labour Hours= Labour cost/ Labour rate per hour {b}	Overheads Per Hour = Overheads/ Labour hours {c}	Overheads per Batch = {b} × {c} {d}
April 2005	20,000÷10=2,000	60,000÷4,000=15	30,000
May 2005	24,000÷10=2,400	45,000÷4,500=10	24,000
June 2005	16,000÷10=1,600	75,000÷5,000=15	24,000

Overall Profit position of the order for 6,000 units

Details	Amount (₹)
Sales Value (6,000 units @ ₹ 35 per unit)	2,10,000
Less: Total Cost (6,000 units @30 per unit)	1,80,000
PROFIT	30,000

Problem 7. *Standard Manufacturing Company uses a job order cost system and compiled the following data for the month of August, 2008 for Job 430:*

Details	*Amount (₹)*
Work-in-progress Inventory on August 1,2008	*1,75,000*
Transactions for the month of August, 2008:	
1. Raw Materials Purchased on credit	*2,25,000*
2. Materials Issued (Indirect materials)	*1,75,000*
3. Payroll (Indirect ₹ 50,000)	*2,50,000*
4. Factory Overhead Incurred	*3,00,000*
5. Applied factory overhead (120% of direct labour costs)	
6. Jobs with a cost of ₹ 5,50,000 were completed in August,2008	
7. Jobs costing ₹ 7,00,000 were shipped out and billed at a mark up of 25% on cost	

Prepare the general entries for the above transactions. Compute the work-in-progress Inventory account at August 31, 2008.

Solution :

No.	Details		Debit Amount (₹)	Credit Amount (₹)
1.	Materials Inventory A/c	Dr	2,25,000	
	To Accounts Payable A/c			2,25,000
2.	Work-in-Progress A/c (Job No. 430)	Dr	1,50,000	
	Factory overhead Control A/c	Dr	25,000	
	To Materials Inventory A/c			1,75,000
3.	Work-in-Progress A/c (Job No. 430)	Dr	2,00,000	
	Factory overhead Control A/c	Dr	50,000	
	To Payroll Payable A/c			2,50,000
4.	Payroll Payable A/c	Dr	2,50,000	
	To Bank A/c			2,50,000
5.	Factory overhead Control A/c	Dr	3,00,000	
	To Accounts Payable A/c			3,00,000
6.	Work-in-Progress A/c (Job No. 403)	Dr	2,40,000	
	To Factory Overhead (Applied)A/c [2,00,000 × 1.2]			2,40,000
7.	Finished Goods Stock A/c	Dr	5,50,000	
	To Work-in-Progress A/c (Job No. 430)			5,50,000
8.	Cost of Goods Sold A/c	Dr	7,00,000	
	To Finished Goods Stock A/c			7,00,000
9.	Accounts Receivable	Dr	8,75,000	
	To Sales A/c [7,00,000 × 1.25]			8,75,000

Dr **Work-in-Progress Inventory Account** Cr

Details	Amount (₹)	Details	Amount (₹)
To Balance b/d	1,75,000	By Jobs completed A/c	5,50,000
To Direct Materials	1,50,000	By Balance c/d	2,15,000
To Direct Labour	2,00,000		
To Factory Overheads	2,40,000		
Total	7,65,000	Total	7,65,000
To Balance b/d	2,15,000		

Problem 8. *In Engineering Company, the factory overheads are recovered on a fixed percentage basis on direct wages and the Administration overheads are absorbed on a fixed percentage basis on works cost.*

The company has furnished the following data relating to two jobs undertaken by it in a period:

Details	*Job 501 Amount (₹)*	*Job 502 Amount (₹)*
Direct Materials	*75,600*	*52,500*
Direct Wages	*58,800*	*42,000*
Selling Price	*2,33,310*	*1,79,550*
Profit percentage on total cost	*10%*	*20%*

Required:

(i) Computation of percentage recovery rates of factory overheads and administration overheads.

(ii) Calculation of the amount of factory overheads, administration overheads and profit for each of the two jobs.

(iii) Using the above rates of recovery, fix the selling price of Job No. 503, the additional data being:

Direct Materials	*₹ 30,400*
Direct Wages	*₹ 25,000*
Profit percentage on selling price	*12%*

Solution : Working Notes:

Job 501: 2,33,310 ÷1.1=> ₹ 2,12,100

Job 502: 1,79,550 ÷1.2=> ₹ 1,49,625

Computation of Absorption rates of factory overheads:

Let the Factory overhead Absorption rate as a percentage of direct wages be 'x'

Administration overhead Absorption rate as a percentage of Factory cost be 'y'

Factory cost of Jobs:

Job 501: ₹ 75,600 + ₹ 58,800 + ₹ 58,800 x

Job 502: ₹ 52,500 + ₹ 42,000 + ₹ 42,000 x

Total cost of Production of jobs:

Job 501:

[₹1,34,400 + ₹ 58,800 x] + [₹1,34,400 + ₹ 58,800 x] y = 2,12,100 ...(1)

Job 502:

[₹94,500 + ₹ 42,000 x] + [₹94,500 + ₹ 42,000 x] y =1,49,625 ...(2)

1,34,400 + 58,800 x + [1,34,400 + 58,800 x] y = 2,12,100 ...(1)

94,500 + 42,000 x + [94,500 + 42,000 x] y = 1,49,625 ...(2)

58,800 x + [1,34,400 + 58,800 x] y = 77,700 ...(1)

94,500 + 42,000 x + [94,500 + 42,000 x] y = 55,125 ...(2)

58,800 x + 1,34,400y + 58,800 x y = 77,700 ...(1)

42,000 x + 94,500y + 42,000 x y = 55,125 ...(2)

Multiplying (1) by 5 and (2) by 7, we get

2,94,000 x + 6,72,000y + 2,94,000 x y = 3,88,500 ...(3)

2,94,000 x + 6,61,500y + 2,94,000 x y = 3,85,875 ...(4)

Deducting (4) from the (3) we get

10,500y = 2,625

y = 2,625÷10,500 => 0.25 i.e. 25%

Putting the value of y in Equation (1)

58,800 x + (1,34,400× 0.25) + (58,800× 0.25) x = 77,700

58,800 x + 33,600 + 14,700 x = 77,700

73,500 x = 44,100

x= 44,100 ÷ 73,500 => 0.6 i.e. 60%

Statement of Cost and Profit of each Job

Details		Job 501 Amount (₹)	Job 502 Amount (₹)
Direct Materials		75,600	52,500
Direct Wages		58,800	42,000
Prime cost		1,34,400	94,500
Factory Overheads	[58,800 × 0.6] [42,000 × 0.6]	35,280	25,200
Factory Cost		1,69,680	1,19,700
Administration Overheads	[1,69,680 × 0.25] [1,19,700 × 0.25]	42,420	29,925
Total Cost		2,12,100	1,49,625
Profit (Balancing figure)		21,210	29,925
Selling Price		2,33,310	1,79,550

Ascertainment of Selling Price for Job No.503

Details	Job 503 Amount (₹)
Direct Materials	30,400
Direct Wages	25,000
Prime cost	55,400
Factory Overheads [25,000 × 0.6]	15,000
Factory Cost	70,400
Administration Overheads [70,400 × 0.25]	17,600
Total Cost	88,000
Profit [88,000 × (0.12 ÷ 0.88)]	12,000
Selling Price	1,00,000

Problem 9. *You are given below the following information relating to a factory for the year, 2008:*

Item of Expense	***Amount*** (₹)
Direct Material	*25,00,000*
Direct labour	*15,00,000*
Direct factory expenses	*10,00,000*
Factory overheads	*16,00,000*
Office & Administration Overheads	*9,00,000*

During February 2008, the factory receives an enquiry for a job which requires:

Item of Expense	***Amount*** (₹)
Direct material cost	*8,200*
Direct labour cost	*3,200*
Direct factory expenses	*1,100*

It has been decided that factory overheads should be recovered on the basis of a percentage to prime cost. Office & Administration Overheads are to be recovered on the basis of percentage to cost of production with an increase of 14% for the cost hikes in the current year.

Prepare cost sheet for the job in each of the following three cases:

1. *Profit is 10% of the quotation price and selling and distribution expenses are 25% of quotation price.*
2. *Profit is 10% of cost of sales and selling and distribution expenses are 25% of cost of sales.*
3. *Profit is 10% of sales and selling and distribution expenses are 25% of cost of sales.*

Solution : **Job cost sheet for the factory for 2008**

Details	Amount (₹)
Direct Material	25,00,000
Direct labour	15,00,000
Direct factory expenses	10,00,000
Prime cost	50,00,000
Factory overheads	16,00,000
Works cost	66,00,000
Office and Administration Overheads	9,00,000
Cost of production	75,00,000

Working note:

Computation of Recovery Rates of Overheads:

1. Factory overheads as a percentage of prime Cost:

$$= (16,00,000 \div 50,00,000) \times 100 = 32\%$$

2. Office & Administration overheads as a percentage of cost of production:

$$= (9,00,000 \div 75,00,000) \times 100 = 12\%$$

Job cost sheet for Job No……

Case I: Profit is 10% of the quotation price and selling and distribution expenses are 25% of quotation price.

Details	Amount (₹)
Direct Material	8,200
Direct labour	3,200
Direct factory expenses	1,100
Prime cost	12,500
Factory overheads @ 32% of Prime cost (12,500 × 0.32)	4,000
Works cost	16,500
Office & Administration Overheads @ 12% of Cost of production raised by 14%	2,565
Cost of production	19,065
Selling & Dist. Exp. @ 25% of sales value (29,331× 0.25)	7,333
Cost of sales	26,398
Profit @ 10% of sales value (29,331× 0.1)	2,933
Sales	29,331

Working note:

Cost of production (Pre-Revised) = Works cost/ 0.88

= 16,500/ 0.88 =>18,750

Office and Administration Overheads:

$$= (18{,}750 \times 0.12) \times (1.14) \Rightarrow ₹\ 2{,}565$$

Cost of production (Post -Revised):

= Works cost + Office and Administration Overheads

$$= 16{,}500 + 2{,}565 \Rightarrow ₹\ 19{,}065$$

Let sales be = x

$$x = 19{,}065 + 0.25x + 0.1x$$

$$0.65x = 19{,}065$$

$$x = 19{,}065 / 0.65 = 29{,}331$$

Case II: Profit is 10% of cost of sales and selling and distribution expenses are 25% of cost of sales.

Details	Amount (₹)
Cost of production	19,065
Selling & Dist. Exp.	6,355
Cost of sales	25,420
Profit	2,542
Sales OR Quotation Price	27,962

Working note: let sales be = x

Selling & Dist Expenses = 0.25x

$$x = 19{,}065 + 0.25x$$

$$0.75x = 19{,}065$$

$$x = 19{,}065 \div 0.75 = 25{,}420$$

Case III: Profit is 10% of sales and selling and distribution expenses are 25% of cost of sales.

Details	Amount (₹)
Cost of production	19,065
Selling & Dist. Exp.	6,355
Cost of sales	25,420
Profit	2,824
Sales	28,244

Working note: let cost of sales be = x

Selling & dist exp = 0.25x

$$x = 19{,}065 + 0.25x$$

$$0.75x = 19{,}065$$

$$x = 19{,}065 \div 0.75 = 25{,}420$$

Profit 10% of sales = 1/9 th of cost of sales

Profit = {25,420 × (1/9)} =>₹ 2,824

Sales = 25,420 ÷ 0.9 = 28,244.

Problem 10. *The following information for the year ended December 31, 2004 is obtained from the books and records of a factory:*

Details	*Completed Jobs (₹)*	*W.I.P (₹)*
Raw Materials supplied from stores	*1,18,800*	*43,200*
Chargeable expenses	*13,500*	*5,400*
Materials returned to stores	*1,350*	
Wages	*1,35,000*	*54,000*

Factory overheads are 120% of Wages. Office Overheads are 40% of factory cost and Selling Distribution Overheads are 10% of cost of Production.

The completed Jobs realised ₹ 7,25,000. Write up:

(i) Work-in-Progress Ledger Control Account;

(ii) Completed Job ledger Control Account; and

(iii) Cost of Sales Account.

Solution :

Dr **Work-in-Progress Ledger Control A/c** Cr

Details	Amount (₹)	Details	Amount (₹)
Materials	43,200	Balance c/d	2,34,360
Wages	54,000		
Chargeable Expenses	5,400		
Prime Cost	1,02,600		
Factory overheads: (54,000 × 1.2)	64,800		
Factory Cost	1,67,400		
Office Overheads: (1,67,400 × 0.4)	66,960		
Total	2,34,360	Total	2,34,360

Dr **Completed Job ledger Control A/c** Cr

Details	Amount (₹)	Details	Amount (₹)
Materials 1,18,800 Less: Returns (1,350)	1,17,450	Cost of Sales A/c	5,99,130

Wages	1,35,000		
Chargeable Expenses	13,500		
Prime Cost	2,65,950		
Factory overheads	1,62,000		
Factory Cost	4,27,950		
Office Overheads	1,71,180		
Total	5,99,130	Total	5,99,130

Dr **Cost of Sales A/c** Cr

Details	Amount (₹)	Details	Amount (₹)
Completed Jobs A/c	5,99,130	Sales A/c	7,25,000
Selling Distribution Overheads (5,99,130 × 0.1)	59,913		
Profit	65,957		
Total	725000	Total	725000

Problem 11. *The following information for the year ended 31.12.2008 is obtained from the books and records of a factory:*

Details	*Completed Jobs (₹)*	*Work-in-Progress (₹)*
Raw Materials supplied from stores	*3,08,000*	*80,000*
Wages	*4,00,000*	*1,20,000*
Chargeable Expenses	*40,000*	*10,000*
Materials Returned to stores	*8,000*	*NIL*

Factory overheads are 75% of wages. Office overheads are 30% of factory cost and selling distribution overheads are 12.5% of the cost of production.

The completed jobs realized ₹ 18, 00,000. Write up:

(i) Work-in-Progress Ledger control Account;

(ii) Completed Jobs Ledger control Account;

(iii) Cost of Sales Account.

Solution :

Dr **Work-in-Progress Ledger control Account** Cr

Details	Amount (₹)	Details	Amount (₹)
To Raw Materials	80,000	By Balance c/d	3,90,000
To Wages	1,20,000		
To Chargeable expenses	10,000		

To Factory overheads [0.75 × 1,20,000]	90,000		
Factory Cost	3,00,000		
To Office overheads [0.3 × 3,00,000]	90,000		
Total	3,90,000	Total	3,90,000

Dr **Completed Jobs Ledger control Account** Cr

Details	Amount (₹)	Details	Amount (₹)
To Raw Materials 3,08,000 Less: Returns 8,000	3,00,000	By Cost of Sales A/c	13,52,000
To Wages	4,00,000		
To Chargeable expenses	40,000		
To Factory overheads [0.75 × 4,00,000]	3,00,000		
Factory Cost	10,40,000		
To Office overheads [0.3 × 10,40,000]	3,12,000		
Total	13,52,000	Total	13,52,000

Dr **Cost of Sales Account** Cr

Details	Amount (₹)	Details	Amount (₹)
To Completed Jobs A/c	13,52,000	By Sales A/c	18,00,000
To Selling & Distribution Overheads A/c [0.125 × 13,52,000]	1,69,000		
To Profit	2,79,000		
Total	18,00,000	Total	18,00,000

Problem 12. *In a factory following the job costing system, an abstract from the work-in-process as on September 30, 2008 was prepared as under:*

Job No.	*Materials Amount (₹)*	*Direct Labour Amount (₹)*		*Factory Overhead applied Amount (₹)*
1015	*5,300*	*400 hours*	*6,000*	*3,600*
1018	*3,240*	*250 hours*	*7,500*	*4,500*
1020	*3,060*	*300 hours*	*3,000*	*1,800*
Total	*11,600*		*16,500*	*9,900*

Materials used in October were as under:

Material Requisition No.	***Job No.***	***Cost (₹)***
101	*1018*	*1,200*
102	*1018*	*1,700*
103	*1018*	*2,060*
104	*1020*	*2,660*
105	*1021*	*3,640*
106	*1024*	*2,880*
Total		*14,140*

A summary of Labour hours deployed during October is as under:

Details	***Job No.***	***Number of Hours***	
		Shop-I	***Shop-II***
	1015	*25*	*25*
	1018	*90*	*30*
	1020	*75*	*10*
	1021	*65*	——-
	1024	*20*	*10*
	Total	*275*	*75*
Indirect Labour:			
Waiting for Material		*20*	*10*
Machine break down		*10*	*5*
Idle time		*5*	*6*
Overtime premium		*6*	*5*
Total		*316*	*101*

A shop credit slip was issued in October that material issued under Requisition NO. 101 was returned back to the stores as not being suitable. A Material transfer Note issued in October indicated that material issued under Requisition No. 102 for Job No. 1018 was directed to Job No. 1024.

The labour rate in Shop-I per labour hour is ₹ 30 per hour while at shop- II it is ₹ 20 per hour. The factory overhead is applied at the same rate as in September. Jobs No. 1015, 1018 and 1020 were completed in October.

You are asked to compute the factory cost of the completed jobs. It is the practice of the management to put a 10% on the factory cost to cover administration and selling overheads and invoice the job to the customer on a total cost plus 25% basis. What would be the price of these three jobs?

Solution :

Details	Job Number					
	1015		1018		1020	
	Amount (₹)	Amount (₹)	Amount (₹)	Amount (₹)	Amount (₹)	Amount (₹)
Material:						
September	5,300		3,240		3,060	
October	———	5,300	2,060	5,300	2,660	5,720
Labour:						
September	6,000		7,500		3,000	
October	1.250	7.250	3.300	10.800	2.450	5.450
Overheads:						
September	3,600		4,500		1,800	
October	750	4,350	1,980	6,480	1,470	3,270
Works Cost		16,900		22,580		14,440

Working Notes:

(1) Computation of labour cost incurred in October:

Details	Amount (₹)
Job Number 1015:	
Shop-I: 25 × 30 = 750	
Shop-II: 25 × 20 = 500	1.250
Job Number 1018:	
Shop-I: 90 × 30 = 2,700	
Shop-II: 30 × 20 = 600	3.300
Job Number 1020:	
Shop-I: 75 × 30 = 2,250	
Shop-II: 10 × 20 = 200	2.450

(2) Overheads rate: In September, overheads are recovered @ 60% of direct Labour cost. In October also the same pattern of charging overheads is maintained.

Details	Job No. 1015 Amount (₹)	Job No. 1018 Amount (₹)	Job No. 1020 Amount (₹)
Works cost	16,900	22,580	14,440
Administration and Selling Overheads [10% on works cost]	1,690	2,258	1,444
Total cost	18,590	24,838	15,884
Profit (25% on Sales or 20% on cost of sales)	3,718	4,968	3,177
Total	22,308	29,806	19,061

Problem 13. *Following information for the month of April is extracted from the cost records of Hilton Limited which specializes in the manufacture of automobile parts. The parts are manufactured in department D-I and assembled in department D-II:*

Details	*Total*	*Department D-I*	*Department D-II*
Direct Labour Hours worked	*1,00,000*	*37,500*	*62,500*
Machine Hours worked	*37,500*	*31,250*	*6,250*
Machine Horse power (H.P.)	*500*	*400*	*100*
Book Value of Machines (₹)	*2,00,000*	*1,60,000*	*40,000*
Floor Area (Sq. Feet)	*30,000*	*15,000*	*15,000*
Direct Material (₹)	*3,25,000*	*2,50,000*	*75,000*
Direct Labour (₹)	*4,50,000*	*2,00,000*	*2,50,000*
Factory Rent(₹)	*90,000*	———	———
Supervision (₹)	*48,000*	*20,000*	*28,000*
Depreciation on Machines (₹)	*25,000*	———	———
Power (₹)	*40,000*	———	———
Repairs to Machines (₹)	*10,150*	*8,150*	*2,000*
Indirect Labour (₹)	*25,050*	*12,550*	*12,500*

The prime cost of batch B-2048 has been booked as under:

Details	*Total Amount (₹)*	*Department D-I Amount (₹)*	*Department D-II Amount (₹)*
Material	*20,500*	*16,875*	*3,625*
Labour	*47,928*	*18,750*	*29,178*

Direct Labour hours worked on batch B-2048 were 3,000 in department D-I and 7,500 in department D-II. Machine hours worked on this batch were 1,500 in department D-I and 900 in department D-II. Allocate overhead expenditure and calculate the cost of each unit in the batch B-2048 which consists of 1,250 units.

Solution : Statement showing allocation of overhead expenditure to Departments D-I and D-II

Details	**Basis of Allocation**	**Total Amount (₹)**	**Depart-ment D-I Amount (₹)**	**Depart-ment D-II Amount (₹)**
Machine Costs:	Book value of machines (4:1)	25,000	20,000	5,000
Depreciation	Horse Power (21:4)	40,000	33,600	6,400
Power	(Actual)			
Repairs to Machines		10,150	8,150	2,000
Total		75,150	61,750	13,400

Other Overhead Costs:	Floor Area (1:1)			
Factory Rent	(Actual)	90,000	45,000	45,000
Supervision	(Actual)	48,000	20,000	28,000
Indirect Labour		25,050	12,550	12,500
Total		1,63,050	77,550	85,500

Computation of Overheads Absorption Rates:

Machine Hour Rate:

Department D-I: ₹ 61,750 ÷ 31,250 = ₹ 1.976

Department D-II: ₹ 13,400 ÷ 6,250 = ₹ 2.144

Labour Hour Rate:

Department D-I: ₹ 77,550 ÷ 37,500 = ₹ 2.068

Department D-II: ₹ 85,500 ÷ 62,500 = ₹ 1.368

Cost Sheet of Batch 2048
(Number of Units: 1,250)

Details	Total Amount (₹)	Department D-I Amount (₹)	Department D-II Amount (₹)
Material	20,500	16,875	3,625
Labour	47,928	18,750	29,178
Overhead costs	21,572	9,168	12,404
Total	90,000	44,793	45,207

Cost per unit of the batch: ₹ 90,000 ÷1,250 units =>₹72.

Working Notes:

Details	Amount (₹)
Department D-I:	
Machine cost (1,500 Machine Hours × ₹ 1.976)	2,964
Other Overheads (3,000 Labour Hours × ₹ 2.068)	6,204
Total	9,168
Department D-II:	
Machine cost (1,000 Machine Hours × ₹ 2.144)	2,144
Other Overheads (7,500 Labour Hours × ₹ 1.368)	10,260
Total	12,404

OBJECTIVE TYPE EXERCISES

I. Fill in the blank spaces with suitable word/s :

1. .... costing and .... costing are the variants of job costing.

2. In pharmaceutical formulation factory, method of costing used is .... costing.

3. Under job costing system, each job is assigned one identifying job ....

4. In job costing, each .... is a cost unit.
5. A .... contains all relevant information regarding production and other detailed particulars of the job.
6. Production order is prepared by the .... Department.
7. .... is that size of the batch of production where total cost is minimum.
8. In industries where batch costing is employed, an important point is the determination of ....
9. In determining economic batch size , two types of cost involved are .... and ....
10. Determination of economic batch size helps to .... cost and .... profits.
11. Economic Batch quantity depends on .... and .... costs.

Answers :

1. Batch, Contract	**2.** Batch	**3.** Job
4. number	**5.** Production order	
6. production department	**7.** economic batch size	
8. economic batch size	**9.** Set up cost, carrying cost	
10. minimize, maximize	**11.** Set up , Storage	

II. Indicate whether the following statements are True or False :

1. In job costing, a cost sheet is prepared for each job.
2. A production order is an order received from a customer for a particular job.
3. In job costing, the cost of each job is ascertained by dividing the total cost of all the jobs by the number of jobs.
4. Job cost sheet may be prepared for estimating profit in the job.
5. Job costing cannot be used in industries using standard costing.
6. Job costing can be applied only in small concerns.
7. Job costing cannot be used in conjunction with marginal costing.
8. Job costing can be more suitably used in concerns producing uniformly any specific product.
9. Batch costing is a variant of job costing.
10. Batch costing may be used in a boiler house.
11. In determining economic batch size, cost and time in setting up the machines is not considered.
12. The concept of economic batch size is similar to that of economic order quantity.

Answers :

1. True	**2.** False	**3.** False	**4.** True
5. False	**6.** False	**7.** False	**8.** False
9. True	**10.** False	**11.** False	**12.** True

THEORETICAL EXERCISES

1. Explain Job costing. What are its advantages? **[B.Com, Madras]**
2. What are the main features of job costing? Give a proforma cost sheet under such a system.
3. What is a job cost sheet? What kind of data usually appear on job cost sheet?
4. Describe in brief the procedure of recording costs under job order costing. **[B.Com., Kerala; M.com, Mysore]**
5. What do you understand by Batch costing? In which industries is it applied? **[C. A. (inter)]**
6. Explain in brief the following concepts:
   (i) Batch costing; **[DU, B.Com (Hons.) 2001]**
   (ii) Job costing.
7. Describe briefly the nature of accounting problems associated with job costing. **[DU, B.Com (Hons.) 2002]**
8. Specify the ledgers and forms which are normally necessary in job costing system. Briefly discuss the purpose of each.
9. Discuss the importance of estimating in job costing.
10. Describe the concept of Economic batch size with the help of a simple formula.

NUMERICAL EXERCISES

1. Lomex Limited undertakes to supply 2,500 units of a component per month for three months of October, November and December 2008. Every month a batch order is opened against which materials and labour costs are booked at actual. Overheads are levied at a rate per labour hour. The selling price is contracted at ₹ 50 per unit.

   From the following data, present the cost and profit per unit of each batch order and the overall position of the order for 7,500 units.

Month	Batch Output (Number)	Material cost (₹)	Labour cost (₹)
October 2008	2500	20000	30000
November 2008	3000	33000	36000
December 2008	2400	19200	28800

Labour is paid at rate of ₹ 12 per Labour hour. The details are:

Month	Overheads (₹)	Total Labour Hours
October 2008	140000	10000
November 2008	66000	6000
December 2008	112000	8000

[Ans. ₹ 60000]

2. You are given below the following information relating to a factory for the year 1999:

Details	Amount (₹)
Direct Material	10,00,000
Direct labour	6,00,000
Direct factory expenses	4,00,000
Factory overheads	5,00,000
Office and Admn. Overheads	2,00,000

During February 2008, the factory received an enquiry for a job which requires:

Details	Amount (₹)
Direct material cost	5,000
Direct labour cost	2,000
Direct factory expenses	1,000

It has been decided that factory overheads should be recovered on the basis of percentage to prime cost. Office & Administration Overheads should be recovered on the basis of percentage to cost of production with an increase of 10% for the cost hikes in the current year.

Prepare cost sheet for the job in each of the following three cases:

1. Profit is 10% of the quotation price and selling and distribution expenses are 20% of quotation price.
2. Profit is 10% of cost of sales and selling and distribution expenses are 20% of cost of sales.
3. Profit is 10% of sales and selling and distribution expenses are 20% of cost of sales.

[Ans. Total sale value of job [(1) ₹ 15,543; (2) ₹14, 960; (3) ₹ 15,111]

3. From the following details, prepare the cost sheet for Job No. 67 and find out the value of the job.

Details	Amount (₹)
Materials issued for the Job	25,000
Direct Wages	20,000
Direct Expenses	4,200

Provide 60% on direct wages for works on cost and 15% on Works Cost for Office-on-cost. Profit to be realized on the selling price is 10%. **[Ans. 78,200]**

4. Prepare a quotation for a job which requires direct Materials ₹ 25,000, Direct Labour ₹ 30,000 and direct factory expenses ₹ 5,000.

The job passes through three Machines: Machine I for 10 hours, Machine II for 20 hours, Machine III for 5 hours. Machine Hour Rate for three machines is ₹ 80, ₹ 100, and ₹ 120 respectively. Administrative overheads are 25% of Prime Cost; Selling Overheads are 12.5% of cost of production. The Manufacturer desires to earn a profit of 20% on the Quotation Price. Prepare Job cost sheet. **[Ans. ₹ 1,10,250]**

5. The under mentioned costs were incurred on Job No. 541of Quality Ltd.

Materials ₹ 8,050

Direct Wages:

Department: X80 Hours @ ₹ 5 per Hour

Y 50 Hours @ ₹ 3 per Hour

Z 30 Hours @ ₹ 8 per Hour

Overhead Expenses for these departments were estimated as follows:

Variable Overheads:

Department: X ₹ 9,000 for 6000 Labour Hours

Y ₹6,000 for 3000 Labour Hours

Z ₹ 4,000 for 1000 Labour Hours

Fixed Overheads estimated at ₹ 30,000 for 10,000 normal working hours.

You are required to calculate the cost of Job NO. 541 and calculate the price to five profit of 25% on selling price. **[Ans. ₹12, 880]**

6. Compute the Economic Batch Size of Production for a firm using batch costing with the following information:

Annual Demand for the Component: 8000 units

Setting up and order processing costs: ₹ 40

Cost of manufacturing one unit: ₹ 200

Annual Inventory Holding cost per unit per annum: 8%. **[Ans. 200 units]**

7. Batch No. M-13/06 incurred the following costs:

Department P: 500 Labour hours @ ₹ 14

Department T: 700 Labour hours @ ₹ 12

Direct Materials ₹ 10800

Factory overheads are recovered on Labour and the rates are ₹ 30 per hour for department P and ₹ 20 per hour for department T.

The firm uses a cost plus system for fixing selling prices and expects a 25% gross profit (Sales value minus factory cost). Administrative overheads recovered @ 10% of Selling Price. 800 units were produced in Batch No. M-13/06, calculate

(a) The Selling Price per unit;

(b) Total Amount of Administrative overheads recovered by Batch No.M-13/06; and

(c) The notional profit per unit. **[Ans. ₹ 92; ₹ 7360; and ₹13.80]**

8. The following information for the year ended 31.12.2000 is obtained from the books and records of a factory:

Details	Completed Jobs (₹)	Work-in-Progress (₹)
Raw Materials supplied from stores	88,000	32,000
Wages	1,00,000	40,000
Chargeable expenses	10,000	4,000
Materials returned to stores	1,000	———

Factory overheads are 80% of wages. Office overheads are 25% of factory cost and selling distribution overheads are 10% of the cost of production.

The completed jobs realized ₹ 4, 10,000. Write up:

(i) Work-in-Progress Ledger control Account;

(ii) Completed Jobs Ledger control Account;

(iii) Cost of Sales Account. **[DU, B.Com (Hons), 2001]**

[Ans. WIP Control A/c ₹ 1, 35,000; Completed Jobs Control a/c ₹ 3, 46,250; Cost of Sales A/c : Profit ₹ 29,125]

9. Compute the Economic Batch Size of Production for a firm using batch costing with the following information:

Annual Demand for the Component: 20,000 Kg.

Setting up and order processing costs: ₹ 256

Cost of manufacturing one kg. of output: ₹ 80

Annual Rate of Interest 10 %;

The annual Warehouse rent is ₹ 100 per sq. ft. and a sq. ft. space can accommodate 20 Kg. of the output.

Other carrying costs are estimated at ₹ 3 per kg. per annum. **[Ans. 800 Kg.]**

10. In Engineering Company, the factory overheads are recovered on a fixed percentage basis on direct wages and the Administration overheads are absorbed on a fixed percentage basis on works cost.

The company has furnished the following data relating to two jobs undertaken by it in a period:

Details	Job 101 Amount (₹)	Job 102 Amount (₹)
Direct Materials	54,000	37,500
ts11 Direct Wages	42,000	30,000
Selling Price	1,66,650	1,28,250
Profit percentage on total cost	10%	20%

Required:

(i) Computation of percentage recovery rates of factory overheads and administration overheads.

(ii) Calculation of the amount of factory overheads, administration overheads and profit for each of the two jobs.

Using the above rates of recovery, fix the selling price of Job No. 103. the additional data being:

Direct Materials ₹ 24,000

Direct Wages ₹ 20,000

Profit percentage on selling price 12.5% **[C.A.Inter, May 1995]**

[Ans. Rates of recovery: Factory Overheads 60% and Administration Overheads 25%; Selling Price of Job NO. 103 ₹ 80,000]

specific order costing which applies where work is undertaken to customers special requirements and each order is of long –term duration (compared with those to which job costing applies). The work is usually constructional and in general the method is similar to job costing". It includes engineering projects, construction of bridges and roads, railway line contracts, civil construction etc. The work is done on sites and mainly involves construction activity. Contract costing is essentially a form of job costing. Under this method of costing, the cost of each contract is calculated separately. The contracts are of long duration and the completion of the same takes more than one accounting period. Each contract is a mini profit and Loss account. It gives costs, revenues and profit/loss from each contract which is transferred to General Profit and Loss account.

Features of Contract costing

The under mentioned are the salient features of the contract costing:

1. Contract is executed as per the requirements and specifications of the customer i.e. the contractee.
2. A contract requires three parties: (i) Contractor, who executes the contract; (ii) Contractee, who grants the contract to the contractor; and (iii) Certifier/Evaluator, who periodically examines the progress of work and certifies the value of work done up to a certain point of time.
3. Each contract is an independent unit for the purpose of costing. Separate accounts are made to ascertain the profitability of each contract.
4. A contract takes long time to complete, generally more than one accounting year.
5. A contract is of large size and involves large costs.
6. A big chunk of the total cost is in the nature of direct costs. Most of the purchases of materials and others are specific costs.
7. Contract is executed away from contractor's premises usually at Contractee's site. Control of materials, labour and other costs is very difficult as the execution of the contract is at a place far away from the contractor's premises and work on contracts may take place simultaneously at different sites.
8. At times sub-contractors are engaged to perform specialized jobs involved in a contract. Sanitary fittings, electricity fittings and welding etc. are some of the specialized works involved in a contract.
9. The contractor is entitled to get payment for execution of the contract in installments based on the stage of completion of contract work as certified by the architect/ valuer.
10. The contract involves valuation of work-in-progress at the end of each accounting year.

11. There is a need to estimate profit on incomplete contract at the end of each accounting year.
12. A contract usually involves imposition of penalties for faulty/defective work and undue delay in the execution of work.
13. Each contract in itself is a complete Profit and Loss account. The profit or loss is transferred to the general Profit and Loss Account.

Principles of Accounting for Contract Costs

1. Each contract is treated as an independent cost unit. However, in terms of costs analysis and control, costs relating to each part of the contract are computed separately.
2. The costing department provides information for the purpose of estimation of cost and submission of bid tender price. Where the value of the contract is high, estimation becomes crucial. The split-up of the total contract into sub-units facilitates the estimation of costs for the submission of quotation. Actual costs collected against these sub-units prove useful for comparison purposes.
3. There is trade-off between the accounting concepts of 'prudence' and 'matching costs with revenue' while recognizing profit each year for the purpose of credit to profit and loss account during the execution of a contract.
4. The actual cost of the contract does not include abnormal costs. Abnormal costs are those, which fulfill the under noted conditions:
   (a) There is no chance of such costs to recur.
   (b) The estimates did not take into consideration such costs.
   Abnormal costs should be directly transferred to Costing Profit and Loss Account.
5. Progress Reports that show progress and effectiveness in the utilization of resources are prepared for the management.

Job and Contract Costing : A comparison

Similarities:

1. Under both work is executed as per the requirements and specifications of the customer.
2. Each job and each contract is a separate cost unit, and are costed separately. Thus, profitability of each job and contract is determined separately.
3. Quotation for price is asked before the final order from the customer.
4. Production is not for stock.

11. Two fitters, a labourer and a boy undertake a job on piece rate basis for ₹ 13,500. The time spent by each of them is 220 ordinary working hours. The rates of pay on time rate basis are ₹ 15.00 per hour for each of the two fitters, ₹ 10.00 per hour for the labourer and ₹ 5.00 per hour for the boy. Calculate:

(i) The amount of piece work premium and the share of each worker, when the piece work premium is divided proportionately to the wages paid and

(ii) The selling price of the above job on the basis of following additional data:

Cost of direct material ₹ 22,500; Works overhead @ 20% of prime cost, selling overhead @ 10.0% of works cost and profit @ 25% on cost of sales.

[I.C.W.A. Inter (Modified)]

[Ans. Sharing of Piece work premium: ₹ 2,400, ₹ 800 and ₹ 400; Selling Price of Job No. 103 ₹ 59,400]

❑❑❑

16

Contract Costing

Learning Objectives

It attempts to explain the process of contract costing. In this chapter you will learn :

1. Meaning, nature and objectives of contract cost accounting.
2. Comparison between job costing and contract costing.
3. Costing procedure.
4. Types of contract.
5. Treatment of profit or loss on incomplete contracts.
6. Treatment of escalation clause in the terms of contract.

INTRODUCTION

Contract costing is a form of specific order costing. Work is done as per the requirements and specifications of the customer and each contract is a separate cost unit. Each contract is different from the other and like a job each contract is costed separately. Contracts are usually executed at the customer's site, take longer time to complete and involve much larger costs than in case of jobs. Contracts are usually of constructional and repair nature. This type of costing is necessary in construction industry. Building of dams, bridges and roads, ship building, and plant erection etc. are some of the examples of contract costing.

Meaning of Contract Costing

CIMA terminology defines contract as "the aggregated costs relative to a single contract designated a cost unit". CIMA also states contract as " that form of followed for plant, which is sent to the site. The written down value is determined using revaluation method.

Another method is to debit depreciation charge to the contract account. There may be difficulty in determining the reasonable rate of depreciation considering the difficult conditions in which equipments may be required to work.

2. In respect of plant taken on hire, the hire charges are charged to the contract for which it was taken on hire.
3. Contract account is debited with the amount of depreciation. Such practice is usually adopted when the plant is used on the contract only for a short period. Mobile crane or bulldozer used in a contract may be charged on this basis.

Illustration 16.2 : Plant costing ₹ 2,00,000 issued to Contract No. 503 on June1, 2008. Plant worth ₹ 5,000 was returned to store; Plant costing ₹ 10,000 was sold for ₹ 11,500. Plant worth ₹ 2,000 was stolen and worth ₹ 6,000 destroyed by fire. Plant at site at the end of the year was ₹ 40,000.

Dr **Contract No. 503 Account (Skeleton)** Cr

Details	Amount (₹)	Details	Amount (₹)
To Plant Issued to Contract site	2,00,000	By Plant returned to Stores	5,000
To Profit and Loss A/c:		By Bank A/c (Plant sold)	11,500
Profit on Plant sold (11,500 – 10,000)	1,500		
		By Profit and Loss A/c: Plant stolen 2,000 Plant destroyed (by fire) 6,000	8,000
		By Plant at site	40,000

(C) Accounting for Labour:

1. Labour, which has worked at site or is presently at work on the site, is known as direct labour and such should be charged to that contract for which it works.
2. Supervisors and other administrative personnel, who work at site, devote their time to a particular contract. Their salaries and allowances should be charged to the contract.
3. There should be accurate time keeping records and some system of control. It is essential to introduce some system of internal check for the

preparation of wage sheets and payment of wages because of the distinct possibility of payment to ghost workers.

4. The contract account should show chargeable wages whether paid or not. It means that outstanding wages are also shown in the contract account.
5. Wages are credited to Contract Account:
   (a) When there is abnormal loss of labour due to idle time, payment of wages for the period of strike, machine break-down etc.
   (b) When a section of labour is transferred to other contract/s.
6. No entry need to be made in the contract Account as there is normal loss (wastage) of labour due to normal factors.

(D) Accounting for Overheads: A suitable basis is used for apportioning overhead costs to each contract. Generally it is done on the basis of sales value. Other bases could be percentage of materials or a percentage of labour. The overheads so apportioned are charged to the relevant contract account.

(E) Accounting for Payment made to the Sub-Contractors: Most of the times, some part of the work relating to the contract is given to the petty contractors (generally specialists) and they are paid at the agreed rates. Payment made to such sub-contractors is charged to the respective contracts based on value in sub-contractors' invoice and architect's or surveyor's certificate. There should be proper system for the accounting and control of materials issued to sub-contractors where they supply only the labour.

(F) Extra work: At times a contractor is asked to make additions/ alterations in the work originally agreed to be done under the contract. As it is the additional work outside the original contract, the contractor is to charge extra money besides the original contract amount. If the extra work is substantial, the contractor may treat it as another contract and will make records accordingly. If the extra work is not substantial, the contractor will combine its expenses and the price charged with the original contract account. The cost of extra work will be debited to the contract account and the price charged for the extra work will be credited to the contract account.

(G) Payment by the contractee to the contractor: Payment by the contractee is always linked to the value of work certified. Generally, the monthly/quarterly payment is on the predetermined percentage of work certified, which is usually mentioned in the contract. In case the contractee periodically pays 75% of the work certified then the cash ratio is 75% and the retention money is 25%. On the completion of the contract the entire balance amount is paid to the contractor. Any of the following methods may be adopted by the contractor for receipt of cash from the contractee:

Dissimilarities:

1. The fundamental difference between a job and a contract is of size.
2. Job is performed in the workshop of the producer while the contract is usually executed at customer's site.
3. A contract takes longer time to complete than a job.
4. A contract involves much larger cost compared with the job.
5. Most of the costs in case of a contract are direct as compared to a job. However, the proportion of overhead costs is much less in case of a contract as compared to a job.
6. Payment is made to the producer on the completion of the job while in case of a contract payment is made in installments during the process of execution of the contract.
7. A contract involves a larger work-in-progress spread over a much larger period of time.
8. In case of a job, profit is ascertained on the completion of the job. In case of a contract estimated profit is ascertained even on incomplete contract at the end of the accounting year.
9. In case of a job work there is no problem of keeping profit in reserve/suspense. However, In case of a contract reserve is kept on work-in-progress.

Costing Procedure

The cost of each contract has to be determined individually. And for this following procedure is adopted-

- **Allotment of Unique Number:** Each contract is given a separate job number. This is to be done for the sake of proper accounting and administrative purposes.
- **Maintenance of a separate contract account:** A separate contract account is maintained for each contract.
- **Charging costs to individual Contract Account:** All costs relating to a particular contract are charged to respective contract accounts. This is done in order to ascertain the cost correctly and fix responsibility.

Collection of costs :

(A) Materials:

1. Accounting for Material: Materials, which are sent to the site, are charged to the specific contract on the basis of requisitions.
2. Purchases of materials for a particular contract are charged to the particular contract on the basis of values given in the invoices.
3. Transfer of materials from one contract to another is credited to the transferor-contract account and charged to the transferee-contract account on the basis of Material Transfer Note.

4. Returns of materials to stores are credited to the transferor-contract account on the basis of Material Returns Note.
5. At the end of accounting period, materials, which are in stock, are valued and duly credited to the relevant contract account.
6. Surplus materials and defective items are sold from time to time. The amount so realized is credited to the contract account.
7. Materials lying unused on the site after the completion of the contract is valued and credited to the contract account.

Illustration 16.1 : Quality Builders Limited undertook a contract No. 503 for the construction of a building. Materials purchased ₹ 5,00,000. Materials supplied from stores ₹ 40,000. Materials returned to stores ₹ 5,000. Materials costing ₹ 10,000 were sold for ₹ 8,000.Materials costing ₹ 6,000 were stolen and materials worth ₹ 15,000 destroyed by fire. Materials worth ₹ 70,000 were received from contract No. 502 which was completed. Materials of ₹ 48,000 were at site. Materials of ₹ 18,000 were transferred to other contracts.

Show the above details in contract No. 503 account.

Dr **Contract No. 503 Account (Skeleton)** Cr

Details	Amount (₹)	Details	Amount (₹)
To Materials Purchased	5,00,000	By Materials returned to Stores	5,000
To Materials supplied from stores	40,000	By Materials transferred to other contracts	18,000
To Materials received from contract No. 502	70,000	By Materials sold	10,000
		By Profit and Loss A/c: Loss on Sale of Materials (10,000 – 8,000) = 2,000 Materials Stolen 6,000 Loss by fire (Materials destroyed) 15,000	23,000
		By Materials at Site	48,000

(B) Accounting for use of Plant:

1. Plant purchased for the specific purpose of a contract is charged to that Contract only. At the end of each accounting period, the written down value of the plant is credited to the contract account. The difference between debit and credit of such plant is the cost of use of the plant i.e. depreciation on plant used for the contract. Similar method is to be

1. Contractee's personal account is debited with the value of the work certified and the contract is credited. On the receipt of the payment, Contractee's account is credited and Cash/Bank A/c is debited. The balance in the contractee A/c shows the amount of the retention money. The entries are:

Details		Amount (₹)
1. Contractee A/c	Dr	(Value of the work certified)
To Contract A/c		
2. Bank A/c	Dr	(Receipt of cash)
To Contractee A/c		

2. The Contract A/c is credited with the value of work certified. The Contractee A/c is debited with the money immediately payable by him and Retention Money A/c is debited by the amount of retained money. The entries are:

Details		Amount (₹)
1. Contractee A/c	Dr	(Money immediately payable)
Retention Money A/c	Dr	(Amount of retained money)
To Contract A/c		(Value of the work certified)
2. Bank A/c	Dr	(Receipt of cash)
To Contractee A/c		

3. The Contract A/c is credited with the value of work certified. As and when the payment is received, the Contractee A/c is credited. In this manner, the amount paid by the contractor is treated as an advance towards the final payment. Such advance is shown by way of deduction from the value of work-in-progress in the Balance Sheet. On the completion of the contract, the Contractee's A/c is debited by the contract price and the Contract A/c is credited; the balance payment made by him is credited to his account so as to get it closed. The entries are:

Details		Amount (₹)
1. Work-in-Progress A/c	Dr	(Value of the work certified)
To Contract A/c		
2. Bank A/c	Dr	(Receipt of cash)
To Contractee A/c		
3. (On the completion of the contract)		(Contract price)
Contractee A/c	Dr	
To Contract A/c		
4. Bank A/c	Dr	(Receipt of Balance payment)
To Contractee A/c		

(H) Retention Money: Usually, in terms of the contract, full amount of the work certified is not paid to the contractor. A certain proportion of the amount is retained by the contractee and is paid after the completion of the contract. The sum of money thus retained for some time is known as retention money. The retained amount exerts a pressure on the contractor to complete the work as per schedule and according to specifications. This money could even be used for imposing penalties for defective or delayed work.

(I) Work certified: Work certified means the work which has been completed by the contractor and certified by the contractee's architect or surveyor/ valuer. It becomes the basis of payment made by the contractee to the contractor. A contractee may pay only 75% or 80% of the work certified. Work certified is composed of cost of work done and certified and profit element thereon.

Work certified = Cash Received ÷ (1– Proportion of Retention Money)

(J) Uncertified work: The work which has been done by the contractor but not certified by the architect on the date of accounting due to insufficient progress is known as uncertified work. It is a part of work-in-progress. It may arise due to the fact that by the end of accounting period, certain work may not have reached the stipulated stage of completion. Work uncertified is valued at cost and no profit is considered in respect of such work. The contract account is credited with the cost of uncertified work and work-in-Progress account is debited with the same. Unlike work certified, the work uncertified does not accumulate. Work uncertified at the end of the next year may be more or less than that at the end of the current year.

Ascertaining the value of work uncertified: It can be estimated on the basis of total cost incurred and the quantum and value of work certified. We can explain it by taking an example:

Example: Total cost incurred on a contract till the end of the current year is ₹ 15, 00,000 which is 60% of the total cost of the contract. The architect has certified that work done is worth only 50% of the total contract price of ₹ 32,00,000. The cost of Work done but not yet certified is estimated as under:

A. Cost of work done till date= ₹ 15, 00,000
B. Total estimated cost of the complete contract= 15, 00,000÷0.6=> ₹ 25, 00,000.
C. Estimated cost of work certified= 0.5×25, 00,000=> ₹ 12, 50,000
D. Cost of work Uncertified [(A) – (C)] = 15, 00,000 – 12, 50,000=>₹ 2,50,000
E. Profit amount in the work Certified = Value of work certified – Cost of work certified = (0.5×32, 00,000) – 12,50,0000 = 16,00,000 – 12,50,000 =>₹ 3,50,000.

(K) Work-in-Progress Account: Work-in-Progress means work is still not complete in all respects, and something is yet to be done. The contractor may prepare 'work-in-Progress account' by debiting the account with the value of work certified and the cost of work uncertified and by crediting the profit not transferred to Profit and Loss account (i.e. profit in suspense/reserve). The difference between the two sides of the account is the value of work-in- progress which is shown in the Balance Sheet. The cash received on account of such uncompleted contract should be shown in the Balance Sheet as a deduction from work in progress.

Dr **Work-in-Progress Account (Pro-forma)** Cr

Details	Amount (₹)	Details	Amount (₹)
To Contract A/c: Work Certified Work Uncertified		By Contract A/c (Profit in suspense/reserve) By Balance c/d	
Total		Total	
To Balance b/d			

Balance Sheet (Relevant)

Liabilities	Amount (₹)	Assets	Amount (₹)
		Work-in-Progress A/c: Work Certified *Add:* Work Uncertified *Less:* Reserve for Unrealized Profit *Less:* Amount received from contractee on account	

TYPES OF CONTRACTS

Contracts may be of Three Types

(1) *Fixed Price Contract:* A fixed price of the contract is agreed upon between the contractor and the contractee. It is an amount of consideration for work awarded to the contractor. It is to be executed as per the terms of the contract .The contractor receives payment of execution of contract in installments based on the quantum of work done and certified by the authorized architect. The payment of the contractor is always linked to the value of work done and certified. The agreed price is paid by the contractee to the contractor. The contractee is permitted to

make deductions on account of defectives and penalties for delay; he is required to make extra payment for the additional work.

(2) *Contract with Escalation and/or de-escalation Clause:* The contract has a special provision of escalation in the cost of materials, labour rates and other major costs. This escalation is applied according to mutually pre-determined formula. Escalation clause is a clause under which the fixed contract price is subject to modification due to likely increase in the prices of materials and labour beyond a certain percentage. This clause protects the interests of the contractor.

Following are the circumstances which make it desirable to have an escalation clause in the contract:

(i) Contract is to run for a long period.

(ii) Cost of raw material is likely to go up.

(iii) Wage rates are subject to frequent upward revisions by the regulatory authorities.

(iv) Power fuel and other inputs are subject to frequent price rise.

(v) It is difficult to estimate the quantity of materials and labour to be used for the contract with reasonable accuracy.

De-escalation clause entitles the contractee to a rebate in the event of prices going down beyond a certain percentage. It implies downward adjustment in the contract piece. It protects the interests of the contractee as the benefit of decline in the prices is passed on to the contractee.

(3) *Cost plus Contracts:* It is the reverse of a fixed price contract. No fixed contract price is settled with the contractor. It involves an agreement as to the items of cost to be included in the actual cost and the percentage of profit to be added to the actual cost, no price could be pre-determined for the contract. The contractee reimburses the contractor for all the admissible costs incurred by him. Over and above such costs, the contractor is paid a fixed amount or percentage of cost as profit or a lump sum charge of profit.

Following are the circumstances which make it desirable to have cost plus contract:

(i) It is not possible to estimate its cost with a reasonable degree of accuracy due to long period of time, wide fluctuations in prices of materials and labour rates etc.

(ii) There is an emergency and there is no time to negotiate a contract price.

(iii) Work is more important than its cost.

(iv) Work is of new character and design which has no precedence.

(v) Frequent modifications are required in the allotted work.

Illustration 16.3. *Prepare contract account and Contractee's account assuming that the amount due from the contractee was duly received by a Crossed "Account Payee" Cheque drawn on SBI.*

Details		*Amount (₹)*
Direct Material		*85,000*
Direct Wages		*62,000*
Materials Issued from Stores		*42,000*
Loose Tools		*11,000*
Tractor Expenses:		
Fuel, Oil etc.	*10,000*	
Wages of Drivers	*13,000*	*23,000*
Other Direct Charges		*12,250*

The contract price was ₹ 4, 00,000 and the contract took just three months time. The value of Loose Tools and Stores returned at the end of the period was ₹ 1,100 and ₹ 12,000 respectively. The Plant was also returned at a value of ₹ 85,500 after charging depreciation @ 20% p.a. for a period of three months. The value of the tractor was ₹1, 00,000 and the depreciation was to be charged to the contract @ 15% p.a. The Administrative overheads are to be provided @ 20% of works cost.

Solution :

Dr **Contract Account** Cr

Details	Amount (₹)	Details	Amount (₹)
To Direct Material	85,000	By Stores Returned	12,000
To Direct Wages	62,000	By Loose Tools Returned	1,100
To Stores Issued	42,000	By Plant Returned	85,500
To Plant Issued	90,000	By Balance c/d (Works Cost)	2,30,400
To Loose Tools	11,000		
To Tractor Expenses:			
Fuel, oil etc. 10,000			
Wages to Drivers 13,000	23,000		
To Depreciation On tractor: [(1,00,000 × 0.15) × (3/12)]	3,750		
To Other Direct Charges	12,250		
Total	3,29,000	Total	3,29,000
To Balance b/d	2,30,400	By Contractee's A/c	4,00,000

To Administrative Overheads @ 20% on Works Cost: (0.2 × 3,29,000)	65,800		
To Profit & Loss A/c	1,03,800		
Total	4,00,000	Total	4,00,000

Dr **Contractee's account** Cr

Details	Amount (₹)	Details	Amount (₹)
To Contract A/c	4,00,000	By Bank A/c	4,00,000
Total	4,00,000	Total	4,00,000

Note: Depreciation on Plant:

= Quarterly rate of depreciation is 20/4 =5%

Value of plant and machinery after charging depreciation is ₹ 85,500 which is 95% of the original value of plant and machinery issued for the contract. Thus, the issued value of the plant and machinery is ₹ 90,000 (i.e. 85,500/0.95)

Illustration 16.4. *The contract price of a contract undertaken by PV Limited on September 1, 2008 was ₹ 6,00,000. Following expenses were incurred on the contract:*

Item of Expenses	***Amount (₹)***
Materials consumed	*2,25,000*
Materials at site (31.3.2009)	*50,000*
Direct Wages	*1,00,000*
Direct Expenses	*80,000*
Plant Purchased	*1,00,000*

The contract was completed on 31.3.2009 and the contract price duly received by bank draft. Provide depreciation on Plant @ 18% p.a. and charge indirect expenses @ 25% on wages.

Prepare contract account and contractee account in the books of PV Limited.

Solution :

Dr **Contract Account** Cr

Details	Amount (₹)	Details	Amount (₹)
To Material Issued: Materials consumed 2,25,000 Materials at site 50,000	2,75,000	By Materials at site	50,000

To Direct Wages	1,00,000	By Plant at site: Cost 1,00,000 *Less:* Depreciation* 10,500	89,500
To Direct Expenses	80,000	By Contractee's A/c	6,00,000
To Indirect Expenses (1,00,000 × 0.25)	25,000		
To Plant Purchased	1,00,000		
To Profit & Loss A/c	1,59,500		
Total	7,39,500	Total	7,39,500

*Depreciation: {(1,00,000 × 0.18× (7/12)} = ₹ 10,500

Dr **Contractee's account** Cr

Details	**Amount (₹)**	**Details**	**Amount (₹)**
To Contract A/c	6,00,000	By Bank A/c	6,00,000
Total	6,00,000	Total	6,00,000

Loss on Contract

Every loss on contract, whether completed or incomplete, should be transferred to Profit and Loss account in its entirety. In case of Loss the prudence concept gets operative.

Illustration 16.5. *The contract price of a contract undertaken by AV Limited on April 1,2008 was ₹ 11,25,000. the contractor at the end of the year as on 31.3.2009 received ₹ 4,50,000 representing 80% of the amount of work certified. Following expenses were incurred on the contract:*

Item of Expenses	***Amount (₹)***
Materials issued	*2,25,000*
Materials at site (31.3.2009)	*9,375*
Direct Wages	*3,00,000*
Direct Expenses	*41,250*
Plant installed at site	*2,25,000*
Overheads allocated to this contract	*20,625*
Work finished but not yet certified at cost	*18,750*
Plant to be depreciated @ 12.5%	

Prepare contract account in the books of AV Limited.

Solution :

Dr **Contract Account** Cr

Details	Amount (₹)	Details	Amount (₹)
To Material Issued	2,25,000	By Work-in-progress: Work certified 5,62,500 Work uncertified 18,750	5,81,250
To Direct Wages	3,00,000	By Materials at site	9,375
To Direct Expenses	41,250	By Plant at site (2,25,000 – 28,125)	1,96,875
To Overheads	20,625	By Profit & Loss A/c (Loss)	24,375
To Plant installed at site	2,25,000		
Total	8,11,875	Total	8,11,875

Profit on Incomplete Contracts

Usually, a contract takes more than one accounting year to complete. There arises a question whether profit on such contracts should be worked out only on the completion of the contract or at the end of each accounting year on the partly completed contract work. If profit is determined only on the completion of the contract, profit will be high in the year of completion of the contract, whereas in other years of working on contracts, it will be NIL. This would give a distorted picture of the profit pattern and also higher tax liability in the year of completion of the contract. In view of the foregoing exposition, it becomes necessary to take into account the profit earned (or loss incurred) on the work done during each accounting year. There are two aspects of computation of profit:

(i) Ascertainment of Notional profit or Estimated profit;

(ii) Ascertainment of that portion of such profit which is to be transferred to Profit and Loss Account.

Notional Profit: It is the difference between the value of work-in-Progress certified plus cost of work done but not yet certified AND the cost of work done to date. It is ascertained as under:

Details	Amount (₹)
Value of Work Certified	5,00,000
Add: Cost of work done but not yet certified	1,00,000
Less: Cost of work Done to date	4,80,000
Notional Profit	1,20,000

OR

Details	Amount (₹)
Value of Work Certified	5,00,000
Less: Cost of work Certified [(Cost of work Done to date) – (Cost of work done but not yet certified)] i.e.(4,80,000 – 1,00,000)	3,80,000
Notional Profit	1,20,000

Note: If in any accounting year, the cost of work done exceeds the value of work-in-Progress certified plus cost of work done but not yet certified, the resultant figure would be Notional Loss.

Estimated Profit: Estimated profit is the Difference between the Contract Price and the estimated total cost of the contract. It is ascertained as under:

Details		Amount (₹)
Contract Price		50,00,000
Less:		
(a) Total cost of work incurred to date	38,00,000	
(b) Estimated Further cost to complete the contract	4,00,000	42,00,000
Estimated Profit		8,00,000

Transfer of Notional profit or estimated profit to Profit and Loss Account: The portion of Notional Profit or Estimated Profit to be transferred to Profit and Loss Account depends upon the stage of completion of the contract. It means the ratio of Value of certified work-in-Progress and the Value of the Total contract work (Contract Price). As a normal practice, some portion of the notional profit is withheld as a reserve to meet any unforeseen future expenses or contingencies. Thus, the entire amount of the notional profit is not transferred to the Profit and Loss account. The under mentioned rules usually adopted in practice may be followed in this regard:

Ratio of Work Certified to Contract Price (I)	Transfer to Profit and Loss Account (II)	Balance of Profit in Suspense or in Reserve (III)
I. Less than 25%	No Profit is transferred	None
II. 25% or less than 50%	1/3 of the Notional Profit	Notional Profit –Transfer made in column No. II.
III. 50% or less than 90%	2/3 of the Notional Profit	Notional Profit –Transfer made in column No. II.
IV. Contract is near completion	Proportion of the Estimated Profit	Estimated Profit –Transfer made in column No. II.
V. Loss on Uncompleted Contract	The Entire Loss	None

Note:

1. In General, this 1/3 or 2/3 of the Notional Profit to be transferred to Profit and Loss account is subject to CASH Ratio. This is calculated as under: Transfer to Profit and Loss Account is
   = [(1/3) or (2/3) × (Notional Profit) × (Cash Received/Work certified)]
2. The proportion of the estimated profit to be transferred to Profit and Loss account is ascertained as under:
   (a) [(Estimated Profit) × (Work Certified/ Contract price)]
   (b) [(Estimated Profit) × (Work Certified/ Contract price) × (Cash Received/Work Certified)]
   (c) (Estimated Profit) × (Cost of work to Date/ Estimated Total Cost of work)]
   (d) [(Estimated Profit) × (Cost of work to Date/ Estimated Total Cost of work) × (Cash Received/Work certified)]

It may be observed that the above mentioned rules are not hard and fast rules. They are usually put in practice. The application of these rules may depend upon the nature of work involved, degree of risk in the business and quantum of work completed. Whatever method is adopted, it should be applied uniformly from year to year.

Illustration 16.6. *Given : Contract Price: ₹ 10, 00,000.*

Details	*Case I Amount (₹)*	*Case II Amount (₹)*	*Case III Amount (₹)*	*Case IV Amount (₹)*
Notional Profit	*60,000*	*1,05,000*	*1,80,000*	*3,00,000*
Work certified	*2,00,000*	*4,00,000*	*6,00,000*	*8,00,000*
Cash received	*1,50,000*	*3,00,000*	*4,50,000*	*6,40,000*

Determine the amount of profit to be transferred to the Profit and Loss account in each case.

Solution : Case I:

Stage of completion: [Work certified/ Contract Price] × 100
= [2, 00,000/10, 00,000] × 100 =>20%

Rule I is applicable i.e. Nothing is transferred to Profit and Loss Account.

Case II:

Stage of completion: [Work certified/ Contract Price] × 100
= [4,00,000/10,00,000] × 100 =>40%

Rule II is applicable i.e. 1/3 of the Notional profit is transferred to Profit and Loss Account.

Transfer to Profit and Loss Account is

= [(1/3) × (Notional Profit)]

= [(1/3) × 1, 05,000] => ₹ 35,000

Alternatively,

Transfer to Profit and Loss Account is

= [(1/3) × (Notional Profit) × (Cash received/Work certified)]

= [(1/3) × (1, 05,000) × (3, 00,000/4, 00,000)] => ₹ 26,250.

Case III:

Stage of completion: [Work certified/ Contract Price] × 100

= [6, 00,000/10, 00,000] × 100 =>60%

Rule III is applicable i.e. 2/3 of the Notional profit is transferred to Profit and Loss Account.

Transfer to Profit and Loss Account is

= [(2/3) × (Notional Profit)]

= [(2/3) × 1, 80,000] => ₹ 1, 20,000

Alternatively,

Transfer to Profit and Loss Account is

= [(2/3) × (Notional Profit) × (Cash received/Work certified)]

= [(2/3) × (1, 80,000) × (4, 50,000/6, 00,000)] => ₹ 90,000.

Case IV:

Stage of completion: [Work certified/ Contract Price] × 100

= [8, 40,000/10, 00,000] ×100 =>84%

Rule III is applicable i.e. 2/3 of the Notional profit is transferred to Profit and Loss Account.

Transfer to Profit and Loss Account is

= [(2/3) × (Notional Profit)]

= [(2/3) × 3, 00,000] => ₹ 2, 00,000

Alternatively,

Transfer to Profit and Loss Account is

= [(2/3) × (Notional Profit) × (Cash received/Work certified)]

= [(2/3) × (3, 00,000) × (6, 40,000/8, 00,000)] => ₹ 1,60,000.

Illustration 16.7. *From the following information suggest the amount of profit to be taken on Contract No. 404 which is nearly 62% complete.*

Details	*Amount (₹)*
Total cost of contract to date	*4,60,000*
Cost of contract not yet certified	*26,000*
Value of contract certified	*5,00,000*
Cash received to date	*4,50,000*

Solution : As the contract has reasonably advanced to about 62%, the profit to be taken should be based on the following formula:

= [(2/3) × (Notional Profit) × (Cash received/Work certified)]

Item	Amount (₹)
Value of Work Certified	5,00,000
Add: Cost of work done but not yet certified	26,000
Less: Cost of work Done to date	4,60,000
Notional Profit	66,000

OR

Item	Amount (₹)
Value of Work Certified	5,00,000
Less: Cost of Work Certified	
[Cost of work Done to date) – (Cost of Work not yet Certified)]	4,34,000
i.e. (4,60,000 – 26,000)	
Notional Profit	66,000

So, Profit to be taken to general Profit and Loss Account:

= [(2/3) × (66,000) × (4, 50,000÷5, 00,000)] = ₹ 39,600.

The balance of notional Profit i.e. ₹ 26,400 may be put as 'Profit in Suspense'.

Illustration 16.8. *Compute a conservative estimate of profit on a contract (which has been 80% complete) from the following details. Illustrate the four methods of ascertaining the profit to be transferred to the Profit and Loss account.*

Details	*Amount (₹)*
Total Expenditure to date	*17,00,000*
Estimated Further expenditure to complete the contract (including contingencies)	*5,50,000*
Contract Price	*30,00,000*
Work certified	*21,00,000*
Work done but not yet certified	*1,70,000*
Cash received	*16,80,000*

Solution : Notional Profit:

= Work certified + Work done but not yet certified – Total Expenditure to date

= 21, 00,000 + 1, 70,000 – 17, 00,000 = ₹ 5, 70,000.

Estimated Profit:

Item	Amount (₹)
Contract Price	30,00,000
Less:	
(a) Total cost of work incurred to date	17,00,000
(b) Estimated Further cost to complete the contract	5,50,000
Estimated Profit	7,50,000

Methods of ascertaining the amount of estimated profit to be transferred to the profit and Loss account:

(a) [(Estimated Profit) × (Work certified/ Contract price)]

= [(7, 50,000) × (21, 00,000 ÷ 30, 00, 000)]

= ₹ 5, 25,000.

(b) [(Estimated Profit) × (Work certified/ Contract price) × (Cash received/Work certified)]

= [(7,50,000) × (21,00,000 ÷ 30,00,000) × (16,80,000 ÷ 21,00,000)]

= ₹ 4, 20,000.

(c) [(Estimated Profit) × (Cost of work to date/ Estimated total cost of work)]

= [(7,50,000) × (17, 00,000 ÷22, 50,000)]

= ₹ 5,66,667.

(d) [(Estimated Profit) × (Cost of work to date/ Estimated total cost of work) × (Cash received/Work certified)]

= [(7,50,000) × (17,00,000 ÷ 22,50,000) × (16,80,000 ÷ 21,00,000)]

= ₹ 4, 53,333.

Illustration 16.9. *The contract price was ₹ 39, 37,500. Actual expenditure for the period 01.11.2003 to 31.10.2004 and estimated for the period 01.11.2004 to 31.3.2005 is given below:*

Details	***November 01, 2003 to October 31, 2004 Actual (₹)***	***November 01, 2004 to March 31, 2005 Estimated (₹)***
Materials Issued	*6,75,000*	*12,37,500*
Labour: Paid	*4,50,000*	*5,62,000*
Prepaid	*25,000*	—
Outstanding	—	*2,500*
Plant Purchased	*3,75,000*	—

Expenses: Paid	*2,00,000*	*3,50,000*
Outstanding	*50,000*	*25,000*
Plant returns to store	*75,000*	*3,00,000*
	On March 31,2004	*On March 31,2005*
Work certified	*20,00,000*	*F U L L*
Work uncertified	*75,000*	———
Cash received	*17,50,000*	———
Materials at site	*75,000*	*37,500*

The plant is subject to annual depreciation @ 100/3% on written down value method. The contract is likely to be completed on March 31, 2005. It was decided to estimate the total profit on the contract and to the credit of P& L A/c that portion of estimated profit on cash basis, which work completed bore to the total contract. Prepare contract A/c. **[B.Com (Hons.) DU, 2009]**

Solution : **Contract Account**

Dr (November 01, 2003 to October 31, 2004) Cr

Details	Amount (₹)	Details	Amount (₹)
To Materials Issued	6,75,000	By Materials at site	75,000
To Wages Paid 4,50,000 *Less:* Pre-paid 25,000	4,25,000	By Plant Returned to store on 31.10.2004: Cost 75,000 *Less:* Depreciation 10,417	64,583
To Plant Purchases	3,75,000	By Plant at site on 31.10.2004: Cost 3,00,000 *Less:* Depreciation 1,00,000	2,00,000
To Expenses Paid 2,00,000 *Add:* Outstanding 50,000	2,50,000	By Work-in-Progress A/c: Work Certified 20,00000 Work Uncertified 75,000	20,75,000
To Notional Profit c/d	6,89,583		
Total	24,14,583	Total	24,14,583
To Profit and Loss A/c	1,48,580	By Notional Profit b/d	6,89,583
To Profit in Suspense transferred to Work-in-Progress A/c	5,41,003		
Total	6,89,583	Total	6,89,583

Working Notes:

Depreciation:

(1) = 75,000 × (100/3) × (5/12) × (1/100) = ₹ 10,417.

(2) (a) = 3, 00,000 × (100/3) => ₹ 1, 00,000.

(b) =2, 00,000× (100/3) × (5/12) × (1/100) = ₹ 27,778.

Estimated cost and Profit on the contract to be completed on 31.3.2005:

Details	**Cost up to 31.10.2004 Amount (₹)**	**Estimated cost between 01.11.2004 and 31.3.2005 Amount (₹)**	**Total Cost up to 31.3.2005 Amount (₹)**
Materials Issued	6,75,000	13,12, 500	18,75,000
Less: Materials at Site	(75,000)	(37,500)	
Labour Paid and Outstanding	4,25,000	5,90,000	10,15,000
Expenses Paid and Outstanding	2,50,000	3,25,000	5,75,000
Depreciation on Plant	1,00,000	38,195	1,38,195
Total	13,75,000	22,28,195	36,03,195
Estimated Profit (Balancing figure)			3,34,305
Contract Price			39,37,500

Profit to be taken to Profit and Loss account:

[(Estimated Profit) × (Work certified/ Contract price) × (Cash received/Work certified)]

= [(3,34,305) × (20,00,000÷39,37,500) × (17,50,000÷20,00,000)]

= ₹ 1, 48,580.

Illustration 16.10. *From the details of expenditure on a contract No. 101 for ₹ 15,00,000, prepare contract account for the year 2007–08. [The date of commencement of this contract is April1, 2007.]*

Details	***Amount (₹)***
Materials	*3,00,000*
Wages	*2,60,000*
Plant	*3,00,000*
Overheads	*21,600*
Work Uncertified	*10,000*

Cash received on account of the contract as on 31.3.2008 was ₹ 6, 00,000, being 80% of the work certified. The value of the materials in hand was ₹ 15,000. The plant had undergone 25% depreciation.

Solution : **Contract Account**

Dr (For the year ending on 31.3.2008) Cr

Details	Amount (₹)	Details	Amount (₹)
To Materials	3,00,000	By Materials in Hand	15,000
To Wages	2,60,000	By Plant in Hand (300000- 75000)	2,25,000
To Plant	3,00,000	By Work-in-Progress: Work Certified (6,00,000/0.8) = 7,50,000 Work Uncertified: 10,000	7,60,000
To Overheads	21,600		
To Notional Profit c/d	2,18,400		
Total	10,00,000	Total	10,00,000
To Profit and Loss A/c [2,18,400× (2/3) × 0.8]	1,16,480	By Notional Profit b/d	2,18,400
To Profit in Suspense transferred to Work-in-Progress A/c	1,01,920		
Total	2.18.400	Total	2.18.400

ESCALATION CLAUSE

It aims at safeguarding the interest of the contractor against unforeseen rise in cost. This clause is usually provided in long term contracts with a view to protecting both the contractor as well as the contractee against vacillations in the input prices. It provides for modification in the price of contract to cover changes in the price of raw materials and labour or changes in the utilisation factor of plant and machinery. Suitable indices are selected to which both the material and the labour cost is linked. The contract price is revised in an agreed proportion to the changes in the price of the specified inputs.

Circumstances necessitating the Escalation clause:

- The term of the contract is very long.
- The price of the raw material is expected to rise significantly.
- Labour rates are subject to frequent changes by the regulatory authorities.
- The price of fuel and power is subject to frequent changes.
- There may be a project for the completion of which the quantum of raw material and labour cannot be accurately estimated.

The de-escalation Clause provides for a decrease in contract price due to decrease in the price of inputs so that the benefit of price decreases is passed on to the contractee.

Illustration 16.11. *A Contractor undertook a contract for ₹ 6, 00,000 on 1.4.2007 for the construction of a Library building for a public school in Patna. On 31.3.2008, when the accounts were closed, the following details about the contract were gathered:*

Details	*Amount (₹)*
Materials Purchased	*1,50,000*
Wages Paid	*56,000*
General Expenses	*12,900*
Plant Purchased	*80,000*
Materials on Hand on 31.3.2008	*30,000*
Wages accrued on 31.3.2008	*4,000*
Work Certified	*2,40,000*
Work Uncertified	*20,000*
Cash Received	*1,80,000*
Plant as on 31.3.2008	*72,000*

The above contract contained an escalation clause which reads as follows: "In the event of prices of materials and rates of wages increase by more than 5%, the contract price would be increased accordingly by 30% of the rise in the cost of materials and wages beyond 5% in each case."

It was found that since the date of signing the agreement, the prices of materials and wage rates increased by 20%. The value of work certified does not take into account the effect of the above clause.

Prepare the contract account. Working should form part of your answer.

[I.C.W.A. Inter; CA Inter (Modified)]

Solution : Working Notes:

Calculation of Amount of Escalation:

Details	Amount (₹)
Materials consumed (1,50,000 – 30,000) = 1,20,000 Increase in Material cost = [1,20,000×(20/120)]	20,000
Wages Incurred (56,000 + 4,000) = 60,000 Increase in Wages cost = [60,000×(20÷120)]	10,000
Total Increase	30,000

Since the increase in materials and wage is more than 5%, the escalation Clause will apply. Escalation is 20% of the rise in the cost of materials and wages which is beyond the stipulated minimum 5%.

Details	Amount (₹)
20% Increase	30,000
Less: 5% Increase (5/20 × 30,000)	7,500
Increase beyond 5%	22,500

Alternatively,

Element of cost	Total Increase (₹)	Up to 5% Increase (₹)	Increase Beyond 5% (₹)
Material	[1,20,000 × (20÷120)] = 20,000	[1,20,000 × (5÷120)] =5,000	15,000
Wages	[60,000×(20÷120)] = 10,000	[60,000 × (5÷120)] =2,500	7,500
Total	30,000	7,500	22,500

Escalation = 22,500 × 0.3 =>₹ 6,750

Contract Account

Dr (For the year ending on 31.3.2008) Cr

Details		Amount (₹)	Details		Amount (₹)
To Materials		1,50,000	By Materials in Hand		30,000
To Wages	56,000		By Plant in Hand		72,000
Add: Accrued	4,000	60,000			
To Plant		80,000	By Work-in-Progress:		
			Work Certified	2,40,000	
			Work Uncertified	20,000	2,60,000
To General Expenses		12,900	By Contract Escalation		6,750
To Notional Profit c/d		65,850			
Total		3,68,750	Total		3,68,750
To Profit and Loss A/c [65,850× (2/3) ×0.75]		32,925	By Notional Profit b/d		65,850
To Profit in Suspense A/c transferred to Work-in-Progress A/c		32,925			
Total		65,850	Total		65,850

Illustration 16.12. *M/s Construction Bulls Limited secured a contract to supply and erect machinery for a sum of ₹ 45, 00,000. It was to receive payment on account from time to time equal to 90% of the certified value of work done. The work commenced on April 1, 2007 and the following expenditures were incurred during the year:*

Plant and Tools ₹ 4, 20,000; Machinery and Stores ₹ 12,00,000; Wages ₹ 9,00,000; Sundry expenses ₹ 2,40,000 and establishment charges ₹ 3,00,000. A part of the machinery costing ₹ 1, 20,000 was unsuited to the contract and was immediately sold at a profit of ₹ 30,000. The value of the plant and tools on March 31, 2008 was ₹ 2, 00,000 and the value of machinery and stores then on hand was ₹1, 50,000. By April 30, 2008 the company had received payments on account amounting to ₹ 27,00,000 being 90% of the certified value of work done up to the preceding March 31, 2008.

In order to compute profit made on the contract till 31.3.2008, the contractor- company estimated further expenditure that would be incurred in completing the contract, and took to the credit of the Profit and Loss account for the year that proportion of the estimated profit to be realized on the contract which the certified value of work done bore to the contract price. The company estimated:

(i) That the Contract would be completed in the next eight months;

(ii) That plant and tools would have a residual value of ₹ 40,000 upon the completion of the contract;

(iii) That the cost of machinery and stores required , in addition to those in stock as on 31.3.2008 would be ₹ 3,00,000 and that further Sundry expenses of ₹ 1,20,000 would be incurred;

(iv) That the wages on the contract for the eight months on 30.11.2008 would amount to ₹ 5,00,000;

(v) That establishment would cost the same sum per month as in the preceding year; and

(vi) That 2% of the total cost of the contract (Excluding this percentage) should be provided for contingencies.

Prepare the contract account for the year ended on 31.3.2008 and show your calculations of the profit to be credited to the Profit and Loss account for the year.

Solution :

Contract Account

Dr (For the year ending on March 31, 2008) Cr

Details	Amount (₹)	Details	Amount (₹)
To Plant and Tools	4,20,000	By Sale of Plant	1,50,000
To Machinery and Stores	12,00,000	By Plant and Tools in hand c/d	2,00,000

To Wages	9,00,000	By Machinery and Stores in hand c/d	1,50,000
To Sundry expenses	2,40,000	By Work-in-Progress (Value of work certified)	30,00000
To Establishment charges	3,00,000		
To Profit & Loss A/c (Profit on Plant sold)	30,000		
To Balance c/d	4,10,000		
	35,00,000		35,00,000
To Profit & Loss A/c (Profit credited)	2,80,000	By Balance b/d	4,10,000
To Work in Progress A/c (Profit in suspense transferred)	1,30,000		
Total	4,10,000	Total	4,10,000
To Work in Progress b/d: Work certified 30,00,000 *Less:* Profit in Suspense A/c 1,30,000	28,70,000		
To Plant and Tools in hand b/d	2,00,000		
To Machinery and Stores in hand b/d	1,50,000		

Working Notes:

Total Net Expenditure till March 31, 2008:

Details		Amount (₹)
Plant and Tools		4,20,000
Machinery and Stores		12,00,000
Wages		9,00,000
Sundry expenses		2,40,000
Establishment charges		3,00,000
Gross Expenditure		30,40,000
Less:		
Cost of Plant sold	1,20,000	
Plant and Tools in hand	2,00,000	
Machinery and Stores in hand	1,50,000	4,70,000
Total Net Expenditure		25,70,000

Add:		
Further expenditure(Estimated) For the next Eight Months:		
Plant and Tools in hand	2,00,000	
Less: Residual Value	40,000	1,60,000
Machinery and Stores in hand	1,50,000	4,50,000
Add: Further Machinery and Stores Required	3,00,000	1,20,000
Sundry expenses wages		5,00,000
Establishment charges(for Eight Months)		2,00,000
Total Further cost		14,30,000
Total cost of the contract excluding Contingency reserve		40,00,000
Add: Contingency reserve (0.02× 40,00,000)		80,000
Total Estimated cost		40,80,000

Contract Price	45,00,000
Less: Estimated cost	40,80,000
Estimated Total Net Profit	4,20,000

That Proportion of ₹ 4, 20,000 which the certified value of the work done bore to the contract price is to be credited to the Profit and Loss Account:

Certified work: 30, 00,000

Contract Price: 45, 00,000

Thus, [(30, 00,000/4500000) of ₹ 4, 20,000] = ₹ 2, 80,000 credited to Profit and Loss Account, i.e. {(2/3) × 4,20,000 = ₹ 2, 80,000}

Note: In the given illustration (2%) of the total cost of the contract excluding this percentage has been provided for contingencies. But if instead it is given:

"Provide 2% of the total cost of the contract for contingencies." OR

"Provide 2% of the total cost of the contract including this percentage for contingencies."

In that case reserve for contingencies would be:

$$[40,00,000 \times (0.02/(1-0.02))] = ₹\ 97,561.$$

COST PLUS CONTRACTS

Circumstances Necessitating Cost Plus Contract

Under the following conditions such a contract is entered into between the parties:

1. It is not possible to estimate the cost of contract in advance with reasonable accuracy.
2. Contract will take long time to complete and the conditions are expected to be uncertain.
3. The nature of work is entirely new, and the design, specifications like of which has not been undertaken earlier.

4. Quality is the essence of the performance of such work.
5. Market conditions in regard to the availability and price of materials, labour etc. are unstable and unpredictable.
6. There is an urgency to start the work and there is no time to prepare an advance estimate of the proposed work.
7. The contractee is not sure of the details of the work to be done till the commencement of the work.
8. Frequent modifications are required to be done in the work.
9. Cost incurred by the contractor can be monitored and the contractor's accounts are subject to rigorous scrutiny.

Advantages:

- All costs are fully covered. There is no risk of loss due to fluctuation in price and under-estimation of costs.
- There is an automatic escalation clause so that upward-cost changes are duly recovered.
- Contractee pays only the reasonable price based on actual cost incurred.
- Contractee gets the benefit of fall in price of materials and wage rates etc.

Disadvantages:

- The contractor is denied the benefit of efficiency improvement due to savings in cost.
- Wherever agreed profit is a percentage of costs, every step in cost reduction results in lower profit. There is no incentive for the contractor to go for cost reduction programme during the performance of the contract.
- The contractor has to maintain detailed cost records, get them audited and show them to the contractee for settling the claims. This leads to the loss of confidentiality of cost records.
- There is a scope for dispute regarding the costs actually incurred by the contractor.
- The final price payable to the contractor by the contractee remains uncertain making his budgeting exercise very difficult.

Illustration 16.13. *Modern Engineers Limited undertook several contracts during the year 2008. The following information relates to contract No. 405:*

Details	***Amount (₹)***
Direct Materials	*1,01,250*
Direct Wages	*77,500*
Stores Issued	*52,500*
Loose Tools	*12,000*

Tractor Expenses:		
Running material	*11,500*	
Wages of driver	*15,000*	*26,500*
Other Direct Charges		*16,275*

The contract took three months in its completion. The value of loose tools and stores returned at the end of the period were ₹ 1, 000 and ₹ 15,000 respectively. The plant was also retuned at a value of ₹95, 000 after charging depreciation @ 5% for the contract period. The value of the tractor was ₹ 1,00,000 and the depreciation was to be charged to the tractor @ 12.5% p.a. The administration and office expenses are to be provided at 10% on works cost. Profit is to be charged at 20% of the total cost.

Prepare the aforesaid Contract Account assuming the balance of the contract was duly received from the contractee.

Solution : **Modern Engineers Limited**

Contract Account

Dr (For the year ending on December 31, 2008) Cr

Details	Amount (₹)	Details	Amount (₹)
To Direct Materials	1,01,250	By Loose Tools Returned	1,000
To Direct Wages	77,500	By Stores Returned	15,000
To Stores	52,500	By Contractee's A/c (Balancing figure)	3,67,158
To Loose Tools	12,000		
To Tractor Expenses	26,500		
To Depreciation on Tractor	3,125		
To Depreciation on Plant	5,000		
To Other Direct charges	16,275		
To Administration and Office Expenses (2,78,150 × 0.1)	27,815		
To Profit & Loss A/c (3,05,965 × 0.2)	61,193		
Total	3,83,158	Total	3,83,158

Working Notes:

Works cost

= (1,01,250 + 77,500 + 52,500 + 12,000 + 26,500 + 3,125 + 5,000 + 16,275) – (1,000+15,000)

= 2, 94,150 – 16,000 = 2,78,150.

Total cost = Works cost + Administration and office cost

= 2,78,150 + 27,815 => ₹3, 05,965.

Amount to be credited to the Contractee's account:

$$= 3,05,965 \times 1.2 = ₹\ 3,67,158$$

Illustration 16.14. *The following is the summarised information relating to Contract Account Number 301:*

Details	*Amount (₹)*
Contract Price	*19,20,000*
Wages	*5,24,800*
General Expenses	*27,520*
Materials	*3,84,000*
Cash received (80% of the work certified)	*7,68,000*
Materials at Site	*32,100*
Plant	*64,000*

Note: *Included in the above information are wages ₹ 11,200, materials ₹ 12,800 and other expenses ₹ 8,000 which were incurred since certification.*

Depreciate Plant @ 12.5% p.a.

Prepare Contract Account Number 301.

Solution :

Dr **Contract Account Number 301** Cr

Details	**Amount (₹)**	**Details**	**Amount (₹)**
To Materials	3,84,000	By Work-in-Progress A/c:	
		Certified 9,60,000	
		Uncertified 32,000	9,92,000
To Wages	5,24,800	By Closing Balance at Site:	
		Materials 32,100	
		Plant 52,000	84,100
		(64,000 – 8,000)	
To General Expenses	27,520		
To Plant	64,000		
To Profit and Loss A/c 40,416			
To Profit in Suspense A/c 35,364	75,780		
Total	10,76,100	Total	10,76,100

Work certified: 50% of the contract price (i.e. 9, 60,000÷19, 20,000)

Profit to be carried to the Profit and Loss account:

$$= [(2/3) \times (75{,}780) \times (08)] = ₹\ 40{,}416.$$

The balance of notional Profit i.e. ₹ 35,364 may be put as 'Profit in Suspense'.

Illustration 16.15. *The Haryana Contractors limited obtained a contract to build a long portion of the road in Ambala district at a Contract price of ₹ 250, 00,000. The work commenced on October2, 2006 and cost of work completed up to March 31,2007 was ₹ 96, 00,000 and a sum of ₹ 10, 00,000 was on that date credited to Profit and Loss Account in respect of the contract. The other items on that date relating to this contract were as under:*

Details	*Amount (₹)*
Value of work certified	*100,00,000*
Cash Received	*75,00,000*
Cost of Work uncertified	*16,00,000*
Materials on site	*2,00,000*
Plant at site	*8,00,000*
Accrued wages	*1,00,000*

During the year 2007-08 the following amounts were spent in respect of this contract:

Details	*Amount (₹)*
Materials	*40,00,000*
Wages	*65,00,000*
Establishment charges	*2,00,000*
Plant and Tools	*5,00,000*
Sundry Expenses	*1,00,000*

Materials for ₹ 5, 00,000 and Plant for ₹ 1, 00,000, purchased during the year 2006-07were found unsuitable for the contract and were sold during the current year for ₹ 5, 40,000 and ₹ 80,000 respectively. The value of Plant and Tools on site on 31.3.2008 was estimated at ₹ 7,50,000 and that of materials at ₹ 10, 00,000; this work was certified next year for ₹ 12, 00,000. Value of work certified during the year 2007-08 was ₹ 125, 00,000 and the company received 75% of it in cash during the same year.

Prepare the contract account for the year ended on 31.3.2008. It was estimated that the contract would be completed by 31.5.2008 requiring further payments of ₹ 8,20,000 (Materials ₹ 3,00,000, Wages ₹ 5,00,000 and

Establishment charges ₹ 20,000) and the company would be able to realize after the completion of the contract ₹ 3,20,000 by the sale of materials and ₹ 7,00,000 by the sale of Plant and Tools. Also show how the various assets and liabilities relating to this contract will be shown in Company's Balance Sheet as at 31.3.2008.

Solution : **Haryana Contractors limited**

Contract Account

Dr (For the year ending on March 31, 2008) Cr

Details	Amount (₹)	Details		Amount (₹)
To Work-in-Progress (Opening) b/d	10,600,000	Accrued wages b/d		1,00,000
To Materials on site b/d	2,00,000	By Materials sold		5,40,000
To Plant at Site b/d	8,00,000	By Plant sold		80,000
To Materials	40,00,000	By Profit & Loss A/c (Loss on sale of Plant)		20,000
To Wages	65,00,000	By Closing Balances:		
		Plant at Site	7,50,000	
		Materials on site	6,50,000	14,00,000
To Establishment charges	2,00,000	By Work-in-Progress (Closing) c/d:		
		Work Certified	225,00,000	
		Work Uncertified	10,00,000	235,00,000
To Plant and Tools	5,00,000			
To Sundry Expenses	1,00,000			
To Profit & Loss A/c (Profit on sale of materials)	40,000			
To Balance c/d	27,00,000			
Total	256,40,000	Total		256,40,000
To Profit & Loss A/c (Profit credited)	20,25,000	By Balance b/d		27,00,000
To Work in Progress A/c (Profit in suspense transferred)	6,75,000			
Total	27,00,000	Total		27,00,000

Working Notes:

I. Cost of work Certified:

Cost of Completed work	96,00,000
Less: Cost of work Uncertified	(16,00,000)
Cost of work Certified	80,00,000

II. Work-in-Progress (Opening):

Cost of work Certified	80,00,000	
Cost of work Uncertified	16,00,000	
Add: Profit taken to the		
Credit of Profit and Loss A/c	10,00,000	
Work-in-Progress	106, 00,000	

III. Estimated cost of contract on completion:

Cost of contract to date (229, 40,000 – 21,40,000)		208,00,000
Add: Estimated Expenses:		
Materials (6, 50,000 + 3, 00,000)		9,50,000
Plant		7,50,000
Wages		5,00,000
Establishment charges		20,000
Less: Value of Material at the end	3,20,000	
Value of Plant at the end	7,00,000	(10,20,000)
Total cost of the contract		220,00,000
Profit		30,00,000
Value of contract		250,00,000

IV. Value of certified up to 31.3.2008:

Value of work certified (till 31.3.2007)	100,00,000
Value of work certified (done during the Year 2007-08)	125,00,000
Total certified work till 31.3.2008	225,00,000

V. Cash received up to 31.3.2008:

Cash received till 31.3.2007	75,00,000
Cash received (during the Year 2007-08)	93,75,000
Total Cash Received till 31.3.2008	168,75,000

VI. Profit to be credited to Profit and Loss account:

[Notional Profit × (Work certified/Contract Price) × (Cash received/ Work certified)]

[30,00,000 × (225,00,000÷250,00,000) × (168,75,000÷225,00,000)

= ₹ 20,25,000.

Illustration 16.16. (Value of work Uncertified is not given)

A Contractor, who prepares his accounts on December 31 each year, commenced a contract on April1, 2008. The costing records concerning the said contract reveal the following information on december31, 2008:

Details	***Amount*** **(₹)**
Materials charged to site	*5,16,200*
Labour engaged	*8,96,800*
Foremen's Salaries	*5,55,100*

Plants costing ₹ 13, 00,000 had been on site for 146 days. Their working life is estimated at seven years and the final scrap value at ₹ 75,000. A supervisor, who is paid ₹ 20,000 p.m., has devoted approximately 80% of his time to this contract. The administrative and other expenses amount to ₹ 3,50,000. Materials in hand at site on 31.12.2008 cost ₹ 50,800. Some of the material costing ₹ 9,000 was found unsuitable and was sold for ₹ 8,000 and part of the plant costing ₹ 11,000 (on 31.12.2008) unsuited to the contract was sold at a profit of ₹ 2,000.

The contract price was ₹ 48, 00,000 but it was accepted by the contractor for ₹ 45,00,000. On 31.12.2008 two-third of the contract was complete. Architect's certificate had been issued covering 50% of the contract price and ₹ 16,87,500 had so far been paid on contract. Prepare contract account and state how much profit or loss should be included in the financial accounts on 31.12.2008. Workings should be clearly given. Depreciation is charged on time basis.

Also prepare the contractee's account and show how these accounts would appear in the Balance Sheet as on 31.12.2008. **[C.A.; C.S. (Modified)]**

Solution : Working Notes:

Contract completed for the period ended 31.12.2008	2/3
Contract certified for the period ended 31.12.2008	1/2
Contract Uncertified {(2/3) – (1/2)}	1/6
Cost of 2/3 contract work	₹ 24,72,600
Cost of FULL Contract (3/2 × 24,72,600)	₹ 37,08,900
Cost of 1/6 contract work (i.e. uncertified work) (1/6 × 37, 08,900)	₹ 6,18,150

Contract Account

Dr (For the year ending on March 31, 2008) Cr

Details	Amount (₹)	Details	Amount (₹)
To Materials	5, 16,200	By Materials at Site	50,800
To Wages	8, 96,800	By Materials sold	8,000
To Supervisor's Salary [20,000 × 0.80 × 9)	1,44,000	By Profit & Loss A/c (Loss on sale of Material)	1,000
To Depreciation of Plant [{(13,00,000 – 75,000) ÷ 7} × (146 ÷ 365)]	70,000	By Cost of work done c/d	24,72,600
To Administrative and Other expenses	3,50,000		
To Foremen's salaries	5,55,100		
Total	25,32,400	Total	25,32,400

To Cost of work done b/d	24,72,600	By Work-in-Progress: Work certified Work uncertified	 22,50,000 6,18,150
To Profit & Loss A/c (Profit credited) [(3,95,550) × (2/3) × 0.75]	1,97,775		
To Work in Progress A/c (Profit in suspense transferred)	1,97,775		
Total	28,68,150		28,68,150

Accounting of Contracts for more than One Accounting Year

When contract work is completed in more than one accounting year, the first year's contract account is prepared as incomplete contract. Accordingly, work-in-progress, materials at site and plant at site will be credited to that year's contract account. These closing balances in the first year will be carried as opening balances in the following year's contract account. Work-in- Progress account is shown in all the years other than the final year when the contract is 100% complete. The last year's contract account will be credited by the amount of contract consideration.

Illustration 16.17. *Prepare the contract account from the following information relating to a contract for ₹ 60,00,000, the contractee paying 80% of the value of work done as certified by the architect and the balance on completion:*

Details	***Year***		
	2006-07 Amount (₹)	***2007-08 Amount (₹)***	***2008-09 Amount (₹)***
Materials	*7,20,000*	*8,80,000*	*5,04,000*
Direct Wages	*6,80,000*	*9,20,000*	*6,80,000*
Direct Expenses	*28,000*	*1,00,000*	*36,000*
Indirect Expenses	*12,000*	*16,000*	*NIL*
Work certified	*14,00,000*	*45,20,000*	*60,00,000*
Work done but yet to be certified	*NIL*	*80,000*	*NIL*
Plant	*80,000*	*NIL*	*NIL*

The value of the plant at the end of the year 2006-07, 2007-08 and 2008-09 was ₹ 64,000, ₹ 40,000, and ₹ 16,000 respectively.

Solution :

Dr **Contract Account** Cr

Date	Details	Amount (₹)	Date	Details	Amount (₹)
2006			2007		
1-Apr	To Materials	7,20,000	31-Mar	By work-in-Progress: Certified 14,00,000 Uncertified N I L	14,00,000
	To Wages	6,80,000		By Plant	64,000
	To Direct expenses	28,000		By Costing Profit and Loss A/c	56,000
	To Indirect Expenses	12,000			
	To Plant	80,000			
	Total	15,20,000		Total	15,20,000
2007			2008		
1-Apr	To Work-in-Progress: Certified 14,00,000 Uncertified N I L	14,00,000	31-Mar	By work-in-Progress: Certified 45,20,000 Uncertified 80,000	46,00,000
	To Materials	8,80,000		By Plant	40,000
	To Wages	9,20,000			
	To Direct expenses	1,00,000			
	To Indirect Expenses	16,000			
	To Plant	64,000			
	To costing profit and Loss A/c	6,72,000			
	To Work-in-Progress: Profit in Suspense A/c	5,88,000			
	Total	46,40,000		Total	46,40,000
2008			2009		
1-Apr	To Work-in-Progress: Certified 45,20,000 Uncertified 80,000 46,00,000 *Less:* Profit in suspense 5,88,000	40,12,000	31-Mar	By Plant	16,000
				By Contractee's A/c	60,00,000
	To Materials	5,04,000			
	To Wages	6,80,000			
	To Direct expenses	36,000			
	To Indirect Expenses	N I L			
	To Plant	40,000			
	To costing profit and Loss A/c	7,44,000			
	Total	60,16,000		Total	60,16,000

Profit for the year 2007-08:

= [Notional Profit × (2/3) × (Cash Received / Work Certified)]

= [12,60,000 × 2/3 × 0.8]

= ₹ 6,72,000.

LET US RECAPITULATE

1. Contract costing is a form of specific order costing. Work is done as per the requirements and specifications of the customer and each contract is a separate cost unit.
2. The cost of each contract is calculated separately.
3. The contracts are of long duration and the completion of the same takes more than one accounting period.
4. Each contract is a mini profit and Loss account. It gives costs, revenues and profit/loss from each contract which is transferred to General profit and Loss account.
5. A big chunk of the total cost is in the nature of direct costs. Most of the purchases of materials and others are specific to costs.
6. At times sub-contractors are engaged to perform specialized jobs involved in a contract.
7. The contractor is entitled to get payment for execution of the contract in installments based on the stage of completion of contract work as certified by the architect/valuer.
8. There is a need to estimate profit on incomplete contract at the end of each accounting year.
9. There is trade-off between the accounting concepts of 'prudence' and 'matching costs with revenue' while recognizing profit each year for the purpose of credit to profit and loss account during the execution of a contract.
10. Job is performed in the workshop of the producer while the contract is usually executed at customer's site.
11. A contract involves a larger work-in-progress spread over a much larger period of time.
12. Plant purchased for the specific purpose of a contract is charged to that contract only. At the end of each accounting period, the written down value of the plant is credited to the contract account.
13. Contract account is debited with the cost of the amount of depreciation. Such practice is usually adopted when the plant is used on the contract only for a short period.

14. Payment made to such sub-contractors is charged to the respective contracts based on value in sub-contractors' invoice and architect's or surveyor's certificate.

15. The cost of extra work will be debited to the contract account and the price charged for the extra work will be credited to the contract account.

16. Payment by the contractee is always linked to the value of work certified.

17. A certain proportion of the amount is retained by the contractee and is paid after the completion of the contract. The sum of money thus retained for some time is known as retention money.

18. Work certified means the work which has been completed by the contractor and certified by the Contractee's architect or surveyor/ valuer.

19. The work which has been done by the contractor but not certified by the architect on the date of accounting due to insufficient progress is known as uncertified work. It is a part of work-in-progress.

20. Work-in-Progress means work is still not complete in all respects, and something is yet to be done.

21. The contractor may prepare 'work-in-Progress account' by debiting the account with the value of work certified and the cost of work uncertified and by crediting the profit not transferred to Profit and Loss account.

22. In the Fixed Price contract, the agreed price is paid by the contractee to the contractor. The contractee is permitted to make deductions on account of defectives and penalties for delay; he is required to make extra payment for the additional work.

23. Escalation clause is a clause under which the fixed contract price is subject to modification due to likely increase in the prices of materials and labour beyond a certain percentage. This clause protects the interests of the contractor.

24. The Cost plus Contract involves an agreement as to the items of cost to be included in the actual cost and the percentage of profit to be added to the actual cost, no price could be pre-determined for the contract.

25. Every loss on contract, whether completed or incomplete, should be transferred to Profit and Loss account in its entirety.

26. Notional Profit is the difference between the value of work-in-Progress certified plus cost of work done but not yet certified AND the cost of work done to date.

27. Estimated Profit is the Difference between the Contract Price and the estimated total cost of the contract.

28. The portion of Notional Profit or Estimated Profit to be transferred to Profit and Loss Account depends upon the stage of completion of the contract.

SOLVED PROBLEMS

Problem 1. *Engineers Limited undertook several contracts during the year 2008. The following information relates to contract No. 701:*

Details	*Amount (₹)*
Direct Materials	*1,21,500*
Direct wages	*93,000*
Stores Issued	*63,000*
Loose Tools	*14,400*
Tractor Expenses:	
Running Material 13,800	
Wages of driver 18,000	*31,800*
Other Direct charges	*15,900*

The contract took 13 weeks on its completion. The value of Loose Tools and Stores returned at the end of the period were ₹ 1,200 and ₹ 18,000 respectively. The Plant was also returned at a value of ₹ 96,000 after charging depreciation at 20%. The value of the tractor was ₹ 20,000 and the depreciation was to be charged to the tractor @ 16% p.a. The administration and office overheads are to be provided at 12.5% on works cost. Profit is to be charged at 22% of the total cost.

Prepare the aforesaid contract account assuming the balance of the contract was duly received from the contractee.

Solution :

Dr **Contract Account** Cr

Details	Amount (₹)	Details	Amount (₹)
To Direct Material	1,21,500	By Stores Returned	18,000
To Direct Wages	93,000	By Loose Tools Returned	1,200
To Stores Issued	63,000	By Plant Returned	96,000
To Plant Issued	1,20,000	By Balance c/d (Works Cost)	3,44,400
To Loose Tools	14,400		
To Tractor Expenses:			
Fuel, oil etc. 13,800			
Wages to Drivers 18,000	31,800		
To Depreciation On Tractor: [(20,000 × 0.16) × (13/52)]	800		
To Other Direct Charges	15,900		
	4,59,600		4,59,600

To Balance b/d	3,44,400	By Contractee's A/c	4,72,689
To Administrative Overheads @ 12.5% on Works Cost: (0.125 × 3,44,400)	43,050		
To Profit & Loss A/c @ 22% on Cost: (0.22 × 3,87,450)	85,239		
Total	4,72,689	Total	4,72,689

Dr **Contractee's Account** Cr

Details	Amount (₹)	Details	Amount (₹)
To Contract A/c	4,72,689	By Bank A/c	4,72,689
Total	4,72,689	Total	4,72,689

Problem 2. *From the following information suggest the profit to be taken on a contract which is 95% complete. Illustrate the different methods of computing the profit and compare the profit, had it not been nearly complete.*

Details	***Amount*** (₹)
Total cost of contract to date	*10,00,000*
Estimated additional expenditure	*96,000*
(Including Provision for contingencies)	
Contract Price	*12,50,000*
Value of contract certified	*12,00,000*
Cost of Work not certified	*10,000*
Cash Received	*10,80,000*

Solution : As the contract is almost complete, the calculation of profit may be made as under:

Estimated Profit:

Contract Price	12,50,000
Estimated total expenditure	10,96,000
Estimated total Profit	1,54,000

(a) [(Estimated Profit) × (Work certified/ Contract price)]

= [(1, 54,000) × (12, 00,000 ÷12, 50,000)]

= ₹ 1, 47,840.

(b) [(Estimated Profit) × (Work certified/ Contract price) × (Cash Received/Work certified)]

= [(1, 54,000) × ((12, 00,000 ÷12, 50,000)]) × (10, 80,000 ÷ 12, 00, 000)]

= ₹ 1, 33, 056.

(c) [(Estimated Profit) × (Cost of work to date/ Estimated Total cost of work)]

= [(1, 54,000) × (10, 00,000 ÷10, 96,000)]

= ₹ 1,40,511.

(d) [(Estimated Profit) × (Cost of work to date/ Estimated Total cost of work) × (Cash Received/Work certified)]

= [(1, 54,000) × ((10, 00,000 ÷10, 96,000)]) × (10, 80,000 ÷12, 00, 000)]

= ₹ 1,19, 750.

Assuming the contract has reasonably advanced but not almost complete, the computation of profit to be transferred to the Profit and Loss account is as under:

Item	Amount (₹)
Value of Work Certified	12,00,000
Less: Cost of Work Certified [Cost of work Done to date) – (Cost of Work not yet certified)] i.e.(10,00,000 – 10,000)	9, 90,000
Notional Profit	2,10,000

= [(2/3) × (Notional Profit) × (Cash Received/Work certified)]

= [(2/3) × (2, 10,000) × (1 0, 80,000 ÷12, 00,000)]

= ₹ 63,000.

Problem 3. *Three contracts were commenced on the following months April1, October1, and January1, 2007. They were undertaken by the Build-well Limited and their accounts as on 31.3.2008 showed the following:*

Details	*Contract I Amount (₹)*	*Contract II Amount (₹)*	*Contract III Amount (₹)*
Contract Price	*20,00,000*	*13,50,000*	*15,00,000*
Expenses:-			
Materials	*3,60,000*	*2,90,000*	*1,00,000*
Wages Paid	*5,50,000*	*5,62,000*	*70,000*
General Charges	*20,000*	*14,000*	*5,000*
Plant	*1,00,000*	*80,000*	*60,000*
Materials on Hand	*20,000*	*20,000*	*10,000*
Wages accrued	*20,000*	*20,000*	*9,000*
Work Certified	*10,00,000*	*8,00,000*	*1,80,000*
Cash Received in respect thereof	*7,50,000*	*6,00,000*	*1,35,000*
Work completed but not yet certified	*30,000*	*40,000*	*10,500*

The Plant was installed on the date of the commencement of each contract. Depreciation is to be charged at 12.5% p.a. You are required to prepare contract Accounts.

Solution : **Contract No. I Account**

Dr For the year ending on March 31, 2008 Cr

Details	Amount (₹)	Details	Amount (₹)
To Materials To Wages To Wages Accrued To General charges	3,60,000 5,50,000 20,000 20,000	By Work-in-Progress (Closing) c/d: Work Certified 10,00,000 Work Uncertified 30,000	10,30,000
To Plant To Balance c/d	1,00,000 87,500	By Closing Balances: Plant at Site 87,500 Materials on site 20,000	1,07,500
Total	11,37,500	Total	11,37,500
To Profit & Loss A/c (Profit credited) To Work in Progress A/c (Profit in suspense transferred)	43,750 43,750	By Balance b/d	87,500
Total	87,500	Total	87,500
To Closing Balance: Work-in-Progress b/d: Work Certified 10,00,000 Work Uncertified 30,000	10,30,000	By Closing Balance: Wages Accrued 20,000 Work in Progress A/c (Profit in suspense transferred) 43,750	63,750
To Closing Balances: Plant at Site 87,500 Materials on site 20,000	1,07,500		

Contract No. II Account

Dr For the year ending on March 31, 2008 Cr

Details	Amount (₹)	Details	Amount (₹)
To Materials To Wages To Wages Accrued To General charges	2,90,000 5,62,000 20,000 14,000	By Work-in-Progress (Closing) c/d: Work Certified 8,00,000 Work Uncertified 40,000	8,40,000

To Plant	80,000	By Closing Balances: Plant at Site 75,000 Materials on site 20,000	95,000
		By Profit & Loss A/c (Loss debited)	31,000
Total	9,66,000	Total	9,66,000

Note: The entire Loss has been transferred to Profit and Loss account.

Contract No. III Account

Dr For the year ending on March 31, 2008 Cr

Details	Amount (₹)	Details	Amount (₹)
To Materials	1,00,000	By Work Done (Balancing figure)	1,90,875
To Wages	70,000	By Closing Balances: Plant at Site 58,125 Materials on site 10,000	68,125
To Wages Accrued	9,000		
To General charges	20,000		
To Plant	60,000		
Total	2,59,000	Total	2,59,000
To Balance b/fd: Work-in-Progress (Work Done)	1,90,875	By Balance b/fd: Work-in-Progress : Wages Accrued	9,000

Note: Work certified in Contract No. III Account represents a small proportion of contract price; the entire expenditure has been treated as work-in-Progress.

Problem 4. *The Standard Firm undertook a contract for construction of a large building complex. The construction work started on April 1, 2007 and the following data are available for the year ended on March 2008.*

Details	*Amount (₹)*
Materials Issued to Site	*105,00,000*
Planning and Project Estimation Cost	*14,00,000*
Direct wages Paid	*56,00,000*
Materials Returned from Site	*3,50,000*
Plant Hire charges	*24,50,000*

Other Labour costs	*7,00,000*
Site Office Costs	*9,49,200*
Head Office Expenses Apportioned	*5,25,000*
Direct Expenses Incurred	*12,62,800*
Work certified	*280,00,000*
Work Done but not yet certified	*2,08,600*
Progress Payments received	*224,00,000*
Contract Price	*500,00,000*

The firm owns a plant, which originally costed ₹ 28 Lakhs, has been continuously in use in this contract throughout the year. The residual value of this plant after five years of life is expected to be ₹ Seven lakhs. Straight Line Method of depreciation is applied to the plant

As on 31.3.2008 the direct wages due and payable amounted to ₹ 3, 78,000 and the Cost of Materials estimated to be ₹ 2, 80,000.

You are required to:

(1) Prepare the Contract Account for the year ended on 31.3.2008.

(2) Show the calculation of profit to be taken to the Profit and Loss account of the year.

(3) Show the Relevant Balance Sheet as on 31.3.2008.

Solution :

Dr **Contract Account** Cr

Details	Amount (₹)	Details	Amount (₹)
To Materials Issued to Site 105,00,000 *Less:* Materials returned to Site 3,50,000	101,50,000	By Work-in-Progress A/c: Certified 280,00,000 Uncertified 2,08,600	282,08,600
To Planning and Project Estimation Costs	14,00,000	By Closing Balance at Site: Materials 2,80,000 Plant: (28,00,000 – 4,20,000) = 23,80,000	26,60,000
To Direct wages: Paid 56,00,000 Outstanding 3,78,000	59,78,000		
To Direct Expenses Incurred	12,62,800		
To Plant	28,00,000		
To Plant Hire Charges	24,50,000		

To Other Labour Costs	7,00,000		
To Office Overheads: Site Office Costs 9,49,200 Head Office 5,25,000	14,74,200		
To Profit c/d	46,53,600		
Total	308,68,600	Total	308,68,600
To Profit & Loss A/c	24,81,920	By Profit b/d	46,53,600
To Work-in-Progress A/c (Profit in Suspense)	21,71,680		
Total	46,53,600	Total	46,53,600

Working Notes:

Profit to be taken to the Profit & Loss A/c:

(i) Cash Ratio = (Payments Received/ Work certified) × 100

= (224, 00,000 ÷280, 00,000) ×100= 80%.

(ii) Work certified Ratio = (Work Certified/ Contract Price) ×100

= (280, 00,000 ÷500, 00,000) ×100= 56%

[Work certified Ratio comes in the category of 50% or more, so 2/3 proportion of the notional profit would be considered]

(iii) To be transferred to Profit and Loss A/c= Notional Profit ×2/3 × 0.8

= 46, 53, 600 × 2/3 × 0.8= ₹ 24, 81,920.

(iv) To be kept in suspense and transferred to Work-in Progress A/c:

Profit Transferred to work-in-progress A/c: (46, 53,600 – 24, 81,920) = ₹ 21,71,680.

Balance Sheet (Relevant) as on 31.3.2008

Liabilities	Amount (₹)	Assets	Amount (₹)
Direct Wages Outstanding	3,78,000	Work-in-Progress: Certified 280,00,000 Uncertified 2,08,600 282,08,600 Less: Profit in Suspense 21,71,680 260,36,920 Less: Amount Received 224,00,000	36,36,920

Profit & Loss A/c (Relevant)	24,81,920	Closing Balance at Site: Materials 2,80,000 Plant 23,80,000	26,60,000

***Problem 5.** The following information related to building contract for ₹ 80,00,000 for which 80% of the value of work-in-Progress as certified by the architect is being paid by the contractee:*

Details	*2005-06*	*2006-07*	*2007-08*
Materials Issued	*9,60,000*	*11,60,000*	*6,72,000*
Direct Wages	*8,80,000*	*12,40,000*	*8,80,000*
Direct Expenses	*40,000*	*1,36,000*	*48,000*
Indirect Expenses	*16,000*	*20,700*	*4,000*
Work certified	*18,80,000*	*60,00,000*	*80,00,000*
Uncertified Work	*22,400*	*64,000*	———
Plant Issued	*1,12,000*	———	———
Materials at Site	*16,000*	*40,000*	*64,000*

The value of the plant at the end of the year 2005-06, 2006-07 and 2007-08 was ₹ 89,600, ₹ 56,000 and ₹ 24,000 respectively. Prepare contract account for these three years, taking into account such profit as you deem fit on incomplete contracts.

Solution :

Contract Account

Dr (For the year ending on March 31, 2006) Cr

Details	Amount (₹)	Details	Amount (₹)
To Materials Issued	9,60,000	By Work-in-Progress A/c: Certified 18,80,000 Uncertified 22,400	19,02,400
To Direct Wages	8,80,000	By Closing Balances: Plant at Site 89,600 Materials on site 16,000	1,05,600
To Direct Expenses	40,000		
To Indirect Expenses	16,000		
To Plant Issued	1,12,000		
Total	20,08,000	Total	20,08,000

Contract Account

Dr For the year ending on March 31, 2007 Cr

Details	Amount (₹)	Details	Amount (₹)
To Work-in-Progress A/c (Opening): Certified 18,80,000 Uncertified 22,400	19,02,400	By Work-in-Progress A/c: Certified 60,00,000 Uncertified 64,000	60,64,000
To Plant at the Beginning	89,600	By Closing Balances: Plant at Site 56,000 Materials on site 40,000	96,000
To Materials at the Beginning	16,000		
To Materials Issued	11,60,000		
To Direct Wages	12,40,000		
To Direct Expenses	1,36,000		
To Indirect Expenses	20,700		
Profit & Loss A/c(Profit: (16,11,300 ×2/3 × 0.8)	8,59,360		
To Work-in-Progress A/c (Profit in Suspense)	7,51,940		
Total	61,60,000	Total	61,60,000

Contract Account

Dr For the year ending on March 31, 2008 Cr

Details	Amount (₹)	Details	Amount (₹)
To Work-in-Progress A/c (Opening): Certified 60,00,000 Uncertified 64,000	60,64,000	By Contractee's A/c	80,00,000
To Plant at the Beginning	56,000	By Plant at Site (Transferred to Head Office)	24,000
To Materials at the Beginning	40,000	By Materials on site (Transferred to Head Office)	64,000
To Materials Issued	6,72,000		
To Direct Wages	8,80,000		
To Direct Expenses	48,000		

To Indirect Expenses	4,000		
Profit & Loss A/c	3,24,000		
Total	80,88,000	Total	80,88,000

Problem 6. *Following are the items of expenses in connection with a contract for ₹ Fifteen lakhs:*

Details	***Amount (₹)***
Materials issued to Contract	*2,08,125*
Plant used for Contract	*75,000*
Wages	*2,96,000*
Other Expenses	*37,500*

Cash received on account up to 31.3.2008, amounted to ₹ 6, 75,000 which were 90% of the work certified. Of the Plant and materials charged to contract, plant which cost ₹ 15,000 and materials cost ₹ 11,250 were lost on July12007. The cost of work done but yet to be certified was ₹ 60,000 and materials costing ₹10, 000 was at the site. On the last day of the accounting year Plant costing ₹11, 250 were returned to the Stores. Charge 20% depreciation on Plant.

Prepare

(i) Contract Account of M/s Brilliant Contractors who commenced this contract on April 1, 2007;

(ii) Contractee's Account; and

(iii) Balance Sheet from the above details furnished.

Solution : **Contract Account**

Dr For the period ending on 31.3.2008 Cr

Details	**Amount (₹)**	**Details**	**Amount (₹)**
To Materials issued to Contract	2,08,125	By Profit and Loss A/c: Loss of Plant 15,000 Loss of Materials 11,250	26,250
To Plant used for Contract	75,000	By Work-in-Progress A/c: Work Certified 7,50,000 Work done but not yet Certified 60,000	8,10,000

To Wages	2,96,000	By Balance c/d: Materials 10,000 Plant in Store 11,250 Plant at Site 36,750	58,000
To Other Expenses	37,500		
To Notional Profit c/d	2,77,625		
Total	8,94,250	Total	8,94,250
To Profit and Loss A/c	1,66,575	By Notional Profit b/d	2,77,625
To Work-in-Progress A/c (Profit in Suspense/Reserve)	1,11,050		
Total	2,77,625	Total	2,77,625

Dr **Contractee's A/c** Cr

Details	Amount (₹)	Details	Amount (₹)
To Contract A/c	6,75,000	By Bank A/c	6,75,000
Total	6,75,000	Total	6,75,000

Balance Sheet (Relevant)

As on 31.3.2008

Liabilities	Amount (₹)	Assets	Amount (₹)
Reserves and surpluses: Profit & Loss on contract: 1,43,175 *Less:* Loss of Plant 15,000 Loss of Materials 11,250	1,16,925	Work-in-Progress: Certified 7,50,000 Uncertified 60,000 8, 10,000 *Less:* Profit in Suspense 1,11,050 6,98,950 *Less:* Amount Received 6,75,000	23,950
		Closing Balance at Site: Materials 10,000 Plant in Store 11,250 Plant at site 36,750	58,000

Problem 7. *The following particulars relate to two houses which a firm of builders had in course of construction under contract:*

Details	*Amount (₹)*	*Amount (₹)*
Work-in-Progress on April, 2004 excluding ₹ 4,000 estimated Profit which was taken to Profit and Loss account in 2003-04.	*70,000*	*NIL*
Materials purchased	*1,15,000*	*83,000*
Wages	*1,00,000*	*70,000*
Electrical services	*7,000*	*1,500*
Road making charges	*44,000*	*NIL*
Contract price (inclusive of Road Making)	*3,00,000*	*2,00,000*
Cash Received up to 31.3.2005	*3,00,000*	*1,50,000*
Percentage of cash received to work certified	*100*	*75*
Value of materials in hand on 31.3.2005	*2,000*	*2,700*
Work done but yet to be certified	*NIL*	*12,500*
Value of Plant used on sites	*60,000*	*30,000*
Period of Plant remained on site during the year (Month)	*10*	*8*

The total administrative expenses incurred during the current accounting year amounted to ₹ 61,200. These are to be charged to the two contracts in proportion to wages. Depreciation of Plant is to be taken at the Rate of 12.5% per annum.

Prepare the two contract accounts (in columnar form) showing the profit or loss on each house for the year 2004-05 and the sums which you consider appropriately transferable to the Profit and Loss account.

Solution : **Contract Account**

Dr (For the year 2004-05) Cr

Details	House A (₹)	House B (₹)	Details	House A (₹)	House B (₹)
To Work-in-Progress (excluding estimated Profit)	70,000	———	By Work-in-Progress (Closing): Work Certified Work Not Yet Certified	3,00,000 ———	2,00,000 12,500
To Materials purchased	1,15,000	83,000	By Profit & Loss A/c (Loss debited)	76,250	———
To Wages	1,00,000	70,000	By Materials in hand (Closing)	2,000	2,700
To Electrical services	7,000	1,500			
To Road making charges	44,000	———			
To Administrative expenses (10:7)	36,000	25,200			
To Depreciation of Plant	6,250	2,500			
To Notional Profit c/d	———	33,000			
Total	3,78,250	2,15,200	Total	3,78,250	2,15,200

To Profit & Loss A/c	———	16,500	By Notional Profit b/d	———	33,000
To Profit in Suspense A/c (33,000×2/3×3/4)	———	16,500			
Total	———	33,000	Total	———	33,000

Problem 8. *A contractor, who prepares his account on December 31, every year, commenced a contract on 1.4.2005. The costing records concerning the said contract reveal the following information on 31.12.2005:*

Material charged to Site	*2,58,100*
Labour Engaged	*5,60,500*
Foreman's Salary	*79,300*

Plant costing ₹ 2, 60,000 has been on site for 146 days. Their working life is estimated at seven years and their final scrap value at ₹ 15,000. A supervisor, who is paid ₹ 20,000 p.m., has devoted approximately two-fifth of his time to this contract. The administrative and other expenses amounted to ₹ 1, 40,000. Material in hand at the site on 31.12.2005 cost ₹ 25,400. Some of the material costing ₹ 4,500 was found unsuitable and was sold for ₹ 4,000 and part of the plant costing ₹ 5,500 (on 31.12.2005) unsuited to the contract was sold at a profit of ₹ 1,000.

The contract price was ₹ 20, 00,000. On 31.12.2005, two-third of the contract was completed. Architect's certificate has been issued covering 50% of the contract price. ₹ 7, 50,000 has so far been paid on account. Prepare contract account and Contractee's account. Show how these accounts would appear in the balance Sheet as on 31.12.2005. Depreciation is charged on time basis.

[B. Com (Hons.) DU, 2006(Modified)]

Solution : **Contract Account**

Dr (For the year ending on March 31, 2005) Cr

Details	Amount (₹)	Details	Amount (₹)
To Materials	2,58,100	By Materials on site	25,400
To Wages	5,60,500	By Loss on Sale of Material	500
To Foreman's Salary	79,300	By Materials Sold	4,000
To Supervisor's Salary	72,000	By Cost of WIP(Balancing Figure)	10,94,000
To Depreciation of Plant	14,000		
To Administrative and other expenses	1,40,000		
Total	11,23,900	Total	11,23,900
To Cost of WIP	10,94,000	By WIP Certified	10,00,000
To P & L A/c (1,79,500×2/3 × 0.75)	89,750	By Work Uncertified	2,73,500
To Profit in Suspense A/c	89,750		
Total	12,73,500	Total	12,73,500

Balance Sheet (Relevant)

As on 31.12.2006

Liabilities	Amount (₹)	Assets	Amount (₹)
Reserves and surpluses:	1,06,625	Work-in-Progress:	
Net Profit on contract		Work Certified 10,00,000	
Less: Loss on Sale of Material	(500)	Work Uncertified 2,73,500	
	1,000	12,73,500	
Add: Profit on Sale of Plant	1,07,125	*Less:* Profit in Suspense A/c	
		(89,750)	
		11,83,750	
		Less: Cash Received	
		7,50,000	4,33,750
		Plant less Depreciation	
		(2,60,000 – 14,000) =	
		2,46,000	
		Less: Sold 5,500	2,40,500
		Stock of Materials(At site)	25,400

Working Notes:

I. Cost of Full Contract = 10, 94,000 × 3/2 => ₹ 16, 41,000.
Cost of 50% of Contract WIP certified
= 0.5 × 16, 41,000 => ₹ 8, 20,500.
Cost of Uncertified Work
= (Cost of WIP) – (Cost of 50% of Contract WIP certified)
= 10, 94,000 – 8, 20,500 => ₹ 2, 73,500.

II. Depreciation of Plant
= [{(2, 60,000 – 15,000)/7} × (146/365)] = ₹ 14,000.

III. Supervisor's Salary = (20,000 × 12) × (9/12) × (2/5) =>72,000.

Problem 9. *The contract Ledger of M/s XYZ showed the following expenditure on account of contract on December 31, 2006:*

Details	*Amount (₹)*
Materials issued to Contract	*2,10,000*
Wages	*2,93,000*
Plant	*70,000*
Sundry Expenses	*15,000*
Establishment Charges	*10, 000*

The contract was started on January 1, 2006 and the contract price was ₹ 10, 00,000. Cash received on account to date was ₹ 4, 80,000 representing 80% of work certified, remaining 20% being retained until completion. Value of Plant on December 31, 2006 was ₹ 20,000 and the value of materials was ₹ 6,000. The cost of work finished but not certified on the said date was ₹ 50,000.

Some of the materials costing ₹ 20,000 were found unsuitable and were sold at a profit of ₹ 1,000. The contractor estimated a further expenditure that would be incurred in completing the contract and took to the credit of P & L A/c for the year 2006. The preparation of estimated net profit on contract which the value of work certified bears to the contract price. This is to be further reduced by proportion of cash received that bears to the work certified. The estimates of further expenditure were as follows:

(i) That the contract would be completed by June 30, 2007.

(ii) That a further sum of ₹ 30,000 would have to be spent on the plant and its residual value on completion of the contract would be ₹ 12,000.

(iii) That materials in addition to that in hand on 31.12.2006 would cost ₹ 1,00,000 and that further sundry expenses of ₹ 7,000 would be incurred.

(iv) That the wages for the completion of contract would amount to ₹ 1,69,900.

(v) That the establishment charges would cost the same amount per year as in the previous year.

(vi) That ₹ 18,000 would be sufficient to provide for contingencies.

Prepare contract account for the year ended on December 31, 2006 and show the amount to be credited to P & L A/c for the year. Also sow the relevant figures that would appear in the Balance Sheet on that date.

[B.Com (Hons.) DU, 2007]

Solution :

Contract Account

Dr (For the year ending on March 31, 2006) Cr

Details	Amount (₹)	Details	Amount (₹)
To Materials	2,10,000	By Plant in Hand	20,000
To Wages	2,93,000	By Materials in Hand	6,000
To Sundry Expenses	15,000	By Loss on Materials	4,000
To Establishment Charges	10,000		16,000
To Materials	70,000		6,000
To Profit on Sale of Plant	1,000	By Work-in-Progress A/c:	
		Certified 6,00,000	
		Uncertified 50,000	6,50,000
Notional Profit c/d	1,03,000		
Total	7,02,000	Total	7,02,000
To P & L A/c (1,09,100 × 0.6)	65,460	By Notional Profit b/d	1,03,000

To Profit in Suspense A/c	37,540		
Total	1,03,000	Total	1,03,000

Working Notes:

Calculation of Estimated Profit:

1. Cost already incurred: (Materials + Wages + Sundry Expenses + Establishment Charges + Plant) – (Materials Sold + Plant Sold + Materials in Hand + Plant in Hand)
   = (2,10,000 + 2, 93, 000 + 15,000+10,000 + 70,000) – (20,000 + 5,000 +6,000+20,000)
   = 5,98,000 – 51,000 => 5,47,000
2. Estimated Further Expenditure:

Details	Amount (₹)
Sundry Expenses	7,000
Establishment Expenses	5,000
Plant(30,000 +20,000 –12,000)	38,000
Materials (6,000 + 1,00,000)	1,06,000
Wages	1,69,000
Provision for contingencies	18,000

Total Estimated Further Expenditure:	3,43,900
Total Estimated Cost	8,90,900
Estimated Profit (Balancing Figure)	1,09,100
Contract Price	10,00,000

Balance Sheet (Relevant)

As on 31.12.2006

Liabilities	Amount (₹)	Assets	Amount (₹)
		Work-in-Progress: Work Certified 6,00,000 Work Uncertified 50,000 6,50,000 Less: Profit in Suspense A/c (37,540) 6,12,460 Less: Cash Received 4,80,000	1,32,460
		Materials in Hand	6,000
		Plant in Hand	20,000

Problem 10. *ABC Ltd. began to trade on January 1, 2006. During 2006 the company was engaged on only one contract of which the contract price was ₹*

5,00,000. Of the plant and materials charged to the contract, plant which cost ₹ 5,000 and materials which cost ₹ 4,000 were lost in an accident. On December 31,2006 plant which cost ₹ 5,000 was returned to the store, the cost of work done but uncertified was ₹ 2,000 and materials costing ₹ 4,000 were in hand on site. Charge 10% depreciation on plant. Compute contract A/c and the Balance Sheet from the following:

Trial balance as on December 31, 2006

Details	*Amount (₹)*	*Amount (₹)*
Share Capital		*1,20,000*
creditors		*10,000*
Cash received (80% of work certified)		*2,00,000*
Land and Building	*43,000*	
Bank Balance	*25,000*	
Charged to Contract:		
0Materials	*90,000*	
Plant	*25,000*	
Wages	*1,40,000*	
Expenses	*7,000*	

[B.Com (Hons.) DU, 2007{Correspondance}]

Solution : **Contract Account**

Dr (For the year ending on March 31, 2006) Cr

Details	Amount (₹)	Details	Amount (₹)
To Materials	90,000	By Work-in-Progress A/c:	
		Certified 2,50,000	
		Uncertified 2,000	2,52,000
To Wages	1,40,000	By Plant Lost	5,000
To Expenses	7,000	By Materials Lost	4,000
To Plant	25,000	By Materials Returned (5,000 × 0.9)	4,500
To Notional Profit c/d	21,000	By Closing Balances:	
		Plant at Site (15,000 × 0.9) 13,500	
		Materials on site 4,000	17,500
Total	2,83,000	Total	2,83,000
To P & L A/c (21,000 ×2/3 × 0.8)	11,200	By Notional Profit b/d	21,000

To Profit in Suspense A/c	9,800		
Total	21,000	Total	21,000

Balance Sheet as on 31.12.2006

Liabilities	Amount (₹)	Assets	Amount (₹)
Share capital	1,20,000	Land and Building	43,000
Reserves and surpluses:		Work-in-Progress:	
Net Profit on contract 11,200		Work Certified 2,50,000	
Less: Loss 9,000	2,200	Work Uncertified 2,000	
		2,52,000	
		Less: Profit in Suspense A/c	
		(9,800)	
		2,42,200	
		Less: Cash Received	
		2,00,000	42,200
Creditors	10,000	Bank	25,000
		Plant:	
		In Store 4,500	
		At site 13,500	18,000
		Stock of Materials(At site)	4,000
Total	1,32,200	Total	1,32,200

Problem 11. *Surya construction limited with a paid up capital of ₹ 50 Lakh under took a contract to construct MIG apartments. The work commenced on the contract on April1, 2002. The contract price was ₹ 60 Lakh. Cash received on account of the contract up to March 31, 2003 was ₹ 18 Lakh (being 90% of the work certified). Work completed but not certified was estimated to be Rupees one Lakh. As on March 31, 2003 material at site was estimated at ₹ 30,000, machinery at site costing ₹ 2, 00,000 was returned to stores and wages outstanding were ₹ 5,000. Plant and Machinery at site is to be depreciated at 5%.*

The following were the ledger balances (Dr) as per trial balance as on March 31, 2003:

Details	***Amount (₹)***
Land and Building	*23,00,000*
Plant and Machinery(60% at site)	*25,00,000*
Furniture	*60,000*
Materials	*14,00,000*
Fuel and power	*1,25,000*
Site Expenses	*5,000*

Office Expenses	*12,000*
Rates and Taxes	*15, 000*
Cash at Bank	*1,33,000*
Wages	*2,5 0,000*

Prepare the contract account and the Balance Sheet.

[B. Com (Hons.) DU, 2002]

Solution : **Contract Account**:

Dr (For the year ending on March 31, 2003) Cr

Details	Amount (₹)	Details	Amount (₹)
To Materials	14,00,000	By Work-in-Progress A/c: Certified 20,00,000 Uncertified 1,00,000	21,00,000
To Wages	2,50,000	By Plant Returned (2,00,000 – 10,000)	1,90,000
To Wages Outstanding	5,000	By Plant at Site (13,00,000 – 65,000)	12,35,000
To office Expenses	12,000	By Materials at Site	30,000
To Plant and Machinery	15,00,000		
To Fuel and Power	1,25,000		
To Site Expenses	5,000		
To Rates and Taxes	15,000		
To Notional Profit c/d	2,43,000		
	35,55,000		35,55,000
To P & L A/c (2,43,000 ×1/3 × 0.9)	72,900	By Notional Profit b/d	2,43,000
To Profit in Suspense A/c	1,70,100		
Total	2,43,000	Total	2,43,000

Balance Sheet as on March 31, 2003

Liabilities	Amount (₹)	Assets	Amount (₹)
Share capital	50,00,000	Land and Building	23,00,000
Reserves and surpluses: Net Profit on contract	72,900	Plant and Machinery: In Store 10,00,000+1,90,000 = 11,90,000 At site 12,35,000	24,25,000
Wages Outstanding	5,000	Bank	1,33,000
		Stock of Materials(At site)	30,000
		Furniture	60,000

		Work-in-Progress: Work Certified 20,00,000 Work Uncertified 1,00,000 21,00,000 Less: Profit in Suspense A/c (1,70,100) 19,29,900 Less: Cash Received 18,00,000	1,29,900
Total	50,77,900	Total	50,77,900

Problem 12. *Compute a conservative estimate of profit on a contract (which has been 90% complete) from the following particulars. Illustrate four methods of computing the profit transferable to Profit& Loss account.*

Details	***Amount (₹)***
Total Expenditure to Date	*4,50,000*
Estimated further expenditure to complete the contract (including contingencies)	*25,000*
Contract Price	*6,12,000*
Work Certified	*5,50,800*
Work Uncertified	*34,000*
Cash Received	*4,40,640*

[B.Com (Hons.) DU, 2008]

Solution :

Details	**Amount (₹)**
Notional Profit:	
WIP:	
Work Certified	5,50,800
Add: Uncertified	34,000
	5,84,800
Less: Cost	4,50,000
	1,34,800

Estimated Profit:	
Contract Price	6,12,000
Less: Cost	4,50,000
Less: Estimated further Cost	25,000
	1,37,000

Methods of computing profit transferable to Profit and Loss A/c:

Method I: Notional Profit × 2/3

= 1, 34,800 × 2/3

= ₹89867.

Method II: Notional Profit × 2/3 × Cash Ratio

= 1,34,800 × 2/3 × 0.8

= ₹71,894.

Method III: Estimated Profit × Work completed Ratio

= 1,37,000 × 0.9

= ₹ 1,23,300.

Method IV: Estimated Profit × Work completed Ratio × Cash Ratio

= 1,37,000 × 0.9 × 0.8

= ₹ 98,640

Working Note:

Cash Ratio = Cash received / work Certified

= 4,40,640/ 5,50,800 = 0.8

Work completed Ratio = work Certified/ Contract Price

= 5,50,800/ 6, 12,000 = 0.9

Problem 13. *SV Engineers are engaged in construction and erection of a bridge under a long term contract. The cost incurred up to 31.3.2008 was as under:*

Details	***Amount (₹ Lakhs)***
Fabrication:	
Direct materials	*700*
Direct Wages	*240*
Overheads	*150*
Total Fabrication cost	*1,090*
Erection cost to date	*310*
Total	*1,400*

The contract price is ₹ 2,800 Lakhs and the cash received on account till 31.3.2008 was ₹ 1,560 lakhs. A technical estimate of the contract indicates the following degree of completion of work:

(i) Fabrication: Direct materials *70%;*

Direct Wages and Overheads *60%;*

(ii) Erection: *40%.*

Prepare a statement of cost on contract and estimate the profit that could be taken to the Profit and Loss account against this partly completed contract as on 31.3.2008 based on cost to date and total estimated cost of the contract. Also estimate the overall degree of completion of contract to date.

[C.A. (inter) Modified]

Solution : Statement of Cost on contract to date and in the next period

Details	Cost to Date		Cost in the Next Period		Total Cost	
	% of completion	Amount (₹ Lakhs) (A)	% of completion in the next period	Computations	Amount (₹ Lakhs) (B)	Amount (₹ Lakhs) [(A)+(B)]
Fabrication costs:	70	700	30	(700/.7) ×30	300	1,000
Direct materials	60	240	40	(240/.6) ×40	160	400
Direct Wages	60	150	40	(150/.6) ×40	100	250
Overheads						
Total Fabrication cost		1,090			560	1,650
Erection cost		310	60	(310/.4) ×60	465	775
Total cost		1,400			1,025	2,425
Profit		216.5			158.5	375
Total		1,616.5			1,183.5	2,800

Working Notes:

1. Profit to Date (Notional Profit):

   [Estimated Total Profit (on entire contract) × (Cost to date/ Total cost)]

   = [375 × (1,400 ÷2,425)] =₹ 216.5 Lakhs

2. Value of work Certified to Date:

   Cost to Date + Profit to Date = 1,400 + 216.5 => ₹ 1,616.5 lakhs

3. Overall Degree of Completion of work to Date:

   = (Value of work Certified / Total value of contract) ×100

   = (1,616.5 ÷2,800) ×100 => 57.73 %.

4. Profit to be taken to the credit of Profit and Loss A/c:

   = [Notional Profit × 2/3 × (Cash Received/ Work Certified)]

   = [216.5 × 2/3 × (1,500 ÷1,616.5)] => ₹ 133.93 Lakhs

5. Profit in Suspense account:

   = Notional Profit – Profit to be credited to the profit and Loss A/c

   = 216.5 –133.93 =₹ 82.57 Lakhs

OBJECTIVE TYPE EXERCISES

I. Fill in the blank spaces with suitable word/s :

1. When there is a loss on an incomplete contract, it is treated as ...... transferred to ....
2. Two examples of industries in which contract costing is used are .... and ....
3. A job is a .... Contract and a contract is a .... job.
4. .... is that part of the work-in-progress which is not approved by the architect or engineer.
5. Work certified is valued at contract price, the work uncertified is valued at ....
6. In contract costing, the cost unit is ....
7. Work-in-progress appears on the .... side of the contract.
8. Cost of the work of subcontract is ...... to the contract account.
9. .... is a contract in which the price of the contract is determined by adding a percentage margin of profit to the costs of the contract.
10. The escalation clauses in contract are usually provided as safeguards against any likely changes in ....
11. .... in a contract provides that in the event of a specified contingency occurring, the contract price would be suitably enhanced.
12. When 60% of the contract price is certified work-in-progress, the profit to be credited to profit and Loss account will be equal to ....
13. Two variants of job order costing are .... And ....
14. The estimated profit is ₹ 90,000 and the contract is almost 65% complete. If the cash ratio is 80%, the profit to be transferred Profit in Suspense account is ₹ ....

Answers :

1. Loss, Costing Profit and Loss A/c **2.** Building construction, Ship building
3. small, big **4.** Work uncertified
5. Cost **6.** Contract
7. Credit **8.** debited
9. Cost plus contract
10. price and utilization of material and labour
11. escalation clauses
12. {(2/3) × Notional profit × (Cash received/ work certified)}
13. Contract costing, batch costing **14.** ₹ 42,000

II. Indicate whether the following statements are True or False :

1. In contract costing, the cost unit is a contract.
2. Contract costing is only a variant of job costing.
3. In cost-plus contracts the contractor runs a risk of incurring a loss.

4. More costs are direct in contract costing than in job costing.
5. Cost of the work of sub contract is debited to contract account.
6. Escalation clause in a contract provides that contract price is fixed.
7. Final contract price to be paid is not certain in cost-plus contracts.
8. The estimated profit is ₹ 84,000and the contract is almost two-third complete. If the cash ratio is 85%, the profit to be transferred to Profit and Loss Account is ₹ 71,400.
9. When cash ratio is 85%, the retention money is 25%.
10. In contract costing, each contract is a cost unit.
11. When a contract is 95% complete at the end of the accounting year, entire amount of profit is transferred to Profit and Loss account.
12. A job is a small contract and contract is a big job.
13. Escalation clause in a contract is often provided as safeguards against any likely changes in the price of materials and labour rates.
14. When there is a notional loss on an incomplete contract, transfer to Profit and Loss Account depends upon the degree of completion of the contract.
15. There is no difference between notional profit and estimated profit, in relation to contracts.
16. Profit on each contract is computed every year on incomplete portion of the contract.
17. When a contract is 50% complete, 50% of its profit on cash basis is generally transferred to Profit and Loss Account at the end of each year.

Answers :

1. True	**2.** True	**3.** False	**4.** True
5. True	**6.** False	**7.** True	**8.** False
9. False	**10.** True	**11.** False	**12.** True
13. True	**14.** False	**15.** False	**16.** True
17. False			

THEORETICAL EXERCISES

1. What is cost-Plus contract? Discuss this from the point of view of (a) The manufactures, (b) The buyer.
2. Distinguish between job costing and contract costing. State the special features of contract costing.
3. Give your views regarding justification in charging profit on incomplete contracts and explain methods of charging profit on incomplete contracts.
4. Explain in brief the following concepts:
   (i) Escalation clause **[DU, B.Com (Hons.) 2001]**
   (ii) Cost Plus contracts
5. How will you treat profit on incomplete contracts in cost accounts? **[DU, B.Com (Hons.) 2004]**

6. Discuss the methods of ascertaining profit on the following contracts:
(a) When contract is completed;
(b) When contract is not completed;
(c) When the contract is nearing completion.

7. Indicate how you would deal with the following Items:
(a) Plant and machinery purchased and used on contract work;
(b) Amounts received from the contractee;
(c) Materials lying unused at site.

8. How are profits computed in respect of incomplete contracts when (a) the work has not advanced reasonably, (b) the work has reasonably advanced, (c) the work has sufficiently advanced but not in final stages of completion. **[I.C. W.A. (Inter)]**

NUMERICAL EXERCISES

1. Shruti Construction Limited with a paid-up capital of ₹ 80 Lakh undertook a contract to construct MIG Apartments. The work commenced on the contract on April 1, 2004. The contract price was ₹ 85 Lakh. Cash received on account of the contract up to March 31, 2005 was ₹ 25 Lakh (being 80% of the work certified). Work completed but not certified was estimated at ₹ 220000/-. As on 31.3.2005 Materials at site was estimated at ₹ 65000, Machinery at site costing ₹ 500000 was returned to stores and wages outstanding were ₹ 25000. Plant and Machinery at site is to be depreciated at 6%.

The following were the Ledger balances (Dr) as per Trial Balances as on 31.302005:

Details	Amount (₹)
Land and Building	35,00,000
Plant and Machinery (75% at Site)	40,00,000
Furniture	2,50,000
Materials	19,00,000
Fuel and Power	1,80,000
Site Expenses	12,000
Office Expenses	28,000
Rates and Taxes	20,000
Cash at Bank	2,80,000
Wages	3,30,000

Prepare the Contract account and Balance Sheet.

[Ans. Notional Profit ₹ 7,35,000; Balance Sheet Total ₹ 82,21,000]

2. M/s Kathuria Constructions have entered into a contract to build a factory complex for ₹ 600 Lakhs. The work started in April 2002 and it is estimated that the contract will take 15 months to be completed. Work has progressed as per schedule and the actual cost charged till March 2003 is as follows:

	(₹ in Lakhs)
Materials	168.30
Labour	243.00
Hire Charges for equipments and other expenses	54.00
Establishment Charges	48.60
	513.90

The following information is available:

	(₹ in Lakhs)
Materials in hand (March 31, 2003)	9.90
Work certified (of which ₹ 486 Lakhs have been paid) till March 31, 2003	600.00
Work not yet certified at March 31, 2003 (at cost)	11.25

As per management estimates, the following further expenditure will be incurred to complete the work:

	(₹ in Lakhs)
Materials	15.75
Labour	24.00
Sub-contractor	30.00
Equipments hire and other charges	4.50
Establishment Charges	10.35

You are required to compute the value of work-in-progress as on March 31, 2003 after considering a reasonable margin of profit and show the appropriate accounts. Make a provision for contingencies amounting to 4% of total costs.

3. One of the marketing complex contracts currently engaged in by a construction company commenced 15 months ago and remains unfinished. The following information relating to the work on the contract has been prepared for the year just ended:

Details	Amount (₹)
Contract Price	1,50,00,000
Value of work certified at the end of year	1,32,00,000
Cost of work not yet certified at the end of year	2,40,000
Costs incurred**:**	
(a) Opening balances:	
(1) Cost of work completed	18,00,000
(2) Materials on site (physical stock)	60,000
(b) During the year:	
(1) Material delivered to site	36,60,000
(2) Wages	34,80,000
(3) Hire of plant	6,60,000
(4) Other expenses	5,40,000
(c) Closing balance:	
(1) Materials on site (physical stock)	1,20,000

[Ans. ....]

4. (Contracts which run for more than one accounting year)
The following information relates to a building contract for ₹ 10,00,000.

Details	Year 2006 (₹)	Year 2007 (₹)
Materials issued	3,00,000	84,000
Direct wages	2,30,000	1,05,000
Direct expenses	22,000	10,000
Indirect expenses	6,000	1,400
Work certified	7,50,000	10,00,000
Work uncertified	8,000	-
Material at site	5,000	7,000
Plant issued	14,000	2,000
pnumCash received from contractor	6,00,000	10,00,000

The value of plant at the end of 2006 and 2007 was ₹ 7,000 and ₹ 5,000 respectively. Prepare (a) contract account; and (b) Contractee account for two years 2006 and 2007 taking into consideration such profit for transfer to Profit and loss account as you deem fit. **[Ans. ....]**

5. M/s Construction Bulls Limited secured a contract to supply and erect machinery for the sum of ₹ 45,00,000. It was to receive payment on account from time to time equal to 90% of the certified value of work done. The work commenced on April 1, 2007 and the following expenditures were incurred during the year:
Plant and Tools ₹ 4,20,000; Machinery and Stores ₹ 12,00,000; Wages ₹ 9,00,000; sundry expenses ₹ 2,40,000 and establishment charges ₹ 3,00,000. A part of the machinery costing ₹ 1,20,000 was unsuited to the contract and was immediately sold at a profit of ₹ 30,000. The value of the plant and tools on March 31, 2008 was ₹ 2,00,000 and the value of machinery and stores then on hand was ₹1,50,000. By April 30, 2008 the company had received payments on account amounting to ₹ 28,00,000 being 80% of the certified value of work done up to the preceding March 31, 2008?
In order to compute profit made on the contract to 31.3.2008, the contractor company estimated further expenditure that would be incurred in completing the contract, and took the credit of the Profit and Loss account for the year that proportion of the estimated profit to be realized on the contract which the certified value of work done bore to the contract price. The company estimated:
(i) That the Contract would be completed in the next eight months;
(ii) That plant and tools would have a residual value of ₹ 40,000 upon the completion of the contract;
(iii) That the cost of machinery and stores required, in addition to those in stock on 31.3.2008 would be ₹ 3,00,000 and that further Sundry expenses of ₹ 120000 would be incurred;
(iv) That the wages on the contract for the eight months on 30.11.2008 would amount to ₹ 5,00,000;

(v) That establishment would cost the same sum per month as in the preceding year; and

(vi) That 2.5% of the total cost of the contract (Excluding this percentage) should be provided for contingencies.

Prepare the contract account for the year ended on 31.3.2008 and show your calculations of the profit to be credited the Profit and Loss account for the year.

[Ans. ....]

6. A Contractor undertook a contract for ₹ 5,00,000 on 1.4.2207for the construction of a Library building for a public school in Palamu district of Himachal Pradesh. On 31.3.2008, when the accounts were closed, the following details about the contract were gathered:

Details	Amount (₹)
Materials Purchased	1,00,000
Wages Paid	55,000
General Expenses	9,000
Plant Purchased	60,000
Materials on Hand on 31.3.2008	25,000
Wages accrued on 31.3.2008	5,000
wrapdefaultWork Certified	2,00,000
Work Uncertified	15,000
Cash Received	1,50,000
Plant as on 31.3.2008	54,000

The above contract contained an escalation clause which reads as follows: "In the event of prices of materials and rates of wages increase by more than 5%, the contract price would be increased accordingly by 25% of the rise in the cost of materials and wages beyond 5% in each case."

It was found that since the date of signing the agreement, the prices of materials and wage rates increased by 25%. The value of work certified does not take into account the effect of the above clause.

Prepare the contract account. Working should form part of your answer.

[I.C.W.A. Inter; CA Inter (Modified)]

[Ans. Escalation ₹ 5,000; profit in suspense ₹ 60,000.]

7. A contractor, who prepares his account on December 31, every year, commenced a contract on 1.4.2005. The costing records concerning the said contract reveal the following information on 31.12.2005:

Material charged to Site	2,58,100
Labour Engaged	5,60,500
Foreman's Salary	79,300

Plant costing ₹ 2,60,000 has been on site for 146 days. Their working life is estimated at seven years and their final scrap value at ₹ 15,000. A supervisor, who is paid ₹ 4,000 p.m., has devoted approximately three-fourth of his time to this contract. The administrative and other expenses amounted to ₹ 1, 40,000. Material in hand at the site on 31.12.2005 cost ₹ 25,400. Some of the material costing ₹ 4,500 was found unsuitable and was sold for ₹ 4,000 and part of the plant costing ₹ 5,500 (on 31.12.2005) unsuited to the contract was sold at a profit of ₹ 1,000.

The contract price was ₹ 20, 00,000. On 31.12.2005, two-third of the contract was completed. Architect's certificate has been issued covering 50% of the contract price. ₹ 7, 50,000 has so far been paid on account. Prepare contract account and Contractee's account. Show how these accounts would appear in the balance Sheet as on 31.12.2005. Depreciation is charged on time basis. **[B. Com (Hons.) DU, 2006]**

[Ans. Profit in Suspense A/c: ₹ 1, 06,625; Value of Work-in-Progress for Balance Sheet purposes ₹ 4, 05,625; Value of Plant ₹ 2, 40,500; Profit in Balance sheet ₹ 1, 07,125]

8. The following is the trial balance of Premier Construction Company engaged on the execution of contract No. 1047 for the year 31.12.2005:

Details	Dr. Amount (₹)	Cr. Amount (₹)
Contractee's Account (Amount received)		3,00,000
Buildings	1,60,000	
Creditors		72,000
Bank Balance	35,000	
Capital Account		5,00,000
Materials	2,00,000	
Wages	1,80,000	
Expenses	47,000	
Plant	2,50,000	
Total	8,72,000	8,72,000

The work on Contract No. 1047 was commenced on January 1, 2005. Material costing ₹ 1, 70,000 were sent to the site of the contract but those of ₹ 6,000 were destroyed in an accident. Wages of ₹ 1, 80,000 were paid during the year. Plant costing ₹ 50,000 was used on the contract all through the year. Plant with a cost of ₹ 2 Lakh was used from January 1, 2005 to September 30, 2005 and was then returned to stores. Materials of the cost of ₹ 4,000 were at site on 31.12.2005.

The contract was for ₹ 6, 00,000 and the contractee pays 75% of the work certified. Work certified was 80% of the total contract work at the end of 2005. Uncertified work was estimated at ₹ 15,000 on 31.12.2005. Expenses are charged to contract at 25% of wages. Plant is to be depreciated at 10% p.a.

Prepare Contract No. 1047 account for the year 2005 and make out the Balance Sheet as on 31.12.2005 in the books of Premier Construction Company.

[B. Com (Hons.) DU, 2006: Correspondance]

[Ans. Profit in Suspense A/c: ₹ 52,500; Balance Sheet total ₹ 5,96,500; Value of Work-in-Progress for Balance Sheet purposes ₹ 1,42,500]

9. The following are the details relating to a contract which has begun on January 1, 2007.

Details	Amount (₹)
Contract Price	8,00,000
Machinery	48,000
Materials	2,73,000
Wages	2,38,000
Direct Expenses	8,600
Outstanding wages	10,100
Uncertified work	14,400
Overheads	13,200
Materials Returned	2,540
Materials on hand 31.12.2007	5,960
Machinery on hand 31.12.2007	35,200
Value of Work certified	6,24,000
Cash Received	5,61,600

Prepare the contract account for the year 2007 showing the profit that may be taken to the credit of Profit and Loss account for the year. **[Ans. ₹ 54,720]**

10. XP construction limited took a contract in 2007 for road construction. The contract price was ₹ 35, 00,000 and its estimated cost of completion would be ₹ 32, 20,000. At the end of 2007 the company has received ₹ 12, 60,000 representing 90% of work certified. Work not yet certified has cost ₹ 35,000. Expenditure incurred on the contract during 2007 was as follows; Materials ₹ 1, 75,000; Labour ₹ 10, 50,000; Plant ₹ 87,500.

Materials costing ₹ 17,500 were damaged and had to be disposed of for ₹ 3,500. Plant is considered as having depreciated by 20%.

Prepare contract account for the year 2007 in the books of XP construction limited. Also show all the possible figures that can be reasonably credited to Profit and Loss Account in respect of the contract.

[Ans. ₹ 70,000; ₹ 63,000; ₹ 1, 12,000; ₹ 1, 00,800]

11. Surya construction limited with a paid up capital of ₹ 80 Lakh under took a contract to construct MIG apartments. The work commenced on the contract on April1, 2002. The contract price was ₹ 96 Lakh. Cash received on account of the contract up to March 31, 2003 was ₹ 28.80 Lakh (being 90% of the work certified). Work completed but not certified was estimated to be Rupees one Lakh sixty thousand. As on March 31, 2003 material at site was estimated at ₹ 48,000, Machinery at site costing ₹ 3, 20,000 was returned to stores and wages outstanding were ₹ 8,000. Plant and Machinery at site is to be depreciated at 5%.

The following were the ledger balances (Dr) as per trial balance as on March 31, 2003:

Details	Amount (₹)
Land and Building	36,00,000
Plant and Machinery(60% at site)	40,00,000
Furniture	1,76,000
Materials	22,40,000
Fuel and power	2,00,000
Site Expenses	8,000
Office Expenses	18,200
Rates and Taxes	25, 000
Cash at Bank	2,12,800
Wages	4,0 0,000

Prepare the contract account and the Balance Sheet.

[B. Com (Hons.) DU, 2002(Modified)]

[Ans. Profit Credited: ₹ 1, 16,640; Balance Sheet Total ₹ 81, 24,640]

12. Engineers Limited undertook several contracts during the year 2006. The following information relates to contract No. 504:

Details	Amount (₹)
Direct Materials	81,000
Direct Wages	62,000
Stores Issued	42,000
Loose Tools	9,600
Tractor Expenses:	
Running material 9,200	
Wages of driver 12,000	21,400
Other Direct Charges	13,000

The contract took 13 weeks in its completion. The value of loose tools and stores returned at the end of the period were ₹ 800 and ₹ 12,000 respectively. The plant was also retuned at a value of ₹64, 000 after charging depreciation at 20%. The value of the tractor was ₹ 80,000 and the depreciation was to be charged to the tractor @ 15% p.a. The administration and office expenses are to be provided at 10% on works cost. Profit is to be charged at 20% of the total cost.

Prepare the aforesaid Contract Account assuming the balance of the contract was duly received from the contractee. **[B. Com (Hons.) DU (Modified)]**

[Ans. Profit Credited: ₹ 51,172]

13. The following is the summarised information relating to Contract Account Number 100:

Details	Amount (₹)
Contract Price	6,00,000
Wages	1,64,000
General Expenses	8,600
Materials	1,20,000
Cash received (80% of the work certified)	2,40,000
Materials at Site	10,100
Plant	20,000

Included in the above information are wages ₹ 3,500, materials ₹ 4,000 and other expenses ₹ 2,500 which were incurred since certification.

Depreciate Plant at 10%.

Prepare Contract Account Number 100. **[B. Com (Hons.) DU, 2004 (Modified)]**

[Ans. Profit Credited: ₹ 13,600]

14. Engineers Limited undertook several contracts during the year 2008. The following information relates to contract No. 107:

Details	Amount (₹)
Direct Materials	20,250
Direct wages	15,500
Stores Issued	10,500
Loose Tools	2,400
Tractor Expenses:	5,300
Running Material 2,300	
Wages of driver 3,000	
Other direct charges	2,650

The contract took 13 weeks on its completion. The value of Loose tools and stores returned at the end of the period were ₹ 200 and ₹ 3,000 respectively. The Plant was also returned at a value of ₹ 16,000 after charging depreciation at 20%. The value of the tractor was ₹ 20,000 and the depreciation was to be charged to the tractor @ 15% p.a. The administration and office overheads are to be provided at 10% on works cost. Profit is to be charged at 20% of the total cost.

Prepare the aforesaid contract account assuming the balance of the contract was duly received from the contractee. **[B.Com (Hons.) DU, 2002]**

[Ans. Profit Credited: ₹ 12,793]

❑❑❑

17 Operating/Service Costing

Learning Objectives

It attempts to explain the process of ascertaining the cost of service in various industries. In this chapter you will learn :

1. Meaning, nature of operating/service costing.
2. Unit costing and service costing.
3. Concept of composite cost unit.
4. Treatment of normal and abnormal loss.
5. Transport costing.
6. Boiler-house costing.
7. Power-house costing.
8. Hotel costing.
9. Hospital costing.

INTRODUCTION

Service Costing, also known as operating costing, is used where services are provided /rendered and articles are not produced. According to Institute of Cost and Management Accountants (UK) operating Costing is "that form of operation costing which applies where standard services are provided either by an undertaking or by a service center within an undertaking". Service costing is especially suitable for the costing of road and rail transport services, electricity undertakings and hospitals, etc. Operating costing is not to be confused with operation costing. Operating costing is used to ascertain the cost of providing or rendering service; operation costing is a refinement and more detailed application of process costing.

Service costing (Nature and Problem): Service or operating cost is the cost of providing service. The term service costing is applied to describe the system used to find the cost of performing a service such as transport, gas or electricity.

(i) Services rendered to customers are of unique and standardized type.

(ii) Distinction between fixed cost and variable cost is of special importance as the scale of operations considerably affects the cost per unit of service rendered.

(iii) A large chunk of total capital is invested in fixed assets and relatively less working capital is required.

(iv) The method of costing is different from that used in connection with production, and the difference lies mainly in the manner of accumulating the cost data and finally in its allocation to cost units.

UNIT COSTING AND SERVICE COSTING: (PRINCIPLES INVOLVED)

Unit costing is the method of costing used when the cost units are identical, and identical cost units should have identical costs and this concept of costing is the fundamental feature of Unit costing. Following is the basic computation in all unit costing methods:

Cost per unit =Total cost / Number of units

Output costing and service/Operating costing are the sub-divisions of Unit Costing method.

Cost Accumulation

The principle of operating/service costing is to accumulate costs under suitable headings and to express them in terms of the unit of service rendered.

Service cost is usually collected under the following categories:

1. Standing Charges (Fixed)
2. Maintenance Charges (Semi-fixed)
3. Running Charges (Variable)

Most of the costs are of fixed in nature.

Cost Unit

One of the problems of operating costing is the selection of a suitable cost unit. To select a proper cost unit, the cost accountant needs to be highly skilled and technically sound. Two types of cost units are applied in operating costing:

(i) Simple cost unit, and

(ii) Composite cost unit.

Simple cost unit could be per kilometer, per passenger in transport undertakings, per room in hotels, per bed in hospitals. In the composite cost unit, more than one variable is considered. It could be passenger-kilometer, tonne-kilometer, patient-day, room-day, and patient-bed-day.

The following composite cost unit is applied for different services:

Nature of Service/ Business	Cost unit
Transport	Per Passenger-km, Per Tonne-km
Electricity	Per kilowatt hour
Hospital	Per patient day, Per bed, Per Operation
Hotel	Per Room
Canteen	Per Meal
Road/Rail Maintenance	Per km of road, Per km of rail-track
Road lighting	Per Pole-Lamp
Cinema Hall	Per Seat per Show

TRANSPORT COSTING

Transport companies may be railways, roadways, shipping or airways. Main objectives of transport costing are:

(i) Ascertaining the rates of carriage of goods/passengers on the basis of operating costs.

(ii) Ascertaining the price at which a vehicle should be hired out.

(iii) Comparing the cost of using own motor vehicles and that of using alternative forms of transport.

(iv) Ascertaining what should be charged against the departments, or others, using the service.

The total cost consists of standing charges, running charges (variable) and maintenance charges. *Standing Charges* consist of (a) Licence fee and insurance (b) Garage costs and administrative expenses (c) Wages of Drivers, Conductors and Cleaners (d) Depreciation (e) Tax. *Running Charges* compose of (a) Petrol, (b) Oil, and (c) Grease/Lubricants. *Maintenance Charges* include (a) Repairs and maintenance (b) Tubes and Tyres and (c) Garage charges.

Cost Unit: Passenger-kilometer or Tonne-kilometer is usually the cost unit. After collecting total cost, the cost per unit is ascertained. The cost per unit is calculated as under:

= Number of vehicles × Distance traveled × Number of Days × Number of trips per day × Passenger/Weight actually carried.

Cost Accumulation: The information about the costs of each vehicle is obtained through Daily Log Sheet and the operating cost sheet. A specimen of Daily Log Sheet is given hereunder:

Daily Log Sheet

Vehicle Number : Month:
Registration Number: Date and time of leaving the Garage:
Name and Emp-ID number of the driver: Date and time of returning:

Trip No.	From	To	Tons or packages carried Outward	Collected enroute	Distance (Kms)	Time Outward	Return	Remarks

Supplies	Worker's time	Loss of time
Petrol	Driver	Loading
Oil	Conductor	Unloading
Grease	Mechanic	Traffic delays
Others	Cleaner	Accidents
		Others

Operating Cost Sheet

It is a statement which throws light on standing charges and running expenses. Cost accounting department prepares a separate cost sheet for each vehicle. Total standing/fixed charges are divided by number of units of the cost unit. By this we get standing charges per unit. Running charges are calculated per unit of cost.

Operating Cost Sheet

(For the month of ....)

Vehicle No. .... Number of cost Units.........

Details	Total (₹)	Per unit (₹)
A. Standing Charges:		
1. Garage Rent		
2. Supervision		
3. Insurance		
4. Driver's Wages		
5. Interest on Capital		
6. Office and Administration Overheads		
7. Licence fee		
8. Road Tax		
Total Standing Charges		

B. Running and Maintenance Charges:		
1. Depreciation		
2. Petrol/Diesel		
3. Repairs and Maintenance		
4. Tyres and tubes		
5. Lubricants/ Grease		
Total Running Charges		
C. Total Operating cost [(A) + (B)]		

Illustration 17.1 : *DPT Ltd. runs five buses between two towns, which are 125 kms apart; the seating capacity of each bus is 50 passengers and 84 per cent of this capacity is actually occupied. Each bus makes two round trips daily and the buses ply on the road on an average of 25 days a month. Determine the cost per passenger-km, if the total operating cost for the five buses is ₹ 94,50,000.*

Solution :

Passenger-km

= Number of buses × distance per trip × capacity of each bus × Number of trips × 2 × Number of operating days in a month × Occupancy Rate.

= 5 × 125 × 50 × 2 × 2 × 25 × 0.84 = 26,25,000 Passanger-kms

Cost per Passenger-km

= Total operating cost divided by total Passenger-kms.

= 94,50,000/26,25,000 = ₹ 3.60.

(**Note:** When the transport undertaking owns vehicles having different capacities, cost unit should be determined with reference to varying capacities.)

Illustration 17.2 : *A transport Undertaking operates the following fleet: 25 trucks of 10- tonne capacity, 15 trucks of 5-tonne capacity, and 10 mini-trucks of 2- tonne capacity each. In a fortnight, the following distances were covered by each of the trucks: 10-tonne capacity truck 1,000kms; 5- tonne capacity truck, 800 kms; 2-tonne capacity truck, 500kms.*

If the total cost is ₹ 16,00,000, determine the cost per tonne-km, assuming that all vehicles worked to their respective full capacity during the period.

Solution : **Determination of total tonne-kms**

Vehicles (Number)	Capacity (tonne)	Distance (kms)	Tonne-kms
25	10	1,000	2,50,000
15	5	800	60,000
10	2	500	10,000
		Total	3,20,000

Cost per tonne-km= 16,00,000 ÷ 3,20,000=₹ 5.

Concept of Absolute and Commercial Tonne-Kilometer

The composite cost unit may be computed in two ways:

(a) Absolute tonne-Kilometer; and

(b) Commercial tonne-Kilometer.

In absolute tonne-Kilometer, travel distance in tonne-kilometers between two stations is considered individually and then summed up. However, in commercial tonne-Kilometers, the trip is considered as a *whole* and it is arrived at by multiplying the total distance in kilometer by the average load quantity carried. The above distinction is made clear by taking the following two Illustrations:

Illustration 17.3 : *A truck starts from Delhi with a load of 15 tons for B, a distance of 200 kms, where it unloads 5 tons. From there it goes to C, a distance of 60 kms and unloads 7 tons there. At C 4 more tons of loads are put in the truck with which it comes to D, a distance of 125 kms and unloads 3 tons. Then the truck comes back to its head office at Delhi with 4 tons already picked up at C. Distance between D and Delhi is 45 kms. Calculate 'Absolute ton-kms' and 'commercial ton-kms'.*

Solution :

Absolute ton-kms = Actual Load × Actual Distance

= (15 × 200) + (10 × 60) + (7 × 125) + (4 × 45)

= 3,000 + 600 + 875 + 180

= 4,655 ton-kms.

Commercial ton-kms = Average Load × Total Distance covered

= {(15+10+7+4)/ (4)} × (200+60+125+45)

= 9 × 430 = 3,870 ton-kms.

Note: While calculating the absolute tons-kms, the travel between any two stations is considered individually, but in case of commercial tons-kms., the trip is considered as a whole.

Illustration : *A lorry starts with a load of 20 tonnes of goods from station A. It unloads 8 tonnes at station B and rest of the goods at station C. It reaches back directly to station A after getting reloaded with 16 tonnes of goods at station C. the distances between A to B, B to C and then C to A are 80 Kms, 120 kms, and 160 kms respectively. Compute Absolute tonne-kms, and Commercial tonne-kms.* **[C.A.]**

Solution : Absolute tonne-kms:

Absolute tonne-kms

= Actual Load × Actual Distance

= (20 tonne × 80 Kms) + (12 tonne × 120 Kms) + (16 tonne × 160 Kms)

= 1,600 tonne-Kms + 1,440 tonne-Kms + 2,560 tonne-Kms

= 5,600 tonne-Kms

Commercial tonne-kms:

Commercial tonne-kms

= Average Load × Total Distance covered

= {(20+12+16)/ (3)} × (80+120+160) = 16 × 360 = 5,760 tonne-kms.

Illustration 17.4 : *Joy Returns limited operates a haulage business with three vehicles. The following estimated cost and performance data are available:*

Petrol *₹3.20 per kilometer on average*

Repairs *₹2.00 per kilometer*

Depreciation *₹ 2.50 per kilometer, plus ₹300 per week per vehicle*

Driver's wages *₹800 per week per vehicle*

Supervision and general expenses ₹1,400 per week

Loading costs *₹11 per tonne*

During week No. 17 it is expected that all five vehicles will be used, 470 tonnes will be loaded and a total of 6,600 kilometers traveled (including return journeys when empty) as shown in the following table:

Journey	*Tones carried (one way)*	*Kilometers (one way)*
1	*57*	*300*
2	*47*	*443*
3	*67*	*652*
4	*54*	*192*
5	*44*	*368*
6	*67*	*802*
7	*49*	*150*
8	*44*	*168*
9	*41*	*225*
	470	*3,300*

Requirement: Calculate the average cost per tonne -kilometer for week No. 17.

Solution : Computation of Cost per tonne-kilometer for

Joy Returns limited
Operating Cost Sheet
(For the week No. 17)

Vehicle No. … 1,85,866 tonne-kilometers

Details	Total (₹)	Per unit (₹)
A. Standing Charges:		
1. Depreciation (5×300)	1,500	
2. Supervision	1,400	

3. Driver's Wages (5×800)	4,000	
Total Standing Charges	6,900	
Standing Charges per unit (6,900 ÷ 1,85,866)		0.0371
B. Running Charges:		
1. Loading (470 × ₹11)	5,170	
2. Petrol/Diesel (6,600× 3.20)	21,120	
3. Repairs (6,600× 2.00)	13,200	
4. Depreciation (6,600× 2.50)	16,500	
Total Running Charges (55,990÷ 1,85,866)	55,990	0.3012
C. Total Operating cost [(A) + (B)		0.3383

Average cost per tonne-kilometer =0.3383@ ₹0.34

Working Notes: Computation of Tonne kilometers

Journey	Tones carried (one way)	Kilometers (one way)	Tonne-km
1	57	300	17,100
2	47	443	20,821
3	67	652	43,684
4	54	192	10,368
5	44	368	16,192
6	67	802	53,734
7	49	150	7,350
8	44	168	7,392
9	41	225	9,225
Total	470	3,300	1,85,866

Normal and Abnormal Losses

All normal costs/losses must be considered at the time of ascertaining cost per unit. Cost per unit must not be influenced by abnormal gains / losses. If a taxi has usually 30% running without fair, this cost of 30% idle running is to be recovered from 70% normal running with fare. On the same pattern, if a 40-seater bus has generally 90% occupancy, all fixed and variable costs relating to the operation of such a bus should be divided by passenger-kilometers based on 36 seats so as to find out the cost per passenger-kilometer. In the same way, in case of goods transport, one way running without fare is common and is treated as normal loss.

If there is abnormal loss, such as, loss on account of accident, it should not form part of the operating cost sheet. If the idle capacity or idle running is more than normal, excess idle running or idle capacity implies abnormal loss and the cost per service unit need not get affected.

Actual and Effective kms/ ton-kms

Actual kms or actual ton-kms refer to the actual kms run or actual ton-kms of freight carried. Effective kms or ton-kms refer to the kms or ton-kms over which normal total operating costs (Fixed as well as variable) are to be recovered from. This concept becomes clear from the following illustration:

Illustration 17.5 : Daya Singh owns a fleet of five taxies, three Buses and two 20-tonne capacity trucks. Relevant information relating to three types of vehicles is given hereunder:

(1) Each taxi runs on the average 3,200 kms in a month out of which 16% is normal running without fare. Variable cost per kilometer run is ₹ 6.30.

(2) Three buses operate between Delhi and Chandigarh, one-way distance being 250 kms. Each bus has 50 seats of which 90% are in general occupied, and make 25 round trips in a month. Variable cost per kilometer is ₹ 12.60.

(3) Each truck operates between Delhi and Rohtangpass, one-way distance being 900 kms. Each truck earns fare only on onward journey and on return journey without any freight. It makes 12 trips in a month. Occupancy rate of each truck is 80%. Variable cost per kilometer is ₹12.

You are required to compute:

(i) For the fleet of five Taxies: Total variable cost, effective kilometers, and variable cost per effective kilometer.

(ii) For buses: Total variable cost for the three buses, total effective passenger-kms for the buses, and variable cost per effective passenger-km.

(iii) For trucks: Total variable cost for the trucks, total effective ton-kms, and variable cost per effective ton-km.

Solution :

(1) For fleet of five taxies:

Actual Distance run: 3,200 × 5=16,000

Total Variable cost = 16,000 × 6.30 = ₹ 1,00,800.

Effective Kilometer = 16,000 × 0.84 = 13,440.

Variable cost per effective km = 1,00,800 ÷ 13,440 = ₹ 7.50 per km.

(2) For three Buses:

Actual Distance run: Number of buses × 2 × Number of trips × Distance per trip

= 3 × 2 × 25 × 250 = 37,500kms.

Total Variable cost = 37,500 ×12.60 = ₹ 4,72,500.

Effective Passenger-kms

= Actual Distance run X Number of seats X Occupancy rate

= 37,500 × 50 × 0.9 = 16,87,500.

Variable cost per passenger-km = 4,72,500 ÷ 16,87,500 = ₹0.28.

(3) For two trucks:

Actual Distance run: One-way distance × Number of trucks × 2 × Number of trips

= 900 × 2 × 2 × 12 = 43, 200 kms.

Total Variable Cost = 43,200 × 12 = ₹ 5,18,400.

Effective ton-kms

= (Actual Distance run) × (Maximum Capacity × Occupancy rate)

= (43,200) × (20 × 0.8) = 43,200 × 16 = 6, 91, 200.

Cost per ton-km = Total variable cost divided by Effective ton-kms

= 5,18,400 ÷ 6,91,200 = ₹ 0.75.

BOILER-HOUSE COSTING

In large undertakings, boiler house is treated as separate department and the departmental operating statement indicates the efficiency of the use of each element of cost. Cost of steam produced is obtained by relating the total costs to net quantity produced. The costs are usually categorised under the following heads: (a) Fuel and Labour; (b) Treated Water; (c) Maintenance services; and (d) Other overheads. A specimen of the Boiler House cost statement is given as under:

Boiler-House Cost Statement

Maximum capacity: .... Period: ....

Standard capacity: .... Actual output: ....

Details	Total cost		Cost per 1,000 lbs of steam		Remarks
	Current period	Previous period	Current period	Previous period	percentage increase/decrease
Fuel:					
Fuel					
Fuel-handling					
Ash removal					
Electric power					
Stokers					
Direct Labour:					
Fuel handling					
Ash handling					
Stoker					

Water:
Water purchased
Water softening
Indirect Labour:
Supervision
Foreman
Sweepers
General labour
Boiler cleaner
Maintenance:
Fixed Plant
Meters
Boilers
Ash washer Plant
Economisers
Other accessories
Coal bunkers
Furnace
Service materials
Fixed overhead:
Rent, rates, etc.
Depreciation:
Plant
Building
Allocatioon of
General factory
Expenses
Total

Steam consumption: .... Remarks: ....
Steam losses: .... Entered by: ....
Main factors responsible for losses: ....

The objective of boiler house costing is to ascertain cost per pound (lb) of steam produced. The fundamental principles of cost finding remain unchanged. Total cost incurred during a particular period divided by pounds of steam produced gives cost per pound of steam. Total cost may be divided into fixed cost and variable cost or as per the classifications given in the specimen proforma of operating cost statement. In case of boiler house, the proportion of fixed cost is quite large. Therefore larger the quantity of steam produced, lower is the cost per unit of steam.

POWER-HOUSE COSTING

The cost of electricity generated can be obtained from the steam production cost as well as other costs regarding electricity generation. A Specimen of the operating statement of the power house is given below:

Power-House Cost Statement

Maximum capacity: .... Power generation capacity: ....
Standard capacity: .... Power generated: ....
Steam used for power generation: .... Power used in generating department:...

Details	Total cost		Cost per 1,000 lbs of steam		Remarks
	Current period	Previous period	Current period	Previous period	percentage increase/decrease
Boiler house costs:					
Coal					
Water					
Water softener					
Coal handling					
Wages					
Ash removal					
Storage costs					
Depreciation					
Stoking					
Supervision					
Total					
Less: Cost of steam used in boiler house					
Steam used in Power generation					
Generating station costs:					
Steam					
Coal					
Oil					
Gas					
Wages					
Repairs and maintenance					
Depreciation of Plant					
Interest on Investment					
General overheads:					
Apportioned Supervision costs					

Depreciation of Building
Total
Power Losses: ....
Factors of Losses: ....
Remarks: .... Entered by: ....

There are two options of finding out the cost of power generated in the power house:

(1) A separate cost sheet is prepared for the boiler house and costs of steam produced and used in generation of power is transferred to cost sheet meant for power generation as an input cost.

(2) Cost of steam production and power generation is combined into one operating cost statement. Costs of the Boiler house as well as the Generating Station may be distinctly accumulated and stated, or the two may be combined and shown in the category of fixed and variable costs, or fuel, labour and overheads, etc.

There may be losses of power consumed and/or some power may be consumed by the power house itself in the process of production. In such cases, the total cost incurred for power generation is for the Net number of power units available for consumption. The cost of power generated may be calculated 'per kilowatt' or per kilowatt-hour (kwh).

Illustration 17.6 : *GPS Power House produced 40,000 therms of steam out of which 20% was used for heating purposes of its own steam plant. Followings are the expenses of the two plants in the month of August, 2008:*

Details	*Boiler Plant (₹)*	*Electricity Plant (₹)*
Coal	*2,10,000*	
Water	*2,500*	
Water softener	*1,500*	
Operator's Wages:		
Coal Handling	*15,000*	
Stocking	*36,000*	*29,000*
Repairs and Maintenance	*18,000*	*12,800*
Stores	*10,000*	*6,000*
Depreciation	*5,000*	*17,200*
Supervision	*42,000*	*15,000*

Find out cost per unit of electricity generated during August, 2008.

Solution :

Power-House Cost Statement

Cost centre: ………… Month: August, 2008

Steam produced 40,000 therms

Steam used for generation: 32,000 therms

Units of electricity generated: 3,20,000 units

Details	Total cost current Month (₹)	Cost per therm (₹)	Remarks
Coal	2,10,000		
Water	2,500		
Water softener	1,500		
Wages:	15,000		
Coal Handling	36,000		
Stocking			
Repairs and Maintenance	18,000		
Stores	10,000		
Depreciation	5,000		
Supervision	42,000		
Total cost of production of 40,000 therms	3,40,000	8.50	
Less: Allocated to heating 8,000 therms @ ₹	68,000		
Cost of steam used for generation of 32,000 therms	2,72,000	8.50	
	Total (₹)	**Cost per unit (₹)**	
Electricity generation costs:			
Cost of Steam used	2,72,000		
Operator's Wages	29,000		
Stores	6,000		
Repairs and Maintenance	12,800		
Depreciation	17,200		
Supervision	15,000		
Total cost for generation of 3,20,000 units	3,52,000	1.10	

Remarks ……… Checked by ……..

CANTEEN AND HOTEL COSTING

Costs are recorded in Canteen Operating Statement, a Specimen of which is given as under and corresponding number of meals for the period is determined by the canteen manager. Company subsidy is deducted from the total costs incurred. Amount realized from sale is then compared with the total costs and the net operating profit or loss is determined.

Canteen Operating Statement

Details	Total cost (₹)		Cost per meal (₹)	
	Current month	Year to date	Current month	Year to date
Wages and Salaries:				
Supervisors				
Cooks				
Helpers				
Provisions:				
Vegetables				
Mutton				
Fish				
Eggs				
Fruits				
Bread				
Biscuits				
Milk				
Groceries				
Miscellaneous:				
Rent				
Gas				
Electricity				
Steam				
Consumable Stores				
Towels				
Crockery and Glassware				
Depreciation on non-consumbale items				
Total cost				
Deduct:				
Company subsidy				
Profit /loss				
Sales				

Remarks .... Checked by ....

Costing for Hotels involve some additional computations. Hotels need to do costing on the basis of less than 100% occupancy as normal. Further, there are peak seasons and slack seasons. Generally room rates are high during the peak season and low during the slack season. Certain costs, such as power, differ in winter and summer season. Some costs are related to room occupancy while most other costs are incurred irrespective of occupancy. All these problems are involved in Hotel costing.

Illustration 17.7 : *From the following information relating to a hotel, calculate the room rent to be charged to give a profit of 20% on cost excluding interest.*

- *Salaries of staff: ₹ 42,00,000 p.a.*
- *Wages of room Attendant ₹ 120 per day.*
- *There is one room attendant for each room. He is paid wages only when the room is occupied.*
- *Lighting , heating and power:*
  - *(a) The normal lighting expenses for a room for the whole month is ₹ 800, when occupied.*
  - *(b) Power is used only in winter and the charges are ₹ 350 per month for a room, when occupied.*
- *Repair to Buildings: ₹ 5,40,000 p.a.*
- *Linen, etc. ₹ 2,85,000 p.a.*
- *Sundries ₹ 2,00,000 p.a.*
- *Interior decoration and furnishings ₹ 1,60,000 p.a.*
- *Depreciation @ 5% on investment in buildings costing ₹ 120,00,000.*
- *Depreciation @ 15% on Equipments.*
- *Interest @ 6% on investment in buildings and equipments costing ₹ 150,00,000.*
- *There are 125rooms in the hotel. 80% of the rooms are generally occupied in summer. A month may be assumed to be of 30 days, and 40% in winter. The period of summer and winter may be considered to be six months in each case.*

Solution : Working Notes:

1. Room Days:

   Summer: 125 rooms × 6 months × 30 days × 0.8 = 18,000

   Winter: 125 rooms × 6 months × 30 days × 0.4 = 9,000

   Total Room Days: 27,000

2. Room Attendant's wages:

   Summer: ₹ 120 × 125 rooms × 6 months × 30 days × 0.8

   = ₹ 21,60,000

   Winter: ₹ 120 × 125 rooms × 6 months × 30 days × 0.4

   = ₹ 10,80,000

   Total Wages of the room attendants: ₹ 32,40,000

3. lighting, heating and Power:
   (i) Lighting and heating:
   Summer: ₹800 × 125 rooms × 6 months × 0.8 = ₹ 4,80,000
   Winter: ₹800 × 125 rooms × 6 months × 0.4 = ₹ 2,40,000
   Total Wages of the room attendants: ₹ 7,20,000
   (ii) Power:
   Winter: ₹ 350 × 125 rooms × 6 months × 0.4 = ₹ 1,05,000
   Total lighting, heating and Power:
   7,20,000 + 1,05,000 => ₹ 8,25,000

Operating cost statement of a Hotel

(Room Days: 27,000)

Details (Annual Total cost)		Amount (₹)
Staff Salaries		42,00,000
Room Attendants' Wages		32,40,000
Lighting, heating and Power		8,25,000
Repairs to Building		5,40,000
Linen, etc.		2,85,000
Sundries		2,00,000
Interior decoration and furnishings		1,60,000
Depreciation:		
Building @ 5% (120,00,000 × 0.05)	6,00,000	19,50,000
Equipments @ 11% (30,00,000 × 0.15)	4,50,000	
Interest @ 6% (150,00,000 × 0.06)	9,00,000	
Total cost		114,00,000
Profit @ 20% on cost excluding Interest i.e. {(114,00,000 - 9,00,000) × 0.2}		21,00,000
Total revenue		135,00,000

Room Rent per day = Total revenue/ Total room days
= 135,00,000/ 27,000 => ₹ 500.

Illustration 17.8 :

Anushka Transport Company has been given a route 25kms long to run a bus. The bus costs the company a sum of ₹4, 50,000. It has been insured at 3% p.a. and the annual tax will amount to ₹4, 500, garage rent is ₹1,000 p.m., annual repairs will be ₹6,000 and the bus is likely to last for 5 years.

The driver's salary will be ₹3, 000 per month and the conductor's salary will be ₹2, 500 per month in addition to 10% of the takings as commission (to be shared by the driver and the conductor equally). Cost of stationery will be ₹ 5,820 p.a. Manager cum accountant's salary is ₹5, 000 p.m.

Petrol and oil will be ₹40 per 100 km. the bus will make 3 round trips carrying on an average 40 passengers on each trip. Assuming 15% profit on takings, calculate the bus fare to be charged from each passenger. This bus will run on an average 25 days in a month.

Solution : Statement showing the fare to be charged from one passenger for one Km. travelled

Details	Total (₹)	Per Month (₹)
A. Standing Charges:		
1. Garage Rent	12,000	
2. Cost of stationery	5,820	
3. Insurance	12,000	
4. Driver's Wages	36,000	
5. Conductor's salary	30,000	
6. Manager – cum – accountant's salary	60,000	
7. Road Tax	4,500	
Total Standing Charges	1,60,320	
Standing charges per month (1,60,320 ÷ 12)		13,360
B. Running Charges:		
1. Depreciation	90,000	7,500
2. Petrol/Diesel*		1,500
3. Repairs and Maintenance	6,000	500
4. Commission**		3,048
C. Total cost per month [(A) + (B)		25,908
D. Profit 15% on takings		4,572
E. Total takings		30,480
F. Fare per passenger – km (30,480 ÷ 1,50,000)		0.2032
G. Fare per passenger – km for one round trip (0.2032 × 2×25)		10.16

Working Notes:

1. Total effective passenger- kms per month:

   $$= (3\times2\times25\times25\times40) \Rightarrow 1,50,000$$

2. * Cost of Petrol: (3×2×25×25×0.40) = > ₹ 1,500

3. **In order to compute the amount of commission payable to the driver and the conductor, total takings will have to be calculated.

Let total takings be 'X'

Commission: $X \div 10 = 0.1\,X$

Profit to be charged: $3\,X \div 20 = 0.15\,X$

costs per month excluding commission: ₹22, 860

$$X = 22{,}860 + 0.15X + 0.1\,X$$

$$X - 0.25\,X = 22{,}860$$

$$0.75\,X = 22{,}860$$

$$X = 22{,}860 \div 0.75 = ₹\ 30{,}480$$

LET US RECAPITULATE

1. Operating costing is used to ascertain the cost of providing or rendering service; operation costing is a refinement and more detailed application of process costing.
2. Service or operating cost is the cost of providing service.
3. Services rendered to customers are of unique and standardized type.
4. Distinction between fixed cost and variable cost is of special importance as the scale of operations considerably affects the cost per unit of service rendered.
5. A large chunk of total capital is invested in fixed assets and relatively less working capital is required.
6. The method of costing is different from that used in connection with production, and the difference lies mainly in the manner of accumulating the cost data and finally in its allocation to cost units.
7. Simple cost unit could be per kilometer, per passenger in transport undertakings, per room in hotels, per bed in hospitals.
8. In the composite cost unit, more than one variable is considered. It could be passenger-kilometer, patient-day, room-day, and patient-bed-day.
9. The total cost consists of standing charges, running charges (variable) and maintenance charges.
10. The information about the costs of each vehicle is obtained through Daily Log Sheet and the operating cost sheet.
11. Operating Cost Sheet is a statement which throws light on standing charges and running expenses.
12. In absolute tonne-Kilometer, travel distance in tonne-kilometers between two stations is considered individually and then summed up.
13. In commercial tonne-Kilometers, the trip is considered as a whole and it is arrived at by multiplying the total distance in kilometer by the average load quantity carried.
14. All normal costs/losses must be considered at the time of ascertaining cost per unit.
15. Cost per unit must not be influenced by abnormal gains / losses.
16. Actual kms or actual ton-kms refer to the actual kms run or actual ton-kms of freight carried.

17. Effective kms or ton-kms refer to the kms or ton-kms over which normal total operating costs (Fixed as well as variable) are to be recovered from.
18. Cost of steam produced is obtained by relating the total costs to net quantity produced.
19. The objective of boiler house costing is to ascertain cost per pound (lb) of steam produced.
20. The cost of electricity generated can be obtained from the steam production cost as well as other costs regarding electricity generation.
21. The total cost incurred for power generation is for the Net number of power units available for consumption.
22. Costs are recorded in Canteen Operating Statement. Company subsidy is deducted from the total costs incurred. Amount realized from sale is then compared with the total costs and the net operating profit or loss is determined.
23. Hotels need to do costing on the basis of less than 100% occupancy as normal.

SOLVED PROBLEMS

Problem 1. *A Transport Company maintains a fleet of Lorries for carrying goods from Delhi to Panipat, 100 kms off. Each Lorry, which operates 25 days on an average in a month starts every day from Delhi with a load of 5 tonnes and returns from Panipat with a load of 3 tonnes. Compute the total commercial tonne-kms and cost per commercial tonne-km when the total monthly charges for a lorry are ₹ 72,000. What rate per tonne should the company charge if it plans to earn a gross profit of 25% on the freightage?*

Solution : Computation of Commercial tonne-kms.:

= Average Load × Total Distance covered × Number of days

= {(5+3)/ (2)} × (100+100) × (25) = 4 × 200 × 25= 20,000 tonne-kms.

Cost per tonne-km.:

= Total Monthly Charges / Total tonne-kms.

= 72,000 ÷ 20,000 => ₹ 3.60

Calculation of freight rate per tonne to earn a gross profit of 25% on freightage:

Details	**Amount (₹)**
Cost per tonne-km.	3.60
Profit [25% on freightage or 100/3% on cost]	1.20
Freight rate per tonne	4.80

Problem 2. *Mr. Babu Lal started business with a fleet of Eight Taxis. Expenses incurred by him are given below:*

Item	*Amount (₹)*	*Item*	*Amount (₹)*
Cost of each Taxi	*4,00,000*	*Salary of office staff p.m.*	*16,000*
Road Tax and Repairs p.a. per taxi	*21,600*	*Salary of garage staff p.m.*	*8,000*
Insurance Premium@ 4.5% of cost p.a.		*Driver's salary (per Taxi) per month*	*3,000*
Rent of garage p.m.	*5,600*		

The life of taxi is 3,00,000 km. at the end of which it is estimated to be sold at `40,000. A taxi on an average runs 5,000 kms. per month of which 20% it runs empty. Petrol consumption is 10 km. per liter of petrol costing ₹ 38 per liter. Oil and other sundry expenses amount to ₹ 65 per 25 kms.

Compute the effective cost of running taxi per kilometer. Also find out the profit for the first year if the hire charge is ₹ 15 per km.

Solution : Statement of Operating Cost (Per Taxi p.m.)

Item of Expense	Total Amount (₹)	Per effective km. Amount (₹)
Standing Charges:		
Salary of office staff (16,000 ÷ 8)	2,000	
Salary of garage staff	1,000	
Rent of garage	700	
Driver's salary	3,000	
Road Tax and Repairs	1,800	
in0Insurance Premium: {(0.045×4, 00, 000) ÷ (12)}	1,500	
Total Standing Charges	10,000	2.50
Running Charges:		
Depreciation (5, 000) × (4, 00, 000 – 40, 000) ÷(3, 00, 000)	6,000	1.50
Petrol (5, 000) ×(38 ÷ 10)	19,000	4.75
Oil and other Sundries (5,000) ×(65 ÷ 25)	13,000	3.25
Total Running Charges	38,000	9.50
Total Standing Charges and Running Charges	48,000	12.00
Profit per month per Taxi	12,000	3.00
Monthly Fare 4,000×15	60,000	15.00
Total Annual Profit (4,000 × 15× 12 × 8) = ₹57 60 000		

Note: Effective cost of running a taxi has been calculated by dividing monthly cost by 4,000 = (5,000 × 0.8).

Computation of Effective-kms:
A taxi runs in a month = 5,000 kms
Less: Empty running (0.2 × 5,000) = 1,000
Effective Distance per a month = 4,000 kms

Problem 3. *Mr. Madhvan has been promised a contract to run a tourist car on a 25 km. long route for the chief executive of a standard Firm. He buys a car costing ₹3,60,000. The annual cost of insurance and taxes are ₹ 10,800 and ` 2,160 respectively. He is required to pay ₹ 1,200 per month for a garage where he keeps the car when it is not in use. The annual repair costs are estimated at ₹ 9,600. The car is estimated to have a life of 10 years at the end of which the scrap value is likely to be ₹ 60,000.*

He hires a driver who is to be paid ₹ 1,000 p.m. plus 10% of the takings as commission. Other incidental expenses are estimated at ₹ 500.

Petrol and oil will cost ₹ 400 per 100 kilometres. The car will make four round trips each day. Assuming that a profit of 15% on takings is desired and that the car will be on the road for all the days of the month, determine the charge per round trip?

Solution : Statement showing the per Round-trip charge

Details	Annual Amount (₹)	Monthly Amount (₹)
Standing Charges:		
1. Insurance Charges	10,800	
2. Taxes	2,160	
3. Garage Rent	14,400	
4. Driver's Salary	12,000	
	39,360	3,280
Running Expenses:		
1. Depreciation		2,500
2. Repairs		800
3. Petrol		20,000
4. Commission		3,544
Total cost per Month		30,124
Profit @15% on takings		5,316
Total Takings		35,440
Charge per Round-trip (35,440 /200)		177.20

Working Notes:

1. Number of round trips in one month of 25 working days:
= 4 × 2 × 25 => 200

2. Traveling distance in one month of 25 days:

   = 4 × 2 × 2 5 × 25 => 5,000 Kms.

3. Petrol and oil cost:

   = Total distance traveled in one month of 25 days × Rate per Km.

   = 5,000 × (400 ÷ 100)

   = ₹ 20,000.

4. Depreciation (Monthly):

   = [(3,60,000 – 60,000) ÷ (10 × 12)]

   = ₹ 2,500.

5. Commission: Let total Takings be 'X'

   Commission = 0.1X

   Profit = 0.15X

   Total Costs per month without commission are ₹ 26,580

   X = 26,580 + 0.1X + 0.15X

   X – 0.25X = 26,580

   0.75X = 26,580

   X = (26,580 ÷ 0.75) => ₹ 35,440

Problem 4. *Mr. Himmat Rai uses his own car and his office reimburses him at ₹ 14 per Km. Mr. Himmat Rai claims that he needs ₹ 16 per kilometer just to break-even. A scrutiny of his expenses by the office reveals the following:*

Item	*Amount (₹)*
Oil Charge every 3,000 Km	*200*
Maintenance (other than Oil) every 1,000 Km	*600*
Annual Insurance (Comprehensive with accident benefits)	*8,000*
Cost of a Car, with an average residual value of ₹ 80,000 and with Useful life of 4 years	*4,00,000*

Petrol in ₹ 40 a liter and Himmat Rai gets 12 kms per liter for his car. When Himmat Rai is on the road, he averages 200 km a day. He works five days a week, has 11 days vacation in a year besides 7 holidays and spends 14 working days in a month in the office. Determine: (I) an equitable rate for reimbursement on the basis of the schedule he presently follows and (ii) the number of kilometers a year he would have, to travel, to break-even at the current rate of reimbursement.

Solution : Working Note:

Details	Days
Total Days in a Year	365
Less: Non-Working Days (52×2)	104
Number of working Days in a Year	261

Less: Vacation 11 Holidays 7 Office Work days 14×12 = 168	186
Days on Travelling	75

Kms. On Work = 75 × 200 = 15,000 in a year.

Statement of Travel Cost per Kilometer

Details	Amount p.a. (₹)	Amount Per Km. (₹)
Fixed Charges:		
Depreciation (4,00,000 – 80,000) ÷ 4	80,000	
Annual Insurance	10000	
Total Fixed Charges	90000	
Fixed Charge per Km. (90,000÷15,000)		6.0000
Variable Charges:		
Oil Expense (200÷3,000) × 15,000	1000	0.0667
Maintenance (600÷1,000) × 15,000	9000	0.6000
Petrol (40÷12) × 15,000	50000	3.3333
Total Variable Charges	60000	4.0000
Total Cost: Fixed + Variable	150000	10.0000

(1) Equitable Rate of Reimbursement per Km. ₹ 10

(2) Current Reimbursement Rate= ₹ 9

Less: Variable Cost = ₹ 4

Contribution per Km. (9 – 4) = ₹5

Break-Even Kms with Current Rate = (Fixed Cost ÷ Contribution per Km.)

= 90,000÷5=18,000kms.

For this his average traveling per day must be

= (18,000÷75) =240 kms. i.e. An increase by 40 kms per day.

Problem 5. *The truck starts with a load of 10 tonnes of goods from a place P. It unloads 6 tonnes at a place R and rest of the goods at place S. It reaches back directly to the place P after getting reloaded with 7 tonnes of goods at a place S. The distances between P to R, R to S and then from S to P are 50 km, 80 km and 100 km respectively. Compute absolute tonne/km and commercial tonne/km.*

Solution : Absolute tonne-km:- The travel distance between any two places is considered individually.

Distance P ←50 km→ R ←50 km→ P ←80 km→ S ←100 km→ P

Absolute tonne-km

= (10 tonne × 50 km) + (4 tonne × 80 km) + (7 tonne × 100 km)

= 1,520 Tonne-km

Commercial tonne-km:- The trip is considered as a whole.

Commercial tonne-km = Average load × Total kms. Traveled

= {(10+4+7) ÷ 3)} × (230)

= 1,610 Tonne-km

Problem 6. *City Bus Service Ltd. runs the following fleet of buses within the limits of Ajmer city of Rajasthan:*

Bus (Number)	*Carrying capacity (passengers)*
10	*50*
15	*40*

On an average, each bus makes 10 trips a day covering a distance of 8 kms. In each trip, and 75% of the seats are occupied. The annual records show that 5 buses are generally required to be kept away from road each day for repairs.

The following expenses were incurred by the company during March 2005:

Item of expense	*Amount (₹)*	*Item of expense*	*Amount (₹)*
Garage Rent & Rates, and Insurance	*2,500*	*Consumable Stores*	*4,500*
Road and Vehicle Tax	*500*	*Petrol*	*24,400*
Salary: Chief Operating Manager	*1,500*	*Lubricants*	*5,500*
3 Assistant Managers	*800 each*	*Replacement of Tyres and Tubes*	*1,750*
4 Supervisors	*400 each*	*Gas and Electricity*	*350*
25 Drivers	*240 each*	*Miscellaneous*	*1,850*
30 Cleaners	*100 each*	*Repairs*	*3,500*
Office Staff	*4,000*		

The Cost Clerk of the Company prepared a Cost Sheet using the actual figures for various expenses and writing off ₹ 6,500 for depreciation. Show the Cost Sheet in proper form as might have been prepared by the Cost Clerk.

Also advise the Cost Clerk about those expenses which should be included in the Cost Sheet on the basis of annual estimate of those expenses (in place of the actual amount spent during this month in respect of the same) and point out to him how he should arrive at this month's share of each of those expenses.

Solution : **Operating Cost Sheet of City Bus Service Ltd.**

Fixed Expenses	Amount (₹)	Amount (₹)
Garage Rent, Rates and Insurance	2,500	
Road and Vehicle Tax	500	
Salary : Chief Operating Manager	1,500	
3 Assistant Managers @ ₹ 800 each	2,400	
4 Supervisors @ ₹ 400 each	1,600	
25 Drivers @ ₹ 240 each	6,000	
30 Cleaners @ ₹ 100 each	3,000	
Office Staff	4,000	
Consumable Stores	4,500	
Lubricants	5,500	
Gas and Electricity	350	
Miscellaneous Expenses	1,800	33,650
Variable Expenses:		
Depreciation	6,500	
Repairs	3,500	
Petrol	24,000	
Replacement of Tyres and Tubes	1,750	35,750
Total Expenses		69,400

Effective Passenger-Kms.:

$(10 \times 50) + (15 \times 40) = 500 + 600 = 1{,}100$ effective passengers.

$1{,}100 \times 10 \times 8$ km. $\times 0.75 \times 0.8 \times 31 = 16{,}36{,}800$ passenger-kms.

Cost per passenger-km. = 69,400 ÷ 16, 36,800 = ₹ 0.042

Expenses like road and vehicle tax, repairs, replacement of tyres and tubes and miscellaneous expenses should be estimated by the cost accountant for the year as a whole and then charged to the month concerned on an equitable basis (generally equally on 12 months' basis). The estimates about those expenses can be made on the basis of past experience and the possible increase or decrease in the current period.

Problem 7. *MV Limited owns a fleet of ten trucks each costing ₹ 3, 00,000. The company has employed one manager to whom it pays ₹ 27,000 p.m., an accountant who gets ₹ 15,000 p.m. and a peon who gets ₹ 6,000 p.m. The company has got its trucks insured @ 2.5% per annum. The annual total tax is ₹ 6,000 per truck. The other expenses are as under:*

Driver's Salary	*₹ 12,000 per month*
Cleaner's Salary	*₹ 5,000 per month*

Mechanic's salary ₹ *18,000 per month*
Repairs and maintenance ₹ *6,000 per month for one truck*
Diesel consumption: *3 kms. per litre @* ₹ *27 per litre*
Estimated life of the truck *5 years*

Other information:

1. Distance travelled by each truck per day: 240 kms.

2. Normal Loading capacity: 100 quintals

3. Wastage in Loading capacity: 10%

4. Percentage of truck laid up for repair: 5%

5. Effective days in a month: 25

Calculate (a) cost per quintal kilometer, (b) cost per kilometer of running a truck.

Solution : Working Note:

(I) Total number of Quintal Kilometers of a Truck

Quintal Capacity = 100	Distance per day = 240	Effective days in a month = 25	Loading capacity = 90%	Percentage of truck available = 95%

= 100 × 240 × 25 × 0.9 × 0.95 => 5, 13,000 Quintal Kilometers

(II) Total Number of Kilometers covered during a month by one truck

Distance traveled = 240	Effective days per month = 25	Percentage of truck available = 95%

= 240 × 25 × 0.95 = >5,700 Kilometers

Operating Cost Statement

Details	**Amount (₹)**	**Amount (₹)**
Fixed Expenses per month (For 10 trucks):		
Manager's Salary	27,000	
Accountant's Salary	15,000	
Peon's Salary	6,000	
Mechanic's Salary	18,000	
Total for ten trucks	66,000	
Fixed Expenses per month (For one truck): (66,000 ÷ 10)		6,600

Other fixed cost:		
Driver's salary per truck	12,000	
Cleaner's salary	5,000	
Repairs and maintenance	6,000	
Insurance [(3,00,000 × 0.025) ÷12]	625	
Total tax (6,000÷12)	500	
Depreciation (3,00,000 ÷ (5 × 12)	5,000	
	29,125	
Fixed Expenses		35,725
Variable Expenses per truck: Diesel charges (27÷3) × (5,700)		51,300
Total charges		87,025
Operating expenses Per kilometer per truck:[87,025 ÷ 5,700]	Per Km.	Per quintal-
Operating expenses Per Quintal- kilometer per truck: [87,025 ÷ 5, 13,000]	15.2675	Km. 0.1697

Problem 8. *Mount Carmel is a public school having eight buses, each plying in different direction for the transport of its school students. In view of a large number of students availing of the bus service, the buses work two shifts in the morning and two in the after noon: One shift for senior students and other for junior students.*

The distance travelled by each bus one way is 10 kms. The school works 25 days in a month and remains closed for vacation in May, June, and December. Bus fee, however, is payable by the students for all the 12 months in a year. The details of expenses for a year are as under:

Driver's salary	*₹4, 500 per month per driver*
Cleaner's salary	*₹ 3,000 per month*

(Salary payable for all 12 months, two cleaners employed for all the eight buses)

Licence fee, taxes, etc.	*₹ 4,500 per bus per annum*
Insurance	*₹6, 000 per bus per annum*
Repairs and maintenance	*₹ 22,500 per bus per annum*
Purchase price of the bus	*₹ 4, 50,000 each*
Life	*10 years*
Scrap value	*₹ 30,000*
Diesel cost	*₹28 per litre*

Each bus gives an average of 5 km per litre of diesel. The seating capacity of each bus is 50 students. Students picked up and dropped within a range up to 4 km. of distance from the school are charged half fare and fifty percent of students travelling in each trip are in this category. Ignore interest. Since the charges are to be based on average cost, you are required:

(i) Prepare a statement showing the expenses of operating a single bus.

(ii) Work-out the average cost per student per month in respect of:

(a) Students coming from a distance of up to 4 kames from the school, and

(b) Students coming from a distance beyond 4 kames from the school.

Solution :

Distance travelled in a day 10 kms one way by each in 4 round trips:

$$= (2 \times 4 \times 10) = 80 \text{ kms.}$$

Distance in a month of 25 days = 80 × 25 = 2,000 kms. For 9 months in a year:

$$= 2{,}000 \times 9 = 18{,}000 \text{ kms.}$$

Number of half- fare students: 50 % of 50 capacity in each trip = 25 half and 25 full.

When full fare students are converted to half fare students, the number = [2{(2×25) + (25)}] = 150 half fare in 2 trips and 75 full fare students.

Operating Cost Statement of School Bus

Details	Per Bus (Annual) Amount (₹)	8 Buses (Annual) Amount (₹)
Operating and maintenance charges:		
Repair and maintenance	22,500	1,80,000
Diesel cost: = (18,000 kms÷5) × 28	1,00,800	8,06,400
(a) Total annual operating cost	1,23,300	9,86,400
Standing Charges:		
Depreciation = (4,50,000 – 30,000) ÷ 10	42,000	3,36,000
Driver's salary (4,500 × 12)	54,000	4,32,000
Two Cleaner's salary (3,000 × 2 × 12) = 72,000 72,000 ÷ 8	9,000	72,000
Licence fee, taxes etc.	4,500	36,000
Insurance	6,000	48,000
(b) Total annual standing charges	1,15,500	9,24,000
Total annual cost (a + b)	2,38,800	19,10,400
(i) Operating cost per month (divided by 12)	19,900	1,59,200
(ii) (A) Per Half fare student (divided by 150; and 8 ×150)	132.67	132.67
(b) Per Full fare student	265.34	265.34

Problem 9. *Navneet owns a bus, which runs according to the following schedule:*

(i) Delhi to Chandigarh and back, the same day.

Distance covered: 180 km one way.

Number of days running each month: 9

Seating capacity occupied: 90%

(ii) Delhi to Agra and back, the same day.

Distance covered: 150 km one way

Number of days running each month: 11

Seating capacity occupied: 85%

(iii)Delhi to Jaipur and back, the same day.

Distance covered: 300 km one way.

Number of days running each month: 5

Seating capacity occupied: 100%

Other details are as under: *Cost of the Bus: ₹7, 50,000; Salary of the driver ₹ 4,500 p.m.; Salary of conductor ₹ 3,500 p.m.; Salary of part-time accountant ₹1, 000 p.m.; insurance of the Bus ₹6, 000 p.a.; diesel consumption 4 km per litre at ₹28 per litre; road tax ₹4, 200 p.a.; lubricant oil ₹25 per 100 km; Permit fee ₹720 p.m.; Repairs and Maintenance ₹ 4,415 p.m.; Depreciation of the Bus 20 % p.a.; Seating capacity of the Bus 50 persons; Passenger tax is 12% of the total takings.*

Calculate the fare per passenger - km and Bus fare to be charged from each passenger to earn a profit of 28 % on total takings. The fares are to be indicated per passenger for the journeys:

(i) Delhi to Chandigarh. (ii) Delhi to Agra, and (iii) Delhi to Jaipur.

Solution : Computation of Total passenger kms

(i) Delhi – Chandigarh – Delhi: (2 × 180×50×9×0.90)	1,45,800
(ii) Delhi – Agra – Delhi: (2 × 150 × 50× 11× 0.85)	1,40,250
(iii) Delhi –Jaipur – Delhi: (2 × 300× 50×5×1)	1,50,000
Total passenger- km :	4,36,050

Computation of Total kms

(i) Delhi – Chandigarh – Delhi: (2×180×9)	3,240
(ii) Delhi – Agra – Delhi: (2×150×11)	3,300
(iii) Delhi – Jaipur – Delhi: (2×300×5)	3,000
Total kms:	9,540

Operating cost sheet for Bus No: ....

Monthly operating and maintenance charges	Per month (₹)	Total (₹)
Repairs and maintenance	4,415	
Petrol / diesel (28×9,540) ÷4	66,780	
Lubricant oil (0.25×9,540)	2,385	
Total variable charges		73,580
Monthly standing charges		
Depreciation [(7,50,000 ÷ 5) × 12)]	12,500	
Salaries:		
Driver (4,500)		
Conductor (3,500)		
Part time accountant (1,000)	9,000	
Insurance of the bus	500	
Road tax	4,200	
Permit fee	720	
Total standing charges		26,920
(a) Total cost	1,00,500	1,00,500
(b) Profit (28% of 1,67,500)	+0.28X	46,900
Net takings		1,47,400
(c) Passenger tax (12% of 1,67,500)	+0.12X	20,100
Total takings or total fare collection (i.e. a + b + c)	X	1,67,500

Fare per passenger – km =1, 67,500 ÷ 4, 36,050 =₹ 0.38413

Fare to be charged:

(I) Delhi – Chandigarh trip: (180 × 0.38413) = ₹ 69.14 one-way

(ii) Delhi – Agra trip: (150 × 0.38413) = ₹ 57.62 one-way

(iii) Delhi – Japer trip: (300 × 0.38413) = ₹ 115.24 one-way

Ascertainment of total takings: Let total taking be 'X' therefore passenger tax is {(12 X) ÷ 100} and profit is {(28 X) ÷ 100} as both are on total takings. Accordingly, total takings = total operating cost excluding passenger tax, i.e. ₹73, 580 plus total standing charges ₹26, 920, plus passenger tax, plus profit. Thus,

$$X = 1{,}00{,}500 + 0.12\,X + 0.28\,X$$

$$0.6\,X = 1{,}00{,}500$$

$$X = (1{,}00{,}500 \div 0.6) \Rightarrow ₹\ 1{,}67{,}500.$$

Problem 10. *A transport company is running five buses between Delhi and Tilliar (a Picnic spot in Haryana), covering a distance of 125 kms. The seating capacity of each bus is 50 passengers. The following particulars are obtained from its books for the month of November, 2007:*

Details	*Amount (₹)*
Wages of drivers, conductors	*32,000*
Salaries of office staff	*14,000*
Honorarium of Accountant	*5,000*
Diesel, oil etc.	*1,50,000*
Repairs and Maintenance	*6,500*
Road Tax and Insurance	*10,000*
Depreciation	*30,000*
Interest and Other Charges	*22,500*

Actual passengers carried were 80% of the seating capacity. All the buses ran for 30 days. Each bus made one round trip per day. Find out the fare the company should charge per passenger/km if it wants a profit of 25% on the takings.

Solution : **Operating Cost Statement**

Details	Amount (₹)
Wages of drivers, conductors	32,000
Salaries of office staff	14,000
Honorarium of Accountant	5,000
Diesel, oil etc.	1,50,000
Repairs and Maintenance	6,500
Road Tax and Insurance	10,000
Depreciation	30,000
Interest and Other Charges	22,500
Total Cost	2,70,000

Cost per Passenger Km.:

= (2, 70,000 ÷ 15, 00,000) =₹ 0.18

Fare to be charged:

Cost per Passenger Km =	0.18
Profit 25% or ¼ th of takings or {(1/3) × (0.18}	0.06
Fare per passenger km.	0.24

Fare per Round trip:

= (125 × 2) × 0.24 => ₹60

Working Notes:

Passenger-kilometers:

[Number of Buses × Capacity Available × Capacity Utilized × Number of Days × Distance covered per trip × Number of Trips per day]

= (5 × 50 × 0.80 × 30 × 125 × 2) =>15, 00,000 Passenger-kilometers

Problem 11. *Mr. Singh started transport business with a fleet of 8 taxis. Expenses of operating the fleet are given below:*

Details	***Amount (₹)***
Cost of each Taxi	*4,35,000*
Driver's Salary per taxi per month	*5,000*
Salaries of office and Garage staff per month	*48,000*
Rent of Garage per month	*16,000*
Insurance , Tax and sundry expenses per taxi p.a.	*93,000*

The life of a taxi is 2, 50,000 kms at the end of which it is sold at ₹ 35,000. A taxi is expected to run on an average 5,000 kms per month. Petrol consumption is 12 kms per litre of petrol costing ₹ 54 per litre. You are required to:

(i) Calculate the cost of running a taxi per km by preparing a statement of operating cost; and

(ii) Find out the profit Mr. Singh may expect to earn during the first month of operations if the hire charges is ₹ 16 per km. assume that during the month each taxi runs on an average 5,000 kms of which 20% it runs empty.

Solution :

Operating cost Sheet

Details	**Per Taxi (per month) (₹)**	**Per km. (₹)**
Fixed Expenses:		
Rent (16,000 ÷ 8)	2,000	
Salary of office and Garage Staff (48,000 ÷ 8)	6,000	
Salary of Driver	5,000	
Insurance etc. (93,000 ÷ 12)	7,750	
Total	20,750	
Fixed expenses per km. (20,750 ÷ 5,000)		4.15
Variable Expenses:		
Depreciation {(4,35,000 – 35,000) ÷ (2,50,000)}		1.60
Petrol		4.50
Total Expenses		10.25

Calculation of Profit:

Takings: (4,000 × 8 × 16) =>	₹ 5,12,000
Less: Cost of (5,000 × 8 × 10.25) =>	₹ 4,10,000
Profit:	₹ 1,02,000

Problem 12. *A truck with maximum capacity of 10 tons operates between Delhi and Mussoorie. The one- way distance is 360 kms. Truck gets fare only one way, the return journey being without fare. The truck completes 10 to and fro trips every month. Monthly fixed cost is ₹ 25,000 and variable cost is ₹9 per km run by the truck. During September the truck could make only 8 trips due to an accident, which resulted in an additional repair cost of ₹ 12,000. The truck generally operates at 84% capacity. Calculate the fare per effective ton- km and per trip if the operator wants to make a profit of 25% on his fare.*

Solution :

With fare normal ton km in a month

$$= (10 \times 360) \times (10 \times 0.84) = 30{,}240 \text{ ton-kms}$$

Effective normal ton- kms in a trip

$$= (360) \times (10 \times 0.84) = 3{,}024 \text{ ton- kms.}$$

Actual running in September

$$= (8 \times 360 \times 2) = 5{,}760 \text{ kms.}$$

Actual ton – kms in September

$$= (8 \times 360) \times (10 \times 0.84) = 24{,}192 \text{ ton-kms}$$

Details	Total absorbed cost (₹)	Cost per effective ton-km (₹)
Monthly fixed cost:		
(25000× 8) ÷ (10) =(20,000 ÷ 24,192)= ₹0.827	20,000	0.827
Variable cost for the month (5,760 × 9)	51,840	2.143
Total cost	71,840	2.970
Profit 25%on fare i.e. {(1/3) × (71,840)	23,947	0.990
Total collection as fare per ton - kms	95787	3.960
Rate per trip: (3.96× 2,880=11,404.8 = ₹ 11,405		

Unabsorbed Standing Cost:

₹25, 000 – ₹ 20,000 = ₹ 5,000 or

Monthly standing charge × unavailable trips/total normal trips =
₹ {(25,000 × 2) ÷ (10)} = ₹ 5,000

Additional cost due to accident also debited to costing profit and loss account ₹12,000

Total debit to costing profit and loss account= ₹5, 000 + ₹12,000 ₹17,000

Problem 13. *A company is considering three alternative proposals for conveyance facilities for its sales personnel who have to do considerable travelling, approximately 20,000 kilometers every year.*

The proposals are as follows:

(i) Purchase and maintain its fleet of cars: The average cost of a car is ₹ 3,00,000.

(ii) Allow the executive use his own car and reimburse expenses at the rate of ₹ 5.00 per kilometer and also bear insurance costs.

(iii) Hire cars from an agency at ₹ 60,000 per year per car. The company will have to bear costs of petrol, taxes and tyres.

The following further details are available:

Petrol ₹ 4 per kilometer

Repairs and maintenance ₹ 1.20 per kilometer

Tyre ₹ 0.60 per kilometer

Insurance ₹ 6,000 per car per annum

Taxes ₹ 4,000 per car per annum

Life of the Car: 5 years with annual mileage of 20,000 kilometers

Resale value: ₹ 50,000 at the end of the fifth year.

You are required to work out the relative costs of the three proposals and rank them. **[B.Com (Hons.) DU, 2001(Modified)]**

Solution :

Détails	Proposal I Amount (₹)	Proposal II Amount (₹)	Proposal III Amount (₹)
Fixed Cost: per Year.			
Taxes	4,000	……..	4,000
Depreciation	50,000	……..	…….
Insurance	6,000	6,000	……..
Fixed Cost : Total	60,000	6,000	4,000
Fixed Cost : per km.	3.00	0.30	0.20
Reimbursement	…….	5.00	3.00

Variable Cost: per km.			
Petrol	4.00	4.00	4.00
Repairs	1.20	……	……
Tyre	0.60	……	0.60
Total Variable Cost : per km.	5.80	4.00	4.60
Total Cost : per km.	8.80	9.30	7.80
Ranking	II	III	I

Problem 14. *In view of increasing cost of operation of own fleet of cars, your company is presently considering two proposals, viz.*

1. *To hire cars with drivers from an agency @ ₹4, 500 per month. The company will bear the cost of petrol, oil, and tyres.*
2. *The executives will be given ₹ 1, 00,000 interest free loan (repayable in 5 years) to buy their own cars. The company will, however, provide them with free petrol and ₹ 1,500 per month for maintenance and driver's wages.*

If the present cost of a car is ₹2,60,000 and monthly average is 1,920 kilometers, find out the most economic way with the help of the following data: Petrol 320 paisa per km ; oil 40 Paisa per km; Tyre 35 paisa per km; repair 50 paisa per km ; tax and insurance ₹3072 per year; driver's wages and bonus ₹4,000 p.m.; life of a car 5 years; resale value at the end of 5th year ₹ 20,000; assume interest @ 15% p.a.

Solution : Monthly Operating Cost Statement

(Under present condition of monthly average of 1920 km)

Details	**Per month (₹)**	**Per km (₹)**
Tax and insurance (3072 ÷ 12)	256	
Driver's wages and bonus	4,000	
Depreciation (2,60,000 – 20,000)¸ 5 = 48,000	4,000	
= 48,000 ÷ 12 = 4,000		
Total Monthly Standing Cost	8,256	
Total Standing Cost per km. (8,256 ÷ 1,920)		4.30
Variable cost:	8,544	4.45
Petrol : (3.20 × 1,920) = 6,144		
Oil: (0.40 ×1,920) = 768		
Tyre, &(0.35 ×1,920) = 672		
repairs (0.50×1,920) = 960		
OR (4.45 × 1,920) = 8,544		
Total cost / per km cost	16,800	8.75

Monthly operating cost statement

Proposal (1):

Item	**Amount (₹)**
Hire charges	4,500
Petrol, oil, and tyre3.20+0.40+0.35 = 3.95 (3.95 × 1,920)	7,584
Total operating cost per month	12,084

Proposal (2): Interest @ 15 % p.a. on diminishing balance on ₹1, 00,000 repayable in 5 years

Total interest for 5 years comes to ₹45, 000

Item	**Amount (₹)**
Average interest p.m. (45,000 ÷ 5) × (1/12)	750
Petrol (3.20 × 1,920)	6,144
Maintenance and driver's wages (3,000+1,200)	4,200
Total operating cost per month	11,094

Since operating cost per month of ₹11,094 in case of proposal (2) is less, therefore proposal (2) is recommended.

Problem 15. *An employee of Ritz Hotels limited has started using his personal automobile for company's business purpose with effect from 1st January 2004. he would be reimbursed by the company at the rate of 25 Paise km. determined on the basis of the operating costs for 2003 which were as follows:*

Operating Cost	*Amount (₹)*
Depreciation – straight line	*1,000*
Licence fee	*100*
Insurance	*700*
Gas, Oil, Repairs and other variable cost	*1,200*
Total	*3,000*
Kms driven	*12,000*
Cost per km	*25 Paise*

During the year 2004, the car is estimated to be used by the employee as thus:

Mode of Use	***Distance (kms)***
Personal	*15,000*
Business	*10,000*
Total	*25,000*

You are required to:

(a) Calculate the estimated annual operating cost for 2004 and the estimated cost per km to be driven in 2004

(b) *Calculate the amount the employee would be required to pay every km driven on account of personal use in 2004;*

(c) *Indicate whether it would be less expensive for the company to furnish an automobile to the employee.*

Note: *operating cost would be same in 2004 as in 2003.*

Solution :

(a) Estimated cost for 2004

Item of Expenses	Amount (₹)
Depreciation	1,000
Licence fee	100
Insurance	700
Gas, oil, repairs and other variable costs = (1200 ×25,000) ÷ (12,000)	2,500
Total operating cost	4,300

Cost per km. = (4,300 ÷ 25,000) = ₹0.172

(b) Calculation of cost per km for Personal Use:

Item of Expenses	Amount (₹)
Total estimated operating cost	4,300
Less: Reimbursement for business use (10,000 × 0.25)	2,500
Cost the employee has to bear	1,800

Cost per km = (1,800 ÷ 15,000) = ₹ 0.12 on the assumption of the existing level of business use and personal use.

(c) Evaluation of the company furnishing an automobile to the employee.

Annual cost if owned:

Details	Amount (₹)
Standing Charges	1,800
Variable (10,000×0.1) based on ₹1,200 for 12,000 Kms)	1,000
Total	2,800
Less: Reimbursement for business use (10,000 × 0.25)	2500
Net saving in cost to company	300

Decision: It is advisable for the company not to own a car but reimburse the employee for business use of his personal car.

Problem 16. *A Transport Company has been given a 20 km long route to run a bus. The Bus costs ₹ 50,000 and has been insured @6% p.a. while annual taxes amount to ₹ 2,000. Garage rent is ₹ 100 p.m. Yearly repairs will be ₹ 2,000, and the Bus is likely to last for 5 years.*

The driver's salary will be ₹ 3,000 p.a. and that of conductor's ₹ 1,800 p.a. is in addition to 10% of the takings as commission (to be shared by the driver and the conductor equally). Cost of stationery will be ₹ 600 p.a., manager's salary is ₹ 400 p.m. who also looks after accounts.

Diesel and oil will be ₹ 25 per 100 km. the bus will make 3 trips carrying on the average 40 passengers on each trip. Assuming 25% profit on takings, calculate the bus fare to be charged from each passenger. The Bus runs on an average 25 days in a month. **[B.Com (Hons.) DU, 2008]**

Solution : **Operating Cost Statement**

Details	Amount (₹)
Annual Standing Charges:	
Taxes	2,000
Insurance (50,000 × 0.06)	3,000
Garage Rent (100 × 12)	1,200
Repairs	2,000
Salary of Driver	3,000
Salary of conductor	1,800
Stationery	600
Salary of Manager (400 ×12)	4,800
Total	18,400
Monthly Standing Charges (18,400 ÷ 12)	1,533.33
Depreciation [(50,000÷5) ÷(12)]	833.34
Diesel and Oil [(3×2×20×25) ×(0.25)]	750.00
Total Cost Before commission	3,116.67
Commission (0.1×4794.87)	479.49
Total Cost	3,596.16
Profit (0.25×4794.87)	1,198.72
Takings	4,794.88

Working Notes:

1. Total km run by the Bus: (3 ×2 ×20×25×40)= 1,20,000 kms
2. Calculation of Commission and Profit:

Suppose Takings = X

Commission = 0.1X

Profit = 0.25X

X = 3116.67 +0.1X + 0.25X

0.65X = 3,116.67

X = 3,116.67 ÷ 0.65 => ₹ 4,794.88

Problem 17. *A transport company charges ₹ 120 per ton for a 5 tons lorry load from A-station to B- station. The charges for return trip are ₹ 110 per ton. In the month of July, 2006, a truck has made 10 outward journeys with full load out of which 3 tons were unloaded twice at C-station on the way. It returned without any load once only from C-station to A-station.*

The expenses incurred were:

Annual fixed charges:	*₹ 38,400*
Annual maintenance:	*₹ 19,200*
Monthly running charges:	*₹ 2,404*

You are required to find the cost per-ton-kilometer (absolute) and the profit for the month of July, 2006 assuming that no concession is made for delivery at the intermediate stations.

Distance from A-station to B-station is 210 kms, and from A-station to C-station 120 kms. The truck carried a load of 8 tons 5 times while returning from B-station was once caught by the police and was fined ₹ 2,000.

[B.Com (Hons.) DU, 2009]

Solution : **Transport Company**

Operating Cost and Profit Statement

(July, 2006)

Details	**Amount (₹)**
Fixed Cost: (38,400÷12)	3,200
Maintenance Charges (19,200÷12)	1,600
Running Costs	2,404
Total Operating Cost	7,204
Cost per Absolute ton Km (7,204÷19,860)	0.36
Net Revenue Received	10,550
Less: Total Operating Cost	7,204
Profit	3,346

Working Notes:

	Ton-kms
1. Absolute Ton-Kms for outward journey:	
From A-station to B-station: (8 × 210 × 5)	8,400
From A-station to C-station: (2 × 120 × 5)	1,200
From C-station to B-station: (2 × 90×2)	360
Total ton-kms	9,960
2. Absolute Ton-Kms for return journey:	
From B-station to A-station: (9 × 210 × 5)	9,450
From B-station to C-station: (1 × 90×5)	450
Total ton-kms	9,900

3. Total Absolute Ton-Kms [(1) + (2)] 19,860
4. Net Revenue Received Amount (₹)

	Amount (₹)
From A-station to B-station: (10 × 5 × 120)	6,000
From A-station to B-station: (5 × 8 ×110)	4,400
From A-station to B-station: (4×4 × 100)	1,600
From A-station to B-station: (1×5 ×110)	550
Total revenue received	12,550
Less: Fine Paid	2,000
Net Revenue	10,550

Problem 18. *The following cost data pertaining to the year 2009 has been collected from the books of ABC Power Company limited. Prepare a cost sheet showing the cost of generation of power per unit of kwts.*

Total units generated: 25,00,000 kwts

Details	Amount (₹)	Details	Amount (₹)
Operating labour	*57,750*	*Repairs and maintenance*	*73,500*
Plant supervision	*37,750*	*Administrative overheads*	*31,500*
Lubricants and supplies	*36,750*	*Capital cost*	*6,00,000*

Coal consumed per kwts is .680Kg. and cost of coal delivered to the Power station is ₹ 125 per metric ton. Depreciation rate chargeable is 5% and interest on capital is to be taken at 8%.

Solution :

Details			Total Cost Amount (₹)	Cost per kwts Amount (₹)
Fixed costs:				
Plant Supervision	37,750			
Administration overheads	31,500			
Depreciation (6,00,000 × 0.05)	30,000			
Interest (6,00,000 × 0.08)	48,000		1,47,250	
Total fixed cost				0.0589
Variable costs:				
Coal (0.680 × 25,00,000 × 125) / 1,000 =		2,12,500		
Operating labour		57,750		
Lubricant and supplies		36,750		
Repairs and maintenance		73,500	3,80,500	
Total fixed cost				0.1522
Total			5,27,750	0.2111

Problem 19. *From the following information relating to a hotel, calculate the room rent to be charged per day both during the season and the off-season months, so as to give a profit of 20% on cost excluding interest.*

- *Salaries of staff: ₹ 42,00,000 p.a.*
- *Wages of room Attendant ₹ 120 per day.*
- *There is one room attendant for each room. He is paid wages only when the room is occupied.*
- *Lighting , heating and power:*
  - *(a) The normal lighting expenses for a room for the whole month is ₹ 800, when occupied.*
  - *(b) Power is used only in winter and the charges are ₹ 350 per month for a room, when occupied.*
- *Repair to Buildings: ₹ 5,40,000 p.a.*
- *Linen, etc. ₹ 2,85,000 p.a.*
- *Sundries ₹ 2,00,000 p.a.*
- *Interior decoration and furnishings ₹ 1,60,000 p.a.*
- *Depreciation @ 5% on investment in buildings costing ₹ 120,00,000.*
- *Depreciation @ 15% on Equipments.*
- *Interest @ 6% on investment in buildings and equipments costing ₹ 150,00,000.*
- *There are 125rooms in the hotel. 80% of the rooms are generally occupied in summer. A month may be assumed to be of 30 days, and 40% in winter. The period of summer and winter may be considered to be six months in each case. During off-season months, half of the full-room rent is to be charged.*

Solution : Working Notes:

1. Room Days:
   Summer: 125 rooms × 6 months × 30 days × 0.8 = 18,000
   Winter: 125 rooms × 6 months × 30 days × 0.4 = 9,000
   Total effective Room Days: 27,000
2. Full room Rent Days:
   Room-days on full rent during season: 18,000 × 1= 18,000
   Room-days on half rent during off-season: 9,000 × 0.5= 4,500
   Equivalent Full room rent days: 18,000 + 4,500 = 22,500
3. Room Attendant's wages:
   Summer: ₹ 120 × 125 rooms × 6 months × 30 days × 0.8
   = ₹ 21,60,000
   Winter: ₹ 120 × 125 rooms × 6 months × 30 days × 0.4
   = ₹ 10,80,000
   Total Wages of the room attendants: ₹ 32,40,000

4. lighting, heating and Power:
   (i) lighting and heating:
   Summer: ₹800 × 125 rooms × 6 months × 0.8 = ₹ 4,80,000
   Winter: ₹800 × 125 rooms × 6 months × 0.4 = ₹ 2,40,000
   Total Wages of the room attendants: ₹ 7,20,000
   (ii) Power:
   Winter: ₹ 350 × 125 rooms × 6 months × 0.4 = ₹ 1,05,000
   Total lighting, heating and Power: 7,20,000 + 1,05,000
   = ₹ 8,25,000

Operating cost statement of a Hotel
(Equivalent Full room rent days: 22,500)

Details (Annual Total cost)		Amount (₹)
Staff Salaries		42,00,000
Room Attendants' Wages		32,40,000
Lighting, heating and Power		8,25,000
Repairs to Building		5,40,000
Linen, etc.		2,85,000
Sundries		2,00,000
Interior decoration and furnishings		1,60,000
Depreciation:		
Building @ 5% (120,00,000 × 0.05)	6,00,000	
Equipments @ 11% (30,00,000 × 0.15)	4,50,000	
Interest @ 6% (150,00,000 × 0.06)	9,00,000	19,50,000
Total cost		114,00,000
Profit @ 20% on cost excluding Interest i.e. {(114,00,000 - 9,00,000) × 0.2}		21,00,000
Total revenue		135,00,000

Full Room Rent per day = Total revenue/ Total room days
= 135,00,000/ 22,500 => ₹ 600.

Half Room Rent per day during off-season: ₹ 300 (i.e. 600 × 0.5)

Verification:

Season days' rent: 18,000 × 600 = ₹ 108,00,000
Off-season days' rent: 9,000 × 300 = ₹ 27,00,000
Total = ₹ 135,00,000.

Problem 20. *SPA limited plans to start a lodging house at a tourist centre with a capacity of 40 single occupancy rooms. Cost per day per room has been estimated as under:*

Details	*Amount (₹)*
When Occupied:	
Dusting, sweeping and cleaning	*10*
Electricity and utilities	*25*
Linen and laundry	*55*
When Unoccupied:	*10*

Over and above these costs, following expenses represent the estimate of fixed charges p.a. (i.e. 365 days):

Staff Salaries etc. ₹ *9,00,000*

Administrative Expenses (Excluding salaries) ₹ *2,69,000*

Rates, taxes, Insurance, Maintenance and depreciation ₹ *1,74,200*

***Note:** 100% occupancy means all the 40 rooms fetch revenue for all the 365 days.*

You are required to find the followings assuming the plan period is one year:

(a) Tariff per day per room in order to reach break-even at an occupancy level of 60%.

(b) Profit, if the occupancy is (i) 75% ; and (b) 85%.

(c) Profit, if the tariff per day is reduced by 10% from the answer in (a) above and the occupancy level is 100%.

Solution : (Point-wise)

Point No. (a):

Variable cost per day per room when occupied: 10 + 25 + 55 => ₹ 90

Variable cost at 60% Occupancy Level:

40 rooms × (.6 × 365) × ₹ 90 7,88,400

Add: variable cost for the balance 40% when unoccupied:

40 rooms × (.4 × 365) × ₹ 10 58,400

Total Variable cost in a year at 60% occupancy 8,46,800

Add: fixed charges per year 13,43,200

Total cost in a year 21,90,000

Break-even tariff = Total cost in a year/ Occupied room days at 60% level

Occupied room days at 60% level = 40 × 0.6 × 365 = 8,760

= 21,90,000 / 8,760 => ₹ 250 per day per room

Point No. (b):

(i) At 75% Level of occupancy:

Details	Amount (₹)
Revenue: (40 rooms × 0.75 × 365 days × 250)	27,37,500
Less:	
Variable cost when occupied (40 × 0.75 × 365 × 90)	9,85,500
Variable cost for the balance 25% (40 × 0.25 × 365 × 10)	36,500
	10,22,000
Contribution	17,15,500
Less: Fixed costs	13,43,200
Profit	3,72,300

(ii) At 85% Level of occupancy:

Details	Amount (₹)
Revenue: (40 rooms × 0.85 × 365 days × 250)	31,02,500
Less:	
Variable cost when occupied (40 × 0.85 × 365 × 90)	11,16,900
Variable cost for the balance 15% (40 × 0.15 × 365 × 10)	21,900
	11,38,800
Contribution	19,63,700
Less: Fixed costs	13,43,200
Profit	6,20,500

Point No. (c):

At 100% Level of occupancy provided tariff is reduced by 10% i.e. new tariff would be ₹ 225.

Details	Amount (₹)
Revenue: (40 rooms × 1 × 365 days × 225)	32,85,000
Less: Variable cost when occupied (40 × 1 × 365 × 90)	13,14,000
Contribution	19,71,000
Less: Fixed costs	13,43,200
Profit	6,27,800

Inference: Profit is highest if 10% reduction in tariff results in 100% occupancy.

OBJECTIVE TYPE EXERCISES

I. Fill in the blank spaces with suitable word/s :

1. The method of costing used in undertakings like electricity, gas supply, cinema house, power house etc is known as ....
2. In transport company, ... book is maintained for each vehicle to record details of trips during a specified period.
3. In cinema halls, composite cost unit is ....
4. In a Nursing Home, composite cost unit is ....
5. In those industries where operating costing is used, relatively .... working capital is required.
6. In operating cost sheet, costs are classified into .... and ....
7. In transport costing, two examples of fixed costs are .... and ....
8. Service costing is applied in the organizations which are engaged in the production or distribution of ....
9. Under service costing normally .... Unit of cost is applied.
10. In service costing, fixed charges are also known as ....
11. Service costing is also known as ....
12. If a Lorry carries 5 tons of goods for 16 kms, 3 tons of goods for 10 kms and 2 tons of goods for 5 kms, the absolute ton-kms will be...........

Answers :

1. Operating costing	**2.** daily Log
3. a seat per show	**4.** per patient per day or per bed day
5. small	**6.** fixed, variable or running cost
7. insurance, Licence fee	**8.** services
9. Composite	**10.** standing charges
11. Operating costing	**12.** ton-kms :120

II. Indicate whether the following statements are True or False :

1. An example of a composite cost unit in transport costing is 'a passenger-kilometer' or 'Tonne-Kilometer'.
2. In those industries where service costing is used, relatively large working capital is required.
3. The method of costing used in undertakings like electricity, gas supply, cinema house etc. is known as operating or service costing.
4. Operating costing can be used in internal transport department of a factory.
5. In transport companies Daily Log sheet is maintained for each vehicle to record details of trips made by vehicles during a specified period.
6. Operating costing is part of specific order costing.
7. Operating costing deals with costing of services.

8. Operating costing is a form of process costing.
9. Cost of each operation in manufacture of a product is ascertained under Operating costing.
10. Generally fixed cost constitutes a large part of total cost under Operating costing.
11. Cost unit involved in Operating costing is generally composite.
12. Absolute ton-kms and commercial ton-kms are same.
13. In case of a bus hired for a procession, the cost unit is generally simple.
14. Cost of normal idle running of a taxi is charged to passengers by including it in cost per kilometer.
15. Operating cost sheet is always prepared with reference to actual capacity used.
16. Operating costing is also used for evaluating alternatives.
17. Operating costing can be used both for services produced for internal use and those for sale.
18. A 50-seater bus has a normal occupancy of 80%. On a particular trip it had only 50% occupancy. Cost per passenger-km is to be calculated on the basis of 50% occupancy.
19. A truck operates on a route it generally gets freight only on one way running. Total cost of two ways running is to be charged to one way normal ton-kms.
20. Log sheet is prepared for each vehicle.
21. In a passenger transport company, if buses run full capacity, the cost per passenger will be higher than that if buses do not run full capacity.
22. There is no difference between service costing and output costing.
23. In Transport Company, salaries to drivres are a fixed charge.
24. Service costing is applied in the organizations which are engaged in the production of goods.
25. Fare in case of a taxi is generally based on cost per passenger-km.

Answers :

1. True	**2.** False	**3.** True	**4.** True
5. True	**6.** False	**7.** True	**8.** False
9. False	**10.** True	**11.** True	**12.** False
13. True	**14.** True	**15.** False	**16.** True
17. True	**18.** False	**19.** True	**20.** True
21. False	**22.** False	**23.** True	**24.** False
25. False			

THEORETICAL EXERCISES

1. What is operating costing? To what industries is this method of costing applied?
2. State the salient features of service costing.
3. Write short note on "operating costing".

4. What is Power House Costing? Give a proforma Cost sheet under this method.
5. What is Hotel costing? Give its proforma Cost sheet.
6. Distinguish between:
   (i) Absolute and Commercial ton-miles;
   (ii) Actual and effective tons-miles;
   (iii) Simple and Composite Cost unit;
   (iv) Operation costs and operating costs.
7. Explain in brief the following concepts:
   (i) Composite unit in operating costing; **[DU, B.Com (Hons.) 2001]**
   (ii) Normal idle time running of a taxi;
   (iii) Operating cost;
   (iv) Daily Log sheet'

NUMERICAL EXERCISES

1. From the following information calculate the total kilometers and total passenger kilometers:
   Number of buses: 6
   Days operated in the relevant month: 25
   Trips made by each bus: 4
   Distance of route (One side): 20 Kilometers
   Capacity of bus (Passenger): 50
   Normal Passenger travelling: 85% Capacity
   [Ans. Total kilometers: 24,000; Total passenger kilometers: 10, 20,000]
2. A truck starts with a load of 10 tonnes of goods from station R. It unloads 4 tonnes at station S and rest of the goods at station T. It reaches back directly to station R after getting reloaded with 8 tonnes of goods from station T. The distances between R to S, S to T and then from T to R are 60 Kms. and 80 kms. and 100 kms. respectively. Compute 'Absolute tonne-km.' and 'Commercial tonne-km.'
   [Ans. Absolute tonnes-Kms.: 1,880; Commercial tonnes-Kms.: 1,920]
3. The Road transport company which keeps a fleet of Lorries provides the following information:

Kilometers run for April 2008	50,000
Wages for April 2008	3,00,000
Petrol, oil etc. for April 2008	6,00,000
Original cost of Vehicles	15,00,000
Depreciation to be allowed @ 20% per annum on original cost	
Repairs for April 2008	30,000
Garage Rent etc. for April 2008	15,000
License, insurance etc. for the year	60,000

[Modified I.C. W.A., Inter]
[Ans. ₹ 19.50 per kilometer]

4. The truck starts with a load of 15 tonnes of goods from a place P. It unloads 9 tonnes at a place R and rest of the goods at place S. It reaches back directly to the place P after getting reloaded with 12 tonnes of goods at a place S. The distances between P to R, R to S and then from S to P are 50 km, 80 km and 100 km respectively. Compute absolute tonnes/km and commercial tonnes/km. **[Ans. 2,430; 2,530]**

5. 'Jea-Travels' owns a Deluxe Bus and operates a tourist service on daily basis. The bus starts from New-city to Relax-village and returns back to New-city the same day. Distance between New-city to Relax-village is 280 kms. This trip operates for 11 days in a month. The bus also plies for another 11 days between New-city and Madhopur and returns back to New-city the same day; distance between these two places is 250 Kms. The bus makes local sight-seeing trips for six days in a month, covering a total distance of 75 Kms per day. The following data are given:

Details	Amount (₹)
Cost of Bus	7,50,000
Depreciation	20%
Driver's Salary (per Month)	6, 000
Conductor's Salary (per Month)	5, 000
Part-time Administrative Personnel Salary	2, 000
Insurance (per Year)	24,000
Diesel Consumption 5 Kms per Litre @ ₹ 22 per Litre	
Token Tax (per Year)	12,000
Permit fee (per Quarter)	5,400
mLubricant Oil ₹ 260 for every 200 Kms	
Repairs and Maintenance (per Month)	15,000
Normal Capacity (Persons)	50

While plying to and fro Relax-village the bus occupies 92% of the capacity and 84% when it plies between New-city and Madhopur (both ways). In the city the bus runs full capacity. Passenger Tax is 20% of the net takings of the Travels' firm. Calculate the rate to be charged to Relax-village and Madhopur from New-city per passenger, if the profit required to be earned is 30% of net takings of the firm.

[Ans. Rate per Passenger-Km= 0.365. Charges per Passenger: New-city to Relax-village ₹ 102.20; New-city to Madhopur ₹ 91.25; and Local ₹ 27.38]

6. Anamika Transport Company has been given a route 25kms long to run a bus. The bus costs the company a sum of ₹4, 50,000. It has been insured at 3% p.a. and the annual tax will amount to ₹4, 360, garage rent is ₹1, 000 p.m., annual repairs will be ₹6, 000 and the bus is likely to last for 5 years. The driver's salary will be ₹3, 000 per month and the conductor's salary will be ₹ 2, 500 per month in addition to 10%of the takings as commission (to be shared by the driver and the conductor equally). Cost of stationery will be ₹5, 000 p.a. Manager cum Accountant's salary is ₹5, 000 p.m.

Petrol and oil will be ₹40 per 100 km. the bus will make 3 round trips carrying on an average 40 passengers on each trip. Assuming 20% profit on takings, calculate the bus fare to be charged from each passenger. This bus will run on an average 25 days in a month. **[Ans. 0.217paise per Passenger Km.]**

7. The Meghdoot Transport Company supplied the following details of a truck of 5 ton capacity:

Cost of truck	₹ 3,60,000
Estimated life	10 years
Diesel, oil, grease	₹ 32 per trip each way
Repairs and maintenance	₹ 3,900 per month
Cleaner's wages	₹ 3,000 per month
Insurance	₹ 12,600 per month
Tax	₹ 7,500 per month
Driver's wages	₹ 5,000 per month
General's supervision	₹ 27,600 per year

The truck carries goods to and from city covering a distance of 50 miles away. While going to the city, freight is available to the extent of full capacity and on return 30% of the capacity. Assuming that the truck runs on average 25 days a month, work out:

(1) Operating cost per ton – mile, and

(2) Rate per ton trip that the company should charge, if a profit of 40% on freightage is to be earned. **[Ans. (1) ₹ 2.10, (2) ₹ 210]**

8. A Transport Company maintains a fleet of Lorries for carrying goods from Delhi to Panipat, 100 kms off. Each Lorry, which operates 25 days on an average in a month starts every day from Delhi with a load of 4 tonnes and returns from Panipat with a load of 2 tonnes. Compute the total commercial tonne-kms and cost per commercial tonne-km when the total monthly charges for a lorry are ₹ 27,000. What rate per tonne should the company charge if it plans to earn a gross profit of 20% on the freightage?

[B.Com (Hons.) DU, 2000]

[Ans. ₹ 2.25 freight per tonne-km]

9. A City Municipality arranges for removal of its garbage by means of motor vehicle transport. The following vehicles are maintained:

No. of Vehicles	**Specification**
20	5 tonne Lorries
30	4 tonne Lorries
50	3 tonne Lorries
40	2 tonne Lorries

On an average each lorry makes six trips a day and in each trip covers an average distance of five kms. Each lorry carries garbage of 60% its capacity. On an annual average, 20% of Lorries are laid up for repairs. The conservancy work is carried out daily. Calculate tonne-kms utilised for the removal of garbage per month.

[Ans. 1, 94,400 tonne km]

[B.Com (Hons.) DU, 2007]

10. A City Municipality arranges for removal of its garbage by means of motor vehicle transport. The following vehicles are maintained:

No. of vehicles	Specification
20	5 tonne Lorries
30	4 tonne Lorries
60	3 tonne Lorries
50	2 tonne Lorries

On an average each lorry makes five trips a day and in each trip covers an average distance of eight kms. Each lorry carries garbage of 70% its capacity. On an annual average, 15% of Lorries are laid up for repairs. The conservancy work is carried out daily. Calculate tonne-kms utilised for the removal of garbage per month.

[Ans. 3,57,000 tonne- km]

11. A City Municipality arranges for removal of its garbage by means of motor vehicle transport. The following vehicles are maintained:

No. of Vehicles	Specification
20	5 tonne Lorries
30	4 tonne Lorries
50	3 tonne Lorries
40	2 tonne Lorries

On an average each lorry makes five trips a day and in each trip covers an average distance of six kms. Each lorry carries garbage of 50% its capacity. On an annual average, 10% of Lorries are laid up for repairs. The conservancy work is carried out daily. Calculate tonne-kms utilised for the removal of garbage per month.

[Ans. 1, 82,250 tonne km]

[B.Com (Hons.) DU, 2007 : Correspondance]

12. Globasl Transport Ltd, charges ₹ 90/tonne for its 6 tonnes lorry load from city ‘A’ to city ‘B’. the charges for the return journey are ₹ 84/tonne. No concession or reduction in these rates is made for any delivery of goods at the intermediate station ‘C’. In January 2005, the truck made 12 outward journeys for city ‘B’ with full load out of which 2 tonnes were unloaded twice in the way at city ‘C’. The truck carried a load of 8 tonnes in its return journey for 5 tonnes but once caught by the police and ₹ 1200 was paid as fine. For the remaining trips the truck carried full load out of which all the goods on load were unloaded once at city ‘C’. The distance from city ‘A’ to city ‘C’ and city ‘B’ are 140 km and 300 km respectively. Annual fixed costs and maintenance charges are ₹ 60,000 and ₹ 12,000 respectively. Running charges spent during January 2005 are ₹ 2,944. You are required to find out the cost per absolute tonne-km and the profit for January 2005.

[B.Com (Hons.) DU, 2006: Correspondance]

[Ans. 20 Paise; ₹ 3,224. Note: Fine imposed by police is assumed to be abnormal]

13. From the following information calculate the bus fare to be charged from each passenger for the journeys:

(1) Delhi to Agra;

(2) Delhi to Bhiwani;

(3) Delhi to Chandigarh.

(i) Distance: (Absolute)

Delhi to Agra	200 Km
Delhi to Bhiwani	120 Km
Delhi to Chandigarh	250 Km

(ii) Distance: (effective Passenger Km) 3,72,000

(iii) Total operating cost (Excluding Conductor's commission @ 15% and Passenger tax @ 5% of total takings) ₹ 1,48,800

(iv) Desired Profit: 30% on total takings. **[B.Com (Hons.) DU, 2002]**

[Ans. Fare per passenger Km. 80 Paise; Fare: Delhi to Agra ₹ 160; Delhi to Bhiwani ₹ 96; Delhi to Chandigarh ₹ 200]

14. A bus started from Delhi for Mussoorie with 50 passengers on board. 20 passengers got off at Dehradun and the bus proceeded with the remaining passengers. In the evening the same bus left Mussoorie with 50 passengers, 10 passengers got off at Dehradun and the bus resumed its journey with remaining g passengers for Delhi. The distance between Delhi and Dehradun is 280 km and between Dehradun to Mussoorie it is 20 km.

Compute the cost per passenger km, if the total cost of running the bus comes out to be ₹ 5,000. **[B.Com (Hons.) DU, 2003]**

[Ans. Fare per passenger Km. 19 Paise; Total Passenger kms: 26,800]

15. A transport company is running four buses between Delhi and Alwar, covering a distance of 100 kms. The seating capacity of each bus is 40 passengers. The following particulars are obtained from its books for the month of October, 2003:

Details	Amount (₹)
Wages of drivers, conductors	9,600
Salaries of office staff	3,000
Honorarium of Accountant	1,000
Diesel, oil etc.	16,000
Repairs and Maintenance	3,200
Road Tax and Insurance	6,400
Depreciation	10,400
Interest and Other Charges	8,000

Actual passengers carried were 75% of the seating capacity. All the buses ran for 30 days. Each bus made one round trip per day. Find out the fare the company should charge per passenger/km if it wants a profit of 20% on the takings.

[DU, B.Com (Hons.) 2004 (External)]

[Ans. Fare per passenger Km. 10 Paise; Total Passenger kms: 7, 20,000]

16. Mr. Singh started transport business with a fleet of 10 taxis. Expenses of operating the fleet are given below:

Details	Amount (₹)
Cost of each Taxi	3,80,000
Driver's Salary per taxi per month	4,000
Salaries of office and Garage staff per month	38,000
Rent of Garage per month	12,000
Insurance , Tax and sundry expenses per taxi p.a.	55,200

The life of a taxi is 3, 00,000 kms at the end of which it is sold at ₹ 20,000. A taxi is expected to run on an average 4,000 kms per month. Petrol consumption is 12 kms per litre of petrol costing ₹ 51 per litre. You are required to:

(i) Calculate the cost of running a taxi per km by preparing a statement of operating cost; and

(ii) Find out the profit Mr. Singh may expect to earn during the first month of operations if the hire charges is ₹ 16 per km. assume that during the month each taxi runs on an average 4,000 kms of which 20% it runs empty.

[DU, B.Com (Hons.) 2004 (Modifiedl)]

[Ans. Cost per Passenger km. ₹ 8.85; Profit ₹ 1, 58,000]

17. A truck starts with a load of 10 tonnes of goods from station P. It unloads 4 tonnes at station Q and rest of the goods at station R. It reaches back directly to station P after getting reloaded with 8 tonnes of goods at station R. The distance between P to Q, Q to R and then from R to P are 40 kms, 60kms and 80 kms respectively. Compute absolute tonne-km. **[Ans. Total absolute tonne-kms 1,400]**

[DU, B.Com (Hons.) 1998]

18. A company is considering three alternative proposals for conveyance facilities for its sales personnel who have to do considerable travelling, approximately 20,000 kilometers every year.

The proposals are as follows:

(i) Purchase and maintain its own fleet of cars: The average cost of a car is ₹ 1, 00, 000.

(ii) Allow the executive use his own car and reimburse expenses at the rate of ₹ 1.60 per kilometer and also bear insurance costs.

Hire cars from an agency at ₹ 20,000 per year per car. The company will have to bear costs of petrol, taxes and tyres.

The following further details are available:

Petrol Re. 0.60 per kilometer

Repairs and maintenance Re. 0.20 per kilometer

Tyre Re. 0.12 per kilometer

Insurance ₹ 1,200 per car per annum

Taxes ₹ 800 per car per annum

Life of the Car: 5 years with annual mileage of 20,000 kilometers

Resale value: ₹ 20,000 at the end of the fifth year.

You are required to work out the relative costs of the three proposals and rank them.

[B.Com (Hons.) DU, 2001]

[Ans. Proposal I: ₹ 1.82; Proposal II: ₹ 1.66; Proposal III: ₹ 1.76]

19. The following cost data pertaining to the year 2000 has been collected from the books of a Thermal Power Station. Prepare a cost sheet showing the cost of generation of power per unit of kwh.

Total units generated: 10,00,000 kwh.

Details	Amount (₹)	Details	Amount (₹)
Operating labour	65,000	Repairs and maintenance	55,000
Plant supervision	40,000	Administrative overheads	25,000
Lubricants and supplies	50,000	Capital cost	2,00,000

Coal consumed per kwh. for the year is 2.5 kg @ Es. 0.05 per kg. Charge depreciation depreciation @ 10% on capital cost. **[B.Com. Tirupati (Adapted)]**

[Ans. ₹ 0.38 per kwh]

20. From the following data, find out, in an appropriate cost sheet from, the generating cost of electricity per unit in an Iron and Steel works during the month of April 2009.

1. Fuel: Coal at the beginning of the month 500 tons
   Supply during the month 1,100 tons
   Balance at the end of the month 400 tons
   Annual contract for supply of coal F.O. R. colliery is at ₹ 250 per ton. Add 10% to cover freight and handling charges.
2. Oil 10 tons @ ₹ 2,500 per ton.
3. Water: 50,000 gallons, pumping charges @ ₹ 2.50 per 100 gallons.
4. Depreciation of Steam Boiler: Capital Value ₹ 3,00,000 and the rate of depreciation 12% p.a.
5. Salaries and Wages of the Boiler-house: 10 men @ ₹ 5,000 p.m., each, 40Coolies @ ₹ 2,000 p.m., each
6. Recovery on account of sale of ash: 100 tons @ ₹ 25 per ton.
7. Salaries and Wages of the Generating station: 50 men @ ₹ 5,000 p.m., each, 20Coolies @ ₹ 2,000 p.m., each
8. Repairs and maintenance of the generating equipment ₹ 13,000.
9. Depreciation of Generating Plant: Capital Value ₹ 15,00,000 and the rate of depreciation 12.5% p.a.
10. Share of Administration charges ₹ 27,625.
11. Number of units generated: 2,50,000.
12. Loss in the process: 5,000 units generated.

[Ans. ₹ 3.40 per unit (8,33,000/2,45,000)]

❑❑❑

18 Process Costing

Learning Objectives

It attempts to explain the process of production of standardized goods. In this chapter you will learn :

1. Meaning, nature and objectives of process costing.
2. Industries where it is usually applied.
3. Difference between :
   (a) Unit costing and process costing,
   (b) Job costing and process costing
4. Advantages and limitations of process costing.
5. Procedure of process costing.
6. Elements of production cost.
7. Treatment of normal loss, abnormal loss/gain.
8. Treatment of empties.
9. Inter-process profits.
10. Work-in-progress and effective production.

INTRODUCTION

Process costing refers to costing of one or more processes involved in converting a raw material into finished product. The word 'Process' denotes process or operation in this chapter. Process costing is suitably employed where goods are made for stock and production is continuous; or goods although made to customer's order are, owing to the continuous nature of production, lost sight of in the volume of production. It can be used in all those industries where job, batch, contract or unit or operating costing system cannot be applied. Thus process-costing method is applied in the following industries:

(1) Chemicals (Pharmaceuticals, paints, ink, varnishing, soap etc.)

(2) Steel/ Rubber

(3) Distilleries

(4) Dairy food processing, and Confectioneries

(5) Canneries

(6) Paper

(7) Textiles weaving, spinning etc

(8) Oil Refineries.

This method is applied where it is not possible to trace the items of prime cost to a particular order, as its identity is lost in the volume of continuous production. In oil refining factory, one cannot trace the prime cost of a specific order for say, 250 litres of refined coconut oil where thousands of litres of oil are being produced at the same time. So the procedure would be to divide the cost of production during a certain period by the total number of units produced during that certain period in order to determine the cost per litre of coconut oil.

Process costing method is used to ascertain the cost of the product at each process, operation of a manufacturing process, which involves a sequence of continuous or repetitive operations and processes. Plant and Machinery is so arranged that production of a standard product continues for a long period without any hindrance/ interruption. Continuous operation/process has one or more of the following features:

(i) The product is produced in single process/operations.

(ii) If manufacture of saleable products involves more than one process/operation, output of one process/operation becomes the input for the next process/operation.

(iii) During the continuity of the process/operation, products or materials are not distinguishable from one another. If more than one product is produced in a single process/operation, each can be identified separately, only when they emerge as finished products.

Because of the above features following points arise:

(a) Records for cost per unit of finished product cannot be built up, as there is an indistinguishable homogeneous mass during the production process.

(b) At the end of each accounting period there is work-in-progress. The process cost for a period is apportioned between completed outputs and work-in-progress at the end of the accounting period.

(c) Loss of materials due to scrapping, chemical reactions and evaporations is unavoidable and accounting for such losses assumes greater significance in the process costing method.

(d) The output of one operation/process is transferred to the next process/operation either at cost or at a predetermined transfer price.

(e) More than one product may emerge at the end of different process/operation depending upon the sale value of the product, which is termed as joint products or by-products.

Job Order and Process-costing Methods: A Comparison

(1) Each job can be identified from the beginning to the end of the manufacturing process. The job physically moves from one workstation to another. However, the process of manufacturing is continuous and a particular unit cannot be identified at any point in the manufacturing process. Usually, more than one product results from a process.

(2) Costs are accumulated for each job. Job cost is computed only when the job is complete. In process costing method costs are accumulated for each process. Cost per unit is determined by averaging the process cost. Costs are compiled on time basis.

(3) In general, there is no transfer from one job to another. If necessary, only surplus work or excess production is transferred. But output of one process is transferred to the next process as raw materials until the product is finally manufactured.

(4) There may or may not be any job-in progress at the end of an accounting period but in process costing there is usually work-in-progress at the conclusion of an accounting period.

(5) As each job is unique and peculiar in nature, accounting for and control of costs require more intensive managerial attention and involve more paper work. As all output units are uniform and production process is continuous, accounting for and control of costs is relatively comfortable.

Elements of Production Cost

Materials: Raw materials are introduced in the very first process and after processing they are transferred to the next process or to the warehouse. Conversion of raw materials into finished products involves only one process or more than one process. The preceding process costs are termed as transferred-in-costs. Additional materials put in the subsequent/second process/does not add to the quantity of basic inputs introduced in the initial process/process no. one Raw materials and sundry supplies needed for each process are requisitioned from the stores in the routine manner. Material requisitions are used for issuing materials even from departmental stock. In order to control waste and spoilage, actual consumption is compared with the normal consumption.

Labour: In industries for which process-costing method is quite suitable, the cost of direct labour constitutes a small part of the total cost of production because such industries are capital intensive. With increasing automation the direct labour cost decreases while the manufacturing overhead increases. In such a situation workers are kept to keep a close watch on the process /operation; they cannot directly influence the productivity. Therefore, the time rates are applied to compute their remuneration. If a worker is uninterruptedly engaged in one process, the time spent by him is analysed and his wages are directly charged to that process only. However, if a worker looks after more than one process/operation, the time spent by him is apportioned on the basis of time sheet.

Direct Expenses and Overheads: Expenses attributable to a particular process should be treated as a direct charge to that process. The Manufacturing overhead is allocated to different processes on some equitable basis. The proportionate Administrative overheads are also allocated to each process on reasonable criterion.

Illustration 18.1 : *A product passes through three unique processes P-1, P-2, and P-3 before it is complete. During a certain week ended on June 30, 2004 it produced 420 units of output. The following information is available from the records of the company:*

Details	*Process P-I (₹)*	*Process P-II (₹)*	*Process P-III (₹)*
Material	*37,800*	*18,900*	*12,600*
Wages	*31,500*	*25,200*	*31,500*
Direct Expenses	*6,300*	*1,260*	*6,300*

Production overheads for the period amounted to ₹ 17,640. This is to be apportioned to various processes on the basis of wages. There is no work-in-progress either at the beginning or at the end of the week.

Solution :

Dr **Process: P-1 A/c** Cr

Details	Units	Amount (₹)	Details	Units	Amount (₹)
To Material (@ ₹ 90)	420	37,800	By Process: P-2 A/c (@ ₹ 195)	420	81,900
To wages (@ ₹ 75)		31,500			
To Direct Expenses (@ ₹ 15)		6,300			

To Production Overheads (@ ₹ 15)		6,300			
Total	420	81,900	Total	420	81,900

Dr **Process: P-2 A/c** Cr

Details	Units	Amount (₹)	Details	Units	Amount (₹)
To Process: P-1 A/c (@ ₹ 195)	420	81,900	By Process: P-3 A/c Account (@315)	420	1,32,300
To Material (@ ₹ 45)		18,900			
To wages (@ ₹ 60)		25,200			
To Direct Expenses (@ ₹ 3)		1,260			
To Production Overheads (@ ₹ 12)		5,040			
Total	420	1,32,300	Total	420	1,32,300

Dr **Process: P-3 A/c** Cr

Details	Units	Amount (₹)	Details	Units	Amount (₹)
To Process: P-2 A/c (@315)	420	1,32,300	By Finished Stock A/c (@450)	420	1,89,000
To Material (@30)		12,600			
To wages (@75)		31,500			
To Direct Expenses (@15)		6,300			
To Production Overheads (@15)		6,300			
Total	420	1,89,000	Total	420	1,89,000

Note: Production overheads have been apportioned in the ratio of wages i.e. 31,500:25,200: 31,500 or in the ratio of 5:4:5 respectively.

Accounting of Normal loss, Abnormal loss, and Abnormal Gain

The basic principle of cost accounting is to value completed units at normal cost and exclude abnormal costs from the product cost. In process accounting the total cost is divided by normal output i.e. the cost of normal loss is absorbed by Good Units. The Normal Product Cost so determined is applied to evaluate

Abnormal Loss or Abnormal Gain or Abnormal Effectives. Normal output is the difference between Process input Units and Normal loss Units.

Normal Output =Process Input Units – Normal Loss in Units

In most of the manufacturing processes some loss of material is unavoidable. Consequently, usually, expected yield is less than the input quantity. Such loss inherent in the productive process is normal loss and must be distributed over normal output. The loss may be in the form of (a) weight loss or scrap which may be physically available but may not have realizable value, or (b) the scrap may have realizable value. The normal loss gets reduced by the amount of realizable value of the scrap.

It may be noted that from the point of sale of scrap, there is no difference between normal scrap and abnormal scrap, as scrap is just scrap only. The distinction is made for the purpose of ascertaining cost per unit of normal output and the value of abnormal loss is to be transferred to the Costing Profit and Loss Account.

▣ **Example 1.** *In a workshop monthly input of material @ ₹ 60 per Kg. is 12,500 Kgs Other expenses in the workshop amount to ₹ 4,80,000. Normal loss is 4% of input and it realizes nothing. Actual output is equal to normal Output i.e. 12,000 units. Prepare Process account.*

Solution : Working Notes:

Cost per unit

$$= \frac{\text{(All Normal process costs – Realizable value of Normal Scrap)}}{\text{(Process Input Units – Normal Loss in Units = Normal Output)}}$$

$$= \frac{[(7,50,000 + 4,80,000) – \text{NIL}]}{(12,500 – 500 = 12,000)}$$

= 12,30,000/12,000 => ₹ 102.50

Process Account

Dr Cr

Details	Unit	Amount (₹)	Details	Unit	Amount (₹)
To Input of Material (@ ₹60)	12,500	7,50,000	By Normal Loss A/c	500	———
To Other expenses		4,80,000	By Output transferred to Next process (@ ₹102.50)	12000	12,30,000
	12,500	12,30,000		12,500	12,30,000

▣ **Example 2.** *In a workshop monthly input of material @ ₹ 60 per Kg. is 12,500 Kgs. Other expenses in the workshop amount to ₹ 4, 86,250. Normal* *loss is 4% of input and it realizes @ ₹ 12.50 per unit. Actual output is equal to normal Output i.e. 12,000 units. Prepare Process account and Normal Loss account.*

Solution : Working Notes:

Cost per unit

$$= \frac{\text{(All Normal process costs – Realizable value of Normal Scrap)}}{\text{(Process Input Units – Normal Loss in Units)}}$$

$$= \frac{[(7,50,000 + 4,86,250) - 6250]}{(12,500 - 500 = 12,000)}$$

= 12,30,000/12,000 => ₹ 102.50

Process Account

Dr Cr

Details	Unit	Amount (₹)	Details	Unit	Amount (₹)
To Input of Material (@ ₹ 60)	12,500	7,50,000	By Normal Loss A/c (@ ₹ 12.50)	500	6,250
To Other expenses		4,86,250	By Output transferred to Next process (@ ₹ 102.50)	12,000	12,30,000
	12,500	12,36,250		12,500	12,36,250

Normal Loss Account

Dr Cr

Details	Unit	Amount (₹)	Details	Unit	Amount (₹)
To Process A/c (@ ₹ 12.50)	500	6,250	By Cash/ Debtors A/c	500	6,250
	500	6,250		500	6,250

▣ **Example 3.** *Same as example 2 except that due to an accident in the workshop the actual output is found to be 11,000 units. Prepare Process account, Normal Loss account and Abnormal Loss account.*

Solution : Working Notes:

Cost per unit

$$= \frac{\text{(All Normal process costs – Realizable value of Normal Scrap)}}{\text{(Process Input Units – Normal Loss in Units)}}$$

$$= \frac{[(7,50,000 + 4,86,250) - 6,250]}{(12,500 - 500 = 12,000)}$$

= 12,30,000/12,000 => ₹ 102.50

Process Account

Dr Cr

Details	Unit	Amount (₹)	Details	Unit	Amount (₹)
To Input of Material (@ ₹ 60)	12,500	7,50,000	By Normal Loss A/c (@ ₹ 12.50)	500	6,250
To Other expenses		4,86,250	By Abnormal Loss A/c (@ ₹ 102.50)	1,000	1,02,500
			By Output transferred to Next process (@ ₹ 102.50)	11,000	12,30,000
	12,500	12,36,250		12,500	12,36,250

Normal Loss Account

Dr Cr

Details	Unit	Amount (₹)	Details	Unit	Amount (₹)
To Process A/c (@ ₹ 12.50)	500	6,250	By Cash/ Debtors A/c	500	6,250
	500	6,250		500	6,250

Abnormal Loss Account

Dr Cr

Details	Unit	Amount (₹)	Details	Unit	Amount (₹)
To Process A/c (@ ₹ 102.50)	1,000	1,02,500	By Cash/ Debtors A/c (@ ₹ 12.50)	1,000	12,500
			Costing Profit and Loss A/c		90,000
	1,000	1,02,500		1,000	1,02,500

▣ **Example 4.** *Same as example 2 except that the actual output is found to be 12,300 units. Prepare Process account, Normal Loss account and Abnormal Gain/Effectiveness account.*

Solution : Working Notes:

Cost per unit

$$= \frac{\text{(All Normal process costs – Realizable value of Normal Scrap)}}{\text{(Process Input Units – Normal Loss in Units)}}$$

$$= \frac{[(7,50,000 + 4,86,250) - 6,250]}{(12,500 - 500 = 12,000)}$$

= 12,30,000 ÷ 12,000 => ₹ 102.50

Process Account

Dr Cr

Details	Unit	Amount (₹)	Details	Unit	Amount (₹)
To Input of Material (@ ₹ 60)	12,500	7,50,000	By Normal Loss A/c (@ ₹12.50)	500	6,250
To Other expenses		4,86,250	By Output transferred to Next process (@ ₹ 102.50)	12,300	12,60,750
To Abnormal Gain A/c (@ ₹ 102.50)	300	30,750			
	12,800	12,67,000		12,800	12,67,000

Normal Loss Account

Dr Cr

Details	Unit	Amount (₹)	Details	Unit	Amount (₹)
To Process A/c (@ ₹ 12.50)	500	6,250	By Cash/ Debtors A/c (@ ₹ 12.50)	200	2,500
			By Abnormal Gain A/c (@ ₹ 12.50)	300	3,750
	500	6,250		500	6,250

Abnormal Gain Account

Dr Cr

Details	Unit	Amount (₹)	Details	Unit	Amount (₹)
To Normal Loss A/c (@ ₹ 12.50)	300	3,750	By Process A/c (@ ₹ 102.50)	300	30,750
To Costing Profit and Loss A/c		27,000			
	300	30,750		300	30,750

Empties

In most of the cases materials are packed in gunny bags, tins, cartons, etc when bought. On getting emptied, these packs are sold. Such sale of empties is a normal feature and their expected sale proceeds are a normal deduction in cost of the process. Thus, normally realizable value of empties should be deducted from the total cost while computing cost per unit, the illustration of which is given below.

Illustration 18.2 : *In a workshop monthly input of material @ ₹ 60 per Kg. is 12,500 Kgs packed in gunny bags of 100 kg each. Other expenses inclusive of additional cost of ₹ 37,000 due to an accident in the workshop amount to ₹ 5,35,000. Normal loss is 4% of input and it realizes @ ₹14 per unit and each bag is sold @ ₹ 40. Actual output is 12,300 units of which 3,000 units were sold @ ₹ 125 per Kg of output. Prepare Process account, Normal Loss account, Abnormal Gain account, Empties account and the Statement of Profit.*

Solution : Working Notes:

Cost per unit

= {(All Normal process costs – Realizable value of Normal Scrap and Normal empties)} ÷ {(Process Input Units – Normal Loss in Units)}

= {(7,50,000 + (5,35,000 – 37,000)) – [(7,000 + 5,000)} ÷ (12,500 – 500)

= 12,36,000 ÷ 12,000 => ₹ 103.

Process Account

Dr Cr

Details	Unit	Amount (₹)	Details	Unit	Amount (₹)
To Input of Material (@ ₹ 60)	12,500	7,50,000	By Costing Profit and Loss A/c (Loss due to an accident)		37,000
To Other expenses		5,35,000	By Normal Loss A/c (@ ₹ 14)	500	7,000
To Costing Profit and Loss A/c (Gain on Sale of Output of this Process @ ₹22)	3,000	66,000	By Empties A/c (125bags @ ₹ 40 per bag)		5,000
To Abnormal Gain A/c (@ ₹ 103)	300	30,900	By Bank (Sale) @ ₹ 125 per unit of output	3,000	3,75,000
			By Output transferred to Next process (@ ₹ 103)	9,300	9,57,900
	12,800	13,81,900		12,800	13,81,900

Normal Loss Account

Dr Cr

Details	Unit	Amount (₹)	Details	Unit	Amount (₹)
To Process A/c (@ ₹ 14)	500	7,000	By Cash/ Debtors A/c (@ ₹14)	200	2,800
			By Abnormal Gain A/c (@ ₹ 14)	300	4,200
	500	7,000		500	7,000

Abnormal Gain Account

Dr Cr

Details	Unit	Amount (₹)	Details	Unit	Amount (₹)
To Normal Loss A/c (@ ₹ 14)	300	4,200	By Process A/c (@ ₹ 103)	300	30,900
To Costing Profit and Loss A/c		26,700			
	300	30,900		300	30,900

Empties Account

Dr Cr

Details	Unit	Amount (₹)	Details	Unit	Amount (₹)
To Process A/c (@ ₹ 40)	125	5,000	By Cash/ Debtors A/c (@ ₹40)	125	5,000
	125	5,000		125	5,000

Statement of Profit:

Gain on sale of Process output (3,000 × 22)		66,000
Abnormal Gain		26,700
		92,700
Less: Abnormal Loss due to Accident	37,000	
		(37,200)
Net Gain		55,500

Illustration 18.3 : *The Petra Refining Works manufacture products, which pass through various processes of manufacture. The following information is available for the preceding accounting period:-*

1. *Input Material 1,250 Liters @ 61.92 per Liter*
2. *Direct Labour = ₹ 51,000*

3. Production Overhead Rate of Recovery is @ 48% of Direct Labour.

4. Completed Units transferred to Process No.2:

Case (i) 1,200 units, Case (ii) 1,185 units, and Case (iii) 1,220 units.

5. There was no work-in-process either at the beginning or at the end

6. Normal Loss is @ 4% of the Input.

Prepare Process No 1 Account under the assumption that the scrap has value: (a) NIL; (b) ₹ 24 per Liter.

Solution to Illustration : 3 (a) (i)

(Assumption that the scrap has value: NIL)

Dr **Process No.1 Account** Cr

Details	Units	Amount (₹)	Details	Units	Amount (₹)
To Direct Materials @ ₹ 61.92	1,250	77,400	By Normal Loss A/c	50	——
To Direct Wages		51,000	By Process: No.2 A/c @ ₹ 127.40	1,200	1,52,880
To Production Overheads		24,480			
Total	1,250	1,52,880	Total	1,250	1,52,880

Solution to Illustration : 3 (a) (ii)

(Assumption that the scrap has value: NIL)

Dr **Process No.1 Account** Cr

Details	Units	Amount (₹)	Details	Units	Amount (₹)
To Direct Materials @ ₹ 61.92	1,250	77,400	By Normal Loss A/c	50	——
To Direct Wages		51,000	By Abnormal Loss A/c @ ₹ 127.40	15	1,911
To Production Overheads		24,480	By Process: No.2 A/c @ ₹ 127.40	1,185	1,50,969
Total	1,250	1,52,880	Total	1,250	1,52,880

Dr **Abnormal Loss Account** Cr

Details	Units	Amount (₹)	Details	Units	Amount (₹)
To Process: No.2 A/c	15	1,911	By Costing Profit & Loss A/c @ ₹ 127.40	15	1,911
Total	15	1,911	Total	15	1,911

Solution to Illustration : 3 (a) (iii)

(Assumption that the scrap has value: NIL)

Dr **Process No.1 Account** Cr

Details	Units	Amount (₹)	Details	Units	Amount (₹)
To Direct Materials @ ₹ 61.92	1,250	77,400	By Normal Loss A/c	50	—
To Direct Wages		51,000	By Process: No.2 A/c @ ₹ 127.40	1,220	1,55,428
To Production Overheads		24,480			
To Costing Profit & Loss A/c @ ₹ 127.40	20	2,548			
Total	1,270	1,55,428	Total	1,270	1,55,428

Dr **Abnormal Gain Account** Cr

Details	Units	Amount (₹)	Details	Units	Amount (₹)
Normal Loss A/c	20	—	By Costing Profit & Loss A/c @ ₹ 127.40	20	2,548
To Costing Profit & Loss A/c		2,548			
Total	20	2,548	Total	20	2,548

Solution to Illustration : 3 (b) (i)

(Assumption that the scrap has value: ₹ 24 per Liter)

Dr **Process No.1 Account** Cr

Details	Units	Amount (₹)	Details	Units	Amount (₹)
To Direct Materials @ ₹ 61.92	1,250	77,400	By Normal Loss A/c (@ ₹ 24)	50	1,200
To Direct Wages		51,000	By Process: No.2 A/c @ ₹ 126.40	1,200	1,51,680
To Production Overheads		24,480			
Total	1,250	1,52,880	Total	1,250	1,52,880

Dr **Normal Loss Account** Cr

Details	Units	Amount (₹)	Details	Units	Amoun (₹)
To Process: No.1 A/c (@ ₹ 24)	50	1,200	By Bank/Drs. A/c (@ ₹ 24)	50	1,200
Total	50	1,200	Total	50	1,200

Solution to Illustration : 3 (b) (ii)

(Assumption that the scrap has value: ₹ 24 per Liter)

Dr **Process No.1 Account** Cr

Details	Units	Amount (₹)	Details	Units	Amount (₹)
To Direct Materials (@ ₹ 61.92)	1,250	77,400	By Normal Loss A/c (@ ₹ 24)	50	1,200
To Direct Wages		51,000	By Abnormal Loss A/c (@ ₹ 126.40)	15	1,896
To Production Overheads		24,480	By Process: No.2 A/c (@ ₹ 126.40)	1,185	1,49,784
Total	1,250	1,52,880	Total	1,250	1,52,880

Dr **Normal Loss Account** Cr

Details	Units	Amount (₹)	Details	Units	Amount (₹)
To Process: No.1 A/c (@ ₹ 24)	50	1,200	By Bank/Drs. A/c (@ ₹ 24)	50	1,200
Total	50	1,200	Total	50	1,200

Dr **Abnormal Loss Account** Cr

Details	Units	Amount (₹)	Details	Units	Amount (₹)
To Process: No.2 A/c (@ ₹ 126.40)	15	1,896	By Bank/Drs. A/c (@ ₹ 24)	15	360
			By Costing Profit & Loss A/c		1,536
Total	15	1,896	Total	15	1,896

Solution to Illustration : 3 (b) (iii)

(Assumption that the scrap has value: ₹ 24 per Liter)

Dr **Process No.1 Account** Cr

Details	Units	Amount (₹)	Details	Units	Amount (₹)
To Direct Materials @ ₹ 61.92	1,250	77,400	By Normal Loss A/c (@ ₹ 24)	50	1,200
To Direct Wages		51,000	By Process: No. 2 A/c (@ ₹ 126.40)	1,220	1,54,208
To Prod. Overheads		24,480			
To Costing Profit & Loss A/c	20	2,528			
Total	1,270	1,55,408	Total	1,270	1,55,408

Dr **Abnormal Gain Account** Cr

Details	Units	Amount (₹)	Details	Units	Amount (₹)
Normal Loss A/c (@ ₹ 24)	20	480	By Process A/c (@ ₹ 126.40)	20	2,528
To Costing Profit & Loss A/c		2,048			
Total	20	2,528	Total	20	2,528

Dr **Normal Loss Account** Cr

Details	Units	Amount (₹)	Details	Units	Amount (₹)
To Process: No.1 A/c (@ ₹ 24)	50	1,200	By Bank/Drs. A/c (@ ₹ 24)	30	720
			Abnormal gain A/c (@ ₹ 24)	20	480
Total	50	1,200	Total	50	1,200

Illustration 18.4 : *Three Processes are to be gone through before Product M is manufactured. The following information is available for determining the cost of the product M: -*

Details	*Total (₹)*	*Process-1 (₹)*	*Process-2 (₹)*	*Process-3 (₹)*
Direct Material	*14,680*	*6,960*	*4,920*	*2,800*
Direct Wages	*22,500*	*9,000*	*9,300*	*4,200*
Production Overhead	*13,500*			

400 units @ ₹ 12 per unit were introduced in Process-1. Production Overheads are recovered as a percentage of direct wages. The actual output and normal loss of the respective processes are:

Details	Output (Units)	Normal Loss (% of Input)	Value of Scrap (₹) per unit
Process-1	360	10	6
Process-2	272	20	15
Process-3	216	25	25

There is no stock or work-in-progress in any process. Prepare process and relevant accounts with workings.

Solution :

Dr **Process No. 1 Account** Cr

Details	Unit	Amoun (₹)	Details	Unit	Amoun (₹)
To Units Introduced @ ₹ 12	400	4,800	By Normal Loss A/c @ ₹ 6	40	240
To Direct Material		6,960	By Process No. 2 A/c @ ₹ 72	360	25,920
Direct Wages		9,000			
To Production Overhead (60% of Direct Wages		5,400			
Total	400	26,160	Total	400	26,160

Dr **Process No. 2 Account** Cr

Details	Unit	Amoun (₹)	Details	Unit	Amoun (₹)
To Process No. 1 A/c @ ₹ 72	360	25,920	By Normal Loss A/c @ ₹ 15	72	1,080
To Direct Material		4,920	By Abnormal Loss A/c (@ ₹ 155)	16	2,480
To Direct Wages		9,300	By Process No. 3 A/c @ ₹ 155	272	42,160
To Production Overhead (60% of Direct Wages)		5,580			
Total	360	45,720	Total	360	45,720

Dr **Process No. 3 Account** Cr

Details	Unit	Amount (₹)	Details	Unit	Amount (₹)
To Process No. 3 A/c @ ₹ 155	272	42,160	By Normal Loss A/c @ ₹ 25	68	1,700
To Direct Material		2,800	By Finished Goods Stock A/c @ ₹ 245	216	52,920
Direct Wages		4,200			
To Production Overhead (60% of direct Wages)		2,520			
To Abnormal Gain A/c @ ₹ 245	12	2,940			
Total	284	54,620	Total	284	54,620

Dr **Normal Loss Account** Cr

Details	Unit	Amount (₹)	Details	Unit	Amount (₹)
To Process No. 1 A/c	40	240	By Cash/Drs A/c	168	2,720
To Process No. 2 A/c	72	1,080	By Abnormal Gain A/c	12	300
To Process No. 3 A/c	68	1,700			
Total	180	3,020	Total	180	3,020

Dr **Abnormal Loss Account** Cr

Details	Unit	Amount (₹)	Details	Unit	Amount (₹)
To Process No. 2 A/c @ ₹ 155	16	2,480	By Cash/Drs A/c @ ₹ 15	16	240
			By Costing Profit and Loss A/c		2,240
Total	16	2,480	Total	16	2,480

Dr **Abnormal Gain Account** Cr

Details	Unit	Amount (₹)	Details	Unit	Amount (₹)
To Normal Loss A/c @ ₹ 25	12	300	By Process No. 3 A/c @ ₹ 245	12	2,940
To Costing Profit and Loss A/c		2,640			
Total	12	2,940	Total	12	2,940

Working Notes : *Process No. 1 Account:*

Cost per unit:

$$= \frac{\text{(All Normal process costs – Realizable value of Normal Scrap)}}{\text{(Process Input Units – Normal Loss in Units = Normal output)}}$$

$$= \frac{[(4,800 + 6,960 + 9,000 + 5,400) - 240]}{(400 - 40 = 360)}$$

= 25,920 ÷ 360 => ₹ 72

Process No. 2 Account

Cost per unit:

$$= \frac{\text{(All Normal process costs – Realizable value of Normal Scrap)}}{\text{(Process Input Units – Normal Loss in Units = Normal output)}}$$

$$= \frac{[(25,920 + 4,920 + 9,300 + 5,580) - 1,080]}{(360 - 72 = 288)}$$

= 44,640 ÷ 288 => ₹ 155

Process No. 3 Account

Cost per unit:

$$= \frac{\text{(All Normal process costs – Realizable value of Normal Scrap)}}{\text{(Process Input Units – Normal Loss in Units = Normal output)}}$$

$$= \frac{[(42,160 + 2,800 + 4,200 + 2,520) - 1,700]}{(272 - 68 = 204)}$$

= 49,980 ÷ 204 => ₹ 245

INTER PROCESS PROFIT

As a matter of policy, some manufacturing organizations transfer the output of one process to the other, not at cost to the process, but at the prevailing market price, at the standard cost plus profit, at the process cost plus profit, or any other basis considered appropriate. This results in profit, at different processes, in addition to profit or loss at the time of sale of the finished goods. The price at which the output of one process is transferred to the other processes in the concern is called transfer price. The practices of recognizing profit or loss at different processes is called inter process profit or internal process profit.

Objectives of Recognizing Inter Process Profit

1. The system of transfer pricing facilitates the decision regarding 'Make or Buy' before each process, or 'Further process or Sell' after the process.
2. Process-wise profitability is ascertained.
3. Process-wise contribution to the overall profitability of the organization.
4. No transfer of efficiency/inefficiency of one process to the other.
5. Transfer prices have a positive impact on the motivation of employees working at different processes.

Problems in Recognizing Inter Process Profit

Recognition of Internal profit i.e. inter process profit gives rise to the following problems:

1. It is difficult to find out the most appropriate basis of transfer price for a process out of many available bases for determining the transfer prices.
2. It gives rise to unearned profit hidden in the value of stock at process and the finished stock.
3. Inefficiency gets percolated.

Segregation of process Stock: It is a fact that the transfer from one process to another within an organization is not a sale, and as such the organization has not earned any profit on account of stocks at processes and stock of finished Goods. This unearned or unrealized profit in stocks at processes except the first one or finished goods need to be segregated because as per the accounting principle, 'the value of stocks is to be at cost or market price, whichever is less'. Correct ascertainment of profit and correct valuation of stocks for balance sheet purposes makes it obligatory to segregate true cost and profit in total value of stock.

Three columns on each side of the process account are inserted. Closing stock at process is deducted on the debit side of the process account for convenience purposes. The basis of calculations is the ratio of the cost incurred at the process to the cost transferred from the preceding process. The formula applied to this effect is as under:

Closing Stock (at cost) = [(Value of Closing Stock) ×
(Sum of Cost column)/ Sum of Total column)]

The difference between the value of closing stock and the closing stock (at cost) is the unearned profit hidden in the value of the closing stock. This unearned profit is adjusted in the profit figure so as to arrive at the figure of true profit. The complete procedure of arriving at the correct figure of true profit is explained in the succeeding illustration No. 5.

Illustration 18.5 : (Concept of Unrealized profit)

A product passes through three processes A, J and S to completion. The output of each process is charged to the next –process at a price calculated to give a profit of 25% on the transfer price. The output of Process s is charged to finished stock on similar basis. There is no partly finished work in any process on March 31, on which date the following information was made available for analysis:

Details	*Process*		
	A (₹)	***J (₹)***	***S (₹)***
Material	*6,000*	*11,000*	*4,000*
Labour	*8,000*	*9,000*	*11,000*
Closing stock as on 31.3.2010	*2,000*	*4,500*	*6,000*

Stock in each process is valued at cost to that process.

There was no stock in hand on April 1, 2009 and the question of overhead was ignored. Of the goods passed into finished stock, ₹ 4,000 remained in hand on March 31, 2010 and the balance has been sold for ₹ 80,000. Show process accounts and calculate reserve for unrealized profits.

Solution :

Dr **Process 'A' Account** Cr

Details	Amount (₹)			Details	Amount (₹)		
	Total	Cost	Profit		Total	Cost	Profit
To Materials	6,000	6,000	—	By Process 'J 'A/c (Transfer)	16,000	12,000	4,000
To labour	8,000	8,000	—				
Total	14,000	14,000	—				
Less: Closing Stock c/d	2,000	2,000	—				
Prime cost	12,000	12,000	—				
Profit (1/3 of cost)	4,000	—	4,000				
Total	16,000	12,000	4,000	Total	16,000	12,000	4,000

Dr **Process 'J' Account** Cr

Details	Amount (₹)			Details	Amount (₹)		
	Total	Cost	Profit		Total	Cost	Profit
To Process 'J 'A/c (Transfer)	16,000	12,000	4,000	By Process 'S 'A/c (Transfer)	42,000	28,000	14,000
To Materials	12,000	11,000	—				
To labour	8,000	9,000	—				
Total	36,000	32,000	4,000				
Less: Closing Stock c/d	4,500	4,000	500				
Prime cost	31,500	28,000	3,500				
Profit (1/3 of cost)	10,500	—	10,500				
Total	42,000	28,000	14,000	Total	42,000	28,000	14,000
To Stock b/d	4,500	4,000	500				

Dr **Process 'S' Account** Cr

Details	Amount (₹)			Details	Amount (₹)		
	Total	Cost	Profit		Total	Cost	Profit
To Process 'J 'A/c (Transfer)	42,000	28,000	14,000	By Finished Goods Stock A/c (Transfer)	68,000	38,474	29,526
To Materials	4,000	4,000	—				
To labour	11,000	11,000	—				
Total	57,000	43,000	14,000				
Less: Closing Stock c/d	6,000	4,526	1,474				
Prime cost	51,000	38,474	12,526				
Profit (1/3 of cost)	17,000	—	17,000				
Total	68,000	38,474	29,526	Total	68,000	38,474	29,526
To Stock b/d	6,000	4,526	1,474				

Dr **Finished Goods Stock Account** Cr

Details	Amount (₹)			Details	Amount (₹)		
	Total	Cost	Profit		Total	Cost	Profit
To Process 'S' A/c (Transfer)	68,000	38,474	29,526	By Sales	80,000	36,211	43,789
Less: Closing Stock c/d	4,000	2,263	1,737				
Output sold	64,000	36,211	27,789				
Profit (1/3 of cost)	16,000	—	16,000				
Total	80,000	36,211	43,789	Total	80,000	36,211	43,789
To Stock b/d	4,000	2,263	1,737				

Working Notes :

1. Profit of 25% (i.e. ¼) of transfer price is equal to 1/3 of cost.
2. Cost of closing Stock at processes is ascertained on the basis of ratio of Total Cost to the Total Value which includes profit component taken into account till a particular stage. Thus

   Closing Stock (at cost) = [(Value of Closing Stock) × (Sum of Cost column)/ Sum of Total column)]
3. Profit figure on the credit side of the process account shows accumulated amount of profit till that stage.

4. Computation of closing stock at cost and unearned profit in closing stock at processes:

Process	Closing stock		Unearned profit (₹)
	Value (₹)	Cost (₹)	NIL
A	2,000	2,000	500
J	4,500	4,000	1,474
S	6,000	4,526	1,737
Finished Goods Stock	4,000	2,263	NIL
Total for Balance Sheet Purposes		12789*	

* Closing Stock (at cost) = Aggregate of all costs – Cost of sales

* 12,789 = 49,000 – 36,211

Verification of realized profit:

Process (I)	Process Profit (₹) (II)	Unearned Profit in Closing stock (₹) (III)	Actual Profit (₹) (IV) = (II) – (III)
A	4,000	NIL	4,000
J	10,500	500	10,000
S	17,000	1,474	15,526
Finished Goods Stock	16,000	1,737	14,263
Total	47,500	3,711	43,789

WORK-IN-PROGRESS AND THE CONCEPT OF EFFECTIVE PRODUCTION

Work-in-progress at the process implies materials which had entered the process, on which some production activity has been performed, but work is not yet fully completed at the process; i.e. something still needs to be done. Existence of such partly completed units of output leads to a problem of determining cost per unit at the process, cost of completed units of output and the cost of closing inventory of work-in-progress at the process. The problem is solved by using the concept of Effective Production or Equivalent Production.

Equivalent Production refers to estimating the equivalence of partly completed units in comparison with the completed units i.e. incomplete units are more or less equal to how many units in terms of cost spent on incomplete units and total cost to be spent on completed units. For example, 4,000 incomplete units are on an average 75% complete i.e. they have consumed that much cost which is required for 4,000 × 0. 75 = 3,000 completed units of output. Thus, 4,000 incomplete units are equivalent to 3,000 completed units. Such equivalence requires an estimation which can be reasonably correct for a producer who is regularly involved in certain types of production processes. However, in actual practice, details regarding material cost, labour cost and overheads are available in cost records. To be more exact, the producer tries to ascertain equivalence NOT in terms of entire product but in terms of each element of cost, i.e. the incomplete units have consumed materials equivalent to how many completed units, labour compared to how many completed units, and overheads spent on incomplete units are equivalent to that required for how many completed units. Following illustration explains the entire process of equivalence.

Illustration 18.6 : (Concept of Equivalence)

During a costing period the manufacturer has produced 6,000 completed units and 3,000 units are incomplete at the end of the period. Costs incurred during that costing period on both categories of output are as under:

Details	*Amount (₹)*
Direct Material	*5,19,750*
Direct wages	*3,58,800*
Overheads	*2,70,000*
Total	*11,48,550*

Incomplete units are complete equivalent to various elements of costs are as under:

Details	*Percentage*
Direct material	*75*
Direct wages	*60*
Overheads	*50*

Prepare a Statement of Equivalent Production, Statement of Cost per unit, Statement of Apportionment of Cost, and Process Account. Make explanatory statements.

Solution : Direct Material: 6,000 units are 100% complete, and therefore, they have consumed 100% material required for 6,000 units. 3,000 units are 75% complete as regards materials cost, i.e. they have consumed that much direct material cost which is required for 2,250 complete units (3,000 × 0. 75). So 6,000 completed units plus 3,000 incomplete units with 75% material costs incurred on them are equivalent to 6,000 + 2,250 = 8,250 equivalent or effective completed units (EQP units) as regards direct material cost. Thus, direct material cost per unit amounts to ₹ 63 as per following formula:

Direct Material Cost per Unit:
= (Total direct material cost/ Equivalent units of output in terms of material cost)

= ₹ 5,19,750 ÷ 8,250 EQP units => ₹ 63

Direct Wages: Similarly, 6,000 units are 100% complete, and therefore, they have consumed 100% labour required for 6,000 units. 3,000 units are 60% complete as regards labour cost, i.e. these incomplete units are equivalent to 3,000 × 0.6 = 1,800 complete units. As regards labour cost, total output is equal to 6,000 + 1,800 = 7,800 complete units (EQP units). Thus, direct labour cost per unit amounts to ₹ 46 as per following formula:

Direct Labour Cost per Unit:
= (Total direct Labour cost/ Equivalent units of output in terms of Labour cost)

= ₹ 3,58,800 ÷ 7,800 EQP units => ₹ 46

Overheads: In the same way, 6,000 units are 100% complete, and therefore, they have consumed 100% overhead costs required for 6,000 units. 3,000 units are 50% complete as regards overhead costs, i.e. these incomplete units are equivalent to 3,000 × 0.5 = 1,500 complete units. As regards overhead costs, total output is equal to 6,000 +1,500 = 7,500 complete units (EQP units). Thus, overheads cost per unit amounts to ₹ 36 as per following formula:

Overheads cost per Unit:
= (Total overheads cost / Equivalent units of output in terms of overhead costs)

= ₹ 2,70,000 ÷ 7,500 EQP units => ₹ 36

Per unit of cost of completed units:

Cost of Complete unit of Output

= Direct material cost per unit + Direct labour cost per unit + Overheads cost per unit

= ₹ 63 + ₹ 46 + ₹ 36 => ₹ 145.

Cost of uncompleted 3,000 units:

Details	Computations (Cost per unit × EQP units)	Amount (₹)
Direct material	63 × 2,250 =	1,41,750
Direct wages	46 ×1,800 =	82,800
Overheads	36 × 1,500 =	54,000
Total		2,78,550

Following statements are being prepared as per the requirements of the Illustration:

Statement of Equivalent Production

Input units	Details	Output units	EQP Units		
			Material	Labour	Overhead
9,000	Introduced				
	Finished and transferred	6,000	6,000	6,000	6,000
	Work-in-Progress	3,000	2,250	1,800	1,500
9,000	Total	9,000	8,250	7,800	7,500

Statement of Cost

Element of Cost	Cost (₹)	EQP (Units)	Cost per EQP Unit (₹)
Direct Material	5,19,750	8,250	63
Direct wages	3,58,800	7,800	46
Overheads	2,70,000	7,500	36
Total Cost	11,48,550		145

Statement of Evaluation

Details	Element of Cost	EQP Units	Cost per EQP Unit (₹)	Element-Wise Cost (₹)	Total Cost (₹)
Finished Production	Material	6,000	63	3,78,000	
	Labour	6,000	46	2,76,000	
	Overhead	6,000	36	2,16,000	8,70,000
Work-in-Progress	Material	2,250	63	1,41,750	
	Labour	1,800	46	82,800	
	Overhead	1,500	36	54,000	2,78,550
Total					11,48,550

Dr **Process Account** Cr

Details	Units	Amoun (₹)	Details	Units	Amoun (₹)
To Direct Material	9,000	5,19,750	By Process-2: A/c (Transfer)	6,000	8,70,000
To Direct wages		3,58,800	By Work-in-Progress A/c	3,000	2,78,550
To Overheads A/c		2,70,000			
Total	9,000	11,48,550	Total	9,000	11,48,550

Valuation of Opening and Closing Work-in-Progress

The valuation of work-in-progress may be made either according to First –in-first-out (FIFO) or Average cost method. The choice of the method depends upon the extent to which identification of the output transferred to the succeeding process can be made. If the output transferred to the succeeding process can be differentiated and identified with the work-in-progress and fresh units introduced in the process, the FIFO method is preferable, else average cost method be adopted.

(a) First-in First-out Method

The closing work-in-progress is valued at the current costs. It is based on the assumption that whatever remains partly finished is out of the lot introduced afresh during the current period. Thus, the cost incurred during the current period is spread over to the opening stock of work-in-progress (Now completed), work introduced and completed during the current period and the closing stock of work-in-progress. The cost incurred during the current period id divided by the relevant equivalent production quantity so as to arrive at the cost per unit of EQP.

Example (FIFO Method) :

Details	*Number/ Amount (₹)*
Units Introduced during the current period	*8,000*
Units Completed during the current period	*6,000*
Closing Stock of work-in-progress (40% complete)	*2,000*
Costs incurred during the current period	*34,000*

Solution :

Equivalent Production Units: 6,000 units + (2,000 × 0.4)

= 6,000 + 800 => 6,800 units

Cost per unit of EQP = ₹ 34,000 ÷ 6,800 => ₹ 5

Value of closing stock of Work-in-Progress = 800 × 5 => ₹ 4,000.

Illustration 18.7 : (FIFO Method)

Details	*Number/Amount (₹)*	
Opening Stock of work-in-progress (40% complete)	*2,000*	*4,000*
Units Introduced during the current period	*8,000*	
Units Completed during the current period (Transferred to the Next Process)	*9,200*	
Closing Stock of work-in-progress (50% complete)	*800*	
Costs incurred during the current period		*57,200*

Solution : Statement of Equivalent (effective) Production

Input units	Details	Output units	EQP Units
8,000	Introduced		
2,000	Opening work-in-progress (40% Complete)	2,000	1,200
	Introduced and completed during the current period (100% Complete)	7,200	7,200
	Closing Work-in-Progress (50% Complete)	800	400
10,000	Total	10,000	8,800

Cost per unit of EQP = ₹ 57,200 ÷ 8,800 => ₹ 6.50

Statement of Evaluation

Details	EQP Units	Cost per EQP Unit (₹)	Total Cost (₹)
Opening Work-in-Progress (Additional cost for the completion of these units)	1,200	6.50	7,800
Introduced and completed during the current period	7,200	6.50	46,800
Closing Work-in-Progress	400	6.50	2,600
Total	9,200	6.50	57,200

Cost of Units transferred to the Next Process

Details	Amount (₹)	Amount (₹)
Value of Opening work-in-Progress:		
(a) Cost incurred during the previous period (2,000 units)	4,000	
(b) Cost incurred during the current period (2,000 units)	7,800	11,800
Introduced and completed during the period (7,200 units)		46,800
Total (9,200 units)		58,600

Dr **Process Account** Cr

Details	Unit (lbs)	Amoun (₹)	Details	Unit (lbs)	Amount (₹)
To Opening Stock of work-in-Progress	2,000	4,000	By Next Process A/c	9,200	58,600
To Costs incurred during the period	8,000	57,200	By Closing work-in-Progress A/c	800	2,600
Total	10,000	61,200	Total	10,000	61,200

(b) Average Cost Method

This method is applied on the assumption that it is not possible to identify or first complete the opening work-in-progress. The work is carried on all units simultaneously and the units to be transferred to the next process may not necessarily contain all the units of the opening work-in-progress. It implies that the closing work-in-progress at the end of the current period need not be out of the units introduced during the current period. Further, the degree of completion of opening work-in-progress may not be known. Under all such circumstances, average cost method is to be used.

The cost of opening work-in-progress and the costs incurred during the period are added up. The units completed and transferred, and the equivalent units of closing work-in-progress on the basis of degree of completion are added to arrive at the total EQP units. The total cost is divided by the total EQP units to obtain the cost per unit. Based upon the availability of details in regard to various elements of cost, the valuation may be done cost-element wise as per the completion stage reached in respect of the cost element.

The main difference between the two methods is that of inclusion of complete costs of the units of opening work in progress under average cost method while under FIFO method only the remaining work done during the current period is considered.

Illustration 18.8. (Average cost Method) : *Solve the preceding Illustration by using Average cost method.*

Solution : **Statement of Equivalent (effective) Production**

Input units	Details	Output units	EQP Units
10,000	Available for Processing during the current period		
	Finished and Transferred (100% Complete)	9,200	9,200
	Closing Work-in-Progress (50% Complete)	800	400
10,000	Total	10,000	9,600

Statement of Cost

Details	Amount (₹)
Cost of Opening work-in-Progress	4,000
Cost incurred during the current period	57,200
Total cost	61,200
EQP units: 9,600	
Cost per unit of EQP = ₹ 61,200 ÷ 9,600=> ₹ 6.375	

Statement of Evaluation

Details	EQP Units	Cost per EQP Unit (₹)	Total Cost (₹)
Finished and Transferred	9,200	6.375	58,650
Closing Work-in-Progress	400	6.375	2,550
Total	9,600		61,200

Process Account

Dr Cr

Details	Unit (lbs)	Amoun (₹)	Details	Unit (lbs)	Amount (₹)
To Opening Stock of work-in-Progress	2,000	4,000	By Next Process A/c	9,200	58,650
To Costs incurred during the period	8,000	57,200	By Closing work-in-Progress A/c	800	2,550
Total	10,000	61,200	Total	10,000	61,200

Treatment of Loss/Wastage

Normal percentage of loss is predetermined. The actual loss may be more or less than the predetermined norm; it may result in abnormal loss or abnormal gain. The realizable value of the normal wastage is generally deducted from the cost of materials. Net cost of materials is divided by the effective units of production. Abnormal loss is valued at full cost of such production. Units of abnormal gain would also be taken as 100% complete but its value would be deducted out of the total cost of production. If the loss of output occurred during the course of manufacture is complete as regards materials, labour and overheads in different degrees, the degree of completion must be given due consideration while computing effective production in regard to abnormal loss. However, normal loss will not be taken as equal to any equivalent units while abnormal effective would always be taken as 100% complete as regards all the elements of cost.

Concept of Material II

Material received from the previous process should be separately recorded. The opening work-in-progress does not require this material during the current period of production and hence there is no equivalent units of opening work-in-progress in regard to this material. The units which have been introduced and completed during the current period, abnormal Loss and closing work-in-progress would be 100% complete as regards the material received from the previous process. Abnormal effective is obviously 100% complete. Normal loss has no equivalents. *The realizable value of normal wastage is deducted out of the material cost brought forward from the previous process only* instead of prorating it to this material and material added during the process for the sake of convenience. Material received from the previous process is termed as Material I and material added during the current process is termed as Material II.

Illustration 18.9 : (Concept of Material II)

1. *Opening Work-in-progress: 2,000 units costing ₹ 15,200 (transferred in cost ₹ 3,000, materials ₹ 3,950, Labour ₹ 4,350, and overheads ₹ 3, 900).*
2. *Transferred from previous Process I: 30,000 units costing ₹ 68,125.*
3. *Cost incurred in Process II:*
   Materials ₹ 50,375; Labour ₹ 1, 30,000 and Overheads ₹78, 000.
4. *Normal Loss in process II: 10%.*
5. *Scrap realized @ ₹ 4.00 per unit*
6. *Closing Work-in-progress: 4,500 units*
7. *Transfer to Next process: 24,250 units*
8. *Degree of completion:*

Details	*Opening Work-in-Progress (%)*	*Closing Work-in-Progress (%)*	*Scrapped Units (%)*
Material	*60*	*60*	*100*
Labour	*40*	*52*	*42*
Overheads	*40*	*52*	*42*

From the information given above, prepare:

(i) Statement of Equivalent production;

(ii) Statement of element of cost/unit;

(iii) Statement of apportionment of cost; and

(iv) Process II Account under FIFO method.

Solution : **Statement of Equivalent Production**

Input	Details	Output	Material I		Material II		Labour& Overhead	
			(%)		(%)		(%)	
2,000	Opening W.I.P.	2,000	—	—	40	800	60	1,200
30,000	Transferred from previous process I							
	Received and completed	22,250	100	22,250	100	22,250	100	22,250
	Normal Loss	2,750	—	—	—	—	—	—
	Abnormal Loss	500	100	500	100	500	42	210
	Closing W.I.P.	4,500	100	4,500	60	2,700	52	2,340
32,000	Total	32,000		27,250		26,250		26,000

Statement of Element of Cost

Details		Amount (₹)	EQP Unit	Per unit (₹)
Material I		68,125	27,250	2.50
Material II	50,375			
Less: Scrap	11,000	39,375	26,250	1.50
Labour		1,30,000	26,000	5.00
Overhead		78,000	26,000	3.00
Total				12.00

Statement of Apportionment of Cost

Details	Element of Cost	EQP Unit	Cost per unit (₹)	Cost (₹)
Opening Work-in-Progress	Material I	—	2.5	—
	Material II	800	1.5	1,200
	Labour	1,200	5.0	6,000
	Overhead	1,200	3.0	3,600
Total				*10,800*
Units Completed	—	22,250	12.0	*2,67,000*
Units Transferred to Process III:				
Opening Work-in-Progress:				
Existing		2,000		15,200
New				10,800
Units Completed		22,250		2,67,000
Total		24,250		**2,93,000**
Abnormal Loss	Material I	500	2.5	1,250
	Material II	500	1.5	750
	Labour	210	5.0	1,050
	Overhead	210	3.0	630
Total				**3,680**
Closing Work-in-Progress	Material I	4,500	2.5	11,250
	Material II	2,700	1.5	4,050
	Labour	2,340	5.0	11,700
	Overhead	2,340	3.0	7,020
Total				**34,020**

Dr **Process II Account** Cr

Details	Unit	Amount (₹)	Details	Unit	Amount (₹)
To Opening Work-in-Progress A/c	2,000	15,200	By Normal Loss A/c @ ₹ 4.00	2,750	11,000
To Process I (Transfer)	30,000	68,125	By Abnormal Loss A/c	500	3,680
To Material		50,375	By Process III	24,250	2,93,000
To Labour		1,30,000	By Closing Work-in-Progress A/c	4,500	34,020
To overheads		78,000			
Total	32,000	3,41,700	Total	32,000	3,41,700

Illustration 18.10 : *During a particular month 2,500 units at a cost of ₹ 1,24,000 were introduced into Process-1.The normal loss was estimated at four percent. At the end of the month 1,750 units had been produced and transferred to the next process, 600 units were partially complete and 150 units had been scrapped.*

It was estimated that the Closing work-in-progress had reached the following stages of production:

Materials 100% complete, Labour 60% complete, and Overhead 50% complete.

Additional costs incurred during the month were: Materials: ₹ 36,000 Labour: ₹ 60,480 Overheads: ₹ 35,700.

The units scrapped realized ₹ 16 each. Prepare the process-1 Account.

Note: *Workings form part of your answer.*

Solution : Process-1: Statement of Equivalent Production

Input units	Details	Output units	EQP Units		
			Material	Labour	Overhead
2,500	Introduced				
	Normal Loss	100	—	—	—
	Finished and transferred	1,750	1,750	1,750	1,750
	Abnormal Loss	50	50	50	50
	Work-in-Progress	600	600	360	300
2,500	Total	2,500	2,400	2,160	2,100

Process-1: Statement of Cost

Element of Cost	Cost (₹)	EQP (Units)	Cost per EQP Unit (₹)
Direct Material	1,24,000		
Additional Materials	36,000		
Less: Scrap value of Normal	(1,600)		
Total Materials	1,58,400	2,400	66
Labour	60,480	2,160	28
Overheads	35,700	2,100	17
Total Cost	2,54,580		111

Process-1: Statement of Evaluation

Details	Element of Cost (₹)	EQP Units	Cost per EQP Unit	Cost (₹)	Total Cost (₹)
Finished Production	Material	1,750	66	1,15,500	
	Labour	1,750	28	49,000	
	Overhead	1,750	17	29,750	1,94,250
Abnormal Loss	Material	50	66	3,300	
	Labour	50	28	1,400	
	Overhead	50	17	850	5,550
Work-in-Progress	Material	600	66	39,600	
	Labour	360	28	10,080	
	Overhead	300	17	5,100	54,780

Dr **Process-1: Account** Cr

Details	Units	Amount (₹)	Details	Units	Amount (₹)
To Basic Input Material A/c	2,500	1,24,000	By Normal Loss A/c	100	1,600
To Additional Material A/c		36,000	By Abnormal Loss A /c	50	5,550
To Labour A/c		60,480	By Process-2: A/c (Transfer)	1,750	1,94,250
To Overhead A/c		35,700	By Work-in-Progress A/c	600	54,780
Total	2,500	2,56,180	Total	2,500	2,56,180

Dr		Normal Loss Account			Cr
Details	**Units**	**Amount (₹)**	**Details**	**Units**	**Amount (₹)**
To Process A/c	100	1,600	By Cash/Drs A/c	100	1,600
Total	100	1,600	Total	100	1,600

Illustration 18.11 : *From the following data, find out the equivalent units of production to determine the per unit processing cost, which was incurred evenly during the month of January, 2008:*

Opening work-in-progress: 12,500 Units (40% completed)

Fresh Units introduced: 40,000 units

Finished goods: 30,000 units

Closing work-in-progress: 20,000 Units (75% completed)

The entire stock of Opening work-in-progress was completed during January, 2008 without any loss/rejection.

Solution :

Input Units	Details	Output Units	EQP Units
12,500	Opening Work-in-Progress	12,500	7,500
40,000	Introduced		
	Introduced and Finished (30,000 – 12,500)	17,500	17,500
	Abnormal Loss	2,500	2,500
	Closing Work-in-Progress	20,000	15,000
52,500	Total	52,500	42,500

Illustration 18.12 : *In a manufacturing unit, raw material passes through four processes I, II, III, IV and the output of each process is the input of the subsequent process. The loss of the four processes I, II, III, IV are respectively 25%, 20%, 20%, and 12.5% of the input. If the end product of Process IV is 21,000 Kgs., what is the quantity of materials required along with its cost to be fed at the start of Process I when the cost of the same is ₹ 30 per Kg.*

Solution :

Output of Process IV is 21,000 Kg. which is 87.5%
= 24,000 Kg. (i.e. 21,000 ÷ 0.875)

Output of Process III is 24,000 Kg. which is 80.0%
= 30,000 Kg. (i.e. 24,000 ÷ 0.80)

Output of Process II is 30,000 Kg. which is 80.0%
= 37,500 Kg. (i.e. 30,000 ÷ 0.80)

Output of Process I is 37,500 Kg. which is 75.0%

= 50,000 Kg. (i.e. 37,500 ÷ 0.75)

Alternatively, Output in a process is input minus loss in process.

Suppose input in Process I = 100Kg.

Output in Process I: 100 – 25 % of 100 = 75 Kg.

Output in Process II: 75 – 20% of 75 = 60 Kg.

Output in Process III: 60 – 20% of 60 = 48 Kg.

Output in Process IV: 48 – 12.5% of 48 = 42 Kg.

Output of Process IV is 21,000 Kg and the Input in Process I will be:

= 21,000 × (100/42) => 50,000 Kg.

Thus cost of material introduced in Process I:

₹ 15,00,000 (i.e. 50,000 × 30)

LET US RECAPITULATE

1. Process costing refers to costing of one or more processes involved in converting a raw material into finished product.
2. Process costing is suitably employed where goods are made for stock and production is continuous.
3. This method is applied where it is not possible to trace the items of prime cost to a particular order, as its identity is lost in the volume of continuous production.
4. Raw materials are introduced in the very first process and after processing they are transferred to the next process or to the warehouse.
5. Records for cost per unit of finished product cannot be built up, as there is an indistinguishable homogeneous mass during the production process.
6. Costs are accumulated for each process. Cost per unit is determined by averaging the process cost. Costs are compiled on time basis.
7. At the end of each accounting period there is work-in-progress. The process cost for a period is apportioned between completed outputs and work-in-progress at the accounting period.
8. As all output units are uniform and production process is continuous, accounting for and control of costs is relatively comfortable.
9. The cost of direct labour constitutes a small part of the total cost of production because such industries are capital intensive.
10. The total cost is divided by normal output.
11. From the point of sale of scrap, there is no difference between normal scrap and abnormal scrap.
12. Normally realizable value of empties should be deducted from the total cost while computing cost per unit.

13. The price at which the output of one process is transferred to the other processes in the concern is called transfer price.
14. The practices of recognizing profit or loss at different processes is called inter process profit or internal process profit.
15. Correct ascertainment of profit and correct valuation of stocks for balance sheet purposes makes it obligatory to segregate true cost and profit in total value of stock.
16. Work-in-progress at the process implies materials which had entered the process, on which some production activity has been performed, but work is not yet fully completed at the process.
17. Equivalent Production refers to estimating the equivalence of partly completed units in comparison with the completed units.
18. In F I F O method the closing work-in-progress is valued at the current costs.
19. In the average method the cost of opening work-in-progress and the costs incurred during the period are added up.
20. The total cost is divided by the total EQP units to obtain the cost per unit in the average method.
21. Net cost of materials is divided by the effective units of production.
22. Material received from the previous process is termed ad as Material I and material added during the current process is termed as Material II.

SOLVED PROBLEMS

Problem 1. *In a certain process, material is mixed and cooked in batches of 1.25 kg. each. Cooking results in 10% loss of weight of the mixture. Since the cooking requires considerable skill and constant watching, there is generally a further loss from spoilage which is discovered only on the completion of the process. Also, past experience shows that normally two batches out of every ten started in the process are spoiled in this way. In a given period, the production records show:*

(i) Production started in process: 140 batches of 1.25 Kg. each.

(ii) Production completed and transferred to finished goods is

In a workshop monthly input of material @ ₹ 60 per Kg. is 12,500 Kgs packed in gunny bags of 100 kg each. Other expenses inclusive of additional cost of ₹ 37,000 due to an accident in the workshop amount to ₹ 5, 34,600. Normal loss is 4% of input and it realizes @14 per unit and each bag is sold @ ₹ 40. Actual output is 12,270 units of which 3,000 units were sold @ ₹ 125 per Kg of output. Generally 8% of containers get so damaged that they fetch nothing in value. Actually only 110 containers were in saleable position and were sold. Prepare Process account, Normal Loss account, Abnormal Gain account, Empties account and the Statement of Profit.

Solution : Working Notes:

Cost per unit

$$= \frac{\text{(All Normal process costs – Realizable value of Normal Scrap and Normal empties)}}{\text{(Process Input Units – Normal Loss in Units)}}$$

$$= \frac{[(7{,}50{,}000 + (5{,}34{,}600 - 37{,}000)) - [7{,}000 + 4{,}600]}{(12{,}500 - 500 = 12{,}000)}$$

= 12, 36,000 ÷ 12,000 => ₹ 103

Process Account

Dr | Cr

Details	Unit	Amount (₹)	Details	Unit	Amount (₹)
To Input Material @ ₹ 60	12,500	7,50,000	By Normal Loss @ ₹ 14	500	7,000
To Other Expenses		5,34,600	By Normal Empties (115 × 40)		4,600
To Abnormal Gain A/c @ ₹ 103	270	27,810	By Cash/Drs @ ₹ 125	3,000	3,75,000
To Costing Profit and Loss A/c (Gain on sale) (3,000 × 22)		66,000	By Transfer to next process @ ₹ 103	9,270	9,54,810
			By Costing Profit and Loss A/c (Loss due to accident)		37,000
Total	12,770	13,78,410	Total	12,770	13,78,410

Normal Loss Account

Dr | Cr

Details	Unit	Amount (₹)	Details	Unit	Amount (₹)
To Process A/c @ ₹ 14	500	7,000	By Cash/Drs @ ₹ 14	230	3,220
			By Abnormal Gain A/c	270	3,780
Total	500	7,000	Total	500	7,000

Abnormal Gain Account

Dr Cr

Details	Unit	Amount (₹)	Details	Unit	Amount (₹)
To Normal Loss A/c @ ₹ 14	270	3,780	By Process A/c @ ₹ 103	270	27,810
To Costing Profit and Loss A/c		24,030			
Total	270	27,810	Total	270	27,810

Empties Account

Dr Cr

Details	Unit	Amount (₹)	Details	Unit	Amount (₹)
To Process A/c @ ₹ 40	115	4,600	By Cash/Drs @ ₹ 40	110	4,400
			By Costing Profit and Loss A/c	5	200
Total	115	4,600	Total	115	4,600

Statement of Profit:

Details		Amount (₹)
Gain on sale of Process output (3,000 ×22)		66,000
Abnormal Gain		24,030
		90,030
Less:		
Abnormal Loss due to Accident	37,000	
Abnormal Loss of empties (5 × 40)	200	
		(37,200)
Net Gain		52,830

Problem 2. *A Producer of cotton yarn purchases 2,500 kg of cotton in bags of 50 kg. each at ₹ 30 per kg. Other costs at the processing are ₹ 46,150. Normal Loss is 6% of input. 40% of the input loss disappears and the balance is available for sale @ ₹ 10 per kg. Each Empty bag sells for ₹ 20. Actual Output is:*

(i) 2,250 kg, and *(ii) 2,430 kg.*

Solution : Working Notes:

Cost per unit = (All Normal process costs – Realizable value of Normal Scrap and Normal empties) ÷ (Process Input Units – Normal Loss in Units = Normal Output)

$$= \frac{[(75{,}000 + 44{,}400) - [(150 \times 0.6 \times 10) + (50 \times 20)]}{(2{,}500 - 150 = 2{,}350)}$$

$= 1{,}17{,}500 \div 2{,}350 \Rightarrow$ ₹ 50.

Case (i) :

Process Account

Dr Cr

Details	Unit	Amount (₹)	Details	Unit	Amount (₹)
To Input of Material (@ ₹ 30)	2,500	75,000	By Weight Lost A/c	60	—
To Other expenses		44,400	By Normal Loss A/c @ ₹ 10	90	900
			By Empties A/c (50bags @ ₹ 20 per bag)		1,000
			By Abnormal Loss A/c @ ₹ 50	100	5,000
			By Output transferred to Next process @ ₹ 50	2,250	1,12,500
	2,500	1,19,400		2,500	1,19,400

Normal Loss Account

Dr Cr

Details	Unit	Amount (₹)	Details	Unit	Amount (₹)
To Process A/c @ ₹ 10	90	900	By Cash/Debtors A/c @ ₹ 10	90	900
	90	900		90	900

Abnormal Loss Account

Dr Cr

Details	Unit	Amount (₹)	Details	Unit	Amount (₹)
To Process A/c (@ ₹ 50)	100	5,000	By Cash/Debtors A/c @ ₹ 10	60	600
			By Weight Lost	40	—
			By Costing Profit and Loss A/c		4,400
	100	5,000		100	5,000

Case (ii) :

Process Account

Dr Cr

Details	Unit	Amount (₹)	Details	Unit	Amount (₹)
To Input of Material @ ₹ 30	2,500	75,000	By Weight Lost	60	—
To Other expenses		44,400	By Normal Loss A/c @ ₹ 10	90	900
To Abnormal Gain A/c @ ₹ 50	80	4,000	By Empties A/c (50 bags @ ₹ 20 per bag)		1,000
			By Output transferred to Next process @ ₹ 50	2,430	1,21,500
	2,580	1,23,400		2,580	1,23,400

Normal Loss Account

Dr Cr

Details	Unit	Amount (₹)	Details	Unit	Amount (₹)
To Process A/c @ ₹ 10	90	900	By Abnormal Gain A/c (80 × 0.6) (@ ₹ 10)	48	480
			By Cash/Debtors A/c @ ₹ 10	42	420
	90	900		90	900

Abnormal Gain Account

Dr Cr

Details	Unit	Amount (₹)	Details	Unit	Amount (₹)
To Normal Loss A/c @ ₹ 10	48	480	By Process A/c @ ₹ 50	80	4,000
To Costing Profit and Loss A/c		3,520			
	80	4,000		80	4,000

Problem 3. *In a certain process, material is mixed and cooked in batches of 1,000 lbs each. Cooking results in ten percent loss of weight of the mixture. Since the cooking requires considerable skill and constant watching; there is generally a*

further loss from spoilage which is not discovered until the process has been completed. Also, past experience shows that normally five batches out of every twenty started in the process are spoiled in this way.

In a given quarter, the production records show:

(i) Production started in the process: 200 batches of 1,000 lbs each.

(ii) Production completed and transferred to finished goods is 1, 25,000 lbs.

(iii) There is no inventory of work-in-progress at the start or at the end of the quarter.

Costs recorded during the quarter amounted to ₹ 6, 75,000 of which Input cost was ₹ 3, 00,000.

Prepare the Process Account for the quarter and determine the cost per pound of finished product.

Solution : **Process Account**

Dr Cr

Details	Unit (lbs)	Amount (₹)	Details	Unit (lbs)	Amount (₹)
To Cost of material and processing	2,00,000	3,00,000	By Weight Lost	20,000	—
To Labour and Overheads		3,75,000	By Norma Loss A/c [(0.25) × (2,00,000 – 20,000) = 0.25]	45,000	—
			By Abnormal Loss A/c (@ ₹5 per lb	10,000	50,000
			By Finished Goods Stock A/c (Output transferred)	1,25,000	6,25,000
	2,00,000	6,75,000		2,00,000	6,75,000

Problem 4. *The following particulars related to two processes M an S for the month of January 2005:*

Details	*Process M*	*Process S*
Total Input (Units)	*80,000 (@ ₹ 5 per unit)*	*2,000*
Normal Loss (% of Input)	*10*	*4*
Additional Costs Incurred:		
Material	*—*	*20,000*
Direct Labour	*70,000*	*2,50,000*
Overheads	*50,000*	*2,20,500*
Realisable Value of scrap per unit (₹)	*2.00*	*8.00*
Output (Units)	*70,000*	*70,000*

The entire output of Process M was transferred to Process S. The entire output of Process S was sold at ₹ 20 per unit. Assume there was no opening or closing stock of any type in the process of M or S.

You are required to prepare the necessary accounts for the period.

Solution :

Process M Account

Dr Cr

Details	Unit (lbs)	Amount (₹)	Details	Unit (lbs)	Amount (₹)
To Material Introduced	80,000	4,00,000	By Normal Loss A/c [(0.10)×(80,000)	8,000	16,000
To Direct Labour		70,000	By Abnormal Loss A/c (@ ₹7 per unit	2,000	14,000
To overheads		50,000	By Process S A/c	70,000	4,90,000
	80,000	5,20,000		80,000	5,20,000

Process S Account

Dr Cr

Details	Unit (lbs)	Amount (₹)	Details	Unit (lbs)	Amount (₹)
To Process M A/c	70,000	4,90,000	By Normal Loss A/c [0.04 × 72,000]	2,880	23,040
To Material Introduced	2,000	20,000	By Finished Goods Stock A/c (Output transferred @ ₹ 13.85 per unit)	70,000	9,69,500
To Direct Labour		2,50,000			
To overheads		2,20,352			
To Abnormal Gain A/c @ ₹ 13.85 per unit	880	12,188			
	72,880	9,92,540		72,880	9,92,540

Abnormal Wastage A/c

Dr Cr

Details	Unit (lbs)	Amount (₹)	Details	Unit (lbs)	Amount (₹)
To Process M	2,000	14,000	By Bank/Drs A/c	2,000	4,000
			By Costing profit & Loss Account		10,000
	2,000	14,000		2,000	14,000

Abnormal Gain A/c

Dr | Cr

Details	Unit (lbs)	Amount (₹)	Details	Unit (lbs)	Amount (₹)
To Normal Loss A/c	880	7,040	By Process S A/c	880	12,188
To Costing profit & Loss A/c		5,148			
	880	12,188		880	12,188

Costing Profit & Loss Account

Dr | Cr

Details	Amount (₹)	Details	Amount (₹)
To Cost of Process S	9,69,500	By Sales A/c (70,000 × 20)	14,00,000
To Abnormal Wastage A/c	10,000	By Abnormal Gain A/c	5,148
To Net profit	4,25,648		
	14,05,148		14,05,148

Problem 5. *A product passes through three processes—-P, Q, and R. The details of expenses incurred on the three processes during the year 2006 were as under:*

Details	*Process P*	*Process Q*	*Process R*
Units issued	*40,000*		
Cost per unit (₹)	*250*		
Sundry Materials	*1,00,000*	*1,50,000*	*50,000*
Labour (₹)	*3,00,000*	*8,00,000*	*6,50,000*
Direct Expenses (₹)	*60,000*	*1,81,500*	*2,72,000*
Sale price of output per unit (₹)	*300*	*420*	*640*

Management Expenses during the year amounted to ₹ 8, 00,000 and selling expenses were ₹ 5, 20,000. Both these are not allocable to the processes.

Actual output of the three processes was as under:

Process P: 37,200 units

Process Q: 21,600 units

Process R: 8,400 units

Two thirds of the output of Process P and one-half of the output of Process Q was passed on to the next process and the balance was sold. The entire output of Process R was sold.

The normal wastage of the three processes calculated on the input of every process was:

Process P: 5%; Process Q: 15%; Process R: 20%.

The wastage of Process P was sold at ₹ 5 per unit, that of Process Q at ₹ 12.50 and that of Process R at ₹ 25 per unit.

Prepare the three process Accounts and a statement of Income for the year 2006 showing fully the accounting treatment of process wastage.

Solution :

Process P Account

Dr Cr

Details	Unit	Amount (₹)	Details	Unit	Amount (₹)
To Input of Basic Material @ ₹ 250	40,000	100,00,000	By Normal Loss A/c (@₹ 5)	2,000	10,000
To Sundry Materials		1,00,000	By Abnormal Loss A/c @₹ 275	800	2,20,000
To Labour		3,00,000	By Bank (Sale) @ ₹ 300 per unit of output	12,400	37,20,000
To Direct expenses		60,000	By Output transferred to process Q @ ₹ 275	24,800	68,20,000
To Costing Profit and Loss A/c (Gain on Sale of Output of this Process @ ₹25)		3,10,000			
	40,000	107,70,000		40,000	107,70,000

Process Q Account

Dr Cr

Details	Unit	Amount (₹)	Details	Unit	Amount (₹)
To Transferred from Process P	24,800	68,20,000	By Normal Loss A/c @ ₹ 12.5	3,720	46,500
To Sundry Materials		1,50,000	By Bank (Sale) @ ₹ 420 per unit of output	10,800	45,36,000
To Labour		8,00,000	By Output transferred to Process R @ ₹ 375	10,800	40,50,000
To Direct expenses		1,81,500			
To Abnormal Gain A/c (@ ₹ 375)	520	1,95,000			
To Costing Profit and Loss A/c (Gain on Sale of Output of this Process (@ ₹45)		4,86,000			
Total	25,320	86,32,500	Total	25,320	86,32,500

Process R Account

Dr Cr

Details	Unit	Amount (₹)	Details	Unit	Amount (₹)
To Transferred from Process Q	10,800	40,50,000	By Normal Loss A/c @ ₹ 25	2,160	54,000
To Sundry Materials		50,000	By Abnormal Loss A/c @ ₹ 575	240	1,38,000
To Labour		6,50,000	By Output transferred to Finished Goods @ ₹ 575	8,400	48,30,000
To Direct expenses		2,72,000			
	10,800	50,22,000		10,800	50,22,000

Normal Loss Account

Dr Cr

Details	Unit	Amount (₹)	Details	Unit	Amount (₹)
To Process P A/c @ ₹ 5	2,000	10,000	By Cash/Debtors A/c :		
			Process P (@ ₹ 5)	2,000	10,000
			Process Q (@ ₹ 12.5)	3,200	40,000
			Process R (@ ₹ 25)	2,160	54,000
To Process Q A/c @₹ 12.5	3,720	46,500	By Abnormal Gain A/c @ ₹ 12.50	520	6,500
To Process R A/c @₹ 25	2,160	54,000			
	7,880	1,10,500		7,880	1,10,500

Abnormal Gain Account

Dr Cr

Details	Unit	Amount (₹)	Details	Unit	Amount (₹)
To Normal Loss A/c (@₹ 12.5)	520	6,500	By Abnormal Gain A/c @ ₹ 375	520	1,95,000
To Costing Profit and Loss A/c		1,88,500			
	520	1,95,000		520	1,95,000

Abnormal Loss Account

Dr Cr

Details	Unit	Amount (₹)	Details	Unit	Amount (₹)
To Process P A/c @₹ 275	800	2,20,000	By Cash/Debtors A/c		
			By Process P @₹ 5	800	4,000
			By Process R @₹ 25	240	6,000
To Process R A/c @₹ 575	240	1,38,000	By Costing Profit and Loss A/c		3,48,000
	1,040	3,58,000		1,040	3,58,000

Finished Goods Account

Dr Cr

Details	Unit	Amount (₹)	Details	Unit	Amount (₹)
To Process R A/c @ ₹ 575	8,400	48,30,000	By Cash/Debtors A/c @ ₹ 640	8,400	53,76,000
To Costing Profit and Loss A/c		5,46,000			
	8,400	53,76,000		8,400	53,76,000

Costing Profit and Loss Account

Dr Cr

Details	Amount (₹)	Details	Amount (₹)
To Abnormal Loss A/c	3,48,000	By Process P(12,400×25)	3,10,000
To Management Expenses	6,00,000	By Process Q (10,800×45)	4,86,000
To Selling Expenses	4,20,000	By Finished Goods A/c (8,400×60)	5,46,000
To Net Profit	1,62,500	By Abnormal Gain A/c	1,88,500
	15,30,500		15,30,500

Working Notes:

1. Cost per unit of output of Process P:

$$[(104,60,000 - 10,000) \div (40,000 - 2,000)$$

$$104,50,000 \div 38,000 = ₹\ 275.$$

2. Cost per unit of output of Process Q:

[(79, 51,500 – 46,500) ÷ (24,800 – 3,720)

7905000 ÷ 21,080 = ₹ 375.

3. Cost per unit of output of Process R:

[(50, 22,000 – 54,000) ÷ (10,800 – 2,160)

49, 68,000 ÷ 8,640 = ₹ 575.

Problem 6. *The following data are available pertaining to a product after passing through.*

Two processes I and II: Output transferred to Process III from Process II 8500 units for ₹ 96,985.

Expenses incurred in Process III:

Details	***Amount (₹)***
Sundry Materials	*1,900*
Direct Wages	*8,000*
Direct Expenses	*2,100*

The wastage of Process III is sold at ₹ 1.25 per unit. The overhead charges were 175% of direct wages. The final product was sold at ₹ 20 per unit fetching profit of 25% on sales.

Find the percentage of wastage in Process III and Prepare Process III account.

Solution :

Dr **Process III Account** Cr

Details	**Units**	**Amount (₹)**	**Details**	**Units**	**Amount (₹)**
To Process II A/c	8,500	96,985	By Normal Loss A/c @ ₹ 1.25	340	425
To Sundry Materials		1,900	By Finished Goods A/c @ ₹ 16	8,160	1,30,560
To Direct Wages		8,000			
To Direct Expenses		2,100			
To Overheads		22,000			
Total	8,500	1,30,985	Total	8,500	1,30,985

Percentage of Normal Loss in Process III: (340/8,500) × 100=>4%.

Working Notes:

Let the Units of Normal Loss be= X

Number of units of Finished goods = (8500 – X)

Value of Normal Loss@ ₹ 1.25 per unit = ₹ 1.25 X

Cost of Finished Goods per unit = ₹ 20 – (0.25 × 20) => ₹ 16.

Cost of Finished Goods = (8500 – X) × 16= ₹ 1, 36,000 – 16 X

Thus,

₹ 1.25 X + 1, 36,000 – 16 X] = ₹ 1, 30,985

1, 36,000 – 14.75 X = 1, 30,985

14.75 X = 1, 36,000 – 1, 30,985

14.75 X = 5,015

X = 5,015/14.75 = 340units

Units of Finished Goods = 8,500 – 340 => 8,160

Cost of Finished Goods = 8,160 × 16 = ₹ 1, 30,560.

Problem 7. *From the following details prepare Statement of Equivalent Production and Statement of cost by using FIFO:*

Opening work-in-progress (Units)		*2,000*
Materials (100% complete)	*₹ 7,500*	
Labour (60% complete)	*₹ 3,000*	
Overhead (60% complete)	*₹ 1,500*	
Introduced into the Process (Units)		*8,000*

There are 2,000 units in closing work-in-progress and the stage of completion is estimated to be:

Materials 100%, Labour 50% and Overhead 50%, 8000 units are transferred to next process.

The process cost for the period are:

Details	***Amount (₹)***
Material	*1,00,000*
Labour	*78,000*
Overhead	*39,000*

[B.Com (Hons.) DU, 2009]

Solution : **Statement of Equivalent Production**

Input Units	Details	Output units	Equivalent Production			
			Material		Labour & Overheads	
			%	Unit	%	Unit
2,000	Opening work-in-Progress	2,000			40	800
8,000	Introduced and completed during the period	6,000	100	6,000	100	6,000
	Closing work-in-Progress	2,000	100	2,000	50	1,000
10,000	Toal	10,000		8,000		7,800

Statement of Cost

Details	Cost (₹)	EOQ Units	Cost per unit (₹)
Material	1,00,000	8,000	12.50
Labour	78,000	7,800	10.00
Overheads	39,000	7,800	5.00
Total	2,17,000		27.50

Statement of Apportionment of Cost

Details	Element of cost	EOQ Units	Cost per unit (₹)	Cost (₹)	Total Cost (₹)
I(a). Opening work-in-Progress (Work done during the preceding Period)	Material			7,500	
	Labour			3,000	
	Overheads			1,500	12,000
I(b). Opening work-in-Progress (Work done during the current Period)	Material	—	12.50	—	
	Labour	800	10.00	8,000	
	Overheads	800	5.00	4,000	12,000
I. [(I(a) + I(b)] Total Value of Opening work-in-Progress		—	—	—	24,000
II. Introduced and completed during the period	Material	6,000	12.50	75,000	
	Labour	6,000	10.00	60,000	
	Overheads	6,000	5.00	30,000	1,65,000
III. Closing work-in-Progress	Material	2,000	12.50	25,000	
	Labour	1,000	10.00	10,000	
	Overheads	1,000	5.00	5,000	40,000

Statement of Cost of Output Transferred

Details	Amount (₹)
Value of Opening work-in-Progress	24,000
Introduced and completed during the period	1,65,000
Total	1,89,000

Problem 8. *The Global Limited has a single process.*

Work-in-process (Opening) 8,000 units; cost: Materials ₹ 37,000; Wages ₹ 8,250; Overhead ₹ 7,250.

During the period the input was 32,000 units.

Additional costs were: Materials ₹ 1,41,000; Wages ₹ 42,900; Overhead ₹ 37,700.

At the end of the year 28,000 units were fully processed and 12,000 units were in process. The value of the closing stock includes full cost of materials and only one fourth of the cost of wages and overheads. Tabulate the production and cost figures to give quantities, unit values, total value of completed output and detailed values for the closing work-in-process.

Solution :

Note: Degree of completion of opening work-in-process is NOT given. Therefore, it has been averaged over completed output and process.

Stastement of Equivalent Production

Input Units	Details	Output units	Equivalent Production			
			Material		Labour & Overheads	
			%	Unit	%	Unit
8,000	Opening work-in-Progress					
32,000	Units introduced					
	Units Completed	28,000	100	28,000	100	28,000
	Closing work-in-Progress	12,000	100	3,000	25	3,000
40,000	Total	40,000		31,000		31,000

Statement of Cost Per unit (₹)

Details	Material	Labour	Overhead	Total
Opening work-in-Progress	37,000	8,250	7,250	52,500
Additional cost incurred in the process	1,41,000	42,900	37,700	2,21,600
a. Total cost of entire output	1,78,000	51,150	4 4,950	2,74,100
b. Equivalent Production (Units)	40,000	31,000	31,000	
c. Cost per unit (a / b)	4.45	1.65	1.45	7.55

Statement of Apportionment of Cost

Details	Computations	Total Cost (₹)
I. Cost of completed Units	28,000 × 07.55	2,11,400
II. Cost of closing work-in-Progress	Material: 12,000 × 4.45 = 53,400 Labour: 3,000 × 1.65 = 4,950 Overheads: 3,000 × 1.45 = 4,350	62,700
Total		2,74,100

Process Account

Dr Cr

Details	Units	Amount (₹)	Details	Units	Amount (₹)
To Cost of Opening work-in-Progress A/c (37,000 + 8,250 + 7,250)	8,000	52,500	By Units completed	28,000	2,11,400
To Materials	32,000	1,41,000	By Closing work-in-Progress	12,000	62,700
To Direct Wages		42,900			
To Overheads		37,700			
Total	40,000	2,74,100	Total	40,000	2,74,100

Problem 9. *From the following details, prepare statement of Equivalent Production, statement of cost and Find out the value of: (a) Output transferred; and (b) closing work-in-progress.*

I. Opening work-in-progress: 2,500 units

Materials (100%) complete) ₹ 30,000; Labour (60% complete) ₹ 12,000; Overheads (50% complete) ₹ 6,800.

II. Introduction in the Process: 10,000 units

III. Closing work-in-progress: 2,500 units

Materials (100%) complete); Labour (50% complete); Overheads (40% complete).

IV. Transferred to the Next Process: 10,000 units

V. Process costs for the period are Materials ₹ 4,00,000; Labour ₹ 3,12,000; Overheads ₹ 1,56,000.

Also prepare Process account using (i) Average Method, and (ii) FIFO Method.

Solution : (Method Wise):

(i) Average Method:

Statement of Equivalent Production

Input Units	Details	Output units	Equivalent Production					
			Material		Labour		Overheads	
			%	Unit	%	Unit	%	Unit
2,500	Opening work-in-Progress							
10,000	Units introduced							

	Finished and transferred including Opening WIP	10,000	100	10,000	100	10,000	100	10,000
	Closing work-in-Progress	2,500	100	2,500	50	1,250	40	1,000
12,500	Total	12,500		12,500		11,250		11,000

Statement of Cost Per unit (₹)

Details	Material	Labour	Overhead	Total
Opening work-in-Progress	30,000	12,000	6,800	48,800
Additional cost incurred in the process	4,00,000	3,12,000	1,56,000	8,68,000
a. Total cost of entire output	4,30,000	3,24,000	1,62,800	9,16,800
b. Equivalent Production (Units)	12,500	11,250	11,000	
c. Cost per unit (a / b)	34.40	28.80	14.80	78.00

Statement of Apportionment of Cost

Details	Computations	Total Cost (₹)
I. Cost of completed and transferred Units	10,000 × 78.00	7,80,000
II. Cost of closing work-in-Progress	Material 2,500 × 34.40 = 86,000 Labour 1,250 × 28.80 = 36,000 Overheads 1,000 × 14.80 = 14,800	1,36,800
Total		9,16,800

Process Account

Dr Cr

Details	Units	Amount (₹)	Details	Units	Amount (₹)
To Cost of Opening work-in-Progress A/c (30,000 + 12,300 + 6,000)	2,500	48,800	By transfer to Next Process A/c	10,000	7,80,000
To Materials A/c	10,000	4,00,000	By Closing work-in-Progress A/c	2,500	1,36,800
To Direct Wages A/c		3,12,000			
To Overheads A/c		1,56,000			
Total	12,500	9,16,800	Total	12,500	9,16,800

(ii) FIFO Method:

Statement of Equivalent Production

Input Units	Details	Output units	Equivalent Production					
			Material		Labour		Overheads	
			%	Unit	%	Unit	%	Unit
2,500	Opening work-in-Progress	2,500	NIL	NIL	40	1,000	50	1,250
10,000	Units introduced							
	Introduced and Completed	7,500	100	7,500	100	7,500	100	7,500
	Closing work-in-Progress	2,500	100	2,500	50	1,250	40	1,000
12,500	Total	12,500		10,000		9,750		9,750

Statement of Cost Per unit (₹)

Details	Material	Labour	Overhead	Total
a. Cost incurred during the current period	4,00,000	3,12,000	1,56,000	8,60,000
b. Equivalent Production (Units)	10,000	9,750	9,750	
c. Cost per unit (a / b)	40.00	32.00	16.00	88.00

Statement of Apportionment of Cost

Details	Element of cost	EOQ Units	Cost per unit (₹)	Cost (₹)	Total Cost (₹)
I(a). Opening work-in-Progress	Material			30,000	
(Work done during the preceding	Labour			12,000	
Period)	Overheads			6,800	48,800
I(b). Opening work-in-Progress	Material	—	40.00	—	
(Work done during the current	Labour	1,000	32.00	32,000	
Period)	Overheads	1,250	16.00	20,000	52,000
I. [(I(a) + I(b)] Total Value of Opening work-in-Progress					1,00,800
II. Introduced and completed during the period	Material	7,500	40.00	3,00,000	
	Labour	7,500	32.00	2,40,000	
	Overheads	7,500	16.00	1,20,000	6,60,000
III. Closing work-in-Progress	Material	2,500	40.00	1,00,000	
	Labour	1,250	32.00	40,000	1,56,000
	Overheads	1,000	16.00	16,000	

Statement of Cost of Output Transferred

Details	Amount (₹)
Value of Opening work-in-Progress	1,00,800
Introduced and completed during the period	6,60,000
Total	7,60,800

Process Account

Dr Cr

Details	Units	Amount (₹)	Details	Units	Amount (₹)
To Cost of Opening work-in-Progress A/c (30,000 + 12,000 + 6,800)	2,500	48,800	By Transfer to Next Process A/c	10,000	7,60,800
To Materials A/c	10,000	4,00,000	By Closing work-in-Progress A/c	2,500	1,56,000
To Direct Wages A/c		3,12,000			
To Overheads A/c		1,56,000			
Total	12,500	9,16,800	Total	12,500	9,16,800

Problem 10. *At the end of process P, carried on in a factory during the month ending March 31, 2007 the number of units produced was 10,200 excluding 600 units damaged at the very end of the process. The damaged units realized ₹ 15 per unit as scrap. A normal wastage of 10% occurs during the process, the wastage realized was ₹ 10 per unit. A unit of raw materials cost ₹ 25. The other expenses for the week were:*

Details	*Amount (₹)*
Direct Wages	*50,000*
Power	*30,000*
General Expenses	*1,00,000*

30% of the output is sold so as to show a profit of 20% on the selling price; the rest of the output is transferred to Process B.

Solution : Working Notes:

I. Material Introduced:

= (10,200 + 600) ÷ 0.9 => 12, 000 units

II. Total Cost of 10,200 units:

= (3, 00,000 + 50000 + 30,000 + 1, 00,000) – (12,000 + 9,000)

= 4, 80,000 – 21,000 => ₹ 4, 59,000

Cost per unit of finished goods:

= 4, 59,000 ÷10,200 => ₹ 45.

III. Cost of 3,060 units (after damage):

= (4, 59,000) × 3,060) ÷10,200 => ₹ 1, 37,700

Sale Price of 3,060 units:

= (1, 37,700) × (5/4) => ₹ 1, 72,125

Note: 1/5 (or 20%) of selling price is ¼ (25%) of cost.

Process: P Account

Dr Cr

Details	Units	Amount (₹)	Details	Units	Amount (₹)
To Materials Introduced @ ₹ 25	12,000	3,00,000	By Normal Loss A/c @ ₹ 10	1,200	12,000
To Direct Wages A/c		50,000	By Damaged Goods A/c @ ₹ 15	600	9,000
To Power A/c		30,000	By Bank A/c @ ₹56.25	3,060	1,72,125
To General Expenses A/c		1,00,000	By Process B A/c @ ₹45	7,140	3,21,300
To Costing Profit & Loss A/c (3,060 × 11.25)		34,425			
Total	12,000	5,14,425	Total	12,000	5,14,425

Problem 11. *The following data are available in respect of process I for March, 2007:*

(i) Opening work-in-Progress 800 Units at accost of ₹ 4,000.

(ii) The degree of completion Opening work-in-Progress:

Details	*%*
Materials	*100*
Labour	*60*
Overheads	*60*

(iii) Input of materials at a total cost of ₹ 36,800 for 9,200 units.

(iv) Direct Wages incurred ₹ 16,740.

(v) Production overheads ₹ 8,370.

(vi) Units scrapped 1,200 units. The stage of completion of these units was:

Details	*%*
Materials	*100*
Labour	*80*
Overheads	*80*

(vii) Closing Work-in-Progress 900 Units. The stage of completion of these units was:

Details	*%*
Materials	*100*
Labour	*70*
Overheads	*70*

(viii) 7,900units were completed and transferred to the next process.

(ix) Normal Loss: 8% of the total input (opening stock plus units put into the process.

(x) Scrap value is ₹ 4 per unit.

You are required to:

1. *Compute Equivalent Production*
2. *Calculate Cost per equivalent unit*
3. *Calculate the cost of abnormal loss (or gain), closing work-in-progress and units transferred to the next process using FIFO method.*
4. *Show the Process account for March 2007.* **[B.Com (Hons.) DU, 2007]**

Solution : **Statement of Equivalent Production**

Input units	Details	Output units	EQP (Units)		
			Material	Labour	Overhead
9,200	Introduced				
800	Work-in-Progress (Opening)	800	—	320	320
	Normal Loss	800	—	—	—
	Finished	7,100	7,100	7,100	7,100
	Abnormal Loss	400	400	320	320
	Work-in-Progress (Closing)	900	900	630	630
10,000	Total	10,000	8,400	8,370	8,370

Process-I: Statement of Cost

Element of Cost	Cost (₹)	EQP (Units)	Cost (₹) (EQP Unit)
Direct Material	36,800		
Scrap value of Normal Loss	(3,200)		
Total Materials	33,600	8,400	4.00

Labour	16,740	8,370	2.00
Overheads	8,370	8,370	1.00
Total Cost	58,710		7.00

Process-I: Statement of Evaluation

Details	Element of Cost (₹)	EQP Units	Cost per EQP Unit	Cost (₹)	Total Cost (₹)
Work-in-Progress (Opening)	Material	—	—		
	Labour	3200	2.00	640	
	Overhead	320	1.00	320	960
Finished Production	Material	8,400	4.00	33,600	
	Labour	8,370	2.00	16,740	
	Overhead	8,370	1.00	8,370	49,700
Abnormal Loss	Material	400	4.00	1,600	
	Labour	320	2.00	640	
	Overhead	320	1.00	320	2,560
Work-in-Progress (Closing)	Material	900	4.00	3,600	
	Labour	630	2.00	1,260	
	Overhead	630	1.00	630	5,490

Completed and Transferred to the Next Process:

(i) Opening Work-in-progress (800 Units): (Existing cost + Current cost)
= 4,000 + 960=> 4,960

(ii) Introduced and completed (7,100 Units): 49,700

Total (7,900 Units): 54,660

Process-I Account

Dr Cr

Details	Units	Amount (₹)	Details	Units	Amount (₹)
To Work-in-Progress (Opening)	800	4,000	By Normal Loss A/c	800	3,200
To Materials A/c	9,200	36,800	By Transfer to Process II A/c	7,900	54,660
To Labour A/c		16,740	By Abnormal Loss A/c	400	2,560
To Overheads A/c		8, 370	By Work-in-Progress A/c (Closing)	900	5,490
Total	10,000	65,910	Total	10,000	65,910

Problem 12. *The accountant of a chemical company provides you the following data:*

Details	*Unit*	*Amount (₹)*
Work-in-Process (Beginning period)	*2,000*	
Direct Materials		*4,200*
Direct Labour and Manufacturing Overheads		*1,950*
Addition to Work-in-Process in January	*4,000*	
Direct Materials		*36,000*
Direct Labour and Manufacturing Overheads		*30,000*
Total		*72,150*
Work-in-Process (End of period)	*1,500*	

Further, Work-in-Process at the beginning of the period is complete to the extent: Materials 100% and labour and manufacturing overheads 75%. Work-in-Process at the end of the period is complete to the extent: Materials 100% and labour and manufacturing overheads 50%.

You are required to:

(i) Calculate the number of units of product transferred to finished goods stock during the period. Assume no units are lost in process.

(ii) Calculate the number of equivalent whole units of work completed during the period.

(iii) Calculate the unit cost for materials during the month of January using a FIFO method of inventory issue.

Solution :

(i) Number of units of product transferred to Finished Goods Stock:

= Units in the beginning + Units added – Units at the end

= 2,000 + 4,000 – 1,500 = 4,500 Units

(ii) Statement of Equivalent Production (EQP (Units)

Input units	**Details**	**Output units**	**Material**	**Labour**	**Overhead**
4,000	Introduced				
2,000	Work-in-Progress (Opening)	2,000	—	500	500
	Finished	2,500	2,500	2,500	2,500
	Work-in-Progress (Closing)	1,500	1,500	750	750
6,000	Total	6,000	4,000	3,750	3,750

(iii) Direct Material Cost:

= Direct Material Cost/ Equivalent Production

= 36,000/4,000 = ₹ 9 per EQP unit

Problem 13. *The following data relate to process Q:*

(i) Opening work-in-Progress 4,000 Units

Degree of completion:

Details	%	Amount (₹)
Materials	100	24,000
Labour	60	14,400
Overheads	60	7,200

(ii) Received during the month of April from Process P:

40,000 Units ₹ 1,71,000

(iii) Expenses incurred in Process Q during the month:

Details	Amount (₹)
Materials	79,000
Labour	1,38,230
Overheads	69,120

(iv) Closing Work-in-Progress 3,000 Units

Degree of Completion:

Details	%
Materials	100
Labour	50
Overheads	50

(v) Units scrapped 4,000 units

Degree of completion:

Details	%
Materials	100
Labour	80
Overheads	80

(vi) Normal Loss: 5% of current input

(vii) Spoiled goods realized ₹ 1.50 each on sale.

(viii) Completed units are transferred to warehouse.

Prepare, using FIFO method:

1. Statement of Equivalent Production

2. Statement of Cost per equivalent unit

3. Statement of Evaluation

4. Process Q account. **[B.Com (Hons.) DU, 2008]**

Solution : Process-Q: Statement of Equivalent Production

Input units	Details	Output units	EQP (Units)		
			Material	Labour	Overhead
40,000	Transferred from Process P				
4,000	Work-in-Progress (Opening)	4,000	—	1,600	1,600
	Normal Loss	2,000	—	—	—
	Finished and transferred	33,000	33,000	33,000	33,000
	Abnormal Loss	2,000	2,000	1600	1,600
	Work-in-Progress (Closing)	3,000	3,000	1500	1,500
44,000	Total	44,000	38,000	37,700	37,700

Process-Q: Statement of Cost

Element of Cost	Cost (₹)	EQP (Units)	Cost (₹) (EQP Unit)
Direct Material	1,71,000		
Additional Materials	79,000		
Scrap value of Normal Loss	(3,000)		
Total Materials	2,47,000	38,000	6.50
Labour	1,38,230	37,700	3.67
Overheads	69,120	2,100	1.83
Total Cost	4,54,350		12.00

Process-Q: Statement of Evaluation

Details	Element of Cost (₹)	EQP Units	Cost per EQP Unit	Cost (₹)	Total Cost (₹)
Work-in-Progress (Opening)	Material	—	—	—	
	Labour	1,600	3.67	5,872	
	Overhead	1,600	1.83	2,928	8,800

Finished Production	Material	33,000	6.50	2,14,500	
	Labour	33,000	3.67	1,21,110	
	Overhead	33,000	1.83	60,390	3,96,000
Abnormal Loss	Material	2,000	6.50	13,000	
	Labour	1,600	3.67	5,872	
	Overhead	1,600	1.83	2,928	21,800
Work-in-Progress (Closing)	Material	3000	6.50	19,500	
	Labour	1500	3.67	5,505	
	Overhead	1500	1.83	2,745	27,750

Process-Q Account

Dr Cr

Details	Units	Amount (₹)	Details	Units	Amount (₹)
To Work-in-Progress A/c (Opening)	4,000	45,600	By Normal Loss A/c	2,000	3,000
To Process P A/c	40,000	1,71,000	By Abnormal Loss A/c	2,000	21,800
To Materials A/c		79,000	By Transfer to Warehouse A/c	37,000	4,50,400
To Labour A/c		1,38,230	By Work-in-Progress A/c (Closing)	3,000	27,750
To Overheads A/c		69,120			
Total	44,000	5,00,950	Total	44,000	5,00,950

Normal Loss Account

Dr Cr

Details	Units	Amount (₹)	Details	Units	Amount (₹)
To Process-Q A/c @ ₹ 1.50	2,000	3,000	By Bank/Drs A/c @ ₹ 1.50	2,000	3,000
Total	2,000	3,000	Total	2,000	3,000

Dr **Abnormal Loss Account** Cr

Details	Units	Amount (₹)	Details	Units	Amount (₹)
To Process-Q A/c @ ₹ 10.90	2,000	21,800	By Bank/Drs A/c @ ₹ 1.50	2,000	3,000
			By Costing Profit and Loss A/c		18,800
Total	2,000	21,800	Total	2,000	21,800

Problem 14. *The product of a manufacturing concern passes through two processes: A and B. the normal losses and abnormal losses are defective units having a scrap value of ₹ 2 and ₹ 5 per unit in process A and B respectively. The following information relates to the month ending 31.3.2010:*

Details	*Process A*	*Process B*
Raw Materials issued @ ₹ 5	*300 units*	—
Normal Loss	*10% of input*	*5% of input*
Output	*280 units*	*260 units*
Additional Components	*₹ 1,000*	*₹ 780*
Direct Wages	*₹ 4,000*	*₹ 3,000*
Direct Expenses	*₹ 10,000*	*₹ 14,000*
Production Overhead (as a percentage of direct wages)	*75%*	*125%*

There was no opening or closing work-in-progress but opening and closing stocks of finished goods were ₹ 20,000 and ₹ 23,000 respectively.

Prepare Process accounts, Finished Stock A/c, Normal Loss A/c, Abnormal Loss A/c and Abnormal Gain A/c. **[B.Com (Hons.) DU, 2010]**

Solution :

Process A Account

Dr Cr

Details	Unit	Amount (₹)	Details	Unit	Amount (₹)
To Input of Basic Material @5	3,000	15,000	By Normal Loss A/c (@₹ 2)	300	600
To Additional components		1,000	By output transferred to process B @ ₹ 12	2,800	33,600
To Direct Wages		4,000			
To Direct Expenses		10,000			
To Production Overheads		3,000			
To Abnormal Gain A/c @ ₹ 12	100	1,200			
	3,100	34,200		3,100	34,200

Working Note:

Cost per Unit = (33,000 – 600) ÷ 2,700 = ₹ 12 per unit

Process B Account

Dr | Cr

Details	Unit	Amount (₹)	Details	Unit	Amount (₹)
To Transferred from Process A	2,800	33,600	By Normal Loss A/c @ 5	140	700
To Additional components		780	By Abnormal Loss A/c @ ₹ 20.46	60	1,228
To Direct Wages		3,000	By transferred to Finished Stock A/c	2,600	53,202
To Direct Expenses		14,000			
To Production Overheads		3,750			
Total	2,800	55,130	Total	2,800	55,130

Working Note:

Cost per Unit = (55,130 – 700) ÷ 2,660 = ₹ 20.46 per unit

Finished Goods Account

Dr | Cr

Details	Amount (₹)	Details	Amount (₹)
To Balance b/d	20,000	By Cost of Sales A/c	50,202
To Process B A/c	53,202	By Balance c/d	23,000
Total	73,202	Total	73,202
To Balance b/d	23,000		

Normal Loss Account

Dr | Cr

Details	Unit	Amount (₹)	Details	Unit	Amount (₹)
To Process A A/c @ ₹ 2	300	600	By Cash/Debtors A/c:		
			Process A (@ ₹ 2)	200	400
			Process B (@ ₹ 5)	140	700
To Process B A/c @ ₹ 5	140	700	By Abnormal Gain A/c @ ₹ 2	100	200
Total	440	1,300	Total	440	1,300

Dr **Abnormal Gain Account** Cr

Details	Unit	Amount (₹)	Details	Unit	Amount (₹)
To Normal Loss A/c (@₹ 2)	100	200	By Process A A/c	100	1,200
To Costing Profit and Loss A/c		1,000			
Total	100	1,200	Total	100	1,200

Dr **Abnormal Loss Account** Cr

Details	Unit	Amount (₹)	Details	Unit	Amount (₹)
To Process B A/c @ ₹ 20.46	60	1,228	By Cash/Debtors A/c	60	300
			By Costing Profit and Loss A/c		928
Total	60	1,228	Total	60	1,228

OBJECTIVE TYPE QUESTIONS

I. Fill in the blank spaces with suitable word/s :

1. In process costing, normal loss is not transferred to .... Account.
2. Abnormal Loss appears on the .... side of the process account.
3. Abnormal Gain appears on the .... side of the process account.
4. Normal loss does .... per unit cost of production.
5. When actual loss in process is more than normal loss, the difference between the two is called ....
6. Two main methods of calculating equivalent production are .... and ....
7. When actual process loss is 95 units and normal loss is 100 units, then there is .... Of 5 units.
8. Two items that appear on the credit side of a process account are .... and ....
9. Two of the special problems that arise in process costing are .... and ....
10. Two items that appear on the debit side of a process account are .... and ....
11. Sale proceeds from abnormal process loss are credited to .... account.
12. In inter-process profits, the output of one process is transferred from one process to the next process not at .... but at ....
13. In .... Method of computing equivalent production, the cost of opening work-in-progress is not kept separate but is added to the costs incurred during the period.

14. The main objective of inter-process profit is to ....
15. Two of the special problems that arise in process costing are .... and ....
16. In process costing, total process cost is divided by .... to arrive at eh cost per unit.

Answers :

1. Costing profit and Loss account
2. Credit
3. Debit
4. increase
5. Abnormal Loss
6. FIFO, Average method
7. Abnormal gain
8. Normal loss, Abnormal loss
9. Process loss, Valuation of work-in-Progress
10. material cost, Labour cost
11. Abnormal loss
12. Cost, Market price
13. Average
14. Show the profitability of each process
15. Process losses, valuation of work-in-progress
16. Number of un its produced

II. Indicate whether the following statements are True or False :

1. Abnormal process loss is transferred to factory overhead account.
2. Cost per unit remains same in case of abnormal loss as well as abnormal gain.
3. Process costing is a specific order costing.
4. In process industries there is a flow of materials from one operation to the next operation.
5. Process input less normal loss less actual output gives output abnormally lost (all in units).
6. 'Make' or 'Buy' decisions are involved before and after different processes.
7. Various units produced at a process are not homogeneous.
8. The standard system of costing cannot be applied to process accounts.
9. Each process is a separate cost centre.
10. There are no work-in-progress inventories at processes.
11. Process output is usually for stock.
12. Costs incurred at preceding processes get accumulated in next process.
13. All normal losses are charged to the product in process costing.
14. Abnormal losses increase cost per unit in process accounts.
15. In process industries output at a process is always equal to input in units.
16. Cost per unit at a process is equal to total normal costs incurred at the process divided by normal output of the process.
17. Realizable value of normal loss is deducted from cost incurred at a process.
18. Abnormal gain results in higher scrap than the normal.
19. Entire input lost at the process is available in the form of scrap.
20. Determination of equivalent production gives precise values of output and work-in-progress, not estimated values.

21. Computation of equivalent production is required only where there is opening and/or closing work-in-progress at processes.
22. In case of work-in-progress at process, production is measured in terms of equivalence of fully complete units.
23. Statement of Equivalent production gives normal equivalent units of output.
24. In case of work-in-progress at process, realizable value of normal scrap is deducted from total cost incurred at the process for computing cost per unit.
25. In process industries materials move down the production line in a continuous stream.
26. Process cost system is applicable to Paper mills and Textile mills.
27. In industries using process costing, production is against orders from customers.
28. In process costing, costs are compiled process-wise.
29. Waste has no realizable value.
30. Process costing is usually used in small scale industries.
31. In process costing, cost per unit is the average cost.
32. Normal loss is transferred to costing profit and Loss account.
33. In calculating equivalent production, the main difference between FIFO and Average methods is the treatment given to opening work-in-progress.

Answers :

1. False	**2.** True	**3.** False	**4.** True
5. True	**6.** True	**7.** False	**8.** False
9. True	**10.** False	**11.** True	**12.** True
13. True	**14.** False	**15.** False	**16.** True
17. False	**18.** False	**19.** False	**20.** False
21. True	**22.** True	**23.** True	**24.** False
25. True	**26.** True	**27.** False	**28.** True
29. True	**30.** False	**31.** True	**32.** False
33. True			

THEORETICAL EXERCISES

1. What are the basic differences between job order and process cost systems.
2. Describe the general features of process costing. In what type of industries is process costing generally adopted? Discuss with figures the method of treatment of process loss and wastage in process costing system.
3. How will you deal with (i) Normal wastage, (ii) Abnormal wastage, and (iii) abnormal effectives in process cost accounts? Explain the effect of each of them on the ascertainment of cost of an article.
4. What are normal and abnormal process losses? Explain the possible causes. How are these dealt with in cost accounts?

5. Write short notes on:
   (i) Inter process profits;
   (ii) Equivalent production, and mode of computation.
6. Distinguish between Job costing and process costing **[DU, B.Com (Hons.) 2000]**

NUMERICAL EXERCISES

1. (Processing) Products limited in the course of refining crude oil obtains four joint products A, B, C and D. the total cost till the split-off point was ₹ 97,600. The output and sales in the year 2006 were as follows:

Product	Output (Gallons)	Sales (₹)	Separate costs (₹)
A	5,00000	1,15,00,000	30,00,000
B	10,000	10,00,000	6,00,000
C	5,000	4,00,000	
D	9,000	30,00,000	1,00,000

You are required to:

(a) Calculate the net income for each of the products if the joint costs are apportioned on the basis of net realizable values at split-off point of the different products.

(b) What would be the net income of company from each product if it decides to sell the products at the split- of point itself A @ ₹ 15, B @ ₹ 50, C @ ₹80, and D @ ₹300 per gallon.

(c) In case the company expects to operate at the same level of production and sales in the year 2007, could the company increase net income by altering its processing decisions? If so, what would be the expected overall net income? Which products should be processed further and which should be sold at split-off? Assume that all costs incurred after the split-off are variable.

2. A company within the food industry mixes powdered ingredients in two different processes to produce one product. The output of process I becomes the input of the process II and the output of process II is transferred to the packing department.

From the information given below you are required to open accounts for Process I, Process II, Abnormal loss and packing department and to record the transactions for the week ended 11th may,2006:

Process I

Input:

Material A	6,000 kilograms @ ₹ 50 per kilogram
Material B	4,000 kilogram @ rupee 1 per kilogram
Mixing labour	430 hours @ ₹ 20 per hour
Normal loss	5% of weight input, disposed off @ ₹ 16 per kilogram
Output	9,200 kilograms

Note: No work in process at the beginning or end of the week.

Process II

Input:

Material C	6,600 kilograms @ ₹ 12.5 per kilogram
Material D	4,200 kilograms @ Re. 7.5 per kilogram
	₹ 3,300
Mixing Labour	370 hours @ ₹ 20 per hour
Normal Waste	5% of weight input with no disposal value
Output	18,000 kilograms

No work in process at the beginning of the week but 1000 kilograms in process at the end of the week and estimated to be only 50% complete so far as labour and overhead were concerned.

Overheads of ₹ 32000 incurred by the two processes are to be absorbed on the basis of mixing labour hours.

3. Process Management Limited makes product X using two processes- 1 and 2. The following details are available for the last period:

Process 1

No Opening work-in-progress

Input materials	24,000 kg. Costing	₹ 168,000
Labour		₹ 52,800
Overheads		₹ 13,200

There were no process losses and 19,000 kgs were transferred to process 2. The unfinished production was complete as to materials and 60% complete as to labour and overheads.

Process 2

No Opening work-in-progress

Completed good production	15,200 kg
Labour	₹ 45,752
Overheads	₹ 27,353

The normal process loss is 5% of input which was exactly achieved in the period. The unfinished production was estimated to be 40% complete as to labour and overheads.

Requirements:

(a) Prepare a process account for process 1.

(b) Prepare a process account for process 2.

4. A product passes through three processes P-1, P-2 and P-3 to completion. The output of each process is charged to the next –process at a price calculated to give a profit of 20% on the transfer price. The output of Process s is charged to finished stock on similar basis. There is no partly finished work in any process on March 31, on which date the following information was made available for analysis:

Details	Process		
	P-1 (₹)	P-2 (₹)	P-3 (₹)
Material	4,000	6,000	2,000
Labour	6,000	4,000	8,000
Closing stock as on 31.3.2010	2,000	4,000	6,000

Stock in each process is valued at cost to that process.

There was no stock in hand on April 1, 2009 and the question of overhead was ignored. Of the goods passed into finished stock, ₹ 4,000 remained in hand on March 31, 2010 and the balance has been sold for ₹ 36,000. Show process accounts and calculate reserve for unrealized profits. **[Ans. Total profit ₹ 19,083]**

5. Navodya Chemicals manufacture Wonderchem using two processes- mixing and distillation. The following details relate to the distillation process for a period.

Opening work-in-progress (WIP)		NIL
Input from mixing	36,000 kgs. at a cost of	₹ 1,66,000
Labour for period		₹ 43,800
Overheads for period		₹ 29,200

Closing WIP of 8,000 kg. was 100 per cent of fully complete production. Actual loss in the period was 3,600 kg. Fully complete, which was scrapped.

Requirements:

(a) Calculate whether there is a normal or abnormal loss or abnormal gain for the period.

(b) Prepare the distillation process account for the period, showing clearly weights and values.

(c) Explain what changes would be required in the accounts if the scrapped production had a resale value, and give the accounting entries.

6. From the following data, find out the equivalent units of production to determine the per unit processing cost, which was incurred evenly during the month of March, 2008:

Opening work-in-progress: 12,500 Units (20% completed)

Fresh Units introduced: 40,000 units

Finished goods: 30,000 units

Closing work-in-progress: 20,000 Units (60% completed)

The entire stock of Opening work-in-progress was completed during March, 2008 without any loss/rejection. **[Ans. 42,000 Units]**

7. Find out the Equivalent Production from the following data under the FIFO method:

Details	Cost Element	Unit/%
Opening Work-in Progress		2,000
Degree of completion:	Materials	80
	Labour	60
	Overheads	60
Units Introduced		8,000
Closing Work-in Progress		3,000
Degree of completion:	Materials	80
	Labour	60
	Overheads	60

Assume there are no process losses.

[Ans. EQP: Materials 7,800 units, Labour and Overheads 7,600 units]

8. The accountant of a chemical company provides you the following data:

Details	Unit	Amount (₹)
Work-in-Process (Beginning period)	5,000	
Direct Materials		10,500
Direct Labour and Manufacturing Overheads		9,750
Addition to Work-in-Process in May	10,000	
Direct Materials		90,000
Direct Labour and Manufacturing Overheads		75,000
Total		1,85,250
Work-in-Process (End of period)	3,750	

Further, Work-in-Process at the beginning of the period is complete to the extent: Materials 100% and labour and manufacturing overheads 80%. Work-in-Process at the end of the period is complete to the extent: Materials 100% and labour and manufacturing overheads 60%.

You are required to:

(i) Calculate the number of units of product transferred to finished goods stock during the period. Assume no units are lost in process.

(ii) Calculate the number of equivalent whole units of work completed during the period.

(iii) Calculate the unit cost for materials during the month of January using a FIFO method of inventory issue.

[Ans. (i) 11, 250 Units; (ii) EQP: Materials 10,000 units, Labour and Overheads 9500 units; (iii) ₹ 9 per EQP unit]

9. The following data pertain to Process I for March, 2003 of Beta Ltd.:

Details	Unit	Amount (₹)
Work-in-Progress (Beginning period)	1,500	15,000
Input of Direct Materials	18,500	52,000
Direct Labour		14,000
Manufacturing Overheads		28,000
Work-in-Progress (End of period)	5,000	
Units transferred to the next process	15,000	
Total		1,09,000

Further, Work-in-Process at the beginning of the period is complete to the extent: Materials 100% and labour and manufacturing overheads 100/3%. Work-in-Progress at the end of the period is complete to the extent: Materials 90% and labour and manufacturing overheads 30%. Normal Loss is 10% of total input (Opening Work-in-Progress + Units put in). Scrap value ₹ 2 per unit

You are required to:

(i) Compute the number of equivalent units of production.

(ii) Compute cost per equivalent unit for each cost element, i.e., materials, Labour and Overheads.

(iii) Compute the cost of finished output and closing work-in-progress.

(iv) Prepare the Process and other Accounts.

[Ans. (i) EQP: Materials 16,000 units, Labour and Overheads 14,000 units; (ii) cost per EQP unit: Materials ₹ 3, Labour ₹ 1 , Overheads ₹ 2 (iii)Cost of Finished Output ₹ 99,000 (15,000 units)] and Closing Work-in-Progress ₹ 18,000; Abnormal Gain ₹ 8,000 (2,000 units)]

10. A product passes through three processes—-I, II, and III. The details of expenses incurred on the three processes during the year 2007 were as under:

Details	Process I	Process II	Process III
Units issued	10,000		
Cost per unit (₹)	100		
Sundry Materials	10,000	15,000	5,000
Labour (₹)	30,000	80,000	65,000
Direct Expenses (₹)	6,000	18,150	27,2 00
Sale price of output per unit (₹)	120	165	250

Management Expenses during the year amounted to ₹ 80,000 and selling expenses were ₹ 50,000. Both these are not allocable to the processes.

Actual output of the three processes was as under:

Process I: 9300 units

Process II: 5400 units

Process III: 2100 units

Two thirds of the output of Process I and one-half of the output of Process II was passed on to the next process and the balance was sold. The entire output of Process III was sold.

The normal wastage of the three processes calculated on the input of every process was:

Process I: 5%; Process II: 15%; Process III: 20%.

The wastage of Process I was sold at ₹ 2 per unit, that of Process II at ₹ 5 and that of Process III at ₹ 10 per unit.

Prepare the three process Accounts and a statement of Income for the year 2007 showing fully the accounting treatment of process wastage.

[Ans. Cost per unit of normal output of Process I ₹ 110, Process II ₹ 150 Process III ₹ 230; Abnormal Loss (Total) ₹ 34,800; Abnormal Gain 18,850 ; Total Loss for the year 2007 ₹ 32,450]

11. The following data are available pertaining to a product after passing through Two processes A and B: Output transferred to Process C from Process B 9,120 units for ₹ 49,263.

Expenses incurred in Process C:

Details	Amount (₹)
Sundry Materials	1,480
Direct Wages	6,500
Direct Expenses	1,605

The wastage of Process C is sold at Re. 1.00 per unit. The overhead charges were 168% of direct wages. The final product was sold at ₹ 10 per unit fetching profit of 20% on sales.

Find the percentage of wastage in Process C and Prepare Process C account.

[B.Com (Hons.) DU, 1999]

[Ans. Cost of normal output of Process C ₹ 456; 5% wastage in Process C.]

12. In a certain process, material is mixed and cooked in batches of 1,000 lbs each. Cooking results in ten percent loss of weight of the mixture. Since the cooking requires considerable skill and constant watching; there is generally a further loss from spoilage which is not discovered until the process has been completed. Also, past experience shows that normally two batches out of every ten started in the process are spoiled in this way.

In a given quarter, the production records show:

(1) Production started in the process: 50 batches of 1,000 lbs each.

(2) Production completed and transferred to finished goods is 34,200 lbs.

(3) There is no inventory of work-in-progress at the start or end of the quarter.

Costs recorded during the quarter amounted to ₹ 45,000.

Prepare the Process Account for the quarter and determine the cost per pound of finished product. **[B.Com (Hons.) DU, 2000]**

[Ans. Cost of Finished Goods per unit ₹ 1.25.]

13. At the end of process A, carried on in a factory during the week ending July 31, 2002 the number of units produced was 850 excluding 50 units damaged at the very end of the process. The damaged units realized ₹3 per unit as scrap. A normal wastage of 10% occurs during the process, the wastage realized was ₹ 2 per unit. A unit of raw materials cost ₹ 4. The other expenses for the week were:

Details	Amount (₹)
Wages	500
Power	200
General Expenses	450

40% of the output is sold so as to show a profit of (50/3) % on the selling price; the rest of the output is transferred to Process B. **[B.Com (Hons.) DU, 2002]**

[Ans. Profit ₹ 384]

14. The following particulars are extracted from the books of Y Ltd. for the month of August 1998:

Details	Percentage	Unit
Opening stock of W.I.P. (units)		200
Degree of completion:		
Materials	100	
Labour	40	
Overheads	40	
Units introduced in August 1998		1,050
Completed Units in August, 1998		1,100
Closing W.I.P. (Unit)		150
Degree of completion:		
Materials	100	
Labour	70	
Overheads	70	

Prepare a statement of Equivalent production. **[B.Com (Hons.) DU, 2003]**

[Ans. EQP Units: Material 1,050; Labour and Overheads 1,125]

15. The Vega Manufacturing company uses FIFO method of inventory valuation in process costing. The following data relate to Process I for the month of April, 2004:

Details	Quantity (units)	Amount (₹)
Beginning Work-in-process	1,500	4,500
Introduced during the month	5,000	
Transfer to Process II	5,500	
Ending Work-in-process	1,000	
Degree of completion:		
Opening:		
Materials 100%		
Conversion costs 80%		
Closing:		
Materials 100%		
Conversion costs 60%		
Costs added during the month:		
Materials		10,000
Labour		9,800
Overheads		4,900

[B.Com (Hons.) DU, 2004]

[Ans. EQP Units: Material 5,000; Labour and Overheads 4,900; Cost per Unit: Materials ₹ 2, Labour ₹ 2, overheads Re. 1]

16. During the month of April, 2003, 4,000 units were introduced into Process 'A' at the cost of ₹ 23,200. At the end of the month, 3,000 units were completed and transferred to Process 'B' A/c. 720 units were still in process and 280 units were scrapped. A normal wastage of 5% was expected. It was estimated that the incomplete units have reached a stage in production as follows:

Materials: 75%;

Labour and Overheads: 50%.

The additional costs incurred were:

Details	Amount (₹)
Materials	6,160
Wages	13,760
Overheads	6,880

Units scrapped realized at ₹ 2 per unit.

Prepare:

(a) A statement showing equivalent production;

(b) Statement showing cost per unit. **[B.Com (Hons.) DU, 2004(External)]**

[Ans. EQP Units: Material 3,620; Labour and Overheads3, 440; Cost per Unit: Materials ₹ 8, Labour ₹ 4, overheads ₹ 2]

17. The following particulars related to two processes X an Y for the month of January 2005:

Details	Process No. I	Process No. II
Total Input (Units)	50,000 (@ ₹ 1.50 per unit)	1,000
Normal Loss (% of Input)	10	5
Additional Costs Incurred:		
Material	—	3,600
Direct Labour	35,000	45,000
Overheads	27,500	39,500
Realisable Value of scrap per unit (₹)	0.50	2.00
Output (Units)	43,000	43,000

The entire output of Process X was transferred to Process Y. The entire output of Process Y was sold at ₹ 6 per unit. Assume, there was no opening or closing stock of any type in the process of X or Y.

You are required to prepare the necessary accounts for the period.

[B.Com (Hons.) DU, 2005]

[Ans. Value of Transfer from Process X to Process Y: ₹ 1, 29,000 and from Process to Finished Goods Stock A/c ₹ 2, 18,806; Profit ₹ 37,900.]

18. From the following information prepare:
(i) Statement of Equivalent production;
(ii) Statement of element of cost/unit;
(iii) Statement of apportionment of cost;
(iv) Process No. II Account under FIFO method.

1. Opening Stock: 800 units costing ₹ 6,038 (transferred in cost ₹ 1,200, materials ₹ 1,578, Labour ₹ 1,710, and overheads ₹ 1,550).
2. Transferred from previous Process I: 12,000 units costing ₹ 16,350.
3. Cost incurred in Process II: Materials ₹ 11,600; Labour ₹ 20,760 and Overheads ₹ 15,570.
4. Normal Loss in process II: 10%.
5. Scrap realized @ ₹ 10/10 units
6. Closing stock: 1,800 units
7. Transfer to Next process: 9,700 units
8. Degree of completion:

Details	Opening Stock (%)	Closing Stock (%)	Scrapped Units (%)
Material	60	60	100
Labour	40	51	41
Overheads	40	51	41

[B.Com (Hons.) DU, 2006 (External)]

[Ans. EQP Units: Material I 10,900; Material II 10,500; Labour and Overheads 10,380; Cost per Unit: Materials I ₹ 1.50, Materials II ₹ 1.00 Labour ₹ 2, overheads ₹ 1.50; Abnormal Loss ₹ 787 for 200 EQP units; Value of transferred units ₹ 61,438.]

19. Two products A and B are obtained in a crude form and require further processing at a cost of ₹ 5 for A and ₹ 4 for B per unit before sales. Assuming a net margin of 25% on cost, their sale price is fixed at ₹ 13.75 and ₹ 8.75 per unit respectively. During the period, the joint cost was ₹ 88,000 and the outputs were:
A: 8,000 units; and B; 6,000 units.
Ascertain the joint cost per unit. **[B.Com (Hons.) DU, 2002]**

[Ans. ₹ 8 for Product A, and ₹ 4 for Product B.]

20. In a manufacturing unit, raw material passes through four processes I, II, III, IV and the output of each process is the input of the subsequent process. The loss of the four processes I, II, III, IV are respectively 25%, 20%, 20%, and 50/3 % of the input. If the end product of Process IV is 21,000 Kgs., what is the quantity of materials required along with its cost to be fed at the start of Process I when the cost of the same is ₹ 28 per Kg. **[Ans. ₹ 14,70,000 for 52,500 Kg.]**

21. In a manufacturing unit, raw material passes through four processes I, II, III, IV and the output of each process is the input of the subsequent process. The loss of the four processes I, II, III, IV are respectively 25%, 20%, 20%, and 50/3 % of the input. If the end product of Process IV is 16,000 Kgs., what is the quantity of materials required along with its cost to be fed at the start of Process I when the cost of the same is ₹ 25 per Kg. **[B.Com (Hons.) DU (Modified)]**

[Ans. ₹ 10,00,000 for 40,000 Kg.]

22. In a workshop monthly input of material @ ₹ 48 per Kg. is 500 Kgs packed in containers of 50 kg each. Other expenses inclusive of additional cost of ₹10,000 due to an accident in the workshop amount to ₹ 38,760. Normal loss is 5% of input and it realizes @ 6 per unit and each container is sold @ ₹ 40. Actual output is 480 kg. Generally 10% of containers get so damaged that they fetch nothing in value. Actually only 7 containers were in saleable position and were sold. Prepare Process account, Normal Loss account, Abnormal Gain account, Empties account and the Statement of Profit. **[Ans. Net Loss: ₹ 9,560]**

❑❑❑

19

Joint Product and By-Product Costing

Learning Objectives

It attempts to explain the costing of Joint product and By-products. In this chapter you will learn :

1. Meaning, nature of joint products.
2. Split off point, joint costs and subsequent costs.
3. Methods of apportionment of joint costs.
4. Meaning and nature of by-products.
5. Distinction between joint products, main product and by-products.
6. Accounting for by-products.

INTRODUCTION

Up to a stage two or more products of varying importance are produced simultaneously with the help of common manufacturing processes. Before the simultaneously produced products are separated, they do not have independent identity and the costs incurred are also common to them. Having separated these jointly produced products, additional costs may or may not be incurred to make them saleable

Nature of Joint Products

When two or more products are simultaneously produced with the help of common processes and common costs and these products have significant value individually, they are known as joint products. Up to a stage in manufacturing these products do not have independent identity. After they get separated further costs may or may not be necessary for making them saleable. Oil refining, dairy production and sugar manufacturing are glaring examples of joint products.

Salient Features of Joint Products

1. They are produced from the same basic raw material.
2. During pre-separation they are produced simultaneously.
3. Till separation, they have no individual identity.
4. Manufacturing processes are common till the point of split-off.
5. All costs are common till the point of split-off.
6. Each joint product has significant value.
7. They may be saleable immeditately after separation or further costs need to be incurred on some or all of them for converting them into saleable or to produce the improved product.

Objectives of Joint Product Costing

Main objectives of analyzing joint costs are:

- Ascertaining cost of products jointly produced;
- Determining selling price of joint products;
- Determining profitability of each product;
- Determining the most profitable product mix;
- Determining whether to sell joint product/s immediately after split off or incur further costs for improving them or transforming them into new products;
- Taking strategic market decisions.

Joint products and co-products

Both relate to same line of production but they differ in their productive process, their identification and cost characteristics. Following points of distinction are worth considering:

1. Co-products such as cars, jeeps, trucks, buses, in an automobile industry are separately produced. Skimmed milk and butter which are joint products in dairy industry are simultaneously produced. In meat packing unit, the quantity of various joint products remains almost the same and cannot be changed without accepting the quantity of the rest of the items.
2. Co-products maintain their separate identity from the very beginning. Joint products have no identity till the point of spilt-off.
3. In the case of joint products all costs before the point of separation are joint or common. There are no or minor joint costs in the case of Co-products.

4. The level of output of Co-products can be changed depending upon managerial decision. The proportion of various joint products is determined on the basis of nature of products and processes.
5. The ascertainment of cost of joint products involves estimation but the computation of cost of Co-products is relatively easy and precise.

Sell at Split off or Further Process

In most of the cases a firm has to decide whether to sell a by-product immediately after the split off or to process further. Such decisions are based on analysis of incremental cost and incremental revenue. If incremental revenue on account of further processing exceeds incremental cost, such further processing should be taken up.

Illustration 19.1 : *The plant of a Processing Limited processes 7,50,000 kg of raw material in a month to produce two products, Allex and Ballex. The cost of Raw material is ₹ 24 per kg. The process costs per month are:*

Details	***Amount*** (₹)
Direct materials	*6,65,000*
Direct Wages	*15,00,000*
Variable overheads	*9,90,000*
Fixed Overheads	*12,00,000*

The loss in process is 5% of input and the output ratio of Allex and Ballex which emerge simultaneously is 1:2. The selling prices of the two products at the point of split-off are: Allex ₹ 30 per Kg and Ballex ₹ 40 per Kg.

A proposal is available to process Allex further by mixing it with other purchased materials. The entire current output of the factory can be so processed to obtain a new Product PA. The price per kg of PA is ₹ 50 and each Kg of output of PA will require one Kg of input of Allex. The cost of processing of Allex into PA including other materials is ₹ 19,25,000 per month.

Alternatively, another proposal available is to introduce a new raw material for the manufacturing of Allex and Ballex. The new raw material will bring down the process loss to 4% and change the output mix of Allex and Ballex to 2:3. The company's capacity to process the new raw material is also 7,50,000 Kg per month. The cost of new raw material is ₹ 22.60 per Kg. All other costs will remain the same.

Required:

(i) Present a statement showing the monthly profitability based on the existing manufacturing operations.

(ii) Evaluate the two proposals independently and present statements showing the respective monthly profitability.

Solution : Statement showing the monthly profitability based on existing manufacturing operations

Details	Product Allex Amount (₹)	Product Ballex Amount (₹)	Total Amount (₹)
Sales volume (Kg)	2,37,500	4,75,000	7,12,500
Selling Price per kg	30	50	
Sales Value	71,25,000	237,50,000	308,75,000
Less: Joint Cost(2:7)	51,58,860	171,96,200	223,55,060
Current Profit	13,92,000	46,40,000	85,19,940

Proposal I: Processing product allex into Product PA:

Details	**Amount (₹)**
Cost of Product Allex	51,58,860
Additional cost for Product PA	19,25,000
Total cost of Product PA	70,83,860
Sales of Product PA (2,37,500 × 40)	95,00,000
Profit of Product PA	24,16,140
Add: Profit of Product Ballex	46,40,000
Total profit under this proposal	70,56,140

Statement showing the monthly profitability based on Proposal II

Details	Product Allex Amount (₹)	Product Ballex Amount (₹)	Total Amount (₹)
Sales volume (Kg)	2,88,000	4,32,000	7,20,000
Selling Price per kg	30	50	
Sales Value	86,40,000	216,00,000	302,40,000
Less: Joint Cost(2:7)	60,87,160	152,17,900	213,05,060
Current Profit	25,52,840	63,82,100	89,34,940

Comment: Proposal II should be accepted as it improves the overall profit by ₹ 4,15,000. The recommendation is based on the assumption that the products will be acceptable in the market.

Working Notes:

Materials (Kg)	7,50,000	
Less: 5% Loss	37,500	
Total Output		7,12,500
Product-wise Share:		
Allex> [7,12,500 × (1/3)]		2,37,500
Ballex> [7,12,500 × (2/3)]		4,75,000

Total Joint cost:

₹ 223,55,060 = [180,00,000 + 6,65,060 + 15,00,000 + 9,90,000 + 12,00,000]

For Proposal II:

Materials (Kg)	7,50,000	
Less: 4% Loss	30,000	
Total Output		7,20,000
Product-wise Share:		
Allex> [7,20,000 × (2/5)]		2,88,000
Ballex> [7,20,000 × (3/5)]		4,32,000

Total Joint cost:

₹ 213,05,060 = [169,50,000 + 6,65,060 + 15,00,000 + 9,90,000 + 12,00,000]

Costing of By-Products

By-Products are products of limited sales value produced simultaneously with a product of greater sales value. The Main product is usually produced in much greater quantities than the by-products.

By-products are of secondary importance; therefore, cost allocation differs from that of joint products. The costing of by-products falls into one of two categories:

Category 1: By-Products are recognized when "Sold." By-products are considered to be of little importance, so no production costs are allocated to them. However, net by-product income (net of actual additional processing costs and marketing and administration expenses) is shown on the income statement in one of the two ways:

(A) As an addition to income, either

(i) Part of other sales, or (ii) Other income

(B) As a deduction from cost of Goods sold of the main product

Category 2: By-Products are recognised when "Produced." By-products are considered important and the net by-product income is significant. Therefore, production costs are allocated to by-products. On the Income Statement, the production costs of the main products produced are reduced by the expected value of the by-products "produced." The amount deducted from production costs is computed in one of the two ways:

(i) *Net Realisable Value Method:* The expected sales value of the by-product produced is reduced by the expected additional processing costs and marketing and administrative expenses.

(ii) *Reversal Cost Method:* The expected sales value of the by-product is reduced by the expected additional processing costs and normal gross profit on the by-product (or by the marketing and administrative expenses and net income).In such computation (revenue less additional cost less gross profit), the amount remaining represents the portion of joint costs allocated to the by-product.

Upon the sale of the by-product, the inventory account must be modified and the cost of by-products sold must be recognized.

From the above, it is obvious that this is the only method where a portion of joint costs is actually allocated to the by-product. This method must be used when by-product is considered significant.

Joint Costs: Methods of Allocation

Market Value: Joint costs are apportioned on the basis of ratio of sales value of respective products. This results in uniform gross profit ratio for each product. So this method is based on the logic that products that have the highest market value should bear the largest share of the joint costs.

Notional Market value/ Net Realisable Value: This is applicable only when one or more products require additional processing either because there is no ready market or it would be more profitable to process it further. These additional /identifiable processing costs are subtracted from the sale prices and the resultant net product contribution at the split-off point is then applied to production to provide the basis for allocating joint costs.

Physical Measure Method/ Physical Unit Method: Relative proportion at the split-off point using a common physical measure (Volume or Weight) is the criterion for apportionment of joint costs. This method requires that the products should be homogenous. Output of all joint products is measured using the same unit of measurement e.g. Kilogram, Litre etc.

(1) *Simple Average Method:* Average unit cost is calculated by dividing the total manufacturing cost by total number of units produced. This is so when all products can be measured in terms of the same unit.

(2) *Weighted Output Method (Homogenous Products):* This method overcomes the difficulty encountered under the Physical Method by assigning weight factors, such as Quantum of materials used, Difficulty of manufacture, Time consumed and difference in type of labour used, and their relative weights are usually combined in a single value i.e. Factor of conversion is determined and used based on (A) weights or points assigned on the basis of survey (B) their relative weights.

(3) *Working Back (Reverse Gear)/Standard method:* Pre-determined standards are used. Sales value is estimated from which is deducted the profit margin, selling and distribution expenses and conversion cost. Thus, the price that can be paid for raw material is obtained.

Illustration 19.2 : (Market Value Method)

A, B, C, and D are four joint products manufactured at a total manufacturing cost of ₹ 15,00,000 and in quantities as given below:

Joint Product	*Selling Price (₹)*	*Quantity (Unit)*
A	*1.60*	*2, 50, 000*
B	*40.00*	*30, 000*
C	*40.00*	*15, 000*
D	*60.00*	*30, 000*

Find out joint cost apportioned to each joint product using Market Value Method.

Solution :

Joint Product	Selling Price (₹)	Quantity (Unit)	Sales Value (₹)	Proportion (%)	Joint Cost (₹)
A	1.60	2,50,000	4,00,000	10	1,50,000
B	40.00	30,000	12,00,000	30	4,50,000
C	40.00	15,000	6,00,000	15	2,25,000
D	60.00	30,000	18,00,000	45	6,75,000
		Total	40,00,000	100	15,00,000

Illustration 19.3 : *Two products M-1 and M-2 are obtained in a crude form and require further processing at a cost of ₹ 25 for M-1 and ₹ 20 for M-2 per unit before sales. Assuming a net margin of 100/3% on cost, their sale price is fixed at ₹ 60 and ₹ 40 per unit respectively. During the period, the joint cost was ₹ 2, 72,000 and the outputs were:*

M-1: 12,000 units; and M-2: 10,000 units.

Ascertain the Joint cost per unit.

Solution : **Apportionment of Joint Cost**

Details	Product M-1 Amount (₹)	Product M-2 Amount (₹)
Selling Price	60.00	40.00
Less: Profit 100/3% on cost OR 25% of selling Price	15.00	10.00
Total cost	45.00	30.00
Less: Further Processing cost	25.00	20.00
Share in Joint cost	20.00	10.00
Output in Units	12,000	10,000
Ratio = 2,40,000 : 1,00,000	=12,000 × 20 = 2,40,000. 12	=10,000 × 10 = 1,00,000. 5
Joint cost of ₹ 2,72,000 in the ratio of 12:5	1,92,000	80,000
Joint Cost per unit: =Allocated Joint cost/ Number of units	16	8

JOINT PRODUCTS

The term 'joint product' is used for more than one product of almost equal value which is simultaneously produced from the same manufacturing process and the same raw material.

Accounting of Joint Products

Apportionment of costs to joint products may affect the profitability of individual products but the total profit or loss remains unchanged. The following are some of the methods used in apportioning joint costs:

(1) Apportionment by Physical measurement : Some Physical coefficient (Unit or weight of products) Proportion of raw material Input, Volume of output becomes the basis of apportionment of joint cost. Valuation of inventory shall be assessed on the basis of joint cost apportioned plus further cost of processing. This method is unsuitable if the joint products are in different units of measurement.

Illustration 19.4 : *The following data have been extracted from the books of PV Works:*

Product	***Output (Kg) (Per 1,000 Kg of Input)***
A-1	*700*
A-2	*150*
A-3	*80*
A-4	*50*
A-5	*20*

The price of the basic raw material is ₹ 1,800 per 100 Kg. direct labour and overhead costs up to the point of split off are ₹ 22,000 and ₹10, 000 respectively per tonne of the basic raw material. Compute material, labour, overhead and total cost of each product on the basis of weight.

Solution : **Appointment of Cost**

Product	Output per tonne of basic raw material	Weight (%)	Basic raw material (₹)	Direct labour (₹)	Overhead (₹)	Total cost (₹)
A-1	700	70	12,600	15,400	7,000	35,000
A-2	150	15	2,700	3,300	1,500	7,500
A-3	80	8	1,440	1,760	800	4,000
A-4	50	5	900	1,100	500	2,500
A-5	20	2	360	440	200	1,000
Total	1,000	100	18,000	22,000	10,000	50,000

(2) Survey Method: Sometimes joint costs are apportioned on Average Unit Cost basis. To attain better accuracy, it is distributed amongst the joint products on the basis of technical evaluation, such as quantity of material used, labour operations performed, time taken for production, technical difficulties in manufacture and a combination of such factors. Weightage is given by means of Technical Evaluation Points. This is explained by taking the following illustration:

Illustration 19.5 : *In the timber industry, the milling operations to the split-off point during a certain period amounted to ₹ 24,600 with the following production:*

Timber	***Unit***
A-1 Grade	*600*
A-2 Grade	*1,000*
A-3 Grade	*400*
Total	*2,000*

Apportion the joint cost (i) On average unit cost method; (ii) On technical Evaluation with points 5, 4, and 3 for A-1, A-2 and A-3 grade Timber respectively.

Solution : **Average Unit cost method**

Average cost per Unit: 24,600 ÷ 2,000 = ₹ 12.30

Timber (Grade)	Unit	Average Unit cost (₹)	Apportioned cost (₹)
A-1	600	12.30	7,380
A-2	1,000	12.30	12,300
A-3	400	12.30	4,920
Total	2,000		24,600

Technical Evaluation Method

Cost per Equivalent Unit: 24,600 ÷ 8,200 = ₹ 3

Timber	Unit (1)	Point (2)	Equivalent Unit (3)= (1) × (2)	Cost per Equivalent unit (₹) (4)	Apportioned cost (₹) (5) = (3) × (4)	Cost per Unit (₹) (6) = (5) ÷ (1)
A-1 Grade	600	5	3,000	3	9,000	15
A-2 Grade	1,000	4	4,000	3	12,000	12
A-3 Grade	400	3	1,200	3	3,600	9
Total	2,000		8,200		24,600	

(3) Apportionment on the basis of Market Value at the point of split-off: Market value of the joint products is ascertained at the point of split-off and the joint cost is apportioned in the ratio of sales value or selling price. However, the use of selling price results in erroneous apportionment and as such sales value becomes the equitable basis.

Illustration 19.6 : *The joint cost of making 80 units of Product A, 200 units of Product B and 400 units of product C is ₹ 13,800. The respective selling price of products A, B, and C is ₹ 5, 8, and 10. The products did not require any further processing after split-off point. You are required to apportion the joint cost*

(a) On the basis of selling price; and

(b) On the basis of sales value.

Solution : **On the Basis of Selling Price**

Product	Selling Price (₹)	Apportionment Ratio	Apportioned Joint Cost (₹)
A	5	5/23	3,000
B	8	8/23	4,800
C	10	10/23	6,000
Total	23		13,800

On the Basis of Sales Value

Product	Quantity sold (Unit)	Selling Price (₹)	Sales Value (₹)	Apportion-ment Ratio	Apportio-ned Joint cost (₹)
A	80	5	400	1	920
B	200	80	1,600	4	3,680
C	400	10	4,000	10	9,200
Total			6,000		13,800

(4) Apportionment on the basis of Market Value after further processing: In case it is difficult to ascertain the market value of the joint products at the point of split-off, the joint cost is apportioned in the ratio of selling price or market value of joint products after further processing. This method is useful in those circumstances where additional processing costs are proportional to selling prices or sales values and detailed records of subsequent processing costs are not kept.

Illustration 19.7 : *Kumar limited manufactures two joint products JP-1 and JP-2and sells them at ₹ 200 and ₹ 250 per unit respectively. During the quarter ended on December31, 2007, 750 units of JP-1 and 500 units of JP-2 were produced and sold. The joint cost amounted to ₹1, 76,000 and no record has been kept of subsequent processing cost. Apportion joint cost on 'after further processing market value'.*

Solution :

Product	Quantity Produced and sold (Unit)	Selling Price (₹)	Sales Value (₹)	Apportion-ment Ratio	Apportio-ned Joint cost (₹)
JP-1	750	200	1,50,000	6/11	96,000
JP-2	500	250	1,25,000	5/11	80,000
Total			2,75,000		1,76,000

Illustration 19.8 : *Continuing with the preceding illustration, if the subsequent processing cost is ₹ 18,750 and ₹ 31,250 respectively for the two products JP-1 and JP-2, apportion the joint cost.*

Solution :

Product	Quantity Produced and sold (Unit)	Selling Price (₹)	Sales Value (₹)	Subsequent Processing cost (₹)	Sales Value less Subseq-uent Proce-ssing cost (₹)	Apportio-nment Ratio	Apportio-ned Joint cost (₹)
JP-1	750	200	1,50,000	18,750	1,31,250	7/12	1,02,667
JP-2	500	250	1,25,000	31,250	93,750	5/12	73,333
Total			2,75,000				1,76,000

(5) Reverse Gear Method (Sales to Estimated Cost): Estimated Cost at the point of split-off is ascertained by deducting estimated net profit and subsequent processing cost from the sales value of every joint product. Joint cost is then apportioned to the joint products on the basis of estimated cost thus computed. This is explained by taking the following illustration.

Illustration 19.9 : *In the course of manufacture of the main product 'M', By-products 'B-1' and 'B-2' also emerge. The joint expenses of manufacture amount to ₹ 5,97,750. All the products are processed further after separation and sold as per details furnished below:*

Details	*Main Product*	*By-Product*	
	M (₹)	*B-1 (₹)*	*B-2 (₹)*
Sales	*4,50,000*	*3,00,000*	*2,00,000*
Cost Beyond split off stage	*30,000*	*25,000*	*20,000*
Profit as percentage of sales	*25*	*20*	*15*

Selling and administration overheads are absorbed as percentage of cost of sales. Prepare a statement showing the apportionment of joint cost to the main product and By-products. Also prepare Main product 'M' A/c.

Solution : **Statement of Apportionment of Cost**

Details	Main Product	By-product		Total (₹)
	M (₹)	B-1 (₹)	B-2 (₹)	
Sales	4,50,000	3,00,000	2,00,000	9,50,000
Less: Profit (25%; 20%; and 15%)	1,12,500	60,000	30,000	2,02,500
Cost of sales	3,37,500	2,40,000	1,70,000	7,47,500
Less: Selling & Distribution Expenses	33,750	24,000	17,000	74,750
Less: Cost beyond split off	30,000	25,000	20,000	75,000
Share in Joint Cost	2,73,750	1,91,000	1,33,000	5,97,750

Dr **Main Product 'M' Account** Cr

Details	Amount (₹)	Details	Amount (₹)
Share in Joint costs	2,73,750	Sales	4,50,000
Post split-Off costs	30,000		
Selling & Distribution Expenses	33,750		
Profit	1,12,500		
Total	4,50,000	Total	4,50,000

Limitations of Joint Cost Analysis

Analysis of Joint cost suffers from the following limitations:

(i) Arbitrary: True cost of various individual products remains unknown as the apportionment of joint cost is mainly arbitrary. Further, inter-firm comparison becomes difficult.

(ii) Unrealistic Assumptions: Apportionment of joint cost is based on certain assumptions which are usually unrealistic or at times misleading.

(iii) Basis of Classification: Different firms may adopt different criterion to classify the simultaneous products as joint products or by-products. Thus, there is no clear cut distinction between joint products and by-products.

(iv) Decision making: It does not facilitate any decision making in regard to processing the products beyond the point of split-off. Decision is taken on the basis of comparative study of the incremental revenue and incremental cost on further processing. So long the incremental revenue exceeds the incremental cost on further processing of a joint product or a by-product , it is beneficial to further process the product.

(v) Purpose of classification: the purpose of classification stands defeated in case the value of the by-product is negligible.

LET US RECAPITULATE

1. When two or more products are simultaneously produced with the help of common processes and common costs and these products have significant value individually, they are known as joint products.
2. Oil refining, dairy production and sugar manufacturing are glaring examples of joint products.
3. Till separation, they have no individual identity.
4. Co-products maintain their separate identity from the very beginning.
5. If incremental revenue on account of further processing exceeds incremental cost, further processing should be taken up.
6. By-Products are products of limited sales value produced simultaneously with a product of greater sales value.
7. Cost allocation of By-Products differs from that of joint products.
8. In the Net realisable method, the expected sales value of the by-product produced is reduced by the expected additional processing costs and marketing and administrative expenses.
9. In the Reverse cost method, the amount remaining represents the portion of joint costs allocated to the by-product.
10. For homogenous products relative proportion at the split-off point using a common physical measure (Volume or Weight) is the criterion for apportionment of joint costs.
11. Apportionment of costs to joint products may affect the profitability of individual products but the total profit or loss remains unchanged.
12. In the survey method, weightage is given by means of Technical Evaluation Points.
13. The use of selling price results in erroneous apportionment and as such sales value becomes the equitable basis.
14. True cost of various individual products remains unknown as the apportionment of joint cost is mainly arbitrary.
15. Different firms may adopt different criterion to classify the simultaneous products as joint products or by-products.

SOLVED PROBLEMS

Problem 1. (Apportionment of Joint cost)

Bright Chemicals Limited electrolyses common salt to obtain three joint products: Caustic Soda, Chlorine, and Hydrogen. During a costing period, the expenditure relating to the inputs for the common process amounted to ₹ 14,40,000. After separation, expenses amounting to ₹ 5,00,000, ₹ 2,50,000 and ₹ 50,000 were incurred for Caustic Soda , Chlorine and Hydrogen respectively.

The entire production was sold and ₹ 15,00,000, ₹ 10,00,000 and ₹ 3,00,000 were realized for Caustic Soda, Chlorine and Hydrogen respectively. The selling expenses were estimated at 8% of realizations from sale. The management expected profits @ 16%, 10% and 6% of realizations from sale of Caustic Soda, Chlorine and Hydrogen respectively.

Draw a columnar statement showing the apportionment of joint costs and the profitability of each product.

Solution : Statement showing the Apportionment of Joint Costs to the Joint products and their Profitability

Details	Total (₹)	Caustic Soda (₹)	Chlorine (₹)	Hydrogen (₹)
Realisation from Sale	28,00,000	15,00,000	10,00,000	3,00,000
Less: Expected profit (16%, 10% and 6% on Realisation)	3,58,000	2,40,000	1,00,000	18,000
Less: Selling Expenses (8% on Realisation)	2,24,000	1,20,000	80,000	24,000
Estimated cost of Production	22,18,000	11,40,000	8,20,000	2,58,000
Less: Post -separation cost	8,00,000	5,00,000	2,50,000	50,000
Estimated Joint cost and their respective proportion	14,18,000 100%	6,40,000 45.13%	5,70,000 40.20%	2,08,000 14.67%
Actual joint cost apportioned in the ratio of estimated joint cost (45.13: 40.20: 14.67)	14,40,000	6,49,872	5,78,880	2,11,248
Add: Post -separation cost	8,00,000	5,00,000	2,50,000	50,000
Actual Cost of Production	22,40,000	11,49,872	8,28,880	2,61,248
Add: Selling Expenses	2,24,000	1,20,000	80,000	24,000
Actual Cost of Sales	24,64,000	12,69,872	9,08,880	2,85,248
Profit Realized (Balancing figure)	3,36,000	2,30,128	91,120	14,752
Realisation from Sale	28,00,000	15,00,000	10,00,000	3,00,000

Problem 2. (Apportionment of Joint cost)

Three joint products are produced by passing chemicals through two successive processes. Output from Process I is transferred to process II from which three products are produced and immediately sold. The data regarding the process of September, 2009 is given below:

Details	*Process I*	*Process II*
Direct material (4,000 kg @ ₹ 12.50)	*50,000*	———
Direct Wages	*32,600*	*34,500*
Overheads	*22,500*	*34,500*

Normal Loss	*10% of Input*	*N I L*
Scrap value of loss (@ ₹ 6.25 per Kg)		
Output (Kg)	*3,680*	*Joint products:* *JP-I: 1,440;* *JP-II: 1,280;* *JP-III: 960;*

There were no opening or closing inventory in either process and the selling prices of the output from process I were:

Joint product JP-I: ₹ 40 per kg

Joint product JP-II: ₹ 30 per kg

Joint product JP-III: ₹ 20 per kg

Required:

(i) Prepare an account for Process I together with any Loss or gain accounts you consider necessary to record the month's activities.

(ii) Calculate the profit attributable to each of the joint products by apportioning the total costs from Process II:

(a) According to weight of output;

(b) By the market value of the production.

Solution : Working Notes:

Cost per unit:

$$= \frac{\text{(All Normal process costs – Realizable value of Normal Scrap)}}{\text{(Process Input Units – Normal Loss in Units)}}$$

$$= \frac{[(50{,}000 + 32{,}600 + 22{,}500) – 2{,}500]}{(4{,}000 – 400 = 3600)}$$

= 1,02,600 ÷ 3,600 => ₹ 28.50

Process I Account

Dr Cr

Details	Unit	Amount (₹)	Details	Unit	Amount (₹)
To Input of Material (@ ₹ 12.50)	4,000	50,000	By Normal Loss A/c @ ₹ 6.25	400	2,500
To Direct Wages		32,600	By Output transferred to Process II (@ ₹ 28.50)	3,680	1,04,880
To Overheads		22,500			
To Abnormal Gain A/c (@ ₹ 28.50)	80	2,280			
	4,080	1,07,380		4,080	1,07,380

Normal Loss Account

Dr Cr

Details	Unit	Amount (₹)	Details	Unit	Amount (₹)
To Process A/c @ ₹ 6.25	400	2,500	By Cash/Debtors A/c (@ ₹ 6.25)	320	2000
			Abnormal Gain A/c @ ₹ 6.25	80	500
	400	2,500		400	2,500

Abnormal Gain Account

Dr Cr

Details	Unit	Amount (₹)	Details	Unit	Amount (₹)
To Normal Loss A/c @ ₹ 6.25	80	500	By Process A/c @ ₹ 28.50	80	2,280
To Costing Profit and Loss A/c		1,780			
	80	2,280		80	2,280

Statement showing the calculation of profit when joint costs are apportioned on Weight basis and Market Value Basis

Product	Output (Kg)	Selling Price per unit (₹)	Sales Value (₹)	Weight Basis (₹)	(Profit/ (Loss) (₹)	Sales Value Basis (₹)	Profit/ (Loss) (₹)
JP-I	1,440	62.50	90,000	68,040	21,960	79,843	10,157
JP-II	1,280	50.00	64,000	60,480	3,520	56,777	7,223
JP-III	960	43.25	42,000	45,360	(3,360)	37,260	4,740
Total	3,680		1,96,000	1,73,880	22,120	1,73,880	22,120

Joint Cost: (1,04,880 + 34,500 + 34,500) =>₹ 1,73,880

Apportionment on Weight Basis: 1,440: 1,280: 960 i.e. 9: 8:6

Share of Joint Product JP-I: {(1,73,880) × (9/23)} => ₹68,040

Share of Joint Product JP-I: {(1,73,880) × (8/23)} => ₹60,480

Share of Joint Product JP-I: {(1,73,880) × (6/23)} => ₹45,360

Apportionment on Sales Value Basis: 90,000: 64,000: 42,000 i.e. 45: 32:21

Share of Joint Product JP-I: {(1,73,880) × (45/98)} => ₹79,843

Share of Joint Product JP-I: {(1,73,880) × (32/98)} => ₹56,777

Share of Joint Product JP-I: {(1,73,880) × (21/98)} => ₹37,260

Problem 3. (By-Product)

A factory is engaged in the production of a chemical X and in the course of its manufacture a by-product Y is produced, which after a separate process has a commercial value. For the month of March 2007 the following are summarised cost data:

Details	*Joint Expenses (₹)*	*Separate Expenses X (₹)*	*Separate Expenses Y (₹)*
Materials	*19,200*	*7,360*	*780*
Labour	*11,700*	*7,680*	*2,642*
Overheads	*3,450*	*1,500*	*544*

The output of the month was 142 tonnes of X and 49 tonnes of Y. The selling price of Y averaged ₹ 280 per tonne.

Assuming the profit on Y is estimated at 50% of selling price; calculate the cost of X per tonne. **[B.Com (Hons.) DU, 2007]**

Solution : **Share of BY-Product Y in Joint Cost**

Details	Amount (₹)
Sale (49 units @ ₹ 280 per unit)	13,720
Less: Profit 50% (i.e. 0.5 × 13,720)	6,860
Cost of By-Product Y	6,860
Less: Subsequent Expenses (780 + 2,642 +544)	3,966
Share in Joint Cost	2,894

Cost of Product X

Details	Amount (₹)
Material Cost (19,200 + 7,360)	26,560
Labour (11,700 + 7,680)	19,380
Overheads(3,450 +1,500)	4,950
Total	50,890
Less: Share of By-Product Y in Total Joint cost	(2,894)
Cost of Product X (Balance)	47,996
Cost of Product X per tonne (47,996÷142)	338

Problem 4. (Joint Product)

In an Oil Mill in Maharastra Four Products emerge from a refining process. The total cost of input during the quarter ending December, 2007 is ₹ 3, 00,000. The output/sales and additional processing costs are as follows:

Product	*Output (Litre)*	*Additional processing cost beyond split-off point (₹)*	*Sales value (after further processing) (₹)*	*Selling price (at the point of split-off) (₹)*
M	*4,000*	*1,00,000*	*3,50,000*	*60*
P	*2,000*	*20,000*	*50,000*	*24*
S	*1,000*	———	*12,000*	*12*
T	*2,000*	*7,000*	*90,000*	*30*

Prepare a Statement of profitability based on:

(1) If products are sold after further processing.

(2) If the products are sold at the point of split-off.

Solution : Statement of Profitability for the Quarter ending December, 2007

(After further processing)

Product	Sales value (after further processing Cost) (₹) (a)	Share of Joint cost 20:4:1:5 (₹) (b)	Further processing Cost (₹) (c)	Total Cost (₹) (d)= (b)+(c)	Profit (Loss) (₹) (e):=(a) – (d)
M	3,50,000	2,00,000	1,00,000	3,00,000	50,000
P	50,000	40,000	20,000	60,000	(10,000)
S	12,000	10,000	———	10,000	2,000
T	90,000	50,000	7,000	57,000	33,000
Total	5,02,000	3, 00,000	1,27,000	4,27,000	75,000

Working Notes:

Sales Value at the point of Split-off:

$$M = 4000 \times 60 = ₹\ 2{,}40{,}000$$

$$P = 2000 \times 24 = ₹\ 48{,}000$$

$$S = 1000 \times 12 = ₹\ 12{,}000$$

$$T = 2000 \times 30 = ₹\ 60{,}000$$

Sharing Ratio:

2,40,000 : 48,000 : 12,000 : 60,000. OR 20 : 4 : 1 : 5.

Statement of Profitability for the Quarter ending December, 2007

(At the split-off Point)

Product	Selling price (at the point of split-off) (₹) (a)	Output (unit) (b)	Sales value at split-off Point (₹) (c)=(a)×(b)	Share of Joint cost 20:4:1:5 (₹) (d)	Profit at split-off Point (₹) (e)
M	60	4,000	2, 40,000	2,00,000	40,000
P	24	2,000	48,000	40,000	8,000

S	12	1,000	12, 000	10,000	2,000
T	30	2,000	60,000	50,000	10,000
Total			3,60,000	3, 00,000	60,000

Problem 5. (Joint Product)

Three joint products are produced by passing chemicals through two consecutive processes. Output from Process- I is transferred to Process- II from which three joint products are produced and immediately sold. The information regarding the processes for July 2007 is given hereunder:

Details	*Process I (₹)*	*Process II (₹)*
Direct Material (6,000 Kgs. @ ₹ 5 per Kg)	*30,000*	———
Direct Labour	*18,750*	*31,050*
Overheads	*14,250*	*31,050*
Normal Loss (% of Input)	*10*	*NIL*
Scrap Value of Loss	*6*	———

Joint product X : 2,160 Kgs, Joint product Y : 1,920 Kgs, Joint product Z : 1,440 Kgs.

Output: 5,520 Kgs.

There were no opening or closing stocks in either process or the selling price of the output of process II were:

Joint product X: ₹50.00 per Kg

Joint product Y: ₹ 37.50 per Kg

Joint product Z: ₹ 25.00 per Kg

Required:

(1) Prepare an account for Process-I together with any loss or gain accounts you consider necessary to record month's activities.

(2) Calculate the profit attributable to each of the joint products by apportioning the total costs from Process II:

(i) According to weight of output; and

(ii) By the market value of production.

Solution :

Dr **Process I Account** Cr

Details	**Unit (Kg)**	**Amount (₹)**	**Details**	**Unit (Kg)**	**Amount (₹)**
Input of Material @ ₹ 5 per Unit = (6,000 × 5)	6,000	30,000	Normal Loss A/c (@ ₹ 6 per unit)	600	3,600

Direct Labour		18,750	Output transferred to Process-II @₹ 11 per unit	5,520	60,720
Overheads		14,250			
Abnormal Gain @₹ 11 per unit	120	1,320			
	6,120	64,320		6,120	64,320

Normal Cost per Kg:

= (Total cost – Sales Value of Scrap) ÷ Normal Output

= (63,000 – 3,600) ÷ (6,000 – 600)

= 59,400 ÷ 5,400 = ₹ 11

Abnormal Gain Account

Dr Cr

Details	Kg	Amount (₹)	Details	Kg	Amount (₹)
To Normal Loss A/c @₹ 6 per unit	120	720	By Process I A/c @₹ 11 per unit	120	1,320
To Costing Profit and Loss A/c		600			
	120	1,320		120	1,320

Normal Loss Account

Dr Cr

Details	Kg	Amount (₹)	Details	Kg	Amount (₹)
To Process I A/c @₹ 6 per unit	600	3,600	By Cash/Drs A/c @₹ 6 per unit	480	2,880
			By Abnormal Gain A/c @₹ 6 per unit	120	720
	600	3,600		600	3,600

Statement of Profit

(Apportionment of Joint cost According to Weight of Output)

Joint Product	Output (Kg) (a)	Selling Price (₹) (b)	Sales Value (₹) (c)=(a) × (b)	Joint Cost (₹) (d)	Profit (Loss) (₹) (e): (c) – (d)
X	2,160	50.00	1,08,000	48,060	59,940
Y	1,920	37.50	72,000	42,720	29,280
Z	1,440	25.00	36,000	32,040	3,960
Total	5,520		2,16,000	1, 22,820	93,180

Statement of Profit

(Apportionment of Joint cost According to Market Value of Output)

Joint Product	Output (Kg) (a)	Selling Price (₹) (b)	Sales Value (₹) (c)=(a) × (b)	Joint Cost (₹) (d)	Profit (₹) (e): (c) – (d)
X	2,160	50.00	1,08,000	61,410	46,590
Y	1,920	37.50	72,000	40,940	31,060
Z	1,440	25.00	36,000	20,470	15,530
Total	5,520		2,16,000	1, 22,820	93,180

Working Notes:

A. Joint cost of the products under Process II:

Details	Amount (₹)
1. Transfer of output from Process I	60,720
2. Direct Labour	31,050
3. Overheads	31,050
Total	1,22,820

B. Apportionment of Joint cost based on ratio of Output i.e. 9:8:6 which is X: 2,160 Kgs., Y: 1,920 Kgs., Z: 1,440 Kgs.

C. Apportionment of Joint cost based on ratio of Sales i.e. 3:2:1 which is X: ₹ 1, 08,000, Y: ₹ 72,000, Z: ₹ 36,000.

Problem 6. *In a factory, engaged in chemical processing 4,000 litres of a certain type of raw material Cz are used for each production cycle(Batch). Four joint products are obtained after processing. Estimated output and sale price for joint products are as under:*

Product	*Output (per 4,000 litres)*	*Selling Price (per Litre) (₹)*
JP-1	*300*	*50*
JP-2	*1,200*	*40*
JP-3	*600*	*60*
JP-4	*1,800*	*25*

The estimated processing cost per production cycle (Batch) is ₹ 20,800. Selling and distribution cost is estimated at 20% of sales. Management's expected rate of return is 10% on sales. The unaccounted raw material is taken as normal waste.

You are required to work out:

(i) The purchase price per litre of the raw material with a view to achieving the above outcome and

(ii) The unit cost of sales of JP-1, JP-2, JP-3, and JP-4 on the basis of their sale value. **(ICWA- Inter)**

Solution : (i)

Product	Output (per 4,000 litres)	Selling Price (per Litre) (₹)	Sale Value (₹)
JP-1	300	50	15,000
JP-2	1,200	40	48,000
JP-3	600	60	36,000
JP-4	1,800	25	45,000
Total	3,900	———	1,44,000
Less:	1. Expected Profit		14,400
	2. Selling & Distribution cost		28,800
Balance	Total cost		1,00,800
Less:	Processing cost		20,800
Balance	Total Cost of Raw Material Consumed		80,000
	Per unit Cost of Raw Material Consumed	80,000 ÷ 4,000 = ₹ 20	

(ii) Computation of unit cost of sales:

Details	Product JP-1 (₹)	Product JP-2 (₹)	Product JP-3 (₹)	Product JP-4 (₹)
Sale value	15,000	48,000	36,000	45,000
Less: Profit @ 10% of sale value	1,500	4,800	3,600	4,500
Cost of Sale	13,500	43,200	32,400	40,500
Cost of Sale per unit= [Cost of Sale/ No. of units]	45	36	54	22.50

Problem 7. *JB Limited produces four joint products A, B, C, and D, all of which emerge from the processing of one raw material. The following are the relevant data: Production for the period:*

Joint Product	*Number of Units*	*Selling Price per Unit (₹)*
A	*500*	*18.00*
B	*900*	*8.00*
C	*400*	*4.00*
D	*200*	*11.00*

The company budgets for a profit of 10% of sales value. The other estimated costs are:

Item of Cost	*Amount (₹)*
Carriage Inward	*1,000*
Direct Wages	*3,000*
Manufacturing Overhead	*2,000*
Administrative Overhead (10% of sales value)	

You are required to:

(a) Calculate the maximum price that may be paid for the raw material.

(b) Prepare a comprehensive cost statement for each of the products allocating the materials and other cost based upon:
(i) number of units; and (ii) Sales value **{C.A. Inter}**

Solution : Computation of raw material Cost

Joint Product	Number of units	Selling Price per Unit (₹)	Sale Value (₹)
A	500	18.00	9,000
B	900	8.00	7,200
C	400	4.00	1,600
D	200	11.00	2,200
Total	2,000	——	20,000
Less:	Expected Profit		2,000
Balance	Total Cost		18,000
Less:	1. Other Cost: (a) Carriage Inward 1,000 (b) Direct Wages 3,000 (c) Manufacturing Overhead 2,000 (d) Administrative Overhead 2,000		8,000
Balance	Cost of Raw Material Consumed		10,000

Cost Statement

Details	Product A (₹)	Product B (₹)	Product C (₹)	Product D (₹)	Total (₹)
Number of units 5:9:4:2	4,500	8,100	3,600	1,800	18,000
Sales value 45:36:8:11	8,100	6,480	1,440	1,980	18,000

Problem 8. *Work out the estimated pre-separation cost per ton of by-products Y and Z from the following data:*

Cost of manufacture before separation ₹ 25, 60,000. Main product is X. There are two by-products Y and Z whose selling price are as under:

Sale price of Y: ₹ 500 per ton, and

Sale price of Z: ₹ 800 per ton.

Selling and distribution expenses have between estimated to be 25% of selling price and net profit is expected to be 10% of selling price. Cost to manufacture each ton after separation from the product re:

₹ 95 for by-product Y; and ₹ 145 for product Z. Assume equal weight for Y and Z. **[B.Com (Hons.) DU, 2009]**

Solution : **Computation of pre-separation Cost**

Details	By-Product	
	Y (₹)	Z (₹)
Selling Price per ton	500	800
Less: (i) Selling and Distribution Expenses:	(125)	(200)
(ii) Net profit: [Y: (125 + 50); Z: (200 + 80)]	(50)	(80)
Cost of Production	325	520
Less: Post-separation cost	95	145
Pre-separation Cost per ton	230	375

Problem 9. *During August 1,250 units of main product were produced at total cost of ₹ 1,05,000. The production also resulted in 5,000 units of a by-product which was sold @ ₹ 3 per unit. However, this sale of by-product led to additional selling expenses of ₹ 800. 1,000 units were sold at a price of ₹ 105 per unit. Calculate the amount of gross profit after crediting the realization from by-product (a) to cost of production, and (b) to cost of sales.*

Solution : (a) Realization from by-product credited to cost of production:

Details			Amount (₹)
Sale of Main product during August (1,000 units @ ₹ 105)			1,05,000
Less: cost of sales:			
Total cost of 1,250 units		1,05,000	
Sale of by-product: 5,000 × 3 =	15,000		
Less: Selling Expenses	800		
Less: Net realization from by-product		14,200	
Net Production cost of 1,250 units		90,800	
Less: Closing Stock: 250 × 72.64		18,160	
Less: cost of sales of 1,000 units			72,640
Gross Profit			32,360

(b) Realization from by-product credited to cost of sales:

Details			Amount (₹)
Sale of Main product during August (1,000 units @ ₹ 105)			1,05,000
Less: cost of sales:			
Total cost of 1,250 units	1,05,000		
Less: Closing Stock: 250 × 84	21,000	84,000	
Sale of by-product: 5,000 × 3 =	15,000		
Less: Selling Expenses	800		
Less: Net realization from by-product		14,200	69,800
Gross Profit			35,200

Note: The difference in gross profit of ₹ 2,840 is due to the difference in the value of closing stock which is ₹ 18,160 in the first method and ₹ 21,000 in the second method. In the first method the net realization from the sale of by-product of ₹ 14,200 has been deducted from the entire cost of production of 1,250 units whereas in the second method it has been deducted from the cost of goods sold of 1,000 units.

Problem 10. *In a sugar producing factory along with sugar two by-products: Molasses, and Bagasse, are also produced. The cost details are furnished hereunder:*

Total cost before split-off: ₹ 16,50,000

Details	*Sugar*	*Molasses*	*Bagasse*
Sale of Entire Output (₹)	*25,00,000*	*9,60,000*	*6,00,000*
Post split-off cost (₹)	*4,00,000*	*60,000*	*37,500*
Estimated Profit on sales (%)		*20*	*12.5*
Estimated Selling expenses on sales (%)	*10*	*20*	*15*

Prepare comparative profit and Loss statement for the three products using reverse cost method of Joint product accounting.

Solution : Reverse Cost Statement for By-Products

Details	Molasses		Bagasse	
	Amount (₹)	Amount (₹)	Amount (₹)	Amount (₹)
Sales		9,60,000		6,00,000
Less: Estimated profit: 20% and 12.5%	1,92,000		75,000	
Selling Expenses:20% and 15%	1,92,000		90,000	
Post Split-off Cost	60,000	4,44,000	37,500	2,02,500
Share in Joint costs		5,16,000		3,97,500

The share of main product in Joint cost is ₹7,36,500 i.e. the difference between Total Joint cost and the sum of share in Joint costs of Molasses and Bagasse [(16,50,000) – (5,16,000 + 3,97,500)].

Comparative Statement of Profit and Loss

Details	Sugar Amount (₹)	Molasses Amount (₹)	Bagasse Amount (₹)	Total Amount (₹)
Sales	25,00,000	9,60,000	6,00,000	40,60,000
Less: Cost of sales				
Cost of Production:				
Joint cost	7,36,500	5,16,000	3,97,500	16,50,000
Post split-off cost	4,00,000	60,000	37,500	4,97,500
	11,36,500	576,000	4,35,000	21,47,500
Add: Selling Expenses	2,50,000	1,92,000	90,000	5,32,000
Cost of sales	13,86,500	7,68,000	5,25,000	26, 79,500
Profit	11,13,500	1,92,000	75,000	13,80,500

Problem 11. (Sell at Split off or further process)

A Standard Firm has manufactured four joint products: JP-1, JP-2, JP-3 and JP-4.Total cost till the point of separation amounted to ₹ 18,00,000. The output and sales during the preceding year were as under:

Product	*Output (Units)*	*Sales (₹)*	*Post-Split off cost (₹)*
JP-1	*1,50,000*	*21,40,000*	*1,60,000*
JP-2	*25,000*	*10,00,000*	*96,000*
JP-3	*5,000*	*3,08,000*	*48,000*
JP-4	*12,500*	*8,72,000*	*1,76,000*

Required:

(i) Calculate the net income from each product if the joint costs are apportioned on the basis of sales value at split off point.

(ii) What would be the net income if all joint products are sold at split off point@ ₹ 11, ₹33, ₹ 19.25 and ₹ 66 per unit?

(iii) Which of these products should be further processed if the above information remains true in the current year.

Solution : (i) **Statement of Income**

(Joint costs apportioned based on sales at Split off point)

Product (A)	Sales (₹) (B)	Post-Split off cost (₹) (C)	Sales at split off point (₹) (D)= [(B) – (C)]	Share in Joint cost (₹) (E)	Net Income (₹) (F) =[(D) – (E)]
JP-1	21,40,000	1,60,000	19,80,000 (51.5625%)*	9,28,125**	10,51,875
JP-2	10,00,000	96,000	9,04,000 (23.5417%)	4,23,751	4,80,249
JP-3	3,08,000	48,000	2,60,000 (6.7708%)	1,21,874	1,38,126
JP-4	8,72,000	1,76,000	6,96,000 (18.125%)	3,26,250	3,69,750
Total	43,20,000	4,80,000	38,40,000	18,00,000	20,40,000

(51.5625%)* = (19,80,000 ÷ 38,40,000) × 100

9,28,125** = (18,00,000 × 0. 515625)

(ii) **Statement of Income**

(Sales at Split off point)

Product (A)	Sales at split off point (₹) (B)	Apportionment of Joint cost (₹) (C)	Net Income (₹) (F) =[(B)- (C)]
JP-1	16,50,000 (0.4858)* (1,50,000 ×11)	8,74,440**	7,75,506
JP-2	8,25,000 (0.2429) (25,000 × 33)	4,37,220	3,87,753
JP-3	96,250 (0.0284) (5,000 ×19.25)	51,120	45,238
JP-4	8,25,000 (0.2429) (12,500 × 66)	4,37,220	3,87,753
Total	33,96,250	18,00,000	15,96,250

*= (16,50,000/33,96,250) × 100 => (0.4858)

**= (0.4858 ×18,00,000) => ₹ 8,74,440

(iii)

Product (A)	Sales after procgessing (₹) (B)	Sales at split off point (₹) (C)	Incremental sales (₹) (D)	Post-Split off Cost (₹) (E)	Incremental Gain or Loss (₹) (F) =[(D) – (E)]
JP-1	21,40,000	16,50,000	4,90,000	1,60,000	3,30,000
JP-2	10,00,000	8,25,000	1,75,000	96,000	79,000
JP-3	3,08,000	96,250	2,11,750	48,000	1,63,750
JP-4	8,72,000	8,25,000	47,000	1,76,000	(1,29,000)
Total	43,20,000	33,96,250	9,23,750	4,80,000	4,43,750

Decision: The Standard Firm should further process JP-1, JP-2 and JP-3 but NOT JP-4. It can raise its profits by ₹ 1,29,000 if JP-4 is sold immediately after split off point.

Problem 12. *SV Limited produces a main product M and a by-product Bp upon which further-costs are incurred to render it saleable. The joint costs of manufacture are given below:*

Materials ₹ 8,00,000; Labour ₹ 3,00,000 and Overheads ₹ 1,80,000. Subsequent costs are:

Cost Element	***Product M Amount (₹)***	***Product Bp Amount (₹)***
Materials	*3,50,000*	*1,75,000*
Labour	*1,80,000*	*1,30,000*
Overheads	*70,000*	*55,000*
Total	*6,00,000*	*3,60,000*
Selling Value	*20,00,000*	*10,00,000*
Estimated profit on Selling Price	*25(%)*	*20(%)*

Selling Expenses were also incurred on the products.

Prepare statement showing apportionment of Joint costs and Process account M and Bp to show cost of production.

Solution : Statement of Apportionment of Cost

Details	**Product M Amount (₹)**	**Product Bp Amount (₹)**	**Total Amount (₹)**
Sales Value	20,00,000	10,00,000	30,00,000
Less: Profit (25%; 20%)	5,00,000	2,00,000	7,00,000
Total Cost	15,00,000	8,00,000	23,00,000
Less: Subsequent production cost	6,00,000	3,60,000	9,60,000

Estimated total Joint cost including Selling and Distribution expenses	9,00,000	4,40,000	13,40,000
Less: Selling and Distribution expenses*	40,000	20,000	60,000
Joint cost	8,60,000	4,20,000	12,80,000

***Note:** Total cost before separation given is ₹ 12,80,000 {i.e. . 8,00,000 + 3,00,000+ 1,80,000}. The excess of ₹ 60,000 as per estimate represents selling and distribution costs: 13,40,000 – 12,80,000 = 60,000 to be apportioned in the ratio of Sales value of ₹ 20,00,000 : ₹ 10,00,000 i.e. 2:1.

Main Product M A/c

Dr Cr

Details	Amount (₹)	Details	Amount (₹)
Materials (8,00,000 +3,50,000)	11,50,000	Product Bp A/c (Transfer of Joint cost)	4,20,000
Labour (3,00,000 +1,80,000)	4,80,000	Sales	20,00,000
Overheads (1,80,000 +70,000)	2,50,000		
Selling & Distribution Expenses	40,000		
Profit	5,00,000		
Total	24,20,000	Total	24,20,000

By- Product Bp A/c

Dr Cr

Details	Amount (₹)	Details	Amount (₹)
Product M A/c (Transfer of Joint cost)	4,20,000	Sales	10,00,000
Materials	1,75,000		
Labour	1,30,000		
Overheads	55,000		
Selling & Distribution Expenses	20,000		
Profit	2,00,000		
Total	10,00,000	Total	10,00,000

OBJECTIVE TYPE EXERCISES

I. Indicate whether each of the following statements is 'True' by writing T :

1. True Joint costs are indivisible.
2. Meat packing industry is a classic example of joint product costing.
3. There is no clear cut distinction between joint products and by- products,
4. There is no difference between joint products and co- products,
5. By products may be sold in their original form without further processing.
6. Apportionment of joint cost to joint and by- products does not affect overall profit or loss.
7. Management may treat a joint product as a by-product.

Answers :

1. True	**2.** True	**3.** True	**4.** False
5. True	**6.** True	**7.** True	

II. Fill in the blank spaces :

1. Two instances of industries producing joint products are .... and ....
2. Differentiation between joint products and byproducts tends to be based on factors like .... and .... and ....
3. The stage of production at which joint and by products are identified is known as ....
4. Costs incurred after split-off point are called .... costs,
5. The main purpose of accounting of joint and byproducts is to ....
6. Various grades of coal should be treated as .... products,
7. In sugar industry .... is the main product and .... is the by-product.
8. In process industries, the accountant classifies multiple products according to their relative importance. The principal product is called .... and incidental products of lesser value are usually called .... and products of nearly equal value are called ....
9. The costs incurred up to the point at which individual products are separated from the common raw material and common process are called ....
10. The .... of the products is the most important criterion to distinguish between scrap, by-products and main product.
11. The .... product is usually produced in greater quantity than the by-product.
12. .... are products of less sales value produced simultaneously with the products of greater value.

Answers :

1. Meat and Petroleum

2. relative sales value, purpose of manufacture, profit pattern desired

3. Separation stage

4. subsequent costs

5. determine profit or loss product-wise

6. joint

7. sugar, bagasse
8. main product' by-product and joint product
9. joint costs
10. Sales value
11. Main
12. By-products

THEORETICAL EXERCISES

1. What do you mean by by-products and joint products? What is the distinction between them? Give appropriate examples.
2. State the main objectives of analysis of costs and accounting of joint and by-product costs.
3. What is the basic cost accounting problem in dealing with joint products? Mention the various methods of accounting for joint products.
4. What are by-products and joint products?
5. How would you deal with by –products in costing
   (i) Where they are of small total value,
   (ii) Where they are of considerable total value,
   (iii) Where they require further processing.
6. Distinguish between the followings:
   (1) Joint Product and by-products with reference to the (i) method of accounting, and (ii) method of valuation. **[B.Com (Hons.), DU, 1998]**
7. Explain in brief the following concepts:
   (i) Split off Point; **[DU, B.Com (Hons.) 2001]**
   (ii) Equivalent production

NUMERICAL EXERCISES

1. One tonne of Basic raw material put into a common process yields four products P, T, S, and M, their weights being 72 kgs, 117 kgs, 171kgs and 540 kgs respectively. Normal loss is 10% of the input of raw material. Total processing cost of this material is ₹ 50,000 per tonne of raw material input. Apportion the joint cost to products P, T, S, and M. **[Ans. P ₹4, 000, T ₹6, 500, S ₹9, 500, and M ₹30, 000]**
2. A coke manufacturing company produces the following products by putting 8,000 tonnes of coal @ ₹ 50 per tonne into common process:

Product	Output (Tonne)
Coke	5,700
Coal Tar	1,710
Sulphate	133
Benzol	57

Apportion the joint cost amongst the products on the basis of physical unit method.

[Ans. ₹ 3,00,000, ₹ 90,000, ₹ 7,000, ₹ 3, 000]

3. In an Oil Mill in Andhra Pradesh Four Products emerge from a refining process. The total cost of input during the quarter ending March, 2007 is ₹ 1,50,000. The output/sales and additional processing costs are as follows:

Product	Output (Litre)	Additional processing cost beyond split-off point (₹)	Sales value (after further processing) (₹)	Selling price (at the point of split-off) (₹)
M	8,000	45,000	1,72,500	15.00
P	4,000	10,000	25,000	6.00
S	2,000	———	6,000	3.00
T	4,000	3,500	45,000	7.50

Prepare a Statement of profitability based on:

(1) If products are sold after further processing.

(2) If the products are sold at the point of split-off. **(C.A. Inter)**

[Ans. (1) Total Profit ₹ 40,000, after adjusting a loss of ₹ 5,000 incurred by Product P ; (2)Total Profit ₹ 30,000]

4. Three joint products are produced by passing chemicals through two consecutive processes. Output from Process I is transferred to process II from which three joint products are produced and immediately sold. The information regarding the processes for April 2007 is given below:

Details	Process I (₹)	Process II (₹)
Direct Material (2,500 Kgs. @ ₹ 4 per Kg.	10,000	———
Direct Labour	6,250	6,900
Overheads	4,500	6,900
Normal Loss (% of Input)	10	NIL
Scrap Value of Loss	2	———

Joint product A : 900 Kgs, Joint product B : 800 Kgs, Joint product C : 600 Kgs. Output: 2,300 Kgs.

There were no opening or closing stocks in either process or the selling price of the output of process II were:

Joint product A: ₹24 per Kg

Joint product B: ₹ 18 per Kg

Joint product C: ₹ 12 per Kg

Required:

(1) Prepare an account for Process I together with any loss or gain accounts you consider necessary to record month's activities.

(2) Calculate the profit attributable to each of the joint products by apportioning the total costs from Process II:

(i) According to weight of output; and

(ii) By the market value of production. **(C.A. Inter)**

[Ans. Joint cost ₹ 34,500; Profit (according to weight) for product A ₹ 8,100, for product B ₹ 2,400, Loss for product C ₹ 1,800; Profit (according to Market value) for product A ₹ 4,350, for product B ₹ 2,900, for product C ₹ 1,450]

5. The yield of a certain process is 75% as to the main product, 20% as to the by-product and 5% to the process loss. The material input (8000 units) costs @ ₹ 85.50 per unit and all other charges are ₹ 51,300, of which power cost accounted for 100/3%. It is ascertained that power is chargeable as to the main product and by-product in the ratio of 10:9. Draw up a statement showing the cost of the by-product.

[Ans. ₹ 1,59,300]

6. A refinery has a single compact unit for refining crude oil. The cost of processing 250 litres of crude oil is ₹ 1200. The standard yield per 250 litres of crude oil and the selling price of each product are given below:

Product Basket	Standard yield (in litres per 250 litres of crude)	Selling Price (per litre) (₹)
Motor Spirit (Petrol)	64.0	45
Diesel Oil	50.0	28
Fuel Oil	50.0	24
Kerosene	64.0	12
Gas (M3 converted into litres	9.5	8
Process loss	12.5	——

7. In a process line of MILAN limited the following data for the month of June 2007 are available for the joint products:

Details	Product JP-1 (₹)	Product JP-2 (₹)	Product JP-3 (₹)
Selling Price per Kg	10	23	50
Subsequent cost	10,000	11,000	35,000
Output in Kg	2,500	1,000	1,500

Pre-separation cost amounted to ₹ 50,000.

The joint products are manufactured in one common process, after which they are separated and may undergo further individual processing. The pre-separation point costs are apportioned to joint products according to weight. You are required to prepare a statement showing the estimated profit or loss for each product and in total.

[(I.C.W.A. –Inter (modified)]

[Ans. Loss ₹10, 000 for JP-1; Profit ₹ 2,000 for JP-2; and Profit ₹ 25,000 for JP-3; and Total Profit ₹ 17,000]

8. In a factory, engaged in chemical processing 5,000 Kgs. of a certain type of raw material Cx are used for each production Batch. Four joint products are obtained after processing. Estimated output and sale price for joint products are as under:

Product	Output (Per 5,000 Kgs.)	Selling Price (Per Kg.) (₹)
JP-1	400	80
JP-2	1,500	64
JP-3	750	100
JP-4	2,250	40

The estimated processing cost per production Batch is ₹ 72,775. Selling and distribution cost is estimated at 20% of sales. Management's expected rate of return is 12.5% on sales. The unaccounted raw material is taken as normal waste.

You are required to work out:

(1) The purchase price per litre of the raw material with a view to achieving the above outcome and

(2) The unit cost of sales of JP-1, JP-2, JP-3, and JP-4 on the basis of their sale value. **[Ans. (1) ₹ 25 per kg.; (2) Unit cost of sales: ₹ 70, ₹ 56, ₹ 87.50, and ₹ 35]**

9. AV Limited produces four joint products A, B, C, and D, all of which emerge from the processing of one raw material. The following are the relevant data: Production for the period:

Joint Product	Number of Units	Selling Price per Unit (₹)
A	600	50.00
B	1,000	25.00
C	500	10.00
D	400	20.00

The company budgets for a profit of 15% of sales value. The other estimated costs are:

Item	Amount (₹)
Carriage Inward	6,000
Direct Wages	10,000
Manufacturing Overhead	5,000
Administrative Overhead (10% of Sales Value)	

You are required to:

(a) Calculate the maximum price that may be paid for the raw material.

(b) Prepare a comprehensive cost statement for each of the products allocating the materials and other cost based upon:
(i) Number of units; and (ii) Sales value

[Ans. (a) `30,000 ; (b) (i) ₹13,872; ₹23,120; ₹11,560; ₹9,248; (ii) ₹25,500; ₹21,250; ₹4,250; ₹6,800;]

10. In the course of manufacture of the main product 'P', by products 'A' and 'B' also emerge. The joint expenses of manufacture amount to ₹ 1,19,550. All the products are processed further after separation and sold as per details furnished below:

Details	Main Product	By-Product	
	P (₹)	A (₹)	B (₹)
Sales	90,000	60,000	40,000
Cost Beyond split off stage	6,000	5,000	4,000
Profit as percentage of sales	25	20	15

Selling and administration overheads are absorbed as percentage of cost of sales. Prepare a statement showing the apportionment of joint cost to the main product and by-products. Also prepare Main product 'P' A/c. **[B.com (Hons.), DU , 2001]**

[Ans. Profit ₹ 22,500]

11. During July 1,000 units of main product were produced at total cost of ₹ 40,000. The production also resulted in 4,000 units of a by-product which was sold @ ₹ 2 per unit. However, this sale of by-product led to additional selling expenses of ₹ 500. 800 units were sold at a price of ₹ 60 per unit. Calculate the amount of gross profit after crediting the realization from by-product (a) to cost of production, and (b) to cost of sales. **[Ans. Profit (a) ₹ 22,000; (b) ₹ 23,500]**

12. In a sugar producing factory along with sugar two by-products: Molasses, and Bagasse, are also produced. The cost details are furnished hereunder:

Total cost before split-off: ₹ 2,50,000

Details	Sugar	Molasses	Bagasse
Sale of Entire Output (₹)	4,00,000	1,60,000	80,000
Post split-off cost (₹)	60,000	10,000	5,000
Estimated Profit on sales (%)		20	10
Estimated Selling expenses on sales (%)	10	20	20

Prepare comparative profit and Loss statement for the three products using reverse cost method of Joint product accounting.

[Ans. Share in joint cost: ₹ 1,13,000; ₹ 86,000; ₹ 51,000; Profit: ₹ 1,87,000; ₹ 32,000; ₹ 8,000.]

13. A Standard Firm has manufactured four joint products: JP-1, JP-2, JP-3 and JP-4.Total cost till the point of separation amounted to ₹ 2,25,000. The output and sales during the preceding year were as under:

Product	Output (Units)	Sales (₹)	Post-Split off (₹)
JP-1	60,000	2,00,000	20,000
JP-2	10,000	80,000	12,000
JP-3	2,000	16,000	6,000
JP-4	5,000	64,000	22,000

Required:

(i) Calculate the net income from each product if the joint costs are apportioned on the basis of sales value at split off point.

(ii) What would be the net income if all joint products are sold at split off point@ ₹ 2, ₹6, ₹ 3.50 and ₹ 12 per unit?

(iii) Which of these products should be further processed if the above information remains true in the current year.

[Ans. (i) ₹ 75,000; (ii) ₹ 22,000; (iii) Product JP-4 should not be processed further]

14. PV Limited produces a main product M and a by-product Bp upon which further-costs are incurred to render it saleable. The joint costs of manufacture are given below:

Materials ₹ 1,50,000; Labour ₹ 90,000 and Overheads ₹ 60,000. Subsequent costs are:

Cost Element	Product M Amount (₹)	Product Bp Amount (₹)
Materials	90,000	45,000
Labour	42,000	30,000
Overheads	18,000	15,000
Total	1,50,000	90,000
Selling Value	4,80,000	2,40,000
Estimated profit on Selling Price	25(%)	20(%)

Selling Expenses were also incurred on the products.

Prepare statement showing apportionment of Joint costs and Process account M and Bp to show cost of production. **[Ans. Profit ₹ 1,20,000 ; ₹ 48,000]**

15. Z Limited manufactures Product A which yields two by-products X and Y. In a period, the amount spent up to the point of separation was ₹ 20,600. Subsequent expenses were:

Elements of cost	Product A Amount (₹)	Product X Amount (₹)	Product Y Amount (₹)
Materials	300	200	150
Direct Wages	400	300	200
Overheads	300	270	280
Total	1,000	770	630

Gross sales value of products A, X and Y were ₹ 15,000, ₹ 10,000and ₹ 5,000 respectively. It was estimated that the net profit as percentage of sales in case of X and Y would be 25 percent and 20 percent respectively.

[B.com. (Kerala); M.Com. (Osmania)]

[Ans. ₹ 3,500]

16. JB limited produces four products, A, B,C, D, all of which emerge from the processing of one raw material . the following are the relevant data:

Joint Product	Number of units	Selling Price per unit (₹)
A	500	18
B	900	8
C	400	4
D	200	11

The company budgets for a profit of 10% on sales value. The other estimated costs are:

Details	**Amount (₹)**
Carriage Inwards	1,000
Direct Wages	3,000
Manufacturing Overheads	2,000
Administrative overheads	10% of Sales value

You are required to:

(a) Calculate the maximum price to be paid for the raw material;

(b) Prepare a comprehensive statement for each of the products allocating the materials and other costs based upon: (i) Number of units, and (ii) Sales Value.

[C.A.]

[Ans. Maximum Price for raw material ₹ 10,000]

17. The yield of a certain process is 80% as to the main product, 15% as to the by-product and 5% as to the process loss. The material put in process (5,000 units) cost ₹ 23.75 per unit and all other charges are ₹ 14,250, of which power cost accounted for 100/3%. It is ascertained that power is chargeable as to the main product in the ratio of 10:9.

Draw up a statement showing the cost of the by-product. **[C.A.]**

[Ans. Total cost of the by-product ₹ 22,500]

18. Bright Chemicals Limited electrolyses common salt to obtain three joint products: Caustic Soda, Chlorine, and Hydrogen. During a costing period, the expenditure relating to the inputs for the common process amounted to ₹ 3,50,000. After separation, expenses amounting to ₹ 1,60,000, ₹ 75,000 and ₹ 10,000 were incurred for Caustic Soda , Chlorine and Hydrogen respectively. The entire production was sold and ₹ 3,75,000, ₹ 2,50,000 and ₹ 60,000 were realized for Caustic Soda, Chlorine and Hydrogen respectively. The selling expenses were estimated at 5% of realizations from sale. The management expected profits @ 15%, 10% and 5% of realizations from sale of Caustic Soda, Chlorine and Hydrogen respectively.

[I.C.W.A. (Inter)]

[Ans. Actual Profit/ Loss (Product- wise): Caustic Soda ₹ 44,000; Chlorine ₹ 12,700; and Hydrogen (₹ 950)]

19. In the course of manufacture of the main Product 'P', by-products 'A' and 'B' also emerge. The joint expenses of manufacture amounted to Rupees 1, 19,550. All the products are processed further after separation and sold as per details given below:

Details	Main Product	By-Products	
	P (₹)	A (₹)	B (₹)
Sales	90,000	60,000	40,000
Cost beyond Split-Off	6,000	5,000	4,000
Profit as percentage of sales	25	20	15

Selling and Administration overheads are absorbed as percentage of cost of sales. Prepare a statement showing the apportionment of joint cost to the main product and by-products. Also prepare main product 'P' account. **[B.Com (Hons.) DU, 2001]**

[Ans. Joint Cost. P: ₹ 54,750, A: ₹ 38,200, B: ₹ 26,600; Profit on Main product P: ₹ 22,500]

❑❑❑

20 Integral Accounting

Learning Objectives

It attempts to explain the operation of integral system of accounting. In this chapter you will learn :

1. Meaning, nature, advantages and limitations of integral system of accounting.
2. Essentials for the execution of the integral system of accounting.
3. Difference between inter-locking and integration of cost and financial accounts.
4. Make appropriate entries in the books of account under integral system.
5. Concept of cost ledger control (memoranda) account.

INTRODUCTION

Integrated accounting implies a system of accounting where both Cost and financial accounts are maintained in one set of books. The system provides information for ascertaining the cost of each product/process/ job in addition to making it possible the ascertainment of marginal cost, variances, abnormal losses and gains etc. It also makes it feasible for the management to have full control over its assets and liabilities and prepares the Profit and Loss Account and the Balance Sheet as per the requirements of the Companies Act, 1956 and other relevant statutes.

INTEGRAL ACCOUNTING SYSTEM

Integral or Integrated accounting is the recording of cost and financial transactions in one consolidated ledger. In practice, the system is similar to that of non-integral system except that it eliminates duplicate entries and keeping of some unnecessary accounts, such as Cost ledger Control Account, and General Ledger Adjustment Account, Purchases account as well as Stores ledger Control account, etc.

An integrated account is defined as a "single set of accounts which provides financial and cost accounting information". Under the system, cost and financial accounts are kept in one self-contained ledger known as Integrated Ledger. This system does not recognize the necessity of preparing separate set of accounts.

Advantages: The system of integral accounting has the under-mentioned advantages:

1. It is simple and economical as there is *no duplication* of recording and effort.
2. As cost accounts are posted straight from the books of original entry, there is *no delay* in obtaining cost data.
3. As there is only one set of accounts, there will be one figure for profit or loss and as such the question of *reconciliation* does not arise. As there is automatic check on the *correctness* of the cost data, the cost figures create confidence in the management.
4. This system tends to co-ordinate the functions of different sections of the accounting which leads to *economy*.
5. It ensures better coordination between cost and financial staff. The fact that Cost Accounting and Financial Accounting are *complementary* to each other is properly appreciated.
6. Centralization of accounting function results in economy.
7. This system is essential in *mechanized* accounting.

Limitations:

1. The system does not suit large concerns which require detailed cost and financial data on continuing basis.
2. As 100% integration is not possible, the need for preparing Reconciliation Statement is still felt.
3. Merger of financial books and cost books into a single set of books makes it complicated; it fails to serve both the financial as well as costing requirements of the organization.

Salient features: It has the following salient features:

1. Cost ledger Control Account is dispensed with.
2. Subsidiary Ledgers i.e. Stores Ledger, Work-in-Progress Ledger and Finished goods Ledger are maintained. In addition a Sales Ledger (containing personal accounts of all customers) and a Bought ledger (containing personal accounts of all suppliers) are also maintained. Overhead Ledger is maintained to contain separate accounts for factory, administration and selling & distribution overheads.

3. For each subsidiary ledger, a control account is opened in the General Ledger.
4. Balance in various overhead control accounts represent over/under recovery of overhead costs which is transferred to Profit and Loss Account.
5. Balance in Profit and Loss Account represents profit or loss which is transferred to Profit and Loss (Appropriation) Account.
6. A suitable coding system is generally developed to serve the purposes of both cost accounts and financial accounts.

Installation of an Integrated Cost Accounting System

Following factors should be considered before installing the system:

1. *Degree of integration:* It must be decided in advance in regard to the degree of integration, which could be up to the stage of Prime Cost or Factory cost. Some firms prefer to integrate the entire records.
2. *Control Accounts:* Control accounts may be prepared for each of the elements of cost, such as: (a) Material Control Account, (b) Direct Labour Control Account, (c) Factory Overhead Control Account, (d) Administrative Overhead Control Account, (e) Selling and Distribution Overhead Control Account. Some of these control accounts may be split into fixed and variable depending on the requirements of the firm.
3. *Cost Accumulation Purposes:* Complete details regarding cost data are provided to the cost accounting department so as to achieve the following objectives:
   (a) To provide the necessary costing data.
   (b) To form the basis of journal entries so that the control accounts can be cleared to suitable revenue accounts resulting into cost of sales account.
4. *Suspense Accounts:* Items relating to Provisions for accrued expenses, prepayments and stocks should be dealt with by transfers to suitable suspense account, so that the balance remaining in each control account represents the charges for the period.
5. *Coding:* As the integrated accounts have to provide information both for financial as well as costing purposes, a meaningful system of coding should be used. Coding should be easily comprehensible, exhaustive and well understood by every one in the Accounts Department. The system of coding should be such as to permit a meaningful consolidation and analysis. The Coding system is an integral part of a mechanized system of accounting.

6. *Items to be considered separately:*
   (a) Items of pure finance: Items of financial nature such as, cash discount, interest on capital etc. which are not considered in cost accounts but taken into account while preparing Financial Statements should be considered separately.
   (b) Appropriation of profits: Items such as Dividend paid, transfer to reserves etc. should also be considered separately.
   (c) Abnormal profits and Losses: A proper distinction is to be made between normal loss and abnormal Losses for costing purposes.
   (d) Valuation of stock: Different criteria of valuation of stock of finished goods and work-in-progress are adopted in the case of cost and financial books. In financial books, usually the basis of valuation is cost price or market price which ever is lower, whereas in cost accounts, the valuation may be made at prime cost or works cost or total cost of production.

PRINCIPAL ACCOUNTS

Under the integral system of accounting the following accounts are primarily made and maintained:

Stock Control Account

This account is prepared for each of the following cost items:

- *Raw Material:* This account has opening stock and purchases on the debit side and material issued on the credit side.
- *Work-in-Progress:* The debit side has opening stock as well as factory overhead charged to production. It is credited with finished goods stock account and the balance is carried forward to the next period.
- *Finished Goods Stock:* It is debited with goods completed and credited with cost of sales.

The above stock accounts are usually used in place of the stock and purchase account, which is maintained in the financial books.

Cost of Sales Account

It is debited with cost of goods sold, and selling and distribution overheads, and credited with costing profit and loss account.

Asset Account

Individual accounts are kept for each item of asset. These individual asset accounts are prepared in the usual way and any capital expenditure incurred is debited to the respective asset account.

Debtors and Creditors Control Account

Credit transactions with the customers and suppliers are recorded. The balance in creditors account should tally with the balance of the Bought Ledger. Similarly, the Debtors Control account should tally with the Sales Ledger.

Prepayments Account and Outstanding Account

The advance payment made is debited to the Prepaid Account and credited to Overhead Control Account. Thus, the expense, which is related to the period, is charged to the work-in-progress account. In case of an expense due but not paid, the Expense Due account is credited and the overhead control account is debited. When the amount is actually disbursed, the Expense Due account is debited and cash/bank account is credited or it can be adjusted through the overhead control account.

Wages Control Account

Total Payment on account of remuneration to employees is debited to this account and the account is credited with the charge to Work-in-Progress and appropriate amount to Production overhead/Administration Overhead/ Selling and Distribution Overhead control account. Thus, there is neither opening nor closing balance in this account.

Overhead Control Account

The actual amount incurred is debited to the relevant overhead control account. The Production Overhead Control Account is credited with the work-in-Progress account. The Selling & distribution account is credited with the Cost of Sales account. Similarly, The Administration Overhead control account is credited either with the Finished Goods stock account or Costing Profit and Loss account. The Charging of such overhead control accounts may be on actual basis or at the pre-determined rates of recovery. There may be balance at the end of the period because of under or over recovery of overheads and the same may be transferred directly to the Costing Profit and Loss Account or through Overhead suspense account. Some times costing Profit and Loss account is not charged with under/over recovery of overheads and this may be carried forward to the next period.

Cash/Bank Account

All cash receipts are debited and cash disbursements are credited.

PRE-REQUISITES OF INTEGRATED ACCOUNTING

Some of the essential points may be kept in mind:-

1. A confirmed decision is required to be made in regard to the level of Integration. whether cost and financial accounts are to be fully integrated or to be integrated upto a particular stage like prime cost or factory cost.
2. All accounts are to be suitably coded so as to facilitate understanding and analysis.
3. A separate record should be maintained in respect of such items which are treated differently in cost and financial accounts.

4. Proper coordination must be ensured between the staff responsible for financial and cost aspects of the accounts for generating correct information and using it effectively.

DISTINCTION BETWEEN 'INTERLOCKING' AND 'INTEGRATING' OF COST AND FINANCIAL ACCOUNTS

When two separate sets of books are maintained, they are interlocked by CONTROL ACCOUNTS maintained in the two sets of books. Cost Ledger Control Account is maintained in the financial books and a General Ledger Adjustment Account is maintained in the Cost books. In Cost books, all entries relating to external world are posted in General Ledger Adjustment account. It may be pointed out that the Cost Ledger Control Account and General Ledger Adjustment accounts are contra accounts.

Integrating requires the preparation and maintenance of only one set of books in which all transactions are recorded. The Cost Ledger is dispensed with, and all the control accounts are maintained in the General Ledger.

From the point of view of economy, integration is preferable but due to practical difficulties, interlocking becomes essential. It may be very difficult to organize such a big set of integrated books. In the modern days cost accounting has assumed considerable importance in the planning and control of business operations and hence the management sets up a separate Cost Accounting department. Thus, in general, 'integral' system can be employed with efficiency only in small business units.

Illustrative Journal Entries

Transactions	Entry
Materials	
1. Cash Purchase for Stock	1. Stores Ledger Control A/c Dr To Cash/Bank A/c
2. Credit Purchase for Stock	2. Stores Ledger Control A/c Dr To Total Creditors A/c OR To Bought Ledger Control A/c
3. Materials Issued (Direct Materials)	3. Work-in-Progress Control A/c Dr To Stores Ledger Control A/c
4. Materials Issued (Indirect Materials)	4. Factory Overhead Control A/c Dr To Stores Ledger Control A/c
5. Materials Purchased for Specific Jobs	5. Work-in-Progress Control A/c Dr To Trade Creditors A/c/ To Cash/ Bank A/c
6. Materials Returned from Production	6. Stores Ledger Control A/c Dr To Work-in-Progress Control A/c
7. Indirect Materials Returned from Production	7. Stores Ledger Control A/c Dr To Factory Overhead Control A/c

8. Materials Returned to the Supplier	8. Trade Creditors A/c/ Bought Ledger Control A/c Dr To Stores Ledger Control A/c
9. Materials transferred from one Job to another Job **Note:** Some do not recommend any entry rather a separate record is kept in the form of a note.	9. (i) Transferee Job A/c Dr To Work-in-Progress Control A/c (ii) Work-in-Progress Control A/c Dr To Transferor Job A/c
10. Payment to creditors	10. Trade Creditors A/c Dr To Cash/Bank A/c
11. Normal Loss of Material on Physical stock taking	11. Factory Overhead Control A/c Dr To Stores Ledger Control A/c
12. Abnormal Loss of Material on Physical stock taking	12. Profit and Loss A/c Dr To Stores Ledger Control A/c
Wages	
1. Payment of Wages	1. Wages Control A/c Dr To Cash/Bank/Wages Payable A/c
2. Direct Wages allocated to Production	2. Work-in-Progress Control A/c Dr To Wages Control A/c
3. Indirect Wages allocated to Production/ Administration/ Selling & Distribution	3. Factory Overhead Control A/c Dr Administration Overhead Control A/c Dr Selling & Distribution Overhead Control A/c Dr To Wages Control A/c
Direct Expenses	Work-in-Progress Control A/c Dr To Cash/Bank/ Trade Creditors A/c
Overheads	
1. Overheads Incurred	1. (Relevant)Overhead Control A/c Dr To Cash/Bank/ Trade Creditors A/c
2. Production Overheads Absorbed	2. Work-in-Progress Control A/c Dr To Factory Overhead Control A/c
3. Administration Overheads Absorbed	3. Finished Goods (Stock) Control A/c Dr To Administration Overhead Control A/c
4. Selling & Distribution Overheads Absorbed	4. Cost of Sales A/c Dr To Selling & Distribution Overhead Control A/c

5. Under-Recovery of overheads	5. Overhead Adjustment A/c Dr To (Relevant) Overhead Control A/c
6. Over-Recovery of overheads	6. (Relevant) Overhead Control A/c Dr To Overhead Adjustment A/c
Others	
1. Finished Goods Produced	1. Finished Goods (Stock) Control A/c Dr To Work-in-Progress Control A/c
2. Finished Goods sold at: (a) Factory cost	2. (a) Cost of Sales A/c Dr To Finished Goods (Stock) Control A/c
(b) Sales Value	(b) Trade Debtors A/c Dr To Finished Goods (Stock) Control A/c
3. Sales Returns	3. Cost of Sales A/c Dr To Trade Debtors A/c
4. Repairs and Maintenance	4. Factory Overhead Control A/c Dr To Work-in-Progress Control A/c
5. Capital Work	5. Asset A/c Dr To Work-in-Progress Control A/c
6. Specific Jobs Completed and Billed at: (a) Factory cost	6. (a) Cost of Sales A/c Dr To Work-in-Progress Control A/c
(b) Selling Price	(b) Trade Debtors A/c Dr To Cost of Sales A/c
7. Abnormal wastage in production	7. Profit & Loss A/c Dr To Work-in-Progress Control A/c
8. Balance of Profit	8. Profit & Loss A/c Dr To Profit & Loss (Appropriation) A/c

Illustration 20.1 : *Journalise the following transactions in the integrated books of accounts:*

Transaction	***Amount (₹)***
1. Purchases on Credit	*2,50,000*
2. Production Wages Paid	*1,50,000*
3. Stores Issued to Production Orders	*1,60,000*
4. Production Expenses charged to Production	*80,000*

5. Administration Expenses Charged to Production	*30,000*
6. Finished Goods transferred from Production Orders	*3,60,000*
7. Production Expenses Incurred	*25,000*
8. Production Expenses Outstanding	*95,000*

Solution : Journal Entries (Under Integral System of Accounting)

Transaction		Amount (₹)	Amount (₹)
1. Stores Ledger Control A/c	Dr	2,50,000	
To Total Sundry Creditors A/c			2,50,000
(Being purchase of Stores on credit)			
2. Wages control A/c	Dr	1,50,000	
To Cash/Bank A/c			1,50,000
(Being Wages paid by cash/cheque)			
3. Work-in-Progress Control A/c	Dr	1,60,000	
To Stores Ledger Control A/c			1,60,000
(Being the issue of stores against production orders)			
4. Work-in-Progress Control A/c	Dr	80,000	
To Production Overhead control A/c			80,000
(Production Expenses allocated to Production)			
5. Work-in-Progress Control A/c	Dr	30,000	
To Administration Overhead control A/c			30,000
(Administration Expenses allocated to Production)			
6. Finished Goods Stock Control A/c	Dr	3,60,000	
To Work-in-Progress Control A/c			3,60,000
(Being the transfer of goods produced during the period)			
7. Production Overhead control A/c	Dr	95,000	
To Cash/Bank A/c			95,000
(Being Production expenses paid in cash/cheque)			
8. Production Overhead control A/c	Dr	25,000	
To Production Expenses Payable A/c			25,000
(Being Production expenses incurred during the period but still to be paid)			

Illustration 20.2 : *Prepare a Quarter's cost accounts from the following relevant information for a firm, which operates a batch costing system fully integrated with the financial accounts.*

Transaction	*Amount* (₹)
Balance at the beginning of the Quarter:	
Stores Ledger Control Account	*60,000*
Work-in-Progress Control account	*48,000*
Finished Goods Stock Control Account	*84,000*
Prepaid Production Overheads brought forward from the preceding Quarter	*15,400*
Transactions during the current Quarter:	
A. Materials Purchased	*2,50,000*
Materials issued:	
To Production	*1,00,000*
To Factory Maintenance	*15,000*
Materials transferred between batches	*18,000*
B. Total Wages Paid:	
To Direct Workers	*1,25,000*
To Indirect Workers	*25,000*
Direct Wages charged to Batches	*1,10,000*
Recorded non-productive time of direct workers	*15,000*
C. Selling and Distribution Overheads Incurred	*26,000*
Other Production Overhead Incurred	*72,000*
Sales	*4,28,000*
Cost of Finished Goods Sold	*3,70,000*
Cost of goods completed and transferred into Finished Goods during the current Quarter	*2,30,000*
Physical value of Work-in-Progress at the end of the Quarter	*1,20,000*
Production Overhead Rate of Absorption is 160% of Direct wages charged to Work-in-Progress.	—

Required: *Prepare the following accounts for the Quarter:*

(a) Stores Ledger Control Account;

(b) Work-in-Progress Control Account;

(c) Finished Goods Stock control Account;

(d) Production Overhead control account; and

(e) Profit and Loss account.

Solution :

Dr **Stores Ledger Control Account** **Cr**

Details	Amount (₹)	Details	Amount (₹)
To Opening Balance	60,000	By Work-in-Progress Control A/c	1,00,000

To Creditors/Bank	2,50,000	By Production Overhead Control Account By Closing Balance	15,000 1,95,000
Total	3,10,000	Total	3,10,000

Dr **Work-in-Progress Control Account** **Cr**

Details	Amount (₹)	Details	Amount (₹)
To Opening Balance	48,000	By Finished Goods Stock Control A/c	3,30,000
To Stores Ledger Control A/c	1,00,000	By Closing Balance	1,20,000
To Wages Control A/c	1,10,000		
To Production Overhead Control A/c (1,10,000 × 1.6)	1,76,000		
To Profit and Loss A/c (Gain on Stock)	16,000		
Total	4,50,000	Total	4,50,000

Dr **Finished goods Stock Control Account** **Cr**

Details	Amount (₹)	Details	Amount (₹)
To Opening Balance	84,000	By Cost of Sales A/c	3,70,000
To Work-in-Progress Control Account	3,30,000	By Closing Balance	44,000
Total	4,14,000	Total	4,14,000

Dr **Production Overhead Control Account** **Cr**

Details	Amount (₹)	Details	Amount (₹)
To Opening Balance	15,400	By Work-in-Progress Control A/c (1,10,000 × 1.6)	1,76,000
To Stores Ledger Control A/c	15,000		
To Wages Control A/c:			
Direct wages	15,000		
Indirect wages	25,000		
To Bank A/c	72,000		
To Profit and Loss A/c: (Over-Recovery as Balancing Figure)	33,600		
Total	1,76,000	Total	1,76,000

Dr **Cost of Sales Account** Cr

Details	Amount (₹)	Details	Amount (₹)
To Finished Goods Stock Control A/c	3,70,000	By Total Debtors/Bank A/c (Sales)	4,28,000
To Selling & Distribution Overhead Control A/c	26,000		
To Profit and Loss A/c	32,000		
Total	4,28,000	Total	4,28,000

Dr **Profit and Loss Account** Cr

Details	Amount (₹)	Details	Amount (₹)
To Closing Balance	81,600	By Cost of Sales A/c (Profit)	32,000
		By Production Overhead Control A/c	33,600
		By Work-in-Progress Control A/c (Gain on stock)	16,000
Total	81,600	Total	81,600

Notes:

1. Materials transferred between batches do not affect the Control accounts.
2. Non-Production time of direct workers is an item of Production Overhead and hence transferred to Production Overhead Control Account.
3. Excess Physical value of stock over book value is a gain on stock and so transferred to Profit and Loss account.

COST LEDGER CONTROL (MEMORANDA) ACCOUNT

Third Entry is made in respect of all items of cost. All items of cost are collected under the caption Cost Ledger Control (Memoranda) Account. Whenever any cost is incurred, it is debited to this account. Total cost shown by this account is analysed into direct and indirect material/labour and various types of overheads. Total of these accounts is transferred to Work-in-Progress account, Finished Goods Stock account and Profit & loss account etc. and the Cost Ledger Control (Memoranda) Account is credited. The record keeping is illustrated as under:

Transaction	Journal Entry			
Materials Purchased (80% on Credit Basis) ₹ 45,000	Purchases A/c	Dr	45,000	
	Cost Ledger Control (Memoranda) A/c	Dr	45,000	
	To Bank A/c			9,000
	To Trade Creditors A/c			36,000
Wages Paid ₹ 18,000	Wages A/c	Dr	18,000	
	Cost Ledger Control (Memoranda) A/c	Dr	18,000	
	To Cash/Bank A/c			18,000
Depreciation on Plant and Machinery ₹ 11,500	Depreciation A/c	Dr	11,500	
	Cost Ledger Control (Memoranda) A/c	Dr	11,500	
	To Plant and Machinery A/c			11,500

Note: The Third entry for the Cost Ledger Control (Memoranda) A/c appears to be superfluous and therefore, usually this approach to Cost book keeping is avoided.

LET US RECAPITULATE

1. Integral or Integrated accounting is the recording of cost and financial transactions in one consolidated ledger.
2. An integrated account is defined as a single set of accounts which provides financial and cost accounting information.
3. This system is essential in mechanized accounting.
4. The system does not suit large concerns which require detailed cost and financial data on continuing basis.
5. When two separate sets of books are maintained, they are interlocked by CONTROL ACCOUNTS maintained in the two sets of books. Cost Ledger Control Account is maintained in the financial books and a General Ledger Adjustment Account is maintained in the Cost books.
6. Integrating requires the preparation and maintenance of only one set of books in which all transactions are recorded. The Cost Ledger is dispensed with, and all the control accounts are maintained in the General Ledger.
7. Third Entry is made in respect of all items of cost. All items of cost are collected under the caption Cost Ledger Control (Memoranda) Account. The Third entry for the Cost Ledger Control (Memoranda) A/c appears to be superfluous and therefore, usually this approach to Cost book keeping is avoided.

SOLVED PROBLEMS

Problem 1. (Stock Discrepancy: Journal Entry)

The following discrepancies have been observed between book stock and physical stock during the course of annual stock taking:

Item	*Bin card/Stock Card (Unit)*	*Stores Ledger (Unit)*	*Physical Count (Unit)*	*Cost per Unit (₹)*
K	*900*	*900*	*860*	*30*
P	*650*	*650*	*670*	*25*
S	*840*	*865*	*820*	*12*

Make necessary journal entries to record the above situation under different circumstances.

Solution :

Details		**Debit Amount (₹)**	**Credit Amount (₹)**
Item K:			
Case (1): If shortage of 40 units × 30=1,200 is due to abnormal reasons:			
Costing Profit and Loss A/c	Dr	1,200	
To Stores Ledger Control A/c			1,200
Case (2): If shortage of 40 units × 30=1,200 is due to normal reasons:			
Factory Overheads A/c	Dr	1,200	
To Stores Ledger Control A/c			1,200
Case (3): If shortage is due to non-recording or short-recording of issue of materials:			
Work-in-Progress A/c	Dr	1,200	
To Stores Ledger Control A/c			1,200
Item P:			
Case (1): In this case there is abnormal gain of (670 – 650) = 20 units @ ₹ 25 valued at ₹ 500.			
Stores Ledger Control A/c	Dr	500	
To Costing Profit and Loss A/c			500
Case (2): If abnormal gain is due to normal factors:			
Stores Ledger Control A/c	Dr	500	
To Factory Overheads A/c			500

Case (3): If excess stock is due to excess recording of issue of materials:		
Stores Ledger Control A/c Dr	500	
To Work-in-Progress A/c		500
Item S: In this case shortage is (865 – 820) =45 units @ ₹12 valued at ₹ 540.		
Case(1) If shortage is due to abnormal factors:		
Costing Profit and Loss A/c Dr	540	
To Stores Ledger Control A/c		540
Case (2): If shortage is due to normal factors		
Factory overheads A/c Dr	540	
To Stores Ledger Control A/c		540
Case (3): If shortage is due to non-recording or short recording of issue of materials:		
Work-in-Progress A/c Dr	540	
To Stores Ledger Control A/c		540

Problem 2. *V Enterprises operates an integral system of accounting. You are required to pass the Journal entries for the following transactions that took place for the year ended March31, 2004.*

Details	*Amount (₹)*
1. Raw Materials Purchased (60% on Credit)	*2,50,000*
2. Materials Issued to Production	*2,00,000*
3. Wages Paid (40% Indirect)	*1,50,000*
4. Wages charged to Production	*80,000*
5. Production Overheads Incurred	*1,10,000*
6. Production Overheads charged to production	*1,20,000*
7. Selling & distribution Overheads Incurred	*25,000*
8. Finished Goods at cost	*2,50,000*
9. Closing Stock	*NIL*
10. Sales (80% Credit)	*3,75,000*
11. Receipts from Debtors	*90,000*
12. Payments to Creditors	*1,40,000*

Solution : **Journal Entries**

Details		Debit Amount (₹)	Credit Amount (₹)
1. Stores Ledger Control A/c	Dr	2,50,000	
To Trade Creditors A/c			1,50,000
To Bank A/c			1,00,000
(Raw Materials purchased)			
2. Work-in-Progress Control A/c	Dr	2,00,000	
To Stores Ledger Control A/c			2,00,000
(Direct Materials issued to production)			
3. (i) Wages Control A/c	Dr	1,50,000	
To Bank A/c			1,50,000
(Payment of Wages)			
(ii) Production Overhead Control A/c	Dr	60,000	
To Wages Control A/c			60,000
(Indirect wages apportioned to Production Overhead)			
4. Work-in-Progress Control A/c	Dr	80,000	
To Wages Control A/c			80,000
(Direct wages charged to production)			
5. Production Overhead Control A/c	Dr	1,10,000	
To Bank A/c			1,10,000
(Production expenses incurred)			
6. Work-in-Progress Control A/c	Dr	1,20,000	
To Production Overhead Control A/c			1,20,000
(Production expenses charged to Production)			
7. Selling & Distribution Overhead control A/c	Dr	25,000	
To Bank A/c			25,000
(Selling & Distribution Overhead control Incurred and Paid)			
8. (i) Finished Goods Stock Control A/c	Dr	2,50,000	
To Work-in-Progress Control A/c			2,50,000
(Finished Product at cost transferred from Work-in-Progress Account)			
(ii) Cost of Sales A/c	Dr	2,50,000	
To Finished Goods Stock Control A/c			2,50,000
(Cost of products transferred to Cost of Sales)			

9. Cost of Sales A/c	Dr	25,000	
To Selling & Distribution Overhead control A/c			25,000
(Incurred selling expenses charged)			
10. Bank A/c	Dr	75,000	
Trade Debtors A/c	Dr	3,00,000	
To Sales A/c			3,75,000
(Finished Goods Sales Value)			
11. Bank A/c	Dr	90,000	
To Trade Debtors A/c			90,000
(Receipts from debtors)			
12. Trade Creditors A/c	Dr	1,40,000	
To Bank A/c			1,40,000
(Payment made to Creditors)			

Problem 3. *From the following details, make journal entries in an integrated accounting system:*

(i) *Issued Materials ₹ 15,00,000 of which ₹ 13,00,000 direct material.*

(ii) *Net wages paid ₹ 3,70,000 deductions being ₹ 30,000.*

(iii) *Gross salaries payable for the period is ₹ 1,50,000, deductions ₹ 15,000.*

(iv) *Sales (Credit) ₹ 40,00,000.*

(v) *Discount allowed ₹ 25,000.*

(vi) *Salaires and Wages allocation: ₹ 3,00,000 direct and out of the balance, 45% production, 35% administration and 20% selling and distribution overheads.* **[M.Com (Osmania) {Modified}]**

Solution : **Journal Entries**

Details		Debit Amount (₹)	Credit Amount (₹)
1. Work-in-Progress Control A/c	Dr	13,00,000	
Production Overhead Control A/c	Dr	2,00,000	
To Stores Ledger Control A/c			15,00,000
(Issue of Direct Materials and Indirect Materials to production)			
2. Wages Control A/c	Dr	4,00,000	
To Bank A/c			3,70,000
To Employees Deduction A/c			30,000
(Payment of Wages after deduction)			

3. Salaries Control A/c	Dr	1,50,000	
To Salaries Payable A/c			1,35,000
To Employees Deduction A/c			15,000
(Salaries Payable after deduction)			
4. Trade Debtors A/c	Dr	40,00,000	
To Sales A/c			40,00,000
(Credit sales made)			
5. Discount A/c	Dr	25,000	
To Trade Debtors A/c			25,000
(Production expenses incurred)			
6. Work-in-Progress Control A/c	Dr	3,00,000	
Production Overhead Control A/c	Dr	1,12,500	
Administration Overhead control A/c	Dr	87,500	
Selling & Distribution Overhead control A/c	Dr	50,000	
To Wages Control A/c			4,00,000
To Salaries Control A/c			1,50,000
(Allocation of wages and salaries to various overheads)			

Problem 4. *The following transactions are extracted from the books of XYZ Ltd. You are required to make journal entries under Integrated Accounts system:*

Details	***Amount (₹)***
1. Purchase of Raw materials on credit	*4,00,000*
2. Carriage Inward	*3,000*
3. Paid to creditors	*3,00,000*
4. Stores Issued	*2,50,000*
5. Productive Wages Paid	*2,00,000*
6. Unproductive wages paid	*70,000*
7. Works overhead incurred	*3,60,000*
8. Materials Issued for repairs	*2,000*
9. Selling Expenses Paid	*10,000*
10. Office Expenses Paid	*4,000*
11. Works Overhead Absorbed	*4,10,000*
12. Cost of Completed Jobs	*8,60,000*

Solution : **Journal Entries**

Details		Debit Amount (₹)	Credit Amount (₹)
1. Stores Ledger Control A/c	Dr	4,00,000	
To Trade Creditors A/c			4,00,000
(Raw Materials purchased)			
2. Stores Ledger Control A/c	Dr	3,000	
To Cash			3,000
(Carriage Inward Paid for)			
3. Trade Creditors A/c	Dr	3,00,000	
To Bank A/c			3,00,000
(Payment made to Creditors)			
4. Work-in-Progress Control A/c	Dr	2,50,000	
To Stores Ledger Control A/c			2,50,000
(Direct Materials issued to production)			
5. Wages Control A/c	Dr	2,00,000	
To Bank A/c			2,00,000
(Payment of productive Wages)			
6. Wages Control A/c	Dr	70,000	
To Bank A/c			70,000
(Payment of Unproductive Wages)			
7. Works Overhead Control A/c	Dr	3, 60,000	
To Bank A/c			3, 60,000
(Works Overhead Incurred and Paid)			
8. Works Overhead Control A/c	Dr	2,000	
To Stores Ledger Control A/c			2,000
(Materials Issued for repairs)			
9. Selling & Distribution Overhead control A/c	Dr	10,000	
To Bank A/c			10,000
(Selling & Distribution Overhead control Incurred and Paid)			
10. Administration Overhead control A/c	Dr	4,000	
To Bank A/c			4,000
(Administration Overhead control Incurred and Paid)			
11. Work-in-Progress Control A/c	Dr	4,10,000	
To Works Overhead Control A/c			4,10,000
(Absorption of Works Overhead)			
12. Finished Goods Stock Control A/c	Dr	8,60.000	
To Work-in-Progress Control A/c			8,60,000
(Finished Product at cost transferred from Work-in-Progress Account)			

Problem 5. *Following are the extracts of balances of SV Ltd. in its integrated Ledgers on April1, 2008:*

Ledger A/c	*Debit Amount (₹)*	*Credit Amount (₹)*
Stores Control A/c	*93,600*	
Work-in-Progress A/c	*88,400*	
Finished Goods A/c	*67,600*	
Cash at Bank	*52,000*	
Creditors control A/c		*41,600*
Fixed assets A/c	*2,86,000*	
Debtors Control A/c	*62,400*	
Share Capital A/c		*4,16,000*
Depreciation Provision A/c		*26,000*
Profit and Loss A/c		*1,66,400*
Total	*6,50,000*	*6,50,000*

Transactions for the twelve months ended March 31, 2009 were as:

Details	*Amount (₹)*
Wages: Direct	*4,52,400*
Wages: Indirect	*26,000*
Stores Purchased on Credit	*5,20,000*
Stores issued to Repair Order	*10,400*
Stores Issued to Production	*5,72,000*
Goods finished during the period at cost	*11,18,000*
Goods sold at sales value (on credit)	*15,60,000*
Goods sold at cost	*11,44,000*
Production Overhead recovered	*24,9,600*
Production Overhead Paid by cheque	*2,08,000*
Administration Overhead Paid by cheque	*62,400*
Selling & Distribution Overhead Paid by cheque	*72,800*
Depreciation (Works)	*6,760*
Payment made to Suppliers by Cheque	*5,25,200*
Payments Received from customers by Cheque	*15,08,000*
Rates prepaid included in production Overhead incurred	*1,560*
Purchase of Fixed assets	*10,400*
Charitable Donation	*5,200*
Fines Paid	*2,600*
Interest on Bank Loan	*520*
Income-Tax	*1,04,000*

Write up the accounts in the Integral Ledger and make out a Trial Balance. The Administration Overhead is written off to Profit and Loss Account.

Solution : **Integral Ledger of S.V. Ltd.**

Dr **Stores Control A/c** **Cr**

Details	Amount (₹)	Details	Amount (₹)
To Opening Balance	93,600	By Work-in-Progress A/c	5,72,000
To Creditors Control A/c	5,20,000	By Production Overhead A/c	10,400
		By Closing Balance	31,200
Total	6,13,600	Total	6,13,600

Dr **Wages Control A/c** **Cr**

Details	Amount (₹)	Details	Amount (₹)
To Bank A/c	4,78,400	By Work-in-Progress A/c	4,52,400
		By Production Overhead A/c	26,000
Total	4,78,400	Total	4,78,400

Dr **Production Overhead A/c** **Cr**

Details	Amount (₹)	Details	Amount (₹)
To Wages Control A/c	26,000	By Prepayment (Rent) A/c	1,560
To Stores Control A/c	10,400	By Work-in-Progress A/c	2,49,600
To Bank A/c	2,08,000		
To Depreciation Provision A/c	6,760		
Total	2,51,160	Total	2,51,160

Dr **Administration Overhead A/c** **Cr**

Details	Amount (₹)	Details	Amount (₹)
To Bank A/c	62,400	By Costing Profit and Loss A/c	62,400
Total	62,400	Total	62,400

Dr **Selling &Distribution Overhead A/c** **Cr**

Details	Amount (₹)	Details	Amount (₹)
To Bank A/c	72,800	By Cost of Sales A/c	72,800
Total	72,800	Total	72,800

Dr **Work-in-Progress A/c** Cr

Details	Amount (₹)	Details	Amount (₹)
To Opening Balance	88,400	By Finished Goods A/c	11,18,000
To Wages Control A/c	4,52,400	By Closing Balance	2,44,400
To Stores Control A/c	5,72,000		
To Production Overhead A/c	2,49,600		
Total	13,62,400	Total	13,62,400

Dr **Finished Goods A/c** Cr

Details	Amount (₹)	Details	Amount (₹)
To Opening Balance	67,600	By Cost of Sales A/c	11,44,000
To Work-in-Progress	11,18,000	By Closing Balance	41,600
Total	11,85,600	Total	11,85,600

Dr **Cost of Sales A/c** Cr

Details	Amount (₹)	Details	Amount (₹)
To Finished Goods A/c	11,44,000	By Costing Profit and Loss A/c	12,16,800
To Selling & Distribution Overhead A/c	72,800		
Total	12,16,800	Total	12,16,800

Dr **Costing Profit and Loss A/c** Cr

(For the period ended on March 31, 2009)

Details	Amount (₹)	Details	Amount (₹)
To Cost of Sales A/c	12,16,800	By Debtors Control A/c	15,60,000
To Administration Overhead A/c	62,400		
Profit and Loss A/c	2,80,800		
Total	15,60,000	Total	15,60,000

Dr **Profit and Loss A/c** Cr

(For the period ended on March 31, 2009)

Details	Amount (₹)	Details	Amount (₹)
To Charitable Donation A/c	5,200	By Opening Balance	1,66,400
To Fines A/c	2,600	By Costing Profit & Loss A/c	2,80,800
To Interest on Bank Loan A/c	520		
To Income-Tax A/c	1,04,000		
To Net Profit Balance	3,34,880		
Total	4,47,200	Total	4,47,200

Dr **Prepayment A/c** Cr

Details	Amount (₹)	Details	Amount (₹)
To Production Overhead A/c	1,560	By Closing Balance	1,560
Total	1,560	Total	1,560

Dr **Depreciation Provision A/c** Cr

Details	Amount (₹)	Details	Amount (₹)
To Closing Balance	32,760	By Opening Balance	26,000
		By Production Overhead A/c	6,760
Total	32,760	Total	32,760

Dr **Creditors Control A/c** Cr

Details	Amount (₹)	Details	Amount (₹)
To Bank A/c	525200	By Opening Balance	41600
To Closing Balance	36400	By Stores Control A/c	520000
Total	561600	Total	561600

Dr **Debtors Control A/c** Cr

Details	Amount (₹)	Details	Amount (₹)
To Opening Balance	62,400	By Bank A/c	15,08,000
To Cost of Sales A/c	15,60,000	By closing Balance	1,14,400
Total	16,22,400	Total	16,22,400

Dr **Bank A/c** **Cr**

Details	Amount (₹)	Details	Amount (₹)
To Opening Balance	52,000	By Wages Control A/c	47,8,400
To Debtors control A/c	15,08,000	By Fixed assets A/c	10,400
		By Production Overhead A/c	2,08,000
		By Administration Overhead A/c	62,400
		By Selling &Distribution Overhead A/c	72,800
		By Creditors control A/c	5,25,200
		By Fines A/c	2,600
		By Charitable donations A/c	5,200
		By Interest on Bank Loan A/c	520
		By Income- Tax A/c	1,04,000
		By Closing Balance	90,480
Total	15,60,000	Total	15,60,000

Dr **Fixed assets A/c** **Cr**

Details	Amount (₹)	Details	Amount (₹)
To Opening Balance	2,86,000	By Closing Balance	2,96,400
To Bank A/c	10,400		
Total	2,96,400	Total	2,96,400

Dr **Share Capital A/c** **Cr**

Details	Amount (₹)	Details	Amount (₹)
To Opening Balance	4,16,000	By Closing Balance	4,16,000
Total	4,16,000	Total	4,16,000

Trial Balance as on March 31, 2009

Ledger account	Debit Amount (₹)	Credit Amount (₹)
Stores Control A/c	31,200	
Work-in-Progress A/c	2,44,400	
Finished Goods A/c	41,600	
Cash at Bank A/c	90,480	

Creditors control A/c		36,400
Fixed Assets A/c	2,96,400	
Debtors Control A/c	1,14,400	
Share Capital A/c		4,16,000
Depreciation Provision A/c		32,760
Prepayment A/c	1,560	
Profit and Loss A/c		3,34,880
Total	8,20,040	8,20,040

Problem 6. *Some of the accounting records of SJ Ltd. have been destroyed by fire. You have been able to collect the following information from the spoilt papers/records as a result of consultation with accounting staff in respect of November, 2008:*

(A) Incomplete Ledger Entries:

Dr **Raw Material A/c** ***Cr***

Details	*Amount (₹)*	*Details*	*Amount (₹)*
Opening Balance	*40,000*		

Dr **Work-in-Progress A/c** ***Cr***

Details	*Amount (₹)*	*Details*	*Amount (₹)*
Opening Balance	*10,000*	*Finished Goods stock A/c*	*1,82,000*

Dr **Creditors A/c** ***Cr***

Details	*Amount (₹)*	*Details*	*Amount (₹)*
Closing Balance	*23,000*	*Opening Balance*	*18000*

Dr **Production Overheads A/c** ***Cr***

Details	*Amount (₹)*	*Details*	*Amount (₹)*
Amount Incurred	*34,000*		

Dr **Finished goods Stock A/c** ***Cr***

Details	*Amount (₹)*	*Details*	*Amount (₹)*
Opening Balance	*32,000*		
		Closing Balance	*41,000*

(B) Additional Information:

1. *The Cash Book showed that an amount of ₹ 1,02,000 has been paid to creditors for raw material.*
2. *Closing Inventory of Work-in-Progress included material ₹ 8,700 on which 400 direct labour hours have been booked against wages and overheads.*
3. *Job card showed that workers have worked for 7,500 hours. The wage rate is ₹ 12 per labour hour.*
4. *Overhead absorption rate was ₹ 5 per direct labour hour.*

You are required to complete the above accounts in the General Ledger of the Firm.

Solution :

Dr **Raw Material A/c** **Cr**

Details	Amount (₹)	Details	Amount (₹)
Opening Balance	40,000	Work-in-Progress A/c	60,000
Creditors A/c (Purchases)	1,07,000	Closing Balance	87,000
Total	1,47,000	Total	1,47,000

Dr **Work-in-Progress A/c** **Cr**

Details	Amount (₹)	Details	Amount (₹)
Opening Balance	10,000	Finished Goods Stock A/c	1,82,000
Wages A/c (7,500 × 12)	90,000	Closing Balance:	
		Material 8700	
		Wages (400 × 12) 4800	
		Overheads (400 × 5) 2000	15,500
Overheads A/c (7,500 × 5)	37,500		
Raw Material A/c (Balancing figure)	60,000		
Total	1,97, 500	Total	1,97,500

Dr **Creditors A/c** **Cr**

Details	Amount (₹)	Details	Amount (₹)
Bank A/c	1,02,000	Opening Balance	18,000
Closing Balance	23,000	Raw Material A/c (Purchases: Balancing figure)	1,07,000
Total	1,25,000	Total	1,25,000

Dr **Production Overheads A/c** **Cr**

Details	Amount (₹)	Details	Amount (₹)
Bank A/c	34,000	Work-in-Progress A/c	37,500
Closing Balance (Over-Recovery)	3,500		
Total	37,500	Total	37,500

Dr **Finished Goods Stock A/c** **Cr**

Details	Amount (₹)	Details	Amount (₹)
Opening Balance	32,000	Cost of sales A/c (Balancing figure)	1,73,000
Work-in-Progress A/c	1,82,000	Closing Balance	41,000
Total	2,14,000	Total	2,14,000

Problem 7. *GCJ Limited operates an integrated accounting system and the following details are given for the year ended March 31, 2008.*

Trial Balance

Ledger A/c	*Debit Amount (₹)*	*Credit Amount (₹)*
Stock:	*3,20,000*	
Raw Material	*80,000*	
Work-in-Progress	*1,05,000*	
Finished Goods		
Debtors	*2,80,000*	
Bank	*3,20,000*	
Plant and Machinery	*10,00,000*	
Buildings (at Cost)	*15,00,000*	
Paid up Capital		*25,00,000*
Reserves and Surplus		*5,00,000*
Creditors:		*3,25,000*
For Purchases		*40,000*
For Expenses		
Provision for Depreciation on Plant and Machinery		*2,40,000*
Total	*36,05,000*	*36,05,000*

The following data for the First Quarter ending on June 30 are given:

Details	***Amount (₹)***	***Details***	***Amount (₹)***
Raw Materials purchased on credit	*14,80,000*	*Depreciation for the month on Plant and Machinery*	*85,000*
Raw Material returned to suppliers	*50,000*	*Sales (20% non-credit)*	*30,00,000*
Materials issued to production	*13,00,000*	*Cash received from debtors*	*25,00,000*
Materials returned from the Shop floor	*30,000*	*Paid the following by Cheque:*	
		Creditors for Purchases	*16,25,000*
		Creditors for Expenses	*6,90,000*
Factory Wages Paid:		*Production Overhead applied to Production*	*6,40,000*
Productive	*4,00,000*		
Non-Productive	*80,000*		
Salaries Paid:		*Administration overhead applied to Finished Goods*	*2,90,000*
Administration	*2,00,000*		
Selling & Distribution	*1,30,000*		
Overhead Expenses Incurred but not Paid:		*Selling & distribution applied to Cost of Sales*	*3,00,000*
Production	*5,00,000*		
Administration	*1,00,000*		
Selling & distribution	*1,50,000*		
		Closing Stock:	
		Work-in-Progress	*2,60,000*
		Finished Goods	*3,25,000*

Dividend @8% on the Paid-up Capital was paid for the preceding year.

Prepare (1) Appropriate Ledger Accounts; (2) Profit and Loss account for April, 2008; and (3) Balance Sheet as on June30, 2008.

Solution :

Dr **Stores Ledger Control A/c** **Cr**

Details	**Amount (₹)**	**Details**	**Amount (₹)**
To Opening Balance	3,20,000	By Creditors (Purchase) A/c	50,000
To Creditors (Purchase) A/c	14,80,000	By Work-in-Progress A/c	13,00,000
To Work-in-Progress A/c	50,000	By Closing Balance	5,00,000
Total	18,50,000	Total	18,50,000

Dr **Wages Control A/c** **Cr**

Details	Amount (₹)	Details	Amount (₹)
To Bank (Salaries and wages) A/c	8,10,000	By Work-in-Progress A/c	4,00,000
		By Production Overhead Control A/c	80,000
		By Administrative Overhead Control A/c	2,00,000
		By Selling & Distribution Overhead Control A/c	130000
Total	8,10,000	Total	810000

Dr **Production Overhead Control A/c** **Cr**

Details	Amount (₹)	Details	Amount (₹)
To Wages Control A/c	80,000	By Work-in-Progress A/c	6,40,000
To Creditors (Expenses) A/c	5,00,000	By Overhead Suspense A/c (Under Recovery)	25,000
To Provision for Depreciation (Plant and Machinery) A/c	85,000		
Total	6,65,000	Total	6,65,000

Dr **Work-in-Progress Control A/c** **Cr**

Details	Amount (₹)	Details	Amount (₹)
To Opening Balance	80,000	By Stores Ledger Control A/c	50,000
To Stores Ledger Control A/c	13,00,000	By Finished Goods Ledger Control A/c	21,10,000
To Wages Control A/c	4,00,000	By Closing Balance	2,60,000
To Production Overhead Control A/c	6,40,000		
Total	24,20,000	Total	24,20,000

Dr **Finished Goods Ledger Control A/c** **Cr**

Details	Amount (₹)	Details	Amount (₹)
To Opening Balance	1,05,000	By Cost of Sales A/c	21,80,000
To Administrative Overhead Control A/c	2,90,000	By Closing Balance	3,25,000
To Work-in-Progress A/c	21,10,000		
Total	25,05,000	Total	25,05,000

Dr Administrative Overhead Control A/c Cr

Details	Amount (₹)	Details	Amount (₹)
To Wages Control A/c	2,00,000	By Finished Goods Ledger Control A/c	2,90,000
To Creditors (Expenses) A/c	1,00,000	By Overhead Suspense A/c (Under Recovery)	10,000
Total	3,00,000	Total	3,00,000

Dr Selling & Distribution Overhead Control A/c Cr

Details	Amount (₹)	Details	Amount (₹)
To Wages Control A/c	1,30,000	By Cost of Sales A/c	3,00,000
To Creditors (Expenses) A/c	1,50,000		
To Overhead Suspense A/c (Over Recovery)	20,000		
Total	3,00,000	Total	3,00,000

Dr Provision for Depreciation (Plant and Machinery) A/c Cr

Details	Amount (₹)	Details	Amount (₹)
To Closing Balance	3,25,000	By Opening Balance	2,40,000
		By Production Overhead Control A/c	85,000
Total	3,25,000	Total	3,25,000

Dr Cost of Sales A/c Cr

Details	Amount (₹)	Details	Amount (₹)
To Selling & Distribution Overhead Control A/c	3,00,000	By Costing Profit & Loss A/c	24,80,000
To Finished Goods Ledger Control A/c	21,80,000		
Total	24,80,000	Total	24,80,000

Dr Creditors (Purchase) A/c Cr

Details	Amount (₹)	Details	Amount (₹)
To Stores Ledger Control A/c (Returns)	50,000	By Opening Balance	3,25,000

To Bank A/c	16,25,000	By Stores Ledger Control A/c	14,80,000
To Closing Balance	1,30,000		
Total	18,05,000	Total	18,05,000

Dr **Creditors (Expenses) A/c** **Cr**

Details	Amount (₹)	Details	Amount (₹)
To Bank A/c	6,90,000	By Opening Balance	40,000
To Closing Balance	1,00,000	By Production Overhead Control A/c	5,00,000
		By Administrative Overhead Control A/c	1,00,000
		By Selling & Distribution Overhead Control A/c	1,50,000
Total	7,90,000	Total	7,90,000

Dr **Debtors Control A/c** **Cr**

Details	Amount (₹)	Details	Amount (₹)
To Opening Balance	2,80,000	By Bank A/c	25,00,000
To Sales A/c	24,00,000	By Closing Balance	1,80,000
Total	26,80,000	Total	26,80,000

Dr **Bank A/c** **Cr**

Details	Amount (₹)	Details	Amount (₹)
To Opening Balance	3,20,000	By Wages Control A/c	8,10,000
To Debtors Control A/c	25,00,000	By Creditors (Purchases) A/c	16,25,000
To Sales A/c (cash)	6,00,000	By Creditors (Expenses) A/c	6,90,000
djustright		By Dividend Paid	2,00,000
		By Closing Balance	95,000
Total	34,20,000	Total	34,20,000

Dr **Overhead Suspense A/c** **Cr**

Details	Amount (₹)	Details	Amount (₹)
To Production Overhead Control A/c	25,000	By Selling & Distribution Overhead Control A/c	20,000
To Administrative Overhead control A/c	10,000	By Costing Profit & Loss A/c	15,000
Total	35,000	Total	35,000

Dr **Costing Profit and Loss A/c** **Cr**

Details	Amount (₹)	Details	Amount (₹)
To Cost of Sales A/c	24,80,000	By Sales A/c	30,00,000
To Overhead Suspense A/c	15,000		
To Profit & Loss (Appropriation)A/c	5,05,000		
Total	30,00,000	Total	30,00,000

Dr **Sales A/c** **Cr**

Details	Amount (₹)	Details	Amount (₹)
To Costing Profit & Loss A/c	30,00,000	By Bank A/c	6,00,000
		By Debtors Control A/c	20,00,000
Total	30,00,000	Total	30,00,000

Dr **Profit and Loss (Appropriation) A/c** **Cr**

Details	Amount (₹)	Details	Amount (₹)
To Dividend Paid	2,00,000	By Opening Balance	5,00,000
To Closing Balance	8,05,000	By Costing Profit & Loss A/c	5,05,000
Total	10,05,000	Total	10,05,000

Trial Balance
(As on June30, 2004)

Ledger A/c	Debit Amount (₹)	Credit Amount (₹)
Stock:		
Raw Material	5,00,000	
Work-in-Progress	2,60,000	
Finished Goods	3,25,000	
Debtors	1,80,000	
Bank	95,000	
Plant and Machinery	10,00,000	
Buildings (at Cost)	15,00,000	
Paid up Capital		25,00,000
Reserves and Surplus		8,05,000

Creditors:		
For Purchases		1,30,000
For Expenses		1,00,000
Provision for Depreciation on Plant and Machinery		3,25,000
Total	38,60,000	38,60,000

Balance Sheet
(As on June 30, 2004)

Liabilities	Amount (₹)	Assets		Amount (₹)
Share Capital	25,00,000	Building		15,00,000
Reserve and Surplus	8,05,000	Plant and Machinery		
			10,00,000	
		Less: Provision	3,25,000	6,75,000
Creditors (Purchase)	1,30,000	Debtors		1,80,000
Creditors (Expenses)	1,00,000	Stock:		
		Raw Materials	5,00,000	
		Work-in-Progress	2,60,000	
		Finished Goods	3,25,000	10,85,000
		Bank		95,000
Total	35,35,000	Total		35,35,000

Problem 8. *Shivam Enterprises operates an integral system of accounting. You are required to pass journal entries for any four of the following transactions that took place for the year ended 31.3.2009.*

Details	*Amount (₹)*
1. Raw Materials purchased (60% on credit)	*10,00,000*
2. Materials Issued to Production	*8,00,000*
3. Factory Overhead Incurred	*1,50,000*
4. Sales (50% on credit)	*14,00,000*
5. Receipt from Debtors	*5,00,000*
6. Payment to Creditors	*4,00,000*

Solution : Journal Entries under Integral System of Accounting

Details		Debitr Amount (₹)	Credit Amount (₹)
Stores Ledger Control A/c	Dr	10,00,000	
To Trade Creditors A/c			6,00,000
To Bank A/c			4,00,000
(Raw Materials purchased)			

Work-in-Progress Control A/c	Dr	8,00,000	
To Stores Ledger Control A/c			8,00,000
(Direct Materials issued to production)			
Works Overhead Control A/c	Dr	1,50,000	
To Bank A/c			1,50,000
(Works Overhead Incurred and Paid)			
Bank A/c	Dr	7,00,000	
Debtors A/c	Dr	7,00,000	
To Sales A/c			14,00,000
(Sales actualized)			
Bank A/c	Dr	5,00,000	
To Debtors A/c			5,00,000
(Payment received from debtors)			
Trade Creditors A/c	Dr	4,00,000	
To Bank A/c			4,00,000
(Payment made to Creditors)			

Problem 9. *Give journal entries for the following transactions under integrated accounting:*

(i) Materials purchased on credit;

(ii) Payment to creditors;

(iii) Issue of Direct materials for production;

(iv) Payment of wages; and

(v) Charging wages for production.

Solution :

Date/ S.No.	Details		Dr Amount (₹)	Cr Amount (₹)
1.	Stores Ledger Control A/c	Dr		
	To Creditors A/c			
	(Materials purchased on credit)			
2.	Creditors A/c	Dr		
	To Bank A/c			
	(Payment to creditors)			
3.	WIP Ledger Control A/c	Dr		
	To Stores Ledger Control A/c			
	(Issue of Direct materials for production)			

4.	Wages Control A/c To Bank A/c (Payment of wages)	Dr		
5.	WIP Ledger Control A/c To Wages Control A/c (Charging wages for production)	Dr		

OBJECTIVE TYPE EXERCISES

I. Fill in the blank spaces with suitable word/s :

1. Under integral system, the accounting entry for recording depreciation on machinery is to debit .... Account and credit ...... account.
2. .... is a system of cost book keeping in which cost and financial accounts are contained in one set of books of account.
3. In .... ledger, an account is maintained for each job.
4. Integral system of accounting eliminates the necessity of maintaining ....account.
5. Abnormal loss of materials in case of Integral system of accounting is charged to .... account.
6. Third Entry method may be used in case of .... system of accounting.
7. Mechanized system of accounting can be used with .... system of accounting.

Answers :

1. Factory overhead, Machinery **2.** Integral accounting
3. Work-in-progress **4.** General ledger Adjustment
5. Profit and Loss **6.** Integral
7. Integral

II. Indicate whether the following statements are True or False :

1. Integral system of accounting implies maintenance of same set of books for both cost and financial accounts.
2. Mechanized system of accounting can not be used with integral system of accounting.
3. Integral system of accounting is more useful in case of small concerns.
4. Integral accounts eliminate the necessity of generating cost ledger control accounts.
5. In integral system, no entry is passed for issuing materials to production by stores department.
6. Under integral system, no accounts are opened for debtors and creditors.
7. Loss on sale of capital asset is included in accounts under integral system.
8. Cost and financial accounts are reconciled under integrated system.

Answers :

1. True **2.** False **3.** True **4.** True
5. False **6.** False **7.** True **8.** False

THEORETICAL EXERCISES

1. What is integrated cost accounting?
2. State the need for Integral Accounts.
3. What do you understand by "Integrated" accounts, and what are the principles involved? State the advantages of "Integrated" accounts.
4. Write a short essay on "Integration of cost and financial accounts".
5. Explain the nature of integral accounting. What are its special features?
6. State the essential pre-requisites of Integrated Accounting System.
7. Explain the basic requirements of an Integrated Accounting System.
8. What is integrated accounting? Briefly describe its advantages.
9. What is integrated accounting? What are its advantages?
[B Com (Hons.), DU, 1997]
10. What is integrated accounting? Briefly describe the merits of integration.
11. Enumerate the advantages of integrated cost accounts. **[DU, B.Com (Hons.) 2000]**
12. Enumerate the advantages of integrated cost and financial accounts.
[DU, B.Com (Hons.) 2004]
13. Distinguish between Integral and Non-integral system of accounts.
[DU, B.Com (Hons.) 2001; M.Com, Madras, 1995]

NUMERICAL EXERCISES

1. Prepare a Month's cost accounts from the following relevant information for a firm, which operates a batch costing system fully integrated with the financial accounts.

Transaction	Amount (₹)
Balance at the beginning of the month:	
Stores Ledger Control Account	30000
Work-in-Progress Control account	24000
Finished Goods Stock Control Account	42000
Prepaid Production Overheads brought forward from the preceding quarter	3600
Transactions during the current month:	
A. Materials Purchased	100000
Materials issued:	
To Production	40000
To Factory Maintenance	5000
Materials transferred between batches	6000

B. Total Wages Paid:	
To Direct Workers	35,000
To Indirect Workers	7,000
Direct Wages charged to Batches	30,000
Recorded non-productive time of direct worker	5,000
C. Selling and Distribution Overheads Incurred	8,000
Other Production Overhead Incurred	16,000
Sales	1,38,000
Cost of Finished Goods Sold	1,00,000
Cost of goods completed and transferred into Finished Goods during the current Quarter	80,000
Physical value of Work-in-Progress at the end of the Quarter	50,000
Production Overhead Rate of Absorption is 140% of Direct wages charged to Work-in-Progress.	N.A.

Required: Prepare the following accounts for the Quarter:

(a) Stores Ledger Control Account;

(b) Work-in-Progress Control Account;

(c) Finished Goods Stock control Account;

(d) Production Overhead control account; and

(e) Profit and Loss account.

2. Following are the extracts of balances of UV Ltd. in its integrated Ledgers on April1, 2003:

Ledger A/c	Amount (₹)	Amount (₹)
Stores Control A/c	45,000	
Work-in-Progress A/c	42,500	
Finished Goods A/c	32,500	
Cash at Bank	25,000	
Creditors control A/c		20,000
Fixed assets A/c	1,37,500	
Debtors Control A/c	30,000	
Share Capital A/c		2,00,000
Depreciation Provision A/c		12,500
Profit and Loss A/c		80,000
Total	3,12,500	3,12,500

Transactions for the twelve months ended March 31, 2005 were as:

Details	Amount (₹)
Wages: Direct	2,17,500
Wages: Indirect	12,500

Stores Purchased on Credit	2,50,000
Stores issued to Repair Order	5,000
Stores Issued to Production	2,75,000
Goods finished during the period at cost	5,37,500
Goods sold at sales value (on credit)	7,50,000
Goods sold at cost	5,50,000
Production Overhead recovered	1,20,000
Production Overhead Paid by cheque	1,00,000
Administration Overhead Paid by cheque	30,000
Selling & Distribution Overhead Paid by cheque	35,000
Depreciation (Works)	3,250
Payment to Suppliers by Cheque	2,52,500
Payments from customers by Cheque	7,25,000
Rates prepaid included in production Overhead incurred	750
Purchase of Fixed assets	5,000
Charitable Donation	2,500
Fines Paid	1,250
Interest on Bank Loan	250
Income-Tax	50,000

Write up the accounts in the Integral Ledger and make out a Trial Balance. The Administration Overhead is written off to Profit and Loss Account.

3. PV Enterprises operates an integral system of accounting. You are required topass the Journal entries for the following transactions that took place for the year ended March31, 2003.

Details	Amount (₹)
Raw Materials Purchased (60% on Credit)	8,00,000
Materials Issued to Production	6,00,000
Wages Paid (75% Direct)	4,00,000
Wages charged to Production	3,00,000
Production Overheads Incurred	1,20,000
Production Overheads charged to production	1,50,000
Selling & distribution Overheads Incurred	60,000
Finished Goods at cost	15,00,000
Sales (50% Credit)	24,00,000
Closing Stock	NIL
Receipts from Debtors	6,00,000
Payments to Creditors	5,00,000

4. Record the following transactions in the Ledger under the Integral System and prepare the Trial Balance. The balance at the beginning of the period is as under:

Ledger account	Debit Balance (₹)	Credit Balance (₹)
Bank	60,000	
Stock:		
Finished Goods	80,000	
Work-in-Progress	1,30,000	
Raw Materials	1,20,000	
Creditors		40,000
Debtors	20,000	
Fixed Assets	20,50,000	
Depreciation Provision		50,000
Share Capital		22,00,000
Profit and Loss		1,70,000
Total	24,60,000	24,60,000

Transactions during the period were as under:

Details	Amount (₹)	Amount (₹)
Materials purchased on credit		2,00,000
Materials issued to production:		
Direct	1,40,000	
Indirect	20,000	1,60,000
Payments to Creditors		1,20,000
Wages Paid:		
Direct	2,00,000	
Indirect	40,000	2,40,000
Finished Goods Produced		6,00,000
Cost of Finished Goods Sold		6,40,000
Sales Value		8,00,000
Receipt from Debtors		7,00,000
Overhead Incurred:		
Production	1,20,000	
Administration	20,000	
Selling and distribution	20,000	1,60,000
Depreciation (in addition to overheads)		10,000

5. Some of the accounting records of SJ Ltd. have been destroyed by fire. You have been able to collect the following information from the spoilt papers/records as a result of consultation with accounting staff in respect of September,2003:

(A) Incomplete Ledger Entries:

Raw Material A/c

Debit side	Amount (₹)	Credit side	Amount (₹)
Opening Balance	32,000		

Work-in-Progress A/c

Debit side	Amount (₹)	Credit side	Amount (₹)
Opening Balance	9,200	Finished Goods stock A/c	1,51,000

Creditors A/c

Debit side	Amount (₹)	Credit side	Amount (₹)
		Opening Balance	16,400
Closing Balance	19,200		

Production Overheads A/c

Debit side	Amount (₹)	Credit side	Amount (₹)
Amount Incurred	29,600		

Finished goods Stock A/c

Debit side	Amount (₹)	Credit side	Amount (₹)
Opening Balance	24,000		
		Closing Balance	30,000

(B) Additional Information:

1. The Cash Book showed that an amount of ₹ 89,200/- has been paid to creditors for raw material.
2. Closing Inventory of Work-in-Progress included material ₹ 5,000 on which 300 direct labour hours have been booked against wages and overheads.
3. Job card showed that workers have worked for 7,000 hours. The wage rate is ₹ 10 per labour hour,.
4. Overhead absorption rate was ₹4 per direct labour hour.

You are required to complete the above accounts in the General Ledger of the Firm.

6. Shivalika Enterprises operates an integral system of accounting. You are required to pass journal entries for any four of the following transactions that took place for the year ended 31.3.1997. (Narration is not required).

S.No.	Details	Amount (₹)
1.	Raw Materials purchased (50% on credit)	6,00,000
2.	Materials Issued to Production	4,00,000
3.	Factory Overhead Incurred	80,000
4.	Sales (50% on credit)	7,50,000
5.	Receipt from Debtors	2,00,000
6.	Payment to Creditors	2,00,000

[DU, B.Com (Hons.) 1998]

7. Rex Enterprises operates an integral system of accounting. You are required to pass the Journal entries for the following transactions that took place for the year ended June 30, 2002:

Details	Amount (₹)
Raw Materials Purchased (50% on credit)	6,00,000
Materials issued to production	4,00,000
Wages paid to workers	2,00,000
Factory Overhead incurred	80,000
Factory overheads charged to production	1,00,000
Selling and distribution Overhead incurred	40,000
Finished goods at cost	5,00,000
Sale (50% credit)	7,50,000

[DU, B.Com (Hons.) 2002]

❑❑❑

21 Non-Integral Accounts

Learning Objectives

It attempts to explain the process of making separate accounts in financial books and cost books. In this chapter you will learn :

1. Meaning and nature of control accounts in cost ledger and financial ledger.
2. Comparison of journal entries in cost ledger and financial ledger.
3. Preparation of control accounts.

NON-INTEGRATED SYSTEM

In cost Accounting the cost books are mainly maintained under the following two systems: (1) Non-Integral or non-integrated cost accounting; (2) Integral or integrated cost accounting.

The system is known as non-integral when cost and financial transactions are kept separately. However, when the cost and financial transactions are integrated, the accounting system is known as integrated or integral.

Under the system of non-integral accounting, separate ledgers are kept for cost and financial transaction. The financial accountants look after financial transactions and the cost accountants are responsible for cost accounting transactions.

Financial Ledgers

The financial accounting department maintains the following :

1. *General Ledger:* It contains all real, nominal and personal accounts except trade debtors and trade creditors' accounts.
2. *Debtors Ledger:* It has details of credit transactions on personal basis of trade debtors. (Credit Customers)

3. *Creditors Ledger:* It has details of credit transactions on personal basis of trade creditors. (Credit suppliers of goods and materials)

Cost Ledgers

The cost accounting department maintains the following cost ledgers:

1. *Stores Ledger:* It keeps item-wise records of raw materials and other supplies.
2. *Work-in-Progress Ledger:* All costs of material, wages and overhead for each job or work-in-progress are posted to the respective job accounts in this ledger.
3. *Finished Goods/Stock ledger:* This ledger records details of finished goods and jobs.
4. *Cost Ledger:* This is the main ledger, which records impersonal accounts, i.e. accounts relating to income and expenditure. It has General Ledger Control or Adjustment account. The following accounts are maintained in cost ledger.

(A) Cost Control Accounts

They summarise all detailed information contained in the subsidiary ledgers and also help in reconciliation of cost and financial accounts. Such accounts are maintained to exercise control over the three subsidiary ledgers and also to complete double entry in cost accounts.

The important cost control accounts are as under:

(a) *Stores Ledger Control Account:* The total of materials received in stores (which can be found in Purchases Journal also) is shown on the debit side of this account. Total of materials issued out of stores (Refer Materials Abstract) is credited in this account. The balance of this account shall tally with the individual totals of stores account. Some times separate ledgers are kept for raw materials and other stores. In that eventuality, there will be two separate Control ledgers:(i) Materials Ledger Control Account, (ii) Stores Ledger Control Account.

(b) *Work-in-Progress Ledger Control Account:* This account gives total value of work-in-progress at any point of time. On the debit side of this account following items are recorded:

(1) All costs incurred on all products/jobs;
(2) Opening balance of work-in-progress;
(3) Direct material, direct labour and direct expenses chargeable to output/jobs
(4) Factory overheads chargeable to output/jobs.

The balance of this account gives the value of incomplete works done. This balance should be equal to the sum of all the balances of individual accounts in the job ledger. Cost data for this account is available from the schedule of material requisitions, bills of materials, wage abstract and overhead summary, etc.

(c) *Wages Control account:* This account records wage transactions in aggregate. Postings are made from the wages analysis sheet. This account is debited with gross wages and is closed by transfer of direct wages to work-in-progress and indirect wages to factory, administration and selling and distribution overhead control accounts.

(B) Other Accounts

They include all other impersonal accounts (Real as well as Nominal) which effect cost, e.g., wages Control Account, Factory Overhead Control Account, Administration Overhead Control Account, Selling and distribution Control Account, Cost of Sales Account. Sometimes, following additional accounts are also opened:

(a) *Overhead suspense account:* While valuing semi-finished jobs, Production overheads may not be considered. Similarly, while valuing closing stock of finished goods, Administration overheads are not included. In such cases, at the end of the accounting period, the estimated amount of such overheads is debited to Production or Administration Overhead Suspense account are credited to Production or Administration Overheads Account. In the beginning of the next period, the entries are reversed to close the suspense accounts.

(b) *Capital Orders:* For each item of capital nature work to be performed in the factory itself, e.g. Producing tools and equipments, certain expenditures of materials, wages and other expenses shall be incurred. Such expenditures should be recorded in the Capital Order Account or Capital Work-in-Progress account and later on capitalized.

(c) *Service Orders:* If repairs and maintenance work is done in the factory, the cost is debited to Repairs and Maintenance Account and later transferred to various Overheads account, because the expenditure might have been incurred on Production, Administration and Selling and distribution departments

No separate account is maintained for direct expenses since they are directly charged to work-in-progress account.

When sales of finished goods are effected, they are transferred to Cost of Sales Account. At the end, a Costing Profit and Loss Account can be prepared with the help of all the above accounts.

Control accounts are maintained on double entry system of book-keeping. They provide a check on the accuracy of postings to individual accounts. Separate trial balance can also be prepared for each ledger independently. Operation of non-integral accounts with the help of control accounts is explained hereunder starting with journal entries.

Journal entries

Part A: External

Transactions	Entries in Financial Books	Entries in Cost Ledger
Materials: 1. Cash/Credit purchase of materials for stock	Purchases A/c Dr Cost Ledger A/c (Memorandum) Dr To Bank/Suppliers A/c	Stores Ledger Control A/c Dr To General Ledger Adjustment A/c
2. Cash/Credit purchase of materials for direct issue to production	Purchases A/c Dr Cost Ledger A/c (Memorandum) Dr To Bank/Suppliers A/c	Work-in-Progress Ledger A/c Dr To General Ledger Adjustment A/c (Individual Jobs for which materials have been procured will be debited in Job Ledger)
3. Materials returned to suppliers	Creditors A/c Dr To Purchase returns A/c To Cost Ledger Control A/c (Memorandum)	General Ledger Adjustment A/c Dr To Stores Ledger Control A/c (Individual Stores A/c will be credited in Stores Ledger)
Labour: Payment of Wages	Wages A/c Dr Cost Ledger Control A/c (Memorandum) Dr To Bank/Cash	Wages Control A/c Dr To General Ledger Adjustment A/c
Direct Expenses:	Expense A/c Dr Cost Ledger Control A/c (Memorandum) Dr To Bank/Cash	Work-in-Progress Ledger Control A/c Dr To General Ledger Adjustment A/c
Production Overheads: (Paid or Outstanding)	Expense A/c Dr Cost Ledger Control A/c (Memorandum) Dr To Bank/Personal A/c	Production Overheads Control A/c Dr To General Ledger Adjustment A/c
Administration Overheads: (Paid or Outstanding)	Expense A/c Dr Cost Ledger Control A/c (Memorandum) Dr To Bank/Personal A/c	Administration Overheads Control A/c Dr To General Ledger Adjustment A/c
Selling & Distribution Overheads: (Paid or Outstanding)	Expense A/c Dr Cost Ledger Control A/c (Memorandum) Dr To Bank/Personal A/c	Selling & Distribution Overheads Control A/c Dr To General Ledger Adjustment A/c
Sales	Bank/Debtors A/c Dr To Sales To Cost Ledger Control A/c (Memorandum)	General Ledger Adjustment A/c Dr To Cost of Sales A/c

Part B : Internal (no entry in financial ledger; entries in cost ledger only)

Transactions	Entries in Cost Ledger
Materials:	
1. Issue of Materials for Production as per Material Requisition Slip	Work-in-Progress Ledger Control A/c Dr To Stores Ledger Control A/c
2. Issue of Indirect Materials	Production/Factory Overhead Control A/c Dr To Stores Ledger Control A/c
3. Returns from Jobs to stores	Stores Ledger Control A/c Dr To Work-in-Progress Ledger Control A/c
4. Transfer from one job to another	Transferee Job A/c Dr To Transferor Job A/c
Labour: 1. Charge to Production as per wages Abstract	Work-in-Progress Ledger Control A/c Dr To Wages Control A/c
2. Charging of indirect labour for Production	Production Overhead Control A/c Dr To Wages Control A/c
Production Overheads: 1. Absorption of Production overhead from output	1. Work-in-Progress Ledger Control A/c Dr To Production Overhead Control A/c
2. Under Absorption	2. Overhead Suspense A/c OR Costing Profit & Loss A/c Dr To Production Overhead Control A/c (Overhead Suspense A/c is carried forward to the next year and reversed at the beginning of the next year)
3. Over Absorption	3. Production Overhead Control A/c Dr To Overhead Suspense A/c OR Costing Profit & Loss A/c (Overhead Suspense A/c is carried forward to the next year and reversed at the beginning of the next year)
Administration Overheads:	
1. Issue of Indirect Materials for office	1. Administration Overhead Control A/c Dr To Stores Ledger Control A/c
2. Absorption of Production overhead from output	2. Finished Goods Ledger Control A/c Dr To Administration Overhead Control A/c
3. Under Absorption	3. Overhead Suspense A/c OR Costing Profit & Loss A/c Dr To Administration Overhead Control A/c (Overhead Suspense A/c is carried forward to the next year and reversed at the beginning of the next year)
4. Over Absorption	4. Administration Overhead Control A/c Dr To Overhead Suspense A/c OR Costing Profit & Loss A/c (Overhead Suspense A/c is carried forward to the next year and reversed at the beginning of the next year)

Selling & Distribution Overheads:	
1. Issue of Indirect Materials for Selling & Distribution	1. Selling & Distribution Overhead Control A/c Dr To Stores Ledger Control A/c
2. Absorption of Selling & Distribution overhead from output	2. Cost of Sales A/c Dr To Selling & Distribution Overhead Control A/c
3. Under Absorption of Selling & Distribution	3. Overhead Suspense A/c OR Costing Profit & Loss A/c Dr To Selling & Distribution Overhead Control A/c (Overhead Suspense A/c is carried forward to the next year and reversed at the beginning of the next year)
4. Over Absorption	4 Selling & Distribution Overhead Control A/c Dr To Overhead Suspense A/c OR Costing Profit & Loss A/c (Overhead Suspense A/c is carried forward to the next year and reversed at the beginning of the next year)
Normal Loss/Wastage: 1. Normal loss of Materials	1. No Entry if normal loss has been recovered by inflating unit cost of materials. Otherwise Production Overhead Control A/c Dr To Stores Ledger Control A/c
2. Normal Idle Time	2. No Entry if normal Idle Time has been recovered by inflating unit cost of labour. Otherwise Production Overhead Control A/c Dr To Wages Control A/c
Abnormal Loss/Wastage:	
1. Abnormal Loss of Materials	1. Costing Profit & Loss A/c Dr To Stores Ledger Control A/c
2. Abnormal Loss of Materials	2. Costing Profit & Loss A/c Dr To Wages Control A/c
Finished Stock, Sales and Profit and Loss:	
1. Cost of Production of Finished Goods	1. Finished Goods Ledger Control A/c Dr To Work-in-Progress Ledger Control A/c
2. Cost of Goods sold	2. Cost of Sales A/c Dr To Finished Goods Ledger Control A/c
3. Profit on Sale	3. Cost of Sales A/c Dr To Costing P & L A/c
4. Loss on Sale	4. Costing P & L A/c Dr To Cost of Sales A/c
5. Transfer of net profit as per costing P&L A/c	5. Costing P & L A/c Dr To General Ledger Adjustment A/c
6. Transfer of net loss as per costing P&L A/c	6. General Ledger Adjustment A/c Dr To Costing P & L A/c

Illustration 21.1 : *During the physical verification of stores of SV Limited it was found that 400 units of raw material 'Margin' returned to the supplier has not been recorded. Its purchase price is ₹ 30 per unit while the current standard cost is ₹ 25 per unit. Make necessary journal entry to record the adjustment in the Cost ledger of SV Limited.*

Solution :

Details		Debit Amount (₹)	Credit Amount (₹)
General Ledger Adjustment A/c	Dr	12,000	
To Stores Ledger Control A/c			10,000
To Material Price Variance A/c			2,000
(Being the recording of materials returned to supplier, earlier ignored)			

Illustration 21.2 : *During September 2004, the following transactions took place in Laxmi Limited.*

(1) Materials Purchased:	
(a) Credit purchases	*72,000*
(b) Credit purchases for Special Job	*10,000*
(c) Cash purchases	*18,000*
(2) Returns to Suppliers	*8,000*
(3) Direct Materials issued to production	*50,000*
(4) Indirect Materials issued	*5,000*
(5) Materials returned from production to stores	*800*
(6) Materials transferred from Job No. 36 to Job No. 37	*1,600*

You are required to enter the transactions in the financial and Cost Books.

Solution : **Financial Books**

Details		Debit Amount (₹)	Credit Amount (₹)
Purchases A/c	Dr	72,000	
Cost Ledger Control A/c (Memorandum)	Dr	72,000	
To Sundry Creditors A/c			72,000
(Being the amount of credit purchases)			
Purchases A/c	Dr	10,000	
Cost Ledger Control A/c (Memorandum)	Dr	10,000	
To Sundry Creditors A/c			10,000
(Being the amount of special purchases)			

Purchases A/c	Dr	18,000	
Cost Ledger Control A/c (Memorandum)	Dr	18,000	
To Cash A/c			18,000
(Being the Cash purchases)			
Sundry Creditors A/c	Dr	8,000	
To Purchase Returns A/c			8,000
To Cost Ledger Control A/c (Memorandum)			8,000
(Being the return of materials)			

Cost Books: From the above entries in the cost ledger control account, the cost accounting department makes corresponding entries in the cost books as under:

Details		Debit Amount (₹)	Credit Amount (₹)
1.(a) Stores Ledger Control A/c	Dr	72,000	
To General Ledger Adjustment A/c			72,000
(Being the Credit Purchases made)			
(b) Work-in-Progress Ledger Control A/c	Dr	10,000	
To General Ledger Adjustment A/c			10,000
(Being the amount of special purchases)			
(c) Stores Ledger Control A/c	Dr	18,000	
To General Ledger Adjustment A/c			18,000
(Being the Cash Purchases made)			
2. General Ledger Adjustment A/c	Dr	8,000	
To Stores Ledger Control A/c			8,000
(Being the return of materials)			
3. Work-in-Progress Ledger Control A/c	Dr	50,000	
To Stores Ledger Adjustment A/c			50,000
(Being the issue of direct materials to production)			
4. Production Overhead A/c	Dr	5,000	
To Stores Ledger Adjustment A/c			5,000
(Being the issue of indirect materials)			
5. Stores Ledger Control A/c	Dr	800	
To Work-in-Progress Ledger Control A/c			800
(Being the return of materials from production to stores)			
6. Job No. 37A/c	Dr	1,600	
To Job No. 36 A/c			1,600
(Being the transfer of materials from job No 36 to job No.37)			

Illustration 21.3 : *From the following figures ascertained from the costing records and financial books of a factory you are required to pass necessary journal entries in the cost journal (Assume that a system of maintaining control accounts prevails in the organization).*

Details	*Amount (₹)*	*Details*	*Amount (₹)*
Cost of completed Jobs	*15,36,800*	*Stores issued*	*5,40,600*
Purchases	*5,78,000*	*Direct Wages*	*4,35,600*
Carriage Inward	*7,200*	*Indirect Wages*	*1,46,000*
Materials used in repairs	*3,750*	*Works on Cost*	*4,18,200*

Solution : **Cost Journal**

Details		Amount (₹)	Amount (₹)
Finished Goods Ledger Control Account	Dr	15,36,800	
To Work-in-Progress Ledger Control Account			15,36,800
(Completed jobs transferred to finished stock)			
Stores Ledger Control account	Dr	5,78,000	
To General Ledger Adjustment Account			5,78,000
(Materials purchased)			
Stores Ledger Control account	Dr	7,200	
To General Ledger Adjustment Account			7,200
(Carriage inwards charged to materials)			
Works Overhead Control Account	Dr	3,750	
To Stores Ledger Control account			3,750
(Materials used for repairs)			
Work-in-Progress Ledger Control Account	Dr	5,40,600	
To Stores Ledger Control account			5,40,600
(Being the issue of materials for production)			
Work-in-Progress Ledger Control Account	Dr	4,35,600	
Works Overhead Control Account	Dr	1,46,000	
To Wages Control A/c			5,81,600
(Wages allocated to production and works overhead)			
Works Overhead Control Account	Dr	4,18,200	
To General Ledger Adjustment Account			4,18,200
(Being the incurrence of works overhead)			

Illustration 21.4 : *Cost Ledger of Vidya Limited shows the following balances as on March 31, 2009.*

Ledger Account	*Debit Amount ₹ (in Lakh)*	*Credit Amount ₹ (in Lakh)*
Stores Ledger Control A/c	*400*	
Work-in-Progress Ledger Control A/c	*100*	
Finished Stock Ledger Control A/c	*2150*	
Building Construction A/c	*50*	
General Ledger Control A/c		*2,700*
Total	*2,700*	*2,700*

During the first Quarter of the following year, the under-mentioned transactions took place:

Details	*Amount ₹ (in Lakh)*	*Details*	*Amount ₹ (in Lakh)*
Materials Purchased	*200*	*Works Overhead*	
Issued to production	*250*	*Actual amount Incurred*	*800*
Issued to general maintenance	*30*	*(Excluding items shown above)*	
Issued to building construction	*20*	*Absorbed in building construction*	*100*
		Under absorbed	*40*
		Royalty paid	*25*
Wages		*Selling, Distribution and Administration Overheads*	*125*
Gross Wages Paid	*750*		
Indirect Wages	*200*		
For Building construction	*50*		
		Sales	*2,250*

At the end of the quarter, the stock of raw materials and works-in-progress was ₹ 275 Lakhs and ₹ 125 lakhs respectively. The loss arising in the raw materials account is treated as factory overheads. The building under construction was completed during the quarter. Company's gross profit margin is 20% on sales.

Prepare the relevant control accounts to record the above transactions in the cost ledger of the company. **[C.A. (Inter) Modified]**

Solution : **Cost Ledger**

Dr **General Ledger Control Account** Cr

Details	Amount ₹ (in Lakh)	Details	Amount ₹ (in Lakh)
To Sales	2,250	By Balance b/d (Opening Balance)	2,700
To Balance c/d (Closing Balance)	2,635	By Stores Ledger Control A/c	200
		By Wages Control A/c	750
		By Works Overhead Control A/c	800
		By Royalty A/c	25
		By Selling, Distribution and Administration overheads control A/c	125
		By Costing Profit and Loss A/c	285
Total	4,885	Total	4,885

Dr **Stores Ledger Control A/c** Cr

Details	Amount ₹ (in Lakh)	Details	Amount ₹ (in Lakh)
To Balance b/d (Opening Balance)	400	By Work-in-Progress Ledger Control A/c	250
To General Ledger Control A/c	200	By Works Overhead Control A/c	30
		By Building construction A/c	20
		By Works Overhead Control A/c (loss)	25
		By Balance c/d (Closing Balance)	275
Total	600	Total	600

Dr **Work-in-Progress Ledger Control A/c** Cr

Details	Amount ₹ (in Lakh)	Details	Amount ₹ (in Lakh)
To Balance b/d (Opening Balance)	100	By Finished Stock Control account (Balancing Figure)	1,665
To Stores Ledger Control A/c	250	By Balance c/d (Closing Balance)	125

To Wages Control account	500		
To Works Overhead Control A/c	815		
To Royalty A/c	25		
Total	1,790	Total	1,790

Dr **Finished Stock Ledger Control A/c** Cr

Details	Amount ₹ (in Lakh)	Details	Amount ₹ (in Lakh)
To Balance b/d (Opening Balance)	2,150	By Cost of Sales A/c (2,250 × 0.8)	1,800
To Work-in-Progress Ledger Control A/c	1,665	By Balance c/d (Closing Balance)	2,015
Total	3,815	Total	3,815

Dr **Wages Control A/c** Cr

Details	Amount ₹ (in Lakh)	Details	Amount ₹ (in Lakh)
To General Ledger Control A/c	750	By Work-in-Progress Ledger Control A/c	500
		By Works Overhead Control A/c	200
		By Building Construction A/c	50
Total	750	Total	750

Dr **Works Overhead Control A/c** Cr

Details	Amount ₹ (in Lakh)	Details	Amount ₹ (in Lakh)
To General Ledger Control A/c	800	By Work-in-Progress Ledger Control A/c	915
To Stores Ledger Control A/c	30	By Building Construction A/c	100
To Wages Control A/c	200	By Costing Profit and Loss A/c (Under recovered overheads)	40
To Stores Ledger Control A/c (Loss)	25		
Total	1,055	Total	1,055

Dr **Selling, Distribution and Administration overheads control A/c** Cr

Details	Amount ₹ (in Lakh)	Details	Amount ₹ (in Lakh)
To General Ledger Control A/c	125	By Cost of Sales A/c	125
Total	125	Total	125

Dr **Cost of Sales A/c** Cr

Details	Amount ₹ (in Lakh)	Details	Amount ₹ (in Lakh)
To Finished Stock Ledger A/c	1,800	By Costing Profit and Loss A/c	1,925
To Selling, Distribution and Administration overheads control A/c	125		
Total	1,925	Total	1,925

Dr **Royalty A/c** Cr

Details	Amount ₹ (in Lakh)	Details	Amount ₹ (in Lakh)
To General Ledger Control A/c	25	By Work-in-Progress Ledger Control A/c	25
Total	25	Total	25

Dr **Building Construction A/c** Cr

Details	Amount ₹ (in Lakh)	Details	Amount ₹ (in Lakh)
To Balance b/d (Opening Balance)	50	By Balance c/d (Closing Balance)	220
To Stores Ledger Control A/c	20		
To Wages Control A/c	50		
To Works Overhead Control A/c	100		
Total	220	Total	220

Dr **Costing Profit and Loss A/c** Cr

Details	Amount ₹ (in Lakh)	Details	Amount ₹ (in Lakh)
To Cost of Sales A/c	1,925	By General Ledger Control Account (Sales)	2,250
To Works Overhead Control Account (Under recovered)	40		
To General Ledger Control Account (Profit)	285		
Total	2,250	Total	2,250

Trial Balance as on 30.6.2010

Ledger Account	Debit Amount ₹ (in Lakh)	Credit Amount ₹ (in Lakh)
Stores Ledger Control A/c	275	
Work-in-Progress Ledger Control A/c	125	
Finished Stock Ledger Control A/c	2,015	
Building construction A/c	220	
General Ledger Control A/c		2,635
Total	2,635	2,635

LET US RECAPITULATE

1. Under the system of non-integral accounting, separate ledgers are kept for cost and financial transaction.
2. Cost control accounts summarize all detailed information contained in the subsidiary ledgers and also help in reconciliation of cost and financial accounts.
3. Stores Ledger Control account records the total of materials received in stores on the debit side and the total of materials issued out of stores on its credit side.
4. Work-in-Progress Ledger Control Account provides total value of work-in-progress at any point of time.
5. Wages Control account records wage transactions in aggregate.
6. No separate account is maintained for direct expenses since they are directly charged to work-in-progress account.
7. Control accounts are maintained on double entry system of book-keeping.
8. Control accounts provide a check on the accuracy of postings to individual accounts. Separate trial balance can also be prepared for each ledger independently.

SOLVED PROBLEMS

Problem 1. *From the following details show the necessary accounts in the cost ledger:*

Item	*Materials*	*Work-in-Progress*	*Finished Goods*
Opening Balance	*10,000*	*6,000*	*12,750*
Closing Balance	*13,250*	*12,000*	*15,000*

Transactions during the period:

Item	*Amount (₹)*
Materials Purchased	*32,000*
Wages Paid (including ₹ 2,500 Indirect)	*12,500*
Overhead Incurred	*10,000*
Sales	*62,000*
Overhead Recovered	*12,000*

Solution : Opening Trial Balance to ascertain opening balance of General Ledger Control Account

Ledger Account	Debit Amount (₹)	Credit Amount (₹)
Stores Ledger Control Account	10,000	
Work-in-Progress Ledger Control Account	6,000	
Finished Stock Ledger Control Account	12,750	
General Ledger Control Account		28,750
Total	28,750	28,750

Cost Ledger

Dr **General Ledger Control account** Cr

Details	Amount (₹)	Details	Amount (₹)
Sales	62,000	Opening Balance	28,750
Closing Balance	40,250	Stores Ledger Control account	32,000
		Wages Control account	12,500
		Overhead Control account	10,000
		Costing Profit and Loss Account	19,000
Total	1,02,250	Total	1,02,250

Dr **Stores Ledger Control account** Cr

Details	Amount (₹)	Details	Amount (₹)
Opening Balance	10,000	Work-in-Progress Ledger Control account	28,750
	32,000	Closing Balance	13,250
Total	42,000	Total	42,000

Dr **Work-in-Progress Ledger Control account** Cr

Details	Amount (₹)	Details	Amount (₹)
Opening Balance	6,000	Finished Stock Control account (Balancing Figure)	44,750
Stores Ledger Control account	28,750	Closing Balance	12,000
Wages Control account	10,000		
Overhead Control account	12,000		
Total	56,750	Total	56,750

Dr **Finished Stock Ledger Control account** Cr

Details	Amount (₹)	Details	Amount (₹)
Opening Balance	12,750	Cost of Sales account (Balancing Figure)	42,500
Work-in-Progress Ledger Control account	44,750	Closing Balance	15,000
Total	57,500	Total	57,500

Dr **Wages Control account** Cr

Details	Amount (₹)	Details	Amount (₹)
General Ledger Control account	12,500	Work-in-Progress Ledger Control account	10,000
		Overhead Control account	2,500
Total	12,500	Total	12,500

Dr **Overhead Control account** Cr

Details	Amount (₹)	Details	Amount (₹)
General Ledger Control account	10,000	Work-in-Progress Ledger Control account	12,000
Wages Control account	2,500	Costing Profit and Loss A/c	500
Total	12,500	Total	12,500

Dr **Cost of Sales account** Cr

Details	Amount (₹)	Details	Amount (₹)
Finished Stock Ledger account	42,500	Costing Profit and Loss account (Sales)	42,500
Total	42,500	Total	42,500

Dr **Costing Profit and Loss account** Cr

Details	Amount (₹)	Details	Amount (₹)
Cost of Sales account	42,500	General Ledger Control Account (Sales)	62,000
Overhead Control Account (Under recovered)	500		
General Ledger Control Account (Profit)	19,000		
Total	62,000	Total	62,000

Closing Trial Balance to ascertain opening balance of General Ledger Control Account

Ledger Account	Debit Amount (₹)	Credit Amount (₹)
Stores Ledger Control Account	13,250	
Work-in-Progress Ledger Control Account	12,000	
Finished Stock Ledger Control Account	15,000	
General Ledger Control Account		40,250
Total	40,250	40,250

Problem 2. *The Profit and Loss accounts as shown in the financial books of a company for the year ended on 31.3.2004 together with a statement of reconciliation between the profit as per financial and cost accounts is given below:*

Debit Side	*Amount (₹)*	*Credit Side*	*Amount (₹)*
Opening stock: *Raw Materials 1,20,000* *Work-in-Progress 65,000* *Finished Stock 95,000*	*28,0000*	*Sales*	*2,78,0000*

Purchase of Raw Materials	*9,30,000*	*Closing stock:* *Raw Materials 1,30,000* *Work-in-Progress 73,000* *Finished Stock 1,02,000*	*3,05,000*
Direct Wages	*4,20,000*	*Miscellaneous Receipts*	*1,60,000*
Factory Overheads	*5,10,000*		
Administration Expenses	*2,85,000*		
Selling and Distribution Expenses	*4,05,000*		
Preliminary Expenses written off	*30,000*		
Goodwill Written off	*70,000*		
Debenture Interest Paid	*50,000*		
Net Profit	*2,65,000*		
Total	*32,45,000*	*Total*	*32,45,000*

Statement of Reconciliation of Profit as per Financial and Cost account

Details	***Amount (₹)***	***Amount (₹)***
Profit as per Financial Accounts		*2,65,000*
(I) Difference in valuation of stock:		
Add: Raw Materials (Closing Stock)	*3,200*	
Work-in-Progress (Opening Stock)	*2,500*	
Finished Goods (Opening Stock)	*3,500*	
Finished Goods (Closing Stock)	*2,800*	
Total (I)	*12,000*	
(II) Less: Work-in-Progress (Closing Stock)	*1,600*	
Raw Materials (Opening Stock)	*3,600*	
Total (II)	*5,200*	*6,800*
(I)-(II)	*6,800*	
Other Items:		
Add: Preliminary expenses written off	*30,000*	
Goodwill Written off	*70,000*	
Debenture Interest	*50,000*	
Total	*1,50,000*	
Less: Miscellaneous Receipts	*1,60,000*	*(10,000)*
Profit as per cost Accounts		*2,61,800*

You are required to prepare the following accounts, as they would appear in the cost ledger:

(i) Raw Material Control Account;

(ii) Work-in-Progress Control Account;

(iii) Finished Goods Control Account;

(iv) Cost of Sales Account;

(v) Costing Profit & Loss Account.

Solution : **Derivation of Cost Accounts Value of Stocks**

Details	Financial Accounts (₹)	Adjustment in Value (₹)	Cost Accounts (₹)
Raw Materials: Opening	1,20,000	3,600	1,23,600
Raw Materials: Closing	1,30,000	3,200	1,33,200
Work-in-Progress: Opening	65,000	(2,500)	62,500
Work-in-Progress: Closing	73,000	(1,600)	71,400
Finished Goods: Opening	95,000	(3,500)	91,500
Finished Goods: Closing	1,02,000	2,800	1,04,800

Dr **Raw Material Control Account** Cr

Debit Item	Amount (₹)	Credit Item	Amount (₹)
Opening Balance	1,23,600	Work-in-Progress Control Account (Transfer)	9,20,400
General Ledger Control Account	9,30,000	Closing Balance	1,33,200
Total	10,53,600	Total	10,53,600

Dr **Work-in-Progress Control Account** Cr

Debit Item	Amount (₹)	Credit Item	Amount (₹)
Opening Balance	62,500		
Raw Material Control Account	9,20,400	Closing Balance	71,400
General Ledger Control Account (Wages)	4,20,000	Finished Goods Control Account	18,41,500
General Ledger Control Account (Factory Overhead	5,10,000		
Total	19,12,900	Total	19,12,900

Dr **Finished Goods Control Account** Cr

Debit Item	Amount (₹)	Credit Item	Amount (₹)
Opening Balance	91,500	Cost of Sales Account	21,13,200
Work-in-Progress Control Account	18,41,500	Closing Balance	1,04,800
General Ledger Control Account (Administration)	2,85,000		
Total	22,18,000	Total	22,18,000

Dr **Cost of Sales Account** Cr

Debit Item	Amount (₹)	Credit Item	Amount (₹)
Finished Goods Control Account	21,13,200	Costing Profit and Loss Account	25,18,200
General Ledger Control Account (Selling Overheads)	40,5000		
Total	25,18,200	Total	25,18,200

Costing Profit and Loss Account

Debit Item	Amount (₹)	Credit Item	Amount (₹)
Cost of Sales Account	25,18,200	General Ledger Control Account	27,80,000
Profit	2,61,800		
Total	27,80,000	Total	27,80,000

Problem 3. *Following figures have been extracted from the cost records of a manufacturing segment of a firm:*

Items	*Amount (₹)*	*Items*	*Amount (₹)*
Stores:		*Work-in-Progress:*	
Opening Balance	*75,000*	*Opening Balance*	*1,500,00*
Purchases	*2,40,000*	*Direct Wages Applied*	*1,80,000*
Transfer from Work-in-Progress	*1,20,000*	*Overheads Applied*	*6,50,000*
		Closing Balance	*1,30,000*
Issues to Work-in-Progress	*2,40,000*		
Issues to repairs and manufacturing	*50,000*		
Shortages in stock-taking	*15,000*		

Finished Product: *Entire Output is sold at a profit of 10% on actual cost from Work-in-Progress*			

Others: *Wages incurred ₹ 2,00,000; Overheads incurred ₹ 7,10,000.*

Items not included in Cost Records: Income from Investments ₹ 50,000; Loss on sale of Capital Assets ₹ 30,000.

Draw up Stores Control A/c, Work-in-Progress Control A/c, Costing Profit and Loss A/c, Financial Profit and Loss A/c and Reconciliation A/c.

Solution :

Stores Ledger Control Account

Debit Side	Amount (₹)	Credit Side	Amount (₹)
Opening Balance	75,000	WIP Ledger Control A/c	2,40,000
General Ledger Control A/c	2,40,000	Overhead Control A/c	50,000
WIP Ledger Control A/c	1,20,000	Overhead Control A/c	15,000
		Closing Balance	1,30,000
Total	4,35,000	Total	4,35,000

Wages Control Account

Debit Side	Amount (₹)	Credit Side	Amount (₹)
General Ledger Control A/c	2,00,000	WIP Ledger Control A/c	1,80,000
		Overhead Control A/c (Balance assumed to be Indirect Wages)	20,000
Total	2,00,000	Total	2,00,000

Overhead Control Account

Debit Side	Amount (₹)	Credit Side	Amount (₹)
General Ledger Control A/c	7,10,000	WIP Ledger Control A/c	6,50,000
Stores Ledger Control Account	50,000	Closing Balance (Un-recovered Overhead)	1,45,000
Stores Ledger Control Account (Deficiency in Stock)	15,000		
Wages Control A/c	20,000		
Total	7,95,000	Total	7,95,000

Work-in-Progress Ledger Control Account

Debit Side	Amount (₹)	Credit Side	Amount (₹)
Opening Balance	1,50,000	Stores Ledger Control Account	1,20,000
Stores Ledger Control Account	2,40,000	Costing Profit and Loss A/c (Balancing Figure)	9,70,000
Wages Control A/c	1,80,000	Closing Balance	1,30,000
Overheads Control A/c	6,50,000		
Total	12,20,000	Total	12,20,000

Costing Profit and Loss Account

Debit Side	Amount (₹)	Credit Side	Amount (₹)
WIP Ledger Control A/c	9,70,000	General Ledger Control A/c (Sales)	10,67,000
General Ledger Control A/c (Net Profit)	97,000		
Total	10,67,000	Total	10,67,000

Financial Profit and Loss Account

Debit Side	Amount (₹)	Credit Side	Amount (₹)
Opening Stock:		Sales	10,67,000
Stores	75,000		
WIP	1,50,000		
Purchases	2,40,000	Income from Investments	50,000
Wages	2,00,000	Closing Stock:	
		Stores	1,30,000
		WIP	1,30,000
Overheads	7,10,000	Loss (Balancing Figure)	28,000
Loss on sale of Capital Assets	30,000		
Total	14,05,000	Total	14,05,000

Statement of Reconciliation of Profit as per Financial and Cost account

Details	Amount (₹)	Amount (₹)
Profit as per Financial Accounts		(28,000)
Add: Under recovery of overheads	1,45,000	1,75,000
Loss on sale of capital assets	30,000	
Less: Income from Investments		(50,000)
Profit as per Cost Accounts		97,000

OBJECTIVE TYPE EXERCISES

I. Fill in the blank spaces with suitable word/s :

1. Finished Goods Ledger Control Account will invariably have a .... balance.
2. When production overheads are over absorbed, the Production Overhead Account will show a .... balance.
3. When stores are issued to Repairs and Maintenance Account, the accounting entry is to .... Production Overhead Account and .... Stores Ledger control account.
4. The balance in cost of sales account is transferred to ....
5. In .... Ledger, an account is maintained for each job.
6. .... is the Principal ledger of the costing department in which impersonal accounts are maintained.
7. The closing balance of Costing Profit and Loss account represents the ....
8. When materials are returned to the supplier, accounting entry is to debit .... Control account and credit to .... Account.
9. The main function of Cost Ledger control account is to make the cost ledger ....
10. Postings in Wages control account are made from ....

Answers :

1. Debit	**2.** Credit
3. Debit, Credit	**4.** Costing Profit and Loss account
5. Work-in-progress	**6.** Cost Ledger
7. Profit or Loss	**8.** Cost ledger, Stores ledger
9. Self-balancing	**10.** Wages Analysis Sheet

II. Indicate whether the following statements are True or False :

1. Non-integrated accounts are based on double entry system of accounts.
2. In case normal loss of materials has been recovered by inflating unit cost of materials, there is no need for an adjustment entry in cost ledger.
3. Materials purchased for specific jobs are debited to work-in-progress control account.
4. Cost ledger control account in financial books is a memorandum account.
5. Transfer entries in cost ledger are also entered in 'Financial ledger control account'.
6. Credit balance of factory overhead control account represents under absorption of production overheads.
7. Control accounts are total accounts.
8. Materials and labour used for creating capital asset are debited to work-in-progress control account.
9. Debit balance of selling and distribution overhead control account represents over absorption of selling and distribution overheads.

10. Cost ledgers are maintained on self-balancing principle.
11. There is no need to reconcile profit as per financial books and as per cost ledger on non-integral system.
12. Data for wage control account is derived from wage analysis sheet.
13. Cost ledger control account serves as a link between financial accounts and cost accounts.
14. Balances of 'Cost Ledger Control Account' in financial books and of 'General Ledger Adjustment account' in cost ledger do not agree with each other.
15. Income tax and dividends paid are recorded on the debit side of the cost ledger.
16. Non-integral accounting is also called interlocking accounting system
17. Cost control accounts always integrate cost and financial accounts.
18. Indirect labour is debited directly to work-in-progress control account.
19. Selling and distribution overheads recovered are debited to cost of sales account.
20. Only those entries appear in 'General Ledger Control account' which influences both financial and cost books.

Answers :

1. True	**2.** True	**3.** True	**4.** True
5. False	**6.** False	**7.** True	**8.** False
9. False	**10.** True	**11.** False	**12.** True
13. True	**14.** False	**15.** False	**16.** True
17. False	**18.** False	**19.** True	**20.** True

THEORETICAL EXERCISES

1. Explain the system of non-integrated accounting and state the principal ledgers that are to be maintained and the principal accounts that are to be maintained.
2. Explain the nature and contents of the 'Cost Ledger'. What are the advantages of cost Ledger?
3. What is 'Control Account'? Describe its advantages.
4. "Control accounts are summary accounts". Discuss.
5. Explain the treatment of normal and abnormal loss of materials and over / under recovery of overheads in cost ledger.
6. What is the function of Cost ledger Control Account?
7. What is the source of entries in Factory Overhead Control Account?
8. What is the source of entries in Stores Ledger Account?
9. What is the source of entries in Wages Control Account?
10. What is meant by interlocking system and integrated system of maintaining cost and financial accounts? Which one would you adopt and why?

NUMERICAL EXERCISES

1. The Balance in a Firm's Work-in-Progress Control A/c as on March 31, 2004 was ₹7,20,000. During the preceding month, the transactions that took place were as under:

Details	Amount (₹)	Details	Amount (₹)
Direct Wages Incurred	1,20,000	Sub-Contract Charges	13,000
Direct Materials issued	5,40,000	Direct Expenses	15,000
Completed Work billed at cost	8,60,000	Special Purchases for jobs	20,000
Factory overhead Incurred	1,90,000	Materials Returned to Stores	8,000

Write up the Work-in-Progress Control A/c and state its initial Balance.

[Ans. 6,90,000]

2. From the following details show the necessary accounts in the cost ledger:

Item	Materials	Work-in-Progress	Finished Goods
Opening Balance	8,000	5,000	10,000
Closing Balance	11,000	9,000	12,000

Transactions during the period:

Item	Amount (₹)
Materials Purchased	25,000
Wages Paid (including ₹ 2,000 Indirect)	10,000
Overhead Incurred	8,000
Sales	50,000
Overhead Recovered	9,000

[Ans. Profit : 16,000]

3. The Profit and Loss accounts as shown in the financial books of a company for the year ended on 31.3.2004 together with a statement of reconciliation between the profit as per financial and cost accounts is given below:

Debit Side		Amount (₹)	Credit Side	Amount (₹)
Opening stock:			Sales	15,00,000
Raw Materials	90,000			
Work-in-Progress	50,000			
Finished Stock	70,000	2,10,000		

Purchase of Raw Materials	5,00,000	Closing stock: Raw Materials 98000 Work-in-Progress 53000 Finished Stock 72000	2,23,000
Direct Wages	2,00,000	Miscellaneous Receipts	45,000
Factory Overheads	2,00,000		
Administration Expenses	1,70,000		
Selling and Distribution Expenses	2,20,000		
Preliminary Expenses written off	30,000		
Goodwill Written off	50,000		
Debenture Interest Paid	25,000		
Net Profit	1,63,000		
Total	17,68,000	Total	17,68,000

Statement of Reconciliation of Profit as per Financial and Cost account

Details	Amount (₹)	Amount (₹)
Profit as per Financial Accounts		1,63,000
(I) Difference in valuation of stock:		
Add: Raw Materials (Closing Stock)	1,200	
Work-in-Progress (Opening Stock)	1,300	
Finished Goods (Opening Stock)	2,000	
Finished Goods (Closing Stock)	1,000	
Total (I)	5,500	
(II) Less: Work-in-Progress (Closing Stock)	750	
Raw Materials (Opening Stock)	1,650	
Total (II)	2,400	3,100
(I)-(II) [i.e. 5,500-2,400]	3,100	
Other Items:		
Add: Preliminary expenses written off	30,000	
Goodwill Written off	50,000	
Debenture Interest	25,000	
Total	1,05,000	
Less: Miscellaneous Receipts	45,000	60,000
Profit as per cost Accounts		2,26,100

You are required to prepare the following accounts, as they would appear in the cost ledger:

(i) Raw Material Control Account
(ii) Work-in-Progress Control Account
(iii) Finished Goods Control Account
(iv) Cost of Sales Account
(v) Costing Profit & Loss Account.

4. Following figures have been extracted from the cost records of a manufacturing segment of a firm:

Items	Amount (₹)	Items	Amount (₹)
Stores:		Work-in-Progress:	
Opening Balance	30,000	Opening Balance	60,000
Purchases	1,60,000	Direct Wages Applied	75,000
Transfer from Work-in-Progress	80,000	Overheads Applied	2,60,000
		Closing Balance	50,000
Issues to Work-in-Progress	1,60,000		
Issues to repairs and manufacturing	20,000		
Shortages in stock-taking	6,000		
Finished Product: Entire Output is sold at a profit of 12.5% on actual cost from Work-in-Progress			

Others: Wages incurred ₹ 80,000; Overheads incurred ₹ 2,80,000.

Items not included in Cost Records: Income from Investments ₹ 20,000; Loss on sale of Capital Assets ₹ 10,000.

Draw up Stores Control A/c, Work-in-Progress Control A/c, Costing Profit and Loss A/c, Financial Profit and Loss A/c and Reconciliation A/c.

[Ans. Financial Profit: 12,125; Costing Profit: 53,125]

5. From the following information prepare various accounts in the cost ledger and trial balance as on March 31, 2004:

Balance as on April 1, 2003:

Details	Amount (₹)
Material Control	12,40,000
Work-in-Progress	6,25,000
Finished Goods	12,40,000
Production Overhead	84,000Dr
Administration Overhead	1,20,000Cr
Selling & Distribution Overhead	65,000Dr
General Ledger Control	3,13,4000

Transactions for the year ended March 31,2004:

Details	Amount (₹)	Details	Amount (₹)
Materials: Purchases	48,01,000	Production Overhead:	
Issued to:		Incurred	24,23,000
Jobs	47,74,000	Absorbed	3,591

Maintenance Works	4,12,000	Sales Overhead:	
Administrative office	34,000	Incurred	6,42,000
Selling department	72,000	Absorbed	8,20,000
		Production Overhead:	
		Incurred	7,40,000
		Allocated to Production	5,29,000
		Allocated to Sales	1,48,000
Direct Wages	14,93,000	Indirect Wages	6,50,000
Carriage Inward	84,000	Finished Goods Prod.	95,84,000
Sales Realisation	1,24,30,000	Finished Goods Sold	97,73,000

[Ans. Closing Balance> Materials Control 7,49,000; Work-in-Progress Control 8,99,000; Finished Goods Control 15,80,000; Overhead Adjustment Control A/c 2,000Cr]

6. From the following information gathered from the Cost Records of an industrial unit, prepare:

(a) A work-in-progress Account

(b) A Cost of Sales Account, and

(c) A Costing Profit and Loss Account.

Details	Amount (₹)	Amount (₹)
Opening Balances:		
Work-in-Progress	3,800	
Materials	22,000	
Finished Stock	17,000	42,800
		58,000
Materials Purchased		21,000
Direct Labour		20,000
Electricity Charges		27,000
Factory Overhead Expenses-Incurred		26,000
Factory Overhead Expenses Applied to production		28,000
Selling, Distribution and Administration Expenses		
Selling, Distribution and Administration Expenses charged to Finished Stock		29,000
Sales		1,86,000
Closing Balances :		
Work-in-progress	2,500	
Materials	15,000	
Finished Stock	32,000	49,500

❑❑❑

22 Reconciliation of Cost and Financial Accounts

Learning Objectives

It attempts to explain the method of reconciling profits shown by financial books and costing books. In this chapter you will learn :

1. Need for reconciliation of costing profit and financial profit.
2. Factors for divergence of profit as per two sets of books.
3. Steps required for making a reconciliation statement.
4. Format of a reconciliation statement.

INTRODUCTION

The need for reconciliation of profits as per Cost books and financial books arises because of two separate sets of books being kept under Non-Integral System with different bases of stock valuation, under- or over-recovery of overhead and disregarding some items of expenses in cost or financial accounts, by the same organization. The management requires cost data for decision-making, and it is essential that such cost data should be correct. For this very reason and to check the arithmetical accuracy of both sets of accounts as well as to explain the difference in profits, a reconciliation of cost and financial profits is to be done necessarily at regular intervals. However, under the integral System of accounting the problem of reconciliation does not occur. If both sets of books are interlocked thoroughly, reconciliation work will be facilitated. If under/over recovered overhead balances are adjusted to costing profit and Loss account during the same period, there will be no divergence in profit due to under/over recovery of overhead. Similarly, if a notional expenditure, such as rent charge, is considered in cost accounts only, the profit will be same if corresponding credit is also given to costing profit and loss account, by the following journal entry:

Dr Production Overhead Control account

Cr Costing Profit and Loss account.

Advantages of Reconciliation

1. It facilitates the checking the arithmetical accuracy of both the sets of accounts.
2. It makes the difference in profits in two sets of books explicit.
3. It causes co-ordination between cost and financial departments.

FACTORS RESPONSIBLE FOR DIVERGENCE IN PROFITS

Following factors cause the divergence in profits of two sets of accounts:

(A) Items included in one set of accounts only.

(B) Under/Over Recovery of Overheads.

(C) Different bases of stock valuation.

(D) Depreciation may be charged differently in two sets of books.

Items Included in One Set of Accounts Only

Some transactions are recorded exclusively either in financial accounts/books or in the cost accounts/books. Following is the list of items recorded only in financial accounts/book

(I) *Items recorded only in financial accounts/books:* Such items relate to

(i) Appropriation of Profits

(ii) Financial Charges

(iii) Financial Income, and

(iv) Items appearing only in cost accounts.

Items relating to the Appropriation of Profit include the followings:

(a) The sum transferred to Debenture Redemption Fund Account for the purpose of repayment of debentures or any other sum transferred to any other such account created with a view to discharge long-term liability.

(b) Dividends paid to, or proposed for Preference shareholders and Equity Shareholders.

(c) Amounts transferred to various accumulated profit reserves (General Reserve, Dividend Equalization Reserve etc.).

(d) Creation of additional provision for depreciation on Plant and Machinery and other fixed assets besides additional provision for bad and doubtful debts on sundry debtors.

(e) Issue of bonus shares to the equity shareholders out of the current year's Profit and Loss (appropriation) account.

(f) Income Tax

(g) Dividend distribution tax

Items exclusively related to Financial charges include the followings:

(a) Damages payable by Law
(b) Loss due to scrapping of machinery before the expiry of its life i.e. Obsolescence Loss
(c) Loss on sale of Investments, Building etc.
(d) Loss of capital assets arising from sale/exchange or uninsured destruction.
(e) Penalty payable for late completion of contracts.
(f) Interest on bank loans, mortgages, debentures and other borrowed money, if interest on capital is ignored in cost accounts.
(g) Goodwill written off
(h) Underwriting commission and debenture discount written off
(i) Fines and Penalties

Purely Financial Income

(a) Rental Income
(b) Transfer fees
(c) Interest, Dividend Income on investments
(d) Profit on sale of Fixed Assets /Investments
(e) Interest received on bank deposits.

Items Appearing Only in Cost Accounts (i.e. Imputed Cost Items)

(a) Notional Interest on Capital
(b) Notional Rent on Premises owned
(c) Notional Salary of the Proprietor/Partner

RECONCILIATION IN COMPUTER ERA

The functioning of computers reduces the necessity for reconciliation of cost and financial accounts due to following reasons:

(a) It can bring out different financial accounting and cost accounting statement/reports pointedly and precisely.
(b) The reasons for difference in profits as per cost and financial books can be presented on comparative format at one place by the computer.

Keeping in view the above, it can be stated that the work of the accountant has been greatly reduced in computing the two amounts of profits. However, the main reason for divergence in profits shown by financial and cost accounts is the presence of certain items in financial books only and not in cost books. Similarly, there may be some items which appear in cost books only but do not find any place in financial books. Hence, the need to reconcile the profits still remains essential even in the computer era.

RECONCILIATION STATEMENT

Reconciliation statement is a statement which reconciles the profit/loss as per cost accounts with the profit/loss as per financial accounts by showing all causal factors of differences between the two. It is prepared to reconcile the profit/loss as per Cost accounts with the profit/loss as per financial accounts by showing all the causal factors of differences between the two and to take the necessary follow up action, if any required.

Preparation of Reconciliation statement can be avoided provided the Cost and Financial accounts are integrated i.e. only one set of books is maintained for recording both cost and financial transactions. Integration means that the same set of accounts fulfills the requirements of both i.e. Cost and Financial accounts.

Steps Required for Making Reconciliation

To reconcile financial and cost profits, either a Reconciliation Statement or a Memorandum Reconciliation Account is prepared. Except for the Format, there is no difference between the two. The following steps are usually adopted for reconciling profit/loss as per cost records and profit/loss as per financial records:

1. Debit side of the Costing Profit & Loss Account should be compared with the Debit side of the Financial Profit & Loss Account, and Credit side of the Costing Profit & Loss Account should be compared with the Credit side of the Financial Profit & Loss Account.
2. Points of difference between cost and financial profit/loss should be identified and ascertained.
3. A Reconciliation Statement is made at a point of time and NOT for a period of time. The purpose of making such a statement is *to reconcile* and *not to rectify* the differences.

The process of reconciliation may start with financial profit/loss at the beginning or costing profit/loss. If the starting point is financial profit/loss, adjustments are made to arrive at the costing profit/loss at the end, and vice versa. If the starting point is financial profit/loss, for each point of difference we make addition to or subtraction from the financial profit only so as to make it at par with that of the costing profit. Similarly, if the starting point is costing profit/loss, for each point of difference we make addition to or subtraction from the costing profit only so as to make it at par with that of the financial profit.

In order to make a Reconciliation Statement, following steps are necessary (Assuming the starting point is Profit as per *cost accounts*):

(I) Add the following items:

(a) Purely financial incomes shown only in financial books.

(b) Notional items of expenses included in cost accounts only.

(c) Over- Recovery of overheads in cost accounts.

(d) Depreciation overcharged in cost accounts.
(e) Under-Valuation of closing stock in cost accounts.
(f) Over-Valuation of opening stock in cost accounts.

(II) Deduct the following items:

(a) Purely financial charges shown only in financial books.
(b) Appropriation of profit shown in financial accounts only.
(c) Under- Recovery of overheads in cost accounts.
(d) Depreciation undercharged in cost accounts.
(e) Under-Valuation of opening stock in cost accounts.
(f) Over-Valuation of closing stock in cost accounts.

Format No. I: (Additions and Subtractions Method)

Reconciliation Statement (Format)

Details	Amount (₹)	Amount (₹)
Net profit as per Cost accounts		
ADD:		
1. Purely financial Incomes not recorded in cost accounts		
2. Notional items of expenses included only in cost accounts		
3. Over-Recovery of overheads in cost accounts		
4. Over-valuation of Opening stock in cost accounts		
5. Under-valuation of Closing stock in cost accounts		
6. Excess charging of Depreciation in cost accounts		
DEDUCT:		
1. Purely financial Charges shown in financial accounts		
2. Under-recovery of overheads in cost accounts		
3. Under -valuation of Opening stock in cost accounts		
4. Over-valuation of Closing stock in cost accounts		
5. Under charging of Depreciation in cost accounts		
6. Appropriations of profit appearing only in financial accounts		
Net Profit as per financial accounts		

Format No. II: (Separate Columns for Additions and Subtractions)

Reconciliation Statement (Format)

Details	PLUS Amount (₹)	MINUS Amount (₹)
Net profit as per Cost accounts		
ADD:		
1. Purely financial Incomes not recorded in cost accounts		
2. Notional items of expenses included only in cost accounts		

3. Over-recovery of overheads in cost accounts		
4. Over-valuation of Opening stock in cost accounts		
5. Under-valuation of Closing stock in cost accounts		
6. Excess charging of Depreciation in cost accounts		
DEDUCT:		
1. Purely financial Charges shown in financial accounts		
2. Under-recovery of overheads in cost accounts		
3. Under -valuation of Opening stock in cost accounts		
4. Over-valuation of Closing stock in cost accounts		
5. Under charging of Depreciation in cost accounts		
6. Appropriations of profit appearing only in financial accounts		
Total (Column-wise)		
Net Profit as per financial accounts (Balancing figure)		
Grand Total		

MEMORANDUM RECONCILIATION ACCOUNT

(i) It is basically presentation of Reconciliation statement in 'T' account form.

(ii) It is not a part of double entry system as all items posted in this account do not have their corresponding debits/credits in the books of accounts.

Format No. III: (Memorandum Reconciliation Account)

Dr **Memorandum Reconciliation Account** **Cr**

Details	Amount (₹)	Details	Amount (₹)
Items to be Deducted: 1. Purely financial Charges shown in financial accounts 2. Under-recovery of overheads in cost accounts 3. Under -valuation of Opening stock in cost accounts 4. Over-valuation of Closing stock in cost accounts 5. Under charging of Depreciation in cost accounts 6. Appropriations of profit appearing only in financial accounts		Profit as per Costing P&L A/c	

Profit as per Financial P&L A/c		Items to be Added: 1. Purely financial Incomes not recorded in cost accounts 2. Notional items of expenses included only in cost accounts 3. Over-recovery of overheads in cost accounts 4. Over-valuation of Opening stock in cost accounts 5. Under-valuation of Closing stock in cost accounts 6. Excess charging of Depreciation in cost accounts	
Total		Total	

Illustration 22.1 : *Net Profit as per costing accounts is ₹ 73,800. The following points of difference were noted:*

(i) Income tax ₹ 52,000;

(ii) Opening stock as per costing books ₹ 20,000 and as per financial books ₹ 18,500;

(iii) Notional rent of the business premises ₹ 36,000;

(iv) Overheads recovered in costing books ₹ 32,500 while Actual Overheads incurred ₹ 35,000;

(v) Dividends on investment received ₹ 25,000;

(vi) Closing stock as per costing books ₹ 24,800 and as per financial books ₹ 28,000.

Prepare a reconciliation Statement explaining the logic behind treatment of each item.

Solution : **Reconciliation Statement (Format I)**

Details	Amount (₹)	Amount (₹)
Net profit as per Costing accounts		73,800
ADD:		
1. Notional Rent of the business premises	36,000	
2. Over-valuation of Opening stock in costing accounts (20000 – 18500))	1,500	
3. Under-valuation of Closing stock in cost accounts (28000 – 24800)	3,200	
4. Dividends on investment received	25,000	65,700
DEDUCT:		
1. Income tax	52,000	
2. Under-Recovery of overheads in cost accounts (35,000 – 32,500)	2,500	(54,500)
Net Profit as per financial accounts		85,000

Format No. II: (Separate Columns for Additions and Subtractions)

Reconciliation Statement (Format II)

Details	PLUS Amount (₹)	MINUS Amount (₹)
Net profit as per Costing accounts	73,800	
ADD:		
1. Notional Rent of the business premises	36,000	
2. Over -valuation of Opening stock in cost accounts (20000 – 18500)	3,200	
3. Under-valuation of Closing stock in cost accounts (28000 – 24800	1,500	
4. Dividends on investment received	25,000	
DEDUCT:		
1. Income tax		52,000
2. Under-recovery of overheads in cost accounts (35,000 – 32,500)		2,500
Total (Column-wise)	1,39,500	54,500
Net Profit as per financial accounts (Balancing figure)		85,000
Grand Total	1,39,500	1,39,500

Format No. III: (Memorandum Reconciliation Account)

Dr Memorandum Reconciliation Account Cr

Details	Amount (₹)	Details	Amount (₹)
Income tax Not charged in cost accounts	52,000	Profit as per Costing P&L A/c	73,800
Under-recovery of overheads in cost accounts (35000 – 32500)	2,500	Notional Rent of the business premises	36,000
		Over-valuation of Opening stock in cost accounts (20000 – 18500)	1,500
		Under-valuation of Closing stock in cost accounts (28000-24800)	3,200
Profit as per Financial P&L A/c (1,39,500 – 54,500)	85,000	Dividends on investment received	25,000
Total	1,39,500	Total	1,39,500

Item-wise Explanation

We are given costing profit of ₹ 73,800. For each point of difference the costing profit is to be adjusted in such a manner that it is at par with that of the financial profit. Item-wise explanation is given as under:

1. Income tax of ₹ 52,000 does not appear in costing Profit and Loss account resulting in higher costing profit. Therefore, deduct ₹ 52,000 from costing profit to make it at par with that of financial profit.
2. Opening stock being a debit side item, higher value of opening stock results in lower profit and vice versa. Opening stock in cost books is valued higher by ₹1, 500. Add back this amount in costing profit.
3. Notional Rent of the business premises of ₹ 36, 000 appears in cost books only resulting in lower costing profit. Add ₹ 36, 000 to the costing profit and loss account so that it is at par with that of the financial profit.
4. There is Under-Recovery of overheads in cost accounts by ₹ 2,500 resulting in higher profit as compared with financial profit. Reduce costing profit by ₹ 2,500 so that it is at par with that of the financial profit.
5. Dividends on investment received being a financial item of income has raised the financial profit by ₹ 25,000. Therefore, Increase the costing profit by ₹ 25,000 so as to make it at par with that of the financial profit.
6. Closing stock being a credit side item, higher value of closing stock results in higher profit and lower value of it leads to lower profit. In costing books the value of the Closing stock is lower by ₹ 3,200 resulting in lower profit. Therefore, Add ₹ 3,200 to the costing profit and loss account so that it is at par with that of the financial profit.

Illustration 22.2 : *The profit of a company appeared at ₹ 64,377 as per financial records for the year ended 31.03.2007. The cost books, however, showed a net profit of ₹ 86,200 for the same period. Both the sets of accounts reveal the following data:*

- *Selling overheads over-recovered in cost accounts: ₹ 850, and factory overheads under-recovered in cost accounts: ₹ 1,560.*
- *Interest on investments not included in cost accounts: ₹ 4,000.*
- *Loss due to obsolescence charged in financial records ₹ 2,850.*
- *Depreciation charged in financial accounts ₹ 5,600 and recovered in cost accounts ₹ 6,250.*
- *Income tax paid: ₹ 20,150.*
- *Bank interest and transfer fees: ₹ 375.*
- *Loss due to depreciation in stock values charged in financial accounts: ₹ 3,375.*
- *Stores adjustment (credited in financial records): ₹ 237.*

Prepare a Reconciliation statement to reconcile the cost and financial records.

Solution : **Reconciliation Statement**

Details		Amount (₹)	Amount R₹)
Net profit as per Cost accounts			86,200
Add:			
1. Selling overheads over-recovered		850	
2. Receipts and gains credited in Financial accounts:			
(a) Interest on investments	4,000		
(b) Bank interest and transfer fees	375		
(c) Stores adjustment (credited)	237		
	4,612	4,612	
3. Depreciation Over-charged in cost accounts		650	6,112
Less:		1,560	
1. Factory overheads under-recovered			
2. Expenses and losses debited in financial books:			
(a) Loss due to obsolescence	2,850		
(b) Loss due to depreciation in stock values	3,375		
(c) Income tax paid	20,150		
	26,375	26,375	(27,935)
Net Profit as per Cost accounts			64,377

Illustration 22.3 : *Following is the summarised Trading, Profit and Loss Account of Mekins Industries (P) Ltd. for the year ended on 31.3.2008:*

Dr ***Cr***

Details	*Amount (₹)*	*Details*	*Amount (₹)*
To Materials	*1,40,625*	*By Sales (12,000 Units)*	*3,36,000*
To Wages	*1,03,125*	*Closing Stock(3,000 Units)*	*63,750*
To Manufacturing Expenses	*84,000*		
To Administrative expenses	*38,750*		
To Net profit	*33,250*		
Total	*3,99,750*		*3,99,750*

The cost records of the company reveal the followings:

(a) Manufacturing overheads have been absorbed at ₹ 7 per unit produced; and

(b) Administration overheads have been absorbed @ ₹ 3 per unit produced.

There is no opening or closing work-in-progress and there is no opening stock of finished goods.

Prepare:

(1) A statement of cost indicating the net profit; and

(2) A statement reconciling the profit as per disclosed by cost accounts and that shown in financial accounts.

Solution :

Statement of Cost
(For the year ended on 31.3.2008)

Details	Amount (₹)
Direct Materials	1,40,625
Direct Wages	1,03,125
PRIME COST	2,43,750
Manufacturing Overheads (@ ₹ 7 per unit produced) i.e. (7 × 15,000) i.e. (12,000 + 3,000)	1,05,000
WORKS COST	3,48,750
Administration overheads (@ ₹ 3 per unit produced) i.e. (3 ×15,000)	45,000
COST OF PRODUCTION	3,93,750
Less: Closing Stock of finished goods [(3,93,750 × 3,000) ÷ (15,000)]	78,750
COST OF GOODS SOLD (12,000 Units)	3,15,000
PROFIT (Balancing figure)	21,000
SALES	3,36,000

Reconciliation Statement

Details	Amount (₹)	Amount (₹)
Net profit as per Cost accounts		21,000
ADD:		
1. Over-recovery of Administrative overheads in cost accounts (45,000 – 38,750)	6,250	
2. Over-recovery of Manufacturing overheads in cost accounts (1,05,000 – 84,000)	21,000	27,250
DEDUCT:		
1. Over-valuation of Closing stock in cost accounts (78,750 – 63,750)		(15,000)
Net Profit as per financial accounts		33,250

Illustration 22.4 : *Following is the summarised Trading, Profit and Loss Account of SV Industries (P) Ltd. for the year ended on 31.3.2008:*

Dr ***Cr***

Details	Amount (₹)	Details	Amount (₹)
Purchases	*1,13,550*	*Sales (12,500 Units @ ₹ 30 per unit)*	*3,75,000*
Less: Closing Stock	*(20,400)*		
	93,150		
Direct Wages	*52,500*	*Discount Received*	*2,100*
Manufacturing Expenses	*60,650*	*Profit on sale of a plot of Land*	*57,000*
Selling Expenses	*35,500*		
Administrative expenses	*38,750*		
Depreciation	*6,500*		
Net profit	*1,47,050*		
Total	*4,34,100*		*4,34,100*

The Profit as per cost accounts was only ₹ 98,900. Reconcile the financial and cost profits using the following information:

(a) Value of closing stock as per Cost accounts was ₹ 22,450.

(b) The Manufacturing Expenses in the cost accounts were taken as 100 per cent of Direct Wages.

(c) Selling and Administration Expenses were charged in the cost accounts @ 10 percent of sales and ₹ 3 per unit respectively.

(d) Depreciation in the cost accounts was ₹ 5,000.

Solution : Alternative No. I

Reconciliation Statement

Details	Amount (₹)	Amount (₹)
Net profit as per Cost accounts		98,900
ADD:		
1. Over-Recovery of Selling overheads in cost accounts (37,500 – 35,500)	2,000	
2. Profit on sale of Land	57,000	
3. Discount received	2,100	61,100

DEDUCT:		
1. Over-valuation of Closing stock in cost accounts (22,450 – 20,400)	2,050	
2. Under recovery of Manufacturing Overheads (60,650 – 52,500)	8,150	
3. Under recovery of Administration Overheads (38,750 – 37,500)	1,250	
4. Depreciation under charged in cost accounts (6,500 – 5,000)	1,500	(12,950)
Net Profit as per financial accounts		1,47,050

Alternative No. II

Reconciliation Statement

Details	Amount (₹)	Amount (₹)
Net profit as per Financial accounts		1,47,050
ADD:		
1. Over-valuation of Closing stock in cost accounts (22,450 – 20,400)	2,050	
2. Under recovery of Manufacturing Overheads (60,650 – 52,500)	8,150	
3. Under recovery of Administration Overheads (38,750 – 37,500)	1,250	
4. Depreciation under charged in cost accounts (6,500 – 5,000)	1,500	12,950
DEDUCT:		
1. Over-recovery of Selling overheads in cost accounts (37,500 – 35,500)	2000	
2. Profit on sale of Land	57,000	
3. Discount received	2,100	(61,100)
Net Profit as per cost accounts		98,900

Illustration 22.5 : *The following information is available from the financial books of a company having a normal production capacity of 60,000 for the year ended 31.3.2005:*

(i) Sales ₹ 10,00,000 (50,000 units)

(ii) There was no opening or closing stock of finished goods.

(iii) Direct material and direct wages cost were ₹ 5, 00,000 and ₹ 2, 50,000 respectively.

(iv) Actual factory expenses were ₹ 1, 50,000 of which 60% are fixed.

(v) *Actual administrative expenses were ₹ 45,000 which is completely fixed.*

(vi) *Actual selling and distribution expenses were ₹ 30,000 of which 40% are fixed.*

(vii) *Interest and dividend received ₹ 15,000.*

You are required to:

(a) *Find out the profit as per financial books for the year ended 31.3.2005.*

(b) *Prepare a statement of cost and profit to ascertain the profit as per cost accounts for the year ended 31.3.2005 assuming that the indirect expenses are absorbed on the basis of normal production capacity.*

(c) *Prepare a reconciliation statement.* **[B.Com (Hons.) DU, 2006]**

Solution :

Financial Profit and Loss Account

(For the year ended 31.3.2005)

Dr **Cr**

Details	Amount (₹)	Details	Amount (₹)
To Direct Materials	5,00,000	By Sales (50,000 Units)	10,00,000
To Direct Wages	2,50,000	By interest and dividends	15,000
To Factory Expenses	1,50,000		
To Administrative expenses	45,000		
To selling and distribution expenses	30,000		
To Net profit	40,000		
Total	10,15,000		10,15,000

Statement of Cost

(For the year ended on 31.3.2005)

Details		Amount (₹)
Direct Materials		5,00,000
Direct Wages		2,50,000
PRIME COST		7,50,000
Manufacturing Overheads		
Fixed: [(90,000) × (50,000/60,000)]	75,000	
Variable: (1,50,000 × 0.4)	60,000	1,35,000
WORKS COST		8,85,000
Add: Administration overheads Fixed: [(45,000) × (50,000 ÷ 60,000)]		37,500
COST OF PRODUCTION		9,22,500
Add: Selling and Distribution overheads		
Fixed: [(12,000) × (50,000 ÷ 60,000)]	10,000	
Variable: (30,000 × 0.6)	18,000	28,000

COST OF Sales (Total Cost of Produced and sold)	9,50,500
PROFIT(Balancing figure)	49,500
SALES	10.00,000

Reconciliation Statement

Details		Amount (₹)	Amount (₹)
Net profit as per Cost accounts			49,500
ADD: Purely Financial Income Item: interest and dividends			15,000
DEDUCT: Under recovery of overheads:			
(i) Manufacturing	15,000		
(ii) Administration	7,500		
(iii) Selling and Distribution	2,000		(24,500)
Net Profit as per financial accounts			40,000

Illustration 22.6 : *The following figures have been extracted from the books of PV Limited for the year ending on 31.3.2008:*

Details		*Amount (₹)*
Direct Materials Consumption		*75,000*
Productive Wages		*45,000*
Production Overheads		*30,000*
Administration Overheads		*25,000*
Selling and distribution Overheads		*28,000*
Bad Debts Written Off		*1,200*
Preliminary Expenses Written Off		*600*
Legal Charges		*150*
Dividend Received		*1,500*
Interest Received on Bank Deposits		*300*
Sales (15,000units)		*2,70,000*
Closing Stock:		
Finished Goods (600 units)	*9,600*	
Work-in-progress	*3,600*	*13,200*

The cost accounts for the same period show that Direct Materials Consumption was ₹ 84,000. Factory overheads are recovered at 20% of Prime Cost. Administration overheads are recovered @ ₹1.50 per unit of production. Selling and distribution overheads are recovered or charged ₹ 2 per unit sold.

Prepare the manufacturing cum Trading and Profit &Loss Account as per financial records and cost sheet. Also reconcile the profit shown by the two records.

Solution : **Financial books Of PV Limited**

Dr Trading and profit and loss account for the year ended........ Cr

Details	Amount (₹)	Details	Amount (₹)
To Direct Materials consumption	75,000	By Sales (15000 Units @ ₹ 18 per unit)	2,70,000
To Productive Wages	45,000	By Closing stock (600 units)	7,200
To Production Overheads	30,000	By Work-in-Progress	3,600
To Gross profit c/d	1,30,800		
	2,80,800		2,80,800
To Administration Overheads	25,000	By Gross profit b/d	1,30,800
To Selling and distribution Overheads	28,000	By Dividend Received	1,500
To Bad Debts Written Off	1,200	By Interest Received on Bank Deposits	300
To Preliminary Expenses Written Off	600		
To Legal Charges	150		
To Net Profit	77,650		
Total	1,32,600		1,32,600

Cost Sheet

Details	Amount (₹)
Direct Materials	84,000
Productive Wages	45,000
Prime Cost	1,29,000
Production Overheads @ 20% of Prime Cost [1,29,000 × 0.2]	25,800
Works cost (Gross)	1,54,800
Less: Work-in-Progress (closing)	3,600
Works cost (Net)	1,51,200
Administration Overheads @ ₹ 1.50 per unit of production [15,600 × 1.5]	23,400
Cost of Production (15,600 units)	1,74,600
Less: Closing stock of Finished Goods [(600/15600) × 1,74,600]	6,715
Cost of Goods sold (15,000 Units)	1,67,885
Selling and distribution Overheads @ ₹ 2 per unit [15,000 × 2]	30,000
Cost of sales	1,97,885

Profit	72,115
Sales	2,70,000

Reconciliation Statement

Details		Amount (₹)	Amount (₹)
Profit as per Cost Accounts			72,115
Less:			
1. Items not charged in Cost Accounts:-			
(a) Preliminary Expenses written Off	600		
(b) Bad Debts Written Off	1,200		
(c) Legal Charges	150	1,950	
2. Under-absorption of Production Overheads (30,000 -25,800)		4,200	
3. Under-absorption of Administration Overheads (25,000-23,400)		1,600	(7,750)
Add:			
1. Over-recovery of Selling and distribution overheads in cost accounts (30,000 – 28,000)		2,000	
2. Under-valuation of Closing stock in cost accounts (7,200 - 6,715)		485	
3. Over recovery of Material cost (84,000-75,000)		9,000	
4. Non-operating Incomes:			
Dividend Received	1,500		
Interest Received on Bank Deposits	300	1,800	13,285
Profit as per Financial Accounts			77,650

Illustration 22.7 : *A manufacturing company disclosed a net loss of ₹ 4, 05,000 as per their cost accounts for the year ended March 31, 2003. The financial accounts, however, disclosed a net loss of ₹ 6, 30,000 for the same period. The following information was revealed as a result of scrutiny of the figures of both sets of accounts:*

Details	*Amount (₹)*
Factory Overheads under-absorbed	*85,000*
Administration Overheads over-absorbed	*75,000*
Depreciation charged in financial accounts	*4,20,000*
Depreciation charged in cost accounts	*3,40,000*
Interest on Investments not included in cost accounts	*1,00,000*
Income Tax provided	*60,000*

Interest on Loan funds in financial accounts	*2,67,000*
Transfer fees (Credit in financial books)	*30,000*
Stores Adjustment(Credit in financial books)	*16,000*
Dividend Received	*46,000*

Prepare a Memorandum Reconciliation Account.

Solution :

Dr **Memorandum Reconciliation Account** **Cr**

Details	Amount (₹)	Details	Amount (₹)
To Net loss as per Cost Accounts	4, 05,000	By Administration Overheads over-absorbed	75,000
To Factory Overheads under-absorbed	85,000	By Interest on investments	1,00,000
To Depreciation under-absorbed (4,20,000-3,40,000)	80,000	By Transfer fees	30,000
To Income Tax	60,000	By Stores Adjustment	16,000
To Interest on Loan funds	2,67,000	By Dividend Received	46,000
		By Net loss as per financial Accounts	6, 30,000
Total	8,97,000		8,97,000

Illustration 22.8 : *The following figures have been extracted from the Financial Accounts of S. V. Limited, for the year ending on March 31, 2009 :*

Details	*Amount (₹)*	*Details*	*Amount (₹)*
Direct Material Consumed	*60,000*	*Discount on issue of debentures Written off*	*500*
Direct Wages	*36,000*	*Interest Received*	*260*
Factory Overhead	*19,200*	*Sales (3,000 Units)*	*1,80,000*
Administrative Overhead	*9,000*	*Dividend received*	*1,200*
Selling & Distribution Overheads	*12,500*	*Closing Stock:* *Finished Goods (100Units)*	*3,840*
		Work in Progress	*2,900*
Bad debts written Off	*1,000*		

The cost accounts for the same period reveal that direct material consumption was ₹ 68,000. Factory overhead is recovered at 25% on prime cost. Administrative overheads are recovered @ ₹3 per unit of production; Selling and distribution overheads are recovered @₹4 per unit sold.

Prepare Profit and Loss Account both as per financial books and as per costing books. Also, reconcile the profit as per two books of accounts at the end of the year.

Solution : Format No.1 : Plus-Minus Items (1) Costing Profit as the Starting Point, (2) Financial Profit as the Starting Point.

This is the most convenient form because each item can be taken up one by one in the order the information is given. In case, the starting point is 'Loss' figure, and then it is entered in the 'Minus' column. The excess of the total of 'Plus' column over that of 'Minus' column implies profit at the end and the excess of the total of 'Minus' column over that of 'Plus' column implies loss at the end.

Profit and Loss Account for the year ending on March 31, 2009

Dr Cr

Details	Amount (₹)	Details	Amount (₹)
Direct Material Consumed	60,000	Sales (3000 Units)	1,80,000
Direct Wages	36,000	Closing Stock: Finished Goods (100Units)	3,840
		Work in Progress	2,900
Factory Overhead	19,200	Dividend received	1,200
Administrative Overhead	9,000	Interest Received	260
Selling & Distribution Overheads	12,500		
Discount on issue of debentures Written off	500		
Bad debts written off	1,000		
Profit	50,000		
Total	1,88,200	Total	1,88,200

Statement of Cost and Profit for the year ending on March 31, 2009

Details	Amount (₹)
Direct Materials	68,000
Direct Wages	36,000
Prime Cost	1,04,000
Factory Overhead (25% of prime cost i.e. 0.25×1,04,000)	26,000
Gross Factory Cost	1,30,000
Less: Closing stock of Work-in-Progress	2,900
Net Factory Cost	1,27,100

Administrative Overhead (@ ₹3 per unit produced):	9,300
Produced= Sale+ Closing Stock i.e. 3,000+100=3,100 units	
Cost of Production of 3,100 Units	1,36,400
Less: Closing Stock of Finished Goods valued at cost = (1,36,400 ÷ 3,100=44/-) i.e. (100@44)	4,400
Cost of Goods Sold (3000 Units)	1,32,000
Selling and Distribution Overhead (3000@₹4)	12,000
Cost of Sales	1,44,000
Profit (Balancing Figure)	36,000
Sales	1,80,000

(1) Cost Books' Profits as the Starting Point: Statement of Reconciliation of Profits as at the year ending on March 31, 2009

Details	Amount (₹) : (Plus)	Amount (₹) : (Minus)
Profit as per Costing Books	36,000	
Add: Materials over-recovered in Cost Books (68,000 – 60,000)	8,000	
Add: Factory overheads over- recovered (26,000 –19,200)	6,800	
Add: Administrative overheads over-recovered (9,300 – 9,000)	300	
Less: Selling &Distribution overheads under- recovered (12,000 –12,500)		500
Less: Discount on issue of debentures Written off in Financial Books only		500
Add: Bad debts written off in Financial Books only		1,000
Less: Over valuation of Closing Stock of Finished Goods in Cost Books (4,400 – 3,840)		560
Add: Income Items excluded from costing Books:		
Dividends Received	1,200	
Interest Received	260	
Total	52,560	2,560
Total Profit as per Financial Books	50,000	

(2) Financial Books' Profits as the Starting Point: Statement of Reconciliation of Profits as at the year ending on March 31, 2009

Details	Amount (₹) : (Plus)	Amount (₹) : (Minus)
Profit as per Financial Books	50,000	
Less: Materials over-recovered in Cost Books (60,000 – 68,000)		8,000
Less: Factory overheads over- recovered (19,200 – 26,000)		6,800
Less: Administrative overheads over-recovered (9,000 – 9,300)		300
Add: Selling &Distribution overheads under- recovered (12,000 – 12,500)	500	
Add: Over valuation of Closing Stock of Finished Goods in Cost Books (4,400 – 3,840)	560	
Add: Bad debts written off in Financial Books only	1,000	
Add:: Discount on issue of debentures Written off in Financial Books only	500	
Less: Income Items excluded from costing Books:		
Dividends received		1,200
Interest Received		260
Total	52,560	16,560
Profit as per Cost Books	36,000	

Format No. 2 : Additions and Subtractions Format: Under this format first all items requiring addition are added to the given profit figure and then all items requiting subtraction are subtracted from the given profit figure.

Reconciliation statement as at March 31, 2009

Details			Amount (₹)
Profit as per Financial Books			50,000
Less: Materials over-recovered in Cost Books (60,000 – 68,000)		8,000	
Factory overheads over- recovered (19,200 – 26,000)		6,800	
Administrative overheads over-recovered (9,000 – 9,300)		300	
Income Items excluded from costing Books:			
Dividends received	1,200		
Interest Received	2,60		
		1,460	(16,560)
Add: Selling &Distribution overheads under- recovered (12,000 – 12,500)		500	
Over valuation of Closing Stock of Finished Goods in Cost Books (4,400 – 3,840)		560	

Discount on issue of debentures Written off in Financial Books only	500	
Bad debts written off in Financial Books only	1,000	2,560
Profit as per Cost Books		36,000

LET US RECAPITULATE

1. The need for reconciliation of profits as per Cost books and financial books arises because of two separate sets of books being kept under Non-Integral System with different bases of stock valuation, under/over-recovery of overhead and disregarding some items of expenses in cost or financial accounts, by the same organization.
2. The functioning of computers reduces the necessity for reconciliation of cost and financial accounts.
3. The main reason for divergence in profits shown by financial and cost accounts is the presence of certain items in financial books only and not in cost books. Similarly, there may be some items which appear in cost books only but do not find any place in financial books.
4. Memorandum Reconciliation Account is basically presentation of Reconciliation statement in 'T' account form.
5. Memorandum Reconciliation Account is not a part of double entry system as all items posted in this account do not have their corresponding debits/credits in the books of accounts.
6. For each point of difference the costing profit is to be adjusted in such a manner that it is at par with that of the financial profit.

SOLVED PROBLEMS

Problem 1. *Net Profit as per financial accounts is ₹ 85,000. The following points of difference were noted:*

(a) Income tax: ₹ 52,000;

(b) Opening stock as per financial books ₹ 18,500 and as per costing books ₹ 20,000;

(c) Notional rent of the business premises: ₹ 36,000;

(d) Actual Overheads incurred ₹ 35,000 while recovered in costing books ₹ 32,500;

(e) Dividends on investment received ₹ 25,000;

(f) Closing stock as per financial books ₹ 28,000 and as per costing books ₹ 24,800.

Prepare a reconciliation Statement explaining the logic behind treatment of each item.

Solution : **Reconciliation Statement (Format)**

Details	Amount (₹)	Amount (₹)
Net profit as per financial accounts		85,000
ADD:		
1. Income tax	52,000	
2. Under-recovery of overheads in cost accounts (35,000-32,500)	2,500	54,500
DEDUCT:		
1. Notional Rent of the business premises	36,000	
2. Over-valuation of Closing stock in financial accounts (28,000-24,800)	3,200	
3. Under-valuation of Opening stock in financial accounts (20,000 – 18,500)	1,500	
4. Dividends on investment received	25,000	(65,700)
Net Profit as per Costing accounts (Balancing figure)		73,800

Format No. II : (Separate Columns for Additions and Subtractions)

Reconciliation Statement (Format)

Details	PLUS Amount (₹)	MINUS Amount (₹)
Net profit as per financial accounts	85,000	
ADD:		
1. Income tax	52,000	
2. Under-recovery of overheads in cost accounts (35,000-32,500)	2,500	
DEDUCT:		
1. Notional Rent of the business premises		36,000
2. Over-valuation of Closing stock in cost accounts (28,000-24,800)		3,200
3. Under-valuation of Opening stock in financial accounts (20,000 – 18,500)		1,500
4. Dividends on investment received		25,000
Total (Column-wise)	1,39,500	65,700
Net Profit as per costing accounts (Balancing figure)		73,800
Grand Total	1,39,500	1,39,500

Format No. III : (Memorandum Reconciliation Account)

Details	Amount (₹)	Details	Amount (₹)
Notional rent of the business premises	36,000	Profit as per Financial P&L A/c	85,000
Over-valuation of Closing stock in cost accounts (28,000-24,800)	3,200	Income tax	52,000
Under-valuation of Opening stock in financial accounts (20,000 – 18,500)	1,500	Under-recovery of overheads in cost accounts (35,000-32,500)	2,500
Dividends on investment received	25,000		
Profit as per Costing P&L A/c	73,800		
Total	1,39,500	Total	1,39,500

Note:

Item-wise Explanation: We are given financial profit of ₹ 85,000. For each point of difference the financial profit is to be adjusted in such a manner that it is at par with that of the costing profit. Item-wise explanation is asunder:

1. Income tax of ₹ 52,000 does not appear in costing Profit and Loss account and it appears only in financial profit and Loss account. As a result financial profit has come down by ₹ 52,000. Therefore, add ₹ 52,000 to financial profit to make it at par with that of the costing profit.
2. Opening stock being a debit side item, lower value of opening stock results in higher profit and vice versa. Opening stock in financial books is valued lower by ₹1,500 resulting in higher financial profit. So, deduct this amount in financial profit.
3. Notional Rent of the business premises of ₹ 36,000 appears in cost books only resulting in Lower costing profit. There is no such charging of expense in financial profit. Thus, deduct ₹ 36,000 in the financial profit and loss account so that it is at par with that of the costing profit.
4. In financial books, overheads are recorded at a higher value of ₹ 2,500 i.e. (35,000-32,500).It results in lower profit in financial books. Therefore add ₹ 25,000 to financial profit to make it at par with that of the costing profit.
5. Dividends on investment received being a financial item of income has raised the financial profit by ₹ 25,000 while costing profit remains unaffected. Thus, deduct ₹ 25,000 in the financial profit and loss account so that it is at par with that of the costing profit.

6. Closing stock being a credit side item, higher value of closing stock results in higher profit and lower value of it leads to lower profit. In financial books the value of the Closing stock is higher by ₹ 3,200 resulting in higher profit. Therefore, deduct ₹ 3,200 in the financial profit and loss account so that it is at par with that of the costing profit.

Problem 2. *State with reasons, in each of the following circumstances, whether costing profit will be higher or lower than the financial profit:*

Details	*Cost Valuatio (₹)*	*Financial Valuation (₹)*
Raw Materials (Opening)	*50,000*	*60,000*
Work-in-Progress (Closing)	*60,000*	*50,000*
Finished Stock (Closing)	*50,000*	*60,000*
Finished Stock (Opening)	*60,000*	*50,000*

[B.Com (Hons.) DU, 2007]

Solution :

1. Costing Profit would be higher because value of opening Stock of raw materials is lower in Cost accounts as compared to financial Accounts.
2. Costing Profit would be higher because value of Work-in-Progress (Closing) is higher in Cost accounts as compared to financial Accounts.
3. Costing Profit would be lower because value of Finished Stock (Closing) is lower in Cost accounts as compared to financial Accounts.
4. Costing Profit would be lower because value of opening Stock of Finished Stock is higher in Cost accounts as compared to financial Accounts.

Problem 3. *The Manufacturing, Trading and Profit and Loss, and Profit and Loss Appropriation Accounts of UV Ltd. for the year ended March 31, 2004 are as under:*

Debit Side		*Amount (₹)*	*Credit Side*	*Amount (₹)*
To Raw Materials:			*By Trading A/c (Cost of Goods Manufactured)*	*2,28,000*
Opening stock	*19,880*			
Purchases	*94,780*			
Available for Consumption	*1,14,660*			
Less: Closing Stock	*20,860*			
Raw Materials Consumed		*93,800*		

To Wages	*83,200*		
To Factory Overhead:			
Indirect Wages 10,000			
Rent and Rates 4,000			
Power and fuel 8,500			
Depreciation 15,500			
Other Expenses 14,460			
Total Factory-On- Cost	*52,460*		
Gross Works Cost	*2,29,460*		
Add: Opening Work-in-Progress	*13,620*		
Less: Closing Work-in-Progress	*(15,080)*		
Net Works Cost 2,28,000			
Total	*228000*	*Total*	*2,28,000*
To Finished Goods:		*By Sales*	*3,40,000*
Opening Stock 14560			
Add: Manufactured 228000			
Less: Closing Stock (16100)	*2,26,460*		
To Gross Profit c/d	*1,13540*		
Total	*3,40,000*	*Total*	*3,40,000*
To Administration Overhead:		*By Gross Profit c/d*	*1,13,540*
Office Salaries 21,700			
Office Expenses 5,660	*27,360*		
To Selling and Distribution Overhead:	*16,000*	*By Dividends Received*	*1,460*
Salesmen's Salaries 10,000			
Selling Expenses 2,000			
Distribution Expenses 4,000			
To Loss on Sale of Machinery	*1,100*		
To Fines	*440*		
To Net Profit for the year	*70,100*		
Total	*1,15,000*	*Total*	*1,15,000*
To Income-Tax	*14,000*	*By Balance b/d*	*42,300*
To General Reserve	*7,000*	*By Net Profit for the year*	*70,100*
To Dividend	*17,000*		
To Goodwill written off	*4,100*		
To Balance c/d	*70,300*		
Total	*1,12,400*	*Total*	*1,12,400*

The cost accounts revealed a profit of ₹ 97,305. In preparing this figure stocks have been valued in cost accounts as follows:

Item	*Opening stock*	*Closing stock*
Raw Materials	*19,740*	*20,930*
Work-in-Progress	*13,825*	*14,840*

Administration Overhead has been ignored in cost accounts. Prepare a reconciliation statement.

Solution : **Reconciliation Statement**

Details	**Amount (₹)**	**Amount (₹)**
Profit as per Cost Accounts		97,305
Less:		
1. Items not charged in Cost Accounts:-		
(a) Administration Overhead	27,360	
(b) Loss on sale of Machinery	1,100	
(c) Fines	440	
2. Under-valuation of Opening Stock of Raw Materials	140	
3. Over-valuation of Closing Stock of Raw Materials	70	(29,110)
Add:		
1. Over-valuation of Opening Stock of Work-in-Progress	205	
2. Under-valuation of Closing Stock of Work-in-Progress	240	
3. Items not credited in cost accounts:		
Dividends Received	1,460	1,905
Profit as per Financial Accounts		70,100

Problem 4. *The Profit as per cost accounts is ₹ 6,00,000. The following information is ascertained on comparison of cost and financial accounts:*

	Details	***Cost Accounts Amount (₹)***	***Financial accounts Amount (₹)***
(a)	*Opening Stock:*		
	Materials	*60,000*	*90,000*
	Finished Goods	*1,10,000*	*95,000*
(b)	*Closing Stock:*		
	Materials	*70,000*	*80,000*
	Finished Goods	*1,20,000*	*1,05,000*

(c) *Interest charged but not paid ₹ 50,000;*

(d) *Dividends received from U T I ₹ 5,000;*

(e) *Indirect expenses charged to Financial Accounts ₹ 4,00,000 but ₹ 3,75,000 absorbed in cost accounts.*

Find out the profit as per financial Accounts by preparing a Reconciliation statement.

Solution : **Reconciliation Statement as on.........**

Details		Amount (₹)
Profit as per Cost Accounts		6,00,000
Add:		
Over-valuation of Opening Stock Finished goods in Cost books (1,10,000 – 95,000)	15,000	
Dividends from UTI ignored in cost Books	5,000	
Under-valuation of Closing Stock Materials in Cost books (80,000 – 70,000)	10,000	30,000
Less:		
Under-valuation of Opening Stock of Materials in cost books (90,000 – 60,000)	30,000	
Under-absorption of Indirect Expenses (4,00,000 – 3,75,000)	25,000	
Interest charged in financial books but not in cost books	50,000	
Over-valuation of Closing Stock of Finished goods in cost books (1,20,000 – 1,05,000)	15,000	1,20,000
Profit as per Financial Accounts		5,10,000

Problem 5. *The following transactions have been extracted from the financial records of PV enterprises:*

Details		*Amount (₹)*	*Unit*
Sales		*5,00,000*	*10,000*
Materials		*2,00,000*	
Wages		*1,00,000*	
Production Overheads		*90,000*	
Office and administration Overheads		*52,000*	
Selling and distribution Overheads		*36,000*	
Closing stock:			
1. Finished Goods		*27,060*	*615*
2. Work-in-Progress:			
(a) Materials	*6,000*		
(b) Wages	*4,000*		
(c) Production Overheads	*4,000*	*14,000*	
Goodwill written Off		*30,000*	
Interest on Capital		*4,000*	

In costing Books Factory Overheads are charged at 100% on wages. Administration Overheads @ 10% of factory cost and selling and distribution overheads @ ₹ 4 per unit sold. Prepare a Statement reconciling the Profit as per cost and financial accounts.

Solution : **Financial books Of PV Enterprises**

Dr Trading and profit and loss account for the year ended........ Cr

Details	Amount (₹)	Details	Amount (₹)
To Materials	2,00,000	By Sales (10,000 Units @ ₹ 50 per unit)	5,00,000
To Wages	1,00,000	By Closing stock (615 units)	27,060
To Production Overheads	90,000	By Work-in-Progress	14,000
To Gross profit c/d	1,51,060		
	5,41,060		5,41,060
To Office and administration Overheads	52,000	By Gross profit b/d	1,51,060
To Selling and distribution Overheads	36,000		
To Goodwill written Off	30,000		
To Interest on Capital	4,000		
To Net Profit	29,060		
Total	1,51,060		1,51,060

Cost Sheet

Details	Amount (₹)
Direct Materials	2,00,000
Direct Wages	1,00,000
Prime Cost	3,00,000
Production Overheads @ 100% of Direct Wages	1,00,000
Works cost (Gross)	4,00,000
Less: Work-in-Progress (closing)	14,000
Works cost (Net)	3,86,000
Office and administration Overheads @ 10% of Works cost (Net)	38,600
Cost of Production	4,24,600
Less: Closing stock of Finished Goods [(615/10615) *4,24,600]	24,600
Cost of Goods sold (10,000 Units)	4,00,000
Selling and distribution Overheads @ ₹ 4 per unit	40,000
Cost of sales	440,000
Profit	60,000
Sales	5,00,000

Reconciliation Statement

Details		Amount (₹)	Amount (₹)
Profit as per Cost Accounts			60,000
Less:			
1. Items not charged in Cost Accounts:-			
(a) Goodwill written Off	30,000		
(b) Interest on Capital	4,000	34,000	
2. Under recovery of Administration Overheads (52,000 – 38,600)		13,400	(47,400)
ADD:			
1. Over-recovery of Manufacturing overheads in cost accounts (1,00,000 – 90,000)		10,000	
2. Over-recovery of Selling and distribution overheads in cost accounts (40,000 – 36,000)		4,000	
3. Under-valuation of Closing stock in cost accounts (27,060 -24,000)		3,060	17,060
Profit as per Financial Accounts			29,060

Problem 6. *During the year the profits of AV Limited were estimated from the costing system to be ₹ 2,30,630 whereas the final accounts prepared by the accountants disclose a profit of ₹ 1,71,240. Given the following information, you are required to prepare a reconciliation statement showing clearly the reasons for the difference:*

Profit and Loss Account

Dr ***(For the Year ended on 31.3.2008)*** ***Cr***

Details		*Amount* (₹)	*Details*	*Amount* (₹)
To Opening Stock	*24,71,790*	*25,42,120*	*By Sales*	*34,65,000*
Add Purchases	*8,21,540*			
	32,93,330			
Less Closing Stock	*7,51,210*			
To Direct Wages		*2,31,330*		
To Production Overheads		*2,08,260*		
To Gross profit c/d		*4,83,290*		
		34,65,000		*34,65,000*
To Administration Expenses		*98,450*	*By Gross profit b/d*	*4,83,290*
To Selling Expenses		*2,21,760*	*By Sundry Incomes*	*8,160*
To Net Profit		*1,71,240*		
Total		*4,91,450*		*4,91,450*

1. *Stock Ledger Closing Balance is of ₹7,81,970;*
2. *Credit balance in Wages Control Account is ₹ 2,48,670;*
3. *Credit balance in Production Overheads Control Account is ₹ 1,97,140;*
4. *Administration Expenses are charged to sales at 3% of selling price in cost accounts;*
5. *Selling price includes 5% (on sales) provision for selling expenses;*
6. *Sundry Incomes are not considered in Cost Accounts.*

Solution : **Reconciliation Statement**

Details	Amount (₹)	Amount (₹)
Profit as per Cost Accounts		2,30,630
Less:		
1. Difference in Stock valuation	30,760	
2. Under recovery of Production Overheads (2,08,260 – 1,97,140)	11,120	
3. Under-recovery of Selling Overheads (2,21,760 – 1,73,250)	48,510	(90,390)
ADD:		
1. Over-Charged in Cost Accounts:		
(i) Direct Wages	17,340	
(ii) Administration Overheads	5,500	
2. Sundry Incomes not taken in costing records	8,160	31,000
Profit as per Financial Accounts		1,71,240

Problem 7. *Prepare a Reconciliation Account from the following details:*

Profit as per cost accounts were ₹ 60,000, while the profits as per financial accounts were of ₹ 61,400. The values pf opening and closing stock as shown in cost accounts and financial accounts were as under:

Details	*Financial Accounts (₹)*	*Cost Accounts (₹)*
Raw Materials:		
Opening	*52,300*	*51,200*
Closing	*40,000*	*39,400*
W.I.P:		*17,500*
Opening	*16,000*	*19,600*
Closing	*20,000*	

Solution :

Dr **Reconciliation Account** **Cr**

Details	Amount (₹)	Details	Amount (₹)
To undervaluation of Opening Stock of Raw Materials	1,100	By Costing Profit	60,000
To Financial Profit	61,400	By undervaluation of Closing Stock of Raw Materials	600
		By undervaluation of Closing Stock of Work-in-Progress	400
		By Overvaluation of Opening Stock of Work-in-Progress	1,500
Total	62,500	Total	62,500

Problem 8. *Following information is available in respect of AV Enterprises for the year ended on 31.3.2008:*

Details	*Financial Accounts (₹)*	*Cost Accounts (₹)*
Opening stock:		
Raw Material	*32,000*	*27,000*
Work-in-Progress	*37,000*	*34,500*
Finished goods	*27,000*	*24,500*
Closing stock:		
Raw Material	*23,000*	*24,500*
Work-in-Progress	*18,000*	*21,500*
Finished goods	*32,500*	*34,000*
Purchases	*2,10,000*	
Direct Wages	*1,05,000*	
Indirect Wages	*17,000*	
Factory Expenses	*90000*	*1,10,000 (Absorbrd)*
Sales	*560000*	
Administration Expenses	*16000*	*13500 (Absorbrd)*
Selling Expenses	*21,000*	*25,000 (Absorbrd)*
Financial Expenses	*11,000*	
Interest and dividends received	*8,000*	
Transfer to Reserve	*25,000*	
Dividends	*50,000*	

Compute Profit in Financial Accounts as well as in Cost Accounts and prepare a Reconciliation statement. Previous year's profit was ₹ 40000.

Solution :

Dr Trading and profit and loss account for the year ended 31.3.2008 Cr

Details	Amount (₹)	Details	Amount (₹)
To Opening stock:		By Closing stock :	
Raw Material	32,000	Raw Material	23,000
Work-in-Progress	37,000	Work-in-Progress	18,000
Finished goods	27,000	Finished goods	32,500
To Purchases	2,10,000	By Sales	5,60,000
To Wages	1,05,000		
To Production Overheads	90,000		
To Gross profit c/d	1,32,500		
	6,33,500		6,33,500
To Indirect Wages	17,000	By Gross profit b/d	1,32,500
To Office and administration Overheads	16,000	By Interest and dividends received	8,000
To Selling and distribution Overheads	21,000		
To Financial Expenses	11,000		
To Net Profit	75,500		
	1,40,500		1,40,500
To Dividends	50,000	By Profit of Last Year	40,000
To General Reserve	25,000	By current Year Profit	75,500
To Profit after Appropriation	40,500		
	1,15,500		1,15,500

Cost Sheet

Details	Amount (₹)
Direct Materials (27,000 +2,10,000 – 24,500)	2,12,500
Direct Wages	1,05,000
Prime Cost	3,17,500
Production Overheads	1,10,000
Indirect Wages	17,000
Works cost (Gross)	4,44,500
Add: Work-in-Progress (Opening)	34,500
Less: Work-in-Progress (closing)	(21,500)

Works cost (Net)	4,57,500
Office and administration Overheads	13,500
Cost of Production	4,71,000
Add: Opening stock of Finished Goods	24,500
Cost of goods available for sale	4,95,500
Less: Closing stock of Finished Goods	(34,000)
Cost of Goods sold	4,61,500
Selling and distribution Overheads	25,000
Cost of sales	4,86,500
Profit	73,500
Sales	5,60,000

Reconciliation Statement

Details	Amount (₹)	Amount (₹)
Profit as per Cost Accounts		73,500
Less:		
1. Financial Expenses not shown in costing books	11,000	
2. Under recovery of Office and administration Overheads (16,000 – 13,500)	2,500	
3. Under-valuation of Opening stock in cost accounts (96,000 – 86,000)	10000	
4. Over-valuation of Closing stock in cost accounts (80,000 – 73,500)	6,500	(30,000)
ADD:		
1. Over-recovery of Manufacturing overheads in cost accounts (110000 – 90000)	20,000	
2. Over-recovery of Selling and distribution overheads in cost accounts (25,000 – 21,000)	3,500	
3. Interest and dividends received	8,000	31,500
Profit as per Financial Accounts (Before Appropriation)		75,500

Problem 9. *The following information is available from the books of a company having a normal production capacity of 60,000 units for the year ended on 31.3.2005:*

(i) Sales ₹ 10,00,000 (50,000 units)

(ii) There was no opening or closing stock of finished goods.

(iii) Direct material and direct wages cost were ₹ 5, 00,000 and ₹ 2, 50,000 respectively.

(iv) Actual factory expenses were ₹ 1, 50,000 which 60% are fixed.

(v) Actual Administrative expenses were ₹ 45,000 which is completely fixed.

(vi) Actual selling and distribution expenses were ₹ 30,000 of which 40% are fixed.

(vii) Interest and dividend received ₹ 15,000.

You are required to:

(a) Find out the profit as per financial books for the year ended 31.3.2005.

(b) Prepare a statement of cost and profit to ascertain the profit as per cost accounts for the year ended 31.3.2005 assuming that the indirect expenses are absorbed on the basis of normal production capacity.

(c) Prepare a reconciliation statement.

Solution :

Dr Financial Profit and loss account for the year ended 31.3.2005 Cr

Details	Amount (₹)	Details	Amount (₹)
To Direct material	5,00,000	By Sales	10,00,000
To Direct Wages	2,50,000	By Interest and dividends received	15,000
To Factory expenses	1,50,000		
To Administration expenses	45,000		
To Selling and distribution expenses	30,000		
To Net Profit	40,000		
	10,15,000		10,15,000

Cost Sheet

Details		Amount (₹)
Direct Materials		5,00,000
Direct Wages		2,50,000
Prime Cost		7,50,000
Factory Overheads:		1,35,000
Fixed: [(90,000)×(50,000÷60,000)]	75,000	
Variable: (1,50,000 – 90,000)	60,000	
Works cost		8,85,000
Administration Overheads: [(45,000) × (50,000÷60,000)]		37,500
Cost of Production		9,22,500

Selling and distribution Overheads:		
Fixed: [(12,000) × (50,000÷60,000)]	10,000	
Variable: (30,000 – 12,000)	18,000	28,000
Cost of sales		9,50,500
Profit		49,500
Sales		10,00,000

Reconciliation Statement

Details	Amount (₹)	Amount (₹)
Profit as per Cost Accounts		49,500
Less: Under recovery of Overheads:		
1. Factory Overheads (1,50,000 – 1,35,000)	15,000	
2. Administration Overheads (45,000 – 37,500)	7,500	
3. Selling and distribution Overheads (30,000 – 28,000)	2,000	(24,500)
ADD: Interest and dividends received	15,000	15,000
Profit as per Financial Accounts		40,000

Problem 10. *The following figures are available from financial accounts for the year ended 31st March, 2008:*

Details	*Amount (₹)*	*Details*	*Amount (₹)*
Direct Material consumption	*2,50,000*	*Legal charges*	*5,000*
Direct Wages	*1,50,000*	*Dividend Received*	*50,000*
Factory Overheads	*3,80,000*	*Interest on deposits Received*	*10,000*
Administration overheads	*2,50,000*	*Sales 25,000 units*	*12,50,000*
Selling and Distribution Overheads	*4,80,000*	*Closing stock:*	
		Finished Goods Stock (8,000 units) 2,40,000	
		Work-in-Progress 77,500	*3,17,500*
Bad Debts	*20,000*		
Preliminary Expenses (written Off)	*10,000*		

The cost accounts reveal:

Direct Material consumption ₹ 2,80,000

Factory Overheads recovered @ 60% on Prime cost

Administration overheads @₹ 12 per unit of Production

Selling and Distribution Overheads @₹ 20 per unit sold

Required: Prepare:

(1) Costing Profit and Loss Account;

(2) Financial Profit and Loss Account;

(3) Reconciliation statement to reconcile the profits disclosed by Costing Profit and Loss Account and Financial Profit and Loss Account.

Solution :

Dr **Financial Profit and loss account for the year ended 31.3.2005** Cr

Details	Amount (₹)	Details	Amount (₹)
To Direct Material Consumed	2,50,000	By Sales	12,50,000
To Direct Wages	1,50,000	By Dividends received	50,000
To Factory Overheads	3,80,000	By Interest on Deposit	10,000
To Administration Expenses	2,50,000	By Closing Stock:	
		Finished goods	2,40,00
		Work-in-Progress	77,500
To Selling and Distribution Expenses	4,80,000		
To Bad Debts	20,000		
To Preliminary Expenses written Off	10,000		
To Legal Charges	5,000		
To Net Profit	82,500		
	16,27,500		16,27,500

Cost Sheet (33,000 Units)

Details	Amount (₹)
Direct Materials	2,80,000
Direct Wages	1,50,000
Prime Cost	4,30,000
Factory Overheads@ 60% on Prime cost (4,30,000 × 0.6)	2,58,000
Works cost(Gross)	6,88,000
Less: Work-in-Progress	(77,500)
Works cost(Net)	6,10,500
Administration Overheads@ ₹ 12 per unit produced (33,000) × 12)	3,96,000
Cost of Goods Produced@ 30.5	10,06,500
Less: Closing Stock	(2,44,000)
Cost of Goods sold	7,62,500
Selling and distribution Overheads: (25,000) × 20)	5,00,000
Cost of sales	12,62,500
Loss	(12,500)
Sales	12,50,000

Reconciliation Statement

Details	Amount (₹)	Amount (₹)
Loss as per Cost Accounts		(12,500)
Less: Under recovery of Factory Overheads:	1,22,000	
(3,80,000 – 2,58,000)	20,000	
Bad Debts NOT included in Cost Accounts	10,000	(1,61,000)
Preliminary Expenses NOT included in Cost Accounts	5,000	
Legal charges NOT included in Cost Accounts	4,000	
Over Valuation of Closing Stock		
ADD: Over-charging of Materials in Cost Accounts	30,000	
Over- recovery of Administration Overheads:		
(3,96,000 – 2,50,000)	1,46,000	
Over- recovery of Selling and Distribution Overheads:		
(5,00,000 – 4,80,000)	20,000	
Dividend and Interest NOT included in Cost Accounts	60,000	2,56,000
Profit as per Financial Accounts		82,500

Problem 11. *Following are the figures extracted from the cost ledger of a manufacturing unit of PV Limited:*

Stores:

(a) Opening balance ₹ 15,000;

(b) Purchases ₹ 80,000;

(c) Transfer from work-in-progress ₹ 40,000;

(d) Issued to work-in-progress ₹ 80,000;

(e) Issued repairs and maintenance ₹ 10,000;

(f) Sold some quantity as a special case at cost ₹ 5,000 and

(g) Shortages in the year ₹ 3,000.

Work-in-progress:

(a) Opening balance ₹ 30,000;

(b) Direct Labour cost charged ₹ 30,000;

(c) Overhead cost charged ₹ 1,20,000;

(d) Closing balance ₹ 20,000.

Finished Product: Entire output is sold at 12.5% profit on actual cost from work-in-process.

Others: Wages of the period ₹ 40,000; overheads ₹ 1,25,000.

Find out profit or loss as per financial account and cost accounts and reconcile the same.

Solution : Working Notes:

(I) Stores Account

Receipts	Amount (₹)	Issues	Amount (₹)
Opening Balance	15,000	Issued to work-in-progress	80,000
Purchases	80,000	Issued repairs and maintenance	10,000
Transfer from work-in-progress	40,000	Sold some quantity (as a special case)	5,000
		Shortages	3,000
		Balance	37,000
	1,35,000		1,35,000

In the financial account, the stores have been charged as under:

Opening Balance and Purchases:	₹ 95,000
Less: Closing Stock:	₹ 37,000
Available for sale:	₹ 58,000
Sold at cost	₹ 5,000
	₹ 53,000*

(II)

* Sum of

(a) Materials consumed:	₹ 40,000
(b) Materials for repairs and Maintenance:	₹ 10,000
(c) Shortage in Materials:	₹ 3,000

(III) In cost Accounts, the stores have been charged to the tune of ₹ 40,000; and therefore, materials for repairs and maintenance of ₹ 10,000 and shortage in materials of ₹ 3,000 have not been charged assuming that they have recovered as Overheads.

Financial Books of PV Limited

Dr Trading and profit and loss account for the year ended........ Cr

Details	Amount (₹)	Details	Amount (₹)
To Opening stock 15,000 *Add:* Purchases 80,000	95,000	By Sales (Finished Stock)	22,5000
To Work-in-Progress: Opening 30,000 *Less:* Closing 20,000	10,000	By Sales (Other items at cost)	5,000
To Wages	40,000	By Closing stock (615 units)	37,000
To Production Overheads	1,25,000	By Loss	3,000
	2,70,000		2,70,000

Cost Sheet

Details	Amount (₹)
Direct Materials	80,000
Direct Wages	30,000
Prime Cost	1,10,000
Production Overheads	1,20,000
Works cost (Gross)	2,30,000
Adjustment for work-in-Progress	10,000
Less: Work-in-Progress (Transferred to stores)	(40,000)
Works cost (Net)	2,00,000
Profit @12.5% of cost	25,000
Sales	2,25,000

Reconciliation Statement

Details		Amount (₹)	Amount (₹)
Profit as per Cost Accounts			25,000
Less:			
1. Items not charged in Cost Accounts:-			
(a) Repairs and Maintenance	10,000		
(b) Shortage in Materials	3,000	13,000	
2. Under recovery of Administration Overheads (1,25,000 – 1,20,000)		5,000	
3. Wages Under charged in cost accounts (40,000 – 30,000)		10,000	(28,000)
Loss as per Financial Accounts			3,000

Problem 12. *The Profit and Loss A/c of XYZ Ltd. for the year ended 31.3.2007 is as follows:*

Details	*Amount (₹)*	*Details*		*Amount (₹)*
To Materials	*4,80,000*	*By Sales*		*9,60,000*
To Wages	*3,60,000*	*By Closing stock*		*1,80,000*
To Factory Expenses	*2,40,000*	*By Work-in-Progress;*		*60,000*
		Materials	*30,000*	
		Wages	*18,000*	
		Factory Expenses	*12,000*	
To Gross Profit	*1,20,000*			
	12,00,000			*12,00,000*
To Administration Expenses	*60,000*	*By Gross Profit*		*1,20,000*
To Net Profit	*66,000*	*By Dividend Received*		*6,000*
	1,26,000			*1,26,000*

As per the costing records the indirect factory overheads have been absorbed @ ₹ 30 per kg. and administrative overheads @ ₹ 15 per kg. during the year 6,000 kgs. were manufactured and 4,800 kgs were sold. Prepare a statement as per costing records and reconcile the costing profit and loss account with the financial profit. **[B.Com (Hons.) DU, 2007]**

Solution : **Statement of Cost and profit as on 31.3.2007**

(as per cost Accounts)

Details		Amount (₹)
Materials		4,80,000
Wages		3,60,000
Prime Cost		8,40,000
Indirect Factory Expenses (6,000 × 30)		1,80,000
Factory Cost (Gross)		10,20,000
Less: Closing Stock of Work-in-Progress:		
Materials	30,000	
Wages	18,000	
Factory Expenses	9,000	57,000
Factory Cost (Net)		9,63,000
Administration Expenses (6,000 × 15)		90,000
Cost of Production		10,53,000
Less: Closing Stock of Finished Goods [(10,53,000) × (1200÷6000)]		2,10,600
Cost of Goods Sold		8,42,400
Profit (Balancing figure)		1,17,600
Sales		9,60,000

Reconciliation Statement

Details	Amount (₹)	Amount (₹)
Profit as per Cost Accounts		1,17,600
Less:		
1. Under recovery of Factory overheads (2,40,000 – 1,80,000)	60,000	
2. Difference in stock Value (2,10,600 – 1,80.000)	30,600	(90,600)
Add:		
1. Over recovery of Administration Overheads (90,000– 60,000)	30,000	
2. Difference in Value of Factory Expenses in WIP	3,000	
3. Dividends received	6,000	39,000
Profit as per Financial Accounts		66,000

Working Notes:

Factory Expenses in the Closing Work-in-Progress are arrived at as under:

= 12,000 × (1, 80,000÷2, 40,000)

= ₹ 9,000.

Problem 13. *The following is the Trading and Profit & Loss account of Omega Ltd.*

Dr *Cr*

Details	Amount (₹)	Details		Amount (₹)
To Materials Consumed	23,01,000	By Sales (30,000 Units)		48,75,300
To Direct Wages	12,05,750	By Finished Goods Stock (1000 Units)		1,30,000
To Production Overheads	6,92,250	By Work-in-progress:		
		Materials	55,250	97,500
		Wages	26,000	
		Production overheads	16,250	
To Administration Overheads	3,10,375	By Dividends Received		3,90,000
To Selling & Distribution Overheads	3,68,875	By Interest on Bank Deposits		65,000
To Bad Debts Written Off	22,750			
To Goodwill Written Off	45,500			
To Fines	3,250			
To Interest on Mortgage	13,000			
To Loss on Sale of Machine	16,250			
To Taxation	1,95,300			
To Net Profit	3,83,500			
Total	55,57,500	Total		55,57,500

The Cost Accounting records of Omega Ltd. which manufactures a standard unit show the following:

(i) *Production Overheads have been charged at 20% of Prime cost.*

(ii) *Administration Overheads have been recorded at ₹ 9.75 per finished unit.*

(iii) *Selling & Distribution Overheads have been recorded at ₹ 13 per unit sold.*

Required:

(i) *Prepare a Costing Profit and Loss account, indicating net profit.*

(ii) *Prepare a Statement reconciling the profit disclosed by cost records with that shown in financial accounts.* **[B.Com (Hons.) DU, 2008]**

Solution :

Dr **Costing Profit & Loss Account** Cr

Details	Amount (₹)	Details	Amount (₹)
Materials Consumed	23,01,000	Sales	48,75,300
Direct Wages	12,05,750		
Prime cost	35,06,750		
Production Overheads (35,06,750 × 0.2)	7,01,350		
Less: Closing Work-in-Progress	97,500		
Works cost	41,10,600		
Administration Overheads (31000 × 9.75)	3,0,2,250		
Cost of Production	44,12,850		
Less: Finished Goods Stock (1000 × 142.35)	1,42,350		
Cost of Goods Sold	42,70,500		
Add: Selling & Distribution Overheads (30,000 × 13)	3,90,000		
Cost of Sales	46,60,500		
Add: Net Profit (Balancing figure)	2,14,500		
Sales	48,75,300		
Total	48,75,300	Total	48,75,300

Note: Value of Closing Finished Goods Stock

= Cost of Production/ Number of units produced

= 44,12,850 ÷ 3,100 => ₹ 142.35 per unit

Reconciliation Statement

Details		Amount (₹)	Amount (₹)
Profit as per Cost Accounts			2,14,500
Less:			
1. Items not charged in Cost Accounts:-			
(a) Bad Debts	22,750		
(b) Goodwill	45,500		
(c) Fines	3,250		
(d) Interest on Mortgage	13,000		

(e) Loss on Sale of machine 16,250		
(f) Taxation 1,95,000	2,95,750	
2. Under recovery of Administration Overheads (3,10,375 – 3,0,2,250)	8,125	
3. Difference in stock Value (1,42,350 – 1,30.000)	12,350	(3,16,225)
Add:		
1. Over recovery of Production Overheads (7,01,350– 6,92,250)	9,100	
2. Over recovery of Selling & Distribution Overheads (3,90,000 – 3,68,875)	21,125	
3. Dividends received	3,90,000	
4. Interest on Bank Deposits	65,000	4,85,225
Profit as per Financial Accounts		3,83,500

Problem 14. *The cost accountant of a company has arrived at a profit of ₹ 73,24,150 based on cost accounting records for the year ended 31.3.2007. As cost auditor, you find the following differences between financial accounts and cost accounts.*

Details	*Amount (₹)*
Decrease in value of WIP and finished goods as per F/A	*1,28,21,995*
As per cost accounts	*1,31,04,220*
Profit on sale of fixed assets	*61,500*
Loss on sale of investments	*11,200*
Voluntary retirement compensation included in salaries and wages in F/A	*16,75,000*
Donation Paid	*25,000*
Major repairs and maintenance written off in F/A	*13,26,000*
Amount in cost accounts	*6,08,420*
Insurance claim relating to previous year received during the year	*14,29,000*
Profit from retail trading activity	*7,12,300*

You are required to prepare a reconciliation statement between the profit figures as per costing and financial accounts. Calculate the profit as per financial books. **[B.Com (Hons.) DU, 2009]**

Solution :

Details	PLUS Amount (₹)	MINUS Amount (₹)
Profit as per cost accounts	73,24,150	
Add: Difference in Decrease in Value of WIP and Finished Goods (1,31,04,220 – 1,28,21,995)	2,82,225	
Add: Profit on sale of fixed assets recorded in cost accounts	61,500	

Less: Loss on sale of investments recorded in cost accounts		11,200
Less: Voluntary retirement compensation not recorded in cost accounts		16,75,000
Less: Donation Paid not recorded in financial accounts		25,000
Less: Excess repairs and maintenance in financial accounts (13,26,000– 6,08,420)		7,17,580
Add: Insurance claim received relating to previous year received during the year	14,29,000	
Add: Profit from retail trading activity	7,12,300	
Total	98,09,175	24,28,780
Profit as per financial accounts (98,09,175– 24,28,780)	73,80,395	

Problem 15. *The following information is available from the financial books of PV Limited for the year ended on 31.12.2009:*

Details	Amount (₹)	Details	Amount (₹)
Direct material consumed	6,00,000	Sales (40,000 units)	16,00,000
Direct wages	4,00,000		
Works Expenses	2,40,000		
Office expenses	80,000		
Selling and distribution expenses	1,60,000		
Net Profit	1,20,000		
Total	16,00,000	Total	16,00,000

Normal Output of the factory is 50,000 units. Factory overheads are fixed upto ₹ 1,20,000 and office expenses are fixed for all practical purposes. Selling and distribution expenses are fixed to the extent of 1,00,000, the rest are variable.

Prepare a statement recoding the profits as per cost and financial accounts assuming that indirect expenses are absorbed on the basis of normal production capacity in cost accounts.

Solution : Working Notes:

Computation of Fixed overhead rates of recovery:

Works Overhead:

= 1,20,000 ÷ 50,000 => ₹ 2.40

Office Overhead:

= 80,000 ÷ 50,000 => ₹ 1.60

Selling and distribution overhead:

= 1,00,000 ÷ 50,000 => ₹ 2.00

Computation of Variable overheads:

Works Overhead:

Variable Overhead = Total Overhead Amount – Fixed overhead Amount
= 2,40,000 – 1,20,000 =>₹ 1,20,000

Selling and distribution overhead:

Variable Overhead = Total Overhead Amount – Fixed overhead Amount
= 1,60,000 – 1,00,000 =>₹ 60,000

Statement of cost for the year ending on 31.12.2009

Details		Amount (₹)
Direct material consumed		6,00,000
Direct wages		4,00,000
Prime cost		10,00,000
Works Expenses:		
Variable	1,20,000	
Fixed (40,000 × 2.40)	96,000	2,16,000
Works Cost		12,16,000
Office expenses Fixed (40,000 × 1.60)	64,000	64,000
Office cost		12,80,000
Selling and distribution expenses:		
Variable	60,000	
Fixed (40,000 × 2.00)	80,000	1,40,000
Cost of Sales		14,20,000
Profit (Balancing figure)		1,80,000
Sales		16,00,000

Reconciliation statement as on 31.12.2009

Details		Amount (₹)
Profit as per financial books		1,20,000
Add:		
Under Recovery of Works overheads: (2,40,000 – 2,16,000)	24,000	
Under Recovery of Office overheads: (80,000 – 64,000)	16,000	
Under Recovery of Selling and Distribution overheads: (1,60,000 – 1,40,000)	20,000	60,000
Profit as per Cost books		1,80,000

Problem 16. *Shiva Engineering Company manufactures two sizes of machine components, size A-20 and A-25. The following data refer to the year ending March 2004:*

Details	*Size : A-20*	*Size : A-25*
Production	*500*	*1600*
Sales	*475*	*1500*
Wages cost per unit	*25*	*20*
Material cost per unit	*60*	*50*
Sale price per unit	*200*	*150*

All expenses other than wages and materials are analysed under 'Works overhead' which during the year amounted to ₹ 34,000 and 'Office overheads which amounted to ₹ 69,500. In fixing selling price, it was estimated that works overheads are charged @ 60% on wages and Office Overheads @40% on works cost.

You are required to compute:

(a) The total cost of each unit on the basis of the above overhead percentages.

(b) The net profit for the year shown by the financial accounts, valuing unsold stocks at actual materials and wages cost plus works overhead @ 60% on wages.

(c) The reconciliation of net profit in (b) above with estimated total net profit based on cost figures.

Solution : **(A) Statement of Cost**

Details	Product A Per Unit	Product A Total	Product B Per Unit	Product B Total	Product : A+B Total
Material	60.0	30,000	50.0	80,000	1,10,000
Wages	25.0	12,500	20.0	32,000	44,500
Prime Cost	85.0	42,500	70.0	1,12,000	1,54,500
Works Overhead @ 60% of Direct wages	15.0	7,500	12.0	19,200	26,700
Works Cost	100.0	50,000	82.0	1,31,200	1,81,200
Office Overheads @ 40% of Works Cost	40.0	20,000	32.8	52,480	72,480
Cost of Production	140.0	70,000	114.8	1,83,680	2,53,680
Less: Closing Stock	140.0	(3,500)	114.8	(11,480)	(14,980)
Cost of Goods Sold	140.0	66,500	114.	1,72,200	2,38,700
Profit (Balancing Figure)	60.0	28,500	35.2	52,800	81,300
Sales	200.0	95,000	150.0	2,25,000	3,20,000

(B) Financial Profit and Loss Account for the year ending March31, 2004.

Debit Items	Amount (₹)	Credit Items	Amount (₹)
Materials:		Sales:	
A: 500 × 60 = 30,000		A: 475 × 200 = 95,000	
B: 1600 × 50 = 80,000	1,10,000	B: 1500 × 150 = 2,25,000	3,20,000
Wages:		Closing stock at Works Cost:	
A: 500 × 25 = 12,500		A: 25 × 100 = 2,500	
B: 1600 × 20 = 32,000	44,500	B: 100 × 82 = 8,200	10,700
Works Overheads	34,000		
Office Overheads	69,500		
Net Profit	72,700		
Total	3,30,700	Total	3,30,700

(C) Reconciliation Statement

Details	Plus Amount	Minus Amount
Profit as per Financial Profit& Loss account	72,700	
Add: Under-Recovered Works Overhead (26,700-34,000)	7,300	
Add: Over-Valuation of Closing stock	1,000	
A: (3,500-2,500)	3,280	
B: (11,480-8,200)		
Less: Office Overhead Over-recovered (72,480-69,500)		2,980
Profit as per Cost Accounts		81,300
Total	84,280	84,280

Problem 17. *The following information is available from the books of a company having normal production capacity of 50,000 units for the year ended March 31, 2004:*

(i) Sales ₹ 16,00,000 (40,000 units)

(ii) There was no opening and closing stock of finished goods.

(iii) Direct Material and direct labour cost were ₹ 8,00,000 and 4,00,000 respectively.

(iv) Actual factory expenses: ₹ 2,50,000 of which 60% are fixed.

(v) Actual administrative expenses were ₹ 75,000 which are fully fixed.

(vi) Actual selling & distribution expenses: ₹ 50,000 of which 40% are fixed.

(vii) Interest and dividends received ₹ 45,000.

You are required to:

(a) Find out profit as per financial books for the year ended March 31, 2004;

(b) Prepare the cost sheet and ascertain the profit as per cost accounts assuming that the Overheads are absorbed on the basis of normal production capacity;

(c) Prepare a Memorandum Statement of Reconciliation of profits shown by financial and cost books.

Solution : (A) Profit and Loss Account for the year ending March 31, 2004

Debit Items	Amount (₹)	Credit Items	Amount (₹)
Direct Materials	8,00,000	Sales (40,000 Units)	16,00,000
Direct Wages	4,00,000	Interest and Dividends	45,000
Factory Expenses	2,50,000		
Administrative Expenses	75,000		
Selling and Distribution Expenses	50,000		
Profit	70,000		
Total	16,45,000		16,45,000

(B) Cost Statement for the year ending on March 31,2004

Details	Amount (₹)
Direct Materials	8,00,000
Direct Wages	4,00,000
Prime Cost	12,00,000
Factory Expenses:	
Variable (40% of 2,50,000) 1,00,000	
Fixed Absorbed [1,50,000(40,000/50,000)] 1,20,000	2,20,000
Works Cost	14,20,000
Administrative Expenses Absorbed [75,000(40,000/50,000)]	60,000
Cost of Production	14,80,000
Selling and Distribution Expenses:	
Variable (60% or 50,000) = 30,000	
Fixed Absorbed [20,000(40,000/50,000)] = 16,000	46,000
Cost of Sales	15,26,000
Profit (Balancing Figure)	74,000
Sales	16,00,000

(C) Memorandum Reconciliation Account

Details	Amount (₹)	Details	Amount (₹)
Under-absorbed Overheads: Factory 30,000 Administration 15,000 Selling &Distribution 4,000	49,000	Profit as per Cost statement	74,000
Financial Profit	70,000	Income from Interest and Dividends	45,000
Total	1,19,000	Total	1,19,000

Problem 18. *Costing Profit is Rupees 2,25,000. Following relevant details are ascertained on comparison of the cost and financial accounts:*

Details	*Cost accounts (₹)*	*Financial accounts (₹)*
Opening Stocks:		
Materials	*40,750*	*41,250*
Work-in-Progress	*25,000*	*26,250*
Closing Stocks:		
Materials	*45,000*	*43,000*
Work-in-Progress	*20,000*	*19,000*
Finished Goods	*10,000*	*11,250*

Directors' Fees paid ₹ 2,000, Interest Paid ₹ 1,600; Reserve for Bad Debts ₹ 800, Transfer fees collected ₹ 500 and dividends received ₹ 400 are exclusively taken in Financial Accounts; but not considered in cost accounts.

Rent charged in cost accounts but not in financial accounts ₹ 8,000.

Preliminary expenses written off: ₹ 17,000, but not charged in cost accounts.

Overheads charged in financial books ₹ 1,31,700, but recovered in cost accounts ₹ 1,46,700.

Solution : **Prepare Reconciliation Account**

Debit Side	Amount (₹)	Credit Side	Amount (₹)
Opening Stock Under-valued in Cost Books:		Profit as per Cost Accounts	2,25,000
Materials	500		
Work-in-Progress	1,250		

Closing Stock Over-valued in Cost Books:		Closing Stock of Finished Goods undervalued in Cost Books	1,250
Materials	2,000		
Work-in-Progress	1,000		
Items of Expenses considered in Financial Books but ignored in Cost Books:	4,400	Financial Income Items ignored in Cost Books:	
Director's fees 2,000 + Interest Paid 1,600 + Reserve for Bad debts 800 = 4,400		Dividends Received	400
		Transfer Fees	500
Preliminary Expenses Written off in Financial Books.	17,000	Cost Expenditure Item ignored in Financial Books:	
		Rent charged in cost Accounts	8,000
Profit as per Financial Accounts	2,24,000	Over-Recovery of Overheads in Cost Accounts	15,000
Total	2,50,150	Total	2,50,150

OBJECTIVE TYPE EXERCISES

I. Fill in the blank spaces with suitable word/s :

1. ……… and ………. and ……… are purely financial incomes and thus not included in cost accounts.
2. ……… system eliminates the necessity of operating Cost ledger control account and of reconciliation of cost and financial accounts.
3. Notional rent is an item included in ……… accounts but not in ……… accounts.
4. ……… and ……… are items which represent appropriation of profit and thus not included in costing books.
5. ……… and ……… are two such items which are shown only in cost accounts and not in financial accounts.
6. When costing profit is ₹ 48,000 and the amount of production overhead under-recovered is ₹ 3,000, the financial profit is ₹ ………

Answers :

1. Dividend received, rent income, interest income
2. Integrated
3. Cost, financial
4. Transfer to reserves, income tax
5. Notional interest on capital employed, charge in lieu of rent
6. ₹ 45,000

II. Indicate whether the following statements are True or False :

1. Reconciliation of cost and financial accounts ensures the accuracy of the two sets of accounts.
2. Amount of loss due to theft is added back to costing profit to reconcile it with financial profit.
3. Profit or loss on sale of fixed assets is included only in financial accounts but not in cost accounts.
4. Over-absorption of overhead results in lower profit in cost accounts.
5. Under non-integral system of accounting, cost and financial accounts do not need to be reconciled.
6. Works overhead under recovered is to be added in costing profit to reconcile it with financial profit.
7. Need for reconciliation arises only in case of integrated accounts.
8. Figure of sales needs to be same in cost as well as financial books.
9. Capital losses are debited in both cost as well as financial profit and Loss account.
10. Income tax is recorded in financial books only.
11. Reconciliation statement is always prepared at a point of time.
12. Notional costs appear both in cost and financial books.
13. Higher value of opening stock in cost books results in higher cost profit.
14. Large number of entries in cost and financial books is similar.
15. Items of pure financial character are excluded for cost ascertainment,
16. Reconciliation statement aims at rectifying errors in cost records.
17. The need to reconcile cost and financial profit arises if cost accounts and financial accounts are independent of each other.
18. Items of pure financial nature usually do not appear in cost books.
19. Higher value of closing stock in financial books results in higher financial profit.
20. Carry forward of under and over recovery of overheads does not lead to mismatch between cost and financial profit.
21. Transfers to 'General reserve' are excluded from cost books.
22. In case abnormal losses and gains are debited and credited to Costing Profit & Loss account, it will lead to disagreement between cost and financial profit.

Answers :

1. False	**2.** False	**3.** True	**4.** True
5. False	**6.** False	**7.** False	**8.** True
9. False	**10.** True	**11.** True	**12.** False
13. False	**14.** True	**15.** True	**16.** False
17. True	**18.** True	**19.** True	**20.** False
21. True	**22.** False		

THEORETICAL EXERCISES

1. What is reconciliation statement?
2. What is a memorandum reconciliation statement?
3. Describe in brief the conditions which necessitate the reconciliation of financial and cost accounts.
4. Why is it necessary to reconcile the Profit as shown by the Cost and Financial Accounts? Explain the reasons for the difference in profit also. **[B.Com (Hons.), DU, 1997]**
5. Briefly explain the reasons why it is necessary to reconcile the cost and financial accounts of an organisation?
6. What is the purpose of reconciling cost and financial accounts? Indicate the possible sources of difference between them. Illustrate your answer with examples.
7. Describe the procedure adopted to reconcile the profit shown by cost accounting and financial accounting.
8. Explain the importance of reconciling cost and financial accounts.

NUMERICAL EXERCISES

1. Prepare a reconciliation statement from the details given below:-

Details	Amount (₹)
Profit as per cost accounts	25,000
Works Overheads under charged in cost accounts	2,000
Interest on capital included in financial accounts	2,000
Dividend received	3,000
Rent for owned building charged in cost accounts	1,600
Profit as per financial accounts	25,600

2. The manufacturing, Trading and Profit and Loss, and Profit and Loss Appropriation Accounts of AV Ltd. for the year ended March 31, 2004 are as under:

Debit Side		Amount (₹)	Credit Side	Amount (₹)
To Raw Materials:			By Trading A/c (Cost of Goods Manufactured)	1,61,500
Opening stock	14,200			
Purchases	67,700			
Available for Consumption	81,900			
Less: Closing Stock	14,900			
Raw Materials Consumed		67,000		
To Wages		58,000		

To Factory Overhead:	37,400		
Indirect Wages 7,000			
Rent and Rates 3,000			
Power and fuel 6,000			
Depreciation 11,000			
Other Expenses 10,400			
Total Factory On Cost			
Gross Works Cost			
Add: Opening Work-in-Progress	1,62,400		
Less: Closing Work-in-Progress	9,800		
Net Works Cost 1,61,500	(10,700)		
Total	1,61,500	Total	1,61,500
To Finished goods:	1,60,400	By Sales	2,40,000
Opening stock 10,400			
Add: Manufactured 1,61,500			
Less: Closing stock (11,500)			
To Gross Profit c/d	79600		
Total	240000	Total	2,40,000
To Administration Overhead:	19500	By Gross Profit c/d	79,600
Office Salaries 15500			
Office Expenses 4000			
To Selling and Distribution Overhead:		By Dividends Received	1,000
Salesmen's Salaries 6,000			
Selling Expenses 1,000			
Distribution Expenses 3,000	10,000		
To Loss on Sale of Machinery	800		
To Fines	300		
To Net Profit for the year	50,000		
Total	80,600	Total	80,600
To Income-Tax	10,000	By Balance b/d	30,200
To General Reserve	5,000	By Net Profit for the year	50,000

To Dividend	12,000		
To Goodwill written off	3,000		
To Balance c/d	50,200		
Total	80,200	Total	80,200

The cost accounts revealed a profit of ₹ 69575. In preparing this figure stocks have been valued in cost accounts as follows:

Item	Opening stock	Closing stock
Raw Materials	14,100	14,950
Work-in-Progress	9,875	10,600

Administration Overhead has been ignored in cost accounts. Prepare a reconciliation statement.

3. The profit of a company appeared at ₹ 1,28,755 as per financial records for the year ended 31.03.2007. The cost books, however, showed a net profit of ₹ 1,72,400 for the same period. Both the sets of accounts reveal the following data:
   - Selling overheads over-recovered in costs ₹ 1,700 and factory overheads under-recovered in costs ₹ 3,120.
   - Interest Received on investments not included in costs ₹ 8,000.
   - Loss due to obsolescence charged in financial records ₹ 5,700.
   - Depreciation charged in financial accounts ₹ 11,200 and recovered in cost accounts ₹ 12,500.
   - Income tax provided in financial books ₹ 40,300.
   - Bank interest and transfer fees ₹ 750.
   - Loss due to depreciation in stock values charged in financial accounts ₹ 6,750.
   - Stores adjustment (credited in financial records) ₹ 475.

   Prepare a Reconciliation statement to reconcile the cost and financial records.

4. Following is the summarised Trading, Profit and Loss Account of Medak Industries (P) Ltd. for the year ended on 31.3.2008:

Dr Cr

Details	Amount (₹)	Details	Amount (₹)
To Materials	45,000	By Sales (4800 Units)	96,000
To Wages	33,000	Closing Stock(1200 Units)	20,400
To Manufacturing Expenses	24,000		
To Administrative expenses	6,00		
To Net profit	8,400		
	1,16,400		1,16,400

The cost records of the company reveal the followings:

(a) Manufacturing overheads have been absorbed @ ₹ 3 per unit produced; and

(b) Administration overheads have been absorbed @ ₹ 1.50 per unit produced.

There is no opening or closing work-in-progress and there is no opening stock of finished goods.

Prepare

1. A statement of cost indicating the net profit; and
2. A statement reconciling the profit as per disclosed by cost accounts and that shown in financial accounts.

5. Find out whether costing profit will be higher or lower than financial profit:-

Item of Stock	Valuation	
	Cost Books (₹)	Financial Books (₹)
Opening Raw material	60,000	80,000
Closing work-in-Progress	80,000	60,000
Closing Finished goods stock	60,000	80,000
Opening Finished goods stock	80,000	60,000

[Ans. (Costing Profit: (1) Higher, (2) Higher, (3) Lower, (4) Lower]

6. Following information is available in respect of AV Enterprises for the year ended on 31.3.2008:

Details	Financial Accounts (₹)	Cost Accounts (₹)
Opening stock:		
Raw Material	32,000	27,000
Work-in-Progress	37,000	34,500
Finished goods	27,000	24,500
Closing stock:		
Raw Material	23,000	24,500
Work-in-Progress	18,000	21,500
Finished goods	32,500	34,000
Purchases	2,10,000	
Direct Wages	1,05,000	
Indirect Wages	17,000	
Factory Expenses	1,20,000	1,10,000 (Absorbed)
Sales	5,90,000	
Administration Expenses	16,000	23,500 (Absorbed)

Selling Expenses	22000	20000 (Absorbed)
Financial Expenses	10,000	
Interest and dividends received	12,000	
Transfer to Reserve	25,000	
Dividends	50,000	

Compute Profit in Financial Accounts as well as in Cost Accounts and prepare a Reconciliation statement. Previous year's profit was ₹ 40,000.

[Ans. (Financial Profit: ₹ 75,500; Costing Profit: ₹ 98,500)]

7. The following information has been obtained from the records of M/s Modern Electronics Ltd., a manufacturer of T.V. sets.

Details	Amount (₹)
Materials cost per T.V. Set	5,000
Wages per T.V. Set	2,500
Charge 80% of wages as Production Overheads	130,00,000 (Incurred)
Charge 25% of Prime cost as Administration Overheads	140,00,000 (Incurred)
Charge 10% of Production cost as Selling and distribution Overheads	65,00,000 (Incurred)
Number of units manufactured and sold	6,000
Selling price per T.V. Set	14,000

Note: There was no opening stock or closing stock of raw material, work-in-progress and finished goods.

Prepare a cost sheet showing profit as per costing records, and a statement showing profit as per financial records.

Prepare a reconciliation statement of profit as per costing records and profit as per financial records.

[Ans. (Financial Profit: ₹ 55,00,000; Costing Profit: ₹ 56,25,000)]

8. Net Profit as per financial accounts is ₹ 85,000. The following points of difference were noted:

(a) Income tax ₹ 52,000;

(b) Opening stock as per financial books ₹ 20,000 and as per costing books ₹ 18,500;

(c) Notional rent of the business premises ₹ 36,000;

(d) Actual Overheads incurred ₹ 35,000 while recovered in costing books ₹ 32,500;

(e) Dividends on investment received ₹ 25,000;

(f) Closing stock as per financial books ₹ 28,000 and as per costing books ₹ 24,800. Prepare a reconciliation Statement explaining the logic behind treatment of each item. **[Ans. (Costing Profit: ₹ 73,800)]**

9. (Reconciliation) From the accounts of Tata Production Ltd., the following Manufacturing, Trading and Profit and Loss Account for the year ended 31st December, 2004 is extracted:

Tata Production Ltd.
Manufacturing, Trading and Profit and Loss Account
For the year ended 31st December, 2003

Details	Amount (₹)	Details	Amount (₹)
To Raw Materials:	59,000	By Raw Materials:	64,000
Opening Stock	3,73,000	Closing Stock	
Purchases	5,62,000	By Work-in-progress	8,000
To Wages paid	34,000	Material	11,000
To Wages Accrued	3,81,500	Wages	6,600
To Factory expenses		Factory expenses	
		By Cost of Goods Manufactured	13,19,900
	14,09,500	(18,000 units)	14,09,500
To Cost of Goods Manufactured (18,000 units)	13,19,900	By Sales (15,200 units)	18,24,000
	2,45,000	By Finished Stock (2,800 units)	2,35,200
To Administration expenses		By Interest on Investments	2,600
To Selling and distribution expenses	3,28,000	By Dividend earned	11,000
To Preliminary expenses (written off)	20,000		
To Goodwill (written off)	15,000		
To Net Profit transferred to Profit and Loss (Appropriation) A/c	1,44,900		
	20,72,800		20,72,800

The following procedure is adopted in connection with the costing of the product:

(a) Factory expenses are allocated to production at 60% of direct labour cost.

(b) Administration expenses are applied at ₹ 12 per unit over the units produced.

(c) Selling and distribution expenses are charged so as to work out 20% of selling price.

Prepare Costing Profit and Loss Account and the Statement of Reconciliation between the profit and loss as per two sets of accounts. **[B.Com (Hons.) DU, 2004]**

[Ans. (Costing Profit: ₹1, 82,400)]

10. (Reconciliation) The Caliber Chip Manufacturing Co. Ltd., which commenced manufacturing chips from 1st October, 2003, supplies the following information and asks you to prepare a cost sheet showing profit per chip sold:

(1) Materials and wages are to be charged at actual cost.

(2) Works on cost at 75% of the wages.

(3) Office on cost at 20% of the works cost.

(4) Two types of chips are manufactured :

Patterns "Monolithic" and "Hybrid".

(5) There was no stock of chips unsold nor there any in course of manufacture by 30th September.

(6) Number of chips sold during the year pattern "Monolithic" 720 and pattern "Hybrid" 504.

(7) Other particulars are :

Details	Pattern Monolithic (₹)	Pattern Hybrid (₹)
Material per chip	38	64
Wages per chip	24	32
Selling price per chip	120	180

Prepare necessary statement showing the actual profit for the year if the actual works expenses were ₹ 28,000 and office expenses ₹ 22,000.

You are required to prepare a statement reconciling the profits as shown by the cost accounts with the Profit of Loss as shown by the financial accounts for the year ended 30th September, 2004.

11. A firm of sports Equipments commenced business on April 1,2007 for manufacturing two varieties of 'Leg Pads'., LP-1 and LP-2.The following information has been extracted from the accounts for the year ended on 31.3.2008:

Details	Amount (₹)
Average Material cost per unit of LP-1	200
Average Material cost per unit of LP-2	150
Average labour cost per unit of LP-1	350
Average labour cost per unit of LP-2	275
Finished Goods sold:	
LP-1 : 300 units	
LP-1 : 700 units	
Selling price per unit:	
LP-1 :	1,250
LP-2 :	975
Works expenses incurred during the year	3,00,000
Administration expenses	1,70,000

You are required to prepare a statement showing:

(a) Per unit of 'Leg Pads' of each variety; Charge Labour and material at actual average cost. Works overheads at 100% on labour cost and Administration Overheads at 25% of works cost.

(b) Financial profit for the year 2007-08;

(c) Reconciliation between profits as shown by cost accounts and financial accounts.

[Ans. Profit as per cost books ₹ 1,07,500 and as per financial books ₹ 1,25,000]

12. From the following prepare reconciliation statement:

Details	Amount (₹)
Profit as per cost accounts	1,45,500
Work overheads under recovered	9,500
Administrative overheads under recovered	22,750
Selling overheads over recovered	19,500
Overvaluation of Opening stock in cost accounts	15,000
Overvaluation of Closing stock in cost accounts	7,500
Interest earned during the year	3,750
Rent received during the year	27,000
Bad debts written off during the year	9,000
Preliminary expenses written off during the year	18,000

[B.Com (Hons.) DU, 2006 (External)]

[Ans. Financial Profit ₹ 1, 44,000]

13. The following figures have been extracted from the books of PV Limited for the year ending on 31.3.2008:

Details		Amount (₹)
Direct Materials Consumption		50,000
Productive Wages		30,000
Production Overheads		16,000
Administration Overheads		7,000
Selling and distribution Overheads		9,600
Bad Debts Written Off		800
Preliminary Expenses Written Off		400
Legal Charges		100
Dividend Received		1,000
Interest Received on Bank Deposits		200
Sales (12,000units)		1,20,000
Closing Stock:		
Finished Goods (400 units)	3,200	
Work-in-progress	2,400	5,600

The cost accounts for the same period show that Direct Materials Consumption

Was ₹ 56,000? Factory overheads are recovered at 20% of Prime Cost. Administration overheads are recovered @ 60 Paise per unit of production. Selling and distribution overheads are recovered or charged 80 Paise per unit sold.
Prepare the manufacturing cum Trading and Profit &Loss Account as per financial records and cost sheet. Also reconcile the profit shown by the two records.

[Ans. Financial Profit ₹ 12, 900; Profit as per costing statement ₹ 5,652]

14. The financial records of M/s Modern Manufactures ltd. reveal the following data for the year ended March 31, 2008:

Details		Amount (₹ In Thousands)
Sales (20,000 units)		4,000
Materials		1,600
Wages		800
Factory Overheads		720
Office and Administration Overheads		416
Selling and distribution Overheads		288
Goodwill Written Off		320
Interest on Capital		32
Closing Stock Finished Goods (1,230 units)		240
Work-in-progress (Closing) : (₹'000)		
Materials	48	
Labour	32	
Overheads (Factory)	32	112

In the costing records, factory overheads are charged at 100% of wages, administration overheads at 10% of works cost and selling and distribution overheads at ₹ 16 per unit sold.
Prepare a statement reconciling the profit as per cost records with the profit as per financial records of the company. All workings should form part of your answer.

[Ans. Financial Profit ₹ 1, 76,000; Profit as per costing statement ₹ 4,80,000]

15. In reconciliation between Cost and Financial accounts one of the areas of differences is different method of stock valuation. State in each of the following circumstances, whether costing profit will be higher or lower than the financial profit.

Items of stock	Cost Valuation (₹)	Financial Valuation (₹)
(1) Raw material (Opening)	50,000	60,000
(2) Work-in-Progress (Closing)	60,000	50,000
(3) Finished Goods (Closing)	50,000	60,000

[Ans. (Costing Profit: (1) Higher, (2) Higher, (3) Lower]

16. The Profit as per cost accounts is ₹ 1,50,000. The following information is ascertained on comparison of cost and financial accounts:

Details	**Cost Accounts Amount (₹)**	**Financial accounts Amount (₹)**
(a) Opening Stock:		
Materials	10,000	15,000
Finished Goods	18,000	16,000
(b) Closing Stock:		
Materials	12,000	13,000
Finished Goods	20,000	17,000

(c) Interest charged but not paid ₹ 10,000;

(d) Dividends received from SBI (Mutual fund) ₹ 1,000;

(e) Indirect expenses charged to Financial Accounts ₹ 80,000 but ₹ 75,000 absorbed in cost accounts.

Find out the profit as per financial Accounts by preparing a Reconciliation statement.

[Ans. Financial Profit ₹ 1,31,000]

17. **Profit and Loss account**

(For the year ending on 31.3.2010)

Dr Cr

Details	**Amount (₹)**	**Details**	**Amount (₹)**
Materials consumed	2,50,000	Sales	6,20,000
Carriage Inwards	1,70,000		
Works Expenses	60,000		
Direct wages	5,000		
Administrative Expenses	22,500		
Selling & Distribution Expenses	32,500		
Debenture Interest	5,000		
Net Profit	75,000		
	6,20,000		6,20,000

Net profit as per cost accounts ₹ 80,850. On comparison it was found (a) works over heads recovered ₹ 58,000, (b) Administrative overheads recovered ₹ 22,950, (c) selling and distribution overheads recovered ₹ 33,200, (d) No Debenture interest is charged in cost accounts.

18. In a factory, works overheads are absorbed at 60% of labour cost and office overheads are 20% of works cost. Prepare (i) Cost Sheet, (ii) Trading and Profit & Loss Account, and (iii) Reconciliation Statement if Total Expenditure consists of materials ₹ 2,00,000; Wages ₹ 1,50,000; Factory Expenses ₹ 1,00,000; and office Expenses ₹ 85,000. 10% of the output is stock at the end and sales are ₹ 5, 20,000.

[B.Com (Hons.) DU, 2000]

[Ans. Financial Profit ₹ 30,000; Profit as per costing statement ₹ 44,800]

19. The Profit and Loss Account of Oil India (Pvt.) ltd. for the year ending 31.3.2003 is as follows:

Details	Amount (₹)	Details		Amount (₹)
To Materials	4,80,000	By Sales		9,60,000
To Wages paid	3,60,000	By Work-in-progress		
To Direct Expenses	2,40,000	Material	30,000	
To Gross Profit	1,20,000	Wages	18,000	
		Direct expenses	12,000	60,000
		By Closing Stock		1,80,000
	12,00,000			12,00,000
To Administration exp.	60,000	By Gross Profit		1,20,000
To Net Profit	60,000	By Dividends Received		6,000
	1,20,000			1,20,000

As per the costing records the direct expenses have been estimated at a cost of ₹ 30 per kg. and administration expenses at ₹ 15 per kg. During the year production was 6,000 kg. and sales were 1,200 kg.

Prepare a statement of Costing Profit & Loss Account and reconcile the costing profit with financial profit. **[B.Com (Hons.) DU, 2001]**

[Ans. Profit as per costing statement ₹ 1,10,400]

20. The following information is made available to you from the financial books of SV Limited for the year ended December 31, 2002:

Details	Amount (₹)	Details	Amount (₹)
To Direct Materials Used	3,00,000	By Sales (2,00,000 Units)	7,50,000
To Direct Wages	2,00,000		
To Factory Expenses	1,20,000		
To Office Expenses	40,000		
To Selling and Distribution Expenses	80,000		
To Net Profit	10,000		
Total	7,50,000	Total	7,50,000

Normal output of the factory is 2, 50,000 units. Factory overheads are fixed up to ₹ 60,000 and office expenses are fixed for all purposes. Selling and Distribution expenses are fixed to the extent of ₹ 50,000; the rest are variable.

Prepare a statement reconciling the profits as per cost and financial accounts assuming that indirect expenses are recovered on the basis of Normal production capacity in cost accounts. **[B.Com (Hons.) DU, 2002]**

[Ans. Profit as per costing statement ₹ 40,000]

21. Prepare a Reconciliation Account from the following details:

Profit as per cost accounts were ₹ 60,000, while the profits as per financial accounts were of ₹ 59,700. The values pf opening and closing stock as shown in cost accounts and financial accounts were as under:

Details	Financial Accounts (₹)	Cost Accounts (₹)
Raw Materials:		
Opening	25,300	25,000
Closing	30,000	29,600
W.I.P:		
Opening	16,000	15,500
Closing	20,000	19,900

[B.Com (Hons.) DU, 2002]

22. From the following data prepare a reconciliation statement:

Details	Amount (₹)	Details	Amount (₹)
Net Loss as per costing records	1,72,500	Stores Adjustment (credit) in Financial books	500
Works overhead under recovered in Cost	3,120	Depreciation charged in financial records	11,200
Administration overhead over recovered in excess	1,700	Depreciation recovered in costing	12,500
Interest income received not included in costing	8,000	Obsolescence loss charged in financial records	5,700
Income tax provided in financial books	40,300	Bank interest credited in financial books	750
Value of Opening Stock :		Value of Closing Stock :	
Cost books	52,600	Cost books	51,000
Financial books	54,000	Financial books	49,600
Interst charged in cost books but not in financial books	6,000	Provision for doubtful debts in financial accounts	800
Preliminary Expenses written off in financial accounts	150		

[Ans. Net Loss as per financial accounts ₹ 2,07,170]

23. A manufacturing company disclosed a net loss of ₹ 3, 47,000 as per their cost accounts for the year ended March 31, 2003. The financial accounts however, disclosed a net loss of ₹ 5, 10,000 for the same period. The following information was revealed as a result of scrutiny of the figures of both sets of accounts:

Details	Amount (₹)
Factory Overheads under-absorbed	40,000
Administration Overheads over-absorbed	60,000
Depreciation charged in financial accounts	3,25,000
Depreciation charged in cost accounts	2,75,000
Interest on investments not included in cost accounts	96,000
Income Tax provided	54,000
Interest on Loan funds in financial accounts	2,45,000
Transfer fees (Credit in financial books)	24,000
Stores Adjustment(Credit in financial books)	14,000
Dividend Received	32,000

Prepare a Memorandum Reconciliation Account

[B.Com (Hons.) DU, 2005(External)]

24. A Company maintains separate cost and financial accounts, and the costing profit for 2006 differed to that revealed in the financial accounts, which was shown as ₹ 80,000. The following information is available:

(I)

Details	Cost Accounts (₹)	Financial Accounts (₹)
Raw Materials:		
Opening	8,000	8,800
Closing	6,400	8,480
Finished Goods:		
Opening	19,200	24,000
Closing	22,400	25,600

(II) Dividends of ₹ 2,000 were received by the company.

(III) A machine with net book value of ₹ 16,000 was sold during the year for ₹ 13,000.

(IV) The company charged 8% interest on its opening capital employed of ₹ 1, 50,000 to its process costs.

You are required to determine the profit figure which was shown in the cost accounts. And also prepare Reconciliation account.

[Ans. Profit as per costing statement ₹ 69,320]

25. A Company maintains separate cost and financial accounts, and the costing profit for 2006 differed to that revealed in the financial accounts, which was shown as ₹ 80,000. The following information is available:

(I)

Details	Financial Accounts (₹)	Cost Accounts (₹)
Raw Materials:		
Opening	5,500	5,000
Closing	5,300	4,000
Finished Goods:		
Opening	15,000	12,000
Closing	16,000	14,000

(II) Dividends of ₹ 1,000 were received by the company.

(III) A machine with net book value of ₹ 10,000 was sold during the year for ₹ 8,000.

(IV) The company charged 10% interest on its opening capital employed of ₹ 80,000 to its process costs.

You are required to determine the profit figure which was shown in the cost accounts. And also prepare Reconciliation account.

[Ans. Profit as per costing statement ₹ 43,200]

26. Following is the summarised Trading, Profit and Loss Account of Moderation Industries (P) Ltd. for the year ended on 31.3.2008:

Details	Amount (₹)	Details	Amount (₹)
To Materials	27,40,000	By Sales (48,000 units)	60,00,000
To Wages	15,10,000	Closing Stock: (1,600 units)	1,60,000
To Manufacturing Exp.	8,30,000	By Work-in-Progress : Materials 64,000 Wages 36,000 Manufacturing Expenses 20,000	1,20,000
To Administrative exp.	3,82,400	By Dividend Received	18,000
To Selling expenses	4,50,000		
To Preliminary expenses written off	60,000		
To Net profit	3,25,600		
	62,98,000		62,98,000

The cost records of the company reveal the followings:

(i) Manufacturing overheads have been absorbed @ 20% of Prime cost; and

(ii) Administration overheads have been absorbed @ ₹ 7.50 per unit produced

(iii) Selling Expenses @ ₹ 10 per unit sold.

Prepare

1. A statement of cost indicating the net profit; and
2. A statement reconciling the profit as per disclosed by cost accounts and that shown in financial accounts.

Hint: Closing stock in cost accounts:

= (Material cost+ Wages + Manufacturing Expenses + administrative expenses)/49,600

= (53,52,000 ÷ 49,600) => ₹ 1,72,645

[Ans. Profit as per costing statement ₹ 3,40,645]

27. Costing Profit is Rupees 1,65,300. Following relevant details are ascertained on comparison of the cost and financial accounts:

Details	Cost accounts (₹)	Financial accounts (₹)
Opening Stocks:		
Materials	32,600	33,000
Work-in-Progress	20,000	21,000
Closing Stocks:		
Materials	36,000	34,400
Work-in-Progress	16,000	15,200
Finished Goods	8,000	9,000

Directors' Fees paid ₹ 1,000, Interest Paid ₹ 800; Reserve for Bad Debts ₹ 500, Transfer fees collected ₹ 300 and dividends received ₹ 200 are exclusively taken in Financial Accounts; but not considered in cost accounts.

Rent charged in cost accounts but not in financial accounts ₹ 6,000.

Preliminary expenses written off: ₹ 13,000, but not charged in cost accounts.

Overheads charged in financial books ₹ 1,21,200, but recovered in cost accounts ₹ 1,26,200 Prepare Reconciliation Account..

[Ans. Profit as per Financial Accounts: 1,58,700]

28. Following is the certified financial accounts of Vishnu Ltd.:

Trading and Profit& Loss account

Debit Items	Amount (₹)	Credit Items	Amount (₹)
To Opening Stock	1,06,600	By Sales	4,50,500
To Purchases	3,21,360	By Closing Stock	97,500
To Direct Wages	29,900		
To Factory Overheads	27,300		
To Gross Profit c/d	62,840		
	5,48,000		5,48,000

To Administrative Expenses	12,400	By Gross Profit b/d	62,840
To Selling Expenses	29,200	By Other Income	650
To Net Profit	21,890		
	63,490		63,490

The costing records show:

(a) Profit as per cost records ₹ 31,300.

(b) Book value of closing Stock ₹ 1,01,500.

(c) Factory overheads have been absorbed to the extent of ₹ 24,700.

(d) Other income is not considered.

(e) Administration expenses are recovered to the extent of 2.4% of selling Price.

(f) Total absorption of Direct Wages amounted to ₹ 32,000.

(g) Selling Price includes 5.6% for selling expenses.

Prepare a reconciliation statement.

29. The following information is available from the books of Shakti Ltd. for the year ended March 31, 2004:

Items	Financial accounts	Cost accounts
Stock on 1.4.2003:		
Raw Materials	12,000	10,000
Work-in-Progress	14,000	13,000
Finished Goods	10,000	9,000
Stock on 31.3.2004:		
Raw Materials	8,000	9,600
Work-in-Progress	6,000	7,400
Finished Goods	11,800	12,400
Purchases	80,000	
Direct Wages	40,000	
Indirect Wages	6,000	
Other Factory expenses	34,000	42,000
Sales	2,20,000	
Administrative Expenses	6,000	4,600
Selling Expenses	8,000	9,000
ightFinancial Expenses	2,000	
Dividend Received	3,200	
Net Profit	37,000	

Prepare a cost sheet and reconcile costing profit with financial books profit.

[Ans. Costing Profit: 34,800]

30. The net profit of Narain Ltd. appeared at Rupees 60,700 as per financial records for the year ending on March 31, 2005. However, the cost books showed a net profit of ₹ 86,500 for the same period. A scrutiny of the figures from both the sets pf accounts revealed the following facts:

Details	Amount (₹)
Works Overhead under recovered in cost accounts	1,760
Administrative Overheads over-recovered in cost accounts	850
Depreciation charged in financial accounts	5,600
Depreciation recovered in cost accounts	6,250
Interest on Investments not included in cost accounts	4,000
Obsolescence Loss charged in financial accounts	2,850
Income Tax provided in financial accounts	20,150
Bank interest and transfer fee in financial books	425
Stores adjustment (credit in financial accounts)	235
Opening stock in cost accounts	24,800
Opening stock in financial accounts	26,300
Closing stock in Financial accounts	25,000
Closing stock in cost accounts	23,000
Interest charged in cost accounts	2,000
Goodwill written off	5,000
Loss on sale of old furniture	700

Prepare a statement showing the reconciliation between net profit as per cost accounts and net profit as shown in the financial books.

31. The following information is available from the books of a company having normal production capacity of 60,000 units for the year ended March 31, 2004:

(i) Sales ₹ 10,00,000 (50,000 units)

(ii) There was no opening and closing stock of finished goods.

(iii) Direct Material and direct labour cost were ₹ 5,00,000 and 2,50,000 respectively.

(iv) Actual factory expenses were ₹ 1,50,000 of which 60% are fixed.

(v) Actual administrative expenses were ₹ 45,000 which are fully fixed.

(vi) Actual selling & distribution expenses were ₹ 30,000 of which 40% are fixed.

(vii) Interest and dividends received ₹ 15,000.

You are required to: (a) Find out profit as per financial books for the year ended March 31, 2004; (b) Prepare the cost sheet and ascertain the profit as per cost accounts assuming that the Overheads are absorbed on the basis of normal production capacity; (c) Prepare a Memorandum Statement of Reconciliation of profits shown by financial and cost books.

[Ans. Financial Profit: ₹ 40,000; Costing Profit: 49,500]

32. Prepare Memorandum Reconciliation Account showing the profit as per cost accounts from the given Profit and Loss Account.

Profit & Loss Account.

Debit Side	Amount (₹)	Credit Side	Amount (₹)
Office Salaries	16,924	Gross Profit	81,970
Office Expenses	9,770	Dividends Received	800
Salesmen's Salaries	7,389	Interest on Bank deposits	377
Sales Expenses	13,950		
Distribution Expenses	4,485		
Loss on Sale of machinery	2,925		
Fines	500		
Discount on Debentures	300		
Net Profit	26,904		
Total	83,147	Total	83,147
Income Tax	12,000		26,904
Reserve	2,000		
Dividends	5,000		
Balance	7,904		
Total	26,904	Total	26,904

The Cost accountant has ascertained a Profit of ₹ 29,452 as per Cost Books.

❑❑❑

Solved Question Paper (2010)
B.Com. (Hons.) IInd Year (DU)

Q.1. *The particulars obtained from the records of M/s. Jeevan Industries for the year 2009 are given below:*

Item	***Amount (₹)***
Opening Stock:	
Raw materials	*1,40,000*
Finished goods (1,000 units)	*20,000*
Purchases	*2,10,000*
Factory wages	*3,80,000*
Factory Overheads	*70,000*
Office overheads	*40,000*
Selling overheads	*9,600*
Sales (3,200 units)	*9,28,000*
Closing Stock:	
Raw materials	*19,600*
Finished goods (900 units)	*1,64,080*

Prepare a cost sheet showing prime cost, factory cost, and cost of production, total cost and sales per unit.

During 2010 the industry expects to receive an order for 5,000 units. It is estimated that

(i) The prices of raw materials and factory wages will rise by 15% and 10% respectively.

(ii) There will be no change in the total factory overheads and office overheads,

(iii) Selling overheads per unit will remain the same.

Prepare an estimated cost sheet. The factory intends to earn the same rate of profit on cost.

Solution : **Cost Sheet for the year 2009**

(3,100 Units)

Details		Amount (₹)	Amount (₹)
Opening Stock of Materials		1,40,000	
Add: Purchases		2,10,000	
Less: Closing Stock		(19,600)	
Materials Consumed			3,30,400
Factory Wages			3,80,000
Prime Cost			**7,10,400**
Factory overheads			70,000
Works Cost			**7,80,400**
Office overheads			40,000
Cost of Goods Poduced			**8,20,400**
Add: Opening Stock of Finished Goods	(1,000 units)		20,000
Cost of Goods Available for Sale	**(4,100 units)**		**8,40,400**
Less: Closing Stock of Finished Goods	(900 units)		1,64,080
Cost of Goods Sold	**(3,200 units)**		**6,76,320**
Selling Overheads @ ₹. 3 per unit			9,600
Cost of Sales = Total Cost			**6,85,920**
Profit (Balancing figure)			2,42,080
Sales	**(3,200 units)**		**9,28,000**

Working Notes :

1. Units produced in Year 2009:

   = Sales + Closing Stock – Opening stock

   = 3,200 + 900 – 1,000 = 3,100 units

2. Cost of Raw material consumed per unit in Year 2009 :

   = 3,30,400 ÷ 3,100 = ₹ 106.58

   Add: 15% increase in 2010:

   = 106.58 × 1.15 = ₹ 122.57

3. Factory Wages per unit in Year 2009 :

   = 3,80,000 ÷ 3,100 = ₹ 122.58

   Add: 15% increase in 2010:

   = 122.58 × 1.10 = ₹ 134.83

4. Profit as a percentage of total cost:

   = (2,42,080 ÷ 6,85,920) × 100 = 35.29 %.

5. Sales per unit in 2010:

   = 19,10,295 ÷ 5,000 = ₹ 382.06

Estimated Cost Sheet for the year 2010

(5,000 Units)

Details	Per unit Amount (₹)	Total Amount (₹)
Raw Materials	122.57	6,12,850
Factory Wages	134.83	6,74,150
Prime Cost	**257.40**	**12,87,000**
Factory overheads		70,000
Works Cost		**13,57,000**
Office overheads		40,000
Cost of Goods Produced		**13,97,000**
Selling Overheads @ ₹. 3 per unit		15,000
Cost of Sales = Total Cost		**14,12,000**
Profit @ 35.29% (14,12,000 × 0.3529)		4,98,295
Sales		**19,10,295**

Q.2. *The following data are available in respect of material X for the year ended 31st March, 2009:*

Item	*Amount (₹)*
Opening Stock	*90,000*
Purchase during the year	*2,70,000*
Closing Stock	*1,10,000*

Calculate:

(i) Inventory ratio, and

(ii) The number of days for which the average inventory is held.

Solution :

Cost of materials Consumed

= Opening Stock + Purchases – Closing Stock

= 90,000 + 2,70,000 – 1,10,000 = ₹ 2,50,000

Average Stock

= (Opening Stock + Closing Stock) ÷ 2

= (90,000 + 1,10,000) ÷ 2 = ₹ 1,00,000

Inventory Turnover Ratio

= (Cost of materials Consumed ÷ Average Stock)

= 2,50,000 ÷ 1,00,000 = 2.5 times

Number of days for which the average inventory is held:

= (Number of Days in a Year / Inventory Turnover Ratio)

= 365 ÷ 2.5 = 146 Days

Q.3. *Show how the items given ahead relating to purchases and issue of a raw material will appear in the Stores Ledger using LIFO, FIFO and Weighted average Methods of pricing of materials issue:*

2010	*Details*	*Unit*	*Price per unit (₹)*
Feb. 1	*Opening Balance*	*300*	*20*
Feb. 5	*Purchases*	*200*	*22*
Feb. 11	*Issue*	*150*	*?*
Feb. 22	*Purchases*	*200*	*23*
Feb. 24	*Issue*	*150*	*?*
Feb. 28	*Issue*	*200*	*?*
Feb. 28	*Shortage*	*5*	*?*

Solution :

Stores Ledger (LIFO Method)

Date 2010	Receipts			Issues			Balance		
	Unit	Rate (₹)	Amount (₹)	Unit	Rate (₹)	Amount (₹)	Unit	Rate (₹)	Amount (₹)
Feb. 1							300	20	6,000
Feb. 5	200	22	4,400				{300	20	6,000
							{200	22	4,400
Feb. 11				150	22	3,300	{300	20	6,000
							{50	22	1,100
Feb. 22	200	23	4,600				{300	20	6,000
							{50	22	1,100
							{200	23	4,600
Feb. 24				150	23	3,450	{300	20	6,000
							{50	22	1,100
							{50	23	1,150
Feb. 28				{50	22	1,100	200	20	4,000
				{50	23	1,150			
				{100	20	2,000			
Feb. 28				5	20	100	195	20	3,900

Stores Ledger (FIFO Method)

Date 2010	Receipts			Issues			Balance		
	Unit	Rate (₹)	Amount (₹)	Unit	Rate (₹)	Amount (₹)	Unit	Rate (₹)	Amount (₹)
Feb. 1							300	20	6,000
Feb. 5	200	22	4,400				{300	20	6,000
							{200	22	4,400
Feb. 11				150	20	3,000	{150	20	3,000
							{200	22	4,400
Feb. 22	200	23	4,600				{150	20	3,000
							{200	22	4,400
							{200	23	4,600

Feb. 24				150	20	3,000	{200 {200	22 23	4,400 4,600
Feb. 28				200	22	4,400	200	23	4,600
Feb. 28				5 Shortage	23	115	195	23	4,485

Stores Ledger (Weighted Average Price Method)

Date 2010	Receipts			Issues			Balance		
	Unit	Rate (₹)	Amount (₹)	Unit	Rate (₹)	Amount (₹)	Unit	Rate (₹)	Amount (₹)
Feb. 1							300	20	6,000
Feb. 5	200	22	4,400				500	20.80	10,400
Feb. 11				150	20.80	3,120	350	20.80	7,280
Feb. 22	200	23	4,600				550	21.60	11,880
Feb. 24				150	21.60	3,240	400	21.60	8,640
Feb. 28				200	21.60	4,320	200	21.60	4,320
Feb. 28				5 Shortage	21.60	108	195	21.60	4,212

Working Note :

Weighted average Price

as on Feb.5, 2010:

= 10,400 / 500 = ₹ 20.80 per unit

as on Feb.22, 2010:

= 11,880 / 550 = ₹ 21.60 per unit

Q.4. *Three workers Govind, Ram and Shyam produced 80,100 and 120 pieces of a product X on a particular day of eight hours in may 2009 in a factory. The time allowed for 10 units of Product X is one hour and their hourly rate is ₹ 4.*

Calculate for each of these workers the following:

(i) Earnings for the day

(ii) Effective rate of earnings per hour under:

(a) Straight piece- rate Plan

(b) Halsey premium bonus plan (50% sharing)

(c) Rowan premium bonus plan of labour remuneration.

Solution : Working Notes :

Straight piece-rate of earning:

Hourly Rate: ₹ 4

Time allowed for 10 units: One hour

Piece Rate: (Hourly Rate / Time allowed for 10 units) = ₹ 0.40

Halsey Bonus Plan:

Wages = (Time Taken + 0.5 Time Saved) × Time Rate

Govind: (8 + 0) × 4 = ₹ 32.00

Ram: (8 + 1) × 4 = ₹ 36.00

Shyam: (8 + 2) × 4 = ₹ 40.00

Rowan Bonus Plan:

Wages = (Time Taken × Time Rate) + {(Time Saved / Time Allowed) × (Time Taken × Time Rate)}

Govind: (8 × 4) + {(0/8) × (8 × 4)} = ₹ 32.00

Ram: (8 × 4) + {(2/10) × (8 × 4)} = ₹ 38.40

Shyam: (8 × 4) + {(4/12) × (8 × 4)} = ₹ 42.67

Statement of Daily Earnings (₹)

Details	Straight piece-rate	Halsey Bonus Plan	Rowan Bonus Plan
Govind	(80 × 0.4) = 32.00	32.00	32.00
Ram	(100 × 0.4) = 40.00	36.00	38.40
Shyam	(120 × 0.4) = 48.00	40.00	42.67

Statement of Effective Earnings per Hour (₹)

Details	Straight piece-rate	Halsey Bonus Plan	Rowan Bonus Plan
Govind	(32.00 ÷ 8) = 4.00	(32.00 ÷ 8) = 4.00	(32.00 ÷ 8) = 4.00
Ram	(40.00 ÷ 8) = 5.00	(36.00 ÷ 8) = 4.50	(38.40 ÷ 8) = 4.80
Shyam	(48.00 ÷ 8) = 6.00	(40.00÷ 8) = 5.00	(42.67 ÷ 8) = 5.33

Q.5. *A truck starts with a load of 10 tonnes of goods from station P. It unloads 4 tonnes at station Q and rest of the goods at station R. It reaches back directly to station P after getting reloaded with 8 tonnes of goods at station R. The distances between P to Q, Q to R and then from R to P are 40 km, 60 km and 80 km respectively. Compute Absolute tonne-km and commercial tonne-km.*

Solution : Absolute tonne km: (Absolute Load × Distance)

= (10 × 40) + (6 × 60) + (8 × 80)

= 400 + 360 + 640 = 1,400 tonnes km

Commercial tonne km: (Average Load × Total Distance)

Average Load = (10 + 6 + 8) ÷ 3 = 8 tonees

Total Distance = 40 + 60 + 80 = 180 kms.

Commercial tonne km = (8 × 180) = 1,440 tonnes km

Q.6. *The following information relates to the activities of a production department for the month of January, 2010:*

Details		***Amount (₹)***
Materials used		*72,000*
Direct Wages		*60,000*
Machine Hours	*20,000*	
Labour Hours	*24,000*	
Overheads chargeable to the department		*48,000*

On one order to be carried out in the month of February 2010, the relevant data were:

Materials		*4,000*
Direct Wages		*3,300*
Machine Hours	*1,200*	
Labour Hours	*1,650*	

Calculate the cost of this order by using the following methods of absorption of overheads:

(i) Direct labour hour Rate;

(ii) Percentage of Direct Wages; and

(iii) Machine Hour Rate.

Solution : Working Notes :

Direct labour hour Rate = (Overheads ÷ Labour Hours)
= 48,000 ÷ 24,000 = ₹ 2

Percentage of Direct Wages = (Overheads ÷ Direct Wages) × 100
= (48,000 ÷ 60,000) × 100 = 80%

Machine Hour Rate = (Overheads ÷ Machine Hours)
= 48,000 ÷ 20,000 = ₹ 2.40

Computation of the Cost of Order

Details	Direct labour hour Rate (₹)	% of Direct Wages (₹)	Machine Hour Rate (₹)
Materials	4,000	4,000	4,000
Direct Wages	3,300	3,300	3,300
Factory Overheads	3,300 = (1,650 × 2)	2,640 = (3,300 × 0.8)	2,880 = (1,200 × 2.4)
Total	10,600	9,940	10,180

Q.7. *A transport company is running 4 buses between Delhi and Meerut covering a distance of 100 kms. The seating capacity of each bus is 40 passengers. The following particulars are obtained from the books for the month of march, 2010:*

Details	*Amount* (₹)
Wages of Drivers and Conductors	*19,200*
Salaries of office staff	*6,000*
Honorarium to Accountant	*2,000*
Diesel, Oil, etc	*32,000*
Repairs and Maintenance	*6,400*
Road Tax and insurance	*12,800*
Depreciation	*20,800*
Interest and other charges	*16,000*

Actual passengers carried were 75% of the seat9ing capacity. All the buses ran for 30 days. Each bus made one round trip per day. Find out the cost per passenger-km.

Solution : Working Notes :

Total Passenger Km:

= Number of buses × Distance × Number of Passengers × Capacity utilized × Number of days

= 4 × 200 × 40 × 0.75 × 30 = 7,20,000.

Operating Cost Sheet

Details	Total (₹)	Per unit (₹)
A. Standing Charges:		
1. Wages of Drivers and Conductors	19,200	
2. Salaries of office staff	6,000	
3. Honorarium to Accountant	2,000	
4. Road Tax and insurance	12,800	
5. Interest and other charges	16,000	
Total Standing Charges	56,000	
Standing Charges per unit (56,000 ÷ 7,20,000)		0.0777
B. Running Charges:		
1. Repairs and Maintenance	6,400	
2. Diesel, Oil, etc.	32,000	
3. Depreciation	20,800	
Total Running Charges (59,200 ÷ 7,20,000)	59,200	0.0822
C. Total Operating cost [(A) + (B)]		0.1599

Average cost per Passenger-kilometer = 0.1599 @ ₹ 0.16.

Q.8. *The following is the summarised information relating to contract No. 101:*

Details	***Amount (₹)***
Contract Price	*9,00,000*
Wages	*2,46,000*
General Expenses	*12,900*
Materials	*1,80,000*
Cash received (80% of work certified)	*3,60,000*
Plant Issued	*30,000*
Materials at site	*15,000*
Plant at site	*27,000*

Included in the above information are wages ₹ 5,250, materials ₹ 6,000 and other expenses ₹ 3,750 which were incurred since certification.

Prepare Contract No.101 A/c and calculate the amount of profit which should reasonably be transferred to Profit & Loss A/c.

Solution :

Dr **Contract No. 101 Account** Cr

Details	Amount (₹)	Details	Amount (₹)
To Material	1,80,000	By Materials at site	15,000
To Wages	2,46,000	By Plant at site	27,000
To Plant Issued	30,000	By Work certified (3,60,000 ÷ 0.8)	4,50,000
To General Expenses	12,900	By Work Uncertified (5,250 + 6,000 + 3,750)	15,000
To Notional Profit c/d	38,100		
	5,07,000		5,07,000
To Profit in Suspense A/c	17,780	By Notional Profit b/d	38,100
To Profit & Loss A/c	20,320		
	38,100		38,100

Working Note :

Profit to be transferred to Profit & Loss A/c:

= (Notional Profit × 2/3 × Cash Ratio)

= (38,100 × 2/3 × 0.8) = ₹ 20,320

Q.9. *Meerut Manufacturing Company makes several product lines which are processed through three production departments: X, Y and Z. The information concerning the relevant data for a year is as under:*

Department	*Factory overheads (including share of service department) (₹)*	*Direct Labour hours*	*Direct Labour Cost (₹)*
X	1,24,000	80,000	1,60,000
Y	2,30,000	1,15,000	2,41,500
Z	5,46,000	1,05,000	1,99,500

Production records at the end of the year indicated the following for the product line 'Krish':

Units Produced: 20,000

Details	*Department X (₹)*	*Department Y (₹)*	*Department Z (₹)*
Prime cost	45,000	10,500	59,500
Direct Labour hours	10,000	5,000	30,000

You are required to

(a) *Calculate the departmental and Plant-wise, overhead rate based on direct labour hours;*

(b) *Compute the cost of 'Krish' line for the year by using (i) Plant-wise rate and (ii) departmental rates; and*

(c) *Comment on the results.*

Solution : Working Notes :

Computation of Rates:

(I) Departmental :

Department	Factory overheads	Direct Labour hours	Rate of Absorption: (Factory overheads ÷ Direct Labour Hours) (₹.)
X	1,24,000	80,000	1.55
Y	2,30,000	1,15,000	2.00
Z	5,46,000	1,05,000	5.20

(II) Plant Wise Overhead Rate:

= Total Factory Overheads ÷ Total Direct labour hours

Total Factory Overheads

= 1,24,000 + 2,30,000 + 5,46,000 = ₹ 9,00,000

Total Direct labour hours

= 80,000 + 1,15,000 + 1,05,000 = 3,00,000 Hours

= ₹ 9,00,000 ÷ 3,00,000 Hours = ₹ 3 per direct labour hour

Computation of cost of "krish" line: Using departmental rates

Details	Department X (₹)	Department Y (₹)	Department Z (₹)	Total (₹)
Prime cost	45,000	10,500	59,500	1,15,000
Factory Overheads	15,500 = (10,000 × 1.55)	10,000 = (5,000 × 2.00)	1,56,000 = (30,000 × 5.20)	1,81,500
Factory cost	60,500	20,500	2,15,500	2,96,500

Using Plant-wise rates:

Details	Total (₹)
Prime cost Department X :45,000 Department Y :10,500 Department Z : 59,500	1,15,000
Factory Overheads (45,000 × 3)	1,35,000
Total	2,50,000

❑❑❑